Armageddon in Stalingrad

The Stalingrad Trilogy, Volume 2

Armageddon in Stalingrad

SEPTEMBER–NOVEMBER 1942

David M. Glantz

with

Jonathan M. House

University Press of Kansas

Published by the University Press of Kansas (Lawrence, Kansas 66045), which
was organized by the Kansas Board of Regents and is operated and funded by
Emporia State University, Fort Hays State University, Kansas State
University, Pittsburg State University, the University of Kansas, and
Wichita State University

Library of Congress Cataloging-in-Publication Data

Glantz, David M.
    Armageddon in Stalingrad : September–November 1942 / David M. Glantz,
Jonathan M. House.
        p.   cm. — (Modern war studies) (Stalingrad trilogy ; v. 2)
    Includes bibliographical references and index.
    ISBN 978-0-7006-1664-0 (cloth : alk. paper)
    1. Stalingrad, Battle of, Volgograd, Russia, 1942–1943. 2. Soviet Union. Raboche-
Krestﬁanskaia Krasnaia Armiia—History—World War, 1939–1945. 3. Germany. Heer.—
History—World War, 1939–1945. I. House, Jonathan M. (Jonathan Mallory), 1950–
II. Title.
    D764.3.S7G588 2009
    940.5421747—dc22   2009016234

British Library Cataloguing-in-Publication Data is available.

Printed in the United States of America

10 9 8 7 6 5 4 3 2 1

The paper used in this publication is recycled and contains 30 percent
postconsumer waste. It is acid free and meets the minimum requirements of
the American National Standard for Permanence of Paper for Printed Library
Materials Z39.48-1992.

To my daughter Susan Mangan and her husband, Darin,
for inspiring me with the wondrous gift of
my granddaughter, Elizabeth

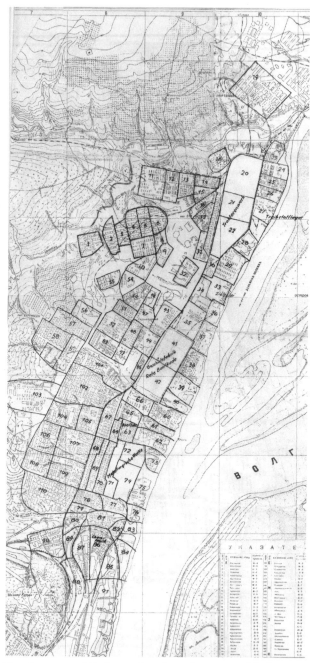

Russian map of Stalingrad with grid sectors added
by Germans

Contents

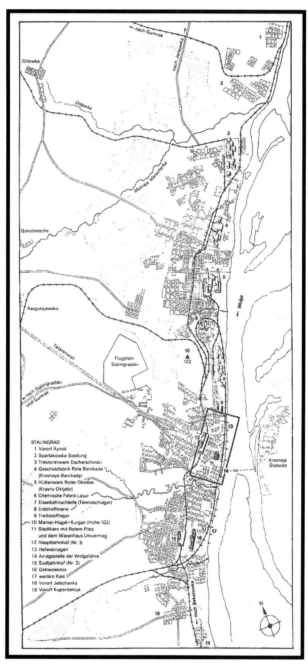

STALINGRAD
1 Vorort Rynok
2 Spartakowka-Siedlung
3 Traktorenwerk Dscherschinski
4 Geschützfabrik Rote Barrikade
  (Krasnaya Barrikady)
5 Hüttenwerk Roter Oktober
  (Krasny Oktjabr)
6 Chemische Fabrik Lasur
7 Eisenbahnschleife (Tennisschläger)
8 Erdölraffinerie
9 Treibstofflager
10 Mamai-Hügel=Kurgan (Höhe 102)
11 Stadtkern mit Rotem Platz
   und dem Warenhaus Univermag
12 Hauptbahnhof (Nr. 1)
13 Hafenanlagen
14 Anlegestelle der Wolgafähre
15 Südbahnhof (Nr. 2)
16 Getreidesilos
17 weitere Kais
18 Vorort Jelschanka
19 Vorort Kuporosnoje

German map of Stalingrad identifying key points in
the city

Maps, Tables, Illustrations

Tables

ILLUSTRATIONS

Following page 20:
General of Panzer Troops Friedrich Paulus, commander of Sixth Army,
    meeting with his commanders.
Colonel General Andrei Ivanovich Eremenko, commander of Southeastern
    and Stalingrad Fronts.
Nikita Sergeevich Khrushchev, Member of the Military Council
    (Commissar) of the Stalingrad Front.
Lieutenant General Konstantin Konstantinovich Rokossovsky, commander
    of Don Front.
Lieutenant General V. I. Chuikov, commander of 62nd Army.
Major General Mikhail Stepanovich Shumilov, commander of 64th Army.

Following page 156:
The southern part of Stalingrad city with Railroad Station No. 2 in the
    upper center, the Grain Elevator to the left of SU 83131, and the railroad
    line and El'shanka River on the left.
The region north and south of Tsaritsa River with Railroad Station No. 2
    and the Grain Elevator at the lower left.
Red Army soldiers swearing allegiance to their Motherland before crossing
    the Volga River into Stalingrad. The banner reads, "For our Soviet
    Motherland."
Red Army soldiers and naval infantry fighting in the streets of southern
    Stalingrad.

Following page 264:

Members of Stalingrad Front's Military Council: (from left to right)
N. S. Khrushchev, member; A. S. Chianov, secretary of the Stalingrad
city Communist Party Committee; and General A. I. Eremenko,
commander.

(From left to right) Major General N. I. Krylov, chief of staff of 62nd Army;
Lieutenant General V. I. Chuikov, commander of 62nd Army; Lieutenant
General K. A. Gurov, member of 62nd Army's Military Council
(commissar); and Major General A. I. Rodimtsev, commander of 13th
Guards Rifle Division.

Lieutenant General V. I. Chuikov, commander of 62nd Army (on the right),
and Division Commissar K. A. Gurov, member of 62nd Army's Military
Council (on the left).

Colonel I. I. Liudnikov, commander of 138th Rifle Division (on the
right), with S. Ia. Tychinsky, V. I. Shuba, and N. I. Titov, the 138th Rifle
Division's chief of artillery, chief of staff, and political officer, respectively
(on the left).

Major General V. A. Glazkov, commander of 35th Guards Rifle Division.

Colonel V. A. Goryshnyi, commander of 95th Rifle Division.

Major General F. N. Smekhotvorov, commander of 193rd Rifle Division.

Major General S. S. Gur'ev, commander of 39th Guards Rifle Division.

Colonel L. N. Gurt'ev, commander of 308th Rifle Division.

Major General V. G. Zholuder, commander of 37th Guards Rifle Division.

Following page 362:

The southern third of the Factory District (looking west from the Volga
River). The "Tennis Racket" and Bannyi Ravine on the left (south),
Vishnevaia *Balka* from left to right across the top, the Krasnyi Oktiabr'
village and Factory from top to bottom in the center, and the *balka* with
the "twin gullies" from top to bottom on the right.

The central third of the Factory District (looking west from the Volga River
bottom). The *balka* with the "twin gullies" from top to bottom on the
left, the Silikat Factory, the *balka* with "the narrows," Skul'pturnyi Park,
and the Barrikady Factory from top to bottom in the center, and the
Mechetka River, upper Tractor Factory village, Zhitomirsk Ravine, and
Minusinsk region from top to bottom on the right.

The northern third of the Factory District (looking west from the Volga
River). The Mechetka and Mokraia Mechetka Rivers diagonally from top
left to bottom right, the Silikat and Barrikady Factories on the left, the
Tractor Factory village in the center and right center, and the Tractor
Factory on the lower right.

Soviet troops fighting in the upper Krasnyi Oktiabr' village.

Panorama of the Factory District in flames.

People's militiamen participating in the defense of the Krasnyi Oktiabr'
Factory.

Several of the tens of thousands of civilians who endured the fighting in
Stalingrad city.

Following page 586:

Colonel General Ewald von Kleist, commander of First Panzer Army and
Army Group A.

Army General Ivan Vladimirovich Tiulenev, commander of Trans-Caucasus
Front.

Red Army cavalrymen in the High Caucasus Mountains.

Soviet submachine gunners fighting in the northern Caucasus region.

Red Army machine gunners fighting in the Mozdok region.

Red Army submachine gunner and antitank rifleman fighting in the
northern Caucasus region.

Following page 694:

Colonel I. I. Liudnikov, commander of 138th Rifle Division, at his
command post.

Soldiers of 138th Rifle Division defending in buildings in "Liudnikov's
Island"

Soviet communications trenches in "Liudnikov's Island."

A Soviet mortar crew defending "Liudnikov's Island."

Soldiers of 138th Rifle Division leave a bunker to repulse a German attack
during the fight for "Liudnikov's Island."

The oil storage farm southeast of the Barrikady Factory, which was the
scene of heavy fighting during the first half of November 1942 to rescue
the forces isolated on "Liudnikov's Island."

Preface

The Battle of Stalingrad remains one of the epic struggles of human courage and ferocity. Millions of people who are otherwise unaware of the Soviet-German struggle, through histories, novels, and motion pictures, have at least a vague impression of the misery and sacrifice that led to Adolf Hitler's first great strategic defeat.

Yet despite the vast and growing literature about Stalingrad, many misunderstandings remain. In the first volume of this trilogy, for example, we have traced the manner in which a German offensive aimed at seizing the Caucasus oil fields was sidetracked by the unintended objective of seizing the Soviet dictator's namesake city. Volume 1 also demonstrated that, contrary to general belief, the German attacks experienced great difficulty and suffered considerable attrition before they ever reached the city.

This second volume focuses on the actual battle within the confines of the city and again argues that the course of the battle was significantly different from that described in most previous accounts. In large measure, this was due to the absence of detailed records for the campaign. The politics of the Cold War compounded the excessive secrecy of the Soviet state to ensure that few documents were available until the 1990s. Most historians, therefore, chose to rely upon the memoirs of Vasilii Ivanovich Chuikov, the commander of Soviet 62nd Army, the principal tactical defender of Stalingrad. Although Chuikov's memoirs were remarkably detailed and honest when they appeared in the 1960s, he had to write without complete access to the official Soviet records of the battle. Working largely from memory and limited intelligence reports from the period, Chuikov committed several unintentional errors in describing the locations, composition, and combat actions of both the German Sixth Army and Soviet 62nd Army, errors that carried over into most subsequent histories. Western sources were equally scarce, because the Soviets captured the records and the eyewitnesses of Sixth Army in 1943. Many of the traditional German accounts written by Walter Goerlitz, Paul Carell, and others, though superb efforts at the time of publication, were therefore as prone to error as were Chuikov's memoirs.

This study, by contrast, goes well beyond the traditional accounts to include two major groups of additional sources. First, we compare the daily official records of both sides, using a considerable number of primary documents.

The records of the People's Commissariat of Internal Affairs (NKVD), which provided Moscow with an independent and often critical view of the battle, have never been exploited before. The same applies to the records of Soviet 62nd Army and many of its subordinate units. Second, a number of Soviet memoirs and German divisional histories have accumulated over the past 65 years, adding greater texture to earlier views of the battle. Finally, an emerging generation of new Russian historians, unfettered from the restraints and shibboleths of former Soviet times, has given us fresh, detailed, and candid accounts of many aspects of the fighting.

In order to describe what really happened in the streets and rubble of Stalingrad, this second volume must, of necessity, include immense details of the battle. At the same time, to keep this battle in operational context, we will examine the ongoing battles in the Caucasus and elsewhere along the Soviet-German front. The rest of the story, beginning with the Soviet counteroffensive of 19 November 1942 and ending with the German maneuver battles that temporarily restored their front lines in the late winter of 1943, will be the subject of the third volume.

Based on these new sources, this study offers unprecedented detail and fresh perspectives, interpretations, and evaluations of the Stalingrad campaign, superseding all previous historical accounts. Both the German offensive and the Soviet defense emerge as being markedly different from our traditional understanding of the 1942 campaign.

Any research effort of this magnitude incurs obligations of gratitude for the support provided by numerous individuals and agencies. In this regard, we must again thank Jason Mark, both for his generous personal assistance and for the groundbreaking tactical accounts of Stalingrad published by Leaping Horseman Books in Pymble, Australia. Likewise, Michael Jones, the British author of the book, *Stalingrad: How the Red Army Triumphed*, an insightful study of the psychology of Soviet commanders and soldiers in the battle, generously provided us with many Russian archival documents from his collection of sources. William McCrodden, who has spent a lifetime compiling detailed and definitive orders of battle for German forces during the war, shared with us the numerous draft volumes produced by his research.

Finally, we are indebted for the usual prodigies of effort provided by the staffs of the Military History Institute in Carlisle, Pennsylvania, the Combined Arms Research Library at Fort Leavenworth, Kansas, and the Hightower Library of Gordon College in Barnesville, Georgia. As with our previous efforts, we gratefully acknowledge the crucial role Mary Ann Glantz played in editing this manuscript.

David M. Glantz   *Jonathan M. House*
Carlisle, PA   *Leavenworth, KS*

Armageddon in Stalingrad

CHAPTER 1

The Germans at the Gates

WHO'S BESIEGING WHOM?

In the late afternoon of 23 August 1942, Hyazinth, *Graf* [Count] Strachwitz von Gross-Zauche und Camminetz, led his *kampfgruppe* [battle group] of 16th Panzer Division into the northern suburbs of the industrial city of Stalingrad. The advance halted only when the Germans stood atop the high banks overlooking the Volga River. This breakthrough had been so rapid that the only opposition the Germans encountered near the river had been from antiaircraft guns manned by female factory workers. Strachwitz's *kampfgruppe*, composed of tanks from 2nd Panzer Regiment and truck-mounted infantry of 2nd Battalion, 64th Panzer Grenadier Regiment, was the arrow-slim point of XIV Panzer Corps, which in turn was the leading element of General of Panzer Troops Friedrich Paulus's Sixth German Army. Strachwitz's men stared down with understandable pride at the river and the city, thrilled to have achieved such a remarkable advance.[1]

Behind this *kampfgruppe*, its parent division, Major General Hans Hube's 16th Panzer, and the other two major elements of General of Infantry Gustav von Wietersheim's XIV Panzer Corps—3rd and 60th Motorized Divisions—were strung out in a long corridor along the high ground leading westward to the German bridgehead over the Don River at Vertiachii (see Map 1). That night these three divisions formed a series of temporary hedgehog defenses to wait for the German fighter-bombers that would return at dawn to resume the attack. On the large-scale operations maps in German higher headquarters, the panzer spearhead appeared poised to complete its mission of interdicting the Volga River barge traffic and occupying the northern industrial suburbs of Stalingrad. Far to the south, 29th Motorized and 14th Panzer Divisions of Colonel General Hermann Hoth's Fourth Panzer Army were engaged in a mirror-image advance to the northeast. Together, Paulus's and Hoth's troops hoped to catch the Stalingrad metropolitan area in a pincers.

Yet it soon became evident that the Germans, rather than their Soviet opponents, were the ones under siege. Wietersheim's headlong advance had brushed aside the threadbare 62nd Red Army on 23 August, but that army's commander, Lieutenant General Anton Ivanovich Lopatin, made every effort to shore up his defenses on the southern side of the German corridor,

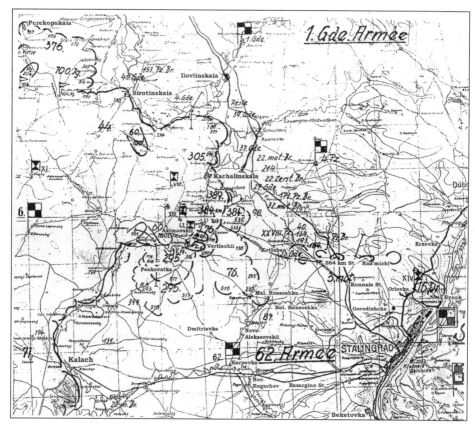

Map 1. Sixth Army's situation, 22–23 August 1942

while other elements of Colonel General Andrei Ivanovich Eremenko's Stalingrad Front (equivalent in size to a small German army group) besieged the Vertiachii bridgehead from which Wietersheim had advanced. None of these Soviet counterattacks made headway against the Germans with their Stuka dive-bomber support, but they did prevent Sixth Army from reinforcing XIV Panzer Corps. Meanwhile, Eremenko used every available force, from a regiment of NKVD internal security troops to the Red Navy's Volga River Flotilla, to build an internal defensive arc along the northern flank of the city. (NKVD, or "secret police," is the acronym for *Narodnyi Kommissariat Vnutrennih Del*—the People's Commissariat of Internal Affairs.) The improvised defense was under the command of Lieutenant General Nikolai Vladimirovich Feklenko, a man who had earlier been disgraced in fighting west of the Don. Other Soviet forces, including the 2nd and 23rd Tank Corps and 315th Rifle Division, gathered themselves to attack from the north and south, seeking to interdict the long German salient in the Kotluban' area.[2]

On 24 August, 16th Panzer Division was unable to make progress against the suburbs of Rynok and Spartanovka. At one point, using unpainted T-34 tanks that had come directly off the assembly lines of this area, Feklenko's men overran the headquarters of 64th Panzer-Grenadier Regiment and forced Hube's troops to withdraw to defensive positions south of Rynok. The German *Luftwaffe* failed in its attempts to airdrop supplies on the night of 24–25 August, leaving the three divisions of XIV Panzer Corps almost out of ammunition and fuel. That night, Hube decided to use his 16th Panzer in a breakout to the west, despite explicit orders, direct from Adolf Hitler, to hold the banks of the Volga. Gathering his staff and regimental commanders together, Hube, a one-armed veteran of both world wars, was blunt:

> The shortage of ammo and fuel is such that our only chance is to break through to the west. I absolutely refuse to fight a pointless battle that must end in the annihilation of my troops, and I therefore order a break-out to the west. I shall personally take responsibility for this order, and will know how to justify it in the proper quarters. I absolve you, gentlemen, from your oath of loyalty, and I leave you the choice of either leading your men in this action or handing over your command to other officers who are prepared to do it. It is impossible to hold our positions without ammunition. I am acting contrary to the Führer's orders.[3]

On 25 August, a supply column from 3rd Motorized Division fought its way forward to resupply 16th Panzer, giving Hube a breathing space, but Paulus as Sixth Army commander rejected all requests to withdraw. At the same time, Paulus had to keep one nervous eye over his left shoulder, where the poorly equipped Hungarian Second and Italian Eighth Armies had been pressed into service to defend the ever-lengthening German left flank. After a week of constant fighting with up to 500 casualties per day, 16th Panzer Division abandoned Rynok on 31 August, pulling back 2 kilometers.[4] Ultimately, XIV Panzer Corps fought off the uncoordinated Soviet counterattacks and survived to fight again, but the Germans had lost their best chance to seize Stalingrad from the march, before the Soviet defenses were ready.

THE STRATEGIC CONUNDRUM

The enduring, German-sponsored myth of the Soviet-German conflict is that the *Wehrmacht* advanced triumphantly from the initial invasion of 22

June 1941 until the Soviet strategic counteroffensive of 19 November 1942. Supposedly, the only hiccup in this advance came in December 1941, when severe winter weather enabled the Red Army to push the Germans back from the gates of Moscow; once the weather improved, the Germans resumed their phenomenal advance as far as Stalingrad and beyond. Then in November 1942, so the alibi version goes, a combination of overwhelming Soviet numbers, incompetent interference from Hitler, vast distances, and extreme winter weather slowed and eventually overwhelmed the German Armed Forces.

The reality is somewhat different. It is true that the Red Army, in the initial battles of 1941, lacked competent leadership at every level, allowing the Germans to achieve encirclement battles that eliminated up to 4 million men from the Soviet muster rolls in less than six months. Yet even in this first campaign (Operation Barbarossa), the German mobile forces frequently outran their own logistics and their foot- and horse-mobile infantry support echelons. The German mechanized spearheads had to stop every 100–150 kilometers to wait for fuel, ammunition, and infantry support to catch up. During these pauses, many Soviet troops escaped the loose German encirclements to reorganize for another battle. On at least two occasions during 1941, German panzer or motorized divisions found themselves completely surrounded by the Soviets, and incidents such as XIV Panzer Corps' corridor battle became increasingly common. These stranded German units survived only through a combination of superior training and the inability of Soviet commanders to coordinate large-unit counterattacks.

With each battle that the Germans won, they lost irreplaceable veterans. With each battle that the Soviets lost, they learned new lessons and gradually combined that hard-won experience with their own prewar concepts of mechanized warfare.[5] Much of this Soviet improvement was invisible at national command levels, so that both Hitler and Stalin came to believe that their subordinates were lacking in aggressiveness. Franz Halder, the German Army Chief of Staff, recorded rainy weather and other practical problems in his diary in 1942, yet even he seemed to believe that the Red Army was "soft."[6] In fact, the two opposing armies were rapidly evolving in the direction of a tactical equality that would make future German exploitations far more problematical.

As for strategic and operational command, Hitler and Stalin did indeed interfere with their field commanders on occasion, but, when they did so, the dictators were often correct in their assessments. For the first year and a half of the Soviet-German conflict, Hitler generally followed his commanders' advice, even when his instincts told him otherwise. Moreover, he often tolerated quiet dissent. General Hube, for example, not only did not suffer for his planned breakout in August 1942 but was actually promoted to command XIV Panzer Corps the next month. As late as 3 July of that year, Hitler joked with his generals about the British tendency to fire commanders in North Africa after a single defeat, thereby paralyzing the generals' freedom of decision.[7]

More fundamentally, the entire German campaign against the Soviet Union displayed a lamentable disconnect between strategic ends and operational and tactical means. The initial Barbarossa plan assumed that, once the Red Army was destroyed in a series of encirclement battles in western Russia, the Soviet regime would collapse and the captive nationalities would welcome the Germans as liberators. This assumption underestimated both the Soviet capacity to reconstitute new units from a vast pool of reservists and the ability of the Soviet regime to maintain itself in power. Moreover, German racial prejudices against Slavs, coupled with plans for the economic and political rape of the occupied territories, drove many potential collaborators into the arms of the Soviet government.

Germany was simply unprepared for the sustained, attritional struggle necessary to defeat a larger, implacable foe. The Germans were, in fact, the very model of what Geoffrey Parker and others have termed "the Western Way of War"—the belief that superior training, discipline, and technology can produce a rapid, decisive, offensive victory, thereby minimizing the strain on one's economy and society.[8] Yet when they invaded the Soviet Union, the Germans had less than 20 percent of their ground force in mechanized and motorized formations. Even those few mobile divisions were equipped with a hodgepodge of German, Czech, and French equipment that was tactically incompatible and logistically unsustainable over long distances. The remainder of the German force marched on foot and moved its guns and supplies with draft animals, much as it had done in the previous world war.[9]

After the initial failure of December 1941, the Germans made some gestures toward increased production, but they still did not fully mobilize for war. Instead, only one of the three major army formations in the east—Army Group South—was reequipped prior to the 1942 campaign, and even in Army Group South the divisions were typically manned and equipped to no more than 85 percent of authorized strength.[10] By the time 16th Panzer Division reached the Volga after two months of campaigning, for example, it probably had no more than 75 functioning tanks, and its motorized infantry had already suffered significant casualties. Elite units such as the *Waffen* (Combat) SS were the only exceptions, receiving almost full equipment and replacements before the second offensive began. All of these issues of logistics and geography, it must be noted, weakened the offensive before the first German soldier set foot on the streets of Stalingrad.

OPERATION BLAU, 1942

The 1941 Barbarossa campaign had sought to overthrow the Soviet regime and occupy most of European Russia. By contrast, the 1942 Blau (Blue) plan called for a simpler but ultimately more ambitious goal—the seizure of the Caucasus oil fields to remedy one of Germany's most pressing resource shortages. Hitler was probably correct to choose these oil fields over another attempt on the political capital of Moscow. Still, the distances involved made the 1941 logistical issues appear minor in comparison to those of the new campaign. Ironically, the original plan for Operation Blau, issued in Führer Directive No. 41 on 5 April 1942, barely mentioned the city of Stalingrad, indicating that it should be neutralized by fire as the German advance passed by en route to the oil fields.[11]

Still, the 1942 campaign began auspiciously for the Germans. Between 8 May and 3 July, the understrength German Eleventh Army and its Romanian allies cleared the Crimean Peninsula and captured the fortress city of Sevastopol', a feat that earned Eleventh Army's commander, Erich von Manstein, a field marshal's baton. Meanwhile, excessive Soviet optimism had led to the disastrous Second Battle of Khar'kov in which Marshal Semen Konstantinovich Timoshenko, Stalin's old comrade from the Russian Civil War, sacrificed two field armies—1,249 tanks and nearly 267,000 casualties—in a vain attempt to strike preemptively at the gathering German force.[12] In his first battle as commander of Sixth Army, General Paulus had been typically cautious in his tactics, but the resulting German counterattacks placed Army Group South in an excellent position to launch the main Blau offensive on 28 June.

The Soviet *Stavka* [headquarters, Supreme High Command] played into German hands by focusing on Moscow as the most likely goal of the new German offensive. As a result, the *Stavka* concentrated its best units for the defense of that city, leaving the southern flank relatively weak. As late as 5 July, Soviet intelligence estimates still considered Blau to be a deception operation in preparation for a subsequent offensive toward Moscow.

Therefore, when the Blau offensive began at the end of June 1942, its initial progress rivaled the triumphal advances of the previous summer. Paulus's Sixth Army and Colonel General Maximilian von Weichs's temporary army group (consisting of the German Fourth Panzer and Second Armies, supported by the Hungarian Second Army) rolled forward at considerable speed in the early days of July. In some instances, Soviet troops panicked, and Soviet commanders proved unable to coordinate the mechanized (tank) units that had been reconstituted over the winter and the new tank corps and armies that were formed in the spring and early summer. The attacking Germans completely destroyed four of the Red Army's new tank "corps"—actually the size of small armored divisions—in the first ten days of operations and seriously damaged five more. However, although Stalin ordered his armies in the south to stand and fight and the Germans encircled and destroyed most that did, the *Wehrmacht* took far fewer prisoners in 1942 than in 1941. In the first month of Operation Blau, the four Soviet *front* commands opposite the advance lost 370,522 men killed or captured—a colossal number equal to about one-quarter of their initial strength but far less than the disasters of the previous year.[13] Instead, most of the encircled Soviet troops escaped into the countryside, some going to ground, joining or forming partisan bands, or ultimately making their way back to Red Army lines and others falling back in good order, all the while inflicting casualties on their pursuers.

Worse still for the Germans, egged on by Stalin and his *Stavka,* who were impatient to defeat the new German offensive, the Red Army began an incessant series of counterattacks at every level of command. Many of these early attacks failed because of poor command and control, complicated by well-meaning interference from the *Stavka* in Moscow. Inexperienced Soviet commanders often tried to lead from the rear, using written orders because of an obsessive concern for radio communications security. Cumulatively, however, the Red defenders slowed and in some instances halted the German advance while continuing to weaken their opponents. In particular, the Soviet Briansk and Voronezh Fronts hammered away at the Axis defenders around the Don River city of Voronezh, the left shoulder of the steady German advance southeastward, deflecting German forces from the point of their main attack farther south. These offensives recurred frequently throughout the summer and fall. Although the Soviet attacks always failed, they nonetheless gave German commanders cause for concern and pinned down critical troop units in the Voronezh region along the Don.

Hitler and Stalin each underestimated his opponent's armies, refusing to recognize the reasons why offensive plans were so often stymied. Stalin's solution was to constantly change commanders and commit more reserve forces until he found leaders whom he could trust to stem the invading tide. Hitler, however, had no strategic reserves to send except his lightly equipped Axis allies. This lack of reserves and the resulting inability to influence affairs undoubtedly contributed to the dictator's increasing frustration with his subordinates. As early as 3 July, Hitler had disagreements with Bock and his other commanders, insisting that they move faster to prevent the supposed escape of enemy forces that Hitler thought were fleeing in disorder. Field commanders such as Hoth and Paulus, on the other hand, felt compelled to move cautiously and protect their flanks from the newly effective foe.

Marshal Fedor von Bock, the army group commander who initially commanded the entire campaign, was caught in an unenviable position between national and tactical viewpoints. On the one hand, the field marshal understood his subordinates' caution and sometimes defended them from criticism by Hitler and Halder. On the other hand, however, Bock was sufficiently out of contact with tactical reality that he shared Hitler's belief that the Germans must accelerate their advance to prevent the enemy from fleeing. His diary of the early days of the offensive is replete with statements of frustration about the slow pace of advance:

> [3 July 1942]—The enemy . . . had gradually learned from past experience. The enemy will withdraw in time, as he tried to do, though so far not altogether successfully in all the battles this year. It is therefore important that we attack as soon as possible. . . .
>
> [5 July 1942]—[When Bock urged Paulus to redeploy infantry units to relieve the panzers at Voronezh] The answer came that the right wing of the 6th Army can only attack when the enemy is gone! . . . Hoth's old aversion against the attack was expressed in an intercepted radio communication. . . .
>
> [8 July 1942]—At noon I submitted a telex to Halder, in which I said that the enemy was without any doubt retreating in front of the 6th Army's entire front and also south of it, and that, as presently deployed by the Army Command [Halder], the double-sided envelopment will probably hit nothing.[14]

Although Bock fundamentally agreed with Halder and Hitler, the two headquarters worked at cross-purposes during July, with Halder (on Hitler's orders) second-guessing the field commanders. This friction, born of differing viewpoints of the same situation, continued to build through July and August until it led to wholesale dismissals of German general officers in September 1942. Ironically, the field army commanders most responsible for the slowness of the advance survived, while higher-level officials such as Halder and Bock were relieved. Thus, in the course of the 1942 campaign, Hitler gradually lost faith in his generals, while Stalin increasingly came to trust selected subordinates.

TO STALINGRAD

Hitler's dissatisfaction with Bock contributed to his decision, effective 7 July, to divide the offensive forces of Operation Blau into two different army groups (see Table 1).

In planning for Operation Blau, the German staffs had foreseen the need for two different army groups to control the vast new territories, with Bock's Army Group B protecting the ever-lengthening eastern flank while List's Army Group A focused on the ultimate prize of the Caucasus oil fields. Bock

Table 1. The General Organization of Army Groups B and A on 7 July 1942

Army Group B – Field Marshal Fedor von Bock
   Armeegruppe von Weichs – Colonel General Maximilian von Weichs
      Headquarters, Second Army
      LV Army Corps
      Fourth Panzer Army – Colonel General Hermann Hoth
         XIII, VII, and XXIX Army Corps; and
         XXIV, XXXXVIII Panzer Corps.
      Hungarian Second Army – Colonel General Gusztav Jany
         Hungarian III Army Corps
      Sixth Army – General of Panzer Troops Friedrich Paulus
         VIII, XVII, and LI Army Corps; and
         XXXX Panzer Corps.
   VIII Air Corps
   Reserve – Hungarian IV Army Corps
Army Group A – Field Marshal Wilhelm List
   First Panzer Army– Colonel General Ewald von Kleist
      XI and XXXXIV Army Corps;
      III and XIV Panzer Corps; and
      Romanian VI Army Corps.
   Seventeenth Army (*Armeegruppe* Ruoff) – Colonel General Richard Ruoff
      IV and LII Army and XXXXIX Mountain Army Corps;
      LVII Panzer Corps; and
      Italian Expeditionary Corps.
   Reserve
      V Army Corps;
      Headquarters, Italian Eighth Army, with Italian II Army Corps; and
      Hungarian IV and VI Army Corps.

had argued bitterly against this violation of the unity of command, and his continued disagreements about the operational needs of the campaign contributed to his dismissal on 13 July. Weichs, the able commander of a temporary group built around his Second Army, moved up to command Army Group B.[15]

Quite apart from these personnel changes, in bureaucratic terms the creation of two army groups led almost inevitably to the development of two different operational missions at a time when German logistical capabilities were once again hard-pressed to support a single advance southward. Although the creation of these two headquarters did not make German overextension inevitable, this decision moved the *Wehrmacht* a long way toward that mistake. On 13–14 July, the German Army headquarters (*Oberkommando des Heeres*, or OKH) transmitted new teletype orders to Weichs. Without mentioning Stalingrad, these orders modified the existing operations plan (Blau III, or Operation Braunschweig): Fourth Panzer Army and two corps of Sixth Army were to join Army Group A for the advance southward while the remainder of Sixth Army was to turn eastward, becoming a flank guard toward the Don River (see Map 2).[16]

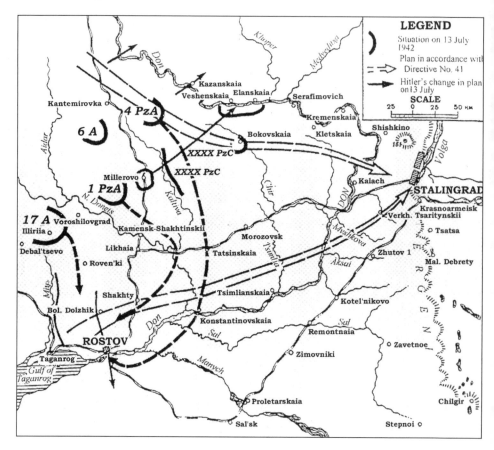

Map 2. Hitler's change in plan, 13 July 1942

By 27 July, Army Group A had cleared Rostov on the lower Don River, the next step on the long road to the Caucasus. In the process, the Germans wrecked the Soviets' Southwestern Front and seriously damaged their Southern Front. Pleased to finally see progress, the German dictator had already issued Führer Directive No. 45 on 23 July. In essence, Hitler tried to continue the victorious advance of Army Group A while redirecting much of its forces eastward. So the two German army groups would advance on two divergent axes—Stalingrad and the Caucasus—while defending in a third direction—the Voronezh shoulder. Army Group B's role was not only to protect Voronezh and the lengthening eastern flank but to deal with "a concentration of enemy force groups [that] has been detected in the Stalingrad

region, which [Marshal Timoshenko] apparently intends to defend stubbornly" (see Map 3).[17]

The city of Stalingrad, almost ignored in the original planning, now became, almost inevitably, a magnet pulling Army Group B eastward. Stalingrad was situated at the point where the Don and Volga Rivers came closest
to each other, making it a major communications hub as well as a significant
industrial center that produced Soviet tanks and artillery. Indeed, had the
Germans been able to take Stalingrad and interdict the Volga River traffic,
they would have significantly reduced Soviet tank production while subjecting Soviet north-south logistical communications to strains at least as great as
those going on behind the German lines. Moreover, the Volga River appeared
to be a more defensible flank guard position than the Don. Yet the clinching
argument, at first unspoken, was the name of the city. In an ideological, na-
tionalistic war to the death, the side that possessed a great city named for one
of the two dictators would have an unparalleled advantage in terms of morale
and propaganda. Thus, Stalingrad came to have an emotional value out of all
proportion to its actual strategic and economic worth.

Sixth German Army assumed this new task. In addition to XXIX, XVII,
VIII, and LI Army Corps, it now controlled XIV Panzer Corps, with the
three divisions mentioned above, plus XXIV Panzer Corps' headquarters
with 24th Panzer Division attached.

Meanwhile the Soviet dictator took his own actions to defend Paulus's
objective. Late on 22 July, Stalin ordered the creation of two new headquarters—1st and 4th Tank Armies—within Stalingrad Front. The nuclei for these
new formations were the staffs of the destroyed 38th and 28th Armies.[18] The
creation of these two armies clearly indicated Stalin's intention to employ
these armies in a concerted counterstroke. Each of the new tank armies received control of two fresh tank corps plus three rifle divisions transferred
from Far Eastern Front and two antitank and antiaircraft artillery regiments.
Stalin assigned Lieutenant General Vasilii Dmitrievich Kriuchenkin, former
commander of 28th Army, to command 4th Tank Army, and Major General Kirill Semenovich Moskalenko, who during July had conducted a tough
if unsuccessful maneuver defense against Army Group A, to command 1st
Tank Army.

Josef Stalin and his chief of staff, General Aleksandr Mikhailovich Vasilevsky, chose this occasion to end the previous policy of defending along
successive lines and conducting fighting withdrawals in favor of a more rigid
defense. On 28 July 1942, the People's Commissariat of Defense issued an
order drafted by Vasilevsky and rewritten by Stalin. Officially labeled Order
No. 227, the decree became famous for its title, *Ni Shagu Nazad!* (Not a Step
Back!). This remarkably frank document provided a reasoned explanation
for the need to stand and fight the overextended invaders. Stalin ordered all

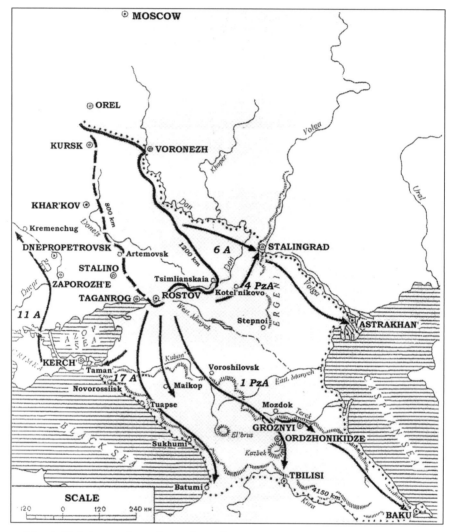

Map 3. Hitler's new plans of 23 and 30 July 1942

commanders to "unconditionally liquidate the mood of retreat in the forces and halt the propaganda that we must and can supposedly retreat farther to the east and that such a retreat will supposedly not be harmful." Soviet commanders were to "relieve from their posts . . . commanders and their commissars who permit unauthorized retreats by their forces from occupied positions without an order from [their senior commanders] and send them to the *Stavka* [or *fronts*] for trial by military court."[19] In short, the time for strategic withdrawals had ended, and the Soviet dictator expected his armies to defend in place.

While Stalin and the *Stavka* were adjusting their defenses along the Stalingrad and Caucasus axes, on 27 July the forward elements of Paulus's Sixth Army began advancing eastward across the Chir River toward the Don. As they crossed the Chir, Sixth Army's advancing panzers encountered forward detachments of Major General Vladimir Iakovlevich Kolpakchi's 62nd Army, precipitating a weeklong battle that intensified steadily as the Germans advanced.

This set the pattern for three subsequent attacks over the next month. Each time that the Germans gathered their forces to advance eastward, they encountered new Soviet defenses. Each time Paulus's men prevailed, shattering the Soviet defenders and warding off attempted counterstrokes by 1st and 4th Tank Armies. Still, after each success the Germans had to stop, reshuffle available troops, reassemble fuel and ammunition, and launch another deliberate attack. Instead of an easy advance, the march eastward into the Great Bend in the Don River and finally to the northern suburbs of Stalingrad consumed more and more of the resources of Army Group B. The German forces and logistics were simply insufficient to conduct simultaneous major advances to the east and south, and Paulus's men paid a steady toll for this weakness.

Army Group A was equally overextended. Field Marshal Ewald von Kleist's First Panzer Army had begun the summer offensive with a lower level of equipment than the other elements of Army Group South because it originally had only a supporting role in the offensive. Now, however, First Panzer and Seventeenth Armies were leading the effort to reach the oil fields. By the time they reached Rostov in late July, the one Slovak and six German mobile divisions in these two armies totaled only 235 functioning tanks, for an average of 38 per division. The problems were compounded by the fact that even the equipment that *was* available in quantity, including the basic greatcoat, high boots, and type 98 rifle of the infantry units, proved unsuited for fighting in the Caucasus mountains.[20]

GERMAN LEADERSHIP

A host of famous names commanded in both armies during the 1942 campaign. However, the focus of this volume is on the tactical operations of the two armies in Stalingrad and those on the immediate flanks; thus it is appropriate to start with the field commanders for that struggle.

As head of German Sixth Army, the ultimate loser in this struggle, Friedrich Paulus has become a controversial figure in German military history.[21] Born in 1890, the son of a minor civil servant, Paulus advanced in army and society because he was both bright and hardworking, if somewhat withdrawn and high-strung. Slender, tall, and perfectly dressed, he appeared to be the model officer. He spent World War I as a staff captain at battalion and regimental level. Between the world wars, Paulus pursued the standard career of a German General Staff specialist, interrupted only twice for brief, obligatory assignments with troops. After the 1940 campaign, Paulus reached the penultimate position in his career field as *Oberquartiermeister* I, or Deputy Chief of the Army General Staff, under General Franz Halder. As such, Paulus drafted the original plan for Operation Barbarossa, although he later claimed to have doubts about the outcome of the campaign.[22]

The refined, introverted Paulus was never comfortable arguing with rough and assertive men such as Hitler, but he recognized the considerable ability of such leaders, and they in turn valued his loyal service as a meticulous subordinate. Given Hitler's growing desire for minions who would faithfully execute their Führer's orders, it was perhaps inevitable that Friedrich Paulus would receive a starring role in the 1942 campaign. On 5 January 1942, the man who had never commanded anything larger than a battalion was promoted to colonel general and appointed to head the German Sixth Army, one of the spearheads of Plan Blau. The quintessential staff officer had become a major field commander, a position to which he was suited by education and intelligence but not, perhaps, by temperament.

If Paulus had the starring role in the German assault on Stalingrad, Colonel General Herman Hoth was his supporting actor as commander of the neighboring Fourth Panzer Army. Born in 1885, Hoth became one of Germany's most experienced armored tacticians. He commanded a panzer corps in France in 1940 with such skill that in 1941 he began the invasion of the Soviet Union as commander of Third Panzer Group, then shifted to command Seventeenth Army. In 1942, as we have already seen, his Fourth Panzer Army was often the bill-payer for changes in mission, including providing a steady stream of units to support Paulus's attack on Stalingrad.

Many of the senior German commanders between Paulus and Hoth in the field and Adolph Hitler at the national level found themselves, like Bock, unemployed when the dictator finally lost patience with what he perceived as foot-dragging. One exception was Colonel General Maximilian, *Freiherr* [Baron] von Weichs, commander of Army Group B throughout the fall of 1942. Born in 1881, Weichs was a gaunt, bespectacled cavalryman from a family of soldiers. He commanded German Second Army from the start of Operation Barbarossa until he succeeded Bock in July 1942. His army group eventually grew to include not only Fourth Panzer, Second, and Sixth Armies but also a host of satellite formations, including Hungarian Second, Italian Eighth, and Romanian Third and Fourth Armies. Despite this apparent wealth of resources, Weichs's problem throughout the Stalingrad campaign was to protect his long left flank while constantly reshuffling units to provide the combat power needed to sustain Paulus's advance. Despite his usual competence, Weichs found himself shunted aside once the Soviets counterattacked in November, with most of Army Group B being either shattered by the Soviets or resubordinated under Field Marshal Manstein for the vain attempt to save Sixth Army.

If Weichs, Paulus, and Hoth planned and supervised the battle for Stalingrad with Hitler's intimidating presence influencing their every move, the generals commanding Sixth Army's and Fourth Panzer Army's corps in and around the city directed the increasingly complex and frustrating day-to-day and hour-to-hour tactical struggle. These included Generals Seydlitz and Kempf, the commanders of LI Army and XXXXVIII Panzer Corps, whose infantry and panzer corps faced the daunting task of clearing Russian forces from the city, and Generals Heitz and Wietersheim, the leaders of VIII Army and XIV Panzer Corps, whose infantry and tanks fought prolonged battles north and northwest of the city to keep counterattacking Soviet forces at bay.

Born in 1888, General of Artillery Walter von Seydlitz-Kurzbach, scion of a Prussian Junker family, fought as a junior officer in World War I and rose to the rank of colonel in command of 22nd Artillery Regiment in 1936. Promoted to major general in 1940 and lieutenant general in 1941, Seydlitz led 12th Infantry Division throughout Operation Barbarossa. After Soviet forces encircled II Army Corps in the Demiansk region in January 1942, Seydlitz headed a Special Corps that carved a corridor through to the encircled corps. Appointed general of artillery in June 1942, Seydlitz led LI Army Corps during Sixth Army's advance to Stalingrad. During the ensuing fall, Seydlitz's infantry were responsible for uprooting Soviet 62nd Army's forces from the city's ruins.[23]

General of Panzer Troops Werner Kempf, who shared with Seydlitz the awesome task of seizing Stalingrad, was born in 1886 and had served as an infantry officer before transferring to the German Army's panzer arm in the late 1930s. Rising rapidly in command, he led 4th Panzer Brigade in 1937, composite "Division Kempf" during the Polish campaign in 1939, 6th Panzer Division during the Western campaign in 1940, and XXXXVIII Motorized Corps during Operation Barbarossa. Kempf's panzers spearheaded First Panzer Army's advance during the summer and fall of 1941 and Hoth's Fourth Panzer Army's drive to the lower Don River and Stalingrad in the summer of 1942. Presumably, Kempf's three armored divisions, 14th and 24th Panzer and 29th Motorized, were to provide Hoth and, later, Paulus with the shock power necessary to overcome 62nd Army's defenses in and around Stalingrad city.[24]

General of Artillery Walter Heitz was born in 1878 and served as an artillery officer during World War I. A teacher in an artillery school and artillery battalion commander in the 1920s, he commanded the Juterbog Artillery School and served as commandant of the Konigsberg Fortress and as president of the Reich's War Court during the 1930s. A general of artillery by 1937, Heitz received field command on 25 October 1939 when he was assigned command of VIII Army Corps. He led this corps in the French campaign of 1940, in Operation Barbarossa, and, under Sixth Army, in Operation Blau, when his infantry shared responsibility for defending Stalingrad's northern flank with XIV Panzer Corps.[25]

The commander of XIV Panzer Corps, General of Infantry Gustav Anton von Wietersheim had led his corps since late 1938 except for a brief stint when he served as chief of staff of German Forces in the West. Born in 1884 and an infantry officer early in his military career, Wietersheim commanded 29th Infantry Division (Motorized), one of the army's finest mobile divisions, from 1936 to 1938, earning a reputation as one of the army's premier specialists in motorized operations. In command of XIV Army Corps (Motorized), he participated in the Polish campaign in 1939, Operation Barbarossa in 1941, and Operation Blau. Despite Wietersheim's stellar performance in corps command, Hitler denied him command of an army, probably because he had openly questioned the Führer's plan for operations in the West.[26]

SOVIET COMMANDERS

On the Soviet side, the closest counterpart to Paulus was Lieutenant General Vasilii Ivanovich Chuikov, the 41-year-old commander of 64th Army in July 1942 and then 62nd Army in September.[27] The son of a peasant, Chuikov had risen to command a regiment during the Russian Civil War but had earned temporary disgrace as commander of 9th Army during the ill-fated 1939–1940 war with Finland. As a result, Chuikov found himself relegated in 1940 to an obscure role as the Soviet military attaché to China. Eventually, he talked his way back to an assignment in European Russia after the German invasion, but an automobile accident took him out of action for more than a year. Thus he did not meet the Germans in battle until the summer of 1942, when he salvaged something from the repeated defeats of that summer. Chuikov proved to be the type of commander that Stalin had called for in *Not a Step Back!*—energetic, profane, technically competent, and utterly ruthless, sacrificing commanders and whole units with a calculated rather than impulsive mind. In the long, attritional struggle for Stalingrad, Chuikov's stamina and iron nerve proved more effective than Paulus's high-strung brilliance.

The Soviet command structure shifted repeatedly during the Battle of Stalingrad, but for most of the time Chuikov fell under Stalingrad Front, newly formed from the remnants of the shattered Southwestern Front. At this level, two figures reigned supreme: Lieutenant General Andrei Ivanovich Eremenko, the *front* commander, and his Member of the Military Council commissar, Nikita Sergeevich Khrushchev. Whereas Khrushchev later became legendary as head of the Soviet Union, Eremenko is familiar only to specialists. Eremenko had joined the Tsarist Army in 1913 and the Red Army in 1918, serving as the chief of staff of a cavalry brigade and deputy commander of a cavalry regiment during the Civil War. Between the world wars, he followed a standard progression of military schooling and commands, including extensive experience with mechanized forces.[28]

In early July 1941, shortly after the war began, the *Stavka* recalled Eremenko from the Far East and appointed him deputy commander of Western Front, followed by command of the ill-fated Briansk Front in the defense of Moscow. In December, after Eremenko recuperated from wounds he had suffered during this campaign, Stalin reassigned him as commander of the newly formed 4th Shock Army, one of three such armies destined to spearhead the Red Army's counteroffensive in the Moscow region. Eremenko's success in this role led the dictator to appoint him commander of Stalingrad Front in August 1942.

In his new capacity, Eremenko had to be even more ruthless than Chuikov, allocating just enough men and munitions so that 62nd Army could prevent German victory in Stalingrad while holding back most of his strength for the coming great counteroffensive. Thus Eremenko and his commissar, Khrushchev, remained east of the Volga, surrounded by the constant roar of Chuikov's artillery (which was located on the far bank for lack of depth on the battlefield). Had Stalingrad Front's leaders actually lived in Stalingrad rather than visiting it on rare occasions, they might have become involved personally in the day-to-day struggle and thus lose their objectivity about the larger issues of the campaign.

Between Stalingrad Front and Stalin himself, two other generals appear repeatedly in this story: Zhukov and Vasilevsky.

Army General Georgii Konstantinovich Zhukov was Stalin's favorite general even before the 1942 campaign. During the Russian Civil War, Zhukov had become a junior member of Stalin's "cavalry clique" of officers who had served with the future dictator. In August 1939, Zhukov defeated the Japanese Kwantung Army in an undeclared war in the Far East, a victory that led to his rapid advancement to senior command and staff positions in the Red Army. Once the war broke out, he became one of the first "representatives of the *Stavka*," Stalin's designated troubleshooters (or "fixers") whenever a field commander faltered.

As a commander, Zhukov earned lasting fame for his tenacious defense of Leningrad in September 1941 and Moscow in October–November 1941. He then planned and conducted the Red Army's counteroffensive in the Moscow region from December 1941 through April 1942. In all these endeavors, he displayed a ruthless determination, although the Red Army still lacked the combat power to completely defeat the Germans.

In August 1942, at the culminating moment of the German Blau offensive, Stalin rewarded Zhukov by anointing him as Deputy Supreme Commander. Zhukov subsequently played a key role in planning the Red Army's strategic counteroffensives at Stalingrad (Operation Uranus) and in the Rzhev region (Operation Mars). In the latter offensive, he coordinated the operations of his Western Front and the neighboring Kalinin Front in a vain attempt to build upon the German defeat at Stalingrad.[29]

If Zhukov was Stalin's favorite field commander, his best staff officer was 47-year-old Aleksandr Mikhailovich Vasilevsky. A former infantry officer, Vasilevsky advanced through merit alone and joined the General Staff after his graduation from the General Staff Academy in the class of 1937, a course that was shortened by the start of Stalin's massive purges of the Red Army. A brilliant planner, Vasilevsky had gained Stalin's trust when he remained in Moscow during the 1941 German attacks on the capital while most of the government had evacuated the city. Rising from colonel to colonel-general in four years, Vasilevsky became Chief of the General Staff in June 1942 and a deputy People's Commissar of Defense in October.[30] Despite these responsibilities in Moscow, Vasilevsky, like Zhukov, frequently visited forward headquarters as a representative of the *Stavka*.

Although history has accorded Chuikov, who planned and supervised his 62nd Army's skillful defense of Stalingrad city, much of the credit for defeating Operation Blau, five other army commanders played an indirect though equally decisive role in the ensuing Soviet victory. These generals were K. A. Moskalenko, V. D. Kriuchenkin, D. T. Kozlov, and R. Ia. Malinovsky, whose 1st Guards, 4th Tank, 24th, and 66th Armies figured prominently in the Stalingrad and Don Fronts' counterstrokes in the Kotluban' region northwest of Stalingrad, and M. S. Shumilov, whose 64th Army did the same from its bridgehead at Beketovka, south of the city.

The first of these five generals was Kirill Semenovich Moskalenko, an experienced 40-year-old officer when the *Stavka* assigned him command of 1st Guards Army in August 1942. After joining the Red Army in 1920, he fought as a cavalryman in the Civil War and rose to lead 1st Special Cavalry Division in the Far East and a rifle regiment in the Kiev Special Military District's 2nd Mechanized Corps during the 1930s. A 1939 graduate of the Dzerzhinsky Political-Military Academy, Moskalenko fought in the Finnish War of 1939–1940 and the invasion of Romanian Bessarabia in the spring of

1940. During Operation Barbarossa, he commanded 1st Motorized Antitank Artillery Brigade in June and July 1941 and led 5th Army's 15th Rifle Corps in September 1941, miraculously escaping the Kiev encirclement. When the Red Army launched its successful counteroffensive in the winter of 1941–1942, Moskalenko headed 13th Army's Cavalry-Mechanized Group during its victory at Elets in December 1941 and Southwestern Front's 6th Army and 6th Cavalry Corps during the Barvenkovo-Lozovaia offensive in January and February 1942. Recognized for his audacity and keen skills as a tactician, despite leading 38th Army's unsuccessful defense during the initial stages of Operation Blau and 1st Tank Army during its fierce but failed counterstroke in the Great Bend in August, Moskalenko was assigned to command the Red Army's 1st Guards Army on the eve of the struggle for Stalingrad city.[31]

The second of the five Stalingrad generals was Vasilii Dmitrievich Kriuchenkin, who was assigned command of 4th Tank Army in late July 1942. Born in 1894, Kriuchenkin was a veteran of World War I and the Civil War who joined the Red Guards in 1917 and the Red Army in 1918. A graduate of cavalry courses in 1926 and 1935 and the Frunze Academy in 1941, he commanded 14th Cavalry Division during the Soviet invasion of eastern Poland in September 1939 and during the first few months of Operation Barbarossa, when his cavalrymen fought skillfully during Southern Front's withdrawal across the Ukraine and Donbas regions. Kriuchenkin then commanded 5th Cavalry Corps during Southwestern Front's victory at Elets in December 1941 and the Barvenkovo-Lozovaia offensive in January and February 1942. Although his 3rd Guards Cavalry Corps suffered defeat during the disastrous Khar'kov operation in May 1942, Kriuchenkin received command of 4th Tank Army on 22 July 1942, just in time to lead it in its failed counteroffensive in August against Paulus's Sixth Army in the Great Bend.[32]

Dmitri Timofeevich Kozlov, the third of these army commanders, was a former *front* commander who received command of 9th Reserve (24th) Army in August 1942 at age 41. Born in 1893, he fought in World War I and the Civil War and against the Basmachi insurgency in Central Asia. A graduate of the *Vystrel'* Officers Course and Frunze Academy in the 1920s, he commanded a rifle corps during the Finnish War in 1939–1940. Promoted to lieutenant general in June 1940, Kozlov headed the Trans-Caucasus Military District from January through June 1941 and the Trans-Caucasus and Crimean Fronts from August 1941 through January 1942. While a *front* commander, Kozlov secured the Soviet Union's southern borders with Turkey and Iran during the first six months of war and conducted the successful amphibious operation at Kerch' in December 1941. Although Kozlov was disgraced because of his *front*'s disastrous defeat at Kerch' in May 1942, Stalin nevertheless retained him as an army commander.[33]

The fourth Stalingrad general was Rodion Iakovlevich Malinovsky, ultimately one of the Red Army's most successful senior commanders, who took command of 66th Army in August 1942 at age 43 after being demoted from *front* command. Malinovsky was a veteran of World War I and the Civil War who commanded a machine-gun crew in the Russian Expeditionary Corps in France and served in a foreign regiment of the French Army from 1916 to 1918. Returning to Russia in 1919, he led a platoon and battalion during the Civil War and rose to command 3rd Cavalry Corps in the mid-1930s. After service as a "volunteer" on the Republican side in the Spanish Civil War, Malinovsky taught briefly at the Frunze Academy, was promoted to major general in June 1940, and commanded the Kiev Special Military District's 48th Rifle Corps from March to August 1941 when his corps performed credibly during fighting in the Ukraine. Thereafter, he led 6th Army from August to December 1941, when his forces helped defeat First Panzer Group at Rostov, as well as Southern Front from December 1941 through the initial stages of Operation Blau. Although Malinovsky lost his command because of his defeat during Blau, Stalin nevertheless valued him enough to assign him command of 66th Army.[34]

The last of these five army commanders was Mikhail Stepanovich Shumilov, who was assigned command of 64th Army in early August 1942 and in early September found his army isolated in a narrow bridgehead on the eastern bank of the Volga River south of Stalingrad. Born in 1895, Shumilov was a veteran of World War I, joined the Red Army in 1918, and was a company, battalion, and regimental commander during the Civil War. A graduate of a Command-Political Course in 1924 and the *Vystrel'* Officers Course in 1929, Shumilov commanded a rifle regiment and a rifle division in the 1920s and 1930s before receiving his baptism of fire leading a rifle corps during the invasion of eastern Poland in September 1939 and the Finnish War in 1939–1940. During Operation Barbarossa, Shumilov led Northwestern Front's 8th Army during the summer of 1941 and was deputy commander of 55th Army during the battle for Leningrad in the fall of 1941. After Shumilov led Briansk Front's 21st Army in spring of 1942 and the initial stages of Operation Blau, in August the *Stavka* chose him to command 64th Army along the southern approaches to Stalingrad.[35]

THE SOLDIERS

Although many of the generals commanding in the Stalingrad campaign are now famous, the young men they commanded seem far removed from the present day, as if relegated to the basement of time. Photographs of the German and Soviet troops show us groups of fit, usually slender figures

General of Panzer Troops Friedrich Paulus, commander of Sixth Army, meeting with his commanders.

Colonel General Andrei Ivanovich Eremenko, commander of Southeastern and Stalingrad Fronts.

Nikita Sergeevich Khrushchev, Member of the Military Council (Commissar) of the Stalingrad Front.

Lieutenant General Konstantin Konstantinovich Rokossovsky, commander of Don Front.

Lieutenant General V. I. Chuikov, commander of 62nd Army.

Major General Mikhail Stepanovich Shumilov, commander of 64th Army.

struggling in the heat and later the cold of southern Russia. On the German side in particular, the expressions of these young men still reflect well-justified confidence in the prowess of German arms, despite the fact that the German Army's supply of veteran troops was ebbing quickly. While rebuilding their strength during the spring of 1942, some divisions had received soldiers with as little as two months of training under their belts.[36] An army that had always prided itself on its training and tactical skill now had to deal with half-trained recruits and less-than-effective units. On 12 July, for example, General Halder wrote in his diary about the report of a general staff observer who had returned from observing Fourth Panzer and Sixth Armies: "His attention was mostly struck by the poor training apparent in our rehabilitated Armd. Divs., the inadequacies of materiel and the deficiencies of signal communications. The complaints are in part justified, [but] in part they derive from the fact that our troops are spoiled from earlier campaigns."[37]

This began a downward spiral that continued for the rest of the war—inexperienced soldiers with inferior equipment were more likely to die than experienced, well-equipped ones, which only increased the demand for replacements. This, in turn, meant that the new recruits received even shorter periods of training before joining their units, which only reinforced the tendency of German units to suffer from reduced effectiveness and high casualties.

The high turnover in German troops, with its resulting influx of younger men, also contributed to another ongoing trend: the increasing Nazification of the German Army. Most German senior commanders were still the products of the conservative, professional army of World War I and the Weimar Republic and, as such, claimed to be apolitical professionals who would uphold the laws of war. This was true even though some famous generals such as Manstein tended to a blind anti-Semitism that caused them to accept mass murder as necessary to suppress partisan resistance.[38] More generally, by 1942 junior officers and the rank-and-file had grown up under the Nazi regime and often reflected Nazi attitudes.[39] Whatever the generals believed, or claimed to believe, at the tactical level many Germans accepted the racial theories of their Führer, which regarded opponents as uncivilized subhumans. This attitude encouraged Germans to fight with great bravery because they feared capture more than death. Yet the same belief structure had a darker side, making German soldiers guilty of thoughtless abuse and intermittent atrocities against Soviet civilians as well as prisoners of war.

As the training level of the average German soldier declined after 1941, that of his counterpart rose. During Operation Blau, thousands of Soviet soldiers still died for lack of training, but these losses gave the surviving troops and their commanders a growing measure of experience and competence.[40]

The Communist regime had indoctrinated its youth for at least a decade longer than had the Nazi state, and postwar Soviet histories tend to glorify the Socialist spirit of the Red Army soldier. Yet, if anything, the average Soviet soldier may have been less influenced by ideology compared to his Nazi counterpart. Many Red Army men and women of various nationalities were more inspired by the traditional motives of loyalty to comrades and defense of the nation than by their healthy fear of the oppressive Marxist dictatorship and its minions, the commissars and secret police. In fact, beginning in 1941 the Soviet state consciously identified itself with Mother Russia in the struggle against the invaders, an identification that motivated the troops even when they had little use for the Communist Party and for the ethnic Great Russians who dominated the Red officer corps.

Thus, by training, experience, and motivation the Soviet soldier was gradually becoming the equal of his opponent and the superior of many poorly motivated Axis satellite troops. This growing improvement in the Red Army, when combined with declining German combat power and the vast distances of southern Russia, was evolving slowly toward a stalemate in which the Germans could advance no farther.

CHAPTER 2

The Battle in Stalingrad's Suburbs, 3–12 September 1942

AREA OF OPERATIONS

The city of Stalingrad in 1942 was a long, thin strand of urban areas, factory districts, and associated workers' settlements and apartment houses that snaked for more than 40 kilometers along the western bank of the Volga (see Map 4). The city center, at the southern extremity of this strand, was flanked on the north by the factories and factory settlements and, farther to the north, by more towns and villages, the largest of which was Rynok, on high ground north of the Orlovka River. This entire strip was nestled along the eastern slopes and at the base of the heights looming above the river's western bank. To the east, numerous islands in the Volga River and the steppe lands beyond were on far lower ground than the heights to the west.

Once the battle reached into Stalingrad itself, the Soviet defenders had to bring every replacement soldier, every round of ammunition, and every loaf of bread across this broad river, exposed to interdiction by German air and artillery fire from the heights west of the city. For the other side, the terrain in the Stalingrad region made it impossible for the Germans to encircle the city's defenders completely. Therefore, the attackers were eventually forced to conduct costly frontal attacks in an effort to break up the long city into less-defensible segments. Moreover, because the Germans on the heights above the river's western bank were not able to depress their artillery enough to bring intensive direct fire to bear against Soviet forces in the narrow strip of land below, the defenders were able to unload supplies and construct command posts in relative safety.

By Soviet standards, Stalingrad was a model city, with many modern white apartment buildings as well as extensive gardens and parks. A series of landmarks, both man-made and natural, dominated the skyline. Inevitably, these landmarks became military objectives, the goals of both attackers and defenders. In the northern half of the city, four huge factories—from north to south, the Dzerzhinsky Tractor Factory, the Barrikady [Red Barricade] Gun Factory, the Krasnyi Ok'tiabr [Red October] Iron Works, and the Lazur Chemical Factory—would become veritable fortresses and the focal point of intense combat. During the initial days of the fighting in the city's suburbs, the Dzerzhinsky Tractor Factory continued producing T-34

Map 4. Stalingrad and its environs

tanks that went directly into battle. Due west of the Barrikady Factory was Skul'pturnyi Park, a large rectangular relatively open area, and, several hundred meters beyond, the Silikat Factory. Between these larger factories were smaller ones, such as the Brick Factory, just south of the Tractor Factory, and the Bread Factory, one block south of Barrikady.

Northwest and west of these factories were workers' villages, one per factory, flanked on the west by the Mechetka River and its associated Vishnevaia *Balka*, a deep ravine suitable for defense of the factory district against attack from the west. On higher ground farther to the west were two outlying towns, Orlovka and Gorodishche, and the city's airport at Gumrak, which was situated about 10 kilometers northwest of the city.

The most prominent terrain feature in Stalingrad is the Mamaev Kurgan, an ancient Tartar burial mound situated midway between the city's center and its northern factory district. Both sides coveted this 102-meter hill as an observation post. On the northern and southern flanks of Mamaev Kurgan, three deep *balkas* [ravines], the Bannyi to the north and the Krutoi and Dolgii to the south, extend eastward to the Volga, forming formidable barriers to north-south movement and protecting their defenders from observation and artillery fire. West of Mamaev Kurgan and the three ravines were an airfield and associated flying school. Beyond them was a hospital situated on the heights south of Razgulaevka Station on the main railroad line into the center city. Farther south in the city proper stood its main railroad station (Station No. 1), often a site of conflict because it lay just west of the city's Red Square and the principal ferry landing across the river.

The southern end of Stalingrad was separated from the center city by the Tsaritsa River, which flowed through a deep gorge that divided the city itself in half and provided a natural axis for east-west movement, terminating at the Volga River. This part of the city, which was bounded on the south by the El'shanka River, contained another railroad station (Station No. 2) and the huge Grain Elevator (silo) several hundred meters to the southeast. The railroad line from Voroponovo and Sadovaia Station ran eastward along the northern bank of the El'shanka River and then swung northward through the southern section of Stalingrad past Station No. 2 and across the Tsaritsa River to Station No. 1 in Stalingrad's center city. Between the elevator and the railroad was a large collection of factory buildings and warehouses belonging to the city's Food Combine. A cemetery and large barracks complex were on slightly higher ground west of the southern part of the city, and a farm and garden complex with an associated leather factory and Motor Tractor Station were on the heights farther west.

South of the El'shanka River were the suburbs of Minina and Kuporosnoe. The former contained several brick factories on the southern bank of the El'shanka River and a lumber factory and the "Elektroles 25 October" Power Plant on the western bank of the Volga River. The latter, located on a narrower strip of land between the Volga and open agricultural country to the west, included Lumber Factory No. 2.

The terrain around Stalingrad favored three possible approaches into the city. The first ran southward along the western bank of the Volga River from Rynok through Spartanovka, across the Mokraia Mechetka River, and into the city's factory district. The second approach extended southeastward along the road and railroad line from Konnaia Station through Gorodishche and Gumrak Station and then west of Mamaev Kurgan into Stalingrad's center city, terminating at Station No. 1 and Red Square. The third stretched eastward along the railroad and roads north of the El'shanka River from Voroponov Station and Peschanka into the southern part of the city, ending at Station No. 2. Sixth Army's XIV Panzer and LI Army Corps attempted to exploit the first two axes while Fourth Panzer Army's XXXXVIII Panzer Corps entered the city along the third axis.

OPPOSING FORCES

Beginning on 3 September, when the Germans began their assaults on Stalingrad's western and southwestern suburbs, the strength and composition of the two antagonists in and around the city changed constantly, as each side fed troops into what would become the meat grinder of city combat.

On 3 September the strength of Army Group B was roughly 980,000 men, including 580,000 German and 400,000 Allied troops, as opposed to Army Group A's strength of approximately 300,000 German and Allied troops (see Table 2).[1]

Along the Stalingrad axis—that is, the sector of the front from Babka on the Don River southward to Lake Sarpa, which extended from the Italian Eighth Army's left boundary to the right boundary of Fourth Panzer Army's IV Army Corps—on 3 September Army Group B fielded roughly 425,000 troops subordinate to its Italian Eighth, German Sixth, and German Fourth Panzer Armies. Of this number, approximately 30,000 combat troops belonging to Sixth Army's LI Army Corps (389th, 295th, and 71st Infantry Divisions) and 50,000 men of Fourth Panzer Army's XXXXVIII Panzer and IV Army Corps (24th and 14th Panzer, 29th Motorized, 94th Infantry, and Romanian 20th Infantry Divisions), for a total of 80,000 combat soldiers, participated in the initial assault on Stalingrad city.[2] These were later reinforced or replaced in the assault by 100th Jäger, 305th Infantry Divisions, and, in November, two regiments of 79th Infantry Division.

The remainder of Sixth Army, upward of two-thirds its strength, occupied defenses north and northward of the city or farther west along the southern bank of the Don River. The army's XVII and XI Army Corps, with 35,000 and 45,000 troops, respectively, faced the Soviet 21st and 4th Tank Armies along the Don River from the Serafimovich bridgehead eastward to Kachalinskaia. Farther south, VIII Army Corps, with roughly 32,000 men, and XIV Panzer Corps, also with 32,000 men, faced the Soviet 24th, 1st Guards, and 66th Armies between the Don and Volga Rivers. Although the bulk of their forces faced north, because they occupied the narrow corridor to the Volga

Table 2. The Dispositions and Relative Strengths of Army Group B's Forces, 3 September 1942

- **Second Army** (Livny to south of Voronezh) – four army corps, 14 infantry divisions, one panzer division, and roughly 180,000 men;
- **Second Hungarian Army** (south of Voronezh to Babka) – three Hungarian army corps and XXIV Panzer Corps, with nine Hungarian light infantry divisions, one Hungarian armored division, and roughly 100,000 men. In addition, two German infantry divisions (168th and 336th), with roughly 20,000 men in support;
- **Eighth Italian Army** (Babka to Serafimovich) — two Italian and one German army corps, with seven infantry divisions, two cavalry brigades, and about 100,000 men. In addition, two German infantry divisions (294th and 62nd) with about 20,000 men in support;
- **Sixth Army** (Serafimovich to Voroponovo) – one panzer and four army corps and 11 infantry, two panzer, and one motorized divisions, with roughly 200,000 men;
- **Fourth Panzer Army**, two army (one German and one Romanian) and one panzer corps, seven infantry (three German and four Romanian), two panzer, and one motorized division, with about 150,000 men;
- **16th Motorized Division**, with 14,000 men, screening the army group's southern flank;
- **Army group reserves** – one German infantry division (298th), the Italian Alpine Corps, with two mountain divisions and 20,000 men, and Romanian forces, including two army corps, controlling seven infantry, one armored, and two cavalry divisions, with roughly 100,000 men.[1]

---

[1] Estimates of Sixth Army's and Fourth Panzer Army's combined strength vary considerably. For example, the Russian official history, Zolotarev, *VOV*, Book 1: 361, asserts that on 21 August, even before the heavy fighting later in the month, the combined strength of the German Sixth Army and Fourth Panzer Army was 236,000 men, 400 tanks, and 2,800 guns and mortars, and the combined strength of Stalingrad Front's 4th Tank and 62nd and 64th Armies was 148,000 men, 270 tanks, and 1,888 guns and mortars. Of course, the actual combat (line) strengths of these forces were considerably lower. According to Walter Goerlitz, in *Paulus and Stalingrad*, 273, quoting a Sixth Army report dated 0700 hours 22 December 1942, 249,600 German and Romanian troops were encircled at Stalingrad, including 13,000 Romanians and 19,300 *Hiwis* (*Hilfswillige* — Russian volunteer auxiliaries), meaning the combined strength of Sixth Army and Fourth Panzer Army was 227,300 men. If roughly 34,000 German troops were killed during the encirclement battle and about 39,000 escaped, the total strength of the encircled elements of Sixth Army and Fourth Panzer Army in early November was roughly 300,000 men, as opposed to 340,000 men in early September.

River XIV Panzer Corps' three divisions deployed with two-thirds of their forces facing north and the other third facing south toward the city of Stalingrad. Ironically, although history has focused on Sixth Army's struggle for Stalingrad, much more than half of the army's forces did not participate in the battle for the city but were instead involved in the equally, if not more, decisive fighting north and northwest of the city.

At the same time, the Stalingrad and Southeastern Fronts defended the sector from Babka on the Don to Lake Sarpa with a force of eight armies and roughly 550,000 men, roughly 470,000 of which were assigned to their combat armies (see Table 3).

Table 3. The Dispositions and Relative Strengths of the Stalingrad and Southeastern Fronts' Forces, 3 September 1942

Stalingrad Front:

- **63rd Army** (Babka to the Khoper River) – six rifle divisions with about 45,000 men;
- **21st Army** (The Khoper River to the Ilovlia River) – 11 rifle divisions, one destroyer brigade, and three separate tank battalions, with roughly 60,000 men;
- **4th Tank Army** (The Ilovlia River to Kotluban') – five rifle divisions and one tank and one motorized rifle brigade, with about 40,000 men;
- **24th Army** (Kotluban' to 564 km Station) – five rifle divisions and one tank brigade, with about 50,000 men;
- **1st Guards Army** (564 km Station to the Motor Tractor Station) – eight rifle divisions and three tank corps, with roughly 80,000 men; and
- **66th Army** (The Motor Tractor Station to the Volga River) – six rifle divisions and four tank brigades, with about 60,000 men.
  Armor strength – 350–400 tanks

Southeastern Front:

- **62nd Army** (Rynok to Staro-Dubovka) – eight rifle divisions, three rifle brigades, one destroyer brigade, one fortified region, two tank corps, one tank brigade, and two motorized rifle brigades, with 54,000 men;
- **64th Army** (Staro-Dubovka to Ivanovka) – eight rifle divisions, two rifle brigades, one fortified region, and six student officer regiments, with roughly 50,000 men; and
- **57th Army** (Ivanovka to Lake Sarpa) – three rifle divisions and one fortified region, with about 30,000 men.
  Armor strength – about 200–250 tanks[1]

[1] Isaev, *Kogda vnezapnosti uzhe ne bylo*, 80, states that 62nd Army's strength was 54,000, opposed by 100,000 German forces fighting in the city. Rokossovsky, *Velikaia pobeda na Volga*, 154, places 62nd Army's strength at 44,970 men, opposed by 80,240 Germans committed to the city fight. However, Isaev mistakenly includes 76th Infantry Division in his figures, which, if subtracted, brings his count close to Rokossovsky's. The relative strengths of the armies of Stalingrad and Southeastern Fronts cited here are based on the relative strengths of the armies' component divisions and brigades and whether or not they were fresh or had been eroded in previous combat.

In terms of armor support, Sixth and Fourth Panzer Armies were able to muster between 250 and 300 tanks on 3 September, including 35–40 tanks each in 14th and 24th Panzer Division, 60–70 in 16th Panzer Division, and 66 in 22nd Panzer Division, plus 20–30 each in the 3rd, 60th, and 29th Motorized Divisions. These were augmented by 30–40 assault guns, which the Soviets counted as tanks, in 177th, 244th, and 245th Assault Gun Battalions assigned to Army Group B and its subordinate armies and corps.[3] These were opposed by 550–650 tanks in the Stalingrad and Southeastern Fronts. The 350–400 tanks available to Stalingrad Front included about 300 tanks in 4th, 7th, and 16th Tank Corps and 50–100 tanks in 22nd and 28th Tank Corps, seven tank brigades, and four separate tank battalions. The 200–250 tanks in Southeastern Front included 146 tanks supporting 62nd and 64th Armies (with about 50 tanks in 28th Tank Corps and 13 in 23rd Tank Corps), and the remainder in the *front's* 2nd Tank Corps and its tank brigades and separate tank battalions.[4]

The Stalingrad and Southeastern Fronts outnumbered Sixth Army's and Fourth Panzer Army's forces along the Stalingrad axis in terms of personnel and armor, which was nothing new. But with roughly 950 aircraft as opposed to the Soviets' 226, the Germans maintained air superiority.[5]

The actual numbers of troops, tanks, and aircraft available on the battlefield on any given day were affected by factors such as the logistical difficulties experienced by the Germans and the challenge the Soviets faced in bringing weapons and manpower across the Volga River. To cite but one example, *Luftflotte* 4, the air force headquarters supporting Operation Blau, had begun the campaign with 1,600 aircraft but by September had only 950, of which perhaps 550 were operational on any given day.[6] In addition, tanks were constantly entering and exiting each side's active tank park as the fighting proceeded.

Despite this rough correlation of opposing forces, the actual troop deployments on both sides changed constantly to reflect the ebb and flow of combat. Between them, the German Sixth Army and Fourth Panzer Army on 3 September controlled 21 German and four Romanian divisions deployed from the Soviet bridgehead across the Don River at Serafimovich southward to the lake region west of the Volga River south of Stalingrad (see Table 4).

On 3 September XI Army Corps' four infantry divisions were defending the Kletskaia bridgehead. The VIII Army Corps' 305th and 76th Infantry Divisions and XIV Panzer Corps' 3rd and 60th Motorized and 16th Panzer Divisions were defending Paulus's left (northern) wing between the Don and Volga Rivers. However, small elements of XIV Panzer Corps' three mobile divisions were also pressing into Stalingrad's northern suburbs. Meanwhile, Seydlitz's LI Army Corps was assaulting Stalingrad's northwestern and western suburbs with its 389th, 295th, and 71st Infantry Divisions. To the south, Fourth Panzer Army's XXXXVIII Panzer Corps was advancing into the southern third of the city with its 24th Panzer, Romanian 20th, 14th Panzer, and 29th Motorized Divisions and IV Army Corps' 94th Infantry Division.[7]

Thus, slightly in excess of 80,000 German troops initially assaulted the city's defenses, primarily from the northwest, west, and southwest. Initially, the attackers had hoped to roll up the city from the flanks, with XIV Panzer Corps pressing down from the north, XXXXVIII Panzer Corps advancing from the southwest, and LI Corps advancing from the west. However, the counterstroke that Stalingrad Front's armies launched in the Kotluban' region in late August made this plan impossible by drawing XIV Panzer Corps' attention and forces away from the northern approaches to Stalingrad. Thereafter, Sixth Army's LI Corps and Fourth Panzer Army's XXXXVIII Panzer

Table 4. The Organization of Sixth Army and Fourth Panzer Army and Cooperating Army Group B Forces, 3 September 1942 (from north to south)

Sixth Army – General of Panzer Troops Friedrich Paulus
  XVII Army Corps – General of Infantry Karl Hollidt
    79th Infantry Division – Lieutenant General Richard von Schwerin
    113th Infantry Division – Lieutenant General Hans-Heinrich Sixt von Arnim
    22nd Panzer Division – Lieutenant General Wilhelm von Apell
  XI Army Corps – General of Infantry Karl Strecker
    376th Infantry Division – Lieutenant General Alexander Edler von Daniels
    100th Jäger Division – Lieutenant General Werner Sanne
    44th Infantry Division – Lieutenant General Heinrich Deboi
    384th Infantry Division (transferred from VIII Army Corps in early September)
  VIII Army Corps – Lieutenant General Walter Heitz
    384th Infantry Division (transferred to XI Army Corps in early September) —
      Lieutenant General Eccard *Freiherr* von Gablenz
    305th Infantry Division – Lieutenant General Kurt Oppenländer
    76th Infantry Division (transferred from LI Army Corps in early September) –
      Lieutenant General Carl Rodenburg
  XIV Panzer Corps – General of Infantry Gustav von Wietersheim
    60th Motorized Division – Major General Otto Kohlermann
    3rd Motorized Division – Lieutenant General Helmuth Schlömer
    16th Panzer Division – Major General Hans-Valentin Hube
  LI Army Corps – General of Artillery Walter von Seydlitz-Kurzbach
    76th Infantry Division (transferred to VIII Army Corps in early September)
    389th Infantry Division – Lieutenant General Erwin Jänecke
    295th Infantry Division – General of Artillery Rolf Wuthmann
    71st Infantry Division – General of Infantry Alexander von Hartmann

Fourth Panzer Army – Colonel General Hermann Hoth
  XXXXVIII Panzer Corps – General of Panzer Troops Werner Kempf
    24th Panzer Division – Major General Bruno *Ritter* von Hauenschild
    Romanian 20th Infantry Division
    14th Panzer Division – Lieutenant General Ferdinand Heim
    29th Motorized Division – Lieutenant General Max Fremerey
  IV Army Corps – General of Infantry Viktor von Schwedler
    94th Infantry Division – General of Artillery Georg Pfeiffer
    297th Infantry Division – General of Artillery Max Pfeffer
    371st Infantry Division – Lieutenant General Richard Stempel
  Romanian VI Army Corps (Romanian Fourth Army) – Lieutenant
      General Corneliu Draglina
    Romanian 2nd Infantry Division
    Romanian 1st Infantry Division
    Romanian 4th Infantry Division

Army Group B's control:

Italian Eighth Army – Colonel General Italo Gariboldi
  Italian II Army Corps
    294th Infantry Division (German) – General of Infantry Johannes Block
    Italian 5th Infantry Division Cossaria
    Italian 3rd Infantry Division Ravenna

Table 4. (continued)

Italian XXXV Army Corps
    Italian 9th Infantry Division Pasubio Italian 3rd Mobile Division Celere
    Italian 2nd Infantry Division Sforzesca
    Italian 2nd Alpine Division Tridentina
    Italian Cavalry Brigade Barbo
    Italian Blackshirt Cavalry Brigade 3 January
XXIX Army Corps – General of Infantry Hans von Obstfelder
    Italian 52nd Infantry Division Torino
    62nd Infantry Division (German) – Lieutenant General Rudolf Friedrich,
        Major General Richard-Heinrich von Reuss on 15 September

Army Group Control
    Romanian II Army Corps (headquarters only)
    Romanian V Army Corps (headquarters only)
    Romanian 1st Armored Division
    Romanian 1st Cavalry Division
    Romanian 5th Infantry Division
    Romanian 7th Cavalry Division
    Romanian 13th Infantry Division
        16th Motorized Division (German) – (screening the flank in the Elista region by
          early September) – General of Panzer Troops Sigfrid Henrici
        298th Infantry Division (German) – Lieutenant General Arnold Szelinski

Corps conducted a series of frontal attacks against the city, trying to break up the defending Soviet 62nd Army into small pockets while seizing key terrain such as the Mamaev Kurgan and the main ferry sites along the riverbank.

Although almost half of the attackers—initially nine and ultimately 12 out of Sixth Army's and Fourth Panzer Army's 25 divisions—became directly involved in the city fighting, Stalingrad Front's forces and most forces in Southeastern Front remained outside of Stalingrad (see Table 5).[8]

By 3 September, only Lopatin's 62nd Army and less than half of Shumilov's 64th Army, supported by various NKVD and militia troops, were defending the approaches to the city proper. However, even these armies were incomplete because most of their artillery remained on the Volga's eastern bank, shelling the city without actually entering it. This separation was necessary to address two problems: The shallow depth of the Soviet bridgeheads in the city did not leave room for artillery positions, and all troops inside the city had to be resupplied by ferry. Thereafter, 62nd Army's combat strength ebbed and flowed drastically as the battle progressed but probably never exceeded its initial strength of roughly 54,000 men. As further discussed below, the bulk of 64th Army's initial force of 50,000 men was driven from the city entirely, ending up in the Beketovka bridgehead south of the city.

Although psychological and political factors required the Soviet regime to do everything in its power to prevent the city from falling into German hands, military necessity dictated that the Red Army make its main effort

Table 5. The Organization of the Stalingrad and Southeastern Fronts, 3 September 1942 (from north to south)

Stalingrad Front – Colonel General A. I. Eremenko
  63rd Army – Lieutenant General V. I. Kuznetsov
    14th Guards, 1st, 127th, 153rd, 197th, and 203rd Rifle Divisions
  21st Army – Major General A. I. Danilov
    4th and 40th Guards, 23rd, 63rd, 76th, 96th, 124th, 278th, 304th, 321st, and
      343rd Rifle Divisions and 5th Separate Destroyer Brigade
    646th, 647th, and 652nd Separate Tank Battalions
  4th Tank Army – Major General V. D. Kriuchenkin
    27th and 37th Guards, 18th, 214th, and 298th Rifle Divisions,
    193rd Tank Brigade, 22nd Motorized Rifle Brigade, and 40th Armored Train
      Battalion
  24th Army – Major General D. T. Kozlov
    173rd, 207th, 221st, 292nd, and 308th Rifle Divisions
    217th Tank Brigade
  1st Guards Army – Major General of Artillery K. S. Moskalenko
    38th, 39th, and 41st Guards, 24th, 64th, 84th, 116th, and 315th Rifle Divisions
    4th Tank Corps
    7th Tank Corps
    16th Tank Corps
  66th Army – Lieutenant General R. Ia. Malinovsky
    49th, 99th, 120th, 231st, 299th, and 316th Rifle Divisions
    10th, 69th, 148th, and 246th Tank Brigades
  8th Air Army – Lieutenant General of Aviation V. N. Zhdanov
    206th, 226th, and 228th Assault Aviation Divisions
    220th, 268th, 269th, 287th, and 288th Fighter Aviation Divisions
    270th, 271st, and 272nd Fighter Bomber Aviation Divisions
    23rd, 282nd, 633rd, and 655th Mixed Aviation Regiments
    8th Reconnaissance, 714th Light Bomber, and 678th Transport Aviation
      Regiments
  Front Forces:
    3rd Guards Cavalry Corps (5th and 6th Guards and 32nd Cavalry Divisions)
    147th and 184th Rifle Divisions
    13th and 22nd Separate Destroyer Brigades
    54th Fortified Region
    22nd Tank Corps
    28th Tank Corps
    176th Tank Brigade, 648th Separate Tank Battalion, 59th Separate Armored
      Train, and 377th Antiaircraft Armored Train Battalions

Southeastern Front – Colonel General A. I. Eremenko
  62nd Army – Lieutenant General A. I. Lopatin (Lieutenant General
    V. I. Chuikov on 12 September)
    33rd and 35th Guards, 87th, 98th, 196th, 229th, 309th, and 10th NKVD Rifle
      Divisions, 115th, 124th, and 149th Rifle and 20th Separate Destroyer
      Brigades, and 115th Fortified Region
    2nd Tank Corps
    23rd Tank Corps
    20th and 38th Separate Motorized Rifle Brigades
    169th Tank Brigade

Table 5. (continued)

64th Army – Lieutenant General M. S. Shumilov
 36th Guards, 29th, 38th, 126th, 138th, 157th, 204th, and 208th Rifle Divisions, 66th and 154th Naval Rifle Brigades, 10th Reserve (160th Separate) Rifle Brigade, 6 student rifle regiments from the Vinnitsa, Zhitomir, Groznyi, 1st and 2nd Ordzhonikidze Infantry Schools and the Krasnodar Machine Gun-Mortar School, and 118th Fortified Region
 13th Tank Corps
 28th Separate Armored Train Battalion
57th Army – Major General F. I. Tolbukhin
 15th Guards, 244th, and 422nd Rifle Divisions and 76th Fortified Region
 6th Tank Brigade
51st Army – Major General T. K. Kolomiets
 91st and 302nd Rifle Divisions
 115th Cavalry Divisions and 255th Separate Cavalry Regiment
 125th Separate Tank Battalion and 51st Separate Armored Train Battalion
Front Forces:
 77th, 78th, and 116th Fortified Regions and 132nd Destroyer Detachment
 40th, 134th, 135th, 137th, and 255th Tank Brigades, 644th Separate Tank Battalion, and 30th Separate Armored Train Battalion

---

outside the flaming city. Therefore, both the *Stavka* and Eremenko treated the battle in the city like a blazing fire they needed to keep burning, if only to consume German strength and divert German attention from the region in which the decisive battle would be fought—that is, along the Don River and Volga River fronts. Therefore, whenever the Germans seemed to be on the verge of capturing the city and 62nd Army's manpower seemed about to ebb away, the *Stavka* and the *front* commander fed new units into the army—new fuel for the fire—to keep the defense alive and deny victory to the Germans. All the while, however, the Soviet command carefully marshaled its reserves along the Don and Volga Rivers northwest and south of the city, where the decisive battle would occur along increasingly vulnerable flanks of Sixth Army and Fourth Panzer Army.

Just as he had done in the fall of 1941, Stalin worked to ensure there were sufficient forces to implement this strategy as well as other planned offensive operations. He issued numerous directives creating new armies and corps and marshaling fresh reserves, primarily for employment along the Moscow and Stalingrad axes. For example, after forming 66th and 24th Armies on 24 and 26 August and assigning them to Stalingrad Front on 28 August for immediate commitment in the region, early on 31 August the dictator issued virtually identical directives to the Volkhov, Northwestern, Western, Briansk, Voronezh, and Stalingrad Fronts, requiring each to dispatch a specific number of rifle divisions and rifle brigades from their forces to the *Stavka*'s reserve (see Table 6).[9]

Table 6. The Formation of *Stavka* Reserves, 31 August 1942

	Number of Formations and Effective Dates	
Front	10 September	20 September
Volkhov	Two rifle brigades	Four rifle divisions and two rifle brigades
Northwestern	One rifle division and five rifle brigades	One rifle division and three rifle brigades
Western	Five rifle divisions and three rifle brigades	Five rifle divisions and three rifle brigades
Briansk		One rifle brigade
Voronezh	Two rifle divisions and one rifle brigade	Three rifle divisions
Stalingrad	Five rifle divisions	
TOTAL	13 rifle divisions and 11 rifle brigades	13 rifle divisions and nine rifle brigades

Exploiting these forces and other formations already in the *Stavka*'s reserve, Stalin also ordered the formation of five new reserve armies, 4th from the headquarters of 65th Army, which it had already formed only days before, and 10th, 1st, 3rd, and 2nd from scratch (see Table 7).[10]

The 4th and 10th Reserve Armies were situated for employment, either as armies or reinforcing formations, in the Stalingrad region, and 1st Reserve Army was positioned for use in the Voronezh sector. The 3rd and 2nd Reserve Armies were clearly earmarked to reinforce the Kalinin and Western Fronts along the Moscow axis.

In addition, Stalin ordered the Stalingrad Military District transformed into a new 28th Army, effective on 5 September. The new army was to operate on Southeastern Front's left flank and also control the Astrakhan' Military Commissariat and its adjacent territory.[11] To plug the gap between Southeastern Front and 28th Army after it formed at Astrakhan', the *Stavka* also organized a new 7th Rifle Corps, made up of 169th Rifle Division, 141st Rifle Brigade, and three unspecified rifle brigades, and deployed it in the Verkhnii Baskunchak region on the Volga River, 100–120 kilometers southeast of Stalingrad.[12]

Meanwhile, Zhukov sought to keep his offensive options open in the Moscow region, where the armies of his Western and Konev's Kalinin Front were still attacking German Army Group Center's forces in the Rzhev-Viaz'ma salient. To reinforce these forces, Zhukov issued a directive on 31 August reestablishing 43rd Army, whose headquarters had been dormant under the *Stavka*'s control, effective on 10 September. Headed by Lieutenant General

Table 7. The Composition of *Stavka* Reserve Armies, 31 August 1942

Army	Composition	Location
4th (65th)	9th Guards, 193rd, 252nd, 226th, 284th, and 333rd Rifle Divisions	Borisoglebsk, Uriupinsk, Elan', and Arkadak (250–350 kilometers northwest of Stalingrad)
10th	13th Guards, 300th, 62nd, 277th, 45th, and 21st Rifle Divisions	Atkarsk, Balanda, Krasnyi Iar, Kamyshin, and Saratov (180–320 kilometers north of Stalingrad)
1st	293rd and 387th Rifle Divisions, 3 unspecified rifle divisions, and 1 unspecified rifle brigade	Tambov, Rasskazovo, Michurinsk, and Morshansk (200–250 kilometers northeast of Voronezh)
3rd	4 unspecified rifle divisions and 2 unspecified rifle brigades	Vyshnii Volochek, Torzhok, Kalinin, and Klin (80–210 kilometers northwest of Moscow)
2nd	256th and 381st Rifle Divisions, 3 unspecified rifle divisions, and 25th Rifle Brigade	Vologda, Cherepovets, Danilov, and Bui (300–320 kilometers north-northeast of Moscow)

Konstantin Dmitrievich Golubev, who had led 10th, 13th, and 43rd Armies during Operation Barbarossa, 43rd Army consisted of 21st Guards and 262nd Rifle Divisions and 262nd, 32nd, 238th, 279th, and 306th Rifle Divisions from the former 10th Reserve Army.[13] Golubev's army was to assemble in the Volokolamsk, Mozhaisk, Vereia, and Naro-Fominsk regions west of Moscow where, together with the newly formed 2nd and 3rd Reserve Armies, it would be in positions to reinforce either the Kalinin or Western Fronts.[14]

By issuing these directives, Stalin, Zhukov, and the *Stavka* began assembling vital reserves that could be employed to either reinforce 62nd and 64th Armies' sagging defenses around Stalingrad or reinforce planned counterstrokes or counteroffensives in the Stalingrad region, along the Moscow axis, or both. As Stalin and the *Stavka* marshaled fresh strategic reserves, the fighting at Stalingrad reached a new crescendo of violence. Paulus's and Hoth's armies pounded the city's outer defenses, and Stalingrad Front's armies north and northwest of the city desperately tried to smash their way through the Germans' corridor to the Volga River and rescue the city's defenders.

ZHUKOV'S KOTLUBAN' OFFENSIVE, 3–12 SEPTEMBER

The fighting in the Stalingrad region during the first two weeks of September took two forms. First, Sixth Army and Fourth Panzer Army began a concerted assault to pierce 62nd and 64th Armies' defenses protecting

Stalingrad's suburbs and penetrate into the city proper. Second, and simultaneously, Stalingrad Front orchestrated an offensive designed to penetrate the narrow German corridor extending eastward from the Don River to the Volga River north and northwest of the city and reestablish contact with 62nd Army in Stalingrad. Paulus's and Hoth's forces commenced their assaults on Stalingrad's suburbs at dawn on 3 September. Stalingrad Front's armies north of the corridor, now led by Zhukov, attacked German defenses between the Don and Volga Rivers, albeit delayed by a day and ultimately in piecemeal fashion.

Less than a week before, on 26 August, Stalin had appointed Zhukov to the unprecedented position of Deputy Supreme Commander and, to ensure everything possible was being done to defend Stalingrad, dispatched him southward to assume control of Stalingrad's defenses. During the next 48 hours, the dictator formed 24th and 66th Armies, directed they be employed to attack Sixth Army's northern flank, and assigned them to Eremenko's Stalingrad Front. Meanwhile, en route to his new assignment, Zhukov stopped briefly in Moscow to consult with his master and the State Defense Committee. Zhukov reached Eremenko's headquarters in Malaia Ivanovka late on 29 August. Then, pursuant to Stalin's guidance, the Deputy Supreme Commander ordered General Moskalenko to shift the headquarters of his 1st Guards Army from the Kletskaia bridgehead eastward across the Don River to the village of Sadki, 25 kilometers northeast of Kotluban', and his army's forces to the nearby Loznoe region so that they could participate in a new offensive: "Regroup General Moskalenko's 1st Guards Army to the Loznoe region. On the morning of 2 September, it must attack the enemy grouping which has penetrated to the Volga River and link up with 62nd Army. Under the cover of Moskalenko's army, direct the 24th and 66th into their jumping-off regions and immediately commit them into battle; otherwise we can lose Stalingrad."[15]

Moskalenko received Zhukov's order early on 30 August, leaving him only three days to move his forces eastward and make the necessary preparations for the offensive. Once in position, Moskalenko's army was flanked by Malinovsky's 66th Army on its left and Kozlov's 24th Army and Kriuchenkin's 4th Tank Army on its right. Moskalenko's guardsmen were to spearhead a fresh offensive against Sixth Army's VIII Corps. First, however, Moskalenko had to transfer most of his forces and the sectors they occupied to Danilov's 21st Army, transfer his army's 38th and 41st Guards Rifle Divisions to the Loznoe region, and integrate former Group Kovalenko's 39th Guards, 24th, 64th, 84th, 116th, and 315th Rifle Divisions and 4th and 16th Tank Corps, as well as the fresh 7th Tank Corps, into his army.[16] As of 31 August, the three tanks corps in 1st Guards Army fielded 36, 104, and 169 tanks, respectively, for a total of 309 armored fighting vehicles.[17] However, as was the case with other

Soviet tank corps, the tank corps' motorized rifle brigades were woefully understrength, typified by 7th Tank Corps' 7th Motorized Rifle Brigade, which had only 30 percent of its required infantrymen.

From the very start, Moskalenko faced almost insurmountable problems. First, forces being transferred to his army from Group Kovalenko had suffered heavy losses during their intense struggle with Sixth Army's VIII Corps and XIV Panzer Corps in the region south and southeast of Kotluban' from 26 to 28 August. The six rifle divisions had lost up to one-third of their strength, the two tank corps more than 250 of their 350 tanks.[18] By late on 31 August, German counterattacks had driven Kovalenko's forces back to their original jumping-off positions along the 17-kilometer front from north of 564 km Station eastward through Kuz'michi and Hill 139.7 to the dry riverbed of the Sukhaia Mechetka River.[19]

Second, 1st Guards Army and its supporting artillery units were experiencing an acute shortage of artillery pieces. For example, 39th Guards Rifle Division fielded only 19 guns, 24th Rifle Division 42 guns, and 315th Rifle Division 54 guns; making matters worse, half of their surviving antitank guns were weak 45mm models. Third, the relatively fresh reinforcements promised to Moskalenko's army, 38th and 41st Guards Rifle Divisions and Rotmistrov's full-strength 7th Tank Corps, would have to travel up to 200 kilometers to reach their new concentration areas, meaning that many, including Rotmistrov's tanks, did not arrive in their jumping-off positions until late on 2 September, the very eve of the planned attack.[20]

Despite the daunting challenges Moskalenko and his fellow army commanders faced, orders were orders, and at this stage of the war it was not healthy to question superiors. As he had done at Leningrad in September 1941 and at Moscow in November 1941, Zhukov had no choice but to carry out Stalin's orders; he did so with characteristic ruthlessness and abandon.

Even Zhukov, however, could not alter the factors of time and space. Since Moskalenko was not able to concentrate his army fully in its designated jumping-off positions on the night of 1–2 September, during the evening Zhukov authorized him to postpone the start time for the attack from 0500 hours to 1030 hours on 2 September. When these difficulties persisted, at Moskalenko's urging, after midnight on 2 September, Zhukov notified the *Stavka*:

> Because of shortages of fuel and delays in occupying their jumping-off positions, the units making up 1st Guards Army cannot attack on the morning of 2 September. 7th Tank Corps and the M-30 guards-mortar units are also without fuel. The fuel supply departments of the *front* and the armies are not operating [properly]. I cannot conduct the intended attack at 1030 hours. I am taking all measures for the rapid dispatch of

fuel so that the forces can reach their jumping-off positions and attack during the second half of the day, but I am not convinced of the combat readiness of the forces. If the situation permits, I request the attack be postponed to the morning of 3 September 1942.[21]

After receiving the *Stavka's* approval, several hours later Zhukov notified Moscow:

> The 1st Guards Army will begin its operations at 0500 hours on 3 September 1942. The army could not begin its offensive today, 2 September, because the units have not yet managed to reach their jumping-off positions, brought up their fuel and ammunition, and organized themselves for battle. To avoid a disorganized commitment of the forces into combat and consequent unnecessary losses, after a personal inspection on the ground, I decided to postpone the attack until 0500 hours on 3 September.
>
> I have set the offensive of 24th and 66th Armies for 5 or 6 September. At the moment the entire command is engaged in drawing up detailed objectives. We are also taking steps to ensure material support for the operation.[22]

To this message Zhukov mistakenly added, "We have information that the enemy are transferring an additional four infantry divisions to the crossing region [on the Don River], two of them from 1st Guards Army's previous area of operations."[23] This was in error because the Germans were moving only two divisions eastward across the Don on 1 and 2 September. The first, 389th Infantry Division, was destined to reinforce LI Corps' assault on Stalingrad. The second, 305th Infantry Division, was to replace 384th Infantry Division, which had suffered heavy casualties during the previous week's fighting east of the Don. The "castling" of 305th and 384th placed the stronger of the two divisions south of Kotluban' astride one of the most likely Soviet attack axes. Once relieved, 384th Infantry took over 305th's former positions west of the Don. After Paulus juggled his forces, VIII Corps' 305th and 76th Infantry Divisions and one-third of XIV Panzer Corps' 60th and 3rd Motorized and 16th Panzer Divisions defended the corridor's northern face against any future assaults by Stalingrad Front's 4th Tank, 24th, 1st Guards, and 66th Armies. This was the same number of divisions that had defended this sector in late August.[24] With Sixth Army's northern flank secured, two-thirds of XIV Panzer Corps' three mobile divisions prepared to support LI Corps' assault on Stalingrad by penetrating 62nd Army's defenses at Orlovka and Rynok in Stalingrad's northern suburbs, cross the Mokraia Mechetka River, and capture Stalingrad's northern factory district.

Once Paulus reshuffled his divisions, Sixth Army protected the northern face of its corridor from the Don River eastward to the Volga with its VIII Army and XIV Panzer Corps deployed from west to east. Heitz's VIII Corps defended the 26-kilometer sector from the Don River eastward to south of Kotluban' Station with its 384th and 76th Infantry Divisions. Both of these divisions defended with all three of their regiments forward, with their companies and battalions forming interconnected strongpoints constituting an elaborate hedgehog defense backed up by small mobile reserves and protected by preplanned artillery concentrations along each likely enemy axis of advance.

On Heitz's right, Wietersheim's XIV Panzer Corps defended the 29 kilometers from south of Kotluban' Station eastward to the Volga River with its 60th and 3rd Motorized and 16th Panzer Divisions deployed in similar hedgehog defenses facing both north and south. On XIV Corps' left, Kohlermann's 60th Motorized Division defended the sector from the village of Borodkin eastward past 564 km Station to the ancient Tatar Ditch just north of the village Kuz'michi with 60th Pioneer (Engineer) and Reconnaissance Battalions, 9th Machine Gun Battalion (attached from Sixth Army), and 120th Grenadier Regiment arrayed from west to east. The division's 92nd Grenadier Regiment was split, with part of its forces facing south toward Orlovka and the remainder reinforcing the forces facing north. On 60th Motorized Division's right, Lieutenant General Helmuth Schlömer's 3rd Motorized Division defended the sector from the Tatar Ditch eastward past several hills (Hills 111.1 and 129.6) to Hill 131.2 east of the Sukhaia Mechetka River with its 8th Grenadier Regiment, 53rd Motorcycle Battalion, and 29th Grenadier Regiment deployed abreast from left to right. On 3rd Motorized Division's right, Hube's 16th Panzer Division manned hedgehog defenses in the 10-kilometer sector at the eastern end of the corridor. Its 79th Grenadier Regiment occupied defenses facing north from Hill 139.5, 6 kilometers west of Erzovka, southeastward to the village of Akatovka on the Volga. Its 64th Grenadier Regiment, facing both east and south, defended the sector along the western bank of the Volga and then westward from the Volga north of Rynok to Hill 145.1, north of Orlovka.[25]

On 2 September, the day before Moskalenko's planned assault, the forces on 4th Tank Army's left wing attacked VIII Corps' defenses. This was to divert attention from 1st Guards Army's assault the next day and to support and protect Moskalenko's right flank once he began his assault. However, this attack by the tank army's 214th, 27th Guards, and 298th Rifle Divisions against the defenses of VIII Corps' 384th and 76th Infantry Divisions failed miserably in the face of effective German counterattacks, thereby depriving Moskalenko of his required support.[26]

Nevertheless, Moskalenko's army began its offensive at 0530 hours on 3 September after firing a weak and ineffective 30-minute artillery preparation (see Map 5). Its mission was to penetrate the Germans' defenses from Hill 139.7 westward to Kuz'michi, destroy the enemy, and link up with 62nd Army's 23rd Tank Corps near Konnaia Station, 10 kilometers to the south. Moskalenko launched his main attack in his army's center. The 116th Rifle Division, supported by more than 150 tanks from General Rotmistrov's 7th Tank Corps, attacked the defenses of 3rd Motorized Division's 8th Grenadier Regiment at Konnaia *Balka* and along the northern slope of Hill 139.7. On 116th Rifle Division's right, 24th Rifle Division, supported by a composite brigade of roughly 50 tanks from General Pavelkin's 16th Tank Corps, attacked 9th Machine Gun Battalion's defenses along the northern and northeastern approaches to the village of Kuz'michi. Fortunately for the defending Germans, this sector was reinforced by *Luftwaffe* 88mm antiaircraft guns firing over open sights.[27]

Farther east, on the left wing of Moskalenko's army, 84th Rifle Division, supported by 50 tanks from a composite brigade of General Mishulin's 4th Tank Corps, attacked the sector defended by 3rd Motorized Division's 29th Grenadier Regiment and 53rd Motorcycle Battalion along the northern edge of Sukhaia Mechetka *Balka*. East of the *balka* [ravine], 39th Guards and 315th and 64th Rifle Divisions manned defenses opposite 16th Panzer Division's left wing. The 38th and 41st Guards and 84th Rifle Divisions constituted 1st Guards Army's second echelon.[28]

The fighting on 3 September was as fierce as it was costly and indecisive for Zhukov's forces. Moskalenko's riflemen and tanks attacked across terrain that was billiard-table flat, treeless, and crisscrossed with numerous *balkas* and smaller dry streambeds and gullies, which offered ideal concealment for the defending infantry, tanks, and supporting artillery, and funneled his advancing forces into deadly fire sacks in between numerous German strongpoints. Despite an acute shortage of supporting artillery, especially antitank and antiaircraft guns, Moskalenko's attacking forces bit into the Germans' defenses, in places penetrating up to 4 kilometers deep and reducing the width of the 8-kilometer corridor between his army and 62nd Army by half. Ultimately, however, the assault bogged down against the effective German strongpoint and antitank defenses.

Opposite Moskalenko's main attack, 3rd Motorized Division's 8th Grenadier Regiment reported an assault by 140 tanks (from 7th Tank Corps) under the cover of heavy artillery and *Katiusha* [multiple-rocket launcher] fire. This assault also included at least two rifle divisions in the sector from 1 kilometer north of Kuz'michi eastward to Hill 139.7, although *Luftwaffe* aircraft and the 88mm guns destroyed many of the Soviet tanks.[29] Because 1st Guards Army lacked most of the field and antiaircraft artillery support promised by Eremenko, the *Luftwaffe* pummeled its attacking forces unmercifully from the moment they departed from their jumping-off positions and throughout

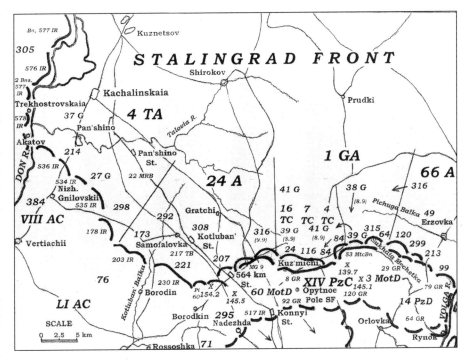

Map 5. Stalingrad Front's Kotluban' offensive, 3–12 September 1942

the entire assault. Despite this intense fire, infantrymen from Colonel I. M. Makarov's 116th Rifle Division, supported by Rotmistrov's tanks, succeeded in reaching the northern and northeastern slopes of Hill 139.7 before their attack stalled in a welter of blood and destroyed tanks.[30]

The Red Army General Staff's daily operational summary described the day's action:

> **1st Guards Army** went over to the attack southward from the Kuz'michi-Hill 112.7 (3 kilometers northeast of Kuz'michi)-Molochnaia Farm "13 Year of October" (14 kilometers west of Erzovka)-Hill 141.2 (6 kilometers west of Erzovka) line at 0530 hours on 3 September.
>
> 39th Gds. RD [guards rifle division], with units of 315th RD [rifle division], was defending its previous positions.
>
> 24th RD, with a mixed brigade from 16th TC [tank corps], was engaged in offensive fighting with the enemy defending on the northern and northeastern outskirts of Kuz'michi and the northeastern outskirts of Opytnoe Pole.

116th RD was fighting along the line Konnaia _Balka_-northern slope of Hill 139.7.

84th RD, with a mixed brigade from 4th TC, was fighting on the northern edge of Sukhoi Mechetka _Balka_.

64th RD was defending its previous positions.

41st Gds. RD concentrated in the Sukhaia Karkagon _Balka_-Hill 132.9-Hill 126.0 region at 1700 hours on 3 September.

38th Gds. RD reached the vicinity of Hills 131.6-Hill 124.7.[31]

Although Moskalenko's inexperienced troops achieved only meager success, their offensive did divert German aircraft and artillery forces to this region, forces that would otherwise have supported the main attack on the city. It also forced 3rd and 60th Motorized Divisions to shift forces from their southern flanks adjacent to the city northward to reinforce their defenses against Zhukov's resolute assaults. Over the next three days, 3rd Motorized Division replaced its battle-worn 8th Grenadier Regiment with the fresher 92nd Grenadier Regiment and, ultimately, with 60th Motorized Division's 120th Grenadier Regiment. Likewise, 60th Motorized Division reinforced 3rd Motorized Division's 29th Grenadier Regiment with its 79th Grenadier Regiment. This meant that neither division had significant forces available to support the ongoing assault on Stalingrad by Seydlitz's LI Corps.[32]

As the Germans resumed their heavy air strikes against downtown Stalingrad on 3 September, Eremenko convinced Stalin that defeat was imminent, prompting the Soviet leader to send a panicky telegram to Zhukov late in the day:

> The situation at Stalingrad has worsened. The enemy is situated three _versts_ [3 kilometers] from Stalingrad. He can take Stalingrad today or tomorrow unless the Northern Group of Forces [66th, 1st Guards, 24th, and 4th Tank Armies] renders immediate assistance. Demand the commanders of the forces standing north and northwest of Stalingrad attack the enemy immediately and go to the assistance of the Stalingraders [Stalingrad's defenders]. No sort of delay is permissible. Procrastination now is equivalent to a crime. Throw all of your aircraft in to assist the Stalingraders. Very few aircraft remain in Stalingrad itself. Immediately report receipt and measures taken.[33]

When Zhukov protested by telephone, Stalin asked sarcastically whether his newly chosen deputy thought that the Germans would wait until he was ready. The most that the dictator would concede was a delay until 5 September. Even then he added: "If the enemy starts a general offensive against the city, you must attack at once, even if you are not fully prepared. Your main task now is to divert the German forces from Stalingrad and, if possible, wipe out the corridor separating the Stalingrad and South-Eastern Fronts."[34]

For his army's attack on 4 September, Moskalenko altered his offensive plan slightly by reinforcing the shock group in his army's center (24th and 116th Rifle Divisions and 7th Tank Corps) with 84th Rifle Division. On the left wing, he instructed 38th Guards Rifle Division, supported by 4th Tank Corps' composite brigade, to assault the defenses of 3rd Motorized Division's 53rd Motorcycle Battalion south of the Motor Tractor Station. However, the army's forces began their assault at 0830 hours instead of 0630 as planned because the Germans fired a 90-minute counter-preparation, which overwhelmed Moskalenko's supporting artillery and wrought carnage in the ranks of the 116th Rifle Division's infantrymen as they formed for attack. This deprived 7th Tank Corps of virtually all of its infantry support.

Regardless of these problems, closely supervised by Zhukov, who was observing the action at Moskalenko's headquarters, 1st Guards Army resumed its assaults at 0830 hours on 4 September without any support from the armies on its flanks, which were still frantically concentrating their forces for the offensive. As the Red Army General Staff reported:

> **4th Tank Army** occupied and was strengthening its previous positions.
>
> 22nd MRB [motorized rifle brigade] was concentrated in the vicinity of Kotluban' State Farm.
>
> **1st Guards Army**, overcoming strong enemy fire and resistance, continued to engage in stubborn offensive fighting all day on 4 September and, after approaching close to the southern grouping of our forces defending the Hill 145.1-Hill 143.6 (8 kilometers northwest of Orlovka) line, reached the Hill 145.1-Hill 139.7 (both heights 4–6 kilometers northwest of Orlovka)-Sukhaia Mechetka *Balka* line by day's end on 4 September.
>
> 39th Gds. RD, with units of 315th RD, continued to defend its previous positions.
>
> 24th RD was fighting to capture Kuz'michi and Opytnoe Pole State Farm.
>
> 116th RD and 16th TC, encountering stubborn enemy resistance and continuous air attacks, were fighting along the Hill 145.1-southern spurs of Konnaia *Balka* line at 1700 hours on 4 September.
>
> 84th RD was fighting along the eastern slope of Hill 139.7-western spur of Sukhaia Mechetka *Balka* line at 1700 hours on 4 September.
>
> 64th RD was defending its previous positions.
>
> 38th Gds. RD, constituting the army's second echelon, reached the Motor Tractor Station (10 kilometers southwest of Erzovka)-1.5 kilometers southwest of Hill 141.2 (5 km west of Erzovka) line by 1700 hours on 4 September.

The units of **24th and 66th Armies** were moving into their jumping-off positions for the start of their attack.[35]

Overall, the two days of bloody fighting cost 7th Tank Corps a total of 77 burned or destroyed tanks, including 21 KVs, 40 T-34s, and 16 T-60s, essentially rendering the corps only marginally combat-effective.[36]

Although Kozlov's 24th, Malinovsky's 66th, and Kriuchenkin's 4th Tank Armies failed to join Zhukov's offensive, on 4 September 304th and 124th Rifle Divisions of Danilov's 21st Army launched heavy diversionary assaults against XVII Army Corps' 79th Infantry Division south of Serafimovich. This attack was intended to tie down German forces in this region. Simultaneously, the same army's 321st Rifle Division attacked XI Army Corps' defenses northeast of Kletskaia to prevent Lieutenant General Wilhelm von Apell's 22nd Panzer Division from moving eastward to reinforce Paulus's main shock group at Stalingrad.

Army Group B's daily situation report early on 5 September acknowledged Moskalenko's assault but denied it influenced Paulus's advance: "The panzer and motorized formations located north of Stalingrad attacked and, despite strong enemy counterattacks, reached the heights north of Stalingrad. A massive enemy offensive from the north, which began after an artillery preparation, was disrupted with the help of large formations of our aircraft. Of the 120 attacking enemy tanks, 30 were destroyed during the first half of the day."[37]

A conversation between Major General Grigorii Fedorovich Zakharov, Southeastern Front's chief of staff, and Colonel I. I. Boiko, on the General Staff, illustrated 1st Guards Army's dilemma in the aftermath of the 4 September fighting:

> **Zakharov**—Comrade Boiko, I request you inform me, even if briefly, what is happening to Moskalenko?
> **Boiko**—I am informing you briefly [on the situation] as of 1400 hours. Moskalenko renewed the attack with his forces performing their previous missions at 0630 hours [actually, at 0830 hours]. Simultaneously, large groups of enemy aircraft, up to hundreds of aircraft, constantly attacked the combat formations of 24th, 116th, and 84th Rifle Divisions and prevented the infantry from going on the attack. For this reason, the units made very little progress by 1400 hours, particularly in the Kuz'michi region. With Comrade Zhukov present, the army commander took measures to protect the attacking units' combat formations from the air more reliably and strengthen our actions against enemy aircraft to support the advancing infantry and tanks.[38]

Unfortunately, Moskalenko later admitted these measures "did not provide the hoped-for cover from the air." As a result, the assaults in his army's center expired by day's end with few gains, and 38th Guards Division, on the army's left wing, was unable to maneuver its forces into position to launch its supporting attack. At the same time, Schlömer's 3rd Motorized Division quickly reinforced its defenses south of the Motor Tractor Station with a battalion from its 92nd Grenadier Regiment.[39] A thoroughly frustrated Moskalenko later noted that the forward elements of 62nd Army, which were defending Hills 145.1 and 143.6, situated only a few kilometers to the south, had watched helplessly as 1st Guards Army's attacks faltered. An equally frustrated Zakharov reported to the General Staff: "All day long the enemy stormed the region of Hill 139.7, Kuz'michi, and to the north—apparently against our forces which were attacking from the north. I ordered Shumilov [the commander of 64th Army] to dispatch a tank company with submachine gunners to the north, penetrate to our forces at any cost, and lead them to the south."[40]

To Moskalenko's everlasting relief, 66th and 24th Armies finally completed their attack preparations late on 4 September—or so he thought. Overnight, however, it became apparent neither army was completely ready to attack. Malinovsky, the commander of 66th Army who visited 1st Guards Army's Command Post (CP) on the afternoon of 4 September, informed Moskalenko and Zhukov that his divisions would not complete their concentration by 0630 hours the next day, the H-hour for the new offensive. Nor was Kozlov able to concentrate the forces of his 24th Army forces on time. Pressured by Stalin to begin the offensive come what may, Zhukov nevertheless ordered Malinovsky (and, later in the evening, Kozlov and Kriuchenkin) to begin their assaults at 0900 hours on 5 September with whatever forces they could muster and then feed their remaining forces into combat as they arrived on the battlefield.[41]

Eremenko's new offensive plan, which Zhukov personally approved, required Moskalenko's 1st Guards and Kozlov's 24th Armies to conduct the *front*'s main attack in the Hill 137.9 and Kuz'michi sector and Malinovsky's 66th and Kriuchenkin's 4th Tank Armies to support and protect the main shock group's left and right flanks:

- **66th Army** will cut off and destroy the enemy grouping which has penetrated to the Volga River by an attack [southward] toward Orlovka;
- **1st Guards Army**, cooperating with 24th Army, will attack toward Basargino Station [25 kilometers west of Stalingrad] and subsequently reach the Novyi Put' [50 kilometers west-southwest of Stalingrad]-Verkhne-Tsaritsynskii [55 kilometers southwest of Stalingrad] line;

- **24th Army** will attack toward Karpovka [35 kilometers west of Stalin-grad] and, after destroying the opposing enemy, reach the Marinovka [45 kilometers west of Stalingrad]-Novyi Put' [50 kilometers west-southwest of Stalingrad] line; and
- **4th Tank** Army will attack toward Vertiachii [on the Don River, 50 ki-lometers northwest of Stalingrad] with its left wing, throw the enemy back across the Don River, and reach the Lake Peschanoe [55 kilometers northwest of Stalingrad]-Marinovka [45 kilometers west of Stalingrad] line.[42]

The plan required the four attacking armies to penetrate the German defenses along the northern face of their corridor to the Volga River, capture the bulk of the land bridge between the Don and Volga Rivers north and east of Kalach-on-the-Don, and encircle and destroy the German forces attacking Stalingrad proper west of the city. In retrospect, and probably at the time, Moskalenko considered this plan totally unrealistic given the results of the previous three days of fighting. Not only had his army already lost as many as half its original 300 tanks; its infantry had also suffered grievous losses. With their strength of six and four rifle divisions, respectively, and only minimal armor support, 66th and 24th Armies could not be expected to add much weight to Moskalenko's offensive, even if they committed all forces simulta-neously, which they already declared they could not do.[43]

Regardless of these stark realities, the offensive began as Zhukov had de-manded. As they had done on the two previous days, the exhausted soldiers of Moskalenko's army resumed their assaults at 0630 hours on 5 September, after another weak artillery preparation. On Moskalenko's left, Malinovsky's 66th Army joined battle at 0900 hours, attacking 16th Panzer Division's de-fenses between the Volga River at Akatovka and Sukhaia Mechetka *Balka*; on his right, Kozlov's 24th and Kriuchenkin's 4th Tank Armies began their assaults at 1500 hours against the defenses of VIII Corps' 305th and 76th In-fantry Divisions. This attack struck the Germans from just west of Kuz'michi to the Don River, with entirely predictable results. Moskalenko's assault fal-tered almost immediately against "clearly increasing resistance," and the armies on the flanks recoiled under withering German fire by day's end.

From 16th Panzer Division's vantage point:

On 5 September the Russians managed to penetrate the northeastern stretch between 6th Company, 64th Panzer Grenadier Regiment, and 7th Company, 64th Panzer Grenadier Regiment, with a regimental-size force, encircled the 6th of the 64th under Senior Lt. Rieger, and burst through the 7th of the 64th under Lt. Richter. Mues' battalion and the MTW [armored personnel carrier] company of 16th Motorcycle Battalion under Captain Georg succeeded in freeing the encircled regiment, cleared Akatovka of enemy, and brought the blown up vehicles back to the former front lines. That night the Russians took revenge with a bombardment by all calibers.[44]

The Red Army General Staff's daily summary stoically recorded the action:

4th Tank Army attacked toward the Verkhne-Gnilovskii and Nizhne-Gnilovskii regions with its left wing units at 1100 hours on 5 September.

37th Gds. RD was defending its previously occupied positions.

214th RD attacked and reached the left bank of the Don River in the Lake Kalach-Lake Krivoe sector by 2000 hours 5 September. Fighting was raging on the northeastern and southern outskirts of Verkhne-Gnilovskii.

27th Gds. RD was fighting at the eastern outskirts of Nizhne-Gnilovskii and in the Kul'turnyi Station region.

Information has not been received about 298th RD's positions.

24th Army went over to the attack at 1500 hours on 5 September with the units of its 173rd, 221st, and 207th RDs and, after dislodging the enemy's security, reached the forward edge of his defenses along the northwestern slopes of Hill 93.1-the village 4 kilometers southwest of Samofalovka-the northwestern slopes of Hill 13.4 line by 1700 hours, wedging into the forward edge of the enemy's defenses in several sectors.

1st Guards Army resumed its offensive on the morning of 5 September but, after encountering stubborn enemy resistance, had no success and fought in its previous positions all day.

39th Gds. RD was fighting along the Hill 133.4-564 km Station-the junction of the paths 1.5 kilometers west of Kuz'michi line.

24th RD was fighting to capture the Kuz'michi-Opytnoe Pole State Farm region but had no success.

The units of 116th RD, encountering heavy enemy fire, were fighting for the northern slope of Hill 143.6 at 1500 hours on 5 September.

41st Gds. RD approached the railroad at 1500 hours on 5 September and was fighting along the northwestern slopes of Hill 143.6 and the southeastern slopes of Hill 145.1.

38th Gds. RD was fighting on the northern slopes of Hill 139.7.

The positions of the units of 84th RD are being verified.

66th Army went over to the attack southward from the Hill 141.2-Hill 134.0-Tatarkino *Balka* line at 0900 hours on 5 September and was occupying [the following] positions by 1200 hours:

299th RD was fighting along the line Hill 139.7-southwestern branch of Sukhaia Mechetka *Balka* line.

120th RD was fighting along the southern branch of Sukhaia Mechetka *Balka*-the grove 1 kilometer south of Hill 112.2 line.

231st RD was attacking and reached the Motor Tractor Station (6 kilometers northeast of Orlovka)-Hill 111.2 (8 kilometers northeast of Orlovka) line at 1300 hours on 5 September.

The positions of the army's remaining units are unchanged.[45]

As the General Staff's operational summary indicated, the bitter truth was that Zhukov's entire offensive had stalled—and done so irrevocably. As Moskalenko later wrote, "On this and subsequent days, the enemy offered exceptionally stubborn resistance," although he should have added "effective" to his choice of adjectives. Nevertheless, driven on by Stalin's entreaties and threats, Zhukov insisted the four armies continue their assaults, if only to slow Paulus's advance into Stalingrad. The armies did so woodenly through 13 September, even though Zhukov had already decided two days before that any further action would be futile.

Once again, Hube's 16th Panzer Division experienced incessant assault, which kept the division off balance and prevented it from committing any additional forces to the battle in Stalingrad's suburbs:

On 9 September they chased 7th Company, 64th Panzer Grenadier Regiment, out of their positions once again. Panzers and the MTW [armored personnel carriers] of Lenz's company launched a counterattack and formed blocking positions right behind the firing line during the night. The enemy's artillery fire became more and more intense, while the batteries of 16th Panzer Division remained silent due to a lack of ammunition. Under the protection of their guns, the Russians managed to concentrate more and more of their troops. KG Krumpen had to release some of its companies that had been fighting at Rynok and Orlovka to reinforce the northern blocking positions and fill in the gaps from the rear. Friedrich's panzer company and MTW companies of Lenz and Hölterhoff joined the effort. They reached Hill 1.1 but were held up by field and antiaircraft guns and antitank rifle fire outside of Akatovka. The Russian artillery fire intensified into drum fire. On 11 September the intense struggle for Hill 1.6 began once again. Stuka attacks against the [so-called] Tomato *Balka* south of Erzovka in front of 7th Company, 64th Panzer Grenadier Regiment, brought relief. However, the resistance of the companies was at an end. They had melted down, and the losses were in no way comparable to their success. The rest of the men despaired and were exhausted by the continuous fighting.

On the night of 12 September, 7th Company, 64th Panzer Grenadier Regiment, was relieved by 6th and 7th Companies of 79th Panzer Grenadier Regiment. The very next day, however, the enemy broke through again. Incessantly, his superior forces pressed forward against 16th Panzer Division's lines, the fighting continued without a break.

Stalingrad had to fall and only then, when its back was free, could the superior forces of the enemy be held back and thrown back.[46]

Despite Zhukov's and Eremenko's frustration and their armies' heavy losses, their offensive was indeed having a beneficial effect on the outcome of the fighting in Stalingrad. For example, the ferocity of Zhukov's assaults forced Paulus to call a temporary halt to the advance by Seydlitz's LI Army Corps into Stalingrad at midday on 5 September and divert most of the army corps' air support to his northern front. Meanwhile, Wietersheim's XIV Panzer Corps hastily shifted its forces to and fro to block potential or partial Soviet penetrations, all the while admitting it was suffering "perceptible losses in men and material and a heavy expenditure of ammunition."[47]

Although a detailed account of the fighting on the northern flank of the Germans' corridor has yet to be written, the Red Army General Staff's daily reports provide ample evidence of the ferocity of the fighting as well as its constantly diminishing scope. For example, the journal entries describing the fighting on 6 September indicate all four of Zhukov's armies were stubbornly continuing their assaults with virtually all of their forces but with only negligible gains. The divisions on 24th Army's right wing and center managed to eke out an advance of 2–4 kilometers during the day, but 1st Guards, 4th Tank, and 66th Armies were simply fighting "along previous lines."

Once again, however, the crisis in the north had an adverse impact on Paulus's assault on the city. On the afternoon of 6 September, Wietersheim informed Sixth Army's commander that his front was "strained to the limit" and that he needed more infantry and stronger air support "even if it meant putting off the attack into Stalingrad indefinitely," because Stalingrad could be taken after the northern front was secure.[48] Disagreeing sharply, Paulus reversed Wietersheim's priorities by asserting that the capture of Stalingrad was a necessary precondition for shoring up the northern front. Therefore, said Wietersheim, XIV Panzer Corps must hold until the city fell.

On 7 September 24th Army's assaults stalled once again, 1st Guards Army's forces "dug in along existing lines" but regrouped to resume the offensive, and 4th Tank and 66th Armies simply failed to "achieve any success." The following day, the General Staff reported 4th Tank and 24th Armies had also "dug in along [their] existing positions," but it added that 66th Army and 1st Guards Armies were continuing their fruitless assaults, the latter with only its left wing. Egged on by Zhukov and Eremenko, all four armies resumed their attacks on 9 September but only in selected sectors, once again with little or no success.

Late in the evening, in response to Zhukov's request to withdraw 4th and 16th Tank Corps from combat for rest and refitting, Stalin responded, "I consider the restoration of 4th and 16th Tank Corps as pointless" because "the commanders of the tank corps, Pavelkin and Mishulin, are not in keeping with their duties."[49] Instead, Stalin recommended the two tank corps be withdrawn to the Moscow region and be replaced by 20 September with eight tank brigades being formed in the Saratov region. Zhukov responded on 11 September by agreeing to Stalin's decision. However, he held the two tank corps in his sector so they could be replenished with 94 T-34 tanks due to reach Kamyshin on 15–16 September. The crews for these T-34s came from the tank brigades forming in Saratov. Zhukov also relieved Pavelkin and Mishulin, replacing the former with Major General Aleksei Gavrilovich Maslov on 14 September and the latter with Major General Andrei Grigor'evich Kravchenko on 18 September.[50] Zhukov intended to employ the refitted corps and the eight new tank brigades in yet another offensive after midmonth.[51]

Once again, on 10 September 24th, 1st Guards and 66th Armies attacked relentlessly, the heaviest fighting being in 1st Guards Army's sector, where Moskalenko's infantry struck repeatedly at 60th Motorized Division's defenses on Hill 139.7. Meanwhile, Rotmistrov's tanks assaulted 3rd Motorized Division's defenses near the Motor Tractor Station. And so the bloodletting went on with scarcely a pause as Zhukov fulfilled Stalin's orders and his perceived duty to the defenders of Stalingrad.[52]

Despite Zhukov's resolve to penetrate the corridor at all costs or at least draw German forces away from the fight at Stalingrad proper, on 11 September he allowed Moskalenko to withdraw Rotmistrov's decimated 7th Tank Corps from battle and place it in second echelon to rest and refit. The next day Zhukov authorized all four of the armies to go over to the defense. However, this respite would be short because all four armies and Rotmistrov's tank corps received new attack orders on 16 September.[53]

While the four armies on the left wing of Eremenko's Stalingrad Front were battering themselves bloody against VIII Army and XIV Panzer Corps' defenses in the sector from the Don River eastward to Sukhaia Mechetka *Balka*, the two defending German corps reshuffled their forces frantically to parry the incessant attacks. On 5 September, for example, Kohlermann's 60th Motorized Division moved its 92nd Grenadier Regiment and part of its 120th Grenadier Regiment northward from the Orlovka sector, where it had been participating in Paulus's assault on Stalingrad, to reinforce 8th Grenadier Regiment near Hill 139.7 and Kuz'michi. By 11 September two battalions of 120th Panzer Grenadiers and the entire 8th, 92nd, and 29th Grenadier Regiments were occupying defenses in the sector from Kuz'michi eastward to Sukhaia Mechetka *Balka*, leaving just 60th Motorized Division's

160th Motorcycle (Reconnaissance) Battalion and 1st Battalion, 120th Grenadier Regiment, in the region north of Orlovka.[54]

At the eastern end of XIV Panzer Corps' corridor, Hube's 16th Panzer Division was just as hard-pressed as its neighbors to the west, particularly after Malinovsky's 66th Army joined the assault on 5 September. During its fight, the growing weight of Soviet artillery almost overwhelmed the German gunners, who were still short of ammunition after their previous defensive battles. The 16th Panzer reported that Malinovsky committed large numbers of T-34 tanks and even American M-3 Lend-Lease tanks. Although their crews were inexperienced and the American tanks were poorly armored, these attacks strained 16th Panzer to the utmost, forcing it to reshuffle panzer-grenadier companies from the southern flank of the salient to plug gaping holes on the northern front.[55] Ultimately 16th Panzer left just two panzer-grenadier battalions facing the Soviet defenses north of Stalingrad, while the remainder of the division's three regiments faced 66th Army's onslaught from the north.[56]

Consequently, Orlovka and Rynok remained in Soviet hands, and the planned advance by XIV Panzer Corps into Stalingrad's northern factory district never materialized. As subsequent fighting would indicate, the panzer corps' failure to capture the factory district would have immensely negative ramifications for Paulus's efforts to capture the city.

Amid the appalling bloodletting southeast of Kotluban', after inspecting his battle-worn armies on 10 September, the next day Zhukov informed Stalin:

> With the forces at the disposal of the Stalingrad Front, we shall not be able to penetrate the corridor and join up with the troops of the Southeastern Front in the city. The Germans' defensive front has been considerably strengthened by reinforcements brought up from around Stalingrad. Further attacks by the same forces in the same order will be pointless, and our troops will inevitably suffer heavy losses. Additional forces and time to regroup are needed for a more concentrated thrust by the Stalingrad Front. The armies' attacks lack the capability to overturn the enemy.[57]

Stalin immediately ordered Zhukov to persist in his offensive and, to emphasize the point, summoned him to Moscow, where the two met with Vasilevsky on 12 September to discuss future offensive options. On the eve of this meeting, Zhukov and his commissar, Malenkov, dispatched a more comprehensive message to Stalin, explaining why the multiple attacks had failed but pointing out the vital contributions they made to the successful defense of the city.

To Comrade Stalin

1. We received both of your directives about speeding up the northern group's advance.

2. We are not ceasing 1st, 24th, and 66th Armies' offensive, and we will conduct it persistently. As we reported to you, all on-hand forces and weapons are taking part in the ongoing operation. We have not been able to link up with the Stalingraders because we have proven to be weaker than the enemy in terms of artillery and aircraft. Our 1st Guards Army, which began the offensive first, has neither a single reinforcing artillery regiment nor a single antitank or antiaircraft artillery regiment.

The situation at Stalingrad forced us to commit 24th and 66th Armies into action on 5 September without waiting for them to concentrate fully or for their reinforcing artillery to arrive. The rifle divisions went into battle straight after a 50-kilometer march.

Such a commitment of the armies to combat piecemeal and without reinforcing weaponry did not provide them with the opportunity to penetrate the enemy's defense and link up with the Stalingraders, but, on the other hand, our rapid attack forced the enemy to turn his main grouping from Stalingrad against our grouping, by doing so easing the situation in Stalingrad, which, without this attack, would have been taken by the enemy.

3. We will not assign any mission whatsoever the *Stavka* has not informed us of. We intend to prepare a new operation on 17 September, about which Comrade Vasilevsky must have informed you. This operation and the time it will be conducted will depend on the approach of new divisions, the refitting of our tank units, the strengthening of the artillery, and the ammunition supply.

4. Just as in previous days, today our attacking units have advanced negligibly and have suffered heavy losses from enemy artillery fire and aircraft; but we do not consider it possible to stop the offensive, since this will untie the enemy's hands for operations against Stalingrad.

We consider it obligatory for us, even in this difficult situation, to continue the offensive, grind down the enemy, who are suffering losses no less than ours, and, simultaneously, to prepare a better organized and stronger blow.

5. Based on the combat, we have determined that six divisions, including three infantry, two motorized, and one tank, are operating in the first line against the northern group. No fewer than two infantry divisions and up to 150–200 tanks have been concentrated in the second line in reserve against the northern group.

Zhukov, Malenkov[58]

Zhukov's message clearly exaggerated the impact his offensive was having on Paulus's forces by asserting his northern group now faced six to eight German divisions at a time when it faced only five. Still, this report contained far more than a grain of truth. In fact, by tying down the bulk of Wietersheim's XIV Panzer Corps in combat between Kuz'michi and the Volga River, Zhukov's offensive had seriously disrupted both the form and the timing of Paulus's assault on Stalingrad. In addition to being delayed for at least one day, when the assault finally began, it forced Paulus to orient the advance of Seydlitz's LI Corps northwestward toward Orlovka to take the pressure off XIV Panzer Corps instead of due eastward into the city proper. This left less than one-half of Seydlitz's corps to participate with Hoth's Fourth Panzer Army in the assault on the city.[59]

Upon arriving in the Kremlin on 12 September, Zhukov assured Stalin that 24th, 1st Guards, and 66th Armies were effective fighting formations whose Achilles' heels were their lack of sufficient artillery and armor support. When asked by the dictator what Eremenko's *front* needed to be able to succeed, Zhukov responded, "At least one full-strength field army, a tank corps, three tank brigades, and not less than 400 howitzers," and "not less than one air army."[60] After further exchanges, Zhukov and Vasilevsky adjourned to the General Staff, where they studied their offensive options. The next morning they presented Stalin with a general concept for a new counteroffensive, which, based on their experiences with previous offensive actions, "concentrated on the possibility of a large-scale operation that would enable us to avoid squandering our prepared and half-prepared reserves on isolated operations."[61] Tentatively, the two generals recommended no such action until October, when "we should be completing the formation of the strategic reserves," and "our industry would have substantially increased its output of the latest types of aircraft and ammunition for the artillery."[62] In the meantime, Zhukov and Vasilevsky recommended the Red Army conduct an active defense to wear down the enemy.

As Zhukov, Vasilevsky, and Stalin discussed grand strategy in Moscow, Zhukov's and Eremenko's Kotluban' offensive ran its course. By day's end on 12 September, Zhukov permitted the four armies in Eremenko's northern shock group to halt their attacks and go over to the defense—a fact duly noted in the General Staff's daily report for 14 September.[63] However, this respite would be brief.

The Russians have yet to release casualty figures for the four armies participating in the first offensive at Kotluban'. Nonetheless, the costs were staggering, likely approaching one-third of the approximately 250,000 men taking part in the action and as many as 300 of the four armies' 400 tanks. Throughout the fighting, however, the *Stavka* and NKO (Narodnyi Komissariat Oborony—People's Commissariat of Defense) were feeding a steady stream of troops (organized as march-companies and battalions) and tanks into the region to reinforce the attacking armies. Assessing the nature of the fierce and bloody struggle south of Kotluban', Rokossovsky later wrote, "As a result [of attacking along the same axes in stereotypical fashion], the forces delivered frontal attacks and fought in unaltered groupings, persistently, in linear fashion, and unskillfully, for 12 days without achieving success."[64] As for the offensive's consequences:

> The operations by the forces on the left wing of the Stalingrad Front did not essentially alter the conditions in the Southeastern Front. However, the enemy's Sixth Army command was forced to reinforce its defenses between the Don and Volga Rivers by transferring the forces of 3rd Motorized and the greater part of 60th Motorized Divisions to there from the northwestern approaches to the city, which weakened the enemy grouping breaking through toward Stalingrad and eased the situation of its defenders.[65]

Rokossovsky concluded Zhukov's offensive failed because:

> Despite their superiority in troops and weapons at the beginning of the offensive operations, the grouping on the left wing of the Stalingrad Front was not suited to the existing conditions and did not have a clearly expressed main attack axis to resolve the important mission—linking up with 62nd Army. The armies attacked in sectors 12 kilometers wide, in dispersed combat formations, and within army sectors whose boundaries were strictly defined. The formations of the armies did not have time to orient themselves on the open terrain to the required degree and organize cooperation and command and control. They were not able to determine the enemy's grouping and his defensive system before the start of the offensive and during its course. As a result, lacking complete information, during the artillery preparation for the attack, the artillery and multiple rocket launchers were forced to suppress secondary targets, leaving the most important targets unengaged. The infantry's jumping-off positions for the attack were located an excessive distance from the enemy's forward edge.
>
> The poor employment of tank formations, which were committed to combat in the first echelon, in some instances directly from the march and without reconnoitering the enemy and the terrain, played a negative role. While organizing the offensive, the *front* and army commanders did not realize the enemy had sufficient time to organize defenses along this line. Specifically, in some sectors he exploited our defensive works and created a strong and well-organized system of fires, especially antitank.

The Germans adapted inoperable Soviet tanks and his own as armored firing points.

Dominating the skies, the enemy's air forces, operating in groups of 20–40 aircraft, bombed the combat formations of our infantry and tanks continuously. Small groups of enemy bombers were located over the battlefield throughout the entire day. And since an effective struggle with German aircraft was not conducted because of the weak antiaircraft cover and shortages of fighters, our bombers and assault aircraft could not remain long over the battlefield. At the time, the *front*'s air armies had only around 100 operable aircraft, and the enemy about 400. If Soviet air forces (not counting long-range aviation) were able to conduct 500–700 aircraft sorties per day, the German aircraft conducted 1,500–2,000 sorties.[66]

Moskalenko later paid homage to those soldiers who survived their ordeal: "Displaying a sense of selfless bravery and self-sacrifice in the name of destroying the enemy, the soldiers of 1st Guards Army, including the attached units and formations, literally gnawed their way through the enemy's defenses."[67] Rotmistrov, the commander of 7th Tank Corps, seconded this sentiment: "During seven days of fierce combat, the corps' units advanced a total of four kilometers. For us and for the enemy, these few kilometers were indeed a field of death."[68]

In his own memoirs, Rotmistrov recorded:

In the course of this most intense and bloody battle, the forces advanced 6–7 kilometers during the day and this owning to unprecedented obstinacy, bordering on self-sacrifice, of the *tankists*, who were attacking under continuous Fascist air strikes. We suffered heavy losses, particularly in T-60 and T-70 light tanks, which had weak armor defenses. We calculated that, in the course of a single day, the enemy conducted up to 2,000 air sorties against us with the main forces of Fourth Air Fleet. Furthermore, knowing well what the Soviet forces delivering the blows on Stalingrad from the north were striving to do, the German-Fascist command withdrew some tank and motorized divisions from the Stalingrad axis and threw them to meet us. On a majority of the heights, the Fascists dug their tanks and assault guns into the earth and organized powerful strong points, saturated to the limits with antitank artillery.

The units of our corps advanced a total of 4 kilometers during the next seven days in uncommonly fierce combat, primarily not far from Kotluban' State Farm, but those were kilometers won at a cost of heavy losses. We lost 156 of the 191 tanks we had at the start of military operations at Stalingrad in these battles. Many soldiers and commanders perished or were wounded.[69]

Rotmistrov admitted that his tank corps lost 400 men killed and wounded from 3 to 10 September but claimed his soldiers destroyed 50 German tanks, 69 artillery pieces and mortars, and more than 100 vehicles.[70]

German sources more fully substantiate just how costly the fighting near Kotluban' was for Zhukov's four armies. For example, 3rd Motorized Division, which absorbed the main force of 1st Guards Army's assaults, claimed the division destroyed 355 Soviet tanks, 61 guns, 67 *Katiushas*, and 117 machine guns while capturing 3,939 prisoners, at a cost of 710 casualties of its own during the period from 3 to 15 September.[71]

SIXTH AND FOURTH PANZER ARMIES' ASSAULT ON STALINGRAD'S SUBURBS, 3–9 SEPTEMBER

As the vicious struggle raged along the northern face of VIII Army and XIV Panzer Corps' corridor, north and northwest of the city Paulus and Hoth made final preparations to unleash their assault on the city itself at dawn on 3 September (see Map 6). As they did so, 62nd and 64th Armies completed withdrawing their forces back to the city and its southern suburbs, wherever possible anchoring their new defensive lines on the city's previously prepared battalion strongpoints and other fortifications. On 1 September Eremenko had ordered Lopatin's 62nd Army "to withdraw to the Rynok, Hills 144.4 and 143.5, Novaia Nadezhda Collective Farm, Gonchar, and the railroad in the vicinity of Alekseevka Station line," "occupy a defense no later than 0500 hours on 2 September 1942," and establish the army's CP at the hospital, 4 kilometers northeast of Opytnaia Station, on the high ground west of the Krasnyi Oktiabr' workers' village.[72] This defense incorporated Battalion Fortified Regions Nos. 78, 96, 80, 81, 82, 69, 84, 87, and 89, which were arrayed in an arc around the northern and western approaches to the city from the Rynok region westward to Orlovka and then southward just west of Gumrak airfield to the Stalingrad-Kalach railroad south of the Tsaritsa River (see Map 7).

Likewise, Shumilov's 64th Army was to withdraw and occupy defenses extending from the Tsaritsa River southwest through Voroponovo Station, Staro-Dubovka, and Elkhi to the Chervlennaia River near Ivanovka. Tolbukhin's 57th Army would defend the sector from Ivanovka southward to Tundutovo Station and then eastward and northeastward to the Volga River south of Krasnoarmeisk.

As Lopatin was conducting his withdrawal, on 2 September Eremenko ordered his forces "to prevent a penetration by enemy tanks and infantry into the city of Stalingrad by destroying them on the approaches to the forward edge [of his defenses]. Pay particular attention to the Voroponovo-Stalingrad

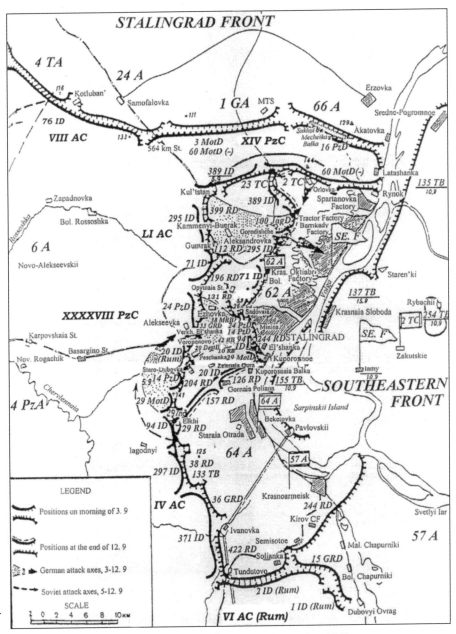

Map 6. Operations along the Stalingrad axis, 3–12 September 1942

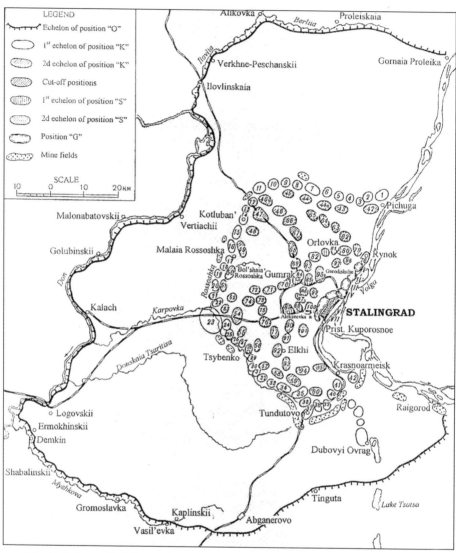

Map 7. Stalingrad's defensive lines and fortified positions

axis."[73] This was a particularly difficult mission to accomplish because part of Lopatin's forces found themselves south of the Tsaritsa River, the line previously designated as the boundary between his 62nd and Shumilov's 64th Army. Nonetheless, 62nd Army occupied its assigned defensive positions by late on 2 September (see Table 8).

Table 8. The Composition, Commanders, Dispositions, and Missions of 62nd Army, 3 September 1942 (from north to south) [tank strengths, where available, in brackets]

- **Operational Group Gorokhov** (Colonel. S. F. Gorokhov) (124th and 149th Rifle Brigades, 282nd Rifle Regiment NKVD, motorized infantry detachment, and 227th Separate Machine Gun-Artillery Battalion, 115th Fortified Region). Firmly defend the Rynok-Hill 185.4 sector and, by relying on antitank regions in Spartanovka and the Tractor Factory village, prevent an enemy penetration into Stalingrad from the north. Prepare a counterstroke toward Orlovka with no less than one rifle brigade and tanks. Dig your tanks into the ground to provide all-round fire.
  - ○ 124th Rifle Brigade – Rynok-northern and northwestern parts of Spartanovka.
  - ○ 149th Rifle Brigade – south of the Rynok-Spartanovka road.
  - ○ 282nd Rifle Regiment NKVD – Hill 101.3 and Hill 135.5.
  - ○ Boundary on the left – Tractor Factory village, Hill 85.1, Hill 144.2, and Hill 129.6.
- **2nd Tank Corps** (Major General A. G. Kravchenko) (26th, 99th, and 27th Tank Brigades, 2nd Motorized Rifle Brigade, 98th Rifle Division, and 115th Rifle Brigade). Relying on prepared positions and with the main groupings on your flanks, continue to defend the Hill 135.4, Hill 144.2, Hill 147.6, and Hill 143.6 line and prevent an enemy penetration toward the south and southeast.
  - ○ 26th Tank Brigade (Lieutenant Colonel P. V. Piskarev). Fulfill combat mission in the Nizhnaia Peschanka region in accordance with the *front's* orders.
  - ○ 99th Tank Brigade (Lieutenant Colonel P. S. Zhitnev, Major M. I. Gorodetsky on 14 September) [with 31 tanks] – in Operational Group Gorokhov. Deployed along the line Rynok and the road to the southern outskirts of the airfield, prepare counterattacks toward Rynok and Gorodishche with your tanks and echelon them in depth and dig them in for all-round fire.
  - ○ 27th Tank Brigade (Major P. G. Popov). In reserve [with 31 tanks].
  - ○ 115th Rifle Brigade (Colonel K. M. Andriusenko). Defend the Hill 135.4-Hill 147.6, and the crossing south of Hill 145.1 line.
  - ○ 724th Rifle Regiment (315th Rifle Division). Defend the Orlovka, western slopes of Hill 144.2, and the *balka* south of Hill 145.1 line.
  - ○ 2nd Motorized Rifle Brigade. Defend the crossing south of Hill 145.1 and the railroad line.
- **23rd Tank Corps** (Major General A. F. Popov) — 189th (Major F. I. Bystrik), 169th (Colonel A. P. Kodenets), and 39th Tank Brigades (Lieutenant Colonel M. I. Popov), 20th Motorized Rifle Brigade, and 399th Rifle Division (Colonel N. G. Travnikov). Firmly defend the occupied positions with the main grouping on your left wing to prevent an enemy penetration into Stalingrad and prepare counterattacks toward Kuz'michi and Bol'shaia Rossoshka. Pay special attention to preparing a counterstroke toward Pitomnik [airfield] and dig your tanks into the ground echeloned in depth.
  - ○ 169th and 39th Tank Brigades and 20th Motorized Rifle Brigade. Fulfill special combat missions on order of the *front's* and army's headquarters.
- **112th Rifle Division** (Colonel I. E. Ermolkin), with 157th and 158th Separate Machine Gun-Artillery Battalions, and 115th Fortified Region. Relying on prepared positions, occupy a defense in the vicinity of Hill 156.1, the barn at Gumrak, Kammenyi Buerak, and Uvarovka to prevent an enemy penetration toward Aleksandrovka and Opytnaia Station and prepare counterattacks toward Orlovka and Talovoi.
- **196th Rifle Division** (Colonel V. P. Ivanov), with 50th Machine Gun-Artillery Battalion, 115th Fortified Region, 398th Tank Destroyer Regiment (four guns), and 236th Rifle Regiment. Defend prepared positions along the Talovoi, Ezhovka, Babaevo, and Opytnaia Station line to prevent an enemy penetration toward the southeast and prepare counterattacks [toward] Opytnaia Station, Gumrak, Ezhovka, and Voroponovo.

Table 8. (continued)

- **33rd Guards Rifle Division** (Colonel A. I. Utvenko), with 52nd Separate Machine Gun-Artillery Battalion, 115th Fortified Region (three batteries) and 651st Tank Destroyer Regiment. Firmly defend the Ezhovka, Kruten'kii suburb, and Hill 153.2 (incl.) line to destroy the enemy in front of the forward edge, deny the enemy the Minina suburb, and prepare a counterattack toward Peschanka.
- **20th Motorized Rifle Brigade** (commander unknown), with 160th, 174th, and 175th Separate Machine Gun-Artillery Battalions, 115th Fortified Region. Firmly defend the road junction in the vicinity of Hill 151.7, Hill 135.1, and Alekseevka to prevent enemy tanks from penetrating toward Kuporosnoe, organize a system of strong flanking fires toward Talovoi, Hill 103.3, and the Motor Tractor Station, and prepare a counterattack toward Talovoi.
- **Shock Groups:**
    a) **87th Rifle Division** (Colonel A. I. Kazartsev), with 139th Separate Machine Gun-Artillery Battalion, 115th Fortified Region. Occupy the Aleksandrovka, Kammenyi Buerak, Opytnaia Station, and Stalingrad defensive region and be prepared to counterattack along the Aleksandrovka-Gorodishche-Orlovka, Aleksandrovka-Hill 185.2, and Stalingrad-Talovoi axes.
    b) **35th Guards Rifle Division** (Major General V. A. Glazkov, Colonel V. P. Dubiansky on 8 September), with two batteries of 651st Tank Destroyer Regiment. Occupy the Opytnaia Station, Hill 76.8, and Hospital [*Bol'n*] defensive region and be prepared to attack along the Hospital-Krasnyi Oktiabr', Hospital-Gorodishche, and Hill 76.8-Verkhniaia El'shanka axes.
    c) **131st Rifle Division** (Colonel M. A. Pesochin). Occupy the Hill 115.8, Hill 144.9, and Verkhniaia El'shanka (incl.) defensive region and prepare counterattacks along the Babaevo, Peschanka, Zelenaia Poliana axes.
    d) **169th Tank Brigade** (Colonel A. P. Kodenets). Concentrate in the Minina suburb region and, while protecting the axes in the southern part of Stalingrad and Kuporosnoe, prepare counterattacks along the Opytnaia Station, Gumrak, Verkhniaia El'shanka, Alekseevskaia, Minina suburb, and Peschanka axes.
- **Artillery Group** (Chief, General of Artillery Pozharsky). Will consist of 103rd Gun Artillery Regiment (six guns), 1105th Gun Artillery Regiment (three guns), 83rd Guards-Mortar Regiment (12 M-8 launchers), 17th Guards-Mortar Regiment (four M-13 launchers), and 110th Guards-Mortar Battalion (two M-8 launchers). . . .[1]

---

[1] *62nd Army Combat Journal*; and "Boevoi prikaz no. 114. Shtarm 62. 2. 9. 42. 10.30" [Combat order no. 114, headquarters, 62nd Army, 1030 hours 2 September 1942], in Ibid. By this time 2nd Tank Corps' 98th Rifle Division consisted of less than a battalion's worth of survivors commanded by Colonel Ivan Fedotovich Seregin, who had replaced the former division commander, Colonel Iosef Fedorovich Barinov, on 3 September 1942. Seregin had led 299th Rifle Division from 10 July to 3 December 1941 and 18th Rifle Division between 28 February and 25 August 1942. He survived the fighting at Stalingrad to lead 98th Rifle Division, redesignated as 86th Guards Rifle Division on 16 April 1943, until 27 May of that year. Thereafter Seregin's fate remains unknown. His predecessor, Barinov, born in 1891, was older than many of his fellow division commanders. After relinquishing command to Seregin, he commanded 233rd Rifle Division from 24 September 1942 to 5 February 1943 and later became deputy commander of 65th Army. A survivor of the war, he served as commandant of the Suvorov Military School in Kalinin from 1946 to 1948. The commander of the Artillery Group, General of Artillery Pozharsky, who commanded 62nd Army's artillery, was born in 1899 and rose through artillery ranks during the interwar years. He survived the battle for Stalingrad and continued to serve as 62nd (later 8th Guards) Army's chief of artillery until his death from illness in 1945. Pozharsky was a lieutenant general at the time of his death. For tank strengths, see Isaev, *Stalingrad*, 153. The 27th Tank Brigade's 31 tanks included 9 T-34s, 7 T-70s, and 15 T-60s, while 99th Tank Brigade's 31 tanks included 23 T-34s, 7 T-70s, and 1 T-60.

As sound as 62nd Army's defensive configuration seemed on paper, there were major weaknesses, particularly on the army's left wing. Group Gorokhov, 23rd and 2nd Tank Corps, and 112th Rifle Division anchored the defenses on the army's right and in its center by manning more or less contiguous defenses extending from the Volga River at Rynok westward through Orlovka to Konnaia Station and then southward through Kammenyi Buerak to the vicinity of the hospital. South of the hospital, however, the army's defenses were far more threadbare. The 196th Rifle and 33rd Guards Rifle Divisions and 20th Motorized Rifle Brigade, which occupied the defenses bulging westward from the hospital southward through Opytnaia Station and then across the Tsaritsa River to Talovoi and the Motor Tractor Station north of the Stalingrad-Kalach railroad line, were only shells of their former selves, with their regiments numbered in the hundreds of men instead of thousands and their battalions in the tens of soldiers rather than hundreds.

Although Lopatin had directed 87th Rifle Division and 35th Guards Rifle Divisions to counterattack in this sector, it was by no means certain they would arrive in time to shore up the army's sagging forward defenses. Nor was there any guarantee that, when they arrived, 35th Guards and 131st Rifle Divisions would be able to anchor the army's defenses in the El'shanka, Sadovaia Station, Minina, and Kuporosnoe regions, where the withdrawal of Shumilov's 64th Army had left the defenses on 62nd Army's extreme left wing virtually unprotected. In the interim, Lopatin could do no more than dispatch 38th Motorized Rifle Brigade to back up the depleted 196th Rifle and 33rd Guards Rifle Divisions.

Lopatin did receive more positive news on the evening of 2 September when Eremenko informed him that he was reinforcing his army with Colonel M. S. Batrakov's 42nd Rifle Brigade, which would cross the Volga later in the evening, and with Major General G. A. Afanas'ev's 244th Rifle Division and supporting 20th Destroyer Brigade, which he was transferring from Shumilov's 64th Army. Eremenko urged Lopatin to use these forces to reinforce his army's left wing. The 4,500-man 42nd Brigade consisted largely of sailors from the White Sea Military Flotilla but was not completely filled out. Transferred to Stalingrad from Northwestern Front, it had reached the eastern bank of the Volga on 31 August and began crossing the river less than 48 hours later. This brigade's first assignment had been to bolster the army's defenses at Bol'shaia El'shanka in Stalingrad's southern suburbs. However, Lopatin soon diverted Batrakov's unit to the vicinity of the hospital and Defensive Sector No. 6 (Battalion Region No. 100) north of the Stalingrad-Kalach railroad, where it reinforced 38th Motorized Rifle Brigade's defenses. Forty-one years old when he was assigned command of 42nd Rifle Brigade in late 1941, Matvei Stepanovich Batrakov was born in Gor'ki, joined the Red Army in 1919, and fought in the Civil War. An experienced and battle-hardened commander, he had earned the title of Hero of the Soviet Union while commanding 107th Rifle Division's 765th Regiment during the battle for El'nia in August 1941 and 211th Rifle Division during the fall of 1941.[74]

When Afanas'ev's 244th Rifle Division reached Stalingrad before dawn on 3 September, Lopatin directed it to concentrate in the bulging sector defended by 196th and 33rd Guards Rifle Division southeast of the hospital and Opytnaia Station, with one-third of its forces deployed north of the Tsaritsa River and two-thirds to the south. Before assuming command of the 244th on 30 June 1942, Colonel Georgii Afanas'evich Afanas'ev had led 297th Rifle Division from 4 August 1941 to 15 April 1942, fighting throughout virtually all of Barbarossa and the ensuing winter campaign.[75] Once forward, 244th Division, supported on the right by 42nd Rifle Brigade, 2nd Tank Corps' 26th Tank Brigade, and the separate 38th Motorized Rifle Brigade, was to defend its sector stoutly and also organize a counterattack toward the north and west.[76] Within hours, however, Seydlitz's LI Corps resumed its assaults, thoroughly disrupting all of Lopatin's complex but frenetic planning.

Weichs's original plan called for the armor of Sixth Army's XIV Panzer Corps and Fourth Panzer Army's XXXXVIII Panzer Corps to envelop Stalingrad from the north and south, respectively, while the infantry of Sixth Army's LI Corps advanced into the city from the northwest and west. Attacking from the north, 16th Panzer and 3rd and 60th Motorized Divisions of Wietersheim's panzer corps left only a small portion of their forces to defend the northern flank of the corridor isolating Stalingrad from the north. The remainder of these three divisions was to advance southward to capture Rynok, Orlovka, and Gorodishche, cross the Mokraia Mechetka River, and penetrate into and capture Stalingrad's northern factory district. These forces would engage the forces of 62nd Army's Group Gorokhov and roughly half of 2nd Tank Corps.

In the south, 24th Panzer, Romanian 20th Infantry, 14th Panzer, 29th Motorized, and 94th Infantry Divisions of Kempf's panzer corps, deployed abreast from north to south, were to attack eastward from Voroponovo Station and northeastward from Elkhi. Their objective was to reach the Volga River and seize the half of the city south of the Tsaritsa River. Kempf's advancing divisions would strike at the junction between 62nd and 64th Armies, ultimately pressing the former's 33rd Guards and reinforcing 35th Guards, 87th, 244th, and 131st Rifle Divisions and supporting tank and destroyer brigades back toward El'shanka, Sadovaia Station, and Kuporosnoe. The 64th Army's 157th, 204th, and 126th Rifle Divisions and 10th Rifle Brigade had to withdraw eastward toward Gornaia Poliana and the Volga River south of Kuporosnoe.

As Paulus's and Hoth's panzers raced into the city by the shortest and least difficult routes, 295th and 71st Infantry Divisions of Seydlitz's LI Corps, joined on the left by 389th Infantry Division once it deployed forward, were to advance on the city's suburbs from the northwest and west. Their mission was to capture Gumrak Station and Gorodishche and then penetrate into the city proper to seize Mamaev Kurgan and Railroad Station No. 1. Thereafter, Seydlitz's infantry would cooperate with Wietersheim's panzer-grenadiers to clear Soviet forces from the factory district and with Kempf's corps to crush remaining resistance in southern Stalingrad. As they advanced toward the city, Seydlitz's infantry faced 62nd Army's 399th Rifle Division, 23rd Tank Corps, 112th and 196th Rifle Divisions, 42nd Rifle, 38th Motorized Rifle, and 2nd Tank Corps' 27th and 99th Tank Brigades and the portion of 244th Rifle Division north of the Tsaritsa River.

As for the assault's timing, XXXXVIII Panzer Corps was to attack at dawn on 3 September before LI Corps completed assembling its infantry in its designated attack positions. Simultaneously, VIII Air Corps' aircraft, reinforced by most of IV Air Corps' planes transferred from the Caucasus region, were to commence a 24-hour round-the-clock raid on the city itself, during which XIV Panzer and LI Corps would join the assault.[77]

At dawn on 3 September, General of Panzer Troops Bruno *Ritter* von Hauenschild's 24th Panzer, Heim's 14th Panzer, and Fremerey's 29th Motorized Divisions of Kempf's XXXXVIII Panzer Corps edged forward along and south of the railroad line at Voroponovo Station, overrunning 33rd Guards Rifle Division's and 20th Destroyer Brigade's defenses. From there, Kempf's men captured the eastern approaches to Peschanka and threatened the southwestern sector of the city's defenses (see Map 8).

From 24th Panzer Division's perspective:

After regrouping, preparations, and detailed orientation about the enemy, 24. Panzer-Division set out at 0800 hours from Hill 151.7 with a sharply concentrated attack led by Gruppe Broich. The right wing moved past the left of Pestshanka [Peschanka], holding themselves to the left of the railway line. Gruppe Edelsheim would only feint attack on a broad front for the time being, later to follow staggered rearwards to the right. Romanians covered the northern flank. The first objective of Panzergrenadier-Regiment 21 was a hill on the ring railway; the second was the village of Alexeyevka [Alekseevka]. The attack progressed well, quickly reaching the hill in front of the circular railway of Stalingrad. The railway line stretched out into the distant naked steppe and joined up with the tracks coming from the north and south. Rifle pits studded the area. The armoured Gruppe pushed forward over this railway embankment.[78]

Marring an otherwise successful advance in fighting the division described as "particularly difficult and costly," General Hauenschild was lightly wounded by an enemy shell fragment but remained in command; however,

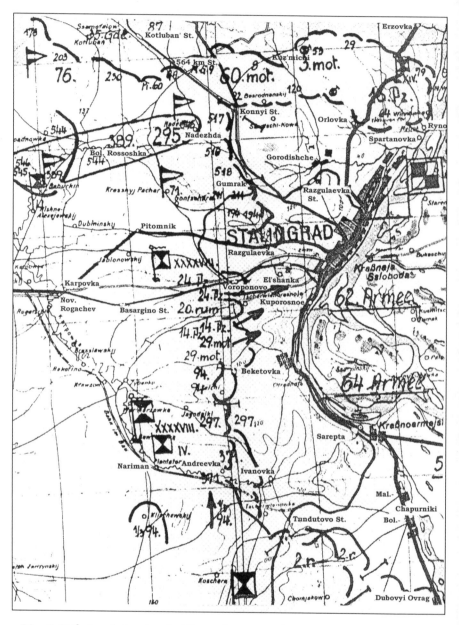

Map 8. Sixth Army's situation, 3–4 September 1942

Colonel Gustav von Nostitz-Wallwitz, commander of 89th Panzer Artillery Regiment, was wounded more severely.[79]

Continuing its assault, XXXXVIIII Panzer Corps' 24th Panzer Division forced Major General Vasilii Andreevich Glazkov's reinforcing 35th Guards Rifle Division and 20th Motorized Rifle Brigade on 62nd Army's left wing to withdraw to the outskirts of Voroponovo.[80] However, despite losing some ground west of Peschanka, Colonel M. A. Pesochin's reinforcing 131st Rifle Division of 62nd Army and 20th Tank Destroyer Brigade of Shumilov's 64th Army still managed to hold on to coherent defenses in the Voroponovo and Peschanka sectors and at Staro-Dubovka to the south. Farther south, 64th Army's 126th, 204th, 157th, and 29th Rifle Divisions succeeded in repelling the attacks by XXXXVIII Panzer Corps' 14th Panzer and 29th Motorized Divisions in the sector from west of Peschanka southward to Elkhi.[81]

Proceeding as planned, Seydlitz also unleashed his infantry divisions at dawn on 3 September before they had finished concentrating their forces. With small *kampfgruppen* in the lead, General Rolf Wuthmann's 295th and Alexander von Hartmann's 71st Infantry Divisions drove eastward and southeastward, pressing the units of Major General A. F. Popov's 23rd Tank Corps and Colonel Nikolai Grigor'evich Travnikov's supporting 399th Rifle Division eastward toward Konnaia Station, capturing Gumrak Station from elements of Kravchenko's 2nd Tank Corps and Colonel Ivan Efimovich Ermolkin's 112th Rifle Division and positioning their main forces for the advance toward Gorodishche and Mamaev Kurgan later in the day (see Map 9).[82] During this fighting, advancing abreast from left to right (north to south), 295th Infantry Division's 517th, 516th, and 518th Regiments smashed the defenses of Travnikov's 399th Rifle Division and 23rd Tank Corps' 189th Tank Brigade west and southwest of Konnaia Station while 71st Infantry Division's 211th and 194th Regiments, also arrayed from north to south, savaged the defenses of Ermolkin's 112th Rifle Division, the remnants of 2nd Tank Corps's 27th and 99th Tank Brigades, and Colonel Aleksandr Ignat'evich Kazartsev's reinforcing 87th Rifle Division in the Gumrak region.[83] Simultaneously, on 71st Infantry Division's right wing, its 191st Regiment demolished the defenses of Colonel Vasilii Polikarpovich Ivanov's 196th Rifle Division and captured Talovoi, Opytnaia Station, and Ezhovka, inflicting heavy losses on the Soviet defenders before a counterattack by reserves from 196th, 87th, and 112th Rifle Divisions halted 71st Division's further progress west of the hospital.[84] This fighting, during which the 71st drove a deep wedge into 62nd Army's defenses south of Gumrak Station, so decimated 87th and 196th Rifle Divisions that they literally disappeared from 62nd Army's order of battle within a matter of days.

Meanwhile, despite being increasingly distracted by the ongoing Soviet attacks in the Kotluban' region, Wietersheim on 3 September also unleashed

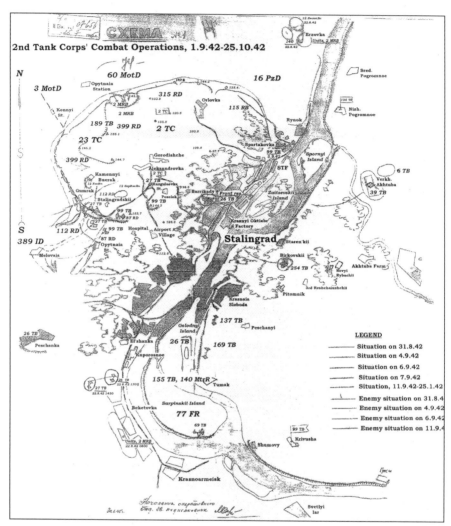

Map 9. 2nd Tank Corps' situation, 1 September–25 October 1942

a small portion of his XIV Panzer Corps in the assault along Stalingrad's northern approaches. Advancing at dawn, small *kampfgruppen* from 16th Panzer and 3rd and 60th Motorized Divisions pressed against the defenses of Group Gorokhov's 124th and 149th Rifle Brigade and 282nd NKVD Regiment in the Rynok region and those of 115th Rifle Brigade, 2nd Tank Corps' 2nd Motorized Brigade, and the remnants of 315th Rifle Division's 724th Regiment in the sector from Orlovka westward to Konnaia Station. However, the weakness of these assaults prevented any substantial advance as 62nd Army's right wing held firm. As a result, within days a large Soviet-occupied salient began forming west of Stalingrad's northern factory district. Worse still from Sixth Army's perspective, not only did Weichs's northern pincer fail; until it was eliminated the Orlovka salient separated XIV Panzer and LI Army Corps, destroying the coherence of any future German assault on the city.

Southeastern Front's daily situation report for 3 September, for example, claimed its forces were engaged in "fierce defensive fighting, with enemy tanks and infantry advancing from the west and northwest against the positions of the Stalingrad Fortified Region's internal defensive line." As a result, 62nd Army was forced "to abandon Voroponovo, Ezhovka, Opytnaia Station, and Elkhi . . . under the pressure of superior enemy forces."[85]

62nd Army also recorded the day's action with remarkable clarity:

> The enemy went over to the offensive beginning on the morning of 3 September. Up to an infantry division (presumably 295th ID) attacked the sector from Novaia Nadezhda Collective Farm and Hill 120.0 with two regiments and reached the line of the western slopes of Hill 143.3 and 144.1. Up to one enemy ID (presumably 76th ID) attacked in the Hill 144.1 and Gonchar sector. Up to an enemy ID with 50 tanks attacked toward Gumrak from the southwest at 1400 hours.
>
> Up to an enemy ID, supported by 30–40 tanks, captured Opytnaia Station and Ezhovka.
>
> Up to 30 enemy tanks reached Bol'shaia Peschanka from the south (southern Peschanka).
>
> Enemy aircraft in groups of 10–15 planes operated constantly against the combat formations of [our] infantry and artillery along the line of the central and southern sector of the front.[86]

The three corps of Paulus's and Hoth's armies continued their advance toward Stalingrad on 4 September, although XIV Panzer Corps' efforts were even feebler than the previous day. In fact, preempting Wietersheim's assaults, a composite combat group from Kravchenko's 2nd Tank Corps attempted a counterattack against 60th Motorized Division, 8 kilometers northwest of Orlovka.[87] Although it surprised the Germans, the attack failed to break through the corridor and link up with Moskalenko's 1st Guards Army.

Farther to the south, in LI Corps' sector, General Rolf Wuthmann's 295th Infantry Division turned over its sector south of Konnaia Station to Lieutenant General Erwin Jänecke's 389th Infantry Division, which had just completed its five-day movement from VIII Corps' defensive sector along the Don River. Wuthmann then castled his regiments southward into the vicinity

of Gumrak airfield, where they completed clearing elements of Ermolkin's
112th Rifle Division (285 riflemen) from the airfield and Gumrak Station
to the east.[88] General Richard von Hartmann's 71st Infantry Division, concentrating its regiments on its left wing, pushed the remnants of Ermolkin's
112th, Ivanov's 196th, and Kazartsev's 87th Rifle Divisions out of the Gumrak region. Ermolkin and Kazartsev withdrew their divisions and supporting
27th and 99th Tank Brigades (a total of 35 tanks) northeastward toward the
village of Stalingradskii, 5 kilometers southwest of Gorodishche, while the
remnants of the 196th Rifle and 33rd Guards Rifle Divisions fell back southeastward toward Opytnaia Station and the wooded northern slopes of the
Tsaritsa River valley. There they reinforced the defenses of Batrakov's 42nd
Rifle Brigade. In addition to splitting the defense of 62nd Army's left wing,
71st Infantry Division's advance propelled the forward elements of LI Corps
to within 5 kilometers of Stalingrad's western outskirts. Later in the day, Lopatin reported that his army was organizing a counterattack with Afanas'ev's
244th Rifle Division to contain any attempt by 71st Division to lunge eastward down the Tsaritsa River valley.[89]

Meanwhile, on the right wing of Weichs's assaulting forces at dawn on
4 September, XXXXVIII Panzer Corps began fulfilling its simple order to
"push into the city." Spearheading Kempf's assault, Hauenschild's 24th Panzer Division was to "attack east on 4 September, press into the city of Stalingrad, and clear out the city sectors between the dividing line to 14th Panzer
Division [sic] and the Tsaritsa Gully."[90] During the day, 24th Panzer Division
managed to edge forward and capture Voroponovo from 35th Guards Rifle
Division and 20th Tank Destroyer Brigade despite suffering unnecessary casualties from an attack by their own supporting Stuka aircraft. However, the
attacks by Heim's 14th Panzer Division stalled short of Peschanka in the
face of stout resistance by 64th Army's 126th and 204th Rifle Divisions. The
advance by Hauenschild's panzer-grenadiers ultimately stalled short of the
division's objectives in the face of heavy flanking delivered by Soviet forces
still lodged in the town of El'shanka. Still farther south, XXXXVIII Panzer
Corps' 29th Motorized and 94th Infantry Divisions forced 64th Army's 157th
and 29th Rifle Divisions and 154th Naval Rifle Brigade to abandon Elkhi and
give ground north of the town, although 64th Army reported it was organizing a counterattack with its reserve 66th Naval Rifle Brigade to recapture
the region.[91]

Reflecting on the day's action, 62nd Army reported accurately:

During the day the army conducted an intense battle with the attacking
enemy, and, simultaneously, the army went over to a counteroffensive
with part of its forces in the general direction of Opytnaia Station, Talovoi, and Ezhovka.

The enemy, as a result of his offensive on 4 September 1942, captured the Opytnaia Station, Poliakovka, and Voroponovo line with a force of up to one tank division (presumably 24th TD [Panzer Division]). Simultaneously, he launched a secondary attack from the direction of Bol'shaia Rossoshka with a force of up to an infantry division and tanks and pushed our units to the line of the railroad and *Traktorizatsiia* [Tractor] State Farm (4 kilometers north of Gumrak).

Beginning on the morning of 4 September, the enemy's Rossoshka Grouping, consisting of up to two infantry divisions (295th and 76th), with tanks (up to 80), and units of 60th MotD [Motorized Division], and Basargino Grouping, consisting of 24th TD, 14th TD, and units of 29th MotD, supported by aircraft dominating the skies, conducted fierce offensive fighting in the general direction of Sadovaia Station, while limiting themselves to covering actions along the Latashanka and Konnaia line.

His aircraft, constantly having 25–30 planes in the air, actively operated against the combat formations of the infantry and artillery.[92]

At this point, however, despite Seydlitz's and Kempf's notable successes, Zhukov's offensive against Paulus's northern flank began to unravel Weichs's carefully orchestrated offensive plan. By nightfall on 4 September, 1st Guards Army's furious assaults against XIV Panzer Corps' defenses southeast of Kotluban' had already forced Paulus to divert aircraft from Stalingrad to support Wietersheim's forces. Causing even more consternation in Sixth Army, the even larger-scale assault by three of Stalingrad Front's armies on 5 September further disrupted Weichs's plan, forcing Paulus to order Seydlitz to postpone LI Corps' assault on Stalingrad and divert virtually all his supporting aircraft to assist the beleaguered XIV Panzer Corps. Therefore, Stalingrad Front's counterstroke south of Kotluban' resulted in a two-day delay in LI Corps' advance. Nevertheless, 62nd and 64th Armies' daily situation reports, as well as those of Sixth Army, indicate that, although the advance by Kempf's XXXXVIII Panzer Corps into Stalingrad from the north indeed slowed, LI Corps' two divisions, reinforced by the 389th on 4 September, did push steadily eastward toward Stalingrad's western outskirts.

Nor did the Germans' assaults on the city totally end on 5 September, the day that all four of Eremenko's armies went into action in the Kotluban' region (see Map 10).

For example, although complaining about "large enemy forces concentrating in well-prepared positions west of the bend in the Volga River south of Stalingrad [the Beketovka bridgehead]," more optimistically, Army Group B reported, "the panzer and infantry divisions are conducting attacks 4 kilometers from the Volga, advancing toward the city center from the west and overcoming strong enemy resistance."[93] Seconding this claim, Southeastern

Map 10. Sixth Army's situation, 5–6 September 1942

Front recorded that 62nd Army was "holding on to its existing positions and successfully repelling all enemy attacks on the approaches to Stalingrad."[94] As German records indicate, Army Group B's description of the day's progress was a bit optimistic, because LI and XXXXVIII Panzer Corps' forward progress did slow perceptibly in all of their attack sectors. For example, Hauenschild's 24th and Heim's 14th Panzer Divisions encountered stiff resistance, supported by heavy Soviet artillery and rocket fire:

> During the night [of 4–5 September], violent enemy artillery fire lay on the sector of the Division. Near 14. Panzer-Division and 24. Panzer-Division, there were barrages by Stalin Organs, and enemy aircraft attacked with bombs and onboard weapons several times during the night. Enemy pressure was unchanged in front of 24. Panzer-Division, but the enemy strengthened in the bushy terrain south of Square Forest. The momentary condition of 24. Panzer-Division's forces permitted no further attacks for the time being, so all the Division could do was defend the attained positions. The enemy smothered the Wäldchen at irregular intervals with heavy barrages by artillery, Stalin organs and, above all, by mortars in unheard-of concentrations. It caused high casualties, in many cases by direct hits on the foxholes. Strong enemy air attacks also followed. The [squadrons] prepared for more trouble from the repeated enemy infantry assaults so, with the Division in precarious bulges thrust deep into the Russian lines, the other divisions of XXXXVIII. Panzerkorps were ordered to move up to the same level as 24. Panzer-Division and through this, the Division would at least have its southern flank covered. In accordance with Korps instructions, 29. Infanterie-Division (mot) and 20. Romanian Division set off at 0400 hours, 14. Panzer-Division an hour later at 0500 hours. . . .
>
> The attack of 29. Infanterie-Division (mot) and 14. Panzer-Division eventually broke down with only small gains of ground, stalling in front of considerable enemy resistance and strong flanking fire. Casualties were not inconsiderable for the minimal amount of territory gained.[95]

Confirming the adverse effects of the Soviet bombardment and the day's fighting, 24th Panzer Division by nightfall reported its armor strength had fallen to 34 tanks.[96] The 62nd and 64th Armies reported most of their forces were either digging in along existing positions or organizing local attacks to improve their defenses.

Reflecting these reports, during the day 62nd Army launched a counterattack with Afanas'ev's 244th Rifle Division straight into the teeth of 71st Infantry Division's 191st Regiment, which had advanced eastward down the northern edge of Tsaritsa River valley to within 4 kilometers of the city's center. At the end of the day, Lopatin reported—mistakenly, as it turned out—that Afanas'ev's forces had destroyed much of the German regiment. Still later in the day, as insurance should his army lose Stalingrad, Lopatin deployed five more tank brigades (135th, 137th, 155th, 254th, and 169th), all without tanks, into reserve defensive positions along the eastern bank of the Volga opposite Stalingrad.[97] Meanwhile, Shumilov's 64th Army worked hard to erect impenetrable defenses protecting the approaches to Kuporosnoe, Beketovka, and Krasnoarmeisk on the Volga's eastern bank and maintain contact with Lopatin's 62nd Army in Stalingrad. While the forces on his army's right wing (204th, 126th, 157th, and 29th Rifle Divisions) clung to their defenses from Peschanka southward to Elkhi, the forces on his army's center and left wing (38th, 36th Guards, and 422nd Rifle Divisions) kept Fourth Panzer Army's IV Army and Romanian VI Army Corps at bay from Elkhi southward to Tundutovo and westward to the Volga River. All the while, Shumilov assembled a reserve in the Beketovka region, including Colonel I. D. Driakhlov's 10th Reserve (160th Separate) Rifle Brigade, which he intended to employ to shore up the defenses on his army's right wing.[98]

By day's end on 5 September, Group Gorokhov's 124th and 149th Rifle Brigades and 282nd NKVD Regiment, together with Colonel K. M. Andriusenko's 115th Rifle Brigade and remnants of Travnikov's 399th Rifle Division, were fortifying their defenses from Rynok westward to Orlovka, opposite XIV Panzer Corps' 16th Panzer and 60th Motorized Divisions. On their left, 315th Rifle Division's 724th Rifle Regiment, 2nd Tank Corps' 2nd Motorized Rifle Brigade, and 23rd Tank Corps' 189th Tank Brigade were defending the front from Orlovka westward to Konnaia Station, opposite small elements of XIV Panzer Corps' 3rd Motorized Division and LI Corps' newly arrived 389th Infantry Division. From Konnaia Station southward to Stalingradskii (east of Gumrak), Travnikov's 399th and Ermolkin's 112th Rifle Division, reinforced by 2nd Tank Corps' 27th and 99th Tank Brigades, faced LI Corps' 295th Infantry Division. On the 112th's left flank, Kazartsev's 87th Rifle Division had counterattacked and recaptured a foothold in Opytnaia Station from the 295th Infantry's 517th Regiment and Batrakov's 42nd Rifle Brigade. The remnants of Ivanov's 196th Rifle Division and the northern third of Afanas'ev's 244th Rifle Division clung to their defenses on the northern bank of the Tsaritsa River northeast of Ezhovka. From the Tsaritsa southward to Voroponovo, the remnants of Colonel A. I. Utvenko's 33rd Guards Rifle Division and 20th Tank Destroyer Brigade, reinforced by Glazkov's 35th Guards and Pesochin's 131st Rifle Divisions, were holding their own against XXXXVIII Panzer Corps' 24th Panzer Division. In the sector from Peschanka southward through Staro-Dubovka to Elkhi, 64th Army's 204th,

126th, 157th, and 29th Rifle Divisions were facing XXXXVIII Panzer Corps' 14th Panzer, 29th Motorized, and 94th Infantry Divisions.[99]

Despite the continuing crisis on the corridor's northern face, Weichs's forces assaulting Stalingrad registered some gains on 6 September, principally in the sector from Orlovka westward to Konnaia Station and from the station southward to the Gumrak region, but made scant progress elsewhere. Here, LI Corps' 389th Infantry Division, supported on the left by a small *kampfgruppe* from XIV Panzer Corps' 3rd Motorized Division, attacked along converging axes. This collapsed the defenses of 23rd Tank Corps' 399th Rifle Division and 189th Tank Brigade, forcing them to withdraw about 5 kilometers to new defenses protecting the approaches to Gorodishche.[100] Regardless, Lopatin insisted Popov's tank corps hold on to its positions in the Orlovka region come what may since they were the closest forces to Zhukov's armies still trying to break through to 62nd Army from the north. Despite the 389th's advance, Lopatin's forces continued to hold firmly to the large salient jutting northward to Orlovka that separated Wietersheim's XIV Panzer Corps from Seydlitz's LI Corps to the south. All in all, the fighting west of Stalingrad remained desultory on 6 September, largely due to the heavy fighting in the Kotluban' region to the north.[101]

Once Paulus was certain that Wietersheim's corps had stabilized the situation in the Kotluban' region, on 7 September Sixth Army's commander unleashed Seydlitz's LI Corps for what he hoped would be its final assault to capture the city and the western bank of the Volga River (see Map 11). Advancing abreast at dawn, Jänecke's 389th and Wuthmann's 295th Infantry Divisions, supported by 30–40 assault guns and groups of 40–50 Stuka dive-bombers, ground their way due eastward across the steppe toward the bluffs overlooking the city. Simultaneously, on the corps' right wing, Hartmann's 71st Infantry Division drove eastward along the high ground north of the Tsaritsa River valley.

This combined assault forced 399th, 112th, and 87th Rifle Divisions and 2nd and 23rd Tank Corps' supporting 189th, 27th, and 99th Tank Brigades to give ground steadily (see Map 12). Withdrawing rapidly in intense fighting, Travnikov's 399th Rifle Division and Bystrik's 189th Tank Brigade dug in on the western outskirts of Gorodishche and Aleksandrovka, and Ermolkin's 112th Rifle Division, with the remnants of Major P. G. Popov's 27th and Lieutenant Colonel P. S. Zhitnev's 99th Tank Brigades, did the same along the railroad line south of Aleksandrovka. By this time, 27th and 99th Tank Brigades were virtually "tankless," the commander of 27th Brigade, Popov, had been wounded, and the commander of 99th Tank Brigade, Zhitnev, had been killed in action. As a result, Eremenko ordered Kravchenko to turn over the few remaining inoperable tanks in his corps' 27th and 99th Tank

Map 11. Sixth Army's situation, 7–8 September 1942

Brigades to Popov's 23rd Tank Corps and withdraw the remnants of his tank corps back across the Volga River. On 11 September, Kravchenko's corps would assume responsibility for defending the 84-kilometer-wide sector on the river's eastern bank with the new or reconstituted 135th, 137th, 155th, 254th, 169th, and 99th Tank Brigades.[102]

Meanwhile, on Ermolkin's left, Kazartsev withdrew the remnants of his shattered 87th Rifle Division to new defenses northeast of Opytnaia Station. Southward to the northern bank of the Tsaritsa River, the remnants of Ivanov's 196th Rifle Division, Batrakov's 42nd Rifle Brigade, and the

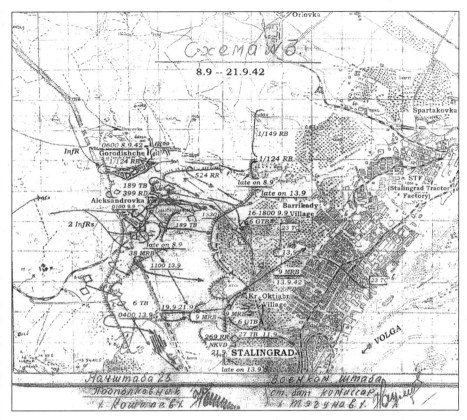

Map 12. 23rd Tank Corps' situation, 8–21 September 1942

northern third of Afanas'ev's 244th Rifle Division repelled several assaults by 71st Infantry Division eastward from Opytnaia Station and managed to contain the German drive at Sadovaia and Razgulaevka Stations, only 8–10 kilometers northeast of Mamaev Kurgan. Decimated in previous combat, by this time 399th, 112th, and 87th Rifle Divisions numbered only 195, 300, and 180 bayonets (fighters), respectively, with slightly more in the 196th.[103] That evening Southeastern Front admitted that its forces "were continuing intense defensive fighting with enemy infantry and tanks along the approaches to Stalingrad and, under this pressure, had abandoned the Gorodishche and Aleksandrovka regions."[104]

On 62nd Army's left wing, 24th and 14th Panzer and 29th Motorized Divisions of Kempf's XXXXVIII Panzer Corps remained relatively inactive and regrouped their forces on 7 September. The two regiments of Afanas'ev's 244th Rifle Division south of the Tsaritsa River clung firmly to their defenses

east of Poliakhovka and Pesochin's 131st Rifle and Glazkov's 35th Guards
Rifle Divisions, supported by what little was left of 20th Tank Destroyer
Brigade, also held their own along the railroad line east of Voroponovo.
However, Colonel Glazkov was seriously wounded in the fighting and was
replaced by his deputy, Colonel Vasilii Pavlovich Dubiansky, an experienced
officer who had served as deputy commander of 7th Motorized Rifle Division during Operation Barbarossa.[105]

Despite LI Corps' successful advance on 7 September, when General
Seydlitz and his chief of staff went to Sixth Army headquarters that evening,
they found Paulus seriously concerned. Zhukov's offensive in the Kotluban'
region was continuing to strain XIV Panzer Corps to the north, while in the
south Hoth's Fourth Panzer Army had halted its attacks temporarily because
of the flanking threat posed by 64th Army's forces, which were lodged se-
curely in the large bridgehead east of Beketovka and Krasnoarmeisk.[106] Un-
decided as to his next course of action—whether to continue the attack into
the city or assist Wietersheim's beleaguered forces to the north—Paulus finally ordered Seydlitz to wheel the left wing of his corps northeastward on 9
September to mop up the Soviet forces in Wietersheim's rear area and eliminate the persistent Soviet salient at Orlovka. At the same time, Hoth was
to reorient the attack by Kempf's XXXXVIII Panzer Corps southeastward,
away from the city and toward the northern flank of 64th Army's Berezovka
bridgehead.[107] During the heavy fighting that preceded this regrouping,
however, General Hauenschild, commander of 24th Panzer Division, was severely wounded while directing operations at the front, and the commander
of the division's 4th Motorcycle Battalion, Colonel von Gröben, was killed
by exploding Soviet shells. Colonel Broich then took temporary command of
24th Panzer Division until he was replaced by Major General Arno Lenski
on 14 September.[108]

If Paulus's change in plans provided any respite to the defenders of the
narrow strip of territory west of the city, it was clearly not evident to 62nd
Army's soldiers. On 8 September combat raged along the entire sector from
Gorodishche southward to Peschanka, engulfing 62nd Army's southern wing
and the northern wing of 64th Army. As Southeastern Front reported, "[The
front's] forces continued intense defensive fighting with large forces of enemy infantry and tanks, supported by constant air strikes, along the immediate approaches to Stalingrad and, under their pressure, abandoned a number
of positions."[109] The only saving grace was the fact that 62nd Army's right
wing remained relatively quiet. There, Group Gorokhov's 124th and 149th
Rifle Brigades (the former less one of its battalions, which had reinforced
112th Rifle Division's defenses at Gorodishche), 10th NKVD Rifle Division's 282nd Regiment, and a battalion of 115th Rifle Brigade defended the
sector from Rynok westward to Orlovka. The remainder of Andriusenko's

115th Rifle Brigade, 2nd Motorized Rifle Brigade, and 315th Rifle Division's 724th Rifle Regiment (the only surviving regiment of this division) manned defenses along the northern and western faces of the Orlovka salient. Of course, this was the case only because XIV Panzer Corps was fully occupied with Zhukov's offensive, and LI Army Corps was regrouping its forces for an assault on the salient from the west.

On 62nd Army's left wing, however, on 8 September LI Corps' 295th and 71st Infantry Divisions attacked eastward toward Gorodishche and Razgulaevka Station on the main railroad line from Gumrak into Stalingrad. The 295th Division's assault pressed Travnikov's 399th Rifle Division, Ermolkin's 112th Rifle Division, and 23rd Tank Corps' tattered supporting tank brigades back into Gorodishche, Aleksandrovka, and across the railroad line at Razgulaevka Station to the south. In desperation, Lopatin reinforced this sector with 38th Motorized Rifle Brigade and Lieutenant Colonel S. A. Khopko's 6th Tank Brigade. To the south, 71st Infantry Division pushed the few hundred men of Kazartsev's 87th Rifle Division, Batrakov's 42nd Rifle Brigade, and the northern regiment of Afanas'ev's 244th Rifle Division back to the vicinity of the hospital and a motor tractor station north of the Tsaritsa River.

While heavy fighting raged on in the sectors of LI Corps' 71st Infantry Division south of Razgulaevka Station, late in the day Seydlitz reshuffled the regiments of Jänecke's 389th and Wuthmann's 295th Infantry Divisions so that Jänecke's division could occupy jumping-off positions for an attack northeastward toward Orlovka. Meanwhile, Wuthmann's division was to continue its eastward advance on Gorodishche and Stalingrad's northern factory district.

On Sixth Army's right, Hoth's Fourth Panzer Army also activated its forces on 8 September, when it unleashed the three armored divisions of Kempf's XXXXVIII Panzer Corps in heavy assaults against 62nd Army's left wing south of the Tsaritsa River. On Kempf's left, Broich's 24th Panzer Division assaulted the defenses of the two regiments of Afanas'ev's 244th Rifle Division from the Tsaritsa River southward through Sadovaia Station to the northern outskirts of Minina suburb. At the same time, Heim's 14th Panzer Division struck the defenses of Pesochin's 131st Rifle and Dubiansky's 35th Guards Rifle Divisions and 20th Tank Destroyer Brigade from northeast of Voroponovo Station southward to Peschanka. While barely managing to contain furious attacks by a *kampfgruppe* from Broich's panzer division, Afanas'ev saw two of his division's battalions destroyed to the last man in the heavy fighting northwest of Minina.[110] By day's end, a distraught Lopatin directed Colonel Driakhlov's 10th Rifle Brigade, transferred to his reserve from 64th Army, to shore up 244th Rifle Division's defenses at Sadovaia Station and Minina and prepare to counterattack against Kempf's panzers along the railroad line south of the Tsaritsa River.

Still farther to the south, Fremerey's 29th Motorized Division of Kempf's panzer corps, now supported by a *kampfgruppe* from Heim's 14th Panzer Division, wheeled south and struck the defenses on 64th Army's extreme right wing southeast of Voroponovo Station. This attack, supported by an estimated 50 tanks and assault guns, pressed 204th and 126th Rifle Divisions and the reinforcing 138th Rifle Division and 133rd Tank Brigade back to new defenses extending southwestward from the western outskirts of Peschanka. Evidencing the ferocity of this fighting, 64th Army reported, "As a result of the enemy tank attack, [138th Rifle Division's] 343rd Rifle Regiment was almost completely destroyed," although "18 enemy tanks were destroyed and burned" during the fighting.[111] Later in the day, Shumilov withdrew his army's 126th Rifle Division, which was seriously weakened in the previous fighting, to his army's second-echelon defenses at Gornaia Poliana, with orders to protect the northern approaches to Beketovka.

Capitalizing on their previous day's success, Sixth Army's LI Army Corps and Fourth Panzer Army's XXXXVIII Panzer Corps continued their assaults on 9 September. Seydlitz began the day's action by unleashing Jänecke's 389th Infantry Division, which had reoriented its regiments toward the northeast the day before, in a concerted drive on Orlovka from the southwest. Attacking northwestward from southwest of Gorodishche at dawn, Jänecke's forces engaged an enemy, which in Seydlitz's words "tenaciously defended every single bunker." Nevertheless, throughout the day the division's 545th, 546th, and 544th Regiments cut deeply into the left wing of Travnikov's 399th Rifle Division and 2nd Tank Corps' 189th Tank Brigade, threatening 115th Rifle and 2nd Motorized Rifle Brigades, whose main forces were still defending the northeastern extremity of the Orlovka salient under Colonel Andriusenko's command. Thrusting forward, the three regiments captured Gorodishche from the remnants of 399th Rifle Division and 23rd Tank Corps' supporting tank brigades.

Meanwhile, on 389th Infantry Division's right, the 516th Regiment of Wuthmann's 295th Infantry Division assaulted and captured the western section of Aleksandrovka village from Ermolkin's 112th Rifle Division, which reported it had only 82 riflemen left in its ranks. At the same time, 295th Division's 517th and 518th Regiments pushed eastward from Razgulaevka Station, smashing the defenses of 38th Motorized Brigade, the remnants of Kazartsev's 87th Rifle Division, and 6th Tank Brigade, although Khopko's tanks managed to launch a vigorous but futile counterattack during the afternoon. By the end of the day, however, 38th Motorized Rifle Brigade was reeling back eastward from the railroad south of Razgulaevka Station, and Kazartsev reported his 87th Rifle Division had only 140 surviving bayonets.

Farther south on LI Corps' right wing, the three regiments of Hartmann's 71st Infantry Division pressed eastward and southeastward in the sector between the hospital and the Tsaritsa River but registered only modest gains in heavy fighting against Batrakov's 42nd Rifle Brigade and the northern regiment of Afanas'ev's 244th Rifle Division. Although Seydlitz reported optimistically later in the day that the defending Soviets had suffered heavy losses, he was forced to admit that "our own were not inconsequential."[112] Confirming Seydlitz's judgment, Southeastern Front reported, "Along the immediate approaches to Stalingrad, on 9 September the forces of the Southeastern Front continued heavy defensive fighting with enemy infantry and tanks and withdrew from a number of points under heavy pressure."[113]

South of the Tsaritsa River, Hoth's Fourth Panzer Army continued its incessant attacks with the three armored divisions of Kempf's XXXXVIII Panzer Corps in an attempt to penetrate into the southern section of Stalingrad. Broich's 24th Panzer Division spearheaded Kempf's drive despite the fact that its armored strength had fallen to only 24 tanks. Advancing shortly after dawn, Broich's panzers captured Sadovaia Station from 244th Rifle Division, although the latter, now reinforced by 10th Rifle Brigade, counterattacked repeatedly in vain to recapture the station. Farther south, part of Heim's 14th Panzer Division, with even fewer tanks than Broich, nonetheless forced Pesochin's 131st Rifle and Dubiansky's 35th Guards Rifle Divisions and the supporting 20th Destroyer Brigade to abandon Peschanka. These Soviet formations withdrew to new defensive positions extending from just west of El'shanka southward along the southern outskirts of Kuporosnoe, both on the western bank of the Volga River south of Stalingrad's city center.[114]

Meanwhile, on XXXXVIII Panzer Corps' right, 29th Motorized Division, still supported by a *kampfgruppe* from 14th Panzer Division, drove southward west of Kuporosnoe, forcing 64th Army's 204th, 138th, and 157th Rifle Divisions to abandon Staro-Dubovka. The three Soviet divisions withdrew to the new defense line east and west of Gornaia Poliana, which was already manned by the army's 126th Rifle Division. During the day, Heim shifted the remainder of his 14th Panzer Division southward from the Peschanka region to reinforce the assault by Fremerey's panzer-grenadiers. Although Shumilov's forces were able to contain the Germans' assault short of Kuporosnoe and the western bank of the Volga, all four of his army's divisions were literally eroding away before their commander's eyes.[115]

From the perspective of Weichs, Army Group B's commander, the heavy fighting along the western approaches to Stalingrad from 5 through 9 September had the beneficial effect of halving the distance between the advancing LI Army and XXXXVIII Panzer Corps and the Volga River. The fighting had also significantly reduced the danger that Stalingrad Front's four armies posed to XIV Panzer Corps' 60th and 3rd Motorized and 16th Panzer Divisions in the fragile corridor to the Volga River north of Stalingrad. From Eremenko's perspective, however, the situation had become far more precarious in two key respects. First, the successful advances by LI Army and XXXX-VIII Panzer Corps threatened to split apart 62nd and 64th Armies in the relatively undeveloped southern suburbs of the city. Second, the *front* commander harbored serious doubts concerning Lopatin's ability to lead 62nd Army successfully in such a crisis. Therefore, on Eremenko's advice, late on 9 September, the *Stavka* appointed General Chuikov to replace Lopatin as commander of 62nd Army.

CHANGES OF COMMAND

Weichs's forces moved cautiously, almost timidly, into the city, obviously impressed by the ferocity of the Soviets' resistance. Colonel General Wolfram *Freiherr* von Richthofen in particular was frustrated by the slow pace set by Sixth Army, complaining of "the jitters and poor leadership of the Army."[116] Yet this caution was not evident to Stalin, the *Stavka*, Zhukov, or Eremenko, who were becoming increasingly desperate over Stalingrad's fate. By the end of the first week in September, General D. N. Nikishov, former commander of Southern Front's 9th and 57th Armies but now Eremenko's chief of staff, was exhausted by the effort to coordinate operations when even his headquarters staff was split between four locations. Lopatin, who had commanded 62nd Army since the chaotic days of late July, became so despondent that he began to withdraw troops from the city. Concerned over Lopatin's resiliency under such trying circumstances, Eremenko late on 7 September requested that Stalin relieve Lopatin of his post. The dictator did so early the next morning but failed to appoint a successor for another 36 hours.[117]

When Stalin finally acted late on 9 September, he selected Chuikov, deputy commander of 64th Army, as Lopatin's replacement, with Major General N. I. Krylov as his chief of staff. Lopatin's current deputy and by trade an engineer, Nikolai Ivanovich Krylov had previously served with distinction as the Coastal Army's chief of staff during the sieges of Odessa and Sevastopol'.[118] As for Chuikov, the ongoing combat in the Stalingrad region prevented him from reaching Southwestern Front's headquarters east of the Volga River for almost three days.[119] During the intervening period of almost three days, Krylov tackled the arduous task of sorting out the army's forces and preparing to meet the Germans' final assaults into the city.

In this crisis, Eremenko, his chief of staff, Nikishov, and Stalingrad Front's Member of the Military Council (commissar), Nikita Sergeevich Khrushchev, turned to Vasilii Ivanovich Chuikov because he was a proven fighter who had displayed unusual doggedness and determination during the fighting in late July and August. Exasperated by his commanders' repeated failures to halt Army Group B's juggernaut, Stalin agreed to the change of command only after Eremenko personally vouched for Chuikov. The new commander of 62nd Army reported to Southeastern Front's headquarters, across the river from the stricken city, at 1000 hours on 12 September. In a brief conversation, Chuikov received his new command and a rudimentary outline of the tactical situation. At the end, Khrushchev asked Chuikov how he interpreted his mission: "'We cannot surrender the city to the enemy,' I replied, 'because it is extremely valuable to us, to the whole Soviet people. . . . All possible measures will be taken to prevent the city from falling. I don't ask for anything now, but I would ask the [Southwestern Front's] Military Council not to refuse me help when I ask for it, and I swear I shall stand firm. We will defend the city or die in the attempt.'"[120]

In retrospect, these words seem so stilted and melodramatic that one is tempted to question Chuikov's recollection of his speech. Yet the determined, almost fatalistic attitude he expressed undoubtedly reflected the mind-set of many Soviet soldiers at the time and certainly his own resolve.

That evening, after darkness had halted the German air attacks, Chuikov and his aides crossed the Volga River by ferry. In a truck with covered head-lights, he drove through a dead city, a set of burned-out ruins where civilians dug through the rubble searching for lost possessions. His way was lit by the fires started by German bombers. Eventually, Chuikov located his new head-quarters on the slope of Mamaev Kurgan:

I find myself in the dugout of the Army Chief of Staff, General N. I. Krylov, who has been Acting Commander. He is a thick-set, stocky man with a determined face.

Krylov's dugout, strictly speaking, is not a dugout at all, but a broad trench with a bench made of packed earth along one side, a bed made of earth on the other, and a table made of earth at the end of the bed. The roof is made of brushwood, with bits of straw sticking through it, and on top of the straw a layer of soil about twelve to fifteen inches thick. Shells and mortar bombs are exploding nearby. The explosions make the dugout shake, and soil runs down through the ceiling onto the spread-out maps and onto the heads of the people inside.

There are two people in the dugout—General Krylov, with a telephone in his hand, and the telephonist [telephone operator] on duty, Elena Bakarevich, a blue-eyed girl of about eighteen. Krylov is having strong words with someone or other. His voice is hard, loud, angry. The telephonist is sitting near the entrance with headphones on, answering someone: 'He is speaking on the other telephone. . . .'

I take out my papers and put them in front of Krylov. Continuing to tell somebody off, he glances at the papers, then finishes the conversation, and we introduce ourselves. In the poor light of a paraffin lamp, I see a

vigorous, stern, and, at the same time, friendly face. . . . The telephone
rings continually. Elena Bakarevich hands the telephone to Krylov. He is
giving instructions for the following day. . . . I listen to Krylov and at the
same time study his working map, the marks and arrows on it, trying to
feel my way into the events taking place. I realize that he has no time to
give me a report on the situation.[121]

As a veteran of the defenses of Odessa and Sevastopol', Krylov had extensive experience in organizing a desperate defense against German assaults.
Together with Chuikov, Krylov formed two-thirds of the troika that alter-
nately cajoled and threatened 62nd Army to hang on to Stalingrad despite
enormous German efforts and unimaginable human hardships. Krylov was
intellectual and precise; Chuikov, although equally analytical, gave the appearance of being more down-to-earth, alternating between joviality and
cold ruthlessness. The third member of the command team was 62nd Army's
Member of the Military Council, Kuz'ma Akimovich Gurov, by rank a divisional commissar and later a lieutenant general.[122] At this stage of the conflict, commissars were still more hatchetmen than cheerleaders, motivating
by fear more than by patriotic fervor. Even Gurov's bald head and contrasting dark, thick, threatening eyebrows conveyed a sense of menace. Gurov
had earned his spurs as a commissar in Western Front's 29th Army and in
Southwestern Front from January 1942. Together, Chuikov and Gurov used
encouragement, embarrassment, fear, and ruthless punishment to motivate
any whose faith wavered. NKVD guards at the ferry landings closely questioned anyone who sought to leave the city.[123]

The chief task facing Chuikov and the other members of his troika was to
restore a semblance of order to the almost shattered 62nd Army and trans-
form it into a force that could indeed defend Stalingrad to the last man.
As of 11 September, "to the last man" meant Chuikov's army had roughly
54,000 men and 115 tanks to expend before it would totally exhaust its fighting strength (see Tables 9 and 10).[124] However, since many of these troops
were assigned to the divisions' and brigades' rear-services organs, their combat regiments, battalions, and companies were significantly understrength.

THE FALL OF STALINGRAD'S SUBURBS, 10–12 SEPTEMBER

The *Stavka*'s concerns became a stark reality on 10 September when XXXX-
VIII Panzer Corps' 29th Motorized Division finally broke through to the
Volga River at Kuporosnoe (see Map 13).

Attacking overnight on 9–10 September in the wake of 24th Panzer Division, which had carved a corridor through the Soviet defenses, Fremerey's

Table 9. The Personnel Strength of 62nd Army's Rifle Formations on 11 September 1942

- 33rd Guards Rifle Division – 864 men
- 35th Guards Rifle Division – 454 men
- 87th Rifle Division – 1,819 men
- 98th Rifle Division – 465 men
- 112th Rifle Division – 2,297 men
- 131st Rifle Division – 2,540 men
- 196th Rifle Division – 1,004 men
- 229th Rifle Division – 192 men
- 244th Rifle Division – 3,685 men
- 315th Rifle Division – 2,873 men
- 399th Rifle Division – 565 men
- 10th Rifle Division NKVD – 8,615 men
- 10th Rifle Brigade – 1,912 men
- 115th Rifle Brigade – 4,868 men
- 149th Rifle Brigade – 4,125 men
- 124th Rifle Brigade –3,607 men
- 42nd Rifle Brigade – 5,032 men
- 9th Motorized Rifle Brigade – 1,073 men
- 38th Motorized Rifle Brigade – 2,370 men
- **Total** – 48,360 men

Source: Aleksei Isaev, *Stalingrad: Za Volgoi dlia nas zemli net* [Stalingrad: There is no land for use beyond Stalingrad] (Moscow: Iauza, Eksmo, 2008), 161–162, citing *TsAMO RF*, f. 345, op. 5487, d. 6, l. 3.

Table 10. The Combat Strength of Southeastern Front's Armored Units in Stalingrad on 10 September 1942

Force	Personnel		Vehicles			Tanks		
	Auth.	Present	Light	Trucks	Special	Heavy	Medium	Light
133rd TB	1,107	1,117	4	92	42	22	—	—
23rd TC	7,592	5,494	12	331	53	—	38	10
27th TB°	1,181	768	2	71	19	—	13	32
Total	9,880	7,379	18	494	114	22	51	42

Source: Isaev, *Stalingrad*, 64, citing *TsAMO RF*, f. 48, op. 468, d. 25, ll. 33, 35.
° Attached to 23rd Tank Corps on 12 September 1942.

division pierced the defenses at the junction of 62nd and 64th Armies and reached the Volga River:

On 4 September, 24th Panzer Division pushed along the Stalingrad-Kalach railroad line, through the western edge of the city, against weak enemy resistance. It appeared that the enemy was unable to hold the segment from the Volga west along the railroad line. After a brief regrouping, on 9

Map 13. Sixth Army's situation, 9–10 September 1942

September the [29th Motorized] Division as part of [XXXXVIII] Panzer
Corps moved along the southern side of the road to the approaches of the
Volga bridgehead near Verkhniaia El'shanka. . . . [The Germans advanced]
in bitter house-to-house fighting against the defending elements of 35th
Guards [Rifle] Division and 38th Motorized Infantry Brigade [should read
20th Tank Destroyer Brigade]. . . . Early on 10 September, 71st Infantry

Regiment of the [29th Motorized] Division became the first German troops to reach the Volga on the southern side of the city, near Kuporosnoe.[125]

If this crisis was not sufficiently serious, 62nd Army now faced assaults along its entire front from the Orlovka region southward to Kuporosnoe. The question was, after shifting its forces to and fro frantically during the previous week, Would the army's defenses be capable of holding the Germans short of the western bank of the Volga River (see Table 11)?

At dawn on 10 September, both wings of Weichs's assault forces resumed their advance on Stalingrad city, Sixth Army's LI Corps in the north and Fourth Panzer Army's XXXXVIII Panzer Corps in the south. In Seydlitz's LI Corps, Jänecke's 389th Infantry Division continued gnawing its way through the defenses of Colonel Andriusenko's composite force made up of 4th Battalion, 115th Rifle Brigade, 1st Battalion, 149th Rifle Brigade, and 1st Battalion, 124th Rifle Brigade, southwest of Orlovka, all the while fending off counterattacks by the remnants of General Popov's 23rd Tank Corps northeast of Gorodishche. On Jänecke's left, the three regiments of Wuthmann's 295th Infantry Division pressed eastward in the sector from Gorodishche southward to south of Razgulaevka Station, engaging 38th Motorized Rifle Brigade and elements of 112th Rifle Division east and southeast of Razgulaevka Station, the composite battalion of 6th Guards and 189th Tank Brigades near the hospital, and 6th Tank Brigade near the Motor Tractor Station. Still farther south, the three regiments of Hartmann's 71st Infantry Division continued pounding the defenses of 42nd Rifle Brigade and 244th Rifle Division's lone regiment north of the Tsaritsa River. By now, a portion of 6th Tank Brigade was supporting Batrakov's infantry.

The unrelenting pressure the two infantry divisions of Seydlitz's corps were applying against the center of 62nd Army's defenses in the sector from Gorodishche southward to the Tsaritsa River threatened to create multiple penetrations in the ever-thinning defenses of Chuikov's army west of Stalingrad. By this time, Khopko's 6th and Bystrik's 189th Tank Brigades had lost all of their tanks and were fighting as infantry, and Batrakov's 42nd Rifle Brigade and Ermolkin's and Afanas'ev's 112th and 244th Rifle Divisions were suffering from extreme attrition. To create reserves capable of strengthening 62nd Army's sagging defenses, Chuikov had already ordered the remnants of 399th and 112th Rifle Divisions, which numbered no more than several hundred men each, to withdraw and man new defensive positions along the heights west of the city, the former in the wooded hills west of Krasnyi Oktiabr' village, and the latter on the heights 1.5 kilometers southwest of the city's center. This meant the forces defending 62nd Army's center were situated only 4–6 kilometers west of the city's northern factory district and only 1.5–2 kilometers west of the city's center.

Table 11. The Dispositions and Actions of 62nd Army's Forces Late on 10 September 1942 (from north to south)

- **Northern Operational Sector** (Group Gorokhov)
  - **124th Rifle Brigade** (less 1st Battalion) defending the Rynok, Marker 35.0, and northwestern outskirts of Spartanovka line. Did not conduct combat operations during the day.
  - **149th Rifle Brigade** [less 1st Battalion] defending the (inclusive) Spartanovka, (incl.), separate building 1 kilometer southeast of Marker 93.2, and (incl.) gully northwest of Marker 93.2 line. Did not conduct combat operations.
  - **282nd Rifle Regiment** [**NKVD**] defending the gully (1 kilometer northwest of Marker 93.2), southern slope of Hill 135.4, and Marker 85.1 sector.
- **115th Rifle Brigade** [less 4th Battalion] defending the (incl.) Hill 135.4, southern slope of Hill 144.2, and hollow south of Hill 147.6 line. Attacks from the northwest by two enemy forces of up to a battalion each were repulsed.
- **Composite Rifle Regiment, 196th Rifle Division, 724th Rifle Regiment** (120 men), and **2nd Motorized Rifle Brigade** (up to 150 men) defending the (incl.) hollow southwest of Hill 147.6, Marker 108.8, and Marker 120.5 line. Repelled two enemy attacks during the second half of the day, inflicting heavy losses on submachine gunners filtering through along the hollow toward Orlovka by joint actions with the 115th Rifle Brigade.
- **4th Battalion, 115th Rifle Brigade** defending the (incl.) Hill 120.5 and Marker 128.0 line.
- **1st Battalion, 149th Rifle Brigade** defending the (incl.) Marker 128.0 and unnamed *balka* 2 kilometers south of Marker 128.0 line.
- **1st Battalion, 124th Rifle Brigade**, with its right flank in the *balka* 1.5 kilometers southeast of Hill 106.6 and its left flank 500 meters southeast of the detached farm on the eastern outskirts of Gorodishche, with its front facing toward the southwest.
- **6th Guards Tank Brigade** and **189th Tank Brigade**, formed into a composite battalion defending the Motor Tractor Station and unnamed village east of the Razgulaevka Station line.
- **38th Motorized Rifle Brigade** defending along the (incl.) unnamed village east of Razgulaevka Station and (incl.) Hill 153.7 line.
- **6th Tank Brigade** defending the Hill 153.7 and (incl.) Hospital line.
- **42nd Rifle Brigade** defending the (incl.) Hospital, eastern slope of Hill 133.4, and (incl.) detached building in the valley of the Tsaritsa River (2 kilometers east of Marker 50.7) line. The brigade repelled attempts by small groups of enemy to filter through the forward edge.
- **244th Rifle Division**, with the left flank battalion of 911th Rifle Regiment and the right flank battalion of 10th Rifle Brigade in the sector of the railroad line, withdrew 1 kilometer eastward under pressure from enemy aircraft and tanks.
- **133rd Tank Brigade** and **271st Rifle Regiment NKVD** defending the (incl.) Kuporosnoe and western part of Minina suburb (to the parallel of Marker 120.0) line.
- **35th Guards Rifle Division** repelled repeated attacks on their positions by enemy infantry and heavy tanks and armored transporters, with their force of no more than 150 soldiers and commanders.
- **131st Rifle Division** defending along its previous lines and withdrawing into the command's reserve in the vicinity of the railroad junction in the southern part of Stalingrad by the end of the day.
- **399th Rifle Division** serving as the army's mobile reserve and concentrated in the vicinity of the woods east of Marker 98.9.
- **27th Tank Brigade** concentrated in the woods in the vicinity of Ovrazhnaia Hill.
- **112th Rifle Division** defending the Marker 114.3 and Marker +0.8 line.

Table 11. (continued)

- **87th Rifle Division** transferred its personnel (up to 200 men) to fill out the composite detachment [battalion] of 6th Guards Tank Brigade. . . .
  The army commander has decided:
  a) After reinforcing the units up to 1,000 men at the expense of the rear services and by the commitment of the composite regiment of 399th Rifle Division, to restore the situation at the boundary between the 244th Rifle Division and 10th Rifle Brigade.
  b) Since the units of 131st Rifle Division have made their way into Kuporosnoe, to include them in the army's southern group of forces. After putting its units in order, the division will concentrate at the railroad junction in the Minina suburb in the southern group of forces' reserve, with the mission of occupying defenses in the designated region and be prepared to attack toward the Sadovaia, El'shanka, or Kuporosnoe railroads.[1]

---

[1] "Opersvodka no. 145" [Operational summary no. 145], in *62nd Army Combat Journal*. The personnel strength figures included in this report reflect the number of soldiers and officers in a given formation that were fighting on the western bank of the Volga River. For example, 87th Rifle Division had 120 "fighters" west of the river, although its total strength was roughly 1,819 men. The remaining troops were rear service support troops or artillerymen.

The situation was not much better on 62nd Army's left wing and on 64th Army's right wing, where XXXXVIII Panzer Corps was driving eastward toward the Volga River and, for a time, 29th Motorized Division actually reached the river's western bank. On the panzer corps' left, Lenski's 24th Panzer Division pushed eastward early on 10 September and reached the eastern approaches to Stalingrad's southern suburb of Minina by nightfall. This advance turned the left flank of the bulk of Afanas'ev's 244th Rifle Division, which was defending the sector from just east of Sadovaia Station northward to the Tsaritsa River and forced 10th Rifle and 133rd Tank Brigades to retreat eastward toward the western outskirts of the Minina suburb. Farther south, exploiting 29th Motorized Division's bold thrust the night before, when one of its battalions reached the Volga in a narrow sector south of Kuporosnoe, a combined assault by Heim's 14th Panzer and the main body of Fremerey's 29th Motorized Divisions forced Pesochin's 131st Rifle Division to withdraw to Gornaia Poliana State Farm, south of Minina, and Dubiansky's 35th Guards Rifle Division to man new defensive positions protecting the road extending from east of Sadovaia Station southeastward past Minina to the southwestern outskirts of Kuporosnoe.

Overnight on 10–11 September, however, Hoth's and Kempf's ardor cooled a bit; "the [29th Motorized Division's] battalion [at Kuporosnoe] lost the half mile adjacent to the river . . . when it was overrun by furious charges from the north and south, and the wild melees continued there for four more days."[126] In this case, the offending parties that spoiled 29th Division's success were elements of 131st Rifle and 35th Guards Rifle Divisions, which raced back to Kuporosnoe quickly enough to snuff out the motorized division's precarious foothold on the river before reinforcements arrived. Nevertheless, late on 10 September, the *Wehrmacht* High Command (*Oberkommando der Wehrmacht*—OKW) announced triumphantly, "The battle on the approaches to Stalingrad is continuing. During the course of fierce fighting, German forces penetrated the enemy's defensive positions south of the city and reached the Volga. The enemy's answering blows have been repelled."[127]

As Kempf's 24th Panzer and 29th Motorized Divisions were driving a dangerous wedge between 62nd and 64th Armies' defenses south of Kuporosnoe, after shifting most of its forces southward Heim's 14th Panzer Division drove 64th Army's 204th, 126th, and 138th Rifle Divisions back toward their new defensive line east and west of Gornaia Poliana, where they relieved 131st Rifle Division, allowing it to return northeastward to Kuporosnoe. During the sharp struggle on the approaches to Gornaia Poliana, 64th Army reported that 204th Rifle Division's 704th Regiment, while withdrawing, was encircled and virtually destroyed near Peschanka and that a regiment of 10th NKVD Rifle Division was also encircled and severely damaged south of Kuporosnoe. Although 64th Army's defenses contained 14th Panzer Division well short of Beketovka, by this time Shumilov's defending divisions were as severely worn down as those of 62nd Army.[128]

Encouraged by LI Army's and XXXXVIII Panzer Corps' progress over the previous five days, Weichs late on 10 September ordered Fourth Panzer Army to reorganize its forces and mount an advance northeastward directly into the southern half of Stalingrad city. Hoth, in turn, directed Kempf to begin moving his armor divisions into the southern section of Stalingrad the next day and, thereafter, seize the city "piece by piece."[129] From the perspective of Army Group B's commander, the only other problem Paulus's Sixth Army faced was the dilemma posed by the Orlovka salient, which LI Corps' 389th Infantry Division had still been unable to liquidate. In fact, lacking any substantial assistance from XIV Panzer Corps' armored divisions to the north and any tanks of their own, the infantry of Jänecke's division were still bogged down in an increasingly bloody fight for possession of the Orlovka salient. It was also clear that this dilemma would not go away unless and until Sixth Army found some means to reinforce the 389th's advance. Therefore, after directing Kempf's panzers to initiate their drive on Stalingrad city from the south, Paulus, early on 12 September, ordered Seydlitz to turn responsibility for the Orlovka battle over to Wietersheim's XIV Panzer Corps and get ready to attack "toward the Volga on the 13th."[130]

While Weichs and Paulus were pondering their next moves, fighting continued to rage along the western and southwestern approaches to Stalingrad, although LI Army's and XXXXVIII Panzer Corps' forward progress slowed noticeably. On 11 September LI Corps' 389th, 295th, and 71st Infantry

Divisions, now advancing abreast from north to south, drove eastward toward Orlovka and toward the heights above Stalingrad very slowly against fanatically fierce resistance (see Map 14). To free up 389th Division from the quagmire of Orlovka, during the day Paulus reinforced Seydlitz's army corps with Group Stahel, a *Luftwaffe* combat group formed around the nucleus of Colonel Rainer Stahel's 99th Flak (Antiaircraft) Regiment, and inserted Stahel's Group in the sector previously occupied by 389th Infantry Division's left wing. Stahel's mission was to help lock up Soviet forces in the Orlovka salient, thereby freeing up most of Jänecke's division to participate in LI Corps' climactic assault on Stalingrad city.

As before, on 11 September 62nd Army continued to defend the sector from Rynok westward to the shrinking salient around Orlovka with Group Gorokhov's 124th and 149th Rifle Brigades and 282nd NKVD Rifle Regiment. The salient itself contained 115th Rifle and 2nd Motorized Rifle Brigades, a composite regiment of 196th Rifle Division, and 724th Rifle Regiment, now combined under Andriusenko's command, and the detached battalions from 115th, 124th, and 149th Rifle Brigades. These forces faced scratch forces from XIV Panzer Corps and Group Stahel. Opposite LI Corps' three infantry divisions, Chuikov's army defended the sector stretching from the heights west of Stalingrad and east of Gorodishche southward to the Tsaritsa River with makeshift combat groups formed from 23rd Tank Corps' 6th Guards and 189th Tank and 9th Motorized Brigades, the three decimated regiments of 112th Rifle Division, and 38th Motorized and 42nd Rifle Brigades, reinforced by separate groups from 6th Tank Brigade, as well as one regiment of 244th Rifle Division. South of the Tsaritsa River, 62nd Army defended with the remaining two regiments of 244th Rifle Division, 10th Rifle and 133rd Tank Brigades, and 35th Guards and 131st Rifle Divisions facing XXXXVIII Panzer Corps' 24th Panzer and 29th Motorized Divisions.[131]

South of Stalingrad's suburb of Kuporosnoe, 64th Army's 126th and 138th Rifle Divisions, supported by the fresh 56th Tank Brigade and a student-officer regiment from the Krasnodar Infantry School, manned the Gornaia Poliana defensive line containing the advance of XXXXVIII Panzer Corps' 14th Panzer Division. Therefore, somehow but obviously with extreme exertions, Chuikov and Shumilov had managed to cobble together enough units to constitute a contiguous defensive line protecting the city from north, west, and south. However, the forces in both armies were threadbare at best and lacked adequate artillery support and the effective communications necessary to ensure coherence. Testifying to the appalling state of communications, Shumilov on 12 September reported that the right wing of his army's 126th Rifle Division, still loosely cooperating with elements of 62nd Army's 131st and 35th Guards Rifle Divisions, "had driven the enemy from Kuporosnoe," even though they had actually done so on the night of 10–11 September.[132]

Map 14. Sixth Army's situation, 11–12 September 1942

Meanwhile, on the German side of the front, Paulus and Hoth made final adjustments to their forces before commencing their final assault on the city. As Paulus was completing Group Stahel's relief of 389th Infantry Division, on 10 and 11 September Hoth shifted IV Army Corps' 94th Infantry Division northward from the Beketovka sector to provide infantry support for XXXX-VIII Panzer Corps' thrust into Stalingrad city.[133] The 94th, commanded by General of Artillery Georg Pfeiffer, who had led the division since August

1940, finally relieved 24th Panzer Division late on 11 September. Attesting to the severe attrition 24th Panzer Division had already suffered, by this time the division reported its combat strength was 8,714 men, as compared with its ration strength of 15,401 men, and it had only 14 operable tanks. By now Kempf was already shuttling his corps' precious remaining tanks back and forth between 24th and 14th Panzer Divisions.[134]

The battle for Stalingrad's suburbs reached its climax on 12 September when the divisions of Seydlitz's LI Corps and Kempf's XXXXVIII Panzer Corps completed the arduous process of clearing Soviet forces from most of the high ground west and southwest of the city. The most intense fighting this day took place in the relatively narrow 1.5–3-kilometer-wide strip of terrain west of the bluffs rising above Stalingrad city and its northern factory district. Specifically, it raged along a line extending southward from Orlovka, east of Gorodishche, Aleksandrovka, Razgulaevka Station, and the hospital, across the Tsaritsa River east of Poliakhovka, east of Sadovaia Station and through the western outskirts of Minina and El'shanka, and then westward through the southern outskirts of Kuporosnoe to the Volga River.

On the left wing of Weichs's assaulting force, LI Army Corps' Group Stahel and 389th, 295th, and 71st Infantry Divisions, deployed abreast from Gorodishche in the north to the Tsaritsa River in the south, advanced slowly eastward, pressing the four detached battalions of Group Gorokhov's brigades' deeper into the Orlovka salient and, farther south, the remnants of 23rd Tank Corps' 6th Guards and 189th Tank and 9th Motorized Brigades, parts of 112th Rifle Division, 38th Motorized, 42nd Rifle, and 6th Tank Brigades, and 244th Rifle Division's regiment eastward toward the bluffs west of the factory-district villages, Mamaev Kurgan, and Stalingrad's center city.

South of the Tsaritsa River, the right wing of Weichs's assaulting force, XXXXVIII Panzer Corps' 24th Panzer, 94th Infantry, and 29th Motorized Divisions, struck eastward against the defenses of 244th Rifle Division, 10th Rifle Brigade, 10th NKVD Rifle Division's 271st Regiment, and 35th Guards Rifle Division. These defenders were now reinforced by Colonel N. M. Bubnov's fresh but tankless 133rd Tank Brigade in the sector from the Tsaritsa River southward through the western outskirts of Minina, El'shanka, and Kuporosnoe. Still farther south, XXXXVIII Panzer Corps' 14th Panzer Division, flanked on the right by IV Army Corps' Romanian 20th and 297th and 371st Infantry Divisions, probed the defenses of 64th Army's 126th, 138th, 204th, 157th, and 29th Rifle Divisions, stretched out from the southwestern outskirts of Kuporosnoe southwestward through Gornaia Poliana to Elkhi and Shumilov's 66th and 154th Naval Rifle Brigades and 36th Guards Rifle Division to the army's boundary with 57th Army at Ivanovka.[135]

By this time, Chuikov, who had just assumed command of 62nd Army, had already prudently constituted a new reserve. This consisted of the remnants of Travnikov's 399th Rifle Division concentrated in the woods 4 kilometers southeast of Orlovka, Ermolkin's 112th Rifle Division, and Major Popov's 27th Tank Brigade, positioned in Krasnyi Oktiabr' village and the woods east of Razgulaevka Station, and Pesochin's 131st Rifle Division, assembled in the southern part of Stalingrad city. However, because all of these units had themselves been decimated in the previous fighting, Chuikov was indeed depending for success on slender reeds.

As Weichs's ground forces closed in on downtown Stalingrad and the city's northern factory district, the air battle over the battlefield and the city intensified. The *Luftwaffe's* objectives in this battle included the city's beleaguered defenders and its population. For example, between 5 and 12 September *Luftflotte* 4 conducted an average of 938 sorties per day, the majority of them over Stalingrad. Strapped by aircraft shortages, Major General Timofei Timofeevich Khriukin's 8th Air Army, which was assigned to Stalingrad Front, was able to fly only about 354 sorties per day in response.[136] This air army had only 137 operable aircraft on 3 September. Therefore, on 6 September the *Stavka* ordered Khriukin's air army to give priority support to Zhukov's armies north of Stalingrad and also released Major General Pavel Stepanovich Stepanov's 16th Air Army, then in its reserve, to protect 62nd and 64th Armies struggling in and south of the city. To enable Stepanov's air army to do so, the *Stavka* assigned it two fresh fighter aviation regiments, also from its reserve. In the same directive, Stalin ordered his air force chief, Lieutenant General Aleksandr Aleksandrovich Novikov, to coordinate both of the air army's operations.[137]

By nightfall on 12 September, the battle for Stalingrad's suburbs was virtually over. Weichs's forces were in possession of most of the high ground west and southwest of the city, save for the shrunken salient around Orlovka, and both Seydlitz's LI Corps and Kempf's XXXXVIII Panzer Corps were poised to mount their culminating drive into the city. With a total of four infantry divisions (389th, 295th, 71st, and 94th), two panzer divisions (24th and 14th), and one motorized division (29th), the Germans' Stalingrad assault force still numbered about 80,000 men and roughly 110 tanks and assault guns. These figures did not include the 8,000–10,000 men and additional armor from Wietersheim's XIV Panzer Corps, which could join the action north of the city when and if the fighting in the Kotluban' region ended.[138]

By this time, all of 62nd and 64th Armies' formations and units had suffered severe attrition, which reduced the two armies' total strength from about 104,000 men and 200–250 tanks on 3 September to about 90,000 men and 120 tanks on 12 September.[139] However, many of the armies' divisions were in even sadder state, in danger of losing their cohesion and combat effectiveness. For example, 35th Guards and 131st, 315th, 112th, and 399th Rifle Divisions numbered 20–25 percent of their authorized strength of

10,386 men and far fewer bayonets, and 87th, 98th, and 196th Rifle Divisions fielded about 800, 300, and 400 bayonets, respectively.[140] These and other divisions and brigades suffered the heaviest attrition in their combat units and subunits, meaning strength in terms of riflemen constituted an ever smaller proportion of overall strength. Clearly, if Southeastern Front was to mount an effective defense of the city, additional reinforcements were required.

CONCLUSIONS

The intense fighting around and north of Stalingrad during the first 12 days of September provided the context for and, ultimately, the form of the even more desperate struggle that followed. This expanding struggle would take place in three specific regions: first in Stalingrad city and its northern factory district; second, and simultaneously, in the land bridge between the Don and Volga Rivers along the northern, northwestern, and southern flanks of the battle in Stalingrad; and third along the banks of the Don and Volga Rivers far to the northwest and in the Beketovka bridgehead south of Stalingrad.

Although the fierce assaults by Zhukov's four armies in the Kotluban' region demonstrated the futility of attempting to rescue 62nd and 64th Armies by an offensive directly from the north, they also indicated the limiting effects such an offensive could have on the ability of German forces to mount and sustain a drive to capture Stalingrad. Therefore, Zhukov resolved to continue this offensive action come what may, at least for the foreseeable future. Ultimately, their failed multiple counterstrokes in the Kotluban' region would convince Zhukov, Eremenko, and the *Stavka* that, in order to penetrate, encircle, and destroy Army Group B's forces in the Stalingrad region, it would be necessary to marshal their forces and conduct an even larger-scale offensive, certainly far more distant from Stalingrad, from bridgeheads across the Don and Volga Rivers. Drawing upon his experiences at Leningrad in September 1941 and Moscow in December 1941, Zhukov by mid-September also believed the Germans had committed so much strength to their drive on Stalingrad that conditions might be conducive for the conduct of multiple strategic offensives across the entire German-Soviet front, first and foremost in the Moscow region.

As for the battle in Stalingrad itself, because the Germans appeared preoccupied with capturing Stalin's namesake city, Zhukov, Eremenko, and the *Stavka* were convinced that Hitler would employ whatever forces were required to do so, even at the expense of seriously weakening other sectors of the front. To ensure that 62nd and 64th Armies functioned as meat grinders —chewing up attacking German forces without losing the city—Stalin appointed tough men like Chuikov and Shumilov to command 62nd and 64th Armies. He also reinforced their armies with just enough forces to guarantee they could perform this task without detracting from the assembly and concentration of reserves necessary to conduct counteroffensives. Meanwhile, to facilitate the success of the grander offensive efforts, Stalin directed the armies of the Stalingrad and Southeastern Fronts deployed along the Don River northwest of the city and along the Volga River south of the city to hold firm to the bridgeheads they already controlled in such locations as Serafimovich, Kletskaia, and Beketovka. In fact, Stalin ordered these armies to expand the bridgeheads and capture new ones as well if the opportunity arose.

Regarding the fighting in the Kotluban' region and along the approaches to Stalingrad, clearly the Germans emerged victorious in both struggles. In the former, Paulus's VIII Army and XIV Panzer Corps denied Zhukov's four armies their objective and seriously bloodied them in the process. In the latter, Paulus's LI Army Corps and Hoth's XXXXVIII Panzer Corps reached and penetrated Stalingrad's suburbs, in the process decimating Lopatin's 62nd and Shumilov's 64th Armies. However, for those who thought the subsequent advance into Stalingrad would be easier, they were mistaken because they overlooked two vivid lessons derived from the previous two weeks of fighting. First, despite its failure the Kotluban' offensive succeeded in thwarting Weichs's original plan for seizing the city by reducing German air support for Paulus's shock group advancing on Stalingrad and by preventing Sixth Army's northern pincer, XIV Panzer Corps, from taking part in the assault on the city's factory district. Second, 62nd and 64th Armies' stout resistance along the approaches to Stalingrad indicated that the strength of Weichs's assault group attacking the city was inadequate to the task. Instead of seizing the city from the march as Weichs, Paulus, and Hoth had hoped, the advance by their shock groups had degenerated by mid-September into a grinding and costly struggle for terrain, measured in hundreds of meters per day. If this advance was to continue, additional troops clearly were required.

Despite this positive appreciation of the fighting at Kotluban' and on the approaches to Stalingrad, one Russian historian offers a far more somber and caustic assessment:

> Summarizing the results of the first stage of the battle for Stalingrad, one can say with confidence that the Soviet military leadership performed in undistinguished fashion. Paulus and Hoth, who had at their disposal 18 German and 4 Romanian divisions, including 3 panzer and 3 motorized divisions, conducted a successful offensive for two months. Troubled by Comrade Stalin, during these two months, Generals Gordov, Eremenko, Vasilevsky, and Zhukov were able to commit more than 60 rifle divisions,

8 tank corps, 12 separate tank brigades, and several separate tank battalions, with about 2,500 tanks, into combat in the Stalingrad region. Over the course of three months of combat, during this time 13th Tank Corps alone received four complete sets of combat equipment up to its establishment [table of equipment] requirements and again lost 550 combat vehicles.

And now the enemy stood at the banks of the Volga River and, adorned with numerous stars and kilograms of orders [decorations], the military chiefs are telling us tales about the enemy's four- to six-fold superiority and how the "Soviet military leadership learned much in the difficult school of modern war during the fierce battles on the approaches to Stalingrad."

On the one hand, Comrade Stalin could sympathize with them, on the other—he himself had trained this cadre.[141]

If the Red Army's senior command cadre in the Stalingrad region hoped to prevail in the subsequent fighting, this meant they would have to perform far better than they had during late July, August, and early September. Only time would tell whether they succeeded or not.

CHAPTER 3

The Battle for Central and Southern Stalingrad, 13–26 September 1942

OPPOSING FORCES

As mid-September approached, Hitler, his OKW and OKH, and the *Wehrmacht's* field commanders were convinced that Operation Blau was reaching its culminating point in both Stalingrad and the Caucasus. Along the Stalingrad axis late on 12 September, the main forces of Army Group B were concentrated along the southern bank of the Don River from Verkhnyi Mamon to Vertiachii, eastward astride the land bridge between the Don River at Vertiachii and the northern outskirts of Rynok on the Volga River, southward in an arc extending around the immediate periphery of Stalingrad, and southward west of Beketovka and the lake region south of Stalingrad into the vast expanse of steppe lands east of Elista. The Italian Eighth Army defended the Don River front from Verkhnyi Mamon eastward to the Serafimovich region opposite Stalingrad Front's 63rd Army. On the army group's right wing, the Romanian Fourth Army defended the extended front south of Stalingrad, and 16th Motorized Division screened its extreme right flank against Southeastern Front's 57th, 51st, and 28th Armies. Most important from the Führer's perspective, Weichs's main shock group—Paulus's Sixth and Hoth's Fourth Panzer Armies—were finally poised to assault and capture Stalingrad.

However, because Sixth Army still had to protect its long left wing along the Don River and between the Don and the Volga Rivers, only a portion of it was available to participate in the assault on Stalingrad. Specifically, Sixth Army's XVII Army Corps defended the Don River front from Serafimovich to Kletskaia with its 79th and 113th Infantry and 22nd Panzer Divisions, and XI Army Corps protected the Don River front from Kletskaia to Vertiachii with its 376th, 100th Jäger, 44th, and 384th Infantry Divisions. These two corps faced Stalingrad Front's 21st Army. East of the Don River, 305th and 76th Infantry Divisions of Sixth Army's VIII Army Corps still faced Stalingrad Front's 4th Tank and 24th Armies in the western half of the land bridge between the Don and Volga Rivers. Most of 60th and 3rd Motorized and 16th Panzer Divisions of XIV Panzer Corps protected the eastern section of the land bridge against Stalingrad Front's 1st Guards and 66th Armies.[1]

Therefore, only Seydlitz's LI Army Corps, with Group Stahel, 389th, 295th, and 71st Infantry Divisions, and whatever forces Wietersheim's XIV

Panzer Corps could spare from its front were available to participate in the assault on the city. Stahel's group was a composite force consisting of *Luftwaffe* troops from Flak [antiaircraft] Regiment 99 and other ground support units headed by Colonel Reiner Stahel, the regiment's commander. Stahel's group was formed by 12 September and assigned to LI Corps. Seydlitz and later XIV Panzer Corps employed this *kampfgruppe* as an economy-of-force unit to help contain Soviet forces isolated in the salient around the village of Orlovka, northwest of Stalingrad.[2] This was a precursor to more widespread use of *Luftwaffe* forces in a ground combat role beginning in December 1942 and reflected the *Luftwaffe*'s reluctance to transfer its ground personnel to the control of the understrength German Army.

Only half of Hoth's Fourth Panzer Army was available to take part in the assault on the city proper. The IV Army Corps was containing Southeastern Front's 64th Army in its bridgehead west of Beketovka with its German 297th and 371st Infantry Divisions and Romanian 20th Infantry Division. Farther south, the three infantry divisions of the Romanian VI Army Corps were defending the panzer army's long right wing in the lake region south of Stalingrad against Southeastern Front's 57th and 51st Armies.[3] Therefore, this should have left Hoth with 24th Panzer, 94th Infantry, and 29th Motorized Divisions of Kempf's XXXXVIII Panzer Corps to participate in the assault on the southern part of the city. However, once 29th Motorized Division reached the Volga River south of Kuporosnoe, Hoth turned 14th Panzer southward to operate against the northern flank of the Beketovka bridgehead, thus reducing Kempf's city assault force to just four divisions. Since previous combat indicated that Paulus's and Hoth's shock groups were too weak to seize the city quickly, as mid-September approached Weichs and Paulus were already undertaking measures to reinforce Sixth Army.

As Chuikov was assuming command of 62nd Army and Weichs was preparing for the first major assault on the city, Hitler was also restructuring Army Group B and adjusting its objectives. Reflecting his determination to manage the war personally, the German dictator held a planning conference at *Werwolf*, his headquarters near Vinnitsa in the Ukraine, on 12 September. Accounts of this conference are somewhat suspect considering that the participants tended to blame Hitler for their subsequent defeats. Apparently, however, Friedrich Paulus, as commander of Sixth Army, and Maximilian von Weichs, his superior as commander of Army Group B, arrived at Vinnitsa to find their Führer convinced the battle of Stalingrad was virtually over.[4]

Based on the repeated Soviet defeats of the previous months, combined with optimistic German intelligence estimates about the weakness of the Red Army, Hitler believed his opponents were incapable of launching a major counteroffensive. Paulus and Weichs reportedly expressed concern about the difficulty of capturing the city and the vulnerability of the long German flank north of Stalingrad. Given Hitler's recent dismissal of generals who had expressed similar doubts, his refusal to accept such warnings was entirely in character. Instead, he insisted on the prompt capture of Stalingrad and transferred XXXXVIII Panzer Corps' 24th Panzer, 94th Infantry, and 29th Motorized Divisions to Sixth Army, effective by 15 September, to expedite this process. Hitler also directed Army Group B to conduct a number of minor operations to straighten out its long left wing and further defend Voronezh.

Issued on 13 September, Hitler's new instructions addressed the problems at Stalingrad and also recommended solutions for other potentially threatened sectors of Army Group B:

1. Army Group B must prepare the "average solution" to the matter of its front line trace. If the offensive encounters weakening enemy resistance, you should reinforce your efforts to destroy the enemy by attacks with mobile forces through the final positions designated by the "average solution." Finally, submit timely reports with exact data on the forces being employed and begin the offensive.

2. At the same time, prepare the projected attack toward Astrakhan in the spirit of the previously issued directives. Also submit reports with information about the forces employed and the timing of the offensive.

3. For the time being, you can wait a bit for the improvement of the situation at the junction of Sixth and Eighth Italian Army by means of offensive operations. At first, you can employ 22nd Panzer Division and 113th Infantry Division, which are earmarked for this purpose, for pushing the front back north of Stalingrad. On the contrary, you can deploy 1st Rumanian [Cavalry] Division as rapidly as possible as an immediate reserve behind XVII Army Corps. . . .

4. I agree with the front line trace envisioned by the army group in XXIV Panzer Corps' sector in the Don bend.

5. You should attach special importance to the rapid preparation of positions on the Don west of Voronezh and also cut-off positions behind 387th, 377th, and 385th Infantry Divisions.[5]

Most important, Hitler's instructions specified that Army Group B, if the Soviet defenses north of Stalingrad weakened suddenly, should launch an immediate pursuit to the east.

Fatefully, as it turned out, Hitler permitted Weichs to postpone any action against the Red Army's bridgeheads on the southern bank of the Don River at Serafimovich, instead authorizing him to bolster Sixth Army's defenses in the land bridge between the Don and Volga Rivers with 22nd Panzer and 113th Infantry Divisions and the Hungarian Second Army's defenses with XXIV Panzer Corps. Ever ambitious, the Führer still insisted on the viability of the advance by Hoth's XXXXVIII Panzer Corps on Astrakhan', although this depended on its rapid completion of the battle for Stalingrad city.

By day's end on 12 September, Weichs was already withdrawing 22nd Panzer Division into Army Group B's reserve. More significant, with the OKH's permission the lead elements of the Romanian Third Army's V Corps were deploying forward into the sector of Sixth Army's XVII and XI Army Corps to relieve part of their forces (in particular, 113th Infantry and 100th Jäger Divisions) so that they could regroup eastward into the Stalingrad region. The Romanian 1st Cavalry Division was already occupying forward positions on XI Army Corps' left wing east of Kletskaia, and the Romanian 13th and 6th Infantry Divisions were closing into assembly areas in XVII and XI Army Corps' rear areas. At the same time, Sixth Army's 298th Infantry Division was resting and refitting in the Bokovskaia region in XVII Army Corps' rear, preparing to reinforce that corps' defenses.[6] Two burning questions were: (1) Could these reinforcements reach Stalingrad in time to make a difference? and (2) Once they occupied defenses along the southern bank of the Don River, could the Romanians defend their sector effectively?

Hitler had previously agreed to transfer General Petre Dumitrescu's Romanian Third Army from the Caucasus to the Kletskaia and Elanskaia sector of the Don River front, northwest of Stalingrad. At least initially, the purpose of this movement was more political than military. Hitler had apparently planned to give his loyal Romanian ally, Marshal Ion Antonescu, the appearance of a field command as part of a proposed Romanian army group on the relatively quiet flank. As Dumitrescu would complain to the OKH on 24 September, however, his Third Army of 69 battalions had to defend a sector of 168 kilometers, or more than 2.4 kilometers per battalion.[7] Even more tellingly, the threadbare Romanian forces lacked the antitank weapons necessary to halt any serious mechanized attack.

By day's end on 12 September, the combatants and their commanders who would conduct the first stage of the assault on Stalingrad were in position to commence Hitler's climactic battle (see Tables 12 and 13).[8]

According to most Soviet and Russian sources, 62nd and 64th Armies fielded a combined total of roughly 90,000 men, with 54,000 in the former and 36,000 in the latter, facing a German force totaling 170,000 men.[9] However, because this figure includes XIV Panzer Corps and other forces the Germans did not commit to the battle for the city, Weichs's shock groups attacking the city proper actually numbered about 80,000 men, supported by about 100 tanks and assault guns.

As far as the armor strength of the opposing forces in the Stalingrad region was concerned, Southeastern Front's tank park contained roughly 150 tanks on 13 September, with about 100 in 62nd Army and 44 in 64th Army.[10] Most of these tanks were assigned either to General Popov's 23rd Tank

Table 12. The Dispositions of Opposing Forces along the Stalingrad Axis Late on 12 September 1942

GERMAN		SOVIET	
Force	Sector	Force	Sector
The Land Bridge between the Don and Volga Rivers			
Sixth Army		**Stalingrad Front**	
VIII Army Corps			
305th Infantry Division	Vertiachii-Samofalovka	4th Tank Army (27th, 37th Gds., 18th, 214th, 292nd, and 298th Rifle Divisions, 193rd Tank Brigade, and 22nd Motorized Rifle Brigade)	Vertiachii-Samofalovka
76th Infantry Division	Samofalovka-564 km Station	24th Army (173rd, 207th, 221st, 308th, and 315th Rifle Divisions and 217th Tank Brigade)	Samofalovka-564 km Station
XIV Panzer Corps			
60th Motorized Division	564 km Station-7 kilometers east of Kuz'michi	1st Guards Army (38th, 39th, 41st Gds., 24th, 64th, 84th, 87th, and 116th Rifle Divisions, and 4th, 7th, and 16th Tank Corps)	564 km Station-Sukhaia Mechetka *Balka*
3rd Motorized Division	7 kilometers east of Kuz'michi-Sukhaia Mechetka *Balka*		
16th Panzer Division	Sukhaia Mechetka *Balka*-Akatovka on the Volga River	66th Army (49th, 99th, 120th, 231st, 299th, and 316th Rifle Divisions and 10th, 69th, 148th, and 246th Tank Brigades)	Sukhaia Mechetka *Balka*-Akatovka on the Volga River

Table 12. (continued)

GERMAN		SOVIET	
Force	Sector	Force	Sector
Sixth Army		**Stalingrad**	
XIV Panzer Corps		**Southeastern Front**	
		62nd Army (33rd Gds. and 229th Rifle Divisions and 129th Rifle Brigade) (refitting)	
16th Panzer Division	Rynok-east of Orlovka	124th (-) and 149th (-) Rifle Brigades and 282nd Rifle Regiment NKVD	Rynok-Spartanovka-Hill 93.2-Hill 135.4 (2 kilometers east of Orlovka)
3rd Motorized Division	North of Orlovka	115th Rifle Brigade (-)	Hill 135.4-Hill 144.2-Hill 147.6 (3 kilometers north of Orlovka)
60th Motorized Division	Northwest of Orlovka	724th Rifle Regiment (196th Rifle Division)	Hill 147.6- Marker 108.8 (northwest of Orlovka)
LI Army Corps			
Group Stahel			
	West of Orlovka	2nd Motorized Rifle Brigade (Battalion), with 399th Rifle Division in reserve.	Marker 108.8-Marker 120.5 (west of Orlovka)
389th Infantry Division	West of Orlovka-east of Gorodishche	2nd Motorized Rifle Brigade (-), 4th Battalion, 115th Rifle Brigade, 1st Battalion, 149th Rifle Brigade, and 1st Battalion, 124th Rifle Brigade,	Hill 120.5-Marker 128.0-farm on eastern outskirts of Gorodishche
295th Infantry Division	Motor Tractor Station (MTC) (1 kilometer northeast of Razgulaevka Station-west of Krasnyi Oktiabr' village	6th Gds. Tank Brigade, with 87th Rifle Division, 189th Tank Brigade, 38th Motorized Rifle Brigade, and 112th Rifle Division, with 27th Tank Brigade in reserve.	MTC (1 kilometer northeast of Razgulaevka Station)-Hill 153.7 (west of Krasnyi Oktiabr' village)
71st Infantry Division	West of Krasnyi Oktiabr' village-Tsaritsa River	6th Tank Brigade, 42nd Rifle Brigade, and one rifle regiment, 244th Rifle Division	Hill 153.7-Hospital-2 kilometers east of Marker 50.7-Tsaritsa River

Table 12. (continued)

GERMAN		SOVIET	
Force	Sector	Force	Sector
Fourth Panzer Army <u>XXXVIII Panzer Corps</u>			
24th Panzer Division	Tsaritsa River-west of Sadovaia Station	Two rifle regiments, 244th Rifle Division, 10th Rifle Brigade, 6th Tank Brigade (-), with dug in tanks and 100 men, and 131st Rifle Division in reserve	Tsaritsa River-railroad Marker 120.0 (west of Sadovaia Station)
94th Infantry Division	West of Sadovaia Station-Minina	133rd Tank Brigade and 271st Rifle Regiment NKVD	Marker 120.0-western part of Minina suburb
29th Motorized Division	Minina-Kuporosnoe	35th Gds Rifle Division	Minina-Kuporosnoe
The Beketovka Bridgehead			
Fourth Panzer Army <u>IV Army Corps</u>		<u>64th Army</u> (66th and 154th Naval Rifle Brigades [refitting] and 118th Fortified Region in Beketovka)	
14th Panzer Division	Kuporosnoe-Gornaia Poliana	126th, 204th, and 138th Rifle Divisions, 13th Tank Corps (-), and Krasnodar Infantry School.	Kuporosnoe-Gornaia Poliana
Romanian 20th Infantry Division	West of Gornaia Poliana	157th Rifle Division	West of Gornaia Poliana
297th Infantry Division	North and south of Elkhi	29th and 38th Rifle Divisions and 133rd Tank Brigade, 13th Tank Corps	North and south of Elkhi
371st Infantry Division	Northwest and southwest of Ivanovka	36th Gds Rifle Division	Northwest of Ivanovka
<u>Romanian VI Army Corps</u> Romanian 2nd Infantry Division	Tundutovo-Dubovoi Ovrag	422nd and 15th Gds, and 244th Rifle Divisions, 6th Tank Brigade, and 76th Fortified Region <u>57th Army</u>	Southwest of Ivanovka-Tundutovo-Dubovoi Ovrag

Note: Notation "(=)" means without some part of the forces

Table 13. The Composition and Commanders of Forces Fighting in Stalingrad City, 12 September–18 November 1942 (from north to south)

Sixth Army – General of Panzer Troops Friedrich Paulus
  XIV Panzer Corps – General of Infantry Gustav Wietersheim, Lieutenant General Hans-Valentin Huge on 15 September
    16th Panzer Division – Lieutenant General Hans-Valentin Hube, Lieutenant General Günther Angern on 15 September
    3rd Motorized Division – Lieutenant General Helmuth Schlömer
    60th Motorized Division – Major General Otto Kohlermann, Major General Hans-Adolf von Arensdorff in November
  LI Army Corps – General of Artillery Walter von Seydlitz-Kurzbach Group Stahel – Colonel Reiner Stahel
    389th Infantry Division – Lieutenant General Erwin Jänecke, Major General Erich Magnus on 1 November
    295th Infantry Division – General of Artillery Rolf Wuthmann, Major General Doctor Otto Korfes on 16 November
    71st Infantry Division – General of Infantry Alexander von Hartmann
  XXXXVIII Panzer Corps – General of Panzer Troops Werner Kempf, Lieutenant General Ferdinand Heim on 1 November
    24th Panzer Division – Major General Bruno *Ritter* von Hauenschild, Major General Arno von Lenski on 12 September
    94th Infantry Division – General of Artillery Georg Pfeiffer
    29th Motorized Division – Lieutenant General Max Fremerey, Major General Hans-Georg Leyser on 28 September

62nd Army – Lieutenant General V. I. Chuikov
  Group Gorokhov – Colonel S. F. Gorokhov
    124th Rifle Brigade – Colonel S. F. Gorokhov
    149th Rifle Brigade
    282nd Rifle Regiment NKVD
  Orlovka Grouping
    115th Rifle Brigade – Colonel K. M. Andriusenko
    724th Rifle Regiment, 196th Rifle Division
    2nd Motorized Rifle Brigade
  399th Rifle Division – Colonel N. G. Travnikov (in reserve)
  23rd Tank Corps – Major General A. F. Popov, Colonel V. V. Koshelev on 16 October
    6th Guards Tank Brigade – Colonel M. K. Skuba
    189th Tank Brigade – Lieutenant Colonel F. I. Bystrik (reorganized as 189th Tank Regiment on 26 October)
    27th Tank Brigade – Major P. G. Popov, Major P. F. Luchnikov on 10 September (in reserve) (reorganized as 18th Tank Regiment on 26 October)
    9th Motorized Rifle Brigade
  38th Motorized Rifle Brigade – Colonel I. D. Burmakov
  112th Rifle Division – Colonel I. E. Ermolkin, Major Ia. D. Filonenko on 16 November
    241st Rifle Regiment (composite) – Captain V. A. Aseev
  6th Tank Brigade – Lieutenant Colonel S. A. Khopko (reorganized as 19th Guards Tank and 73rd Tank Regiments on 12 October)
  42nd Rifle Brigade – Colonel M. S. Batrakov (wounded in action on 23 September)
  244th Rifle Division – Colonel G. A. Afanas'ev
  10th Rifle Brigade – Colonel I. D. Driakhlov
  133rd Tank Brigade (Heavy) – Colonel N. M. Bubnov

Table 13. (continued)

10th NKVD Rifle Division – Colonel A. A. Saraev
   269th Rifle Regiment – NKVD Lieutenant Colonel Kapranov
   270th Rifle Regiment – Major Zhuravlev (subordinate to 269th Rifle Regiment
     NKVD on 8 September and, later, 271st Rifle Regiment NKVD)
   271st Rifle Regiment – NKVD Major Kostenitsyn
   272nd Rifle Regiment – NKVD Major Savchuk
   282nd Rifle Regiment
35th Guards Rifle Division – Major General V. A. Glazkov, Colonel V. P. Dubiansky on
   8 September, and Colonel F. A. Ostashenko on 21 November
131st Rifle Division – Colonel M. A. Pesochin

Refitting in the rear:
87th Rifle Division – Colonel A. I. Kazartsev (combined with 6th Guards Tank Brigade)
33rd Guards Rifle Division – Colonel (Major General on 14 October) A. I. Utvenko
229th Rifle Division – Major General V. N. Martsenkevich
129th Rifle Brigade

Corps, to which many of the units and tanks of former 2nd and 13th Tank Corps had been attached, or the *front's* separate tank brigades. For example, 23rd Tank Corps' 6th Guards Tank Brigade fielded 15 T-34 and 4 T-70 tanks, and its 6th Tank Brigade 18 T-34 tanks. The 133rd Tank Brigade (formerly in 13th Tank Corps but now separate) had 23 KV tanks, and the former 2nd Tank Corps' 26th Tank Brigade had 18 inoperable T-34 tanks, which were partially buried in the ground near Sadovaia Station. The 23rd Tank Corps' 9th Motorized Rifle and 189th Tank Brigades were in reserve near Krasnyi Oktiabr' village, the latter with 8 T-34s and 6 T-70s. Including 27th Tank Brigade, which was attached to 189th Brigade, 23rd Tank Corps fielded a total of 56 operational tanks.[11]

Most Russian sources assert that Sixth Army fielded 500 tanks in the Stalingrad region and committed all of them against 62nd Army. By 13 September, however, Weichs's forces assaulting downtown Stalingrad employed roughly 100 tanks and assault guns, with about 30–40 tanks combined in 24th and 14th Panzer Divisions and no more than 20 in 29th Motorized Division. For example, 24th Panzer Division had only 19 operational tanks on 13 September and 22 on 18 September. Although the division's tank strength increased to 27 on 10 October and 34 on 17 October, during the last week in October and the first two weeks of November its daily tank strength averaged only 14 armored vehicles.[12] In addition, the bulk of 16th Panzer and 3rd and 60th Motorized Divisions' tanks, which totaled no more than 100 armored vehicles, were committed to defending the land bridge between the Don and Volga Rivers, where Stalingrad Front resumed its counteroffensive at dawn on 18 September.

In addition, LI Army and XXXXVIII Panzer Corps were supported by approximately 30–40 assault guns [*sturmgeschutzen*] assigned to special assault-gun battalions, such as the 177th, 244th, and 245th, which the army group or Sixth Army routinely attached to their subordinate corps or divisions. These battalions fielded between five and 17 serviceable guns on any given day.[13] The Soviets routinely counted these guns and other mobile artillery pieces as tanks. In any event, once the opposing forces joined battle in the city's streets and the rubble of its buildings, the assault guns were useful in destroying buildings, but the tanks proved vulnerable in the city's streets.

At the outset of Weichs's assault on Stalingrad, because of the lack of depth between its forces and the Volga River, 62nd Army was defending in a shallow two-echelon formation, with its reserves actually constituting a second echelon 1.5–3 kilometers behind the forward forces and within the city itself. The 64th Army also defended in single echelon formation, with the bulk of its forces and reserves concentrated on its right wing to thwart 14th Panzer Division's advance toward Beketovka. The Volga Flotilla's 1st Brigade of River Ships provided fire support for the forces on the army's right wing.[14]

Given the restrictive depth of their bridgeheads, which ranged from 10 to 12 kilometers in the south and north and far less in the center, both armies would experience difficulty in maneuvering their forces laterally and in the depths. Compounding this problem, the excessive width of the Volga River, which reached up to 1,000 meters in some sectors, made resupplying the forces in the city difficult and treacherous, particularly given German dominance in the skies. Nor was the terrain in the Stalingrad region favorable for effective defense. German control of the dominant heights above the city offered superb observation and fields of fire into the city's blocks and buildings, permitting the Germans to pour effective fire into the defending Soviet soldiers' ranks. Once German infantry reached the Volga, they were able to subject surviving pockets of defenders to devastating flanking fire. Yet once German bombing and artillery reduced the city and its factory district to rubble, the mountains of debris offered excellent concealment for Red Army soldiers resisting the advancing German infantry.

To counter the Germans' advantages in terms of terrain, 62nd and 64th Armies organized special artillery and mortar groups to provide fire support, each with two to four artillery and mortar regiments. The 62nd Army then subdivided its group into northern and southern subgroups. To back up his two forward armies, Eremenko also erected fortifications on the Volga River's eastern bank and, beginning on 11 September, manned these defenses with 2nd Tank Corps from Southeastern Front's reserve. Commanded by General Khasin, who replaced Kravchenko on 14 September when the latter took command of Stalingrad Front's 4th Tank Corps, 2nd Tank Corps deployed

with its 135th, 137th, 155th, and 99th Tank Brigades in first echelon and its
254th and 169th Tank Brigades initially in second echelon. The 254th was in
defensive positions at Rybachii, well to the rear, and the latter on Sarpinskii
Island, in the Volga River east of Beketovka.[15]

On the eve of Weichs's assault, Shumilov's 64th Army was just as understrength as were 62nd Army's formations. For example, at the end of 10
September the army reported that its combat formations numbered 23,078
men (see Table 14).

This meant that the battle in Stalingrad, in addition to being a contest
for possession of the city, was also a manpower race between the Germans
and the Soviets. This race was to determine which side could bring up the
reserves necessary to conquer the city (the Germans) and to defend it (the Soviets). Southeastern Front began this race on the evening of 14 September by
bringing the fresh 13th Guards Rifle Division across the Volga; as Southeastern Front continued to pour reinforcements into the city, Paulus responded
on 19–20 September by shifting 100th Jäger Division eastward from the Don
River front and committing it into the city fight beginning on 25 and 26 September. On 12 September, however, the winner was still unclear.

The ensuing battle for Stalingrad city and its factory district would unfold in three distinct stages encompassing two principal fronts (the city itself as well as the land bridge north and northwest of the city; see Map 15).
The first stage, which lasted from 13 to 26 September, included Paulus's
and Hoth's combined assault on the central and southern parts of the city,
as well as Stalingrad Front's third major counteroffensive in the Kotluban'
region northwest of the city. In the midst of this first stage, to unite German efforts at Stalingrad, Paulus's Sixth Army took control of Fourth Panzer
Army's XXXXVIII Panzer Corps. During the second stage, 27 September to
13 October, Paulus's forces captured the workers' settlements west of Stalingrad's factory district, including the Tractor Factory, Barrikady [Barricade],
and Krasnyi Oktiabr' [Red October] villages, and liquidated the remainder of
62nd Army's salient anchored on Orlovka. Indicative of the difficult fighting,
this stage required two separate phases to complete. In the third and final
stage, from 14 October through 18 November, Sixth Army struggled to capture the city's factory district, beginning with the Tractor Factory and ending
with the fierce fight for the Barrikady Factory and Krasnyi Oktiabr' Factory.
At the same time, Paulus fought to reduce 62nd Army's enclave north of the
city, around Rynok and Spartanovka.

Throughout all of these stages, lesser operations also took place on
Army Group B's left wing along the Don River as Soviet forces positioned
themselves for a fresh counteroffensive, and south of Stalingrad, where
Fourth Panzer Army pondered ways to eliminate 64th Army's bridgehead
at Beketovka.

Table 14. The Personnel Strength of 64th Army's Combat Formations on 10 September 1942

- 29th Rifle Division – 1,856 men
- 36th Guards Rifle Division – 7,149 men
- 38th Rifle Division – 3,435 men
- 121st Rifle Division – 2,036 men
- 138th Rifle Division – 2,123 men
- 157th Rifle Division – 1,996 men
- 66th Naval Rifle Brigade – 1,134 men
- 154th Naval Rifle Brigade – 876 men
- Rifle Regiment, Krasnodar Infantry School – 1,043 men
- 118th Fortified Region – 1,430 men
- **Total** – 23,078 men

Source: Zhilin, *Stalingradskaia bitva*, 549.

THE INITIAL GERMAN ASSAULT, 13–18 SEPTEMBER

Chuikov had no sooner taken command of 62nd Army when Weichs finally launched his long-awaited major effort to seize the city at 0630 hours on 13 September, striking first at the central and southern sectors of the city (see Map 16). Chuikov, based on his previous experiences, was already formulating new tactical concepts to defeat the German war machine, but, at least initially, he struggled to hold together his defenses against the first major German onslaught at Stalingrad.

The core of this effort was Seydlitz's LI Army Corps and Kempf's XXXX-VIII Panzer Corps. Seydlitz's corps—consisting of Group Stahel and 389th, 295th, and 71st Infantry Divisions, concentrated in jumping-off positions from west of Orlovka southward to the northern bank of the Tsaritsa River—was to push eastward toward the bluffs overlooking Stalingrad's workers' villages, Mamaev Kurgan, and the central part of Stalingrad city. During this advance Group Stahel was to contain Soviet forces on the western flank of the Orlovka salient while Jänecke's 389th Infantry Division pushed eastward from Gorodishche region to compress the base of the Orlovka salient. The two infantry divisions on Seydlitz's right wing, Wuthmann's 295th and Hartmann's 71st, sought to advance eastward in the sector from east of Razgulaevka Station southward to the Tsaritsa River, in close cooperation with 24th Panzer and 94th Infantry Divisions on Kempf's left wing, and enter Stalingrad via Krasnyi Oktiabr' village, Mamaev Kurgan, and the heights above the city's center.[16] Thus, Seydlitz's corps would attack the center of Chuikov's 62nd Army, with Group Stahel and 389th Infantry Division engaging 2nd Motorized Rifle Brigade, 4th Battalion, 115th Rifle Brigade, 1st Battalion, 149th Rifle Brigade, 1st Battalion, 124th Rifle Brigade, and 399th

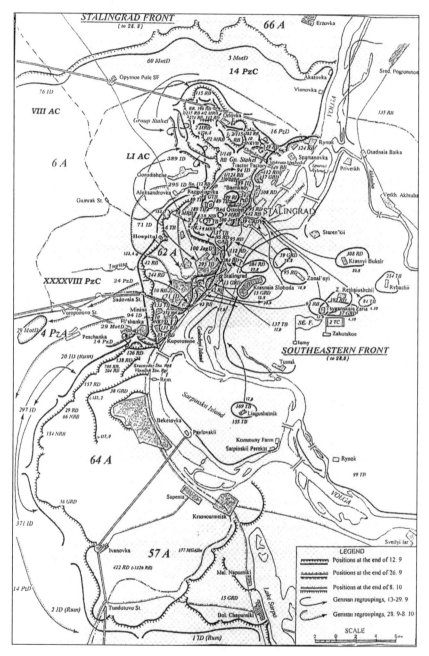

Map 15. Operations along the Stalingrad axis, 13 September–8 October 1942

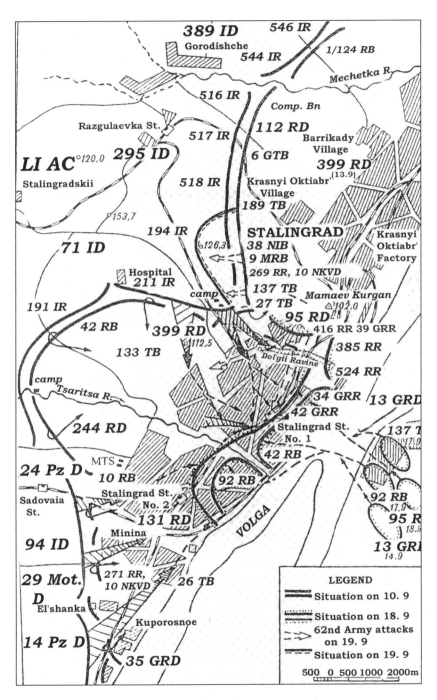

Map 16. The German advance into Stalingrad, 10–18 September 1942

Rifle Division in reserve; 295th Infantry Division attacking 23rd Tank Corps'
6th Guards and 189th Tank Brigades, 38th Motorized Rifle Brigade, 112th
Rifle Division, and 27th Tank Brigade in reserve; and 71st Infantry Division
opposing 42nd Rifle Brigade, 6th Tank Brigade, and the single regiment of
244th Rifle Division north of the Tsaritsa River.

Simultaneously, 24th Panzer, 94th Infantry, and 29th Motorized Divisions of Kempf's XXXXVIII Panzer Corps—concentrated in the sector from
the southern bank of the Tsaritsa River southward to the western outskirts
of Kuporosnoe—were to thrust northeastward and eastward along the railroad line and through the suburbs of El'shanka, Minina, and Kuporosnoe
to crush the left (southern) wing of Chuikov's army and seize the southern
half of Stalingrad. On Kempf's left wing, Lenski's 24th Panzer and Pfeiffer's
94th Infantry Divisions, cooperating closely with LI Corps' two infantry divisions on their left, were to attack from the region west of Sadovaia Station
and Minina. Their goal was to seize the heights above the southern half of
Stalingrad and the Minina suburb and penetrate to Railroad Station No. 2
by advancing along and south of the railroad line and the El'shanka River.
On Kempf's right, Fremerey's 29th Motorized Division, supported by part
of Heim's 14th Panzer Division, was to clear Soviet forces from the suburbs
of El'shanka and Kuporosnoe. So configured, Kempf's panzer corps would
assault the left wing of Chuikov's army, with 24th Panzer Division engaging
two regiments of 244th Rifle Division, 10th Rifle Brigade, and part of 6th
Tank Brigade; 94th Infantry Division striking 133rd Tank Brigade and 271st
NKVD Regiment; and 29th Motorized Division attacking 35th Guards Rifle
Division and 131st Rifle Division in reserve. Thus, the ultimate objective of
these two shock groups was to penetrate to the Volga River and thereby split
62nd Army in half.

On the eve of the German assault, Chuikov was still frantically issuing
orders to strengthen his defenses. Late on 11 September, for example, he
assigned Colonel Andriusenko command of the combined forces of 115th,
124th, 149th Rifle, and 2nd Motorized Brigades, the composite regiment of
196th Rifle Division, and 724th Rifle Regiment and ordered him to defend
the region around Orlovka.[17]

13 September

The Germans preceded their assault with an intense artillery bombardment
and heavy air strikes, during which they dropped at least 856 incendiary
bombs on the city, reportedly killing more than 300 civilians.[18] The Soviets
responded with heavy artillery fire and incessant volleys of *Katiusha* rocket
fire from the eastern bank of the Volga River.[19] However, during the early
stage of the battle, when neither side knew the other's positions in any detail,

this fire support was not well focused but instead discharged at a variety of likely targets. The *Luftwaffe's* bombing was terrifyingly destructive, but that destruction was scattered over a wide area of the city. Moreover, the German bombers generally failed to attack the slow, plodding ferries—the vital supply line that kept 62nd Army in the fight. German artillery was also less than effective, being disrupted by periodic counterbattery fire from the guns and *Katiusha* rockets located across the river. Nevertheless, the German barrage severely disrupted Chuikov's communications, most of which were dependent on field telephone lines strung aboveground. The new commander was able to talk to Eremenko, his superior, only once that afternoon, asking for at least two new divisions to continue the fight. Despite repeated wire repairs made under fire, by 1600 hours the army headquarters had lost contact with most of its subordinates.

This heavy fire, coupled with desperate resistance on the ground, limited the Germans' advance in most sectors to several hundreds of meters. However, the chaos and confusion disrupted 62nd Army's communications, preventing it from effectively monitoring the progress of the fighting. Southeastern Front's summary report on the day's action simply stated, "On 13 September our units were fighting stubborn defensive battles with enemy infantry and tanks."[20] The 62nd Army elaborated:

62nd Army was fighting stubborn defensive battles with enemy forces of up to an infantry division, supported by 40–50 tanks, which attacked in the Aleksandrovka-Hill 126.3 [2.5 kilometers west of Krasnyi Oktiabr' village] sector, all day on 13 September.

The enemy succeeded in capturing the village 1 kilometer southeast of Razgulaevka Station-Hill 126.3-barn 1.5 kilometers southeast of Hill 126.3 line by 1430 hours on 13 September. Individual groups of enemy infantry wedged into the edge of the woods 2 kilometers east of Hill 126.3 and the edge of the woods 1 kilometer east of the barn. Up to 10 enemy tanks reached the railroad in the region 2 kilometers south of Hill 98.9, of which six were destroyed by our units, and the remainder turned back.

An attack by an enemy force of up to a company of infantry, which attacked eastward along the stream from the eastern outskirts of Gorodishche, was repelled by our units.

Information has not been received about the position of the army's units by day's end on 13 September.[21]

Actually, the two German shock groups recorded only limited gains on 13 September (see Map 17). By nightfall, the advance by Jänecke's 389th Infantry Division on the left wing of Seydlitz's army corps ground to a halt before Colonel Andriusenko's defenses east of Gorodishche, composed of the three battalions of 115th, 124th, and 149th Rifle Brigades. To the south, however, Wuthmann's 295th Infantry Division captured Hill 126.3 from 23rd Tank Corps' 6th Guards and 189th Tank and 38th Motorized Rifle Brigades and Hill 153.7 and the region east of the hospital from 112th Rifle Division. These Soviet defenders had to withdraw eastward to the heights above the Vishnevaia *Balka* and the western approaches to the Barrikady and Krasnyi Oktiabr' workers' villages. During this fighting 189th Tank Brigade and the supporting 27th Tank Brigade lost 19 tanks, including 10 T-34s and 9 T-60s and T-70s, and 130 men killed or wounded; 6th Guards Tank Brigade lost 13 of its 15 T-34 tanks and 120 men. However, the tank corps as a whole claimed it killed or wounded 1,260 German troops and destroyed 41 tanks or assault guns, 20 vehicles, 26 antitank guns, 34 mortars, and 8 machine guns in the fierce fighting.[22] The three regiments of Ermolkin's 112th Rifle Division also suffered heavy losses. By nightfall, Wuthmann's right-wing regiment, the 518th, operating north of the railroad, had advanced up to 1.5 kilometers eastward toward Hill 98.9 and Mamaev Kurgan beyond.

On 295th Infantry Division's right, advancing abreast, 194th, 211th, and 191st Regiments of Hartmann's 71st Infantry Division compressed the defenses of Batrakov's 42nd Motorized Rifle Brigade, 6th Tank Brigade, and the regiment of Afanas'ev's 244th Rifle Division eastward toward the heights northwest of the city's center and southward toward the Tsaritsa River. By nightfall, 194th Regiment captured Aviagorodok and advanced up to 2 kilometers along the railroad, reaching the approaches to Hill 112.5 and the heights above the center city, while 211th and 191st Regiments pressed the Soviet defenders back into a salient protruding westward north of the Tsaritsa River. On Hartmann's right, 24th Panzer Division, now commanded by Lenski, and Pfeiffer's 94th Infantry Division of Kempf's XXXXVIII Panzer Corps registered more meager gains south of the Tsaritsa River. These two divisions faced two regiments of 244th Rifle Division, 10th Rifle Brigade, and the supporting 133rd Tank Brigades. By day's end, Lenski's panzergrenadiers captured Sadovaia Station and the Motor Tractor Station 2 kilometers to the east; Pfeiffer's infantry had captured the western outskirts of the Minina suburb. Meanwhile, on 94th Division's right, Fremerey's 29th Motorized Division captured the southwestern section of Minina from Dubiansky's 35th Guards Rifle Division and 10th NKVD Division's 271st Rifle Regiment, which was now backed up by elements of Pesochin's 131st Rifle Division.[23]

However, the progress of Kempf's panzer corps was exceedingly slow:

At 0855 hours, Hauptman Roth, O1 [operations officer] of 24. Panzer-Division, reported to Korps that the north wing had advanced around 100 metres. At 1017 hours, however, he had to call Korps and tell them that the right wing was pinned down in front of bunkers. And there it

Map 17. Sixth Army's situation, 13–14 September 1942

remained; the situation and the forward line unchanged. A connection with the right neighbor [94th Infantry Division] was available along the railway line. As before, the enemy fought toughly and grimly. Strong artillery and mortar fire, as well as air activity, covered the area of the Division. There were no appreciable changes during the further course of the day apart from positions being improved locally. The neighboring division made headway in its assault on Stalingrad but had not been able to reach the same level as 24. Panzer-Division.[24]

Ultimately, the heavy bombardment forced Chuikov to move his command post back from Mamaev Kurgan to the banks of the Tsaritsa River, occupying the dugouts known as the "Tsaritsyn bunker" that had once belonged to the *front* headquarters before it had evacuated the city.[25] Chuikov left an army observation post on the crest of Mamaev Kurgan.

Late on 13 September, Eremenko ordered both Chuikov and Shumilov to mount counterattacks to eliminate the German penetrations, even though they had few resources available with which to do so. At 2230 hours that evening, Chuikov ordered a series of counterattacks to commence at 0330 hours on 14 September from the region east of Razgulaevka Station and west of the Krasnyi Oktiabr' workers' village southward to the Tsaritsa River (see Map 18). These counterattacks sought to eliminate the dangerous penetration by LI Corps' 295th and 71st Infantry Divisions, which aimed like a dagger at Mamaev Kurgan and Stalingrad's center city. On the right wing of Chuikov's counterattack force, Burmakov's 38th Motorized Rifle Brigade, reinforced by a company from 9th Motorized Rifle Brigade, was to counterattack westward from the woods on the western slopes of Hill 98.9 toward a village southeast of Razgulaevka Station. In the counterattack's center, 272nd Regiment of Saraev's 10th NKVD Division was to concentrate in the region southeast of Aviagorodok and counterattack northwestward from Hill 115.4 to recapture Hill 126.3 and then seize Hill 144.3. On 272nd Regiment's left, the composite regiment of 399th Rifle Division, with 6th Tank Brigade attached, was to concentrate south of Aviagorodok and attack through the village to seize Hill 153.7, 2 kilometers northwest of Aviagorodok. In addition, Chuikov also hoped that 92nd Rifle Brigade, commanded by Major V. I. Samodaia and still situated on the Volga River's eastern bank, would be able to cross the river and reinforce the assault toward Aviagorodok and Hill 153.7.[26]

To support the counterattack, Chuikov assigned each of the three shock groups three antitank artillery regiments, three RGK (*Stavka* Reserve) artillery regiments, and three *Katiusha* regiments subordinate to the *front's* southern artillery group, antiaircraft artillery assigned to the Stalingrad PVO (*Protivovozdushnaia Oborona*—Russian air defense) Corps Region, and 2nd Tank Corps' artillery firing from the Volga's eastern bank. However, when the three shock groups began their counterattacks at 0330 hours the next morning, the assaults proved irrelevant because they struck into the teeth of Weichs's advancing shock groups and were pounded by large groups of attacking *Luftwaffe* aircraft. Eremenko did not release Samodaia's 92nd Naval Rifle Brigade to Chuikov's army, as promised, in time to support this counterattack.

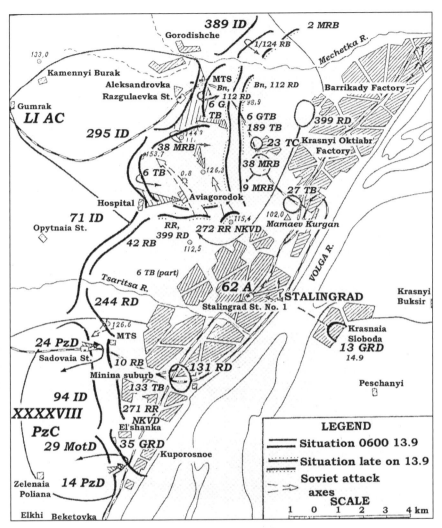

Map 18. 62nd Army's counterattacks, 13–14 September 1942

14 September

At first, the sheer audacity of Chuikov's counterattack took LI Corps' 295th and 71st Infantry Divisions off stride. Once the sun rose, however, attacks by multiple groups of up to 60 Stuka aircraft and well-aimed artillery fire brought the Soviet assaults to an abrupt halt. Thereafter, as 62nd Army reported:

115th RB, 2nd MRB, 724th RR, and composite regiment, 196th RD, were attacked by a battalion of enemy infantry [advancing] from the north toward Orlovka at 1500 hours, and the battalion was destroyed.

23rd TC—the combat formation of the corps was subjected to intense aircraft attacks by enemy dive bombers at 0630 hours. Beginning at 0700 hours, up to one ID with 40–50 tanks went over to the attack in the general direction of the hospital and Krasnyi Oktiabr'. By 1530 hours the enemy succeeded in pressing our units back and captured the line: the railroad (incl.) west of the grove of woods (west of Krasnyi Oktiabr'), eastern slopes of Hill 126.2, and the unnamed village (east of the hospital).

In light of the loss of communications, the positions of the units of the corps were not established by day's end. 16 enemy tanks were burned during the fighting.

42nd RB—was continuing to defend its previous positions, while protecting itself from the right.

244th RD, 10th RB, 271st Regiment NKVD, and 35th Gds. RD continued to hold their occupied positions up to 1400 hours. An attack by the enemy toward Kuporosnoe at 1400 hours is being repelled. Wire communications with the units has been disrupted, and information about the changing situation has not arrived.[27]

Attacking on the left wing of Seydlitz's LI Corps, infantrymen from 194th and 211th Regiments of Hartmann's 71st Infantry Division, spearheaded by a battalion of tanks, broke through the defenses on the right wing of Batrakov's 42nd Rifle Brigade east of the hospital and pushed rapidly southeastward to seize Hill 112.5. On 71st Division's right wing, 191st Regiment demolished the defenses on Batrakov's left wing, forcing the brigade and single regiment of Afanas'ev's 244th Rifle Division defending north of the Tsaritsa River to withdraw eastward into the city or southward toward the river's valley. According to Sixth Army's daily report, the lead elements of 194th Regiment raced down the heights west of the city's center, penetrated into the city's streets, and reached Stalingrad's central railroad station (Station No. 1) at about noon (see Map 16). Confirming this report, Chuikov recorded, "Individual groups of submachine gunners, passing along the *balkas* from the vicinity of Hill 112.5, filtered into the city by 1400 hours and reached the station at 1630 hours. Fighting is going on in the city with enemy submachine gunners."[28] The 71st Division's bold thrust caught Chuikov by surprise, forcing him to assemble whatever forces he could find, principally part of the reserve 6th Tank Brigade, and dispatch them to the city's center.

Even the commitment of some tanks from Khopko's 6th Tank Brigade could not halt the German onslaught. By this time, the advancing Germans had reached within 800 meters of Chuikov's command post. A desperate struggle ensued, with each house becoming the site of a prolonged battle, during which 6th Tank Brigade claimed it had destroyed six German tanks.[29] Joining the tank brigade in defense of the center city were elements of 10th NKVD Division, security troops from 62nd Army's headquarters, and local militia units. Railroad Station No. 1, the governmental and party buildings, and the adjoining Red Square changed hands at least five times on 14 September and continued to be a focus of conflict for days thereafter as Chuikov dispatched 13th Guards Rifle to the rescue. During this chaotic struggle, small groups of German infantry from 71st Division's 194th Regiment boldly infiltrated behind the Soviet forward positions, cutting off communications and reinforcements and, for a brief time, even reaching the Volga.[30]

On the afternoon of 14 September, Chuikov's chief of staff, General Krylov, scraped together two small groups of headquarters staff personnel, the first accompanied by six KV tanks from 62nd Army's last reserve, Colonel Skuba's 6th Guards Tank Brigade, and the second by three KV tanks from the same brigade. These scratch forces succeeded in slowing the advance of 71st Infantry Division's 194th Regiment, whose forces were pressing eastward from Railroad Station No. 1 toward the central landing stage on the Volga. Still later in the afternoon, the German advance actually reached the shoreline, and antitank fire sank two of the precious ferries crossing the river.[31] The only saving grace for Chuikov on 14 September was the fact that Dubiansky's 35th Guards Rifle Division slowed 29th Motorized Division's advance in the streets of Minina, thereby preventing the tide of advancing German forces from sweeping through the entire southern section of the city.

Later that evening, when the situation became clearer, the Red Army General Staff's daily summary recounted the carnage in 62nd Army's sector on 14 September:

62nd Army fought fierce battles with enemy forces of up to an infantry division with tanks attacking the line from Aviagorodok to the northern part of Stalingrad.

124th and 149th RBs and 282nd RR were holding on to their previous positions.

399th RD, 272nd RR, and 6th TB, suffering 70–80 percent losses, withdrew eastward under heavy enemy pressure.

6th Gds. TB (without tanks) was fighting with groups of enemy submachine gunners in the vicinity of the station [Station No. 1] at 1800 hours 14 September.

112th RD, one battalion of 124th RB, 10 tanks (KVs), and 133rd TB [Group Krylov] have been thrown into the region of the breakthrough.

13th Gds. RD began crossing to the western bank of the Volga River at 2000 hours on 14 September.

Our forces [35th Gds. RD] have beaten back the enemy's attacks on Kuporosnoe.[32]

On the same evening, the OKW announced triumphantly, "In the battles at Stalingrad, the attacking units of our ground forces, with powerful support by artillery, penetrated the enemy's positions despite his fierce resistance and seized the commanding heights northwest of the central part of the city. During the course of unsuccessful counterattacks, the enemy lost 29 tanks."[33] Somewhat later, Army Group B reported:

The battle for Stalingrad fortress is distinguished by the enemy's exceptional obstinacy and bitterness. Attacking south of the railroad line, 94th Infantry Division fought its way into the southern suburbs and repelled enemy from the direction of the Volga River. North of the road, one of our panzer divisions [24th] managed to penetrate right up to the water-supply station on the western bank of the Volga River. North of this station, overcoming stubborn enemy resistance, the forces of another division [71st Infantry] penetrated into the city. The attack from the north in the sector between the Volga River and the railroad [by Group Krylov] has been repelled [by 71st Infantry Division] with heavy enemy losses.[34]

Tellingly, this report added, "Attempts by the enemy to cross the Don River in the vicinity of Kazanskaia, on the left flank of the [Italian] 'Pasubio' division, did not achieve success."[35] This underscored the *Stavka*'s growing attention on its buildup of forces along the Don River, far to the northwest of Stalingrad.

Somehow, the desperate defenders of Stalingrad's center city held out until darkness fell on 14 September. As Chuikov took stock of the dwindling strength of his formations, however, it was clear they could not continue to resist unless they received significant reinforcements. For example, his situation report late on 14 September recorded the following strengths: 115th Rifle Brigade—4,185 men, 2nd Motorized Rifle Brigade—666 men, 724th Rifle Regiment—223 men, 196th Rifle Division—548 men, and 1315th Rifle Regiment, 399th Rifle Division—36 men.[36] That evening, with little time to spare, Chuikov received his first effective reinforcements, the almost 10,000 men of 13th Guards Rifle Division, even though many more than 1,000 of these fresh troops lacked rifles.[37] The division's commander, Major General Aleksandr Il'ich Rodimtsev, had crossed in daylight, ahead of his troops, stumbling into the army command post in a uniform covered by dust and mud after repeatedly throwing himself on the ground to avoid German bombs. Rodimtsev was more than willing to fight, but it took all night not only to move his troops across the river but also to find sufficient rifles and ammunition to arm them.

Born in Orenburg *oblast'* in 1905, General Rodimtsev was a 15-year veteran of the Red Army who had commanded at various levels from platoon up to cavalry regiment during the 1920s and 1930s and served as a volunteer in the Republican Army during the Spanish Civil War. There, as a major, he had earned the title of Hero of the Soviet Union, and he graduated from the Frunze Academy in 1939. A colonel when the war began, Rodimtsev commanded the Southwestern Front's 5th Airborne Brigade from June through November 1941, during which he managed to escape with his brigade from the disastrous Kiev encirclement. When 5th Airborne Brigade's parent organization, 3rd Airborne Corps, was converted into 87th Rifle Division in November 1941, Rodimtsev became its first commander. Because of his division's sound performance under 40th Army's control during the winter campaign of 1941–1942, the NKO awarded it the honorific title of 13th Guards Rifle Division in January 1942; Rodimtsev obtained the rank of major general four months later. While subordinate to Southwestern Front's 28th Army, Rodimtsev's guards division was largely destroyed during the heavy fighting in the Donbas region during July (see Chapters 5 and 6). After Southwestern Front evacuated the division's surviving command cadre to the region east of the Don River at the end of July, Rodimtsev's division re-formed during August but, before that re-formation was complete, was dispatched hastily to the Stalingrad region in early September.[38]

When Rodimtsev's rifle division crossed the river, with its artillery firing in support from the river's eastern bank, the 6,000 men of its 39th and 42nd Guards Rifle Regiments, commanded by Majors S. S. Dolgov and I. P. Elin, were to clear German forces from the city's center, in particular the building named the House of "Specialists" and Railroad Station No. 1. At the same time, Major D. I. Panikhin's 34th Guards Rifle Regiment was to occupy defensive positions on Mamaev Kurgan, and the division's training battalion and administrative company would serve as Rodimtsev's reserve.[39] However, the slow and arduous crossing process prevented Elin's 42nd Regiment from crossing the Volga the first night, meaning the division's rifle battalions would enter the battle piecemeal on 15 September. In the meantime, part of Panikhin's regiment would have to reinforce Mamaev Kurgan.

Despite the timely arrival of Rodimtsev's guardsmen, Chuikov, who had lost communications with many of his subordinate formations, could not foresee the disaster that would befall his army the following day when Weichs planned to unleash a lightning strike into the very heart of southern Stalingrad city. In an assault set for dawn on 15 September, Weichs planned to conduct dagger thrusts with Seydlitz's LI Corps toward the heights west of

Krasnyi Oktiabr' village and eastward north of the Tsaritsa River toward Mamaev Kurgan and with Kempf's XXXXVIII Panzer Corps eastward south of
the Tsaritsa River toward the center of the southern half of the city and the
city's southern suburbs of Minina and Kuporosnoe (see Map 19).

In the boldest of these actions, 24th Panzer Division prepared an advance with a strong *kampfgruppe* straight into the heart of southern Stalingrad, which, if successful, would link up with the spearheads of Seydlitz's
corps and likely leave Chuikov's new headquarters at Tsaritsyn bunker almost
surrounded:

> Korps placed particular worth in the fact that 24. Panzer-Division would
> set off the next day with a strong Kampfgruppe and advance to the railway
> station south of the Tsaritsa Gully. At 1220 hours, 71. Infanterie-Division
> of the neighboring LI. Armeekorps reached Stalingrad's central railway
> station. At 1233 hours, Oberst Fangohr from Armee HQ called Oberst
> Friebe: "Establishment of connection with left neighbor advisable. When
> will 24. Panzer-Division advance with [*Kampfgruppe*] Edelsheim?" . . .
>
> At 1645 hours, Major von Menges called Oberst Friebe at Korps head-
> quarters and oriented him about the planned conduct of the attack with
> Gruppe Edelsheim. A battalion would be prepared as an assault group,
> and the main objective was the southern railway station.[40]

Once Lenski's division consolidated its forces in forward positions situated
on the high ground north of the El'shanka River and east of Sadovaia Station,
Kempf informed Lenski's division of its mission for the day:

> 24th Panzer Division will set off at 0330 hours on 15 September with
> tightly concentrated forces in one place in a surprise assault to break
> through the enemy defensive position. Thrust with a *Kampfgruppe* in one
> bound through the city sector west of the station and take that railway sta-
> tion into possession. By the swift penetration, the enemy will be denied
> the possibility of setting up new defenses, as he has previously done. The
> destruction of the enemy and the clearing of the penetrated city sectors
> will follow after the successful breakthrough.[41]

At 2000 hours that evening, Lenski's operations officer issued Division
Order (*Divisionbefehl*) No. 60, which mandated a continuation of the attack on Stalingrad before dawn on the next day with two *kampfgruppen*.
Kampfgruppe Edelsheim, substantially reinforced with heavy weapons, was
to lunge eastward along the railroad line north of the El'shanka River and,
once it reached the junction of the main railroad line and a spur leading to
the Volga River, wheel northward and advance along the main railroad line

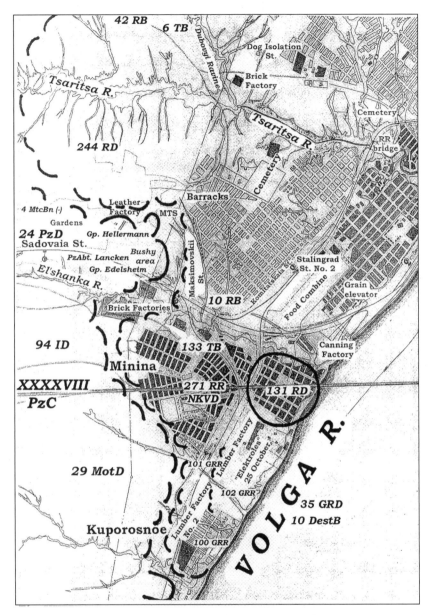

Map 19. XXXXVIII Panzer Corps' situation late on 14 September 1942

and Komitetskaia Street to seize Railroad Station No. 2. *Kampfgruppe* Hellermann was to protect Edelsheim's flank to the east and north. The two *kampfgruppen* were organized as follows:

- **Gruppe Edelsheim:**
  - o 26th Panzer Grenadier-Regiment
  - o 1st Battalion, 21st Panzer Grenadier Regiment
  - o 4th Motorcycle Battalion (less 1st Company)
  - o 1st and 3rd Companies, 40th Panzer Pioneer Battalion
  - o All flamethrowers, 40th Panzer Pioneer Battalion
  - o 89th Panzer Artillery Regiment (less 4th Battery)
  - o Staff and elements of 670th Panzer Jäger [Hunter] Battalion [*Abteilung*] (with five 76.2mm self-propelled guns)
  - o 2nd Company, 40th Panzer Jäger Battalion (less one platoon)
  - o 10 tanks from Panzer *Abteilung* Lancken
- **Gruppe Hellermann:**
  - o 21st Panzer Grenadier Regiment (less 1st Battalion)
  - o 635th Pioneer Battalion
  - o 4th Battalion, 89th Panzer Artillery Regiment
  - o Elements of 670th Panzer Jäger Battalion
  - o One platoon, 2nd Company, 40th Panzer Jäger Battalion

The plan was for Group Edelsheim to break through the enemy's front line in the western part of the city with two rifle battalions, penetrate into the railroad station as quickly as possible, and capture it.[42]

15 September

Weichs's shock groups resumed their assault at dawn on 15 September, accompanied by what Chuikov described as "a colossal air raid."[43] On the left wing of the shock group of Seydlitz's LI Corps, 516 and 517th Regiments of Wuthmann's 295th Infantry Division advanced eastward from the region east of Gorodishche and Hill 126.3 toward the heights above Krasnyi Oktiabr' village, engaging Khopko's 6th Guards Tank and Burmakov's 38th Motorized Rifle Brigades, reinforced by the remnants of 9th Motorized Rifle Brigade (see Map 20). At the same time, on 295th Infantry Division's right wing, 518th Regiment thrust southeastward toward Mamaev Kurgan, attacking 10th NKVD Division's 269th Regiment and Popov's supporting 27th Tank Brigade. Farther to the south, 194th Regiment of Hartmann's 71st Infantry Division continued their struggle in the vicinity of Railroad Station No. 1, while the division's 211th and 191st Regiments also pressed eastward along the northern bank of the Tsaritsa River on LI Corps' left wing. Hartmann's infantry engaged the remnants of Batrakov's 42nd Rifle Brigade and the northern regiment of Afanas'ev's 244th Rifle Division, as well as the lead elements of Rodimtsev's 13th Guards Division as they arrived, in a running block-to-block and building-to-building fight in the city proper.

On LI Corps' right, XXXXVIII Panzer Corps' 24th Panzer and 94th Infantry Divisions pushed eastward, the former south of the Tsaritsa River toward the Motor Tractor Station and Railroad Station No. 2 in southern Stalingrad, and the latter south of the El'shanka River through Stalingrad's southern suburb of Minina. As they did so, they struck the southern two regiments of 244th Rifle Division and 10th Rifle Brigade, supported by 6th Tank Brigade.

The most dramatic German advance during the day was the assault by Lenski's 24th Panzer, which began at 0330 hours, into the heart of southern Stalingrad city (see Map 21). Reinforced by a part of *Kampfgruppe* Heller-mann, Edelsheim's *Kampfgruppe* struck due eastward along and north of the railroad line into southern Stalingrad, leaving the remainder of Hellermann's force to clear bypassed Soviet forces, primarily from 42nd Rifle Brigade and 244th Rifle Division, in the factories and city blocks adjacent to Edelsheim's left flank. On the division's left wing, 4th Motorcycle Battalion pushed eastward toward the barracks on the high ground west of the southern section of the city, which was also defended by a battalion of 42nd Rifle Brigade. On 24th Panzer's right, Pfeiffer's 94th Infantry Division advanced northeastward and eastward south of the El'shanka River to clear Soviet forces from Stalingrad's southern suburbs of Minina and El'shanka and to protect the right flank of Lenski's panzers as they advanced deep into the city.

Enduring "hard combat under difficult terrain conditions," Edelsheim's *kampfgruppe* pushed forward rapidly, seizing a narrow swath of ground along and north of the railroad line and, by midmorning, the railroad junction roughly 2 kilometers west of the Volga River.[44] There, strong Soviet resistance halted the advance briefly, as "brave Russian infantrymen holding out in foxholes on both sides of the tracks defended themselves bitterly," although "most of them, faced with being crushed or blasted by the panzers, gave themselves up."[45]

Once Edelsheim's *kampfgruppe* had established firm contact with 94th Infantry Division on its right and ensured that their and Pfeiffer's artillery suppressed enemy fires against its flank from the factories on the southern bank of the El'shanka River, Edelsheim wheeled 90 degrees to the left and pressed northward through the city's cavernous blocks along Komitetskaia Street and the main north-south railroad line. Advancing another 2 kilometers as "squads of grenadiers and riflemen threaded their way through the warehouses, shacks and buildings along the line of advance, covering the panzers' flanks as well as looking for the enemy," Edelsheim's panzers and

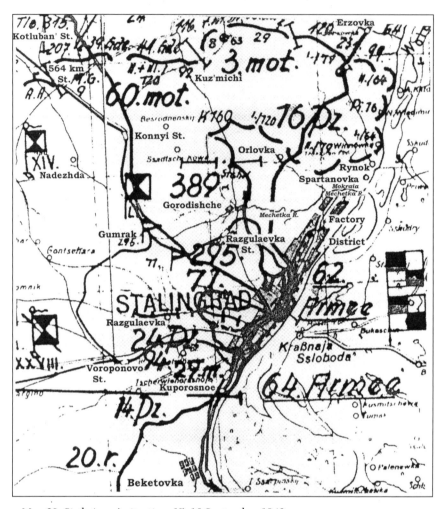

Map 20. Sixth Army's situation, 15–16 September 1942

panzer-grenadiers reached the area just west of Railroad Station No. 2 by
midafternoon. As they advanced, heavy Soviet flanking fires and small groups
of Soviet infantry, which were fighting "toughly" and "had to be individually
thrown out of every street in hard hand-to-hand and close combat," slowed
their forward progress. The advancing Germans were amazed that "the ada-
mantine [Grain] Elevator [the dominant terrain feature in the region less
than 300 meters to their south], menacing and gray," was "always staring
down at them," and they "wondered why such an impregnable strongpoint
was not being defended by the Russians."[46]

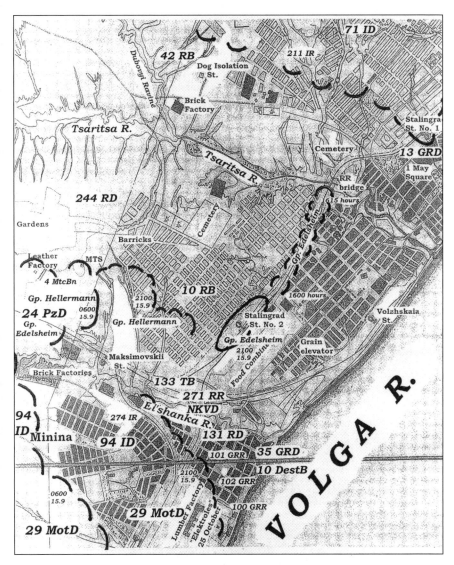

Map 21. XXXXVIII Panzer Corps' advance, 15 September 1942

Pausing to allow supporting artillery and Stukas to soften up the Soviet defenses along its projected line of advance, the main force of *Kampfgruppe* Edelsheim captured the railway station at 1600 hours after a brief fight. Marring what had otherwise been a remarkable advance, the division fell victim to friendly fire:

Stukas had been called in to pummel these defenses, together with other enemy obstructions ahead of the division. The grenadiers, squatting in narrow washaways, gullies and behind bushes, enjoyed watching bombs ploughing up the defenders, causing them grief, but things soon took a nasty turn: the bombs from the Stukas crept back toward them and started exploding among their own lines. Frantic radio messages were sent demanding that the bombings be halted and a few minutes after it had begun, the bombing stopped as word of the error reached the pilots.[47]

Undeterred by this misfortune, Edelsheim left a skeleton force behind to defend the station, while the main body of his *kampfgruppe* resumed its northward advance, scattered small enemy groups, most of which were attempting to withdraw to the east, and reached the southern bank of the Tsaritsa Gulley at 1615 hours. As Edelsheim wheeled his *kampfgruppe* west to help clear enemy forces from the dominating terrain around the barrack's region to his left-rear, at 1830 hours an elated Lenski reported to Kempf's headquarters, "Enemy front-line removed, no more continuous defence after being broken through. Flanking fire from the south very unpleasant. Connection still not completely available with 94th Infantry Division. Railway station not heavily occupied. One enemy company flowing to the east. Tsaritsa no enemy. Our panzer push from Tsaritsa to the west. Precise report will follow."[48] Moments before, at 1810 hours the OKH had informed Fourth Panzer Army that Kempf's XXXXVIII Panzer Corps, for the sake of unity of command, would be subordinated to Paulus's Sixth Army, effective 0000 hours the next day.[49]

The 24th Panzer Division's quick, violent, but brilliantly successful thrust had cost it five of its 25 tanks, reportedly, three being "shot up by the flak of 71st Infantry Division" as they neared their prospective linkup along the Tsaritsa River.[50] That night, *Kampfgruppe* Edelsheim manned hedgehog defenses around its vital but easily won prize, with its panzers defending the railway station after pulling back from the Tsaritsa. In the early evening, 274th Grenadier Regiment of Pfeiffer's 94th Infantry Division seized the railway bridge across the El'shanka River, which flowed eastward into the Volga River south of the railroad station and just north of Kuporosnoe. There Pfeiffer's infantrymen linked up with Lenski's panzer-grenadiers.

However, despite the linkup, the Soviets, primarily elements of 10th Rifle Brigade and NKVD security troops, still held the narrow strip of land between the north-south railroad line and the Volga River. The 24th Panzer's armor cordon through the city's main streets, strung out as it was in hedgehog defenses in a narrow corridor extending southward from just south of the Tsaritsa River to the El'shanka River, remained porous for some time.

After an exchange of messages regarding what to do next, XXXXVIII Panzer Corps issued Lenski new orders at 2050 hours:

Early on 16th September, 24th Panzer Division will thrust forward west of the railway line up to the Tsaritsa Gully, form a bridgehead there, and take up a connection with 71st Infantry Division. Besides that, the task of the division is still to destroy the enemy groups holding out in the western part of Stalingrad and on the hills west of the city and clear out this entire area up to the Tsaritsa. A close connection will be maintained with 94th Infantry Division thrusting up the eastern side of the railway line.[51]

Meanwhile, on XXXXVIII Panzer Corps' right wing, Fremerey's 29th Motorized Division, supported by a few tanks from 14th Panzer Division, assaulted just south of the El'shanka River. Opposite this attack were Dubiansky's 35th Guards Rifle Division, the bulk of Pesochin's 131st Rifle Division, elements of 271st NKVD Rifle Regiment, and 133rd Tank Brigade, which were defending the western approaches to El'shanka and Kuporosnoe. By day's end, with their defenses shattered and in shambles, all of the forces defending on 62nd Army's left wing conducted an often disorganized fighting withdrawal eastward into the southern section of Stalingrad and the narrow strip of land on the Volga's western bank south of the Tsaritsa and El'shanka Rivers.

Summarizing the disasters that befell its left wing, during the evening 62nd reported:

42nd RB, having its right and left flanks driven in, is defending the Lesoposadochnaia, (incl.) Hospital, eastern edge of the woods southeast of Hill 133.4, and (incl.) two buildings 2 kilometers east of Marker 50.7 line.

244th RD, suffering great losses, withdrew its left wing to the western outskirts of the Minina suburb and is occupying the two buildings 2 kilometers east of Marker 50.7, (incl.) Marker 127.6, and the outskirts of Minina suburb line.

10th RB was fighting on the outskirts of Minina suburb, with its right flank along the line of the railroad.

35th Gds. RD, with 131st RD, 10th Destroyer Brigade, 52nd Separate MG-Arty Bn, fought a fierce battle with attacking enemy during the day, suffering losses of up to 75–80 percent of their personnel from aircraft and artillery, and were fighting on the western outskirts of Minina suburb and northern outskirts of Kuporosnoe line by day's end.[52]

Despite the Germans' elation over their relatively easy seizure of Railroad Station No. 2, the paucity of infantry in 24th Panzer and 94th Infantry

Divisions made it impossible for the two divisions to encircle and capture the shattered Soviet forces in the region and occupy all of the important buildings in southern Stalingrad. Therefore, as Kempf's forces manned their hedgehog defenses overnight, the surviving forces on Chuikov's shattered left wing exploited opportunities to occupy and sometimes recapture key buildings and other potential defensive positions. Although some of the soldiers in these defeated and decimated units withdrew in disorder, others, often in small groups, converted key buildings in their path into virtual fortress strongpoints.

For example, after withdrawing from their overrun forward positions, soldiers from the remnants of Batrakov's 42nd Rifle Brigade, Afanas'ev's 244th Rifle Division, and 10th Rifle and 133rd Tank Brigades occupied defenses around the barracks area west of the southern part of the city. Other defenders reoccupied and fortified themselves within the prominent Grain Elevator and other buildings in the vicinity of Railroad Station No. 2. To the south, infantrymen from Dubiansky's 35th Guards and Pesochin's 131st Rifle Division, supported by the remnants of 271st NKVD Rifle Regiment, did likewise in the maze of buildings in Minina and El'shanka, the Lumber Factory No. 2 and Food Combine astride the El'shanka River, and the water tower east of Kuporosnoe. Thus, as they set out to accomplish their new missions in the morning, Lenski's panzer-grenadiers, Pfeiffer's infantry, and Fremerey's panzer-grenadiers would face renewed opposition to their front, flanks, and rear as Soviet soldiers rose phoenix-like from seemingly liberated city blocks and buildings. This would significantly slow the pace of Kempf's advance.

Meanwhile, heavy fighting was also raging in Stalingrad's center and to the north, along the approaches to the Mamaev Kurgan and the heights above Krasnyi Oktiabr' village, where LI Corps' 71st and 295th Infantry Divisions were struggling to reach the Volga's western bank. In these sectors, the arrival of Rodimtsev's 13th Guards Rifle Division eased Chuikov's dilemma considerably. For example, 62nd Army, still out of communication with most of its subordinate units, was able to report that it was "engaged in stubborn fighting to destroy enemy infantry and tanks penetrating into separate regions of Stalingrad city":

> 13th Guards Rifle Division crossed to the western bank of the Volga River on the night of 14–15 September and, on the morning of the 15th, was fighting to destroy enemy submachine gunners who have penetrated into separate regions in the southern part of Stalingrad. By 1500 hours on 15 September, the division had cleared out all parts of the city east of the railroad and reached Hill 102.0 [Mamaev Kurgan] with two of its battalions.

Information has not been received about the positions of the army's remaining units by day's end.[53]

In fact, on 15 September two battalions from Panikhin's 34th Guards Rifle Regiment reinforced the beleaguered 269th NKVD Regiment on Mamaev Kurgan, permitting it to shift northward to reinforce the equally hard-pressed 38th and 9th Motorized Rifle Brigades, which were still holding out against the assaults by 295th Infantry Division's 516th and 517th Regiments east of Hill 126.3. Soon after, the remnants of Group Krylov, including 112th Rifle Division's 416th Regiment, also joined the fight for Mamaev Kurgan.

Within the city itself, 13th Guards Rifle Division's forward detachment, 1st Battalion of Elin's 42nd Guards Rifle Regiment, recaptured Railroad Station No. 1 from 71st Infantry Division's 194th Regiment after the station changed hands several times, but the remainder of Panikhin's 34th Guards Rifle Regiment failed to seize the nearby House of Specialists (see Map 22). Meanwhile, roughly half of Dolgov's 39th Guards Rifle Regiment lunged into the city north and south of Railroad Station No. 1 while the other half, together with part of 34th Guards Rifle Regiment, clung desperately to positions along the western bank of the Volga northward to Dolgii *Ovrag* [ravine] and just south of Mamaev Kurgan. Throughout this fighting, however, the bulk of Elin's 42nd Guards Rifle Regiment remained on the Volga's eastern bank, still awaiting transport across the river.

In the midst of this carnage, on 16 September Senior Major of State Security N. N. Selivanovsky, the chief of Stalingrad Front's Special Department [*Osobyi Otdel'*—OO] (i.e., the NKVD), sent his masters in Moscow, NKVD Chief Lavrenti Beriia and his deputy, V. S. Abakumov, a tellingly candid and revealing report of the real state of affairs in 62nd Army:

> According to the situation at 2400 hours on 15 September, the enemy in Stalingrad occupied the elevator, to which 40 enemy tanks and groups of motorized infantry have penetrated, and the House of Specialists, situated immediately adjacent to the Volga—150–180 meters from the crossings. Here, the enemy brought up more than 20 tanks and groups of submachine gunners and mortar men.
>
> The enemy was occupying the railroad depot, the former State bank building, and a number of other buildings, which they have turned into strong points. The enemy has occupied Mamaev Kurgan (Hill 102), which dominates all of Stalingrad and the left bank of the Volga—a radius of 25–30 kilometers from the Volga by which he has taken under his control all crossings and roads leading to Krasnaia Sloboda.
>
> Arriving here during the night, 13th Guards Rifle Division (commanded by Major General Rodimtsev), which was withdrawn for re-forming in

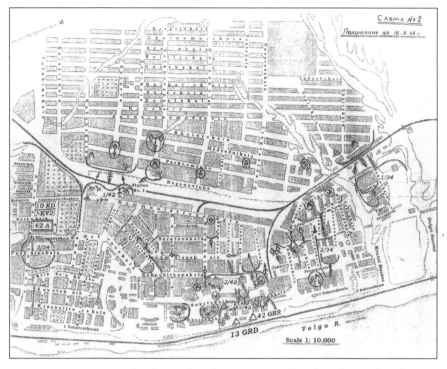

Map 22. Dispositions of 13th Guards Rifle Division's 34th and 42nd Guards Rifle Regiments, 16 September 1942

August and has been on the march constantly for the last two weeks, was fighting with the enemy in Stalingrad on 15 September.

The division's soldiers employ their weapons poorly, and the division reached its positions in Stalingrad without ammunition. The division undertook measures to obtain ammunition.

During combat on 15 September, 13th Guards Rifle Division lost 400 men killed and wounded and expended all of the ammunition for its automatic weapons, and, nevertheless, the division still has not received ammunition and artillery at midnight on 16 September.

The division is experiencing a sharp need for artillery; it needs it to destroy the building where the enemy submachine gunners are lodged.

The matter of transporting wounded to the left bank of the Volga is very bad. The commander of 13th Guards Rifle Division has no means whatsoever for transporting the wounded.

The lightly wounded soldiers are building rafts themselves, carrying the seriously wounded on them, and, while crossing to the left bank, are easily carried by the currents along the Volga, where they disperse into the villages and search for help.

Such is the situation in 62nd Army.

In general, Stalingrad was not prepared for defense. Fortifications were not built in the street in timely fashion, and there were no sorts of warehouses with ammunition, medical supplies, and food dug into the ground in Stalingrad.

The units fought street battles for only a single day, and there was already no ammunition. Now ammunition and food must be delivered across the Volga—across a single working crossing and then only at night.

Through the *front* commander, Comrade Eremenko, the question is asked about the immediate delivery to 13th Guards Rifle Division in Stalingrad during the night of 500,000 rounds for automatic weapons, 10,000 antitank rifles, 10 guns with shells, and the allocation of one–two river trawlers to transport the wounded and the organization of the crossing of 1,500 soldiers who remained without crossing on the night of 14–15 September.

The enemy has been firing on the crossings over the Volga from artillery, mortars, and automatic weapons fire all of the past days and, today, put three of the four operating pairs of ferries out of action.

As before, enemy aircraft are subjecting our units in Stalingrad to constant bombardment and, today, began bombing Krasnaia Sloboda.

Before 13th Guards Rifle Division's arrival in Stalingrad, 62nd Army's obstacle detachment halted the enemy in the vicinity of the railroad station. Many of the comrades in the detachment have been recommended for governmental decorations for displaying valor in battle.

Instances of disorganization and carelessness are continuing to take place. A personal visit to Stalingrad on the night of 15–16 September revealed that 13th Guards Rifle Division's defense CP [command post] and 62nd Army commander's communications post, which are located in the NKVD building on the bank of the Volga, have not been fully tied in with the Volga despite the fact that the enemy is situated 100–150 meters from the CP and the signal center. This has been pointed out to Comrade Rodimtsev, the commander of 13th Guards Rifle Division, and measures for the organization of the defense and strengthening of security of the CP are being taken.

There is still another characteristic instance that reflects on communications work and speaks to the short-sightedness. For example, just now two soldiers who were carrying two accumulators [batteries] from the field radio station of 13th Guards Rifle Division's 42nd Rifle Regiment, met on the street in Krasnaia Sloboda. Having crossed the Volga on improvised boats, they were now bound for the division's rear, and, not knowing where to have the accumulator recharged, all the while the radio stations were not operating.

At 2200 hours on 14 September, after penetrating along Medveditskaia Street, a group of enemy automatic weapons men captured the CP of 8th Separate Company of the City's Commandant's Command, which was located in a mine gallery. While seizing this CP, about 80 men were captured, and now those taken prisoner were used in small groups to transport ammunition to the German automatic weapons men. One such group numbering 6 men was recaptured by NKVD personnel in the vicinity of 13th Guards Rifle Division's CP, of which 4 men were shot in front of the ranks as traitors to the Motherland. An investigation is under way.

During the battle for the NKVD building on 15 September, a woman calling herself Volodina, who spoke the German language and was actively taking part in combat as an automatic weapons man on the German side, was taken prisoner. Because she was wounded, the situation did not permit interrogation, and our worker shot Volodina.

The Special Department [OO] of 62nd Army's NKVD is creating a special group made up of operational Red Army men for arresting all suspicious persons.

At 2300 hours on 15 September, one such group was fired upon from one of the houses in the vicinity of the city's bazaar. During a search of the house, 5 men dressed in Red Army uniforms were discovered in the basement. All 5 men were arrested. An investigation is under way.

From 13 through 15 September, the blocking detachment of 62nd Army's Special Department detained 1,218 men: of these, 21 were shot, 10 were arrested, and the rest were sent to their units. The majority of those detained came from 10th NKVD Division and the associated regiment of 399th Rifle Division, which was abandoned on the battlefield by the regiment's commander and commissar.

For displayed cowardice—fleeing from the field of battle and abandoning units to the mercy of their fate, the commander of the associated regiment of 399th Rifle Division, Major Zhukov, and the commissar— Senior *Politruk* [political worker] Raspopov, have been shot in front of the ranks.[54]

This and other reports attest to the chaotic situation at the front, the brutal nature of the fighting, and the equally ruthless actions the NKVD took to restore order. Among these measures, the most ubiquitous, arbitrary, and unusually cruel were the employment of blocking detachments. These were NKVD or regular troops deployed behind the advancing or defending Red

Army units, whose mission was to maintain order, prevent desertion, and restrain stragglers by whatever means necessary—often by summary execution. In addition, as was the custom, Southeastern Front and 62nd Army continued fielding penal [*shtrafnye*] battalions and companies to punish those guilty of various infractions, employing them to perform the most dangerous of tasks. These included, at the least, a separate penal battalion in 62nd Army and 1st–5th Separate Penal Companies in 64th Army.[55]

Despite these and other daunting problems, the timely arrival of Rodimtsev's 13th Guards Rifle Division ensured that Chuikov could continue to conduct a viable defense in the city at a time when it appeared his army would simply erode away and collapse outright. It also began a process that would continue throughout September and October and, at the most critical times, feed fresh flesh and blood into the Stalingrad meat grinder (see Table 15).

Not counting replacements reaching the city in march-companies and battalions, these eight rifle divisions and separate tank brigades added more than 100,000 men to Chuikov's army and more than matched the strength of German formations sent to the region (see Table 16). This meant that Chuikov, despite the appalling carnage and 62nd Army's immense losses, was able to maintain his army's strength at just more than 50,000 men and to man credible defenses around his ever-shrinking defensive perimeter.

From the German perspective, these reinforcements were sorely needed because Paulus's army was already suffering from severe attrition and without them was in danger of bleeding itself white. Indicative of this sad reality was a status report that Sixth Army prepared at midday on 14 September, which showed the combat strength of all of LI Corps' divisions and many of XIV Panzer and VIII, XI, and XVII Army Corps' divisions was rapidly deteriorating (see Table 17).

Although the average combat rating of the 109 infantry, panzer-grenadier, and jäger battalions Sixth Army fielded on 14 September was rated slightly above "average," this rating is misleading because the army's divisions should have included a total of 132 full-strength combat battalions.[56] The army fielded a lower quantity of battalions than authorized by existing tables of organization because combat attrition had already compelled many of its divisions to consolidate their weakened battalions into new and stronger battalions. For example, by 14 September LI Corps' 389th Infantry Division included six rather than nine battalions, and the 295th Infantry had seven rather than nine. At the same time, XI Corps' 384th Infantry Division fielded six rather than nine battalions and its 100th Jäger Division five rather than six battalions. Thus, in terms of combat battalions alone, Sixth Army was already about 16 percent below its authorized strength by mid-September. Making matters worse, 19 of the army's infantry battalions were rated "weak," that is, barely able to participate in sustained combat, and the 25 rated "strong" and

Table 15. Major Reinforcements Reaching 62nd Army during September and October 1942

Date Crossed the Volga River	Force	Commander
14 September	13th Guards Rifle Division	Major General A. I. Rodimtsev
16 September	92nd Naval Rifle Brigade	Lieutenant Colonel Tarasov (initials unknown)
16 September	137th Tank Brigade	Lieutenant Colonel K. S. Udovichenko
19–20 September	95th Rifle Division	Colonel V. A. Gorishnyi
21–23 September	284th Rifle Division	Colonel N. F. Batiuk
25–27 September	193rd Rifle Division	Major General F. N. Smekhotvorov
29–30 September	39th Guards Rifle Division	Major General S. S. Gur'ev
30 September	42nd Rifle Brigade (reconstituted)	Colonel M. S. Batrakov
30 September	92nd Naval Rifle Brigade (reconstituted)	Lieutenant Colonel Tarasov, Major Shtrigol' by 10 November
30 September	308th Rifle Division	Colonel (Major General, 7 December 1942) L. N. Gurt'ev
3 October	37th Guards Rifle Division	Major General V. G. Zholudev
4 October	84th Tank Brigade	Colonel D. N. Belyi
12 October	524th Rifle Regt, 112th Rifle Division (reconstituted)	
15 October	138th Rifle Division	Colonel (Major General, 27 January 1943) I. I. Liudnikov
26 October	45th Rifle Division	Colonel V. P. Sokolov

Note: Beginning in mid-October, at Chuikov's request, the flow of replacements shifted from primarily fully formed divisions to individual replacements organized into march-battalions and march-companies.

Table 16. Major Reinforcements to and Departures from Sixth Army's Forces Assaulting Stalingrad during September and October 1942

Arrival Date	Force (Commander)
11–12 September	Group Stahel (*Luftwaffe*)
19–20 September	24th Panzer Division (withdrawn)
20–21 September	16th Panzer Division (part)
25–26 September	100th Jäger Division – Lieutenant General Werner Sanne
26 September	24th Panzer Division (recommitted)
29 September	29th Motorized Division (withdrawn)
29 September	14th Panzer Division (part withdrawn)
13 October	14th Panzer Division (recommitted)
13 October	305th Infantry Division – Lieutenant General Kurt Oppenländer, Lieutenant General Bernhard Steinmetz on 1 November
20 October	79th Infantry Division (two regiments) – Lieutenant General Richard von Schwerin

Table 17. The Condition of Sixth Army's Divisions, 14 September 1942

- LI Army Corps
  - 71st Infantry Division
    - Infantry battalions (8) – 8 weak;
    - Pioneer battalion – average.
  - 295th Infantry Division
    - Infantry battalions (7) – 2 medium strong, 3 average, and 2 weak;
    - Pioneer battalion – average.
  - 389th Infantry Division
    - Infantry battalions (6) – 1 medium strong, 3 average, and 2 weak;
    - Pioneer battalion – average.
- XIV Panzer Corps
  - 16th Panzer Division
    - Panzer grenadier battalions (5) – 3 medium strong and 2 average;
    - Pioneer battalion – average.
  - 3rd Motorized Division
    - Panzer grenadier battalions (5) – 2 medium strong, 2 average, and 1 weak;
    - Pioneer battalion – weak.
  - 60th Motorized Division
    - Panzer grenadier battalions (7) – 1 medium strong and 6 average;
    - Pioneer battalion – average.
- VIII Army Corps
  - 76th Infantry Division
    - Infantry battalions (9) – 5 medium strong and 4 average;
    - Pioneer battalion – average.
  - 305th Infantry Division
    - Infantry battalions (9) – 3 strong, 2 medium strong, and 4 average;
    - Pioneer battalion – average.
- XI Army Corps
  - 384th Infantry Division
    - Infantry battalions (6) – 3 strong, 1 medium strong, and 2 average;
    - Pioneer battalion – strong.
  - 44th Infantry Division
    - Infantry battalions (9) – 7 average and 2 weak;
    - Pioneer battalion – average.
  - 100th Jäger Division
    - Jäger battalions (4) – 4 strong;
    - Croat infantry battalion (1) – strong;
    - Pioneer battalion – medium strong.
  - 376th Infantry Division
    - Infantry battalions (7) – 6 average and 1 weak;
    - Pioneer battalion – average.
- XVII Army Corps
  - 113th Infantry Division
    - Infantry battalions (8) – 5 strong and 3 medium strong;
    - Pioneer battalion – average.
  - 79th Infantry Division
    - Infantry battalions (9) – 6 average and 3 weak;
    - Pioneer battalion – average.
  - 298th Infantry Division
    - Infantry battalions (6) – 6 strong;
    - Pioneer battalion – strong.

Table 17. (continued)

---

o 22nd Panzer Division
  ▪ Panzer grenadier battalions (2) – strong;
  ▪ Motorcycle battalion (1) – strong;
  ▪ Pioneer battalion – strong.
o Romanian 13th Infantry Division
  ▪ Infantry battalions (7) – 7 strong.
o Romanian 1st Cavalry Division
  ▪ Cavalry *Abteilung* [battalions] (4) – 4 strong.

Source: Florian *Freiherr* von und zu Aufsess, "Betr.: Zustand der Divisionen, Armee – Oberkommando 6, Abt. Ia, A. H. Qu., den 14 September 42, 12.35 Uhr," in *Die Anlagen-bander zu den Kriegstagebuchern der 6. Armee vom 14.09.1942 bis 24.11.1942, Band I* (Schwabach, Germany: January 2006), 12.

the 45 rated "average" were more than double the number of those listed as "medium strong."

This attrition had exacted its greatest toll on LI Corps, the infantry force that Weichs and Paulus relied most upon to seize Stalingrad. By mid-September Seydlitz was already short six of 27 authorized battalions. Fully 12 of his 21 battalions were considered "weak," and none were judged to be "strong." Six of the remaining battalions were rated "average" and only three "medium strong." These depressing figures alone underscored Sixth Army's urgent need for reinforcements, in particular because the struggle in Stalingrad city had only just begun.

16 September

On 16 September the heaviest fighting in the Stalingrad region took place in the sector from the heights west of the Krasnyi Oktiabr' village southward past Mamaev Kurgan and through downtown Stalingrad to the El'shanka River (see Map 20). According to Chuikov's daily operational summary:

> During the day, the army repelled attacks by small groups of enemy against the northern sector of the front and held on to their positions, and, in the central and southern sectors of the front, the army conducted fierce combat, as 13th Guards Rifle Division, in cooperation with units of the northern combat sector, conducted an attack with part of its forces for possession of Hill 102.0 [Mamaev Kurgan].[57]

The Red Army General Staff's operational summary captured the deteriorating conditions in 62nd Army:

62nd Army continued to fight stubborn street battles in the center of Stalingrad city all day on 16 September.

112th RD, with a battalion of 13th Gds. RD, captured Hill 102.0 [Mamaev Kurgan], north of Stalingrad [city] at 1500 hours on 16 September. The units of 13th Gds. RD cleared the railroad station [No. 1] of the enemy at 1330 hours, and was defending positions along the railroad line along Kurskaia [Kursk] and Korbovaia Streets [south of the station] with one regiment of the division [39th Guards].

10th RB and 133rd TB (in a weakened state) were holding on to the [grain] elevator [northeast of Station No. 2] with difficulty.

The enemy, fighting for possession of the elevator from the front, simultaneously bypassed it from the flanks and advanced toward the northeast.

244th RD was fighting along the line the southern bank of the Tsaritsa River (2 kilometers southeast of Opytnaia Station State Farm)-the road on the western outskirts of Stalingrad, leading from Verkhniaia El'shanka. The enemy, reaching into the division's rear area, captured Stalingrad Station No. 2.

35th Gds. RD, with part of 131st RD's forces, was fighting with enemy submachine gunners in the vicinity of Lesopromyshlennost' No. 2 [Lumber Plant No. 2] and the railroad water tower [on the eastern edge of Kuporosnoe].[58]

During the intense fighting on 16 September, 516th and 517th Regiments of Wuthmann's 295th Infantry Division, deployed on the left wing of Seydlitz's LI Corps, painfully inched their way eastward from Hill 126.3 toward the western edge of Krasnyi Oktiabr' village, battling with 6th Guards and 189th Tank Brigades and 38th Motorized Rifle Brigade, reinforced by the remnants of 87th Rifle Division, 9th Motorized Rifle Brigade, and elements of 10th NKVD Rifle Division's 269th Regiment.[59] The third regiment of Wuthmann's infantry division, the 518th, began its prolonged see-saw struggle with 1st and 2nd Battalions of 13th Guards Rifle Division's 39th Regiment and 1st and 2nd Battalions of 112th Rifle Division's 416th Regiment for possession of Mamaev Kurgan (see Map 23).

Illustrating the intense but chaotic nature of the subsequent fighting, shortly after dawn on 16 September these four Soviet battalions stormed and recaptured the key summit. During the afternoon, however, 295th Infantry Division's 518th Regiment counterattacked and recovered Mamaev Kurgan's summit, providing its soldiers the best observation post in the city. Thereafter, although both sides would claim control of Mamaev Kurgan, in fact the two antagonists shared the hill, fighting desperately along the burial mound's slopes for days over control of the prize.[60] Possession of Mamaev Kurgan took on special meaning for Germans and Soviets alike because both

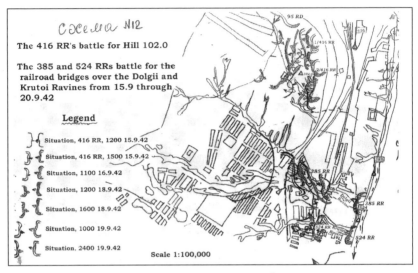

Cxemα №12

The 416 RR's battle for Hill 102.0

The 385 and 524 RRs battle for the railroad bridges over the Dolgii and Krutoi Ravines from 15.9 through 20.9.42

Legend

Situation, 416 RR, 1200 15.9.42

Situation, 416 RR, 1500 15.9.42

Situation, 1100 16.9.42

Situation, 1200 18.9.42

Situation, 1600 18.9.42

Situation, 1000 19.9.42

Situation, 2400 19.9.42

Scale 1:100,000

Map 23. 112th Rifle Division's situation, 15–20 September 1942

sides realized that if the Germans recaptured the hill they would dominate the city, the adjacent workers' settlements, and the approaches to both sides of the Volga River.

Farther to the south, in Stalingrad's center city, after giving back some ground to 13th Guards Rifle Division overnight on 15–16 September, Hartmann's 71st Infantry Division continued pressing into the city with its 194th, 211th, and 191st Regiments advancing abreast from left to right (see Map 22). The 194th Regiment, with a battalion of 295th Division's 518th Regiment on its left, struggled with 112th Rifle Division's 524th and 385th Regiments for possession of the upper reaches of the Dolgii and Krutoi Ravines but were unable to dislodge the Soviet defenders. And farther south, the main forces of 71st Division's 194th Regiment, with the bulk of the division's 211th Regiment on its right, engaged in a swirling and confused street-to-street and building-to-building fight with the battalions of 13th Guards Rifle Division's 34th and 42nd Regiments in a 3.5-kilometer-wide swath of rubbled buildings and bomb-pocked streets extending from the Dolgii Ravine southward past Railroad Station No. 1 to the Tsaritsa River. The heaviest fighting occurred in the vicinity of 9 January Square, where 194th Regiment's lead battalions dueled furiously with 2nd Battalion, 34th Guards Regiment, and 2nd Battalion, 42nd Guards Regiment, for possession of the hulks of buildings flanking the square, and near the railroad station, where 1st Battalion, 42nd Guards Regiment, clung resolutely to the station and adjacent ruined buildings along Kommunisticheskaia Street.

On the right flank of Hartmann's infantry division, in XXXXVIII Panzer Corps' sector, two separate but interconnected struggles were unfolding: the first to capture the entire section of Stalingrad south of the Tsaritsa River, and the second to drive Soviet forces from their remaining footholds in the suburbs of Minina, El'shanka, and Kuporosnoe (see Map 24). The first of these struggles began at dawn when 24th Panzer and 94th Infantry Divisions resumed their attacks. Both divisions expected a more intense fight than the day before because, just before dawn, the corps' Ia (operations) Division had announced, "The enemy has considerably strengthened himself in the tri-angle bounded by the Volga–Tsaritsa Gully railway station."[61]

Advancing in the 4-kilometer-wide sector extending southward from the Tsaritsa River and across the lower reaches of the El'shanka River to the southern outskirts of Minina, Lenski's panzer and Pfeiffer's infantry divisions would encounter the remnants of Batrakov's 42nd Rifle Brigade, Driakhlov's 10th Rifle Brigade, Afanas'ev's 244th Rifle Division, Bubnov's tankless 133rd Tank Brigade, whose *tankists* were fighting as infantry, 271st NKVD Regi-ment, and the right wing of Pesochin's 131st Rifle Division. These forces, which were supposed to be reinforced by Tarasov's fresh 92nd Rifle Brigade during the day, occupied defenses on the high ground south of the Tsaritsa River, in and around the Barracks area on the heights west of the city, in the tangled streets west of the main north-south railroad line and Railroad Sta-tion No. 2, and the lower El'shanka River, backed up by positions to the rear in the vicinity of the Grain Elevator and other prominent buildings between the railroad line and the Volga River. Neither contiguous nor coherent, these defenses consisted of separate strongpoints anchored on the ravines and gul-lies in the open terrain and along the El'shanka River and buildings in the half-ruined city.

The 24th Panzer Division's specific mission on 16 September was to se-cure a bridgehead on the northern bank of the Tsaritsa River, link up with 71st Infantry Division's forces, and liquidate bypassed Soviet forces from the Barracks Hill region and upper Tsaritsa Valley to the west. The 94th Infantry Division's task was to clear Soviet forces from the remainder of the Minina suburb, cross the El'shanka River and the railroad spur from the main line to the Volga River, and clear all Soviet forces from the maze of buildings and streets between the railroad and the Volga River. Both forces were to reach the southern bank of the Tsaritsa by day's end.

Shortly after dawn, *Kampfgruppe* Edelsheim, reinforced by the divi-sion's remaining tanks formed into Panzer Detachment Lancken, pushed northward along the railroad and seized a foothold across the Tsaritsa River against stiffening resistance by elements of Batrakov's 42nd Rifle Brigade. On Edelsheim's left, *Kampfgruppe* Hellermann, screened on its left by the divi-sion's 4th Motorcycle Battalion, swept northwestward against the bypassed

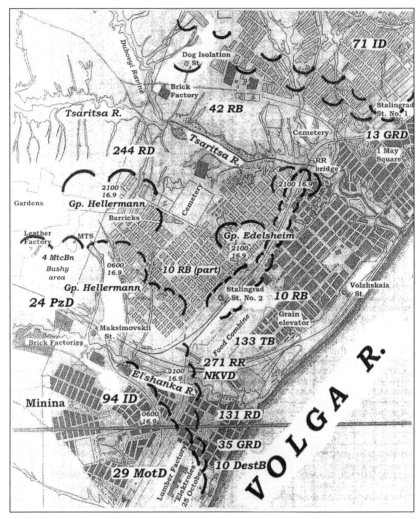

Map 24. XXXXVIII Panzer Corps' advance, 16 September 1942

forces of Afanas'ev's 244th Rifle Division and Driakhlov's 10th Rifle Brigade on Barracks Hill. On 24th Panzer's right (southern) flank, the regiments of Pfeiffer's 94th Infantry Division, which led their assault with four battalion shock groups, attacked successfully northeastward through the northern part of the Minina suburb. This attack forced the defenders from Bubnov's 133rd Tank Brigade, 271st NKVD Rifle Regiment, and Pesochin's 131st Rifle Division to abandon their positions. Once Pfeiffer's grenadiers crossed the

El'shanka River shortly before noon, however, they encountered much stiffer resistance along the gullies on the northern bank of the river and the railroad embankment beyond, where Bubnov's *tankists*, Kostenitsyn's NKVD security troops, and Pesochin's infantry had decided to make their stand.

After grinding their way across the railroad embankment and into the complex of buildings making up Stalingrad's Food Combine, all the while suffering heavy losses, 94th Division's advancing battalions finally ground to a halt in late afternoon, when the grenadiers met even stronger and more determined resistance in the Grain Elevator and adjacent buildings. These formidable strongpoints were defended not only by elements of 133rd Tank Brigade and 271st NKVD Regiment but also by soldiers from 10th Rifle Brigade, which had infiltrated eastward through 24th Panzer's porous armored cordon stretched from north to south along the railroad through the southern half of the city. In addition to failing to accomplish its own mission of the day, 94th Division's slowing advance also left 24th Panzer Division's right flank exposed, in particular *Kampfgruppe* Edelsheim, which had already become more vulnerable because Lenski had transferred Lancken's panzer detachment from Edelsheim's group to reinforce *Kampfgruppe* Hellermann's thrust shortly before midday.

Back in 24th Panzer's sector, although *Kampfgruppe* Hellermann managed to capture the barracks and most of adjacent Barracks Hill from 244th Rifle Division and 10th Rifle Brigade, at midday 42nd Rifle Brigade and NKVD troops subjected *Kampfgruppe* Edelsheim's bridgehead across the Tsaritsa River to heavy assaults from all sides. After Hellermann tried but failed to reach the Tsaritsa and reinforce Edelsheim's forces, the latter had no choice but to abandon the bridgehead shortly after sunset. Compounding matters, because 71st Infantry Division's assaults in Stalingrad's center city were also bogging down against stiffening resistance, Hartmann's grenadiers were unable to offer Edelsheim any support. As a result, the armored strength of Lenski's division dwindled to 19 operational tanks by day's end.[62] When Kempf learned of the situation, he remarked, "The main wish of 24th Panzer-Division, that 94th Infantry Division should cordon [the region] off, was not performable."[63]

The second struggle in XXXXVIII Panzer Corps' sector on 16 September took place in the 2.5-kilometer-wide area extending from the southern outskirts of Minina past the southeastern outskirts of Kuporosnoe to the Volga River. Here, Fremerey's 29th Motorized Division had the mission of rooting the remnants of Dubiansky's 35th Guards Rifle Division and two regiments of Pesochin's 131st Rifle Division out of their strongpoints in the southern part of Minina and Kuporosnoe, capturing the complex of buildings in Lumber Factory No. 2 and the Elektroles Power Plant, and reaching and crossing the El'shanka River near its confluence with the Volga. Thereafter, 29th

Motorized was to provide 94th Division with minimal support but, more important, withdraw its main forces to assembly areas so that it could prepare for its anticipated advance on Astrakhan'. However, 29th Motorized also encountered heavier than anticipated resistance. Although it managed to keep pace with 94th Division, its advance faltered well short of the El'shanka River.

Chuikov, reacting forcefully to the crisis on his army's left wing, at 1230 hours ordered the remnants of 131st Rifle Division, 10th Rifle Brigade, and the remaining forces of 270th NKVD Regiment to join 35th Guards Rifle Division. Under Colonel Dubiansky's command, the reinforced guards division was to "defend the sector: on the right the railroad (Sadovaia Station and Stalingrad Station No. 2) and on the left the Volga River."[64]

The 62nd Army's subsequent daily summary correctly assessed that the Germans were focusing their efforts along two axes by conducting their main attack from the Gorodishche and Aviagorodok regions toward Stalingrad's central city and a secondary thrust from Sadovaia Station toward Minina, Kuporosnoe, and the southern half of the city. It reported, "The forward enemy units reached the Tsaritsa River at 1500 hours, where fighting was going on at the railroad bridge," and powerful columns of enemy tank and infantry columns were moving "from Sadovaia to Stalingrad Station No. 2 and to the east."[65]

The army's summary also provided a detailed description of the positions its subordinate formations and units occupied as of 2400 hours on 16 September:

> The Northern Combat Sector, consisting of 124th and 149th RBs, 115th RB, the remnants of 196th and 315th RDs, and 23rd TC, were continuing to defend their previous positions.
>
> 112th RD was fighting for possession of Hill 102.0 [Mamaev Kurgan] with one regiment and occupied a defense along [the following] line with two regiments: 524th RR-the western edge of the woods (west of marker 35.8), 385th RR-Hill 98.9 and the western edge of the woods (Krasnyi Oktiabr'). 416th RR is fighting on Hill 102.0 and reached the line from 2 kilometers north-east of Marker 102.0 to 0.5 kilometers north of marker 102.0 by 1600 hours.
>
> 39th Gds. RR [13th Gds. RD] is attacking toward Hill 102.0 from the east and captured Hill 102.0 at 1300 hours and is continuing its attack toward the northwest.
>
> 42nd Gds. RR [13th Gds. RD] is fighting for the bank of the Volga along the ravines south of Marker 102.0, and 2nd Bn, 42nd Gds. RR, is conducting street fighting in the vicinity of the northeastern part of Stalingrad.
>
> 34th Gds. RR [13th Gds. RD] is continuing street fighting in the vicinity of the railroad station, and one battalion is fighting in the vicinity of the army's CP.

10th RD NKVD is fighting along the [following] lines: 272nd RR straddles the road to the city southeast of Hill 112.5; 270th RR is fighting along the line from the southern slope of Hill 112.5, Lesoposadochnaia, Marker 20.7, along the western outskirts of Stalingrad, and up to the railroad line; and 275th RR is defending the (incl.) Marker 2.0 and Lesoposadochnaia line.

42nd RB is fighting on the Marker 2.5, Lesoposadochnaia, along the western edge of the grove south of Lesoposadochnaia (incl.), and two buildings 4 kilometers east of Marker 50.7 line. A detachment has been sent to liquidate the penetration at the junction to the left.

244th RD is fighting along the line: (incl.) the two buildings east of Marker 50.7, (incl.) the rectangular woods, the western outskirts of the city, and along the railroad line. The enemy has enveloped the division from the left.

10th RB and 35th GRD—positions are being verified.

CP—Pushkinskaia No. 3, which is being fired on by enemy artillery, machine guns, and automatic weapons. Beginning at 2400 hours on 16 September, the army's headquarters will be in Krasnyi Oktiabr'.[66]

17 September

The fight for the southern half of Stalingrad reached its culminating point on 17 September, when 211th Regiment of LI Corps' 71st Infantry Division linked up with XXXXVIII Panzer Corps' 24th Panzer Division along the Tsaritsa River just south of the city's center, less than a kilometer from Chuikov's command post (see Map 25).

However, the daily operational summary that the Red Army General Staff issued at 0800 hours on 18 September optimistically noted, "The forces of the Southeastern Front continued to fight fierce street battles in Stalingrad city on 17 September and, simultaneously, repelled attacks by the enemy in the Kuporosnoe region with part of its forces."[67] The truth was far grimmer, as indicated by the detail in Chuikov's evening report to the General Staff:

62nd Army fought intense street battles in Stalingrad city all day on 17 September.

13th Gds. RD was fighting on the southwestern slopes of Hill 102.0 [Mamaev Kurgan] with part of its forces [39th Gds. RR] and was fighting with other parts of its forces [34th Gds. RR] along the line of the railroad from Dolgii Ravine to Krutoi Ravine and was withdrawing under enemy pressure to the oil warehouses. 42nd Gds. RR, as a result of attacks by the enemy, abandoned the railroad station [Station No. 1] and was fighting in the vicinity of the House of Specialists with part of its forces.

Map 25. Sixth Army's situation, 17–18 September 1942

272nd RR 10th RD NKVD and 34th TB [erroneous], attacked by superior enemy forces on the morning of 17 September, withdrew and were fighting along the line MTC [Motor Tractor Station]-Height Marker 20.7-Tsaritsa River by day's end.

10th RB and 133rd TB (3 KV tanks) were fighting in the vicinity of the [grain] elevator.

35th Gds. RD and 131st RD were continuing to occupy positions in the southern part of the city in the vicinity of the water tower and to the north. The positions of the remaining units of the army are unchanged.[68]

In fact, during the day Seydlitz's LI Corps continued its slow push eastward, with 545th, 546th, and 544th Regiments of Jänecke's 398th Infantry Division and 517th and 516th Regiments of Wuthmann's 295th Infantry Division gaining ground slowly but steadily against 23rd Tank Corps' 6th Guards and 189th Tank and 38th and 9th Motorized Rifle Brigades in the sector from east of Gorodishche southward past the western edge of Vishnevaia *Balka* to the northern slopes of Mamaev Kurgan. To the south, 295th Division's 518th Regiment continued fencing with 112th Rifle Division's 416th Regiment and 13th Guards Rifle Division's 39th Regiment on the already bloody slopes of the Mamaev Kurgan. Farther south, just north of Stalingrad's center city, 194th Regiment of Hartmann's 71st Infantry Division struggled with 112th Rifle Division's 385th and 524th Regiments for possession of the Dolgii and Krutoi Ravines and the quick access they offered to the Volga River's western bank.

South of the twin ravines, 71st Infantry Division's 211th and 191st Regiments contested with 13th Guards Rifle Division's 42nd and 34th Regiments for control of parks and key buildings along and east of Kommunisticheskaia Street, especially in and around Railroad Station No. 1 and the tactically vital 9 January Square, which lay only three city blocks from the Volga's western bank (see Map 26). By day's end, Hartmann's two regiments controlled virtually all of the city's buildings and streets west of the main railroad line, recaptured Station No. 1 from 1st Battalion, 42nd Guards Regiment, and repelled persistent but futile Soviet counterattacks against their positions in and around the House of Specialists. This fighting saw the railroad station change hands four times, with both sides claiming victory in its ruins. By day's end, Elin's 42nd Regiment reported eight destroyed or burned German tanks, and the bodies of 100 German soldiers were scattered around the railroad station.[69]

Later in the day, the forward elements of 71st Infantry Division's 211th Regiment finally linked up with 24th Panzer Division's *Kampfgruppen* Hellermann and Edelsheim, the former along the upper reaches of the Tsaritsa River and the latter near the railroad bridge across the river. By doing so, Hartmann's infantry and Lenski's panzer-grenadiers encircled most of the remnants of Batrakov's 42nd Rifle Brigade and the bulk of Afanas'ev's 244th Rifle Division in an elongated pocket stretching from west to east along the valley of the Tsaritsa River. By nightfall, Hartmann's 191st Regiment wheeled eastward behind 211th Regiment to join 194th Regiment in the struggle for Stalingrad's center.

While the troops of LI Corps' 295th and 71st Infantry Divisions battled for Mamaev Kurgan and the Dolgii and Krutoi Ravines and edged deeper

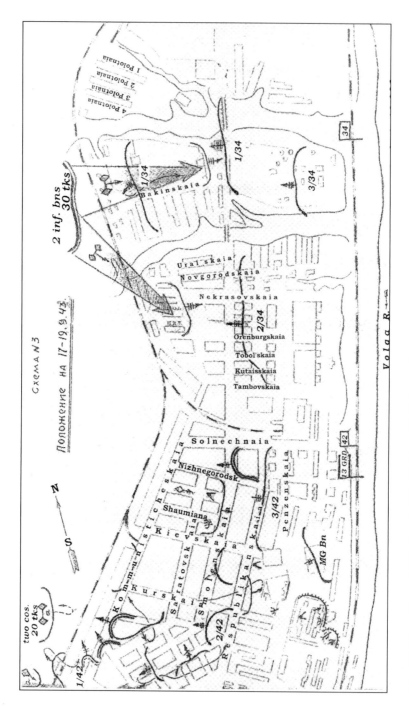

Map 26. Dispositions of 13th Guards Rifle Division, 17–19 September 1942

and deeper into central Stalingrad, XXXXVIII Panzer Corps' 24th Panzer and 94th Infantry Divisions resumed their advance against the remnants of 244th Rifle Division and 10th Rifle and 133rd Tank Brigades in the southern section of the city. In the process, they recaptured Railroad Station No. 2, which 42nd Rifle Brigade had seized earlier in the day. Meanwhile, 24th Panzer Division's *Kampfgruppen* Edelsheim and Hellermann launched converging attacks toward the Tsaritsa River aimed at linking up with 71st Infantry Division's infantry, which was advancing through the streets of the western part of the central city toward the northern bank of the Tsaritsa River. These converging advances, with 94th Infantry Division on their left, established a coherent front along the southern bank of the Tsaritsa River east of Edelsheim's bridgehead (see Map 27).

Advancing northwestward from the main railroad line shortly after dawn, 1st and 2nd Battalions of 24th Panzer Division's 26th Grenadier Regiment (of *Kampfgruppe* Edelsheim) had by 1120 hours cleared elements of 42nd Rifle Brigade and 244th Rifle Division from the maze of streets west of the railroad and south of the Tsaritsa River and had closed on the river's southern bank. On their left, *Kampfgruppe* Hellermann and the division's 4th Motorcycle Battalion swept northward from the barracks' region, pressing the bypassed elements of 244th Rifle Division and 42nd and 10th Rifle Brigades northward toward the valley of the Tsaritsa or eastward into the city's streets through *Kampfgruppe* Edelsheim's still-porous rear. With this task complete, Hellermann's forces advanced northward shortly after noon "through the confused enemy" and seized the hilly region south of the Tsaritsa Gully, where Lenski ordered Hellermann to halt. Still later in the day, a detachment from 21st Grenadier Regiment, the nucleus of Hellermann's *kampfgruppe*, advanced eastward along the southern bank of the Tsaritsa River valley in tandem with forces from 71st Infantry Division's 211th Regiment, which was operating on the right wing of Hartmann's division with orders to secure the Tsaritsa's northern bank.[70]

As the troops from 24th Panzer Division's two *kampfgruppen* advanced on converging axes along the southern bank of the Tsaritsa River, they reported engaging a "desperate enemy" who "resisted in small side gullies and rifts in the steep sides of the Tsaritsa Gully itself until the futility of their situation set in," after which "they slipped off in ones and twos to try their luck in reaching the Volga."[71] Pressed into a pocket formed by 71st Infantry Division's 211th Regiment to the north, parts of 24th Panzer Division's 21st Panzer Grenadier Regiment to the west, and 26th Panzer Grenadier Regiment at the railroad bridge across the Tsaritsa and to the south, the remnants of 42nd Rifle Brigade and 244th Rifle Division were left with only the narrow sector north of the bridge through which they could pass to reach the safety of 13th Guards Rifle Division's defenses in the center city.

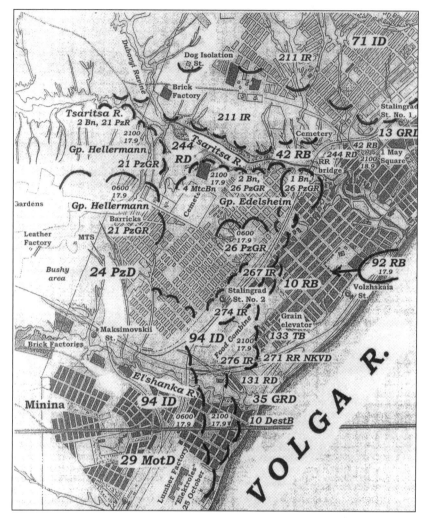

Map 27. XXXXVIII Panzer Corps' advance, 17–18 September 1942

As Batrakov's and Afanas'ev's tired and confused riflemen made their way as best they could through this German cordon, the forces of Lenski's 24th Panzer slowly but steadily cleared the entire region south of the Tsaritsa River and west of the north-south railroad line. On Lenski's right, the troops of Pfeiffer's 94th Infantry Division tried to keep pace by liquidating Soviet forces still defending east of the main railroad line and south of the lower Tsaritsa River and thereby close on the lower Tsaritsa River on 24th Panzer's right flank. However, the 94th found the going far more difficult than anticipated. During the morning, the division's 267th Regiment, with 274th Regiment echeloned to its right rear, managed to advance northward along and east of the main railroad line, leaving its 276th Regiment to clear Soviet forces from the complex of buildings making up the Food Combine.

In exceedingly slow going against stubborn resistance offered by 10th Rifle and 133rd Tank Brigades, 271st NKVD Rifle Regiment, and elements of 131st Rifle Division, a single battalion of 267th Regiment managed to push northward along the railroad and link up with elements of 24th Panzer's *Kampfgruppe* Edelsheim in its bridgehead across the Tsaritsa River. To the rear, however, the remainder of 267th Regiment was still struggling to overcome Soviet forces lodged in the Grain Elevator and other fortified buildings east of the railroad, and 276th Regiment was locked in a vicious fight for the ruined buildings of the Food Combine. In fact, by day's end their forward progress stalled entirely as the regimental commanders paused to configure their forces into *kampfgruppen* task-organized with the proper mix of infantry, sappers, and heavy weapons necessary to destroy the myriad of bothersome and sometimes deadly Soviet strongpoints. All the while, Kempf repeatedly lamented 24th Panzer's failure to secure the Grain Elevator during its initial advance.

To Kempf's partial relief, however, at 1755 hours Lenski informed him that 24th Panzer Division had finally cleared and secured the region south of the Tsaritsa River and west of the main railroad line. By this time, the infantry of 71st Division's 211th Regiment and the panzer-grenadiers of 24th Panzer's two *kampfgruppen* finally formed a continuous line along the Tsaritsa River from its upper reaches eastward to the railroad bridge. Lenski's panzer-grenadiers and infantry of Pfeiffer's 94th Division did the same in the sector extending southward along the railroad from the Tsaritsa River to the vicinity of Railroad Station No. 2 and the Food Combine.

However, 94th Infantry Division's advance east of the railroad first slowed and then stalled in the face of determined resistance. Driakhlov's 10th Rifle and 133rd Tank Brigades, 271st NKVD Rifle Regiment, and the remnants of 131st Rifle Division's right-wing regiment still clung resolutely to the narrow strip of land between the railroad and the Volga River from the southern bank of the Tsaritsa southward through the Food Combine to the northern bank of the El'shanka River.

Nor did Fremerey's 29th Motorized Division register much more progress in its advance through the northwestern section of El'shanka and the northern half of the Lumber Factory and the Elektroles Power Plant. Fremerey's panzer-grenadiers, still supported by a handful of tanks from 14th Panzer Division, drove the survivors of Dubiansky's 35th Guards Rifle Division, reinforced by the remnants of two regiments of 131st Rifle Division and 270th NKVD Regiment, from the northern building of Lumber Factory No. 2, the Elektroles Power Plant, and other buildings south of the El'shanka River, forcing most of the defending troops to withdraw northward across the river or eastward toward the Volga's western bank. By day's end, however, his panzer-grenadiers still faced several Soviet fortified strongpoints on the river's southern bank.

Thus, in addition to clearing the eastern half of Stalingrad's southern city, Kempf's XXXXVIII Panzer Corps by nightfall on 17 September still had to contend with pockets of soldiers from 42nd Rifle Brigade and 244th Rifle Division trapped northwest and north of the railroad bridge over the Tsaritsa River. Kempf first assigned this task to Lenski's 24th Panzer Division. In response, Lenski proposed that the corps ignore this Soviet force and instead conduct a joint operation on 18 September with his division and Pfeiffer's 94th Infantry to clear Soviet forces from the city blocks east of the railroad and reach the Volga River from the Tsaritsa River southward to the El'shanka River.[72] To accomplish this task, Lenski offered to provide artillery support to 94th Infantry Division in its struggle in the vicinity of the Grain Elevator. However, any such proposals were moot, because within 24 hours Paulus would order Kempf to transfer 24th Panzer Division to Seydlitz's LI Corps so that it could lend its weight to the more decisive fight for Stalingrad's northern factory district. This, in and of itself, was a tacit admission that Sixth Army's assault on Stalingrad was not going as well as planned. Nonetheless, 24th Panzer's fight in the southern part of Stalingrad city would soon end.

If Lenski was elated over his panzer division's successes during the previous two days, he was also concerned about its failure to utterly destroy the opposing Soviet forces, the steady erosion of his division's combat strength, and the deteriorating supply situation—and for good reason:

It had been a successful few days for the Division: 400 prisoners taken the previous day, 300 on this day. Two planes had been shot down, and 8 tanks, 2 antitank guns, 55 antitank rifle and 12 mortars were destroyed. The only negative was that the enemy could still retreat to the north-north-east and this was no fault of the Division. It had done all that was asked of it. In the evening, all enemy forces in the attack strips of the Division west of the railway and south of the Tsaritsa sector had been completely destroyed. Found in the Barracks area of Gruppe Hellermann and Viereckwald alone were 46 Russian tanks, among them 23 T-34's, all destroyed by German weapons. The Division's operational panzer strength was 7 Panzer II, 3 Panzer III kz [short], 6 Panzer III lg [long], 1 Panzer IV kz, 4 Panzer IV lg, and 2 Bfwg [command tanks]. The Division had only suffered light casualties: two dead and 37 wounded, fourteen of these wounded men remaining with their units. A severe ammunition shortage caused concern amongst supply officers of all divisions of XXXX-VIII. Panzerkorps. Near 24. Panzer-Division, the critical shortage was in light infantry gun ammunition at 15 percent availability, light howitzers at 25 percent, and antitank shells for the 20mm flak guns, which currently stood at 0 percent. This last figure shows the severity of the fighting. These 20mm antiaircraft guns, mounted on the flatbeds of half-tracks, were attached to the combat groups to support the grenadiers and often formed the only antitank capability in emergency situations.[73]

With attrition like this, it was only a matter of time before Paulus's premier shock force, Lenski's panzer division, would itself become hors de combat.

Chuikov, understanding the potential disaster his army faced, 24 hours before had sent a special appeal to *front* commander Eremenko pleading for reinforcements lest his army lose its grip on the city. Although Chuikov asked for two or three full rifle divisions, late in the day Eremenko promised him Lieutenant Colonel Tarasov's 92nd Naval Infantry Brigade, plus Lieutenant Colonel Udovichenko's 137th Tank Brigade, both of which the *front* finally transferred to 62nd Army's control late on 16 September.[74]

The daily report Chuikov dispatched to Eremenko late on 17 September summed up his army's mounting problems in no uncertain terms:

Beginning in the morning, the enemy continued to introduce motorized infantry and tanks into the fighting, trying to broaden the territory seized in the city.

The army repelled fierce attacks by superior enemy forces. It is holding its previous positions in the northern sector of the front.

112th RD and 39th Gds. RR, 13th Gds. RD, were continuing their attacks since morning, capturing the southwestern slopes of Hill 102.0 [Mamaev Kurgan].

13th Gds. RD was continuing street fighting with enemy infantry and tanks in the center of the city, offering the strongest resistance to the enemy in the vicinity of the NKVD's house of specialists and the railroad station. The division has suffered significant casualties in three days of constant fighting.

In the southern sector of the front, the units have withdrawn to the line: (incl.) railroad station 3 kilometers southeast of Sadovaia, (incl.) the Hospital, (incl.), and the southern outskirts of the Minina suburb.

The positions of the remaining units are unchanged.

The army commander has reported to the *front* commander that the existing reserves have been used up, and it is necessary to reinforce the army immediately with new units, in particular, to prevent the complete exhaustion of 13th Gds. RD.[75]

By day's end on 17 September, along most of the front, Chuikov's defending forces were compressed into a shallow area less than 4 kilometers deep along a 17-kilometer front, with their backs to the Volga River. Only in the north, in the sector from Rynok and Spartakovka southward across the Mokraia Mechetka River to the western outskirts of Krasnyi Oktiabr' village and Mamaev Kurgan, did 62nd Army's forces retain some room for a defense in depth. Even here, however, the troops of XIV Panzer Corps and 389th Infantry Division were gradually compressing Chuikov's bridgehead to the south and east. By this time, the XIV Panzer Corps had a new commander. General von Wietersheim had lost his post on 14 September, apparently because his previous requests to withdraw his corps from its exposed position north of the city, and his suggestions that it was time for Sixth Army to go over to the defense at Stalingrad and that it was also wrong to be employing tanks in the struggle for the city, annoyed the Führer. His replacement was Hans Hube, the unflappable commander of 16th Panzer Division.[76]

Yet the battle for the city was by no means over. Late on 16 September, Eremenko finally acquiesced to Chuikov's repeated requests for desperately needed reinforcements by assigning 92nd Naval Rifle Brigade and 137th Tank Brigade to his army. Tarasov's brigade was composed of sailors from the Northern and Baltic Fleets and had formerly been in the *Stavka*'s reserve. The 137th Tank Brigade, which was commanded by Lieutenant Colonel K. S. Udovichenko and consisted of only 15 T-60 light tanks armed with 45mm guns, had been part of 2nd Tank Corps and had previously occupied defensive positions east of the Volga.[77] Ships of the Volga Military Flotilla ferried both brigades across the river on the night of 16–17 September. Chuikov immediately deployed Tarasov's rifle brigade into the sector from the Tsaritsa River southward to the railroad junction east of the El'shanka River to back up 10th Rifle and 133rd Tank Brigades and reinforced 35th Guards Rifle Division as they defended the buildings and streets between the main railroad line and the Volga River and from the Tsaritsa River in the north to the El'shanka River in the south.

Once across the Volga, Tarasov deployed his brigade's 2nd, 3rd, and 1st Separate Battalions in defensive positions stretching from left to right in the sector from the Food Combine northward east of the main railroad to the southern bank of the Tsaritsa River. His 4th Battalion manned reserve positions on the western bank of the Volga from midway between the El'shanka and Tsaritsa Rivers northward to the Tsaritsa's southern bank (see Map 28). The mission of 92nd Brigade's naval riflemen was to reinforce the remnants of 10th Rifle and 133rd Tank Brigade and 271st NKVD Regiment in the vicinity of the Grain Elevator and adjacent buildings. Thereafter, the combined force was to attack westward along the Tsaritsa to destroy the German bridgehead near the railroad bridge and link up with 42nd Rifle Brigade's

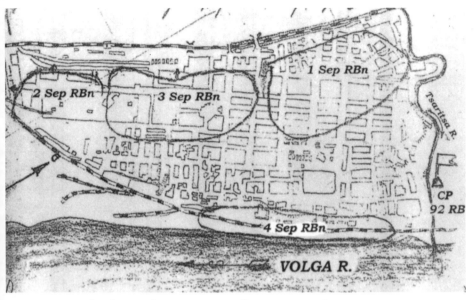

Map 28. 92nd Rifle Brigade's situation, 0600 hours 20 September 1942

and 244th Rifle Division's forces north of the Tsaritsa River. Udovichenko's tanks were to concentrate in the region east of Mamaev Kurgan to back up 112th Rifle and 13th Guards Rifle Divisions' forces fighting on the burial mound. East of the Volga, 2nd Tank Corps' 169th Tank Brigade was to take over Udovichenko's former defensive positions in the Staren'kii and Tumak sectors.[78]

Also on 17 September, the *Stavka* released Major General F. N. Smekhotvorov's 193rd Rifle Division to Southeastern Front. Acting in Chuikov's stead, Krylov, 62nd Army's chief of staff, immediately ordered Smekhotvorov to concentrate his fresh division in the forests east of Tsyganskaia Zaria, 10 kilometers east of the Volga. The 193rd Rifle Division was a "second formation" division created on 3 January 1942 in the Riazan' region southwest of Moscow to replace its predecessor, which had been destroyed in combat a month before.[79] Its new commander, the veteran infantry officer Fedor Nikandrovich Smekhotvorov, had commanded 135th Rifle Division since June 1940 and would lead the division until 18 March 1943. The 193rd had completed its formation and joined the Briansk Front's reserve in June. While assigned to the Briansk Front's Group Chibisov (along with Colonel Batiuk's 284th Rifle Division), Smekhotvorov's division suffered heavy losses in the fighting west of Voronezh during the second half of July when it was encircled and nearly destroyed in the Sukhaia Vereika pocket. After this fighting was over, the division's surviving cadre and soldiers were evacuated to the Ural Military District for re-formation in early August, only to be sent hastily to the Stalingrad region in mid-September. Therefore, like most other divisions sent to reinforce Chuikov's beleaguered army, the 193rd was manned largely by green troops, although with a leavening of cadre from the Perm Machine Gun–Mortar School and sailors from the Pacific Fleet, all led by an experienced commander.[80]

In addition to Smekhotvorov's division, 95th and 284th Rifle Divisions, commanded by Colonels V. A. Gorishnyi and N. F. Batiuk, respectively, were also en route to Stalingrad; both were from the *Stavka's* reserve. The former was due to assemble in the Zonal'nyi region, 6 kilometers east of the Volga, on 18 September, and the latter north of Krasnaia Sloboda on 21 September.[81] Tentatively, Krylov earmarked Gorishnyi's division to reinforce the units fighting on Mamaev Kurgan and Batiuk's division to fill the gap between 13th Guards Rifle Division in the city's center and 95th Division when it reached Mamaev Kurgan.

As Eremenko acted to bolster 62nd Army's defenses in the city, he informed Chuikov on 17 September that he once again intended to activate operations south of Kotluban' by again attacking XIV Panzer and VIII Army Corps' defenses on the land bridge between the Don and Volga Rivers. Zhukov, who had returned on 12 September to Moscow, where he would remain until 26 September, had already concurred with Eremenko's concept for a new offensive.[82] By launching another offensive in the region south of Kotluban', Eremenko sought to break through the German defenses and drive southward to link up with 62nd Army's forces in Stalingrad's ruins. If the offensive failed, he hoped it would at least decrease the pressure on 62nd Army by diverting a portion of Sixth Army's forces away to its northern flank.

To support this offensive, Eremenko ordered Chuikov to conduct a counterattack of his own to halt the German units that were advancing dangerously close to the western outskirts of Krasnyi Oktiabr' village and compel the German force already locked in combat for Mamaev Kurgan and in Stalingrad's center city to retreat. If Chuikov's counterattack succeeded, Eremenko reasoned, it would also facilitate his offensive farther north by cutting off and destroying German forces attacking the western section of the city. In addition, Eremenko also ordered Shumilov to launch a supporting attack with his 64th Army against the Fourth Panzer Army's forces separating his army at Beketovka from Chuikov's 62nd Army in Stalingrad.

While Eremenko was planning his new offensive, Chuikov reorganized his beleaguered forces in the city. He directed Afanas'ev to incorporate the remnants of his 244th Rifle Division fighting north of the Tsaritsa River into Batrakov's 42nd Rifle Brigade. Batrakov's combined force was to protect the right wing of 13th Guards Division in the city center, liquidate the German

The southern part of Stalingrad city with Railroad Station No. 2 in the upper center, the Grain Elevator to the left of SU 83131, and the railroad line and El'shanka River on the left.

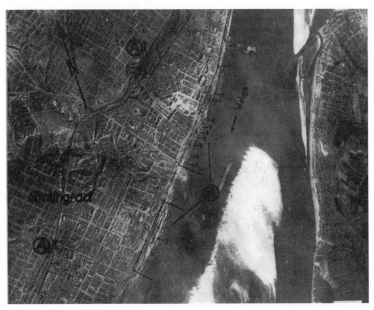

The region north and south of Tsaritsa River with Railroad Station No. 2 and the Grain Elevator at the lower left.

Red Army soldiers swearing allegiance to their Motherland before crossing the Volga River into Stalingrad. The banner reads, "For our Soviet Motherland."

Red Army soldiers
and naval infantry
fighting in the
streets of southern
Stalingrad.

bridgehead over the Tsaritsa River, and, if possible, establish communications with Tarasov's 92nd Rifle Brigade south of the Tsaritsa River. Chuikov also combined all of the forces fighting south of the Tsaritsa River, including the remnants of 10th Rifle and 133rd Tank Brigades, 131st Rifle Division, and 270th and 271st NKVD Regiments, to unite either with Tarasov's 92nd Rifle Brigade or Dubiansky's 35th Guards Rifle Division.[83] Ideally, these orders sought to restore unity of command to all the forces on 62nd Army's left wing by subordinating them to three headquarters, 42nd and 92nd Rifle Brigades and 35th Guards Rifle Division, and to reestablish a contiguous and coherent defensive front in the region. In reality, however, most of these forces were irrevocably intermingled; worse still, XXXXVIII Panzer Corps' planned assault eastward with 94th Infantry Division threatened to split them apart.

As Eremenko rushed reinforcements into the Stalingrad region and Chuikov juggled his army's command structure and disparate forces, XXXXVIII Panzer Corps' forces were already perilously close to Chuikov's army's command bunker, which was located on the Volga's western bank just north of the mouth of the Tsaritsa River. By this time, 24th Panzer Division was shifting its panzer-grenadier regiments eastward into the sector from the Tsaritsa River southward to north of Railroad Station No. 2, from which they could join 94th Infantry Division in an advance to clear Soviet forces from the region between the railroad line and the Volga River. This placed 62nd Army's command post within the range of mortar fire from Lenski's panzer-grenadiers. Chuikov, however, escaped this peril by moving his headquarters to a new and, he hoped, safer location at the ferry stage on the Volga's western bank east of the Krasnyi Oktiabr' Factory. By this time, 62nd Army's hold on the river's western bank was so tenuous that Chuikov actually made the transfer by crossing the Volga opposite the mouth of the Tsaritsa, moving north along the river's eastern bank, and then recrossing the river opposite the Krasnyi Oktiabr' Factory.[84]

18 September

Despite Kempf's stunning victories on 16 and 17 September, XXXXVIII Panzer Corps' struggle in the southern section of the city was prolonged as Soviet forces simply refused to give up. Chuikov, in an attempt to deflect German attention and forces from the fighting in the south, overnight on 17–18 September had ordered Group Gorokhov, which was defending the Rynok and Spartanovka regions north of Stalingrad, "to conduct diversionary attacks beginning at 0500 hours on 18 September with reinforced detachments against 16th Panzer Division's positions on Hill 101.3 and 135.4" north and northwest of Spartanovka.[85] However, as 62nd Army's evening report to the Red Army General Staff indicated, these assaults failed to achieve their desired ends:

62nd Army went over to the offensive with its right wing units at 1500 hours on 18 September and occupied the [following] positions by 1700 hours:

124th RB, while defending the Rynok-(incl.) and Spartanovka line, captured the region of Marker 34.0 (500 meters north of Rynok) with part of its forces.

149th RB, while defending the Spartanovka and Marker 93.2 (4 kilometers west of Rynok) line, attacked toward Hill 101.3 with part of its forces and was slowly advancing forward.

282nd RR NKVD occupied defenses along a line from Marker 93.2 to the separate group of trees (1–2 kilometers southeast of Orlovka).

42nd RB, suffering heavy losses, withdrew to the vicinity of the garden 300 meters south of Station No. 1.

244th RD occupied defenses along the railroad from Turgenevskaia to Liteinaia Streets [400–800 meters northeast of the railroad bridge].

92nd RB, having cleared small groups of enemy from several blocks in Stalingrad south of the Tsaritsa River, reached the line of the railroad from Akhtubinskaia Street [600 meters east of the railroad bridge on the Tsaritsa River] to the [grain] elevator [800 meters east of Railroad Station No. 2].

35th Gds. RD, 10th RB, and 131st RD, after repelled several attacks by the enemy, was continuing to defend the railroad 1 kilometer north of the [grain] elevator, water tower, and L'vov Lane line.

13th Gds. RD repelled fierce attacks by the enemy toward the oil storage tanks and held on to Artemovskaia, Nekrasovskaia, Gogolia, and Respublikanskaia Streets.[86]

The failure of Group Gorokhov's attacks left the Germans free to focus their attentions solely on 62nd Army's shrinking foothold south of the Tsaritsa River and, to a lesser extent, on Stalingrad's center city. Kempf's panzer corps, cooperating with LI Corps' 71st Infantry Division to the north, did so with a vengeance but with only mixed results.

During the day, the three regiments of Hartmann's 71st Infantry Division continued their street fight against 13th Guards Rifle Division's two regiments in Stalingrad's center city in a see-saw struggle for Railroad Station No. 1, the adjacent 9 January Square, and nearby buildings; many buildings changed hands several times. Farther south, the remnants of 42nd Rifle Brigade and 244th Rifle Division, which by now numbered only several hundreds of men under Batrakov's command, escaped the closing pincers of 24th Panzer and 71st Infantry Divisions by infiltrating eastward along both banks of the Tsaritsa River west of the railroad bridge. In the process, the Soviet soldiers crossed the river when necessary and then took up defensive positions in the buildings along Turgenevskaia Street and the gardens to the north. By this time, Batrakov's small force, reinforced by some NKVD troops and local militia, faced 71st Infantry Division's 211th Regiment advancing eastward along the Tsaritsa's northern bank and 24th Panzer Division's forces in the bridgehead at the railroad bridge over the river. Batrakov's forces managed to slow the Germans' advance toward the Volga River, adding to the already dreadful personnel attrition weakening Hartmann's division. ·

While 71st Infantry Division continued its fight north of the Tsaritsa, and 24th Panzer Division consolidated its hold on the Tsaritsa bridgehead and the main railroad line southward toward Railroad Station No. 2, the infantry of Pfeiffer's 94th Infantry Division and the panzer-grenadiers of Fremerey's 29th Motorized Division were left with the painful task of smashing all remaining Soviet resistance in the sector between the railroad line and the Volga from the railroad station southward to the El'shanka River. As simple as this task seemed, it would result in a vicious and often hand-to-hand fight that began on 18 September and would last for another seven days. Initially, the German forces involved in this struggle were Lenski's 24th Panzer Division and Pfeiffer's 94th Infantry and Fremerey's 29th Motorized Divisions. However, within 24 hours Paulus ordered 24th Panzer to leave this region and regroup northward to reinforce LI Corps' advance on Stalingrad's factory district. This would leave only 94th Infantry and 29th Motorized Divisions to clean up the mess in southern Stalingrad.

Before 24th Panzer's departure, however, 94th Division began the fight for this section of the city with its 267th, 274th, and 276th Regiments deployed abreast from the streets east of Railroad Station No. 2 southward to the Food Combine north of the El'shanka River. These regiments were to advance eastward in tandem with 24th Panzer Division's panzer-grenadiers to the north, crush Soviet resistance east of the railroad line, especially in the vicinity of the Grain Elevator, and push the surviving Russians eastward into the Volga. Supporting panzer-grenadiers from 29th Motorized Division were to clear Soviet forces in the sector from the southern edge of the Food Combine southward to the lower El'shanka River.

Lacking a single focal point, the nexus of this operation turned out to be tens of small-scale fights for control of scattered but vital strongpoints. These points included the concrete Grain Elevator, the buildings adjacent to Railroad Station No. 2, the structures in the dense network of city blocks east of the railroad line and south of the Tsaritsa River, the fortified warehouses scattered throughout the Food Combine and other nearby smaller factories and enterprises, and even some buildings situated along the western bank of the Volga south of the El'shanka River. These irksome obstacles were manned by squads, platoons, decimated companies, and, occasionally, small groups of two to five soldiers from a mish-mash of Soviet formations and units; each strongpoint was converted into a miniature fortress.

Troops from the three forward battalions of 92nd Rifle Brigade and the remnants of 10th Rifle and 133rd Tank Brigades and 271st NKVD Rifle Regiment, reinforced by some stragglers from 42nd Rifle Brigade and 244th Rifle Division, defended the most critical sector: from the Food Combine northward past the Grain Elevator and Railroad Station No. 2 to the southern bank of the Tsaritsa River. These forces were under Lieutenant Colonel Tarasov's command (see Map 27). Farther south, similarly configured forces from Dubiansky's reinforced 35th Guards Rifle Division defended the sector from the Volga and El'shanka Rivers to the Food Combine, although some of Dubiansky's troops still clung to strongpoints south of the lower El'shanka River.

The ensuing struggle in this region consisted of a myriad of firefights in which no quarter was asked for or given. German infantry, supported by mortars and PAKS (antitank guns) and artillery firing over open sights from the streets into adjacent blocks and separate buildings, fought with Soviet infantry employing small arms, machine guns, gasoline-filled bottles (known to history as Molotov cocktails), and any other means of destruction at hand. Sometimes better-organized and -supported Soviet troops, such as those from 92nd Rifle Brigade, were fortunate enough to be supported by 76mm field guns, 37mm antitank guns, and 50mm infantry mortars. Blocks of buildings and separate structures became the battlefields, in which individual floors and even rooms changed hands repeatedly.

A naval infantryman (marine) from 3rd Battalion of Tarasov's 92nd Rifle Brigade, which was reinforcing 42nd Rifle Brigade's forces in and around the Grain Elevator, later recorded his impressions of the viciousness:

> Enemy tanks and infantry, approximately ten times our numbers, soon launched an attack from south and west. After the first attack was beaten back, a second began, then a third, while a reconnaissance "pilot" [forward observer] plane circled over us. It corrected the fire and reported our position. In all, ten attacks were beaten off on September 18. . . .
>
> In the elevator, the grain was on fire, the water [coolant] in the machine guns evaporated, the wounded were thirsty, but there was no water nearby. That was how we defended ourselves twenty-four hours a day for three days. Heat, smoke, thirst—all our lips were cracked. During the day many of us climbed up to the highest points in the elevator and from there fired on the Germans; at night we came down and made a defensive ring around the building. . . . At night, during a short lull, we counted our ammunition. There did not seem to be much left. . . . We decided to break out to the south, to the area of Beketovka, as there were many enemy tanks to the north and east of the elevator.
>
> During the night of the 20th . . . we set off. . . . We passed through the gully and crossed the railway line, then stumbled on an enemy mortar

battery which had only just taken up position under cover of darkness. We overturned the three mortars and a truck-load of bombs. The Germans scattered, leaving behind seven dead, abandoning not only their weapons, but their bread and water. And we were fainting with thirst. "Something to drink! Something to drink!" was all we could think about. We drank our fill in the darkness. We then ate the bread we had captured from the Germans and went on.[87]

During this confused, savage fighting, 94th Infantry Division requested support from 24th Panzer Division's attached 88mm antiaircraft guns to pummel Soviet troops defending the irritating Grain Elevator. Although 24th Panzer provided this fire support, its artillery observers noted, "It did not have much of an effect."[88]

In the midst of this struggle, at 1815 hours on 18 September, Sixth Army's chief of staff, General Arthur Schmidt, phoned his counterpart at XXXXVIII Panzer Corps, notifying him that "94th Infantry Division and 24th Panzer Division will be subordinated to LI Army Corps. I will report it to the commanding general. Elements of 24th Panzer Division will soon be pulled out and employed."[89] This order meant that Lenski's panzer division, together with Pfeiffer's infantry division, were destined to be pulled out of line and regrouped northward to reinforce LI Army Corps' faltering assaults against the factory district. A subsequent message sent at 2025 hours confirmed that "24th Panzer Division is subordinated to LI Army Corps from 0800 hours on 19 September." Later in the evening Lenski received instructions to begin moving his division northward promptly after dawn the next day and reassemble it in the Ezovka, Voroponovo, and *Schafzucht* [Sheep Breeding Farm] region by day's end.[90]

This represented a major shift in strategy for General Paulus. By now he believed that XXXXVIII Panzer Corps had already been largely successful in clearing Soviet forces from the southern half of Stalingrad city and would complete the process in a matter of hours. He also appreciated the difficulties LI Corps was likely to encounter during its advance into the northern factory district. Therefore, Sixth Army's commander considered it feasible, if not essential, to reinforce LI Corps with 24th Panzer and 94th Infantry Divisions, not least because the infantry strengths of Seydlitz's three divisions were steadily eroding. However, while reaching these decisions Paulus had not reckoned on two new, and very unpleasant, realities. First, the liquidation of Soviet forces south of the Tsaritsa River was far from complete. In fact, the bulk of 94th Infantry Division had to remain in the south for a week longer before it accomplished its mission. Second, shortly after Paulus reached these decisions, Chuikov threw a wrench into the German commander's plan by ordering Soviet forces in the northern half of the city to launch preemptive counterattacks of their own. In addition to making Seyd-litz's anticipated offensive more difficult, these resulting actions also drew 24th Panzer Division into fresh combat before it could rest and refit for its decisive advance into Stalingrad's factory district.

THE TACTICS OF CITY FIGHTING

During the fight for Stalingrad, units on both sides appeared on operational maps and in written accounts as complete and coherent divisions, brigades, and regiments. Yet with the exception of the set-piece, and essentially linear, fighting along the heights west of Stalingrad's factory district and on the slopes of Mamaev Kurgan, by day's end on 16 September much of the fighting in the city was done by small groups, often no more than 50 men. Particularly for the Soviet defenders, units became hopelessly intermingled in composite combat groups of soldiers pieced together from several formations. When the Germans succeeded in capturing a building, survivors escaped and joined the nearest group of soldiers still capable of fighting. For both sides, the battle began to assume a nightmarish quality. Evening darkness brought a reduction in air and artillery attacks but left German infantrymen and Soviet riflemen marooned within vast expanses of ruins, surrounded on all sides by strange noises and unseen dangers. Snipers and skirmishing became facts of life.

For the Germans, the failure to capture the city in the first daring rush and their subsequent heavy casualties prompted them to adopt a more cautious, methodical approach to the operations. For the Soviets, every day they survived, every day they thwarted the Germans, served to only increase a fatalistic determination. With the Volga River and the ruthless NKVD blocking detachments at his back, the Soviet soldier really had no choice but to fight on. Yet given the heavy attrition to the forces, even blocking detachments sometimes had to fight as ground units on the front lines.

Throughout the chaotic first days of his new command, Chuikov continued to study German tactics with a finely honed analytical mind.[91] He observed, for example, that the usual problems associated with coordinating close air support with the infantry and supporting arms were exacerbated by the terrain of urban warfare. Although Stuka dive-bombers were far more accurate than high-altitude area bombers, their pilots still had only limited control over the exact point of impact of their bombs. Thus, except where a large and visible no-man's-land existed, especially given the previous friendly-fire incident in 24th Panzer's sector, German pilots were understandably reluctant to drop bombs close to their own troops. Moreover, German air operations were confined almost exclusively to daylight attacks in fair weather.

Chuikov quickly reached the obvious conclusions: In order to stay alive, the defenders needed to stay within 100 or even 50 meters of the German infantrymen so that neither Stuka pilots nor artillery observers would dare engage them for fear of causing casualties among their own forces. Moreover, Soviet counterattacks, which were usually conducted during daylight, simply provided more targets for the Germans. Therefore, with the exception of a few nighttime raids, Chuikov ceased launching organized counterattacks unless the threat was so great that he had no choice. Instead, the general encouraged his troops to operate in small combat groups, attacking and defending more like gangs of urban guerrillas than like organized battalions and regiments. These gangs would ambush individual German tanks and small infantry units, then retreat and move through the sewers to take up defensive positions elsewhere. If the Germans captured a fortified house at a corner, they were likely to discover that Soviets were taking up positions *behind* the German spearheads rather than falling back into the confined spaces of the city. Attackers and defenders—often separated only by a single wall within a building—snatched only a few moments of fitful sleep each night.

From these unorthodox beginnings, Chuikov gradually evolved a set of tactics for urban warfare. Although these tactics might not guarantee Soviet success, they would at least make German victory extremely time-consuming and expensive, particularly when combat shifted to the nightmarish fighting in the ruins of Stalingrad's factory district.

STALINGRAD AS A SYMBOL

By mid-September, the *Wehrmacht* and Red Army were locked in a death grip inside the ruins of Stalingrad, a city that had barely figured in the original German plan for Operation Blau. The defenders were only slightly less surprised than the attackers to find their city as the focus of an entire campaign.

Admittedly, Stalingrad had significant military value due to its weapons factories as well as its location astride the remaining river and rail communications that connected Moscow with the Caucasus. Yet the very name: Stalingrad—identifying the city with the Soviet dictator and the beleaguered Communist regime, as well as Stalin's supposed feat in denying Tsaritsyn to the Whites during the Russian Civil War—seemed to the German leadership to give this city a psychological and political importance out of all proportion to its actual military worth. German propaganda reports centered more and more on the titanic struggle for Stalin's namesake city. As the autumn progressed and Army Group A's advance into the Caucasus slowed and then ground to a halt, Stalingrad and the Volga River bend increasingly appeared to be the logical stopping place to conclude Operation Blau. Even before Hitler's speeches made capturing the city a matter of personal prestige, German commanders, soldiers, and citizens began to acquire a kind of tunnel vision about Stalingrad. As one German commander ruefully reflected, "Politics, prestige, propaganda and emotions won the upper hand over sober military judgment."[92]

The defenders fought to the last for many of the same reasons: Stalingrad had become a powerful political and psychological symbol of Soviet resistance. More practically, however, the commanders—from Stalin and Zhukov down to Chuikov—apparently realized that the Red Army, by sucking the German invaders into a prolonged struggle at Stalingrad, could hold the *Wehrmacht* in place, thereby neutralizing its advantages in maneuver warfare and bleeding it white.[93] The daily rate of German advance, once measured in tens of kilometers, was reduced to the city block. Pinning down Sixth Army in this manner also gave the defenders time to launch a series of counteroffensives and counterstrokes on the flanks. Many of these counteractions, as described above, were poorly prepared and generally ineffective, but in the long run such actions contributed to developing the skill of Soviet commanders while further reducing the overstretched Axis forces in southern Russia.

For all these reasons, the struggle for Stalingrad—which the Germans had estimated would take a few weeks to complete— dragged on for month after month after month. As the two sides exhausted themselves, they behaved more and more like a boxer stung hard in the ring: wobbly on their feet, rarely achieving a coordinated series of blows, yet refusing to concede defeat.

THE SECOND KOTLUBAN' OFFENSIVE,
18 SEPTEMBER–2 OCTOBER

Stalingrad Front's third offensive in the region north and northwest of the city was just this sort of counteroffensive. Just as Hitler underestimated the extent of resistance at Stalingrad, so the Soviet leadership believed that its opponents were weakening. It was true that about half of Sixth Army was now decisively engaged in urban warfare, with few reserves available to counter major Soviet actions against its other sectors. However, Sixth Army and its supporting *Luftwaffe* remained immensely strong. Nevertheless, before he departed for Moscow on 12 September, Zhukov directed Eremenko to conduct another major counteroffensive with three armies on Stalingrad Front's left wing, this time beginning on 18 September against a sector of the Germans' defenses considered weaker than the sectors the *front* had assaulted with four armies in late August and early September.

Eremenko was convinced that the previous offensive had failed principally because his *front's* main shock groups had struck German panzer and motorized forces, namely, XIV Panzer Corps' 60th and 3rd Motorized and 16th Panzer Divisions. To avoid doing so again, he decided to shift the axis of his main attack from the Hill 139.7 and Kuz'michi regions north of Orlovka westward to the Samofalovka and 564 km Station regions due south of Kotluban', where infantry, primarily from Sixth Army's VIII Army Corps and XIV Panzer Corps' left flank, defended the main railroad line leading into Stalingrad from the northwest.

There were two reasons why it seemed advantageous to conduct the offensive in this sector. First, the *front's* assaulting shock groups would strike Sixth Army's defenses at the junction between VIII Corps and XIV Panzer Corps, where Eremenko perceived they were weakest. This sector was defended by only one regiment (230th), the reconnaissance battalion of VIII Corps' 76th Infantry Division, the reconnaissance battalion of XIV Corps' 60th Motorized Division, and 9th Machine Gun Battalion, which was attached to XIV Corps. Second, an offensive in this sector would exploit the most trafficable route into Stalingrad: the railroad line leading to its northwestern outskirts. Mitigating against these advantages, as had been the case weeks before, the terrain south of Kotluban' would still require Eremenko's forces to attack across open steppe; only darkness and the numerous *balkas* that crisscrossed the region offered any concealment from enemy fire.

To improve his chances of success at Kotluban', Eremenko directed 62nd and 64th Armies to launch supporting counterattacks, the former from Stalingrad proper and the latter from its bridgehead south of the city. Specifically, Chuikov's army, reinforced by a fresh rifle division, was to strike southwestward from the city to distract Sixth Army's attentions and forces away from the major effort in the north. At the same time, Shumilov's army was to organize a counterattack with the forces on its right wing. This counterattack force was to advance northward from the Gornaia Poliana region, destroy German forces in the Kuporosnoe and El'shanka regions, and link up with 62nd Army's forces defending in the city. To facilitate Shumilov's attack, Eremenko reinforced his army with Colonel I. K. Morozov's 422nd Rifle Division, transferred from Tolbukhin's 57th Army. Eremenko directed all of the artillery groups in his two *fronts*, as well as all of 8th Air Army's aircraft, to support these counterstrokes and counterattacks.[94]

Eremenko chose the 17-kilometer sector from 564 km Station on the main railroad line to Kotluban' *Balka*, 5 kilometers southwest of Samofalovka, as his new offensive target. Because this sector encompassed only Kozlov's 24th Army, which was far too weak to spearhead the effort by itself, Eremenko had no choice but to shuffle his *front's* armies in order to concentrate the necessary forces in the new attack sector. He did this simply by ordering

24th Army and Moskalenko's 1st Guards Army to exchange sectors and then narrowed their combined sectors by turning territory on their left and right wings over to Malinovsky's 66th Army and Kriuchenkin's 4th Tank Army. To avoid a major shift of forces, which the Germans would certainly have identified as preparations for a new Soviet offensive, Eremenko directed Kozlov and Moskalenko to exchange divisions and their sectors rather than move their forces laterally across the front. However, since Moskalenko's guards would make the *front*'s main effort, they did require significant reinforcement, which in and of itself involved extensive troop movements.

Moskalenko's task was challenging because he not only had to move his headquarters and part of his forces westward; he also had to take control of roughly half of 24th Army's divisions and their tactical sectors and, simultaneously, make all necessary preparations for the offensive by nightfall on 17 September. Thus, in the exceedingly brief period of three days, Moskalenko turned his army's former sector and all of its divisions over to 66th and 24th Armies, displaced his command post to the Kotluban' Station region, took control of the 12-kilometer sector from north of 564 km Station westward to south of Samofalovka, and integrated 24th Army's rifle divisions into his army's combat formation. Once he completed this regrouping, with the exception of the attached 4th, 7th, and 16th Tank Corps, 1st Guards Army was an entirely new formation—for the third time in less than 30 days![95]

Although it was new, Moskalenko's army was far from full-strength and anything but fresh (see Table 18). Of its eight newly assigned rifle divisions, four (258th, 260th, 273rd, and 316th) were full-strength or nearly full-strength divisions from the *Stavka*'s reserve, but even they lacked their full complement of mortars, machine guns, and wheeled transports. The remaining five rifle divisions (173rd, 207th, 221st, 292nd, and 308th Rifle) had suffered heavy casualties during 24th and 66th Armies' offensives in early September, and none had received significant replacements.[96]

As for Moskalenko's supporting tank corps, all three had also suffered heavy losses during the previous offensive and were now severely understrength; many of their heavy and medium tanks were under repair, leaving them with many light models. For example, Rotmistrov's 7th Tank Corps fielded 93 tanks, 45 of them light T-60 models. Likewise, 4th and 16th Tank Corps had received only a portion of the 94 T-34 tanks that the *Stavka* had promised on 11 September, and their commanders, Colonel Kravchenko and General Maslov, and most of their new tank crews had reached the corps only days prior to the attack.[97] Ultimately, the three corps fielded 243 tanks, bringing 1st Guards Army's tank strength to 340 armored vehicles (see Table 19).

The mission of Moskalenko's army was to attack southward in the sector from north of 564 km Station westward to the Kotluban' *Balka*, rupture the

Table 18. The Personnel Strengths of 1st Guards Army's Rifle Divisions on 15 September 1942

- 173rd Rifle Division – 7,149 men
- 207th Rifle Division – 4,789 men
- 221st Rifle Division – 5,724 men
- 258th Rifle Division – 13,429 men
- 260th Rifle Division – 13,303 men
- 273rd Rifle Division – 12,770 men
- 308th Rifle Division – 8,671 men
- 316th Rifle Division – 10,495 men
- 292nd Rifle Division – 9,970 men
- **Total – 86,300 men**
- Total army strength – 123,882 men, 611 guns, and 1,956 mortars

Source: Isaev, *Stalingrad*, 184, 192-193, citing *TsAMO RF*, f. 220, op. 220, d. 72, l. 36.

German defenses at the junction of VIII and XIV Corps, and exploit southward along the Borodkin-Nadezhda axis to link up with 62nd Army's forces in the Gumrak region west of Stalingrad (see Map 29). On Moskalenko's left, conducting its main attack on its right wing, Kozlov's 24th Army was to attack and penetrate 60th Motorized Division's defenses east of 564 km Station and exploit southward along the railroad line toward Gorodishche. On Kozlov's left, Malinovsky's 66th Army was to conduct a supporting attack against the German defenses at the boundary between 16th Panzer and 3rd Motorized Divisions north of Hill 139.7, then exploit southward to capture the hill and link up with 62nd Army's forces, defending Orlovka.

Moskalenko formed his army for the offensive into two echelons, with its main shock group on the left wing. Here, 316th, 308th, and 292nd Rifle Divisions, cooperating with 7th Tank Corps' 87th, 67th, and 12th Tank Brigades, were to penetrate the defenses on 60th Motorized Division's left wing in the 3-kilometer sector west of the railroad at 564 km Station and advance southward through the villages of Borodkin and Nadezhda toward the army's final objectives in the Gumrak region. On the shock group's right, 258th and 173rd Rifle Divisions were to advance southward in the sector east of the Kotluban' *Balka*, defeat the forces on 76th Infantry Division's right wing, and exploit southward west of Borodkin to protect the main shock group's right flank. Moskalenko retained Kravchenko's 4th Tank Corps and 221st and 207th Rifle Divisions in his second echelon with orders to reinforce the shock group when appropriate to strengthen its advance toward Gumrak and fend off German counterattacks. His reserve—Maslov's 16th Tank Corps and 260th Rifle Division—was to join the army's offensive whenever required.

Thus, as initially configured, Moskalenko's main attack force included roughly 34,000 men supported by about 90 tanks backed up by another 10,000 men and 80 tanks, from his army's total infantry strength of about

Table 19. The Tank Strength of 1st Guards Army's Tank Corps and Brigades on 18 September 1942

	Tanks				
Force	KV heavy	T-34 medium	T-70 light	T-60 light	Total
4th TC	11	38	—	31	80
7th TC	12	36	—	45	93
16th TC	11	22	—	37	70
148th TB	8	2	—	14	24
12th TB	—	22	13	—	35
3rd TB	—	23	15	—	38
Total	42	143	28	127	340

Source: Isaev, *Stalingrad*, 185, citing *TsAMO RF*, f. 38, op. 11360, d. 120, l. 13.

86,000 men and 340 tanks. These forces faced 76th Infantry Division's 230th Regiment and reconnaissance battalion and 60th Motorized Division's 60th Engineer and 9th Machine Gun Battalions, a force numbering about 6,000 men and few, if any, armored vehicles.[98] However, the defenders were lodged firmly in a dense network of well-prepared defenses.

On 1st Guards Army's left, Kozlov's 24th Army was to attack southward with its 49th, 24th, and 233rd Rifle Divisions deployed abreast in the roughly 10-kilometer sector from north of Kuz'michi westward to 564 km Station. Kozlov's infantry were to be supported by 246th and 69th Tank Brigades, with a total of only 18 tanks.[99] However, it weighted its force more heavily in the 3-kilometer sector on its right wing, where its second-echelon 39th Guards Rifle Division was to reinforce 233rd Rifle Division's assault east of 564 km Station. Thus, Kozlov pitted a force of roughly 18,000 men and a handful of infantry support tanks against the 2nd and 3rd Battalions of 60th Motorized Division's 120th Grenadier Regiment and the right wing of 9th Machine Gun Battalion, a force totaling no more than about 2,500 defending infantry.[100]

On Kozlov's left, Malinovsky planned to conduct the supporting attack by his 66th Army with a shock group consisting of 41st and 38th Guards and 116th Rifle Divisions in a roughly 8-kilometer sector on his army's right wing west of the Sukhaia Mechetka River and north of Hill 139.7. This force of about 18,000 men and a few infantry support tanks faced 60th Motorized Division's 92nd Panzer Grenadier Regiment and 3rd Motorized Division's 8th Panzer Grenadier Regiment—roughly 5,000 men backed up by 30–40 tanks from the two motorized divisions.[101]

Although the three shock groups of Eremenko's three attacking armies, which were assaulting along a front totaling about 14 kilometers, outnumbered the defenders by a factor of more than 6:1 in manpower and 5:1 in tanks, by this time the defenders manned an extensive strongpoint defense

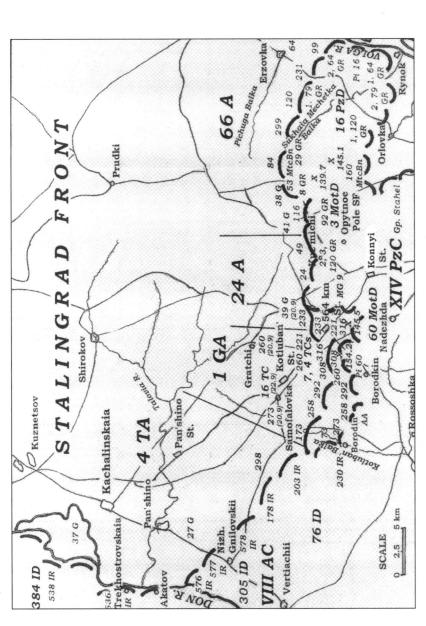

Map 29. Stalingrad Front's Kotluban' offensive, 18–22 September 1942

outfitted with numerous bunkers, dugouts, and firing points protected by elaborate obstacles.[102] In addition, Stalingrad Front's assault was to be supported by 123 aircraft from 16th Air Army (118 fighters, 84 assault planes, and 21 bombers), a force that was far outnumbered by supporting German aircraft.[103] The results were predictable.

In addition to Eremenko's incredibly mistaken optimism concerning the weakness of the German defenses, there were several other problems with his proposed offensive. First, as so often before, Eremenko felt forced by events to rush into an operation using understrength formations manned by either exhausted or inexperienced troops (especially those in 1st Guards Army) and with insufficient time to prepare. The result was predictable: a poorly coordinated operation that wasted the bravery of the soldiers and the production of the armaments factories. Second, the attack frontage of 1st Guards Army was so narrow that the inexperienced units could not maneuver. Third, Eremenko launched the offensive in broad daylight. Although daylight simplified some coordination problems, it also exposed the attackers to air attack at a time when the *Luftwaffe* still outnumbered the Red Army Air Force. And finally, as will be discussed below, 62nd and 64th Armies were in no condition to launch a multidivision offensive to encircle Sixth Army. Their divisions and brigades were in tatters, and by Chuikov's own count his army had only 35 tanks, many of which were fighting as pillboxes because they had been immobilized.[104]

Nonetheless, Eremenko unleashed his third offensive in the Kotluban' region on schedule at 0700 hours on 18 September after firing a 90-minute, but largely ineffective, artillery preparation. The 1st Guards and 24th Armies' shock groups once again attempted to seize the high ground south of Kotluban'. Unfortunately for the attackers, VIII Army and XIV Panzer Corps had established the type of defense-in-depth that had been standard in the German Army since World War I.[105] In defense-in-depth, only a few troops occupied the forward positions to avoid suffering casualties in the event of an enemy assault. Thus, most of the Soviet artillery preparation and initial ground attack fell on thin air; from the rear, the main German positions, situated on higher ground, poured machine-gun, mortar, and artillery fire into the attackers. Soviet infantry, artillery, tanks, and aircraft operated independently, and leaders found it difficult to navigate on the featureless open steppe. By sheer determination, the troops of 1st Guards Army achieved penetrations of up to 3 kilometers in some places but then ground to a halt, leaving the Germans' main defense lines still intact.

Late on 18 September, the Red Army General Staff reported, "The Stalingrad Front went over to the offensive with part of its forces in the general direction of Stalingrad on the morning of 18 September and, after penetrating the forward edge of the enemy's defense, advanced to depths of up to 3 kilometers in a number of points by day's end."[106] The participating armies reported in greater detail:

1st Guards Army went over to the offensive in the general direction of Stalingrad at 0700 hours on 18 September, and, after penetrating the forward area of the enemy's defense with its left wing units, advanced 3 kilometers by 1600 hours.

173rd RD reached the southern slope of Hill 108.4 and the southwestern slope of Hill 107.2 (7–8 kilometers north of Bol'shaia Rossoshka) line by 1600 hours on 18 September. The units of the division captured 25 Germans.

258th RD was fighting along the northern slope of Hill 107.2 and the northwestern slope of Hill 123.6 (7 kilometers northeast of Bol'shaia Rossoshka) line.

292nd RD captured the northern slope of Hill 123.6 and the northern slope of Hill 143.8 (4 kilometers southwest of 564 km Station) line.

308th RD captured the Borodkin region and was fighting along the northern slope of Hill 143.8 and Borodkin State Farm (3 kilometers southwest of 564 km Station) line. The enemy counterattacked against the units of the division from the Podsobnoe Farm axis with a force of 50 tanks. Fighting was going on for Hill 154.2, 2 kilometers southwest of 564 km Station.

316th RD captured the region of Hill 45.5 (3 kilometers southeast of 564 km Station) and was approaching Konnaia Station (5 kilometers southwest of Kuz'michi).

7th TC was fighting jointly alongside the forces of 308th and 316th RDs.

4th TC is being committed into the penetration and was approaching the 564 km Station line at 1530 hours on 18 September.

24th Army went over to the offensive in the general direction of Stalingrad at 0700 hours on 18 September but advanced insignificantly during the day in heavy fighting.

233rd RD captured 564 km Station and the region of the unnumbered height 1 kilometers east of the station by 1030 hours of 18 September. 24th and 49th RDs were fighting for Kuz'michi.

66th Army went over to the offensive at 0800 hours on 18 September with the units on its right wing but, after encountering strong enemy resistance, was unable to advance.[107]

During the day, 1st Guards Army's 316th Rifle Division, commanded by Colonel I. E. Zubarev, and supporting tanks from Colonel I. V. Shabarov's 87th Tank Brigade succeeded in capturing 564 km Station from 60th Motorized Division's 9th Machine Gun Battalion. After clearing German forces from the vicinity of the station while one of Zubarev's regiments pushed southward to attack the defenses of 60th Motorized Division's pioneer battalion on Hill 145.5, the other two regiments wheeled southwest and assaulted the defenses of the 60th's Pioneer Battalion on Hill 152.4, dominating terrain 5 kilometers west of 654 km Station, which the Germans had nicknamed the "*Bol'shoi Greben*" [large crest]. On Zubarev's right, Colonel L. N. Gurt'ev's 308th Rifle Division, supported by tanks from Lieutenant Colonel D. K. Gumeniuk's 62nd Tank Brigade, joined 316th Rifle Division's assault on Hill 154.2 at 1100 hours. Soon after, Shabarov's 87th Tank Brigade caught up with Zubarev's left wing regiment and helped it capture Hill 145.5.

Conducting Moskalenko's secondary attack farther west, Major General S. V. Lishenkov's 292nd Rifle Division, supported by six tanks from Colonel V. M. Badanov's 12th Tank Brigade, succeeded in penetrating the defenses of 76th Infantry Division's 230th Regiment and reconnaissance battalion and advanced southward almost 3 kilometers, reaching the northern part of the Borodkin Farm. The OKW duly reported, "A large enemy tank force (up to three regiments) destroyed the bridge on the road south of Kotluban' and penetrated to Borodkin. The enemy is bringing up fresh forces from the northeast."[108]

However, Moskalenko's assault began to falter during the second half of the day when hastily assembled armored *kampfgruppen* from 60th and 3rd Motorized Divisions, supported by multiple waves of Stuka aircraft flying in groups of 15–20 planes, counterattacked with tanks and motorized infantry from the Bol'shaia Rossoshka region northward toward Hills 154.2 and 145.5 and the Borodkin Farm.[109] This prompted the OKW to add: "Thanks to the brave and decisive actions on the flanks of both divisions [76th Infantry and 60th Motorized] and, as a result of our counterattacks, supported by tanks, assault guns, and antiaircraft artillery [88mm guns], which were brought up to the place of the penetration, the enemy tanks were destroyed, and the former forward edge was restored. The attacks south of Kotluban' are disrupted. A total of 106 enemy tanks have been destroyed, and many prisoners have been captured."[110]

After these German counterattacks brought 1st Guards Army's shock groups to an abrupt halt, at 1400 hours Moskalenko ordered Kravchenko's 4th Tank Corps and his second-echelon 221st and 207th Rifle Divisions, commanded by Colonels P. I. Buniashin and S. S. Guzenko, respectively, to commit their forces to restore momentum to the assault. However, by the time these forces reached the *Bol'shoi Greben* region, it was too late to halt the German counterattacks; a reported force of 50 tanks had swept 308th and 316th Rifle Divisions' infantry from the slopes and crest of Hill 154.2 by 1800 hours. Deprived of tank support by intense *Luftwaffe* air strikes and devastatingly accurate German artillery fire, the soldiers of 308th and 316th Rifle Divisions, which had also failed to dig in along their new positions, "could not resist the enemy's onslaught."[111] Thereafter, the headquarters of the two rifle divisions, as well as the divisions on the army's right wing, lost control of their units. This left the surviving forces no choice but to abandon Borodkin State Farm, Hill 154.2, and 564 km Station and flee northward, in small groups and individually, to new defenses near the original jumping-off positions. Moskalenko later blamed this ignominious defeat on the weakness and exhaustion of his troops and the rank inexperience of their commanders. Whatever the cause, the fact was that the Germans caused his forces to fall back by day's end. Moskalenko later claimed that his forces "assaulted the dominating heights for the following four days almost without interruption," but "the enemy moved forward enough weapons and personnel that it was impossible to capture the 'greben.'"[112]

The intense fighting on 18 and 19 September exacted a terrible toll on Moskalenko's army, including about 36,000 of its original 123,000 troops who were killed, wounded, or missing in action, and, counting replacement tanks received during this period, more than half of its initial 340 tanks. Nor did 24th and 66th Armies escape the bloodletting; the former suffered more than 32,000 casualties, the latter about 20,000 (see Tables 20 and 21).

In its operational summary late on 19 September, the Red Army General Staff admitted that 24th Army had also achieved only meager successes and that 66th Army had no success whatsoever during the previous two days of fighting.[113] Pleased by the results of the two-day fight, the OKW recorded that "the enemy's penetrations on the northwestern flank southeast of Kotluban' have been liquidated. After completing their penetration northeast of Borodkin, the enemy attacked with large forces of infantry and tanks. The tank battle for Height Marker 154.2 is continuing."[114]

With Moskalenko's persistent assault faltering, Stalin intervened once again, instructing Zhukov, who was still in Moscow, to alter the form and direction of Eremenko's offensive:

It seems to me that you ought to shift the main attack from the Kuz'michi axis to the region between Hills 130.7–128.9, six–eight kilometers northeast of Kuz'michi. This would give you the opportunity to link up with the Stalingraders, encircle the enemy group on the western bank of the Volga, and free up 66th Army for active operations toward Stalingrad. To do this, you can reinforce Malinovsky's right wing with three divisions and three tank brigades at the expense of 1st Guards and 24th Armies and go over to an active defense in 24th and 1st Guards Armies' areas of operations. So that the defense along the front of these armies will be firm, you should move two to three divisions here from 63rd and 21st Armies. This is especially possible because the enemy has already taken forces from 63rd and 21st Armies' sector and thrown them into Stalingrad, leaving their weaker Romanian and Italian units which are not capable of active

Table 20. The Condition of 1st Guards Army's Tank Park at 1800 hours on 20 September 1942

Force	KV	T-34	T-70	T-60	Others	Total
			Type of Tanks			
16th TC	13	37	—	36	—	86
7th TC	3/3°	32°°/10	0/2	8/28	—	43/40
4th TC	6/17	14/47	11/1	10/11	0/2+1°°°	41/79
148th TB	1/7	0/2	—	4/13	—	5/22
3rd TB	—	2/4	2/2	—	—	4/6
12th TB	—	2	2	—	—	4
Total	23/27	87/63	15/5	58/52	0/3	183/150

Source: Isaev, *Stalingrad*, 205, citing *TsAMO RF*, f. 38, op. 11360, d. 120, ll. 14, 16, 16. ob.
Notes: Numerator = operational tanks and denominator = tanks needing repair.
° – 7th Tank Corps received 21 T-34 replacement tanks
°° – 4th Tank Corps included 2 BT-5 tanks and 1 Mk III British tank.
°°° – 12th Tank Brigade's strength is as of 21 September.

Table 21. The Personnel Losses of Stalingrad Front's 1st Guards, 24th, and 66th Armies, 1–20 September 1942

Army	Killed	Wounded	Missing in action	Other causes	Total
1st Gds. Army	7,726	26,627	1,267	196	35,806
24th Army	5,747	20,061	6,629	67	32,504
66th Army	3,237	13,125	3,798	245	20,405
Total	16,710	59,803	11,694	508	88,715

Source: Isaev, *Stalingrad*, 206, citing *TsAMO RF*, f. 220, op. 220, d. 72, l. 85.

operations. The rapid link up of the Northern Group with the Stalingrad forces is a condition without which all of your operations will become unsuccessful.[115]

As a result, Zhukov and Eremenko developed a new plan that shifted 1st Guards Army's axis of attack farther west, this time in the sector along both banks of the Kotluban' *Balka*, which was situated on the army's right wing 5 kilometers southwest of Kotluban' Station. Eremenko also insisted Moskalenko maintain unrelenting pressure against the German defenses west of 564 km Station. To improve 1st Guards Army's chances for success, Eremenko reinforced it with several divisions from 4th Tank and 21st Armies. After integrating these fresh forces into his army's ranks, he was to resume his assaults at dawn on 23 September.

In response to Eremenko's directive, Moskalenko formed two shock groups to conduct his attack. The first and stronger group, deployed on the army's right wing, consisted of 258th, 173rd, and 273rd Rifle Divisions, supported on the left by 260th Rifle Division and on the right by 298th Rifle Division, which was transferred from 4th Tank Army. Armor support included about 50 tanks from 148th, 3rd, and 12th Tank Brigades and about 45 tanks from Maslov's 16th Tank Corps.[116] This group was to attack southward east of Kotluban' *Balka* to strike the German defenses at the boundary between 76th Infantry Division's 203rd and 230th Regiments. The 298th Division was to anchor this shock group's right flank by attacking southward west of the *balka*. The second shock group, deployed on the army's left wing, was made up of four rifle divisions, supported by about 30 tanks from Maslov's tank corps. This group, with 207th and 221st Rifle Divisions in first echelon and 316th and 24th Rifle Divisions (transferred from 24th Army) in second echelon, was to assault the defenses of 60th Motorized Division's 9th Machine Gun Battalion at 564 km Station. The following day, after being reinforced by Rotmistrov's 7th Tank Corps and three more rifle divisions from 24th Army, Malinovsky's 66th Army was to join the offensive by attacking 16th Panzer Division's defenses at and west of Erzovka.

Moskalenko completed concentrating his new shock group in the vicinity of Kotluban' *Balka* late on 22 September. His shock groups attacked southward once again the next morning without achieving any more success than they had over the previous six days (see Map 30).[117]

The Red Army General Staff acknowledged this fact in its operational summary late on 23 September:

1st Guards Army resumed its offensive southward with part of its forces at 0630 hours on 23 September and, overcoming strong fire resistance and enemy counterattacks, advanced 2–2.5 kilometers.

173rd RD, with 148th TB, reached the southeastern slope of Hill 108.4.

273rd RD, after repelling counterattacks by up to a company of enemy infantry and tanks, reached the region 1.5 kilometers west of Hill 130.4 at 1300 hours.

258th RD repelled seven counterattacks by the enemy and was fighting along a line from the northeastern slope of Hill 107.2 to a point 2 kilometers northeast of that hill. Up to a battalion of enemy infantry and 35 tanks were destroyed.

207th RD was approaching Hill 145.5 by 1400 hours.

16th TC, which was committed into combat in 273rd RD's offensive sector, was fighting to capture Hill 130.4 (7 kilometers south of Kotluban') at day's end.

24th Army tried to go over to the offensive from its previous positions beginning on the morning of 23 September but had no success after encountering strong enemy fire resistance and constant enemy air strikes.[118]

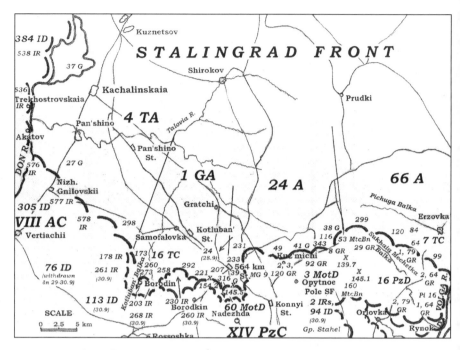

Map 30. Stalingrad Front's Kotluban' offensive, 23 September–2 October 1942

After their failures on 23 September, however, Moskalenko's two shock groups made significantly better progress the next day. Although 24th Army's attacks in the Kuz'michi sector failed dismally, 1st Guards' two shock groups finally succeeded in breaking through the Germans' forward defenses by day's end on 24 September. On the army's right wing, 273rd Rifle Division and 16th Tank Corps' tanks captured Hill 130.4, 2.5 kilometers deep into 76th Infantry Division's defenses, and, on the army's left, 221st Rifle Division captured 564 km Station from 9th Machine Gun Battalion for the second time.[119]

Still farther to the east, Malinovsky's 66th Army joined the fray early on 24 September. The army's shock group, which consisted of 64th and 99th Rifle Divisions (with 7,148 and 8,531 men, respectively), supported by 82 tanks from Rotmistrov's 7th Tank Corps, struck the defenses of 16th Panzer Division's 1st Battalion, 79th Grenadier Regiment, and 2nd Battalion, 64th Grenadier Regiment, west of Erzovka.[120] Although this assault drove roughly a kilometer deep through the panzer division's defenses, as the OKW noted later in the evening, "An answering blow by the enemy against the northern cut-off position was repelled by our forces in fierce fighting during which the enemy lost 36 tanks."[121]

Trying to exploit its previous day's success, 66th Army reported on 25 September that its "left wing units resumed their attacks southward at 0530 hours and, after overcoming stubborn enemy resistance, reached the line extending from the crest of Hill 129.6 through the southern slopes of burial mounds +1.6 and +1.4 to the northern outskirts of Tomilin (3.5–4 kilometers southwest and south of Erzovka)."[122] Contradicting this Soviet report, 16th Panzer Division asserted late the same day that it had destroyed 31 more of Rotmistrov's tanks while "driving off strong enemy attacks in the Erzovka region."[123] Actually, Rotmistrov's two tank brigades lost 75 tanks during the two days of fighting, including 29 totally destroyed.[124] The next day 66th Army reported it fended off eight German counterattacks by infantry supported by up to 40 tanks. Based on subsequent reports by the army, Malinovsky's assaults sputtered to a halt by early October.

Meanwhile, to the west, the attacks by Moskalenko's army also faltered and ground to a halt by late on 26 September, primarily because of the intense German air strikes and strong local counterattacks. Accordingly, the OKW noted 1st Guards Army's local successes but also described the terrible attrition these fights were causing in Maslov's supporting 16th Tank Corps as it reported that "South of Kotluban' the enemy committed a large number of tanks, which overcame our defensive lines in several places. Along the entire northern sector of the front, 35 enemy tanks were destroyed or damaged."[125] Actually, Maslov's tank corps lost 11 KV and 28 T-34 tanks on 24 September and, by day's end on 25 September, reported that it had only 14 operational tanks (3 T34s and 11 T-60s).[126]

Thereafter, Moskalenko's army repeatedly assaulted 76th Division's defenses through 4 October, but with ever weaker forces and sharply diminishing success. By this time, each day's advance was measured in mere hundreds of meters. Despite this continued bloodletting, the personnel losses, though still high, suffered by 1st Guards, 24th, and 66th Armies during the final week of September were significantly lower than they had experienced during the first 20 days of the month (see Table 22).

The attrition in Moskalenko's supporting armor was also appalling. By day's end on 27 September, for example, the army's tank force had dwindled from 340 tanks on 18 September to much less than 100 tanks. Officially, 16th Tank Corps fielded only 6 T-60 light tanks, 4th Tank Corps had only 19 tanks (4 KVs, 8 T-34s, and 7 T-70s), and 7th Tank Corps could muster only 18 tanks (3 KVs, 2 T-34s, and 13 T-70s).[127] Despite these horrendous losses, Eremenko insisted that Moskalenko continue his fruitless assaults, if only to take the slightest pressure off Chuikov's forces struggling in Stalingrad.

Although lost against the backdrop of the cacophonous din of the ongoing struggle in the city, Stalingrad Front's fierce and prolonged assaults in the region south of Kotluban' did have a positive effect on the Soviets' defense

Table 22. The Personnel Losses of Stalingrad Front's 1st Guards, 24th, and 66th Armies, 20–26 September 1942

Army	Killed	Wounded	Missing in action	Other causes	Total
1st Gds. Army	2,009	7,097	1,320	186	10,612
24th Army	1,181	4,700	405	19	6,305
66th Army	432	1,273	99	17	1,821
Total	3,622	13,070	1,824	222	18,738

Source: Isaev, *Stalingrad*, 213, citing *TsAMO RF*, f. 220, op. 220, d. 72, l. 86.

of the city. For example, 3rd Motorized Division's history took note of the heavy fighting south of Kotluban', pointing out that its *kampfgruppen* destroyed 37 of the more than 120 Soviet tanks participating in the action on 30 September and many more in subsequent fighting. Tangentially, it also noted that these destroyed tanks included many American and British Lend-Lease models.[128] This report, as well as others from 16th Panzer Division, underscores the reality that 60th and 3rd Motorized and 16th Panzer Divisions, during this weeklong battle, prevailed only because they dispatched precious tanks and panzer-grenadiers from their southern front north of Orlovka to help bolster their defenses and conduct counterattacks in the region south of Kotluban' and Ezhovka. This, in turn, prevented all three of XIV Panzer Corps' divisions from participating in the fight for Orlovka and Stalingrad proper, at least until the Kotluban' and Ezhovka sectors quieted down after 2 October.

Even more tellingly than its adverse impact on XIV Panzer Corps, Moskalenko's 1st Guards Army captured roughly 20 square kilometers of ground south of Kotluban' Station and the vital 564 km Station itself in the heavy fighting. While doing so, his guards army also inflicted heavy casualties on VIII Army Corps' 76th Infantry Division. This damage was so severe that Paulus, on 29 and 30 September, relieved 76th Division with the stronger 113th Infantry Division, one of the divisions previously earmarked to take part in the assault on Stalingrad city. Thereafter, 76th Infantry Division withdrew to assembly areas well to the rear to rest and refit.[129] The combat ratings shown by Table 23 bear mute testimony to the deleterious effects Zhukov's and, later, Eremenko's offensives in the Kotluban' region had on Sixth Army's divisions defending in the region (see Table 23).

Table 23.   The Combat Rating of Infantry and Pioneer Battalions Subordinate to Sixth Army's Divisions Defending in the Kotluban' Region, 14 September–5 October 1942

	14 September	26 September	5 October
76th Infantry Division			
(9 infantry battalions)	5 medium strong and 4 average	4 medium strong, 3 average, and 2 weak	3 weak and 6 exhausted
(1 pioneer battalion)	average	medium strong	weak
3rd Motorized Division			
(5 infantry battalions)	2 medium strong 2 average, and 1 weak	1 medium strong, 3 average, and 1 weak	3 average and 2 weak
(1 pioneer battalion)	weak	strong	exhausted
60th Motorized Division			
(7 infantry battalions)	1 medium strong and 6 average	6 average and 1 weak	4 average, 2 weak, and 1 exhausted
(1 pioneer battalion)	average	weak	exhausted
16th Panzer Division			
(5 infantry battalions)	3 medium strong and 2 average	3 medium strong and 2 average	3 medium strong 1 average, and 1 weak
(1 pioneer battalion)	average	average	average

Source: Florian *Freiherr* von und zu Aufsess, "Betr.: Zustand der Divisionen, Armee – Oberkommando 6, Abt. Ia, A. H. Qu., den 14 September 42, 12.35 Uhr," "Betr.: Zustand der Divisionen, Armee – Oberkommando 6, Abt. Ia, A. H. Qu., den 26 September 42," and "Betr.: Zustand der Divisionen, erstmalig nach neu festlegter Bestimmung des Begriffes "Gefechsstärke," Armee – Oberkommando 6, Abt. Ia, A. H. Qu., den 5 Oktober 1942," in *Die Anlagenbander zu den Kriegstagebuchern der 6. Armee vom 14.09.1942 bis 24.11.1942, Band I* (Schwabach: January 2006), 12–13, 59–62, and 128–130.

THE STRUGGLE FOR MAMAEV KURGAN AND CENTER CITY, 19-26 SEPTEMBER

All of this was invisible to the defenders of Stalingrad, who had hoped for a major victory to relieve their agony. However, Moskalenko's 18 September attack did divert XIV Panzer Corps and a large portion of German air and artillery support from the city battle, giving 62nd Army a breathing spell to assist its own attack on 19 September. For a day and a half, the *Luftwaffe's* air attacks on the city ceased. Moreover, the heavy fighting in the Kotluban' region made Paulus even more cautious—he slowed the rate of advance of Seydlitz's LI Corps and delayed a planned diversion of additional troops from his northern flank to the city proper.[130]

Pressured by the *Stavka*, Southeastern Front dispatched new orders to Chuikov at 1800 hours on 18 September:

> Under attack by the formations of the Stalingrad Front, which has gone over to a general offensive toward the south, the enemy is suffering heavy losses along the Kuz'michi-Sukhaia Mechetka *Balka*-Akatovka line. With the aim of resisting the offensive of our Northern grouping, the enemy is withdrawing a number of units and formations from the area of Stalingrad and Voroponovo and is transferring them to the north through Gumrak.
>
> With the aim of wiping out the enemy's Stalingrad grouping, by combined operations with the Stalingrad Front, I order:
>
> 1. **62nd Army**, having created a shock group of no fewer than three RDs and one TB in the vicinity of Mamaev Kurgan, will conduct an attack toward the northwestern outskirts of Stalingrad with the mission to destroy the enemy in this region. The mission of the day [immediate mission] is to destroy the enemy in the city of Stalingrad, firmly securing the line— Rynok, Orlovka, Hills 128.0 and 98.9, and the northwestern and western outskirts of Stalingrad.
>
> The chief of the *front*'s artillery will support 62nd Army's attack with a powerful artillery offensive [preparation] in the sector from Gorodishche and Gumrak on the right to the Tsaritsa River on the left.
>
> Include 95th RD [Gorishnyi] in 62nd Army at 1900 hours on 18 September 1942 and ferry the majority of the division's units [regiments] across to Stalingrad via the northern crossings in the Krasnyi Oktiabr' region by 0500 hours on 19 September 1942 and employ it for an attack from the vicinity of Hill 102.0 [Mamaev Kurgan] through the northwestern outskirts of the city.
>
> The 112th RD is ordered to restore its positions during the night and be prepared for the counterattack by the morning of 18 September.
>
> Begin the infantry offensive at 1200 hours on 19 September.[131]

62nd Army then issued its own attack order at 2350 hours. After describing the situation and missions assigned to 62nd Army and adjacent forces, Chuikov assigned missions to his army's subordinate forces:

> 1. The enemy, having committed reserves into the battle and captured the central part of the city of Stalingrad, is attempting to split the army by reaching the Volga River.
>
> 2. The army, while fulfilling the main mission—to defend the city of Stalingrad—is to go over to a counteroffensive with part of its forces on 19 September 1942 with the aim of destroying the enemy penetrating into the city.

3. On the right, the left wing of the Stalingrad Front will conduct an offensive with the mission of destroying the enemy grouping in the region northwest of Rynok and linking up with the units of 62nd Army.

On the left, the units of 64th Army will conduct offensive combat in the Kuporosnoe region.

The boundaries with them are as before.

4. I have decided to cut off and destroy the enemy [forces] which have penetrated into the center of the city by an attack from the vicinity of Hill 102.0 [Mamaev Kurgan] in the general direction of the station [Railroad Station No. 1].

I order:

1. **23rd TC**—attack toward Hill 126.6 and the Hospital with the forces of 9th MRB [three tanks] with the mission to destroy the enemy [389th Infantry Division's 544th Regiment] and capture the line of [Hill] +0.8, while protecting the attacking grouping from the northwest. [269th NKVD RR was in reserve].

The boundary on the left—Hill 107.5, (inclusive) the wagon sheds, and Lesoposadochnaia [forestry station].

2. **137th TB**—attack from the vicinity of the southwestern outskirts of Krasnyi Oktiabr' village toward the wagon sheds, with the mission to destroy the enemy [295th Infantry Division's 517th Regiment] on the western slopes of Hill 102.0 and capture the wagon sheds and Hill 112.5 by nightfall.

The boundary on the left—(incl.) Hill 102.0, (incl.) and the Motor Tractor Station [0.5 kilometers southwest of Hill 112.5].

3. **95th RD**—attack from Hill 102.0 toward the Motor Tractor Station, with the mission to destroy the enemy [295th Infantry Division's 516th Regiment] in the attack sector and capture the northwestern part of the city of Stalingrad by nightfall.

The boundary on the left—(incl.) the Krasnyi Oktiabr' landing site, (incl.) and the railroad station (3 kilometers west of the pump house on the Volga River).

4. **39th Gds. RR (13th Gds. RD)**—attack from the region southeast of Hill 102.0 [southward] along the railroad to the railroad station (Stalingrad No. 1), with the mission to destroy the enemy [295th Infantry Division's 518th Regiment] and link up with the units of 13th Gds. RD, cutting off the enemy's routes of withdrawal to the west.

5. **13th Gds. RD [34th and 42nd Gds. RRs] (less 39th Gds. RR)**—continue to fulfill your previous mission to clear enemy forces [71st Infantry Division's 194th and 191st Regiments] from the center of the city by nightfall.

The boundary on the left—the Tsaritsa River.

6. **112th RD [385th and 524th RRs]**—reach the railroad line in the sector of the bridges across Dolgii and Krutoi Ravines by 1100 hours on 19 September. After the advance of 39th Gds. RR beyond the line of the ravines (south of Hill 102.0)—occupy and defend the western and southern slopes of Hill 102.0.

7. **Group Comrade Gorokhov**—(124th and 149th RBs and 282nd RR NKVD)—continue to attack, cooperating with the left wing of the Stalingrad Front in the destruction of the enemy [16th Panzer Division] in the region northwest of Rynok.

8. **42nd RB, with the attached remnants of 244th RD**—attack from the south along the railroad to the railroad station, in close cooperation with the left wing units of 13th Gds. RD.

The boundary to the left—as before.

9. **92nd RB**—continue fulfilling previously assigned missions [defend the railroad from Akhtiubinskaia Street to the Grain Elevator (against 94th Infantry Division's 267th and 274th Regiments)].

10. The commanders of all remaining units and formations of the army will hold on to the positions they occupy and prevent an enemy penetration into Stalingrad.

11. The chief of army artillery will form an infantry support group from 137th TB and 95th RD. Organize the planned destruction of the enemy by a group of multiple rocket launcher regiments in the region: from the north—the ravine south of Hill 102.2, from the east—the railroad line, and from the south—the Tsaritsa River. Pay special attention to the region of the wagon sheds.

Chuikov, Gurov, Krylov[132]

In accordance with paragraph 10, the army's remaining forces defended as follows:

- **115th RB and 724th RR (196th RD)**—the Orlovka region [against Group Stahel and 389th Infantry Division's 545th and 546th Regiments];
- **2nd MRB, 38th MRB, 6th Gds. TB, and 189th TB**—from east of Gorodishche southward to northwest of Krasnyi Oktiabr' village [against 389th Infantry Division's 544th Regiment and part of 295th Infantry Division's 517th Regiment], with 27th Tank Brigade in reserve near Krasnyi Oktiabr' village;
- **35th Gds. RD and 131st RD, 10th RB and 133rd TB, and 271st RR NKVD**—south of the Tsaritsa River [against 94th Infantry Division and 29th Motorized Division].

19 September

Southeastern Front's 62nd and 64th Armies began their attacks at 1200 hours on 19 September, although Chuikov was under no illusions about German weakness. Once again, a stout ground defense combined with murderous air strikes pummeled Chuikov's attacking forces, either halting them in their tracks or, where they succeeded, severely limiting their forward progress (see Map 31).

The Red Army General Staff's daily operational summary described the action early the next morning:

> **Southeastern Front** went over to the offensive with part of its forces at 1200 hours on 19 September against the enemy's infantry and tank units which have penetrated into Stalingrad and advanced 1–1.5 kilometers in some sectors. . . .
>
> **62nd Army** went over to the offensive along the Hill 35.0, Hill 93.2, Hill 135.4, and Hill 102.0 line and in the center of the city of Stalingrad with the units on its right wing and in its center at 1200 hours on 19 September.
>
> 124th and 149th RBs and 282nd RR NKVD, overcoming stubborn enemy resistance, advanced forward slowly.
>
> 115th RB and composite regiment of 196th RD held their previous positions, while repelling counterattacks by the enemy.
>
> 9th MRB captured Hill 126.3 and was continuing further attacks.
>
> 137th TB attacked from the vicinity of the northwestern slopes of Hill 102.0 and reached the region 1 kilometer east of the wagon sheds (2 kilometers southwest of Krasnyi Oktiabr' village).
>
> 95th RD attacked at 1200 hours and, after reaching the crest of Hill 102.0, was halted by strong enemy artillery and mortar fire.
>
> 112th RD, overcoming stubborn enemy resistance, captured the eastern outskirts of Polotnoe (the 1st, 2nd, 3rd, and 4th lanes) at 1400 hours with one of its regiments; the other regiment was holding on to the bridge across Krutoi Ravine along Artemovskaia Street.
>
> 13th GRD was fighting intense street battles in the center city. The division has suffered heavy losses;
>
> 42nd RB, 244th RD, 35th Gds. RD, 133rd TB and the remnants of 131st RD and 10th RB were continuing to fight street battles in the city. Their positions are being confirmed;
>
> 92nd RB occupied defenses along the [grain] elevator and Valdaiskaia [Valdai] Street up to the unnamed ravine and farther along the right bank of the Volga River.
>
> **64th Army** went over to the offensive with its right wing units along the southern outskirts of Kuporosnoe and northern slope of Hill 145.5 (5 kilometers southwest of Kuporosnoe) line at 1200 hours on 19 September.

Map 31. Sixth Army's situation, 19–20 September 1942

422nd RD (less 1334th RR), encountering heavy fire resistance from the enemy, was fighting along the southern outskirts of Kuporosnoe and southeastern edge of *"Kvadratnyi"* [Quadrilateral] Grove, 1 kilometer southeast of Zelenaia Poliana line.

36th Gds. RD was fighting along the southern edge of the grove (south of Zelenaia Poliana) and the northern slope of Hill 145.5 line.

The remaining units of the army were exchanging fire with the enemy in their previous positions.[133]

Attacking with abandon, the two understrength motorized rifle brigades on the right (northern) wing of Chuikov's shock group—the 9th and 38th—seized Hill 126.3 and a nearby ridge. This forced 295th Infantry Division's 517th Regiment, whose lead units had driven the closest toward Krasnyi Oktiabr' village, to withdraw westward. To the south, near Mamaev Kurgan, the first two battalions of 90th and 161st Regiments of Gorishnyi's 95th Rifle Division, the most recent Soviet reinforcements to have crossed the Volga River, arrived just in time to join the assault by 416th and 385th Regiments of Ermolkin's 112th Rifle Division (against Mamaev Kurgan) and, to the south, 524th Regiment's attack westward up the Dolgii Ravine.

The background of Colonel Vasilii Akimovich Gorishnyi, like most Red Army division commanders, had until recently been relatively anonymous. The commander of 95th Rifle Division, he had led his division since 26 August 1942, after its predecessor division, subordinate to the Coastal Army, had been destroyed in mid-July 1942 during the defense of Sevastopol'. Therefore, when the new 95th went into action at Stalingrad on 20 September, its troops were green, and its commander had been at his new post for less than three weeks. Nevertheless, the division performed well enough in the brutal fighting at Stalingrad to earn the designation of 75th Guards on 3 January 1943 and for Gorishnyi to remain as its commander until war's end.[134]

With no time to plan or coordinate, Gorishnyi's fresh units made little progress in clearing 295th Infantry Division's 518th Regiment from Mamaev Kurgan. However, on 95th Rifle Division's southern flank, 385th and 524th Regiments of Ermolkin's 112th Rifle Division managed to struggle forward and regain control of the railroad embankment extending from Mamaev Kurgan southward to the Dolgii Ravine, 1.5 kilometers south of the burial mound.

Farther south in the city's center, the counterattack by Rodimtsev's 13th Guards Rifle Division on the morning of 19 September had no impact whatsoever on the two regiments of Hartmann's 71st Infantry Division. Nevertheless, Rodimtsev was encouraged when he learned that Colonel Batiuk's 284th Rifle Division, another of Eremenko's long promised reinforcements for Chuikov's army, had finally reached the eastern bank of the Volga River north of Krasnaia Sloboda, opposite the central city and his defending 13th Guards Rifle

Division. However, Batiuk was unable to push his division across the river on 19 September because the Germans were so close to the central ferry landing that this site could not be used. Therefore, because only small parties of troops from Batiuk's division were able to cross the Volga in small boats, Rodimtsev's division had to fight on alone, contesting the area around Red Square and Railroad Station No. 1 against the forces of 71st Infantry Division's 194th and 191st Regiments, in the process "suffering heavy losses."[135]

Meanwhile, on Rodimtsev's left flank north of the Tsaritsa River, the shattered remnants of Batrakov's 42nd Rifle Brigade and Afanas'ev's 244th Rifle Division, now numbering fewer than 200 soldiers each, fought on in the buildings east of the railroad line and around 1 May Square against 71st Infantry Division's 211th Regiment advancing from the west and 94th Infantry Division's forces, which were now firmly lodged along the Tsaritsa River.

Along and south of the Tsaritsa River, XXXXVIII Panzer Corps's 94th Infantry and 29th Motorized Divisions continued their advance, the former painfully slowly eastward down the Tsaritsa Gulley toward the Volga and block by bloody block through the tangle of streets east of the main railroad line south of the Tsaritsa River, and the latter northward across the El'shanka River and eastward past the Food Combine. In the Tsaritsa Gulley, Pfeiffer's grenadiers pressed the battalion's worth of troops from Batrakov's 42nd Brigade and Afanas'ev's 244th Rifle Division eastward north of the Tsaritsa to the vicinity of 1 May Square. South of the river, Tarasov's 92nd Rifle Brigade, together with what was left of Driakhlov's 10th Rifle and Bubnov's 133rd Tank Brigades, withdrew eastward from the railroad line but still fought bitterly for possession of the Grain Elevator and adjacent buildings.

Farther south, although decimated in the previous fighting, Dubiansky's 35th Guards Rifle Division, with the remnants of Pesochin's 131st Rifle Division and 271st NKVD Regiment attached, almost ceased to exist after fighting with 29th Motorized Division for days in the southern section of the city. By this time Dubiansky's entire force numbered only several hundred men defending the buildings along a 1.5-kilometer-wide front from the northeastern corner of the Food Combine (also known as the Canning [*Konservnyi*] Factory) southward to the lower El'shanka River and then eastward to the Volga's western bank. The 101st and 100th Regiments of Dubiansky's division protected the sector from the Food Combine northward to the southern approaches to the Grain Elevator, and the remnants of other forces attached to the division defended 35th Guards Division's left wing to the Volga. After a heavy assault by a *kampfgruppe* from 29th Motorized almost split his forces in half and threatened to encircle his 101st Regiment (about 80 men) along the railroad north of the Canning Factory some 500 meters southeast of Railroad Station No. 2, Dubiansky ordered the regiment to withdraw to new defenses extending westward from the factory's buildings to the houses along the northern bank of the El'shanka River, the nearby ravine, and the bridge across the El'shanka. The division's 100th Regiment continued defending its sector, which faced west between the railroad bridge across the El'shanka to the southern edge of the Grain Elevator southeast of the station.[136]

After repeated German assaults during the afternoon, infantry from 94th Infantry Division's 276th Regiment, supported by about 20 tanks from 29th Motorized Division, broke through Dubiansky's defenses southeast of Railroad Station No. 2. Lacking any artillery or tank support, Dubiansky had no choice but to order a fighting withdrawal, building by building, eastward toward the Volga River and the only remaining ground escape route: crossings over the lower Tsaritsa River, which were now being defended by forces on the left wing of Tarasov's 92nd Rifle Brigade. Although Tarasov's and Dubiansky's forces south of the Tsaritsa made life miserable for their pursuers, their forces, now down to no more than 5,000 men, were slowly but steadily melting away.[137] By late afternoon on 19 September, when Zhukov's offensive had obviously failed, the Stukas returned over the city, making large-scale daylight attacks almost impossible for the Soviets.[138]

However, from the Germans' perspective the struggle in southern Stalingrad was not going as well as planned. Because Lenski's 24th Panzer Division was in the process of redeploying forces northward to support LI Corps, this left Pfeiffer's 94th Infantry Division, supported by tanks from Fremerey's 29th Motorized, to complete the task of mopping up Soviet forces south of the Tsaritsa River. Once 276th Regiment of Pfeiffer's division expelled Tarasov's and Dubiansky's riflemen from the Food Combine, Pfeiffer ordered the regiment to shift northward to the division's left wing and undertake the difficult task of seizing the valley of the lower Tsaritsa River. When and if Pfeiffer's division seized control of the Tsaritsa Gulley all the way to its mouth, all Soviet forces south of the river would be isolated from their comrades to the north. However, it would take several more days of heavy fighting to complete this task. Late on 19 September, Sixth Army reported, "During the second half of the day, in intense street fighting, 94th Infantry Division reached a narrow sector of the front along the western bank of the Volga River south of the Tsaritsa River. North of the Tsaritsa River, 71st Infantry Division was clearing the enemy from the western part of the city up to the railroad."[139] Thus, by day's end on 19 September, Chuikov's shattered units in southern Stalingrad had no choice but to withdraw inexorably, block by block and building by building, back toward the Volga River.

20 September

Stalingrad Front's 1st Guards and 24th Armies persisted in their difficult offensive in the Kotluban' region, and 66th Army had now joined the effort by attacking German defenses in the Erzovka region. Therefore, on 20 September Chuikov ordered his army to continue its assault in the city, even though he saw little to be gained by it. To do so, he reinforced 23rd Tank Corps' 9th Motorized Rifle and 137th Tank Brigades, which were attacking 295th Infantry Division's 517th Regiment on Hill 126.3, with 10th NKVD Rifle Division's 269th Regiment. However, at the same time, 295th Infantry Division's 516th Regiment once again assaulted the crest of Mamaev Kurgan, the perfect observation post for artillery to dominate the city, engaging in an intense fight with the 90th and 161st Regiments of Gorishnyi's 95th Rifle Division, which had just reinforced 112th Rifle Division's 416th and 385th Regiments (see Map 32). During the day, Chuikov also directed Gorishnyi's third regiment, the 241st, which had just crossed the river, to occupy reserve defensive positions east of Mamaev Kurgan and Dolgii Ravine and prepare to conduct counterattacks as necessary.[140]

The intense fight for possession of Mamaev Kurgan that ensued also ended 24th Panzer Division's brief respite in the rear to rest and refit. Because the situation was deteriorating around Mamaev Kurgan, Seydlitz, LI Corps' commander, ordered Lenski's division to dispatch its 26th Grenadier Regiment to reinforce 295th Infantry Division's beleaguered regiment on the burial mound. The panzer-grenadiers began their march from the *Schafzucht* (Sheep Breeding Farm) at 0330 hours, passing along the railroad line toward Gumrak airfield and then wheeling eastward into the area west of the Pilot's School. Soon after, Seydlitz ordered Lenski's panzer division to take over the 295th Infantry Division's sector west of Mamaev Kurgan so that Wuthmann's division could concentrate his forces for a decisive attack on the burial mound and the Volga River beyond.[141] This relief-in-place was to take place on the nights of 20–21 and 21–22 September.

As a result of this regrouping, 24th Panzer Division ultimately assumed responsibility for 295th Division's former sector from the western slope of Mamaev Kurgan westward to the northwestern part of the airfield and associated Pilot's School, where its left flank tied in with the right flank of 389th Infantry Division's 544th Regiment. On Lenski's right wing, his division's 4th Motorcycle Battalion was in contact with 295th Infantry Division's 516th Regiment on the crest of Mamaev Kurgan, 26th Grenadier Regiment manned defenses in the division's center west of the airfield, and *Kampfgruppe* Sälzer (with 2nd Company, 40th Panzer Jäger Battalion, and 3rd Company, 40th Panzer Pioneer Battalion) deployed on the division's left wing east and southeast of Hill 112.0. The remainder of Lenski's division, including 21st Grenadier Regiment and Panzer Detachment Lancken (the rest of 24th Panzer Regiment, now with fewer than 10 operational tanks) remained in division reserve near the *Schafzucht*.

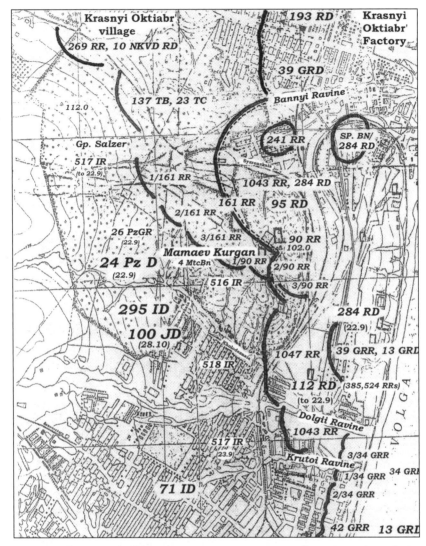

Map 32. The struggle for Mamaev Kurgan, 20 September–5 October 1942

While intense fighting raged for possession of Mamaev Kurgan, the 524th Regiment of Ermolkin's 112th Rifle Division, by now reinforced by the division's 385th Regiment, fended off repeated attacks by the 295th Infantry Division's 517th Regiment along the railroad line south of Dolgii Ravine. This prevented the Germans from advancing eastward across it and the Krutoi

Ravine, which would have split the defenses of the 13th Guards and 95th Rifle Divisions by reaching the Volga's western bank. At the same time, Ermolkin's 416th Regiment also protected the left flank of 95th Rifle Division, fighting on Mamaev Kurgan.

In the city center, Rodimtsev's 13th Guards Rifle Division continued its stout defense against 71st Infantry Division's 194th and 191st Regiments, although "suffering heavy losses" in the process.[142] By this time Rodimtsev's division was defending one to two blocks east of the main railroad line and Railroad Station No. 1, with his 42nd Regiment on the left, the 39th in the center, and the 34th on the right (see Map 33).[143] On Rodimtsev's left, the remnants of Batrakov's 42nd Rifle Brigade and Afanas'ev's 244th Rifle Division were withdrawing eastward from the vicinity of 1 May Square toward the Volga under intense pressure from 71st Infantry Division's 211th Regiment. At the same time, south of the Tsaritsa River, Tarasov's composite 92nd Rifle Brigade was continuing its brutal fight in the web of buildings east of the railroad line, while struggling to hold the railroad bridge over the Tsaritsa River open for the remnants of Dubiansky's 35th Guards Rifle Division to flee northward to safety. Detached from Tarasov's force, Driakhlov's 10th Rifle Brigade was withdrawing eastward from the streets northeast of the Grain Elevator to take up all-round defensive positions to protect the last landing stage on the Volga's western bank south of the Tsaritsa River.

During the day, Chuikov ordered Dubiansky to transfer his defensive sector north of the El'shanka River to Tarasov's rifle brigade and withdraw the remnants of his 35th Guards Rifle Division, together with the few survivors of Pesochin's 131st Rifle Division and 271st NKVD Regiment, into second echelon so they could be evacuated to the Volga's eastern bank. However, before Dubiansky could do so, his forces had to fight their way northward through 92nd Rifle Brigade's rear in what Dubiansky described as "extraordinarily difficult conditions."[144] Subsequently, one group of Dubiansky's guardsmen was encircled by *kampfgruppen* from 94th Infantry Division's 274th Regiment near the Grain Elevator and refused to withdraw despite orders to do so. Only a few of these fighters managed to escape their trap. Dubiansky reported, "At 0700 hours on 21 September, only 80 men remain. I am holding on to the buildings south of the Tsaritsa River with difficulty. I am protecting the junction with 92nd Rifle Brigade only with scouts."[145] After being reinforced by a battalion of naval riflemen from Tarasov's brigade, Dubiansky's forces then cut their way through a battalion of 94th Infantry Division's assault troops and reached 10th Rifle Brigade's defensive line protecting the landing mole on the Volga's western bank.

Once Tarasov's rifle brigade assumed responsibility for defending what little was left of Dubiansky's sector, including the region southeast of the Grain Elevator and a few buildings in the northeastern part of the Food

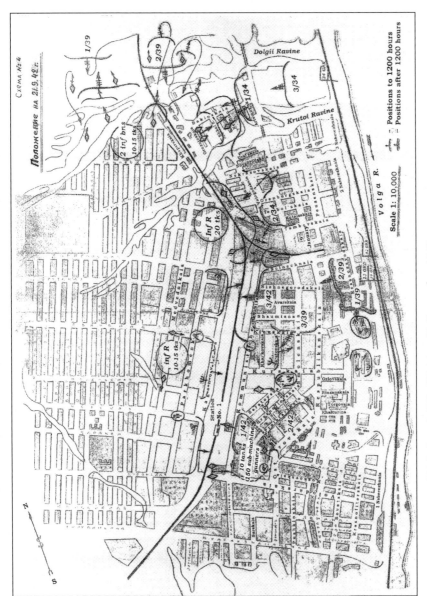

Map 33. Dispositions of 13th Guards Rifle Division, 21 September 1942

Combine, the survivors of Dubiansky's force first attempted to flee northward across the Tsaritsa River above its mouth. By this time, however, the
forward elements of 276th Regiment of Pfeiffer's 94th Infantry Division had
already captured the bridge over the river in this region and were pushing
on eastward toward the river's mouth, effectively blocking Dubiansky's retreat. A heated firefight ensued at day's end on 21 September, during which
35th Guards Rifle Division's 101st Regiment launched a desperate charge
through the German defenders to reach and cross the river. Only a few survived this suicidal charge; both the regimental commander and commissar
were severely wounded in this action.[146] Coincidentally, it would take until
25 September for 276th Regiment of Pfeiffer's division to seize the Tsaritsa
Gulley all the way to its mouth.

As for the survivors of Dubiansky's division and its cooperating forces,
small groups made it across the Tsaritsa River to join up with Batrakov's 42nd
Rifle Brigade in the southern section of Stalingrad's central city while others
either ended up encircled south of the Tsaritsa with 92nd Rifle Brigade or
simply perished in the ruins of the buildings they defended. The division's
headquarters and service-support subunits finally managed to cross the Volga
River on the night of 22–23 September and assembled in the forests near
Zonal'nyi Farm. From there, the division withdrew far to the rear for rest
and refitting on 28 September, a process that produced a new combat-ready
35th Guards Rifle Division by 2 December.[147] Dubiansky's guards division
left more than 9,000 troops in unmarked graves in the ruins of Stalingrad.

An extract from a report by Belousov, a member of Stalingrad Front's
NKVD Special Departments (OO), illustrates the growing problems 62nd
Army was facing in regard to supply, medical support, and, especially, main-
taining discipline and troop morale:

Today the enemy conducted especially intensive fire from artillery and
subjected the city's center and the sites of the crossing berths to bombardment from the air. The two central landing-stages have burned. There are
many casualties. There is continued disorganization at the landing-stage
on the right [eastern] bank of the Volga.

The representatives of 62nd Army's command and its formations are
not receiving the ammunition which has gotten across during the night
in timely fashion, and, as a result, it is lying on the bank and is often
subjected to enemy fire during the day. The seriously wounded are not
receiving help—and they are dying. They are not clearing up their bodies
and coming for them on trucks. There are no doctors. Local women are
rendering help to the wounded.

I have just informed the chief of staff of the *front*, Comrade Zakharov,
about all of these matters. The latter issued orders regarding the dispatch

of medical personnel to Stalingrad and ordered the bodies be gathered up. The commander of 13th Guards Rifle Division gave orders to prepare two berths as fast as possible during the night.

An operational group of 62nd Army's Special Department [OO] has discovered 5 operational guns that belong to 92nd Rifle Brigade on the right bank of the Volga River. The brigade's commander, Colonel Tarasov, explained he left them there because of the absence of crossing means. Workers of the Special Department have found vehicles and loaded and delivered the guns to the crossing.

Today, the chief in charge of the crossing burned to death during a fire on the bank at the berth in Stalingrad. *Osobisti* [Special Department personnel] took measures to save the ammunition, which, to a considerable degree, we managed to accomplish.

Comrade Selivanovsky is today situated in the vicinity of the "Krasnyi Oktiabr'" Factory in Stalingrad.

During 19–20 September, blocking detachments detained 184 men, of whom 21 were shot, including 7 for spying, 5 as traitors to the Motherland, 2 for self-mutilation, 6 for cowardice and panic, and 1 for desertion. Forty men were arrested.

Among those arrested was Colonel Beliakov, the deputy chief of 62nd Army's artillery, who conducted anti-Soviet agitation and was suspected of spying, and the remainder of the detained were sent to their units.

Among those shot for spying, G. A. Pushkov, was a squad leader in 126th Rifle Division, who was taken prisoner by the Germans on 14 September on the outskirts of the city of Stalingrad and, while a prisoner, was recruited and received the mission of determining the locations of the large headquarters, the positions of multiple-rocket launcher sites, and the locations of the workers in the NKVD headquarters and Special Department in Stalingrad. Pushkov was detained today while fulfilling the missions of German intelligence and was shot after a preliminary interrogation.

Among the wounded detained at the crossing is a Red Army soldier of 10th NKVD Division, I. G. Parafonov, who deserted from his unit and feigned being wounded in his head by wrapping bloody rags around his head. Parafonov has been shot in front of the ranks of a number of soldiers who were detained and sent back to their units.[148]

21 September

As the left wing of Chuikov's army crumbled under the weight of 94th Infantry and 29th Motorized Divisions' assaults, desperate fighting raged in the city's center, on the slopes and crest of Mamaev Kurgan, and near Hill 126.3, north of the burial mound, as Chuikov attempted to keep his offensive alive.

On 21 September Udovichenko's 137th Tank Brigade (with nine T-60 tanks) penetrated through the defenses of 295th Infantry Division's 517th Regiment (the day before its relief by 24th Panzer Division's Group Sälzer) along the northern reaches of Bannyi Ravine south of Hill 112.0, but 9th Motorized Rifle Brigade and 269th NKVD Regiment, which were attacking toward Hill 112.0 on their right, could not keep pace, leaving the tank brigade no choice but to withdraw.[149] At the same time, 90th and 161st Regiments of Gorishnyi' 95th Rifle Division captured the eastern slope of Mamaev Kurgan in frenzied assaults against 295th Infantry Division's 516th Regiment and 24th Panzer Division's 4th Motorcycle Battalion. On Gorishnyi's left, 385th and 524th Regiments of Ermolkin's 112th Rifle Division penetrated westward and reached the area 300 meters north of Kolodeznaia Street, just east of the upper reaches of the Dolgii Ravine. Still, neither Gorishnyi nor Ermolkin was able to advance farther in the face of withering enemy fire. Ermolkin's attacking forces, now supported on their left by 13th Guards Rifle Division's 39th Regiment, also stalled along the Dolgii Ravine and south of the railroad line.

Meanwhile, in the center city, 42nd and 34th Regiments of Rodimtsev's 13th Guards Rifle Division were still suffering heavy losses in their fight against 71st Infantry Division's 194th and 191st Regiments (see Map 33). The most intense fighting took place along Kommunisticheskaia [Communist], Respublikanskaia [Republican], Krasnopiterskaia, Stalinskaia [Stalin], and Naberezhnaia Streets, 1.5 kilometers from the Volga on their left flank and even nearer on their right flank.[150] During this dramatic fighting, a *kampfgruppe* reported to consist of 150 German submachine gunners, supported by 10 tanks (more likely assault guns), drove 1st Battalion, 42nd Regiment, from its defensive strongholds in the block of buildings east of Railroad Station No. 1 and half-encircled them in another block of buildings just to the east. Farther north, a second German *kampfgruppe*, reportedly supported by 20 "tanks," but likely including some assault guns, broke through the defenses of 2nd Battalion, 34th Regiment, northwest of 9 January Square but were halted by a vigorous counterattack from Vologodskaia Street.

South of center city, no longer in communication with 62nd Army's headquarters, Batrakov's 42nd Rifle Brigade and the remnants of Afanas'ev's 244th Rifle Division clung to their defenses along Pushkinskaia [Pushkin] Street and along the Tsaritsa River; still farther south, Tarasov's 92nd Rifle Brigade tried frantically to rescue Dubiansky's forces, as well as to hold its own shrinking bridgehead east of the main railroad line and south of the Tsaritsa River. By day's end, the eastward thrust by 94th Infantry Division's 276th Regiment down the Tsaritsa Gulley virtually cut off Tarasov's forces from Batrakov's and Rodimtsev's troops to the north by subjecting all crossings over the Tsaritsa to its mouth to intense small-arms, machine-gun, and mortar fire. To the south, frontal assaults by infantry from 94th Division's 267th Regiment finally snuffed out all Soviet resistance in the Grain Elevator and nearby buildings.[151] By this time, Batrakov's and Tarasov's brigades were the only organized forces still resisting south of the city's center. That night the OKW announced, "The region of the city southeast of the Station [No. 2] and up to the banks of the Volga has been cleared of enemy. The enemy is stubbornly defending the elevator. North of the Tsaritsa River, 71st Infantry Division has occupied part of the buildings to the east of the Party *Obkom* [regional committee] building up to the banks of the Volga River."[152]

Even at this desperate stage in the fighting there was one bright spot for Chuikov. Having *finally* found necessary transport, the first regiment (1043rd) of Batiuk's 284th Rifle Division reached the western bank of the Volga on the night of 21–22 September. Batiuk's division totaled about 10,000 men but lacked many of its authorized weapons. In fact, for a time it had sufficient rifles to arm only one of its three regiments. Once across the Volga, the 1043rd concentrated in the sector from the Krasnyi Oktiabr' Factory southward to east of Mamaev Kurgan to serve as 62nd Army's only reserve.[153] The division's 1045th and 1047th Regiments finally crossed the river overnight on 22–23 September. A Ukrainian by birth (he was born in Akhtyrka in the Sumy region in 1905) and 38 years old in September 1942, Colonel Nikolai Filippovich Batiuk had risen from the ranks during a 15-year military career to take command of 284th Rifle Division on 2 February 1942. Thereafter, he commanded the division with distinction during the heavy fighting west of Voronezh during July, after which the division's survivors were transported to the Urals to rest and refit in early August. Before that process was complete, in early September Batiuk's division received orders to move to Stalingrad.[154]

As Batiuk's division arrived, even though it was short of rifles, Chuikov threw it into combat almost immediately in the sector from Mamaev Kurgan southward to the Krutoi Ravine. The 284th relieved the exhausted troops of Ermolkin's 112th Rifle Division, which Chuikov immediately ordered northward to reinforce the 62nd Army's defenses west of Krasnyi Oktiabr' village.

22 September

Meanwhile, precipitating some of the heaviest fighting to date, 516th and 518th Regiments of Wuthmann's 295th Infantry Division renewed their assaults against 95th and 112th Rifle Divisions' defenses on Mamaev Kurgan and the middle reaches of the Dolgii Ravine to the south in one final lunge to break the stalemate atop the burial mound (see Map 31). Paulus considered this assault by Wuthmann's two regiments against the burial mound as an essential prerequisite to the success of the general assault by Seydlitz's LI Corps against the southern half of Stalingrad's factory district. If the two German regiments pushed the Soviets off the burial mound, the enemy would no longer threaten the corps' right flank. To ensure success on the burial mound, Wuthmann transferred his third regiment, the 517th, from his left to his right wing and ordered it to reinforce the assault on 23 September. The 24th Panzer Division's Group Sälzer took over 517th Regiment's former sector.

After preparatory air strikes by aircraft from VIII Air Corps, and a heavy artillery preparation that began at 0500 hours, 295th Infantry Division's two regiments began their ground assault at 0620 hours under sunny conditions. However, the bombardment failed to achieve major damage on the enemy, who: "From barricaded houses and numerous earth bunkers . . . offered very tough resistance with mortars, artillery and rocket-launchers, in part from the east shore of the Volga, not to mention violent counterthrusts. In costly combat with flamethrowers and concentrated charges, well-supported by assault guns and pioneers, the infantrymen gained ground but their low strengths prevented a large gain of ground."[155]

Despite this fierce resistance by 161st and 90th Regiments of Gorishnyi's 95th Rifle Division, the assault groups from 516th and 518th Regiments pressed Gorishnyi's defending regiments up the southern slope of the mound while suffering heavy casualties. In the process, these Germans pierced the defenses of 385th and 524th Regiments of Ermolkin's 112th Rifle Division along the railroad south of the Dolgii Ravine and drove forward to reach the western bank of the Volga at several points "after difficult fighting."[156] Later in the day, however, 1047th and 1045th Regiments of Batiuk's 284th Rifle Division arrived on the scene just in time to drive 517th Regiment's lead *kampfgruppen* away from tenuous footholds on the Volga's western bank. The 295th Division's attacking forces spent hours trying to clear the Soviets from the nearby blocks of buildings but were able to register only negligible gains. Likewise, on the division's left wing, 516th Regiment was unable to crack 95th Division's defenses and reach the mound's crest. This assault demonstrated that "the Division, with its eroded infantry forces, was no longer equal to the difficult task of house-to-house fighting." Meanwhile, toward day's end, 24th Panzer Division's 26th Panzer Grenadier Regiment, now in position on the mound's western slope, fended off several counterattacks by 1st and 2nd Battalions of 95th Rifle Division's 161st Regiment.

The Red Army General Staff's daily operational summary captured not only the continued ferocity of the fighting and the frustrating lack of progress of Chuikov's offensive but also the positive impact of 284th Rifle Division's arrival on the battlefield:

62nd Army continued to conduct fierce street battles in Stalingrad and continued its offensive from the region of Hill 102.0 toward the southwest with part of its forces.

The enemy resumed his offensive beginning on the morning of 22 September with units of his 295th, 71st, and 94th IDs and 29th MotD, supported by 120–200 tanks [and assault guns], directing his main efforts along the Dolgii Ravine, Donskaia [Don] Street, and the Tsaritsa River, and along the railroad line from Sadovaia to the [grain] elevator. In the city's center, the enemy approached right up to the Oil Storage area. During the second half of the day on 22 September, the enemy continued his attacks along the Dolgii and Krutoi Ravines, from the 9th of January Square region, and along Tambovskaia [Tambov] Street. In the vicinity of 9th of January Square, the enemy succeeded in reaching the Volga River with a force of more than a battalion of infantry with tanks.

The units of the army repelled repeated attacks by the enemy toward the mouth of the Dolgii Ravine in stubborn defensive fighting. We weakened the enemy in this region by 1500 hours.

The attacks by our units from the vicinity of Hill 102.0 [Mamaev Kurgan] toward the southwest had no success.

9th MRB abandoned its positions on the road under heavy enemy pressure and withdrew 200 meters to the northeastern bank [of a ravine].

124th and 149th RBs, 282nd RR, 10th RD NKVD, 115th RB, and 23rd TC [6th Gds., 6th, and 189th TBs] remained in their previous positions, having repelled all attacks by the enemy.

95th RD continued its attacks to the southwest but was twice counterattacked by the enemy and was fighting along the southern and southwestern slopes of Hill 102.0 by day's end.

284th RD, with two regiments [1045th and 1047th], after repelling an attack by the enemy along Dolgii Ravine, was holding the bridge across that ravine on Artilleriiskaia [Artillery] Street and Krutoi Ravine from Artilleriiskaia Street to the Volga River.

13th Gds. RD, suffering considerable losses [200 killed and wounded], held off fierce attacks by enemy infantry and tanks all day on 22 September and withdrew to the vicinity of the 9th of January Square one regiment (34th Gds. RR) by day's end.

The division repelled 12 attacks by the enemy during the day, destroying 42 tanks in the process, and occupied the Krutoi Ravine, 2nd Naberezhnaia Street (incl.), 9th of January Square, Solnechnaia, Kurskaia [Kursk], Orlovskaia [Orel]-Proletarskaia [Proletariat], Gogolia [Gogol], and Kommunisticheskaia [Communist] Streets defensive [line] to the Tsaritsa River by day's end.

42nd RB occupied defenses along the northern bank of the Tsaritsa River in the vicinity of Pushkinskaia [Pushkin] Street.

10th RD NKVD defended the railroad station [No. 2] and railroad bridge across the Tsaritsa River line.

92nd RB withdrew to the line from Kavkaz [Caucasus], Krasnosel'skaia and Kum Streets to the Volga River.[157]

The steady grind of German bombardment and attacks finally took its toll on the defenders around the central ferry site. Rodimtsev's 13th Guards Division, which had already suffered 30 percent casualties during the first few terrible days of fighting, had been reduced to a skeleton force of not many more than 1,000 bayonets by the end of its first week of combat. The remains of his regiments and battalions, often reduced to a handful of men each, were surrounded and, in one instance, buried alive by German fire. In return, 62nd Army's artillery, located east of the river, could easily mass its fires to seriously impede the German advance. Nevertheless, on 22 September the troops of 211th Infantry Regiment of Hartmann's 71st Infantry Division, infiltrating down a drainage sewer, reached the Volga at two points east of Railroad Station No. 1 but had to withdraw that night. During this fighting, Hartmann's troops surrounded 1st Battalion, 42nd Guards Regiment, and 2nd Battalion's 5th Company in the vicinity of Red Square, east of the railroad station, although both forces managed to escape eastward from the encirclement with heavy losses.

23–26 September

When Hartmann's troops resumed their assaults on 23 September, the pressure on Rodimtsev's guardsmen increased immeasurably, in particular on their collapsed left wing, creating a crisis in the ranks of his division and its neighbors to the left and initiating a struggle that would last unabated through 26 September (see Map 34).

As 62nd Army reported:

13th Gds. RD continued to fight intense street battles and was occupying [the following] positions by 1600 hours on 23 September: 34th Gds. RR (730 bayonets) was fighting on 2nd Naberezhnaia Street, 42nd Gds. RR was occupying positions from 2nd Naberezhnaia to Smolensk Streets, and its 1st Battalion manned all-around defenses in the region of the two houses between Volga-Donskaia and Gogolia Streets.

39th Gds. RR (135 bayonets) was fighting along the Respublikanskaia Street from its intersections with Nizhnegorodskaia [Lower City] and Kievskaia [Kiev] Streets line and farther to the southeast to the Volga River.

Map 34. The battle for central Stalingrad, 22–26 September 1942

A detachment of student officers and an armored train are defending the Pristan region [the ferry slips on the Volga River on 13th Gds. RD's left].

42nd RB is defending the region of Pushkinskaia Street along the northern bank of the Tsaritsa River.

92nd RB continued to occupy its previous positions [undefined but south of the Tsaritsa River].[158]

The fierce attacks by the Hartmann's infantry against the defenses of Rodimtsev's beleaguered guardsmen collapsed 13th Guards Rifle Division's defenses along the entire front from the Krutoi Ravine in the north southward to east of Railroad Station No. 1. It also separated the guards division from Batrakov's 42nd Rifle Brigade on its left. Under heavy pressure, Colonel Elin's 42nd Regiment withdrew eastward from its defenses along Kommunisticheskaia Street to Respublikanskaia Street and had to refuse its left flank back to the Volga River near Khersonskaia [Kherson] Street, north of the vital ferry landing. On Elin's right, Colonel Dolgov's 39th Regiment gave ground steadily, withdrawing from Kommunisticheskaia Streets between Solnechnaia and Kievskaia Streets back to Penzenskaia [Penza] Street. On the right wing of Rodimtsev's division, Panikhin's 34th Regiment abandoned its forward positions along Vologodskaia and Artemovskaia Streets and withdrew almost 1 kilometer to new defenses along, and only 500 meters from, the Volga's western bank.

When all was said and done, by nightfall the assaults by 71st Infantry Division's three regiments had compressed the remnants of Rodimtsev's forces into a narrow 500–1,000-meter strip of land extending from the Krutoi Ravine southward to the Volga River at the base of Kievskaia Street.[159] However, Rodimtsev's forces claimed to have killed 500 Germans and destroyed 43 tanks (actually assault guns) in the heavy fighting.[160] More telling still was the sharply declining combat capability of 71st Infantry Division's eight infantry battalions. If all eight of the division's battalions rated "average" on 14 September, then by 26 September, after abolishing one battalion outright, four of its remaining seven battalions rated "average," leaving the other three simply "exhausted."[161]

After additional fighting, 71st Infantry Division on 25 September finally secured the party and governmental buildings near Red Square, but only after those buildings had been reduced to rubble by repeated air and artillery strikes. After weeks of Soviet fighting against an enemy with air superiority, ominous signs appeared that the Red Army's morale and discipline might be beginning to crack. For example, Chuikov discovered that Colonel Tarasov, who commanded the remnants of 92nd Rifle Brigade (and also 42nd Rifle Brigade's remnants after its commander, Batrakov, was severely wounded on 23 September during a German air strike), had deceived the army command by submitting false reports about the locations and actions of his forces. Specifically, while reporting that his forces were continuing their stout defenses south of the Tsaritsa, he had actually abandoned his troops, moved his headquarters onto Golodnyi Island in the Volga River, and thereafter submitted false reports by radio indicating they were still defending actively in the city.[162] Once Chuikov discovered Tarasov's deception, he relieved him of command, later appointing Major Shtrigol' in his stead. In any event, the departure of Tarasov and his forces from the region south of the Tsaritsa River left only Rodimtsev's division to defend the left flank of Chuikov's army.

Although heavy fighting would persist for weeks more in this restricted area, for all practical purposes Rodimtsev's forces were now irrelevant and would remain so unless and until they were reinforced (see Map 35). Indicative of this position, by 28 September Paulus had shifted all three regiments of Pfeiffer's 94th Infantry Division northward to assist in reducing the Orlovka salient, leaving Hartmann's 71st Infantry Division to deal with the remaining pockets of Soviet troops in downtown Stalingrad. And Hartmann's division was certainly not capable of doing much more than simply monitoring Rodimtsev's forces in Stalingrad's center city. Indicative of this fact, by 28 September only one of his seven battalions rated "average," and the remaining seven were "exhausted." Less than a week later, all were hors de combat.

With heavy fighting in Stalingrad's city center, equally heavy combat was taking place in the broad sector extending Hill 126.3 south past the western edge of Krasnyi Oktiabr' village and the slopes of Mamaev Kurgan (Hill 102.0) and the middle reaches of the Dolgii and Krutoi Ravines to the right boundary of 13th Guards Rifle Division along the western bank of the Volga River. There, Chuikov strained to maintain ground links between his forces defending the factory district and Rodimtsev's division in the city's center, all the while trying to fulfill Stalin's and Zhukov's demands that he continue attacking in order to tie down Germans inside the city.

Therefore, without halting 95th Rifle Division's counterattack in the vicinity of Mamaev Kurgan, Chuikov on 23 September ordered Batiuk's 284th Rifle Division, which had just completed its movement across the river the night before, to attack southward across the Dolgii and Krutoi Ravines toward the city center (see Map 32). The goal was to help Rodimtsev's division clear the German 71st Infantry Division from the ferry slips south of the center city and from north of the Tsaritsa River.[163] The right boundary of Batiuk's division extended along Khalturinskaia, Ostrovskaia, and Gogolia Streets. Chuikov was careful to advise the division commander of the special nature and requirements of urban fighting. At the same time, Chuikov dispatched 2,000 reinforcements to Rodimtsev's division so that it could sustain operations.[164]

Meanwhile, north of Mamaev Kurgan, the understrength tank and motorized brigades subordinate to Popov's 23rd Tank Corps had gone over to the defense in the sector from east of Gorodishche southward to the area north of Mamaev Kurgan. These brigades had to rest and refit after the previous week's heavy fighting. With its right flank adjacent to the defenses of 1st Battalion, 124th Rifle Brigade, east of Gorodishche, the tank corps manned thin and shallow defenses extending southeastward along a 13–15 kilometer-wide front to protect the western approaches to Krasnyi Oktiabr' village. Popov held this front with a force of about 50 tanks and little more than 1,000 riflemen.[165] From north to south, Popov's forces included 6th Guards and 189th Tank Brigades deploying west of the northern bank of Vishnevaia *Balka*, northwest of Krasnyi Oktiabr' village; 38th and 9th Motorized Rifle Brigades occupying defenses west of the village and Hill 112.0; and 269th Rifle Regiment, 10th NKVD Rifle Division, and 137th Tank Brigade manning positions northwest of Mamaev Kurgan. These forces faced 389th Infantry Division's 544th Regiment in the north and 24th Panzer Division's

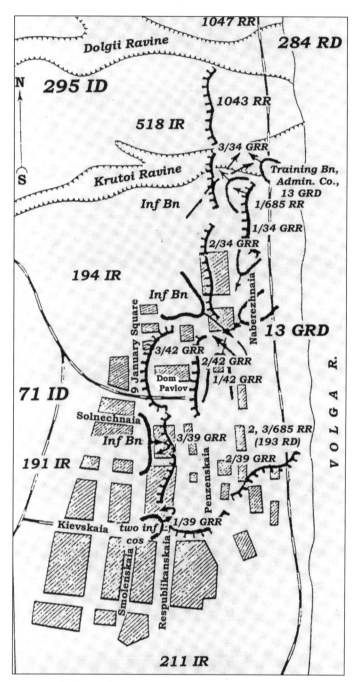

Map 35. The battle for central Stalingrad, 30 September–1 October 1942

26th Grenadier Regiment, which was due to be relieved the next day by the division's 21st Grenadier Regiment, in the south.

The attacks by Chuikov's shock groups at 1000 hours on 23 September, as called for in the plan he articulated several nights before, initiated another 72 hours of heavy combat, described briefly in 62nd Army's summary reports to the Red Army General Staff in Moscow:

[23 September]

62nd Army continued fierce street battles in Stalingrad city on 23 September.

124th and 149th RBs, 282nd RR, 115th RB, and 2nd MRB held on to their previous positions, repelling all attacks by small enemy groups and subunits.

95th RD fought its way to the northern bank of the Dolgii Ravine in the sector from Chernomorskaia [Black Sea] Street to 0.5 kilometers north of Donetskaia [Donets] Street.

284th RD reached the line of the railroad bridge across the Dolgii Ravine, and Zheleznodorozhnaia [Railroad], Artemovskaia, and Nekrasovskaia [Nekrasov] Streets.

[24 September]

62nd Army continued to conduct offensive fighting on 24 September with units of 95th and 284th RDs in their previous regions. The enemy offered fierce resistance to the attacking units of the army, and its air force bombed our units' combat formations in groups of 5–12 aircraft, especially intensely in the vicinity of Hill 102.0 [Mamaev Kurgan] and the Dolgii and Krutoi Ravines.

The units of 95th and 284th RDs were fighting stubbornly along the northern bank of the Dolgii Ravine, on Kolodeznaia Street, along the Krutoi Ravine from the railroad to the Volga River, and in the vicinity of 2nd Naberezhnaia Street.

13th Gds. RD continued intense street fighting in the center of Stalingrad city.

112th RD was defending along the southeastern slopes of Hill 102.0 [Mamaev Kurgan]. The 385th RR of the division was defending the northern bank of the Dolgii Ravine and Artilleriiskaia Street line, and 524th RR the southern bank of the Dolgii Ravine and, further, from Artilleriiskaia Street to the bank of the Volga River.

[25 September]

62nd Army continued to conduct sustained street fighting with part of its forces in Stalingrad city.

124th and 149th RBs, 282nd RR, 115th RB, and composite regiment of 196th RD occupied their previous positions.

95th RD occupied [the following] positions: 241st RR reached the line of Ustiuzhkaia Street in prolonged fighting but withdrew to the line of the Dolgii Ravine, while suffering heavy losses, as a result of counterattacks by an enemy force of up to a battalion of infantry; 161st RR approached right up to the northern block of Belomorskaia [White Sea] and Azovskaia [Azov] Streets but withdrew to Dolgii Ravine under the pressure of heavy enemy flanking fire.

112th RD continued to defend its previous positions.

The units of 284th RD fought with the enemy along the Krutoi Ravine line.

13th Gds. RD continued to conduct street battles in the previous regions of Stalingrad city.

685th RR, 193rd RD, which arrived to reinforce 13th Gds. RD, concentrated in the vicinity of Tambovskaia [Tambov] and 2nd Naberezhnaia Streets by 0900 hours on 25 September.

42nd RB fought fierce street battles in the southern part of Stalingrad city. Fighting was raging along a line from the Tsaritsa River (the Kavkaz region), along Birskaia Street to Kozlovskaia [Kozlov] Street, further along Kum Street to Pugachevskaia [Pugachev] Street, and along Pugachevskaia Street to the fork in the railroad.

[26 September]

62nd Army continued street battles in Stalingrad city, fending off frenzied enemy attacks. After prolonged fighting, the enemy managed to reach the Stalin Quay, subjected it to fire, and kept up the fire on all three berths in the central crossing sites across the Volga River.

The units of the army's northern sector [Group Gorokhov] continued to occupy their former positions.

112th RD (numbering 2,558 men) occupied a second defensive line along the line of the Vishnevaia *Balka* [west of Krasnyi Oktiabr' village].

13th Gds. RD, with 193rd RD's 685th RR, advanced to 9th of January Square and cleared enemy forces out of several buildings on Solnechnaia, Respublikanskaia, Kievskaia, Tobol'skaia, and Tambovskaia Streets.

The remnants of 272nd RR, 10th RD NKVD, 1st Bn, 42nd Gds. RR [13th Gds. RD], as well as units of 42nd and 92nd RBs, fought heavy defensive battles during the day with superior enemy forces, which were attacking toward the mouth of the Tsaritsa River from the south and toward the Central landing-stage [Pristan'] from the railroad station. [Note: The report by Tarasov's 92nd Rifle Brigade and attached 42nd Rifle Brigade was false.] The enemy penetrated the front of these units. The units withdrew toward the east and occupied new positions. Their positions are being verified.[166]

As this fighting unfolded, Paulus readied his forces to resume their advance on the factory district, now planned for 27 September. In the interim, sporadic heavy fighting took place along the entire front, hindering Sixth Army's orderly attack preparations. For example, on 24 September in 24th Panzer and 295th Infantry Divisions' sectors, Gorishnyi's 95th Rifle Division employed all three of its regiments (241st, 161st, and 90th), supported on the right by 137th Tank Brigade, to conduct a fierce assault on the defenses of 24th Panzer's 4th Motorcycle Battalion and 295th Infantry's 516th Regiment (see Map 32). In this instance, the repeated assaults drove the German forces off most of the burial mound's southern and western slopes and penetrated all the way to Kolodeznaia Street along the upper reaches of Dolgii Ravine before the Germans were able to contain them. All the while, Seydlitz's divisions suffered greatly from the incessant Soviet artillery fire. Despite these attacks, LI Corps late on 24 September notified 24th Panzer Division that 100th Jäger Division, newly arrived from the Don River front to join Paulus's new offensive, would begin relieving its forward forces the next day.[167]

As 62nd Army's daily reports and German accounts indicated, Chuikov's counterattacks stalled by 25 September before the attacking forces achieved any of their objectives. Confirming this fact, the OKW announced on 26 September, "In Stalingrad, several fortified buildings, including the building of the Party *Obkom* in the city's center, as well as several bunkers, were captured in the stubbornly defended parts of the city north of the Tsaritsa River."[168] Ever candid, Chuikov was still pleased by his army's performance:

In this fighting, which frequently turned into hand-to-hand skirmishes, the enemy's forward advance from the vicinity of the central landing-stage was halted. But we failed to wipe out the enemy forces which had broken through to the Volga and did not link up with the infantry brigades at the other side of the Tsaritsa River.

At the cost of enormous losses, the enemy won only a partial success. Paulus's plan—to reach the Volga and then strike at the flank and rear of the Army by an attack along the Volga—was frustrated. This plan collapsed when his forces came up against the tenacious actions of Rodimtsev's, Batiuk's, and Gorishnyi's divisions, Batrakov's brigade, and other units.

For the 62nd Army, the crisis was over; it had shown no fear and had not faltered when the enemy made his first breakthrough to the Volga. We still held Mamaev Kurgan. Not one of our units had been completely wiped out. Counterattacks by Batiuk's Siberian division had halted the enemy's advance in the city. The Germans were wallowing in their own blood; the streets were littered with dozens of burnt-out German tanks and thousands of German dead.[169]

Even though Chuikov's counterattacking forces failed to fulfill Zhukov's and Eremenko's high hopes, 95th and 284th Rifle Divisions' furious counterattacks and subsequent stout defense of Mamaev Kurgan and the Dolgii and Krutoi Ravines, coupled with Rodimtsev's resolute defense in the city's center, indeed halted LI Corps' attempts to roll up Chuikov's left flank with its 295th and 71st Infantry Divisions and penetrate into Stalingrad's factory district from the south. However, except for the region around Mamaev Kurgan and the two ravines to the south, Soviet resistance had virtually collapsed in the southern two-thirds of the city, which were now largely under German control. Only the factories and northern suburbs, plus a few pockets in the center, remained in Soviet hands.

But Paulus's victory in the central and southern parts of the city had been costly, and despite the fact that the heavy black lines on his operational maps showed his forces enticingly near the western bank of the Volga in this region, Paulus's position was far weaker than the map symbols indicated. All of the divisions in his shock groups assaulting the city, especially the infantry and pioneer (combat engineer) battalions, were slowly bleeding to death while receiving few replacements. Indeed, LI Corps' 295th and 71st Infantry Divisions, which had assaulted Mamaev Kurgan and the city's center, were seriously depleted. As indicated above, by 26 September four of 71st Division's infantry battalions were rated "weak" and three were "exhausted," and the seven battalions in 295th Division (two of which had been rated "medium strong," three "average," and two "weak" on 14 September) saw their ratings plunge to two "average," four "weak," and one "exhausted" by 26 September.

The same grim pattern existed in XXXXVIII Panzer Corps' 94th Infantry Division, whose seven infantry battalions all had a combat capability rating of "medium strong" on 14 and 26 September but saw the ratings sag to seven "weak" on 28 September, then plummet to seven "exhausted" by 5 October.[170] Nor did 24th Panzer Division escape this attrition. Its four panzer-grenadier battalions fell from two rated "medium strength" and two "average" on 14 and 26 September to two "average" and two "weak" on 28 September, and, finally, one "weak" and three "exhausted," plus an "exhausted" panzer pioneer battalion, on 5 October. And this division was to spearhead Paulus's next major drive into the city!

These appalling ratings meant that the line-infantry regiments and battalions of these divisions had personnel strengths of well below 60 percent for "average," 40 percent for "weak," and 30 percent in their "exhausted" battalions. By this time, the divisions themselves had only one-third to one-half of their authorized assault guns. Expressed in terms of combat infantrymen or engineers, most of the German infantry and panzer-grenadier regiments fielded around 1,000 combat-effective soldiers each; their infantry, panzer-grenadier, and pioneer battalions had 200–250 men if rated "weak" and less than 200 men if categorized as "exhausted." As for the shock group's armor strength, 24th Panzer Division, although supposedly resting and refitting, still had half of its forces in the front lines, with about 30 operational tanks at its disposal; 29th Motorized Division had even fewer tanks.

24th Panzer Division's state typified the condition of Sixth Army's forces as a whole:

> The Division had completely fulfilled the set mission of holding the defensive positions. Every enemy attack was repulsed. This was difficult, as the position in no way aided the defence but resulted in the attacks coming to a standstill. Every step backwards, however, would mean a deterioration in the starting positions for the forthcoming assault. The defence prevailed with the available small combat forces. The troops from the preceding fighting in the central and southern parts of Stalingrad were heavily fatigued and, instead of receiving the promised rest, were again immediately committed in the northern part of Stalingrad.[171]

Even General Richthofen, the *Luftwaffe* commander who was so often critical of the lack of aggressiveness in Paulus and his troops, recognized the problem in his diary:

> 22 September. In the town, some minor progress. Sixth Army attack is suffering from constipation, primarily because such a large portion of its forces is pinned down by constant enemy pressure from the north and because reinforcements—infantry divisions—are coming up so slowly. It's just a filthy slogging match from ruin to ruin and cellar to cellar!
> 3 October. . . . "What we lack," I said, "is some clear thinking and a well-defined primary objective. It's quite useless to muck about here, there and everywhere as we are doing—and doubly futile, with the inadequate forces at our disposal. One thing at a time. . . . But we must first finish off what we've started, of course, especially at Stalingrad and Tuapse."[172]

In fact, the strength of Paulus's shock groups assaulting the city dwindled from six divisions (389th, 295th, 71st, and 94th Infantry, 24th Panzer, and 29th Motorized), with roughly 80,000 men and 100 tanks and assault guns on 13 September to only five and a half divisions (389th, 295th, 71st, and 94th Infantry, 29th Motorized, and half of 24th Panzer), with no more than 65,000 men and fewer than 25 tanks on 26 September. Probably fewer than 40,000 of these soldiers were actually combat-effective infantrymen or panzer-grenadiers. Illustrating the heavy losses that Paulus's shock groups suffered in the city fighting, incomplete data collected by Southeastern Front indicated that 62nd and 64th Armies' ferocious defense from 13 to 26 September killed at least 6,000 German soldiers and destroyed more than 170 tanks (assault guns), 100 artillery pieces and mortars, and 200 aircraft.[173] Fragmentary reports in Sixth Army's records indicate that 71st, 295th, and 389th Divisions alone suffered about 1,000 dead, 3,000 wounded, and 100 missing from 14 to 26 September.

During the same period, although Chuikov's army suffered even greater losses, including at least 69 of its original 100 tanks, it received as many as 40,000 troop reinforcements, including 92nd Rifle and 137th Tank Brigades, 13th Guards, 95th, and 284th Rifle Divisions, several smaller units, and numerous individual replacements. Therefore, despite catastrophic losses Chuikov was able to maintain the strength of his defending forces at about 51,000 men (see Table 24). Overall, the *Stavka* reinforced the Stalingrad and Southeastern Fronts with 10 rifle divisions, two tank corps, and eight tank brigades from its reserve from 13 through 26 September, with five of these rifle divisions going to Chuikov's army.[174]

Although its reinforcing formations and individual replacements suffered heavily from inexperience in urban warfare, gradually 62nd Army devised a system to give experienced leadership to new arrivals. When Chuikov found a unit commander and staff who worked well, he retained that headquarters with him and simply subordinated all troops in an area to it. More commonly, however, once a unit had become depleted he would evacuate the regimental and divisional staffs to the eastern bank, where they would re-form with new replacements and return to the battle at a later date. Survivors of the original unit were then resubordinated to adjacent headquarters.

The task of moving this mass of reinforcements, supplies, casualties, and civilians across the Volga River required the efforts of all available vessels on the river. Rear Admiral D. D. Rogachev commanded the Volga River Flotilla, a combination of brigades of gunboats and minesweepers that provided fire support to the troops while aiding in the actual ferrying. Rogachev formed the special Northern Group of Ships, consisting of two gunships and five armored cutters under the command of Captain 3rd Rank S. P. Lysenko, which took up firing positions near the town of Akhtuba. Most of the transport tasks fell on the civilian fishermen of the region, who were directed by Major General V. F. Shestakov, the commander of the river-crossing sites. These boats, together with those of the Volga Military Flotilla, managed to ferry up to 10,000 troops and 1,000 tons of supplies across the Volga from 12 to 15 September.[175]

Despite the best efforts of the German artillery and *Luftwaffe* to interdict ferry travel, Eremenko was able to send a steady stream of new units and individual replacements across the river into Stalingrad. Once his army lost the southern landing stage, Chuikov ordered additional landing points

Table 24. The Personnel Strengths of 62nd Army's Combat Formations on 25 September 1942

- 13th Guards Rifle Division – 6,906 men
- 95th Rifle Division – 5,455 men
- 112th Rifle Division – 2,557 men
- 193rd Rifle Division – 10,273 men
- 284th Rifle Division – 7,648 men
- 10th Rifle Brigade – 191 men
- 42nd Rifle Brigade – 1,049 men
- 92nd Rifle Brigade – 2,562 men
- 115th Rifle Brigade – 4,023 men
- 124th Rifle Brigade – 4,218 men
- 149th Rifle Brigade – 3,119 men
- 2nd Motorized Rifle Brigade – 883 men
- 20th Motorized Rifle Brigade – 418 men
- 9th Motorized Rifle Brigade – 705 men
- 38th Motorized Rifle Brigade – 1,119 men
- **Total – 51,126 men**

Source: Isaev, *Stalingrad*, 180, citing *TsAMO RF*, f. 48, op. 451, d. 41, l. 129.

established farther north. However, by 15 September the Germans were able to destroy all crossing sites over the river in the heart of the city and by 22 September capture the central ferry docks, isolating 62nd Army's forces in the city center. Thereafter, the 3rd Division of Cutters, commanded by Lieutenant Colonel A. N. Vertiulin, was responsible for supplying this sector and evacuating casualties. Vertiulin's ships were under constant enemy artillery fire and air strikes despite the widespread use of smoke to cover their movements.[176]

After 24 September, when it became impossible to evacuate the wounded by larger ships, the flotilla used fast armored cutters to perform this task, still under withering fire. For example, on the night of 25–26 September, as German forces were advancing toward the lower Tsaritsa River, four armored cutters evacuated 350 wounded from the vicinity of the river's mouth.[177] At one time or another, virtually every large naval or civilian vessel suffered damage and casualties from German air attacks. Only incredible determination enabled these unknown heroes to keep 62nd Army supplied with men and ammunition.[178]

The antiaircraft forces of the Stalingrad PVO (Russian air defense) Corps Region provided whatever protection they could against the incessant German air attacks on the city and its defenders. Deprived of its fixed defenses around the city and its VNOS (*vozdushnoe nabliudenie, opoveshchenie i sviaz'*, Soviet early warning system), the corps region transferred almost all of its units and guns to the river's eastern bank. Eremenko then ordered the region to give priority to protecting the river-crossing sites and the *front's* artillery group. Those few units remaining on the river's western bank used their guns either against enemy aircraft or, more frequently, against ground targets, especially enemy tanks and assault guns.

For example, on 13 September a group of five batteries from 1079th and 1082nd Antiaircraft Artillery Regiments supported 23rd Tank Corps' 6th Guards and 189th Tank Brigades in their defense against 389th Infantry Division's assaults southeast of Gorodishche and the Gumrak airfield. Although four of the five batteries were destroyed in a single day of intense fighting, the batteries reported destroying 15 enemy tanks or assault guns, three aircraft, and up to a battalion of German infantry, primarily by firing over open sights.[179] In addition, a special antiaircraft group, supported by 38 fighter aircraft, including 23 new I-15, I-16, and I-153 models from 102nd Fighter Aviation Division, as well as antiaircraft armored trains, was formed. This group's mission was to prevent the Germans from disrupting vital supply transport along the railroad lines east of the city from Pallasovka to Verbliuzh'ia and Verkhnyi Baskunchak to Akhtuba.[180]

From Paulus's vantage point, Chuikov's proven capability for maintaining his army's strength meant that if Sixth Army was to seize Stalingrad's factory district Paulus had no choice but to reorganize and reinforce his shock group in order to concentrate sufficient strength to take the district by deliberate (and likely costly) storm. In addition, Zhukov's and Eremenko's determined offensives in the Kotluban' region, which continued to prevent Sixth Army from bringing any significant forces from Hube's XIV Panzer Corps to bear on the northern flank of Chuikov's defenses, only exacerbated Paulus's dilemma. In fact, the assaults in the Kotluban' region also diverted 113th Infantry Division, with its seven "strong" and one "medium strong" infantry battalions, from its intended target—Stalingrad city. Underscoring the devastating effects of this fighting, after only two days of operations one of 113th Division's infantry battalions was "exhausted," and by 5 October three more were rated "weak."

Paulus was also under immense pressure from Hitler for results, especially in light of Army Group A's slow advance in the Caucasus region. Sixth Army's commander was acutely aware of the attrition suffered by his infantry units, but during a brief period in late September he became optimistic. Given the reports he received, Paulus could be pardoned for announcing, on the afternoon of 26 September, that the center of the city was secured and that "since noon the German war flag has been flying over the party buildings."[181] However, recognizing the costs thus far and the arduous task that lay ahead, Paulus was already formulating a plan and marshalling his forces for what he believed would be the culminating assaults on the city's factory district to end the battle for Stalingrad.

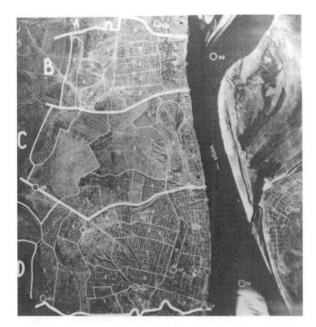

The central part of
Stalingrad from the
Krasnyi Oktiabr'
village and factory
(B) southward past
Mamaev Kurgan and
the "Tennis Racket"
(C) and Stalingrad
center city (D) to
the Tsaritsa River
(to the left of point
750).

The central part of Stalingrad during German 71st Infantry Division's assault on
17 September 1942. The view is oriented from north to south, with the Dolgii
and Krutoi Ravines at the lower left, Railroad Station No. 1 in the center, and the
Tsaritsa River at the upper right.

The central part of Stalingrad under assault, with 9 January Square and Pavlov's House at the upper center, Railroad Station No. 1 at the left center, and Red Square at the lower center.

The central part of Stalingrad in flames.

Street fighting in the central part of Stalingrad.

Railroad Station No. 1 in flames.

General A. I. Rodimtsev, commander of 13th Guards Rifle Division.

Railroad Station No. 1 (left) and central part of Stalingrad.

The central part of Stalingrad east of the railroad line.

NKVD headquarters in the central part of Stalingrad.

Ruins in the central part of Stalingrad.

The northern half of the central part of Stalingrad.

The 9 January Square.

Troops of 13th
Guards Rifle Division
fighting near NKVD
Headquarters in
the central part of
Stalingrad.

The Red Square after the battle.

Red Army soldiers maneuvering through trenches in the central part of Stalingrad.

Pavlov's House (at lower right).

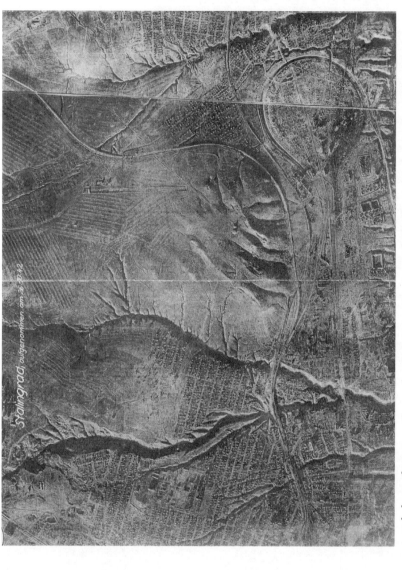

Aerial photo of Mamaev Kurgan (center), Bannyi Ravine and the "Tennis Racket" (right and lower right), and Dolgii and Krutoi Ravines (left center and left) taken on 26 October 1942.

Colonel N. F. Batiuk, commander of 284th Rifle Division, at this command post east of Mamaev Kurgan.

Ships of the Volga Military Flotilla transport naval infantry across the Volga River in October 1942.

A Soviet assault bridge across the Volga in October 1942.

Soviet troops crossing the Volga River on pontoon rafts in late September 1942.

Soviet infantry attacking in the Kotluban' region in late September 1942.

Soviet machine gunners supporting an assault in the Kotluban' region in late September 1942.

N. S. Khrushchev, commissar of Stalingrad Front, and General A. I. Eremenko, commander of Stalingrad Front, addressing Soviet tank crews in the vicinity of Kotluban' in late September 1942.

CONCLUSIONS

The two weeks of bloody fighting in the streets and rubble of Stalingrad from 13 to 26 September established the parameters for the subsequent struggle for possession of the city, as well as the fate of Army Group B and Operation Blau as a whole. Weichs and Paulus had planned for a triumphant march into and through the city, with their tanks, assault guns, and accompanying panzergrenadiers and *landsers* enveloping it from the north and south. Instead, by 26 September the battle for the city had degenerated into a painfully slow, grinding, and immensely costly block-to-block and building-to-building slugging match between Paulus's and Chuikov's troops. German forces had to claw their way through the city's streets—and only from the west and south.

Stalin's decision to defend the city deprived the Germans of their traditional advantages of mobility, maneuver, and precise, overwhelming, and deadly artillery fire and air support. This forced the attackers to gnaw their way through Chuikov's defenses in a battle that resembled the fighting on the Somme and at Verdun in 1916 more than it did the familiar blitzkrieg war during the previous two summers. Although imposed on them by Hitler, Weichs's and Paulus's decision to take Stalingrad by storm negated all of the Germans' traditional advantages and committed Sixth Army to a struggle it could not win, especially because the issue of who possessed Stalingrad was secondary to the *Stavka's* principal aim of mounting a general counteroffensive to destroy Paulus's forces.

Regardless of its ultimate outcome, the fighting in Stalingrad was only one element in the strategy Stalin and his *Stavka* had been pursuing since late July 1942. Their intent was to halt or at least slow the momentum of the German advance sufficiently to permit the Red Army to conduct a massive counteroffensive against Axis forces when they became overextended, something the Soviet leadership saw as inevitable. This strategy had failed to produce victory in late July, August, and early September simply because, at critical moments, Army Group B was able was restore momentum to Sixth Army's advance despite the Red Army's frequent counterstrokes. By mid-September, however, Hitler's decision to seize Stalingrad by storm stripped the momentum from Sixth Army's grasp, putting it instead into the Red Army's hands. From the perspective of Stalin and his *Stavka*, the coldhearted sacrifice of Chuikov's 50,000 men in the streets and ruins of Stalingrad, plus whatever reinforcements were required to keep his army operational, was a small price to pay for victory by the million-plus men who would conduct the Red Army's anticipated counteroffensive, whenever it occurred.

Each piece in the mosaic of military operations taking place from 13–26 September played a vital role in this strategy. Paulus's assault in Stalingrad committed his troops to a paralyzing set-piece battle that, at best, could produce a Pyrrhic victory but at the same time was bound to sap the army's strength. This would force Sixth Army to weaken its defenses in other key sectors by replacing veteran German troops with inexperienced Italian and Romanian troops. The brutal, repetitive offensives by Eremenko's northern group in the Kotluban' region disrupted Paulus's plan for capturing Stalingrad quickly and bloodlessly by depriving him of his planned northern pincer—XIV Panzer Corps. Eremenko did enough damage to VIII Army Corps that Paulus was left with no choice but to divert precious forces earmarked for the battle in Stalingrad (113th Infantry Division) to bolster the defenses on his northern flank. The Kotluban' offensives also left another of Paulus's infantry divisions (76th) essentially hors de combat.

Once locked in the deadly spiral inside the city, Sixth Army's shock groups suffered so many casualties that Paulus was forced to send a steady stream of fresh divisions into the Soviet meat grinder, also at the expense of the defenses on Army Group B's left wing. All the while, the armored strength of Paulus's army—the motive force that had propelled it to Stalingrad in the first place—dwindled dramatically, once again raising the specter of catastrophic defeat when and if the Red Army learned to employ effectively its seemingly endless supply of tanks and tank crews. Sixth Army's readiness report on the condition of its infantry and pioneer battalions revealed the extent of the damage that the urban fighting was having on his army (see Table 25).

As the figure indicates, after two weeks of heavy fighting and the withdrawal of 14th Panzer Division from the struggle, Sixth Army and Fourth Panzer Army no longer fielded any infantry battalions rated "strong," and the number of battalions rated "medium strong" decreased from 25 to 6. In addition, the number of battalions rated either "weak" or "exhausted" increased from 13 and 0 to 23 and 11, respectively. This meant that during this period the overall combat rating of the two armies decreased from between "medium strong" and "average" to "weak."

Facing these grim prospects but not yet fully aware of the ultimate consequences, Paulus late on 26 September prepared his shock groups for their final assaults to capture the remainder of Stalingrad city—the northern factory district. On the other side of the hill, Chuikov's 62nd Army prepared to continue its deadly but vital work in the ruins of Stalingrad's factories and workers' villages.

Table 25. The Combat Rating of Infantry and Pioneer Battalions Subordinate to Sixth Army and Fourth Panzer Armies' Divisions Fighting in Stalingrad, 14–26 September 1942

	14 September	26 September
XIV PANZER CORPS		
3rd Motorized Division		
(5 infantry battalion)	2 medium strong, 2 average, and 1 weak	1 medium strong, 3 average, and 1 weak
(1 pioneer battalion)	weak	strong
60th Motorized Division		
(7 infantry battalions)	1 medium strong and 6 average	6 average and 1 weak
(1 pioneer battalion)	average	weak
16th Panzer Division		
(5 infantry battalions)	3 medium strong and 2 average	3 medium strong and 2 average
(1 pioneer battalion)	average	average
LI ARMY CORPS		
71st Infantry Division		
(8–7 infantry battalions)	8 weak	4 weak and 3 exhausted
(1 pioneer battalion)	average	average
295th Infantry Division		
(7 infantry battalions)	2 medium strong, 3 average, and 2 weak	2 average, 4 weak, and 1 exhausted
(1 pioneer battalion)	average	average
389th Infantry Division		
(6 infantry battalions)	1 medium strong, 3 average, and 2 weak	2 average and 4 weak
(1 pioneer battalion)	average	weak
XXXXVIII PANZER CORPS		
24th Panzer Division		
(4 infantry battalions)	2 medium strong and and 2 average	2 medium strong and 2 average
(1 pioneer battalion)	average	average
14th Panzer Division		
(4 infantry battalions)	4 medium strong	**(not in the city fighting)**
(1 pioneer battalion)	average	
29th Motorized Division		
(6 infantry battalions)	3 medium strong and 3 average	3 medium strong and 3 average
(1 pioneer battalion)	strong	strong
94th Infantry Division		
(7 infantry battalions)	7 medium strong	7 medium strong
(1 pioneer battalion)	average	average

Table 25. (continued)

	14 September	26 September
Totals:		
59–54 infantry battalions	25 medium strong, 21 average, and 13 weak	16 medium strong, 20 average, 14 weak, and 4 exhausted
10–9 pioneer battalions	1 strong, 8 average, and 1 weak	2 strong, 5 average, and 2 weak

Source: Florian *Freiherr* von und zu Aufsess, "Betr.: Zustand der Divisionen, Armee – Oberkommando 6, Abt. Ia, A. H. Qu., den 14 September 42, 12.35 Uhr," and "Betr.: Zustand der Divisionen, Armee – Oberkommando 6, Abt. Ia, A. H. Qu., den 26 September 42," in *Die Anlagenbander zu den Kriegstagebuchern der 6. Armee vom 14.09.1942 bis 24.11.1942, Band I* (Schwabach: January 2006), 12–13 and 59–62.

The Initial Assault on the Workers' Villages and Reduction of the Orlovka Salient, 27 September–3 October 1942

PAULUS'S OFFENSIVE PLAN

By nightfall on 26 September, Paulus concluded that the battle in central and southern Stalingrad was just about over. In central Stalingrad, 194th, 191st, and 211th Regiments of LI Corps' 71st Infantry Division had confined 62nd Army's 13th Guards Rifle Division, now reinforced by the newly arrived 193rd Rifle Division's 685th Regiment, into a narrow corridor one to three blocks deep stretching along the western bank of the Volga River from Krutoi Ravine southward to the base of Kievskaia Street (see Map 36). In the southern part of the city, XXXXVIII Panzer Corps' 94th Infantry Division, assisted by 29th Motorized Division on its right, had pressed the shattered remnants of 62nd Army's 42nd and 92nd Rifle Brigades, together with other decimated Soviet units (244th, 35th Guards and 131st Rifle Divisions, 10th Rifle and 133rd Tank Brigades, and 271st NKVD Rifle Regiment), back toward the western bank of the Volga River. These units were hemmed in north and south of the mouth of the Tsaritsa River, where Chuikov hoped to withdraw them to the eastern bank. With their task almost complete, the grenadiers of Pfeiffer's 94th Infantry Division were preparing to withdraw from the ruins to lick their wounds and prepare for what they hoped would be more decisive action to the north.[1]

North of Stalingrad's center, however, Seydlitz's assaults had faltered well short of their objectives. By late on 26 September, 389th Infantry Division was virtually marking time in front of the makeshift Soviet defenses west and southwest of Orlovka and east of Gorodishche. On Jänecke's right, the three regiments of 295th Infantry Division, now reinforced by half of 24th Panzer Division, had made little headway against the defenses of 23rd Tank Corps and 95th and 284th Rifle Divisions. These Soviet defenses extended from the vicinities of Hills 101.4 and 112.0, west of Krasnyi Oktiabr' village, and then southward along the western and southern slopes of Mamaev Kurgan, to the middle and lower reaches of the Dolgii and Krutoi Ravines. Although Wuthmann's infantry was within a stone's throw of the Volga River in the vicinity of the two ravines, vicious Soviet counterattacks had expelled his forces from most of the burial mound's slopes and nearly to Kolodeznaia Street.

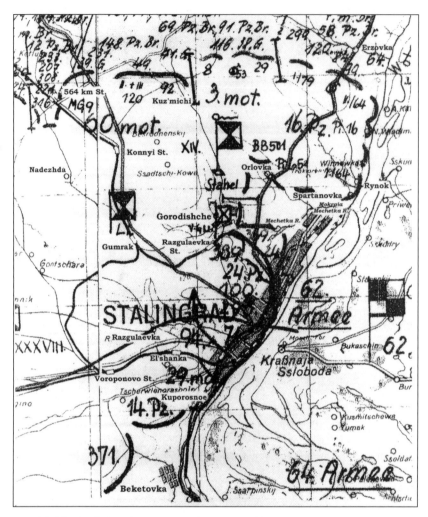

Map 36. The Sixth Army's situation, 27–28 September 1942

Sixth Army did not yet control the city's entire center because of the worn-down state of his army's 295th, 71st, and 94th Infantry Divisions. Still, Paulus believed the price in casualties to achieve complete control of this area simply not worth the effort. Instead, he decided to reorient his army's main forces toward Stalingrad's northern factory district by reinforcing its main shock group, 389th and 295th Infantry Divisions of Seydlitz's LI Corps, with the full-strength 24th Panzer Division and the fresh 100th Jäger Division. He also wanted to shift the shock group's axis of advance northeastward into the very heart of the city's factory district. First, however, Seydlitz's forces had to contend with Chuikov's troops defending the factory workers' villages, a series of settlements lodged in the hills west of the factories proper, as well as the persistent Orlovka salient farther north, which jutted sharply northwestward at the boundary between LI Army and XIV Panzer Corps.

Acknowledging the damage done to his army during its assaults against the central and southern sections of the city, Paulus systematically reconfigured his army and reinforced Seydlitz's LI Corps beginning on 25 September and accelerating the next day. His purpose was to form two shock groups, which together would conduct the army's new main attack—a culminating assault to penetrate and seize the city's factory district. Specifically, Seydlitz's two shock groups would attack northeastward through Krasnyi Oktiabr' village, assault the Soviet defenses on Mamaev Kurgan, and advance eastward along the Dolgii and Krutoi Ravines to reach the Volga River. Farther south, 94th and 71st Infantry Divisions, now fighting under XXXXVIII Panzer Corps' control, were to conduct a supporting attack to eliminate the last vestiges of Soviet resistance in Stalingrad's center city.

The stronger of Seydlitz's two shock groups, which was to operate on LI Corps' left wing, consisted of nine regiments: the 545th, 546th, and 544th of Jänecke's 398th Infantry Division; 24th Panzer and 26th and 21st Panzer Grenadier of Lenski's 24th Panzer Division; and 54th and 227th Jäger Regiments and the Croat 369th Infantry Regiment of Sanne's 100th Jäger Division. With its armored spearhead of about 100 tanks and assault guns concentrated west of Hill 112.0 and the western outskirts of Krasnyi Oktiabr' village, the shock group's jumping-off positions extended from the vicinity of Razgulaevka Station, southeast of Gorodishche, southward to the southern slope of Mamaev Kurgan. This group was to penetrate deep into the workers' villages, clear Soviet forces from Mamaev Kurgan, and, if possible, begin capturing the factories as well. To the south, a second and far smaller shock group, consisting of 516th, 518th, and 517th Regiments of Wuthmann's 295th Infantry Division and 194th Regiment of Hartmann's 71st Infantry Division, was to assault eastward in the sector extending southward from the southern base of Mamaev Kurgan across the middle parts of the Dolgii and Krutoi Ravines to reach the western bank of the Volga River. Once along the Volga, the 295th was to wheel northward and clear Soviet forces from the so-called Tennis Racket, the area of railroad loop east of Mamaev Kurgan, while 71st Division's regiment attacked southward to the Krutoi Ravine to outflank Soviet forces fighting in the center city. If successful, this thrust could cut off Soviet forces defending the center city from those in the factory district to the north and permit an assault on the factory district from the south.

Deployed in the northern shock group's center as its steel tip, 24th Panzer Division's mission was:

Destruction of the enemy south of and on the railway, gaining of Hill 107.5, as well as clearing out city sectors lying northeast and north of there. If the situation allows it, gain the narrows on the northwest edge of the gully in [grid] square 74c and hold it open for a further attack.

On the right, 100th Jäger Division will follow, staggered, and win the southeast part of Krasnyi Oktiabr'. To the left is 389th Infantry Division as flank protection, with a strong right wing, to later roll up the enemy positions from the west.[2]

Lenski's first objective, Hill 107.5, which was roughly 4 kilometers to his front, dominated the open area between upper Krasnyi Oktiabr' village (also called Ovrashnaia) and the section of lower Krasnyi Oktiabr' village west of the main north-south railroad line and Krasnyi Oktiabr' Factory. His final objective was located in the open area between the built-up area known as the Commune House and the northern edge of Krasnyi Oktiabr' village. This gully, located in grid square 74c (a grid square measured 1 kilometer by 1 kilometer), was west of the main railroad line and the northern end of the Krasnyi Oktiabr' village, 2.2 kilometers north of Hill 107.5, and 600 meters south of the Silikat Factory. Prior to assaulting Stalingrad, the Germans had prepared maps of the city, assigning every grid square a specific number (from south to north and west to east) and the four quarter-sections in each grid square the letter *a*, *b*, *c*, or *d* (from west to east across the top and then the bottom) (see Map 37). These designations eased the task of assigning missions and objectives to units fighting in urban terrain, particularly if it was rubbled, as was the case at Stalingrad.

On 24th Panzer Division's left, 389th Infantry Division, with its three regiments abreast, was to attack eastward from the region east and southeast of Gorodishche, cross the main railroad line, advance eastward to the Vishnevaia *Balka*, and then wheel northeastward along both banks of the *balka* to outflank the workers' villages from the west. On 24th Panzer's right, 100th Jäger Division, with its 54th and 227th Regiments forward, would attempt to smash the Soviets' defenses on and northwest of Mamaev Kurgan, capture the burial mound, and then advance northward west of the railroad line and Tennis Racket to cross the Bannyi Ravine and seize the lower section of the Krasnyi Oktiabr' workers' village and Krasnyi Oktiabr' Factory. Once they successfully fulfilled their missions, all three divisions would then be ideally positioned to assault and capture the Tractor, Barrikady, and Krasnyi Oktiabr' Factories from the south and west.[3]

Issued at 1830 hours on 26 September, 24th Panzer Division's order read:

The Division will advance at X-hour with the unarmored assault group under *Oberst* [Colonel] *Reichsfreiherr* von Edelsheim and, at the same

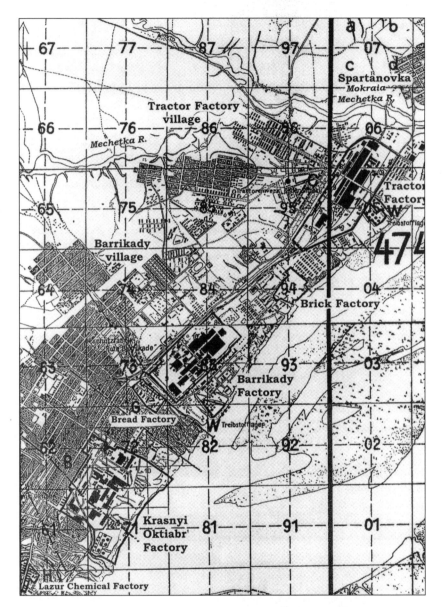

Map 37. German grid square designations in Stalingrad's factory district

time, with the armored assault group on the left under the command of Major von Winterfeld and destroy the enemy south of and on the railway line. Then, after crossing the railway in a totally concentrated mass, gain Hill 107.5 under cover of the east flank and take the city's sectors lying east, northeast and north of there (grid squares 62a, 63c, 63a, 54d [Krasnyi Oktiabr' village west of the railroad]), and clean these out.

With the *Schwerpunkt* [point of main attack] on the right, [*Kampfgruppe* Edelsheim] will break through the enemy positions in the bush terrain and, as 1st attack objective, win the railway line and the 2nd attack objective of Ovrashnaia utilizing the advance of *Gruppe* Winterfeld. The 3rd objective depends upon the situation: advance to Hill 107.5 with the bulk of the group under cover of the east flank or, if Hill 107.5 is already solidly in the hands of *Gruppe* Winterfeld, penetrate into the ordered city sectors (grid squares 62a, 63c, 63a, 54d) as the 3rd objective. These sectors will be cleared of enemy.

[*Gruppe* Winterfeld will] destroy the enemy in the forest south of the railway line and by that, open the way for *Gruppe* Edelsheim to the railway line. As 1st attack objective, win the railway line east of Point 735, whereupon a panzer schwadron will veer off to the east and from this point in time will be subordinated to *Gruppe* Edelsheim. Then, if possible, thrust through Ovrashnaia to Hill 107.5, the 2nd attack objective. The hill is to be taken, the enemy there destroyed. If the situation is favorable, advance up to the group of houses north of Hill 107.5 (63b, 63a) and later, if it comes to question, up to the narrows on the north-west end of the gully in 74c.[4]

In addition, a third and smaller *kampfgruppe*, commanded by Colonel Hellermann and consisting of his 21st Panzer Grenadier Regiment, was to advance due north past the base of Mamaev Kurgan's western slope to reach Bannyi Ravine. Its mission was to protect the panzer division's right flank and maintain contact with 100th Jäger Division on the right.

Paulus allocated much of VIII Air Corps' combat aircraft and most of his army's artillery in support of Seydlitz's advance. This amounted to a total of 17 artillery batteries in support of Lenski's 24th Panzer Division. The artillery was to conduct 12 minutes of preparatory fire before the ground assault and then shift its fires as the panzers and panzer-grenadiers advanced into the depths of the Soviet defenses.[5]

As LI Corps' stronger northern shock group drove into the workers' villages, its smaller southern group, consisting of 295th Infantry Division's three weak regiments reinforced by assault guns and engineers and the equally weak 194th Regiment on 71st Infantry Division's left wing, was to renew its attacks against Soviet defenses between the southern base of Mamaev

Kurgan and the Dolgii and Krutoi Ravines. As Seydlitz's assault progressed, 94th Infantry Division's 276th Regiment, being shifted northward from the southern section of the city, was to reinforce the northern shock group's assaults.[6]

While LI Corps' two shock groups were penetrating into the workers' villages and capturing Mamaev Kurgan and the twin ravines to the south, Hube's XIV Panzer Corps was to attack the Soviet-occupied salient around Orlovka from the west, north, and east. Hube was to conduct his assault with battalion- and company-size *kampfgruppen* formed by 60th Motorized and 16th Panzer Divisions. Since Hube's forces alone were too weak to crush the salient, Paulus intended to provide him with reinforcements. First, the Sixth Army commander directed 94th Infantry Division, once it completed clearing operations in southern Stalingrad, to transfer its 267th and 274th Regiments northward so they could reinforce Hube's thrust. Second, Paulus ordered 389th Infantry Division to support Hube's assaults on Orlovka by orienting the advance of its 545th and 546th Regiments northeastward and eastward to cut off the salient at its base.

Hube's attack plan called for battalion-size *kampfgruppen* from 16th Panzer Division's panzer-grenadier regiments, supported by the attached 654th Engineer and 501st Artillery Battalions, to assault the salient from the east. At the same time, company-size *kampfgruppen* from 60th Motorized Division's 160th Motorcycle Battalion were to advance on Orlovka from the north, and battalion-size *kampfgruppen* formed from 94th Infantry Division's 267th and 274th Regiments were to attack from the west. Group Stahel's *Luftwaffe* ground units were to protect the forward deployment of 94th Infantry Division's two regiments into their jumping-off positions and then cover their flanks and rear as they launched their assaults. In addition, farther south, 389th Infantry Division's 545th and 546th Regiments, also organized into battalion-size *kampfgruppen* deployed northeast of Gorodishche, were to assault northeastward and eastward north of the Mechetka River to seize Hills 109.4 and 97.7, collapse the Soviet defenses along the salient's southwestern flank, and reach the Orlovka River, thereby cutting off the salient at its base.

Despite Hube's careful planning, heavy fighting elsewhere along the front hindered his attack preparations in two important respects. First, the ongoing heavy Soviet assaults against XIV Panzer Corps' defenses in the Kotluban', Kuz'michi, and Erzovka regions prevented Hube from concentrating sufficient forces north of Orlovka to overcome the Soviets' defenses and capture Orlovka in a single, rapid, and decisive thrust.[7] Second, the stronger-than-expected Soviet resistance in the southern section of Stalingrad city delayed the redeployment of 94th Infantry Division northward to reinforce his shock group for several days. Thus, what was planned as a two-day assault to eliminate an irksome salient defended by pitifully weak and utterly fragmented Soviet forces ultimately evolved into a prolonged and bloody weeklong struggle.

Finally, in accordance with Hitler's wishes, once the southern section of Stalingrad city fell into Fourth Panzer Army's hands, Hoth was to withdraw his two mobile divisions from their forward positions—Fremerey's 29th Motorized from southern Stalingrad and Heim's 14th Panzer from the approaches to Beketovka—rest and refit them for about a week, and then unleash them on their long-anticipated thrust to capture Astrakhan' on the lower Volga River.

CHUIKOV'S COUNTERATTACK PLAN

As Paulus's forces prepared for their new assault, 62nd Army's intelligence organs detected the Germans' preparations, concluding that a new wave of German attacks was imminent. Reacting quickly, Chuikov at 2300 hours on 25 September amended the attack orders he had issued days before, ordering 95th and 284th Rifle Divisions to play a more prominent role in his counterattacks. He prefaced his order with a warning: "The enemy, having concentrated up to one infantry division in the Gorodishche and Aleksandrovka region, is preparing an attack in the general direction of Gorodishche, Barrikady." Chuikov ordered 62nd Army "to conduct street fighting to destroy the enemy in the city of Stalingrad with part of its forces, while continuing to hold to the line it occupies."[8] Chuikov then assigned his subordinate units their specific missions:

1. **112th RD** [Ermolkin], with one company of 50mm mortars attached and with 186th Antitank Regiment in support, will occupy and consolidate a second defensive line along the Vishnevaia *Balka* [west of Krasnyi Oktiabr' village] by 0400 hours on 26 September 1942.

[The boundary] on the right—the northwestern corner of the gardens 1 kilometer west of Dizel'naia and the bridge across the Mechetka River, 660 meters north of Barrikady village. [The boundary] on the left—the eastern bank of Vishnevaia *Balka* as far as the railway line and the railroad line from Vishnevaia *Balka* to the southeastern outskirts of Krasnyi Oktiabr' village.

2. Missions:

a) Prevent the enemy from reaching the Barrikady village and Krasnyi Oktiabr' village region.

b) Prevent any advance by enemy units along the valley of the Mechetka River towards the vicinity of the Tractor Factory village.

3. Prepare three garrisons, each consisting of an automatic weapons platoon and submachine gunners, for the conduct of the fighting in the villages. Prepare and defend the buildings of School No. 32 and the stone building on Zherdevskaia Street—Strong point No. 3—with one platoon.

Prepare and defend Strong point no. 10, the buildings of the nursery buildings and the store (Kolpakovskaia [Kolpak] Street in the Barrikady village) with the second platoon.

Prepare and defend Strong point No. 2—the buildings of School No. 20 and the bathhouse (at the crossroads of Kazach'ia [Kazakh] and Dublinskaia [Dublin] Streets) with the third platoon.

The forward edge will be along the eastern side of the Vishnevaia *Balka*. Outfit the Mechetka River and railroad line sector as an antitank line, equipping it with a continuous antitank minefield, and construct escarpments and counter-escarpments in the most threatened sectors.

112th RD's CP—the ravine near the crossroads of Kazach'ia and Dublinskaia Streets.

4. The commander of **284th RD** [Batiuk]—will take over the defensive sector along the northern bank of Dolgii Ravine from 112th RD and will prepare it as an antitank defensive line, allocating no fewer than two battalions for its reliable defense. The division will consolidate firmly along the Sovnarkomovskaia [Sovnarkom] and Khoperskaia [Khoper] Streets line and, farther, along the Krutoi Ravine to the Volga with its remaining forces.

Under no circumstances will the enemy be permitted to reach Artilleriiskaia [Artillery] Street and the bank of the Volga. Be prepared to continue to carry out the task of clearing the city.

5. **95th RD** [Gorishnyi]—will consolidate firmly along the southern edge of the grove (along Kolodeznaia [Kolodez] Street) and prepare a strong point with all-around defenses on the slopes of Hill 102.0 itself with a garrison of one rifle battalion. Under no circumstances allow the enemy to seize the stronghold on Hill 102.0. Be prepared to continue to carry out the task of clearing the city.

5. **13th GRD** [Rodimtsev]—will firmly defend the region of the central landing stage while continuing to destroy the enemy in the center of the city.

6. All of the forces of the Army will be prepared to repel possible enemy attacks, particularly along the Gorodishche and Barrikady axis, by dawn on 26 September 1942.

Chuikov, Gurov, Krylov[9]

The minuscule scale of the fighting inside the city is reflected by the fact that Chuikov's order for this realignment specified individual positions and missions for platoons, units that were five levels below the field army headquarters. In particular, he took great care to organize new defenses in depth in the northern and central sectors of the city. In the north, he reinforced the brigades of Popov's 23rd Tank Corps, which were in contact with LI Corps' 389th Infantry and 24th Panzer Divisions, with Ermolkin's 112th Rifle Division deployed along the eastern edge of the Vishnevaia *Balka*. In the center, he strengthened Gorishnyi's 95th Rifle Division on Mamaev Kurgan, which faced 295th Infantry Division and the newly arrived 100th Jäger Division, with 1045th Regiment of Batiuk's 284th Rifle Division in reserve positions near and in the Tennis Racket. Finally, to the south he solidified his army's hold on the Dolgii and Krutoi Ravines by assigning them to 1043rd and 1047th Regiments of Batiuk's 284th Rifle Division. On the mound itself, the most dominant piece of terrain in the region, Gorishnyi's 95th Rifle Division was defending the base of the burial mound's southern and southwestern slopes, with its 90th, 161st, and 241st Regiments deployed from left to right, the division's training battalion protecting its left flank along the railroad, and the machine-gun battalion dug in to reserve positions on the mound's crest. In the moonscape of gullies, shell craters, and ruined buildings, the defenders constructed a series of camouflaged strongpoints and ambushes to defeat the Germans.

Late on 25 September, about 36 hours before Chuikov's planned counterattacks and Seydlitz's renewed offensive, 62nd Army prepared a lengthy report that, in describing its combat disposition in exquisite detail, also underscored the fragmented and tenuous nature of the army's defenses:

The units of the army occupied the following positions by the morning of 25 September.

Stalingrad's **Northern Sector of Defense**—Group Gorokhov—consisting of 124th, 149th RBs and the 282nd RR is continuing to defend its occupied positions.

124th RB is defending the Rynok, Marker +35.0, and Spartanovka line.

149th RB is [defending] along the (incl.) Spartanovka, separate peasant hut southeast of Marker 93.2, Marker 93.2, and the grove to the southeast line.

282nd RR NKVD is defending the sector (incl.) Marker 93.2, the two southern burial mounds on Hill 135.4, and Marker 85.1.

115th RB, with 893rd RR (196th RD) and 2nd MRB is continuing to defend its previously occupied positions.

1st Bn, 115th RB is defending the region (incl.) of the two burial mounds on Hill 135.4, (incl.) Hill 144.4, and the northeastern outskirts of Orlovka.

3rd Bn, 115th RB is defending the Hill 144.4, southern slope of Hill 147.6, and the hollow sector.

893rd RR (196th RD) is defending the (incl.) northern spur of the hollow, the hollow southwest of Hill 147.6, (incl.) Marker 108.8, (incl.), and Marker 129.1 sector.

2nd MRB is defending the (incl.) Marker 120.5 and (incl.) the burial mound on Hill 129.1 sector.

2nd Bn, 115th RB is defending the southwestern slope of Hill 129.1, Hill 109.4, and Hill 108.8 line.

227th Sep. MG-Arty Bn is defending the Hill 109.4 and slope to the south line.

4th Bn, 115th RB is in the group's second echelon.

23rd TC is occupying a defense along the bridge 1.5 kilometers west of Hill 35.8, Hill 98.9, the southeastern slope of Hill 126.3, and the southern edge of Ovrazhnaia grove line.

6th Gds. TB is [deployed] along the bridge 1.5 kilometers west of Hill 35.8, Hill 98.0, and (incl.) the Viaduct line. It has 21 T-34 tanks, of which 5 tanks and 9th MRB—with 2 tanks, are in the army commander's reserve, and 20 T-70 tanks operational.

189th TB is defending the line along the western side of the Viaduct. It has 7 T-34 tanks and 2 T-70 tanks operational.

38th MRB is defending the northwestern edge of the Fruit Garden and the northern edge of the Ovrazhnaia grove line. It has 4 120mm mortars and 8 82mm mortars.

9th MRB is defending the southeastern slope of Hill 126.7 line. It has 12 76mm guns and 11 82mm mortars.

269th RR NKVD is defending with its first battalion at the junction of 38th and 9th MRBs and its second battalion along (incl.) the southeastern slope of Hill 126.3 and (incl.) the ravine on the southern edge of Ovrazhnaia grove. Operational: 3 45mm guns, 3 82mm mortars, and 8 antitank rifles.

137th TB is defending the line along the northern bank of the southern edge of Ovrazhnaia grove. It has 1 T-34 and 10 T-60 tanks.

27th TB is defending the line along the western edge of the Ovrazhnaia grove with 1 T-34 and 1 T-60 tank operational. Six T-34 tanks and 5 T-60 tanks are [dug in] in the defense.

95th RD continued to attack the defending enemy with its left wing and reached [the following] positions by day's end on 24 September:

241st RR is along the northern bank of the Dolgii Ravine (northern spur).

161st RR captured the northern bank of the ravine in the sector north of Belomorskaia Street.

90th RR is fighting along the southern bank of the hollow, 500 meters south of Hill 102.0 with its 2nd and 3rd Battalions. The 1st Bn, 90th, is approaching to northern bank of the ravine north of Donetskaia Street.

The 499th ATR and two batteries of 141st MR [mortar regiment] are supporting.

112th RD is occupying defenses along [the following] line:

416th RR is along the separate hut southeast of Hill 102.2 and (incl.) the southern siding of the railroad line.

385th RR is along the southern siding of the railroad line and farther along the northern bank of Dolgii Ravine to Divizionnaia Street.

524th RR is along the northern bank of Dolgii Ravine and along the line of the railroad to the bank of the Volga River.

284th RD is continuing attacks against the defending enemy. The division was fighting along [the following] line:

1047th RR is along the northern bank of Krutoi Ravine, with its right flank anchored on the line of the railroad to Artemovskaia Street.

1043rd RR is fighting along the (incl.) Artemovskaia Street line, with its left flank at the line of the railroad to the northern bank of the ravine (east of Nekrasovskaia Street).

1045th RR is in the army's reserve.

13th Gds. RD is fighting in the center of the city.

34th Gds. RR is along the line west of 2nd Naberezhnaia [Street] from Nekrasovskaia [Street] to Tambovskaia Street, with its front toward the west.

2nd Bn, 42nd Gds. RR is along the line of the northern part of Krasnozavodskaia Street, with its front toward the west.

3rd Bn, 42nd Gds. RR is fighting along the line of Solnechnaia Street from the corner of Penzenskaia [Street], including the corner (western) of Smolenskaia [Street], with its front toward the north.

3rd Bn, 39th Gds. RR is defending the line of the three cut off blocks on Respublikanskaia Street.

1st Bn, 39th Gds. RR and 2nd Bn. 39th Gds. RR are defending the southern part of Penzenskaia Street and southern part of Krasnozavodskaia Street line and, farther to the south, to the bank of the Volga at the warehouses 600 meters northeast of the landing stage.

1st Bn, 42nd Gds. RR is fighting along the line of Gogolia Street.

272nd RR NKVD is defending the line of the city garden.

42nd RB is occupying defenses along the northern bank of the Tsaritsa River in the vicinity of Pushkinskaia Street. [Actually, it was already withdrawing to the Volga under 92nd Brigade's control].

92nd RB is defending south of the Tsaritsa River and along Kum Street, operating with its right flank on the Volga River and its left on the Tsaritsa River at Kavkaz Street. [It, too, was already withdrawing to the Volga].[10]

Despite Chuikov's quick reaction to the changing conditions, 295th Infantry Division's successful attacks against Mamaev Kurgan on 26

September, which recaptured part of the mound's southern slope, disrupted the preparations for 62nd Army's counterattacks and once again forced Chuikov to alter his plan. After his army's intelligence department generated a new report indicating that German forces were massing to mount a concerted assault on the workers' villages, Chuikov, at 1940 hours on 26 September, issued revised counterattack orders, this time designed to preempt the German assaults and gain additional room to maneuver by counterattacking with the remaining tanks in Popov's already decimated 23rd Tank Corps:

> 3. **23rd TC** [Popov] will attack in the direction of Hill 112.0 and Rzhevskaia [Rzhev] Street with the forces of 137th TB and 269th RR NKVD. The immediate mission is to capture the bank between Rzhevskaia and Bata-khovskaia Streets. Subsequently, capture the region of the cemetery south of Rzhevskaia Street.
>
> The boundary on the left is the junction of the railroad and the dirt road 500 meters south of Bannyi Ravine and the separate farm 200 meters west of Kashirskaia [Kashira], Irtyshskaia [Irtyshsk], and Chervlennaia Streets. The 397th Antitank Artillery Regiment will support.
>
> 4. **95th RD** [Gorishnyi] will attack toward Mamaev Kurgan and the city park (Chapaevskaia [Chapaev] and Donetskaia [Donetsk] Streets). The immediate mission is to capture the southern spur of the Dolgii Ravine and, subsequently, reach the region of the city park.
>
> The boundary on the left is the separate hut 400 meters south of Hill 102.0 and Sovnarkomovskaia Street. The 651st Antitank Artillery Regiment and 101st Mortar Regiment will support.
>
> 5. **284th RD** [Batiuk] will attack toward Khoperskaia [Khoper] Street, Karabovicha Street, and the railroad station with its right wing. Its immediate mission is to capture the line of the Krutoi Ravine and, subsequently, the region of the railroad station.
>
> The boundary on the left is the Volga.
>
> The 2nd Battery, 457th Gun Artillery Regiment, will support.
>
> 6. **13th Gds. RD** [Rodimtsev] will continue to carry out its previously assigned mission to destroy the enemy in the center of the city. Its immediate mission is to capture the region of the central landing stage and, subsequently, to clear the region as far as the railway station.
>
> 7. The chief of the Army's artillery will employ all of the Army's artillery and rocket artillery regiments for support of the offensive by 95th RD.
>
> Missions:
>
> a) Destroy the enemy's pill-boxes on the southern slope of Hill 102.0;
>
> b) Suppress the enemy's mortar batteries at the upper reaches of the Dolgii Ravine and in the vicinity of the cemetery; and

c) Prevent the approach of reserves from the northwest along the Gumrak-Stalingrad road.

8. The artillery preparation will begin at 0500 hours on 27 September 1942. The infantry attack will be at 0600 hours on 27 September 1942.

9. I again warn the commanders of all units and formations not to carry out operations or battles with whole units like companies and battalions. Organize the offensive primarily on the basis of small groups, with submachine guns, hand-grenades, bottles of incendiary mixture, and anti-tank rifles. Use regimental and battalion artillery to support the attacking groups by firing point-blank into windows, embrasures, and garrets.

Chuikov, Gurov, Krylov[11]

This order required the left wing of Popov's 23rd Tank Corps, now backed up by Ermolkin's 112th Rifle Division, which had just completed its movement from south of Mamaev Kurgan northward to Vishnevaia *Balka*, to assault the forward defenses of Lenski's 24th Panzer Division west of the burial mound. At the same time, Gorishnyi's 95th Rifle Division was to strike the left wing and center of Wuthmann's 295th Infantry Division in the sector from the mound itself southward to the upper reaches of Dolgii Ravine, and Batiuk's 284th Rifle Division was to attack the right wing of Wuthmann's division along the lower reaches of the Dolgii and Krutoi Ravines. When he issued his order, however, Chuikov did not realize that Sanne's 100th Jäger Division was in the process of relieving 24th Panzer and 295th Divisions' forces west and southwest of Mamaev Kurgan. Therefore, when it launched early the next morning, Chuikov's counterattack would become virtually suicidal.

Chuikov dispatched warning orders about the impending counterattack to all participating forces 24 hours before he issued his attack order. But because his forces ran straight into the teeth of the forces Paulus was assembling to conduct his new thrust, 62nd Army's counterattack faltered minutes after it began.

THE INITIAL GERMAN ASSAULT ON THE WORKERS' (FACTORY) VILLAGES, 27–28 SEPTEMBER

27 September

Chuikov's assault groups began the counterattack at 0600 hours on 27 September after firing a one-hour artillery preparation with 220 guns and mortars (see Map 38).

However, before the attacking troops could record any appreciable gains, in Chuikov's words, "At 0800 hours hundreds of dive-bombers swooped on

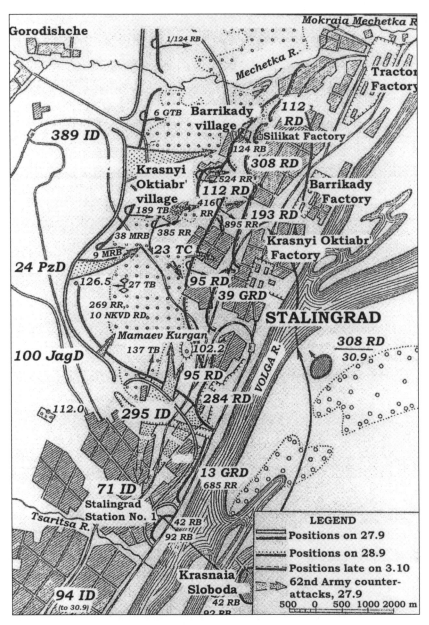

Map 38. The battle for Krasnyi Oktiabr' and Barrikady villages, 27 September–3
October 1942

our formations," forcing the attacking troops "to take cover."[12] The intense German aerial bombardment "utterly destroyed" the strongpoint organized by Gorishnyi's 95th Rifle Division on the crest of Mamaev Kurgan, disrupted 95th Division's and 23rd Tank Corps' counterattack, and subjected Chuikov's command post to constant bombardment, setting fire to the oil tanks in the nearby Oil Syndicate. From 24th Panzer Division's vantage point:

> The Russians attacked with 137th Tank Brigade and 9th Motorized Brigade on and eastward of the airfield at 0600 hours, deploying themselves on a broad front to occupy Hill 102.0. . . . The preparatory fire crushed the attacking Russians. . . . German artillery smothered the front-line with obliterating fire, scything down the attacking Russian troops. . . .
>
> With German shells hammering the Russian lines, the Stukas also swept in, peeling off one by one and with sirens screaming, bombed the forward lines. Ju 88's droned overhead and unloaded their bombs on Hill 197.5. The attack area was enveloped in a murky haze of gunpowder, wafting dust and choking smoke, the flashes of explosions illuminating the fog. To the ground troops ready to push off, it looked and sounded like a storm cloud with cracking thunder and flashing lightning.[13]

After German aircraft pummeled 62nd Army's attacking formations, at 1030 hours the massed infantry of Jänecke's 389th Infantry, Lenski's 24th Panzer, and Sanne's 100th Jäger Divisions began a concerted assault toward the base of the Orlovka salient, Krasnyi Oktiabr' workers' village, and Mamaev Kurgan (see Map 39).

Spearheading 24th Panzer Division's assault, *Kampfgruppe* Edelsheim "had to break obstinate resistance in the brush terrain and eliminate the unpleasant flanking fire from both sides."[14] To do so, Lieutenant Colonel Hellermann's 21st Panzer Regiment assaulted across a Red Army training ground overgrown with low scrub, in the vicinity of the nearby firing range. As vividly described in one account of this action:

> To the right was the rear slope of the menacing Mamayev Kurgan, its bald crown boiling and seething as shell after shell ripped up the ground, sending clods of earth, bits of wood, and smoke high into the air. This was the unpleasant sight to their right as the men plunged into the bushes and pushed toward the shooting range. Encounters came at close range. A burst of fire from the bushes, a man would be hit and then crumble to the ground, his comrades also diving to the ground and opening fire on the suspected area. Grenades were thrown and the bushes stormed, usually ending in the death of the Russians. Then they moved on until fired on again. In this nightmarish terrain, which provided excellent cover and

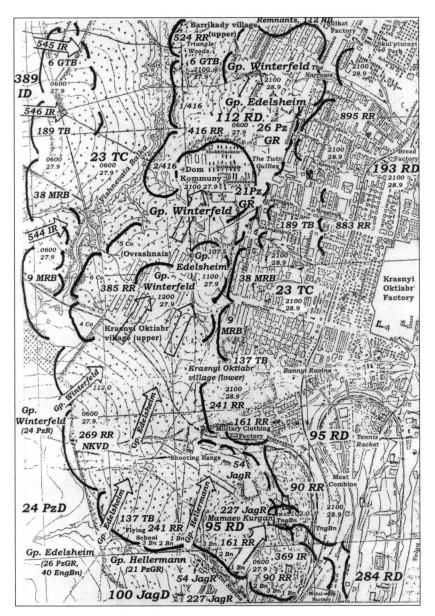

Map 39. LI Army Corps' assault, 27–28 September 1942

camouflage for the Russians, 3. *Schwadron* [3rd Squadron] under *Ober-leutnant* Jurgen Pachnio suffered 11 casualties, including *Oberleutnant* Pachnio himself, who was severely wounded by a shot to the lungs.[15]

Chuikov, too, later recorded the impact of Paulus's assault:

Enemy tanks which had advanced from the vicinity of Gorodishche went straight through the minefields. Infantry crawled forward in waves behind the tanks. Towards noon, telephone communications with the troops began to function erratically, and radio links were put out of action. . . .

Being out of regular communications with our units, we were unable to stay doing nothing at the command post. Although it was no more than a mile and a quarter from the forward positions, we still did not know exactly what was happening at the front and had to go up even closer if we wanted to have any influence on the progress of the fighting.

Taking signal officers with him, Gurov [the army's commissar] went out to the front occupied by the armored formation [23rd Tank Corps], I went to Batiuk's [284th] division, and Krylov [the chief of staff] went to Gorishnyi's [95th] command post.

Even in direct contact with our units, however, we were still unable to clarify the general picture; we were hampered by the constant smoke. When we returned to our command post in the evening, we found that many of our Army staff officers were missing.

Only well into the night were we able to get an exact picture of the position. It was very serious; after crossing the minefield and our forward positions, and in spite of heavy losses, the enemy had in some sectors managed to advance eastward a mile or two.[16]

The OKW's daily report on the evening of 27 September confirmed Chuikov's account of the fighting and validated his own misgivings regarding the ability of his forces to hold on to their shrinking defensive positions:

In the battle for Stalingrad, the buildings on both sides of the Tsaritsa River are being cleared out; therefore, our forces have occupied the entire region of the city to the Volga. North of this region, 100th Jäger and 24th Panzer Divisions have gone over to the attack. Their southern flank is located along the railroad line, and their northern flank—in the outskirts of the city south of the Krasnyi Oktiabr' Factory. To the north of this sector, 398th Infantry Division is clearing out the enemy west of Krasnyi Oktiabr' with its right wing and is attacking this objective. Together with the attacking panzer division [16th], the northern wing of 389th Infantry

Division [545th and 546th] reached the railroad line southeast of Gorodishche. All attacks on the corridor at Kotluban' have been repulsed. In the remaining sectors of the front, local attacks were repelled.[17]

Underscoring the new fixation of Paulus's army on more modest gains, Sixth Army's war diary cryptically reported that the objectives captured included "Height 107.5, the blocks of houses northwest of there, and the gully northwest of Krasnyi Oktiabr' [the workers' settlement]."[18]

Once Chuikov and his staff finally clarified matters late on 27 September, the Red Army General Staff's daily report at 0800 hours the next day reflected Chuikov's perspective on the fighting and the extensive damage done to his defenses:

62nd Army engaged in fierce defensive fighting with enemy forces of up to two infantry divisions and 150 tanks, which attacked eastward and northeastward along the line of the fruit garden 0.5 kilometers west of Krasnyi Oktiabr' village and Dolgii Ravine (up to Sovnarkomovskaia [Sovnarkom] Street on the railroad) at 1030 hours.

6th Gds. TB, with 10–12 tanks, was fighting along the line of the bridge (west of Hill 38.5), Hill 93.3, and the viaduct.

189th TB was fighting in the western part of Vishnevaia *Balka*, with its front toward the south.

112th RD was fighting along the Vishnevaia *Balka* and the grove of trees north of Shakhtinskaia [Shakhtinsk] Street and Narodnaia Street line with two regiments [416th and 385th]. One regiment [524th] of this division has been almost completely destroyed by the enemy.

The remnants of 9th MRB, 137th TB, and 269th RR, 10th RD NKVD, were fighting along the southwestern outskirts of the Krasnyi Oktiabr' village.

A battalion of 1045th RR, 284th RD, was fighting along the line from Narodnaia Street to the railroad line and farther to the east up to Syzranskaia [Syzranka] Street.

95th RD occupied the sector south of the railroad (north of Mamaev Kurgan) and the northeastern slope of Hill 102.0 to the Dolgii Ravine, with its front toward the south and west. 400 soldiers remained in the division.

The units of 284th RD were fighting in the central part of Stalingrad city, while holding on to their previous positions.

13th Gds. RD is fighting unsuccessfully with enemy forces reaching the vicinity of the central landing stage.

92nd and 42nd RBs and the remnants of 270th RR, 10th RD NKVD, after suffering more than 80 percent losses in personnel, abandoned the right bank of the Volga River and were assembling in scattered and unco-ordinated groups on the island opposite the mouth of the Tsaritsa River. The Army's units suffered heavy losses from enemy fire and aircraft. Two tanks each remain in 27th and 189th TBs. The 38th MRB has 120 men, and 112th RD's 416th and 524th RRs have about 300 men. 20 tanks remain in 23rd TC.

Up to two enemy infantry regiments and 50 tanks were destroyed on 27 September.[19]

In this din of heavy fighting, on the left wing of Seydlitz's northern shock group, the infantry and assault guns of Jänecke's 389th Infantry Division advanced eastward across the railroad line and then along and north of Vishnevaia *Balka*. Jänecke advanced with his division's 545th and 546th Regiments on the left and in the center and 544th Regiment on the right. This advance shattered the defenses of 23rd Tank Corps' 6th Guards and 189th Tank and 38th and 9th Motorized Brigades by 1200 hours. All four brigades had to withdraw in considerable disorder and occupy new defensive positions protecting the northern and southern banks of the *balka* and the western approaches to the upper Barrikady village. By day's end, Jänecke's infantry division was employing its 545th and 546th Regiments in the wide swath of open terrain north of the *balka* and its 544th in the vicinity of the *balka* proper. By nightfall on 27 September, the lead elements of Jänecke's division had advanced roughly 3 kilometers, with its right-wing 544th Regiment almost reaching the bridge traversing the *balka*, 1,200 meters west of Hill 107.5 and on the western outskirts of the upper Krasnyi Oktiabr' village (Ovrashnaia). Opposite the division's left wing and center, the remnants of Popov's 6th Guards and 189th Tank Brigades clung desperately to hastily erected defenses protecting the western approaches to the *balka* west of the upper Barrikady village.

In the center of Seydlitz's northern shock group, the two elements making the corps' main attack, 24th Panzer Division's *Kampfgruppen* Edelsheim and Winterfeld, easily repulsed the attempted counterattack by 23rd Tank Corps' 137th Tank and 269th NKVD Rifle Regiment south of Hill 112.0. Crushing both forces, as well as some defending riflemen of 112th Rifle Division's 385th Regiment, which were backing up Popov's forces, the two groups advanced northward in two separate and distinct bounds into and through the upper section of the Krasnyi Oktiabr' village. During the first bound, which ended at roughly 1110 hours, *Kampfgruppe* Edelsheim shattered the defenses of 23rd Tank Corps' 137th Tank Brigade and 269th NKVD Rifle Regiment defending the western end of the shooting range and airstrip northwest of Mamaev Kurgan. Edelsheim crossed the railroad line and captured, first, the open ground between the upper and lower Krasnyi

Oktiabr' villages, and finally, after being reinforced by the tank squadron from *Kampfgruppe* Winterfeld, took his first objective, Hill 107.5. During its advance, Edelsheim's forces also engaged and defeated 23rd Tank Corps 27th Tank Brigade, which had been manning reserve positions in the 269th Regiment's rear. On Edelsheim's left, *Kampfgruppe* Winterfeld sped northward, smashed 23rd Tank Corps' defenses at the boundary between its 269th NKVD Regiment and 9th Motorized Rifle Brigade, and crossed the railroad line. The armored group then seized the western part of the upper Krasnyi Oktiabr' village in a sharp fight with 112th Rifle Division's 385th Regiment, which was supported by several T-34 tanks. Winterfeld then wheeled his forces eastward to reinforce Edelsheim's group on Hill 107.5.

On 24th Panzer Division's right wing, *Kampfgruppe* Hellermann exploited the chaos on Mamaev Kurgan to its right and Edelsheim's dramatic thrust on its left to drive northward toward the eastern edge of the shooting range and airfield. Although it successfully smashed the defenses of 95th Rifle Division's 241st Regiment, the group's numerical weakness prevented it from keeping pace with its partner on the left. By day's end, Hellermann's advance ground to a halt south of the Military Clothing Factory and Bannyi Ravine, where Gorishnyi had created a new defensive strongpoint anchored around the nucleus of 71st Flame Company, a unit from the *Stavka*'s reserve, which Chuikov hastily assigned to his rifle division. Nonetheless, the combined assault by 389th Infantry and 24th Panzer Divisions decimated the brigades of Popov's tank corps and Ermolkin's 112th Rifle Division, in particular its 385th and 524th Regiments.

Thoroughly routed, the defending Soviet forces withdrew eastward toward upper Bannyi Ravine and northeastward through the upper Krasnyi Oktiabr' village, hastily and in considerable disorder. In addition to demolishing 23rd Tank Corps' 137th Tank and 9th Motorized Rifle Brigades and 269th NKVD Regiment and routing 112th Rifle Division's 385th Regiment, the first violent bound by Lenski's panzer division also turned the left flank of 23rd Tank Corps' 38th Motorized Rifle and 189th Tank Brigades, forcing their remnants to refuse their left flank and withdraw into Vishnevaia *Balka*, with their front facing toward the south. Therefore, any further German advance threatened to outflank Popov's forces lodged in the *balka* from both north and south, isolate them from Chuikov's main forces struggling south of the *balka*, and ultimately destroy them piecemeal.

Without waiting for the defending Soviet troops to catch their breath, Lenski's panzer division unleashed its second offensive burst shortly after noon. Leaving *Kampfgruppen* Edelsheim and Hellermann to protect Hill 107.5 and its lengthening right flank as it advanced, Winterfeld's *kampfgruppe* lunged northward another 2.2 kilometers and captured the division's second objective, the built-up area known as Commune House west of the gully on the northern edge of upper Krasnyi Oktiabr' village.[20] This thrust encountered only scattered resistance from the remnants of Popov's shattered tank and motorized rifle brigades and small groups of soldiers from Ermolkin's decimated 112th Rifle Division. By nightfall, therefore, 24th Panzer Division had carved a deep wedge in Chuikov's defenses west of the lower Krasnyi Oktiabr' village and the factory farther east, with its spearhead facing north toward the Barrikady village and its left wing poised on Hill 107.5, in the open ground between the lower and upper Krasnyi Oktiabr' villages.[21] In addition to crushing 62nd Army's defenses west of Krasnyi Oktiabr' village, this bold thrust threatened to isolate the brigades of Popov's 23rd Tank Corps and elements of Ermolkin's 112th Rifle Division along and west of Vishnevaia *Balka*.

From Chuikov's perspective, the only saving grace for Popov's and Ermolkin's forces was that the panzer *kampfgruppe* from Lenski's 24th Panzer Division reportedly had lost more than half its tanks in the fighting. As Chuikov later assessed:

> [The 112th Rifle Division], which had borne the main brunt of the attack, had suffered heavy losses and, at nightfall on 27 September, occupied a front from the bridge over the Mechetka [River], a mile and a half west of the Barrikady settlement, the southwest part of the settlement, and the western outskirts of the Krasnyi Oktiabr' suburb as far as Bannyi Ravine. The Germans had occupied Shakhtinskaia and Zherdevskaia Streets and Hill 107.5.[22]

As the forces on the left wing and in the center of Seydlitz's northern shock group were savaging Chuikov's defenses in Krasnyi Oktiabr' village and north of Mamaev Kurgan, an equally desperate and vicious fight was raging for possession of the burial mound itself and in the sector to the north between it and the shooting range (see Map 39). There, on 24th Panzer Division's right flank, the infantrymen and assault guns of Sanne's 100th Jäger Division exploited the ferocious preliminary artillery and aerial bombardment of the heights, which destroyed 95th Rifle Division's command post and pulverized the defenses of its 241st, 161st, and 90th Regiments deployed on the northern slope of Mamaev Kurgan and to the northwest. Flanked on the left by 24th Panzer's *Kampfgruppe* Hellermann and on the right by Wuthmann's 295th Infantry Division, which was advancing eastward south of Mamaev Kurgan and toward the Dolgii and Krutoi Ravines and the Volga River, Sanne's *jägers* launched a headlong assault against the mound's northern slope and crest.

Attacking with 54th and 227th Jäger Regiments abreast and the Croatian 369th Infantry Regiment in reserve, Sanne's troops managed to clear 95th Rifle Division's 241st and 161st Regiments from the western slope but, at least initially, failed to push forward more than 100 meters up the burial mound's southern slope because of determined resistance offered by Gorishnyi's 90th Regiment. However, intense German artillery fire, coupled with 227th Regiment's vigorous infantry attack in the afternoon, produced mass casualties among Gorishnyi's 161st and 90th Regiments, whose remnants were defending the crest. As the struggle continued unabated throughout the evening, Sanne's *jägers* finally secured the vital crest, although some bypassed Soviet troops continued to hold out for days, dug in along the southern and western slopes.[23] Overnight, still relatively fresh, 100th Jäger Division succeeded in forcing the remnants of 95th Rifle Division's 241st and 161st Regiments to withdraw to new defensive positions south of the Military Clothing Factory, the upper section of Bannyi Ravine, and the burial mound's northern and northwestern slopes. Meanwhile, the rifle division's 90th Regiment, by now bolstered by the division's training battalion, clung resolutely to the eastern slope and the railroad line to the southeast.

As furious fighting raged on the crest and southern and western slopes of the burial mound, on 100th Jäger Division's right wing 369th Croatian Infantry, which Sanne finally committed from his reserve, joined with 516th Regiment on the left wing of Wuthmann's 295th Infantry Division in an assault designed to pierce the defenses of 284th Rifle Division's 1045th Regiment southeast of Mamaev Kurgan, penetrate into the Tennis Racket region, and seize the Meat Combine (slaughterhouse), which was situated just south of the Bannyi Ravine and adjacent to the eastern slope. To the south, 518th and 517th Regiments, in the center and on the right wing of Wuthmann's division, assaulted eastward along Dolgii and Krutoi Ravines in an attempt to crush the defenses of 284th Rifle Division's 1047th and 1043rd Regiments and reach the Volga River. Only stiff and often fanatical resistance by Batiuk's three regiments staved off even greater disaster by preventing 295th Infantry Division from reaching the Volga River and splitting Chuikov's army in half.[24]

While LI Corps' main shock groups pummeled Chuikov's defenses west of the workers' villages and atop and south of Mamaev Kurgan, XXXXVIII Panzer Corps' 71st Infantry Division persisted in its supporting attacks in the city's center. Even though three of Hartmann's seven infantry battalions were now rated "exhausted," his 194th and 191st Regiments renewed their assaults against the defenses of Rodimtsev's 13th Guards Rifle Division and 193rd Rifle Division's reinforcing 685th Regiment in the city's center (see Map 35). On the 71st's right wing, 211th Regiment was now cooperating with 94th Infantry Division's 276th Regiment, which was now operating along the lower reaches of the Tsaritsa River. These two regiments cleared the remnants of 42nd and 92nd Rifle Brigades and other Soviet stragglers from the region north and south of the river's mouth. This produced heavy fighting in several quarters, including 39th Regiment's defense of the House of

Specialists, south of Krasnozavodskaia Street, as well as Pavlov's House. The latter, situated in a vital position adjacent to 9 January Square, was seized, fortified, and stoutly defended by a reconnaissance group from 13th Guards Rifle Division's 42nd Regiment, commanded by Sergeant Iakob F. Pavlov.[25] Pavlov transformed the four-story house into a fortress, manned by 48 men, two heavy and two light machine guns, four antitank rifles, two 50mm mortars, 20 rifles, and eight automatic weapons, which the group successfully defended for 58 days. While the fighting smoldered on in Stalingrad's center city, late in the day General Pfeiffer finally began transferring his 94th Infantry Division's 276th Regiment out of the city's rubble and northward toward Krasnyi Oktiabr' village. There, it was earmarked to provide infantry support for 24th Panzer Division. Soon after, Pfeiffer also began moving 267th and 274th Regiments northward to reinforce XIV Panzer Corps' struggle to reduce the Orlovka salient.

As Pfeiffer deployed his division northward, Paulus directed Hartmann's 71st Infantry Division to assume responsibility for the entire sector along the western bank of the Volga River from Dolgii Ravine southward past the Tsaritsa and El'shanka Rivers and through the suburb of Minina to the northern outskirts of Kuporosnoe. Once he shuffled his regiments to fulfill Paulus's order, Hartmann's 211th Regiment protected the broad sector from the El'shanka River southward to Kuporosnoe, 191st Regiment manned defenses in the sector from the Tsaritsa River southward to the El'shanka River, and 194th Regiment became responsible for controlling the extended sector stretching from the Dolgii Ravine southward to the Tsaritsa River and also for liquidating 13th Guards Rifle Division's bridgehead in the city center. This, too, was an impossible task for a single German regiment, especially since its battalions already rated somewhere between "weak" and "exhausted."

Compounding Hartmann's problems, on 29 and 30 September a fresh Soviet offensive in the lake region south of Stalingrad forced XXXXVIII Panzer Corps to remove its 14th Panzer and 29th Motorized Divisions from reserve assembly areas on the southern flank of Paulus's shock group and to transfer them southward. That day, Southeastern Front's 57th and 51st Armies attacked Romanian forces defending south of Lake Sarpa (see Chapter 5). Thus, in addition to requiring 71st Infantry Division to spread its forces dangerously thin in the central and southern sections of Stalingrad, the departure of the two mobile divisions deprived Paulus of much-needed strength for the final assault on the city's factory district.

As a result of the heavy fighting on 27 September, by nightfall the two shock groups of Seydlitz's LI Corps had forced Chuikov's defending forces back to their second defensive line along the western outskirts of the lower workers' villages, as much as half the distance from the previous front to the Volga. When the fighting died down after nightfall, Seydlitz's forces had already penetrated into the western extremities of Barrikady and Krasnyi Oktiabr' villages and were entrenched on the crest of Mamaev Kurgan. By this time, Chuikov's entire army was compressed into an area less than 20 kilometers long and nowhere more than 2 kilometers in depth, with the bulk of his forces north of Bannyi Ravine (1 kilometer north of Mamaev Kurgan). The only 62nd Army forces in the southern two-thirds of the city were Rodimtsev's reinforced 13th Guards Division, clinging to its shrinking bridgehead in the city's center, and Batiuk's 284th Rifle Division, desperately holding on to the Dolgii and Krutoi Ravines and the narrow link connecting the beleaguered parts of Chuikov's increasingly isolated 62nd Army. Although Chuikov's abortive counterattacks had undoubtedly disorganized Paulus's offensive to some degree, the frustrated commander of 62nd Army thought to himself, "One more battle like that and we'll be in the Volga."[26]

Seydlitz's northern shock group, however, did face one vexing problem resulting from the configuration of LI Corps' assault as it unfolded. Although Jänecke's 389th Infantry Division, deployed on 24th Panzer Division's left, was able to maintain contact with Lenski's panzers as they advanced, the infantry of Sanne's 100th Jäger Division on 24th Panzer's right was unable to do so because the terrain to their front was far more difficult and Soviet resistance was far more organized and resolute. Consequently, as 24th Panzer advanced northward, its right flank became overextended, uncovered, and therefore vulnerable to counterattacks by enemy forces from the dense network of buildings along the western edge of lower Krasnyi Oktiabr' village. Mitigating this problem, because of the weakness of the already shattered Soviet forces, at first Lenski was able to divert small forces from his division's main forces to secure his exposed flank. Ultimately, however, the menacing presence of Soviet reinforcements arriving in the factory district forced Lenski to deploy the reinforcing 276th Regiment (from 94th Infantry Division) along his division's long right wing. When this measure proved inadequate, Lenski requested his corps commander, Seydlitz, to assist him by shifting 100th Jäger Division's sector significantly to the right.[27] For the time being, however, 100th Jäger's slow progress forced 24th Panzer Division to leave precious forces behind to protect its vulnerable flank.

In the wake of the sharp reverse that his forces suffered on 27 September, Chuikov took immediate action overnight to shore up his sagging defenses. First, he ordered General Smekhotvorov, commander of the fresh 193rd Rifle Division, to ferry the last two of his regiments, the 883rd and 895th, across the Volga River via Zaitsevskii [Zaitsev] Island by dawn on 28 September. (The 193rd Division's 685th Regiment was already supporting 13th Guards Rifle Division in the city's center.) Smekhotvorov was to reinforce the sagging defenses of Ermolkin's 112th Rifle Division along the western edge of Krasnyi Oktiabr' and Barrikady villages by occupying positions along the western section of the lower Krasnyi Oktiabr' village from the cemetery situated along the southern outskirts of Barrikady village southward along Promyshlennaia Street to the upper reaches of Bannyi Ravine.[28] At the same time, the army commander directed Popov to withdraw the pitifully weak remnants of his 23rd Tank Corps into reserve defensive positions along the western edge of the Krasnyi Oktiabr' Factory. Finally, Chuikov ordered the remnants of Gorishnyi's 95th Rifle Division (in particular 90th Regiment, reinforced by his second-echelon 241st Regiment and elements of Batiuk's 284th Rifle Division), to mount an assault to recapture the crest of Mamaev Kurgan. While this attack was being organized, Chuikov told his chief of artillery "to shell Mamaev Kurgan non-stop throughout the night with artillery and mortars, so as to prevent the enemy from consolidating his position on the hill."[29]

28 September

Once again, however, Seydlitz's shock groups preempted Chuikov's counterattack by resuming their assault at dawn on 28 September (see Map 39).
     As Chuikov recalled:

> The Luftwaffe kept up a constant, concentrated air attack on our troops, on the ferries, and on the Army H.Q. command post. The German aeroplanes dropped not only bombs, but also pieces of metal, ploughs, tractor wheels, harrows and empty metal casks, which whistled about the heads of our troops.
>   Of six cargo boats operating on the Volga, only one had not been knocked out of action. At H.Q. command post, the heat and smoke were suffocating. Flames from the burning oil tanks had spread to the Military Council's dugout. Every air raid by dive-bombers put radios out of action, took its toll on lives.
>   Even the cook, Glinka, who had established himself and his kitchen in a shell-hole, was injured.[30]

The German assault began at dawn on 28 September when Seydlitz's two shock groups resumed their advance across their entire front. In accordance with LI Corps' attack order, at 0100 hours Lenski told his two *kampfgruppen* to advance toward the northwestern section of the lower Krasnyi Oktiabr' village and the open area between the upper and lower Barrikady villages. His order required *Kampfgruppe* Edelsheim to attack northeastward at 0630 hours; *Kampfgruppe* Winterfeld was first to hold the positions it had already reached and, later, exploit Edelsheim's attack after supporting the latter's advancing forces (Edelsheim's) with its flanking fires. Although Seydlitz shifted

100th Jäger Division's left boundary to the north in an attempt to plug the gap between it and Lenski's panzers, 24th Panzer was essentially left with the distracting task of protecting its own long right flank.[31]

On the left flank of Lenski's panzers, Jänecke's 389th Infantry Division was to continue its advance eastward along and north of the Vishnevaia *Balka*, with its 544th Regiment advancing straight down the *balka* to protect 24th Panzer and reach the western edge of the upper Barrikady village. North of the *balka*, Jänecke positioned his 545th and 546th Regiments for a direct assault against Soviet defenses around the Orlovka salient from the west and southwest. On 24th Panzer's right, Sanne's 100th Jäger Division was to begin shifting its regiments northward past the upper Bannyi Ravine on its left while maintaining heavy pressure on 95th Rifle Division's regiments defending the northern and eastern slopes of Mamaev Kurgan and the Meat Combine and the nearby Military Clothing Factory south of Bannyi Ravine. The most important task Sanne faced was that of pushing his left-wing regiment, 54th Jäger, northward across the upper Bannyi Ravine to the blocks of buildings east of Hill 107.5 in order to close the gap between his infantry and Lenski's panzer-grenadiers. This had to be done before Lenski's forces could safely resume assaults deeper into the workers' villages. Still farther south, the three regiments of Wuthmann's 295th Infantry Division were to consolidate their hold on the southern slope of Mamaev Kurgan and, at the same time, outflank Soviet forces defending the Tennis Racket from the south and the Dolgii and Krutoi Ravines from the north and reach the western bank of the Volga.

The OKW's daily operational summary recorded the progress of its forces' assault:

> In the Stalingrad region, 100th Jäger Division redeployed and began an attack toward the northeast. The division seized two thirds of the Meat Combine. The 24th Panzer Division cleared the enemy from the western portion of the "Red Barricade" Factory, up to 500 meters northwest of the railroad line. The northwestern part of the division penetrated into the region of Barricade village. The 389th Infantry Division reached the stream in Gorodishche with its eastern flank and occupied a group of peasant huts.[32]

Sixth Army's war diary acknowledged that LI Corps indeed seized "about half" of the Barrikady village, "two-thirds" of a block of houses around the Meat Combine at the base of Mamaev Kurgan, and the "western part" of the Krasnyi Oktiabr' works.[33]

The Red Army General Staff's daily operational summary provided an abbreviated description of the fighting on 28 September:

62nd Army continued stubborn street fighting in Stalingrad city, repelling repeated attacks by enemy infantry and tanks. The units of the army remained in their previous positions at day's end on 28 September.

124th and 149th RBs, 282nd RR, 10th RD NKVD, 115th RB, and 2nd MRB continued to hold on to their previous positions while repelling attacks by small groups of enemy.

23rd Tank Corps repulsed an attack by up to two battalions of enemy infantry with 12 tanks and occupied [the following] positions:

6th GTB was defending the northwest corner of the "Treugol'nyi" [Triangle] Woods and the western part of Shakhtinskaia Street line;

38th MRB was defending the western part of Zaraiskaia [Zaraisk] Street and Karusel'naia [Carousel] Street with remnants of its force;

The remnants of 9th MRB were defending the region of the western outskirts of Krasnyi Oktiabr' village, (incl.) Karusel'naia Street, and the northern bank of the Bannyi Ravine;

137th TB was defending along the Bannyi Ravine;

189th TB has deployed its tanks between Tsentral'naia [Central] and Karusel'naia Streets; and

27th TB occupied the entrance to Tsentral'naia Street with its remaining tanks.

895th RR, 193rd RD, repelled an attack by up to a battalion of enemy infantry with eight tanks in the vicinity of the cemetery on the southern outskirts of Barrikady village at 1130 hours on 28 September. Four enemy tanks reached Zhmerinskaia [Zhmerinka] Street. Destroyer groups have been sent to destroy these tanks.

95th RD occupied its previous positions. At 1045 hours on 28 September, eight enemy tanks reached the railroad line 200 meters west of Syzranskaia Street and fired on the division's combat formation. These enemy tanks were scattered by our artillery fire.

The enemy attacked twice from the vicinity of Donskaia Street against the 1047th RR, 284th RD. Both of the enemy attacks were repelled with heavy losses to his forces.

13th Gds. RD and 112th RD were defending their previous positions.[34]

After a short *Luftwaffe* bombardment of the built-up areas to 24th Panzer Division's front and heavy air strikes against the Barrikady Factory, at 0615 hours *Kampfgruppe* Edelsheim dispatched reconnaissance parties into the depths of the lower Krasnyi Oktiabr' village to determine weak points in the Soviets' defenses.[35] After this reconnaissance was completed, the entire *kampfgruppe* moved forward from its positions surrounding Hill 107.5, heading northeast through a gauntlet of small-arms fire from an apartment block 300 meters west. This sector was defended by small groups of riflemen from 112th Rifle Division's 416th and 385th Regiments, backed up by the remnants of 23rd Tank Corps' 38th and 9th Motorized Rifle Brigades. On its right flank, Edelsheim's group took fire from small groups of tanks belonging to 23rd Tank Corps' 27th, 189th, and 137th Tank Brigades, which had withdrawn into positions protecting the western section of the lower Krasnyi Oktiabr' village in the sector from Bannyi Ravine northward to Karusel'naia Street. Otherwise, the Soviet resistance was light. Thoroughly disorganized by the German attack, the three regiments of Ermolkin's decimated 112th Rifle Division could do nothing whatsoever to halt the penetration. By this time, the intense fighting had already reduced the strength of Popov's 23rd Tank Corps to only 150 men and 17 tanks, no match for 24th Panzer Division, with more than 3,000 men and 30 tanks.

At about 1200 hours, Edelsheim's *kampfgruppe* reached and occupied defensive positions between two gullies located due west of the built-up area west of Skul'pturnyi Park, roughly 1 kilometer from the division's final objective, another gully 600 meters south of the Silikat Factory, nicknamed the "narrows" by the Germans. Still receiving fire from a few tanks adjacent to its right flank, Edelsheim's *kampfgruppe* now faced Soviet infantrymen on the left wing of 38th Motorized Rifle Brigade, which had dug in along the gully's northern bank. By this time, Edelsheim's group was due east of the positions that *Kampfgruppe* Winterfeld had seized the night before. The moment Edelsheim's forces arrived forward, Winterfeld's *kampfgruppe*, with the division's remaining tanks, began its assault northward toward the western edge of the lower Barrikady village. As it did so, it overran the remnants of 112th Rifle Division's 416th Regiment and pushed forward about a kilometer, ultimately encountering the defenses of 23rd Tank Corps' 6th Guards Tank Brigade between the northwest corner of the so-called Triangle Woods to the western part of Shakhtinskaia Street and the right wing and center of 38th Motorized Rifle Brigade along the western part of Zaraiskaia and Karusel'naia Streets in the western half of upper Barrikady village:

> Armoured *Gruppe* Winterfeld began their attack into the empty terrain between the two westernmost suburbs [Krasnyi Oktiabr' and Barrikady]. The terrain consisted of coverless steppe pockmarked with shell craters and lines of Russian trenches. Their objective was to take the neck of land that lay between the steep-sided gully in [grid square] 64d and the Barrikady housing estate north-west of there. This was seen as a vital objective because it would allow the panzers easy access to the northern area of the city without the need of passing through congested suburbs or crossing easily-defended gullies.[36]

Attacking in two subgroups, the first wheeling northward to flank Barrikady village from the west and the second heading straight toward a cemetery on the village's southwestern edge, *Kampfgruppe* Winterfeld pressed on rapidly, capturing most of the upper Barrikady village south of the Silikat Factory [Silikat Factory No. 3] by nightfall. During its advance, Winterfeld's southern subgroup encountered 1st Battalion of 193rd Rifle Division's 895th Regiment, which had just deployed forward from the Volga's western bank to defensive positions astride Portal'naia and Zhmerinskaia Streets, 500–600 meters south of the Silikat Factory. Recoiling under Winterfeld's assault, the rifle battalion withdrew eastward into the lower Barrikady village and requested reinforcements from its parent regiment. Hastening forward on Winterfeld's right flank, Edelsheim's *kampfgruppe* secured the division's objective of the day, the southern bank of the gully at the narrows between the upper and lower Barrikady villages.

Advancing another 1–1.5 kilometers by nightfall on 29 September, Lenski's two *kampfgruppen* had advanced more than 6 kilometers in two days and captured the critical narrows. In the process, 24th Panzer Division carved a wedge more than 4 kilometers deep into 62nd Army's defenses that pointed menacingly at the northern section of Stalingrad's factory district. As Winterfeld's panzers secured the built-up area of the upper Barrikady village northwest of the narrows, Edelsheim's panzer-grenadiers dug in around the narrows themselves and the streets extending at a right angle southward through the western section of the lower Krasnyi Oktiabr' village. As Lenski's two *kampfgruppen* advanced, they reported capturing 280 prisoners and destroying or capturing five tanks, nine antitank guns, 32 antitank rifles, seven mortars, two flamethrowers, and four mine dogs at a cost to the panzer division of 25 men killed and 164 wounded.[37] The limited quantities of trophies that 24th Panzer seized were indeed indicative of the weakened state of Chuikov's forces defending this region. The day's fight cost 24th Panzer 28 killed and 94 wounded.

At nightfall, *Kampfgruppe* Winterfeld established all-around defenses to protect its hold on the upper section of Barrikady village. Since 100th Jäger Division had yet to close up on the division's right flank, however, Edelsheim had a significantly longer front to defend. He assigned his 26th Grenadier Regiment responsibility for defending the sector facing north and east from the narrows, 600 meters south of the Silikat Factory, southward to the twin gullies west of Skul'pturnyi Park. The 21st Grenadiers were to defend the broad sector facing toward the east from the twin gullies southward past Hill 107.5.[38] This position was indeed precarious, first because the panzer regiment fielded less than 1,000 fighters, and second because Chuikov was already assembling forces that he hoped could recapture the lost upper sections of the workers' villages.

As 24th Panzer Division lunged ever deeper into the workers' villages, on the division's left 544th Regiment of Jänecke's 389th Infantry Division pushed eastward along and north of the Vishnevaia *Balka,* engaging the remnants of 23rd Tank Corps' 6th Guards Tank Brigade and driving them, together with 112th Rifle Division's 524th Regiment, into the western end of the upper Barrikady village. Jänecke's forces moved eastward another 1,200 meters by day's end, reaching the *balka* opposite the western end of the upper Barrikady village, about 400 meters south of its junction with the Mechetka River. By this time, leaving part of one regiment in the *balka,* Jänecke was already redeploying the bulk of his division northward toward the crossings over the Mechetka River so they could mount an attack on the salient that the Soviets were defending around Orlovka. His progress was hindered, however, by forces Chuikov had detached from Group Gorokhov to defend the Mechetka River and the southern approaches to Orlovka.

Thus, by day's end on 28 September 1st Battalion, 124th Rifle Brigade, flanked on the right by 1st Battalion, 149th Rifle Brigade, defended positions extending southward from just east of Hills 124.9 and 129.1, southwest of Orlovka, and then southeastward to the Mechetka River to protect the salient's western and southwestern perimeters.[39] Despite this obstacle, 389th Infantry Division was to advance eastward from its forward positions east of the railroad line and Gorodishche and north of the Vishnevaia *Balka,* penetrate Soviet defenses along and north of the Mechetka River, and advance northeastward to collapse defenses along the southern perimeter of the Orlovka salient. If successful, Jänecke's attack would cut off the Orlovka salient at its base and prevent the defenders from withdrawing southeastward along the Orlovka River to rejoin Chuikov's forces defending the northern section of Stalingrad's factory district.

Although 24th Panzer Division's left (western) flank was secure, the same could not be said about its right (southern) flank because the light infantry of Sanne's 100th Jäger Division had not been able to keep up with his advance.[40] Resuming their attacks at dawn on 28 September, 54th and 227th Jäger Regiments pressed 95th Rifle Division's 241st and 161st Regiments northward from the Flying School and shooting range but managed to advance only about 800 meters to the railroad line northwest of Mamaev Kurgan before being halted by heavy enemy fire. By this time, Gorishnyi's two regiments were joined by the remnants of 269th NKVD Regiment and a few tanks from 137th Tank Brigade. At the end of the day's fighting, 54th Regiment had captured the southern section of the firing range south of the railroad, and the battalions on 227th Regiment's left wing took the heights overlooking the sector of Bannyi Ravine north of the Mamaev Kurgan and the Military Clothing Factory. There, however, their advance came to a halt because 95th

Rifle Division's 241st and 161st Regiments had converted the factory into a strongpoint bristling with machine-gun positions.

Meanwhile, on 100th Jäger Division's right wing, part of its 227th Jäger and 369th Infantry Regiments parried with 95th Rifle Division's 90th Regiment, reinforced by the division's training battalion, on the eastern section of the crest of Mamaev Kurgan. The remainder of 369th Regiment, cooperating with 516th Regiment on 295th Infantry Division's left wing, tried in vain to expel 284th Rifle Division's 1045th Regiment from the Meat Combine and the Tennis Racket. Still farther south, 518th and 517th Regiments in 295th Infantry Division's center and on its right wing failed to record any progress against the 1047th and 1043rd Regiments of Batiuk's division, which were dug in astride the lower courses of the Dolgii and Krutoi Ravines. Indicative of the heavy fighting on 29 September, 100th Jäger Division reported that it lost 70 men killed, 276 wounded, and 10 missing in action and 295th Division 10 killed and 44 wounded. Although 100th Jäger still rated all five of its battalions as "strong," three of 295th Division's battalions were already "exhausted" and the remaining four "weak."[41]

Thus, despite 389th Infantry and 24th Panzer Divisions' slow but steady forward progress, by day's end on 28 September 100th Jäger and 295th Infantry Divisions had not been able to crack Soviet resistance in their sectors. This left the spearhead of Seydlitz's northern shock group, 24th Panzer Division, in exposed and vulnerable forward positions. In addition to the remnants of Popov's 23rd Tank Corps and Ermolkin's 112th Rifle Division lodged in the depths of the lower Krasnyi Oktiabr' village, Lenski's panzer division now had to contend with 883rd and 895th Regiments of Smekhotvorov's 193rd Rifle Division. These Soviet troops still clung tenaciously to their defensive positions on the northern edge of the upper Barrikady village, the Silikat Factory, and the western edge of the lower Barrikady village east of the narrows. Unless and until 100th Jäger Division was able to shift its forces northwestward toward Hill 107.5, Edelsheim's *kampfgruppe*—in particular the 1,000 men of its 21st Grenadier Regiment on its left wing—were especially vulnerable to counterattacks from the western sections of the lower Krasnyi Oktiabr' and Barrikady villages, a threat that would materialize the next morning.

Despite the damage to his defenses caused by Seydlitz's attacks, Chuikov concluded by day's end that the Germans' forward progress was limited and "they were losing their punch." He went on to explain: "They were uncoordinated, not as rapid and well-organized as they had been. Enemy battalions, supported by tanks, were thrown into battle at different points and not very confidently. This enabled us to mass our fires and beat off all attacks in turn and then go over to the counter-attack ourselves. I would then ask the Air Forces Commander, Khriukin, for help, and he did not refuse—he gave us everything he had."[42]

Members of Stalingrad Front's Military Council: (from left to right) N. S. Khrushchev, member; A. S. Chianov, secretary of the Stalingrad city Communist Party Committee; and General A. I. Eremenko, commander.

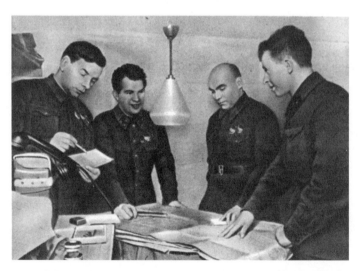

(From left to right) Major General N. I. Krylov, chief of staff of 62nd Army; Lieutenant General V. I. Chuikov, commander of 62nd Army; Lieutenant General K. A. Gurov, member of 62nd Army's Military
· Council (commissar); and Major General A. I. Rodimtsev, commander of 13th Guards Rifle Division.

Lieutenant General V. I. Chuikov, commander of 62nd Army (on the right), and Division Commissar K. A. Gurov, member of 62nd Army's Military Council (on the left).

Colonel I. I. Liudnikov, commander of 138th Rifle Division (on the right), with S. Ia. Tychinsky, V. I. Shuba, and N. I. Titov, the 138th Rifle Division's chief of artillery, chief of staff, and political officer, respectively (on the left).

Major General V. A. Glazkov, commander of 35th Guards Rifle Division.

Colonel V. A. Goryshnyi, commander of 95th Rifle Division.

Major General F. N. Smekhotvorov, commander of 193rd Rifle Division.

Major General S. S. Gur'ev, commander of 39th Guards
Rifle Division.

Colonel L. N. Gurt'ev, commander of 308th
Rifle Division.

Major General V. G. Zholuder, commander of 37th
Guards Rifle Division.

Chuikov claimed that the Germans had lost "at least 1,500 dead," and that "more than thirty of his tanks were burnt out," during the day's fighting: "Nearly 500 German dead littered the slopes of Mamaev Kurgan alone." He admitted, however, that the cost to 62nd Army was high, with Popov's 23rd Tank Corps losing 626 men dead and wounded and Batiuk's 284th Rifle Division suffering about 300 losses; Gorishnyi's 95th Rifle Division was reduced to only a "few men left."[43]

The most serious problem Chuikov now faced, in addition to the severe damage done to his defenses in the city, was the loss of vessels to transport men and materiel across the Volga River. The constant German air strikes threatened to interdict the flow of vital reinforcements while also preventing the evacuation of the mounting casualties to the river's eastern bank. As the Germans regrouped their forces and brought up reinforcements for the assault, it was clear to Chuikov that the battle for the factory district was reaching its culminating point. Therefore, at 1930 hours on 28 September he issued detailed orders to his army:

1. The enemy, while committing fresh reserves into the battle (100th Light Infantry Division), is striving to capture the city of Stalingrad and its suburbs of Krasnyi Oktiabr' and the Tractor Factory village.

2. The army is fulfilling its main and primary mission to hold on to the city and its industrial centers, Krasnyi Oktiabr' and Barrikady, and the Tractor Factory village.

I order:

3. **124th RB** will defend the Rynok, northern outskirts of Spartanovka, and (incl.) Hill 93.2 sector and prevent the enemy from reaching the Spartanovka and Tractor Factory village region.

The boundary to the left is Marker 3.9 (on Zaitsevskii Island), the crossroads 2 kilometers west of Hill 123.4, and Hill 75.9.

Defend the region west of the edge of the woods 2.5 kilometers east of Gorodishche with one battalion. Prevent movement by the enemy along the valley of the Mokraia Mechetka River.

4. **149th RB, with 282nd RR NKVD** attached, will defend the (incl.) Spartanovka, woods west of Spartanovka, the barn, and the burial mounds on the southern slope of Hill 135.4 sector. Prevent the enemy from reaching the northwestern outskirts of the Tractor Factory village.

The boundary on the left is the cemetery (west of Tractor Factory village), Hill 75.9, Hill 135.4, and the Motor Tractor Station.

Defend the region 1 kilometer southwest of Hill 109.4 with one battalion.

Prevent the enemy from reaching the Kazennaia *Balka* in the vicinity of Hill 97.7.

5. **115th RB, with 2nd MRB** attached, will defend the (incl.) Hill 135.4, (incl.) Hill 144.4, (incl.) Hill 147.6, Marker 107.8, Hill 129.1, and Hill 109.4 sector. Prevent the enemy from reaching the Orlovka region, having created a firm all-round defense.

The boundary to the left is Hill 109.4 and Gorodishche.

6. **23rd TC** (6th Gds. TB, 27th, 137th, and 189th TBs and 9th and 38th MRBs) will defend the Mechetka bridge, 1,800 meters south of Hill 109.4, the southern edge of the triangular woods, the southwestern outskirts of Barrikady village, and the cemetery sector. Prevent the enemy from reaching Barrikady village and advancing on it along the valley of the Mechetka. Construct a continuous antitank minefield and anti-infantry obstacles on the western and southern outskirts of Barrikady village. Prepare Barrikady village as a strong point with an all-round defense.

The boundary to the left is Mezenskaia Street, Kaluzhskaia Street, the cemetery, and Zelenaia *Balka*.

7. **193rd RD** (less 685th RR) will defend the southern part of Portal'naia Street, Chernorechenskaia Street, and the Bannyi Ravine sector. Prevent the enemy from reaching the city limit in the division's defensive sector. Prepare strong points and centers of resistance within the city by adapting the stone building for defense according to instructions and schemes previously provided.

Construct continuous antitank and anti-infantry obstacles along Ugol'naia, Promyshlennaia, Narodnaia, and Ovrashnaia Streets in the western outskirts of the city.

The boundary to the left is the mouth of the Bannyi Ravine, the Bannyi Ravine, and Hill 112.0.

8. **95th RD** will defend the (incl.) Bannyi Ravine, the western outskirts of the village 1 kilometer north of Mamaev Kurgan, and the northern slope of Hill 102.0 sector.

The boundary to the left is Gertsen and Griboedova Streets, Hill 102.0, and Belomorskaia.

9. **284th RD** will defend the upper reaches of the ravine 600 meters north of the trigonometric point on Hill 102.0, the eastern slope of Hill 102.0, the railroad bridge, the intersection of Sovnarkomovskaia and Polotninaia Streets, 4th Polotninaia Street, the intersection of Ural'skaia and Artemovskaia Streets, 3rd Naberezhnaia Street, and astride the Krutoi Ravine sector. Prevent the enemy from reaching the Khimicheskaia region [Lazur Chemical Plant] and the bank of the Volga River in the vicinity of the Krutoi Ravine. Prepare the triangle of buildings within Chernomorskaia, Syzranskaia, and Emskaia Streets as a strong point with all-round defense to prevent the enemy from reaching the city between the Bannyi Ravine and its northern slopes and a second strong point with

all-around defenses in the village within the railroad loop [the Tennis Racket].

Create continuous antitank and anti-infantry obstacles in both strong points along their external defensive lines.

The boundary to the left is Nekrasovskaia Street.

10. **13th Gds. RD, with 685th RR and two mortar companies attached**, by holding on to the positions you occupy in the central part of the city, successively destroy the enemy in the buildings he has seized with operations with small assault and blocking groups, while continuing to liberate new blocks.

11. **112th RD**, constituting my reserve, will improve the defenses you occupy in the Barrikady village and be prepared for operations toward the west and south.[44]

Echoing Stalin's early enjoinder to his troops, the last several paragraphs of Chuikov's order contained instructions designed to shape the nature of the forthcoming defense and steel commanders and soldiers alike for what was to come:

12. I expect the commanders of all units to act with all possible haste in carrying out the engineering work to strengthen their positions, in constructing antitank and anti-infantry obstacles along the forward edge and in the depth, and in adapting buildings for defense in the event of street fighting.

Use all available resources for constructing obstacles, right up to dismantling buildings, railroads, and tramlines, while enlisting the services of the civilian population through the local authorities.

The main work should be carried out by the units themselves. Carry out the work around the clock.

Complete the initial work (mainly the antitank obstacles) by the morning on 29 September 1942, making the defenses of the city and its industrial centers impregnable. Every obstacle should be reliably covered by all types of fire.

Explain to all personnel that the Army is fighting on its last line of defense; there can be no further retreat. It is the duty of every soldier and commander to defend his trench, his position—NOT A STEP BACK! The enemy MUST BE DESTROYED AT WHATEVER COST!

Shoot soldiers and commanders who willfully abandon their foxholes and positions on the spot as enemies of THE FATHERLAND.

Chuikov, Gurov, Krylov[45]

SOVIET COMMAND DECISIONS

As Chuikov organized his forces to counter Paulus's next assault, the *Stavka* and Southeastern Front also acted vigorously to stiffen his army's defenses. First, several days before, the *Stavka* had ordered 159th Fortified Region, with its 12 machine gun–artillery battalions, to deploy into the Stalingrad region between 28 September and 1 October. It had already dispatched 37th and 39th Guards Rifle Divisions from 4th Tank and 1st Guards Armies and 308th Rifle Division from 21st Army to Southeastern Front on 25 September. In addition to these divisions, the *Stavka* on 25 September ordered its 4th Reserve Army to release the reconstituted 87th and 315th Rifle Divisions to *Stavka* control to be deployed into Stalingrad Front's rear area, ultimately to the region 70–80 kilometers southwest of Kamyshin on the Volga River.[46] Three days later, 28 September, the *Stavka* directed the chief of the Red Army's Auto-Armored Directorate to transfer 84th and 90th Tank Brigades from the Saratov region to Southeastern Front's control, and the Ural Military District to transfer its 93rd, 96th, and 97th Rifle Brigades to fill out Southeastern Front's newly formed 7th Rifle Corps (see Table 26).[47]

In the wake of these fresh reinforcements to the Stalingrad region, the *Stavka* finally acted on 28 September to end the confusion so prevalent in and damaging to the command and control of Soviet forces fighting in the area. Its new directive read:

In connection with the increasingly complicated situation at Stalingrad, the great extent of the *fronts*, and the growth of the quantity of armies in them, as well as for the sake of convenience in command and control, the *Stavka* of the Supreme High Command orders:

1. Organize two independent *fronts* in the Stalingrad region, with each in direct subordination to the *Stavka* of the Supreme High Command: from the Stalingrad Front—the Don Front, including in it 63rd, 21st, 4th Tank, 1st Guards, 24th, and 66th Armies; and from the Southeastern Front—the Stalingrad Front, including in it 62nd, 64th, 57th, 51st, and 28th Armies.

2. Appoint Colonel General A. I. Eremenko as commander of the forces of the Stalingrad Front.

3. Appoint Lieutenant General K. K. Rokossovsky as commander of the forces of the Don Front, freeing him from his duties as commander of the Briansk Front.

4. Additionally, bring Corps Commissar A. S. Zheltov into the Don Front's Military Council as the member of the Military Council [commissar], freeing him from his duties as the member of the Military Council of 63rd Army.

Table 26. *Stavka* **Reinforcement of Stalingrad and Southeastern Fronts, 25–28 September 1942**

Force	Origin	Place of Deployment
97th Rifle Brigade	Teplaia Gora (Ural Military District)	Vladimirskaia Station, Pristan' (7th Rifle Corps)
93rd Rifle Brigade	Kunar (Ural Military District)	Kharabalinskaia Station (7th Rifle Corps)
96th Rifle Brigade	Zlatousta (Ural Military District)	Verkhnii Baskunchak Station (7th Rifle Corps)
84th Tank Brigade	Saratov (Volga Military District)	Paromnaia Station (Southeastern Front)
90th Tank Brigade	Saratov (Volga Military District)	Paromnaia Station (Southeastern Front)
87th Rifle Division	4th Reserve Army (Ilovlia Station)	Aleshkin Station (*Stavka* reserve), to Zakharovka Station (80 kilometers southwest of Kamyshin) by 2 October
315th Rifle Division	4th Reserve Army (Log Station)	Arkadak Station (*Stavka* reserve), to Zenzevatka Station (70 kilometers southwest of Kamyshin) by 2 October

5. Additionally, bring Comrade Chuianov, the secretary of the Stalingrad *Obkom VKP (B)* [Stalingrad Communist Party District Committee (Bolshevik)], into the Military Council of the Stalingrad Front as the member of the Military Council [commissar].

6. Relieve from their duties Lieutenant General V. N. Gordov, the deputy commander of the Stalingrad Front, and Major General I. N. Rukhle, the chief of the Operations Department of the Stalingrad Front, placing them at the disposal of the People's Commissar of Defense.

7. Appoint Major General K. A. Kovalenko as deputy commander of the Don Front, relieving him of his duties as the chief of staff of the Stalingrad Front.

8. Appoint Major General M. S. Malinin as the chief of staff of the Don Front, freeing him from his duties as the chief of staff of the Briansk Front.

9. Appoint Colonel Boikov as the chief of the Operations Department of the Don Front, freeing him from his duties as chief of the Operations Directorate of the General Staff.

The *Stavka* of the Supreme High Command
I. Stalin, A. Vasilevsky[48]

By transforming Stalingrad Front and Southeastern Front into the new Don Front and Stalingrad Front—each with its own commander and staff—this directive ended the awkward situation in which Eremenko commanded both *fronts* with the entirely undefined assistance of his former deputy,

General Gordov. Although this change later caused considerable confusion among historians, it was not an idle shift in terminology. It recognized that Eremenko's headquarters was now responsible for the defense of the city; for its part Rokossovsky's new Don Front would prepare for future offensive operations along the Don River and in the Kotluban' region northwest of the city.

Shortly after issuing these orders and directives, Stalin on 29 September once again dispatched Vasilevsky and Zhukov to the Stalingrad region, the former to Stalingrad Front's auxiliary command post and the latter to Don Front's command post in Kamyshin, with a side trip to the command post of Moskalenko's 1st Guards Army. Zhukov's task was to inspect the conditions in Rokossovsky's *front* as well as the Axis dispositions in the region, particularly in the vicinity of the Don Front's bridgeheads at Serafimovich and Kletskaia, from which the *Stavka* anticipated launching its future counteroffensive. During this visit Zhukov confirmed Rokossovsky's judgment that Don Front lacked the strength necessary to prevent further German operations in Stalingrad or to mount a credible counteroffensive.[49]

Responding quickly to Zhukov's inspection trip, Stalin on 1 October directed the *Stavka* to issue two new directives designed to significantly bolster the strength of Rokossovsky's *front*. The first ordered Rokossovsky to withdraw Kravchenko's 4th Tank Corps into his *front*'s reserve and, with the assistance of other NKO directorates, "completely fill it out [with authorized personnel and equipment] by 15 October 1942."[50] The second directive reinforced Don Front with seven fresh rifle divisions (277th, 62nd, 252nd, 212th, 226th, 333rd, and 293rd), forces formerly subordinate to 10th Reserve Army that had just completed refitting behind the front. Situated in the Moscow Military District, 10th Reserve Army was to dispatch these fresh divisions to Rokossovsky's control between 7 and 14 October.[51]

Collectively these measures solidified command and control of Soviet forces struggling in the Stalingrad region. They did not, however, immediately relieve the pressure on Chuikov's 62nd Army, which intensified during the next few days, forcing Chuikov's forces to fight literally with their backs to the Volga River as Paulus pressed his offensive deeper into the factory district. To that end, Paulus ordered 24th Panzer Division to continue its offensive thrust toward the Tractor Factory workers' village on 29 September. In order to provide Lenski with necessary forces to sustain his drive, the Sixth Army commander decided to reinforce his panzer division with 94th Infantry Division's 276th Regiment on 30 September so that Lenski could defend his lengthening left wing and reestablish close contact with 100th Jäger Division. Simultaneously, Sixth Army ordered Seydlitz's LI Corps to push its southern shock group, which now consisted of 100th Jäger and 295th Infantry Divisions, across Bannyi Ravine and the Tennis Racket into the southeastern section of Krasnyi Oktiabr' village and the southern part of the Krasnyi Oktiabr'

Factory itself. The southern group was also to clear Soviet forces off the eastern slopes of Mamaev Kurgan and push them out of the Dolgii and Krutoi Ravines and into the Volga River beyond. All the while, the shock groups subordinate to Hube's XIV Panzer Corps and 389th Infantry Division on the left wing of Seydlitz's LI Corps were to conduct their long-awaited assaults against Chuikov's forces defending the exposed Orlovka salient.

THE STRUGGLE FOR MAMAEV KURGAN AND THE WORKERS' VILLAGES, 29–30 SEPTEMBER

29 September

LI Army Corps' northern and southern shock groups resumed their assaults to clear Soviet forces from the remainder of the workers' villages on the morning of 29 September, but not without interference from Chuikov's defenders (see Maps 40–41).

At 0430 hours on 29 September, for example, just before 24th Panzer Division resumed its advance, 193rd Rifle Division's 883rd and 895th Regiments attacked at the defenses of *Kampfgruppe* Edelsheim's 26th Grenadier Regiment, defending the panzer division's right wing just north of the narrows. Attacking from the east, the Soviets struck the regiment's 2nd Battalion, capturing the Germans' attention indeed:

> The grenadiers had established their positions in overgrown vegetable patches, behind paling fences and in half-demolished wooden huts, but, because the line ran through gardens and huts, there was no clear field of fire. In the split-second flash of bursting shells, the grenadiers caught fleeting glimpses of figures flitting through the gardens on the other side of the street. A few even saw the menacing silhouettes of T-34s. Machine guns hammered, and beads of tracers smashed into the huts standing opposite or splashed off remnants of crumbling masonry chimneys. Fires flared and cast a ghastly orange light over the battlefield. The Russians infiltrated the German line and killed several men in their foxholes. The thump of exploding grenades and hoarse Russian voices rang out, and the deep rumbling of diesel engines caused the air to vibrate. Staunch resistance nests held on and prevented the defensive line from collapsing. Calls for help reached Division HQ, and they responded immediately; orders were sent to Major von Winterfeld to dispatch some panzers to the hard-pressed grenadiers, and these arrived a short time later. Officers of the besieged battalion quickly organized a counterattack constructed around the panzers, and soon they pushed into the surprised enemy and swiftly restored the situation.[52]

Map 40. Sixth Army's situation, 29–30 September 1942

This counterattack, which was actually a reconnaissance-in-force conducted by several battalions of the two Soviet regiments, supported by a handful of tanks, collapsed soon after it began. However, it cost Edelsheim's forces one killed, seven wounded, and eight missing.[53] Undeterred by the impetuous but unsuccessful Soviet attack, Lenski's panzer division resumed its advance northward toward the Tractor Factory village shortly after noon. On Lenski's left, 544th Regiment of Jänecke's 389th Infantry Division plowed northeastward along Vishnevaia *Balka* toward the northwestern edge of the Barrikady Factory village, while the remainder of the division crossed the Mechetka River and wheeled northward toward Orlovka. On Lenski's

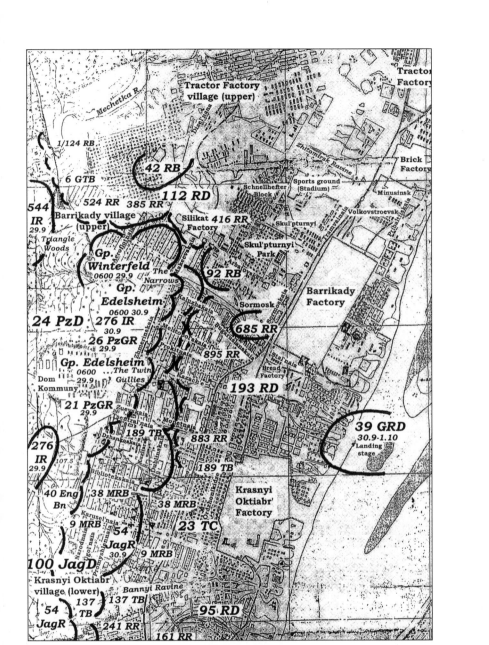

Map 41. LI Army Corps' assault, 29–30 September 1942

right, 100th Jäger and 295th Infantry Divisions renewed their attacks toward Bannyi Ravine, the Volga east of Mamaev Kurgan, and the lower (eastern) sections of the Dolgii and Krutoi Ravines. Providing a fiery backdrop, *Luftwaffe* aircraft pounded the factory district relentlessly, setting the Tractor Factory ablaze.

Advancing northeast along and astride the Vishnevaia *Balka*, 389th Infantry Division's 544th Regiment cleared the remnants of 23rd Tank Corps' 6th Guards and 189th Tank and 9th Motorized Rifle Brigades from the *balka's* eastern extremity, reached and crossed the Mechetka River, and struck the defensive positions of 1st Battalion, 124th Rifle Brigade, and the remnants of 112th Rifle Division's 524th Rifle Regiment defending the northwestern edge of the upper Barrikady village. South of the *balka*, after detaching several tanks to deal with the threat to Edelsheim's *kampfgruppe*, *Kampfgruppe* Winterfeld reassembled its forces and advanced several hundred meters toward the north, capturing the remainder of the upper Barrikady village from the remnants of 112th Rifle Division's 416th Regiment and 193rd Rifle Division's 895th Regiment, which then dug in to protect the southern approaches to the Silikat Factory. Otherwise, the remainder of Lenski's panzer division held its positions until its long right flank was secure.

To the south, opposite 24th Panzer's long right wing, at about midday Sanne's 100th Jäger Division was finally able to overcome the Soviet defenses along the railroad west of Bannyi Ravine and advance its left wing forward toward Hill 107.5. After driving the remnants of 269th NKVD Regiment out of their strong defenses along the railroad line, 54th Jäger Regiment pushed northward toward Hill 107.5, followed shortly by elements of 227th Jäger Regiment, which Sanne shifted to the right after the regiment finally cleared most of 95th Rifle Division's 241st and 161st Regiments from the crest and northern slopes of Mamaev Kurgan. However, no sooner did 227th Regiment vacate the crest than yet another Soviet assault very nearly recaptured the trigonometric mark adjacent to its crest. Ultimately, Sanne's two regiments occupied a new defensive line facing east from Hill 107.5 southward to the Bannyi Ravine, in the process relieving the beleaguered 21st Grenadier Regiment of *Kampfgruppe* Edelsheim. Edelsheim then moved the panzergrenadiers northward to reinforce his main force. As Sanne shifted his front northward to his right, the Croatian 369th Regiment (one reinforced battalion), supported by a battalion from 295th Infantry Division's 516th Regiment, captured the western part of the Meat Combine from 95th Rifle Division's 90th Regiment and 284th Rifle Division's 1045th Regiment, pushing their lines ever closer to the Volga River—but not yet there.[54]

Both Paulus and Weichs visited Lenski's forward positions to observe the progress of Seydlitz's assaults on 29 September. Still, 24th Panzer Division's gains during the day were only minimal—several hundreds of meters—at a cost of 39 killed, 94 wounded, and 8 missing, the highest death toll to date.[55] The 100th Jäger Division reported 346 men killed or wounded.

Meanwhile, on the right wing of Seydlitz's southern shock group, 517th and 518th Regiments of Wuthmann's 295th Infantry Division renewed their assaults against 284th Rifle Division's 1047th and 1043rd Regiments on the southern slope of Mamaev Kurgan and the southern reaches of Dolgii and Krutoi Ravines in an attempt to drive the defenders back into the Volga River (but without any success). At the southern extremity of Paulus's lines, XXXXVIII Panzer Corps' 71st Infantry Division continued its efforts to clear 13th Guards Rifle Division and 193rd Rifle Division's 685th Regiment from the fortified buildings and strongpoints in Stalingrad's center city, especially around 9 January Square. But the single regiment assigned this task (194th) was simply too weak to accomplish its assigned mission.

Despite desperate resistance by Chuikov's hard-pressed troops, by day's end Seydlitz's advancing troops had cleared Soviet forces from most of the upper Krasnyi Oktiabr' and Barrikady villages and captured forward positions just south of the Silikat Factory. In the process, they drove a wedge deep into Soviet defenses along the western reaches of Kazach'ia Street, south of the Silikat Factory, and along the boundary between 112th Rifle Division's 416th and 385th Regiments and the supporting 883rd and 895th Regiments of Smekhotvorov's 193rd Rifle Division. By this time, 24th Panzer Division's two forward *kampfgruppen* were only 1.5 kilometers west of the Krasnyi Oktiabr' landing stage on the Volga River. If they reached this vital crossing point over the Volga, they could then turn south to isolate and destroy Chuikov's 95th and 248th Rifle Divisions defending near Mamaev Kurgan and the Dolgii and Krutoi Ravines, or northward through the Barrikady Factory to envelop and destroy 62nd Army's main forces in the factory district.

Thanks largely to the bravery of Smekhotvorov's soldiers, Chuikov's defenses in this sector held—but only after losing three regimental and battalion commanders killed in action. In the early evening, 193rd Rifle Division reported, "Our attempts to advance to the western outskirts of the village [Krasnyi Oktiabr'] did not succeed. Furthermore, on 29 September we had to repel several powerful counterattacks. The regiments managed to dig in along the line of Aivazovskaia, Dublinskaia [Dublin], and Kuzliarskaia Streets" in the eastern section of Krasnyi Oktiabr' village.[56]

Sixth Army's war-diary entry for the day noted that, even though LI Corps' forces had seized the blocks of houses west of the Bread Factory, situated midway between the Krasnyi Oktiabr' and Barrikady Factories, the corps had lost the houses it had taken around the Meat Combine and lost, and then recaptured, part of the Barrikady settlement.[57]

That evening the Red Army General Staff reported:

62nd Army was continuing to engage in fierce street fighting in Stalingrad city and in the Orlovka region on 29 September. . . .

27th and 137th TBs fought along the Goncharnaia [Gonchar] and Aeroflotskaia [Aeroflot] Streets line. 15 enemy tanks were destroyed.

112th and 193rd RDs fought stubborn defensive battles with an enemy force of up to an infantry division and 60–70 tanks, which reached the vicinity of Goncharnaia Street and the "Silikat" Factory. The enemy captured Barrikady village and the "Silikat" Factory.

193rd RD repulsed two attacks by the enemy. As a result of the third attack, the enemy succeeded in wedging into the combat formation of the units of the division in the vicinity of Kazach'ia Street.

90th RR, 95th RD, captured the area of the trigonometric point [crest] on Hill 102.0 [Mamaev Kurgan].

13th Gds. RD continued to occupy its previous positions and fought street battles in small groups with enemy forces ensconced in separate buildings.[58]

The only good news Chuikov received on 29 September concerned the counterattack by Gorishnyi's 95th Rifle Division against the Germans' defenses on Mamaev Kurgan, which occurred soon after 295th Infantry Division took over responsibility for defending the mound from 100th Jäger Division as the latter shifted its forces to the north. Supported by massive air strikes from 8th Air Army, 95th Rifle Division's 90th Regiment, reinforced by elements of 241st Regiment and two battalions from 1045th Regiment of Batiuk's 284th Rifle Division, almost recaptured the crest of the burial mound from 295th Infantry Division, although at a cost of heavy casualties and without lasting results. As the famed historian A. M. Samsonov later recorded in his history of the battle:

> During the heaviest assault by *front* aviation [units of Major General T. T. Khriukin's 8th Air Army], a regiment of 95th Rifle Division, with two battalions of 284th Rifle Division, launched a counterattack. They secured the trigonometric point on Mamaev Kurgan by a decisive bound. However, they did not succeed in reaching the water tank on the very top. The heights, along which artillery fire constantly rained from this or that side, remained no-one's.[59]

30 September

Seydlitz's two shock groups consolidated their positions on 30 September, in accordance with LI Corps' order to "hold and improve the positions attained."[60] While Lenski shuffled the forces of 24th Panzer Division, he also ordered local advances to improve positions and prepare for a subsequent advance toward the northeast to clear the remainder of the workers' villages (see Map 41). After being reinforced by 94th Infantry Division's 276th Regiment, he ordered it to relieve the southern half of *Kampfgruppe* Edelsheim north of Hill 107.5. Once consolidated south of the narrows in grid square 74c, situated between the upper and lower Barrikady villages, Edelsheim's group was to attack northward to seize a bridgehead north of the narrows. This would place Edelsheim's *kampfgruppe* on line with Winterfeld's to the west.[61]

Seydlitz's attacking divisions had already cleared most Soviet forces from the more open regions along and south of the Vishnevaia *Balka* and the upper sections of Krasnyi Oktiabr' and Barrikady villages. The 100th Jäger Division now faced the arduous task of clearing the lower section of Krasnyi Oktiabr' village south of Hill 107.5, where 95th Rifle Division's 241st and 161st Regiments, the remnants of 23rd Tank Corps' 38th Motorized Rifle and 27th and 137th Tank Brigades and 269th NKVD Regiment, and 193rd Rifle Division's 883rd Regiment had fortified themselves in the densely packed buildings to slow the German assaults. At the farthest point of Seydlitz's penetration to the north, 24th Panzer Division's *Kampfgruppe* Winterfeld was to prepare to penetrate into the Tractor Factory workers' village. This attack had to overcome the defenses of 6th Guards and 189th Tank Brigades and 112th Rifle Division's skeletal regiments, which had just been reinforced by the reconstituted 42nd Rifle Brigade, at dawn on 1 October.

Meanwhile, facing both north and east on the division's right flank, *Kampfgruppe* Edelsheim and 276th Infantry Regiment attacked eastward on 30 September to clear the 193rd Rifle Division's 895th Regiment from the lower sections of Krasnyi Oktiabr' and Barrikady villages north of Hill 107.5 to just north of the narrows. Although its arrival was most welcome, 276th Regiment fielded two weak infantry battalions with a total trench strength of only 160 men.[62] Nor was 24th Panzer Division's dwindling number of tanks ideally suited to operate in this urban terrain. Instead of spearheading lengthy and dramatic advances, the tanks now followed the advancing infantry, often at a snail's pace, to bust bunkers and smash fortified positions and, along with the infantry division's assault and antitank guns, provide direct fire support to the infantry assault groups.

By now, Paulus had shifted the focus of Sixth Army's main attack (*Schwerpunkt*) toward the Orlovka salient, northwest of the city, and Chuikov was beginning to receive fresh reinforcements. However, as the assault on Orlovka developed, heavy fighting continued to rage along the entire factory district front from the northwestern reaches of Barrikady village southward past the Silikat Factory and the western edge of the lower Barrikady and Krasnyi Oktiabr' villages to the eastern bank of Bannyi Ravine and southern slope of Mamaev Kurgan. By this time the struggle had degenerated into a vicious slugfest, with advances and withdrawals by both sides measured in tens and hundreds of meters.

Anchoring the left wing of Seydlitz's merged northern and southern shock groups, the 545th and 546th Regiments of Jänecke's 389th Infantry Division swung northward and northeastward along the northern bank of the Mechetka River to cooperate with the attack by XIV Panzer Corps on the Orlovka salient. The division left most of its 544th Regiment behind in the valley of the Mechetka River to protect 24th Panzer Division's left flank. In Seydlitz's center, the 24th's *Kampfgruppe* Winterfeld clung to its defenses around the upper Barrikady village, while *Kampfgruppe* Edelsheim, flanked on the right by 276th Infantry Regiment (which was deployed southward to just east of Hill 107.5), and 100th Jäger Division's 54th Regiment (which formed up south of Hill 107.5), began advancing into the depths of the lower villages. As they moved, they encountered elements of 23rd Tank Corps' shattered tank and motorized rifle brigades and 193rd Rifle Division's 895th and 883rd Regiments, defending the lower Krasnyi Oktiabr' and Barrikady villages. The 112th Rifle Division's 416th and 524th Regiments manned defenses at and west of the Silikat Factory.

By this time, Popov had subordinated all of 23rd Tank Corps' remaining forces to 6th Guards Tank Brigade (although they were still redeploying to their new positions), bringing the brigade's strength at day's end on 30 September to 21 operational tanks (14 T-34, 1 T-70, and 6 T-60s), 5 inoperable T-34s, 268 "active bayonets," 1 antitank gun, 4 76mm field guns, 6 120mm mortars, and 10 82mm mortars.[63] In addition, Smekhotvorov's 193rd Rifle Division was reinforced by most of its 685th Regiment, which had just returned from 13th Guards Rifle Division's sector in Stalingrad's center city.[64] Upon its arrival, Smekhotvorov ordered the 685th to occupy defensive positions in the streets and buildings west of Sormosk, on the division's right wing. Farther south, on the right wing of Seydlitz's corps, 100th Jäger Division was still completing the task of clearing bypassed remnants of 112th Rifle Division's two regiments from the approaches to the central section of Krasnyi Oktiabr' Factory and capturing the upper Bannyi Ravine and western slopes of Mamaev Kurgan. On Sanne's right, 295th Infantry Division's three regiments continued their struggle to expel 284th Rifle Division's three regiments from the northern and eastern slopes of Mamaev Kurgan, the southern part of the Meat Combine, the Tennis Racket, and the Dolgii and Krutoi Ravines.

The Red Army General Staff's daily operational summary described the day's fighting from its perspective:

62nd Army was continuing to conduct stubborn defensive fighting with enemy infantry and tanks on its right wing in the vicinity of Orlovka and in Stalingrad city on 30 September.

42nd RB [reconstituted] occupied defenses in the area of the woods northeast of Barrikady village with part of its forces (three rifle companies).

6th Gds. TB occupied defenses along the southern edge of the woods north of Barrikady village.

23rd TC transferred all of its remaining equipment and brigade personnel [17 tanks and up to 150 soldiers] to 6th Gds. TB.

112th RD was defending just north of the "Silikat" Factory with the remnants of its 416th and 524th RRs.

92nd RB [reconstituted] occupied defenses along the line from west of the southern outskirts of the "Silikat" Factory past Makeevskaia [Makeevka] Street to the ravine.

193rd RD, operating in small groups, beginning on the morning of 30 September, conducted offensive operations to destroy the enemy in the vicinity of the western outskirts of Krasnyi Oktiabr' village. The division's 685th RR concentrated in the region west of the Barrikady Factory.

95th and 284th RDs remained in their previous positions, repelling attacks by small groups of enemy.

13th Gds. RD continued to hold on to its occupied positions and fought street battles in Stalingrad city with small groups.

39th Gds. RD (3,500 men) and 308th RD, numbering 4,000 men, crossed to the right bank of the Volga River to reinforce the Stalingrad garrison.[65]

In heavy but fragmented fighting throughout the day, Seydlitz's shock groups pushed forward but at a drastically reduced pace, ultimately expanding their 90-degree wedge projecting into Stalingrad's factory district by no more than 250 meters to the east. With *Kampfgruppe* Winterfeld stationary around the upper Barrikady village preparing for its advance on 1 October, *Kampfgruppe* Edelsheim, flanked on the right by 276th Infantry Regiment and the left-wing regiments of Sanne's 100th Jäger Division, pushed slowly and painstakingly into the western sections of the lower Krasnyi Oktiabr' village in block-to-block and house-to-house fighting, with advances measured in the tens of meters per hour. By day's end, Edelsheim's group had secured a 100-meter bridgehead around the narrows.

With both of his *kampfgruppen* aligned, at 1615 hours Lenski ordered them to prepare a concerted advance at dawn on 1 October to "gain the hills on the northeastern edge of Barrikady" by "occupying the ridge in grid squares 84a, 85c, and 75d and c."[66] To the south, 276th Infantry Regiment and 100th Jäger Division's 54th and 227th Regiments clawed their way 150–250 meters eastward into the lower Krasnyi Oktiabr' village toward the railroad line and factory. Still farther south, 100th Jäger Division's Croatian

369th Regiment and 295th Infantry Division's 516th Regiment, now fighting side by side on Mamaev Kurgan, clung tenaciously to the crest and the northern and eastern slopes. However, during the fighting on 30 September, Seydlitz's two shock groups failed once again to capture the Silikat Factory, penetrate into the Krasnyi Oktiabr' Factory, or push the defending Soviets off Mamaev Kurgan and into the Volga.

By day's end, 24th Panzer Division's two *kampfgruppen* faced the remnants of 112th Rifle Division's 416th Regiment, clinging to defensive positions facing to the south at the Silikat Factory, flanked on the right by 385th Regiment of Ermolkin's 112th Rifle Division, which defended the woodland north of Barrikady village. On the right wing of Ermolkin's division, two rifle companies with 132 men from its 524th Regiment and the few remaining tanks and soldiers of Popov's 23rd Tank Corps, now concentrated in 6th Guards Tank Brigade, defended the sector from the western edge of the woods to the Mokraia Mechetka River.

On 112th Rifle Division's left, but facing westward at a right angle to Gorishnyi's defenses, 685th, 895th, and 883rd Regiments of Smekhotvorov's 193rd Rifle Division, now deployed abreast, defended positions extending southward along Zhmerinskaia, Aivazovskaia, Dublinskaia [Dublin], and Kuzliarskaia Streets. They opposed 276th Infantry Regiment and 100th Jäger Division's 54th and 227th Regiments and protected the approaches to the railroad line and Krasnyi Oktiabr' Factory. Opposite 100th Jäger Division's 369th Regiment and 516th Regiment on the left wing of 295th Infantry Division, Gorishnyi's 95th Rifle Division clung to its hard-won footholds on the northern and eastern slopes of Mamaev Kurgan, with its 241st and 161st Regiments on its right wing and in its center lodged on the northern slope of the burial mound and protecting the approaches to the Military Clothing Factory. On Gorishnyi's left wing, the 90th Regiment, reinforced by several battalions from 284th Rifle Division's 1045th Regiment, defended the eastern slopes and the approaches to the Meat Combine.

Finally, south of Mamaev Kurgan, opposite 518th and 517th Regiments on 295th Infantry Division's right wing, 1045th, 1047th, and 1043rd Regiments of Batiuk's 284th Rifle Division, deployed abreast from north to south, defended the narrow strip of land west of the Volga River extending southward from the southern slope of Mamaev Kurgan past the Dolgii and Krutoi Ravines to its left boundary with 13th Guards Rifle Division.

Seydlitz's shock groups had recorded substantial progress in heavy fighting in the workers' villages but only minimal progress on Mamaev Kurgan. Worse yet, the single regiment (194th) of XXXXVIII Panzer Corps' 71st Infantry Division still fighting in Stalingrad's center city proved unable to compress 13th Guards Rifle Division's defenses. There, only three to four city blocks from the Volga River's western bank, Rodimtsev created a virtually impregnable defense based on multiple platoon, company, and battalion strongpoints scattered throughout the dense network of buildings north and south of 9 January Square. So configured, his riflemen proved capable of parrying every blow delivered by Hartmann's grenadiers. By day's end on 30 September, 13th Guards Rifle Division was defending with its 39th Regiment, supported by the reinforced 1st Battalion of 193rd Rifle Division's 685th Regiment, on its left wing along Respublikanskaia and Penzenskaia Streets south of 9 January Square. Its 42nd Regiment was in the center protecting the region around and north of the square; on the right wing, its 34th Regiment clung to Naberezhnaia Street northward to Krutoi Ravine, just one block from the river.[67]

In cooperation with 295th Infantry Division's 517th Regiment on its left, 194th Regiment of Hartmann's 71st Division conducted four assaults in multicompany or battalion strength against Rodimtsev's defenses during the period from 28 September through 1 October. In the north, a 300-man force from 517th Regiment attempted to penetrate the defenses of 3rd Battalion, 34th Guards Regiment, along the southern bank of Krutoi Ravine on the night of 30 September–1 October. However, reinforcements from the regiment's 1st Battalion and 39th Guards Regiment's Training Battalion and Administrative Company helped thwart this assault. Farther south, 194th Regiment also launched unsuccessful attacks against 42nd Guards Regiment's 2nd and 3rd Battalions north of 9 January Square and two more against 39th Guards Regiment's 1st and 3rd Battalions south of the square. Despite Hartmann's best efforts, however, a virtual stalemate existed in Stalingrad's center city by month's end.

Coupled with the enduring, determined, and often fanatical Soviet resistance, Paulus was most depressed by the steady flow of Soviet reinforcements into the city and factory district and his inability to seize the vital landing sites on the river's western bank. Beginning on the night of 29–30 September and for several days thereafter, Chuikov received fresh reinforcements, including the freshly reconstituted and regrouped 42nd and 92nd Rifle Brigades and 37th Guards, 39th Guards, and 308th Rifle Divisions. By committing these additional reinforcements, which initially amounted to roughly 14,000 men but ultimately totaled more than 20,000, Chuikov was able to stabilize his defenses in the most critical and threatened sectors. This was essential, because from 26 September through 30 September Stalingrad Front reported losing 16,174 men, including 3,767 dead, 10,217 wounded, 878 missing in action, and 1,311 who perished for other reasons.[68]

Nor could Paulus match these reinforcements with those of his own. Faced with these difficulties, Seydlitz's assault began to stall. Symptomatic of his problems, the renewed assaults by 295th Infantry Division failed to penetrate 95th and 284th Rifle Divisions' defenses around Mamaev Kurgan and along the Dolgii and Krutoi Ravines. Adding to the problem, a local counterattack by Batiuk's division recaptured part of the Meat Combine at the eastern base of Mamaev Kurgan.

CHUIKOV RECEIVES REINFORCEMENTS, 29 SEPTEMBER– 1 OCTOBER

On 30 September Stalingrad Front assigned Major Generals S. S. Gur'ev's and V. G. Zholudev's 39th and 37th Guards Rifle Divisions and Colonel L. N. Gurt'ev's 308th Rifle Division to Chuikov's army and also ordered Shumilov's 64th Army to mount an attack south of the city to distract German attentions and forces from the fighting in Stalingrad city (see Chapter 5).[69]

No newcomer to the heavy fighting in the Stalingrad region, Gur'ev's 39th Guards Division had fought under 4th Tank and 1st Guards Armies' control during the intense struggle for the Kletskaia bridgehead and Zhukov's counterstrokes in the Kotluban' region during the second half of August and early September.[70] After suffering heavy casualties in these battles, Eremenko on 25 September assigned Gur'ev's division, which now numbered 4,082 men, to Chuikov's army, with instructions that he employ it to reinforce his garrison in Stalingrad.[71]

Although woefully understrength, Gur'ev's division consisted of veteran paratroopers of 5th Airborne Corps, which had been converted into 39th Guards Rifle Division between 25 March and 6 August 1942. Its commander, 40-year-old Stepan Savel'evich Gur'ev, was an experienced combat leader who had commanded 5th Airborne Corps as a colonel since 6 December 1941, was promoted to the rank of major general on 5 March 1942, and had commanded the airborne corps since its conversion into a guards rifle division in the summer of 1942.[72] Gur'ev's division regrouped into the Krasnaia Sloboda region east of the Volga River and Stalingrad city between 25 and 28 September in the expectation of rapid commitment into the city.

The history of Zholudev's 37th Guards Rifle Division, which numbered 6,695 soldiers on 25 September and about the same when it crossed the Volga on the night of 3–4 October, closely resembled that of Gur'ev's division.[73] Formed from 1st Airborne Corps during the same period as 39th Guards Rifle Division experienced its transformation, Zholudev's guards division also consisted of veteran paratroopers who had fought under 4th Tank Army at Kletskaia and Kotluban' during late August and September.[74] Its commander, 37-year-old Viktor Grigor'evich Zholudev, had commanded 1st Airborne Corps as a colonel since 15 December 1941, was promoted to the rank of major general on 19 January 1942, and thereafter had commanded the corps through its transformation into a guards rifle division.[75] Zholudev's division regrouped into the Krasnyi Buksir and Tsyganskaia regions east of the Volga and Stalingrad between 28 September and 2 October for future commitment into the city.

Finally, Gurt'ev's 308th Rifle Division, which numbered 4,248 men on 25 September, was also a veteran force.[76] It had been formed on 12 January 1942 as a second-formation division after its predecessor had been destroyed. Thereafter, the 308th fought under 24th and 21st Armies during the bloody fighting in the Kotluban' region during August and September. Its commander, 51-year-old Leontii Nikolaevich Gurt'ev, served as a regimental commander and rifle-division chief of staff before his assignment to command the second-formation 308th in February 1942.[77] Gurt'ev's division moved into its new assembly areas east of the city on 29 and 30 September.

In addition to the three new rifle divisions, Eremenko also reinforced Chuikov's beleaguered defenders in Stalingrad with 42nd and 92nd Rifle Brigades, which had withdrawn from Stalingrad's center city without proper orders on 24 and 25 September; under new commanders, they were rested, refitted, and relatively combat-ready. The two brigades crossed the Volga and arrived in the city on the night of 29–30 September. The 42nd Brigade reinforced 62nd Army's defenses at the boundary between 193rd Rifle Division's right-wing 685th Regiment and 416th Regiment on 112th Rifle Division's left wing. The brigade manned defensive positions, with its right anchored on the road junction 350 meters northwest of the Silikat Factory and its left in the grove of trees 800 meters northeast of the Barrikady Factory. The 92nd Brigade initially replaced the remnants of Popov's decimated 23rd Tank Corps in the vicinity of the Krasnyi Oktiabr' Factory.[78]

Soon after, beginning on the night of 30 September–1 October, 112th, 117th, and 120th Regiments of Gur'ev's 39th Guards Rifle Division crossed the Volga River on armored cutters and occupied all-around defenses in the vicinity of the Krasnyi Oktiabr' Factory. By the time the division crossed the river, its rifle companies numbered 40–50 men each. Initially, Chuikov planned to deploy Gur'ev's division in defenses extending from the left wing of 112th Rifle Division's defenses around the Silikat Factory on the right to Zuevskaia Street on the left, where it was to link up with 193rd Rifle Division's defenses and prepare to counterattack in order to clear German forces from Barrikady village. However, when 24th Panzer Division's assault on 1 October drove a wedge between the defenses of 112th and 193rd Rifle Divisions south of the Silikat Factory, threatening the Krasnyi Oktiabr' Factory, Chuikov altered Gur'ev's mission.

Henceforth, 39th Guards Division was to form a second echelon behind Smekhotvorov's 193rd Rifle Division. As such, the 39th manned a defensive line extending from the Skul'pturnyi region, east of the Silikat Factory, southward along Arbatovskaia [Arbat] Street to Sormoskaia Street, past the intersection of the railroad line at Buguruslanskaia [Buguruslan] Street, and farther south along Ordzhonikidze Street to Karusel'naia Street and Bannyi Ravine. Once in position, 39th Guards deployed with 112th Regiment on its left, 120th Regiment in its center, and 117th Regiment, the last to arrive in the city, on its right. In addition to defending this line stoutly, Gur'ev's division was to "consolidate itself firmly in the workshops of the Krasnyi Oktiabr' Factory, turning them into powerful strong points."[79]

Chuikov had nothing but praise for Gur'ev and his men. Characterizing him as "short, stocky, and robust—a man, whom, as they say, the enemy would not find easy to budge," he asserted that, like his men, who "did not know the meaning of the word retreat," "Gur'ev himself did not leave his command post even when the grenades of German tommy-gunners were bursting at the entrance."[80]

Beginning on the night of 30 September–1 October, Gurt'ev's 308th Rifle Division also began crossing the Volga, also on cutters, in a process that would last two days. The division's 351st Regiment, reinforced by its supporting antitank and machine-gun battalions, led the crossing on the first night and occupied defensive positions along with 42nd and 92nd Rifle Brigades in the vicinity of the Silikat Factory, west of the Barrikady Factory.[81] By this time, Gurt'ev's lead regiment was flanked on the left (south) by 193rd Rifle and 39th Guards Rifle Divisions, echeloned with one behind the other, and on the right (north) by the remnants of 112th Rifle Division and 42nd Rifle Brigade. Gurt'ev's remaining regiments, the 339th and 347th, crossed the river on the night of 1–2 October and soon joined 351st Regiment in the vicinity of Skul'pturnyi village and park.

Gurt'ev, the commander of 308th Division, appeared to lead a charmed life. "Tall and slim, he did not like to stoop to German shells and bombs"; displaying "unparalleled courage," he encouraged his troops to ever greater efforts, and he survived the entire battle.[82] As soon as Gurt'ev's lead regiment, the 351st, had arrived, it, together with 92nd Rifle Brigade on its left, was to launch a determined counterattack against German forces in the Barrikady workers' village at dawn on 2 October. Striking 24th Panzer Division's *Kampfgruppe* Group Edelsheim, which was just beginning its own headlong attack in the opposite direction, Gurt'ev's riflemen accomplished nothing. Within days, the attrition would be so high in both of the attacking units that Chuikov would have no choice but to dissolve the 92nd Rifle Brigade and incorporate its survivors into the ranks of Gurt'ev's division.

By virtue of these reinforcements, by late on 1 October 62nd Army reported that its combat formations in Stalingrad city fielded 44,201 men (see Table 27).[83]

Table 27.   The Personnel Strength of 62nd Army's Combat Forces at 1800 hours on 1 October 1942

In Stalingrad City:
- 13th Guards Rifle Division – 5,866 men
- 39th Guards Rifle Division – 3,741 men
- 95th Rifle Division – 2,592 men
- 112th Rifle Division – 2,722 men
- 193rd Rifle Division – 4,687 men
- 284th Rifle Division – 3,469 men
- 308th Rifle Division – 4,055 men
- 42nd Rifle Brigade – 1,151 men
- 92nd Rifle Brigade – 1,831 men
- 124th Rifle Brigade – 4,154 men
- 149th Rifle Brigade – 3,302 men
- 2nd Motorized Rifle Brigade – 1,131 men
- 115th Rifle Brigade – 3,464 men
- 6th Guards Tank Brigade – 963 men and 21 tanks (14 T-34s, 1 T-70, and 6 T-60s)
- 282nd Rifle Regiment (NKVD) – 1,073 men
- **Total in City – 44,201 men**
On the eastern bank of the Volga:
- 37th Guards Rifle Division – 6,695 men
- 84th Tank Brigade – 2,500 men (est.) and 49 tanks (5 KVs, 24 T-34s, and 20 T-70s)
- 2nd Tank Corps (re-forming) – 4,000 men (est.)
- 23rd Tank Corps (re-forming) – headquarters only

Source: Entry for 1800 hours, 1 October 1942, in *62nd Army Combat Journal*.

THE REDUCTION OF THE ORLOVKA SALIENT, 29 SEPTEMBER–3 OCTOBER

Beginning on 29 September, as intense fighting raged along the approaches to the factory district and within the remainder of the Krasnyi Oktiabr' and Barrikady workers' villages, Paulus shifted part of his attention to reducing the irritating salient occupied by Soviet forces around the village of Orlovka (see Map 42). This salient jutted almost 10 kilometers to the northwest along the Orlovka River from the junction of the Orlovka and Mokraia Mechetka Rivers and ranged in width from 3 kilometers at its apex to 1.5 kilometers at its waist. The salient was particularly troublesome for Paulus because it separated Hube's XIV Panzer Corps from Seydlitz's LI Corps, its neighbor to the south, and tied down forces that were vitally needed in the assault on Stalingrad proper. Unless and until Sixth Army eliminated the salient, it would continue to tie down these forces and thereby remain a serious impediment to the capture of the factory district.

Prior to 28 September, the fighting around the salient was desultory at best, with both sides carrying out "small-scale attacks resulting in minor fluctuations in the front line, amounting to not more than 100–200 yards."[84] Zhukov's many assaults against XIV Panzer Corps' defenses between Ezhovka

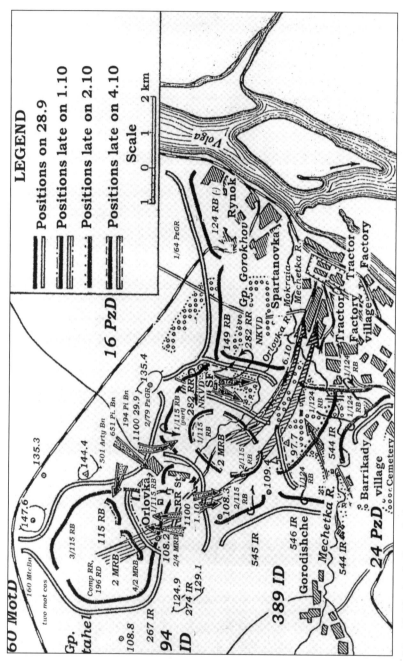

Map 42. The battle for Orlovka, 29 September–3 October 1942

and the Kotluban' region distracted Hube's attentions from the salient. As Chuikov explained, "Apart from limited counter-attacks, we did not and could not wage active operations because we had no forces with which to do so."[85]

As of 28 September, Chuikov defended the increasingly isolated and vulnerable salient with 115th Rifle and 2nd Motorized Rifle Brigades, a composite detachment formed from 196th Rifle Division's 724th Regiment, and another consisting of 250 men from 112th Rifle Division, 1st Battalion, 124th Rifle Brigade, and 1st Battalion, 149th Rifle Brigade. Under the overall command of Colonel K. M. Andriusenko, the commander of 115th Rifle Brigade, this force totaled roughly 6,500 men equipped and supported by 50 76mm field guns, 200 mortars, 36 antitank guns, 72 heavy machine guns, and 150 antitank rifles.

Deployed along the salient's eastern perimeter, 115th Rifle Brigade's 1st and 3rd Battalions occupied defensive positions extending from south of Hill 135.4, 3 kilometers north of the Orlovka River, northward along a 5-kilometer front to south of Hill 147.3, 3 kilometers due north of Orlovka village. The 115th Brigade's right (eastern) flank was protected by Group Gorokhov's 282nd NKVD Rifle Regiment, which was deployed in defensive positions in a State Farm south of Hill 135.4, and by part of 1st Battalion, 149th Rifle Brigade, also subordinate to Group Gorokhov. Farther east, the main forces of Group Gorokhov's 124th and 149th Rifle Brigades defended the Spartanovka and Rynok regions north of the Orlovka and Mokraia Mechetka Rivers and the factory district.

In turn, 115th Rifle Brigade's left flank was protected by 196th Rifle Division's composite 724th Regiment, which defended the sector extending from south of Hill 147.6 to east of Hill 108.8 to protect the northwestern approaches to Orlovka. On 724th Regiment's left, 2nd Motorized Rifle Brigade's 4th and 2nd Battalions, 2nd Battalion, 115th Rifle Brigade, and 1st Battalion, 124th Rifle Brigade, were deployed in defensive positions extending southward east of Hills 124.9 and 129.1 and then southeastward to the Mechetka River to protect the salient's western and southwestern perimeters.[86]

On 28 September Paulus's army was employing forces from three of his army's divisions to contain Soviet forces in the salient. East of the salient, opposite the defenses of 282nd NKVD Rifle Regiment and 1st Battalion, 115th Rifle Brigade, 2nd Battalion, 79th Grenadier Regiment, and 501st Artillery and 651st Pioneer (Combat Engineer) Battalions from Angern's 16th Panzer Division were deployed from left to right (east to west) in positions stretching from Hill 135.4 to Hill 144.4. North of the salient and opposite the defenses of 3rd Battalion, 115th Rifle Brigade, 160th Motorcycle Battalion of Kohlermann's 60th Motorized Division occupied positions in the vicinity of Hill 147.6. On the salient's northwestern and western flanks, opposite the composite 724th Rifle Regiment and 2nd Motorized Rifle Brigade, Group Stahel's *Luftwaffe* forces manned defensive positions extending from west of Hill 147.4 southward past Hill 108.8 to Hills 124.9 and 129.1 northeast of Gorodishche.

Overnight on 28–29 September, 267th and 274th Regiments of Pfeiffer's 94th Infantry Division moved northward from the southern part of Stalingrad city and, screened by Group Stahel, occupied jumping-off positions extending from Hill 108.8 southward to Hills 124.9 and 129.1. Finally, on the salient's southwestern flank, forces from 545th and 546th Regiments of Jänecke's 389th Infantry Division were already deployed in positions extending from northeast of Gorodishche southward to the Mechetka River, facing the defenses of 2nd Battalion, 115th Rifle Brigade, and 1st Battalion, 124th Rifle Brigade.[87]

Paulus's plan for crushing the Orlovka salient required multiple battalion- and company-size *kampfgruppen* from 16th Panzer and 60th Motorized Divisions of Hube's XIV Panzer Corps to attack toward Orlovka from the east and north. However, since all three of Hube's divisions were still actively involved in repulsing the incessant Soviet assaults on their defenses in the Kotluban' and Ezhovka regions to the north, the corps commander could employ only a limited number of units, including a small nucleus of precious panzer-grenadier units, supplemented by artillery, pioneer, and dismounted motorcycle troops, to crush the Soviets' salient defenses. Therefore, his assault force ultimately consisted only of 16th Panzer Division's 2nd Battalion, 79th Grenadier Regiment, supported by 501st Artillery and 194th and 651st Pioneer Battalions, which Sixth Army had attached to his panzer corps. These scratch forces were to assault the salient's defenses in the sector from Hill 135.4 to Hill 144.4 east of Orlovka. On 16th Panzer Division's right flank, 60th Motorized Division's 160th Motorcycle Battalion, supported by several other companies dispatched from the division's motorized regiments, was to assault southward from Hill 147.6 toward Orlovka from the north.

Farther west, with their left flank protected by Group Stahel, the *kampfgruppen* from 94th Infantry Division's 267th and 274th Regiments, their four battalions already rated "weak," were to assault the salient from the vicinity of Hills 108.8, 124.9, and 129.1 and then advance on Orlovka from the west. Finally, operating under LI Corps' control, 545th and 546th Regiments of Jänecke's 389th Infantry Division, whose four infantry battalions were also rated "weak," were to advance eastward from the region east of Gorodishche and north of the Mechetka River to collapse the salient's southern perimeter, cut off its base, and prevent its defenders from withdrawing southeastward along the Orlovka River to rejoin Chuikov's forces defending the northern section of the factory district.

29 September

To soften up the salient's defenses, Paulus orchestrated heavy air strikes against the pocket between 2000 hours on 28 September and 0600 hours on 29 September, during which *Luftwaffe* aircraft dropped as many as 7,000 bombs on the defenders. Then Hube's artillery joined the fray:

> On 29 September the *Nebelwerfer* [rocket launchers] howled aloft; JU-87s dove ceaselessly at Orlovka, [and] artillery shells struck the enemy fortress. Then two companies of the newly-arrived 651st Pioneer Battalion and [8th Company, 79th Panzer Grenadiers] went forward. But the Russians held and broke up the attack until well into the afternoon.
>
> On 30 September once again: Stukas! Columns of brown smoke rose to heaven; the men went forward through the smoke plumes and fought the increasingly-tenacious opponent, taking [part of] Orlovka and mopping up the area.
>
> The attack of 651st and 194th Pioneer Battalions [southward toward Orlovka] . . . [advanced] 100 meters with great difficulty.[88]

62nd Army's daily operational summary cryptically described the fighting on 29 September:

> [Group Gorokhov's] 124th and 149th RBs were continuing to occupy their previous positions.
>
> 282nd RR NKVD repelled enemy attacks from the region of Hill 135.4.
>
> 115th RB engaged in stubborn defensive fighting with attacking enemy units and withdrew its right wing slightly from the positions it occupied.
>
> 2nd MRB fought fierce defensive battles and withdrew to the vicinity of Hill 104.6 (2 kilometers west of Orlovka) under enemy pressure.[89]

After German artillery pounded the salient's defenses from 0700 to 0800 hours, Hube began his attack along two axes, with company-strength reconnaissance groups feeling out the strength of the Soviet defenses. Cooperating with two companies from 651st Pioneer Battalion, 8th Company of 16th Panzer Division's 79th Grenadier Regiment advanced southward toward Orlovka along both sides of the road midway between Hills 134.5 and 144.4 but were halted by the defending 282nd NKVD Regiment and 1st Battalion, 115th Rifle Brigade. Simultaneously, several reinforced companies from 94th Infantry Division advanced eastward from Hills 124.9 and 129.1 toward the railroad station, 500 meters southwest of Orlovka, but were also halted in their tracks by 2nd Motorized Rifle Brigade's defenses.

Once Hube's forces completed their reconnaissances-in-force, at 1000 hours his infantry and combat engineers began their main assaults, this time along three separate axes.[90] The first two axes were north of Hill 135.4 (16th Panzer Division's 2nd Battalion, 79th Grenadier Regiment, and 501st Artillery and 651st Pioneer Battalions) and along the axis from Hills 124.9 and 129.1 (two battalions from Pfeiffer's 94th Infantry Division). Finally, a battalion-size *kampfgruppe* from 60th Motorized Rifle Division struck southward from Hill 147.6 toward Orlovka, reportedly supported by 15 tanks and assault guns. This attack struck the defenses of 3rd Battalion, 115th Rifle Brigade. Although the 60th failed to penetrate Andriusenko's defenses, the assaults by 94th Infantry Division's *kampfgruppen* penetrated the salient's defenses along 2nd Motorized Brigade's front and at the boundary of its defenses with the adjacent 724th Regiment. The advance by Pfeiffer's *kampfgruppen* propelled the lead elements of his 94th Division to within a half-kilometer of the railroad station, 300 meters south of Orlovka, and the railroad bridge over the Orlovka River, 500 meters to the south. The attack also split 2nd Motorized Brigade into two parts, forcing its 4th Battalion to withdraw northward to Hill 108.2, where, together with the composite 724th Regiment, it organized an all-round defense. The 2nd Motorized Brigade's 1st, 2nd, and 3rd Battalions had no choice but to begin withdrawing back to the southern outskirts of Orlovka.

South of 94th Infantry Division's penetration, 2nd Battalion, 115th Rifle Brigade, fought its way southeastward, where it erected new defenses between Hill 108.3, 1.5 kilometers south of Orlovka, and Hill 109.4, 3 kilometers south of Orlovka. However, in addition to having to contend with the 94th's rapid advance from the northwest and west, 2nd Battalion's defenses were struck at 1600 hours by a battalion of infantry from 389th Infantry Division, reportedly supported by an artillery barrage and up to 50 tanks and assault guns. The 389th Division's *kampfgruppe* advanced northeastward across Kazenniaia *Balka*, a ravine that extended northward from the northern bank of the Mechetka River. Pressed from all sides, 2nd Battalion withdrew to all-around defenses on the crest of Hill 108.3 and Hill 109.3.[91]

Meanwhile, pressed hard by 16th Panzer Division's *kampfgruppe* advancing from Hill 135.4, northeast of Orlovka, 1st Battalion, 115th Rifle Brigade, gave ground steadily, ultimately retreating to the northern outskirts of the village. However, 3rd Battalion, 115th Rifle Brigade, which had repulsed all attempts by 60th Motorized Division's *kampfgruppe* to advance on Orlovka from the northwest, and 4th Battalion, 2nd Motorized Rifle Brigade, which had withdrawn to Hill 108.2, managed to cling to their defenses west and northwest of Orlovka throughout the entire day. 16th Panzer and 389th Infantry Divisions' *kampfgruppen* were unable to cut off and encircle the forces in the salient.

30 September–8 October

On 30 September, violent German assaults against the defenses of Andriu-senko's forces from the north, west, and east steadily compressed the two Soviet battalions fighting northwest and west of Orlovka and the parts of the two battalions fighting around Orlovka proper into ever tighter pockets. Andriusenko's defenses held at a heavy cost to the advancing Germans.[92] At nightfall, Group Gorokhov's 282nd NKVD Regiment still clung to its positions south of Hill 135.4, protecting the northern approaches into the salient's narrow base. Within the salient's center, 1st Battalion, 115th Rifle Brigade, now reinforced by most of 2nd Motorized Rifle Brigade's 1st, 2nd, and 3rd Battalions, defended the southern section of Orlovka village, its front facing toward the northeast. Farther north, the main forces of 3rd Battalion, 115th Rifle Brigade, defended positions northwest of Orlovka, with one company protecting the southwestern approaches to the village. To the west, 4th Battalion, 2nd Motorized Rifle Brigade, manned defenses facing westward and southwestward in the sector from Hill 108.2 to just east of Hill 108.8. Farther south, 2nd Battalion, 115th Rifle Brigade, still held its positions on Hills 108.3 and 109.4, while on its left 1st Battalion, 124th Rifle Brigade, covered the southern side of the corridor from Hill 109.3 to the Mokraia Mechetka River. The incessant German assaults during the day had reduced the width of the salient and associated corridor to 1,000–1,200 meters and the strength of each of the defending battalion groups to 200–250 men each.[93]

That night the Red Army General Staff recorded:

124th and 149th RBs and 282nd RR, 10th RD NKVD, continued to hold on to their previous positions.

The left wing subunits of 115th RB and the right wing subunits of 2nd MRB, after repeated attacks by the enemy on Orlovka village from the northeast and the southwest, were pushed back to Peschanaia *Balka* and Vodianaia *Balka* by day's end on 30 September. The fighting is continuing in this region. Individual enemy tanks reached the outskirts of Orlovka.[94]

At 1100 hours on 1 October, 94th Infantry Division's *kampfgruppe* resumed its attack and captured the cemetery 300 meters west of Orlovka. To the east, 16th Panzer Division's *kampfgruppe* captured most of Orlovka village, but only after mounting two determined assaults. In the process, 16th Panzer encircled 3rd Battalion, 115th Rifle Brigade, and 4th Battalion, 2nd Motorized Rifle Brigade, in a narrow pocket extending northwest and west of the village. The remainder of 1st Battalion, 115th Rifle Brigade, and 2nd Motorized Rifle Brigade's remaining three battalions clung desperately to their defenses in the southern part of Orlovka. The Red Army General Staff duly reported, "124th and 149th RBs and 282nd RR NKVD were continuing to occupy their previous positions. 115th RB repelled repeated attacks by up to a regiment of enemy infantry with tanks and continued to hold on to its positions. [No reports were received from 2nd MRB.]"[95]

Beginning on 2 October, heavy fighting erupted south of Orlovka when *kampfgruppen* from 389th Infantry Division's 545th and 546th Regiments repeatedly assaulted the defenses of 2nd Battalion, 115th Rifle Brigade, on and north of Hill 109.4, as well as 1st Battalion, 124th Rifle Brigade, defending north of the Mechetka River. Attacking at 1100 hours, Jänecke's *kampfgruppen*, estimated by the Soviets as a force of up to a full regiment accompanied by 30 tanks and assault guns, struck eastward north of the river. After an intense two-hour fight, 1st Battalion, 124th Rifle Brigade, was forced to withdraw eastward to the woods 1 kilometer southeast of Hill 97.7, only 3 kilometers northwest of Barrikady village.

On 3 October, however, with Orlovka encircled but the advance into Stalingrad's factory district faltering, the commander of Sixth Army shuffled his forces once again to generate the forces necessary for LI Corps' attack toward the Tractor Factory. He did so by replacing the 545th and 546th Regiments of Jänecke's 389th Infantry Division north of the Mechetka River with the 267th and 274th Regiments of Pfeiffer's 94th Infantry Division. Jänecke's two regiments were then to move southward across the Mechetka River and join with the division's 544th Regiment to support 24th Panzer Division's advance by attacking eastward on its left flank. This decision afforded 1st Battalion, 124th Rifle Brigade, a brief respite on 3 October as Paulus regrouped his forces.

After Pfeiffer's 267th and 274th Regiments shifted into their new offensive sectors and resumed their attacks, the renewed German assaults against Andriusenko's forces around Orlovka led to two more days of intense fighting. This struggle decimated the Soviet defenses along the entire southern flank of the Orlovka corridor and threatened Andriusenko's entire force with encirclement and destruction. And the northern flank of the Orlovka corridor was no longer safe, because beginning on 4 October, when Zhukov ceased his assaults in the Kotluban' region, Hube's XIV Panzer Corps was finally able to release additional forces from its 14th Panzer and 60th Motorized Divisions to participate in an all-out assault on the Orlovka salient and also against Group Gorokhov's bridgehead at Rynok and Spartanovka, north of the Mokraia Mechetka River and Stalingrad's factory district.

Acknowledging the loss of Orlovka and the encirclement of two of Andriusenko's battalions, the Red Army General Staff on 2 October recorded:

[2 October]
    124th and 149th RBs and 282nd RR NKVD continued to occupy their previous positions.

    The units of 115th RB and 2nd MRB were fighting in encirclement in the vicinity of Kamennaia [Rocky] *Balka*, the southern bank of Vodianaia *Balka* (incl.), and the railroad line, having repelled attacks by up to a regiment of enemy infantry from Hill 144.2 and up to a battalion of infantry from the region of Hill 108.2. Up to two companies of enemy infantry and 3 tanks were destroyed in the fighting. . . .

    Our units abandoned the village of Orlovka on 2 October under enemy pressure.

[3 October]
    124th and 149th RBs and 282nd RR NKVD continued to occupy their previous positions.

    3rd Bn, 115th RB, and 4th Bn, 2nd MRB, were fighting encircled in their previous region.[96]

Signaling its success, the OKW late on 2 October triumphantly announced, "Northwest of Stalingrad, the powerful strong point of Orlovka—the suburb of Stalingrad—was taken by storm and large groups of enemy were encircled to the west."[97]

After encircling Andriusenko's decimated group in and northwest of Orlovka and completing the reshuffling of his forces, Paulus on 4 October set about reducing the pocket and cutting off any Soviet forces still defending the shrinking corridor between the salient and the factory district. This time Hube decided to attack the remnants of the seven Soviet battalions encircled in the Orlovka region with small *kampfgruppen* from 60th Motorized and 16th Panzer Divisions, supported by Group Stahel, while larger forces from 16th Panzer Division assaulted the corridor's northern face and Group Gorokhov's defenses at Spartanovka. Simultaneously, south of the corridor, *kampfgruppen* from 94th Infantry Division's 267th and 274th Regiments were to advance northeastward north of the Mechetka River to reach the Orlovka River, link up with 16th Panzer's forces, and cut off the Orlovka salient at its base once and for all.

Attacking at 1600 hours on 4 October, 16th Panzer Division's *kampfgruppen* smashed the defenses of 282nd NKVD Rifle Regiment on the grounds of the State Farm south of Hill 135.4, forcing half of the regiment to withdraw southeastward to join Group Gorokhov's 149th Rifle Brigade and the other half to retreat westward, where it joined forces with 1st Battalion, 115th Rifle Brigade, and 2nd Motorized Rifle Brigade's 1st, 2nd, and 3rd Battalions in the southern outskirts of Orlovka. Meanwhile, shortly after noon, *kampfgruppen* from 94th Infantry Division's two regiments assaulted the defenses of 1st Battalion, 124th Rifle Brigade, on the corridor's southern face. This assault forced the battalion to withdraw eastward across the Mechetka River, where it took up positions along the southern bank, on 112th Rifle Division's right flank west of the Tractor Factory village.

By nightfall on 4 October, 16th Panzer and 94th Infantry Divisions' *kampfgruppen* finally linked up just north of the confluence of the Orlovka and Mechetka Rivers. In so doing, they encircled Andriusenko's Orlovka group in two pockets, the first containing 3rd Battalion, 115th Rifle Brigade, and 4th Battalion, 2nd Motorized Rifle Brigade, north of Orlovka, and the second containing 1st and 2nd Battalions, 115th Rifle Brigade, and the remnants of 2nd Motorized Rifle Brigade's 1st, 2nd, and 3rd Battalions south of Orlovka. That night the Red Army General Staff acknowledged the precarious situation facing Orlovka's defenders:

> 149th RB and 282nd RR NKVD withdrew to the southern outskirts of the state farm (2 kilometers northwest of Barrikady village) under heavy enemy pressure.
>
> 115th RB and 2nd MRB were continuing to fight half-encircled along the southern part of Orlovka village, the southern slope of Hill 108.8, and the northern slope of Hill 97.7 (3 kilometers northwest of the Stalingrad Tractor Factory) line up to the railroad.[98]

Hube's advancing *kampfgruppen* tightened their noose around Andriusenko's shrinking defenses north and south of Orlovka on 5 and 6 October. Unable to either reinforce or rescue Andriusenko's shattered groups because his forces in the Tractor Factory workers' village were also facing deadly German attacks, Chuikov limited himself to organizing long-range *Katiusha* barrages against German troop concentrations north of the Mokraia Mechetka River.[99] All the while, his headquarters sent its latest information about the fighting in the twin Orlovka pockets, as well as Group Gorokhov's bridgehead at Spartanovka (Spartakovka), to the Red Army General Staff, which recorded:

> [5 October]
> 124th RB occupied defenses along the northwestern outskirts of Rynok village, (incl.) Marker 123.8, and (incl.) Marker 64.7 line.
>
> 149th RB, with the remnants of 282nd RR NKVD, was located along the Marker 64.7 and the western outskirts of the Spartakovka region line, with covering forces facing south along the Orlovka River and the Mokraia Mechetka River.

115th RB and 2nd MRB were fighting in encirclement in the vicinity of Kamennaia, Vodianaia, and Peschanaia *Balkas*, the southeastern outskirts of Orlovka village, and the railroad bridge.[100]

[6 October]
149th RB, with the remnants of 282nd RR NKVD, repulsed an attack against its left flank from the vicinity of the State Farm (2.5–3 kilometers southeast of Orlovka village) by more than a battalion of enemy infantry and 11 tanks. Up to a company of enemy infantry and 5 tanks were destroyed.

115th RB and 2nd MRB were continuing intense fighting in encirclement in the region northwest and southeast of Orlovka village, while experiencing critical shortages of ammunition and food.[101]

As fighting raged throughout the entire Orlovka salient, late on 6 October a thoroughly frustrated Chuikov finally ordered his forces encircled in the Orlovka region to break out to the southeast and link up with the troops defending the Tractor Factory workers' village. Beset from all sides, the bulk of the soldiers in Andriusenko's northern group perished during their attempts to break out of the salient. However, because of the heavy rocket bombardment organized by Chuikov, a larger proportion of Andriusenko's southern group, fleeing westward individually and in small groups, ultimately made it back to 62nd Army's front lines on the western edge of the Tractor Factory workers' village. The Red Army General Staff's operational summary for that day provided an epitaph for Andriusenko's forces:

[7 October]
124th RB continued to hold on to its previous positions.

149th RB, with the remnants of 282nd RR NKVD repelled several attacks by small groups of enemy infantry while remaining in their previous positions.

115th RB and 2nd MRB were continuing an intense fight in encirclement in their previous regions. The garrison encircled northwest of Orlovka (3rd Bn, 115th RB, and 4th Bn, 2nd MRB) was fighting intense battles with an enemy force of up to two infantry battalions and 22 tanks, which was attacking from the northeast and southwest. The garrison encircled in the region northeast of Orlovka village (the remaining units of the brigade) was fighting fiercely with the enemy beginning on the morning of 7 October. Radio communication with them ceased at 1300 hours.

[8 October]
  3rd Bn, 115th RB, and 4th Bn, 2nd MRB (totaling 220 men), withdrew
  from encirclement and occupied defenses in the vicinity of the confluence of the Orlovka and Mokraia Mechetka Rivers.[102]

Although Soviet accounts vary regarding the number of soldiers who ultimately escaped the Orlovka salient, the most reliable estimate asserts that of
the 6,500 men initially encircled in the region no more than 220 escaped from
the twin pockets.[103] These figures, however, do not include the soldiers of 282nd
NKVD Rifle Regiment and 1st Battalion, 124th Rifle Brigade, even though
those units also suffered heavy casualties (but were ultimately able to withdraw
into 62nd Army's lines north and south of the Mokraia Mechetka River).
  The short but bloody fight for Orlovka was a mere sideshow to the heavy
fighting in Stalingrad city and its factory district. Nevertheless, this struggle,
during which pitifully small and weak Soviet units held off hastily organized
kampfgruppen from parts of four German divisions, typified the larger struggle throughout the region. From an operational standpoint, Paulus's successful elimination of the salient vastly improved his ability to command and
control his forces assaulting the city. However, the stout defense of the region by the two Soviet brigades from 26 September through 4 October severely hindered Sixth Army's operations against the city's factory district by
denying him the forces necessary to achieve quick and decisive victory.

CONCLUSIONS

During the last week of September, German Sixth Army succeeded in seizing
the western half of the Krasnyi Oktiabr' and Barrikady villages in Stalingrad's
northern factory district, encircling the Soviet forces defending the Orlovka
salient, and capturing most but not all of Mamaev Kurgan. Replicating his
army's assault on downtown Stalingrad the week before, Paulus spearheaded
his main attack on the factory district with panzers and panzer-grenadiers
from Lenski's 24th Panzer Division, supported by single infantry regiments
from 389th and 94th Infantry Divisions. Skillfully employing a combination
of shock action and maneuver, Lenski's division advanced more than 6 kilometers in two days of fighting, shattered Chuikov's defenses west of the
workers' villages, and seized ideal jumping-off positions for a subsequent
advance into the western section of the Tractor Factory workers' village, the
lower workers' villages, and the Tractor Factory itself. However, after 48 additional hours of fighting, Lenski's panzer division finally fell victim to the
accumulated attrition it had suffered in weeks of near-constant combat and
was unable to make any further advance.

Paulus was also encouraged by the progress his forces made in the Orlovka region northwest of Stalingrad. By encircling the Soviet force defending the Orlovka salient, Sixth Army's commander hoped to be able to restore closer communication between the forces on his army's left wing and in its center and, perhaps, even concentrate more forces for the final assault on the factory district. However, the victory at Orlovka also proved far less significant than anticipated. Although it did eliminate a thorn in Sixth Army's flesh, the constant threat of new assaults by the armies of Rokossovsky's Don Front against German forces defending the corridor between the Volga and Don Rivers largely negated the positive impact of the victory at Orlovka. Because Paulus expected new attacks against his VIII Army and XIV Panzer Corps at any time, he could ill afford to shift any forces from these corps southward to participate in the culminating assault on the city's factory district. Likewise, the Soviets' assaults against Fourth Panzer Army's defenses in the lake region south of Stalingrad had the same deleterious effect on Sixth Army.

Therefore, despite LI Corps' spectacular initial advance into the workers' villages (especially by 24th Panzer Division), Sixth Army's progress in late September fell far short of its commander's expectations. With only two infantry regiments in support, 24th Panzer Division had no choice but to postpone its advance toward the Tractor Factory workers' village until the end of September. Similarly, the attacks by 100th Jäger and 295th Infantry Divisions bogged down in heavy and costly fighting in the built-up regions west and south of the Barrikady and Krasnyi Oktiabr' Factories, on Mamaev Kurgan, and along the middle reaches of the Bannyi, Krutoi, and Dolgii Ravines. Operating farther to the south, 71st Infantry Division also failed to crush the remnants of Chuikov's forces defending in Stalingrad's center city.

With his army slowly but steadily bleeding to death, Paulus had no choice but to halt its advance through the workers' villages on 1 and 2 October so he could rest and reorganize the forces of Seydlitz's LI Corps and then reinforce them with the remainder of 389th Infantry Division. Once this was done, Paulus hoped that Seydlitz's corps could finally complete its task. As Table 28 indicates, Paulus had every reason to be concerned over the stark toll that combat attrition was having on his army. As the table indicates, whereas the number of battalions rated "medium strong" decreased sharply from 16 to 3, those rated "weak" and "exhausted" increased from 18 to 39. As a whole, the combat rating of Sixth Army's forces fighting in Stalingrad city decreased from "average" to well below "weak."

Undoubtedly, the Soviet 62nd Army suffered a major defeat during the last three days of September and the first three days of October. In addition to preempting and then defeating Chuikov's planned counterattacks, the assault by Seydlitz's corps demolished his defenses west of the workers' villages, captured the upper sections of the Krasnyi Oktiabr' and Barrikady workers'

Table 28. The Combat Rating of Infantry and Pioneer Battalions Subordinate to Sixth Army's Divisions Fighting in Stalingrad, 26 September–5 October 1942

	26 September	5 October
XIV PANZER CORPS		
3rd Motorized Division		
(5 infantry battalions)	1 medium strong, 3 average, and 1 weak	3 average and 2 weak
(1 pioneer battalion)	strong	exhausted
60th Motorized Division		
(7 infantry battalions)	6 average and 1 weak	4 average, 2 weak, and 1 exhausted
(1 pioneer battalion)	weak	exhausted
16th Panzer Division		
(5 infantry battalions)	3 medium strong and 2 average	3 medium strong, 1 average, and 1 weak
(1 pioneer battalion)	average	average
LI ARMY CORPS		
71st Infantry Division		
(7–8 infantry battalions)	4 weak and 3 exhausted	1 weak and 7 exhausted
(1 pioneer battalion)	average	average
295th Infantry Division		
(7 infantry battalions)	2 average, 4 weak, and 1 exhausted	4 weak and 3 exhausted
(1 pioneer battalion)	average	weak
389th Infantry Division		
(6 infantry battalions)	2 average and 4 weak	6 weak
(1 pioneer battalion)	average	exhausted
XXXXVIII PANZER CORPS		
24th Panzer Division		
(4 infantry battalions)	2 medium strong and 2 average	1 weak and 3 exhausted
(1 pioneer battalion)	average	average
29th Motorized Division		
(6 infantry battalions)	3 medium strong and 3 average	**(not fighting in the city)**
(1 pioneer battalion)	strong	
100th Jäger Division		
(5 infantry battalions)	**(not fighting in the city)**	4 average and 1 weak
(1 pioneer battalion)		weak
94th Infantry Division		
(7 infantry battalions)	7 medium strong	7 exhausted
(1 pioneer battalion)	average	average

Table 28. (continued)

	26 September	5 October
Totals:		
54 infantry battalions	16 medium strong, 20 average, 14 weak, and 4 exhausted	3 medium strong, 12 average, 18 weak, and 21 exhausted
9 pioneer battalions	2 strong, 5 average, and 2 weak	4 average, 2 weak, and 3 exhausted

Source: "Betr.: Zustand der Divisionen, Armee – Oberkommando 6, Abt. Ia, A. H. Qu., den 26 September 42," and "Betr.: Zustand der Divisionen, erstmalig nach neu festlegter Bestimmung des Begriffes "Gefechsstärke," Armee – Oberkommando 6, Abt. Ia, A. H. Qu., den 5 Oktober 1942," in *Die Anlagenbander zu den Kriegstagebuchern der 6. Armee vom 14.09.1942 bis 24.11.1942, Band I* (Schwabach: January 2006), 59–62 and 128–132.

villages, seized footholds in their lower sections, and secured ideal jumping-off positions for a subsequent advance on the Tractor Factory. At the same time, Hube's panzer corps encircled and destroyed Chuikov's forces in the Orlovka region, and to the south Seydlitz's forces managed to capture most of Mamaev Kurgan. In the process, the heavy fighting decimated 112th Rifle Division and 23rd Tank Corps. From Chuikov's perspective, then, the only saving grace was the timely arrival in the Stalingrad region of three fresh divisions, 39th and 37th Guards and 308th Rifle, and the release to his control of the refurbished 42nd and 92nd Rifle Brigades. The issue was whether the arrival of these forces could undo the damage done by Lenski's panzers and restore the viability of his army's defenses. From Paulus's perspective, the most burning issues were whether Seydlitz's corps, in its current form, would be able to resume and sustain its advance without significant reinforcements and, if not, where it would obtain fresh forces.

The Final Assault on the Workers' Villages and Battles on Sixth Army's Flanks, 3–13 October 1942

THE FIGHTING FOR THE WORKERS' VILLAGES, 3–7 OCTOBER

Paulus's Plan

As Paulus's northern shock group liquidated the Soviet forces defending the Orlovka salient, a two-day lull interrupted the intense fighting around the periphery of the workers' villages. On 1 and 2 October, Paulus and Seydlitz marshaled the forces necessary to conduct their final drive to capture the city's northern factory district. During this lull, however, sporadic fighting took place as Seydlitz and Chuikov reinforced and repositioned their respective forces. Chuikov also organized counterattacks to keep the Germans at bay (see Maps 43–44).

As late as the evening of 30 September, Paulus still hoped that Seydlitz's LI Corps could continue its thrust the next day with 24th Panzer, 100th Jäger, and 295th Infantry Divisions. Reinforced by 94th Infantry Division's 276th Regiment, all three were to advance along their previous axes in the broad sector from the Mechetka River in the north to the Dolgii and Krutoi Ravines in the south. Once again, 24th Panzer Division was to spearhead this attack. In an order issued at 1615 hours on 30 September, 24th Panzer directed its two *kampfgruppen* to attack northward on 1 October to reach the low hills on the northeastern edge of the lower Barrikady village. The division was to begin its advance at X-hour that day with Edelsheim's *kampfgruppe* on the right and Winterfeld's on the left to seize the ridge stretching from the Dizel'naia section eastward to Zhitomirsk Ravine (grid squares 84a, 85c, and 75a and c). Thereafter, they were to push northward toward the units of Hube's XIV Panzer Corps advancing from the north and squeeze the bottleneck at the eastern end of the Soviets' salient around Orlovka between the two German pincers. The newly arrived 276th Infantry Regiment was to protect the southern flank of the assault.[1]

This plan required Lenski's panzer division to advance in the roughly 1.2-kilometer-wide sector from just east of the Mechetka River eastward to

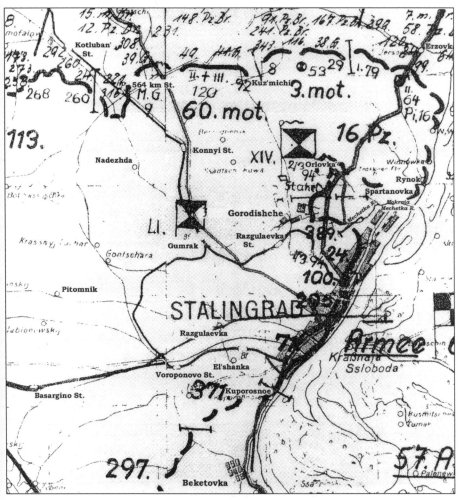

Map 43. Sixth Army's situation, 1–2 October 1942

the Silikat Factory, seize the southwestern approaches to the upper Tractor Factory village and the southern approaches to Hill 97.7, as well as the built-up Dizel'naia area beyond, and capture the Silikat Factory, 600 meters north of the narrows. The 544th Regiment of Jänecke's 398th Infantry Division, operating along and just north of the Mechetka River, was to protect 24th Panzer Division's left flank. The 100th Jäger and 295th Infantry Divisions were to protect its right flank and, if possible, press forward into the lower Krasnyi Oktiabr' village from the west and across Mamaev Kurgan and through the Tennis Racket from the south.

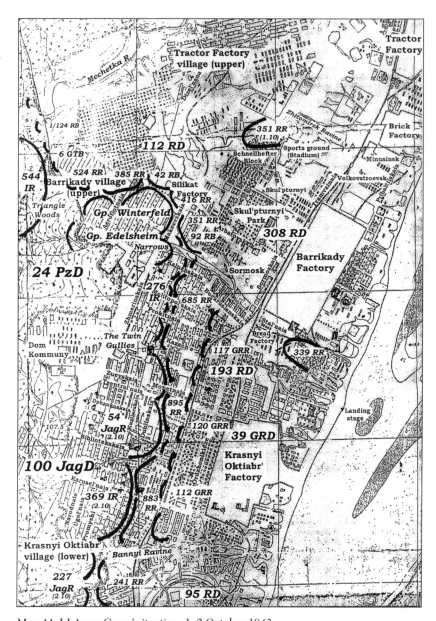

Map 44. LI Army Corps' situation, 1–2 October 1942

By midnight on 30 September, however, the slow progress recorded by Seydlitz's forces, and their increasingly dilapidated state, convinced Paulus that any further advance would be futile unless and until he could reinforce his army corps. The situation report that LI Corps dispatched to Sixth Army headquarters at 2200 hours on 30 September illustrated this problem:

> Along the front of LI Army Corps on 30 September, there were strong enemy counterattacks in the Krasnyi Oktiabr and Barrikady city sectors. After repelling these attacks, 100th Jäger Division was able to reach the railway line in the Krasnyi Oktiabr sector at two places, and 24th Panzer Division won the city sector 74c in Barrikady.
>
> In particular:
>
> On 30 September 100th Jäger Division attacked on its northern wing and reached the railway line in the Krasnyi Oktiabr sector at two places against stiff enemy resistance. Because of an enemy attack on the left flank, some of the ground won on this northern wing had to be relinquished. The connection with 24th Panzer Division has been established.
>
> The 24th Panzer Division made contact with 100th Jäger Division with its 276th Infantry Regiment by attacking in tough house-to-house fighting against strong enemy forces, and rifle squads gained a bridgehead north of the gully in [grid square] 74c as a prerequisite for an intended advance to the north-east. . . .
>
> *Casualties on 30 September:*
> 100th Jäger Division: Killed—15 officers and men.
> Wounded—2 officers and 68 non-commissioned officers and men, and
> Missing—7 men.
> 24th Panzer Division: Killed—5 men.
> Wounded—30 men
> 94th Infantry Division: Wounded—2 officers
> (no other figures available)[2]

Although the corps' losses on 30 September may have seemed modest, as indicated by Table 25, the cumulative losses that Seydlitz's divisions had suffered over the previous month were finally taking a toll on his corps' combat effectiveness. For example, as of 1 October the line-combat strength of 24th Panzer Division had fallen to 6,943 men, as opposed to its ration strength of 13,098 men. More devastating still, the division's most vital combat elements, 24th Panzer and 21st and 26th Grenadier Regiments, reported combat strengths of 1,089, 896, and 923 men, respectively, against ration strengths of 2,064, 1,213, and 1,293. The division's battalion-size combat elements fared no better, with 4th Motorcycle, 40th Panzer Jäger, and 40th

Panzer Pioneer Battalions reporting combat strengths of 586, 368, and 264 men, respectively, compared with ration strengths of 784, 490, and 553.[3] While the panzer division as a whole was operating well below its authorized strength, it fielded an actual combat strength nearing 30 percent of authorized levels. Seydlitz's infantry divisions were in no better shape. Simply stated, both he and Paulus realized that reinforcements were necessary if LI Corps was to continue to pursue its ambitious objectives.

Therefore, Paulus decided to shift some forces participating in the reduction of the Orlovka salient southward to reinforce Lenski's worn-out 24th Panzer Division. Ultimately, this involved 267th and 274th Regiments of Pfeiffer's 94th Infantry Division and 545th and 546th Regiments of Jänecke's 389th Infantry Division, which had been operating against the western perimeter of the Orlovka salient, and the transfer of control over Pfeiffer's two regiments from XIV Panzer to LI Corps. During the next two days, Jänecke transferred the two regiments of the division advancing eastward north of the Mechetka River to the right, south of the river, where they were to form a shock group to operate adjacent to 24th Panzer Division's left flank. The two regiments of Pfeiffer's division then shifted southward, occupying positions facing east on the northern bank of the Mokraia Mechetka River.[4]

Faced with these realities, Paulus had no choice but to postpone any further assaults until the morning of 3 October, allowing Jänecke the time necessary to regroup his forces. Once it arrived, Jänecke's infantry division was to deploy on 24th Panzer Division's left flank and join its assault. Otherwise, Paulus left unchanged the missions he had assigned to the other elements of Seydlitz's army corps on 30 September.

When he postponed Seydlitz's forthcoming assault, Paulus was also paying close attention to Chuikov's opposing forces. As of 2100 hours on 30 September, Sixth Army's intelligence officer reported:

> *Disposition of enemy forces*:
>   A. *Newly established*:
>   1.) West edge of the Barrikady: 193rd Rifle Division with Rifle Regiments 883, 895 (the Division was pulled out near Voronezh in July and sent to Kogan [Chelyabinsk] to be brought up to strength). After replenishment, it crossed the Volga in companies near the Tractor Factory on 28 September. Division commander: Generalmajor Semshatvorov. . . .
>   B. *Confirmed*:
>   1.) . . . .
>   2.) *Krasnyi Oktiabr*: 95th Rifle Division
>   3.) *East of Gorodishche*: 112th Rifle Division (Rifle Regiment 416). 6th Guards Tank Brigade. On 28.9., still has 8 T-34, 3 T-70, awaits 4 to 5

new tanks out of the Tractor Factory. 38th Motorized Rifle Brigade. Replenished mid-September by replacements from Rifle Regiments 178, 190, 390 out of Leninsk, however, was again severely hammered on 25 September by German panzers. . . .[5]

Although this assessment of Chuikov's dispositions was accurate as far as it went, it underestimated the strength of 62nd Army's defending forces. As of nightfall on 30 September, 24th Panzer Division's *Kampfgruppen* Winterfeld and Edelsheim, which were deployed from 300 meters east of the Mechetka River eastward around the northern periphery of the upper Barrikady village to the northern and eastern flank of the narrows, faced 23rd Tank Corps' 6th Guards Tank Brigade, two companies of 112th Rifle Division's 524th Regiment, and the same division's 385th Regiment manning defenses extending from the valley of the Mechetka River southeastward to the western edge of the Silikat Factory. The decimated 416th Regiment of Ermolkin's 112th Rifle Division defended the factory itself. By this time, Colonel Skuba's 6th Guards Tank Brigade fielded 13 tanks, including 9 T-34s and 4 T-70s, with another 8 tanks (5 T-34, 1 T-70, and 2 T-60s) nonoperational, the only tanks left in Chuikov's 62nd Army.[6]

Late on 30 September, however, Chuikov had reinforced Ermolkin's rifle division with the newly arrived and hastily refurbished 42nd Rifle Brigade, which occupied defensive positions in the wooded area south of Dizel'naia, behind 112th Rifle Division's left wing. In addition, early on 1 October Chuikov ordered Gurt'ev's newly arriving 308th Rifle Division to deploy its lead rifle regiment, the 351st, into forward defensive positions at the boundary between Ermolkin's rifle division and the right wing of Smekhotvorov's 193rd Rifle Division, southeast of the Silikat Factory, to protect the approaches to the Barrikady Factory.

When its two remaining rifle regiments (339th and 347th) arrived, Gurt'ev's division would pose a deadly threat to *Kampfgruppe* Edelsheim's positions protecting the infamous narrows, as well as the left wing and center of 276th Infantry Regiment, which was deployed on 24th Panzer Division's right flank. The 276th's defensive positions stretched southward through the western section of the lower Barrikady village, roughly 150–200 meters west of the north-south railroad line, to east of the twin gullies to protect the Barrikady and Bread Factories beyond. In addition to facing forces from Gurt'ev's 308th Rifle Division as they arrived on its left wing and in its center, on its right 276th Regiment faced 193rd Rifle Division's 685th Regiment near the twin gullies.

Farther south, 54th Regiment of Sanne's 100th Jäger Division was now supported on the right by 369th Infantry Regiment, which had regrouped into the region overnight on 30 September from the division's right wing.

These two units faced 883rd and 895th Regiments of Smekhotvorov's 193rd Rifle Division, which were deployed from right to left in defensive positions facing west along Zhmerinskaia Street and Kuzliarskaia Street, several hundred meters west of the railroad, to protect the approaches to the Krasnyi Oktiabr' Factory. Smekhotvorov's soldiers converted the many buildings in the densely built-up area into virtual fortresses to slow the German advance.

Complicating the task facing Sanne's light infantry, on 30 September Major Shtrigol's refurbished 92nd Rifle Brigade reinforced Smekhotvorov's defenses, manning positions in the Krasnyi Oktiabr' Factory; the next day, the three regiments of Gur'ev's 39th Guards Rifle Division moved forward, ultimately occupying second-echelon defenses several blocks to Smekhotvorov's rear. On 100th Jäger Division's right wing, its 227th Regiment, after capturing the railroad line northwest of Mamaev Kurgan, manned positions astride Bannyi Ravine. Opposite the 227th was part of 193rd Rifle Division's 895th Regiment and the three decimated regiments of 95th Rifle Division, deployed in the southern section of the lower Krasnyi Oktiabr' village and on Mamaev Kurgan, west of the Tennis Racket.

Anchoring Seydlitz's right wing and flank, Wuthmann's 295th Infantry Division, which had taken over the crest of Mamaev Kurgan from 100th Jäger Division, was deployed southward along a front of roughly 3.5 kilometers from the eastern slope of the mound and the western edge of the Tennis Racket to the lower Dolgii and Krutoi Ravines, opposite the defenses of Batiuk's 284th Rifle Division, which still clung to the lower sections of both ravines and a section of the Meat Combine.

Because Chuikov was receiving reinforcements, whereas Paulus was not, it would be exceedingly difficult for Seydlitz's shock groups to accomplish their assigned missions—that is, to clear Soviet forces from the entire factory district. As one *Wehrmacht* veteran correctly noted, "At the end of September, General Paulus launched a concerted attack in an attempt to storm the last bulwarks of Stalingrad, one after another. The German forces were insufficient for an all-encompassing attack on the entire industrial complex, however."[7] Instead of employing multiple battalion-size *kampfgruppen* from each regiment to conduct their assaults, as they had done before, henceforth, because of the acute shortage of infantry, Seydlitz's advancing divisions were forced to rely on fewer and weaker battalion-size or multiple company-size *kampfgruppen*, scraped together from whatever combat-ready forces were available at the time, and to reinforce these with engineers (pioneers) and limited numbers of assault guns and tanks. In addition to operating across frontages that were too broad with a limited number of weaker *kampfgruppen*, Seydlitz's shock groups possessed ever fewer assault guns and tanks, which made it difficult to engage successfully defending Soviet rifle divisions.

These defenders routinely converted the numerous houses, buildings, and factories in the heavily built-up area into fortresses. This meant that the ensuing stage of Paulus's offensive would develop at a snail's pace.

Chuikov's Counterattack, 1–2 October

On 1 October, the first day of the lull, Chuikov decided to seize the initiative by employing the reinforcements his army received the day before and overnight to conduct a larger-scale counterattack designed to recapture the narrows region and, if possible, most of the upper Barrikady village from the Germans. Before launching this general counterattack, overnight on 30 September he ordered part of his forces already in position opposite the narrows to conduct strong reconnaissances-in-force the next day. Conducted by reinforced battalions from 112th Rifle Division's 385th and 416th Regiments and 193rd Rifle Division's 685th Regiment, these sorties were designed to improve the jumping-off positions for the 2 October assault, feel out the German defenses, and recapture as much of the region east of the narrows as possible prior to 308th Rifle Division's arrival.

All of these efforts, however, came to naught. As 24th Panzer Division described the attacks, "The enemy attacked the defensive line of the division on a broad front with strong forces, above all on the sectors' boundaries. They were thrown back everywhere. The Division continued to hold the attained line under local improvements."[8] The LI Army Corps seconded this report, adding, "The 24th Pz. Div. held its positions. All attacks were repulsed. The enemy in front of the division's front line is in bunkers and has tanks in strong emplacements."[9]

The Red Army General Staff also described the action—the lull before Chuikov's storm—in its daily operational summary, without even mentioning the reconnaissance:

> **62nd Army** continued to engage in stubborn street fighting in the city of Stalingrad all day on 1 October, repelling repeated enemy attacks. . . .
> 42nd RB, 6th TB, 112th RD, and 92nd RB continued to occupy their previous positions.
> 193rd RD, having repelled attacks by enemy infantry, occupied positions along Ugol'naia [Coal] Street to Kaluzhskaia [Kaluga] Street and farther along Promyshlennaia [Industrial] Street to the Bannyi Ravine.
> 95th RD occupied its previous positions.
> The units of 284th RD repelled attacks by enemy forces of up to two battalions of infantry between the Dolgii and Krutoi Ravines, while continuing to hold on to their previous positions.

13th Gds. RD fought off an attack by an enemy force of up to a battalion of infantry.

39th Gds. RD completed its crossing to the western bank of the Volga River and occupied a defense in the vicinity of the park south of the Skul'pturnyi region from Arbatovskaia [Arbat] Street along Sormoskaia Street, along the intersection of the railroad line with Buguruslanskaia [Buguruslan] Street, and farther along Ordzhonikidze Street to Karusel'naia Street.

308th RD's 351st RR, medical battalion, AT [antitank] battalion, machine gun battalion, and signal battalion crossed to the western bank of the Volga River. The crossing units concentrated in the area of the railroad west of the stadium.[10]

Late on 1 October, 62nd Army reported that Gur'ev's 39th Guards Rifle Division had completed crossing to the western bank of the Volga River and was occupying second-echelon defenses on the lower Krasnyi Oktiabr' village in 193rd Rifle Division's rear. Initially, the division deployed its three regiments to protect the approaches to the Barrikady Factory. Within 24 hours, however, it received new orders requiring it to position its 112th, 120th, and 117th Regiments abreast from left to right from Bannyi Ravine northward to the intersection of the railroad and Buguruslanskaia Street to back up 193rd Rifle Division. In addition, 351st Regiment of Gurt'ev's 308th Rifle Division, with 300 men, crossed the river and reached the vicinity of the ravine west of the Stadium (or Sports Grund, to the Germans).[11] In the same report, 62nd Army reported that its formations in Stalingrad city fielded 44,201 men.

Late in the evening, while Jänecke was redeploying the main force of his 389th Infantry Division southward into the valley of the Mechetka River, Paulus decided once again to postpone the next phase of his offensive, this time to the morning of 3 October.[12]

Although Chuikov's forces in the lower Krasnyi Oktiabr' village held their positions against vigorous German patrolling on 1 October, the army commander was alarmed by the limited success of his reconnaissances-in-force and the Germans' forward progress in the region west and south of the Silikat Factory. Therefore, at 1800 hours on 1 October, he ordered his forces concentrating in the lower Barrikady village to assault the Germans' defenses east of the narrows and in the upper Barrikady village. Their mission was to collapse the right-angle salient projecting toward the Tractor Factory village held by 24th Panzer Division and the supporting 276th Infantry Regiment and to expel German forces from the ground they had seized the week before.

Specifically, beginning at 0600 hours on 2 October, 92nd Rifle Brigade, 351st Regiment of Gurt'ev's 308th Rifle Division, and 42nd Rifle Brigade, deployed from left to right from southeast of the narrows northward to southeast of the Silikat Factory, were to advance westward to clear German forces from the narrows and the upper Barrikady village to the cemetery as far as the eastern bank of Vishnevaia *Balka*. Chuikov retained Ermolkin's understrength 112th Rifle Division in reserve near the Krasnyi Oktiabr' Factory and ordered Gurt'ev to reinforce the attack with his 339th and 347th Regiments as soon as they arrived forward. Finally, 883rd and 895th Regiments of Smekhotvorov's 193rd Rifle Division were to continue their operations to clear German forces from the lower Krasnyi Oktiabr' village and then prepare to attack to capture Hill 107.5 to the west.[13] In his order's final paragraphs, Chuikov told his division and brigade commanders to conduct their assaults with handpicked groups organized and equipped to conduct close-in street fighting and form so-called consolidation echelons to fortify the buildings seized but also prevent unauthorized withdrawals by their troops.

2 October

Chuikov's counterattack indeed materialized on 2 October, but because it was poorly coordinated and only one of 308th Rifle Division's rifle regiments (351st) arrived on the scene in timely fashion, it faltered without achieving its ultimate objectives. Despite 62nd Army's claims to the contrary, 42nd Rifle Brigade failed to dent *Kampfgruppe* Winterfeld's defenses in the northwestern part of the upper Barrikady village, prompting the *kampfgruppe* to report that it repulsed what it described as light "reconnaissance probes."[14] At the same time, to the south, 308th Rifle Division's 351st Regiment probed into the buildings south of the Silikat Factory but recorded only minor gains against *Kampfgruppe* Edelsheim's left flank before being halted by heavy German fire. The division's 339th Regiment finally began reaching the battlefield in the afternoon, but not in time to reinvigorate Gurt'ev's assault. On the southern wing of Chuikov's counterattack force, likewise, 92nd Rifle Brigade's attacks against 276th Infantry Regiment's right wing and the left wing of 100th Jäger Division faltered along Makeevskaia and Vinnitskaia Streets and in the ravines to the southeast.

Meanwhile, all along the front in the western section of the lower Krasnyi Oktiabr' village along Bibliotechnaia and Karusel'naia Streets, 193rd Rifle Division's 895th and 883rd Regiments parried with small groups of infantry and some supporting assault guns from 100th Jäger Division's 54th Jäger and Croat 369th Regiments. This fighting remained desultory because Sanne's two regiments were still in the process of taking over 276th Infantry Regiment's sector, a process that would last until well after dark.[15]

After the fighting died down late on 2 October, the remaining two regiments of Gurt'ev's 308th Rifle Division, the 339th and 347th, began reaching the forward area overnight on 2–3 October. Meanwhile, Chuikov jockeyed

Gurt'ev's division and Smekhotvorov's 193rd Rifle Division into more solid
defensive positions, all the while trying to regain lost ground. Describing the
day's action, the Red Army General Staff reported:

> **62nd Army** continued stubborn street fighting in the city of Stalingrad
> all day on 2 October, repelling repeated attacks by enemy infantry and
> tanks. . . .
>
> 42nd RB, advancing slowly forward, captured the northwestern part of
> Barrikady village by day's end on 2 October.
>
> 351st RR, 308th RD, completely cleared the Silikat village of enemy and
> reached its southern outskirts, where it was halted by heavy enemy fire.
>
> 92nd RB reached the corner of Makeevskaia Street-Vinnitskaia [Vin-
> nitsa] Street line and farther to the southeast along the ravine.
>
> 193rd RD fought with enemy infantry and tanks attacking toward Bib-
> liotechnaia [Bibliotech] and Karusel'naia Streets.
>
> 112th, 95th, and 284th RDs and the 13th Gds. RD continued holding
> on to their occupied positions and repelled attacks by the enemy.
>
> 39th Gds. RD occupied defenses in the second echelon, while prepar-
> ing centers of resistance.
>
> Our units abandoned Orlovka under enemy pressure.
>
> Enemy aircraft in groups of 25 planes bombed our crossings over the
> Volga River in the Stalingrad region on 2 October and damaged up to 90
> percent of them.[16]

As soon as he realized that his counterattacks were faltering, Chuikov
at 1935 hours on 2 October issued new orders to his shock groups, shifting
some of the forces and assigning new attack missions to better resist the anticipated German advance toward the Tractor Factory and its workers' village to the west. In Chuikov's own words:

> At night on October 2, we decided to regroup some of our forces:
>
> —to move Sologub's [Ermolkin's 112th Rifle] division to the left
> flank of Gorokhov's northern group [in the Spartanovka region north
> of the Mokraia Mechetka River], to occupy a line of defense from the
> railway bridge across the stream about 800 yards south of Hill 75.9, to
> point 97.7, and then along the gully to the south-east as far as the River
> Mechetka;
>
> —to move Gurt'ev's 308th Division to a line of defense from the or-
> chards north of the Barrikady settlement to the Silikat Factory, Ma-
> keevskaia Street, and as far as the gully;
>
> —to establish Gur'ev's [39th Guards Rifle] division in defense posi-
> tions along Tsekhovaia, Bibleiskaia, and Severnaia Streets, relieving units

of Smekhotvorov's [193rd Rifle] Division and thereby strengthening the latter and creating partial reserves.[17]

In addition to shifting 112th Rifle Division westward toward the Mechetka River, this relieved 193rd Rifle Division's 883rd Regiment by two regiments from 39th Guards Rifle Division. This permitted 883rd Regiment to shift northward to form a second echelon behind 193rd Division's 895th Regiment.

Amid the heavy fighting on 2 October, *Luftwaffe* bombers did achieve a signal success, which at least temporarily paralyzed 62nd Army's command and control over its forces. In preparation for Seydlitz's assault the next morning, "The *Luftwaffe* bombed selected targets, mainly concentrating along the Volga, without knowing it, almost leaving 62nd Army leaderless."[18] Inadvertently, the attacking German aircraft had bombed Chuikov's command post, which was situated in a gully along the Volga's western bank just below a small reservoir in the northeastern outskirts of the Krasnyi Oktiabr' Factory. Earlier, German bombs had ignited the oil, covering the army command post in "a huge black blanket covering the eastern steppe for a distance of 25 kilometers," "a pillar of smoke" that "remained for several days, providing a perfect orientation point for the attacking troops."[19] The new German air attack struck additional oil tanks near the command post, sending flaming oil down the gully, wrecking the post, and setting aflame nearby barges and the Volga itself. Chuikov's chief of staff, Krylov, quickly took charge and, despite the loss of all wire communication, managed to restore order and direct operations by radio from adjacent dugouts. When Eremenko's headquarters later inquired about the fate of Chuikov and his staff and the location of their headquarters, Chuikov and Krylov responded, "We're where the most flames and smoke are."[20]

Despite these successes on 2 October, Paulus continued fretting over the weakness of his army's forces, especially that of Seydlitz's shock groups. Sixth Army's war diary lamented late on 2 October, "The chief of staff informed the army group, in spite of the most intense efforts by all forces, the low combat strengths of the infantry will prolong the taking of Stalingrad indefinitely if reinforcements cannot be supplied."[21] At the same time, 24th Panzer Division noted, "It came out from enemy statements that the Russians were continually bringing reinforcements over the Volga."[22] Nonetheless, the division concluded, "If [the assault] was still strong, a quick thrust to the Volga could be successful."[23]

Despite these reservations, with the regrouping of Jänecke's 389th Infantry Division progressing well, Paulus persisted in his intent to resume Seydlitz's assault the next morning. Based on the premise that 389th Infantry Division would be able to move into attack positions on 24th Panzer

Division's left flank by dawn on 3 October, Seydlitz ordered Lenski's division to begin its advance at X-hour (still undetermined at this point), with its right flank protected by 276th Infantry Regiment, capture grid squares 74d, 74b, and 84a (the remainder of upper Barrikady village) with its front facing northeast, and then wheel to the southeast. Attacking toward the northeast, *Kampfgruppe* Edelsheim was to capture the "symmetrical group of houses" in grid squares 74b2 and 4 and, later, turn his entire front toward the southeast and seize and hold defensive positions in the favorable terrain in grid squares 74d and 84a. Meanwhile, *Kampfgruppe* Winterfeld would seize the group of separate buildings in grid square 84a while protecting itself against enemy counterattack from the north. After Winterfeld reached his objective, his forces would deploy facing toward the southeast and attack the right flank of enemy forces facing Edelsheim's *kampfgruppe*.[24]

After further refinements, 24th Panzer Division issued its final attack order at 2200 hours that evening.[25] It required *Kampfgruppen* Edelsheim and Winterfeld to conduct a limited-objective assault northeastward toward the Barrikady village on 3 October, but even at this late hour it had not yet set a precise start time. Before Lenski's two *kampfgruppen* began their advance, to their left two regiments of Jänecke's 389th Infantry Division were to begin their attack at 0800 hours from grid square 55 and advance roughly 1.5 kilometers to the line of the north-south gully in grid squares 75a and c, south of the Mechetka River, several hundred meters from the western outskirts of the upper Tractor Factory village. This advance would move the infantry to a position parallel to 24th Panzer Division's jumping-off positions. Lenski's groups were to commence their assaults based only on the progress recorded by Jänecke's infantry.

Prior to its attack, as before, 24th Panzer Division organized its forces into two *kampfgruppen* containing a careful mixture of combat troops and necessary supporting arms (see Table 29).[26]

Once the two attacking regiments of Jänecke's 389th Infantry Division, the 544th and 546th, reached positions on line with 24th Panzer Division's left wing, Lenski's panzer division was to launch LI Corps' main attack with two *kampfgruppen* advancing northward in tandem toward the upper Tractor Factory village. *Kampfgruppe* Winterfeld was to seize the area south of the Tractor Factory village from the railroad east of the Dizel'naia section, eastward through the so-called *Schnellhefter* [Folder] Block of buildings (referred to by the Soviets as the "six-sided block") to the Silikat Factory. On Winterfeld's right, Edelsheim's *kampfgruppe* was to seize the symmetrical block of buildings just south of the *Schnellhefter* Block and the section of lower Barrikady village west of Skul'pturnyi Park. On the panzer division's right, its attached 276th Infantry Regiment was to protect Edelsheim's

Table 29. The 24th Panzer Division's Organization for Combat, 3 October 1942

Kampfgruppe Edelsheim
    21st Panzer Grenadier Regiment
    26th Panzer Grenadier Regiment (less the half-tracks of its 1st Battalion)
    4th Motorcycle Battalion (less its 1st and 2nd Squadrons)
        1st and 2nd Companies, 40th Panzer Pioneer Battalion
        1st Company, 40th Panzer Jäger Battalion
        3rd Battalion, 89th Panzer Artillery Regiment and the heavy rocket-launchers of 2nd
            Battalion, 2nd Heavy *Werfer* Regiment [in support]
Kampfgruppe Winterfeld
    Panzer Detachment Winterfeld, with panzer pioneer and Flak platoons and the
        24th Panzer Regiment's pioneer platoon
    The half-tracks of 1st Battalion, 26th Panzer Grenadier Regiment
    2nd Squadron, 4th Motorcycle Battalion
    1st Battalion, 89th Panzer Artillery Regiment, with 105mm howitzers, 851st Heavy
        Artillery Battalion, with 2 batteries of 105mm howitzers, and 733rd Heavy Artillery
        Battalion, with 2 batteries of 210mm mortars [in support]

extended right flank as his *kampfgruppe* lunged northward past Skul'pturnyi Park. Lenski's division was able to muster 28 tanks for the attack, and 244th and 245th Assault Guns Detachments [*Abteilung*] supported LI Corps' 389th Infantry and 100th Jäger Divisions with 17 and 7 assault guns, respectively, bringing the corps' armored strength to 52 vehicles.[27]

On 24th Panzer Division's right, Sanne's 100th Jäger Division by now had its 54th Jäger, 369th Infantry, and 227th Jäger Regiments deployed abreast from left to right in the western section of the lower Krasnyi Oktiabr' village from the gullies traversing Zhmerinskaia Street southward to upper Bannyi Ravine. The *jägers* had the arduous task of continuing to clear Soviet forces from the densely built-up areas west of the north-south railroad and the Krasnyi Oktiabr' Factory from east of Hill 107.5 south to the Bannyi Ravine. Farther to the south, the left-wing regiment of Wuthmann's 295th Infantry Division was to clear Soviet forces from Mamaev Kurgan, capture the Military Clothing Factory, Meat Combine, and Tennis Racket, and reach the western bank of the Volga River. This regiment was then supposed to wheel northward, cross the lower Bannyi Ravine, and, if possible, capture the southern section of the Krasnyi Oktiabr' Factory in cooperation with 100th Jäger Division. The regiments in 295th Infantry Division's center and on its right wing were to overcome the Soviets' defenses in the lower Dolgii and Krutoi Ravines and wheel south to assist 71st Infantry Division's 194th Regiment in eradicating the final Soviet strongholds in Stalingrad's center city. However, based on previous experiences, Paulus expected 24th Panzer and 389th Infantry Divisions to do the heavy lifting.

3 October

Preceded by a short artillery barrage, 389th Infantry Division's 544th and 546th Regiments began their assault at 0800 hours (see Maps 45–47). With their left flank anchored on the Mechetka River, battalion-size *kampfgruppen* from the two regiments skirted the western edge of the upper Barrikady village, crossing terrain characterized as "basically coverless dry ground with several small orchards scattered throughout the attack area but [with] the axis of advance . . . intersected by several gullies."[28] Resistance by Skuba's 6th Guards Tank Brigade east of the Mechetka River proved stronger than anticipated, in part because, during the previous night, 112th Rifle Division's 416th and 385th Regiments had redeployed into positions along the Mechetka on the tank brigade's right flank, and 112th Division's 524th Regiment and the right wing of 42nd Rifle Brigade manned strong defenses in the upper Barrikady village on Skuba's left flank. Therefore, Jänecke's forces reached their designated objective—the gully south of the Mechetka River—at about noon, later than anticipated and at a cost of 5 killed and 43 wounded.[29] Withdrawing before 389th Infantry Division's advance, 112th Rifle Division's three understrength rifle regiments and the remnants of Skuba's 6th Guards Tank Brigade then occupied new defensive positions protecting the western edge of the upper Tractor Factory village, Hill 97.7, and the western approaches to the Dizel'naia section, located in the bend in the railroad spur about 600 meters north of the Silikat Factory.[30]

Although Lenski thought he might have to postpone his division's assault yet again because of 389th Infantry Division's slow advance, at 1400 hours he unleashed his assault following a two-minute barrage from his division's heavy weapons and close-in air strikes by Stuka dive-bombers, in particular against the Silikat Factory. *Kampfgruppe* Winterfeld, with the division's tanks, advanced northward from the northeastern edge of the upper Barrikady village, according to eyewitnesses, "across terrain that had no buildings on it but the ground was an undulating mish-mash of hollows, hills, and steep-edge depressions [the Silikat Factory]." The tanks, however, "avoided the worst by adhering to a couple of dirt roads that passed through the area, advancing to the edge of the suburb totally devastated by fire and bombs." Although "all that remained were dozens of chimneys and piles of ash, charred wood and shattered masonry, even here, the Russians defended themselves from the cellars and trenches among the rubble."[31] Despite numerous obstacles and determined Soviet resistance, Winterfeld's forces reached their objectives, where they dug in.

On Winterfeld's right, Edelsheim's panzer-grenadiers "worked their way through the shattered streets, creeping through destroyed huts, buildings, and gardens up to the western edge of Skul'pturnyi Park, an overgrown area

Map 45. Sixth Army's situation, 3–4 October 1942

west of the dreaded Barrikady Gun Factory," where they erected defensive
positions anchored on the right in a "solidly constructed" building.[32] The
forces on the *kampfgruppe*'s left wing managed to reach the southwestern
edge of the *Schnellhefter* Block, in the northwestern part of Skul'pturnyi village, and seized the buildings to the south, but were not able to capture the
fortress-like block itself. Thus, by late afternoon Lenski's panzer division had

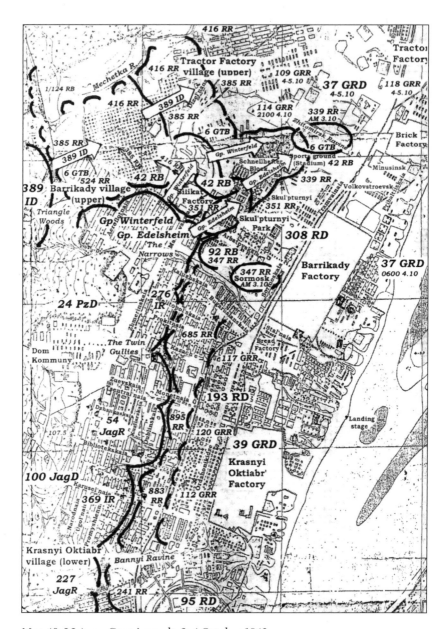

Map 46. LI Army Corps' assault, 3–4 October 1942

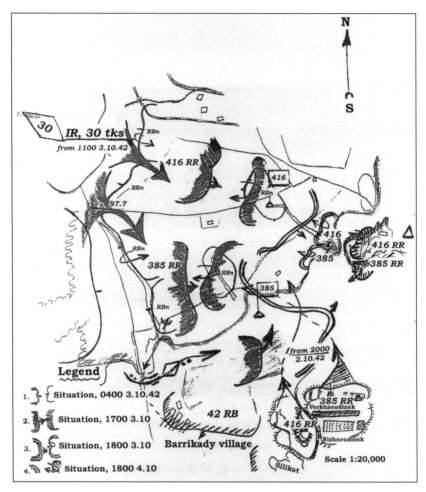

Map 47. 112th Rifle Division's situation, 3–4 October 1942

seized its designated objective, pressing the Soviet defenders back to new defensive positions along the line of grid squares 74d3 and d4, 74b4 and b2, and 75d3. However, by this time his forces had been seriously weakened by the heavy fighting, which was often hand-to-hand.

Lenski's assaulting *kampfgruppen* struck the defenses on the left wing of 42nd Rifle Brigade and 351st Regiment of Gurt'ev's 308th Rifle Division. These Soviet forces were defending the sector west of the Silikat Factory, the factory itself, and the section of the lower Barrikady village north of the ra- vine and the six-sided block (*Schnellhefter*) situated northwest of Skul'pturnyi

Park. This attack inflicted "heavy losses" on Gurt'ev's regiment, forcing it to abandon the Silikat Factory and withdraw to new defenses along the railroad south of Nizhneudinskaia Street. According to 62nd Army's evening report, "The remaining parts of the regiment [less the small groups which withdrew] were destroyed and scattered by the enemy," and "the commander of the regiment, Major Markelov, was severely wounded."[33] The 308th Division's 339th and 347th Regiments, which were now arriving forward, then received orders "to liquidate the enemy [breach] and go over to the defense along the northern edge of Silikat village."[34]

In addition to menacing the Tractor Factory village and the factory beyond, 24th Panzer Division's thrust also threatened to split apart Chuikov's defenses at the boundary between 112th and 308th Rifle Divisions, located in and west of the Silikat Factory and, in the sector of 193rd Rifle Division, defending to the south. By doing so, German forces were poised to march due eastward toward the vital landing stage on the Volga River just north of the Krasnyi Oktiabr' Factory.

As the forces of Jänecke's 389th Infantry and Lenski's 24th Panzer Divisions thrust northeastward to secure their objective, the western and southern parts of the upper Tractor Factory village and the *Schnellhefter* Block—the gateway to both the lower Tractor Factory village and the factory itself— 276th Infantry Regiment and Sanne's 100th Jäger and Wuthmann's 295th Infantry Divisions continued pressing against Chuikov's defenses along the extended front from the Silikat Factory southward to the Krutoi Ravine. But the going was tough, with forward progress measured in terms of individual buildings.

Multiple smaller *kampfgruppen* from 54th Jäger and the Croat 369th Regiments of Sanne's 100th Jäger Division painstakingly worked their way through the complex of buildings west of Bibliotechnaia and Karusel'naia Streets and east of the railroad in the lower Krasnyi Oktiabr' village, only to become enmeshed in heavy street and building-to-building fighting against the left wing of 685th Regiment and 883rd and 895th Regiments of Smekhotvorov's 193rd Rifle Division. The defenders paid dearly for resisting, with the division's regiments reduced in strength to roughly 200 riflemen each. In heavy but fragmented fighting throughout the day, Sanne's grenadiers recorded gains measured only in the tens and hundreds of meters. By nightfall, Sanne's grenadiers pressed back Smekhotvorov's troops several city blocks (685th and 895th Regiments along Bibliotechnaia and Karusel'naia Streets to Bibleiskaia Street, and 883rd Regiment to Martovskaia and Tsekhovaia Streets).[35] Running short of ammunition, Smekhotvorov's troopers frequently engaged the advancing Germans with bayonet charges and hand-to-hand combat. As the hard-pressed 193rd Rifle Division withdrew, by early evening elements of Gur'ev's 39th Guards Rifle Division moved forward to support them.

On the right (southern) flank of 100th Jäger Division, the *kampfgruppen* of Wuthmann's 295th Infantry Division experienced similarly slow progress against Gorishnyi's 95th Rifle Division on the eastern slopes of Mamaev Kurgan and west of Bannyi Ravine and against Batiuk's 284th Rifle Division east and south of Mamaev Kurgan and southward along the Dolgii and Krutoi Ravines. Wuthmann's infantry finally cleared Soviet forces from the northern slopes of Mamaev Kurgan, although it made little progress eastward toward the Meat Combine and Volga River. *Kampfgruppen* organized by the regiment on the division's left wing pressed 95th Rifle Division's 241st Regiment, still reinforced by a battalion of 284th Rifle Division's 1045th Regiment, off the northern slope of Mamaev Kurgan and through the Military Clothing Factory to new defensive positions adjacent to the southern bank of the Bannyi Ravine.

However, the forces in 295th's center and on its right wing had less success. In its center, the remnants of 161st and 90th Regiments of Gorishnyi's 95th Rifle Division, now reduced to strengths of roughly 100 men each, clung tenaciously to their defenses along the railroad line south of Bannyi Ravine. On the right, Wuthmann attempted to replicate the temporary success that a 300-man *kampfgruppe* from his division had achieved on 1 October against 13th Guards Rifle Division's right-wing 34th Regiment in Krutoi Ravine. Wuthmann's assaults also failed in the face of determined resistance by Batiuk's 284th Rifle Division. In this especially fierce fighting, 1047th and 1043rd Regiments of Batiuk's division, reinforced by the division's second-echelon 1045th Regiment, successfully parried all of Wuthmann's attempts to pierce Batiuk's formidable defenses in the narrow strip of land along the Volga's western bank from the Meat Combine southward through the Dolgii and Krutoi Ravines. For Seydlitz, the fighting in these sectors produced nothing but continuous frustration. Given the reduced strength of his attacking divisions and regiments, however, he could expect nothing more.[36]

Undeterred by the devastating attack on his command post and by the limited forward progress of his counterattack force, Chuikov ordered all of his forces to greet the Germans' attacks on 3 October with counterattacks of their own. So that they could do so, he fed the remaining regiments of Gurt'ev's 308th Rifle Division into the fighting as soon as they reached the front. The Red Army General Staff's daily operational summary described the frenzied fighting that day:

> **62nd Army** continuing stubborn defensive fighting on 3 October, repelling attacks by enemy infantry and tank. . . .
> 112th RD conducted intense defensive fighting with enemy forces of up to a regiment of infantry and 17 tanks in the vicinity of Hill 97.7 [the Dizel'naia section]. Suffering heavy losses, the division abandoned Hill

97.7 by day's end. Fighting was raging along the eastern slopes of this hill.

42nd RB, 351st RR, 308th RD, and 92nd RB, after suffering heavy losses as a result of an attack by an enemy force of up to two regiments with tanks, withdrew to the western and southwestern edge of the garden (northeast of Barrikady village), the northern outskirts of Silikat village, and the western corner of Skul'pturnyi Gardens line.

39th Gds. RD was defending [the following] line: 112th RR from the southwestern corner of Skul'pturnyi Gardens along the ravine with its front to the southwest; 120th RR from the ravine at Manezhnaia Street to Feodosievskaia Street; and 117th RR along Bibliotechnaia Street to Mendeleev Street.

883rd RR, 193rd RD, occupied defenses in the vicinity of Martovskaia [Martov] and Tsekhovaia Streets.

241st RR, 95th RD, and a battalion of 1045th RR, 284th RD, occupied defenses along the southern bank of Bannyi Ravine.

37th Gds. RD crossed to the western bank of the Volga River with two regiments and concentrated in the area 1 kilometer south of Stalingrad's Tractor Factory village.[37]

Attesting to the ferocity of Chuikov's counterattacks, all conducted in the wake of the Germans' dramatic advance, during the evening *Kampfgruppe* Winterfeld had to fight hard to retain its forward positions, in what one eye-witness described as "stressful and draining work" for the panzer crewmen:

The battlefield around the destroyed workers huts and hollows was illuminated by burning buildings, the flickering flames causing shadows to move and dance, making it almost impossible to determine if Russian tank-killers were sneaking up with Molotov cocktails. Engagements would flare up with frightening speed; someone would notice a movement in the shadows, a flare would be fired, climbing a hundred meters into the dark sky with a trail like a rocket, bursting into a brilliant white star which then fell gracefully earthward, brilliantly illuminating everything within a circle of several hundred meters.[38]

After suffering heavy losses as a result of Seydlitz's new onslaught, Chuikov's counterattacking forces, their flanks now threatened with envelopment, broke off their attacks late in the evening and withdrew to new defensive positions. Ermolkin's 112th Rifle Division, whose decimated regiments had no choice but to abandon defenses on Hill 97.7, west of the Dizel'naia section, withdrew its shattered regiment to all-around defenses on the eastern slope of the hill. To the southeast, Skuba's 6th Guards Tank and 42nd Rifle

Brigades, the two reinforcing regiments of Gurt'ev's 308th Rifle Division, and Shtrigol's 92nd Rifle Brigade broke off their assaults and withdrew northeastward and eastward to new defenses along Manezhnaia and Feodosievskaia Streets. The 42nd Rifle Brigade moved to positions in the park northeast of Barrikady village, 308th Rifle Division to the northern and eastern outskirts of the Silikat Factory and *Schnellhefter* Block, and 92nd Rifle Brigade to positions around Skul'pturnyi Park, southeast of the Silikat Factory.[39] Tanks from 6th Guards Tank Brigade provided support north and east of the Silikat Factory.

On this group's southern flank, the 117th Regiment, on the right wing of Gur'ev's 39th Guards Rifle Division, occupied defensive positions along Bibliotechnaia Street to Mendeleev Street to protect 92nd Rifle Brigade's left flank. Still farther south, together with the three rifle regiments of Smekhotvorov's 193rd Rifle Division (685th, 895th, and 883rd), 112th and 120th Regiments of Gur'ev's division successfully contained the assaults by Sanne's 100th Jäger Division among the street rubble and the buildings west of the railroad line and the Krasnyi Oktiabr' Factory. According to Chuikov, "Smekhotvorov's division fought the whole day for the bath-house and the kitchens. The bath-house changed hands several times, but finally remained in ours. The regiments in the division now contained 100–150 men each."[40]

Thus, by day's end on 3 October, 389th Infantry Division and 24th Panzer Division's two *kampfgruppen* had shattered Chuikov's defenses in the sector of the Silikat Factory and to the northwest, pushing 112th Rifle Division, 42nd Rifle Brigade, and 308th Rifle Division back toward the north and east. Lenski's forces were now poised to advance into the Tractor Factory village and the Tractor Factory beyond—but only if they could muster the strength necessary to do so. By this time, reflecting its excellent repair capabilities, Lenski's panzer division counted 36 operational tanks, but its grenadier regiments fielded fewer than 1,000 combat troops each. The 244th and 245th Assault Gun Battalions, which were supporting 389th Infantry and 100th Jäger Divisions, respectively, fielded seven and 13 assault guns, respectively.[41]

Nevertheless, Seydlitz insisted that the offensive continue and thus directed 389th Infantry and 24th Panzer Divisions to capture "the dominating heights on the western edge of the northern part of Stalingrad" by late on 3 October. Accordingly, Lenski issued Division Order No. 71, which required his panzer division to conduct a limited attack northeastward on 4 October to reach and hold the plateau on the northern edge of the Barrikady village. While 276th Infantry Regiment continued to protect the division's right flank, *Kampfgruppen* Edelsheim and Winterfeld were to advance in tandem at 0900 hours, the former to seize the southeastern part of the *Schnellhefter* Block, the latter the block's northwestern section. After capturing the block, Edelsheim was to wheel his force to the southeast to form a barrier against expected counterattacks. Before beginning this assault, however, Winter-feld's group was to take over responsibility for defending the northern edge of the *Schnellhefter* Block by 0630 hours.[42]

As 389th Infantry and 24th Panzer Divisions were preparing to resume their northward advance toward the Tractor Factory and its village, Sanne's 100th Jäger and Wuthmann's 295th Infantry Divisions strove to maintain pressure on Chuikov's forces along the western half of the lower Krasnyi Ok-tiabr' village, Bannyi Ravine and Mamaev Kurgan, and the sector southward through the Dolgii and Krutoi Ravines.

In the wake of the day's bloody fighting, the only forces that Chuikov had available to block the German advance toward the upper Tractor Factory village, the *Schnellhefter* Block, and the lower Tractor Factory village were the decimated remnants of Ermolkin's 112th Rifle Division, supported by the few remaining tanks of Skuba's 6th Guards Tank Brigade, 42nd Rifle Brigade, and roughly one-half of Gurt'ev's 308th Rifle Division. Therefore, the night before (2–3 October), Chuikov had requested Stalingrad Front to release Zholudev's 37th Guards Rifle Division to his control. Once Eremenko agreed to do so late on 3 October, Chuikov decided to ferry the division across the Volga as soon as possible and place it on 308th Rifle Division's right flank to block any German advance toward the Tractor Factory. Although Chuikov managed to ferry the division's three regiments across the Volga by the next morning, a shortage of cutters prevented him from transporting the division's headquarters and antitank artillery. This meant that Chuikov had to assign officers from his staff to guide the arriving regiments to their new positions. After doing so successfully, Zholudev's forces went into action almost imme-diately on 4 October, reinforcing 112th and 308th Rifle Divisions' sagging defenses in piecemeal fashion during the next 12 hours.[43]

While Zholudev's division was deploying forward, Ermolkin, on Chui-kov's instructions, began regrouping the remnants of his 112th Rifle Division into new defensive positions facing west at the extreme western end of the upper Tractor Factory village on Zholudev's right flank.[44] The division's 385th Regiment deployed along Shchelkovskaia Street, facing the lead elements of 389th Infantry Division, with its left flank to be supported by 37th Guards Rifle Division's 109th Regiment.[45] The 42nd Rifle Brigade and the remaining tanks of 6th Guards Tank Brigade bolstered 308th Rifle Division's defenses north of the Silikat Factory, in the northwestern part of the Skul'pturnyi dis-trict, and west of Skul'pturnyi Park.

Seydlitz's assaults on 3 October had broken the back of Chuikov's coun-terattacks in the vicinity of the Silikat Factory and now threatened to carve an even deeper wedge in 62nd Army's defenses toward the Tractor Factory village and the Volga east of the Krasnyi Oktiabr' Factory. Yet the heavy at-trition in Paulus's shock groups reminded the army commander how hard it would be for his shock groups to fulfill their missions without additional reinforcements. Paulus expressed these concerns to Weichs late on 3 October, complaining, "At present, even the breaking out of individual blocks of houses can only be accomplished after lengthy regroupings to bring together the few combat-worthy assault elements that can still be found."[46] Because Weichs had no additional troops available, the army group commander had no choice but to inform Paulus that he must prevail with the forces he had at hand. Thereby left to his own devices, Paulus resolved to settle the issue on his own by resuming assaults against more limited objectives. With its left flank protected by 94th Infantry Division's two regiments north of the Mechetka River and its right by 100th Jäger Division's two regiments in the western half of lower Krasnyi Oktiabr' village, Jänecke's 389th Infantry and Lenski's 24th Panzer Divisions were to drive an even deeper wedge into Chuikov's defenses west of the Tractor and Barrikady Factories.

4 October

Early on 4 October, Winterfeld and Edelsheim reorganized their groups to resume their assaults. Part of 4th Motorcycle Battalion assigned to *Kampfgruppe* Winterfeld relieved the northern sector of *Kampfgruppe* Edelsheim by 0630 hours, and at 0815 hours Lenski manned his command post to monitor the attack. The *Luftwaffe* softened up the Soviet defenses until 0900 hours, concentrating its strikes against the defensive positions of 308th Rifle Division's 339th Regiment in the *Schnellhefter* Block and 351st Regiment, with 92nd Rifle Brigade now attached, in and around Skul'pturnyi Park. After a 10-minute artillery preparation by 89th Panzer Artillery Regiment, the two *kampfgruppen* unleashed their assault, spearheaded by Winterfeld's force of 36 tanks. Supported by artillery, whose fires were directed by forward observers in the ranks of the *kampfgruppen*, the two forces ran a gauntlet of small-arms, mortar, and artillery fire as they pressed northward. Apparently catching the Soviet defenders by surprise, Winterfeld's panzers destroyed several T-34 tanks and reached the southern edge of the six-story *Schnellhefter* Block, whose "dozens of blank windows stared down on the German panzers, any of which could contain a Russian sniper."[47] After several hours of fighting with numerous Soviet machine-gun nests and under constant enemy artillery fire, the two *kampfgruppen* secured their objectives, Winterfeld's, the *Schnellhefter* Block, and Edelsheim's, the Sports Ground (Stadium), due east of the immense block. During this fight, 24th Panzer Division reported destroying nine Soviet tanks, including seven T-34s, presumably from the remnants of 6th Guards Tank Brigade.

Simultaneously, *kampfgruppen* from Jänecke's 389th Infantry Division thrust northeastward from the gullies southwest of the upper Tractor Factory village, striking the forward security outposts of 112th Rifle Division's 385th Regiment and driving them back into the regiment's main defense line along Shchelkovskaia Street. Pressing forward slowly but steadily, the 389th penetrated several blocks into the upper Tractor Factory village before its assault stalled late in the day. By this time, the forces on the division's right wing had advanced eastward south of the Dizel'naia section, capturing part of the block of buildings several hundred meters northwest of the *Schnellhefter* Block.

The concentrated thrusts by 389th Infantry and 24th Panzer Divisions' *kampfgruppen* smashed the defenses of 385th Regiment of Ermolkin's 112th Rifle Division along Shchelkovskaia Street in the western section of the Tractor Factory village. They also crushed the defenses of 42nd Rifle Brigade and 351st Regiment of Gurt'ev's 308th Rifle Division, as well as the division's reinforcing 339th Regiment, in and around the *Schnellhefter* Block. In the process, the Germans destroyed more than half of 6th Guards Tank Brigade's remaining tanks and captured the Sports Ground (Stadium) to the east. While *Kampfgruppe* Winterfeld pressed the right wing of 42nd Rifle Brigade and its supporting tanks northward into the gullies on the southern outskirts of the lower Tractor Factory village, *Kampfgruppe* Edelsheim forced 351st and 339th Regiments on the right wing of 308th Rifle Division eastward from Mytishchi, Aviatornaia, and Petrozavodskaia Streets, southwest of the Silikat Factory, toward the railroad and ever deeper into Skul'pturnyi village.

During this intense fighting the bulk of 308th Rifle Division's 351st Rifle Regiment was encircled and destroyed. An entry in the division's combat journal for 4 October stated:

> The 351st Rifle Regiment, excepting 30 men who were situated in the region of the ravines north of Silikat, repelled strong attacks by enemy infantry and tanks from Vogul'skaia, Koppashevskaia, Ushimaskaia, Makeevskaia, and Vinnitskaia [Streets] for several hours. While in full encirclement, the soldiers and their commanders staunchly defended their positions and heroically perished south of Silikat, together with its staff and commissar Frolov, while destroying a considerable number of Fascist soldiers, officers, and their equipment.[48]

Meanwhile, on 308th Rifle Division's right, the left wing of 42nd Rifle Brigade and remnants of 6th Guards Tank Brigade occupied new defenses in the vicinity of Zhitomirskaia Street, near Hill 97.7. Late in the day, Chuikov directed Gurt'ev to move the smashed regiments of his 308th Rifle Division southward into new defensive positions from Skul'pturnyi Street southward past Petrozavodskaia Street to Buguruslanskaia Street, where they were to protect the western approaches to the Barrikady Factory. Finally, once it arrived on the Volga's western bank, Zholudev's 37th Guards Rifle Division was to take over 308th Division's former sector north of the *Schnellhefter* Block and east of the Sports Ground.

Exploiting the Soviets' discomfiture, after Lenski's grenadiers completed clearing Soviet troops from the *Schnellhefter* Block house by house, *Kampfgruppe* Edelsheim tried to thrust eastward toward the main north-south railroad line and the gap between the Tractor and Barrikady Factories. However, stiffening Soviet defenses, now bolstered by lead elements of Zholudev's 37th Guards Rifle Division, halted the thrust and forced Edelsheim to withdraw his forces back to the eastern edge of the Sports Ground.[49] Thus, by day's end Winterfeld's *kampfgruppe* had seized the key terrain of the *Schnellhefter* Block and, supported by Edelsheim's group, consolidated its hold on its objective: the sector extending from the northeastern corner of grid square 84a northward to the right flank of 389th Infantry Division at the crossroads in grid square 85c4 on the southern edge of the upper Tractor Factory village. The 389th had reached the block of buildings from grid square 85c to the western edge of 85b in the western third of the village. However, by this time German intelligence had detected the presence of "new enemy concentrations [37th Guards Rifle Division]" in front of the right wing of 24th Panzer Division's 21st Grenadier Regiment. Coupled with the steady erosion of 24th Panzer Division's combat strength, this increasing Soviet resistance prevented Lenski's division from exploiting its successes further. On the contrary, this resistance compelled both of his *kampfgruppen* to withdraw their forces "a little."[50]

As fighting continued east of the Sports Ground, ultimately forcing Edelsheim to pull his forces back to more defensible positions late in the day, Chuikov once again reorganized his defenses, this time inserting the regiments of Zholudev's 37th Guards Rifle Division into the fight to reinforce the sagging defenses of 112th Rifle Division, 42nd Rifle Brigade, and 308th Rifle Division. In succession, Zholudev deployed his 114th Regiment forward on 4 October, in addition to his 109th and 118th Regiments on the following night, with all three going into action literally from the march.

After it crossed the Volga River during the day on 4 October, 114th Regiment advanced due west into the teeth of the attacking Germans. As it did so, it ran into the lead elements of the *kampfgruppe* on 389th Infantry Division's right wing just as the Germans were reaching their designated objective, in the rear of 42nd Rifle and 6th Guards Tank Brigades' defenses east of Hill 97.7, several hundred meters northwest of the *Schnellhefter* Block. The timely arrival of 114th Regiment enabled 385th and 416th Regiments of Ermolkin's 112th Rifle Division to repulse 389th Infantry Division's assault toward the lower Tractor Factory village at 1200 hours. After this encounter brought the 389th's advance to a halt, 114th Regiment's three battalions relieved the decimated forces of 23rd Tank Corps' 6th Guards Tank Brigade and 42nd Rifle Brigade and occupied defenses along an 800-meter front along Zhitomirskaia Street and the nearby Zhitomir Ravine from just north of Hill 97.7 southward past the eastern side of the Stadium to the northeastern edge of Skul'pturnyi village.

Meanwhile, on the extreme right (northern) wing of Ermolkin's 112th Division, its 416th Regiment repelled several attempts by submachine gunners from the lead elements of 94th Infantry Division to force their way across the Mechetka River. With the defenses of its 416th Regiment along the river threatened and with its 385th Regiment under immense enemy pressure in the western part of the upper Tractor Factory village, Ermolkin's division anxiously waited for assistance from 37th Guards Rifle Division's 109th Regiment, which was supposed to reinforce its defenses.[51]

Crossing the Volga on the night of 4–5 October, 109th Regiment reached its assigned sector along the Mechetka River by dawn, where it reinforced 112th Rifle Division's depleted 416th Regiment, early on 5 October. The guards regiment then placed its 1st Battalion in defensive positions along the eastern bank of the Mechetka River to protect the northwestern face of the Tractor Factory village and its 3rd Battalion in positions to reinforce the sagging defenses of 112th Rifle Division's 385th Regiment at the village's western extremity. It retained 2nd Battalion in reserve several blocks to the rear. By virtue of its timely arrival, 109th Regiment managed to halt any further German advance in this sector. Zholudev's third regiment, the 118th Guards, which also crossed the Volga on the night of 4–5 October, successfully occupied second-echelon defenses about 1,000 meters to 114th Regiment's rear to protect the approaches to the Tractor Factory from the southwest.[52]

Meanwhile, desultory fighting and patrolling activity continued to the south. East of the Silikat Factory, 308th Rifle Division's 339th Regiment, once it shifted southward into its new defensive positions, blocked the forces on the right wing of *Kampfgruppe* Edelsheim from advancing into Skul'pturnyi Park. Farther south, on 308th Division's left wing, 347th Regiment, with the remnants of 92nd Rifle Brigade attached, defended the buildings from Skul'pturnyi Street southward to Petrozavodskaia and Buguruslanskaia Streets, contesting any further advance by 24th Panzer Division's *Kampfgruppe* Edelsheim and 276th Infantry Regiment eastward toward the Barrikady Factory. Still farther south, the three regiments of Smekhotvorov's 193rd Rifle Division, now backed up by Gur'ev's 39th Guards Rifle Division, Gorishnyi's 95th Rifle Division, and Batiuk's 284th Rifle Division successfully prevented Sanne's 100th Jäger and Wuthmann's 295th Infantry Divisions from registering any significant gains in Krasnyi Oktiabr' village, on Mamaev Kurgan, and along the Dolgii and Krutoi Ravines, slowing their forward progress to a snail's pace.

The Red Army General Staff kept track of the confused fighting and the Germans' advances in its daily combat summary:

62nd Army conducted fierce defensive fighting with enemy forces of up to one infantry division with 50–60 tanks, which were attacking along the front from the Mechetka River to Barrikady village all day on 4 October.
. . .
6th Gds. RB, suffering significant losses in personnel and weapons, withdrew to the vicinity of Zhitomirskaia [Zhitomir] Street.

308th RD fought fierce battles along the line of Skul'pturnaia Street and Petrozavodskaia [Petrozavodsk] and Buguruslanskaia Streets.

193rd RD, 39th Gds. RD, 95th and 284th RDs, and 13th Gds. RD were holding on to their previous positions.

37th Gds. RD was fighting along the Nogin Street and Stadium line.

42nd and 92nd RBs, suffering heavy losses, withdrew to the western part of the Tractor Factory village and the northeastern part of Skul'pturnyi Park.[53]

From the German perspective, the OKW's daily summary remarked:

In Stalingrad, 24th Panzer Division captured the area of the railroad station. An advance of tanks and infantry toward Tsigeliaia [Street] did not succeed because of shortcomings in the employment of our infantry. Parts of the division's northern wing penetrated to the eastern block of the buildings west of the Tractor Factory and captured this block by day's end. Developing the attack toward the north, our forces reached the line of the railroad and captured local sectors by attacks from the north and south. In the northern sector of the front, the shock groups conducted fighting of local importance.[54]

Still frustrated over the slow forward progress of Seydlitz's forces, Sixth Army's chief of staff late on 4 October underscored the army's foremost problem, when he wrote in the army's war diary, "Without reinforcements, the army is not going to take Stalingrad very soon. The danger exists, were the Russians to make fairly strong counterattacks, our front might not hold because there are no reserves behind it."[55]

Confirming the chief of staff's concerns, fresh reserves continued to pour in to reinforce Chuikov's army overnight on 4–5 October. In addition to the last two regiments of Zholudev's 37th Guards Rifle Division, Eremenko began dispatching 84th Tank Brigade across the river to bolster Chuikov's decimated tank force. The tank brigade consisted of 49 tanks, including 5 KV-1s, 24 T-34s, and 20 T-70s, which outnumbered the tank force mustered by the entire 24th Panzer Division.[56] The brigade's commander, Colonel Daniil Nikitovich Belyi, was an experienced armor officer who had commanded his brigade since 1 February 1942.[57] Again, however, lack of large vessels meant that only 20 light T-70 tanks could cross the river; these were broken up into small units to provide fire support for Gurt'ev's 308th Rifle Division, fighting on the western outskirts of Skul'pturnyi Park, and Zholudev's 37th Guards, struggling in Skul'pturnyi village and around the *Schnellhefter* Block to the northwest. These nocturnal transfers strained the resources of the Volga Flotilla, which also had to move the fresh 45th Rifle Division to defend Golodnyi and Sarpinskii Islands in the middle of the Volga River opposite Stalingrad's southern suburb of Beketovka.

As a result of Eremenko's and Chuikov's exertions, 62nd Army overnight on 4–5 October was able to muster the following forces to defend the factory district:

- **124th and 149th RBs and 282nd RR, 10th RD NKVD** (Group Gorokhov) defending Spartanovka village north of the Mokraia Mechetka River and the northern and northwestern approaches to the Tractor Factory against 16th Panzer Division.
- **115th RB** and **2nd MRB** defending encircled in Orlovka.
- **112th RD** [416th RR—97 men, 385th RR—124 men], **42nd RB**, and **37th Gds. RD** defending the sector from the Mechetka River eastward to the northwestern edge of Skul'pturnyi village and the approaches to the Tractor Factory village and Tractor Factory against one regiment of 94th Infantry Division west of the Mechetka River, 389th Infantry Division between the Mechetka River and east of Hill 97.7, and 24th Panzer Division's *Kampfgruppe* Winterfeld in the *Schnellhefter* Block.
- **308th RD** and **92nd RB** [50 men] defending eastern edge of the Stadium (Sports Ground), Skul'pturnyi village, Skul'pturnyi Park, and the approaches to the Barrikady Factory against 24th Panzer Division's *Kampfgruppe* Edelsheim and 276th Infantry Regiment.
- **193rd RD** [528 men] and **39th Gds. RD** defending the lower Krasnyi Oktiabr' village and the approaches to the railroad and Krasnyi Oktiabr' Factory against 100th Jäger Division's 54th Jäger and Croat 369th Regiment.
- **95th RD** defending the middle reaches of the Bannyi Ravine, northern and eastern slopes of Mamaev Kurgan, and southern approaches to Krasnyi Oktiabr' Factory against 100th Jäger Division's 227th Regiment and one regiment of 295th Infantry Division.
- **284th RD** defending the lower reaches of the Bannyi Ravine, the Meat Combine, the lower Dolgii and Krutoi Ravines, and the approaches to the Volga River against two regiments of 295th Infantry Division.

- **13th Gds. RD** defending the center city from Kievskaia Street northward past 9 January Square to the lower reaches of Krutoi Ravine against 71st Infantry Division's 194th Regiment.[58]

After losing another 23 killed and 89 wounded in the fighting on 4 October, Lenski informed Seydlitz late in the day that the combat strength of his panzer division was insufficient to continue active offensive operations. During eight days of fighting, his division had indeed accomplished its assigned mission by thrusting northward in nearly constant fighting. However, by 5 October three of its four panzer-grenadier battalions and its pioneer battalion were rated "exhausted," leaving the division with one "weak" panzer-grenadier battalion. By the end of this period, the six "weak" battalions of Jänecke's 389th Infantry Division had established contact with Hube's XIV Panzer Corps by thrusting northward along the Mechetka River and seizing the hills south of the Orlovka River. However, on 24th Panzer's right, 100th Jäger Division had not been able to match his division's forward progress. Therefore, Lenski's panzer division now had to protect an ever lengthening right wing, all the while protecting itself from likely enemy counterattacks against its front and flanks. This situation, coupled with the deadly toll that combat attrition was taking on his forces, left the division unable to exploit its previous successes.[59]

By this time, the line-combat strength of 24th Panzer Division's 21st and 26th Grenadier Regiments had fallen to 265 and 319 men, respectively, and 4th Motorcycle and 40th Panzer Pioneer Battalions to 160 and 94 men; the division's panzer regiment fielded only 27 operational tanks.[60] Thus, 24th Panzer Division was able to generate a force of only about 800 combat troops at a time when Chuikov was in the process of reinforcing his forces in the factory district with about 8,000 fresh troops from 37th Guards Rifle Division. Because all of Seydlitz's infantry divisions were suffering similar deficiencies in infantry, Paulus had no choice but to end this phase of his assault on Stalingrad's factory district unless and until his army received additional reinforcements.

LI Army Corps' Limited-Objective Attacks, 5–7 October

Acquiescing to both Lenski's and Seydlitz's entreaties for a pause, Paulus ordered the bulk of his army's shock groups to go over to the defense. At the same time, however, he directed 389th Infantry Division, which was still lagging behind 24th Panzer Division's forward lines, to conduct a series of limited-objective assaults to align its forward positions with those of Lenski's division. This initiated three days of somewhat limited but nonetheless bloody fighting as both sides prepared for more decisive operations to come (see Map 48). As Paulus's forces were organizing these attacks, Eremenko at 0500 hours ordered Chuikov's army "to attack at 0700 hours on 5 October to destroy the enemy penetrating into the Tractor Factory village and reach the Mechetka River and Barrikady village line."[61] Given the situation, this order was as superfluous as it was unrealistic.

In accordance with Paulus's decision, Lenski, at 1245 hours on 5 October, ordered his 24th Panzer Division to hold and consolidate the positions it had occupied in the northern part of Barrikady village until further notice. Without knowing exactly when they would resume offensive operations, Lenski's forces dug in, intent on improving their defensive positions. On the division's left wing, *Kampfgruppe* Winterfeld's forces were to maintain close connections with 389th Infantry Division in the gully on the southwestern edge of the upper Tractor Factory village, while focusing its defenses on the northern edge of the *Schnellhefter* Block and its right boundary. Group Edelsheim was to hold firm to the positions it occupied in the center. On the division's right, 276th Infantry Regiment was to establish close contact with 1st Battalion of 100th Jäger Division's 54th Regiment, although at this stage its neighbor's left boundary was still unclear.[62]

Seydlitz dispatched similar orders to other elements of LI Corps deployed around the periphery of the factory district. Despite the general lull, Seydlitz's forces continued suffering casualties. 24th Panzer Division, for example, reported 25 killed and 95 wounded on 5 October.[63]

Confirming Weichs's approval of Paulus's decision, Sixth Army's war diary stated the next day that "the army's attack into Stalingrad had to be temporarily suspended because of the exceptionally low infantry combat strengths." In its divisions, the average battalion strengths were down to 3 officers, 11 noncommissioned officers, and 62 men. Although the army could scrape together enough replacements from the supply service to make small advances, it admitted that "the occupation of the entire city is not to be accomplished in such a fashion."[64]

Beginning on 5 October, in accordance with Paulus's instructions and despite the cessation of Seydlitz's general assault, Jänecke's 389th Infantry Division, supported by a panzer squadron detached from Lenski's panzer division, continued combat operations to straighten out its forward lines in and south of the upper Tractor Factory village. To that end, on the morning of 5 October and again on 7 October, 389th Infantry Division launched repeated attacks northward from the vicinity of Hill 97.7 toward the southern reaches of the upper Tractor Factory village.

The assault by Jänecke's division on 5 October, which Chuikov estimated was supported by 700 aircraft sorties, propelled the forces on the division's left wing forward about 400 meters, where it secured positions west of but adjacent to the *Schnellhefter* Block. This attack overcame the defenses of 37th

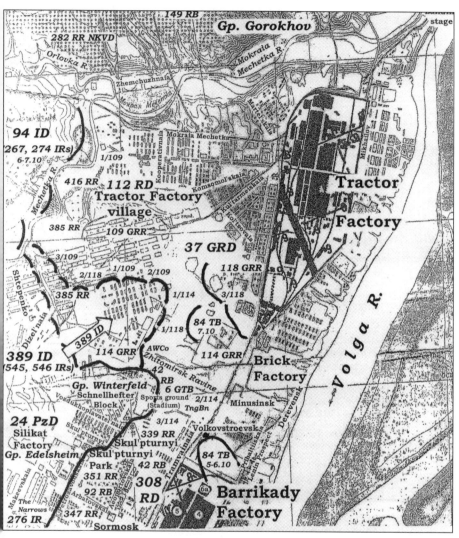

Map 48. LI Army Corps' limited objective attacks, 5–7 October 1942

Guards Rifle Division's 114th and 109th Regiments, backed up by the remnants of 112th Rifle Division's 385th Regiment. Zholudev's regiments were able to contain the attack in reportedly "fierce fighting" only because of effective support it received from 499th Antitank, 11th Artillery, and 85th Howitzer Regiments.[65] In addition, the light tanks from Colonel Belyi's 84th Tank Brigade finally reached the scene to bolster 37th Guards Rifle Division's defenses.

Overhead, *Luftwaffe* aircraft blanketed the entire combat area from Spartanovka to the ravines south of Mamaev Kurgan with a dense carpet of bombs. In Chuikov's words: "On October 5, in the city's factory area alone, about 2,000 sorties were counted. At daybreak all troop movements came to a halt, because anything that moved was hammered by the Luftwaffe. The wounded did not leave their dug-outs or trenches until nightfall and crawled to the evacuation points on the bank of the Volga under cover of darkness."[66]

The Red Army General Staff's daily operational summary for 5 October reflected the ferocity of these limited-objective assaults:

62nd Army conducted fierce defensive fighting with enemy infantry and tanks all day on 5 October. . . .

112th RD occupied defenses along the cemetery-western outskirts of the Tractor Factory village line.

37th Gds. RD engaged in fierce defensive fighting with enemy forces of up to two infantry regiments and tanks, which attacked toward the Dizel'naia-Zhitomirsk region. 12 enemy tanks penetrated into the Zhitomirsk region. The units of the division are located along the line of Shtepenko Street to Vozdukhoplavatel'naia [Aeronautic] Street.

The remnants of 42nd RB occupied defenses in the vicinity of the group of buildings northeast of Zhitomirsk.

The remnants of 92nd RB [50 men] occupied defenses in the region east of Skul'pturnyi Park.

308th RD defended the line from Vozdukhoplavatel'naia Street and along Petrozavodskaia, Glovskaia, and Buguruslanskaia Streets to the railroad line.

193rd RD [with 528 active bayonets] occupied defenses along the line from the ravine along Ochakovskaia [Ochakov] Street to Prokitnaia Street, Kazach'ia Street, and Glovskaia Street to Dzhankoiskaia Street.

39th Gds. RD defended the Tsekhovaia, Belebeiskaia, and Severnaia Streets line to the Bannyi Ravine.

95th RD occupied a defensive line from the railroad along the southern bank of the Bannyi Ravine to Tovarishcheskaia [Comrade] Street and from here southward along the railroad and, farther, along Syzranskaia Street to the trigonometric point 102.0 [crest of Mamaev Kurgan].

284th RD occupied defenses along the line from (incl.) the trigonometric point 102.0 to 4th Polotnaia Street, along the northern bank of the Dolgii Ravine to Artilleriiskaia Street, and farther to south along the Krutoi Ravine to 3rd Naberezhnaia Street.

13th Gds. RD occupied its previous defensive positions.[67]

Although Chuikov's headquarters had survived its harrowing experience with the burning oil only days before, German mortar fire against his command post became so precise and damaging that he had no choice but to move his staff to new quarters. He did so on the night of 4–5 October, relocating to the former headquarters of 10th NKVD Division, about 500 meters farther north along the western bank of the Volga, so that he would be closer to the fighting near the Tractor Factory.

As if to provide Chuikov and his troops with a brief respite, 389th Infantry Division suspended operations on 6 October so it could shift sufficient forces to its left wing and resume its line-straightening operations on 7 October. The Red Army General Staff duly reported this brief lull:

Units of **62nd Army**, repelling fierce enemy attacks, continued to hold on to their previous positions in all sectors of the front on 6 October. . . .

37th Gds. RD, repelling attacks by small groups of enemy infantry, defended its previous positions.

193rd RD, remaining in its previous positions, repulsed attacks toward Dublinskaia [Dublin] Street by small groups of enemy with part of its forces.

84th TB reached the line from the northeastern outskirts of the Krasnyi Oktiabr' Factory and Iamy to 0.5 kilometers north of this factory with its motorized rifle battalion on the night of 6 October.

The positions of the army's remaining units are unchanged.

The enemy continued to bring new forces forward from the Gumrak and Gorodishche regions to the vicinity of Dizel'naia [Street], Barrikady village, and Silikat. We have identified the presence of 40 enemy tanks and a large number of vehicles with infantry in the vicinity of Dizel'naia Street.

Enemy aircraft bombed the Stalingrad Tractor Factory village and our crossings over the Volga River in the Stalingrad region with massive raids.[68]

Although Seydlitz halted 389th Infantry Division's assaults on 6 October, the Germans continued intense air strikes during the lull, in one instance attacking the headquarters of 308th Rifle Division's 339th Regiment in the eastern section of Skul'pturnyi village, killing the entire regimental staff, including its commander and commissar.

As a result of this lull in the ground action, as well as fresh intelligence reports underscoring the likelihood that the Germans would soon resume their assaults toward the Tractor Factory, Eremenko pressed Chuikov to conduct yet another counterattack. This time the *front* commander hoped to drive German forces from their positions threatening the Tractor Factory

village, specifically the Dizel'naia and Zhitomirsk regions and Hill 97.7 to
the south. Under what he described as "great pressure," Chuikov reluctantly
agreed to organize a counterattack to clear German forces from these areas.[69] The counterattack would come from the forces on the adjoining flanks
of Zholudev's 37th Guards Rifle and Gurt'ev's 308th Rifle Divisions, with the
former's 114th and reserve 118th Regiments and the latter's 339th Regiment
concentrated north of Skul'pturnyi Park.[70]

German actions, however, preempted Eremenko's ambitious plans:

> We decided to launch the attack during the afternoon of October 7, reck-
> oning that the enemy would not have time to parry our blow before night-
> fall and would not be able to bring in his aircraft.
>
> I [Chuikov] signed the order to counterattack at 4 A.M., but we were
> unable to implement it. At 11:20 A.M. the enemy launched a new, power-
> ful attack. We met the attackers with fire from previously prepared and
> well-camouflaged positions.[71]

This German assault represented the culminating attempt by Jänecke's
389th Infantry Division to straighten out Sixth Army's forward lines south of
the upper Tractor Factory village. Late in the morning, the 389th, supported
by a panzer squadron from 24th Panzer Division with ten tanks and 245th
Assault Gun Battalion with about 10 assault guns, thrust northward against
the center and right wing of 37th Guards Rifle Division's defenses. Several
battalion-size *kampfgruppen* from two of 389th Division's regiments assaulted from the vicinity of Verkhneudinskaia Street along the railroad spur
northwest of the *Schnellhefter* Block, and a third attacked directly into the
western end of the Tractor Factory village. Although this attack involved only
parts of two regiments, supported by roughly 20 armored vehicles, Chuikov
later exaggerated its strength, writing:

> It was a full-scale attack. From the vicinity of Verkhneudinskaia Street,
> they threw in two divisions and more than 500 tanks. The first attacks
> were thrown back. The units of Zholudev's division inflicted heavy losses
> on the enemy. The Germans brought up reserves and repeated their at-
> tacks several times. After bitter fighting, they managed to penetrate our
> lines in the evening, seize a block of the tractor workers' settlement, and
> approach close to the stadium. Prospect Stakhonovtsev and Skul'pturnyi
> Park remained in our hands.[72]

More accurately than Chuikov's later recollections, 62nd Army had
reported:

The enemy, having concentrated large forces (up to two infantry division and 80–90 tanks) in the Dizel'naia, Barrikady village, and Hill 107.5 region, went over to the attack at 1130 hours in the general direction of the Tractor Factory village. . . .

37th GRD and 84th TB fought intense battles with up to two attacking enemy regiments and 45–50 tanks. The enemy attacked along other axes: the Verkhne-Udinsk and Tractor Factory village and the Verkhne-Udinsk and Zhitomirsk. The initial enemy attacks were repelled with heavy losses to the enemy.[73]

Regardless of their strength, these attacks smashed the defenses of 37th Guards Rifle Division's 114th Regiment, compelling its forces to withdraw roughly 300 meters to the east. There the 114th halted the German advance after being reinforced by 1st Battalion, 118th Regiment, a machine-gun company, and a tank battalion from 84th Tank Brigade. During the German assault, Zholudev also redeployed 1st and 2nd Battalions of his 109th Regiment, the former from the Mechetka River line and the latter from its reserve positions, to contain the German advance 500 meters north of the *Schnellhefter* Block. Meanwhile, on 389th Infantry Division's left wing, *kampfgruppen* from its third regiment advanced only two blocks eastward through the built-up area north of Dizel'naia Street. During this fighting, 94th Infantry Division's 267th and 274th Regiments, which were on 389th Infantry Division's left flank north of the Mechetka River, tried but failed to capture a crossing over the river south of the railroad bridge from 112th Rifle Division's 385th Regiment. As Chuikov described the attack, "At [1800 hours] a reinforced battalion of enemy infantry attacked west of the railway bridge across the River Mechetka. An accurate '*Katiusha*' salvo destroyed the battalion almost completely."[74] As imposing as these struggles seemed on the opposing forces' operational maps, the participating forces consisted of battalion- and company-size groups often numbering no more than several hundred men each and, on the Soviet side, frequently much less than 100.

The Red Army General Staff's daily operational summary reflected Chuikov's recollections of the actions on 7 October, although not his claims regarding German armored strength:

62nd Army fought fierce defensive battles with an enemy force of up to three infantry divisions and one motorized division, which launched an attack in the general direction of the Stalingrad Tractor Factory village at 1130 hours. . . .

37th Gds. RD, 84th TB, and the remnants of 112th RD fought intense battles with enemy forces attacking toward the Stalingrad Tractor Factory village and Zhitomirsk. By day's end on 7 October, the enemy reached the corner of Surkov and Ustiuzhskaia Streets, the upper reaches of Zhitomirsk, and (incl.) Skul'pturnyi Park (incl.). During the day, up to four battalions of enemy infantry and 16 tanks were destroyed. A further enemy advance was halted along that line.

42nd RB reached the line of the two separate buildings (north of Skul'pturnyi Park) and the northwestern part of Skul'pturnyi Park.

The positions of the army's remaining units remain unchanged.[75]

Regardless of Chuikov's exaggerations, Jänecke's 389th Infantry Division severely dented Chuikov's defenses south of the upper Tractor Factory village but, at the same time, failed to straighten out LI Corps' front lines. The short but violent fight on 7 October cost 24th Panzer Division 51 officers and men wounded and 389th Division 20 killed and 45 wounded. By day's end on 7 October, Jänecke's forces had carved out a new salient extending at right angles northward toward the southern outskirts of the village. This salient was bounded on the north by defenses erected by 37th Guards Rifle Division's 109th Regiment and by 112th Rifle Division's 385th Regiment, which together clung to their positions in the built-up region north of Dizel'naia Street and along the eastern bank of the Mechetka River (see Map 49). On the salient's eastern flank, the defenses of Zholudev's 114th Regiment, now reinforced by part of 118th Regiment, stoutly denied German access to the southern approaches to the Tractor Factory. It was now clear to Seydlitz and Paulus that significant reinforcements were required before their forces could successfully reach and conquer the Tractor Factory.

As a result of their decision, an eerie lull set in along Sixth Army's entire front, punctuated by occasional reconnaissance sorties and raids by both sides, as well as incessant artillery and mortar fire and air strikes against each others' positions.[76] All the while, Chuikov strove to do everything in his power to strengthen his defenses; Paulus assembled his forces for what he hoped would be a decisive end to this prolonged struggle.

THE STRUGGLE ON THE FLANKS, 29 SEPTEMBER–11 OCTOBER

Soviet Planning

As intense fighting raged around the Orlovka salient and in Stalingrad's factory district and center city, the *Stavka* did not sit idly by. Instead, it once again attempted to distract the Germans by organizing attacks against their flanks north and south of the city. In addition to ordering Don Front's 1st Guards, 24th, and 66th Armies to continue heavy attacks against XIV Panzer Corps' defenses between the Don and Volga Rivers north of the city, it

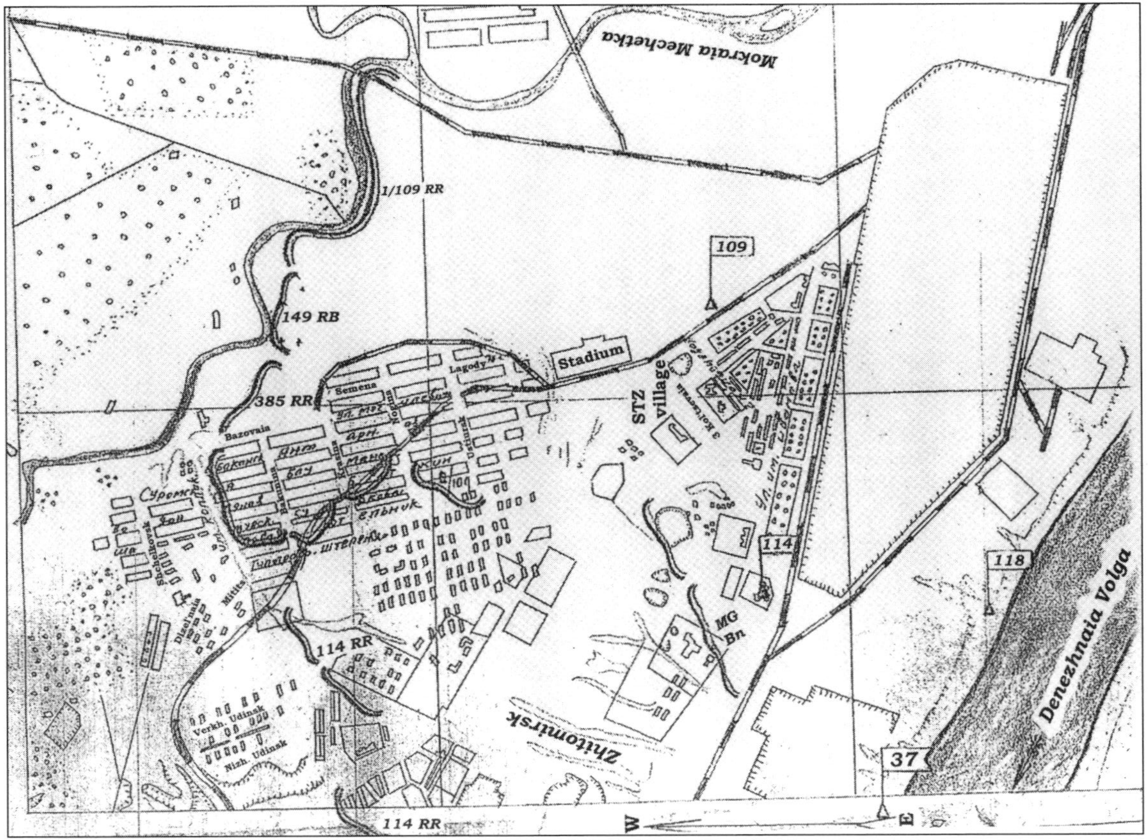

Map 49. 37th Guards Rifle Division's dispositions, 5 October 1942

demanded that Stalingrad Front conduct diversionary offensives south of the
city. As Rokossovsky later wrote:

> In order to divert if only part of the enemy forces from the city, the com-
> mander of the Stalingrad Front decided to conduct local offensive opera-
> tions south of the city on the night of 29 September [28–29 September].
> The aim of this operation was to reach the rear of the southern enemy
> grouping in the vicinity of Tinguta, Abganerovo, and Sadovaia Stations
> and, by doing so, to force the enemy to weaken his forces in the city. The
> 57th and 51st Armies allocated one mixed detachment each, consisting of
> a reinforced rifle regiment, to conduct this operation.
>
> The 8th Air Army was assigned the mission of conducting strikes against
> seven enemy objectives in the city and disorganizing the preparations for
> his next offensive. To eliminate strikes against it by its own aircraft, 62nd
> Army was to reliably mark its forward edge with signal lights.[77]

In addition, Shumilov's 64th Army, which had organized unsuccessful assaults in support of the counterattack by Chuikov's 62nd Army on 27 and 28
September, received orders to support 57th and 51st Armies' assaults with
yet another attack of its own on 2 October.[78]

Dispatched by the *Stavka* to coordinate this attack, Vasilevsky later wrote:

> I flew to the Southeastern [after 29 September the Stalingrad] Front with
> the mission of devoting my main attention to learning about the forces in
> the region of 57th Army and the right wing of 51st Army and the enemy
> operating against them.
>
> Having arrived in the Southeastern Front, I did all of my work in 57th
> Army's headquarters. Upon completing my work, I recommended that
> the commanders of 57th and 51st Armies undertake measures in the
> near future to seize the entrances from the defiles between Lakes Sarpa,
> Tsatsa, and Barmantsak from the enemy and fortify them.[79]

At the time, Axis forces in the region included the Romanian VI Army Corps' 1st
Infantry Division, defending the defile between Lakes Sarpa and Tsatsa, and 4th
Infantry Division, manning defenses between Lakes Tsatsa and Barmantsak.

The Southern Flank: The Battles in the Lake Region and at Beketovka, 29 September–3 October

In accordance with Vasilevsky's instructions, General Tolbukhin, commander of 57th Army, formed a composite detachment consisting of 1334th
and 115th Rifle Regiments and 155th Tank Brigade, supported by 1188th

Antitank Artillery and 18th and 76th Guards-Mortar (*Katiusha*) Regiments. This detachment was to assault the defenses of Romanian 1st Infantry Division south of Lake Sarpa. Simultaneously, a detachment from General Kolomiets' 51st Army, consisting of 254th Tank Brigade reinforced by a rifle battalion from 91st Rifle Division and supported by 80th Guards-Mortar Regiment, all operating under the control of Colonel E. F. Makarchuk, commander of the army's 302nd Rifle Division, was to penetrate the defenses of Romanian 4th Infantry Division south of Lake Tsatsa. Artillery and riflemen from 57th Army's 15th Guards Rifle Division were to support the detachments' assaults.[80]

Tolbukhin and Kolomiets unleashed their forces overnight on 28–29 September, achieving almost immediate success (see Map 50). Catching Romanian 4th Infantry Division by surprise, Kolomiets' detachment penetrated its defenses south of the village of Ungi-Teriachi, reportedly routing its 5th and 21st Infantry Regiments and advancing roughly 18 kilometers to capture the village of Sadovaia. Farther north, Tolbukhin's detachment penetrated Romanian 1st Infantry Division's defenses and advanced roughly 5 kilometers, capturing the villages of Tsatsa and Semkin, nearby Hill 87.0, and the vital Dubovoi Ravine by 1400 hours on 1 October.[81]

The Red Army General Staff's operational summaries described the operations on Stalingrad Front's left wing during the next two days:

[29 September]
64th Army occupied its previous positions.
57th Army. The composite detachment of the army reached the Tsatsa-Semkin region, where it dug in.
51st Army. The composite detachment of the army captured the Sadovaia, Hill 83.1, and Sertin regions and the region 1 kilometer northwest of the village of Dede-Lamin (33 kilometers south Sadovoe) as a result of offensive operations.
28th Army occupied its previous positions.

[30 September]
64th Army occupied its previous positions.
57th Army. The detachment of 15th Gds. RD, overcoming strong enemy fire resistance, captured the northern outskirts of Dubovyi Ravine village by 1500 hours on 30 September. The fighting in that region is continuing.
The **Special Group of the Army** (1334th RR, 155th TB, 1188th ATR, and 18th and 76th Gds.-MRs) engaged in offensive fighting toward Plodovitoe village and reached positions on the un-named hill (9 kilometers east and southeast of Plodovitoe) by 1400 hours on 30

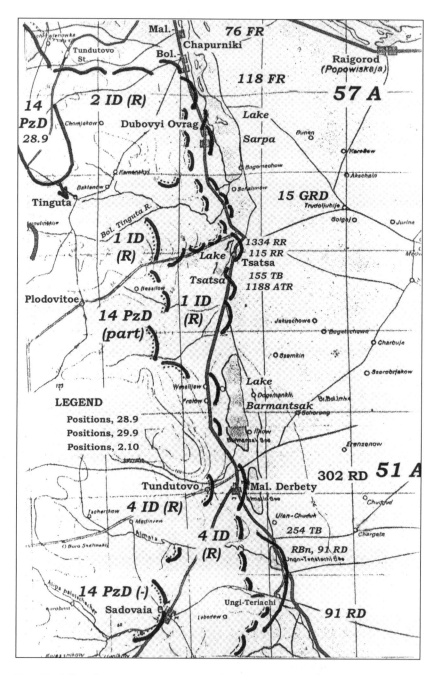

Map 50. 57th and 51st Armies' counterstroke, 28–30 September 1942

September. The positions of the army's remaining forces remain unchanged.

51st Army occupied its previous positions and, with part of its forces, fought with an enemy force of up to a regiment of infantry in the region south of the villages of Mal. Derbety and Tundutovo and a force of up to two battalions on the Dede-Lamin (Magdyn-Kuduk) line.

No new information has been received about the dispositions of **28th Army**'s units.[82]

A history of the Romanian Army confirmed the damage done to the forces of its VI Army Corps during the first two days of the Soviet attack:

> The plight of VI Corps particularly concerned him [Antonescu], as it had suffered heavy casualties and was severely over-extended on open steppe without local provisions or shelter. The 4th Division had to hold 60 kilometers of front and on 29 September suffered heavy losses in a Soviet attack that penetrated to its command post. Throughout October the Red Army mounted a series of generally successful probing attacks on VI Corps which eliminated 1st and 4th Divisions' positions beyond the lake line and exposed their multiple weaknesses.[83]

The defeat that Romanian forces suffered in the vicinity of the lake region, 60–75 kilometers south of Stalingrad, set off alarm bells at Paulus's headquarters. Within hours, he ordered Kempf's XXXXVIII Panzer Corps to dispatch its 14th Panzer Division, which was then in Fourth Panzer Army's reserve along with the 29th Motorized Division awaiting orders to begin a planned thrust toward Astrakhan, southward to rescue the Romanians. Deploying rapidly southward overnight on 30 September, Heim's panzer division went into action east of Plodovitoe on 1 October in support of the shattered Romanian 4th Infantry Division.[84] The Red Army General Staff's daily report for 1 October summed up the effect:

64th Army occupied its previous positions.

57th Army. The units of 15th Gds. RD captured the Dubovyi Ravine region by 1400 hours, where they dug in.

The composite detachment of the army was subjected to a counterattack by an enemy force of up to a battalion of infantry and 50 tanks in the vicinity of Hill 87.0 (9 kilometers southwest of the village of Tsatsa) at 1130 hours on 1 October. The attack was repelled by fire from our artillery and multiple-rocket launchers. 16 enemy tanks were deployed. After a repeat attack, the enemy pushed the units of our detachment back and occupied the Semkin region.

51st Army. 91st RD fought with the enemy in the Dede-Lamin region. The composite detachment of the army approached Tundutovo, where it fought with an enemy force of up to a regiment of infantry.

28th Army occupied its previous positions.[85]

Although Heim's panzers managed to stabilize the situation in the Romanian division's sector, they were unable to dislodge Kolomiets's detachment and restore the original defensive line between Lakes Tsatsa and Barmantsak. As a result, Paulus would be denied the use of Heim's division for the decisive assault on Stalingrad's factory district for another ten days.

Compounding Paulus's dilemma, while 14th Panzer Division was attempting in vain to restore the Romanian defenses in the lake region south of Stalingrad, to the north Shumilov's 64th Army unleashed its attack against German IV Army Corps' defenses northwest of Beketovka (see Map 51). Attacking overnight on 1–2 October, with the bulk of its forces concentrated north and northwest of Beketovka on its right flank, Shumilov's 64th Army struck the German 371st Infantry Division's defenses at and west of Peschanka. Shumilov delivered the attack with five divisions—29th, 138th, 157th, and 422nd Rifle and 36th Guards Rifle—and 66th Naval Rifle Brigade concentrated in the 8-kilometer-wide sector from Elkhi northeastward to Zelenaia Poliana. Later in the day, 204th Rifle Division, in the army's second echelon, went into action alongside 138th Rifle Division in an attempt to capture Staro-Dubovka and Peschanka.

Although this attack failed, it proved to be yet another unpleasant distraction for Paulus. The effect of this action, however, fell short of the *Stavka's* expectations. As described by Major General I. K. Morozov, commander of 422nd Rifle Division, which spearheaded the effort, "Day and night, the divisions of 64th Army fought their way to the north to link up with 62nd Army, but the distance between the armies scarcely diminished."[86] The Red Army's General Staff's daily operational summary described the futile action:

64th Army went over to the attack along the previous axis with the units on its right wing and in its center at 0430 hours on 2 October.

422nd RD attacked from the Zelenaia Poliana region, enveloping the "Topor" woods from the northeast.

36th Gds. RD attacked toward the vicinity of Hill 145.5 (4 kilometers southwest of Peschanka), where it was [still] fighting.

157th RD attacked toward Peschanka. Fighting was raging along the line of the road from Gornaia Poliana State Farm to Hill 136.1 (4 kilometers south of Peschanka).

138th RD attacked toward Staro-Dubovka and was fighting along the southern slope of Hill 136.1.

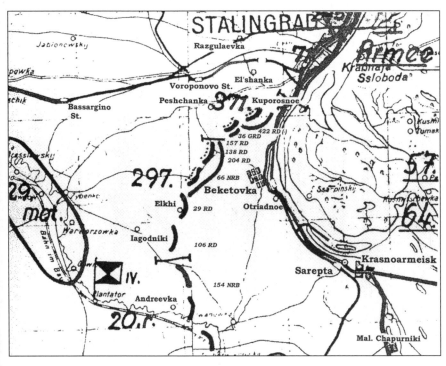

Map 51. 64th Army's counterattack, 1–2 October 1942

66th Naval [Infantry] Brigade attacked along the line from the brush 1 kilometer northeast of Marker 127.5 to the eastern slope of that marker.

29th RD was fighting along the line from the eastern outskirts of the village of Elkhi to Hill 121.7.

204th RD, attacking from behind 138th RD, reached the line from Marker 135.4 to Marker 131.3 (7 kilometers south of Peschanka).

57th Army occupied its previous positions.

The mixed detachment of the army occupied the Semkin region at 1120 hours on 2 October and fought with enemy infantry and tanks attacking toward the region between Lakes Tsatsa and Barmantsak.

51st and 28th Armies continued to occupy their previous positions and conducted reconnaissance.

Providing an epitaph to 64th Army's brief diversionary operation south of Stalingrad, on 4 October the General Staff simply noted, "The 64th Army continued to occupy its previous positions and conducted a partial redeployment of forces to its left flank."[87]

Only at day's end on 4 October, when 389th Infantry and 24th Panzer Divisions' assaults on Chuikov's defenses in the Tractor Factory village faltered, did Paulus finally appreciate the importance of the Soviet attack against Fourth Panzer Army's defenses south of Stalingrad. First, the attack disrupted Hitler's and Army Group B's plan to employ XXXXVIII Panzer Corps' relatively fresh and refitted 14th Panzer and 29th Motorized Divisions for a deep thrust toward Astrakhan' and the lower Volga River. Second, and even more important for Paulus, it also delayed any commitment of either of these two mobile divisions in support of his assault against the factory district. As a result, the army commander would have to wait until 9 October for Heim's panzer division to shift northward from the lake region and spend another four days resting and refitting its forces before it could participate in the final drive on Sixth Army's most vital objective.

The Northern Flank: The Third Kotluban' Offensive, 9–11 October

No sooner did Eremenko's assaults south of the city falter than the *Stavka* once again ordered Rokossovsky's Don Front to resume its attacks in the Kotluban' and Erzovka regions north and northwest of the city. This time, Rokossovsky acted in coordination with the diversionary attacks by Eremenko's armies to the south. As indicated by an order issued by the Red Army General Staff at 2305 hours on 7 October:

> By order of the *Stavka* of the Supreme High Command, by about 20 October, the commander of the forces of the Stalingrad Front will work out a plan for an assault by the reinforced 57th and 51st Armies on its left wing in the general direction of Lakes Tsatsa and Tundutovo to destroy the enemies' forces at Stalingrad.
> Simultaneously with this operation, a meeting blow must be delivered by the center of the Don Front in the general direction of Kotluban' and Alekseevka, for which you are permitted to employ the seven divisions now arriving in the *front*.
> Conduct the operation with a short attack on Stalingrad, which you recently planned, irrespective of your present orders.
> Request you present your decision and remarks regarding this plan to the *Stavka* for approval by 10 October.[88]

Thereafter, the *Stavka*, Rokossovsky, and Eremenko exchanged numerous proposals and counterproposals regarding how best to conduct these coordinated counterstrokes by their forces north and south of the city. As they did so, Rokossovsky reluctantly resumed his attacks in the vicinity of Kotluban'. Without permitting his forces to catch their breath after their failed assaults in late September and the first few days of October, Rokossovsky on 9 October launched the new attacks with his 1st Guards and 24th Armies (see Map 52).

As recorded by the *front*'s daily reports, these assaults were no more productive than before:

[9 October]

1st Guards Army began offensive fighting of local significance with part of its forces at 1400 hours 9 October, encountering strong enemy resistance.

298th RD attacked in the region south of Hill 113.3 (4 kilometers southwest of Kotluban') with part of its forces, advancing 300–400 meters.

258th RD attacked in the vicinity of Hill 123.6, but achieved no success.

207th RD attacked in the vicinity of Hill 123.6 and captured several enemy pill-boxes and foxholes in the Pristan' region.

The positions of the army's remaining units are unchanged.

24th Army conducted attacks of local significance with part of its forces to improve its positions in the vicinity of Hill 130.7 and the Motor Tractor Station (9 kilometers northwest of Opytnoe Pole State Farm) beginning at 1400 hours on 9 October but, encountering strong enemy resistance, had no success.

[10 October]

1st Guards Army held onto its previous positions, while, with part of its forces, it fought to improve the positions it occupied in the vicinity of Hill 123.6 and repelled attacks by small groups of enemy in separate sectors.

258th, 207th, and 173rd RDs tried to resume their attacks against the enemy 2 kilometers north of Hill 123.6 with part of their forces from 1100 to 1130 hours on 10 October but had no success and were fighting in their previous positions.

24th Army continued to hold its previous positions.

343rd RD fought to capture the Mty region (8 kilometers northeast of Kuz'michi) with one regiment.[89]

As the *front*'s subsequent daily reports indicate, Rokossovsky's feeble assaults faltered by 11 October, again without achieving any tangible results. The most that could be said about these futile attacks, as well as Eremenko's far to the south is that collectively they served as constant distractions to Paulus. More important still, they also reminded him that his army's wings, in the north between the Volga and Don, and in the lake district to the south as well, remained terribly vulnerable.

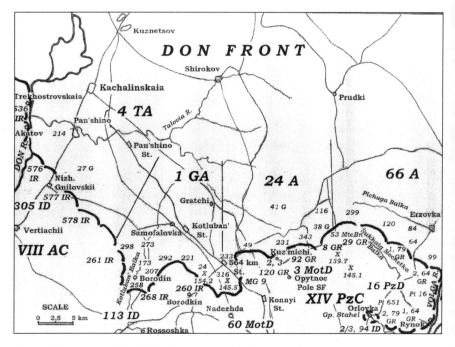

Map 52. Don Front's Kotluban' counterstroke, 9–11 October 1942

THE LULL BEFORE THE STORM, 8–13 OCTOBER

The exhausted and overwrought Paulus could foresee no easy end to the fighting in Stalingrad. On 2 October, Hitler demanded the city be taken immediately; during the subsequent month, his public pledges to do so made any other course of action politically impossible. Indeed, during early October victory at Stalingrad became even more important psychologically in order to offset the Germans' failure in Egypt. Meanwhile, on 6 October the OKH staff informed Hitler that the German Army was a million men below strength. The dictator responded by authorizing the reassignment of 400,000 men from *Luftwaffe* air-defense assignments to the ground forces, but these reassignments would take too long to provide meaningful reinforcements during the autumn of 1942.[90]

Having failed to take the factory district by 7 October, the Germans virtually ceased offensive operations for several days while they prepared for the next major effort. Daily sniping and local firefights resulted from reconnaissance raids and German attempts to strengthen the jumping-off positions for their new offensive, and by Soviet attempts to consolidate their defensive positions or recapture key bits of territory.[91] For example, on 8 October the fight for the Zhitomirsk region, southeast of the upper Tractor Factory village, continued when, at 0830 hours and again at 1300 hours, company-size *kampfgruppen* from 389th Infantry Division attempted to capture the remainder of this region. However, 37th Guards Rifle Division and the remnants of 112th Rifle Division repelled all of these German sorties (see Map 53).

As 62nd Army reported, "The enemy undertook two attacks in 37th Gds. RD's sector during the day but did not display activity with infantry and tanks in the remaining sectors of the front."[92] During the day Chuikov took measures to bolster his army's defenses in the factory district by transferring Gorishnyi's 95th Rifle Division to the region and ordering 37th Guards Rifle Division to conduct a local attack to restore the positions it had lost several days before southwest of the Tractor Factory. Chuikov's order read:

> The Army commander has decided to conduct a partial regrouping of forces on the night of 9 October 1942, with 95th RD to occupy and defend the Zhitomirsk and Skul'pturnyi sector, 284th RD to occupy 95th RD's sector, and, at the expense of shortening the front, to concentrate the combat formation of 37th Gds. RD and create local reserves along that axis for forthcoming offensive operations to restore the positions in 37th Gds. RD's sector.
>
> Prepare an attack by units of 37th Gds. RD, reinforced by tanks and artillery, with the mission to throw the enemy back behind the line of the ravines north of Mytishch and Zhitomirsk. Begin the artillery offensive at 1630 hours and the attack at 1700 hours.[93]

Meanwhile, on 9 October 193rd and 284th Rifle Divisions reported repelling attacks by two German battalions on their defenses at 1900 hours, but otherwise "the army continued its defense of its occupied positions and constructed barriers and obstacles" while "conducting a partial regrouping of its forces: 284th RD occupied the sector of 95th RD's 161st and 241st RRs. The relieved units of 95th RD occupied new designated defensive sectors."[94] However, because of the time it took for 95th Division to complete its movement north, 37th Guards Rifle Division, other than conducting local raids, did not mount a full-scale counterattack until 12 October.

On 11 October, following a quiet day on 10 October, 37th Guards Rifle Division's 114th Regiment reported local attacks, ostensibly by 24th Panzer Division's *Kampfgruppe* Edelsheim, against the defenses on its left wing east of the Stadium. These assaults forced the regiment to withdraw from the six-sided block (*Schnellhefter*) in Skul'pturnyi village south of the Stadium to new defenses extending from the cemetery and along Bakunin, Kotel'nik, and Surkovo Streets to the ravine north of Zhitomirsk village. Farther south, 95th Rifle Division, which had finally occupied its assigned sector, also reported

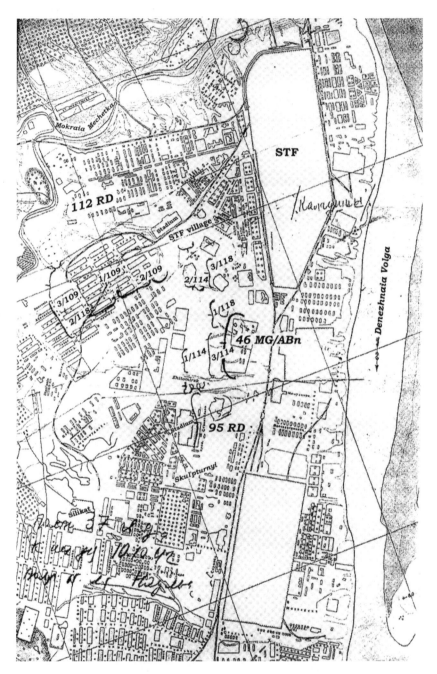

Map 53. 37th Guards Rifle Division's dispositions, 0600 10 October 1942

repelling several local attacks on its positions. Recognizing what the Germans were attempting to accomplish, Chuikov at 2130 hours ordered 37th Guards Rifle Division, this time reinforced by 90th Regiment, 95th Rifle Division, "to deliver a counterattack on the morning of 12 October, with the mission to restore the situation 37th GRD's sector and reliably protect the approaches to the Tractor Factory village"; in addition to recapturing the lost parts of upper Tractor Factory village, Chuikov sought to keep the Germans off balance and disrupt their offensive preparations.[95]

The next morning, 37th Guards Rifle Division's 114th Regiment, supported by 90th Regiment on 95th Rifle Division's right wing, tried to recapture the positions they had lost days before in the vicinity of the six-sided block south of the Stadium. However, Zholudev's counterattack failed, and 90th Regiment advanced only 150–200 meters. While this counterattack was taking place, to the south 308th Rifle Division's 339th Regiment tried but failed to dislodge German troops who had captured buildings 200 meters west of Aeroportovskii [Airport] Park, and 193rd Rifle and 39th Guards Rifle Divisions repelled several sorties by small groups of German infantry.[96]

The jockeying for position in the western and southern sections of the upper and lower Tractor Factory villages continued on 13 October, when 109th Regiment on 37th Guards Rifle Division's right wing reported repelling two separate forays by infantry and tanks from 389th Infantry Division. Meanwhile, the remainder of Zholudev's division clung tenaciously to the six-sided block, with its 114th Regiment capturing two large blocks in Skul'pturnyi village southwest of the six-sided block, and 118th Regiment another block southwest of Zhitomirsk.[97]

While the forward-deployed German divisions consolidated and improved their positions, Sixth Army and Army Group B, during the period from 5 through 13 October, reshuffled their forces to provide Paulus's army with forces they considered strong enough to capture Stalingrad's factory district. At the same time, the two headquarters strove to maintain viable defenses elsewhere along the front, especially in XIV Panzer Corps' sector north of the city and along the Don River farther to the northwest. During this period, largely due to XXXXVIII Panzer Corps' commitment in support of the Romanians to the south, but also because of Paulus's cries for reinforcements, Hitler permitted cancellation of the corps' planned advance on Astrakhan'. Instead, he reluctantly agreed to assign Heim's 14th Panzer Division to Paulus so he could reinforce the shock groups designated to capture the city's factory district.

In addition, Hitler and Weichs agreed to reinforce Paulus's shock group with two additional infantry divisions, the 79th from XVII Army Corps, which had been defending on Sixth Army's left wing opposite Soviet forces in the Serafimovich bridgehead on the Don River, and the 305th from VIII Army

Corps, which had been defending the western half of Sixth Army's defenses facing north between the Don and Volga Rivers.[98] The 305th Division managed to redeploy into its new assembly areas west of Stalingrad in time to participate in Paulus's 14 October assault. However, 79th Infantry Division was not able to close into its assembly areas until days later, and then with only two of its regiments. At the same time, on 30 September and 1 October, Paulus withdrew the battered 76th Infantry Division from its forward positions in VIII Corps' defensive lines south of Kotluban', replacing it with 113th Infantry Division, also from XVII Corps. Once relieved, 76th Infantry, which had consolidated its nine infantry battalions into six to compensate for the attrition it had suffered, moved into rest areas east of the Don River north of Kalach.[99]

This series of regroupings culminated between 1 and 10 October, when Army Group B moved the entire Romanian Third Army into defenses along the southern bank of the Don from the Khoper River eastward to the Kletskaia region (see Map 54).[100] By assigning Third Army so vital a sector, Hitler and Weichs were taking a major gamble—mistakenly as it turned out—that the Red Army would not conduct a major offensive in this critical sector. Army Group B assigned the Romanian Third Army (171,256 men) the sector facing the Red Army's Serafimovich bridgehead and the western end of its Kletskaia bridgehead. Already deployed in exposed positions across open steppe and lacking the firepower necessary to resist a major Red Army offensive, the Romanian forces were short of ammunition and requisite provisions, although their strength and morale was better than that of the Romanian Fourth Army's forces.[101]

Compounding these problems, Hitler denied repeated requests by General Dumitrescu, commander of Romanian Third Army, for permission to conduct operations to eliminate all or part of the Soviets' bridgeheads south of the Don and even to improve his army's defenses:

> On 24 September General Dumitrescu requested German backing to mount an offensive with the still-uncommitted half of 3rd Army to try to recapture the River Don line [the Serafimovich bridgehead], which he badly needed as an anti-tank obstacle. However, the Germans did not want to divert any resources from their assault on Stalingrad and refused, preferring to string 3rd Army ever more thinly along the existing Italian front despite Romanian objections.[102]

Thereafter, beginning on 14 October and on numerous other occasions during October, Soviet forces in the Serafimovich bridgehead subjected Third Army's forces to increasingly intense probing attacks designed to draw German forces away from Stalingrad.[103]

As these shifts took place, Paulus slowly assembled the forces earmarked to participate in the final assault on Stalingrad's factory district. First he transferred the two regiments of Pfeiffer's 94th Infantry Division from Seydlitz's LI Corps to Hube's XIV Panzer Corps, where it was to join Angern's 16th Panzer Division in its assault against Soviet defenses north of the Mokraia Mechetka River. He then assigned Heim's 14th Panzer Division, transferred from Kempf's XXXXVIII Panzer Corps, and General Oppenländer's newly arrived 305th Infantry Division to Seydlitz's LI Corps, where they were to join the corps' 24th Panzer, 389th Infantry, 100th Jäger, and 295th Infantry Divisions in the assault against the factory district. Transferred back to LI Corps from Fourth Panzer Army's XXXXVIII Panzer Corps, Hartmann's 71st Infantry Division was to reduce Soviet remnants in Stalingrad's center city with its 194th Regiment and to defend the western bank of the Volga River southward to Kuporosnoe with its 191st and 211th Regiments. On Paulus's southern flank, Hoth's Fourth Panzer Army would defend the sector from Kuporosnoe southward past the lake district with its IV Army Corps and Romanian VI Army Corps, with the headquarters of XXXXVIII Panzer Corps (without assigned forces) and 29th Motorized Division in reserve.

By virtue of these reinforcements, according to Soviet calculations, Paulus managed to increase the strength of his shock groups operating against Chuikov's 62nd Army to roughly 90,000 men, supported by as many as 2,300 guns and mortars, 300 tanks and assault guns, and 1,000 aircraft subordinate to Fourth Air Fleet.[104] However, these figures are suspect because they include 29th and 60th Motorized and 16th Panzer Divisions' men and tanks in the tally at a time when the bulk of those divisions faced Soviet forces either in the sector between the Don and Volga Rivers north and northwest of Stalingrad or in the lake region south of the city. Furthermore, by this time 14th Panzer Division was able to field no more than 50 tanks on any given day, and 24th Panzer Division only about 30 tanks.[105] Thus, the armored strength of Paulus's shock group facing the factory district numbered fewer than 100 tanks and assault guns, the latter assigned to the supporting 244th and 245th Assault Gun Battalions.[106]

In addition, Soviet (and Russian) sources include 76th Infantry, 29th and 60th Motorized, and 16th Panzer Divisions in calculating the strength of Paulus's forces arrayed against Stalingrad, but few of these forces (if any) participated in Paulus's final assaults on the factory district and other sectors of the city. Moreover, because the attrition rates in Paulus's infantry and panzer divisions were highest for infantrymen and panzer-grenadiers, the actual strength of his army's line-combat forces was much less than 80,000 men and perhaps equal, or even less than, the roughly 55,000 men fielded by Chuikov's army. Underscoring this point, although Sixth Army reported its total ration strength as 334,000 men on 17 October, its actual line strength

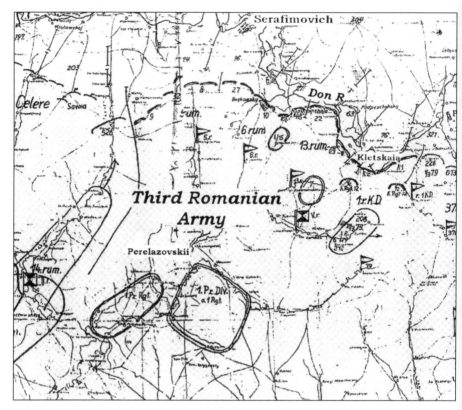

Map 54a. The deployment of Romanian Third Army along the Don River, 1–10 October 1942 (western portion)

for combat troops was only 66,549, many of them north and south of Stalingrad city.[107]

The combat ratings of the battalions in Sixth Army's forces that were poised to continue the offensive against the factory district underscored Paulus's concerns about the ability of his forces to sustain operations to total victory (see Table 30).

Thus, despite increasing the number of infantry battalions fighting in Stalingrad from 54 to 61 and pioneer battalions from 9 to 10, the median combat rating of Sixth Army's forces fighting in the city remained "weak." In addition, combat attrition compelled 389th and 71st Infantry Divisions to consolidate "exhausted" battalions to increase the combat strength of a lesser number of more capable battalions. In essence, then, by 12 October 295th,

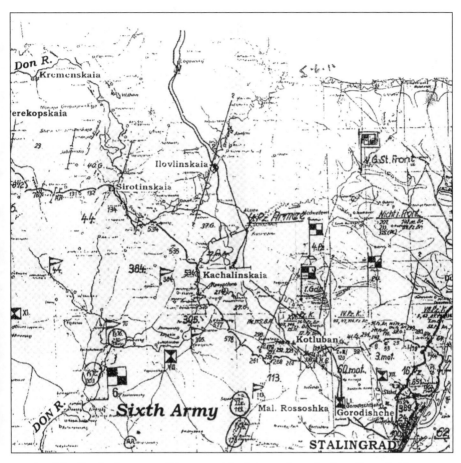

Map 54b. The deployment of Romanian Third Army along the Don River, 1–10 October 1942 (eastern portion)

389th, and 71st Infantry Divisions were hors de combat, and 24th Panzer Division was nearing complete combat exhaustion. This meant that Paulus had to rely on 305th Infantry Division's nine infantry battalions still rated "average" to complete the task at hand.

As Weichs and Paulus assembled their new shock groups for the final assault on the factory district, Chuikov, who was bombarded hour after hour with fresh exhortations and directives from the *Stavka*, readied his defenses. Through Vasilevsky, Stalin set the tone for this new struggle at 1430 hours on 5 October, when he dispatched a scathing rebuke to Eremenko, with a copy going to Rokossovsky at the Don Front:

Table 30. The Combat Rating of Infantry and Pioneer Battalions Subordinate to Sixth Army's Divisions Fighting in Stalingrad, 5–12 October 1942

	5 October	12 October
XIV PANZER CORPS		
3rd Motorized Division		
(5 infantry battalion)	3 average and 2 weak	2 average, 2 weak, and 1 exhausted
(1 pioneer battalion)	exhausted	exhausted
60th Motorized Division		
(7 infantry battalions)	4 average, 2 weak, and 1 exhausted	4 average, 2 weak, and 1 exhausted
(1 pioneer battalion)	exhausted	exhausted
16th Panzer Division		
(5 infantry battalions)	3 medium strong, 1 average, and 1 weak	2 medium strong, 2 average, and 1 weak
(1 pioneer battalion)	average	average
94th Infantry Division		
(7 infantry battalions)	7 exhausted	7 exhausted
(1 pioneer battalion)	average	weak
LI ARMY CORPS		
24th Panzer Division		
(4 infantry battalions)	1 weak and 3 exhausted	1 weak and 3 exhausted
(1 pioneer battalion)	average	exhausted
100th Jäger Division		
(5 infantry battalions)	4 average and 1 weak	4 average and 1 weak
(1 pioneer battalion)	weak	weak
305th Infantry Division		
(9 infantry battalions)	**(not fighting in the city)**	9 average
(1 pioneer battalion)		strong
295th Infantry Division		
(7 infantry battalions)	4 weak and 3 exhausted	4 weak and 3 exhausted
(1 pioneer battalion)	weak	weak
389th Infantry Division		
(6–5 infantry battalions)	6 weak	1 weak and 4 exhausted
(1 pioneer battalion)	exhausted	exhausted
XXXXVIII PANZER CORPS		
71st Infantry Division		
(8–7 infantry battalions)	1 weak and 7 exhausted	7 weak
(1 pioneer battalion)	average	weak

Table 30. (continued)

	5 October	12 October
Totals:		
54–61 infantry battalions	3 medium strong, 12 average, 18 weak, and 21 exhausted	2 medium strong, 21 average, 19 weak, and 19 exhausted
9–10 pioneer battalions	4 average, 2 weak, and 3 exhausted	1 strong, 1 average, 4 weak, and 4 exhausted

Source: Florian *Freiherr* von und zu Aufsess, "Betr.: Zustand der Divisionen, erstmalig nach neu festlegter Bestimmung des Begriffes "Gefechsstärke," Armee – Oberkommando 6, Abt. Ia, A. H. Qu., den 5 Oktober 1942,"and "Betr.: Zustand der Divisionen, Armee – Oberkommando 6, Abt. Ia, A. H. Qu., 12 Oktober 1942, 10.00 Uhr," in *Die Anlagenbander zu den Kriegstagebuchern der 6. Armee vom 14.09.1942 bis 24.11.1942, Band I* (Schwabach: January 2006), 128–132 and 156–160.

I think that you do not see the danger which threatens the forces of the Stalingrad Front. Having occupied the city's center and penetrated to the Volga north of Stalingrad, the enemy intends to take your crossings, encircle 62nd Army and take it captive, and, thereafter, encircle the southern group of your forces, 64th and the other armies, and also take them captive. The enemy can accomplish its intention since he occupies the regions of the crossings over the Volga in the north as well as in the center and to the south of Stalingrad. In order to avert this danger, you must press the enemy back from the Volga and once again seize those streets and buildings in Stalingrad which the enemy has taken from you. To do so, it is necessary to convert every building and every street in Stalingrad into a fortress. Unfortunately, you have not succeeded in doing this and are still continuing to give up block after block to the enemy. This testifies to your poor performance. You have more forces in the Stalingrad region than the enemy, and, in spite of this, the enemy is continuing to press you. I am dissatisfied with your performance in the Stalingrad Front, and I demand you undertake every measure for the defense of Stalingrad. Stalingrad must not be abandoned to the enemy, and those parts of Stalingrad which the enemy has occupied must be liberated.[108]

That same day, Stalin underscored his dissatisfaction with Eremenko and his staff by elevating Major General Georgii Fedorovich Zakharov, the *front*'s chief of staff, to become its deputy commander and by replacing him with Major General I. S. Varennikov, 37th Army's chief of staff. Zakharov, who had been the *front*'s chief of staff since its creation, was a 45-year-old officer with extensive staff experience. Before the Soviet-German War, Zakharov rose to become chief of staff of the Ural Military District from 1939 until the outbreak of war. Thereafter, he served in the same capacity in 22nd Army and Briansk Front in 1941, as deputy commander and chief of staff of Zhukov's Western Front during the winter of 1941–1942, as chief of staff of Budenny's North Caucasus Main Direction Command and North Caucasus Front in early 1942, and finally as deputy commander and chief of staff of Southwestern Front during its defeat in the initial stages of Operation Blau.[109] Zakharov built his career on a reputation as an extremely effective force organizer and an accomplished senior staff officer, traits that would be tested to the extreme during the defense of Stalingrad. Eremenko's new chief of staff, 41-year-old General Ivan Semenovich Varennikov, was also an experienced chief of staff, who had served in that capacity in 26th Army in 1940–1941 and in 37th Army in 1941–1942.[110]

In addition, because he considered Golikov to be a "weak reed," Stalin also relieved him as the *front*'s deputy commander, placing him at the *Stavka*'s disposal for future reassignment.[111] The next day, speaking on behalf of Stalin, Vasilevsky gave Eremenko precise instructions about improving Stalingrad's defenses:

> The *Stavka* of the Supreme High Command orders, while continuing the struggle to clear Stalingrad of enemy, immediately organize the firmest defense of the islands on the Volga River in the vicinity of Stalingrad, paying special attention to the defense of Zaitsevskii and Spornyi Islands.
>
> For the defense of these islands, allocate and deploy on them forces with heavy, divisional, and regimental artillery and air defense [PVO] weapons. To strengthen the forces allocated by the Stalingrad Front, the *Stavka* is placing nine artillery-machine gun battalions at your disposal. Present a plan for defense of the islands to the *Stavka* by 7 October 1942.[112]

On 7 October, the *Stavka* issued two new directives that affected Stalingrad Front. The first placed one air defense artillery regiment at Eremenko's disposal, effective 9 October, with instructions that he deploy it on Golodnyi Island and the northern half of Sarpinskii Island. The second directive "chopped" 45th Rifle Division to Eremenko's *front* with specific instructions that he employ it to erect defenses on Golodnyi Island and the northern half of Sarpinskii Island in the middle of the Volga River.[113] Finally, as insurance in case the city fell to the Germans, the *Stavka* on 10 October issued two more directives designed to strengthen Stalingrad Front's defenses on the eastern bank of the Volga. The first, issued at 1410 hours, transferred 4th Cavalry Corps from Trans-Caucasus Front to Eremenko's *front*; the second, issued at 2345 hours, assigned 300th Rifle Division to his *front*, with instructions that he employ it to reinforce the *front*'s defenses on the Volga's eastern bank.[114] Once in the Stalingrad region, 300th Rifle Division was to be subordinated to General Khasin's 2nd Tank Corps, whose refurbished tank and motorized brigades were already manning defenses on the river's eastern bank but without any tanks.

In addition to reinforcing Stalingrad Front, the *Stavka* also planned new offensive action to relieve pressure on the city and presented proposals for such an offensive to the commanders of the Don and Stalingrad Fronts on 7 October.[115] This plan required 1st Guards, 24th, and 66th Armies of Rokossovsky's Don Front to attack southward along the Kotluban'-Alekseevka axis on or about 20 October to link up with Stalingrad Front's 57th and 51st Armies along the railroad line west of Stalingrad. Simultaneously, Tolbukhin's and Kolomiets's 57th and 51st Armies were to attack once again northwestward along the Lake Tsatsa–Tundutovo axis from the lake region south of Stalingrad. Rokossovsky, however, objected strenuously to the *Stavka*'s proposal on 9 October. First, describing the nature of the Germans' defenses in detail, he asserted that they were simply too strong to penetrate successfully. Then he painted an accurate and depressing picture of the dilapidated condition of his armies after enduring a month of intense fighting:

As a result of months of fighting, the rifle divisions of 1st Guards, 24th, and 66th Armies are severely weakened and consist of no more than a battalion of bayonets in each division. The *front* has no replacements to restore their lost combat readiness. . . . The main force for the penetration and its exploitation include seven rifle divisions that have arrived from the *front*. These forces are completely inadequate for a penetration and the exploitation of the attack recommended by you along the Kotluban'-Alekseevka axis. In this instance, a minimum of four rifle divisions are required to penetrate the front, three rifle divisions to exploit the penetration, and a minimum of three full-blooded rifle divisions are required to protect the shock group against enemy counterattacks from the west and southwest.

In light of the insufficient quantity of rifle divisions, it does not seem possible to organize an operation with the main attack delivered toward Kotluban'.[116]

Based on these judgments, Rokossovsky proposed another, far less ambitious offensive scheme. Instead of deeply enveloping all of German Sixth Army, he recommended that his *front* conduct a far shallower penetration operation designed to link up with 62nd Army somewhere west of Orlovka. Spearheading this offensive, according to his plan, 24th Army would advance southward from the region east of Kuz'michi with a force of seven fresh rifle divisions and link up with 62nd Army's forces in the northern section of Barrikady village. 1st Guards and 66th Armies would simply protect the flanks of the penetration with forces amounting to four and three rifle divisions, respectively.[117]

Annoyed by this unusual challenge to his authority, Stalin rejected Rokossovsky's scheme: "The *Stavka* cannot approve the operational plan presented by you. It is necessary to combine the blow from the north with the Stalingrad Front's blow from the south in regard to their axes, about which additional orders will be given."[118] Instead, the dictator instructed Rokossovsky to "conduct active operations with reinforced detachments from the armies on the *front's* left wing, prevent the enemy from regrouping, attract his forces operating against Stalingrad to you, and seize favorable heights to improve your positions."[119] While doing so, the armies on Don Front's right wing (63rd, 21st, and 4th Tank) were to hold firmly to bridgeheads across the Don River.

Eremenko also responded to Stalin's proposal on 9 October. For his part, the commander of Stalingrad Front bridled at the thought of conducting yet another major attack in the Kotluban' sector, where the strong German defenses would render such an attack futile. Instead, he proposed that Rokossovsky's Don Front conduct a broader envelopment by mounting a major offensive from the Kletskaia and Sirotinskaia bridgeheads on the southern bank of the Don River southward toward Kalach-on-the-Don. He argued that such an attack would take advantage of weaker enemy defenses and 21st Army's previous successes. If properly exploited by mobile forces such as 3rd Guards Cavalry Corps and two or three separate mechanized brigades, such an offensive could penetrate deeply and cut vital German communications routes west of Stalingrad. It might also encircle and destroy Sixth Army. As for his own *front*, he proposed that 57th and 51st Armies conduct their main attacks from the lake region south of Stalingrad toward Kalach-on-the-Don, employing 4th Cavalry Corps and a separate motorized rifle brigade as the exploitation force to effect the linkup with Rokossovsky's forces. 64th Army would conduct local supporting attacks from its bridgehead at Beketovka.[120]

Rokossovsky's objections—entirely justified—convinced the *Stavka* to postpone its new offensive to relieve 62nd Army. Yet the subsequent advance of Paulus's Sixth Army into the factory district forced Moscow to revisit the question of a counteroffensive as early as 15 October. When it did so, it initially adopted Rokossovsky's recommendations. Ultimately, however, Stalin came to appreciate Eremenko's proposal and would use it as the basis for his plan for an even more dramatic and successful counteroffensive a little more than a month later.

While Stalin and his *Stavka* sought ways to ease the pressure on Chuikov's forces, 62nd Army's commander shuffled his forces within the city to improve defensive capabilities. For example, after Gorishnyi's 95th Rifle Division (with 3,075 men) moved from its former positions near Mamaev Kurgan

The southern third of the Factory District (looking west from the Volga River). The "Tennis Racket" and Bannyi Ravine on the left (south), Vishnevaia *Balka* from left to right across the top, the Krasnyi Oktiabr' village and Factory from top to bottom in the center, and the *balka* with the "twin gullies" from top to bottom on the right.

The central third of the Factory District (looking west from the Volga River bottom). The *balka* with the "twin gullies" from top to bottom on the left, the Silikat Factory, the *balka* with "the narrows," Skul'pturnyi Park, and the Barrikady Factory from top to bottom in the center, and the Mechetka River, upper Tractor Factory village, Zhitomirsk Ravine, and Minusinsk region from top to bottom on the right.

The northern third of the Factory District (looking west from the Volga River). The Mechetka and Mokraia Mechetka Rivers diagonally from top left to bottom right, the Silikat and Barrikady Factories on the left, the Tractor Factory village in the center and right center, and the Tractor Factory on the lower right.

Soviet troops fighting in the upper Krasnyi Oktiabr' village.

Panorama of the Factory District in flames.

and Bannyi Ravine to its new sector between the Stadium, Zhitomirsk, and Skul'pturnyi, he directed Gorishnyi to incorporate the 937 survivors of 42nd Rifle Brigade into the ranks of his division.[121] By this time, Gorishnyi's reinforced division formed a second defensive line at the boundary between Zholudev's 37th Guards Rifle Division, defending the approaches to the Tractor Factory on its right, and Gurt'ev's 308th Rifle Division, defending Skul'pturnyi Park and Sormosk on its left. After 95th Rifle Division departed from the Mamaev Kurgan sector, Batiuk's 284th Rifle Division took over responsibility for defending the slopes of Mamaev Kurgan and the southwestern edge of the Krasnyi Oktiabr' Factory, in addition to the division's previous sector protecting the Dolgii and Krutoi Ravines. The next day, Chuikov positioned 524th Regiment of Ermolkin's 112th Rifle Division, which had just crossed the Volga after re-forming and refitting on its eastern bank, in defensive positions extending along the Mokraia Mechetka River and Kooperativnaia Street to and including the Udarnik [Shock Worker] Stadium.[122]

When the remnants of Andriusenko's forces defending the Orlovka salient finally made their way back to 62nd Army's lines, Chuikov on 11 October deployed the weak remnants of 115th Rifle and 2nd Motorized Rifle Brigades in defensive positions facing west along a ravine at the western end of Zhemchuzhnaia Street on the northern bank of the Mokraia Mechetka River. He then withdrew the decimated 282nd NKVD Regiment of Group Gorokhov back across the Volga River for rest and refitting and ordered Gorokhov to employ his 124th Rifle Brigade, less its 1st Battalion, to defend the sector from south of Rynok westward past Spartanovka village to the southeastern slope of Hill 135.4. Finally, after the intense fight for the six-sided block ended, Chuikov on 12 October also adjusted and strengthened his defensive dispositions in this region. First, he shifted 112th Rifle Division's 524th Regiment into new reserve defensive positions extending from the northern edge of the Stadium (Sports Ground) northward east of the six-sided block to the western end of Kul'tarmeiskaia Street. Then he ordered Gur'ev to transfer 117th Regiment of his 39th Guards Rifle Division into new defensive positions along Zhitomirskaia Street to provide defense in depth at the boundary between 37th Guards and 95th Rifle Divisions.[123]

As a result of these adjustments, by the evening of 13 October Chuikov managed to erect what he thought were credible defenses in his army's shrinking perimeter around Stalingrad's center city and factory district. By this time, Group Gorokhov defended the bridgehead north of the Mokraia Mechetka River, which protected the northern approaches to the Tractor Factory and its associated village, with its 124th and 149th Rifle Brigades, less 1st Battalion, deployed in defenses extending from Hill 93.2 eastward north of Spartanovka to the Volga River just north of Rynok. On group Gorokhov's left flank, the remnants of 115th Rifle and 2nd Motorized Rifle

Brigades occupied the ravine from Hill 93.2 southward past the western end of Zhemchuzhnaia Street to the Mokraia Mechetka River.

South of that river, 416th and 385th Regiments of Ermolkin's 112th Rifle Division (re-formed with a total of 2,300 men) and the three regiments of Zholudev's 37th Guards Rifle Division, now backed up by 112th Rifle Division's 524th Regiment and 39th Guards Rifle Division's 117th Regiment, defended the Mechetka River and the western and southwestern approaches to the Tractor Factory. These forces manned defenses extending southward along the eastern bank of the Mechetka River to the western part of the upper Tractor Factory village, from the Mechetka eastward between the Dizel'naia region and the southern edge of the upper Tractor Factory village, and then southward to the western end of Zhitomirsk Ravine.[124] On the left flank of Zholudev's guards division, Gorishnyi's 95th Rifle Division, with 42nd Rifle Brigade attached, defended the sector from the western end of the Zhitomirsk Ravine southward through the western side of Skul'pturnyi village to the northwestern corner of Skul'pturnyi Park, that is, the approaches into the region between the Tractor and Barrikady Factories.

Farther south, the two surviving regiments of Gurt'ev's 308th Rifle Division (339th and 347th) defended the sector from the northwestern corner of Skul'pturnyi Park southward along the western edge of Sormosk to protect the railroad line and western approaches to the Barrikady Factory. On the left flank of Gurt'ev's division, 883rd, 895th, and 685th Regiments of Smekhotvorov's 193rd Rifle Division defended the sector extending southward along Dublinskaia Street from the ravine north of Kaluzhskaia Street (the southwestern corner of Sormosk) southward to Tsentral'naia Street to protect northeastern approaches to the Krasnyi Oktiabr' Factory. Finally, on the left flank of Smekhotvorov's division, 112th and 120th Regiments of Gur'ev's 39th Guards Rifle Division defended the western approaches to the Krasnyi Oktiabr' Factory from Tsentral'naia Street southward two blocks west of the railroad line to the Bannyi Ravine.

At the southern extremity of 62nd Army's defenses protecting the factory district, Batiuk's 284th Rifle Division defended the southern approaches to the Krasnyi Oktiabr' Factory by clinging to positions on the northern half of Mamaev Kurgan and the Meat Combine and the southern neck of the Tennis Racket south of Bannyi Ravine. Batiuk's division also provided a link with 13th Guards Rifle Division's small bridgehead in Stalingrad's center city by holding firmly to the lower reaches of Dolgii and Krutoi Ravines. Finally, Rodimtsev's 13th Guards Rifle Division, on 62nd Army's left wing, stoutly defended its shallow positions extending southward from Krutoi Ravine to the vicinity of 9 January Square.

In addition to 62nd Army's defenses in the city proper, Eremenko's Stalingrad Front, with the *Stavka*'s assistance, erected a formidable network of defensive strongpoints and other positions on the islands in the Volga River and on the river's eastern bank. These were defended primarily by artillery/machine-gun battalions subordinate to 77th Fortified Region and by tank and motorized brigades of 2nd Tank Corps, the latter commanded by General Khasin and, after 15 October, by General Popov, former commander of 23rd Tank Corps (see Table 31).[125]

By 10 October, according to Soviet sources, Chuikov's army totaled 55,000 men, with 44,017 in rifle forces in the city, supported by 1,400 guns and mortars (including 950 artillery tubes of 76mm or greater caliber) and 80 tanks (including 36 T-34 and 33 light T-60 and T-70 tanks) (see Table 32). The tanks were subordinate to 6th Guards and 84th Tank Brigades, plus a separate battalion of 23 tanks (6 KVs, 8 T-34s, 3 T-70s, and 6 T-60s), which occupied dug-in defensive positions amid the ranks of 124th and 149th Rifle Brigades.[126]

For air support, Chuikov relied on 8th Air Army, whose line strength as of 7 October was 188 operational combat aircraft, including 24 fighters, 63 assault planes, and 101 bombers (20 daytime and 81 PO-2 nighttime variants). Given the strength of Paulus's forces and supporting *Luftwaffe* units, this accorded Sixth Army's commander a superiority of 1.7:1 in manpower and artillery, 3.8:1 in tanks and assault guns, and more than 5:1 in aircraft over the Soviets.[127] However, the actual strength of Paulus's divisions in terms of combat-effective infantrymen and panzer-grenadiers was far lower than the 90,000 men that the Soviets estimated. This, plus congenital Soviet overestimation of Sixth Army's armored strength, meant that the real correlation in infantry and armor was far closer to parity than such figures would indicate.

Despite the perceived German advantage in fire support, Chuikov, with Eremenko's assistance, used new techniques for employing his artillery and airpower to disrupt Paulus's preparations for a new offensive. First, he began organizing a new series of far more effective artillery counter-preparations against German troop concentrations. During the first of these counter-preparations, supposedly conducted on 5 October to hinder the line-straightening attacks by LI Corps' 389th Infantry and 24th Panzer Divisions, Chuikov used the artillery of five rifle divisions, two rifle brigades, and the northern artillery subgroup of Stalingrad Front. The latter included four gun-artillery regiments, three antitank artillery regiments, and five *Katiusha* regiments, which together totaled more than 300 guns and many rocket launchers. This artillery struck German troop concentrations in the vicinity of the Silikat Factory and the southwestern section of the Tractor Factory village. The Soviets claimed that this bombardment caused abnormally heavy German casualties.[128] Although Sixth Army's records show no increase in casualties on 5 October, losses did grow on 6 and 7 October, when 24th Panzer and 100th Jäger Divisions reported more than 50 casualties—twice the number lost on

Table 31. Stalingrad Front's Defenses on the Volga River's Islands and the River's Eastern Bank on 13 October 1942

- Volga River Islands:
  - Spornyi and Zaitsevskii Islands – 39th Tank Brigade (part), 2nd Tank Corps, reinforced by two machine gun-artillery battalions, 77th Fortified Region, two divisional artillery regiments, and two antiaircraft artillery battalions;
  - Golodnyi Island – 26th Tank Brigade, 2nd Tank Corps, reinforced by one machine gun-artillery battalion, 77th Fortified Region, one regiment of divisional artillery, and one antiaircraft artillery battalion, joined later by two regiments, 45th Rifle Division; and
  - Sarpinskii Island – Two machine gun-artillery battalions, 77th Fortified Region, reinforced by one antiaircraft artillery battalion, joined later by one regiment, 45th Rifle Division.
- Eastern Bank of the Volga:
  - Srednyi Pogromnaia *Balka* and Osadnaia *Balka* sector – 135th Tank Brigade, reinforced by one machine gun-artillery battalion, 77th Fortified Region, and one separate rifle battalion;
  - Lake Tuzhilkino and the mouth of the Akhtuba River (after 10 October) – 300th Rifle Division, 28th Separate Tank Training Battalion, both controlled by 135th Tank Brigade;
  - Priverkh and Krasnaia Sloboda sector – 39th Tank Brigade (part), 2nd Tank Corps, reinforced by two machine gun-artillery battalions, 77th Fortified Region, and one separate rifle battalion;
  - Krasnaia Sloboda and Tumak sector – 169th Tank Brigade, 2nd Tank Corps, reinforced by one machine gun-artillery battalion, 77th Fortified Region, and one separate rifle battalion;
  - Tumak and Rynok sector – One machine gun-artillery battalion, 77th Fortified Region, and one separate rifle battalion;
  - Rynok and Gromki sector – 99th Tank Brigade, 2nd Tank Corps;
  - Rybachii, 3rd Reshaiushchii ["Decisive"] State Farm, and Tsyganskaia-Zaria sector – Remnants, 6th Guards and 27th Tank and 20th Motorized Rifle Brigades, 23rd Tank Corps, and 133rd Tank Brigade (without tanks); and
  - Svertlyi Iar sector (64th Army) – 90th Tank Brigade.

previous days. In addition, 24th Panzer Division reported that its 89th Artillery Regiment suffered heavier than normal losses in men and weapons on 6 October. One of its junior officers wrote in his diary, "6th October. A black day. The fire emplacements have been recognized in the clear weather by enemy observers and were bombarded. Only in the afternoon had Lindenberg made one gun ready to fire in the new position. Three dead, Leutnant Punge and 12 men more or less severely wounded. An ammunition lorry flew into the air, and three guns were damaged."[129]

During this period, Eremenko also improved the command and control as well as the effectiveness of his *front's* artillery, which by now totaled 250 guns, including 150 tubes between 120mm and 152mm calibers, by dividing his *front's* artillery group into four subgroups, each responsible for concentrating its fires in specific sectors.

Table 32. The Personnel Strengths of 62nd Army's Rifle Divisions and Brigades Fighting in Stalingrad City on 10 October 1942

- 13th Guards Rifle Division – 6,053 men
- 37th Guards Rifle Division – 4,670 men
- 39th Guards Rifle Division – 5,052 men
- 95th Rifle Division – 3,075 men
- 112th Rifle Division – 2,277 men
- 193rd Rifle Division – 4,168 men
- 284th Rifle Division – 5,907 men
- 308th Rifle Division – 3,225 men
- 42nd Rifle Brigade – 760 men
- 92nd Rifle Brigade – 1,050 men
- 115th Rifle Brigade – 1,135 men
- 124th Rifle Brigade – 3,520 men (on 5 October)
- 149th Rifle Brigade – 2,556 men
- 2nd Motorized Rifle Brigade – 569 men
- **Total – 44,017 men**

Source: Isaev *Stalingrad*, 234, citing *TsAMO RF*, f. 48, op. 451, d. 41, l. 136.

Likewise, the air support and associated air defense of Chuikov's forces also markedly improved. General Novikov, the chief of the Red Army Air Force who was in the process of re-forming his forces as a whole, had arrived in Stalingrad in August as a representative of the *Stavka*. He brought with him General P. S. Stepanov, one of his deputies, to organize the city's air defenses. During the early stages of the battle, the Red Army Air Force had almost as many logistical difficulties as did the *Luftwaffe* and, in addition, suffered from lack of experienced pilots. By late September, however, Novikov was beginning to achieve results. Between 27 September and 8 October, for example, 8th Air Army flew 4,000 aircraft sorties in the Stalingrad region, at a time when German air sorties were plummeting in number. Recognizing that his pilots and aircraft could not yet compete on even footing with the Germans, Novikov emphasized nighttime operations, including frequent large raids on German-held sections of the city. These raids further increased the nighttime stress on the German troops, to the point where Sixth Army headquarters asked for *Luftwaffe* attacks to destroy the Red Army Air Forces' bases. Still, the Red Army Air Force had a long way to go before it could dominate the skies over Stalingrad.[130]

Due largely to Stepanov's work, Chuikov's air defenses also improved during the operational lull. Large numbers of light 37mm and medium 85mm antiaircraft guns, many of them with female crews, fired from both banks of the Volga to make German interdiction of the river more difficult. The strongest of these antiaircraft artillery groups, subordinate to the Stalingrad Corps PVO [Air Defense] Region, was deployed on Zaitsevskii, Golodnyi, and Sarpinskii Islands to protect crossing sites over the Volga River. Another special antiaircraft group made up of 56 guns from 748th Antiaircraft Artillery Regiment, eight antiaircraft armored trains, and 19th VNOS [Observation and Early Warning] Battalion, provided air defense for vital railroad stations on the river's eastern bank.[131]

The Volga River Flotilla also struggled during this period to ensure that personnel reinforcements, equipment, and ammunition reached Chuikov's beleaguered army. By great exertions under constant and often devastating German artillery fire and air strikes, the flotilla managed to ferry 42nd and 92nd Rifle Brigades and 308th Rifle and 39th and 37th Guards Rifle Divisions across the river, along with immense quantities of ammunition and other supplies. On their return trips, the flotilla's ships carried wounded and evacuated civilians.

CONCLUSIONS

In the 11 days of heavy fighting between 3 and 13 October, Paulus's Sixth Army solidified its grip on the upper sections of Krasnyi Oktiabr' and Barrikady villages, totally eliminated the Soviet forces encircled at Orlovka, and drove a menacing wedge into the defenses of Chuikov's 62nd Army in the western section of the Tractor Factory village on the southwestern approaches to the Tractor Factory. At the same time, the forces on Sixth Army's left wing fended off the Don Front's repeated assaults in the Kotluban' region with relative ease; Fourth Panzer Army did the same in the lake region south of Stalingrad. However, elsewhere along Paulus's front, combat had degenerated into a virtual stalemate.

After delaying his climactic offensive against Stalingrad's factory district for two days in early October, and with his army steadily weakening, Paulus had no choice but to delay it again, from 8 until 13 October, in order to gain the time necessary to obtain the reinforcements that were essential if Seydlitz's main shock group was to resume its offensive. Sixth Army's commander had to strip forces from other, less threatened sectors of his army's front, as well as to dispatch appeals to Army Group B and the neighboring Fourth Panzer Army for additional assistance. By virtue of these often desperate measures, Paulus was able to reinforce his main shock group with two more divisions, 305th Infantry and 14th Panzer, by 13 October. As Paulus did so, however, Chuikov also reorganized and reinforced his defenses, concentrating as many forces as possible at the approaches to the vital Krasnyi Oktiabr', Barrikady, and Tractor Factories.

In effect, Paulus's Sixth Army during early October had simply replicated the events of late July, August, and September: At the most critical points during its advance, Sixth Army lacked the strength necessary to overcome, defeat, and destroy the opposing Soviet forces decisively without additional reinforcements. In those previous battles, Paulus had received the necessary reinforcements and recorded meaningful victories. In the wake of each of those victories, however, the strength of his army ebbed, especially when it began assaulting Stalingrad city.

Sixth Army's periodic strength and combat capability reports vividly described the army's steady deterioration. For example, including Fourth Panzer Army's XXXXVIII Panzer Corps, Paulus and Hoth committed six full divisions (71st, 94th, 295th, and 389th Infantry, 29th Motorized, and 24th Panzer) and parts of three other divisions (3rd and 60th Motorized and 16th Panzer), which included 54 infantry and panzer-grenadier battalions and nine pioneer battalions, to the city fight by 26 September. Of this force, only one of the divisions, 71st Infantry, had a combat rating below "weak," and only four of its 54 battalions were rated "exhausted." However, by 5 October this force had deteriorated to the point where four of its divisions, 71st, 295th, and 94th Infantry and 24th Panzer, had combat ratings below "weak" and 21 of its 54 battalions were rated "exhausted." This depressing reality compelled Paulus to reinforce his army's LI Corps with two fresher infantry divisions, 305th Infantry and 100th Jäger, which included another 14 infantry and two pioneer battalions. Despite these reinforcements, by 12 October four of Paulus's divisions, 94th, 295th, and 389th Infantry and 24th Panzer, were rated well below "weak," and one, 94th Infantry, was considered totally "exhausted." Therefore, even counting the two divisions that reinforced Paulus's force attacking Stalingrad city, by 15 October fully 19 of its 61 battalions received "exhausted" ratings, and another 19 were rated "weak." In addition, by this time four of this force's 10 pioneer battalions were rated "exhausted" and another four "weak." All of this indicated, unless and until Weichs's Army Group B significantly reinforced Sixth Army, that Paulus's forces would encounter serious difficulties in crushing Soviet resistance in Stalingrad.

Given this seemingly unending process of attrition, Army Group B was facing a most important question on 13 October: Would the reinforcements that Paulus's shock group received prior to its final assault on Stalingrad's factory district be adequate to the task of crushing and destroying Chuikov's army once and for all?

And even though attrition took its toll on the attacking German forces, it also adversely affected Chuikov's defending 62nd Army. In fact, in some ways the ultimate outcome of the struggle in the city depended on which force— Paulus's Sixth Army or Chuikov's 62nd Army—could locate and obtain the reinforcements necessary to counter attrition's negative effects. As a result, then, the contest in the city in a sense became a race to determine which side could best weather and survive the battle of attrition.

Still reeling from its defeats in early October, and despite the reinforcements that it was receiving, Chuikov's army would be hard-pressed indeed to defend the Tractor Factory and its adjacent village successfully. By 13 October 62nd Army's divisions and brigades were also decimated, with some divisions numbering much less than 5,000 men each, with others having only 2,000–3,000 men apiece, and brigades fielding as few as several hundred men each. Consciously fighting a battle of attrition within increasingly cramped quarters, the most vexing question faced by Chuikov was whether his forces could hold out in Stalingrad's center city and factory district before sheer attrition caused his defenses to collapse. The ensuing monthlong struggle for Stalingrad's factory district would provide the answers to both Paulus and Chuikov.

CHAPTER 6

The Struggle for the Tractor Factory and Spartanovka, 14–22 October 1942

COMPETING PLANS

Recognizing the adverse effects of combat attrition on his forces, particularly his landsers, jägers, grenadiers, and panzer-grenadiers, General Paulus did all in his power to muster the strength necessary for his Sixth Army to crush the remainder of Chuikov's 62nd Army once and for all and to push its remnants back the final 400–1,400 meters to the chilly waters of the Volga. However, even after Paulus reinforced Seydlitz's LI Corps with 305th Infantry Division and, soon after, 14th Panzer Division, German victory remained uncertain. The infantry divisions already present in Seydlitz's corps (389th, 100th Jäger, 295th, and 71st) were severely worn down, with scarcely more than 2,000–2,500 bayonets in each of their three combat regiments, making for an average combat strength of 6,000–7,500 men per division. The 94th Infantry Division, whose 267th and 274th Regiments were to operate under XIV Panzer Corps' control, with its 276th Regiment still attached to 24th Panzer Division, showed a combat strength of about 4,500 men out of a ration strength of about 8,000.[1] The new infantry division, the supposedly fresh 305th, was in better shape, with all nine of its infantry battalions rated "average" and its pioneer battalion rated "strong." However, because it had participated in the heavy fighting along the Don River, on the western end of the land bridge to the Volga River, it still showed considerable wear and tear. Compounding Paulus's problems, after more than four months of nearly constant fighting the combat strength of 14th, 16th, and 24th Panzer Divisions had eroded to well below 1,000 men in each combat regiment and a total of 20–50 operable tanks in each division on any given day.

Nevertheless, with Hitler waiting anxiously for positive news, Paulus had no choice but to order Seydlitz's army corps to complete the destruction of Chuikov's forces in the factory district and to order Hube's panzer corps to do the same in the Rynok and Spartanovka regions north of the Mokraia Mechetka River. Paulus's new plan required LI Corps to assault and defeat Soviet forces defending the Tractor Factory, its village, and the brickworks immediately to the south. The specially organized Group [*Gruppe*] Jänecke would conduct this assault. In addition to his own 389th Infantry Division,

Jänecke's group included Lieutenant General Kurt Oppenländer's 305th Infantry Division, panzer squadrons with a total of 83 tanks from Heim's 14th and Lenski's 24th Panzer Divisions, and 31 assault guns from 244th and 245th Assault Gun Battalions.[2]

Operating on Seydlitz's left under XIV Panzer Corps' control, part of Angern's 16th Panzer Division, soon joined by two regiments of 94th Infantry Division, was to defeat and destroy Soviet forces in the Hill 135.4, Spartanovka, and Rynok regions north of the Mokraia Mechetka River and to protect Group Jänecke's left flank. On the right, 24th Panzer Division's panzer-grenadiers, with their right flank protected by the attached 276th Infantry Regiment, were to advance due east through Skul'pturnyi Park toward the Barrikady Factory to protect Group Jänecke's right flank. Paulus's plan called for Seydlitz to begin his attack on 14 October and for Hube to join battle the following day.

Within the context of Sixth Army's attack order, LI Army and XIV Panzer Corps carefully task-organized their forces and assigned them specific objectives (see Table 33).[3]

In addition, while Paulus's shock groups formed for the assault, Sixth Army transferred 94th Infantry Division's 267th and 274th Regiments from LI Corps to XIV Panzer Corps and shifted those two regiments from the region west of the Mechetka River northward across the Mokraia Mechetka River into new jumping-off positions in the vicinity of Hill 135.4, on 16th Panzer Division's right flank. From there it was to join XIV Panzer Corps' attack soon after it began on 15 October. Paulus then assigned 389th Infantry Division responsibility for occupying the sector along the western bank of the Mokraia Mechetka River from the river southward past the western end of the upper Tractor Factory village in addition to its sector east of the Mechetka.

The XIV Panzer Corps also shuffled forces prior to its assault. To free as many of 16th Panzer Division's forces as possible to participate in the attack, Hube reestablished *Luftwaffe* Group Stahel, which had been disbanded shortly after the destruction of the Orlovka salient, and assigned it responsibility for defending the 8-kilometer-wide sector from the Volga River westward south of Erzovka on 16th Panzer Division's former left wing. This left Angern's panzer division responsible for defending the 8-kilometer-wide front along the Volga River and also for attacking Group Gorokhov's bridgehead around Spartanovka and Rynok, along a front of roughly 6 kilometers.

Once formed for their assault, XIV Panzer and LI Army Corps were task-organized as follows (from north to south):

- 16th Panzer Division—*Kampfgruppe* Krumpen (2nd Battalion, 79th Panzer Grenadier Regiment, 1st Battalion, 64th Panzer Grenadier Regiment,

Table 33. XIV Panzer and LI Army Corps' Combat Formations, 14 October 1942 (south to north)

Forces	Jumping-Off Positions
XIV Panzer Corps:	
16th Panzer Division (part) and 651st Pioneer Battalion	Southeast of Point 723 [from Hill 135.4 651st Pioneer eastward north of Spartanovka and Rynok to the Volga River]
LI Army Corps:	
Group Jänecke 389th Infantry Division	Grid squares 76d3-85c3-1, 85a3, and 75b1 [from the Mechetka River eastward through the upper Tractor Factory village to 1,000 meters north of the *Schnellhefter* Block]
576th, 578th Infantry Regiments, 305th Infantry Division	Grid squares 85b4-2 and 1 (east) [1,000 meters north-800 meters northeast of the *Schnellhefter* Block]
14th Panzer Division	Grid squares 85d2 and b4 (east) [800–400 meters northeast of the *Schnellhefter* Block]
577th Infantry Regiment, 305th Infantry Division, and panzer squadron, 24th Panzer Division	Grid squares 85dc (middle) [400–100 meters northeast of the *Schnellhefter* Block]
24th Panzer Division (part)	Grid square 84a2 [the sports ground east of the *Schnellhefter* Block]

one panzer squadron, 16th Panzer Jäger Battalion, and 651st Pioneer Battalion) from north of Rynok and Spartanovka to east of Hill 135.4.

- 94th Infantry Division (267th and 274th Infantry Regiments) regrouping north of the Mokraia Mechetka River to the vicinity of Hill 135.4.
- Group Jänecke
  - o 389th Infantry Division (544th Infantry Regiment north of the Mechetka River and 545th and 546th Infantry Regiments in the western part and southwest of the upper Tractor Factory village).
  - o 576th and 578th Infantry Regiments, 305th Infantry Division, south of the center of the upper Tractor Factory village.
  - o 14th Panzer Division (103rd and 108th Panzer Grenadier Regiments, 36th Panzer Regiment, and 64th Motorcycle Battalion) south of the eastern part of the upper Tractor Factory village.
  - o 577th Infantry Regiment, 305th Infantry Division, and Panzer Squadron Schulte, 24th Panzer Division, southeast of the eastern part of the lower Tractor Factory village.

- 24th Panzer Division—*Kampfgruppe* Edelsheim (26th Panzer Grenadier Regiment, 4th Motorcycle Battalion, less one squadron, Panzer Detachment Winterfeld, less one squadron, 1st Company, 40th Panzer Jäger Battalion, and pioneer and antiaircraft platoons) in the vicinity of the stadium.

Spearheading LI Corps' assault and cooperating closely with 305th Infantry Division's 576th and 578th Regiments, Heim's 14th Panzer Division was to thrust northeastward through the lower Tractor Factory village into the northern and central parts of the Tractor Factory proper while the two infantry regiments cleared the adjacent blocks of buildings in the lower Tractor Factory village. On Heim's left, 389th Infantry Division's 544th and 546th Regiments were to collapse the Soviet defenses in the upper Tractor Factory village and the western part of the lower Tractor Factory village and to clear Soviet forces from the southern bank of the Mokraia Mechetka River west of the Tractor Factory. On Heim's right, 305th Infantry Division's 577th Regiment, supported by a squadron of 10 tanks from 24th Panzer Division, was to advance eastward across the railroad line and penetrate into the southern section of the Tractor Factory. To the south, 24th Panzer Division's *Kampfgruppe* Edelsheim was to protect Group Jänecke's right flank by seizing the remainder of the Sports Ground (Stadium) and suppressing Soviet artillery, mortar, and machine-gun fire against Jänecke's attacking forces.[4]

Seydlitz protected his shock group's extended right flank with 24th Panzer Division's 21st Panzer Regiment, which was deployed from just west of Skul'pturnyi Park, southward to the ravine one block south of Kazach'ia Street, and with the attached 276th Infantry Regiment, which was defending from the ravine southward to the boundary with 100th Jäger Division along Tsentral'naia Street. Still farther south, in the center and along the southern wing of Seydlitz's army corps, 100th Jäger and 295th and 71st Infantry Divisions would remain on the defensive. Opposite these three divisions, Soviet forces were deployed along the western approaches to the Krasnyi Oktiabr' Factory, Mamaev Kurgan, the lower Dolgii and Krutoi Ravines, as well as in the narrow strip of land still occupied by Soviet forces along the Volga's western bank in Stalingrad's center city. When it finally arrived forward on 22 October, presumably after Group Jänecke's forces had already seized the Tractor and Barrikady Factories, the fresh 79th Infantry Division was to cooperate with 100th Jäger Division's 54th Regiment to assault the Krasnyi Oktiabr' Factory from the west in conjunction with an assault on the factory by Group Jänecke's forces from the north.

As Paulus prepared to deliver his coup de grace to Chuikov's beleaguered 62nd Army, Stalin continued discussing with Rokossovsky and Eremenko, the commanders of Don and Stalingrad Fronts, how best to mount counterstrokes to relieve the pressure on Chuikov's forces. As early as 14 October, Stalin had agreed with Rokossovsky's proposal for a concentrated thrust from the north by Don Front's 24th and 66th Armies to link up with Chuikov's army in the northwestern part of Stalingrad's factory district but had yet to work out details for such an attack. The dictator had also authorized Eremenko to orchestrate a supporting attack by 64th Army from the Beketovka bridgehead in the south to threaten Paulus's right wing and divert German forces and attentions from Stalingrad. In this case as well, detailed planning remained to be completed by the time Seydlitz unleashed his assault. Therefore, while Soviet commanders commiserated, Paulus and Seydlitz acted, with the renewed German assault lending urgency to the need for an immediate Soviet counteraction.

THE INITIAL ASSAULTS ON THE TRACTOR AND BARRIKADY FACTORIES, 14–18 OCTOBER

14 October

Group Jänecke began its assault at precisely 0730 hours on Monday 14 October, after conducting a 2.5-hour heavy preparatory bombardment by concentrated artillery and massive carpet bombing by 1,250 aircraft, including many Stuka dive-bombers, against Chuikov's defenses in the northern half of the factory district (see Maps 55–56). Paulus observed the assault from his command post in the eastern outskirts of Gorodishche. Heim's 14th Panzer Division, spearheaded by two panzer squadrons from 36th Panzer Regiment, each cooperating with a single panzer-grenadier battalion from 103rd and 108th Grenadier Regiments, attacked northeastward from its positions 400–800 meters northeast of the *Schnellhefter* Block. Its objectives were the eastern part of the lower Tractor Factory village, the railroad line, and the Tractor Factory beyond. Heim's assault was accompanied and supported by *kampfgruppen* from 305th Infantry Division's 578th and 576th Regiments, echeloned to the left, and the same division's 577th Regiment, supported by Schulte's panzer squadron from 24th Panzer Division, echeloned to the right.

The 14th Panzer and 305th Infantry Divisions' combined assault struck Chuikov's defenses at a vulnerable 90-degree angle, with the apex pointed at the center of the lower Tractor Factory village and Tractor Factory itself. The northern flank of this angle, south of the eastern part of the upper Tractor Factory village, was defended by two battalions of 37th Guards Rifle Division's 109th Regiment and 112th Rifle Division's 416th Regiment (with 600 men). The eastern flank of the angle, from northeast of the *Schnellhefter* Block southward past Zhitomirsk Ravine, was defended by 37th Guards Rifle Division's 114th and 118th Regiments. They were backed up by 112th

Map 55. Sixth Army's situation, 13–14 October 1942

Rifle Division's 524th Regiment, 39th Guards Rifle Division's 117th Regiment, 84th Tank Brigade, and 95th Rifle Division's 90th Regiment in second-echelon defenses and in reserve positions to the rear (see Map 57).

The well-coordinated assault by Heim's panzers and by Oppenländer's infantry utterly demolished Zholudev's guards division and its supporting units. After overrunning the defenses of the 109th Guards and 524th Regiments by 1130 hours, the combined force split 37th Guards Rifle Division's 114th and 118th Regiments away from 109th Regiment on their right. The Germans then encircled and ultimately destroyed two of 109th Regiment's battalions and sliced into and through the second-echelon defenses of 112th

Map 56. LI Army Corps' assault, 14–15 October 1942

Rifle Division's 524th Regiment and 37th Guards Rifle Division's 117th Regiment (see Map 58).

The 37th Guards Division's daily journal entries for 14–15 October recorded the resulting carnage in the division's ranks:

1. An enemy force of more than two infantry regiments supported by more than 60 tanks, with powerful air support and an artillery preparation, penetrated the division's defensive lines and developed an offensive at the boundary between 109th Gds. RR and 114th Gds. RR and the boundary between 117th Gds. RR and 90th RR [95th RD], which was protected by 524th RR [112th RD].

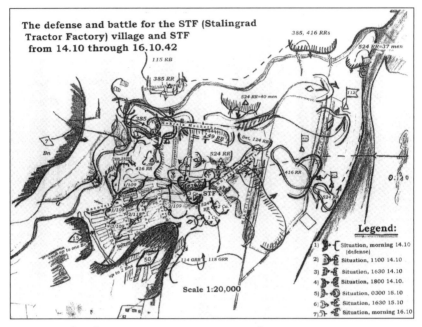

The defense and battle for the STF (Stalingrad Tractor Factory) village and STF from 14.10 through 16.10.42

385, 416 RRs

524 RR=37 men

115 RB

385 RR

524 RR=40 men

Bn

524 RR

416 RR

416 RR

1/109

STF

Scale 1:20,000

Legend:
1) Situation, morning 14.10 (defense)
2) Situation, 1100 14.10
3) Situation, 1630 14.10.
4) Situation, 1800 14.10.
5) Situation, 0300 15.10
6) Situation, 1630 15.10
7) Situation, morning 16.10

Map 57. 112th Rifle Division's situation, 14–16 October 1942

2. While repulsing the enemy attacks, the division suffered great losses in men and weapons.

3. The 2nd Bn, 109th Gds. RR, has been crushed by the enemy tanks and submachine gunners. Twenty-five enemy tanks and up to 200 submachine gunners have penetrated to the north of the stadium.

The 109th Gds. RR has been cut off from the division's main forces and fought in encirclement all day on 15 October 1942 [should read 14 October].

4. The situation of 114th Gds. RR and 118th Gds. RR is grave. Enemy infantry and tanks and dive bombers are inflicting heavy losses in men and weapons.

5. The 524th RR withdrew from its occupied positions, and, as a result, 109th RR's CP was encircled and about 2 enemy tanks were destroyed around the CP.

6. A second group of enemy is penetrating toward the Zhitomirsk Ravine at the boundary between 117th Gds. RR and 90th RR. Communications with 117th Gds. RR were interrupted during the second half of the day.

7. As a result of the 524th RR's and 90th RR's withdrawal, the division and its command post are threatened with encirclement.

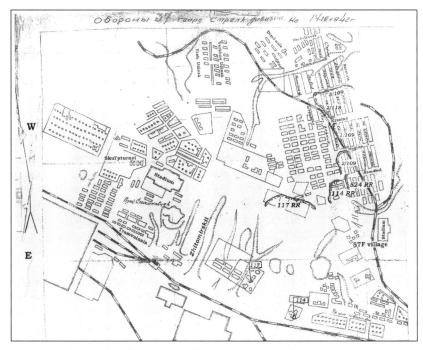

Map 58. 37th Guards Rifle Division's dispositions, 14 October 1942

By direction of the 62nd Army's commander, the division's CP has been transferred to the gully 60 meters west of Marker 80 (at the crossing bridge).

The enemy tanks and infantry reached the bank of the Denezhnaia Volozhka [western channel of the Volga] in the region south of the entrance of Mikhailov Street and across the Zhitomirsk Ravine at Minusinsk Street, and individual tanks reached right up to the water on the southeastern outskirts of the Tractor Factory.[5]

With Zholudev's division literally cut in half, the remnants of 118th Regiment withdrew eastward toward the southern part of the Tractor Factory, and the few survivors of 109th and 114th Regiments fled toward the lower section of the Tractor Factory village.[6] During this withdrawal, the commander of 117th Guards Rifle Regiment, Guards Major Andreev, was killed, and 112th Rifle Division's 416th Rifle Regiment was encircled and virtually destroyed east of the six-sided block. Compounding Zholudev's defeat, German bombers struck his command post, disrupting all communications with his subordinate regiments.[7] The furious panzer assault propelled the *kampfgruppen* of Heim's 14th Panzer and 576th and 578th Regiments of Oppenländer's 305th Infantry Division to and across the railroad line west of the Tractor Factory, into the lower Tractor Factory village, and ultimately into the northern and central parts of the factory itself.

Meanwhile, on the left flank of Heim's and Oppenländer's assaulting forces, multiple battalion–size *kampfgruppen* from Jänecke's own 389th Infantry Division smashed the defenses of 112th Rifle Division's 385th Regiment and the right wing and center of 37th Guards Rifle Division's 109th Regiment, which were defending the line of the Mechetka River and the western section of the upper Tractor Factory village. The remnants of these units conducted a fighting withdrawal either into the depths of the lower Tractor Factory village or northeastward across the Mokraia Mechetka River to join the forces of Group Gorokhov on the river's northern bank. Simultaneously, on Heim's right flank, *kampfgruppen* from 305th Infantry's 577th Regiment, supported by Schulte's small panzer squadron from 24th Panzer Division, swung eastward along Zhitomirsk Street, just north of the Zhitomirsk Ravine, crushing 90th Regiment of Gorishnyi's 95th Rifle Division and separating it from 37th Guards Rifle Division's 118th Regiment on its right (see Map 59). Farther south, 24th Panzer Division's *Kampfgruppe* Edelsheim attacked the defenses of Gorishnyi's 161st Regiment, forcing it to abandon its defenses east of the Stadium and refuse its flank to the north along the southern bank of Zhitomirsk Ravine.[8]

As Group Jänecke's forces demolished Chuikov's defenses in the northern factory district, Sixth Army carefully tracked its progress with periodic reports:

[1200 hours]

The LI Army Corps began its attack at 0730 hours. After breaking through the Russian lines, 14th Panzer Division moved forward to the railroad southwest of the Tractor Factory and broke into the southern section of the factory. To the north, a *kampfgruppe* of the division broke through the Russian defense (grid square 95b2 [200 meters west of the factory's center]) toward the east and resumed its attack toward the southwest. The status of this action is unknown. After heavy house-to-house fighting on its right wing, 305th Infantry Division [576th and 578th Regiments] captured the crossroads on the northwestern edge of the Tractor Factory and, attacking further, occupied the block of buildings at grid square 96d [100 meters west of the factory's center]. From this region, the division attacked toward the northwest. There is still no clear view of the fighting. Parts of 389th Infantry Division attacked and captured building blocks in the northern part of the map (grid squares 86d3 and 4 [the lower section of upper Tractor Factory village].

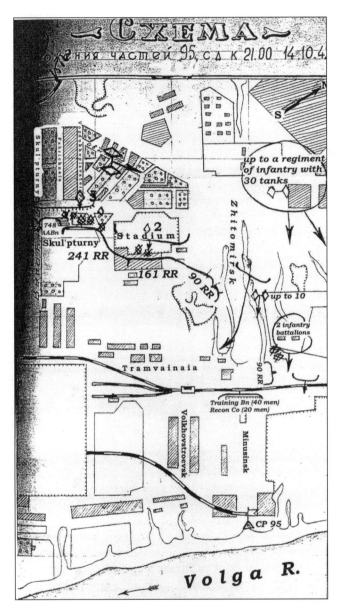

Map 59. 95th Rifle Division's dispositions, 2100 14 October 1942

[1505 hours]

After heavy fighting in places, the following general line was reached by 1500 hours:

24th Panzer Division—The Stadium with the surrounding housing blocks in grid square 84a [east of the Stadium];

14th Panzer Division (reinforced)—The ravine in grid square 84b [Zhitomirsk Ravine]—100 meters northwest of the railroad in grid square 94a [300 meters from the southwestern corner of the Tractor Factory]—southwest of the multiple crossroads in grid square 96d4 [100 meters west of the factory's center];

305th Infantry Division—The housing areas in grid squares 96d4–3 [100–300 meters west of the factory's center]—northern edge of the housing area in 86d [the eastern part of the upper Tractor Factory village].

At 1500 hours 14th Panzer Division's panzer regiment broke into the Tractor Factory at grid square 95a1 [the outbuilding 100 meters west of the main factory]; its subsequent advance south reached the main factory hall in 95d2 [the southern part of the factory] to link up with the armored group [panzer squadron Schulte] coming up from the south. The attack is continuing . . .

[1530 hours]

The commander of 14th Panzer Division reports that elements of his panzer regiment have penetrated into the Tractor Factory.

[2100 hours]

The attack in the northern part of Stalingrad continued in the afternoon against tough Russian resistance. Spearheading with its southern wing, 14th Panzer Division crossed the railroad toward the southern part of the Tractor Factory and has now reached the southern edge of the brick works. Already inside the Tractor Factory, 14th Panzer Division's panzer spearhead was withdrawn to provide the artillery the opportunity to fire on the last Russian defenders inside the factory and to give the next day's attack a full opportunity to occupy the last parts of the factory. The 305th Infantry Division occupied several building blocks during its attack to the northwest. The attack will continue during the night.[9]

Army Group B's daily summary expressed elation over Seydlitz's successes:

The LI Army Corps (Stalingrad) went over to the offensive at 0730 hours and, attacking in cooperation with 14th Panzer Division, seized a group of buildings on the southwestern outskirts of the Tractor Factory. Simultaneously, this panzer division, in cooperation with 305th Infantry Division, penetrated the enemy's defenses north of the indicated group of buildings and captured another group of buildings northeast of the Tractor Factory by storm. During the course of the attack, 389th [Infantry] Division also managed to penetrate farther to the east. The diversionary attacks by a strong enemy group in the Kotluban' region were unsuccessful.[10]

From the perspective of Chuikov and the Red Army General Staff, although the situation was still unclear at day's end, 14 October had certainly brought disaster:

62nd Army engaged in fierce defensive fighting with part of its forces against enemy forces of up to an infantry division with 100 tanks, which went over to an offensive in the vicinity of the Tractor Factory and north of Zhitomirsk at 1030 hours on 14 October.

37th Gds. RD. The right wing units of the division have been pressed back by the enemy. The division's units continued to hold on to the group of large buildings southwest of the "six-sided" building.

The positions of 95th RD's units are being verified.

Under enemy pressure, our units abandoned the Stadium (north) and Kul'tarmeiskaia, Kol'tsevaia No. 2, and Kol'tsevaia No. 1 Streets by day's end on 14 October. The enemy occupied the Tractor Factory with his forward units, and separate groups of his submachine gunners reached Mikhailov Street.

About 1,300 enemy aircraft were noted up to 1400 hours, and more than 5,000 bombs were dropped on our forces' positions in Stalingrad.

The positions of the army's remaining units remain unchanged.[11]

62nd Army's combat journal elaborated in greater detail on the General Staff's report, admitting candidly that its forces "conducted heavy defensive fighting with attacking enemy infantry and tanks in the sector of 112th RD, 37th Gds. RD, and 95th RD," during which "superior enemy forces launching their main attack toward the Tractor Factory captured the factory and split the army's front by day's end."[12] After mounting an intense air and artillery preparation, the Germans attacked with "up to an infantry division and two tank divisions (24th and 14th), more than 110 tanks, and large numbers of accompanying aircraft" toward the Tractor Factory, while "more than an infantry division and 75 tanks" advanced on the Tractor Factory village, and "an infantry regiment and 35 tanks struck out toward Zhitomirsk." Although 62nd Army claimed that its forces "held on to their occupied positions in the remaining sectors of the front," it acknowledged that "the enemy captured the Tractor Factory and Minusinsk by the end of the day and reached the Volga River."[13]

The journal then vividly described the action and resulting carnage in the northern half of the factory district:

112th RD—The enemy began a strong artillery preparation in the division's defensive sector at 0530 hours, and the combat formation of 524th RR was subjected to a fierce bombardment from the skies at 0630 hours. The artillery and mortar bombardment continued until 1815 hours. The enemy once again began shelling and bombing from the air at 2100 hours.

The enemy attacked in the sectors of 109th and 114th Gds. RRs along Iantarnaia, Bauman, and Botkin Streets with a force of up to 2 infantry regiments and 40–50 tanks at 0800 hours.

Up to 50 enemy tanks smashed the left wing of the 524th RR at 1150 hours, seized the church, and approached right up to the Stadium, from where they began to attack in two directions: a) with two battalions with submachine gunners and up to 20 tanks along Kul'tarmeiskaia and Ivanov Streets toward the Tractor Factory; and b) with two battalions and 15 tanks along Kooperativnaia Street, delivering their main attack toward Mokraia Mechetka Street.

The enemy, after crushing the 524th RR's combat formation, committed submachine gunners and reached 416th and 385th RRs' rear areas at 1200 hours but, after reaching Mokraia Mechetka Street by 1630 hours and encountering resistance by our units, began to dig in.

The remnants of 524th RR (up to 40 men) occupied defensive positions along the southern bank of the ravine (200 meters west of Martal'sk Street), with its front facing south.

416th RR is defending the cemetery (450 meters south of the railroad bridge). During the day it delivered fires toward the Oval'naia [Oval] woods, the garden on the eastern slope of Hill 97.7, the railroad siding, and Mokraia Mechetka Street.

385th RR was defending the Mechetka River line in the sector of the railroad bridge and the separate building (450 meters south of the railroad bridge). After leaving 10 men in its defensive region, 80 fighters counterattacked toward the Stadium at 1700 hours but, while advancing, were subjected to a fierce enemy air strikes and strong artillery fire. Suffering heavy losses, the regiment had no success and, together with 524th RR, dug in.

37th Gds. RD—The enemy penetrated the front toward the Tractor Factory at the junction between 109th Gds. RR and 114th Gds. RR, which was protected by 524th RR [112th RD], and at the junction between 117th Gds. RR and 90th RR [95th RD] with more than an infantry division and 75 tanks with powerful air support. The division suffered heavy losses from air strikes, artillery, mortars and, under the pressure of numerically superior enemy infantry forces and tanks, withdrew its remnants to the region southeast of Minusinsk.

109th Gds. RR—The regiment repelled an attack by 8 tanks and two companies of enemy infantry at 1000 hours but was crushed by tanks and submachine gunners at 1200 hours. Up to 125 tanks and up to 200 submachine gunners penetrated to the Stadium, and the regiment was fighting in the vicinity of Nogin and Dvukhkol'tsevaia Streets. The regiment suffered up to 80 percent losses during the day.

117th RR (39th Gds. RD) was fighting encircled in the region 400 meters south of the six-sided block.

114th Gds. RR, which was also attacked by an enemy force of up to two companies of infantry and 8 tanks, suffered heavy losses, but the positions of its subunits were unknown at 2100 hours because communications have been lost with the regiment.

118th Gds. RR fought with 12 enemy tanks and more than two companies of infantry and, as a result, suffered heavy losses. Its remnants of up to 20 men were fighting in the vicinity of the school south of the Tractor Factory at 2100 hours.

As a result of its withdrawal from the positions it occupied, 524th RR and 109th GRR's CP were encircled and were fighting with the enemy under their chiefs of staff.

The enemy reached the southern block on Mikhailov Street and the Volga River with groups and tanks at midnight. The enemy captured Komsomol'skaia and 2nd and 3rd Kol'tsevaia Streets, the park on Kul'tarmeiskaia Street, and the Tractor Factory with large forces. Enemy tanks are continuing to move southward and eastward, and the fighting was continuing at nightfall.

95th RD was engaged in heavy fighting with enemy infantry and tanks advancing toward Zhitomirsk. The enemy opened intense artillery and mortar fire at 0400 hours, and his aircraft began bombing the forward edge of the division's defenses with dive bombers at 0730 hours.

An enemy force of up to a battalion of infantry and 8 tanks destroyed the right flank of 90th RR at the boundary with 117th Gds. RR at 0900 hours and reached the ravine to the Bread Factory village with tanks.

North of the Zhitomirsk Ravine and 300 meters west of the trolley line, the enemy tried to filter through 42nd RB's sector at the boundary with its neighbor to the left from the vicinity of Fabrichnaia Street with a force of up to a company of submachine gunners and 2 tanks but was repelled.

161st RR was attacked by 100 enemy submachine gunners, two medium tanks, and one light tank at 1200 hours in the vicinity of the Stadium, but [they] were repulsed by fire from the regiment, concentrated in close proximity to the forward edge, and resumed their attack by fire.

In 241st RR's defensive sector, two enemy tanks fired repeatedly on the regiment's pillboxes. The enemy captured the ravine north of Zhitomirsk and advanced along Minusinsk Street to the Volga River.

The division occupied the following positions at day's end:

90th RR, because of its heavy losses, could not hold on to its positions and its remnants (11 men) joined the right flank of 161st RR by the end of the day.

161st and 241st RRs repelled attacks by up to two battalions of infantry and tanks and held on to their positions during the day.[14]

Meanwhile, along the southern flank of Group Jänecke's assault, *Luftwaffe* aircraft and artillery and mortars from 24th Panzer and 100th Jäger Divisions pounded the defensive positions of 308th, 193rd, and 39th Guards Rifle Divisions along the entire front from Skul'pturnyi Park southward through the lower Krasnyi Oktiabr' village to Bannyi Ravine. At the same time, the Germans conducted reconnaissances-in-force, ground probes, and raids to prevent Chuikov from shifting forces from these sectors northward to assist their beleaguered comrades to the north.[15]

At day's end on 14 October, Chuikov's defenses in the northern part of Stalingrad's factory district were a shambles. Zholudev's once-strong 37th Guards Rifle Division was now decimated. Largely hors de combat, the remnants of its 109th Regiment, together with the survivors of 112th Rifle Division's 385th Regiment, were in full flight northeastward toward the Mokraia Mechetka River and into the depths of the Tractor Factory village. Utterly smashed, 37th Guards' 114th Regiment, together with 39th Guards' decimated and leaderless 117th Regiment and 112th Rifle Division's hapless 524th and 416th Regiments, were trying to hold out in the depths of the lower Tractor Factory village and west of the factory proper. Both of these groups, however, faced complete encirclement and destruction at the hands of 389th and 305th Infantry Divisions' pincers advancing from west and east.

South of the Tractor Factory, 37th Guards Rifle Division's 118th Regiment, together with the surviving tanks of Belyi's 84th Tank Brigade and stragglers from other shattered units, were fighting in the western part of Minusinsk, striving at all costs to halt the German juggernaut toward the Brick Factory and Volga River south of the Tractor Factory. Still farther south, where the Germans had shattered the defenses of 95th Rifle Division's 90th Regiment in the Zhitomirsk section, Gorishnyi was employing his division's reserves (including its training battalion) to reestablish new defenses along and south of Zhitomirsk Ravine to protect northern approaches to the Barrikady Factory. With Ermolkin's 112th Rifle Division reduced to as few as 1,000 men; Zholudev's guards division dispersed and fielding only one barely combat-effective regiment; and Gorishnyi's rifle division deprived of most of its 90th Regiment, Chuikov faced the formidable task of restoring some semblance of order to his defenses in the region.

Seydlitz's ferocious assault ultimately propelled German forces to within 300 meters of Chuikov's command post on the western bank of the Volga. German bombs then struck his headquarters, killing 30 staff members and totally disrupting the army's wire communications with its subordinate divisions and regiments, many of whose command posts had also been destroyed. This compelled Chuikov to use generally unreliable radio communication to monitor and control his forces. In one of the few positive events during the day, troops from Chuikov's headquarters managed to rescue General Zholudev from his buried command post and return him to the army's headquarters.[16]

Although Chuikov later estimated that Seydlitz's assault cost the Germans more than 3,000 dead, the actual cost to the Germans was only 538 soldiers killed, wounded, and missing on 14 October. Highlighting the relatively low cost of Seydlitz's success, during the day's fighting 24th Panzer lost eight of its 33 tanks and 14th Panzer only one of its 50 tanks; 244th Assault Gun Battalion lost six of its 18 guns and 245th Assault Gun Battalion lost seven of its 13 guns.[17] As usual, the Germans were able to repair many of these vehicles. Therefore, Sixth Army clearly appeared to have regained its stride. After the fact, Chuikov had no choice but to admit that "we also suffered heavy losses, particularly from the bombing. On the night of October 14, 3,500 of our wounded were ferried across to the left bank of the Volga. This was a record figure for the whole period of fighting in the city."[18]

In reality, 62nd Army's casualties on 14 and 15 October probably amounted to many more than 10,000 men. For example, a combat journal of 37th Guards Rifle Division, which suffered the brunt of the army's losses during those two fateful days, recorded on 17 October:

As a result of 15 days of fierce combat, the division suffered 100 percent losses, and, as a result, only the artillery regiment remains. By the evening of 17 October 1942, the division has up to a company and a half of active "bayonets." The division's combat readiness was lost, and it is necessary to give the division a rest. However, the existing conditions demand heroic efforts from the remaining men to defend the Barrikady Factory.

The division's command is undertaking every measure for the improvement of the division's defensive capability. All rear service workers, artillerymen, mortar-men, and the remnants of specialized subunits have been thrown in for the defense of the factory. This has saved the situation. The enemy, having suffered heavy losses, is assembling new forces for an assault on the factory.[19]

By late on 14 October, Chuikov realized that reinforcing the Tractor Factory region would only play into German hands by offering up additional forces for certain destruction. That evening, he discussed the matter with Nikita Khrushchev, Stalingrad Front's commissar, who telephoned him on the *Stavka's* behalf. Khrushchev asked, "What can 62nd Army do to prevent the enemy from taking the Tractor Factory?" Chuikov explained the potentially disastrous implications of doing so, instead urging that his army's subsequent defense be anchored on the Barrikady and Krasnyi Oktiabr' Factories. The commissar agreed. Khrushchev promised to satisfy Chuikov's greatest need—ammunition—but a day later over Chuikov's objections he insisted that the bulk of 62nd Army's headquarters, including his Military Council, remain on the western bank of the Volga River.[20] Providing some additional hope for Chuikov, Eremenko promised to release the fresh 138th Rifle Division to 62nd Army the next day.

Satisfied that he had done all in his power to gain help from Eremenko, Chuikov—at 0100 hours the next morning through his chief of staff, Krylov—made final adjustments to his defense so it could withstand the inevitable onslaught:

1. To the commander of 308th RD—immediately relieve 92nd RB and occupy and firmly defend its defensive sector with one of your units within the boundaries specified in order no. 196 of 14 October 1942.

2. To the commander of 92nd RB—turn the defensive sector you occupy over to the commander of 308th RD and, when alerted, immediately deploy into the Minusinsk region, where you will become operationally subordinate to the commander of 37th GRD and occupy a defense in accordance with his orders.

3. To the commander of 37th GRD and arriving 92nd RB—establish a defense in one of the sectors designated for you along the line of the northern and northwestern outskirts of the village (south of the Tractor Factory) and farther along the railroad to Volkhovstroevsk Street.

4. To the commander of 95th RD, with 1st Bn, 685th RR—occupy the railroad station (northwest of Volkhovstroevsk) and separate building (200 meters northwest of Skul'pturnyi) line.

5. The commanders of the divisions will occupy defenses in the designated sectors and be prepared to repulse attacks by 0500 hours.

Krylov, Eliseev, Zaliziuk[21]

Although Seydlitz's initial attack had deprived Chuikov of more than 50 percent of the forces defending the northern half of the factory district, neither 62nd Army's commander nor his troops lost their nerves. Instead they continued to defend even when lines were broken. In the vast wastes of the lower Tractor Factory village and the rubble-filled buildings of the Tractor Works, small groups of soldiers and armed factory workers persisted in their resistance—street by street, building by building, and room by room—extracting any price for German conquest. The windows and huge skylights of these buildings broke into millions of fragments, which added to the casualties.

15 October

While some of the multiple *kampfgruppen* of Seydlitz's LI Army Corps continued their attacks overnight on 14–15 October, the entire force resumed its concerted assaults against 62nd Army's fragmented defenses in Stalingrad's northern factory district early on 15 October. This time they were joined by a major attack by XIV Panzer Corps against the defenses of Group Gorokhov in its bridgehead north of the Mokraia Mechetka River. Reports prepared by Sixth Army during the early-morning hours of 15 October and at 0930 hours described Seydlitz's progress:

[Before dawn]
In the northern part of Stalingrad, during the hours of darkness, a Panzer Grenadier Regiment of 14th Panzer Division managed to break through the heavily defended Russian positions at the Tractor Factory and, after a daring thrust toward the Volga, reached it south of the fuel dump and dug in.

The attack by 305th Infantry Division west of the northern part of the Tractor Factory was halted due to heavy Russian artillery fire. The LI Army Corps' artillery kept on firing against the strong Russian defenses the remainder of 14 October and on the night of 14–15 October. . . .

There was heavy enemy artillery and Katiusha rocket-fire during the night and heavy Russian aerial bombardment against the northern part of Stalingrad.

[0930 hours]
The battle in Stalingrad during the night and in the early morning yielded hopeful successes. After 14th Panzer Division's 103rd Panzer Grenadier Regiment succeeded in breaking through to the Volga east of the Tractor Factory, and 305th Infantry Division's 577th Infantry Regiment [and panzer squadron] managed to advance across the railroad at the Brick Factory during the night, the Brick Factory (grid square 94), the oil dump east of the Tractor Factory, and the bank of the Volga in between have been captured. The southern half of the Tractor Factory has been in our hands since the morning and the northern half since about

0900 hours. An attack [by 389th Infantry Division and two regiments of 305th Infantry Division] to mop up the salient between the Volga and Orlovka is making good progress. A subsequent regrouping is planned for an attack due south. An attack by elements of XIV Panzer Corps against Spartanovka and Rynok made good progress at first but is now pinned down in front of the flank of the southern bank of the Orlovka stream. The enemy in the northwestern part of the city is still clinging to grid squares 96 and 86 [the northern half of the lower Tractor Factory village], and assault groups are presently attacking them.[22]

From its perspective in Berlin, the OKW announced triumphantly, "In Stalingrad, as a result of a skillful night attack, one panzer division [14th] managed to penetrate down to the Volga and then, together with infantry units, captured the northern part of the factory region, together with the large Dzerzhinsky Tractor Factory, in the course of fierce house-to-house and street fighting."[23] Echoing Sixth Army's report, Army Group B crowed, "The Sixth Army's offensive on 15 October led to the complete seizure of the northern part of Stalingrad, including the Tractor and Brick Factories. Parts of 16th Panzer Division broke through to the edge of Rynok. Diversionary attacks by the Russians southeast of Kotluban' were beaten back."[24] The army group's intelligence officer added:

Despite the stubborn defense of the line of his pillboxes in light of the large number of tanks and flanking fires from the [left] bank of the Volga River and from its islands, the Russians could not prevent the loss of half of the territory in the gun factory [Barrikady]. 16 enemy tanks were destroyed during the tank battle in the northwestern part of the gun factory. An enemy group was cut off west of Spartanovka.[25]

On the other side of the front, the Red Army General Staff grimly reported (with details from 62nd Army's daily reports absent from the General Staff's report placed in brackets):

62nd Army continued to engage in heavy defensive fighting with enemy infantry and tanks in the northern part of Stalingrad.
    The enemy developed his attacks from the vicinity of the Tractor Factory toward the north and south beginning on the morning of 15 October [with a force of up to three infantry divisions and 150 tanks, with powerful air support].
    124th RB repelled several enemy attacks from the north during the day, in the process destroying more than 30 of his tanks. By day's end, the enemy separated 149th and 124th RBs by an attack northward from the

Tractor Factory, captured the landing stage at the mouth of the Mechetka River, and reached the rear of 124th RB's units.

149th RB was cut off from the remaining units of the army by enemy attacks from the north and south. Communication with it has been lost.

[124th RB, 115th and 149th RBs, 2nd MRB, and 112th RD were fighting fiercely in encirclement with enemy infantry and tanks attacking from the north, west, and south. The unit cut off from the crossing, 124th RB (with 12 men), is fighting along Zhemchuzhnaia Street, with its front facing south. 115th RB and 2nd MRB, with 45 men attached from 124th RB, and 416th RR, 112th RD, are fighting in encirclement in the Tractor Factory region].

37th GRD was engaged in intense defensive fighting with the enemy. The enemy, by developing an attack toward Minusinsk and Volkhovstroevsk, cut the remnants of the division off from the remaining units of the army and reached the Volga River in the Pribaltiiskaia region at 1700 hours on 15 October. The division's units continued to fight in the vicinity of the fork in the railroad and the Derevensk region.

95th RD repelled three attacks by enemy infantry and tanks during the day and, after suffering heavy losses, withdrew the units on its right wing to the northern outskirts of the Barrikady Factory. Six enemy tanks reached the region of the two rail-sidings on the northern outskirts of the Barrikady Factory at 1800 hours on 15 October, from which they shelled the 62nd Army's command post and the footbridge across the Volga River. [The remnants of 37th GRD and 95th RD total no more than 148 men, and both divisions have lost their combat capability].

The positions of the army's remaining units were unchanged.

Up to 100 enemy tanks are concentrated in the vicinity of the Tractor Factory. Enemy aircraft heavily bombed the combat dispositions of the army's units. 1,036 enemy aircraft-sorties were noted on 15 October.[26]

Thus, throughout the day on 15 October, supported by 49 tanks in its 36th Panzer Regiment, 14th Panzer Division's 103rd and 108th Grenadier Regiments, flanked on the left by 305th Infantry Division's 576th and 578th Regiments and on the right by the same division's 577th Regiment, completed demolishing Chuikov's fragile defenses in and around the Tractor Factory. In the process, the forward elements of Oppenländer's 305th Division captured the landing stage just south of the junction of the Volga and Mechetka Rivers, cutting off Group Gorokhov in the Rynok and Spartanovka sector from 62nd Army's main forces south of the Tractor Factory. West of the Tractor Factory, *kampfgruppen* from 389th Infantry Division ground their way slowly through the streets and buildings of the lower Tractor Factory village against stout resistance, harried by nearly constant Soviet artillery fire from the Volga River's eastern bank.

By day's end, those elements of 112th Rifle and 37th Guards Rifle Divisions not already encircled and destroyed in the Tractor Factor village withdrew northward to the Mokraia Mechetka River and into buildings in the northern half of the lower village.[27] 112th Rifle Division pulled its 385th Regiment back to defenses along the river's northern bank, opposite the western edge of the lower Tractor Factory village, and its 416th and 524th Regiments, the latter with only 40 men, into the depths of buildings in the northern part of the lower Tractor Factory village. There, they were joined by battalion groups dispatched southward from Group Gorokhov's 149th and 124th Rifle Brigades. By this time, however, Seydlitz's forces had occupied virtually all of the Tractor Factory and its adjacent villages.

South of the Tractor Factory, the assault by 305th Infantry Division's 577th Regiment and cooperating tanks from Schulte's panzer squadron pressed eastward throughout the day, crossing the railroad north of the Barrikady Factory and penetrating to the vicinity of Pribaltiiskaia Street in the heart of Minusinsk. From these positions, Schulte's tanks were able to shell the northern edge of the Barrikady Factory as well as Chuikov's headquarters, situated on the western bank of the Volga, less than 200 meters to the south. Hastily, Chuikov ordered Gorishnyi to deploy the forces on the right wing of his beleaguered 95th Rifle Division to block the northern approaches to the factory. By nightfall, the remnants of 95th Rifle's 90th Regiment and training battalion, reinforced by security troops from Chuikov's headquarters and dug-in tanks from Belyi's 84th Tank Brigade, and flanked on the right by the remnants of 37th Guards Rifle Division's 118th Regiment, succeeded in containing the German advance short of the factory. According to Chuikov:

> Zholudev's [37th Guards] division, which had taken the main brunt of the attack, was split into several sections, fighting as separate garrisons in the tractor settlement and in the vicinity of Minusinskaia Street. Gorishnyi's [95th] division had also suffered heavy losses and was fighting in defence positions along Tramvainaia and Skul'pturnaia Streets. The enemy, moving southward, was threatening to emerge in the rear of Gorishnyi's division and reach the army's command post. Enemy tommy-gunners infiltrated through breaches between our units. The Army H.Q. guard went into action.[28]

Chuikov calculated—correctly as it turned out—that Zholudev's and Gorishnyi's divisions had lost 75 percent of their personnel during the intense fighting on 15 October. However, even as the two divisions were decimated, the determined defense by their remnants slowed the German advance, at least temporarily, and cost the enemy, in Chuikov's estimate, 33 tanks lost and "nearly three battalions of infantry."[29] In reality, during the fighting on

15 October 24th Panzer Division actually increased its tank strength from 25 to 26 vehicles, attesting to its efficient tank-repair capabilities. 14th Panzer Division, which bore the brunt of the day's action, lost 19 of its 40 tanks.[30] According to Sixth Army records, Chuikov's army, in addition to its combat casualties in killed and wounded, also lost 1,028 men captured (including 31 who deserted), 20 tanks, 4 assault guns, 4 antitank guns, 26 machine guns, 8 grenade launchers, and 11 antitank rifles on 15 October.[31]

Compounding Chuikov's mounting dilemma, in addition to contending with the assaults by Seydlitz's LI Army Corps against his defenses in the Tractor Factory region, he also had to reckon on 15 October with a concerted attempt by XIV Panzer Corps' 16th Panzer Division to smash Group Gorokhov's defenses north of the Mokraia Mechetka River (see Map 60). The mission that Hube assigned to Angern's panzer division was simple: crush Soviet defenses at Spartanovka and Rynok and destroy all Soviet forces north of the Mokraia Mechetka. This was no mean task, however, because Gorokhov had been carefully preparing and fortifying his defenses in the region for more than three weeks. 124th Rifle Brigade manned strong defensive positions around Rynok, 149th Rifle Brigade protected approaches to Spartanovka, and the remnants of 115th Rifle and 2nd Motorized Rifle Brigades were deployed facing west in the forested region east of Hill 134.5, west of Spartanovka and north of the junction of the Orlovka and Mokraia Mechetka Rivers.

The strongest parts of Group Gorokhov's defenses were a dense network of bunkers and dugouts on the crests of two knobby hills north and northwest of Spartanovka, which the Germans had nicknamed *Kleinen Pilz* and *Grossen Pilz* [Small Mushroom and Large Mushroom]. Gorokhov, however, had weakened these defenses somewhat on 14 October by dispatching one battalion each from his 124th and 149th Rifle Brigades to reinforce Chuikov's forces fighting in the Tractor Factory village.

Hube decided to assault Gorokhov's bridgehead, with Group Krumpen from Angern's 16th Panzer Division attacking Rynok and Spartanovka, and 94th Infantry Division's 267th Regiment advancing against Spartanovka from the west. Krumpen's group consisted of three composite battalion-size *kampfgruppen*, with roughly 300 men each. The first two were formed from 2nd Battalion, 79th Grenadier Regiment, and 2nd Battalion, 64th Panzer Grenadier Regiment, which were to assault the *Kleinen Pilz* and *Grossen Pilz*, respectively. The third, Battalion Strehlke, was to attack the defenses around Rynok. Each *kampfgruppe* was supported by a small force of about 10 tanks and assault guns from 16th Panzer's pool of 49 operational tanks, the bulk of which were still awaiting renewed Soviet attacks in the Erzovka region to the north.

As described by 16th Panzer Division's history, the struggle was not an easy one:

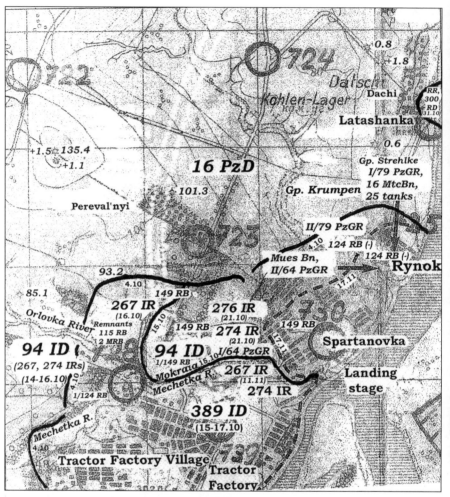

Map 60. The battles for Rynok and Spartanovka, 15 October–17 November 1942

Colonel Krumpen and his men knew the enemy; they recommended not to attack in daylight. Oblivious to the warning of great losses, the units reported they were ready to attack at 0418 hours on 15 October, after a three-minute artillery and *Werfer* preparation. They began to roll at 0420 hours, with grenadiers riding on the tanks and the assault guns. The grenadiers dismounted upon reaching the HKL [main line of the Soviet defense]. When they were attacked by antitank guns and Molotov cocktails during their advance, they retreated back to their original position.

The 2nd Battalion, 79th Panzer Grenadier Regiment, initially made great progress; it reached the crest of the *"Kleinen Pilz"* and the switch line running off the southern railroad fork at around 0500 hours. Here the battalion received heavy flak fire from the *"Grossen Pilz"* to the right and from enemy positions to the left. It came to a standstill and suffered considerable losses. The 2nd Company, 64th Panzer Grenadier Regiment, clawed its way on to the unusually strongly fortified *"Grossen Pilz."* This incredibly high bastion measured 350 meters in length and 120 meters in width. The assault guns rolled toward the right flank, but three were left behind. The 7th Company, 79th Regiment, which had the mission of protecting the left flank, received heavy fire from the interconnected bunker system on the southern edge of Rynok; the company commander, Senior Lieutenant Ingenerff, fell, and the company retreated.

In Rynok, Battalion Strehlke was fighting a bitter battle among the houses. Encased in smoke and fountains of earth, the pioneers were dodging a rain of fragments. Every street and the corner of every building was a scene of bitter fighting.

Every artillery tube and every available combat vehicle was used to help the men assaulting the *"Pilz."* Senior Lieutenant Bloemke's 2nd Company of the 64th advanced again, the tanks dodged the heavy fire, but the attack again came to a standstill.

In the meantime, Strehlke too had been driven out of Rynok and was fighting along its northern outskirts. The 6th Company, 64th, also had to retreat from the Russian HKL they had managed to capture in the morning because of the heavy flanking fire. The enemy pushed after them and recaptured his old HKL from the 6th of the 64th. In spite of the strong enemy defense, the 2nd of the 64th managed to seize some enemy positions right in front of the *"Pilz,"* capturing prisoners and material despite heavy losses in their own ranks. During the evening, the field dressing stations were filled with wounded soldiers, but the really serious cases still lay on the battlefield. Tanks gathered them up during the night. The few survivors sank into a death-like sleep. Field cooks and craftsmen were brought up to take over watch in the [forward] positions. Blood red, the fires in Stalingrad glowed before them.[32]

Frustrated by 16th Panzer Division's failure to crack Group Gorokhov's defenses, Hube, commander of XIV Panzer Corps, ordered Pfeiffer's 94th Infantry Division, which was still shifting its two regiments into attack positions east of Hill 135.4, to accelerate its advance eastward toward Spartanovka and join the assault on 16 October. For his part, Gorokhov, whose communications with Chuikov's main forces and vital supply route across the Volga River were now severed and whose ammunition was beginning to run out, began sending urgent messages to Chuikov and Eremenko, asking for assistance lest his bridgehead totally collapse.

With his army's defenses shattered in the northern factory district and Group Gorokhov's bridgehead north of the Mokraia Mechetka River facing imminent collapse, the only heartening news Chuikov received on 15 October was that Eremenko was about to release 138th Rifle Division to his control. Thus, during the most harrowing days of this siege, it was once again the arrival of fresh reserves that pulled Chuikov out of an untenable position.

The *front* commander had informed Chuikov of this fact late on 14 October, and the army commander had immediately directed the division's lead regiment, the 650th, to cross the Volga River into the Tractor Factory by 0500 on 15 October. However, a shortage of weapons in the regiment forced postponement of this movement, and heavy fighting in the Tractor Factory and intense German bombardment of the Volga crossing sites throughout the day forced another delay in the regiment's arrival. The regiment finally crossed the river overnight on 15–16 October, transported through a hail of fire by boats of the Volga Flotilla's 44th Brigade.[33] Chuikov immediately dispatched it to reinforce 95th Rifle Division's sagging defenses north of the Barrikady Factory. Its orders were to "occupy and firmly defend the line from the southern outskirts of Derevensk to Skul'pturnyi by 0400 hours 17 October 1942. Prevent the enemy from reaching the vicinity of Lenin Prospect and the Barrikady Factory."[34]

The 138th Rifle Division had been assigned to 64th Army prior to 14 October and had participated in that army's defense of the Beketovka bridgehead. As for the division's prior combat experiences, it began wartime service as 138th Mountain Division before being converted into a regular rifle division on 30 March 1942. Thereafter, it fought with 64th Army during the army's difficult defensive operations along the approaches to Stalingrad during July and August and ended up in Stalingrad Front's reserve for rest and refitting on 5 October. Although 138th Rifle Division numbered only 2,646 men and was short of rifles and machine guns, it was strong in artillery, with 11 122mm howitzers, 31 76mm guns, and 21 antitank guns—a critical quantity at this stage of the fighting.[35] The division's commander, 40-year-old Colonel Ivan Il'ich Liudnikov, was an experienced combat veteran who had commanded 200th Rifle Division and 16th Student Rifle Brigade from March 1941 throughout Operation Barbarossa and 138th Rifle Division since 16 May 1942.[36] Ultimately, it would take another 24 hours for Chuikov to bring the full force of Liudnikov's division to bear on the fighting near the Barrikady Factory.

16 October

To exploit the spectacular gains that LI Corps had achieved on 14 and 15 October, Paulus late on 15 October ordered Seydlitz to regroup his forces and conduct a general assault against 62nd Army's defenses north of the Barrikady Factory early the next day (see Maps 61–62). Paulus's new plan called for Seydlitz to employ 14th Panzer and 305th Infantry Divisions, supported on the right by 24th Panzer Division, in a concerted advance southward toward and into the Barrikady Factory. This would leave Group Jänecke's 389th Infantry Division to clear the remnants of Soviet forces from the Tractor Factory village and the Tractor Factory.

To do so, Jänecke was to move 14th Panzer and 305th Infantry Divisions into jumping-off positions extending from the left flank of 24th Panzer Division's forward positions just south of the Sports Ground and three blocks north of Skul'pturnaia Street, northward east of the Sports Ground to the southern bank of the Zhitomirsk Ravine, and then eastward across the railroad line and through the Minusinsk section south of the Brick Factory to the Volga River. Once in position, this force was to attack southward between 24th Panzer Division's positions and the Volga to roll up and destroy the Soviet forces opposite the panzer division's front and capture the Barrikady Factory.

Beginning at 0800 hours, Lenski's 24th Panzer was to support 14th Panzer and 305th Infantry Divisions' advance by fires and feints; once Jänecke's attacking forces passed their positions, the panzer division was to attack eastward, destroy the Soviet forces left in the wake of Jänecke's advance, and occupy positions along the western bank of the Volga between the Brick Factory and the fuel dump just north of the Barrikady Factory.

After conducting a complicated night reorganization, Group Jänecke deployed its new shock group as follows:

- 305th Infantry Division's 576th and 578th Regiments on the left wing between the Volga and the railroad line south of the Brick Factory, with the mission of attacking due south along Pribaltiiskaia Street and Lenin Prospect;
- 14th Panzer Division's 103rd Grenadier and 36th Panzer Regiments deployed astride the railroad line and Tramvainaia Street in the center, with the mission of attacking southward along both corridors;
- 14th Panzer Division's 64th Motorcycle Battalion, with 305th Infantry Division's 577th Regiment on its right wing, positioned from Tramvainaia Street southward past the Sports Ground to the junction with 24th Panzer Division's left flank, with the mission of attacking southward west

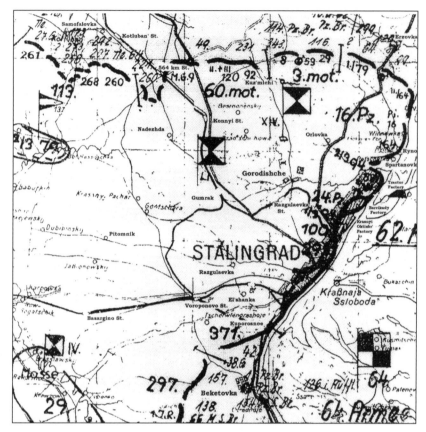

Map 61. Sixth Army's situation, 15–16 October 1942

of Tramvainaia Street and maintaining close contact with 24th Panzer Division; and

• 14th Panzer Division's 108th Grenadier Regiment in general reserve.[37]

Thus configured, Jänecke's force consisted of roughly 10,000 combat troops, supported by about 70 tanks (26 from 24th Panzer and 44 from 14th Panzer) and 18 assault guns (12 from 244th Assault Gun Battalion and 6 from 245th Assault Gun Battalion). This force faced 241st and 161st Regiments of Gorishnyi's 95th Rifle Division (defending from east of the Stadium southward along the western edge of the Skul'pturnyi section), the remnants of 95th Division's 90th Regiment and training battalion, security units from Chuikov's headquarters, and roughly 20 tanks from Belyi's 84th Tank Brigade (defending the Minusinsk section). The remnants of 37th Guards Rifle

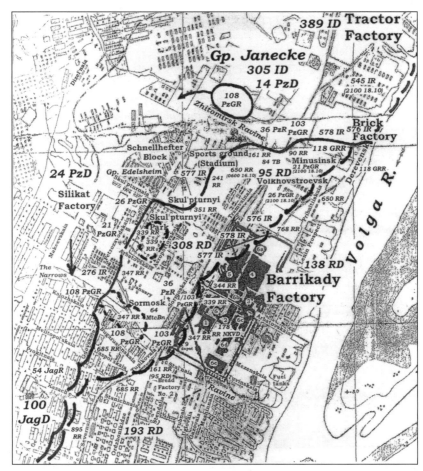

Map 62. LI Army Corps' assault, 16–18 October 1942

Division, now combined under the control of its 118th Regiment, manned defenses from the eastern edge of Minusinsk through the Brick Factory to the Volga River. Most important for the day's fight, the newly arrived 650th Regiment from Liudnikov's 138th Rifle Division now backed up the defenses of 95th Rifle Division's 161st and 241st Regiments east of the Stadium. Although Chuikov's forces defending this sector numbered less than 6,000 men, the defenders occupied well-prepared positions reinforced by Belyi's dug-in tanks. On Group Jänecke's right flank, 24th Panzer Division faced 308th Rifle Division's 339th Regiment in defensive positions along the western edge of Skul'pturnyi Park, and 347th Regiment deployed at the western end of 9 January Street to protect the approaches into the Sormosk section and the Barrikady Factory beyond.

Group Jänecke began its assault at 0800 hours on 16 October after a heavy barrage by its supporting artillery and repeated Stuka strikes against Soviet defensive positions. Despite the devastating artillery preparation and powerful air strikes, Group Jänecke encountered heavier-than-anticipated resistance from Belyi's tanks; dug in along Skul'pturnaia and Tramvainaia Streets, they had survived the bombardment. As one observer recorded:

A tank battle developed at close range, the Russian tanks not firing until the German panzers were large in their sights. Several panzers immediately erupted into flames and confusion reigned when salvoes of Katyusha rockets poured down on the stalled assault. The crewmen of 14th Panzer Division toughed it out for the next few hours, trading blows with the Russian tanks, which presented only their turrets as a consequence of being in hull-down positions. When the ferocity of the fighting caused a temporary halt towards midday, the casualties were surveyed: the Russians lost a total of 16 tanks [1 KV-1, 7 T-34, and 8 T-60, all from 84th Tank Brigade], while 14th Panzer Division suffered 17 panzer casualties. . . .

After a quick regrouping, the attack was relaunched in the afternoon and, with the bulk of the Russian armour now destroyed, the renewed assault led to success, half of the Gun Factory being taken before nightfall.[38]

Chuikov later confirmed this description of Jänecke's assault, although he downplayed the successes that the Germans achieved later in the day:

On 16 October, masses of enemy infantry, supported by tanks, swooped along the road from the Tractor factory to the Barrikady factory. This large-scale, determined attack came up against 84th Brigade's tanks, which had dug in. At and to the west of Tramvainaia Street, our tank crews met an enemy attack with concentrated fire from a distance of 100–200 yards. Ten or more enemy tanks immediately went up in flames. The German attack petered out. At that moment, our artillery on the left bank opened up blistering fire on the enemy's halted infantry and tanks.

Being a long way away from the field of battle and not seeing what was happening on the sector of the main attack, the German generals sent up more and more fresh units, which rolled up our line in waves. Here they were stopped and were pulverized by powerful salvos from our 'Katyushi.' The German tanks, coming under heavy fire from our well-camouflaged T-34s and antitank guns, turned back and abandoned the infantry.[39]

Based on LI Corps' reports, Sixth Army dispatched a message to the OKH at midday confirming Group Jänecke's slow progress. This message also noted that the attack was slowed because of heavy resistance by "partly dug-in Russian tanks" north of the Barrikady Factory and because "much needed re-supply could not reach the troops until late afternoon."[40] However, a subsequent message sent by an OKH observer at Sixth Army headquarters at 1930 hours contained more encouraging news:

> After a heavy tank battle resulting in the loss of 16 enemy tanks in the northeast section of the Gun Factory, 14th Panzer Division attacked at 1600 hours with its left wing along the railroad till it reached the middle lane of the Gun [Barrikady] Factory. The 14th Panzer Division is ready and will push forward during the night. The 305th Infantry Division attacked with its right flank along the railroad and reached the middle lane of the Gun Factory at 1600 hours. In the northeast part of the Gun Factory, fighting is still going on. The left regiment of 305th Infantry Division, after pushing through the not so heavily defended Russian defense line, reached the northeast part of the Gun Factory and pushed forward to the oil tanks. In several *balkas* close to the Volga, there are still some weak Russian units. The fighting of 305th Infantry Division continues.[41]

Based on this report, the OKW's informational bulletin announced to the world:

> In Stalingrad, the infantry and panzer divisions cooperating closely with continuously attacking aircraft and supported by antiaircraft artillery continued their offensive despite desperate enemy opposition, destroyed a great number of strongpoints and dug-in tanks, and penetrated into the grounds of the artillery gun factory "Krasnyi Barrikady." As a result of the attack toward the north, enemy forces were cut off from their communications northwest of Stalingrad and will soon be destroyed.[42]

The Red Army General Staff reported on the deteriorating situation late in the evening (with information from 62nd Army's daily report included in [brackets]):

> **62nd Army**, repelling constant attacks by enemy infantry and tanks along the Rynok-Spartanovka-Barrikady front, continued heavy defensive fighting in the northern part of Stalingrad. The army's units occupied their previous positions and repelled attacks by small groups of enemy along the front from Skul'pturnyi Park and farther to the south.

Up to 40 enemy tanks attacked our units on Tramvainaia Street and Lenin Prospect at 1300 hours on 16 October; and, simultaneously, his infantry and tanks attacked Rynok from the Latashanka region and the southern outskirts of Spartanovka from the Tractor Factory region. The enemy resumed his attack on the Barrikady Factory from the north at 1400 hours [with a force of up to two infantry divisions with 100 tanks]. The enemy reached the line from Derevensk to Minusinsk and from the western part of Volkhovstroevsk section to Tramvainaia and Skul'pturnyi Streets by 1500 hours. [The remnants of 37th Gds. RD, 650th RR, 138th RD, and the remnants of 95th RD and 308th RD engaged in heavy fighting with enemy infantry and tanks along the Derevensk, Minusinsk, Tramvainaia, and Skul'pturnyi line. . . . 37th and 95th RDs suffered losses of up to 85 percent of their personnel, and 42 men remained in 92nd and 42nd RBs]

The units of 37th Gds. RD and 95th and 308th RDs conducted stubborn defensive fighting in their previous positions.

The Northern Group (124th, 149th, and 115th RBs and 2nd MRB) continued to fight in encirclement without ammunition. Measures are being taken to supply them with ammunition.

The Northern Group continued to hold on to the front from Rynok to the southwestern outskirts of Spartanovka and the northern bank of the Mokraia Mechetka [River].

The enemy captured the northern part of the Barrikady Factory by day's end on 16 October.

[The army commander decided to commit 138th RD into combat to halt further movement of the enemy along the Volkhovstroevsk, Barrikady Factory, and Skul'pturnyi line.][43]

By nightfall on 16 October, Group Jänecke captured the northern half of the Barrikady Factory with 14th Panzer Division's 103rd Grenadier Regiment and 305th Infantry Division's 576th Regiment. However, 305th Division's 578th Regiment, on the group's left wing, was still engaged in heavy fighting between Lenin Prospect and the Volga River, 300–500 meters to the rear of the group's forward positions. These assaults pressed the remnants of 37th Rifle Division's 118th Regiment, now reinforced by a march-battalion of replacements, several hundred meters southward along the Volga's western bank. The attacks also decimated Chuikov's security troops defending the southern bank of the Zhitomirsk Ravine and forced 138th Rifle Division's newly arrived 650th Regiment to withdraw to new defensive positions from south of Tramvainaia Street and the railroad line to the northern end of Volkhovstroevsk Street, north of the Barrikady Factory.[44]

In Group Jänecke's center, 14th Panzer's 36th Panzer Regiment penetrated southward along Tramvainaia Street to several blocks south of

Skul'pturnaia Street and thrust several of its tanks into the western half of the Barrikady Factory proper. On the group's right wing, 305th Infantry Division's 577th Regiment expelled 95th Rifle Division's 161st and 241st Regiments from their defensive positions east of the Sports Ground and drove southward to reach Skul'pturnaia Street, where the battalion on its left wing made contact with the battalion on the left wing of 24th Panzer Division's 26th Panzer Grenadier Regiment. In conjunction with 36th Panzer Regiment's bold drive southward along Tramvainaia Street, 577th Regiment's advance also overran the defenses of 95th Rifle Division's 90th Regiment and training battalion and destroyed many of 84th Tank Brigade's dug-in tanks. This forced Gorishnyi to direct his 161st Regiment into new defensive positions protecting the northern and northeastern approaches to Skul'pturnyi Park. However, the damage done to 95th Division essentially rendered it hors de combat and ultimately forced Gorishnyi to combine the division's surviving troops with its 161st Regiment and move the 161st back to defensive positions in the Bread Factory, just south of the Barrikady Factory.

As fragile as Chuikov's defenses in the Barrikady region were, help was already on the way. At 2350 hours on 16 October, 62nd Army ordered Liudnikov's 138th Rifle Division "to occupy and firmly defend the sector from the southern outskirts of Derevensk [along Volkhovstroevsk Street] to Skul'pturnyi" and "prevent the enemy from reaching the vicinity of Lenin Prospect and the Barrikady Factory."[45] Already across the river, the division's 650th Regiment was to "create a network of strongpoints and prevent the enemy from entering the factory."[46]

However, the Germans had already captured most of the division's assigned defensive positions by evening. Therefore, when the Volga Flotilla's 44th Brigade transported the remainder of the division across the river beginning at 0500 hours on 17 October, the division's regiments fanned out to protect the remainder of the Barrikady Factory and the strip of ground between the factory and the Volga. 344th Regiment deployed into positions in the central halls of the Barrikady Factory, and 768th Regiment took up defensive positions along Lenin Prospect northeast of the factory, flanked on the left by the remnants of 95th Rifle Division's 90th Regiment and on the right by the division's 650th Regiment and 37th Guards Rifle Division's 118th Regiment. With suitable terrain exceedingly scarce, Liudnikov, once his division was across the Volga, had to squeeze his command post into the shattered bunkers already occupied by 62nd Army's headquarters' personnel.

While Group Jänecke's forces were pressing southward toward and into the Barrikady Factory, an equally desperate fight was taking place north of the Mokraia Mechetka River, where *kampfgruppen* from XIV Panzer Corps' 16th Panzer Division struggled to seize Rynok and Spartanovka and to destroy Group Gorokhov (see Map 60). After failing to seize the two towns on

15 October, Group Krumpen, at noon the next day, resumed its assaults, this time with greater success:

At midday on 16 October, another shock group of 1st Company, 64th Panzer Grenadier Regiment, advanced toward the southern part of the *Pilzes* [north and northwest of Spartanovka] once again. The enemy was exhausted by the previous fights. The men managed to overcome the enemy in the trench system 80 meters southwest of the fortress. At about 1600 hours, 2nd Company, 64th, continued the attack against the northern part [of the *Pilzes*] with a platoon of Panzer Company Hiller, an assault gun and four Flak [antiaircraft guns] and succeeded in capturing it after an intense fight. The mopping-up continued until late in the evening. The brave enemy left 200 dead, 50 prisoners, and rich booty behind in this location. One part of Spartanovka had been conquered.[47]

At least in part, 124th Rifle Brigade lost some of its fortified positions northwest of Spartanovka simply because the defenders ran out of ammunition.

In the wake of this success, 2nd Battalion, 79th Grenadier Regiment, which had been pulled out of the forward line late on 15 October, maneuvered southwest the next day, linking up with the forward elements of 94th Infantry Division's 267th Regiment farther west of Spartanovka by day's end.[48] When it did so, it slammed shut a ring surrounding Group Gorokhov, with 16th Panzer Division's *kampfgruppen* poised to the north, 267th and 274th Regiments of 94th Infantry Division to the west, and the three regiments of 389th Infantry Division lodged near and along the southern bank of the Mokraia Mechetka River. However, by 15 October all of 94th and 389th Infantry Divisions' infantry battalions were rated "exhausted." Thereafter, as the German ring surrounding Gorokhov's forces tightened, Eremenko worked feverishly to mount a relief effort from across the Volga River—an effort that would take several days to organize.

In addition to having to cope with the renewed German onslaughts against the Barrikady Factory and against Group Gorokhov's defenses north of the Mokraia Mechetka River, Chuikov also had to contend with increasingly impatient and demanding messages from Stalin and the *Stavka*. For example, at 1630 hours on 16 October, at Stalin's insistence, the Red Army General Staff cabled Chuikov, demanding that he "report immediately regarding the reasons why [his] army's forces abandoned the Tractor Factory so rapidly, what the situation was at the moment this cable was received, and about his future intentions" so that it could report on these matters to Stalin.[49] Although Chuikov's rejoinder is still unknown, we do know that 62nd Army's commander responded by asking for permission to move his headquarters back across the Volga. However, through the *Stavka*, Stalin immediately denied this request. With "alarming information coming in" and many of his units "asking for help, wanting to know what to do, and how," Chuikov simply responded with the curt order: "Fight with everything you've got, but stay put."[50]

Amid this slugfest, Stalingrad Front's commander, Eremenko, and his deputy, Lieutenant General M. M. Popov, visited Chuikov's command post on the night of 16–17 October. Stalin, concerned about the danger of losing the battle, had demanded that Eremenko go to Chuikov in person to determine precisely what assistance was required. As Eremenko and Popov crossed a river illuminated by flares and bomb detonations, Chuikov, who went to the landing stage to meet his boss, later described the gruesome scene:

> Gurov, the Member of the Military Council, and I went to the landing-stage to meet them. Everything around us was exploding, the noise was deafening; German six-barreled mortars [*Werfer*] were keeping the Volga under incessant attack. Hundreds of wounded were crawling towards the landing-stage and the ferry. We often had to step over bodies.
>
> Not knowing where the boat with the Front commander would land, we walked up and down the bank, and then returned to the dug-out. . . . To our surprise Generals Yeremenko and Popov were already at the command post.
>
> It was a wretched picture that they had found. The command post dug-outs had been turned into craters with logs sticking out of the ground. Everything on the bank had been covered with ash and dust.
>
> When we said good-bye at dawn, I asked the Front commander to let us have more men, not divisions, but small units, and more ammunition.
>
> "You will have what you want," he said, and, as he left, recommended that, with the arrival of the 138th Division, we should move our Army command post farther south along the bank of the Volga.[51]

During this meeting, General Zholudev, commander of what little was left of the once-proud 37th Guards Division, reportedly broke down emotionally while briefing Eremenko on the enormous casualties suffered by his men. Although Eremenko promised to provide more ammunition, when it arrived the next day it proved to be woefully inadequate for a force that was firing thousands of rounds in vain attempts to halt the German advance. In retrospect, it seems clear that Eremenko and the *Stavka* were already husbanding ammunition for a future counteroffensive, yet the defenders of Stalingrad understandably felt shortchanged at the time.

Although Chuikov refrained from relocating his headquarters for another 24 hours, he did act to shore up his defenses around the Barrikady Factory. Overnight, in addition to ordering Liudnikov's 138th Rifle Division to occupy defenses protecting the Barrikady Factory, he instructed Gorishnyi to consolidate the remnants of his 95th Rifle Division into its 161st Regiment and withdraw it from forward positions along Skul'pturnyi Street back into reserve defensive positions in the eastern part of the Sormosk section, several blocks of streets due west of the central section of the Barrikady Factory.[52] By this time, Chuikov was defending the western approaches to the Krasnyi Oktiabr' Factory and the southern half of the Barrikady Factory with 39th Guards, 193rd, 308th, and 138th Rifle Divisions, reinforced by the remnants of 95th Rifle Division, 42nd Rifle Brigade, and 37th Guards Rifle Division's composite 118th Regiment. These forces manned defenses extending from the middle reaches of Bannyi Ravine northward just west of the main railroad line and along Dublinskaia Street to the eastern outskirts of Sormosk and Skul'pturnyi Park and then sharply eastward through the Barrikady Factory to the Volga south of Volkhovstroevsk Street (see Table 34).[53]

Overnight on 16–17 October, Paulus ordered Seydlitz to reorganize his forces and resume assaults to capture the remainder of the Barrikady Factory and expel Soviet forces from Skul'pturnyi Park and the Sormosk section to the south; seize the bend in the railroad line southwest of the Barrikady Factory; and, if possible, capture the Bread Factory, situated just south of the Barrikady Factory, as well as the entire Barrikady Factory. Seydlitz planned to encircle and destroy Soviet forces in these regions by attacking with two pincers. The first pincer, LI Corps' main shock group, consisted of 14th Panzer Division's 36th Panzer and 103rd Panzer Grenadier Regiments, flanked on the right by 305th Infantry Division's 577th Regiment and on the left by 305th Division's 578th and 576th Regiments. This group was to attack southward to capture the remainder of the Barrikady Factory. The second pincer, LI Corps' supporting attack, consisted of 24th Panzer Division's 26th and 21st Panzer Grenadier and 276th Infantry Regiments, later reinforced on its right wing by 14th Panzer Division's 108th Panzer Grenadier Regiment. This group was to attack eastward in the sector from Skul'pturnyi Park southward past Sormosk to Kaluzhskaia Street—south of the ravine forming the narrows—to destroy Soviet forces in and south of Skul'pturnyi Park and the Sormosk region and penetrate into the southern section of the Barrikady Factory and the Bread Factory from the west.

Forming the left wing of LI Corps' northern pincer, 305th Infantry Division's 578th and 576th Regiments would attack southward to clear Soviet forces from the eastern half of the Barrikady Factory and the narrow strip of ground between that factory and the Volga River. Simultaneously, in the pincer's center, 14th Panzer Division's 103rd Grenadier Regiment, supported by tanks from the division's 36th Panzer Regiment, was to advance due southward along Tramvainaia Street, the railroad, and through the western half of the Barrikady Factory to capture the region east of Skul'pturnyi Park,

Table 34. 62nd Army's Defenses in the Factory District, 17 October 1942

- **284th Rifle Division** (Batiuk), with 1045th, 1047th, and 1043rd Regiments deployed from left to right from the lower reaches of the Krutoi and Dolgii Ravines northward along the eastern slope of Mamaev Kurgan to the Bannyi Ravine defending the approaches to western bank of the Volga River south of the "Tennis Racket" and the southern approaches to the Krasnyi Oktiabr' Factory opposite 295th Infantry Division;
- **39th Guards Rifle Division** (Gur'ev), with 112th and 120th Regiments deployed from left to right in lower Krasnyi Oktiabr' village west of the railroad line from the Bannyi Ravine northward to Tsentral'naia Street, defending the approaches to the Krasnyi Oktiabr' Factory opposite 100th Jäger Division's 227th Jäger and Croat 369th Infantry Regiments;
- **193rd Rifle Division** (Smekhotvorov), with 883rd, 895th, and 685th Regiments deployed from left to right in lower Barrikady village west of the railroad line from Tsentral'naia Street northward to the ravine north of Kaluzhskaia Street, defending the northern approaches to the Krasnyi Oktiabr' Factory and the southern approaches to the Barrikady Factory. They were opposite 100th Jäger Division's 54th Regiment and the right wing of 24th Panzer Division's 276th Infantry Regiment;
- **308th Rifle Division** (Gurt'ev), with 347th and 339th Regiments (the latter with the remnants of 42nd Rifle Brigade) deployed from left to right from the ravine north of Kaluzhskaia Street northward along the western edge of Skul'pturnyi Park to the northeastern corner of the park defending the western approaches to the Barrikady Factory. The 308th was opposite the left wing of 24th Panzer Division's 276th Infantry Regiment and 24th Panzer Division's *Kampfgruppe* Edelsheim (21st and 26th Grenadier Regiments);
- **95th Rifle Division** (Gorishnyi), with its forces consolidated in 161st Regiment, in reserve defensive positions in the eastern part of Sormosk;
- **138th Rifle Division** (Liudnikov), with 344th, 768th, and 650th Regiments, flanked on the right by 37th Guards Rifle Division's composite 118th Regiment, deployed from left to right from the northeastern corner of Skul'pturnyi Park eastward and southeastward to the railroad line, eastward through the central part of the Barrikady Factory, and then northeastward to the Volga River south of the Brick Factory. These forces were opposite 305th Infantry Division's 577th Regiment, 14th Panzer Division's 36th Panzer and 103rd Panzer Grenadier Regiments, and 305th Infantry Division's 578th and 576th Regiments.

Sormosk, and the southwestern part of the factory. Finally, on the northern pincer's right wing, 14th Panzer Division's 64th Motorcycle Battalion and 305th Infantry Division's 577th Regiment were to attack into the depths of Skul'pturnyi Park from the north to clear Soviet forces from the park in co-operation with 24th Panzer Division's forces on their right and, at the same time, maintain contact with and support the forces in the two advancing pincers.

Constituting LI Corps' western pincer, 24th Panzer Division's 26th and 21st Grenadier and 276th Infantry Regiments, deployed abreast from left to right from the northwestern edge of Skul'pturnyi Park southward west of the park and the Sormosk section to the narrows ravine, were to attack due eastward into the park and Sormosk to destroy the defending Soviet forces and drive their remnants toward the Barrikady Factory and the corps' advancing northern pincer. To ensure that the two pincers completely encircled and destroyed the Soviet forces in the park and the Sormosk section, Seydlitz transferred 14th Panzer Division's 108th Grenadier Regiment to 24th Panzer Division's control. He then instructed Lenski to deploy the regiment on his right flank from west of the southwestern corner of Skul'pturnyi Park southward past the ravine to Kaluzhskaia Street. Once in position, the 108th was to attack due eastward along Kaluzhskaia and Buguruslanskaia Streets south of the ravine and link up with the northern pincer's spearhead near the bend in the railroad line in grid square 73c and the southwestern corner of the Barrikady Factory. Together, the united forces were to cut off and encircle Soviet forces near Skul'pturnyi Park and Sormosk. Deployed on 108th's right, 100th Jäger Division's 54th Regiment was to support its assault and protect its right flank. Once this pincer movement was completed, 108th Grenadier Regiment would revert to 14th Panzer Division's control.[54]

If conducted effectively, this maneuver promised to expel 138th Rifle Division and the supporting regiment of 37th Guards Rifle Division from the Barrikady Factory and encircle the entire 308th Rifle Division and 193rd Rifle Division's 685th Regiment in the region west of the Barrikady Factory. However, the thoroughness of the offensive plan and its complexity belied some serious weaknesses among the attacking forces. For example, although official returns showed 24th Panzer Division still fielded 33 tanks, as the division's reports would demonstrate on 18 October, many of these were really in various stages of disrepair. Thus, Senior Lieutenant Hans W. Messerschmidt's panzer squadron from 24th Panzer Division, which was supporting 108th Grenadier Regiment, was able to field only 5 tanks.[55] For its part, 14th Panzer Division was able to support its attacking forces and those of the 305th Infantry Division with 33 tanks and 244th and 245th Assault Gun Battalions, with roughly 12 assault guns. Fortunately for Seydlitz's shock groups, the opposing 84th Tank Brigade had already lost most of its tanks during the previous day's fighting.

Completing Paulus's offensive plans, while Seydlitz's LI Corps focused its efforts on securing the Barrikady Factory, Hube's XIV Panzer Corps was to complete the destruction of Group Gorokhov in the Rynok and Spartanovka regions, this time by combined attacks against the region from the north and west.

17 October

After reorganizing his forces during the early morning on 17 October, Seydlitz launched his pincer movement at 0800 hours. Attacking southward, 103rd Grenadier Regiment and 36th Panzer Regiment's supporting armor made rapid progress, smashing the defenses of 138th Rifle Division's 768th and 650th Regiments at the boundary between the two regiments and forcing both forces to retreat southward toward Sormosk and deeper into the northern and western parts of the Barrikady Factory. Liudnikov's second-echelon regiment, the 344th, was caught up in the melee by 1200 hours (see Maps 63–64). Thereafter, by the end of the day, all three of Liudnikov's regiments fell back while fighting to occupy new defenses covering the western and northern approaches to the factory. In the process, Liudnikov's withdrawal exposed 308th Rifle Division's right wing in the northern section of Skul'pturnyi Park. 36th Panzer Regiment's tanks, accompanied by the lead elements of 103rd Panzer Grenadier Regiment, pursued relentlessly, advancing more than 500 meters by midday to reach the railroad junction west of the southwestern corner of the Barrikady Factory, where they linked up with forward elements of 108th Grenadier Regiment advancing from the west.

Forming 24th Panzer Division's western pincer, 14th Panzer Division's 108th Panzer Grenadier Regiment also began its assault at 0800 hours. Spearheaded by Messerschmidt's five tanks, they smashed through Chuikov's defenses just south of the narrows ravine at the boundary between 308th Rifle Division's 347th Regiment and 193rd Rifle Division's 685th Regiment, then advanced eastward virtually unimpeded along Kaluzhskaia Street. As described by one observer, "The grenadiers of Panzergrenadier-Regiment 108 fought their way through the mesh of streets and shabby wooden huts, blasting the Russians out of their hiding places, but Russian resistance was desperate, especially when they realized they were being caught in an encirclement."[56] Supported on its right by 1st Battalion of 100th Jäger Division's 54th Regiment, 108th Regiment also linked up with 14th Panzer Division's main shock group in the vicinity of the railroad line opposite the southwestern corner of the Barrikady Factory at midday.

As Heim's and Lenski's pincers closed around the 339th and 347th Regiments of Gurt'ev's 308th Rifle Division defending Skul'pturnyi Park and Sormosk, the remainder of Lenski's panzer division faced the arduous task of clearing 339th Regiment from the park itself because the advance by 14th Panzer Division was not "sufficiently far to the west to strike the enemy in front of 24th Panzer Division."[57] Therefore, assault groups from the panzer division's 26th and 21st Grenadier Regiments, supported by 276th Infantry Regiment on their right, attacked the park from the west, in the process striking the dense network of fortified positions manned by 339th Regiment's riflemen. The heavy fighting in the park would endure for nearly three more days before the attacking panzer-grenadiers were finally able to root out the defenders from the vast network of dugouts, foxholes, and interconnected trenches.

Confirming the catastrophic situation, late on 17 October the commander of 308th Rifle Division, Gurt'ev, recorded the day's disastrous events in his division's daily combat journal:

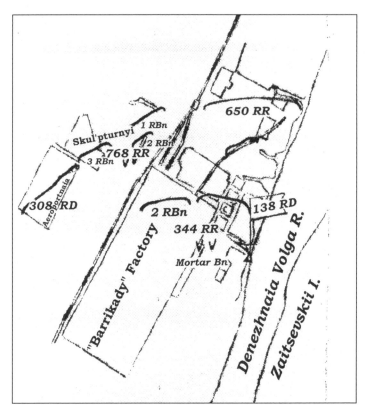

Map 63. Dispositions of the 138th Rifle Division, 1200 17 October 1942

The enemy commenced strong artillery and mortar fire against the combat formations of 339th and 347th RRs and the CP beginning on the morning of 17 October 1942 and began an offensive by exploiting the boundary [between our units] in the region of the ravine in Skul'pturnyi Garden, north of Ochakovaia [Street] and the gap in the vicinity of the three forks in the railroad at the northwestern corner of the Barrikady Factory.

There was up to a battalion of enemy infantry and 17 tanks in the vicinity of the gap at the railroad, up to a battalion of infantry with tanks in the vicinity of Skul'pturnyi Garden, and up to a battalion with tanks in the vicinity of the boundary with 685th RR [193rd RD].

After smashing our reserves in the region northwest of Barrikady and cutting the CPs of 339th and 347th RRs off from their units, [the enemy] encircled 339th RR in the vicinity of Skul'pturnyi Park and 347th RR in the vicinity of Petrozavodskaia and 9 January [Streets].

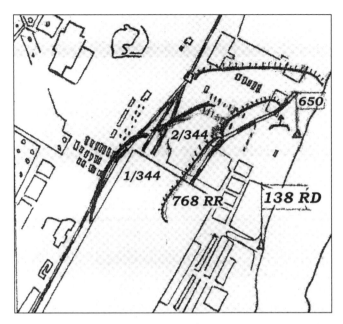

Map 64. Dispositions of the 138th Rifle Division, 2400 17 October 1942

The units in complete encirclement fought fierce battles all day and night on 17 and 18 October. Not a single soldier and commander located in the full encirclement willfully abandoned his position, and none spared his life fighting to destroy the Fascists. Of these, only an insignificant group of people from 339th and 347th RRs, who were sent out as messengers, remained alive. Exploiting success toward the south, the enemy began spreading out toward the Barrikady Factory. A company of 178th Regiment NKVD and a workers' detachment which were located there defended the factory the entire day and only after they ran out of forces in the struggle with superior enemy forces which outnumbered them several times were they forced to retreat to the eastern part of the factory. A total of 5 men remained in the NKVD company and workers' detachment.[58]

Lacking reliable communications with Gurt'ev's division, 62nd Army simply noted in its combat journal that the division repelled two enemy attacks on its right wing but was "holding on to its previous positions."[59]

Ultimately, however, those riflemen in 339th Rifle Regiment of Gurt'ev's division who did not perish in Skul'pturnyi Park ended up fighting individually and in small groups. The survivors withdrew either eastward, toward the Barrikady Factory through the porous cordon of armor erected by 1st Battalion of 14th Panzer Division's 103rd Grenadier Regiment, or southward, into the half-encircled pocket astride and north of the ravine north of Kaluzhskaia Street, which already contained the remnants of the division's 347th Regiment. Thus, in addition to suffering heavy losses in the fighting for Skul'pturnyi Park, many of 308th Rifle Division's riflemen perished while encircled in the ravine and southern part of Sormosk. Those who escaped, less than a quarter of the division's original strength, joined either 95th Rifle Division's 161st Regiment, in the southwestern part of the Barrikady Factory, or the regiments of Liudnikov's 138th Rifle Division, defending from the factory's depths.

As 308th Rifle Division fought for survival west of the Barrikady Factory, 344th and 768th Regiments of Liudnikov's 138th Rifle Division, which had been smashed by 14th Panzer Division's initial assault north and northwest of the Barrikady Factory, conducted a slow but resolute fighting withdrawal into new defensive positions in the western half of the Barrikady Factory.[60]

On 14th Panzer Division's left wing, 305th Infantry Division's 578th and 576th Regiments faced heavier going against 138th Rifle Division's 768th Regiment, 650th Regiment, and 37th Guards Rifle Division's 118th Regiment, which were defending the sector from the northeastern corner of the factory northeastward to the Volga River east of the Brick Factory. During intense fighting, the two infantry regiments pressed back the Soviet defenders several hundred meters before being halted by heavy fire from multiple strongpoints and dugouts stretching northward from the factory's northeastern corner along Baltiiskaia Street and then to the western bank of the Volga east and southeast of the Brick Factory.

Here, too, the chaotic fighting and ruptured communications limited 62nd Army's understanding of events on the ground. Initially, the army reported that "138th RD is fighting with attacking enemy infantry and tanks along the Volga and Skul'pturnyi line due north of the Barrikady Factory. . . . Reserves have been committed. The fighting is continuing."[61] However, later reports began to explain the full scale of 138th Rifle Division's defeat and the fact that German forces were indeed in the Barrikady Factory. Although the Germans failed to capture the factory in one bound, their forward progress posed an immediate threat to Chuikov's command post, enough that he was forced to shift it once again, this time to safer terrain near the Krasnyi Oktiabr' Factory farther south.

Sixth Army reported on the progress of LI Corps' advance to Army Group B and the OKH throughout the day. At midday, for example, it reported that fighting was under way on 100th Jäger Division's northern wing, where its forces (actually 108th Grenadier Regiment) had reached grid square 63d4 (southwest of the Barrikady Factory), and where one panzer-grenadier regiment (103rd) of 14th Panzer Division had penetrated into the southwestern part of the Barrikady Factory.[62] At day's end, it provided a more detailed account of the fighting, claiming that fighting was ongoing in the southern part of the factory and providing specific grid square locations for the precise forward edge of LI Army and XIV Panzer Corps' subordinate units, as follows:

LI Army Corps:
  100th Jäger Division
  —From 62b4 to 63d4 and 63d3 [northeastward along Gdovskaia Street and farther north to the ravine]
  14th and part of 24th Panzer Division
  —From 63d3 to 73c2 and 73d2 [from the ravine eastward to the railroad junction west of the southwestern corner of the Barrikady Factory]; and
  —The "Kessel" [pocket] west of the Gun Factory, from 73c2 to 73a4, 73a2, 73b1, and 73b3 to 73d2 [from the ravine to the Sormosk section and the region south of Skul'pturnyi Park]
  305th Infantry Division
  —From the southwestern edge to the southern edge of the Gun Factory, 93a1, and to the bank of the Volga southeast of the Brick Factory
XIV Panzer Corps:
  94th Infantry Division
  —From 700 meters south of Point 730 [along the southern bank of the Mokraia Mechetka River] to the southern edge of Orlovka, 1.2 kilometers to the southwest, and to the northwestern corner of Spartanovka
  16th Panzer Division
  —From the northwestern corner of Spartanovka to the northwestern edge of Petschetka.[63]

As Seydlitz's forces fought hard to gain the Barrikady Factory, an equally desperate struggle was continuing in the Spartanovka and Rynok regions north of the Mokraia Mechetka River, where parts of XIV Panzer Corps' 16th Panzer and 94th Infantry Divisions were assaulting Group Gorokhov's defenses (see Map 60). On 16 October, Jänecke's 398th Infantry Division assisted Hube's efforts to reduce Group Gorokhov's defenses by clearing bypassed Soviet forces from the Tractor Factory and its lower village and reaching the southern bank of the Mokraia Mechetka River in Group Gorokhov's rear. At this point it appeared that the combined forces of 16th Panzer and 94th and 389th Infantry Divisions would be able to crush Gorokhov's defenses once and for all. However, this was not to be the case, because Paulus was desperate to reinforce Seydlitz's LI Corps so that it could complete its conquest of the factory district. Thus, to Hube's chagrin Paulus, overnight on 16–17 October, ordered Pfeiffer to shift one of the regiments of his 94th Infantry Division to the southern bank of the Mokraia Mechetka. Once there it was to relieve the two regiments of Jänecke's 389th Infantry Division so they could move south to reinforce the assault by Seydlitz's LI Corps on the Barrikady Factory. Accordingly, Pfeiffer moved his division's 274th Regiment southward across the Mokraia Mechetka, leaving his 267th Regiment on the river's northern bank to cooperate with 16th Panzer Division's assault on Spartanovka and Rynok by attacking the region from the west.

While Pfeiffer was shuffling his two regiments, Angern's 16th Panzer Division began a new wave of assaults against Group Gorokhov's defenses at dawn on 17 October. After capturing parts of the imposing twin *Pilzes* on the northern and northwestern outskirts of Spartanovka the day before, late on 16 October Angern had reinforced his division's Group Krumpen with 150 men from 1st Battalion, 64th Panzer Grenadier Regiment, supported by a handful of tanks and assault guns. During the ensuing night, this fresh but severely understrength battalion shifted southward and joined 94th Infantry Division's 267th Regiment in a combined assault on Spartanovka from the southwest. Although the battalion lost 45 men in the attack because it "failed to close ranks" with the infantry regiment on its right, the combined force managed to advance several hundred meters into the western section of Spartanovka by 1530 hours.[64]

This sharp fight prompted Chuikov to acknowledge, "Twenty or more German tanks with tommy-gunners broke through to the southern outskirts of Spartanovka settlement. Here our men were fighting to the death. The slightest weakness or confusion on the part of the commanders could have brought catastrophe to the whole group."[65] True to his fears, Gorokhov, commander of 124th Rifle Brigade and the entire group holding the shrinking bridgehead, requested permission to evacuate his forces to Spornyi Island in the Volga River east of Rynok. Chuikov refused his request, instead sending his operations officer, Colonel Kamynin, to the bridgehead to bolster Gorokhov's resolve.[66]

Once both sides assessed the results of the action on 17 October, it seemed clear that Paulus's forces had prevailed. In addition to smashing Chuikov's defenses west and north of the Barrikady Factory, decimating Gurt'ev's 308th Rifle Division, and forcing Liudnikov's 138th Rifle Division to retreat ignominiously back into the Barrikady Factory, LI Corps reported that the day's fighting produced a bag of 860 Soviet prisoners of war, including 103 deserters, plus a large mass of captured Soviet weapons and equipment.[67] As opposed to Chuikov's vain assertion that his forces had destroyed 40 of Seydlitz's tanks and killed nearly 2,000 of his infantry, the actual toll of German casualties was 576 men. This figure included 91 killed, 469 wounded, and

16 missing.[68] However, Chuikov's tally of destroyed tanks was nearer to the mark: By day's end 24th Panzer Division had four operational tanks out of its original 33, and 14th Panzer Division 19 out of its original 33.[69]

Enthusiastically—but also a bit optimistically—the OKW announced at day's end that the German Army's forces attacking at Stalingrad had "smashed the resistance of the fiercely defending enemy, taken all of the buildings in the artillery gun factory 'Krasnyi Barrikady' by storm, and, after repelling powerful enemy counterattacks during the course of the bloody fighting, dislodged them from the adjacent city blocks"; in addition to claiming that the "immense numbers of aircraft" supporting the attacking forces had "destroyed a large quantity of artillery on the eastern bank of the Volga," the OKW also said that "the Bolshevik forces encircled northwest of the city's Spartanovka region were destroyed."[70]

From Chuikov's perspective, the fight on 17 October simply heaped more disasters upon the calamities of the three previous days. Simply but forthrightly, the Red Army General Staff's daily operational summary stated:

> **62nd Army** continued to conduct fierce defensive fighting with enemy infantry and tanks during the day.
>
> The enemy resumed his offensive at 0900 hours on 17 October with a force of up to one infantry division and tanks toward the Rynok and Spartanovka region from the north, west and south, with a force of up to a regiment of infantry and tanks toward the Barrikady Factory from the north, and with a force of up to an infantry battalion in the vicinity of Kazach'e Street.
>
> The Northern Group (124th, 149th, and 115th RBs and 2nd MRB—2,000 men in all) continued heavy defensive fighting in encirclement, while repelling savage attacks by the enemy. The group continued to hold on to the Rynok-Spartanovka and northern bank of the Mokraia Mechetka line. Five enemy tanks penetrated into the southern outskirts of Spartanovka. Up to 3 battalions of enemy infantry, 28 tanks, 8 guns, 10 mortar batteries, and 10 trucks with infantry were destroyed on 16 October.
>
> The units of 138th RD and remnants of 95th RD conducted fierce defensive fighting with enemy infantry and tanks and occupied the (incl.) Minusinsk, the northern outskirts of the Barrikady Factory, and Skul'pturnyi line. Individual groups of enemy infantry and tanks reached the northwestern outskirts of the Barrikady Factory.
>
> The units of 308th RD repelled attacks by the enemy with a strength of up to an infantry battalion and tanks in the vicinity of Kazach'ia Street.
>
> According to preliminary information, the army's units destroyed 1,200 enemy soldiers and officers and 17 tanks on 17 October.

During the day . . . enemy aircraft bombed the Rynok, Spartanovka, and Barrikady regions and our artillery firing positions on the left bank of the Volga River. From 0800 up to 1000 hours, 524 [enemy] aircraft sorties were noted. Antiaircraft fire downed 5 enemy aircraft.[71]

With his headquarters on the bank of the Volga now subject to machine-gun and small-arms fire as well as constant air assault and artillery and mortar fire, Chuikov finally heeded Eremenko's advice to move it to a safer locale farther south. First, he selected a new site on the river's western bank at the lower end of Bannyi Ravine. However, when this location came under machine-gun fire, he finally shifted to a new site located 800 meters south of Bannyi Ravine, west of the Tennis Racket and about 800 meters east of 284th Rifle Division's forward trenches on Mamaev Kurgan. Here it would remain throughout the rest of the fighting in Stalingrad city.[72]

Although neither Chuikov nor Krylov, his chief of staff, was fully aware of the extent of the day's defeat, to stave off further disasters they nonetheless issued two new orders late on the afternoon of 17 October. The first, distributed only hours after the Germans resumed their assaults, sharply and personally criticized Colonel Liudnikov for his division's failure to defend its assigned defensive sector:

You have not fulfilled my order [no. 209] regarding the occupation of the railroad station and village west of Tramvainaia and Skul'pturnyi. Thus, you failed to protect 308th RD's right flank, and, as a result, a gap developed between your division and the 308th, which permitted the enemy to attack with impunity along the railroad and to threaten to capture the Barrikady Factory and advance further to the south.

Up to this time, you have even failed to report to me about the situation at the front and the actions of your units.

I order:

You, personally, are responsible for liquidating the gap with 308th RD, for protecting its right flank, and, after established elbow-to-elbow communications with it, under no circumstances will you permit penetrations by the enemy into the territory of the Barrikady Factory and into the boundary with 308th RD. You will answer for the boundary.

Report to me promptly about the measures you have taken and their results. Send combat reports to me every three hours (verbally, and duplicated by radio)

Chuikov, Gurov, Krylov[73]

The second order, aimed at ensuring that divisions fighting in and around the Barrikady Factory followed Chuikov's orders to the letter, read:

The Army commander has ordered:
Subordinate the security companies of 178th Regiment NKVD and the armed workers detachment located in the Barrikady Factory to your divisions, operationally, to fulfill unswervingly 62nd Army's order no. 209 about the defense of the Barrikady Factory and its territory with strong points.

Conduct combat operations in close coordination with 38th RD [should read 138th] and the neighbor to the left, 308th RD.

Report to me about the course of combat operations every three hours by messenger and double by radio and telephone.

Krylov, Eliseev[74]

As for Sixth Army, Paulus ordered Seydlitz to reorganize his corps' forces overnight on 17–18 October and to resume assaults to capture the Barrikady Factory and the area immediately south early the next morning. LI Corps' main shock group, with the bulk of 14th Panzer and all of 305th Infantry Divisions, was to push southward to a line extending eastward from grid square 62b2 (the railroad bridge across the ravine near Tsentral'naia Street, northwest of the Krasnyi Oktiabr' Factory), eastward to grid square 82a2–4 (the mouth of the ravine entering the Volga River southeast of the Barrikady Factory) by day's end on 19 October.[75] To their right rear, weaker forces from 24th and 14th Panzer Divisions and 276th Infantry Regiment were to liquidate Soviet forces bypassed in and around Skul'pturnyi Park and encircled in the ravine between the narrows and Sormosk section. At this juncture, Sixth Army's commander began shifting 389th Infantry Division's regiments southward to join the fight and directed 79th Infantry Division to hasten the movements of its regiments into the Stalingrad region.

Seydlitz's main shock group consisted of all three regiments of Oppenländer's relatively fresh 305th Infantry Division, supported by most of 14th Panzer Division's 103rd Grenadier Regiment, 19 tanks from its 36th Panzer Regiment, and 18 assault guns from 244th and 245th Assault Gun Battalions. This group was to seize the blocks southwest of the Barrikady Factory, the remaining halls of the Barrikady Factory, the Bread Factory one block south, and the ravine running into the Volga River southeast of the Barrikady Factory. On the main shock group's right, 100th Jäger Division's 54th Regiment would push eastward to the main railroad line, and on the left 24th Panzer and 389th Infantry Divisions were to crush the last vestiges of Soviet resistance along the Volga's western bank from the Brick Factory southward to Barrikady.

Meanwhile, to the main shock group's right rear, 24th Panzer Division's 21st Grenadier Regiment and attached 276th Infantry Regiment were to liquidate all bypassed Soviet forces still in Skul'pturnyi Park, Sormosk, and the ravine north of Kaluzhskaia Street. Specifically, 276th Infantry Regiment and 14th Panzer Division's 108th Grenadier Regiment were responsible for the region in the immediate vicinity of the bypassed ravine, and 21st Grenadier Regiment and 1st Battalion, 103rd Grenadier Regiment, with a squadron of 10 tanks from 24th Panzer Division, were to cover the area south of Skul'pturnyi Park and the Sormosk region.[76]

As the main shock group pushed south and stay-behind forces eliminated bypassed Soviet forces, 24th Panzer Division was to shift its 26th Grenadier Regiment eastward to the Volga River northeast of the Barrikady Factory. Once there, it was to relieve 305th Infantry Division's 576th Regiment (less one battalion) so that it could join in LI Corps' main attack. After 24th Panzer completed its clearing operations, presumably by 0800 hours on 18 October, it was to move its 21st Grenadier Regiment eastward to join the remainder of the division northeast of the Barrikady Factory and withdraw its attached 276th Infantry Regiment into reserve so that it could rest and refit. Finally, once 94th Infantry Division's 274th Regiment relieved 389th Infantry Division's 545th Regiment south of the Mokraia Mechetka River, the latter was to transfer its grenadiers southward to occupy positions on 24th Panzer Division's left flank along the approaches to the Brick Factory. When in position, the 545th, together with 24th Panzer's 26th and 21st Grenadier Regiments and 10 tanks from 24th Panzer Regiment, was to capture the Brick Factory by the end of the day on 18 October.[77]

18 October

The difficulties inherent in carrying out so complex a plan immediately became apparent shortly after dawn on 18 October. Seydlitz's well-orchestrated assault quickly degenerated into a costly slugfest between attacking Germans and counterattacking Soviets that would endure for several more days and produce only meager German gains. Initiating this contest, 305th Infantry Division's 577th and 578th Regiments, supported by most of 14th Panzer Division's 19 tanks, thrust into the depths of the Barrikady Factory. In response, Liudnikov ordered the bulk of his 138th Rifle Division's 344th Regiment back into the factory to contest every one of its many ruined halls and other buildings (see Maps 65–66). At the same time, fugitives from Gurt'ev's shattered 308th Rifle Division filtered eastward into the factory, where they joined Liudnikov's riflemen. Thereafter, the grenadier of Oppenländer's 305th Division and panzer-grenadiers of Heim's 14th Panzer Division began a tedious and costly process of rooting out Soviet riflemen and sappers from every room, shop, and crevice in the factory's many halls. In this chaotic but often intense fighting, the attackers continued to move forward—but at an excruciatingly slow pace. The closer they approached the Volga River, the more exposed they were to Soviet artillery fires from the opposite bank. Although the Barrikady Factory was ostensibly largely under German control by 17 October, it actually was not. The struggle for the Barrikady and Brick Factories slowly evolved into a vicious building-to-building, room-to-room struggle in which the soldiers on both sides neither sought nor received quarter.

Meanwhile, on 305th Infantry Division's left, 24th Panzer Division's 26th and 21st Grenadier Regiments ultimately reached their assigned positions along the Volga by day's end. Cooperating with 389th Infantry Division's 545th Regiment, which had just arrived from the Mechetka front, they managed to secure the Brick Factory in the face of fierce resistance by the fewer than 200 survivors of 37th Guards Rifle Division's 118th Regiment, supported by 138th Rifle Division's 650th Regiment. On 24th Panzer's right wing, however, 26th Regiment, supported by 1st Battalion of 305th Infantry Division's 576th Regiment, faced far heavier going. Although it managed to seize a small section of the Volga's gully-scarred western bank from 138th Rifle Division's 650th Regiment, its assault soon faltered. The Germans reported that "the Russians were more firmly entrenched," the Soviets conducted "very strong, concentrated fire from the island lying opposite," and they had skillfully "constructed bunker positions on the steep slopes [and in the gullies] which could only be reached with steep fire weapons."[78]

West of the Barrikady Factory, acknowledging that they were suffering "very large" casualties in intense and often hand-to-hand fighting under near-constant Soviet artillery fire, 24th Panzer's attached 276th Infantry Regiment, cooperating with 14th Panzer Division's 108th Grenadier Regiment, 1st Battalion, 103rd Grenadier Regiment, and 64th Motorcycle Battalion, struggled to liquidate the remnants of Gurt'ev's 308th Rifle Division around and north of the ravine and in the Sormosk section. LI Army Corps' combat reports reflected the complexity and difficult nature of the fighting:

[1755 hours]
Today, enemy resistance has come back to life in the districts captured on 16. and 17. 10. . . . Clearing up the gully at 73b3 [east of the "narrows"] has not yet been concluded. On 18 October . . . enemy artillery fire increased on the northern wing of 100th Jäger Division and ahead of 14th Panzer Division. . . .

[2240 hours]
LI AC carried out mopping-up-operations on 18 October with elements of the 24th Panzer Division. In the gully at 73b1–3, the enemy [is] compressed into the narrowest area [but] still holds out.
Prisoners and materiel captured on 18.10.:
537 prisoners, including 10 deserters, 19 machine guns, 2 anti-tank guns, 32 anti-tank rifles, 2 mortars, 10 submachine guns.[79]

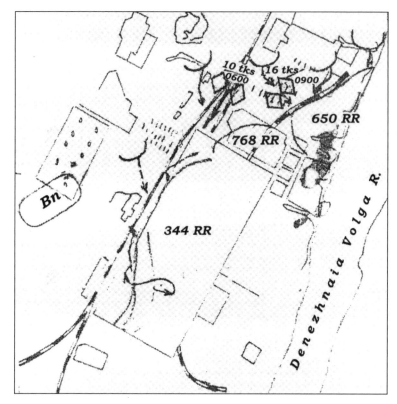

Map 65. Dispositions of the 138th Rifle Division, 1200 18 October 1942

From its perspective, 62nd Army reported:

308th RD has suffered heavy casualties, the division has been fighting with scattered groups of enemy throughout the night and day, and only several men remain in the 339th and 347th RRs. Situated in the Barrikady Factory, during the day, the company of 178th RR NKVD and the workers' detachment fought in the factory and, only after they exhausted their strength in the struggle with an enemy several times superior, were they forced to withdraw to the eastern part of the factory. A total of 5 men remain from the NKVD company and the workers' detachment. By day's end, the enemy smashed through the combat formation of the division and reached the railroad station west of Barrikady Factory.[80]

Despite the difficult fight in the Skul'pturnyi Park and Sormosk regions, at 2245 hours on 18 October 24th Panzer Division ordered 276th Infantry

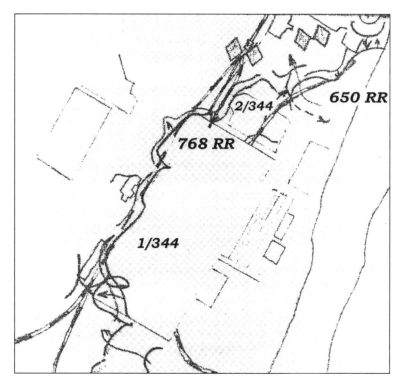

Map 66. Dispositions of the 138th Rifle Division, 2100 18 October 1942

Regiment to complete its clearing operations and revert to division reserve in the region west of the Stadium north of Skul'pturnyi Park.[81]

At day's end, the OKW once again summarized the day's fighting with characteristic optimism, declaring, "In Stalingrad, we cleared the enemy from the civilian and industrial parts of the city seized in the previous fighting. Our aircraft conducted strikes on military objectives in and around Stalingrad and also against enemy columns and rail communications on the eastern bank of the Volga. 11 trains were destroyed, including 2 with fuel."[82]

Belying this optimism, however, Seydlitz's forces clearly had failed to achieve the objectives of the day that Paulus had assigned to them. At day's end, as part of Seydlitz's troops were still struggling to clear Soviet soldiers from their rear area, 14th Panzer Division's 103rd Grenadier Regiment and 64th Motorcycle Battalion, together with 305th Infantry Division's 577th Regiment, were fighting with 138th Rifle Division's 344th Regiment and a few survivors of 308th Rifle Division's 339th and 347th Regiments in the crumbled halls and shops deep inside the Barrikady Factory. Farther east,

305th Infantry Division's 578th Regiment was fencing with 138th Rifle Division's 768th Regiment in the northern section of the factory; still farther east, the 305th's 576th Regiment, flanked on the left by 24th Panzer Division's 26th and 21st Grenadier Regiments, was locked in a virtual stalemate with 138th Rifle Division's 650th Regiment and the remnants of 37th Guards Rifle Division's 118th Regiment in the streets east of the factory and the gullies along the Volga's western bank south of the Brick Factory.

As a result, together with the fighting in and north of the ravine, the intense battle in the factory prevented 14th Panzer and 305th Infantry Divisions from reaching their objectives of the day. Both the Bread Factory and the ravine southeast of the Barriskady Factory remained in the hands of 161st Regiment of Gorishnyi's 95th Rifle Division. Contrary to German reports, the three battalions of Liudnikov's 344th Regiment, as weak as they were, and the pitifully few forces available to Gurt'ev, which now included the 308th's training battalion, still held out in the Barrikady Factory. In fact, in addition to clinging to individual fortified halls and shops within the factory, these troops mounted local counterattacks that seized even more of the factory's halls. Meanwhile, because Liudnikov's division still controlled the strip of ground between the factory and the western bank of the Volga, he was able to feed a steady supply of reinforcements, mostly march-battalions and companies, plus ammunition and new weapons into the factory proper.

The XIV Panzer Corps' battle for Spartanovka and Rynok was not developing any more favorably (see Map 60). Yet another assault by 16th Panzer Division's Group Krumpen and 94th Infantry Division's 267th Regiment against Group Gorokhov's defenses along the western outskirts of Spartanovka failed. On this basis, Colonel Kamynin informed Chuikov that the situation there "was difficult but not hopeless. The enemy troops, which had broken through into Spartanovka, had been destroyed." In fact, reported Kamynin, Gorokhov's group was also successfully defending its positions on the northern outskirts of Rynok and the southern outskirts of Spartanovka, including the vital landing stage near the mouth of the River Mechetka. Although Gorokhov's group had suffered heavy casualties, by 19 October its strength stabilized at 3,953 men, equipped with 95 light and 15 heavy machine guns and 57 antitank rifles and supported by 22 45mm antitank, 20 76mm field guns, and 21 120mm mortars.[83] According to Chuikov, this information reassured him "somewhat . . . we were not so alarmed about the Army's right flank."[84] More encouraging still to the army commander was the news that "ammunition and foodstuffs are being brought forward in sufficient quantities on boats and cutters. The necessity for delivery by air has fallen off."[85]

The Red Army General Staff's daily operational summary reflected Chuikov's increasing optimism that his forces could hold:

62nd Army continued to engage in fierce defensive fighting with enemy infantry and tanks along its entire front and especially stubborn in the vicinity of the Barrikady Factory. All enemy attacks were repelled by day's end.

At 1045 hours on 18 October, the enemy resumed his attack on the Barrikady Factory from the north with a force of more than an infantry regiment with 30 tanks [305th ID and 14th PzD] and toward Skul'pturnyi Garden with a force of more than an infantry regiment [24th PzD]. After stubborn fighting, the enemy succeeded in penetrating from the Skul'pturnyi Garden region to the southern outskirts of the Barrikady Factory by day's end on 18 October. Our units [138th RD and remnants of 308th RD] continued to hold on to the Barrikady Factory. Eighteen enemy tanks were destroyed in the fighting.

The Northern Group (124th, 149th and 115th RB's, the 2nd MRB, and 112th RD), holding on to their previous positions, repelled several enemy attacks. The group's units received ammunition and food.

The positions of the army's remaining units are being confirmed.[86]

However, Chuikov's postwar recollections of the fighting are far more candid. First, he acknowledged, by evening 14th Panzer Division's thrust of infantry and tank southward along Tramvainaia Street reached the railroad west of the Barrikady Factory, and 24th Panzer Division's assault had overrun the right flank regiment (685th) of Smekhotvorov's 193rd Rifle Division and threatened the forces of Gurt'ev's 308th Rifle Division with encirclement. Second, Chuikov admitted, for the first time during the city battle he actually ordered a withdrawal to straighten his army's lines. Avoiding any reference to retreat or withdrawal, his order simply read, "At 0400 hours on 19 October, Gurt'ev's division will occupy defensive positions along Sormoskaia Street and Tupikovskaia Street . . . ," which Chuikov added, "meant moving back from Skul'pturnyi Park."[87]

Estimating the enemy had lost 18 tanks and nearly three battalions of infantry during the heavy fighting on 18 October, although the situation remained critical, Chuikov understood the toll the fighting was taking on German strength and morale:

> We felt not only that our own ranks were thinning and our strength ebbing but also the enemy could not go on indefinitely launching his insane attacks. They were being drowned in their own blood. The enemy's material resources were also being exhausted. The Luftwaffe's sorties had dropped from three thousand to one thousand a day.
>
> Nevertheless, despite his tremendous losses, Paulus did not give up the idea of taking the city. Some inexplicable force drove the enemy to

go on attacking. Fresh infantry and panzer units appeared, and, regardless of losses, they rolled forward toward the Volga. It seemed as though Hitler was prepared to destroy the whole of Germany for the sake of this one city.

But the Germans were no longer what they had been. Even the fresh units and reinforcements knew the meaning of battle by the Volga.[88]

Contradicting Chuikov's assertion, Sixth Army's records indicate Seydlitz's shock group suffered 213 casualties on 18 October, including 45 killed, 165 wounded, and 1 missing in action.[89] Nevertheless, given Sixth Army's steadily dwindling strength, the OKH liaison officer to Sixth Army commented, "The Russians' air superiority over Stalingrad at night has assumed intolerable proportions. The troops cannot rest. Their endurance is strained to the limits. The losses in men and material are unbearable in the long run."[90] In fact, even if the daily casualties were modest, the cumulative numbers were far more dangerous. Sixth Army had suffered 13,343 casualties since 13 September, bringing its total losses since crossing the Don River on 21 August to 40,068 officers and men. Although Paulus's army had captured 57,800 Red Army soldiers since 21 August, including 17,900 since 13 September, these losses were far lower compared to previous fighting.[91] Nevertheless, Paulus remained confident that the battle would not last for more than another two to three days. But because his own strength was diminishing, Soviet resistance was clearly strengthening, and his intelligence organs were reporting the arrival of a steady flow of fresh enemy battalions, Paulus decided to bring 79th Infantry Division forward "to be ready for any eventuality."[92]

As Seydlitz's infantry and tanks continued the fight in the ruins of the Barrikady Factory and the factory district's adjacent blocks, on 18 October he began repositioning his artillery and rocket launchers (Werfer) to bring them to bear against the corps' next objectives, the Bread Factory, which was situated across the ravine due south of the Barrikady Factory, and the Krasnyi Oktiabr' metallurgical factory, which was located 800 meters farther south. However, intermittent heavy rain began overnight, hindering the delivery of vital supplies across the Don River bridges and, ultimately, preventing Paulus from resuming his attacks. Despite hopes for clearing weather, the intermittent rains, sometimes mixed with light snow showers, lasted for two more days, finally ending early on 21 October. While Paulus chafed under the weather-induced delay in his offensive, Chuikov and his superiors reorganized their forces, strengthened their defenses, and, despite the ostensible lull in the fighting, parried occasional German attacks and reconnaissance probes and launched strong local counterattacks of their own within and outside of Stalingrad's factory district.

THE OPERATIONAL LULL, 19–22 OCTOBER

During the subsequent three days of rain, Paulus directed the first two regiments of Lieutenant General Richard von Schwerin's newly arriving 79th Infantry Division, the 208th and 212th, to occupy assembly areas in LI Army Corps' rear (see Map 67). Once there, they were to prepare plans for a concerted assault on the Krasnyi Oktiabr' Factory and the remainder of the Barrikady Factory. General Schwerin was an experienced 40-year-old officer who had commanded 79th Infantry since early 1942.[93] Although the rains ultimately delayed the general assault until early on 23 October, Paulus ordered Seydlitz's units in and adjacent to the Barrikady Factory to continue their assaults, as weather permitted, to clear Soviet forces from the Barrikady and Bread Factories and adjacent regions and to capture favorable positions from which to launch the general assault on the Krasnyi Oktiabr' Factory. Albeit tactical in consequence, the ensuing fighting—from the soldiers' perspective—gave the morbid lie to the casual description "operational lull."

For example, at 2245 hours on 18 October, Seydlitz ordered his corps' forces to attack the next day to seize the objectives they had failed to capture the day before. These included the line from the railroad bridge across the ravine in grid square 62b2 (near the intersection of Monetnaia and Severnaia Streets 400 meters west of the northeastern corner of Krasnyi Oktiabr' Factory) to the mouth of the ravine in 82a2–4 (50 meters from the southeastern corner of the Barrikady Factory) and, beyond, to the bank of the Volga River southeast of the Barrikady Factory. The bulk of Heim's 14th Panzer Division, delivering Seydlitz's main attack, was to capture the Bread Factory and gain the line extending from the multistoried building in grid square 72a (300 meters north of the Krasnyi Oktiabr' Factory) eastward to the middle of the ravine in grid square 82a1 (south of the Barrikady Factory and 500 meters west of the ravines' confluence with the Volga). Heim's forces faced the 1st Battalion of 138th Rifle Division's 344th Rifle Regiment in the southern part of Barrikady Factory, the remnants of 95th Rifle Division's 161st Regiment in the Bread Factory, and the right wing and center of 193rd Rifle Division's 685th Regiment west of the railroad line southwest of Barrikady Factory.

On 14th Panzer Division's left, Oppenländer's 305th Infantry Division, supported by a squadron of tanks from 14th Panzer, was to attack between 0800 and 0900 hours, sweep Soviet forces from the northern and eastern sections of the Barrikady Factory, and then advance southward to reach the line extending from grid square 82a2–5 (in the middle of the ravine south of Barrikady) eastward to the western bank of the Volga southeast of the Barrikady Factory. Oppenländer organized his attacking forces into three *kampfgruppen* formed from his 577th, 578th, and 576th Regiments and directed the first two to assault the northern part of the Barrikady Factory and the third to

Map 67. The Sixth Army's situation, 19–20 October 1942

attack in the sector from the northeastern section of the factory eastward to the Volga's western bank. Oppenländer's forces faced 138th Rifle Division's 768th Regiment and 2nd Battalion of its 344th Regiment in the northern and central halls of the Barrikady Factory.

Simultaneously, on 305th Division's left flank, Lenski's 24th Panzer and Jänecke's 389th Infantry Divisions were to clear Soviet forces from the Volga River's western bank from the Brick Factory southward past the eastern edge of the Barrikady Factory to the corps' objective of the day along the ravine south of Barrikady. Lenski's main attack force was *Kampfgruppe* Below, a composite force consisting of virtually all of 24th Panzer's combat elements, less one panzer squadron, reinforced by one battalion from neighboring 576th Infantry Regiment. Below's group, which numbered roughly 1,500 infantrymen and 19 tanks, was to strike the Soviets' defenses along the western bank of the Volga northeast of the Barrikady Factory.[94] These shock groups faced 138th Rifle Division's 650th Regiment and the attached 118th Regiment from 37th Guards Rifle Division.

Finally, on 14th Panzer Division's right flank, Sanne's 100th Jäger Division was to employ its 54th Regiment, reinforced by a squadron of nine tanks from 24th Panzer Division, to capture the blocks of buildings north of the Krasnyi Oktiabr' Factory and to maintain contact with 14th Panzer's forces east of the railroad. Sanne's single *kampfgruppe* faced the left wing of 193rd Rifle Division's 685th Regiment and most of the same division's 895th Regiment.

Given the weakened state of LI Corps, the combat regiments conducting Seydlitz's attack were able to muster little more than single battalion-size *kampfgruppen* with 1,500–2,000 men each, supported by roughly 10 tanks and assault guns. For example, 14th Panzer Division attacked with two such *kampfgruppen* formed from its 103rd and 108th Grenadier Regiments, supported by roughly 30 tanks and flanked on the right by a single *kampfgruppe* from 100th Jäger Division's 54th Regiment, supported by the small panzer squadron from 24th Panzer Division.

19 October

When Seydlitz's forces began their assault on the Barrikady Factory, the combination of appalling weather conditions, determined Soviet resistance, and devastating Soviet fire brought the assault to an abrupt and bloody halt. Worse still, Chuikov's defending troops had the audacity to exploit the bad weather by conducting strong counterattacks of their own. For example, the *kampfgruppen* from 305th Infantry Division's 576th and 578th Regiments stormed into the northern section of the Barrikady Factory as planned shortly after dawn, pressing back 768th Regiment of Liudnikov's 138th Rifle Division (see Map 68). As they splashed through shell craters filled with runoff and clawed their way over heaps of debris, the advancing German infantry encountered withering flanking small-arms and machine-gun fire from 2nd Battalion of the same rifle division's 344th Regiment, as well as deadly mortar and artillery fire, often firing over open sights, from the supporting 295th Artillery Regiment. Pinned down by this fire and denied air support, after suffering heavy losses the division's assault immediately stalled.

At day's end, 138th Rifle Division reported:

> The 138th RD repulsed repeated attacks by enemy infantry and tanks trying to penetrate the front in the sector of 650th and 768th RRs. The attacks toward the southern outskirts of the factory are continuing. As a result of the active operations to repel the enemy attacks, according to

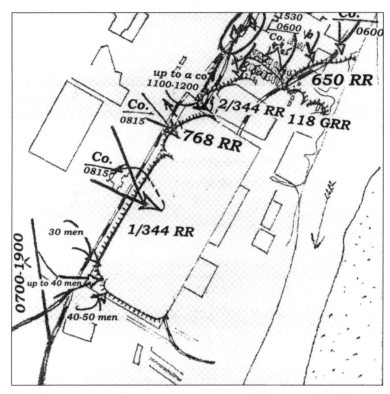

Map 68. Dispositions of the 138th Rifle Division, 1900 19 October 1942

incomplete information, five prisoners (one captain), 5 heavy machine guns, 8 light machine guns, 3 mortars, 17 automatic weapons, and 200 rifles were seized.

The enemy, committing fresh forces, wedged into the southwestern part of the Barrikady Factory at 2000 hours, where the fighting was continuing with mixed success.[95]

And because "it was clear to the commander of 576th Infantry Regiment that the cleansing of Hall 6 (the Manufacturing Hall) and Hall 4 (the Assembly Hall) [in the northern third of the Barrikady Factory] was going to be a bloody and protracted affair," the division commander, Oppenländer, called off further attacks.[96] Soon after, Seydlitz ordered all of his corps' forces to postpone their attacks until further notice.

Hard on the heels of Seydlitz's halt order, the commander of 138th Rifle Division, Liudnikov, ordered his 344th Regiment, supported by the assembled survivors of 339th and 347th Regiments from Gurt'ev's 308th Rifle Division, to counterattack and recapture as much of the Barrikady Factory as possible. As 62nd Army reported, "The 308th RD (the remnants of 339th and 347th RRs), continuing their fire resistance, advanced into the vicinity of the southwestern corner of the Barrikady Factory, with the mission to reach the boundary with 193rd RD."[97] According to German accounts, "After the attack by 305th Infantry Division had been called off, the Russian troops went on the offensive, and, in a surprise attack, the enemy storm troops recaptured the northern part of the Gun Factory and broadened the bridgehead opposite 305th Infantry Division."[98] Concerned about additional Soviet counterattacks, Seydlitz and his division commanders then ordered their troops to dig in wherever they were located, to remain vigilant, and to organize protective artillery and mortar fires opposite their forward positions.

The OKW put the best face on the day's action, announcing, "In the northern part of Stalingrad, German forces seized several more buildings. The fighting to free the grounds of the artillery gun factory 'Krasnyi Barrikady' is still continuing. Tactical support aircraft inflicted their main bombing attacks against the strongly fortified strongpoints on the grounds of the 'Krasnyi Oktiabr'' Factory."[99]

The Red Army General Staff's daily operational summary provided greater detail, acknowledging the perilous situation in Gurt'ev's 308th Rifle Division but otherwise describing the situation in and around the Barrikady Factory accurately (additional information from 62nd Army's daily report is in brackets):

62nd Army continued fierce defensive fighting with enemy infantry and tanks in the northern part of Stalingrad on 19 October.

The units of the Northern Group repelled attacks by the enemy forces of up to a regiment of infantry and 40 tanks toward the southwestern outskirts of the Spartanovka region up to 1300 hours on 19 October. The enemy, committing an additional 30 tanks into combat, attacked the western outskirts of the Spartanovka region at 1300 hours. The fighting was continuing in previous positions at day's end.

The units of 138th RD, together with subunits from 118th RR, 37th Gds. RD, repelled an attack by an enemy force of up to an infantry battalion and 5 tanks along the Volkhovstroevsk-railroad adjacent to the western outskirts of the Barrikady Factory line. The enemy succeeded in wedging into the southwestern part of the Barrikady Factory by the end of the day.

308th RD fought in encirclement in separate strong points in the vicinity of Skul'pturnyi Garden and 9 January Street with part of its forces and fought in the vicinity of the southwestern part of the Barrikady Factory with its remaining forces [to secure the boundary with 193rd RD].

193rd RD, with subunits of 161st RR, 95th RD, repelled attacks by enemy forces of up to an infantry battalion and 30 tanks in the vicinity of the southwestern outskirts of the Barrikady Factory [at 0900 hours], while continuing to hold on to the southwestern corner of the Barrikady Factory and Tupikovaia and Prokitnaia Streets to Gdovskaia Street line.

No changes occurred in the positions of the remaining units of the army.

[Information from captured enemy soldiers and one captain indicate that 305th ID has suffered 70 percent losses in personnel and only 35 men remain in its companies. Without greatcoats, the soldiers and officers are freezing. The 305th ID and 14th TD have the mission to capture the Barrikady Factory and seize the crossing.][100]

According to 62nd Army's daily report, late in the day Chuikov assigned 138th and 308th Rifle Divisions the mission "to drive back the enemy wedging into the southwestern corner of the Barrikady Factory."[101] The army commander also asserted that 45 German tanks were destroyed and about 2,000 German soldiers were killed during the fighting for the factory on 17 October and another 18 tanks and up to two battalions of infantry on 18 October. According to Sixth Army's reports, however, Seydlitz's corps lost 186 men on 19 October, including 34 killed, 137 wounded, and 15 missing, and by day's end 14th and 24th Panzer Divisions fielded 11 and 22 tanks, respectively, meaning their tanks losses for the day were 22 and 7 tanks, respectively.[102]

20 October

With bad weather continuing to preclude the conduct of any sizeable military operations from 20 through 22 October, Paulus and Seydlitz reorganized and replenished their forces, prepared plans for their new assault, and attempted to conduct local attacks to improve their forces' defenses and jumping-off positions. On 20 October, for example, the Germans limited themselves to reconnaissance and patrolling activity, as reflected by the OKW daily informational summary, which announced, "The fighting is continuing in Stalingrad. Antiaircraft artillery sank one cargo boat on the Volga. Our artillery is inflicting strikes on the transport columns, railroad communications, and airfields of Soviet forces on the eastern bank of the Volga River day and night."[103]

Chuikov's account asserted that his forces repelled attacks by enemy infantry and tanks in the northern and central sectors of the front but engaged only small groups of enemy in the southern sector. Continuing their assaults in the northern sector, "The enemy, with a force of up to two battalions and

25–30 tanks, attacked the 138th RD's units twice, at 0630 and 1300 hours," but were repulsed. As a result, Liudnikov's division "reached the vicinity of the southern part of the Barrikady Factory, where it fought with enemy wedging into the southwestern part of the factory" (see Map 69). Meanwhile, 308th Rifle Division "reached Stal'naia Street with its left wing, with the mission to reach the vicinity of the railroad spur," and 193rd Rifle Division and 95th Rifle Division's 161st Regiment defended "the Stal'naia Street, railroad, and Severnaia, Fedoseevskaia, and Tsekhovskaia Streets line," having lost "up to 300 men killed and wounded on 19 October."[104] In addition, Chuikov reported that his army killed more than 500 enemy soldiers on 20 October and destroyed two guns, one vehicle, one mortar, four gun carriages, and two heavy machine guns during the day's fighting.[105] Sixth Army's records once again refuted this claim, reporting that LI Corps lost 147 men, including 45 killed, 95 wounded, and 7 missing, although 79th Infantry Division suffered its first losses in the city—10 killed and 40 wounded.[106]

The Red Army General Staff's daily operational summary reflected these reports:

> **62nd Army** continued to conduct heavy defensive fighting with enemy infantry and tanks on the southwestern outskirts of the Spartanovka region and in the southwestern part of the Barrikady Factory on 20 October.
>
> The units of the Northern Group continued fighting with the enemy that captured two buildings on the southwestern outskirts of the Spartanovka region.
>
> 138th RD repelled two enemy attacks with its right-wing units at 1500 hours on 20 October, the first by a force of up to two infantry companies and 15 tanks toward the Barrikady Factory and the second by a force of up to two infantry battalions and 25 tanks. The division's units remained in their previous positions and fought to destroy small groups of enemy infantry in the southwestern part of the Barrikady Factory.
>
> A rifle battalion of 308th RD reached the southern part of the Barrikady Factory.
>
> 161st RR [95th RD] and 193rd RD held on to their positions along the forward edge in the vicinity of Stal'naia Street-the railroad-Severnaia, Fedoseevskaia, and Gdovskaia Streets.
>
> The positions of the army's remaining units are unchanged.
>
> Up to 1200 hours on 20 October, enemy aircraft (52 planes) bombed the Barrikady Factory.[107]

In the wake of the day's fighting, Chuikov ordered 138th and 308th Rifle Divisions to "drive back the enemy that have wedged into the southwestern corner of the Barrikady Factory, while holding on to the positions you occupy."[108]

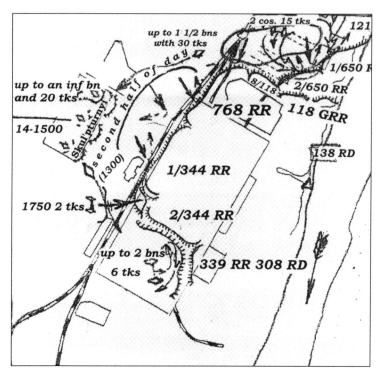

Map 69. Dispositions of the 138th Rifle Division, 2000 20 October 1942

Because 16th Panzer and 94th Infantry Divisions of Hube's XIV Panzer Corps had not been able to make any headway against Group Gorokhov's defenses in the Spartanovka and Rynok region, on 20 October Seydlitz ordered Lenski's 24th Panzer Division to return 276th Infantry Regiment to 94th Infantry Division's control. This regiment moved northward on 21 October, ultimately taking up positions in 94th Infantry Division's center, north of the Mokraia Mechetka River.

Although the lull persisted on 21 October, at 1315 hours the day before Seydlitz had ordered General Schwerin's 79th Infantry Division, whose two regiments had just deployed forward on the left wing of Sanne's 100th Jäger Division, to take control over the left half of Sanne's sector and 100th Jäger's 54th Regiment as well in preparation for the planned general assault. Schwerin was to mount an attack with the jäger regiment the next morning in order to establish a "firm connection" with 14th Panzer Division's forces on the left. The order read: "As a prerequisite for the assault on X-day (23 October), 79th Infantry Division, with the reinforced 54th Jäger Regiment, will break the strong point factory area in grid square 63d4 out of the enemy position and gain a connection with 14th Panzer Division on the railway line on 21 October. For this, the Division will have the Panzer Squadron Schulte of the 24th Panzer Division subordinate."[109]

The objective of this assault was the Cooking Factory, located at the corner of Kommunal'naia and Kizliarskaia Streets just south of the Kazach'ia Ravine and two blocks north of the railroad line, 600 meters northwest of the Krasnyi Oktiabr' Factory. The strongpoint was defended by 1st Battalion of 193rd Rifle Division's 685th Regiment. Conducted by three company-size *kampfgruppen* subordinate to *Kampfgruppe* Weber, named after its regimental commander, 54th Jäger Regiment's assault was to be supported by 10 tanks from Schulte's panzer squadron. In support of 54th Regiment's attack, 2nd Battalion of 14th Panzer Division's 24th Panzer Regiment was to assault the defenses of 138th Rifle Division in and around the southwestern section of the Barrikady Factory well beyond 54th Jäger Regiment's left flank.

21–22 October

Characteristic of the costly fighting during this period, *Kampfgruppe* Weber indeed managed to seize its objectives after a daylong fight. In the process, however, the group lost 20 men killed, 131 men wounded, and 3 men missing in action and 7 of Schulte's 10 tanks, which were destroyed while trying to breach the Soviets' minefields. Schulte's panzer squadron suffered 2 killed, including Schulte himself, and several wounded.[110] That evening, 62nd Army described the action in 193rd Rifle Division's sector: "Up to two battalions of infantry and 12 tanks went over to the attack against the division's left wing along Tsentral'naia and Kommunal'naia Streets at 1100 hours. Two of the enemy tanks succeeded in reaching beyond the forward edge. The infantry were driven back. The attack by the enemy was beaten back by 1500 hours. [The enemy] launched a repeat attack unsuccessfully at 1700 hours and withdrew to his jumping-off positions after suffering losses."[111]

The counterattacking force described in this report consisted of 9th Company, 895th Regiment, the 1st Company of the regiment's machine-gun battalion, and the 2nd Company of 193rd Rifle Division's Training Battalion. In addition, Chuikov reinforced Smekhotvorov's rifle division with a battalion from the 1043rd Rifle Regiment of Batiuk's 284th Rifle Division. Chuikov's flexible employment of reserves drawn from every conceivable sector, whether single companies or entire battalions, literally checkmated all of Paulus's and Seydlitz's local attacks.

As described by 62nd Army's daily report, nor did 14th Panzer Division's forces attacking the 138th Rifle Division's defenses on Weber's left achieve any lasting success, although Chuikov remained anxious over what might follow:

138th RD and 118th RR repulsed an attack by enemy infantry and tanks toward the southwestern corner of the Barrikady Factory at 0640 hours. The enemy suffered heavy losses.

At 1000 hours the enemy threw in a force of more than a battalion with tanks. After a repeat attack, he pushed 1st Battalion, 344th RR back. Hand-to-hand fighting is continuing.

344th RR suffered heavy casualties. The situation in the Barrikady Factory remains serious. The front has nothing with which to reinforce this sector.

308th RD (with 110 bayonets) is continuing to fight for the southwestern corner of the Barrikady Factory. The fighting is continuing with varying success.[112]

Although 138th Division defended its positions successfully, these attacks were simply a sobering portent of things to come.

In the wake of this and other engagements, the OKW announced, "In the fighting at Stalingrad, several fortified firing positions were seized in the course of fierce attacks of local importance. Most strikes by German aircraft were against enemy strongpoints in the northern part of the city."[113] On the other side of the hill, the Red Army General Staff described the assault by 14th Panzer Division and 54th Jäger Regiment, as well as the continuing brutal struggle within the rubble of the Barrikady Factory and elsewhere along 62nd Army's truncated front:

> **62nd Army**. The units of the Northern Group repelled attacks by the enemy on the western outskirts of the Spartanovka region and continued to hold on to their previous positions on 21 October.
>
> 138th RD successfully repelled attacks by the enemy [305th Infantry Division] on the western outskirts of the Barrikady Factory with its right-wing units and, on its left wing, fought fiercely with an enemy force of up to two infantry battalions with 6 tanks [14th Panzer Division] in the southwestern part of the Barrikady Factory. As a result of intense and often hand-to-hand fighting, 344th RR suffered heavy losses.
>
> 308th RD fought with varied success against enemy forces which went over to the defense in the southwestern part of the Barrikady Factory.
>
> 193rd RD held on to its previous positions, having successfully repelled several attacks by an enemy force of up to two infantry battalions with 12 tanks [*Kampfgruppe* Weber].
>
> The positions of the army's remaining units were unchanged.
>
> As a result of the fighting on 21 October, more than a battalion of enemy infantry and 12 tanks were destroyed.[114]

In 62nd Army's daily summary, while describing the local successes, Chuikov also admitted that his army had suffered "heavy losses" and required "immediate reinforcement with personnel and antitank weapons" because "the thinned out combat formations provides opportunities for the enemy to filter through our combat formations." In the meantime, he ordered his beleaguered divisions "to hold on to the positions they occupied and prevent any further enemy advance."[115] As an act of desperation, he ordered his army's flamethrower company to reinforce the approaches to the last landing stage; relieving it of its responsibilities for preventing unauthorized troop withdrawals, he committed the army's 1st Blocking Detachment into active combat.

22 October

As Paulus and Seydlitz finalized their plans for the 23 October assault, the desultory but costly struggle continued for possession of the many separate halls within the Barrikady Factory and the city blocks adjacent to the factory's southwestern and northeastern corners. As described by 62nd Army's daily summary:

> 138th RD, with 118th RR, repelled an attack by two battalions with tanks from Volkhovstroevsk and Sormosk toward the northern and southwestern outskirts of the Barrikady Factory.
> The divisions held on to their occupied positions. 2nd Bn, 344th RR, cooperating with a battalion of 339th RR [308th RD] cleared enemy from individual buildings in the southern part of the Barrikady Factory.
> 308th RD dug in on the territory of the Barrikady Factory.[116]

The intense German aerial bombardment during the day took a heavy toll of Chuikov's forces. In the day's most significant incident, German bombs killed the entire staff of 141st Mortar Regiment, including 19 soldiers, the regiment's commander, his deputy for political affairs, and his pair of deputies, as well as the commander of 37th Guards Rifle Division's 117th Regiment, Lieutenant Colonel Andreev.[117]

Whereas the OKW curtly announced at day's end that "enemy counterattacks were repelled in Stalingrad," at the end of the day the Red Army General Staff's operational summary emphasized 62nd Army's successful defense:

> **62nd Army** continued to hold on to its occupied positions while repelling enemy attacks toward Pribaltiiskaia Street and toward the Barrikady Factory from the west.

124th RB defended its previous positions.

149th RB defended the line (incl.) from the railroad west of Iamy to Tagil'skaia, Izumrudnaia, Krasnozavodskaia, and Asbestovskaia Streets, and farther south from the western outskirts of the Spartanovka region to the Betonnyi [Concrete] Bridge.

1st Bn, 124th RB, defended from the Betonnyi Bridge along the northern bank of the Mokraia Mechetka River to the Volga River.

308th RD dug in on the territory of the Barrikady Factory. In the sector of 118th RR [37th Gds. RD], an attack by an enemy force of up to an infantry battalion with 6 tanks was repelled by fire from all types of weapons at 1700 hours on 22 October.

284th RD repulsed an attempt by enemy infantry to fortify themselves in close proximity to the forward edge of the division's defense.

1047th RR, with 23rd Company and one platoon of 104th Flame-thrower Company, occupied firing positions along the Mezenskaia and Mashinnaia Streets line.

The army's remaining units held on to their previous positions.[118]

REORGANIZATION OF 62ND ARMY'S DEFENSES

Chuikov took advantage of the weather delay to reshuffle his forces once again. His intelligence organs also noted a buildup of German forces in the vicinity of Hill 107.5, in the open terrain between the upper and lower Krasnyi Oktiabr' villages in LI Corps' rear. Based on these reports, 62nd Army's commander concluded that Seydlitz was in the process of reorganizing a more powerful assault on the Krasnyi Oktiabr' Factory and acted accordingly. On the night of 20–21 October, for example, Chuikov withdrew his most badly damaged formations back across the Volga River for rest and refitting. These included the headquarters and remnants of Ermolkin's 112th Rifle Division (416th, 385th, and 524th Regiments), 115th Rifle and 2nd Motorized Rifle Brigades, and the headquarters of Gorishnyi's 95th Rifle and Zholudev's 37th Guards Rifle Divisions.[119] Chuikov had already consolidated the remnants of 95th Rifle and 37th Guards Rifle Divisions in their respective 161st and 118th Regiments. The former was defending the Bread Factory and adjacent blocks under the control of Smekhotvorov's 193rd Rifle Division; the latter, along with 650th Regiment, held the western bank of the Volga northeast of the Barrikady Factory under the control of Liudnikov's 138th Rifle Division. During the same period, Eremenko assigned 87th and 315th Rifle Divisions, which had completed refitting, to 62nd Army. For the time being, however, both of these divisions remained on the eastern bank of the Volga.[120]

The *Stavka* also took advantage of the lull to reorganize its forces in the Stalingrad region, keeping a keen eye on preparations for future offensive operations designed to drive German forces from the region. For example, on 21 October it ordered 1st Guards Army to begin relocating its headquarters and other support organizations by rail from the Ptishchevo region in Don Front's sector to the Novo-Annenskaia region in the Volga Military District, also for rest and refitting.[121] Only days before, the army's commander, General Moskalenko, had reported to Moscow, where the *Stavka* assigned him command of Voronezh Front's 40th Army effective 18 October.[122] Before 1st Guards Army's headquarters began entraining for its trip to the rear, it passed its divisions and supporting tank corps to neighboring armies and *fronts*.[123]

Also on 21 October, the *Stavka* redesignated Don Front's 4th Tank Army as the new 65th Army, effective the next day, and replaced the army's former commander, General Kriuchenkin, with Lieutenant General P. I. Batov, the former deputy commander of Briansk Front. At least in part, the *Stavka's* decision to rename 4th Tank Army was the result of the army's embarrassing lack of tanks. In fact, the army's chief of staff, Colonel I. S. Glebov, had sarcastically nicknamed 4th Tank Army "the four-tank" [*cheryrekhtankovaia*] army because, after losing several hundred tanks during its defeats in the Great Bend of the Don in August and in the Kletskaia bridgehead in September, by mid-October the army fielded only four tanks, all of which were being employed to protect the army's headquarters.[124] By this time, Batov's new army consisted of nine rifle divisions, including the battle-hardened 4th, 27th, and 40th Guards Rifle Divisions and the famous 24th "Iron" Samara-Ul'ianovka Rifle Division.[125]

The 65th Army's new commander, 49-year-old Pavel Ivanovich Batov, was an experienced officer whose record had been severely tarnished: As commander of 51st Army he had presided over the army's catastrophic and embarrassing defeat in the Crimea during November 1941. After weathering this storm, Batov's star rose steadily, as he went on to serve successfully as the commander of Briansk Front's 3rd Army in January and February 1942 and as deputy commander of Briansk Front from February through October 1942 (including three months under Rokossovsky's tutelage). Having rehabilitated himself as a thoroughly competent and respected commander, Batov thereafter commanded 65th Army with distinction until war's end.[126]

On 22 October the *Stavka* took the important step of reorganizing its forces operating north of the Don River to improve command and control and to facilitate the conduct of future offensive operations. In a directive signed by Stalin and Vasilevsky, it formed a new Southwestern Front around the nucleus of the former 1st Guards Army's headquarters and assigned Don Front's 63rd and 21st Armies and Briansk Front's 5th Tank Army to Batov's new *front*:

1. Form the Southwestern Front by 31 October.

2. Include 63rd Army, 21st Army, and 5th Tank Army in the composition of the Southwestern Front. Establish the [following] boundary lines:

a) Between the Voronezh and Southwestern Fronts: from Ptishchevo, Povorino, Novokhopersk, Verkhnyi Mamon, and Kantemirovka to Lisichansk. The first two points are inclusive for the Southwestern Front.

b) Between the Southwestern and Don Fronts: from Atkarsk, Balanda, Rakovka, Kletskaia, and Selivanov to Evseev. All points, except Atkarsk, are inclusive for the Southwestern Front.

3. Deploy the headquarters of the Southwestern Front on the base of the headquarters of 1st Guards Army and station it in the Novo-Annenskaia region.

4. Appoint Lieutenant General Comrade Vatutin as the commander of the Southwestern Front, freeing him from his duties as commander of the Voronezh Front. Appoint Major General Stel'makh as chief of staff of the Southwestern Front. Appoint Lieutenant General Comrade Golikov as commander of the Voronezh Front.

5. The chief of the Main Cadre Directorate and the chiefs of the NKO's main directorates will fill out the headquarters of the Southwestern Front with necessary command and leadership cadre by 28 October in accordance with Tables of Organization [shtat] Nos. 02/206, 02/209, 02/165 and 010/1b.

6. Provide the chief of GLAVUPROFORM [the Main Directorate for the Formation of Red Army Reserves] with instructions concerning the filling out of the proposed support units and service organizations for the headquarters of the front from the tank corps of 1st Guards Army [4th and 16th Tank Corps].

7. The chief of the Main Communications Directorate will dispatch necessary communications units to the commander of the front by 30 October in accordance with the General Staff's instructions.

8. The chief of the Red Army Rear will allocate necessary rear service units and facilities at the expense of reserves and surpluses from other fronts and will send them to the commander of the Southwestern Front by 30 October.[127]

The new Southwestern Front provided unified command over all forces situated in the 130-kilometer-wide sector along the Don River from Verkhnyi Mamon eastward to Kletskaia. Although the front's combat forces along this front on 22 October initially included only 63rd and 21st Armies, the Stavka intended to regroup 5th Tank Army, which had been refitting near Plavsk in Briansk Front's rear since 22 September, first into Southwestern Front's rear and then, at the appropriate juncture, into the Serafimovich region in the *front's* center.[128] The same day, the *Stavka* further reinforced Southwestern Front by transferring 8th Cavalry Corps, one rifle division, and five artillery regiments from Voronezh Front. The cavalry corps was to concentrate in the region 50 kilometers southeast of Veshenskaia by 2 November, the rifle division (with 7,500–8,000 men) in the vicinity of Kalach Voronezh by 2 November, and the artillery regiments in the Sebriakovo region by 3 November.[129] The commander of 8th Cavalry Corps, 42-year-old Mikhail Dmitrievich Borisov, was an experienced cavalryman who commanded 31st Separate Cavalry Division during the Germans' Operation Barbarossa. The division distinguished itself while fighting under 50th Army's control in the Tula region during the battle for Moscow. He later led 9th Cavalry Corps and served as deputy commander of the famed 1st Guards Cavalry Corps before assuming command of 8th Cavalry Corps in October 1942.[130]

The *Stavka* completed the first round of outfitting the new Southwestern Front on 25 October by ordering Rokossovsky's Don Front to transfer 226th, 293rd, 333rd, and 277th Rifle Divisions, 4th Tank and 3rd Guards Cavalry Corps, 11 artillery regiments, 5 antiaircraft artillery regiments, and 2 antiaircraft artillery battalions to Vatutin's *front*, effective 2–3 November.[131] Characteristically, the directive required the NKVD to undertake "measures to cleanse the regions where the divisions were to be situated and their movement routes of all suspicious people."[132]

On 23 October, the day after it formed Southwestern Front, the *Stavka* beefed up its strategic reserves by forming the new 1st and 2nd Guards Armies. The 1st Guards Army, formed on the base of 4th Reserve Army, was to be combat-ready in the Ptishevo, Kirsanov, Balashov, Atkarsk, and Kolyshei regions, 150–190 kilometers north of Serafimovich on the Don, by 10 November 1942. Commanded by Major General I. M. Chistiakov, 1st Guards Army was to consist of 4th Guards Rifle Corps, with 35th and 41st Guards and 195th Rifle Divisions, 6th Guards Rifle Corps, with 38th and 44th Guards and 266th Rifle Division, and 1st Guards Mechanized Corps, which was to be formed from 1st Guards Rifle Division.[133] The army's 42-year-old commander, Ivan Mikhailovich Chistiakov, was an experienced combat veteran who had commanded Western Front's 64th Rifle Brigade and 8th Guards Rifle Division in 1941, the latter with distinction during the battle for Moscow, and Northwestern and (later) Kalinin Fronts' 2nd Guards Rifle Corps in 1942.[134]

The 2nd Guards Army, which was to form in the Tambov region, 100–120 kilometers northeast of Voronezh, around the nucleus of 1st Reserve Army, was to be combat-ready by 25 November. Initially commanded by Major General Ia. G. Kreizer, 2nd Guards Army was to consist of 1st Guards Rifle Corps, with 24th and 33rd Guards and 98th Rifle Divisions, 13th Guards

Rifle Corps, with 3rd and 49th Guards Rifle and 387th Rifle Divisions, and 2nd Guards Mechanized Corps. The 49th Guards Rifle Division was to be formed from the existing 2nd Guards Motorized Rifle Division, and 2nd Guards Mechanized Corps from 22nd Guards Rifle Division.[135] The army's commander, 37-year-old Iakov Grigor'evich Kreizer, had commanded the famous 1st Moscow Motorized Rifle Division during the harrowing battle for Smolensk in the summer of 1941, as well as Southwestern Front's 3rd Army during the Moscow counteroffensive in the winter of 1941–1942. He later served as deputy commander in several armies during 1942.[136]

The *Stavka* earmarked 1st Guards Army to reinforce Southwestern Front and 2nd Guards Army to reinforce either Western Front (operating along the Moscow axis) or Don Front (operating along the Stalingrad axis). Ultimately, the *Stavka* replaced Southwestern Front's 63rd Army along the Don River with 1st Guards Army on 1 November, incorporating 63rd Army's three rifle divisions into Chistiakov's army.[137] 2nd Guards Army, however, remained in the Tambov region through the remainder of October and November, awaiting instructions regarding future employment.

DON FRONT'S COUNTERSTROKE (FOURTH KOTLUBAN'), 20–26 OCTOBER

As Stalin, Rokossovsky, and Eremenko reorganized their forces for possible future offensive operations along the Don River front, they also took immediate measures to counter the violent and successful German assault near the Tractor Factory and to reduce the threat to the remainder of Stalingrad's factory district. As early as the morning of 15 October, when Stalin finally realized the danger posed by the new German advance, the dictator had Zhukov and Vasilevsky prepare a directive ordering Rokossovsky to accelerate his offensive preparations and to implement at least a part of the major counterstroke he had recommended a week before:

> To render immediate assistance to the Stalingraders, the *Stavka* of the Supreme High Command orders you to launch your main attack from the vicinity of Hill 139.7, the MTF [the Motor Tractor Factory], and Hill 128.9 in the general direction of Orlovka and Hill 75.9, where you will link up with the forces of the Stalingrad Front.
>
> Besides the Stalingrad Front's units, employ the services of the four rifle divisions from among those divisions that have arrived along the Bol'shaia Ivanovka and Gornaia Proleika line for the attack. In order to penetrate the enemy's front, create an artillery group on the basis of

no fewer than 60–65 guns per kilometer of front and no fewer than 12 guards-mortar regiments. Employ a quantity of tanks to be determined by the *front* commander.

Launch a supporting attack from the Erzovka region toward Hill 135.4, 2.5 kilometers east of Orlovka. Organize additional artillery support from the eastern bank of the Volga River after coordinating the matter of artillery attached for this purpose with the commander of the Stalingrad Front.

Be prepared to attack by the end of 19 October.

Submit a plan of action in my name by 2300 hours on 15 October.[138]

Minutes later, Zhukov and Vasilevsky sent a second directive to Eremenko, ordering him to mount a similar offensive south of Stalingrad:

To provide assistance to 62nd Army and clear out the central parts of Stalingrad as quickly as possible, the *Stavka* of the Supreme High Command orders you to conduct an attack from the region of Gornaia Poliana State Farm, with the immediate mission of clearing the enemy from the Kuporosnoe and Peschanka regions and the southern part of Stalingrad up to the Tsaritsa River, while protecting your flank toward Peschanka and, subsequently, clearing the central part of the city and linking up with the forces of 62nd Army.

Besides 64th Army's forces, employ 7th Rifle Corps and 90th Tank Brigade. Employ no fewer than·60 guns per kilometer of front and all of 64th and 57th Armies' guards-mortar units to take part in the artillery offensive. Concentrate 61st Cavalry Division in the Solodnikov region and 81st Cavalry Division in the Chernyi Iar region to protect the crossings over the Volga River.

Be prepared to attack by the end of 19 October.

Submit a plan of action . . . by 2200 hours on 17 October.[139]

Rokossovsky responded to Stalin's directive at 1945 hours the same day; Eremenko did so two days later. Rokossovsky's response accepted the *Stavka*'s recommendations and reformulated his *front*'s mission accordingly:

The aim of the operation is to penetrate the defensive belt in the Hill 145.1, Hill 139.7, the MTF, and Hill 128.9 sector and, by developing the attack along the crests of Hills 139.7, 145.1, 147.6, 144.4 and Orlovka, link up with the forces of the Stalingrad garrison in the vicinity of Hill 75.9 and, subsequently, together with the forces on the Stalingrad Front's right wing, destroy the enemy in the Orlovka, Latashanka, Akatovka, and Bol. Sukhaia Mechetka regions.[140]

Rokossovsky's offensive plan required his *front's* shock group, consisting of a strong force deployed on the right wing of Malinovsky's 66th Army and a smaller force deployed on the left wing of 24th Army, to penetrate the German defenses in the 15-kilometer-wide sector north and northeast of Kuz'michi and to advance southeastward toward Orlovka (see Map 70). His forces were to accomplish this mission during a five-day period between 20 and 24 October. By this time, 24th Army was commanded by Lieutenant General I. V. Galanin, who had replaced Kozlov when the latter was appointed assistant commander of Voronezh Front. A veteran of the fighting against the Japanese at Khalkhin-Gol in August and September 1939, when he commanded 57th Rifle Division, Ivan Vasil'evich Galanin then led 18th Rifle Corps and 18th, 59th, and 16th Armies during Operation Barbarossa. He was 43 years old when assigned command of 24th Army.[141]

The shock group of Malinovsky's 66th Army consisted of four relatively fresh rifle divisions, the 62nd, 252nd, 212th, and 226th, just received from the *Stavka's* reserves, supported by the full-strength 91st, 121st, and 64th Tank Brigades, each with a complement of roughly 53 tanks. Attacking in the army's center, in the sector from the upper reaches of Sukhaia Mechetka *Balka* westward to northeast of Kuz'michi, the main shock group had 212th, 252nd, and 62nd Rifle Divisions, each supported by a tank brigade, in first echelon, and 226th Rifle Division in second echelon. Its immediate objectives were Hills 112.7 and 139.7 and, ultimately, Orlovka. Fire support for the assault consisted of 664 guns and mortars and guards-mortars from 12 mortar regiments. The army's remaining nine rifle divisions, including its organic 64th, 84th, 99th, 120th, and 299th Rifle Divisions and 49th, 116th, 231st, and 343rd Rifle Divisions (transferred from 24th Army), were to conduct supporting attacks on the army's left and right flanks. However, these divisions were all severely understrength, with roughly a battalion's worth of bayonets each.

On the left flank of 66th Army's main shock group, 116th and 299th Rifle Divisions, supported by eight tanks from 58th Tank Brigade, were to attack the German defenses west of Erzovka. On the right flank of the army's main shock groups, 49th and 343rd Rifle Divisions, with only minimal armor support, were to attack southward from their jumping-off positions due north of Kuz'michi.

On 66th Army's right, 24th Army's shock group, consisting of 316th, 173rd, and 233rd Rifle Divisions, also seriously understrength, were to support and protect 66th Army's assaults. Rokossovsky's plan assigned specific missions for his attacking forces to achieve on each day of the projected four-day operation.[142]

In light of the previous bloody and frustrating two months of fighting in the Kotluban' region, Rokossovsky later candidly admitted that he expected the assault to achieve very little:

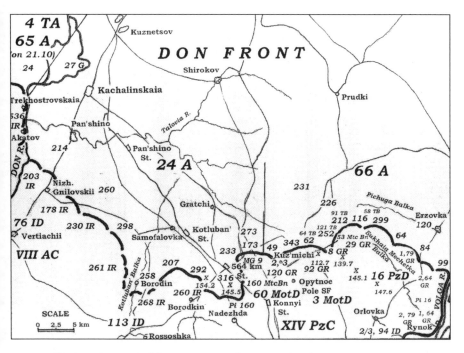

Map 70. Don Front's Kotluban' counterstroke, 20–26 October 1942

Our Don Front had the objective of harassing the enemy from the Don bridgeheads, so as to prevent him from transferring reinforcements to Stalingrad. At the same time, the left flank of our 24th Army, in cooperation with the 66th, was to rout the enemy units north of the city and link up with the 62nd in Stalingrad. We were given permission to use seven infantry divisions from the GHQ Reserve for the operation but received no additional supporting means in the shape of artillery, armour, or aircraft. The chances of success were remote, especially as the enemy had well fortified positions.

Since the main objective in the operation fell to 66th Army, I had a conversation with Malinovsky, who begged me not to commit the seven new divisions to action. "We'll only waste them," he said.

Happily only two [actually four] of the promised seven new divisions arrived by the deadline set by the GHQ and were duly handed over to 66th Army. The others were late, and we relegated them to the Front reserve. Subsequently, they played an important part in the fighting.

As expected, the attack failed. The armies of the Don Front were unable to penetrate the enemy's defenses, and the offensive undertaken by the Stalingrad Front also fell short of its objectives. Still, the enemy was compelled to maintain his group in the area between the rivers, and this greatly influenced the subsequent course of events at Stalingrad.[143]

Rokossovsky's pessimism was justified. Hube's XIV Panzer Corps defended the sector opposite 66th Army's main attack with 3rd Motorized Division's 8th and 60th Motorized Division's 92nd Panzer Grenadier regiments, whose forces were well dug in north and northeast of Kuz'michi. These forces were flanked on the left by 60th Motorized Division's 120th Panzer Grenadier Regiment, whose forces were deployed astride the road and main railroad line from Kotluban' southward to Stalingrad. On the right was 16th Panzer Division's 29th Panzer Grenadier Regiment, which, with *Luftwaffe* Group Stahl in support, defended the sector east of the Sukhaia Mechetka *Balka*, west of Erzovka. All of the German forces occupied fortified defenses protected by extensive artillery fire and interlocking machine-gun and small-arms fire. As in the past, Rokossovsky's mission was sacrificial—if not suicidal.

As if Rokossovsky's task was not sufficiently challenging, Stalin early on 16 October altered his armies' missions and demanded they begin the operation a day earlier than planned:

Make the following changes to the operational plan you submitted:
1. Do not conduct the secondary attack from the Kuz'michi and Hill 112.7 front; envisioning the necessary forces and the turning of your right flank toward Opytnoe State Farm and Kuz'michi after the shock group has penetrated the enemy's defensive front, strengthen the axis of the main attack toward Orlovka at the expense of the freed-up forces.
2. In connection with the worsening situation in Stalingrad, begin your operation on the morning of 19 October instead of 20 October.
Your plan is confirmed in the main.
    Zhukov, Vasilevsky[144]

Although Rokossovsky's reaction to these changes remains unknown, orders were orders, and in the command climate existing in the Red Army during the fall of 1942, commanders did not disobey Stalin's directives. Nevertheless—with or without Stalin's permission—when Rokossovsky unleashed his forces early on 19 October, he did so with a force far weaker than Stalin had anticipated. Attacking in the same rainy weather that forced Paulus and Seydlitz to postpone their assaults against the factory district, once again Rokossovsky's forces stoically replicated the bloody defeats they had experienced during the previous four weeks. The Red Army General Staff's daily operational summary described their fight during the next two days:

[19 October]

66th Army conducted fighting of local importance with part of its forces in separate sectors.

Separate detachments of 64th RD fought to capture Hill 141.5 (5 kilometers west of Erzovka) beginning at 0600 hours 19 October but advanced forward insignificantly after encountering strong enemy resistance.

Units of 84th RD fought defensively with an enemy force of up to a battalion of infantry with 3 tanks and 5 armored personnel carriers, which were attacking from the mound +1.2 toward Hill 129.6 (3.5 kilometers southwest of Erzovka), beginning at 0600 hours. . . . The enemy succeeded in wedging negligibly into the division's defenses.[145]

[20 October]

24th Army, remaining in its previous positions, went over to the offensive with the formations on its left-wing at 0900 hours on 20 October and, overcoming strong enemy fire, advanced negligibly in separate sectors.

316th RD advanced 100–150 meters from its jumping-off positions, encountered strong enemy fire, took to the ground, and exchanged fire.

173rd RD, attacking toward the vicinity of Hill 128.1 (4 kilometers west of Kuz'michi), advanced 150–200 meters, but strong enemy fire prevented further movement.

233rd RD advanced forward insignificantly and exchanged fire from its previous positions.

66th Army went over to the offensive with the units of its right-wing at 0800 hours on 20 October and was fighting within the enemy's defensive belt at 1000 hours. The enemy offered strong resistance and conducted counterattacks.

252nd RD captured the Hill 130.7 (6 kilometers northeast of Kuz'michi) region and the road junction 2 kilometers east of Hill 130.7 as a result of the fighting.

Precise information about the positions of the army's attacking units has not been received by day's end on 20 October.[146]

Commenting on the fighting on 20 October, the OKW's communiqué reported, "In the sector of the front between the Volga and the Don, enemy infantry and tank units transferred to this region launched diversionary attacks from the north which were repulsed by our forces. The enemy suffered significant losses. Forty tanks were destroyed and a great number of prisoners were captured."[147] The Red Army General Staff tracked the fighting on 21 and 22 October, emphasizing the strong German resistance:

[21 October]

24th Army tried to attack toward the south with its left-wing but, after encountering strong enemy resistance, had no success.

66th Army continued to conduct offensive operations along previous axes all day on 21 October.

The enemy offered strong fire resistance, and his air forces bombed the combat formations of the attacking units of the army in groups of 3–5 aircraft.

49th RD tried to attack but, after encountering strong enemy fire from the Kuz'michi region, could not advance.

62nd RD, overcoming strong enemy resistance, captured two lines of foxholes and was fighting in the vicinity of Hill 112.7 (3 kilometers east of Kuz'michi) at 0600 hours on 21 October.

343rd RD, encountering strong enemy fire, fought in the region 4 kilometers northeast of Kuz'michi.

252nd RD fought with the enemy in the region 1.5 kilometers south of Hill 130.7 (6 kilometers east of Kuz'michi).

212th RD, attacking south of Hill 128.9 (10 kilometers northeast of Kuz'michi), advanced 300 meters from its jumping-off positions and, after encountering heavy fire, exchanged fire.

The positions of 116th and 299th RDs' units are being confirmed.

There were no changes in the positions of the army's remaining units.[148]

[22 October]

24th Army, remaining in its previous positions, engaged in offensive fighting on its left wing with assault groups from three divisions (316th, 173rd, and 273rd RDs) on 22 October but, after encountering strong enemy resistance, were unable to advance.

66th Army conducted offensive operations along its previous axes with the units on its right-wing and in its center. The enemy offered strong fire to the attacking units of the army and bombed their combat formations with groups of 2–3 aircraft each.

49th and 343rd RDs fought in their previous positions.

62nd RD engaged in offensive fighting, captured the Hill 112.7 (3 kilometers northeast of Kuz'michi) region, and was fighting for the southern slope of this hill and the road 1.5 kilometers southwest of Hill 130.7 (5 kilometers northeast of Kuz'michi) at 1400 hours on 22 October.

252nd RD captured the region of the Motor Tractor Station (8 kilometers northeast of Kuz'michi) and was fighting for the line from 1.5 kilometers southwest of Hill 130.7 to the fork in the road 1 kilometer south of the Motor Tractor Station at 1400 hours on 22 October.

212th RD, exploiting the success of 252nd RD's left wing, was fighting along a line from the fork in the road 1 kilometer south of the Motor

Tractor Station to Hill 128.9 (8–10 kilometers southeast of Kuz'michi) at 1400 hours on 22 October.

116th RD, with 58th TB, conducted offensive fighting on 22 October. The results are being confirmed.

The positions of 299th RD's units are being confirmed.

64th, 84th, and 99th RDs conducted active operations on 22 October to improve their occupied positions.

120th, 226th, and 231st RDs are situated in their previous positions.[149]

The OKW simply announced, "The enemy's diversionary attacks against the positions of our forces north of Stalingrad were repelled with the support of German and Romanian aircraft."[150] However, 3rd Motorized Division reported extremely heavy fighting was under way in the vicinity of its defenses around Hill 129.6, and the struggle had exacted a heavy toll on its already worn-out units. By this time, the division was defending the hill with 1st Battalion, 8th Grenadier Regiment, and 1st Battalion, 29th Grenadier Regiment, on the right and 2nd Battalion, 29th Panzer Grenadier Regiment, which was deployed in defenses on both flanks of the hill. During this fighting, the division reported destroying 18 enemy tanks on 21 October and another 2 on 22 October, most of them during counterattacks by 3rd Company of the division's 103rd Panzer Battalion. But the attrition during this fighting was also extremely high, with 7th Company, 8th Grenadier Regiment, numbering 1.5 platoons, 4th Company, 53rd Motorcycle Battalion, fielding only 8 men, and the division's panzer strength reduced to a total of 30 tanks, many of which required repair.[151]

In its evening communiqué on 22 October, the OKW played down the importance of the Soviet attacks, stating, "During the evening in the sector between the Volga and the Don, Soviet forces launched several poorly-organized diversionary attacks which were beaten back. The enemy suffered heavy personnel losses."[152] Nonetheless, despite the lack of any appreciable success, the Red Army General Staff reported that Rokossovsky's forces persisted in their assaults on 23 October:

24th Army, defending its existing positions on its right wing and in its center, conducted unsuccessful offensive operations with the units on its left-wing (316th, 173rd, and 273rd RDs) beginning at 1100 hours on 23 October.

66th Army engaged in offensive fighting along its previous axes with the units on its left wing and in its center on 23 October. The enemy offered strong fire to the attacking units of the army.

49th and 343rd RDs fought in their previous positions.

62nd RD, overcoming enemy resistance, fought on the southern slopes of Hill 112.7 (3 kilometers northeast of Kuz'michi) and advanced 300 meters during the day.

252nd RD advanced 700–800 meters, captured Hill 137.8, and fought for the northwestern slopes of Hill 139.7 (8 kilometers east of Kuz'michi).

212th RD advanced 1 kilometer from its jumping-off positions on its right wing and in its center and fought for the northern slopes of Hill 139.7.

84th RD, with a regiment from 120th RD, repelled four attacks by an enemy force of up to a battalion of infantry with 30 tanks in the vicinity of Hill 129.6 (3.5 kilometers southwest of Erzovka) on 23 October. The fighting was continuing. The enemy lost about 70 soldiers and officers, 16 tanks, and 2 armored personnel carriers in the fighting in this region on 23 October.

According to incomplete information, the army's units killed up to 7,000 soldiers and officers, burned or blew up 57 tanks, destroyed more than 100 guns and 70 machine guns, and shot down 26 enemy aircraft on 20–21 October. We seized more than 150 of our tanks and those of the enemy that had been damaged in the previous fighting.[153]

Once again, the OKW announced, "The diversionary attacks by insignificant enemy forces in the northern part of the city were repelled."[154] Driven on by the *Stavka*, Rokossovsky's forces continued to maintain pressure on XIV Panzer Corps' defenses in increasingly futile assaults through 26 October:

[24 October]

24th Army defended its previous positions, fortified them, and conducted reconnaissance.

66th Army, encountering strong enemy fire, continued to conduct offensive operations with the units on its left wing and in its center.

39th [Gds.], 343rd, and 62nd RDs engaged in offensive fighting along their previous axes. The results have not been confirmed.

226th RD passed through 252nd RD's combat formation at 1000 hours on 24 October, dug in along the positions it reached, and fought to capture the region of Hill 139.7 (8 kilometers east of Kuz'michi) with part of its forces.

The positions of 64th, 84th, and 99th RDs are being confirmed.

120th and 231st RDs were located in their previously occupied positions.[155]

[25 October]

66th Army, encountering strong enemy fire, continued to conduct offensive operations along its previous axes with the units on its left wing and in its center on 25 October, but had no success.[156]

[26 October]

66th Army continued to conduct offensive fighting along its previous axis on 26 October. The enemy offered strong fire. The fighting went on along previous lines.[157]

Although the OKW ceased mentioning whatsoever any of the Soviet attacks in the Kotluban' region after 23 October, on 24 October the OKH reported, "On the northern sector of the front between the Volga and the Don Rivers, the enemy repeated his attacks today, committing a total of about 5 battalions and 20–30 tanks. The attacks failed."[158] Considering these actions as minor and irrelevant, the OKH thereafter also ignored them. Acknowledging that any further attacks would be useless, Rokossovsky, with the *Stavka*'s permission, finally ordered his forces to go over to the defense late on 26 October. Confirming this fact, the next day the General Staff reported, "**66th Army** dug in along the positions it attained and put the units on its right wing in order on 27 October. The enemy did not undertake active operations."[159]

As futile as they were, the assaults by Rokossovsky's 24th and 66th Armies were designed to prevent XIV Panzer Corps from transferring any additional forces southward to participate in the fighting in Stalingrad's factory district. However, given the reduced strength of 3rd and 60th Motorized Divisions' forces defending the corridor north of the city, neither of them could have provided significant reinforcements to Seydlitz's LI Corps. In this sense, then, Rokossovsky's attacks were useless and costly gestures.

CONCLUSIONS

The assault by Seydlitz's forces against the Tractor Factory and the lower Tractor Factory village was indeed a bold stroke. It was also the last occasion when Paulus's Sixth Army would be able to exploit surprise and to employ maneuver successfully to seize an objective as large as the Tractor Factory and its associated village in one bound. By deploying 14th Panzer and 305th Infantry Divisions forward in relative secrecy, shifting 389th Infantry Division south of the Mechetka River, and then combining all three divisions into Group Jänecke, Paulus succeeded in concentrating a sufficient force with which to shatter Chuikov's defenses southwest of the factory and its workers' village. This force then sustained an advance to depths of from 2.5 to 3.5 kilometers over the course of two days. As a result, the Tractor Factory was in Seydlitz's hands by day's end on 15 October, and his forces were threatening to cut Chuikov's defenses in half by driving to the Volga River through the Minusinsk area midway between the Tractor and Barrikady Factories.

Caught by the bold German stroke before it could react, Chuikov's army suffered serious losses, including more than three-quarters of its strongest division—Zholudev's fresh 37th Guards—as well as 90th Regiment of Gorishnyi's 95th Rifle Division and the remnants of Ermolkin's 112th Rifle Division, which the German assault rendered hors de combat. The successful German advance also split away Group Gorokhov from 62nd Army's main forces by capturing the line of the Mokraia Mechetka River and Gorokhov's landing stage on the Volga River. Coupled with the gains that XIV Panzer Corps' 16th Panzer Division recorded in the Spartanovka region, especially the seizure of footholds on the twin *Pilzes*, thereafter Gorokhov's forces would fight an increasingly desperate battle while facing encirclement and isolation.

Once in possession of the Tractor Factory, Seydlitz on 16 October attempted to replicate the feat his corps had accomplished on 14 and 15 October by quickly reorganizing Group Jänecke and wheeling its forces southward to seize the Barrikady Factory. As agile and adaptive as these units were, however, the 16 October assault by 14th Panzer and 305th Infantry Divisions failed to repeat their performance of the previous two days.

Clearly taken off balance by late on 15 October, Chuikov was able to right himself, but once again only because his *front* commander, Eremenko, committed fresh reserves into the fray in timely fashion—this time in the form of Liudnikov's 138th Rifle Division. Entering the fight one regiment at a time, Liudnikov's division kept the fight reasonably equal (roughly 2:1 in the Germans' favor), allowed Chuikov to regain his balance, and slowed Group Jänecke's advance before it was able to seize another key objective, this time the Barrikady Factory, in yet another coup de main.

Again, however, on 17 October Seydlitz unleashed another attack, this time a pincer maneuver by 14th Panzer and 305th Infantry Divisions from the north and the reinforced 24th Panzer Division from the west, against Chuikov's defenses in Skul'pturnyi Park and near Sormosk west of the Barrikady Factory. In two more days of heavy fighting, although on a lesser scale than the maneuver that LI Corps conducted on 14–15 October, Seydlitz's skillful pincer attack largely destroyed Gurt'ev's 308th Rifle Division and propelled German forces into the Barrikady Factory and to the northeastern approaches to the Krasnyi Oktiabr' Factory.

However, the tenacious struggle by Soviet forces that were encircled west of the Barrikady Factory so sapped the strength of Seydlitz's corps that its attacks stalled once again by nightfall on 18 October. In fact, the timely arrival of Liudnikov's 138th Rifle Division during this fight enabled his troops to infiltrate back into the Barrikady Factory and to convert much of its ruins into imposing fortified positions. As Paulus brought fresh reserves forward—this time two regiments of 79th Infantry Division in yet another attempt to reinvigorate Seydlitz's depleted army corps—stalemate set in once again as

The Tractor Factory (center), with the Mokraia Mechetka River from left to right across the top and the Tractor Factory village on the left.

The Tractor Factory with its halls and shops.

Spartanovka village, with the Mechetka River and Tractor Factory at the bottom.

Foxholes and shell-holes northwest of Spartanovka village.

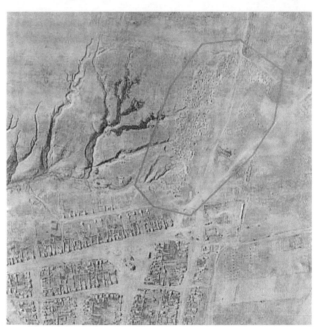

Rynok village with the approaches from the north highlighted.

the two sides jockeyed for position in and around the Barrikady Factory during the next four days.

While LI Corps was registering significant gains in the northern half of Stalingrad's factory district, unknown to the Germans, Stalin and his *Stavka* were reorganizing and reinforcing their forces in the Stalingrad region to better defend the city and to prepare for more extensive and effective offensive operations northwest of Stalingrad. To this end, the *Stavka* formed a new Southwestern Front, assigning it the sector along the Don River between the Don and Voronezh Fronts and formed two new armies, 1st and 2nd Guards, which it earmarked to spearhead offensive operations either near Stalingrad or in the region west of Moscow. These measures gave Southwestern and Don Fronts one bridgehead each on the southern bank of the Don River, the former the Serafimovich bridgehead and the latter the Kletskaia bridgehead, from which they could launch future offensive operations and raised significant reinforcements with which they could conduct those offensives.

Later during this period, the *Stavka* also ordered Don and Stalingrad Fronts to activate offensives against Sixth Army's flanks, the former once again in the Kotluban' region northwest of Stalingrad and the latter from its Beketovka bridgehead south of the city (see Chapter Seven, beginning on page 524). When these assaults materialized, Don Front's assault north of the city on 20 October and 64th Army's attack south of the city six days later seriously distracted Sixth Army's attentions from the fighting in the city's factory district.

By day's end on 22 October, the maneuver phase of Sixth Army's struggle for possession of Stalingrad's northern factory district was clearly over. By conducting two skillful maneuvers within the span of a single week, Seydlitz's forces had been able to capture the Tractor Factory and gain a foothold in the Barrikady Factory. Thereafter, however, there was no further room for maneuver. With all three factory workers' villages and the Tractor Factory in German hands, the cratered but relatively open areas between the factories and their associated workers' village were now in Seydlitz's rear. To his front lay only the Barrikady and Krasnyi Oktiabr' Factories, reduced to grotesquely twisted and gnarled ruins by *Luftwaffe* aircraft and Sixth Army artillery. In turn, Chuikov's beleaguered riflemen, sappers, and snipers converted the ruins into formidable strongpoints and centers of resistance. During the next phase of the struggle, Seydlitz's infantry, panzer-grenadiers, and engineers would have to pry Chuikov's defenders from these ruins like rats from their holes.

Although Paulus managed to reinforce his forces fighting in the city with eight fresh infantry battalions and two pioneer battalions, the tedious and trying urban fighting had an increasingly debilitating effect on the strength and combat capability of Sixth Army. This is evident from a comparison of the combat ratings of Sixth Army's infantry and pioneer battalions on 12 and 19 October 1942 (see Table 35).

Table 35. The Combat Rating of Infantry and Pioneer Battalions Subordinate to Sixth Army's Divisions Fighting in Stalingrad, 12–19 October 1942

	12 October	19 October
XIV PANZER CORPS		
3rd Motorized Division		
(5 infantry battalions)	2 average, 2 weak, and 1 exhausted	3 medium strong and 2 average
(1 pioneer battalion)	exhausted	weak
60th Motorized Division		
(7 infantry battalions)	4 average, 2 weak, and 1 exhausted	2 medium strong, 4 average, and 1 exhausted
(1 pioneer battalion)	exhausted	weak
16th Panzer Division		
(5–4 infantry battalions)	2 medium strong, 2 average, and 1 weak	1 medium strong, 1 average, and 2 weak
(1 pioneer battalion)	average	weak
94th Infantry Division		
(7 infantry battalions)	7 exhausted	7 exhausted
(1 pioneer battalion)	weak	weak
LI ARMY CORPS		
24th Panzer Division		
(4 infantry battalions)	1 weak and 3 exhausted	1 weak and 3 exhausted
(1 pioneer battalion)	exhausted	exhausted
100th Jäger Division		
(5 infantry battalions)	4 average and 1 weak	1 strong, 3 medium strong, and 1 average
(1 pioneer battalion)	weak	medium strong
305th Infantry Division		
(9 infantry battalions)	9 average	9 weak
(1 pioneer battalion)	strong	weak
295th Infantry Division		
(7 infantry battalions)	4 weak and 3 exhausted	4 weak and 3 exhausted
(1 pioneer battalion)	weak	weak
389th Infantry Division		
(5–4 infantry battalions)	1 weak and 4 exhausted	1 average, 1 weak, and 2 exhausted
(1 pioneer battalion)	exhausted	exhausted
14th Panzer Division		
(4 infantry battalions)	**(not fighting in the city)**	4 medium strong
(1 pioneer battalion)		average

Table 35. (continued)

	12 October	19 October
71st Infantry Division		
(7 infantry battalions)	7 weak	2 average, 3 weak, and 2 exhausted
(1 pioneer battalion)	weak	weak
Totals:		
61–63 infantry battalions	2 medium strong, 21 average, 19 weak, and 19 exhausted	1 strong, 13 medium strong, 11 average, 20 weak, and 18 exhausted
10–11 pioneer battalions	1 strong, 1 average, 4 weak, and 4 exhausted	1 medium strong, 1 average, 7 weak, and 2 exhausted

Source: Florian *Freiherr* von und zu Aufsess, "Betr.: Zustand der Divisionen, Armee – Oberkommando 6, Abt. Ia, A. H. Qu., 12. Oktober 1942, 10.00 Uhr"and "Betr.: Zustand der Divisionen, Armee – Oberkommando 6, Abt. Ia, A. H. Qu., 19 Oktober 1942, 12.35 Uhr," in *Die Anlagenbander zu den Kriegstagebuchern der 6. Armee vom 14.09.1942 bis 24.11.1942, Band I* (Schwabach: January 2006), 156–160 and 185–188.

Thus, during the period from 12 to 19 October, Sixth Army increased the number of divisions it committed to the fight in Stalingrad from 10 to 11 and the number of infantry (or panzer-grenadier) battalions from 61 to 63. The addition of some replacements to Paulus's army, together with a reshuffling and consolidation of the battalions in XIV Panzer Corps, enabled the army to reorganize one "strong" and 13 "medium strong" battalions. However, six of these 14 battalions were committed to the fight in the Kotluban' and Erzovka regions north of the city. In the city itself, the balance of "average," "weak," and "exhausted" divisions essentially remained as before. Overall, the number of divisions rated "weak" or "exhausted" increased from five (24th Panzer and 71st, 94th, 295th, and 389th Infantry) to six (with the addition of 305th Infantry). Of the two new divisions added to Seydlitz's LI Corps since 5 October, 305th Infantry fell in its rating from "average" to "weak" and 14th Panzer from "strong" to "medium strong."

The fierce, hellish, and unrelenting struggle, which took place under the worst of conditions, also adversely affected the morale of soldiers on both sides. Describing the scene in and west of the Barrikady Factory on 18 October, a senior noncommissioned officer in 24th Panzer Division's 21st Grenadier Regiment termed Stalingrad an "insatiable abyss of chaos," in which "one can scarcely believe that men can still hold out."[160] Once fighting began in the factories' rubble, "It was a nightmare world for the grenadiers; was that movement a piece of sheet-iron swaying in the wind or a stealthy Russian just waiting for his opportunity to cut some throats?"[161] Most depressing of all was the soldiers' persistent perception that they were fighting against an enemy who never "gives themselves up."[162] Lenski, acknowledging two new constant threats to his men, pointed out that casualties within his panzer-grenadier regiments "were substantial on account of the Soviet snipers and the increasingly unpleasant Stalin Organs," which, the division commander asserted, "caused casualties, on average, of ten men a day. It was thus calculated when the Division would be at the end of its tether with its strength in infantry combatants."[163]

If the combat horrors in such appalling conditions were not concern enough, diseases such as jaundice and infectious hepatitis also "wrecked havoc on the German forces investing Stalingrad"; remarking that he and his comrades were still subsisting on a diet of "dry black bread, canned meat and dried vegetables" when he was struck down by jaundice, one German soldier was transported to the rear "because the illness did not heal in Russia and medication for it did not exist."[164] When he reached the dressing station at Karpovka:

> In the aisles and rooms, the severely wounded men were packed close together on straw. Many could not move themselves, while flies crawled around their faces. The bearded faces were emaciated and filthy and mostly through the loss of blood, were white as a sheet, and several were delirious with fever. In the dressing-station, however, there were still no German sisters to alleviate distress . . . Most of them [the wounded] had head-, stomach- or lung-wounds, but above all they had burns.[165]

Like the other panzer and infantry divisions in Seydlitz's LI Army Corps, even before the fighting in Stalingrad's northern factory district, 24th Panzer Division "had been bled white in the previous months of fighting," and the few replacements they received quickly evaporated "like a drop of water on a hot stone."[166] Soon even senior German commanders were objecting to the bloodletting. Speaking on behalf of Sixth Army's decimated panzer divisions, for example, Lenski, the panzer division's commander, sharply criticized the practice of detaching his tanks for use as assault guns to support infantry assaults, claiming "this unintelligible practice" led to "completely useless casualties."[167]

The situation was not much better from the perspective of Paulus's infantrymen. After hearing a report about the results of 276th Infantry Regiment's assault against Soviet forces defending the ravine south of Skul'pturnyi Park, a soldier in one of the regiment's infantry companies recorded:

> "Pocket eliminated, the 5th, 6th, and 7th Companies together have a combat strength of 23 men. Seven of those belong to the 7th Company. The 3rd Battalion has a total of 21 men in its rifle companies. Our battalion had 8 killed, 14 severely wounded, the rest medium and light wounded. . . ."

I was dumbstruck and couldn't utter a word. What had become of our regiment? Where were the replacements? If no experienced and battle-hardened men arrived—what use was the framework of staff and supply units, as well as units of heavy weapons? We infantrymen were the ones in close contact with the enemy. The day's casualties proved that once again.[168]

Later, when he was told his regiment was to support 24th Panzer Division's assault on the Bread Factory instead of being pulled out of line to rest and refit, the same infantryman complained:

> I couldn't believe what I was hearing. Was this gentleman mad or didn't the Division know the whole picture? . . . I repeated my report and mentioned the number of men still fit for action (two battalions with 44 infantrymen altogether). While doing this, my thoughts were with the dead and wounded. With tears welling up, I ended with the sentence: "Should those few men also serve as cannon-fodder?" . . . That was just so typical when you were "lent" to another unit. You were employed to the last man, then—when you'd served your purpose—you were simply discarded.[169]

Admitting that "at no time had the resistance of the enemy been so obstinate and bitter as it was here . . . ," he still insisted: "The Red Dictator could see his prestige disappearing once Stalingrad fell. And fall it would. I was convinced of that."[170]

If German morale was flagging, at least German forces were still advancing. In sharp contrast, Chuikov's soldiers realized that their situation was rapidly deteriorating, with no letup in the German assaults in sight; facing inevitable death or captivity, many were indeed approaching the limits of their endurance. As the increasing number of desertions indicated, some had already exceeded these limits. All the while, the NKVD's special sections—counterintelligence cells within all Soviet armies and *fronts* that were responsible for monitoring force morale and enforcing discipline within the ranks of the troops—kept close track of declining morale by reading the letters soldiers had sent to families and friends. NKVD reports on the letters' contents provide an accurate if gruesome mosaic of the state and morale of Red Army soldiers as the battle in Stalingrad city reached a crescendo.

For example, rifleman I. V. Shibakov wrote, "We received uniforms while still in Iaroslavl' . . . we walked everywhere in them . . . they are already done for. I have but one pair of underwear, but I can never change them, which is also bad. We can never bathe, there is no soap. We have not bathed since the month of May. We are lice-ridden. We drink when we can. It is now cold. Our boots and our overcoats are in bad shape, [but] nowhere can we obtain others. I don't know what we are to do. We are also eating poorly."[171] Another soldier in an evacuation hospital just east of Stalingrad penned: "Our situation is rotten. As you can see, the enemy is always pushing forward. The advantage is again on his side. The majority of us no longer believe in victory. . . . It strikes me that we have no precision and organization in anything, in the rear as well as in the front."[172]

Rifleman V. T. Iakovlev, en route to Stalingrad by train, sketched an equally depressing description of his likely fate:

> I have been in the south where it is very hot, but I should reach Stalingrad in a day and go into battle against the Germans. This means to offer my head for my family. I am writing this letter on the march, before closing with the Germans, and, no doubt, these are the last minutes of my life because I have news about the front. I want to tell you about a train bringing 4,000 men to the front; out of the 4,000 men and most of its officers, a total of 15–20 men remain alive. The time necessary to destroy this division required a total of only 15 minutes.[173]

Yet another NKVD report contained acerbic comments excerpted from soldiers' letters regarding the severity of the food shortage in Chuikov's army. Machine-gunner Aganov in Batiuk's 284th Rifle Division informed his brother, "I am in a very bad state. Three days have passed since I have eaten. The Germans are bombing us very heavily, and, lying here hungry in my foxhole with a machine gun on my back, I lack the strength necessary to fire and wish only to eat and eat."[174] Seconding this complaint, rifleman Kirilov wrote, "Here, they do not eat, they perish from hunger rather than bullets." And rifleman Lopatin: "Soldiers do not see such products as jam and butter. In the rear area they say that everything is for the front, but I now see that the Red Army soldier, healthy and sick alike, are not offered butter but eat otherwise."[175]

More bitterly still, rifleman Mernuts wrote to his wife:

> Marta! Today, I do not know how I shall live through the day. I go to eat, but, as often happens, it is insufficient. You see, they feed us "well." But mugs such as those who sit in the AKhO [Administrative-Economic section] ought to be pushing guns up to the front. They do manage; one of them butter, another sugar, and the third spirits. It is even simpler in the military store, where its entire staff, in dark blue trousers with bright collars, washed with toilet soap, and putting on airs, walk everywhere at a canter, but nowhere can we get leg bindings, and, like a wolf, you have shortages and hunger everywhere. After the war the workers in the

AKhO and military stores will live, while we will most likely once again receive rations.[176]

Writing to his wife from 149th Rifle Brigade in the Rynok pocket, rifleman Abrosimov added: "I am within a hairbreadth of death. Today, on 15 October, my guts are turning inside out and are severely bloated. The reason for all of this is the accursed dumplings and even the wheat kasha. It would be better to go hungry and not eat this food. They have also given us what passes for flour to eat."[177]

The author of this report, Senior NKVD Major N. N. Selivanovsky, chief of Stalingrad Front's Special Sections, dispatched it directly to V. S. Abakumov, deputy Peoples' Commissar for Internal Affairs in Moscow and chief of the NKVD's Directorate for Special Sections. Selivanovsky endorsed the soldiers' comments, provided stark numerical evidence of the inadequate food supplies, and informed Abakumov that he had already relieved the chief of 64th Army's Food Department, the chief quartermaster in 13th Guards Rifle Division, and others and arrested the chief of 62nd Army's AKhO. Although Selivanovsky suggested measures to improve the situation, the combat conditions themselves made their implementation difficult at best.[178]

Selivanovsky sent a similar report to Abakumov in early November. Prefacing the report with a positive judgment ("An examination of the letters written by soldiers and commanders in the units of the Stalingrad Front has established that the majority of the letters express a positive reaction regarding the issues of the defense of the city of Stalingrad and the struggle with the German invaders"), he then quoted from three letters illustrating what he termed "overt anti-Soviet opinions extolling the Fascist army and lack of faith in the Red Army's victory."[179] For example, rifleman Zorin wrote to his relatives: "It is simply impossible for you to realize how sick I am of military music, and I obey no-one in particular. Perhaps in the rear area, they cry 'everything for the front,' but at the front there is nothing; the feeding of our brothers is bad and little is provided. What they say and chatter is not true."[180] Another soldier named Makeev complained to his wife: "I write you that you cannot even imagine so terrible a front, where hundreds of thousands of persons perish each day. We are now so cornered that there is no possibility of escape, and Stalingrad can be considered as given up."[181] Platoon leader Kucherevenko added: "I took over a machine gun platoon where the men were of one national minority; they were slow-witted, and working with them was very difficult. The German machines [tanks] work very well. The 'Messerschmitt-100' is an impressive plane that we seldom shoot down. The 'Junkers' are also formidable aircraft. German bombers have set fire to the entire city, but our antiaircraft men shoot down few of them. They [the antiaircraft guns] work poorly."[182]

Cataloging the complaints topically with characteristic NKVD efficiency, Selivanovsky reported that within 62nd Army alone there were 35 letters complaining about food shortages, many more about illnesses resulting from these shortages, and 12,747 instances where soldiers violated military secrecy by revealing the designation of their units or formations and spoke of command-and-control matters within the *front* or about the encirclement of their units by the enemy. Regarding the appalling shortage of rations, a rifleman in 1st Separate Rifle Battalion wrote to his aunt, "I want you to come to me and bring me whatever food you can. True, it is embarrassing for me to beg, but hunger compels me."[183] Another soldier wrote, "Dear wife, we sit in the forests and have eaten everything that falls into our hands. The green pumpkin—this is the best nourishment we have. Now we have eaten rotten rinds and home-brewed broth."[184] Rifleman Kurnaev told his son, "They have not provided us with any sort of nourishment for six days. We only dig up potatoes from the kitchen-gardens and eat them." Another soldier named Chelushev wrote to his wife, "I am sick with dysentery. The food is scarce and crude, and we have no tobacco and sugar at all. If this continues further, we cannot escape an epidemic. We already have lice—the initial breeding-ground for disaster." And rifleman Kuratov told his sister, "The summer has passed, but not once have we bathed. We have become lice-ridden, and you try to catch them and simply give up. I myself was sick for two weeks and could scarcely drag my legs."[185]

On the matter of violating military secrecy, Selivanovsky cited many letters. For example, to his relatives in Kazakhstan, a soldier named Karnisakov wrote, "I arrived in Stalingrad with an airborne tank unit. They assigned me as a scout. I was in 99th Tank Brigade on 26 August. I reconnoitered in Razgulaevka as a scout and then withdrew to Stalingrad. I crossed the Volga River on 9 September and am situated along the river on the defense 30 kilometers from Stalingrad."[186] Likewise, a soldier named Zhlob reported to a friend, "I was discharged from the hospital and on 1 October was assigned to 137th Tank Brigade and then transferred to 6th Guards Tank Brigade."[187]

Therefore, as the fighting continued in Stalingrad's factory district, commanders on both sides had far more to worry about than the declining strength of their fighting units. At a time when these survivors' determination to fight would decide the outcome of the battle, morale became ever more important. At this point, however, regardless of whether their morale was good or bad, Paulus's and Chuikov's soldiers had little choice but to persevere.

The Assaults on the Krasnyi Oktiabr' and Barrikady Factories, 23–31 October 1942

PLANNING

Under Paulus's close supervision, Seydlitz's LI Corps completed its attack preparations on 22 October. Two days before, at 1730 hours on 18 October, Sixth Army had "chopped" General Schwerin's 79th Infantry Division, less its 226th Regiment, to Seydlitz's control. Seydlitz directed the division to assemble along the Talovoe-Gumrak line west of the northern half of the city beginning on the evening of 18 October and then to deploy forward on the night of 19–20 October to occupy its new sector, carved from 100th Jäger Division's center and left wing. Because Schwerin's division still lacked its 226th Regiment (occupying a new sector), it assumed control over 54th Jäger Regiment on 100th Jäger Division's former left wing. It then deployed the 54th and its own 208th and 212th Regiments abreast between 14th Panzer Division on its left and 100th Jäger Division's 369th Infantry and 227th Jäger Regiments on its right. According to Paulus's order, 79th Infantry Division's left and right boundaries were:

- With 14th Panzer Division on the left—from the middle of Ovrashnaia [upper Krasnyi Oktiabr' village] (grid square 53b) to the ravine in grid 63a-b [the Twin Gullies] and the railroad, and to the multi-story building (*Hochhaus*) in the middle of grid 72a [200 meters north of the northwestern corner of Krasnyi Oktiabr' Factory]; and
- With 100th Jäger Division on the right—from the northern point of the airfield, south of the street parallel to the broad street in the middle of grid 52, southeastward to the railroad, and along the Great [Bannyi] Ravine from 61d2 to 71c3 [the ravine's confluence with the Volga].[1]

The LI Corps issued its final directive for the 23 October assault at 1315 hours the day before (see Maps 71–72). Conducting the corps' main effort, 14th Panzer and 79th Infantry Divisions were to attack eastward in the sector from the southwestern corner of the Barrikady Factory southward to Karusel'naia Street west of the Krasnyi Oktiabr' Factory. Their objective was to capture the Bread and Krasnyi Oktiabr' Factories and to clear Soviet forces from the narrow strip of land between the two factories and the

Volga's western bank. On 14th Panzer Division's left, 305th Infantry Division and 24th Panzer Division's right wing were to conduct a secondary attack to clear Soviet forces from the remainder of the Barrikady Factory and the Volga's western bank east and northeast of the factory.[2]

Seydlitz's order assigned each of his attacking divisions specific missions, axes of attack, objectives, and boundaries as follows:

Main Attack:

- **14th Panzer Division** (103rd and 108th Grenadier and 36th Panzer Regiments and the 64th Motorcycle Battalion) will break through with its panzer spearhead at the railroad northwest of the Bread Factory as the first objective, seize the general line of the multi-story building [*Hochhaus*] in the middle of grid square 72a to the southern edge of the Bread Factory southeast of the Gun Factory and, with 79th and 305th Infantry Divisions, advance to the western bank of the Volga River;
- **79th Infantry Division** (54th Jäger Regiment, with one panzer squadron of 24th Panzer Division with seven tanks, and 208th and 212th Regiments, with 244th and 245th Assault Gun Battalions, will break into the Metal [Krasnyi Oktiabr'] Factory in the enemy's "bridgehead" and clear the enemy from the region west of the Volga River. With the center of gravity [*Schwerpunkt*] on the left, break through the enemy's position along the railroad and, as the first objective, seize the northwestern edge of the Metal Factory.

Secondary Attack:

- **24th Panzer Division** (*Kampfgruppe* Below, with 21st and 26th Grenadier Regiments) will support 305th Infantry Division's assault by fire and, after 305th Infantry Division clears Soviet forces from the Barrikady Factory, reach the Volga's western bank and, wheeling northward, support [305th's] attack by attacking toward the Volga with 26th Grenadier Regiment.
- **305th Infantry Division** (578th, 576th, and 577th Regiments, with one panzer squadron of 24th Panzer Division with six tanks) will advance with its right wing (578th Regiment) through the Barrikady Factory to the Volga's western bank and wheel northward to destroy the Soviet forces on the Volga's western bank in cooperation with the right wing of 24th Panzer Division's *Kampfgruppe* Below (26th Grenadier Regiment);

Boundaries (from left to right, with the responsible division):

- **Between 24th Panzer and 389th Infantry Divisions**—from the mouth of the ravine in grid 76d4 (389th ID) to the multi-story building in grid 85d2 (24th PzD) and the northern edge of the Brick Factory;

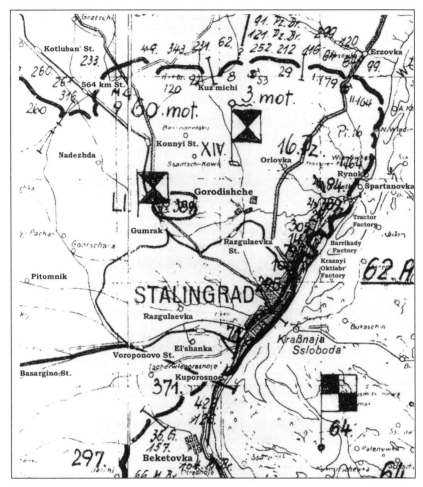

Map 71. Sixth Army's situation, 23–24 October 1942

- **Between 305th Infantry and 24th Panzer Divisions**—from the block of buildings in grid 65 to the northern point of the *Schnellhefter* Block, the southern point of the Sports Ground, and the northeastern edge of the northern face of the Gun Factory to the northern edge of grid 93;
- **Between 14th Panzer and 305th Infantry Divisions**—from the ravine northwest of grid 64 (14th PzD) to the northern point of the massive block of buildings in grid 64b4, the grade on the northwestern edge of the Gun Factory (73b4), and the eastern point of the Bread Factory, and along the ravine from here to the Volga (305th ID);

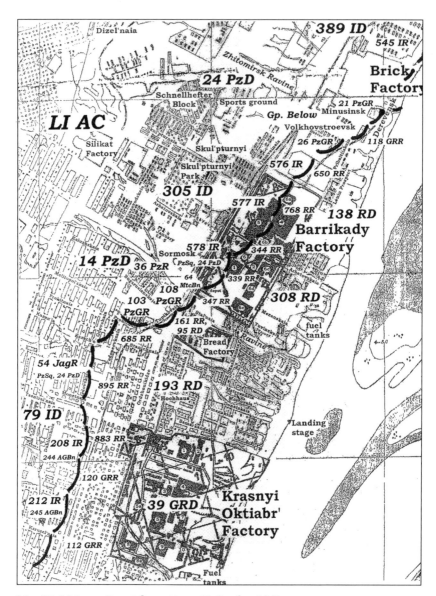

Map 72. LI Army Corps' dispositions, 23 October 1942

- **Between 79th Infantry and 14th Panzer Divisions**—from the ravine in 63a2 to the railroad (79th ID) and the multi-story building in the middle of grid 72a (79th ID) to the Volga 100 meters north of the northeastern point of the Metal Factory;
- **Between 100th Jäger and 79th Infantry Divisions**—from the northern point of the airfield, south of the street parallel to the broad street in the middle of grid 52, southeastward to the railroad and the great [Bannyi] ravine from the [railroad] bridge in grid 61a4 to the ravine's mouth at the Volga (100th JägD);
- **Between 295th Infantry and 100th Jäger Divisions**—unchanged;
- **Between 71st and 295th Infantry Divisions**—unchanged.

As for the configuration of Seydlitz's assaulting forces, 14th Panzer Division formed three *kampfgruppen,* the first from its 64th Motorcycle Battalion and the second and third from its 103rd and 108th Grenadier Regiments, and supported them with two small panzer squadrons from 36th Panzer Regiment, each with roughly 12 tanks. The three *kampfgruppen* were to attack three objectives: the ravine between the Barrikady and Bread Factories, the Bread Factory itself, and the large building in grid square 72a. After seizing these objectives, the combat groups were to drive eastward along the ravine to the Volga River, thereby driving a wedge between the Soviet forces defending the Barrikady and Krasnyi Oktiabr' Factories. Specifically, the *kampfgruppen* from 64th Motorcycle Battalion and 108th Grenadier Regiment, supported by one panzer squadron (the Sauvant squadron) were to attack the ravine and Bread Factory, while 103rd Grenadier Regiment's *kampfgruppe* was to seize the large building to the southwest.[3] The three elements faced the remnants of 308th Rifle Division's 339th and 347th Regiments, supported by a few tanks from 84th Tank Brigade, in the southwestern section of the Barrikady Factory and the ravine to the south; 95th Rifle Division's 161st Regiment in the vicinity of the Bread Factory; and the right wing of 193rd Rifle Division's 685th Regiment in the block of buildings southwest of the Bread Factory and along Prokitnaia Street just west of the railroad line northeast of the Krasnyi Oktiabr' Factory.

Attacking a 2-kilometer-wide sector on 14th Panzer Division's right, 79th Infantry Division was to press eastward across the railroad and engage frontally Soviet forces defending the Krasnyi Oktiabr' Factory, with its attached 54th Jäger and 208th and 212th Regiments deployed abreast from left to right. The division organized three *kampfgruppen* to conduct the assault. On the left, deployed in the narrowest of the division's attack sectors because of its weakness, a battalion-size *kampfgruppe* from 54th Jäger Regiment was supported by a panzer squadron of 24th Panzer Division with seven tanks. This force, supported by consecutive waves of *Luftwaffe* aircraft and advancing in three bounds, was to attack eastward across the railroad line, wheel southward, and penetrate into the northern section of the Krasnyi Oktiabr' Factory, capture Halls 1 and 2 on the factory's grounds, and then advance eastward across the factory's slag heaps to the Volga's western bank.

In 79th Infantry's center, also advancing in three bounds, a *kampfgruppe* made up of 208th Regiment, with a company of assault guns, a company from 179th Pioneer (Engineer) Battalion, and a heavy *Werfer* battalion, was to attack eastward in a gradually widening sector. Its objectives were to capture, first the railroad line, second the Krasnyi Oktiabr' Factory's heavily fortified administrative buildings (called the "H," "Ladder," and "Hook" buildings because of their shape), and third the factory's most important halls (Halls 3–7), situated in the northern half of the factory (see Map 73). On the 79th's right wing, a *kampfgruppe* formed from 212th Regiment included most of the division's 179th Reconnaissance Battalion, a company of assault guns, an antitank company from 179th Antitank Battalion, and a light *Werfer* battalion. The 212th would likewise attack in three bounds, to cross the railroad and enter and capture the southern half of the factory (Halls 8–10 and 8a) and the ravine just south of the factory, and then thrust eastward to the Volga to prevent 62nd Army from reinforcing its forces in the factory.[4] Seydlitz attached the 244th and 245th Assault Gun Battalions, with 13 assault guns between them, to 79th Infantry Division to support the assault by its three *kampfgruppen*.[5]

Typical of the combat formation of the three *kampfgruppen*, the center grouping in each formation formed into two attack wedges of one battalion each. Each wedge, in turn, included two waves of three smaller groups: an assault party armed with machine pistols and hand grenades, reinforced by engineers with satchel charges; a covering party armed with light machine guns, rifles, hand grenades, and mortars, echeloned to the left and right to protect the assault party's flanks; and a cleanup group to clear the captured terrain and bring up additional hand grenades and satchel charges. The first wave was to penetrate the railroad line and then dig in and reorganize; the second wave was to continue its assault through the factory to the Volga beyond; and the third wave followed to clear the remnants of Soviet forces from the factory and also serve as a reserve. The division's attack order categorically forbade its *kampfgruppen* from diverging from the original plan: They were to seize their objectives in the manner and time-frame prescribed and avoid any independent action to take advantage of suddenly arising opportunities—a provision to which some of the regimental commanders objected strenuously.[6]

The 79th Infantry Division's attacking forces faced the entire 39th Guards Rifle Divisions and roughly two-thirds of 193rd Rifle Division. From left to right, 112th and 120th Regiments of Gur'ev's 39th Guards defended

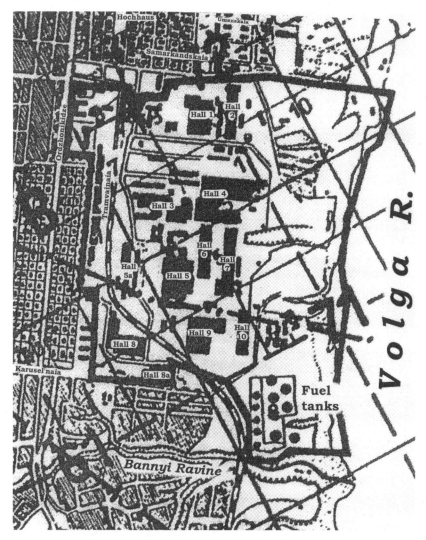

Map 73. The Krasnyi Oktiabr' Factory

the sector from Bannyi Ravine northward to the ravine three blocks south of Tsentral'naia Street opposite 79th Infantry's 212th and 208th Regiments. The mission of Gur'ev's division was to protect western approaches to the southern two-thirds of the Krasnyi Oktiabr' Factory. On the 39th Guards' left, opposite 54th Jäger Regiment, 883rd and 895th Regiments of Sme-khotvorov's 193rd Rifle Division defended the sector from the ravine south of Tsentral'naia Street northward to the railroad and Kazach'ia Ravine northwest of the Krasnyi Oktiabr' Factory. These two regiments had the mission of protecting northeastern approaches to the Krasnyi Oktiabr' Factory.

Conducting a secondary attack on 14th Panzer Division's left, 305th Infantry Division was to clear 62nd Army's forces from the remainder of the Barrikady Factory by employing company- and battalion-size *kampfgruppen* from its 578th, 577th, and 576th Regiments. The strongest of these *kampfgruppen*, 578th Regiment's on the division's right wing, had six tanks from 24th Panzer Division in support and was to attack into the southern part of the factory.[7] The two other *kampfgruppen*, formed in 576th and 577th Regiments on the division's left and in its center, were to advance through the northern and central sections of the factory.

Finally, because it was too weak to attack on its own, 24th Panzer Division's *Kampfgruppe* Below was to join the fight only if and when 305th Infantry Division succeeded in clearing Soviet forces from the factory. Early on 23 October, Lenski's panzer division fielded only 15 tanks, including two command tanks, but no Panzer II or Panzer IV short-barrel models whatsoever.[8]

The 305th Infantry Division's three *kampfgruppen* faced 344th and 768th Regiments of Liudnikov's 138th Rifle Division, reinforced by the remnants of 351st and part of 339th Regiments of Gurt'ev's 308th Rifle Division, supported by a handful of surviving tanks from Belyi's 84th Tank Brigade, which were defending the ruins of the Barrikady Factory. 650th Regiment of 138th Rifle Division, reinforced by the remnants of 37th Guards Rifle Division's 118th Regiment, defended the ravines and gullies along the western bank of the Volga east and northeast of the factory opposite 24th Panzer Division's *Kampfgruppe* Below.

The relatively fresh 79th Infantry Division was able to field *kampfgruppen* numbering as many as 2,500 combat troops in each of its two regiments. Still, because of previous attrition, the formations of the division's 54th Jäger Regiment and 14th Panzer and 305th Infantry Divisions' regiments were far weaker, numbering no more than about 1,000 men each. Thus, Schwerin's assault force totaled about 10,000 infantrymen and panzer-grenadiers. Each of these divisions supported its *kampfgruppen* with between 20 and 30 tanks and assault guns. As for Chuikov's forces, 37th Guards and 193rd Rifle Divisions defended the sector extending northward from Bannyi Ravine past the Krasnyi Oktiabr' Factory with fewer than 5,000 men, and 138th Rifle Division, with the remnants of 308th Rifle and 37th Guards Rifle Divisions, protected the Barrikady Factory and sector to the northeast with a force of fewer than 2,500 men and negligible armor support.

Although Paulus and Seydlitz had high hopes for success, both were concerned about the strength of their attacking forces—and for good reason (see Table 36).

Table 36. The Combat Strength of Sixth Army's (LI Army Corps') Divisions Fighting in Stalingrad on 24 October 1942

LI Army Corps' Main Attack Force

14th Panzer Division

Ration strength	12,070 men	Russians (*Hiwis*) — 523
Combat strength		(Russian auxiliaries)
Panzer-grenadiers	1,640 men	
(4 battalions)		
Motorcycle Battalion	315 men	
Panzer Regiment	829 men	
Artillery	1,184 men	
Flak (AA) Battalion	435 men	
Pioneer Battalion	242 men	
Antitank Battalion	289 men	
Signal Battalion	328 men	
Total combat strength	5,462 men	

79th Infantry Division (two regiments)

Ration strength (est.)	9,000 men
Total combat strength (est.)	4,500 men
Infantry (est.)	2,500 men
(6 battalions)	

LI Army Corps' Secondary Attack Force

24th Panzer Division

Ration strength	11,785 men	Russians (*Hiwis*) – 1,431
Attached units	1,079 men	
Combat strength		
Panzer-grenadiers	1,437 men	
(4 battalions)		
Motorcycle Battalion	453 men	
Panzer Regiment	960 men	
Artillery	1,200 men	
Flak Battalion	349 men	
Pioneer Battalion	313 men	
Antitank Battalion	316 men	
Signal Battalion	359 men	
Total combat strength	5,387 men	

305th Infantry Division

Ration strength	10,578 men	Russians (*Hiwis*) – 1,891
Attached units	988 men	
Combat strength		
Infantry	1,231 men	
(9 battalions)		
Artillery	1,406 men	
Pioneer Battalion	122 men	
Antitank Battalion	none	
Cyclist Battalion	322 men	
Signal Battalion	264 men	
Total combat strength	3,345 men	

LI Army Corps' Supporting Forces

(Left Wing)
389th Infantry Division

Ration strength	8,604 men	Russians (*Hiwis*) – 1,176
Attached units	988 men	

Table 36. (continued)

Combat strength
Infantry	903 men	
(4 battalions)		
Artillery	1,343 men	
Pioneer Battalion	76 men	
Antitank Battalion	none	
Cyclist Battalion	187 men	
Signal Battalion	227 men	
Total combat strength	2,736 men	

(Right Wing)
100th Jager Division

Ration strength	11,700 men	Russians (*Hiwis*) – 1,851
Combat strength		
Infantry	2,806 men	
(5 battalions)		
Artillery	1,542 men	
Pioneer Battalion	365 men	
Antitank Battalion	411 men	
Cyclist Battalion	290 men	
Signal Battalion	351 men	
Total combat strength	5,765 men	

(Other)
295th Infantry Division

Ration strength	10,865 men	Russians (*Hiwis*) – 2,553
Combat strength		
Infantry	1,990 men	
(7 battalions)		
Artillery	1,225 men	
Pioneer Battalion	230 men	
Antitank Battalion	none	
Cyclist Battalion	187 men	
Signal Battalion	255 men	
Total combat strength	2,887 men	

71st Infantry Division

Ration strength	12,277 men	Russians (*Hiwis*) – 1,764
Attached units	5,941 men	
Combat strength		
Infantry	2,235 men	
(7 battalions)		
Artillery	1,607 men	
Pioneer Battalion	218 men	
Antitank Battalion	233 men	
Cyclist Battalion	219 men	
Signal Battalion	211 men	
Total combat strength	4,723 men	

Source: Florian *Freiherr* von und zu Aufsess, "Meldung über Verpflegungs – und Gefechtsstärken der Division, Armee – Oberkommando 6, I a Nr. 4150/42 geh., A. H. Qu., 24. Oktober 1942," in *Die Anlagenbander zu den Kriegstagebuchern der 6. Armee vom 14.09.1942 bis 24.11.1942, Band I* (Schwabach: January 2006), 201–205.

As Table 36 indicates, the strength of LI Army Corps' panzer-grenadier battalions ranged from 350 to 400 men each, and its infantry battalions from as low as 150 men (305th Infantry Division) to almost 500 men (100th Jäger Division). Surprisingly, the number of Russian auxiliaries in many of its divisions (*Hiwis*), which were above and beyond the divisions' ration strength, outnumbered the divisions' German infantrymen and panzer-grenadiers.

As German strength ebbed, so did German morale. For example, when the commander of 79th Infantry Division's 208th Regiment, Lieutenant Colonel Richard Wolf, met with the commander of the neighboring 54th Jäger Regiment, the latter warned him, "You can't expect anything more from my troops. In the long days, we've been completely exhausted and bled dry. The fighting spirit is gone. Just wait till your troops have fought here for fourteen days, you'll be no different." Sadly, Wolf added, "Generally he was proven right."[9]

THE BATTLE FOR THE BARRIKADY AND KRASNYI OKTIABR' FACTORIES, 23–31 OCTOBER

23 October

Despite Paulus's concerns about his army's strength and morale, Seydlitz's forces resumed offensive operations at 0100 hours on 23 October, when assault groups in battalion and company strength from the 305th Infantry Division launched a series of nighttime attacks designed to pry Soviet forces from the numerous gullies and ravines along the western bank of the Volga northeast of the Barrikady Factory and then drive them into the Volga River (see Map 74). Although these assaults generally failed, the sheer novelty of nighttime advances prompted 62nd Army to note, "In distinction from all previous assaults, the enemy launched his attacks beginning at 0100 hours on 23 October, which have yet to cease." Labeling these assaults "unsuccessful," the army's daily report explained that "beginning at 0100 hours on 23 October, the army repelled attacks by enemy infantry and tanks toward the Barrikady and Krasnyi Oktiabr' Factories along the central sector of the front. It fought with small groups of infantry and individual tanks in the remaining sectors of the front."[10]

Yet whatever Soviet elation these minor victories produced was short-lived. With the preliminaries over, Seydlitz's main shock groups began their general assault at 0810 hours on 23 October, preceded by screaming Stuka attacks from 0700 to 0710 and a hail of artillery, *Werfer*, and mortar fire from 0710 to 0810 hours, prompting 62nd Army to admit, "After the unsuccessful night attacks, the enemy repeatedly attacked our positions along the axes of the Barrikady and Krasnyi Oktiabr' Factories with forces of more than one new infantry division (45th or 79th) and heavy tanks, supported by large

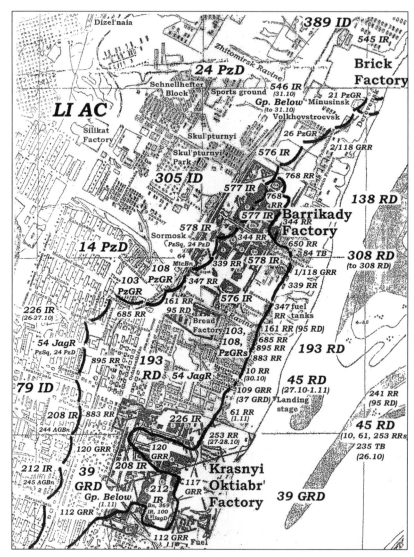

Map 74. LI Army Corps' assault, 23–31 October 1942

groups of aircraft, without regard to their immense losses beginning from 1000 hours."[11] These attacks began what would become yet another disastrous day of fighting.

Against what the Germans termed "determined" resistance, the *kampfgruppen* of Heim's 14th Panzer Division thrust eastward along the ravine south of the Barrikady Factory and southward into the Bread Factory and the block of buildings southwest of the factory. The assaults on 14th Panzer Division's left wing and in the division's center dented the forward defenses of 95th Rifle Division's 161st Regiment and the supporting 347th and 339th Regiments of Gurt'ev's 308th Rifle Division. Even though they stalled after penetrating slightly more than 100 meters eastward along the ravine and gaining a small foothold in the northern part of the Bread Factory, the assault inflicted serious losses on 347th Regiment and destroyed part of its headquarters.[12] Gurt'ev, who was controlling his division's operations from a bunker in the ravine south of the Barrikady Factory, withdrew the remainder of 339th Regiment deeper into the factory and 347th Regiment eastward deeper into the ravine.

On the right wing of Heim's panzer division, the *kampfgruppe* from 103rd Grenadier Regiment pressed back the right wing of 193rd Rifle Division's 685th Regiment several blocks toward the northwestern corner of the Krasnyi Oktiabr' Factory, capturing several buildings before its own assault collapsed. 14th Panzer Division's slow forward progress, coupled with the failure by 79th Infantry Division's 54th Jäger Regiment to penetrate 193rd Rifle Division's stubborn defense along the railroad line farther south, prevented the two divisions from uniting their adjoining flanks and seizing the multistory building in grid square 72a.[13] However, the heavy attacks took a frightful toll on Smekhotvorov's defending riflemen, carving "gaps and intervals in the division's defenses" that, because of the absence of any reserves, could not be plugged.[14]

On 14th Panzer Division's right flank, the two regiments of Schwerin's 79th Infantry Division, together with the attached 54th Jäger Regiment on the division's left wing, advanced to and across the railroad line and into the depths of the Krasnyi Oktiabr' Factory with relative ease. Engaging in a bit of understatement, Chuikov recalled:

> On October 23 the enemy threw into battle the reinforced 79th Infantry Division, together with heavy tanks. They began the attack under mass cover from the air. The main attack was along Tsentral'naia and Karusel'naia Streets toward the Krasnyi Oktiabr' Factory. The center of gravity of the fighting now moved to the sector from the Barrikady Factory to Bannyi Ravine.
>
> In the evening, at a cost of heavy losses, the enemy managed to break through to Stal'naia Street (near the mechanical bakery [the Bread Factory]) and advance along the factory's railroad, piled up with broken trucks. A group of enemy tommy-gunners, nearly a company strong, got through to the northwest of the Krasnyi Oktiabr' Factory.

At dusk our artillery made a heavy attack on enemy tanks and infantry which had concentrated to the northwest of the Krasnyi Oktiabr' Factory.[15]

The 79th Infantry Division's communications officer, Oberleutnant Hubert Mayer, who kept close track of the division's forward progress, provided facts that the 62nd Army commander failed to reveal:

The Soviet first line at the row of wagons [train yard] for the city railroad soon is taken, despite fierce, but short-lived resistance. By 9.30 hours the report comes in that the first objective, the work's [factory] railroad on the western edge of the factory, has been reached. As there is no resistance, the troops ask permission to penetrate the factory and to shift fire to the eastern edge of the factory and the banks of the Volga. It even became clear that individual groups in a quick pursuit had already penetrated into the factory. That was shortly before 11 o'clock. . . .

The right assault wedge quickly penetrated into the factory in the area of Halls 5 and 5a, and by 13.30 had penetrated to the centre of the factory, covering both of its flanks. Then the well-known crisis of the battle occurred. There were no more reports [because all wire communications were lost and radio messages ceased, causing rumors to run rife]. . . .

These are tense hours for the commander. The higher commands demand [but do not receive] new situation reports nearly every 30 minutes. . . .

Then, by 16.00 hours, the relieving news arrives. The good assault troops have done it, they've broken through the work and have penetrated to the steep bank of the Volga. "Reached bank of the Volga east of Hall 7—15.30 hours!" is the proud report of the 5th and 6th Companies. . . . The report is immediately passed on to the left and right assault troops. Infantry Regiment 212 until now had not gotten any similar reports from their troops. . . .

And yet frightening worries set in with me. Only parts of 2nd Battalion (5th and 7th Companies) have achieved this supreme effort. In the factory they ran into elements of the rightmost assault group (Infantry Regiment 212) and now stand on the Volga with them. But the casualties in the advance to the Volga are high . . . there are certainly many scattered stragglers and lost soldiers still in the factory. The clean up is still tying down many parties. The strength of the troops on the river bank is small. They complain of strong flanking fire. . . . Therefore, the 11th Company, the regimental reserve, is ordered to reinforce the bridgehead on the Volga and expand it.[16]

Despite 79th Infantry Division's often spectacular advance, Mayer admitted that after nine hours of fighting the exposed flanks of 208th and 212th Regiments' lead elements threatened the two regiments "like a sword of Damocles." Although the *kampfgruppe* on 212th Regiment's left wing also swept through the factory and captured Halls 8 and 9, intense fighting was ongoing for Hall 10, and the *kampfgruppe* on the regiment's right wing was being chewed up in the fight to protect the *balka* on its right flank while also clearing its rear area of bypassed Soviet troops. Therefore, "decisive success was still lacking" because 212th Regiment was engaged in bitter fighting "for every house, every cellar and every street in the part of the city between the city railway and the factory railway west of the big Hall 8."[17]

In this emerging stalemate, in Mayer's judgment, "The main obstacle to success was the fire of the enemy heavy weapons, which is directed from Height 102.5 [Mamaev Kurgan]." Compounding Schwerin's growing dilemma, even though the combat wedge on 208th Infantry Regiment's right wing had reached the Volga River, after seizing Halls 3 and 6 the attack by the wedge on its left (as well as by 54th Jäger Regiment's *kampfgruppe*) stalled in front of Hall 4. As a result, the regiment's left flank now extended from the western approaches to Hall 4 all the way back to its jumping-off positions and therefore was vulnerable to possible enemy counterattack.[18]

The 79th Infantry Division's combat report at 2310 hours on 23 October substantiated Mayer's account of the day's actions:

The infantry attacked at 0810 hours after an artillery and Stuka preparation. While 208th and 212th Infantry Regiments reached the factory railroad between 61b2 and 63b2 by 0910 hours in one bound, the assault party of 212th Infantry Regiment reached the small ravine in 61b3 [near the southeastern corner of the factory]. However, although maintaining contact with its neighbors on both flanks, 54th Jäger Regiment was not able to cross the railroad bridge over the *balka* in 63b2 [the twin ravine]. This was prevented by strong enemy resistance from bunkers and limited possibilities for the infantry and assault guns to approach. After reorganizing the units and a renewed artillery and Stuka preparation, the attacks continued across the factory railroad at 1000 hours. While they succeeded in penetrating into the Metallurgical Factory itself in their assigned sectors, the assault party on 212th Infantry Regiment's right was not able to get across the *balka* because of determined resistance from a fortified school building. The open right flank, which had resulted from this advance, was being occupied and defended by a police squadron and one company.

Meanwhile, on the left flank, contact with 54th Jäger Regiment was lost because its feeble strength was insufficient to maintain it. After fierce fighting during which the enemy defended himself determinedly, Hall 4 and both Hall 6s were taken. One hour later, Hall 5 was also in our hands. At 1615 hours, reports came in that three companies had reached the steep banks of the Volga. By 1800 hours, it was reported that Hall 4 (the southern one) and the factory southeast of it had also been stormed. Very lively activity by our own Stukas; very little enemy air activity. . . .

The 54th Jäger Regiment, including the light mortar battalion, was released from its current subordination and subordinated to 100th Jäger Division. The subordination of 244th Assault Gun Battalion was also ended. On the other hand, the Croat Regiment (367th of 100th Jäger Division) was subordinated to 79th Infantry Division.[19]

The determined initial assault by Schwerin's 79th Infantry Division indeed shattered the Soviets' defenses west of the Krasnyi Oktiabr' at its most vulnerable point: the adjoining sectors of 112th and 120th Regiments of Gur'ev's 39th Guards Rifle Division and 883rd and 895th Regiments of Smekhotvorov's 193rd Rifle Division. In 79th Infantry Division's center, 208th Regiment's attack drove 39th Guards Rifle Division's 120th Regiment back across the railroad and into the factory's ground, ultimately capturing Halls 5, 5a, 3, 6, and 7 and forcing 120th Regiment to fortify itself inside Hall 4 and to withdraw its forces to Halls 1 and 2 in the northern part of the factory. During this fighting, Major A. Ia. Goriachev, commander of 120th Regiment, was wounded and later evacuated to the rear. On 79th Infantry Division's right, 212th Regiment's assault routed the forces on 112th Guards Rifle Regiment's right wing and center and captured most of Halls 8 and 9 before the regiment's survivors reorganized themselves sufficiently to more stoutly defend Hall 10. By day's end, however, Gur'ev's two guards regiments succeeded in halting the German advance in and around Hall 10 in the eastern third of the factory. They also managed to erect credible defenses along the flanks of 79th Infantry Division's penetration, specifically in Halls 1 and 2 and part of Hall 4 along the northern flank and along the ravine and in the southern part of Hall 8 along the southern flank.[20]

Summarizing the results of this fighting, albeit somewhat optimistically, 62nd Army recorded, "39th Gds. RD is fighting with attacking enemy infantry. The enemy managed to percolate through the forward edge of 112th Gds. RR with individual groups. Measures have been taken to destroy them. One group was almost completely destroyed. The regiments are in their previous defensive positions."[21]

However, on 79th Infantry Division's left wing, according to German accounts, 54th Jäger Regiment's assault failed miserably and in no way kept pace with the advance by its two neighboring regiments to the south. Assaulting the defenses of 193rd Rifle Division's 883rd and 895th Regiments west of the railroad and north of the Krasnyi Oktiabr' Factory, the *jägers'* advance faltered almost immediately after it began. 79th Infantry Division's war diary kept track of the regiment's limited forward progress:

> The 54th Jäger Regiment on the left flank at the railroad bridge across the *Balka* at 62d2 [the twin ravine] is not able to cross the railway due to strong enemy resistance from bunkers and limited avenues of approach. ... The 54th Regiment, due to high losses, leadership casualties, and very strong enemy resistance has gotten pinned down at 11.00 hours. Only the right wing of 54th Regiment in its allotted sector has managed to get past the first railway.[22]

As a result, as early as midday 193rd Rifle Division's 883rd and 895th Regiments still clung to their defenses along and east of the railroad line, thereby preventing 14th Panzer and 79th Infantry Divisions from linking up their adjoining flanks.

The 62nd Army's reports, however, described a far less sanguine picture of 193rd Rifle Division's situation as it tried to fend off 14th Panzer Division's and 54th Jäger Regiment's assaults:

> 193rd RD engaged in intense defensive fighting throughout the day with an enemy force of more than two infantry regiments and 35 tanks (heavy and medium) attacking from Tsentral'naia, Dzhankoiskaia, and Karusel'naia Streets. During the day, the enemy brought reserves forward and committed them into battle.
>
> The division's units continue to remain in their previous places, but gaps and intervals have formed in the combat formations of their units as a result of its heavy losses.
>
> The enemy, resuming his attacks as darkness fell, succeeded in filtering through to the vicinity of Stal'naia Street (the Bread Factory) with 6 tanks, of which two were burned and the remainder continue to fight, into the Profintern and Tsentral'naia Street region with groups of submachine gunners, and into the Krasnyi Oktiabr' Factory area with up to a company of submachine gunners.
>
> The units have suffered heavy losses (according to preliminary data, up to 70 percent of their personnel). The fighting is continuing as the enemy conducts night attacks and intense night shelling.[23]

Thus, by day's end on 23 October, 79th Infantry Division's 208th and 212th Regiments had gained a significant lodgment in the Krasnyi Oktiabr' Factory and an iron grip on many of its buildings, including Halls 3, 5, 6, 7, 8, part of Hall 4, and, after a heavy fight, Hall 10. However, due to the lack of progress on its flanks (in particular that of 54th Jäger Regiment, which failed to keep up with its neighbors to the south), Halls 1, 2, and 3 in the northern part of the factory and the southern part of Hall 8 to the south remained in Soviet hands. These victories were also costly to 79th Infantry Division. Although it assumed that it had inflicted heavy losses on the Soviet defenders while capturing 75 prisoners, the division lost 83 officers and men killed, 364 wounded, and 1 missing—tragically high given the initial strength of the division's *kampfgruppen*.[24]

Meanwhile, on the left flank of LI Corps' main attack force, the three *kampfgruppen* of Oppenländer's 305th Infantry Division began their assault against 62nd Army's defenses in and north of the Barrikady Factory at 0810 hours. Shortly thereafter, 24th Panzer Division's *Kampfgruppe* Below joined the assault north of the factory but with minimal progress against determined Soviet resistance. Supported by their own artillery and by fires from 24th Panzer Division's 89th Artillery Regiment, the division conducted its main effort with 578th Regiment's *kampfgruppen*, supported by six tanks from 24th Panzer Division, on its right wing. This assault struck the railroad yards, smashed adjacent warehouses, and severely damaged halls in the southern half of the Barrikady Factory, which were defended by the remnants, perhaps two weak battalions, of 308th Rifle Division's 347th and 339th Regiments, reinforced later in the day by 138th Rifle Division's 650th Regiment. The *kampfgruppen* from 305th Infantry's 576th and 577th Regiments attacking the northern part of the factory had even less success, advancing only about 100 meters against fierce resistance from 138th Rifle Division's 768th and 344th Regiments (see Map 75).

Thus, as in previous attacks, stiffened Soviet resistance proved too strong for the weakened division to overcome:

Despite the auspicious beginning with beautiful autumn sunshine in the morning, a heavy cover of low-lying clouds rolled in from the northeast at 1030 hours, canceling all *Luftwaffe* operations. The Russians capitalized on this opportunity by launching a strong counterattack in the Gun Factory and wresting Hall 4 from 305th Infantry Division. The strong flanking fire provided by Group Below [24th PzD] could not prevent its loss. With Hall 4 now in enemy hands, the men of 26th Panzer Grenadier Regiment [24th PzD] now formed a salient which would greatly assist in the recapture of the hall, and their fire would hinder Russian movements between the hall and the Volga.

The Russian counterattack and capture of Hall 4 had dealt a heavy blow to the men of 305th Infantry Division. During a visit to his division commander, Colonel General Paulus was informed at 1230 hours that 305th Infantry Division was no longer in a position for large-scale

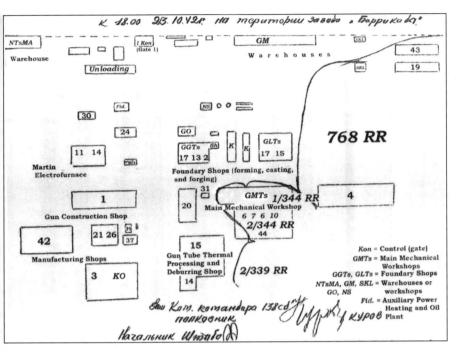

Map 75. Dispositions of 138th Rifle Division's 768th and 344th Regiments in the Barrikady Factory, 1800 23 October 1942

assault. This meant that the right wing of Group Below was not moving forward. . . .

The low-lying clouds that had moved in at 1030 hours cleared up at 1300 hours, and, soon after, the Stukas reappeared in Stalingrad's skies. Hall 4 in the Gun Factory was attacked by Stukas and bombers, as well as by the artillery of 305th Infantry Division and 89th Panzer Artillery Regiment. For the remainder of the day, both sides crouched in foxholes and cellars while the artillery battled it out around them.[25]

Regarding this fight, 62nd Army simply reported, "138th RD, with 118th RR, is repelling attacks by the enemy (305th ID) against the Barrikady Factory from the west and southwest. The forces of 650th RR are fighting intensely with enemy infantry and tanks, which are trying to penetrate through the Barrikady Factory to the Volga."[26]

Assessing the day's action, Paulus and Seydlitz had clearly fallen far short of achieving their desired ends. Not only were Chuikov's forces still holding out in parts of the Barrikady and Krasnyi Oktiabr' Factories; they had also prevented the Germans from thrusting eastward in between the two factories to the Volga so as to split Chuikov's shrinking bridgehead in half. With his defenses in the southern part of the northern factory district still coherent, once again Chuikov had an opportunity to throw fresh reserves into the struggle and to continue bleeding dry Paulus's already weary army—but only if he could find the necessary reserves. Nevertheless, the OKW optimistically reported at day's end:

> In Stalingrad, during the course of fierce street fighting, the attacking infantry and panzer units threw the enemy back, captured part of the grounds of the "Krasnyi Oktiabr" Factory, and reached the Volga River. Bombers, including dive-bombers [Stukas], inflicted massive strikes on enemy positions. In addition, aircraft struck enemy artillery firing positions on the islands and the eastern bank of the Volga day and night.[27]

Army Group B's daily operational summary was a bit more precise and accurate:

> The 79th Infantry Division seized the railroad in the western part of the metallurgical factory [Krasnyi Oktiabr'] (its immediate mission) and, with the help of assault groups, penetrated into the center of the factory. Most of the factory's shops were seized. The fighting is continuing. The 14th Panzer Division liquidated pockets of enemy resistance on the grounds of the Bread Combine. According to unconfirmed information, one assault group from 79th Infantry Division penetrated to the Volga.[28]

Broadening its view to include the continuing fight in Stalingrad's northern suburbs, the army group's intelligence officer added, "In Stalingrad city, the enemy abandoned several buildings in the vicinity of the Metallurgical Factory and Bread Factory. Strong enemy reconnaissance activity had no success. After strong resistance, the enemy abandoned Spartanovka, due north of Stalingrad. He was holding on to only several buildings on the eastern outskirts of that point."[29]

Confirming these Germans' reports, the Red Army General Staff's daily operational summary portrayed a more critical situation as compared to the army commander's:

> **62nd Army** conducted intense fighting with enemy in the Stalingrad region on 23 October. The enemy, after an artillery and aircraft bombardment of our positions, resumed fierce attacks in the sector from the Barrikady Factory to the Bannyi Ravine with a force of up to two infantry divisions with 45 tanks at 1000 hours on 23 October.

138th RD, together with 118th Gds. RR, 37th Gds. RD, repulsed several attacks by the enemy on the Barrikady Factory up to 1800 hours on 23 October. The enemy resumed his attacks at 1800 hours. The fighting degenerated into hand-to-hand combat and continued after nightfall.

308th RD repelled enemy attacks in the southeastern part of the Barrikady Factory.

193rd RD conducted fierce defensive fighting with an enemy force of up to an infantry division with 35 tanks but held on to its positions by day's end. The fighting was continuing. Individual groups of enemy succeeded in penetrating: a group with 6 tanks—in the vicinity of Stal'naia Street; a group of submachine gunners—to the corner of Profintern and Tsentral'naia Streets; and an infantry group of up to one company—to the northwestern corner of the Krasnyi Oktiabr' Factory.

39th Gds. RD repelled several attacks by the enemy and held on to its previous positions.

The army's remaining units held on to their previous positions.[30]

As Chuikov assessed the day's action, his daily situation report acknowledged that his army had suffered more than 60 percent losses and that the combat formations of his units were "sharply weakened over the previous days of fighting."[31] Making matters worse, there was no way to make up for the losses because his reserves "were used up"; as a result, his army faced "the real threat of enemy forces penetrating through to the Volga River in the sector north of the Bannyi Ravine," thereby "cutting off the units of 138th and 308th RDs."[32] He therefore requested that Eremenko provide all possible artillery and multiple rocket launcher support to his beleaguered forces.

The LI Corps, despite the limited gains and heavy losses its forces experienced on 23 October, at 1855 hours ordered 305th Infantry, 14th Panzer, and 79th Infantry Divisions to resume their assault at dawn the next morning against the identical objectives of the previous day. Specifically, Schwerin's 79th Infantry Division, now with one battalion of 54th Jäger Regiment attached, was to clear Soviet forces from the Krasnyi Oktiabr' Factory and "the entire front sector" along the western bank of the Volga, "form a solid front to the south," and be prepared to commit a strong group (at least an infantry battalion from Sanne's 100th Jäger Division) from behind its left wing to thrust northward in support of 14th Panzer Division.

On 79th Infantry Division's left, Heim's 14th Panzer Division (reinforced by the remainder of 54th Jäger Regiment) was to capture the Bread Factory and link up with 79th Infantry Division's left wing southwest of the factory and, later, along the western bank of the Volga. On 14th Panzer's left, Group Jänecke (305th Infantry Division) was to clear the remainder of the Barrikady Factory, link up with 14th Panzer's 64th Motorcycle Battalion southwest of the Bread Factory, and clear the strip of territory between the Barrikady and Bread Factories in cooperation with 14th Panzer Division. The boundary between 79th Infantry and 14th Panzer Divisions was "the wide street [Tsentral'naia] from grid square 63c to grid 62b, north of the Gun Factory, to northern edge of the Gun Factory and, further, to the Volga."[33]

Schwerin decided to focus 79th Infantry Division's efforts on capturing Hall 4 in the Krasnyi Oktiabr' Factory, the hall that the Soviets called the Martenovskii Shop. This shop was defended by elements of 39th Guards Rifle Division's 120th Regiment, whose riflemen were lodged in the shop's tall undestroyed chimneys, where they could rain down fire upon virtually every sector occupied by 79th Infantry Division's forces. Schwerin directed his division's 212th Regiment to defend Halls 9 and 10 in the southern half of the factory against possible counterattacks by 112th Regiment of Gur'ev's 39th Guards Rifle Division, which was deployed to its front and on its right flank. Meanwhile, his division's 208th Regiment, supported by 179th Engineer Battalion, was to conduct a two-phase attack to dislodge 39th Guards Division's 120th Regiment from Hall 4 and the rest of the central and northern sections of the factory.

According to Schwerin's plan, during the first phase of the attack, beginning at 0300 hours, one battalion of 208th Regiment, together with stay-behind forces from 212th Regiment and 3rd Company, 179th Engineer Battalion, was to liquidate Soviet forces in the factory's administrative buildings (Hall 5a), which were bypassed the previous day, in order to shorten the division's front. During the second phase, 208th Regiment's 2nd and 3rd Battalions were to attack eastward from Halls 3, 6, and 7 and seize Hall 4 (the Martenovskii Shop); on the regiment's left wing, its 1st Battalion was to attack northward to seize Halls 1 and 2 and link up with 54th Jäger Regiment, which was to attack from southeastward across the railroad under 14th Panzer Division's control to reach the factory's northern edge and assault Halls 1 and 2 from the north.[34]

Meanwhile, on 79th Infantry Division's left, Heim's 14th Panzer Division was to attack the defenses of 95th Rifle Division's 161st Regiment in and around the Bread Factory with its 64th Motorcycle Battalion, supported by the division's remaining tanks. Simultaneously, 14th Panzer's 103rd and 108th Grenadier Regiments, each fielding a single weak battalion-size *kampf-gruppe*, were to attack eastward along the ravine and Stal'naia Street between the Barrikady and Bread Factories to destroy the remnants of 308th Rifle Division's 347th and 339th Regiments and reach the Volga's western bank at the mouth of the ravine. On 14th Panzer's right wing along the main railroad line, two weak battalion-size *kampfgruppen* from 54th Jäger Regiment were to advance eastward from the railroad and then southeastward toward the Krasnyi Oktiabr' Factory to penetrate the defenses of 193rd Rifle

Division's 883rd and 685th Regiments roughly six blocks northeast and north of the Krasnyi Oktiabr' Factory and link up with 79th Infantry Division's 208th Regiment along the northern edge of the factory.

On 14th Panzer Division's left, Oppenländer, commander of 305th Infantry Division, had declared his division "unfit" to conduct a major attack the day before because three of his seven battalions were rated "exhausted," the remainder were "weak" at best, and his division had only about 1,200 surviving infantrymen. Nonetheless, Seydlitz ordered the 305th to resume its assaults against the remnants of Liudnikov's 138th and Gurt'ev's 308th Rifle Divisions, lodged in the rubble of the northern and eastern sections of the Barrikady Factory and in the numerous ravines and gullies along the Volga's western bank east and northeast of the factory. The corps commander insisted that he do so to protect 14th Panzer Division's left wing. Therefore, with combat forces on both sides reduced to little more than weak battalion and company groups, the ensuing fight turned into a desperate struggle for survival amid the wreckage of the factory's ruined shops, halls, and warehouses, with gains and losses on either side measured in tens of meters.

24 October

Attacking as planned on 24 October, 79th Infantry Division's 208th and 212th Regiments began operations to clear Soviet forces from the Krasnyi Oktiabr' Factory's administrative building (Hall 5a) at 0300 hours. After completing this task by midmorning despite frequent Soviet counterattacks, the two regiments expanded their attacks later in the day to encompass their objectives in the eastern and northern sections of the factory. Once again, Oberleutnant Mayer kept track of the action, providing a vivid description of the chaos and carnage in the ruins of the Krasnyi Oktiabr' Factory. His vivid portrayal of the horror is characteristic of the struggles within every part of Stalingrad's factory district:

> On this day as well, the objectives of the battle were not reached despite strong fire support. However, the front on the eastern edge of the factory held against all Soviet attempts to break through and penetrate into the factory. Hall 4 was encircled from the west and the south. From the factory, Halls 8 and 8a were taken. But the fight for the streets west of the factory [actually northwest and north] only yielded little ground. Tangled with the enemy in the bitterest of close combat, we saw the sun set in the evening of October 24th. I was all the more surprised when the Wehrmacht communiqué in the next days reported the taking of the entire "Red October" factory. When I called division about it, the divisional commander told me he was as amazed, but not guilty of the report, as he

only passed on what was reported to him. This brought the first phase of the battle for "Red October" to a close.

The heavy artillery fire, the rolling bombings by Stukas and close-support aircraft, the salvoes of the rocket batteries surpassed anything seen in battle till then. The giant craters of the heaviest caliber turned the city into a pure lunar landscape. The house high heaps of rubble of the many massive buildings, the giant concrete slabs of the factory halls with their grotesquely heavy and very heavy iron bars [sic] sticking out turned a walk on the terrain into a wearying climb, on which death was waiting in the shape of a bullet from some hidden sniper.[35]

The lieutenant's amazement was entirely justified, for on 24 October the OKW announced, triumphantly (though prematurely):

During the course of fierce fighting of local significance in Stalingrad, German forces completely occupied the grounds of the "Krasnyi Oktiabr'" Factory, with the exception of one shop, captured the enemy's prepared positions, and seized several city blocks, as well as Stalingrad's northern suburb of Spartanovka, with exception to several buildings. The civilian and industrial regions of the city captured the day before have been cleared of the remnants of enemy forces.[36]

Contrary to the OKW's optimistic account, instead of seizing the entire Krasnyi Oktiabr' Factory on 24 October 79th Infantry's two regiments failed to capture all of their objectives. Advancing on the division's left wing, 208th Regiment succeeded in capturing the western half of Hall 4 and the southern sections of Halls 1 and 2 and actually pushed forward some of its forces far enough to reach the Volga's western bank in a narrow sector east of the factory. However, during the afternoon Gur'ev, commander of 39th Guards Rifle Division, committed his reserve 117th Regiment in a counterattack to regain some or all of the lost ground. The 117th attacked from the dense network of gullies and ravines on the Volga's western bank and from scattered strongpoints flanking 208th Regiment's narrow penetration and managed to eliminate the German penetration by nightfall.

Meanwhile, on 79th Infantry's right wing, 212th Regiment tried to expel 39th Guards Rifle Division's 112th Regiment from the southern parts of Halls 8 and 8a. The 212th failed largely because it continued to receive intense and damaging small-arms, machine-gun, and mortar fire from Soviet forces lodged in the ravine due south of the factory as well as devastating artillery fire from the commanding heights of Mamaev Kurgan to the south. Commenting on the day's action, 62nd Army reported:

The 39th Gds. RD held on to its occupied positions. The 117th RR is fighting with the enemy in the Krasnyi Oktiabr' Factory and will subsequently be committed at the boundary between 112th and 120th RRs. The fighting is continuing. The 1st Battalion of 13th Gds. RD's 34th Gds. RR [dispatched from Stalingrad center city] is protecting the boundary on the right and is defending along the railroad line from the FUTB [fuel dump southeast of the Barrikady Factory] to the northwestern outskirts of the Krasnyi Oktiabr' Factory.[37]

Contrasting sharply with 79th Infantry Division's limited successes in the Krasnyi Oktiabr' Factory, to the north the already decimated *kampfgruppen* from 14th Panzer Division's 64th Motorcycle Battalion and 103rd and 108th Panzer Grenadier Regiments proved too weak to capture the Bread Factory and adjacent ravine and to collapse the dangerous salient bulging westward to the railroad between it and 79th Infantry Division. Responding dutifully to Seydlitz's orders, small *kampfgruppen* from Heim's panzer division once again engaged the defenses of 95th Rifle Division's 161st Regiment in the Bread Factory and part of 308th Rifle Division's 347th and 339th Regiments in the ravine south of the Barrikady Factory, while the attached 54th Jäger Regiment assaulted the defenses of 193rd Rifle Division's 685th and 883rd Regiments in the debris-scattered streets and ruined buildings north of the Krasnyi Oktiabr' Factory. However, none of these forces reached their assigned objectives.

In the most dramatic and promising action in 14th Panzer Division's sector, a *kampfgruppe* formed around the nucleus of Captain Erich Domaschk's 2nd Battalion, 103rd Grenadier Regiment, assaulted eastward along the ravine south of the Barrikady Factory. Although this attack succeeded in puncturing the first Soviet defensive line, it, too, faltered after advancing about 100 meters in the face of fierce resistance by the remnants of Gurt'ev's 308th Rifle Division. This action prompted 62nd Army to report cryptically, "308th RD repelled attacks by the enemy in the southeastern part of the Barrikady Factory."[38] Although the assault by 14th Panzer's 64th Motorcycle Battalion initially breached 161st Regiment's defenses on the northern edge of the Bread Factory and gained a small foothold in the factory's main administrative building, it also ended in failure after 161st Regiment mounted a counterattack. Likewise, 54th Jäger Regiment's attacks collapsed less than 100 meters east of the railroad line.

The limited successes registered by his *kampfgruppen* in the vicinity of the ravine and Bread Factory were of little comfort to Heim, whose losses during the two days of fighting prompted him to notify LI Corps' headquarters: "0900 hours—In his command post, the commander of 14th Panzer

Division described the severity of the costly battle at the Bread Factory. The trench [fighting] strength of the division has now been reduced to approximately 750 infantrymen. The Division Commander believes that, without reinforcements, no further significant advances can be achieved."[39]

During the heavy fighting along the ravine and in and around the Bread Factory, one of 14th Panzer Division's *kampfgruppen* drove a wedge between the defenses of 308th and 193rd Rifle Divisions; although shallow, these actually overran Gurt'ev's headquarters and forced him to seek refuge in the rubble at the southern edge of the Barrikady Factory. In response to a direct order from Chuikov, General Smekhotvorov, commander of 193rd Rifle Division, assembled a small group of 10 submachine-gunners and personally led them on a foray to find and rescue Gurt'ev. Smekhotvorov succeeded in his effort and, together with Liudnikov, organized counterattacks that managed to contain 14th Panzer Division's advance.[40]

That evening, 62nd Army provided the General Staff with an abbreviated report summarizing the intense fighting between the southern edge of the Barrikady Factory and the railroad line to the southwest:

193rd RD—161st RR repelled attacks by enemy infantry and tanks on its right wing.

The enemy resumed his attacks with a force of more than an infantry regiment and 30 tanks at 1700 hours, trying to reach the Volga with more than two battalions and 17 tanks [advancing] southward along Krasno-presnenskaia Street toward the northern outskirts of Krasnyi Oktiabr' and more than a battalion with tanks along Stal'naia Street trying to reach the Volga.

In the sector of [193rd RD's] 895th RR, enemy tanks reached its command post, and the infantry following behind wedged into the regiment's fragmented combat formation of the regiment and is fighting within its defensive sector. The division lost more than 300 men. The fighting is continuing.[41]

Finally, on 14th Panzer's left flank, Oppenländer's 305th Infantry Division tried once again to resume its assaults to clear Soviet forces from the Barrikady Factory. However, after seizing part of the factory's main mechanical workshop (identified by the Germans as Hall 6b), this assault also faltered when Liudnikov committed his 344th Regiment to reinforce 768th and 650th Regiments' defenses along the factory's eastern side. Liudnikov's defense was supported by intense artillery fire from the Volga's eastern bank. However, in renewed assaults later in the day, 305th Infantry's 578th Regiment, supported on the left by 577th Regiment, managed to capture the main mechanical workshops and Hall 4 to the north. Although 62nd

Army initially bragged that 138th Rifle Division and 118th Regiment "repelled attacks by enemy infantry and tanks against the Barrikady Factory from the west and southwest," later it grudgingly admitted that "the enemy, by committing reserves into combat, launched a new attack at 1630 hours and captured the central and southwestern part of the Barrikady Factory" (see Map 76).[42]

Reflecting the deadly toll that the day's fighting had on the attackers, the combat strength of 14th Panzer's 103rd Grenadier Regiment fell to 40 men by day's end, which constituted not only "the remains of the battalion" but also "the last panzergrenadiers in the regiment."[43] While Oppenländer continued to assert that his 305th Division was exhausted and not capable of fulfilling any combat missions whatsoever, 14th Panzer reported that its tank strength had decreased to 11 armored vehicles (including 2 Pz. II, 1 Pz. II short, 7 Pz. III long, and 1 Pz. IV long tanks); 24th Panzer reported that its strength was down to 11 tanks (1 Pz. II, 3 Pz. III short, and 7 Pz. III long tanks). Likewise, 244th and 245th Assault Gun Battalions were down to a total of 7 assault guns. In essence, the heavy fighting had pulled LI Corps' "armored teeth."[44]

Reflecting on the action on 24 October, Chuikov later claimed that his forces had beaten back the Germans' initial attacks during the morning, inflicting heavy losses on them; but thereafter things became more difficult:

> The Germans then threw in their second line and their reserves. At 4.30 P.M. they succeeded in over-running the central and southwest parts of the Barrikady Factory.
>
> At 6 P.M. enemy infantry and tanks reached the command post of the 895th Rifle Regiment [193rd Rifle Division]. The Regimental Commander, Major Ustinov, got in touch with us by radio and asked for our "katyushi" to fire a salvo at his command post. "There is no other way" were the final words of his request.
>
> Some two enemy infantry battalions and seventeen tanks approached along Krasnopresnenskaia Street toward the northwest gates of the Krasnyi Oktiabr' Factory. The 117th Regiment of Gur'ev's division waged a bitter battle with them, but small groups of German tommy-gunners managed to get through into the factory workshops.
>
> At the end of the day, we were told that the command post of the 1045th Regiment [284th Rifle Division] had been destroyed by a direct hit from a bomb. The Commander of the regiment, Lieutenant Colonel Timoshin, had been killed.[45]

The Red Army General Staff's daily operational report accurately summarized the day's generally unpleasant fighting in greater detail:

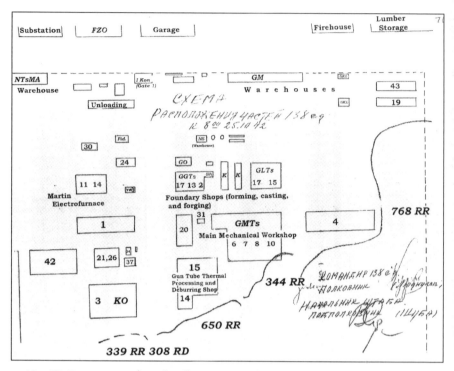

Map 76. Dispositions of 138th Rifle Division in the Barrikady Factory, 0800 25 October 1942

62nd Army continued to engage in fierce defensive fighting with enemy infantry and tanks in the Spartanovka and Barrikady and Krasnyi Oktiabr' Factory regions. Fighting raged on in the southwestern part of Spartanovka and on the territory of the Barrikady Factory.

149th RB's units abandoned Izumrudnaia and Terskaia Streets under heavy enemy pressure.

138th RD and 118th Gds. RR [37th Gds. RD] held on to their previous positions after repelling an attack by an enemy force of up to an infantry battalion with 8 tanks [305th ID's 578th IR].

308th RD repulsed an enemy [14th PzD] attack on the territory of the Barrikady Factory on 24 October.

193rd RD and 161st RR fought with an enemy force of up to two infantry battalions with 17 tanks [14th PzD and 54th Jäger R] in the northern part of the Krasnyi Oktiabr' Factory and a force of up to an infantry battalion with tanks, which was trying to penetrate to the Volga River along Stal'naia Street.

39th Gds. RD continued to hold on to its previous positions and destroyed enemy submachine gunners [79th ID] penetrating into the Krasnyi Oktiabr' Factory with part of its forces.

The positions of the army's remaining units were unchanged.[46]

As a result of the heavy but indecisive fighting on 24 October, on 79th Infantry Division's left wing, 208th Regiment held Halls 3, 5a, 5, 6, 7, and 10 in the central third of the Krasnyi Oktiabr' Factory but was still on the outskirts of Hall 4 in the factory's center and Halls 1 and 2 in the northern third. On 79th Infantry's right wing, 212th Regiment occupied Hall 9 and most of Hall 8 in the factory's southern third but was still outside Hall 8a along the factory's southern edge. By this time, Schwerin's infantrymen faced the remnants of 39th Guards Rifle Division's 112th Regiment in the ravine south of the factory, in the southern half of Halls 8 and 8a, and dug in along the narrow strip of ground between Hall 10 and the Volga's western bank and 120th Regiment, which held most of Hall 4 and all of Halls 1 and 2.

In the swath of ground from the Krasnyi Oktiabr' Factory northward to the Barrikady Factories, 14th Panzer Division's attached 54th Jäger Regiment was dug in along and east of the railroad line several blocks northwest of the Krasnyi Oktiabr' Factory eastward along Dolinskaia Street to roughly Mashinnaia Street. The 54th Regiment was flanked on the left by 14th Panzer's 103rd and 108th Grenadier Regiments and 64th Motorcycle Battalion, which held the ground northward along Mashinnaia Street and through a Soviet-occupied salient jutting westward in the Bread Factory to the middle reaches of the ravine adjacent to the southern edge of the Barrikady Factory. Arrayed from north to south, 62nd Army defended this sector with the remnants of 193rd Rifle Division's 883rd, 895th, and 685th Regiments facing 54th Jäger Regiment and part of 103rd Grenadier Regiment in the streets north of the Krasnyi Oktiabr' Factory, 95th Rifle Division's 161st Regiment in the Bread Factory, and 308th Rifle Division's 347th Regiment in the lower reaches of the ravine. Soon, Chuikov reinforced this sector with a reconstituted detachment of 100–150 men from 37th Guards Rifle Division's previously destroyed 109th Guards Rifle Regiment.

On 14th Panzer Division's left, the three worn-out *kampfgruppen* from 305th Infantry Division's regiments held on to all but the northeastern section of the Barrikady Factory. They were faced by the remnants of 768th, 344th, and 650th Regiments of Liudnikov's 138th Rifle Division (deployed from north to south) diagonally across the factory's eastern face, flanked on the left by 339th and 347th Regiments of Gurt'ev's 308th Rifle Division, which still clung to the rubble along the southeastern face of the factory and the ravine to the south. Finally, at the northern extremity of LI Corps' forward line, 24th Panzer Division's *Kampfgruppe* Below faced the survivors of

138th Rifle Division's attached 118th Guards Rifle Regiment and the right wing of 768th Regiment in the ravines and gullies along the Volga's western bank northeast of the Barrikady Factory.[47]

At day's end on 24 October, Chuikov asserted, because 37th Guards and 308th and 193rd Rifle Divisions "had only a few hundred infantry left between them," and "as a result of the exceptionally tense fighting, the units of 138th and 139th [should read 39th] Gds. RD and the remnants of 308th RD and 37th GRD, after suffering heavy losses, had lost their combat effectiveness as divisions."[48] However, despite such losses, Chuikov informed Eremenko that these forces were prepared "to fight to the last round and to the last man."[49] Considering the number of march-companies and battalions Eremenko's *front* was still sending across the Volga to reinforce Chuikov's shrinking bridgehead, 39th Guards and 138th Rifle Divisions probably still numbered in excess of 2,500 men each. Faced with this situation, Chuikov late on 24 October ordered his forces in the factory district as follows: "Employing the two rifle battalions attached to the army as reinforcements, give (one each) to 193rd and 39th Gds. RDs with the mission to restore the fronts of these divisions along the railroad and hold on to their occupied positions to prevent any further enemy advance."[50]

In fact, by day's end on 24 October, both sides were approaching the limits of their endurance, with neither side able to gain significant advantage over the opposing forces. As one historian later wrote:

For a week after the 24th, LI Corps' effort was totally absorbed, by day, in fighting for what previously would have been considered miniscule objectives—shops number 1, 5, and 10 in the Metallurgical Plant and a furnace [Martenovskii] in the same plant—and, by night, in trying to disrupt boat traffic on the Volga that was bringing Chuikov replacements after dark for his losses in the daylight.[51]

While this seemingly unending and inescapable stalemate discouraged Seydlitz, Paulus, and Hitler, it had the opposite effect on Chuikov, who noted presciently:

It was clear that both the enemy's and our own strength was running out. In ten days of fighting the Germans had again split our army, inflicting heavy losses on us and taken the Tractor Factory but had been unable to wipe out the northern group and the Army's main forces. . . . [Therefore], Paulus could not repeat an attack on the scale of the one on October 14 unless he had 10–15 days to bring up fresh supplies of ammunition, bombs, and tanks as well as reinforcements.[52]

At the time, however, Chuikov erroneously believed that Paulus had two full divisions in reserve in the Gumrak and Voroponovo regions (probably the 76th and 113th), whereas in reality Sixth Army's commander had none. By this time, the only reserve force the Germans had in the entire Stalingrad region was Fourth Panzer Army's 29th Motorized Division, which for good reason was fully occupied backing up Hoth's defenses around the Beketovka bridgehead against counterattacks by Stalingrad Front's 64th Army. Ironically, even though Chuikov's assessment of available German reserves proved incorrect, Paulus was already considering how best to reinforce Seydlitz's corps—although he did not discuss the matter with Weichs and Hitler until a week later. In the meantime, Sixth Army's commander ordered Seydlitz to regroup and reshuffle his forces as best he could and to attack whenever and wherever advantage might be gained.

Following Paulus's guidance, Seydlitz late on 24 October directed 79th Infantry, 14th Panzer, and 305th Infantry Divisions to continue their attacks against Soviet positions in the vicinity of the Barrikady and Krasnyi Oktiabr' Factories come what may the next morning, albeit on a lesser scale. At the same time, Paulus ordered Hube's XIV Panzer Corps to eliminate the Soviet bridgehead in the Spartanovka and Rynok regions north of the Mokraia Mechetka River once and for all. These orders produced numerous intense and nasty but essentially local fights in the vicinity of the Krasnyi Oktiabr' and Barrikady Factories, and they led to far larger fighting north of the Mechetka River.

Egged on by Paulus and Seydlitz, LI Corps' 398th and 24th Panzer Divisions conducted routine reconnaissance, patrolling, and fire-support missions in the broad sector from the Mokraia Mechetka River southward to the Barrikady Factory from 25 through 29 October. To the south, however, 305th Infantry, 14th Panzer, and 79th Infantry Divisions continued a painfully difficult, prolonged, and generally futile struggle to clear 62nd Army's forces from the remainder of the Barrikady and Krasnyi Oktiabr' Factories and the irksome salient between. This generated numerous vicious small-scale attacks designed to expel Soviet forces from the infamous ravine south of the Barrikady Factory, from the Bread Factory, and from the dense network of partially destroyed buildings between the two factories. As this fighting progressed, Chuikov constantly juggled his forces and ordered them to launch frequent counterattacks to keep the Germans at bay. All the while, *front* commander Eremenko fed just enough fresh forces into the blazing cauldron to keep the Germans from extinguishing its fires.

25 October

Schwerin's 79th Infantry Division resumed its assault on the remaining Soviet-held halls in the Krasnyi Oktiabr' Factory on 25 October. Ordering its 212th

Regiment to hold its positions on the division's right wing and flank in the southern half of the factory, Schwerin combined the remainder of the division's combat-effective infantrymen, perhaps as many as 2,500 men, under the command of Lieutenant Colonel Richard Wolf, rocket launcher commander of 208th Infantry Regiment, and ordered Wolf's force to seize Hall 4 (the Martenovskii Shop; see Map 73). However, 208th Regiment's initial assault faltered shortly after its forces penetrated the depths of the hall; the defenders, elements of 120th Guards Rifle Regiment, had hidden in a covered drainage ditch that passed through the hall and, from the hall's ovens, emerged in surprise from hidden positions and delivered withering automatic-weapons and machine-gun fire against the attackers. Schwerin then reinforced Wolf's assault force with a composite battalion-size *kampfgruppe* from 212th Regiment and several hundred men from the division's 179th Reconnaissance Battalion. At the same time, the division commander directed infantry from 100th Jäger Division's Croatian 369th Regiment, which had just been attached to 79th Division but numbered no more than a full battalion, to take over 212th Regiment's defensive positions in Halls 9 and 10. Despite these reinforcements, as Wolf recalled:

The attack launched on Hall 4 from the west, with strong protective fire, at first yielded some successes. We managed to get about halfway through Hall 4. Halls 1 and 2 were retaken. From now on, the forward line of our troops would run along their eastern edge. Unfortunately, the success in Hall 4 was not permanent. Our troops had to yield to Soviet counterattacks [conducted by 39th Guards Rifle Division's 120th Regiment]. Then the forward line of our troops ran from the western facing side [of Hall 4].[53]

From the other side, 62nd Army reported:

The 39th Gds. RD . . . fought with enemy submachine gunners penetrating in the Krasnyi Oktiabr' Factory region. . . . At 1300 hours, while fighting with an enemy force of more than an infantry regiment . . . a group of enemy submachine-gunners managed to reach the vicinity of Samarkandskaia [Street] [one block north of the Krasnyi Oktiabr' Factory] and created a threat to the division's CP. The army's headquarters threw forward a security company to defend the division's CP.[54]

While 79th Infantry Division's assaults inside the grounds of the Krasnyi Oktiabr' Factory were faltering, the *kampfgruppen* from 54th Jäger, and 103rd and 108th Panzer Grenadier Regiments of Heim's 14th Panzer Division, resumed their local assaults against 62nd Army's defenses in the streets and blocks between the Krasnyi Oktiabr' and Barrikady Factories, into the Bread Factory, and eastward along the ravine south of Barrikady. They engaged 193rd Rifle Division's 895th and 685th Regiments, 95th Rifle Division's 161st Regiment, and small forces from 308th Rifle Division's 347th and 339th Regiments, likewise with only limited success. Attacking within the close confines of the Bread Factory, 14th Panzer's 64th Motorcycle Battalion, supported by artillery fire and a few tanks, tried repeatedly to overcome 161st Regiment's defenses in the factory's "second building," in the eastern part of the factory. After the first assault "collapsed in the fierce defensive fire," a second assault finally cleared the building, only to stall on its southern edge.[55] On the motorcycle battalion's left, *kampfgruppen* from 14th Panzer's 103rd and 108th Grenadier Regiments, now eroded in strength to the size of companies, pushed forward against the survivors of Gurt'ev's two regiments, now numbering scarcely more than 200 men, dug in astride the ravine south of Barrikady. Despite best efforts, the panzer-grenadiers managed an advance of only several tens of meters toward the Volga. In the process, all of 103rd Regiment's company commanders perished, and the lead *kampfgruppe* of the regiment eroded to fewer than 20 men.

As 62nd Army described this struggle:

308th RD fought intensely on the territory of the Barrikady Factory during the day. The enemy committed fresh forces and heavy tanks, which we lacked the weapons to fight, in the division's defensive sector.

347th RR suffered heavy losses and had about 36 active bayonets. During the day, the division repelled a series of enemy attacks and exchanged fires in the southeastern corner of the Barrikady Factory while protecting the approaches to the crossing from the northwest.

193rd RD, with [95th RD's] 161st RR, suffered heavy losses in combat on 24 October. The enemy pushed the division's units back and reached the vicinity of the northern parts of Rovnaia, Sevastopol'skaia, and Krasnopresnenskaia Streets [east of the railroad and southwest of the Barrikady Factory].

During the day on 25 October 1942, [the 193rd Division] engaged in heavy fighting with the enemy, [including] a force of up to two infantry regiments with heavy tanks, delivering its main attack with a force of an infantry regiment and 9 heavy tanks toward the southwestern corner of the Barrikady Factory and the landing stage [Pristan'] and, with part of its forces (up to a battalion), from Tsentral'naia Street. Committing his reserves, the enemy wedged into the forward edge and reached the vicinity of the smokestack [*truby*] at 1630 hours. The fighting was continuing at nightfall. While inflicting huge losses on the enemy during the fighting, the division, too, suffered heavy losses in personnel.[56]

Meanwhile, on 14th Panzer Division's left, the *kampfgruppen* from 305th Infantry Division's 576th, 577th, and 578th Regiments, whittled down to company and battalion in strength, succeeded in pushing 138th Rifle Division's 768th, 344th, and 650th Regiments and 308th Rifle Division's 339th Regiment back through the rubble along the eastern edge of the Barrikady Factory but failed to root out their riflemen from cover within all of the factory's many smashed halls and shops. Nevertheless, by the end of the day Oppenländer's ever-weakening forces managed to secure all but the northeastern part of the factory grounds.

The 62nd Army described the day's fighting more optimistically, noting that "138th RD, reinforced by 118th Gds. RR, continued to hold on to its positions overnight and repelled attacks by the enemy on the Barrikady Factory (the northern and eastern parts) during the day, while holding on to their positions."[57] Commenting on what he perceived as the futility of the German assaults, Chuikov later observed, "The units of Liudnikov's and Gurt'ev's divisions, in the army's center sector, fought fiercely in defense of the Barrikady Factory. The Germans' freshly-brought up regiments were obviously incapable of close-quarter fighting. Even though we had only a handful of men in the workshops of the factory, the enemy, with five times as many, could make no progress in the sector occupied by our storm troops."[58] Disingenuously, Chuikov then added, "Paulus was throwing fresh reserves into the battle the whole time. We had none."[59]

Elaborating on Chuikov's brief account, the Red Army General Staff's daily operational summary recorded:

62nd Army conducted stubborn defensive fighting with enemy forces of up to an infantry division with 30 tanks attacking between the Barrikady and Krasnyi Oktiabr' Factories on 25 October.

The Northern Group of Forces repelled several attacks by the enemy in the Spartanovka region and held on to their previous positions.

138th and 308th RDs repelled attacks by the enemy in the vicinity of the Barrikady Factory and occupied their previous positions.

193rd RD conducted heavy defensive fighting against an enemy force of up to an infantry battalion with 9 tanks in the vicinity of Stal'naia Street and against a force of up to an infantry regiment in the vicinity of Tsentral'naia and Dzhankoiskaia Streets with part of its forces on 25 October. The enemy committed his reserves into battle at 1400 hours and reached the corner of Trubnaia and Samarkandskaia Streets [one block northwest of the Krasnyi Oktiabr' Factory].

39th Gds. RD repelled an attack by an enemy force of up to a regiment of infantry and held on to its previous positions.

There were no changes in the positions of the army's remaining units.[60]

In fact, not only did Paulus lack any "fresh troops"; Chuikov would receive "fresh reserves" of his own within 24 hours.

Describing the day's action accurately, the OKW reported that "the forces attacking in Stalingrad suppressed centers of enemy resistance and seized several city blocks. North of the city, continuing their attack, German forces occupied yet another of Stalingrad's suburbs."[61] Underscoring the increasing tendency of Chuikov's forces to conduct incessant counterattacks, Army Group B's report added:

> In Stalingrad proper, powerful enemy counterattacks toward the Metallurgical Factory from the south and northeast were repelled. In the Bread Factory, several more shops have been cleared of enemy. North of the factory, several centers of resistance situated in bunkers and covered passageways in the immediate rear are still being cleared of enemy. North of Stalingrad, 94th Infantry Division captured a group of buildings in the region of the eastern outskirts of Spartanovka.[62]

By far the most dangerous German action on 25 October—at least from Chuikov's perspective—was the progress that Hube's XIV Panzer Corps made against Group Gorokhov's defenses in the Rynok-Spartanovka region, north of the Mokraia Mechetka River (see Map 60). There, Pfeiffer's 94th Infantry Division was reinforced after 21 October by its 276th Infantry Regiment, which Paulus had released from 24th Panzer Division's control. Thereafter, Pfeiffer assaulted and captured much of Spartanovka village, albeit temporarily. As Chuikov recorded:

> His [the enemy's] attack on the Spartanovka settlement, using an infantry division with tanks, created a difficult position on the front occupied by the enemy.
> Backed up from the air, the enemy's tanks and infantry pushed back 149th Brigade's units and occupied an area south of the Gumrak-Vladimirovka railway and the center of Spartanovka settlement. Gorokhov's northern group was helped by ships of the Volga Flotilla, whose artillery caused the heavy losses among the enemy.[63]

In fact, XIV Panzer Corps conducted its assault against Spartanovka, with 94th Infantry Division's 276th and 274th Regiments attacking eastward along the Mokraia Mechetka's northern bank and 16th Panzer Division's 16th Panzer Jäger Battalion, which advanced on 276th Regiment's left. Although 16th Panzer Division's history duly recorded that "on 25 October the infantry managed to mop up the last of the nests of resistance in Spartanovka," it had no choice but to admit that "there were still hundreds of Russians holding out in the lower sections of the *balkas* running west to east between Spartanovka and Rynok. In fact, Group Gorokhov's two rifle brigades defended Rynok with fanatic efforts. They were determined to hang on to their bridgehead on the western bank of the Volga."[64] Giving truth to 16th Panzer Division's concerns, within a matter of days Gorokhov's forces would indeed recapture many of their lost positions in violent counterattacks, and Eremenko would mount an ambitious amphibious assault across the Volga to support and reinforce that beleaguered group.

Summarizing his army's efforts on 25 October, Chuikov lamented that the "backbone" of his 308th, 193rd, and 138th Rifle Divisions and 37th Guards Rifle Division had "lost . . . combat effectiveness" and "only soldiers who arrived as recent reinforcements remain in the divisions." Therefore, he added, "the personnel who have been under constant pressure of artillery and mortar fire and air strikes need relief and rest."[65] On 24 October alone, he reported, his forces had lost 356 soldiers killed in action.

Within this gruesome context, once again the Soviet army commander ordered his remaining forces to hold their occupied positions at all costs and to prevent the Germans from advancing any farther. Ruefully, he added, "I appealed to the *front* commander with a request concerning the relief of 308th, 193rd, and 138th RD's and 37th Gds. RD's personnel, which have suffered great losses in the fighting, by two full-blooded divisions, together with antitank artillery."[66]

Determined to capture its ellusive objectives, Sixth Army ordered Seydlitz's forces to continue assaults against Chuikov's shrinking bridgehead come what may. These assaults continued intermittently from 26 through 30 October, albeit with only limited success, against the Soviet defenses in and east of the Barrikady and Krasnyi Oktiabr' Factories, along the Khvost Ravine to the Volga River south of the former, and along the flanks of the salient jutting westward between the two factories. As such, the field of combat measured a mere 2,000 meters in width and 100–1,000 meters in depth—far less than 1.5 square kilometers. While German and Soviet operational maps displayed a total of seven divisions (one German panzer and two infantry and four Soviet rifle divisions) crowded into this exceedingly small area, the contending forces actually amounted to no more than multiple battalion- and company-sized combat groups fighting for possession of single streets, blocks of buildings, single buildings or parts of buildings, individual rooms in separate factory halls, and separate ravines, gullies, and gully complexes—probably totaling no more than 6,000 German and 3,000 Soviet combat troops. Clearly, as Table 37 and subsequent combat reports indicated, the portion of Paulus's Sixth Army committed to the conquest of Stalingrad had eroded to the point that it was no longer combat-effective. For its part, Chuikov's army was incapable of holding on much longer without additional reinforcements.

Table 37. The Combat Rating of Infantry and Pioneer Battalions Subordinate to Sixth Army's Divisions Fighting in Stalingrad, 19–26 October 1942

	19 October	26 October
XIV PANZER CORPS		
3rd Motorized Division		
(5–4 infantry battalions)	3 medium strong and 2 average	4 medium strong
(1 pioneer battalion)	weak	weak
60th Motorized Division		
(7 infantry battalions)	2 medium strong, 4 average, and 1 exhausted	2 medium strong, 1 average, 3 weak, and 1 exhausted
(1 pioneer battalion)	weak	weak
16th Panzer Division		
(4 infantry battalions)	1 medium strong, 1 average, and 2 weak	1 medium strong, 1 average, and 2 weak
(1 pioneer battalion)	weak	weak
94th Infantry Division		
(7 infantry battalions)	7 exhausted	7 weak
(1 pioneer battalion)	weak	average (with 2 companies and 1 Russian *Hiwi* company attached)
LI ARMY CORPS		
24th Panzer Division		
(4 infantry battalions)	1 weak and 3 exhausted	1 weak and 3 exhausted
(1 pioneer battalion)	exhausted	exhausted
100th Jäger Division		
(5 infantry battalions)	1 strong, 3 medium strong, and 1 average	1 strong, 1 medium strong, 2 average, and 1 weak
(1 pioneer battalion)	medium strong	average
305th Infantry Division		
(9 infantry battalions)	9 weak	5 weak and 4 exhausted
(1 pioneer battalion)	weak	exhausted
295th Infantry Division		
(7 infantry battalions)	4 weak and 3 exhausted	1 average, 4 weak, and 2 exhausted
(1 pioneer battalion)	weak	weak
389th Infantry Division		
(4–5 infantry battalions)	1 average, 1 weak, and 2 exhausted	1 average, 2 weak, and 2 exhausted
(1 pioneer battalion)	exhausted	exhausted
79th Infantry Division		
(6 infantry battalions)	**(not fighting in the city)**	3 average and 3 weak
(1 pioneer battalion)		average

Table 37. (continued)

	19 October	26 October
14th Panzer Division		
(4 infantry battalions)	4 medium strong	4 weak
(1 pioneer battalion)	average	average
71st Infantry Division		
(7 infantry battalions)	2 average, 3 weak, and 2 exhausted	2 average and 5 weak
(1 pioneer battalion)	weak	weak
Totals:		
63–69 infantry battalions	1 strong, 13 medium strong, 11 average, 20 weak, and 18 exhausted	1 strong, 8 medium strong, 11 average, 37 weak, and 12 exhausted
11–12 pioneer battalions	1 medium strong, 1 average, 7 weak, and 2 exhausted	4 average, 5 weak, and 3 exhausted

Source: Florian *Freiherr* von und zu Aufsess, "Betr.: Zustand der Divisionen, Armee – Oberkommando 6, Abt. Ia, A. H. Qu., 19. Oktober 1942, 12.35 Uhr"and "Betr.: Zustand der Divisionen, Armee – Oberkommando 6, Abt. Ia, A. H. Qu., 26. Oktober 1942, 10.15 Uhr,"in *Die Anlagenbander zu den Kriegstagebuchern der 6. Armee vom 14.09.1942 bis 24.11.1942, Band I* (Schwabach: January 2006), 185–189 and 212–216.

Thus, although Sixth Army increased the number of infantry and pioneer battalions in the fight for Stalingrad city to 69 and 12, respectively, the number of infantry battalions rated "strong" and "medium strong" decreased from 1 and 13, respectively, on 19 October to 1 and 8, respectively, on 26 October. During the same period, the number of battalions rated "weak" and "exhausted" changed from 11 "weak" and 20 "exhausted" to 37 "weak" and 12 "exhausted." In the aggregate, the average readiness rating of the army's infantry battalions decreased from below "average" to "weak." The same pattern of attrition applied to the army's 12 pioneer battalions. In essence, by 26 October three of the four divisions in LI Corps' main assault force (14th and 24th Panzer and 305th Infantry Divisions) were rated either "weak" or below, and the fourth, the incomplete 79th Infantry Division, saw its rating decline from 3 "strong," 2 "medium strong," and 1 "average" battalions to well below "average." Compounding these depressing readiness ratings, by 26 October LI Corps could muster only 37 armored vehicles, including 13 tanks in 24th Panzer Division, 15 tanks in 14th Panzer Division, and a total of 9 operational assault guns in 244th and 245th Assault Gun Battalions. These stark realities clearly demonstrated that Sixth Army could not sustain such losses and still fulfill the missions assigned to it unless it received significant reinforcements.

October 26–27

Despite the appalling weakness of his corps' divisions, Seydlitz nevertheless ordered 79th Infantry and 14th Panzer Divisions to resume operations on 26 October, principally in the vicinity of the Bread and Krasnyi Oktiabr' Factories. After another 36 hours of intense fighting, for a brief moment on 27 October it appeared as if the attacking forces might capture the Volga's western bank, thereby splitting apart Chuikov's forces between the Barrikady and Krasnyi Oktiabr' Factories.

During the most successful of these German attacks, on 26 October, a single *kampfgruppe* formed from the remnants of 14th Panzer Division's 103rd and 108th Grenadier Regiments, under the command of Lieutenant Joachim Stempel, managed to capture the second administrative building in the Bread Factory from 95th Rifle Division's 161st Regiment. Taking advantage of the momentary confusion among the Soviet defenses, Stempel's *kampfgruppe* then pushed eastward down Khvost Ravine between Stal'naia Street and the Bread Factory (the Gun Factory Gulley on German maps), striking Soviet defenses at the boundary between 308th Rifle Division's 347th Regiment and 193rd Rifle Division's 685th Regiment. Lunging forward down the ravine another 200 meters, Stempel's group bowled over and scattered the riflemen of Smekhotvorov's 685th Regiment and Gorishnyi's 161st Regiment, forcing them to withdraw southward to new defensive positions facing north along a ravine (Glubokaia *Ovrag*—the Bread Factory Gulley on German maps) north of Matrosnaia Street. Stempel's group then moved farther down Khvost Ravine, striking and dispersing the small reserve force from 109th Guards Rifle Regiment and gaining a narrow lodgment on the Volga's bank at the mouth of the ravine and several hundred meters north of the main ferry.

By this time Stempel's group, which had numbered only 40 men the day before, was fighting against Soviet forces made up largely of staff officers, walking wounded, and sailors from the ferry line. Stempel urgently requested and ultimately received 80 fresh soldiers directly from Sixth Army's replacement center, but all of them were "18 to 19 years old, who haven't fired a shot in anger out here." Yet within 48 hours, most of the men were either wounded or killed, and shortly thereafter fresh Soviet forces appeared, attacked, and forced 103rd Regiment to relinquish its tenuous foothold on the Volga.[67]

The 62nd Army's daily summary accurately described the crisis on 26 October:

193rd RD, with [95th RD's] 161st RR, occupied the line along Mashinnaia and Stal'naia Streets [south of the Barrikady Factory] up to the western bridge on Stendalia Street, to the letter "R" and farther from the railroad line at the smokestack to the railroad (the letter "R" of the northern inscription [name]), and still farther across Gdovskaia Street to Tsentral'naia Street and Ordzhonikidze Street as a result of heavy fighting on 25 October. This line was protected by scattered outposts and small groups. Beginning at 1130 hours, the division fought fierce battles with an attacking enemy force of more than an infantry regiment [Group Stempel] with tanks, which was trying to reach the [ferry] crossing. At 1500 hours the enemy committed his reserves into combat and, after overcoming the resistance of the remaining small groups of our units, reached Bakinskaia and Gazovaia Streets [one block from the river]. The [193rd] division halted any further enemy advance along that line, suffering heavy losses. At day's end, the division was continuing heavy fighting with a numerically superior enemy.

The division's situation was extremely grave, and only several tens of fighters remained in the regiments. All of the antitank rifles and antitank guns were out of action.[68]

Chuikov responded to this crisis by ordering that two reinforcing march-battalions that had just crossed the Volga River be transferred to 193rd Rifle Division's control. Then he demanded that Smekhotvorov's division "prevent the enemy from reaching the vicinity of the crossings."[69]

That evening the OKW simply stated, "In Stalingrad, fierce fighting is continuing in the streets and in the buildings." The Red Army General Staff's daily operational summary provided a far more accurate picture of the day's events:

62nd Army conducted fierce fighting against attacking enemy tanks and infantry in its previous positions with the Northern Group's units during the day on 26 October.

138th RD, reinforced by 118th RR, 37th Gds. RD [in the Barrikady Factory], repelled attacks on its previous positions by small enemy groups [305th ID].

193rd RD engaged in heavy fighting with an attacking enemy force of more than an infantry regiment with tanks [14th PzD's Group Stempel]. Their heavy tanks with assault troops riding on board reached the vicinity of Mashinnaia and Gazov [Gas] Streets [adjacent to Khvost Ravine]. The fighting was continuing.

39th Gds. RD, remaining in its previous positions [in the Krasnyi Oktiabr' Factory], repulsed enemy attacks [79th ID].

284th RD and 13th Gds. RD occupied their previous positions.[70]

German sources claim that, aside from 14th Panzer Division's dramatic thrust toward the landing stage and its disappointing outcome, a general lull prevailed over the remainder of Sixth Army's front on 27 October. 62nd Army reports, however, contradict this claim, instead asserting that the army "engaged in intense fighting during the day in the northern and central sectors" in combat that had an increasingly debilitating effect on the defenders.[71] Specifically:

As a result of the constant heavy fighting, the combat formations of 138th RD's and 39th Gds. RD's units and of the remnants of 308th and 193rd RDs were greatly thinned out. As a result, no continuous front exists in the sectors of the Barrikady and Krasnyi Oktiabr' Factories. Instead, these sectors were being defended by separate centers of resistance hastily created at the expense of recently arrived reinforcements, which had not yet coalesced as combat entities. All of the weight of the recent fighting fell on the headquarters' command cadre and staffs, who very often acted as soldiers while repelling enemy attacks on their headquarters. In this regard, casualties among the command cadre, especially among the commanders and staff officers of battalions, regiments, and, particularly, of divisions and the army, sharply increased.

The periodic infusion into these divisions of reinforcements entering combat from the march did not familiarize them with their command cadre and did not achieve the necessary results.

During the day on 27 October, the enemy continued his attacks with increasing force.[72]

In his memoirs, Chuikov underscored the deteriorating situation between the Barrikady and Krasnyi Oktiabr' Factories on 27 October:

The left flank of Liudnikov's division [138th] and a regiment of Gurt'ev's division [308th] were overrun by the enemy. Enemy tommy-gunners occupied Mezenskaia and Tuvinskaia Streets [near the mouth of the ravine] and began to fire on the area of our last ferry. At the same time, units of Smekhotvorov's [193rd] and Gur'ev's [39th Guards] divisions were beating off attacks by the German 79th Infantry Division, whose main thrust was toward the Krasnyi Oktiabr' Factory.

German tommy-gunners infiltrated through these depleted units. They reached the 39th [Guards] Division's H.Q., and hand grenades were thrown into Gur'ev's dug-out. When I heard this, I rushed a company of the Army's H.Q. guard to Gur'ev's aid. With a rapid attack, they pushed the tommy-gunners back from the divisional H.Q. and, following them, reached the Krasnyi Oktiabr' Factory, where they remained. We incorporated them into Gur'ev's division.

The enemy continued to attack the ferry and Krasnyi Oktiabr'. The attacks were successfully beaten back until 3 P.M., when the Germans managed to occupy Mashinnaia Street [near the mouth of the ravine].

In the sector between the Barrikady and Krasnyi Oktiabr' Factories, German tommy-gunners were only about 400 yards from the Volga. Our last ferry, therefore, was under enemy machine gun fire. The gullies running westward from the Volga were under enemy machine gun and artillery fire. To move along the bank, you had to get down on your knees and elbows. This did not suit us. Our sappers soon managed to construct a double wooden fence across the gullies, filling up the holes with stones, to stop the bullets.[73]

Although it does not contradict Chuikov's account, 62nd Army's daily report provided even more vivid details about this fighting:

308th RD, during the day, engaged in fierce fighting with a numerically superior enemy, who smashed the right wing of 347th RR and reached the eastern part of Mezenskaia and Tuvinskaia Streets with his forward units. The fighting was continuing at day's end. The division has suffered heavy losses. 30 men, riflemen and mortar men, remain in 347th RR, and 53 men, including 22 riflemen, in 339th RR.

193rd RD, with 161st RR, suffered heavy losses as a result of the fighting on 26 October and was holding on to the Mashinnaia Street, Matrosnaia Street, and Malaia Street line by the morning. The division is being reinforced by two battalions of 45th RD, which have crossed to the western bank of the Volga River with a total of 1,588 men (1,127 rifles, 11 heavy machine guns, 42 submachine guns, and 36 antitank rifles).

Beginning in the morning, the [193rd] division engaged in fierce fighting with attacking enemy infantry and tanks. At 1030 hours, up to two battalions and 7 tanks tried to reach the landing stage from the vicinity of the smokestack, and up to a battalion with 12 tanks and assault troops, attacking along Tsentral'naia Street, captured the northwestern part of the Krasnyi Oktiabr' Factory. The fighting was continuing with increasing ferocity at day's end. During the day's fighting, the recently received reinforcements (two battalions) lost up to 70 percent of their personnel.

39th Gds. RD repelled savage attacks by an enemy force of up to an infantry regiment with 6 tanks attacking toward the Krasnyi Oktiabr' Factory from the west and northwest.

The division suffered heavy losses from enemy aircraft, artillery, and mortars. Only 30–40 men remain in its rifle regiments. The enemy, committing reserves into combat and exploiting the division's fragmented combat formation, reached the northwestern part of the Krasnyi Oktiabr' Factory with tanks and infantry. A further enemy advance was halted in bitter combat by day's end.

84th TB repelled attacks by the enemy and held on to its occupied positions, while the left flank group of tanks was cut off from the brigade by penetrating enemy units. The brigade headquarters lost up to 70 percent of its personnel while repelling the penetrating enemy.[74]

Thus, if the Germans seemed somewhat blasé about the day's fighting, 62nd Army certainly was not. With his back to the wall, Chuikov once again simply ordered his remaining forces "to continue to repel the enemy attacks." Reporting losses of 326 men on 24 October (and even heavier losses on 25 and 26 October) from the fighting, Chuikov on 27 October was unable to quantify completely the carnage among his army's ranks.

From its vantage point in Moscow, the Red Army General Staff simply recorded:

> **62nd Army** continued stubborn fighting with enemy infantry and tanks in the Spartanovka region and the Barrikady and Krasnyi Oktiabr' Factories. The enemy succeeded in pushing our units back 250–300 meters in the vicinity of the Barrikady Factory and reached the vicinity of Mezenskaia Street [southeast of the factory] with separate groups. Up to a battalion of infantry with 12 tanks [54th Jäger R] penetrated into the northwestern part of the Krasnyi Oktiabr' Factory. The fighting was still going on. In the southwestern part of the Krasnyi Oktiabr' Factory, our units [112th Gds. RR] repulsed an attack by up to a battalion of infantry [79th ID] and completely destroyed up to a company of enemy motorized infantry.[75]

Apparently ignoring the failure of 14th Panzer Division's *Kampfgruppe* Stempel to hold its hard-won foothold near the landing stage on the Volga, the OKW reported on the evening of 27 October, "In Stalingrad, attacking German forces penetrated to the Volga in the sector east of the Bread Factory and took large regions of the city from the enemy."[76] Army Group B's daily operational summary added more detail—but also without mentioning 14th Panzer's ultimate disappointment. Instead it asserted:

> The 79th Infantry Division captured the remaining territory of the "Krasnyi Oktiabr" Metallurgical Factory. North of the factory, units of 14th Panzer and 305th Infantry Divisions, which attacked from the vicinity of the Bread Factory and the "Krasnyi Barrikady" Factory, reached the

Volga along the entire front to the fuel storage tanks, inclusively. Units of 305th Infantry Division were fighting fiercely in the sector between the gun factory and the Volga, north of the fuel tanks.[77]

The army group's intelligence officer chimed in: "The enemy counterattacks in the southern part of Stalingrad's Metallurgical Factory achieved no success. The enemy abandoned several blocks."[78]

Because the German advance on 26 October propelled its forces to within 400 meters of the landing stage by day's end and threatened the ferry site itself the following day, the flow of reinforcements and supplies to 62nd Army was definitely threatened. Therefore, at midday on 26 October Eremenko decided to release the fresh 45th Rifle Division to Chuikov's control. 45th Shchors Rifle Division—named after a famous partisan leader during the Russian Civil War—was a relatively green division whose predecessor had been nearly destroyed during the fighting in the Donbas region in early July, when it was fighting under the control of Southwestern Front's 40th Army. After refitting with fresh conscripts in the Volga Military District during late July and early August, the 45th was assigned to 4th Reserve Army in late August and, together with 300th Rifle Division, was ultimately transferred to Stalingrad Front.[79] As of 26 October, 45th Division numbered roughly 6,400 men.[80]

A seasoned combat veteran who had commanded 42nd Guards Rifle Regiment in late 1941 and early 1942, 40-year-old General Vasilii Pavlovich Sokolov had commanded the 45th since 10 March 1942. Ironically, General Smekhotvorov, commander of 193rd Rifle Division, which Sokolov was to reinforce, had commanded 45th Rifle Division in late 1941. As was the case with all of the previous Soviet divisions that had reinforced 62nd Army, because of the acute shortage of rifles Chuikov had to move the division across the river a few battalions at a time as they became properly armed.[81]

As the lead battalions of 10th Rifle Regiment of Sokolov's division reached the Volga River's eastern bank at nightfall and received their weapons, Chuikov immediately ferried them across the river, assigning them to Smekhotvorov's 193rd Rifle Division with orders to prevent the Germans from reaching the Volga and the ferry crossing, in particular the base of Khvost Ravine at its confluence with the Volga. However, intense fighting raged along and adjacent to the ravine on 27 October, and strong German artillery and air strikes against what they correctly perceived as arriving reinforcements destroyed the western terminus of the ferry crossing. Chuikov was thus denied its use and forced to transfer the remainder of 45th Rifle Division across the river by other means, which took considerable time:

> The ferrying across of the regiments of Sokolov's 45th Division was going slowly, very slowly. The 62nd Army's landing-stages had been blown up

or gone up in flames. The regiments embarked onto ferries away from the city (in the Akhtuba channel of the river near Tumsk) and set off into the Volga only at night at very great risk (at points under the very noses of enemy troops which had broken through to the Volga) in order to reach the Army's defensive sector.[82]

This slow passage of Sokolov's reinforcing division across the Volga presented Chuikov with a serious dilemma, namely that his forces "would have to hold out for two to three days before Sokolov's 45th Division arrived in full. But where were we going to find forces with which to do so?" Chuikov managed to come up with a solution:

We collected about a dozen men [from the staff and rear services] and put them together with thirty soldiers discharged from the medical centers by the banks of the Volga. And—oh joy!—we had found, or rather had dragged from the battlefield, three broken-down tanks—two light tanks and one with a flame-thrower. We had had them rapidly repaired, and I decided to give the enemy a "shock"—to send the three tanks and fifty infantrymen into an attack . . . [at] the junction point between Smekhotvorov's and Gur'ev's divisions along Samarkandskaia Street, where the enemy had almost reached the Volga. . . .

The counterattack began in the early morning, before dawn. It was supported by artillery from the left bank and by Yerokhin's "katyushi" regiment. We did not manage to advance very far, but the results were impressive. The tank with the flame-thrower sent three German tanks up in flames, and our two light tanks overwhelmed the enemy in two trenches. . . . In this way, we gained a whole day on this sector. . . . In the Barrikady factory area, after repeated attacks, the enemy managed to reach the Volga but were destroyed in hand-to-hand fighting on the bank.[83]

Actually, Chuikov also dispatched 37th Guards Rifle Division's re-formed but still woefully understrength 109th Regiment to man a defensive line facing west along Mashinnaia Street between Novosel'skaia and Donetskaia Street to protect the ferry crossing. He also moved 6th Company of 284th Rifle Division's 1045th Rifle Regiment to reinforce 895th Regiment's defenses facing north along Dolinskaia and Umanskaia Streets. Ultimately, Chuikov's imaginative ersatz measures succeeded in containing 14th Panzer Division's advance down Khvost Ravine and to the ferry crossing on 27 October. By late on 27 October, 1st and 2nd Battalions of 45th Rifle Division's 10th Regiment took up positions on the flanks of 109th Guards Regiment, which by this time had withdrawn two blocks east of Mashinnaia Street, only 500 meters from the Volga's western bank. Still, two days of crisis followed while 45th Rifle

Division's regiments, the 10th, 253rd, and 61st, in succession, moved into their assigned defenses.

A company of tanks from Colonel D. M. Burdov's fresh 235th Tank Brigade followed the two lead battalions, painfully picking their way through the rubble to occupy their assigned positions. Burdov's brigade was new, with relatively green conscripts around a nucleus of veteran junior officers, having been formed in the Moscow Military District on 1 September 1942. The *Stavka* rushed it to Stalingrad in mid-October to ensure that Chuikov's army had necessary armor support. Its commander, 44-year-old Denis Maksimovich Burdov, was an experienced armor officer who had commanded 28th and 129th Tank Regiments from 1938 through 1941 and 26th Tank Brigade from 16 November 1941 to 8 July 1942. Burdov took command of 235th Tank Brigade when it was formed.[84]

As before, the focal points of these fresh crises were the Barrikady and Krasnyi Oktiabr' Factories and the salient between them. Against fierce resistance by the remnants of Liudnikov's 138th and Gurt'ev's 308th Rifle Divisions in and east of the Barrikady Factory and by Gur'ev's 37th Guards Rifle Division within and on the periphery of the Krasnyi Oktiabr' Factory, Schwerin's 79th and Oppenländer's 305th Infantry Divisions persisted in their assaults in the vicinity of the two factories. All the while, Heim's 14th Panzer Division continued to compress the bridgehead being defended by Smekhotvorov's 193rd and the lead elements of Sokolov's 45th Rifle Divisions, located between the two factories.

28–29 October

In his memoirs well after war's end, Chuikov, when describing the fighting on 28 and 29 October, claimed that he considered the fighting at the landing stage (i.e., the ferry crossing) to have been the decisive turning point in the battle:

> On the remaining sectors of the army's front, no great changes took place in these two days. In the Barrikady factory area, after repeated attacks, the enemy managed to advance to Novosel'skaia Street [two blocks east of the factory]. Here, isolated groups of German tommy-gunners managed to reach the Volga but were destroyed in hand-to-hand fighting on the bank.
>
> Units of Liudnikov's [138th] and Gurt'ev's [308th] divisions beat off seven attacks in these days.
>
> Batiuk's [284th] division and the 13th Guards Division beat off hourly attacks on and to the south of Mamaev Kurgan. We used our flame-throwers.[85]

However, as described in 62nd Army's official reports, the fighting in the northern and central sectors of the army's front during this period was "exceptionally heavy"; for example, on the evening of 26 October, the army reported:

> The enemy continued his offensive with forces of up to two infantry divisions with 35–45 tanks. At 0700 hours he attacked toward the northeastern outskirts of Spartanovka with a force of up to a battalion with tanks, and a force of up to five infantry regiments with 25–35 tanks attacked in the Volkhovstroevsk and Karusel'naia sector [north and south of the Barrikady Factory], delivering its main attack from Mashinnaia Street toward the landing stage with the aim of seizing the crossing. At a cost of immense efforts, all of the enemy attacks on the fronts of 138th and 308th RDs were repulsed by day's end. Stubborn fighting is continuing along the Mashinnaia Street line between the Barrikady and Krasnyi Oktiabr' Factories. . . .
>
> 138th and 308th RDs engaged in heavy fighting during the day with an enemy force of up to an infantry regiment with 9–12 tanks, which was attacking from Volkhovstroevsk and Sormosk in an attempt to reach the Volga River, and repelled four attacks. The forward groups of enemy infantry reached the vicinity of the Mezensk Ravine and Novosel'sk.
>
> 193rd RD engaged in heavy fighting with an enemy force of up to 2 infantry regiments and 17 tanks attacking along Samarkandskaia Street toward the landing stage. At day's end, fighting was continuing along the Severnaia Street, northern part of Naberezhnaia, and Bakinskaia and Komissarov Streets line. The units held off the enemy's onslaught at a cost of immense effort.
>
> 39th Gds. RD continued fighting with the enemy on the grounds of the Krasnyi Oktiabr' Factory, repelled an attack by an enemy force of more than an infantry regiment with tanks attacking from the northwestern corner and into the center of the Krasnyi Oktiabr' Factory. The fighting was continuing at day's end. [It is] holding on to its previous positions along the line from the northeastern corner of the factory to the center of Vosstaniia Street and the [separate] building.
>
> 109th Gds. RR (37th Gds. RD), with a total of 40 bayonets, was fighting with a battalion of enemy infantry attacking from Gazov Street and continued to fight along the central part of Novosel'sk and Mostovaia Street line, 300 meters west of the landing stage.
>
> 84th TB occupied defenses in its previous positions with its motorized rifle battalion and the remnants of 339th RR [308th RD] were fighting with enemy infantry and tanks in the vicinity of Tuvinsk, the smokestack, and the railroad.[86]

Reporting the loss of another 226 men, Chuikov repeated his enjoinder to "repel the enemy attacks and prevent him from reaching the landing stage."[87] The Red Army General Staff's daily operational summary also underscored the seriousness of the situation, as well as the importance of the arrival of Sokolov's reinforcements:

[28 October]

62nd Army continued to engage in heavy defensive fighting against an enemy force of up to an infantry division and tanks, which was attacking in the sector between the Barrikady and Krasnyi Oktiabr' Factories with the units on its right wing and in its center on 28 October.

The enemy air force continuously bombed the positions of our units in the vicinity of the Barrikady and Krasnyi Oktiabr' Factories with groups of up to 12 aircraft.

The Northern Group's units held on to their positions, having beaten off three attacks by the enemy.

138th and 308th RDs fought intensely with an enemy force [305th ID] of up to an infantry regiment with 9–12 tanks. The forward groups of enemy infantry reached the vicinity of the Mezensk Ravine and Novosel'sk [east of the Barrikady Factory, 100–200 meters west of the Volga]. The fighting was continuing.

193rd RD fought with two enemy infantry regiments and 17 tanks [14th PzD] along the line of Mashinnaia Street [between the Barrikady and Krasnyi Oktiabr' Factories, 500 meters from the Volga] and the northeastern corner of the Krasnyi Oktiabr' Factory.

39th Gds. RD fought with attacking enemy infantry and tanks [79th ID] in the central and southern parts of the Krasnyi Oktiabr' Factory.

A guards regiment [109th] (with 40 bayonets) from 37th Gds. RD was in heavy fighting with a battalion of enemy infantry along the Novosel'sk-Mostovaia (300 meters west of the landing-stage) [and 200 meters west of the Volga] line.

284th RD, 13th Gds. RD, and 84th TB remained in their previous positions.[88]

From 62nd Army's perspective, the situation did not ease up at all the following day. On 29 October, for example, the army reported heavy fighting in the sector of the Barrikady and Krasnyi Oktiabr' Factories as an enemy infantry division with tanks continued its main attack toward the landing stage:

As a result of especially fierce combat, separate blocks and buildings changed hands several times in hand-to-hand fighting. Separate detachments of enemy with tanks penetrated almost to the bank, where they were destroyed in hand-to-hand combat. New enemy forces committed in the second half of the day succeeded in reaching the eastern outskirts of Tuvinsk and the western edge of the garden (northeast of the outskirts of Krasnyi Oktiabr' Factory) line, at a cost of huge losses, where further enemy movement was halted. A night attack by up to a company of infantry with 4–5 tanks reached the eastern block on Mezenskaia Street, where hand-to-hand fighting was under way. . . .

138th and 308th RDs repelled three attacks by enemy forces of more than an infantry regiment with tanks from the Volkhovstroevsk and Sormosk region. The units held onto their previous positions and conducted night fighting against a penetrating enemy infantry company and tanks in the region east of Mezenskaia.

193rd RD engaged in heavy fighting with an enemy force of more than an infantry regiment and heavy tanks, which was trying to penetrate to the landing stage. The enemy held off the onslaught of a numerically superior enemy. The fighting is continuing along a line from the western edge of the garden south of Dolinskaia Street to the northern part of Severnaia Street, Bakinskaia, and Komissarov Streets.

39th Gds. RD continued to fight with the enemy on the grounds of the Krasnyi Oktiabr' Factory. The division held on to its previous positions.[89]

Again, the Red Army General Staff's account echoed the events as described by 62nd Army:

[29 October]

62nd Army continued stubborn defensive fighting with enemy infantry and tanks in the vicinity of Spartanovka and the Barrikady and Krasnyi Oktiabr' Factories.

The Northern Group of Forces repulsed attacks by the enemy in the Spartanovka region and held on to their occupied positions.

138th and 308th RDs fought defensively with an enemy force of up to a regiment of infantry with 8 tanks [305th ID] in the Barrikady Factory region and held on to their occupied positions.

193rd RD and 84th TB fought with an enemy force of more than a regiment of infantry with 12 tanks [14th PzD], which was striving to reach the landing stage. At a cost of heavy losses, the enemy managed to advance 100 meters by 1700 hours on 29 October. Fighting was raging on the western outskirts of the gardens south of Dolinskaia Street [200 meters north of the Krasnyi Oktiabr' Factory's northeastern corner].

39th Gds. RD repelled enemy attacks [79th ID] on the grounds of the Krasnyi Oktiabr' Factory and held on to its previous positions.

The remaining units of the army occupied their previous positions.[90]

Keeping close track of the fighting during this period, the OKW reported on 28 October that "after repelling several enemy counterattacks, German forces seized several more industrial and civilian regions of the city" and that on 29 October German forces "supported by dive-bombers . . . continued their attacks in Stalingrad. The regions seized during the course of previous fighting are being cleared of enemy. German artillery conducted aimed fire against enemy ferries and cutters on the Volga."[91]

Many accounts of the fighting in Stalingrad play down the action of late October, asserting that the Germans simply jockeyed for position in the Barrikady and Krasnyi Oktiabr' Factories as Paulus intensified his search for fresh forces with which to deliver the coup de grace to Chuikov's 62nd Army. However—as 62nd Army's records and the Red Army General Staff's operational summaries indicate—Seydlitz's corps did all in its sharply diminished power to rid the two factories of the stubborn Soviet defenders. Fighting primarily in company-size and weak battalion–size *kampfgruppen*, usually supported by five to ten tanks or assault guns, LI Corps' 305th Infantry, 14th Panzer, and 79th Infantry Divisions persisted in their assaults despite steadily mounting casualties.

During the heavy fighting on 28 and 29 October, the *kampfgruppen* from Oppenländer's 305th Infantry Division, fighting on the left wing of Seydlitz's weakened main attack force, finally cleared the remainder of the Barrikady Factory of Soviet troops (see Map 77). In innumerable small but vicious actions, arrayed abreast from north to south, the division's 576th, 577th, and 578th Regiments pressed back 138th Rifle Division's 768th, 344th, and 650th Regiments and 308th Rifle Division's 339th and 347th Regiments from the factory's eastern edge and into the maze of buildings, blocks, and streets between the factory and the Volga's western bank. Liudnikov's 138th recorded 12 separate German assaults on 28 October and another eight on 29 October. These assaults pressed the survivors of Liudnikov's and Gurt'ev's divisions into the 500–700-meter-wide strip of ground in the gullies and ravines between the factory and the Volga.

On 305th Infantry's left, Heim's 14th Panzer Division continued pounding 62nd Army's makeshift defenses between the Barrikady and Krasnyi Oktiabr' Factories, in particular the defenses of 37th Guards Rifle Division's 109th Regiment, 45th Rifle Division's 10th Regiment, and 193rd Rifle Division's 685th, 895th, and 883rd Regiments protecting the approaches to 62nd Army's last remaining landing stage and the northern edge of the Krasnyi Oktiabr' Factory. By dint of incessant assaults, 14th Panzer's shrunken *kampfgruppen* drove 193rd Division's regiments back to Umanskaia Street, less than three blocks from the factory's northern edge, and 109th Guards and 10th Rifle Regiments another block farther south of Mashinnaia Street toward the Volga River.

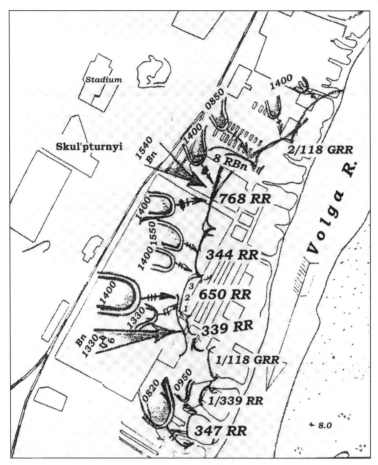

Map 77. Dispositions of 138th Rifle Division, 2000 28 October 1942

These attacks did not come cheap for the advancing Germans. For example, Oppenländer's 305th Division reported 13 men killed and 70 wounded on 27 October; 27 killed, 85 wounded, and 14 missing on 28 October; and another 38 killed, 95 wounded, and 5 missing on 29 October. Fighting on the 305th Infantry's left in the narrow streets and ravines south of the Barrikady Factory, the already decimated 14th Panzer Division reported 13 killed, 77 wounded, and 2 missing on 27 October; 22 killed, 106 wounded, and 7 missing on 28 October; and another 15 killed, 81 wounded, and 10 missing on 29 October. The high toll of missing testified to the close-quarter nature of the fighting and the numerous Soviet counterattacks. And the nearly 300 casualties in 14th Panzer occurred in a division that reported that its strength in panzer-grenadiers was only 1,640 men on 24 October and 750 men on 25 October. During the same period, 305th Infantry Division reported about 300 casualties after reporting its infantry strength at about 1,200 men on 24 October. Completing this mosaic of creeping attrition, by late on 29 October 14th Panzer Division reported that it had only 9 tanks still in action (2 Pz. II, 2 Pz. III short, 2 Pz. III long, 1 Pz. IV long, and 2 command tanks), and 244th and 245th Assault Gun Battalions claimed they had 7 and 3 operational assault guns, respectively.[92]

Meanwhile, in the center of Seydlitz's shock group, Schwerin's 79th Infantry Division was reinforced late on 26 October by its late-arriving 226th Infantry Regiment. Without allowing the regiment to catch its breath, Schwerin immediately threw it into combat on the division's left wing at dawn on 27 October, with orders to capture Halls 1 and 2 in the Krasnyi Oktiabr' Factory. The fresh regiment complied, capturing the two halls in a vicious struggle with 39th Guards Rifle Division's 120th Regiment by late on 27 October. Despite this dramatic gain, during the next two days of heavy fighting Schwerin's reinforced division still proved unable to break the grip of Gur'ev's guardsmen on the factory's now infamous Hall 4.

From the perspective of Lieutenant Colonel Wolf, commander of 79th Division's 208th Regiment:

In the battles that lasted until October 29th, no means of fighting remained unused. Stukas dropped explosive bombs and incendiaries, salvoes of mortar batteries and rocket battalions tore into the halls of the Martin furnaces [Hall 4]. The attacking troops were preceded by a dense bombardment. German assault parties with flamethrowers, attacking concentrically, penetrated the hall at night without any preparatory fire, by surprise. They could not hold it, however. Due to the concentric fire they always ran into after a few minutes, the sudden appearance of a hitherto invisible enemy that seemed to rise up from the earth, their own fighting power that had been reduced considerably, and the tension that was the result of the pauseless [constant] battles, they could not hold on to the territory gained . . . Even when the recently arrived, the 226th IR was committed as [the] neighbor on the left and tried to advance from Halls 1 and 2 across the rubble heaps down to the Volga, this final attempt to take Hall 4 failed. . . .

During the attacks of the 79th Infantry Division on the Metallurgical Factory, it became clear that the hall with the Martin furnaces [Hall 4] was the cornerstone of the enemy resistance. This hall, with the big Martin furnaces with their thick walls, is a natural fortress that till now could neither be destroyed by Stuka bombs or artillery nor taken by infantry and engineers due to its construction that is favorable to the defense.[93]

Schwerin's repeated assaults in the depth of the Krasnyi Oktiabr' Factory were also costly to his division. For example, the division reported it lost 23 killed, 69 wounded, and 1 missing on 27 October; 12 killed, 51 wounded, and 2 missing on 28 October; and another 19 killed, 96 wounded, and 4 missing on the 29th, for a total loss of about 350 men in three days of fighting.[94]

During the heavy fighting on 29 October, Chuikov ordered Sokolov's 45th Rifle Division, the bulk of its forces now on the western bank of the Volga River, to erect a firm defense opposite the German forces lodged in a salient bulging eastward into his army's defenses between the Barrikady and Krasnyi Oktiabr' Factories.[95]

30–31 October

The arrival of the roughly 6,400 men of Sokolov's 45th Rifle Division, albeit only several battalions at a time, tipped the battle in Stalingrad's northern factory district in 62nd Army's favor. Realizing this, Chuikov observed, "On the evening of October 29, the battle began to die down, and on October 30 there were only exchanges of fire; the enemy was utterly exhausted. We knew the Soviet troops were winning the battle."[96] The Red Army General Staff acknowledged as much in its daily reports for the last two days of the month:

[30 October]
62nd Army occupied its previous positions, fortified them, and re-pelled attacks by small enemy groups in the vicinity of Spartanovka, the Krasnyi Oktiabr' Factory, and Artilleriiskaia Street.

The Northern Group's units remained in their previous positions and conducted strong reconnaissance.

138th, 308th, and 193rd RDs defended their previous positions and fortified them.

39th Gds. RD, after repelling two attacks by the enemy [79th ID], fought to improve its positions on the grounds of the Krasnyi Oktiabr' Factory.

284th RD repelled two attacks by up to a company of enemy infantry [295th ID] along Artilleriiskaia Street on the morning of 30 October and repelled attacks by small groups of enemy infantry against its occupied positions beginning at 1400 hours.[97]

[31 October]
62nd Army. A reinforced battalion from 300th RD was fighting to capture the Latashanka region beginning at 0400 hours on 31 October.

The Northern Group of Forces occupied its previous positions.

138th and 308th RDs' subunits repulsed an attack by enemy forces of up to a battalion of infantry [305th ID] but held on to their occupied positions.

193rd RD repelled several attacks by an enemy force of up to two infantry battalions [14th PzD], which were trying to reach the landing stage, and held on to their previous positions.

39th Gds. RD, with a regiment [10th RR] from 45th RD, went over to the attack at 1230 hours on 31 October and, overcoming stubborn enemy resistance [79th ID], [re]occupied several buildings in the Krasnyi Oktiabr' Factory by 1600 hours.

The army's remaining units occupied their previous positions.[98]

As if to underscore the shifting momentum of the struggle, on 31 October 253rd Regiment of Sokolov's 45th Rifle Division, together with elements of 120th Regiment from Gur'ev's 39th Guards Rifle Division, conducted strong counterattacks against 14th Panzer Division's forces, driving eastward toward the Volga between the Barrikady and Krasnyi Oktiabr' Factories, and against 79th Infantry Division's defenses inside the Krasnyi Oktiabr' Factory. By this time, Schwerin's troops had been reinforced by what little was left of Lenski's 24th Panzer Division.[99] During this fighting, 253rd Regiment pressed 79th Division's forces back westward north of the factory, and 39th Guards Rifle Division recaptured Halls 4 and 10, along with other shops in the Krasnyi Oktiabr' Factory. Although Schwerin's infantry managed to drive the attackers out of Hall 10 by nightfall, Chuikov was able to boast:

> Our counterattack took place on October 31 and, in my view, was a great success. In some places we advanced a hundred or so yards, occupied the left side of Novosel'skaia Street and the western fringe of the park, and, in the Krasnyi Oktiabr' Factory, won back the open-hearth [Hall 4—Martenovskii Shop], calibration [Hall 10—Kaliborovnyi Shop], and profiling [Hall 7—Sortovoi Shop] shops and finished products warehouse [Hall 8a south of Hall 10]. But the most important thing was that we had shown the enemy that we could not only defend ourselves but also attack and win back what we had lost. And finally, the last blow, at the end of the fighting from October 14–31, was delivered by us, not the enemy.[100]

The 62nd Army's daily report to the General Staff provided additional details on the fighting:

> The army repelled several attacks by the enemy in the central sector. The 253rd RR (45th RD) and the remnants of 39th Gds. RD went over to a counterattack beginning at 1230 hours with the mission to destroy the enemy in their offensive sectors and restore the situation in the sectors of 193rd RD and 39th Gds. RD. . . .

193rd RD repelled attacks by an enemy force of more than two battalions toward the landing stage. The enemy was thrown back to its jumping-off positions.

253rd RR (45th RD) went over to a counterattack at 1200 hours with the missions to destroy the opposing enemy and reach the line from the railroad to Tupikovaia and Severnaia Streets. Encountering strong resistance by an enemy regiment, which had improved its positions, the regiment reached a line from the western part of Novosel'naia [Street] to the western edge of the garden south of Dolinskaia Street by day's end.

39th Gds. RD had the mission to reach the line of the railroad along Severnaia Street. Overcoming heavy fire resistance, the units captured the Martenovskii, Kaliborovnyi, and Sortovoi Shops and the warehouse for prepared products by day's end.[101]

The recapture of Hall 10 by Schwerin's forces, however, allowed the OKW to put a good face on a bad situation when it announced on 30 October that "German forces are continuing their attacks in Stalingrad with combat reconnaissance groups operating in their first echelon." The next day the OKW noted some exceptional action in the Rynok region, north of Stalingrad, when it reported, "An attempt by several enemy battalions to cross the Volga north of Stalingrad completely miscarried. A large number of cutters were sunk and the main force of Russians was destroyed or taken prisoner."[102]

This fragmentary report reflected a fresh but previously unreported attempt by *front* commander Eremenko to decrease the pressure on Chuikov's beleaguered forces by mounting an amphibious assault across the Volga north of Stalingrad. Evidencing Chuikov's, as well as Eremenko's, newfound optimism, this assault by Eremenko's Stalingrad Front was also aimed at assisting the forces of Gorokhov's Northern Group, which were still confined to the Rynok-Spartanovka region by XIV Panzer Corps' 16th Panzer and 94th Infantry Divisions (see Map 60). Although Chuikov neglected to mention this bold but ill-fated operation in his memoirs—probably because it failed—the Red Army General Staff's daily operational summary kept track of the action in skeletal form. Its account began, "Beginning at 0400 hours on 31 October, a reinforced battalion of 300th RD was fighting to capture the Latashanka region."[103] The General Staff then related the division's subsequent actions correctly, but only in terse summary form, noting on 1 November that "on the army's right flank, as a result of the fighting, 300th RD's [amphibious] assault battalion captured the northeastern part of Latashanka, where it dug in and exchanged fire with up to a battalion of enemy infantry with 14 tanks."[104] After failing to mention 300th Division's fate on 2 November, the General Staff reported on 3 November, "The battalion of 300th RD conducted a fighting withdrawal from the Latashanka region behind the railroad line and continued to fight in the vicinity of the Nizkovodnaia land-ing stage."[105] This report was followed by utter silence.

However, 16th Panzer Division, which was the object of Eremenko's am-phibious assault, did indeed note this bold but ill-fated action. Implying that this was not the first Soviet attempt to cross the river, it recorded:

On the night of 31 October, the Russians made another attempt to gain a firm foothold on Lataschinka as well. As early as the evening of 30 October, the men of *Kampfgruppe* Strehlke were alerted by noise and movement on the other side of the Volga. Around midnight, the can-non and tug boats came closer. Gerke's panzer platoon began firing on the Volga train station. Three boats with 50 Russians each sank, and the others were damaged and turned back. Three boats managed to land at the northeastern edge and southern part of Lataschinka. Their occupants managed to hold their positions on the bank despite machine gun and flak attacks and attacked and entered Lataschinka. Lieutenant Wipperman (16th Panzer Flak) and his Flak crews managed to hold out and inflict losses on the enemy despite the superiority of the attacking forces. The 60 Russians turned south to attack toward Rynok. Under fire from 2nd Company, 16th Panzer Flak, all but a few of these troops were destroyed [along with their commander].

The northern enemy group fought their way to the command post of 3rd Company, 16th Panzer Flak. However, Senior Lieutenant Knoerzer held out with his troops. Under heavy fires, the division prepared a coun-terattack to destroy the enemy that had landed. The Russians were firing from the other side of the river with all of their guns, and the counterat-tack began, but to no avail. At the company's command post, 56 Russians surrendered; another 36 prisoners were taken by 1300 hours.

In the meantime, however, the Russians had landed additional forces and heavy weapons to the north. Although they attacked toward the south with a loud "Urrah," with the help of nine tanks, they were pushed back to the northern edge of Lataschinka.

The next day, the rest of the invaders were destroyed or captured, and the attacks from Rynok were fended off. On the night of 2–3 November, they managed to repel attempts by several large vessels to land. Sub-sequent mopping-up actions cleared the last enemy nests of resistance. Although far inferior to the enemy force numerically, the brave *kampf-gruppe* under the keen leadership of Major Strehlke mastered the task: the 400 men of the Bashkir 300th Division's 1049th Rifle Regiment were held off. Lieutenant Gerke received the *"Ritterkreuz"* [Knight's Cross] for his men's brave defense.[106]

Isaak Kobyliansky, a senior sergeant and gun-crew commander in 300th Rifle Division's 1049th Rifle Regiment, provides a more detailed view of his division's assault, inadvertently also explaining why Chuikov ignored the action in his account of the fighting:

At the end of October, an order came down the chain of command to undertake a landing operation to seize Latashanka in order to draw away some of the enemy's forces from the fighting for Rynok, Spartakovka, and the factory districts in northern Stalingrad and, thereby, relieve the pressure on the defenders. Two battalions of our rifle regiment were designated to form the landing force. By dark night, almost 700 troops embarked on four self-propelled barges that were moored near our bank. There was no strong resistance when they disembarked on the opposite shore at dawn, but the advance along the steep bank was slow. We heard the sounds of fighting from across the river. A report arrived that the landing force had managed to seize only a few peasants' houses by noon. Soon our headquarters lost radio contact with the landing force. Later, before sunset, heavier gunfire was heard, and, in the evening, a lone young soldier swam back across Volga with very bad news. Several German self-propelled guns had arrived in the village and were pressing the landing party back. They needed immediate help.

Our command decided to reinforce the initial landing force. The supporting landing force was our third rifle battalion, reinforced with a field gun platoon and an antitank gun platoon. . . . After sunset, we manhandled both guns of our fire platoon to the embarkation point that was not too far from our emplacements. . . . Well, there were two self-propelled barges moored to the riverbank and waiting to carry us across. We embarked on our barge after the first one had already set off for the opposite bank, sailing slowly with muted engines. But this time the enemy reacted to our crossing. Just after it got dark, the Germans had begun to launch flares. So they discovered us and started shelling ceaselessly. Nevertheless, the first barge managed to reach the far bank, although there were many casualties among the troops it was carrying. But just after our barge left its mooring and its engine had started, a shell exploded beside us, causing a tremendous blast wave that deafened everybody and shook the barge like a small sliver of wood. The engine ceased operating, and the ship started drifting downstream. Several crewmen directed it back to the bank by pressing long poles against the river floor. Fortunately, there were no casualties. That was the end of our battery's participation in the landing operation.

The fate of the troops at Latashanka was tragic. Most of at least nine hundred men were captured, killed, or injured. Only a few survived.[107]

As with the other divisions struggling in the ruins of the factory district, from 16th Panzer Division's perspective "the companies had been bled dry, survivors were weary and exhausted, and weapons and material had worn out. . . . Replenishment was the new task. . . , [but] the situation did not permit it [because] the battle at Stalingrad had not yet been successfully concluded."[108]

Sixth Army's records do indeed indicate that Paulus desisted from continuing his costly assaults after 30 October, and the army's casualty reports after that date confirm this fact. According to LI Corps' daily reports, the casualties in its division decreased from more than 100 men per day prior to 31 October to roughly one-third that number thereafter. Even so, as the desperate fighting in Stalingrad's factory district and in the Rynok and Spartanovka regions north of the Mokraia Mechetka River indicated, neither Seydlitz nor his superiors—Paulus and Weichs—had yet to devise a means for winning this most critical of battles.

64TH ARMY'S COUNTERSTROKE, 25 OCTOBER–2 NOVEMBER

While Seydlitz was conducting his costly but indecisive assault in the southern section of Stalingrad's northern factory district, Eremenko activated offensive operations in 64th Army's sector. Ostensibly, the assault by Shumilov's army was designed to clear German forces from the southern part of Stalingrad. More realistically, however, the aim of this short offensive was to draw away German forces from the far more crucial fighting taking place to the north (see Map 78).

After receiving guidance from Stalin on 15 October, Eremenko dispatched his proposed plan of action to the *Stavka* at 1800 hours on 17 October. He assessed that Shumilov's 64th Army faced the German 71st Infantry and 29th Motorized Divisions, backed up by part of 371st Infantry Division. These forces manned defensive positions extending along a 9-kilometer front from the western bank of the Volga south of Kuporosnoe westward across Peschanka *Balka* to roughly 5 kilometers west of Gornaia Poliana. Eremenko's plan required 64th Army's shock group to penetrate 371st Infantry Division's defenses and advance northward to the Tsaritsa River to link up with 62nd Army's 13th Guards Rifle Division in Stalingrad's central city. Specifically, Shumilov's army was to "conduct a main attack in the 4-kilometer-wide sector along the front from Kuporosnoe to 'Topor' [Axe] Grove (1 kilometer south of Zelenaia Poliana)."[109] Eremenko hoped that an attack on this scale could "attract one infantry and one panzer division from the Stalingrad region."[110]

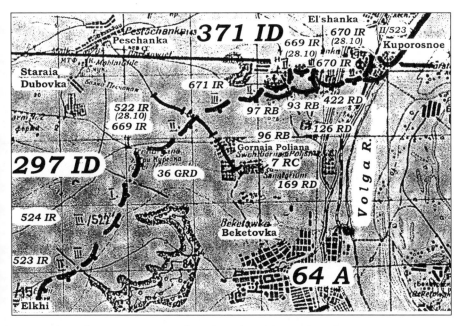

Map 78. 64th Army's counterstroke, 25 October–2 November 1942

Eremenko's plan also required 64th Army to conduct its assault with the relatively fresh 93rd, 96th, and 97th Rifle Brigades of its 7th Rifle Corps, 169th Rifle Division, and the army's 422nd and 126th Rifle Divisions. The total strength of the attacking force was roughly 30,000 men. The attack was to be supported by 80 tanks from 90th, 56th, 13th, and 155th Separate Tank Brigades, 92 rocket launchers from seven guards-mortar regiments, and 243 artillery pieces from 64th Army's artillery. Eighty fighters and 100 assault aircraft from Stalingrad Front's 8th Air Army were to provide Shumilov's attacking forces with air support. Once it assembled its shock group, 64th Army deployed it for the attack in two echelons, with 7th Rifle Corps' 93rd and 97th Rifle Brigades, 422nd Rifle Division, and two supporting tank brigades with 55 tanks in first echelon, and 126th Rifle Division, 96th Rifle Brigade, and two tank brigades with 25 tanks in second echelon. The 169th Rifle Division was retained in general reserve with orders to reinforce the attack whenever and wherever required.[111]

During the first phase of the attack, which was to begin at dawn on 23 October, the shock group's first echelon would assault and destroy 371st Infantry Division's 670th and 671st Infantry Regiments and advance roughly 15 kilometers to reach the Tsaritsa River. After being reinforced by the second echelon and, if necessary, the reserve, the shock group would then continue its advance northeastward, clear German forces from southern Stalingrad, and link up with 62nd Army in Stalingrad's center. Eremenko estimated that Shumilov's force of 30,000 men and 80 tanks would ultimately face as many as two German infantry divisions and one motorized division, with 15,000 men, 100–120 tanks, up to 400 guns, 80 antitank guns, 185 mortars, and 790 machine guns. Therefore, he estimated that the entire operation would take 10 days to complete.[112]

This estimate, however, proved wildly inaccurate, because Shumilov's shock group actually faced only 371st Infantry Division's 670th and 671st Regiments, which were deployed with all three of their battalions on line from the Volga River at Kuporosnoe westward to roughly 2 kilometers southwest of Zelenaia Poliana. 371st Infantry Division's 669th Regiment defended a 5-kilometer sector southwest of Gornaia Poliana, flanked on the right by 297th Infantry Division and a small *kampfgruppe* from 29th Motorized Division—both far away from 64th Army's main attack sector. In addition, 71st Infantry Division was defending along the western bank of the Volga River from Stalingrad's center city southward to Kuporosnoe with its 211th Regiment, and the main forces of 29th Motorized Division were resting and refitting in reserve assembly areas well to the west of the Beketovka bridgehead.[113] This meant that 64th Army's shock group of 30,000 men and 80 tanks faced five battalions of German infantry with well less than 5,000 men in the sector from the Volga to Zelenaia Poliana, although the German forces occupied well-prepared and fortified defensive positions.

The preparations for the operation proved more difficult than anticipated. And as indicated by a scathing rebuke from the *Stavka*, 64th Army apparently neglected to follow mandatory security measures:

> Henceforth, the *Stavka* of the Supreme High Command categorically prohibits you from sending any reports, whatever they may be, concerning the operational plan and issuing and disseminating orders about forthcoming operations by cipher. Dispatch all operational plans demanded by the *Stavka* only by handwriting and with responsible executors. Issue orders about the forthcoming operation to the army commanders only personally on the map.[114]

After delaying the operation for several days to complete necessary offensive preparations, Shumilov's army began its assaults at 0900 hours on 25 October. The army's official history provides a rather perfunctory description of the ensuing action:

The Krasnyi Oktiabr' and Barrikady Factories before the fighting (taken on 21 July 1942).

The view south across the Barrikady Factory at Halls 6 and 2.

The view looking west across Hall 6c in the southern portion of the Barrikady Factory, with Stal'naia Street and the ravine on the left. Note the numerous shell and bomb craters.

The view southwest across Hall 6d in the Barrikady Factory.

Soviet infantry fighting in the Barrikady Factory.

A battered building in the Bread Factory south of the Barrikady Factory.

The famed Red Army sniper, Sergeant V. G. Zaitsev, a soldier in Batiuk's 284th Rifle Division, who wrought havoc in German ranks during the fighting in Stalingrad's factory district.

Sergeant Vasiliy Zaitsev receiving his Party card at a brief ceremony in November 1942.

The Krasnyi Oktiabr' region from west (left) to east (right), with the Volga River running from north (top) to south (bottom) on the extreme right. The lower Krasnyi Oktiabr' village and Bannyi Ravine from top to bottom on the left, the railroad from top to bottom in the center, and the Krasnyi Oktiabr' Factory oil storage tanks and the "Tennis Racket" from top to bottom on the right.

The Krasnyi Oktiabr' Factory (center), with the railroad line across the top, and Bannyi Ravine and oil storage tanks on the left, Samarkandskaia and Donetskaia Streets on the right, and the Volga River at the bottom.

The Krasnyi Oktiabr' Factory under assault in October 1942.

The German bombardment of the oil storage tanks and Krasnyi Oktiabr' Factory in late October 1942.

Combat within the Krasnyi Oktiabr' Factory (looking toward the southwest), with Halls 3 and 4 on the left and Hall 5 on the right.

Soldiers of 39th Guards Rifle Division (on the bank of the Volga) taking an oath "to fight to the death" while defending the Krasnyi Oktiabr' Factory.

Troops of 39th Guards Rifle Division fighting in one of the halls in the Krasnyi
Oktiabr' Factory.

Soldiers of 39th Guards Rifle Division defending a position in the Krasnyi
Oktiabr' Factory.

People's militiamen
participating in the
defense of the Krasnyi
Oktiabr' Factory.

Several of the tens of
thousands of civilians
who endured the fighting
in Stalingrad city.

The forces went over to the offensive on the morning of 25 October after an artillery preparation. On the first day of the operation, the formations of the army captured part of Kuporosnoe. However, strong enemy resistance prevented further development of the offensive.

Fierce fighting in this sector of the front continued from 25 October through 1 November. Despite the fact that the forces participating in the counterstroke advanced only three–four kilometers, the enemy was forced to hold considerable forces here and bring reserves forward. As a result of our counterstroke, the Germans halted their onslaught against 62nd Army in the city's factory district.[115]

Actually, nothing could be farther from the truth. The 371st Infantry Division did indeed lose several hundred meters of ground in downtown Kuporosnoe and suffered a 1- to 2-kilometer-deep dent in its defenses west of the town and southwest of Peschanka. Nevertheless, it was able to stabilize the situation by shifting 669th Regiment from its sector west of Gornaia Poliana into the threatened region, where it established new defenses. The division then stabilized the situation in Kuporosnoe by concentrating its 670th and 676th Regiments in the town and reinforcing them with a battalion from 297th Infantry Division's 523rd Regiment. Therefore, German Sixth Army saw no need to transfer any forces in the vicinity of the factory district southward to the Kuporosnoe region. A reinforced German division had halted the best Shumilov's 64th Army could muster.

Together with periodic German reports, the Red Army General Staff's daily operational summary provides additional detail about 64th Army's struggle in the Kuporosnoe region on 25 October:

64th Army conducted offensive fighting in the Kuporosnoe region with part of its forces beginning at 0900 hours 25 October.

422nd RD, overcoming strong enemy fire resistance, captured the southern part of Kuporosnoe and reached the southern bank of the ravine south of Kozh by 1700 hours on 25 October.

93rd RB captured the grove at Marker 43.8 by 1700 hours on 25 October.

97th RB reached the sandy region 1.5 kilometers southwest of Zelenaia Poliana at the same time, but only after overcoming strong enemy fire.

The army's remaining units occupied their previous positions.[116]

By evening, Army Group B correctly reported, "South of Stalingrad, 30–40 Russian tanks, supported by assault aircraft, attacked the positions of 371st [Infantry] Division after a powerful artillery preparation. The attacks were beaten off, and the enemy suffered heavy losses."[117]

The next day, Stalingrad Front reported, "64th Army resumed its attacks with its shock groups along previous axes at 1130 hours on 26 October . . . and, after overcoming strong enemy fire, advanced forward insignificantly."[118] Specifically, while 422nd Rifle Division, 97th Rifle Brigade, and 36th Guards Rifle Division "fought in their previous positions," and "after a sharp exchange of fire with the enemy, 93rd RB's units once again approached Marker 43.8 (2 kilometers west of Kuporosnoe)."[119] After 422nd Rifle Division resumed its attack on 27 October, that evening Stalingrad Front reported, "64th Army's 422nd RD, having overcome resistance by the enemy's 371st ID, captured the southern portion of Kuporosnoe," and "7th RC's and 36th GRD's units . . . successfully repelled four enemy counterattacks in the Kuporosnoe and Hill 145.5 sector and held on to their occupied positions."[120]

Once again, Army Group B's daily operational summary confirmed Shumilov's limited success:

> South of Stalingrad, yesterday the enemy repeatedly attacked the 371st Infantry Division's positions in the region west of the Volga during the second half of the day. As a result of tank attacks and powerful artillery fire, the sector of the wedge formed the day before by the enemy was broadened. The enemy succeeded in wedging into the southern part of Kuporosnoe. The sector of the wedge has been blocked; measures are being taken to eliminate the wedge.[121]

Elaborating on the situation, the army group's intelligence officer added that in Fourth Panzer Army's sector "after the attack by an enemy force of up to a battalion supported by tanks against the left wing of IV Army Corps south of Kuporosnoe was repelled in the morning, the enemy attacked 371st Infantry Division's front simultaneously from three directions at midday. He succeeded in wedging into the southern part of Kuporosnoe. The fighting is continuing."[122]

By 28 October, however, it was clear to both sides that Shumilov's gambit had stalled irrevocably. At day's end, for example, the Red Army General Staff asserted that although 64th Army was still conducting "offensive fighting in the Kuporosnoe region with units of its shock group beginning at 1300 hours . . . , our units abandoned Kuporosnoe *Balka* and the Kvadratnaia [Quadrilateral] and Topor [Axe] Groves (both groves 0.5–1.5 kilometers west of Kuporosnoe *Balka*) as a result of several enemy counterattacks."[123] The OKW seconded this judgment, adding, "As before, the diversionary attacks by large enemy forces supported by tanks against the German positions south of Stalingrad were repelled. The enemy suffered heavy losses."[124]

Nevertheless, because the situation in Stalingrad's factory district was still in doubt, Eremenko insisted that Shumilov persist in his attacks. Dutifully, Shumilov on 29 October reported that the bulk of his army had "dug in along its occupied positions with the units on its right wing and repelled enemy counterattacks in the Kuporosnoe region," and its 422nd Rifle Division had "repelled a counterattack by an enemy infantry battalion against the southern part of Kuporosnoe." However, pursuant to Eremenko's orders, "36th Gds. RD and the composite Student [Officers] Regiment conducted an unsuccessful attack toward Hill 145.5 (3 kilometers southeast of Peschanka) beginning at 1400 hours."[125] When this action ended, the OKW repeated almost verbatim its report from the day before: "South of Stalingrad, as on the day before, the diversionary attacks which the enemy launched with tank support were repelled by fire from all kinds of weapons in cooperation with aircraft."[126]

Thereafter, the fighting in the Kuporosnoe region went on intermittently for three more days as Shumilov strove to fulfill his *front* commander's orders to the letter. Despite Shumilov's resolve, the defending Germans repelled every attack with apparent ease. Echoing the OKW's terse announcements, the Red Army General Staff's daily operational summaries reflected the sad reality of defeat:

[30 October]
64th Army repelled three attacks by enemy infantry and tanks from the vicinity of "Kvadratnaia" Grove (2 kilometers west of Kuporosnoe) toward the south with the units on its right wing. The enemy withdrew to his jumping-off positions after losing up to 300 men killed and wounded.

7th RC continued to hold the line from the southern part of Kuporosnoe to the Kuporosnoe *Balka* and the center of the sandy region 1 kilometer southwest of Zelenaia Poliana.[127]

The same day, the OKW declared, "The enemy was forced to cease his offensive south of Stalingrad because of heavy losses."[128]

[31 October]
64th Army conducted offensive operations in the region southwest of Kuporosnoe with part of its forces.

97th RB, attacking toward the "Topor" Grove (2 kilometers west of the Kuporosnoe *Balka*), captured the first line of enemy trenches at the southern edge of this grove by 1800 hours on 31 October.

36th Gds. RD, with 108th RR, the composite Student Regiment, and a battalion from 93rd RB, attacked toward Hill 145.5 (5 kilometers southwest of Kuporosnoe) and captured enemy foxholes on the northern slope of this height.

The army's remaining units occupied their previous positions.[129]

The OKW reported: "South of Stalingrad, the enemy once again counterattacked unsuccessfully."[130]

[1 November]

64th Army, remaining in its previous positions, continued offensive operations in the region southwest of Kuporosnoe with part of its forces but, having encountered strong enemy resistance, had no success.

97th TB repulsed an attack by up to two companies of enemy infantry from the "Topor" Grove (2 kilometers west of the Kuporosnoe *Balka*) on 1 November.

A guards regiment of 36th Gds. RD, 1st Bn, 93rd RB, the composite Student Regiment, and 90th TB twice attacked the enemy in the vicinity of Hill 145.5 (4 kilometers southeast of Peschanka) but encountered heavy resistance and had no success.[131]

The OKW echoed, "New enemy attacks supported by tanks were repelled south of Stalingrad."[132]

Although Shumilov's counterstroke barely dented Fourth Panzer Army's defenses along the northern side of the Beketovka bridgehead, the Soviet defeat had a lasting and misleading effect on German decisionmakers at every level of command. Coupled with the multiple failures by Soviet forces to sustain successful offensives in late July and August, and the repeated failed attempts by Rokossovsky's armies to collapse the Germans' defenses in the corridor between the Don and Volga Rivers north of Stalingrad, the relative ease with which Fourth Panzer Army repelled 64th Army's assaults south of Stalingrad left the distinct impression that the *Wehrmacht's* forces— whenever and wherever the Soviets mounted counterstrokes and even a counteroffensive—would be able to fend off the attackers with relative ease. This persistent faith on the part of German senior commanders in the *Wehrmacht's* apparent invincibility would have a particularly telling effect on how these commanders responded to an ever-increasing number of intelligence reports warning them of troop movements indicative of a future Soviet counteroffensive. It also failed to anticipate what might happen if the Soviet counterstroke fell against satellite Axis units rather than German units.

CONCLUSIONS

Sixth Army's struggle to overcome 62nd Army's defenses in the southern section of Stalingrad's factory district was as frustrating as it was difficult. Despite Seydlitz's best efforts, LI Corps failed to accomplish its primary mission—to clear Soviet forces from the Barrikady and Krasnyi Oktiabr' Factories and to seize the Soviets' last remaining ferry site along the Volga to prevent further reinforcement of Chuikov's depleted forces. Compounding this failure, after committing the fresh 79th Infantry Division to the struggle, all of Paulus's divisions fighting in Stalingrad suffered grievous losses, virtually all of his infantry divisions were rated "combat ineffective," and his panzer divisions and assault-gun battalions were shells of their former selves. By 31 October, for example, 14th Panzer mustered 11 tanks; 24th Panzer, despite being rested for almost a week, reported its armor strength was only 16 tanks. Between them, 244th and 245th Assault Gun Detachments fielded only six guns.[133]

Because Hitler still demanded that his army crush the last vestiges of Soviet resistance once and for all, Paulus and Seydlitz would have to do so with company-size rather than battalion- or regiment-size *kampfgruppen*. Because neither commander thought this possible, both began to search for other solutions to this dilemma, principally reinforcements obtained from whatever quarter possible. Unfortunately, this would ultimately mean further denuding the German divisions defending elsewhere along the front.

As if to underscore the adverse effects that this attrition warfare was having on Paulus's Sixth Army, Chuikov on 1 November estimated that 10 German divisions opposed 62nd Army's forces in Stalingrad. He estimated that these divisions (correctly identified as 71st, 79th, 94th, 100th, 295th, 305th, and 389th Infantry and 14th, 16th, and 24th Panzer Divisions) fielded a total of 80 infantry and 28 artillery battalions, with a combat-effective strength of 23,000 fighters and 130–150 tanks and assault guns.[134] Surprisingly, although this estimate of German dismounted strength was close to the mark, Chuikov overestimated the strength of LI Corps' armor and underestimated that of XIV Panzer Corps. Broken down by sector, Chuikov assessed that roughly 40 tanks and assault guns were operating against the Northern Group of Forces (as opposed to an actual figure of 113), that up to 90 were facing his forces in the factory district (as opposed to an actual figure of 32), and that another 20 were deployed opposite his army's southern sector—most, if not all, attached to support infantry divisions. Chuikov also claimed that the Germans were concentrating up to 100 tanks and assault guns (from 29th Motorized and 22nd Panzer Division) in the Gorodishche-Sadovaia region, but this was mistaken.

Quantifying the effects of the fighting on Paulus's infantry forces, 62nd Army estimated that Sixth Army had lost up to 10,000 men killed and wounded and about 50 tanks during the period from 20 October to 1 November, the bulk of these losses suffered by 305th and 79th Infantry, 100th Jäger, and 14th Panzer Divisions. Assessing future German intentions, Chuikov anticipated that they would make the next main effort against the Krasnyi Oktiabr' Factory and Hill 102.0 (Mamaev Kurgan) and that, to this end, they could reinforce their shock groups with one more infantry division and tanks from the Gorodishche region.

After carefully pointing out the Germans' obvious strengths, Chuikov then astutely assessed German tactics, accurately accentuating the difficulties with which Paulus's forces had to contend:

From the perspective of operational principles, one should mention the rapid maneuvering and regrouping and the reinforcing of attacks along separate axes, even at the expense of the splitting up of divisions. . . .

This also manifests itself in the indicator of the exhaustion of enemy forces located in close contact with our forces. The tactical principles of the enemy's actions present themselves in the methodical gnawing through of our defenses, while digging themselves in along their occupied lines. The enemy infiltrates between our combat formations with small groups, which hold on to the last man, and then the enemy develops success along this axis with larger forces of infantry and tanks.[135]

Chuikov's acute appreciation of the problems Paulus faced in no way diminished his concerns for his own army's survival. His assessment acknowledged the intense fighting during the last week of October, which cost his forces 300–500 casualties per day, and indeed tested the limits of his army's endurance. Despite receiving two more divisions as reinforcements, which maintained the overall personnel strength of his army at roughly 50,000 men, the severe attrition affecting his forces on the Volga's western bank had reduced aggregate strength to fewer than 15,000 defenders by 31 October. Making matters worse, the incessant German assaults during this period had chopped his bridgehead into three separate enclaves. Group Gorokhov was isolated north of the Mokraia Mechetka River; 138th, 308th, 193rd, and 45th Rifle and 39th Guards Rifle Divisions were pinned into the shallow bridgehead in and adjacent to the Barrikady and Krasnyi Oktiabr' Factories; and 284th Rifle and 13th Guards Rifle Divisions clung to the eastern half of Mamaev Kurgan, the Tennis Racket, and a narrow sliver of ground on the Volga's western bank in Stalingrad's center city. If this was not bad enough, German forces threatened the last few landing stages in these sectors, and ice floes forming on the partially frozen river would very soon make it more difficult for Chuikov to supply and reinforce his forces.

Yet when all was said and done, Chuikov's task was far simpler than was Paulus's. Hitler demanded that Sixth Army capture the rest of the city with forces no longer capable of conducting sustained operations while simultaneously defending both the city and the army's long flanks. By contrast, Chuikov, if necessary, could accomplish his mission—to tie down German forces fighting in the city—simply by ordering his army to die in place. And by spoon-feeding reinforcements to 62nd Army, Eremenko could see to it that Chuikov's army died for a purpose.

Faced with this familiar dilemma, Paulus and Seydlitz began searching elsewhere in late October for a solution to what by now many, if not
most, German officers and soldiers felt was an impossible task. If Sixth Army
needed reinforcements, then the vital issue was where they could be obtained. In its diminished state, the bulk of the striking power of Paulus's
force was concentrated on Stalingrad, leaving only the fragile armies of its
Axis allies to defend the extended Don River front northwest of Stalingrad
and the expansive lake district south of the city. Quite naturally, therefore,
Paulus turned his gaze to neighboring Army Group A as the only reasonable
source for needed reserves. By this time, however, List's army group was as
overextended as its counterpart to the north and was facing multiple crises
of its own.

CHAPTER 8

The Struggle on the Flanks, 11 September–18 November 1942

THE CAUCASUS IN SEPTEMBER: HITLER TAKES COMMAND

The successful defense that Trans-Caucasus Front mounted at Tuapse, Mozdok, and in the High Caucasus was the immediate cause of a major crisis within the German High Command (OKW). All summer, Adolf Hitler had become increasingly frustrated with his commanders, especially Field Marshal Wilhelm List, whose Army Group A had been conducting operations to seize the Caucasus region and its vital oil fields and ports. Just as Stalin was beginning to trust his staff officers and field commanders, his German counterpart was losing his last ounce of patience with these professionals. From Hitler's point of view, his generals had repeatedly disputed or ignored his wishes, thereby (in his mind) permitting the Red Army to escape a series of encirclements. Hitler, who had so often before succeeded by simple iron determination, rejected the notion that the German forces were inadequate to achieve his strategic goals. In August, as will be discussed below, Soviet offensives against Army Group Center and Army Group North had produced a series of minor crises, absorbing reserve units and resources needed for the offensive in the south as well as an improved defensive posture in Western Europe. Maikop, when captured, proved to be virtually unusable as a fuel source because retreating Red Army troops had destroyed much of its oil facilities. Finally, List had come to a halt in the Caucasus, stopped by a Red Army that Hitler believed he had already destroyed.[1]

For months, Hitler had confined his disparaging remarks to staff assistants, who acted as effective buffers for the field commanders. Then, after consultations on 24 August with Colonel General Richard Ruoff, the commander of Seventeenth Army, the chief of staff of Colonel General Ewald von Kleist's First Panzer Army, and General Rudolf Konrad, the commander of XXXXIX Mountain Corps, List informed the OKH that his army group's operations had "lost their fluidity" because of fuel shortages, casualties, and the enemy's ability to dig in and bring up reserves.[2] Because this retarded the campaign's progress, it was "a cause for serious thought."[3] On 26 August, List acknowledged that his command had fallen behind schedule and reported snowstorms were already impeding XXXXIX Corps at higher elevations, suggesting that his forces, unless he was reinforced by 15 September, might have to go into winter quarters.

Irritated by his army group commander, Hitler summoned List's chief of staff, General Gylenfeldt, to the Führer's forward command complex, *Werwolf*, near Vinnitsa. Dissatisfied by Gylenfeldt's explanations, he ordered List to report on the situation in person on 31 August. By the time this meeting took place, German successes at the port city and naval base of Novorossiisk had mollified Hitler to some degree. Although accounts of this meeting differ, there was only one clear outcome—Hitler diverted sufficient aircraft from Stalingrad to permit Operation Blücher II, Eleventh Army's assault against the Taman' Peninsula, to take place on 2 September. More generally, Hitler apparently believed the field marshal would reenergize the advance toward Tuapse on the Black Sea coast and Grozny in the Caucasus oil fields. List, by contrast, thought he had convinced the dictator that future operations depended on improved logistics.[4]

The understanding lasted for only a week. On 7 September General Alfred Jodl visited Army Group A's headquarters at Stalino. There, List and XXXXIX Mountain Corps' commander, General Konrad, convinced the OKW's operations chief that the mountain corps was exhausted and could not continue its advance over the narrow mountain passes. Instead, List proposed to redeploy most of the mountain corps' forces to the Maikop sector, where it would operate jointly with XXXXIV Army Corps against Tuapse. The next day, Jodl attempted to persuade Hitler on List's behalf. The dictator's response was outrage. "Your orders were to drive the commanders and troops forward, not to tell me that this is impossible."[5] When Jodl insisted that List had only followed orders, Hitler denied it vehemently and instituted a policy of having verbatim stenographic records taken for all his conferences. On 9 September, Hitler directed that List be relieved. He himself assumed command of Army Group A, ordering the two army commanders, Ruoff and Kleist, to report directly to him. In practice, of course, Hitler devoted little attention to his new "command," and Major General Hans von Greiffenberg actually ran operations as the army group chief of staff.[6]

The dictator's anger did not stop with one victim. He refused to shake hands or even to eat meals with his generals, isolating himself from their advice. Hitler spoke openly of replacing all three of his principal assistants— Keitel and Jodl at the OKW, and Halder at the OKH. Emotionally exhausted, Halder acquiesced and turned over his position to Colonel General Kurt Zeitzler effective 24 September. Four days before, Hitler reportedly remarked, "At the moment I have no confidence in any of my generals; I'd [promote] a major up to general and make him Chief of the General Staff if I knew of one."[7] Keitel and Jodl remained, although Paulus was at one time scheduled to replace the latter.

OPPOSING FORCES

During the ensuing two months, in the wake of Army Group A's reorganization in early September, its organizational structure changed significantly as Hitler, Kleist, and Ruoff shifted divisions to and fro among corps to find that magic mix of forces necessary to sustain offensive operations to the depths of their ambitious objectives (see Table 38).

On the other side, the *Stavka* on 1 September had entrusted Army General I. V. Tiulenev's Trans-Caucasus Front with full responsibility for defending the Caucasus region. According to this directive, the former North Caucasus Front, with its 12th, 18th, 47th, and 56th Armies and 5th Air Army, became the Trans-Caucasus Front's Black Sea Group of Forces. Thereafter, Tiulenev reorganized and strengthened his forces to cope with the impending German offensives toward the Black Sea ports and Caucasus oil fields. While the *front* commander raised fresh forces within the bounds of the Caucasus region, the *Stavka* assisted him by dispatching personnel reinforcements across the Caspian Sea and by granting him priority use of Lend-Lease equipment that the Allies sent through Iran. Tiulenev, in turn, employed most of these resources to reinforce his forces resisting the German offensive.

By early September, Tiulenev's *front* consisted of Lieutenant General I. I. Maslennikov's Northern Group of Forces, Colonel General Ia. T. Cherevichenko's Black Sea Group of Forces, and so-called nonoperating forces situated in the Trans-Caucasus region (south of the High Caucasus). Maslennikov's Northern Group consisted of 9th, 37th, 44th, 46th, and 58th Armies and 4th Air Army, and was responsible for defending the regions near the Terek River, Nal'chik, and Groznyi on the approaches to Baku. Cherevichenko's Black Sea Group, which consisted of 18th, 47th, and 56th Armies and 5th Air Army, was to protect the passes through the High Caucasus and the important naval bases on the eastern coast of the Black Sea. Finally, the *front*'s nonoperating forces secured its rear area, in particular the Baku oil fields, the Black Sea port of Batumi, the borders with Turkey and Iran, and the vital Lend-Lease supply routes through Iran. Reflecting the fluid situation in the Caucasus during the fall of 1942, the organization of Tiulenev's *front* and its two subordinate operational groups also changed substantially after early September (see Table 39 at the end of this chapter).

THE MOZDOK-MALGOBEK OPERATION, 2–28 SEPTEMBER

The shakeup in command had only a limited effect upon the advance of Army Group A. At the end of its long logistical tether, the army group had

Table 38. The Organization of Army Group A, 1 September– 20 November 1942

Army Group A – Field Marshal Wilhelm List, Adolf Hitler on 9 September, and Field
    Marshal Ewald von Kleist on 3 November
First Panzer Army – Colonel General Ewald von Kleist, Lieutenant General
    Eberhard von Mackensen on 3 November
III Panzer Corps – Lieutenant General Eberhard von Mackensen
    23rd Panzer Division – Lieutenant General Hans Wilhelm Freiherr von
        Boineburg-Lengsfeld (mid-September)
    13th Panzer Division – General of Panzer Troops Traugott Herr (late September)
    Romanian 2nd Infantry Division (early September) (to Group Steinbauer in
        late September but returned in late October)
    370th Infantry Division (late September) (to LII Corps in mid-November)
    SS "Viking" Motorized Division (late November)
        XXXX Panzer Corps – General of Panzer Troops Leo Freiherr Geyr
            von Schweppenburg
    3rd Panzer Division – General of Panzer Troops Hermann Breith
    13th Panzer Division – General of Panzer Troops Traugott Herr (to LIII
        Army Corps in early September)
    23rd Panzer Division – Lieutenant General Hans Wilhelm Freiherr von
        Boineburg-Lengsfeld (to III Panzer Corps in mid-September)
    Romanian 2nd Infantry Division (to III Panzer Corps in early September)
LII Army Corps – General of Infantry Eugen Ott
    111th Infantry Division (temporarily to Corps Cmd zb V in late November)
    370th Infantry Division (to III Panzer Corps in late September but returned in
        mid-November)
    13th Panzer Division – General of Panzer Troops Traugott Herr (early
        September) (to III Panzer Corps in late September)
    SS "Viking" Motorized Division (late September) (to III Panzer Corps in late
        November)
    50th Infantry Division (-) (late November)
Group Steinbauer (formed in late September and disbanded in late October)
    Romanian 2nd Mountain Division (to III Panzer Corps in late October)
    Army Artillery Command 311
Headquarters Command zb V [For employment] (mid-October)
    111th Infantry Division (temporarily in late November)
    50th Infantry Division (early November) (to LII Corps in late November)

Seventeenth Army – Colonel General Richard Ruoff
    V Army Corps (Group Wetzel in mid-September) – General of Infantry Wilhelm Wetzel
        9th Infantry Division
        73rd Infantry Division
        125th Infantry Division (to LVII Panzer Corps in late September)
        198th Infantry Division (to LVII Panzer Corps in early September)
        Romanian 5th Cavalry Division (in mid-September) (to Army Group B reserve
            in mid-October)
        Romanian 9th Cavalry Division (to Romanian Cavalry Corps in mid-October)
        Romanian 3rd Mountain Division (mid-September) (to Romanian Mountain
            Corps in late September but returned in mid-October)
        Romanian 10th Infantry Division (in mid-October)
    XXXXIV Army Corps – General of Artillery Maximilian de Angelis
        97th Jäger Division
        101st Jäger Division
        46th Infantry Division (late September) (to XXXXIX Mountain Corps in early
            October)

Table 38. (continued)

XXXXIX Mountain Corps – General of Mountain Troops Rudolf Konrad
  1st Mountain Division (one regiment detached from late September to early
    October)
  4th Mountain Division (one regiment detached from late September to early
    October)
  46th Infantry Division (in early October)
LVII Panzer Corps – General of Panzer Troops Friedrich Kirchner
  125th Infantry Division (in late September)
  198th Infantry Division (in early September)
  SS "Viking" Motorized Division (to LII Corps in late September)
  Slovak Mobile Division
Military Commander Crimea
  XXXXII Army Corps (hqs. only)
  Romanian Mountain Corps
    Romanian 1st Mountain Division
    Romanian 4th Mountain Division
    Staff Schröder (to mid-October)
  Reserve
    Romanian 8th Cavalry Division (to Fourth Panzer Army reserve in late
      October)
    50th Infantry Division (to First Panzer Army reserve in early November)
    Romanian 10th Infantry Division (mid-November).
Reserve:
  46th Infantry Division (in mid-September) (to XXXXIV Corps in late September)
  Romanian Third Army – General Petre Dumitrescu (early October to Army Group B)
  Romanian 7th Army Corps (from early October to early November)
Army Group Rear Area Command A
  444th Security Division
  454th Security Division

Source: William McCrodden, *German Ground Forces Orders of Battle, World War Two* (Self-published revised edition, 2002).
Note: Notation "(=)" means without some part of the forces

to exert extreme efforts, often moving forces to and fro across the broad but critical Caucasus front one division at a time, in order to mount operations with genuine promise of success. By the end of the first week of September, its forces reckoned on such success in only two sectors: the axis through the western Caucasus Mountains from the region south of Maikop to Tuapse on the Black Sea, and the Baksan-Nal'chik and Mozdok-Ordzhonikidze axis southward from the Baksan and Terek Rivers. Since it would take days if not weeks for Ruoff to mount his advance on Tuapse, Hitler's and the OKH's attentions in early September turned to the Terek River sector. There, Kleist's forces had captured Mozdok on 25 August and reinforced this sector with 111th and 370th Infantry Divisions of General Eugen Ott's LII Army Corps by the first few days of September.

By 1 September, with Konrad's XXXXIX Mountain Corps having already been transferred to Seventeenth Army, Kleist's First Panzer Army consisted of Lieutenant General Eberhard von Mackensen's III and General

Leo *Freiherr* Geyr von Schweppenburg's XXXX Panzer Corps and Ott's LII Army Corps. On his army's left wing, XXXX Panzer Corps' 3rd and 13th Panzer Divisions, commanded by Generals Hermann Breith and Traugott Herr, respectively, were deployed along the Terek River east of Mozdok. The latter division was already under orders to shift westward and join LII Corps at Mozdok to spearhead Kleist's future offensive southward from the city toward Ordzhonikidze. In the panzer army's center, LII Corps' 111th Infantry Division, commanded by General Hermann Recknagel, occupied positions along the Terek River in and east of Mozdok, and Lieutenant General Dr. Ernst Klepp's (succeeded on 15 September by Lieutenant General Fritz Becker) 370th Infantry Division manned defenses along the Terek River west of the city, with one *kampfgruppe* defending the town of Prokhladnyi farther west.[8] On Kleist's long right wing, III Panzer Corps defended the Baksan River line west of Prokhladnyi with General Hans Wilhelm *Freiherr* von Boineburg-Lengsfeld's 23rd Panzer Division and the Baksan region farther west with Romanian 2nd Mountain Division.[9]

Once the *Stavka*, Tiulenev, and Maslennikov completed reorganizing their forces along and south of the Baksan and Terek Rivers, the Trans-Caucasus Front's Northern Group of Forces was deployed from left to right (west to east) as follows:

- **37th Army** (Major General P. M. Kozlov), with 2nd Guards, 275th, 392nd, and 295th Rifle and 11th NKVD Rifle Divisions defending the Baksan River from Baksan to south of Prokhladnyi to prevent the German III Panzer Corps' Romanian 2nd Mountain and 23rd Panzer Divisions from advancing southward toward Nal'chik;

- **9th Army** (Major General K. A. Koroteev), with 151st, 176th, 389th, and 417th Rifle Divisions, 62nd Naval Rifle Brigade, and 8th, 9th, and 10th Guards Rifle Brigades of 11th Guards Rifle Corps (Major General I. P. Roslyi) defending the Terek River from south of Prokhladnyi eastward south of Mozdok to just northwest of Groznyi. The army's mission was to prevent LII Corps' 370th and 111th Infantry and III Panzer Corps' 13th Panzer Divisions from crossing the Terek River and advancing southward toward Ordzhonikidze;

- **44th Army** (Major General M. E. Petrov), with 223rd, 414th, and 416th Rifle Divisions and 9th, 10th, 60th, 84th, and 256th Rifle Brigades defending the Terek River from northwest of Groznyi northeastward to Kizliar. This army sought to prevent XXXX Panzer Corps' 3rd Panzer Division from advancing southward toward Groznyi. The army's 30th and 110th Cavalry Divisions and three armored trains patrolled the railroad from Kizliar northward to Astrakhan' to defend against LII Corps' forces screening the Germans' long left flank;

- **58th Army** (Major General V. A. Khomenko), with 317th, 328th, and 337th Rifle Divisions, the Makhachkala NKVD Rifle Division, and 3rd Rifle Brigade in second echelon in the Makhachkala region; and
- **Group Reserves**, with 5th, 6th, and 7th Guards Rifle Brigades of 10th Guards Rifle Corps (Major General I. T. Zamertsev), 89th and 347th Rifle Divisions, 52nd Tank Brigade, and 249th, 258th, and 563rd Separate Tank Battalions concentrated in the depths along the Ordzhonikidze and Groznyi axes.[10]

In addition, on 18 September the *Stavka* transferred Major General N. Ia. Kirichenko's 4th Guards Cavalry Corps from the mountains north of Tuapse and subordinated it to Maslennikov's group, replacing it with 328th and 408th Rifle Divisions from 45th and 58th Armies.[11] Kirichenko's cavalry corps was to operate against the Germans' extended left flank in the Kalmyk Steppes south of Elista. This left Maslennikov's forces superior to Kleist's in manpower but with only 45 tanks to oppose Kleist's force of almost 200 tanks in the Mozdok region.[12]

Unlike in previous operations, Kleist's forces mounted their drive toward Ordzhonikidze at a snail's pace, primarily due to the fierce Soviet resistance to LII Corps' efforts to seize a bridgehead over the Terek River south of Mozdok. Kleist's plan called for the corps' 111th and 370th Infantry Divisions to capture the bridgehead opposite Mozdok and 13th Panzer Division, if necessary, supported by *kampfgruppen* transferred from 3rd and 23rd Panzer Divisions, to thrust southwestward from the bridgehead to capture Malgobek, 22 kilometers southwest of Mozdok. Thereafter, Kleist's panzers were to penetrate southward through the Terek and Sunzha Mountains along the valley of the Alkhan-Churt River to clear Soviet forces from the bend south and east of the Terek River. If possible, his panzers were to then push farther southward along the Terek River to Ordzhonikidze and eastward along the Alkhanchurt Canal to Groznyi.[13]

General Ott's LII Corps began its thrust across the Terek River in the Mozdok sector at 0200 hours on 2 September, striking the defenses of General Roslyi's 11th Guards Rifle Corps (see Map 79). General Recknagel's 111th Infantry Division conducted its assault crossing near Predmostnyi, in Mozdok's eastern suburbs, against 11th Guards Corps' 9th Brigade. Simultaneously, General Klepp's 370th Infantry Division attacked 11th Guards Corps' 8th Brigade at the town of Kizliar, just west of Mozdok. Both assaults secured small bridgeheads in heavy fighting in the face of repeated Soviet counterattacks. Late in the day, a reinforced detachment from the guards corps' 9th Brigade organized a counterassault of its own across the Terek River. This assault crossing operation succeeded in seizing a foothold on the river's northern bank at the village of Pavlodol'skii, which threatened

370th Infantry Division's right flank and delayed any subsequent German advance. LII Corps reinforced its bridgeheads overnight on 2–3 September and formed a special *kampfgruppe* from 13th Panzer Division's 66th Grenadier Regiment to eliminate the Soviet bridgehead at Pavlodol'skii.[14]

On 3 September 111th Infantry Division, now supported by 25 tanks from 23rd Panzer Division, resumed its assault and reached the northern outskirts of the village of Terskaia by day's end, in the process expanding its bridgehead to a depth of almost 3 kilometers. Early on 4 September, with its bridgehead secure, the 111th Infantry along with 23rd Panzer's tanks launched a general assault on Terskaia, while a *kampfgruppe* consisting of 3rd Battalion, 117th Grenadier Regiment, and 25 tanks pushed southward along the road to Vosnesenskaia, 10 kilometers south of Mozdok. However, 9th Army's 62nd Naval Rifle Brigade and 249th Separate Tank Battalion struck and halted the *kampfgruppe* in late afternoon, destroying five German tanks at a cost of seven of their own.[15]

The following day, 111th Infantry Division captured Terskaia, and Kleist organized a *kampfgruppe* from 13th Panzer Division to support the 111th's forces fighting north of Vosnesenskaia. Led by Colonel Otto Herfurth, commander of 117th Grenadier Regiment, the expanded *kampfgruppe* consisted of two battalions from Herfurth's regiment and one panzer battalion each from 13th Panzer and 23rd Panzer Divisions, with a total strength of about 40 tanks (100 according to Soviet sources). *Kampfgruppe* Herfurth advanced southward at 0400 hours on 6 September, driving a deep wedge between the defenses of Roslyi's 9th and 8th Guards Rifle Brigades. However, as the *kampfgruppe* approached the northern foothills of the Terek Mountains, it encountered intense artillery, *Katiusha*, and antitank fire, as well as heavy counterattacks by both defending Soviet rifle brigades, 62nd Naval Rifle Brigade and 249th Separate Tank Battalion (with 29 British Valentine and American M-3 tanks), and 417th Rifle Division, with 28 Valentine and M-3 tanks from 258th Separate Tank Battalion. Simultaneously, but farther to the east, 10th Guards Rifle Brigade and 167th Rifle Division struck 111th Infantry Division's defenses at Terskaia.[16] Over the battlefield, aircraft from Major General of Aviation K. A. Vershinin's 4th Air Army conducted as many as 500 sorties per day against German forces and installations in and around Mozdok and German forces advancing to the south.

The intense fighting on 6 September took a terrible toll on both sides. The Soviet 249th Separate Tank Battalion lost 24 of its 29 tanks, and 258th Tank Brigade 22 of its 28 tanks, mostly British Valentine models that caught fire and burned.[17] As for *Kampfgruppe* Herfurth, it also suffered heavy losses, with 2nd Battalion of 111th Infantry Division's 117th Grenadier Regiment emerging from the fight with only 80 men.[18] With his group under assault from all sides and the bridgehead itself facing incessant attacks, Colonel

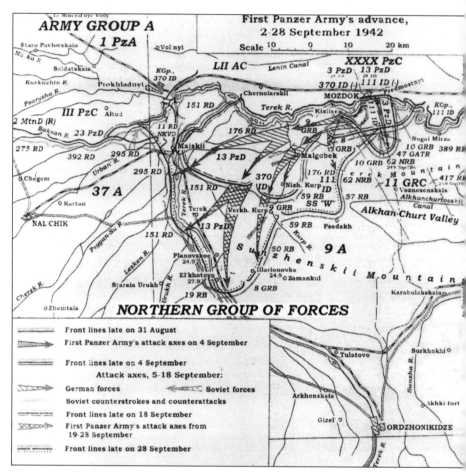

Map 79. The Mozdok-Malgobek operation, 2–28 September 1942

Herfurth was left with no choice but to withdraw his *kampfgruppe* to new positions from which it could bolster the bridgehead's defenses.

Determined to inflict maximum damage on the Germans, Koroteev organized fresh counterattacks on 7 September, this time with 52nd Tank Brigade and 75th Separate Tank Battalion (with a total of 76 tanks), 863rd Antitank Artillery Regiment, and, later, 275th Rifle Division, attacking *Kampfgruppe* Herfurth's defenses from the west. Meanwhile, 11th Guards Rifle Corps' 8th and 10th Guards and 62nd Rifle Brigades and 417th Rifle Division attacked from the east.[19] These joint attacks forced Herfurth's forces to recoil further, even though guns of the supporting 191st Assault Gun Brigade broke the back of the Soviet assault, destroying another 14 T-34s and two KVs.[20] However, the heavy fighting on 7 and 8 September left Kleist with no choice but to withdraw his forces back to their original bridgeheads south of the Terek River at Mozdok. Although Roslyi's 11th Guards Rifle Corps continued its counterattacks from 8 through 10 September, 9th Army was unable to eliminate the Germans' bridgehead on the southern bank of the Terek River. The intensity of the fighting, however, vividly underscored the reality that any further German advance would be hotly contested.

Prodded by Hitler, Kleist persisted in his offensive preparations. On 8 and 9 September, he ordered Breith's 3rd Panzer Division to abandon its bridgehead at Ishcherskaia, east of Mozdok, and transfer its forces back to the Mozdok region. He then formed *Kampfgruppe* Liebenstein, headed by the commander of 3rd Panzer Division's 6th Panzer Regiment, and ordered it to concentrate in 370th Infantry Division's bridgehead at Kizliar. The *kampfgruppe* consisted of 3rd Panzer Division's 6th Panzer and 3rd Grenadier Regiments and a tank battalion from 23rd Panzer Division's 201st Panzer Regiment, with a force of roughly 70 tanks. South of Mozdok proper, after briefly resting its troops, Herr's 13th Panzer Division formed another force, *Kampfgruppe* Crisolli, led by the commander of the division's 93rd Grenadier Regiment. This group, which consisted of elements of 4th Panzer and 93rd Grenadier Regiments with about 25 tanks, was to attack southwestward out of the bridgehead.[21]

However, Maslennikov, commander of the Northern Group, directed General Zamertsev's 10th Guards Rifle Corps, then in reserve, to counterattack and restore 9th Army's defenses.[22] Zamertsev's three guards rifle brigades launched their assaults in the Mekenskaia and Ishcherskaia regions east of Mozdok on 10 September, forcing Kleist to withdraw most of *Kampfgruppe* Liebenstein back north of the Terek River and tying down German forces southeast of the city. Nevertheless, *Kampfgruppe* Crisolli, supported by Klepp's 370th Infantry Division, thrust southwestward out of the bridgehead early on 11 September with a force of about 100 tanks. Exploiting rainy weather, *Kampfgruppe* Crisolli advanced up to 20 kilometers southwestward, capturing Malgobek on 12 September and reaching the Nizhnyi and Verkhnyi Kurp regions, on the Alkhan-Churt River 30 kilometers southeast of Mozdok, by day's end on 14 September. This advance utterly shattered the defenses of Roslyi's 11th Guards Rifle Corps, overwhelming its 9th Brigade and supporting 75th Separate Tank Battalion, and defeated a counterattack by 62nd Rifle and 52nd Tank Brigades, destroying six more Soviet tanks.[23] The German attack temporarily faltered only after Koroteev committed 151st Rifle Division from 37th Army to block the German advance.

Koroteev's 9th Army, however, immediately organized a new series of counterattacks to blunt 13th Panzer Division's offensive, within the context of a new defensive plan issued by Maslennikov. First, Koroteev formed two shock groups, each supported by an army artillery group, to assault the Germans' defenses north of the Terek River east of Mozdok and around the bridgehead south of Mozdok. The first group's 10th Guards Rifle Corps and 417th Rifle Division were to attack 3rd Panzer Division's defenses at Mekenskaia while its 10th Guards Rifle Brigade struck 3rd Panzer Division's defenses near Predmostnyi in the bridgehead southeast of Mozdok. The second group was to employ 275th Rifle Division in an assault against the western flank of the Germans' bridgehead at Kizliar. In addition, a special tank group consisting of 52nd Tank Brigade and 75th Separate Tank Battalion, supported by a third army artillery group, was to block any German advance southward along the Alkhan-Churt River.[24]

Attacking in stages from early on 14 September through the following day, the three counterattacking groups commenced a battle lasting four days before the Germans could muster enough strength to continue their offensive toward the southwest.[25] During this fighting, 13th Panzer Division was forced to abandon Verkhnyi Kurp, and both it and 370th Infantry Division were half-encircled before the counterattacking Soviet forces literally wore themselves out, suffering heavy losses in both tanks and personnel.

After reorganizing their forces late on 17 September, multiple *kampfgruppen* of Herr's 13th Panzer Division burst out of their confinement the following day and raced westward toward the valley of the Terek River and the key crossing site at the town of Arik. Once in the river valley, Herr's panzers were to wheel southward and capture the village strongpoint of El'khotovo and the nearby pass through the Terek Mountains, the gateway to Ordzhonikidze, 55 kilometers farther south. Attacking on 18 and 19 September, Herr was preceded by a Brandenburger detachment, which seized the 1,200-meter-long railroad bridge over the Terek at Arik intact in the early morning hours of 20 September, in the process disarming almost 5 tons of explosives.[26] The 13th Panzer's advance shattered the defenses of 9th Army's 11th Guards Rifle Corps, 275th Rifle Division, and 52nd Tank and 62nd Rifle Brigades. This forced Koroteev to commit 44th Separate Tank Battalion's 14 tanks to contain the German bridgehead on the western bank of the Terek River at Arik and 59th and 60th Rifle Brigades to block the upper Terek River valley south of Arik and the western slopes of the Sunzha Mountains.[27]

After capturing the river line north and south of Arik on 19 September, Herr's panzers reached and captured the town of Terek, 10 kilometers south of Arik, on 21 September. To the west, III Panzer Corps' Romanian 2nd Mountain Division and elements of 23rd Panzer Division finally secured the Baksan Valley by late on 20 September. Farther east, Recknagel's 111th Infantry Division of Ott's LII Corps, supported by a *kampfgruppe* from 3rd Panzer Division, finally broke through the Soviet defenses at the western end of its Mozdok bridgehead late on 18 September. Meanwhile, farther east along the Terek River, the main force of Breith's panzer division continued fending off counterattacks by 9th Army's 10th Guards Rifle Corps, which was now commanded by Colonel I. A. Sevast'ianov, who had replaced General Zamertsev on 15 September.[28]

The 10th Guards Rifle Corps' new commander, Ivan Aleksandrovich Sevast'ianov, was a hardened combat veteran who had experienced both victory and defeat. He began his wartime service as chief of staff of 9th Rifle Corps' 106th Rifle Division during its defense of the Crimea in the fall of 1941. Thereafter, he commanded 51st Army's 276th Rifle Division during the defense of the Taman' Peninsula in November 1941, the bold amphibious assault to seize Kerch' and Feodosiia in the Crimea one month later, and then the embarrassing defeat at Kerch' in May 1942. After a brief interlude serving as deputy commander of 1st Rifle Corps, Sevast'ianov resumed command of the re-formed 276th Division and led it in the defense of the northern Caucasus region before taking command of 10th Guards Rifle Corps on 15 September.[29]

Late on 21 September, extensive Soviet minefields and obstacles in the region north of Planovskoe, 10 kilometers north of its objective at El'khotovo, halted 13th Panzer Division. Thereafter, Kleist paused to reorganize his forces for the final drive to the south. By this time, his forces were stretched along the southern bank of the Terek River westward from southeast of Mozdok through Verkhnyi Kurp to Terek on the Terek River. LII Corps' 111th Infantry Division defended the bridgehead south of Mozdok proper, the corps' 370th Infantry Division was in the Nizhnyi and Verkhnyi Kurp regions, and XXXX Panzer Corps' 13th Panzer Division was deployed in the sector from Verkhnyi Kurp to Terek on the upper Terek River. On Kleist's left wing, under relentless pressure exerted by 9th Army's 10th Guards Rifle Corps and 417th Rifle Division, XXXX Panzer Corps' 3rd Panzer Division was forced to withdraw its forces from the Mekenskaia region to new defenses along the Terek River midway between Mekenskaia and Mozdok. On the right wing, III Panzer Corps' 23rd Panzer Division continued clearing Soviet forces from the Baksan River valley, east and southeast of Prokhladnyi, and prepared to move south along the Terek River to link up with 13th Panzer Division. To its rear, on Hitler's orders, 5th SS "Viking" Motorized Division was redeploying eastward from the Maikop region to reinforce Kleist's panzer spearheads.[30]

At this point, Kleist reshuffled his forces, subordinating 23rd and 13th Panzer and 370th Infantry Divisions to Mackensen's III Panzer Corps and 111th Infantry and, when it arrived, SS "Viking" Divisions to Otto's LII Corps. The next day Mackensen visited 13th Panzer Division's headquarters and ordered Herr's division to attack on 24 September with the objective of breaking through Elkhotovo Pass. German mechanics strained night and day to increase the division's armor strength from 79 tanks on 20 September to 110 on 24 September. Given the rough terrain they would be required to traverse and the noticeable increase in Soviet armor strength, the Germans would indeed need every tank they could muster.

As Herr planned his assault, on 21 September Boineburg-Lengsfeld's 23rd Panzer Division assembled its armor (roughly 80 tanks) south of Prokhladnyi and advanced southward on 23 September, capturing the towns of Maiskoe and Kotliarevskaia on the Terek River by day's end on 24 September. In so doing, 23rd Panzer smashed 295th Rifle and 11th NKVD Rifle Divisions on 37th Army's right wing, occupying the western bank of the upper Terek River and linking up with (and thereafter protecting) 13th Panzer Division's right flank.[31] During this fighting along the Baksan and upper Terek Rivers, the *Chervlennaia* and 42nd NKVD Armored Train Battalions employed four armored trains to block the German advance, albeit temporarily.[32]

Anticipating such a German move and speaking for the *Stavka*, Vasilevsky on 23 September redefined the mission of Maslennikov's Northern Group of Forces:

1. The main and immediate mission of the Trans-Caucasus Front's Northern Group of Forces is to defeat the enemy that has penetrated to the southern bank of the Terek River and fully restore 9th and 37th Armies' initial defensive lines. To do so, immediately set out to liquidate the enemy that have penetrated by delivering your main attack along the southern bank of the Terek River in cooperation with 10th Guards Rifle Corps, which is operating along the northern bank of the Terek River.
2. Under no circumstances weaken the Gudermes and Makhachkala axes, and do not take divisions from the Sulak [River] and Makhachkala defensive lines.[33]

Tiulenev promptly ordered Maslennikov's group to mount two counterstrokes against the flanks of III Panzer Corps' penetration along the upper Terek River; however, Kleist's forces preempted this move by resuming their offensive, forcing Tiulenev to call off the counterstroke.[34]

Herr's 13th Panzer Division thrust southward at dawn on 25 September in groups of five to six tanks supported by panzer-grenadiers, capturing the heavily fortified town of Planovskoe and a neighboring strongpoint at I'llarionovka several kilometers to the east by nightfall. This assault pushed 37th Army's 275th Rifle Division back to the western bank of the upper Terek River and forced 9th Army's 59th and 60th Rifle Brigades to withdraw to new defenses protecting El'khotovo and its adjacent passes.[35] However, the terrain was so rugged that Herr's panzer-grenadiers had to conduct the final assault on the Soviets' numerous bunkers and fortifications, with the tanks laboring forward from behind providing only minimal support. During these assaults, Herr perished from an exploding mine and was succeeded in command by Colonel Crisolli, commander of 13th Panzer's 93rd Grenadier Regiment.

Pausing briefly early on 26 September, Crisolli's forces made extensive preparations to assault the Soviet defenses at El'khotovo and the adjacent El'khotovo Pass.[36] Although the town and pass were only 4 kilometers to the south, both were heavily fortified and surrounded by rugged forested terrain crisscrossed with bunkers and other field positions. The most formidable of these defenses were on Mount Seko and Hill 703, which flanked the pass to the southeast. Crisolli decided to launch his assault through the forests east of El'khotovo to seize the two key terrain features and then envelop the pass and town from the southeast. By this time, Koroteev's 9th Army was defending the region with its 60th and 62nd Rifle, 52nd Tank, and 59th Rifle Brigades deployed from El'khotovo eastward to Nizhnyi Kurt, respectively.

Beginning at midday on 26 September, the battle for El'khotovo town and the adjacent pass lasted for eight days as the German advance slowed to a snail's pace. The initial assaults by 13th Panzer Division's 66th Grenadier Regiment seized the high ground southeast of the pass by nightfall but could advance no farther. After another assault on the pass from the northwest on 28 September, over the next two days 93rd Grenadier Regiment made progress through the deeply layered Soviet defenses south of I'llarionovka. Following another pause to regroup and a day's delay due to heavy fog, in the morning darkness of 3 October 66th Grenadier Regiment finally penetrated into the northeastern section of the town and captured it by 0725 hours, blocking the road and railroad line south of the town as well.[37] However, after this exhausting fight, which reduced its strength to 80 tanks, 13th Panzer Division was incapable of advancing farther.[38]

While 13th Panzer was struggling to overcome Soviet defenses in the El'khotovo Pass, Kleist ordered the SS "Viking" Motorized Division, which reached the northern bank of the Terek River near Mozdok from 15 to 19 September, to join with LII Corps' 370th Infantry Division in a joint attack eastward on 13th Panzer's left flank.[39] Once in position in the vicinity of Nizhnyi and Verkhnyi Kurp on the Alkhan-Churt River, Kleist on 22 September directed Steiner's SS panzer-grenadiers to advance eastward, penetrate the Soviets' defenses blocking access through the passes across the Terek Mountains around the village of Sagopshin, and exploit either eastward toward Grozny or southward toward Ordzhonikidze.[40] At the same time, Recknagel's 111th Infantry Division, supported by part of *Nordland* and *Germania* Regiments from SS "Viking," was to capture Malgobek. Beyond Malgobek and Sagopshin lay Ordzhonikidze, a key junction on the Georgian Military Road, the only significant route in the region. From there, the Germans could turn northeast and capture Grozny, the refinery center of the Caucasus oil region.

Kleist tried to inspire Steiner's troops the night before the attack with the message, "All eyes are on your division. The whole operation depends on its being unsparingly committed."[41]

Simultaneously—but unknown to Kleist and Steiner—their counterpart, Koroteev, had already ordered his 52nd Tank and 59th Rifle Brigades and 75th Separate Tank Battalion, supported by part of 176th Rifle Division, to launch a counterattack against a perceived weak spot in 111th Infantry Division's defenses in the Alkhan-Churt valley. As a result, when Steiner commenced his assault, with his division's *Germania, Nordland,* and *Westland* Regiments and Panzer Detachment [*Abteilung*] "Viking" advancing on Malgobek and Sagopshin abreast from left to right, his forces ran straight into the heavy concentration of Soviet forces. This collision precipitated an intense fight that lasted more than a week before the assault by "Viking" collapsed in the face of fierce Soviet resistance.

During this fighting, a Finnish SS battalion seized Hill 711, overlooking the town of Sagopshin, on 28 September but could go no farther. SS "Viking" Division estimated that it engaged a force of 80 T-34s against its own 40 tanks, although Soviet sources claim that 52nd Tank Brigade fielded 30 tanks (5 KVs, 2 T-34s, 1 MK-III, 8 M-3s, 13 T-60s, and 1 captured German Pz IV), and the separate tank battalion about the same number.[42] As a result of this vicious fighting, SS "Viking" and 111th Infantry Divisions captured Malgobek after considerable difficulty but failed to seize either Sagopshin or the passes through the Terek Mountains. Both divisions suffered heavy casualties in the process. Soviet sources credit the successful defense to their effective employment of antitank weapons, in particular antitank guns and rifles, in dense networks of antitank strongpoints and regions.

Failing to appreciate Koroteev's intent and strength, Kleist blamed the failure of Steiner's division to break through to Ordzhonikidze on the division's poor internal cohesion.[43] The fact was, however, that his forces no longer possessed sufficient strength to advance farther without substantial reinforcements. Kleist seemed to recognize this fact when, on 3 October, he asked Hitler through the OKH "to be informed when and in what strength the army can expect to get reinforcements to continue the advance to Makhachkala via Ordzhonikidze and Groznyy."[44] Because the issue was still in doubt at Stalingrad, and after delaying a week, Hitler informed Kleist on 10 October that he might receive one or two mobile divisions later in the month. Until then, his mission would be "to create the best possible conditions for an advance after the reinforcements arrived."[45]

In the wake of Kleist's seizure of El'khotovo and Malgobek, Maslennikov, commander of the Trans-Caucasus Front's Northern Group of Forces, reported to his *front* commander, Tiulenev. Maslennikov estimated that, in

light of the heavy fighting during Kleist's offensive and the innumerable Soviet counterattacks, without rest and reinforcements his forces were no longer capable of further offensive action and needed to go over to the defense.
On 29 September Vasilevsky in the *Stavka* accepted his decision but also
underscored the extraordinary measures necessary to defend the region:

1. The forces of 9th and 37th Armies will organize a firm defense along
their existing positions.

2. To secure this defense, forestall possible enemy penetrations along
the Groznyi and Ordzhonikidze axes and subsequently transition to a
counteroffensive, concentrate [the following]:

a) The 337th Rifle Division, 256th Rifle and 9th and 10th Guards Rifle Brigades, and 52nd Tank Brigade in the Kalaus, Voznesenskaia, and
Balashov regions [south of El'khotovo, Malgobek, and Mozdok]; and

b) The 414th and 347th Rifle Divisions, 11th Guards Rifle Corps, 84th
and 131st Rifle Brigades, and 5th Guards Tank Brigade in the Nizhnye
Achaluki, Psedakh, and Zamankul regions [south of Mozdok and the
lower Terek River].

3. Concentrate 4th Guards Cavalry Corps, with 9th and 10th Guards
Cavalry Divisions, in the Staro-Shchedrinskii region and, depending on
the situation, subsequently employ it for immediate action in the rear
area of the enemy's Mozdok grouping.

4. For reinforcing the defenses in the Ordzhonikidze region, transfer
276th Rifle Division from Gori to the Redant and Balta regions.

5. For the immediate defense of the city of Groznyi, besides the NKVD
Division, occupy the Groznyi defensive line with 317th Rifle Division.

6. Transfer 43rd Rifle Brigade from Baku to the Gudermes region in
the Northern Group of Forces' reserve.

7. To secure the defenses along the Makhachkala axis:

a) [Occupy] the southern bank of the Terek River from its mouth to
Nogai-Mirzy with 389th, 223rd, and 402nd Rifle Divisions and 3rd and
5th Rifle Brigades, while transferring 402nd Rifle Division from Nakhi-
chevan' to the Gudermes region;

b) [Occupy] a defensive line along the Sulak River with 416th and
319th Rifle Divisions; and

c) [Occupy] the Makhachkala defensive line with the NKVD Division
and 271st Rifle Division.

8. At its discretion, the *front's* Military Council is permitted to reduce
its rear service units and installations to obtain personnel replacements
for the *front's* forces and to form new units.

9. Disband twelve military schools and use the personnel [as follows]:

a) Evacuate permanent personnel from the Trans-Caucasus to locations specified by Comrade Shchadenko, deputy People's Commissar of Defense;

b) Student personnel, first and foremost, are to form antitank detachments and battalions, armed with antitank rifles. To this end and also to strengthen the rifle divisions at the front, 3,000 antitank rifles are being sent. Employ the antitank detachments and battalions to reinforce rifle divisions on likely tank axes.

Use the remaining student personnel for the formation of rifle brigades and also to refill the rifle brigades in the existing guards corps.

10. Employ the contingent obtained from the disbanded rear service units and sapper army, first and foremost, for reinforcing and restoring the existing divisions both located at the front and withdrawn for refitting, first, restoring the Black Sea Group's and 37th Army's divisions. . . .

11. Send 100 tanks, including 69 T-34s and 31 T-70s, to the Trans-Caucasus Front for the Northern Group of Forces. . . .

12. Fully exploit the production of the Tbilisi aircraft factory. At present the *Stavka* cannot allocate additional quantities of aircraft to the Trans-Caucasus Front.[46]

These and other measures that the *Stavka* and Tiulenev implemented in late September guaranteed that Soviet resistance, when and if Kleist's forces resumed their offensive, would be even more formidable than before.

Besides thwarting Kleist's advance toward Ordzhonikidze and Groznyi, Maslennikov's stout defense of the Terek River line also severely undercut Army Group A's efforts to resume offensive operations at Novorossiisk and toward Tuapse. Ultimately, the transfer of SS "Viking" Division eastward to the Mozdok region deprived Ruoff of virtually all of his supporting German armor, which was so necessary to liquidate Soviet forces defending south of Novorossiisk and to strengthen the critical drive through the Caucasus Forest toward the key Black Sea port. In fact, Ruoff's Seventeenth Army had begun its last thrust on Tuapse on 23 September—but without Steiner's panzers and panzer-grenadiers.

THE CAUCASUS IN OCTOBER AND NOVEMBER

When Army Group A failed to break through to the Black Sea coast and penetrate the northern foothills of the Caucasus to Ordzhonikidze and Groznyi in September, Hitler hoped to do so in two simultaneous offensives in October. However, the acute shortage of forces in the region—particularly reserves of any sort—forced Hitler to settle on two separate offensives, the first by Ruoff's Seventeenth Army through the mountains toward Tuapse in late September, and the second by Kleist's First Panzer Army toward Ordzhonikidze in late October. Given the army group's previous problems, as well as the ongoing struggle at Stalingrad, the results were almost predictable.

The Tuapse Operation (Operation Attika), 23 September–31 October

While Kleist's panzer army was maneuvering in the Terek River bend in futile attempts to reach Ordzhonikidze and Groznyi, Ruoff's Seventeenth Army began Operation Attika, its final attempt to reach Tuapse on the Black Sea coast (see Map 80). Ruoff's army began its attack on 23 September with three divisions of General Friedrich Kirchner's LVII Panzer Corps, followed two days later by four divisions of General Maximilian de Angelis's XXXXIV Army Corps and General Konrad's XXXXIX Mountain Corps. Ruoff's objective was to capture Tuapse and encircle the bulk of the defending Soviet 18th Army in the region northeast of Shaumian, 35 kilometers northeast of Tuapse. XXXXIV Army and XXXXIX Mountain Corps were to conduct Seventeenth Army's main attack from the Khadyzhenskii and Neftegorsk regions southwest of Maikop westward toward Shaumian. LVII Panzer Corps was to launch a secondary assault from the Goriachii Kliuch region west of Maikop southward toward Shaumian.

Even though the task of traversing the 50 kilometers between their forward positions west and south of Maikop to the Black Sea coast seemed modest, the tortuously winding mountain roads required the advancing forces to cover at least twice that distance across rough terrain more suited to transit by goats and mules than soldiers with heavy weapons and equipment. Worse still, the Germans had to advance against likely heavy resistance in predictably deteriorating weather conditions. To capture their immediate objective—the town of Shaumian—Ruoff's troops would have to advance along mountain ravines and gorges and uphill through mountain passes, although the remainder of the route to Tuapse was more downhill than uphill.

After the SS "Viking" Division departed for the Mozdok region, Ruoff reorganized his forces, forming an offensive shock group consisting of Lieutenant General Kurt Himer's 46th Infantry Division and Group Lanz of XXXXIX Mountain Corps on the left; Lieutenant General Ernst Rupp's 97th Jäger Division and General of Mountain Troops Emil Vogel's 101st Jäger Division of XXXXIV Army Corps in the center; and the Slovak Mobile and German 125th and 198th Infantry Divisions of LVII Panzer Corps on the right. The 125th and 198th Divisions were commanded by Generals Willi Schneckenburg and Ludwig Müller, respectively. Attacking abreast astride the Tuapse road, 97th and 101st Jäger Divisions of de Angelis's corps were to capture

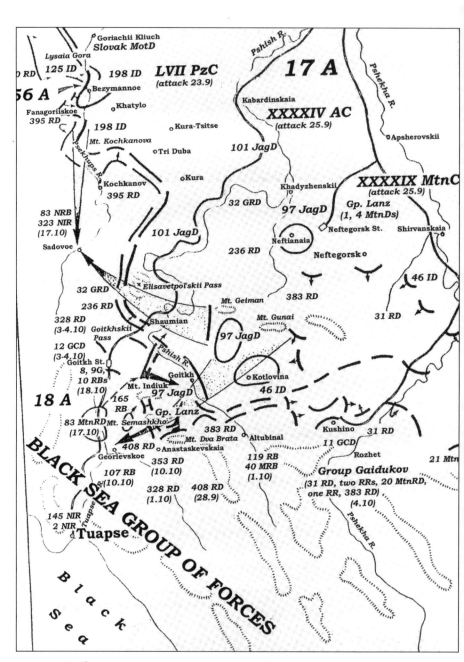

Map 80. The Tuapse operation, 23 September–31 October 1942

Shaumian and then exploit toward Tuapse. On their left was Group Lanz of Konrad's mountain corps, a composite group consisting of 1st Mountain Division's 98th Regiment and 4th Mountain Division's 13th Regiments and artillery and engineer units from the two divisions, all under the command of Major General Hubert Lanz, commander of 1st Mountain Division. Lanz was to thrust eastward through the mountains from the Neftegorsk region to outflank Soviet defenses along the Tuapse road from the south. On Lanz's left, 46th Infantry Division, just regrouped from the Taman' region, was to advance on the Pereval'nyi region to protect Konrad's left flank.

On the right wing of Ruoff's shock group, 198th and 125th Infantry Divisions of Kirchner's now tankless panzer corps were to regroup to the south and attack toward the Tuapse Pass from the north, while the corps' Slovak Mobile Division secured the lateral roads to the rear.[47] If successful, the thrust toward Tuapse would cut off and destroy the Soviet 47th and 56th Armies, shorten Army Group A's front by 200 kilometers, and release up to nine divisions for employment in the vital region south of the Terek River—thereby facilitating Kleist's planned advance on Ordzhonikidze, Groznyi, and Baku.

On the eve of Seventeenth Army's attack, the Black Sea Group of Forces, commanded by Colonel General Ia. T. Cherevichenko, consisted of four armies deployed along the Black Sea coast and along and west of the crest of the western Caucasus Mountains from southeast of Novorossiisk to Pseash-kha Pass northeast of the Black Sea resort city of Sochi:

- **46th Army** (Lieutenant General K. N. Leselidze), with 9th, 20th, and 242nd Mountain Divisions of 3rd Rifle Corps (Colonel G. N. Pere-krestov), 61st, 351st, 394th, and 406th Rifle Divisions, 51st, 107th, 119th, and 155th Rifle Brigades, 63rd Cavalry Division, 1st–10th Mountain Rifle Detachments, a separate naval infantry battalion, 51st Fortified Region, 562nd Tank Battalion, and 11th and 12th Armored Train Battalions defending the approaches to Sukhumi, facing First Panzer Army's XXXXIX Mountain Corps.
- **47th Army** (Major General A. A. Grechko), with 216th and 318th Rifle Divisions, 81st and 83rd Naval Rifle, 255th Naval Infantry, and 163rd Rifle Brigades, and 126th Separate Tank Battalion deployed on the Black Sea Group's left wing southeast of Novorossiisk, with 408th Rifle Division in reserve, facing Seventeenth Army's V Army Corps and the Romanian Cavalry Corps;
- **56th Army** (Major General A. I. Ryzhov), with 339th, 353rd, 349th, and 30th Rifle Divisions deployed in the Back Sea Group's center from Cherkasovskii to Staroobriadcheskii, opposing 125th Infantry Division, part of the Romanian 19th Infantry Division, and Romanian Cavalry

Corps' 6th Cavalry Division of Seventeenth Army's LVII Panzer Corps; and

- **18th Army** (Major General F. V. Kamkov), with the 395th, 32nd Guards, 236th, 383rd, and 31st Rifle Divisions, 12th Guards Cavalry Division, and 76th and 68th Naval Rifle Brigades deployed on the Black Sea Group's right wing from Staroobriadcheskii to Mount Matazyk, 62 kilometers due east of Tuapse, with 328th Rifle and 11th Guards Cavalry Divisions, 145th Naval Infantry Regiment, and 40th Motorized Rifle Brigade in reserve, facing Seventeenth Army's XXXXIV Army Corps and part of XXXXIX Mountain Corps.[48]

Given the importance of retaining the western Caucasus Mountains and the port of Tuapse, Tiulenev reinforced Cherevichenko's group with 10th Rifle Brigade from the Northern Group of Forces and 328th and 408th Rifle Divisions and 119th Rifle Brigade from his *front*'s reserve. In addition, on 29 September the *Stavka* incorporated the remaining personnel from the defunct 12th Army into 18th Army. Weeks before, the *Stavka* had created the Tuapse Defensive Region under the Black Sea Fleet to protect the port city. Meanwhile, Tiulenev, Cherevichenko, and their army commanders constructed fortified strongpoints, bunkers, and other defensive positions in depth along the coast and along every mountain road, pass, and defile.[49] By virtue of this work, 18th Army's defenses protecting Tuapse improved immeasurably. However, the limited road network prevented adequate supply of the forward forces, leaving them short of weapons ammunition and with only five to seven days' worth of foodstuffs.

Seventeenth Army began its Tuapse offensive on 23 September, when LVII Panzer Corps' 125th and 198th Infantry Divisions attacked southward from the region south of Goriachii Kliuch. They were joined on 25 September by XXXXIV Army and XXXXIX Mountain Corps, attacking westward from the Neftegorsk region. Thereafter, the offensive developed in two stages. During the first (25 September through 23 October), Ruoff's forces reached the line of the Pshish River, Mount Semashkho [Semashcho], and the villages of Goitkh [Goich] and Shaumian. In the second stage (23 October through 20 December), the Soviet 18th Army counterattacked to prevent the Germans from reaching the Mount Semashkho and Georgievskoe regions.

During LVII Panzer Corps' initial advance, its 198th Infantry Division, supported by Slovak tanks, assaulted the forward defenses of 395th Rifle Division east of Fanagoriiskoe on 23 and 24 September but recorded only limited gains. 395th Division's commander, 40-year-old Colonel Sabir Umar-Ogly Rakhimov, was an experienced infantryman who led 1149th Rifle Regiment during Operation Barbarossa and had commanded the 395th since 4

September 1942. Rakhimov was one of the highest ranking Uzbek officers in the Red Army and was known for his tenacity and bravery under fire, ultimately becoming a Hero of the Soviet Union twenty years after his death in combat in 1945.[50]

Also on 25 September, XXXXIV Army Corps 97th and 101st Jäger Divisions, the latter reinforced by a regiment from 46th Infantry Division, joined the fight by attacking westward from Khadyzhenskii against 32nd Guards Rifle Division's defenses along the Shaumian road. Particularly heavy fighting raged for possession of a key tunnel through the mountains west of Khadyshenskii. "Fighting like the devil" for three days and making the Germans "pay dearly for each meter of ground," the 32nd Guards gave ground grudgingly, limiting the German advance to only a few kilometers, although the Germans managed to capture the vital tunnel.[51] The commander of 32nd Guards was Colonel Mikhail Fedorovich Tikhonov, a hardened combat veteran who led 4th Airborne Corps' 7th Airborne Brigade during the chaotic fighting in Belorussia during the summer of 1941 and commanded 2nd Airborne Corps during late summer 1941 and, after its conversion into a guards rifle division in May 1942, 32nd Guards Rifle Division throughout the summer of 1942. For the skill and personnel bravery Tikhonov demonstrated during the battles in the High Caucasus, the *Stavka* promoted him to major general in November 1942 and appointed him to command guards rifle corps to war's end.[52]

After shifting the focus of their attack southward, where General Rupp's 97th Jäger Division had achieved greater success than had their neighbor, two *jäger* divisions then assaulted 236th and 383rd Rifle Divisions' defenses on Mount Lysaia, east of Mounts Geiman and Gunai, and captured the mountain in heavy fighting. The commanders of the two divisions, Major Generals N. E. Chuvakov and K. I. Provalov, respectively, were experienced combat veterans who had fought and commanded during Operation Barbarossa. Both ultimately rose to corps command and became Heroes of the Soviet Union.[53] To the north, LVII Panzer Corps' 198th Infantry Division expanded its assaults against 30th and 395th Rifle Divisions' defenses at Fanagoriiskoe, once again without making significant progress, although it was joined by part of the Slovak Motorized Division.[54]

To break the emerging stalemate, Ruoff on 27 September committed Group Lanz in an assault against 383rd Rifle Division's right wing. His goal was to traverse Mount Gunai and reach the Gunaika River and the village of Goitkh beyond in the Soviet division's rear. Once through the Soviet defenses, Group Lanz was to wheel northwestward along the river to outflank 32nd Guards Rifle Division's defenses astride the Shaumian road west of Khadyshenskii. The entire region through which the division was to attack—trackless heavy forests—was dotted with numerous Soviet bunkers, dugouts, and trench lines protected by extensive obstacles.[55] General Himer's truncated 46th Infantry Division was to protect Lanz's left flank. Because it was defending across a broad sector 25 kilometers wide, Provalov had no choice but to withdraw his 383rd Rifle Division westward on 30 September in the face of Group Lanz's determined assault. This, in turn, collapsed the defenses on the right flank of Chuvakov's 236th Rifle Division, forcing it to withdraw as well. As a result, by 5 October Group Lanz's mountain troops captured Mounts Gunai and Geiman, reached the valley of the Gunaika River, and approached the village of Kotlovina, 15–20 kilometers deep into 18th Army's defenses.[56]

On Group Lanz's left, XXXXIX Mountain Corps' 46th Infantry Division attacked westward from the region west of Samurskaia on 28 September, penetrating 18th Army's defenses at the boundary between its 383rd and 31st Rifle Divisions and forcing both divisions to withdraw. By 5 October the infantry of Himer's division had captured the village of Maratuki and Mount Oplepen and approached to within 5 kilometers of the village of Rozhet on 18th Army's right wing. Although 31st Rifle Division and reinforcing 11th Guards Cavalry Division contained 46th Infantry Division's advance short of Rozhet, continued German success in this sector would threaten the Pshekha River valley and the approaches to Lazarevskaia on the Black Sea coast.[57]

Unhappy with Cherevichenko's defense, Vasilevsky, chief of the Red Army General Staff, on 29 September sent Tiulenev a scathing rebuke:

> Despite the sufficient quantity of forces along the Khadyshenskii-Tuapse axis and the lengthy period the forces have had to occupy defensive positions, during the first days of his offensive, the enemy has succeeded in reaching the flank and rear of 18th Army's units defending the Khady-shenskii-Tuapse road.

> The enemy's subsequent intent is to envelop the main forces of our Khadyshenskii grouping by operating from Kotlovina, Mount Gunai, and Mount Geiman and from Fanagoriiskoe along the Psekups River valley to isolate it and, at the same time, to create a genuine threat to reach the coast in the Tuapse region.[58]

Stalin blamed Kamkov, commander of 18th Army, for dispersing his forces and failing to defend its mountain strongholds resolutely enough, conducting necessary counterattacks, and preparing adequate defenses in depth. The dictator added, "I consider it necessary you immediately create shock groups, go over to active operations, and completely restore the situation in the region south of Khadyshenskii and in the Goriachii Kliuch sector, with a view toward preventing the enemy from penetrating into the Tuapse region under any circumstances."[59] At the *Stavka's* direction, Tiulenev then formed an operational group consisting of 31st Rifle and 11th Guards Cavalry Divisions and one regiment of 383rd Rifle Division, all under the command of Major General V. A. Gaidukov, 18th Army's deputy commander. Tiulenev ordered Gaidukov to prevent the Germans from reaching the Pshekha River valley. Vaniamin Andreevich Gaidukov was also an experienced combat veteran who commanded 17th Cavalry Division and 2nd (later 9th) Cavalry Corps during Operation Barbarossa and the Red Army's winter campaign of 1941–1942 and, in the wake of Operation Blau, would command rifle corps to war's end.[60] Counterattacking on 7 October, Gaidukov's forces restored cohesive defenses in the Mount Oplepen region and the village of Maratuki to the west. Simultaneously, Cherevichenko assigned 328th Rifle Division and 40th Motorized Rifle Brigade from his Black Sea Group's reserves to Kamkov's 18th Army, with instructions that it employ them to reinforce the army's center and right flank.[61]

The *Stavka* chimed in once again on 2 October, this time reminding Tiulenev that the Black Sea Group of Forces' mission was to "under no circumstances permit the enemy to penetrate to the Black Sea coast either at Tuapse or along other axes"; therefore "the allocation of forces for the operation to destroy the enemy's Khadyshenskii grouping not be at the expense of weakening the forces defending the Tuapse axis."[62] To that end, Tiulenev was to:

1. Leave 40th Motorized Rifle Brigade in the Kotlovina region with the mission of defending the approaches to the Pshish River valley to prevent the enemy [46th Infantry Division] from reaching the rear of the forces defending the Tuapse road;
2. Concentrate 31st Rifle and 11th Guards Cavalry Divisions and one regiment of 383rd Rifle Division in the Rozhet and Maratuki regions with the mission, after reaching the region south of Samurskaia, to launch a shorter attack toward Cherniakov and Belaia Glina into the flank and rear of the enemy Neftegorsk grouping [Group Lanz]. Attack from the Matazyk region toward Samurskaia with part of 20th Mountain Rifle Division to protect the shock group's flank;
3. Conduct an attack with 119th Rifle Brigade, one regiment of 328th Rifle Division, and part of 68th Rifle Brigade, and 14th Naval Infantry Regiment from the Belaia Glina region toward Pervomaiskii, Khadyshenskii, and Gurievskii to destroy the enemy grouping which has penetrated toward Paportnyi and Kurinskii [101st and 97th Jäger Divisions];
4. Firmly protect the Khadyshenskii-Tuapse road with 32nd Guards, 236th, and 328th Rifle Divisions (the latter, minus one regiment), cooperating actively with the forces attacking from the flanks;
5. Protect the Tuapse region with 145th and 2nd Naval Infantry Regiments, as before;

6. To secure the Fanagoriiskoe axis [against LVII Panzer Corps' 198th Infantry Division] prior to the beginning of the operation, transfer two regiments of 408th Rifle Division from the Novo-Mikhailovskoe region [15 kilometers northwest of Tuapse]; and

7. Undertake measures to further reinforce the Black Sea Group of Forces with additional forces at the *front*'s expense, and simultaneously envision reinforcing the Black Sea Group with march-reinforcements [companies and battalions].[63]

Once Group Lanz penetrated the Black Sea Group of Forces' defenses in the Kotlovina region, Cherevichenko decided to launch a counterattack of his own on 2 October with 328th and 383rd Rifle and 12th Guards Cavalry Divisions and 40th Motorized Rifle Brigade to destroy the penetrating force in the Mount Geiman region. However, Group Lanz preempted this attack with one of its own the day before, in the process capturing Kotlovina. On the same day, General Vogel's 101st Jäger Division also resumed its assaults on the defenses of Tikhonov's 32nd Guards Rifle Division and captured Kurinskii, 10 kilometers west of Khadyshenskii, although a subsequent vigorous Soviet counterattack prevented any further advance.[64]

After recovering his balance in the wake of the Germans' 3 October thrust, Kamkov, commander of 18th Army, orchestrated a counterattack of his own on 7 October, with 236th Rifle and 12th Guards Cavalry Divisions and 40th Motorized and 119th Rifle Brigades attacking Group Lanz's forward positions in the Gunaika Valley. However, because it was hastily planned and poorly organized, this attack also failed to dent Group Lanz's defenses. Cherevichenko then ordered Kamkov to cease these disjointed operations and instead concentrate his forces and conduct successive counterattacks in the Gunaika and Kotlovina regions. These attacks finally brought Group Lanz's advance to a halt on 9 October, barely short of the Khadyshenskii-Tuapse road. By this time, Kamkov's army estimated that it had inflicted at least 10,000 casualties on Ruoff's attacking forces.[65]

Exhausted by two weeks of heavy and complex fighting in the worst terrain conditions, Seventeenth Army halted its operations during 10–13 October to permit its forces to rest, reorganize, and refit. During this period, Ruoff reinforced Group Lanz in the Gunaika Valley and Kotlovina regions and along the Tuapse road by shifting forces from the vicinity of Rozhet to the east.

Tiulenev also exploited the pause to reinforce Cherevichenko's Black Sea Group with 353rd Rifle Division from 18th Army and 107th Rifle Brigade and four artillery regiments from his *front*'s reserve. For his part, Cherevichenko shifted 83rd Naval Rifle Brigade and 137th Naval Infantry Regiment from 47th Army to reinforce Kamkov's defenses in the Tuapse region. These reinforcements shifted the correlation of forces distinctly to Kamkov's advantage. However, before 18th Army could employ its fresh reserves, the *Stavka* on 11 October relieved Cherevichenko of command of the Black Sea Group of Forces, appointing Major General I. E. Petrov, commander of Northern Group of Forces' 44th Army, as his replacement.[66] Major General K. S. Mel'nik replaced Petrov as commander of 44th Army. An experienced cavalryman, 42-year-old Kondrat Semenovich Mel'nik had distinguished himself as commander of 53rd Separate Cavalry Division during Operation Barbarossa and led 15th Cavalry Corps in Iran since March 1942.[67]

Even before Cherevichenko departed his command, Kamkov had prepared a new offensive plan to destroy the enemy's Gunai and Khadyshenskii groupings, meaning Group Lanz, 46th Infantry Division, and 101st and 97th Jäger Divisions, respectively. He planned to encircle and destroy the two German groupings by attacking with one shock group from the Navaginskii region, along the Tuapse road 8 kilometers east of Shaumian, toward Khadyshenskii and with a second shock group from the Maratuki and Rozhet regions toward Neftegorsk. However, this plan was flawed, because the roads were too restrictive to permit concentrating the attacking forces in time to preempt further enemy offensive operations, and it left the army's center too weak.

As if to underscore the flaws in Kamkov's plan, after he conducted his reconnaissance-in-force but before he could launch his main counterattack, the German Seventeenth Army resumed its offensive on 14 October with two blows aimed at encircling 18th Army's main forces and reaching Tuapse. XXXXIX Mountain Corps' Group Lanz conducted the first of these attacks from the Gunaika and Mount Geiman regions westward toward Shaumian. XXXXII Army Corps' 101st and 97th Jäger Divisions mounted the second thrust westward along and north of the Tuapse road toward Shaumian and Sadovoe, 8 kilometers north of Shaumian. Simultaneously, LVII Panzer Corps' 125th Infantry Division, which had regrouped into 198th Division's sector, advanced southwestward from the region east of Fanagoriiskoe toward Sadovoe and Elizavetpol'skii Pass, 6 kilometers north of Shaumian, to support XXXXIV Army Corps' attack.[68] According to the Germans, this assault "completely wiped out" [395th Rifle Division's] 714th and 726th Regiments.[69]

Meanwhile, Group Lanz seized the road and railroad junction 2 kilometers west of Shaumian, once again in heavy fighting. Summing up the cost of these successes, the division's *Kriegstagebuch* [daily journal] noted:

> In 19 days of battle in the trackless mountain forests, Division "Lanz" attacked through 98 bunker groups, taking 1,083 combat positions. In this manner, the *kampfgruppe* of 98th Mountain Jäger Regiment attacked 36 kilometers deep into the 1,000-meter-high mountain forest and the

kampfgruppe of 13th Mountain Jäger Regiment 40 kilometers deep. As a result of the bitter resistance on the extremely difficult terrain, German losses were high. Remaining on the battlefield [dead] were 5 officers, 384 noncommissioned officers and men. 53 officers and 1,417 noncommissioned officers and men were wounded.[70]

Responding to this assault, Petrov, who had just arrived at his new headquarters, on 15 October ordered Provalov to shift his 383rd Rifle Division westward to Goitkh Pass, 8 kilometers west of Shaumian, and 26th NKVD Rifle Regiment to move into and defend Elizavetpol'skii Pass, 10 kilometers to the north.[71] Also alarmed by the Germans' twin thrusts, the *Stavka* reminded Tiulenev not to underestimate the importance of the Black Sea Group of Forces and to provide it with necessary resources:

> Based on your very frequent visits to the Northern Group of Forces and because you have dispatched a significant part of your forces to that group, the *Stavka* perceives you have underestimated the importance of the Black Sea Group and the operational-strategic role of the Black Sea coast.
>
> The *Stavka* explains that the significance of the Black Sea axis is no less important than the Makhachkala axis, since the passage of the enemy through the Elizavetpol'skii Pass to Tuapse will cut off almost all of the Black Sea Group's forces from the *front's* forces, which will undoubtedly lead to their capture; the arrival of the enemy in the Poti and Batumi regions will deprive our Black Sea Fleet of its bases and, simultaneously, present the enemy with the opportunity for further movement through Kutaisi and Tbilisi, as well as from Batumi through Akhaltsikh and Leninakan and along the valleys to reach the rear of the *front's* remaining forces and approach to Baku.[72]

Holding Tiulenev personally responsible for assisting Petrov's forces, the *Stavka* demanded that he reinforce 18th Army with three rifle brigades from the Northern Group's reserves, replacing them with 34th, 164th, and 165th Rifle Brigades in Baku; immediately transfer 46th Army's 63rd Cavalry and 83rd Mountain Rifle Divisions, which were to arrive from the Central Asian Military District, to the Tuapse axis; and employ "the *front's* resources" to raise six new rifle divisions in his *front's* rear area for future employment in key sectors of the *front*.[73]

While the *Stavka* was acting, Ruoff's forces continued their advance, with XXXXIV Army Corps' 97th and 101st Jäger Divisions capturing Navaginskii on 16 October. They captured Shaumian and reached the eastern approaches to Elizavetpol'skii Pass on 17 October. At the same time, Group Lanz approached Shaumian from the south and east. To the north, Müller's

198th Infantry Division penetrated southward about 8 kilometers, on 18 October reaching the northern slope of Mount Kochkanova, 5 kilometers north of Sadovoe and only 9 kilometers north of Elizavetpol'skii Pass. As early as 16 October, Ruoff optimistically wrote in Army Group A's daily journal, "In recent days, enemy resistance in the Tuapse region has become noticeably weaker, leading us to conclude that our constant attacks and also the effective air support have severely eroded the strength of Russian resistance."[74]

Faced with the renewed German advance, Petrov and his staff visited Kamkov's retreating troops on 17 October to check on the situation. There they learned that Kamkov lacked communications with the forces on his army's left wing, was unaware of the fact that the Germans had captured Shaumian, and had fruitlessly tried to maintain a continuous front to the detriment of the defenses in key sectors. Therefore, with the *Stavka's* permission, Petrov relieved Kamkov of his command the next day, replacing him with General Grechko, commander of 47th Army.[75] That same day, the *Stavka* ordered Tiulenev to release 11th and 12th Guards and 63rd Cavalry Divisions to Kirichenko's 4th Guards Cavalry Corps in Maslennikov's Northern Group once Tiulenev concentrated adequate forces to defend Tuapse but not later than 3 November.[76]

Suspecting that the Germans intended to drive a wedge between his 18th Army and General Ryzhov's 56th Army by attacking through Goitkh Pass and Sadovoe, Grechko then adjusted his forces to block the anticipated German thrust. Once this reorganization was complete, Colonel A. A. Luchinsky's fresh 83rd Mountain Rifle Division was concentrated at Indiuk, just north of the pass, and Provalov's 383rd Rifle Division was in reserve in the pass itself and on adjacent mountain peaks. An experienced commander who had led the 83rd since April 1941, Aleksandr Aleksandrovich Luchinsky had fought with distinction throughout Operation Barbarossa and, like so many of his fellow division commanders, had risen to higher command, leading both a corps and several armies through war's end.[77] Meanwhile, 56th Army's 323rd Naval Infantry Regiment and 47th Army's 83rd Naval Rifle Brigade manned defenses around the village of Afanas'evskii Postik north of Goitkhskiai Pass to block 198th Infantry Division's advance on Sadovoe. In addition, 8th and 9th Guards and 10th Rifle Brigades, which had just been transferred to the region from the Northern Group of Forces, were deployed in the Goitkh region just south of the pass, and 165th Rifle Brigade was in reserve at Pereval'nyi, southeast of the pass.

Although Grechko planned to employ these forces to conduct two converging counterattacks against German forces advancing westward from Shaumian, once again Ruoff preempted the 18th Army commander's plan by resuming his advance at dawn on 19 October. By nightfall, Müller's 198th Infantry Division captured Mount Kochkanova from Rakhimov's 395th Rifle

Division on 18th Army's left flank, 101st and 97th Jäger Divisions seized Elizavetpol'skii Pass in the army's center, and Group Lanz pushed Provalov's 383rd Rifle Division southward from Kotlovina on the army's right.

Faced with the impending collapse of the defenses in his army's center and the encirclement of Rakhimov's 395th and Tikhonov's 32nd Guards Rifle Divisions on his army's left wing, Grechko on 20 October ordered the forces on his left to withdraw from the region east of Sadovoe and Elizavetpol'skii Pass. Even though Grechko's resolute actions saved his left wing, on 21 October Group Lanz and Rupp's 97th Jäger Division, supported on the right by Himer's 46th Infantry Division, mounted an attack from the Gunaika River valley toward Goitkh and Georgievskoe on 18th Army's right wing. The twin assaults by 97th Jäger Division and Group Lanz shattered the defenses of the inexperienced 408th Rifle Division and 107th Rifle Brigade, and 46th Infantry Division threatened the defenses of 40th Motorized Rifle Brigade protecting the Pshish River valley. The green 408th Rifle Division had deployed into the region from Turkistan at full strength on 14 October but had already suffered heavy casualties fighting in relative isolation against Group Lanz's previous advance.[78]

After an intense German artillery barrage destroyed the 408th's headquarters near Mount Semashkho, killing and wounding most of its staff, the advancing Germans captured Goitkh and encircled and destroyed most of the division, forcing its remnant to break out in small groups and join the adjacent 353rd and 383rd Rifle Divisions. Meanwhile, Himer's 46th Infantry Division captured Pereval'nyi from 40th Motorized Brigade, forcing the brigade's forces to fall back southward along the Pshish River.[79] The fighting was particularly severe in the village of Pereval'nyi, which changed hands several times but ended up in German control along with Mount Semashkho by day's end on 23 October. The loss of this key mountain peak and the adjacent road severed all of Grechko's lateral communications and propelled Group Lanz into the Tuapsinka River valley, only 30 kilometers from Tuapse.

Anticipating this new disaster, Grechko formulated a plan for another, more formidable counterstroke, once again to be conducted by two shock groups against the flanks of the German penetration. This counterstroke, designated to begin on 25 October, aimed at recapturing Goitkh and encircling and destroying the attacking German 97th Jäger Division and Group Lanz in the Mount Semashkho region. Grechko's plan called for 107th and 109th Rifle and 68th Naval Rifle Brigades and Tikhonov's 32nd Guards Rifle Division to conduct a "resolute" defense on the army's left wing, and 40th Motorized Rifle Brigade to do the same on the army's right flank south of Pereval'nyi; Grechko's two shock groups—10th Rifle Brigade and 383rd and 353rd Rifle Divisions on his army's right wing and 9th Guards Rifle Brigade in his army's center—were to conduct simultaneous converging assaults against German forces (Group Lanz and 97th Jäger Division) in the region around Mount Semashkho from the east, south, and west.[80] An army artillery group and aircraft from 5th Air Army were to support the assault, and 12th Guards Cavalry Division would protect 18th Army's right flank at and south of Altubinal on the Pshish River.

The 353rd Rifle Division commenced the counterstroke at dawn on 23 October by assaulting the defenses of Vogel's 101st Jäger Division and Group Lanz south of Mount Semashkho. This attack captured the mountain in a difficult fight by day's end, in the process encircling part of the *jäger* division's forces.[81] The 353rd Rifle Division was commanded by Major General F. S. Kolchuk, an accomplished officer who had been arrested during Stalin's purges but survived to take command of the division in May 1942 and a rifle corps by war's end.[82] Farther east, on 25 October Provalov's 383rd Rifle Division attacked the defenses of Himer's 46th Infantry Division at Pereval'nyi but failed to capture the village in heavy fighting. Thereafter, the two sides traded counterattacks through 30 October without appreciable gains on either side, although the rifle division did manage to seize a small bridgehead on the northern bank of the Pshish River, in the process cutting the Pereval'nyi-Goitkh road.

The remainder of Grechko's shock group began its assault on 28 October, with 10th Rifle Brigade advancing toward Pereval'nyi and 9th Guards Rifle Brigade toward Goitkh. The former captured its objective on 3 November after an intense fight with Group Lanz, but the latter faltered after gaining a foothold in the village but falling back to its jumping-off positions in the face of heavy German counterattacks.[83] Amid this fighting on 24 October, LVII Panzer Corps' Slovak Motorized Division attacked westward north of the Tuapse road toward Mount Sarai, 5 kilometers northwest of Elizavetpol'skii Pass, and captured the mountain from 68th Rifle Brigade. However, a counterattack by Tikhonov's 32nd Guards and 328th Rifle Divisions against the Slovaks' flanks broke up the advance and recaptured 68th Brigade's original positions.[84]

By early November, more than a month of heavy and complex fighting in difficult terrain conditions had left both sides exhausted and suffering the debilitating effects of attrition, a more serious problem for Ruoff because he had fewer fresh reserves. If sheer exhaustion was not reason enough for both sides to call a halt to active operations, the onset of snowy weather settled the matter. By conducting nearly constant single and multiple counterattacks with its own forces and reserves provided by the Trans-Caucasus Front and *Stavka*, Grechko's 18th Army managed to thwart the first of Hitler's two autumn objectives in the Caucasus.

With the defeat of Ruoff's Seventeenth Army along the Tuapse axis in late October, Hitler's only remaining hope for success in the region rested with

Kleist's panzers operating along the Terek River and the Ordzhonikidze axis farther east. As for the mountain region, quiet prevailed throughout most of November as both sides limited their actions to desultory raids, reconnaissance activity, and ambushes. This self- and weather-imposed operational pause in the High Caucasus region would end at dawn on 26 November, when, on the *Stavka*'s orders, Grechko took advantage of the Germans' misfortune at Stalingrad to launch a fresh offensive to eliminate once and for all the German grouping in the Indiuk and Semashkho regions.

The Nal'chik-Ordzhonikidze Operation, 25 October–12 November

Despite Seventeenth Army's failure to penetrate the High Caucasus and reach Tuapse during Operation Attika, Hitler remained adamant in his insistence that Kleist's First Panzer Army continue its offensive operations to seize Ordzhonikidze and, if possible, Groznyi before the onset of winter. Thus, Hitler considered Kleist's new offensive as one of those realistic local exceptions to his Führer Order No. 1 of 14 October, which announced to the world that the *Wehrmacht*'s summer offensive was at an end.[85]

Prodded by Hitler, Kleist, as early as 14 October, directed Mackensen, commander of III Panzer Corps, to prepare a plan for an offensive toward Ordzhonikidze and the Georgian Military Road via the city of Nal'chik, just more than 100 kilometers northwest of Ordzhonikidze. This plan, once developed by Mackensen and his chief of staff, Lieutenant Colonel von Grenewitz, required the Romanian 2nd Mountain Division to attack southward across the Baksan River east of Baksan and assault the Soviets' defenses at Nal'chik frontally. A day later, III Panzer Corps' 13th and 23rd Panzer Divisions would conduct the main attack from the Maiskii and Kotliarevskaia regions along the upper Terek River to advance on Nal'chik from the northeast and east.[86] Hitler approved Kleist's plan on 16 October, with an attack date set for 25 October.

During the intervening period, Kleist transferred Boineburg-Lengsfeld's 23rd Panzer Division from XXXX Panzer Corps to III Panzer Corps and concentrated it in the Maiskii and Kotliarevskaia regions, with its forward elements in bridgeheads on the western bank of the Terek River west of the two towns. At the same time, Mackensen redeployed Herr's 13th Panzer Division from the El'khotovo and I'llarionovka sectors northward to assembly areas near Arik and Terek on the river's eastern bank and shifted elements of Becker's 370th Infantry Division westward to take over the defense of 13th Panzer's former sector. To the east, Ott's LII Corps was to defend its bridgehead south of Mozdok and the Terek River with Recknagel's 111th Infantry and Steiner's SS "Viking" Motorized Divisions. Once these were concentrated in their new assembly areas, Mackensen designated the Romanian

2nd Mountain Division as Attack Group West and 23rd and 13th Panzer Divisions as Attack Group East. Mackensen screened the 20-kilometer sector between his two attack groups with light security forces (*Feldzugs*), designated as the Security Sector Center.[87] After the extended period of rest and refitting, 13th and 23rd Panzer Divisions fielded a total of roughly 200 tanks, more than twice as many as remained after their Mozdok offensive.[88]

Throughout the month of October, the Trans-Caucasus Front's Northern Group of Forces, commanded by General Maslennikov, also built up its forces to mount a new offensive to drive First Panzer Army out of the Terek region. As a part of this buildup, the *front* commander, Tiulenev, decided to take advantage of the gap, more than 400 kilometers wide, between the left flank of Stalingrad Front and the right flank of his Trans-Caucasus Front. To do so, in late September he transferred Kirichenko's 4th Guards Cavalry Corps into the Staro-Shchedrinskii region, west of Kizliar and north of the Terek River, on his *front*'s extreme right flank. At the time, the Germans were attempting to plug the gap between Army Groups A and B with two forces. In the north, detachments from 16th Motorized Division, which were based at Elista, operated eastward toward Astrakhan' on the lower Volga River. To the south, Special Corps Fermy, an aggregation of 6,000 primarily Muslim soldiers recruited from German prisoner-of-war camps and commanded by Air Force General Helmut Fermy, was based in the Achikulak region, south of the Kuma River roughly 180 kilometers west of Kizliar.[89]

Tiulenev resolved to exploit this weakness on First Panzer Army's left flank by ordering Kirichenko's guards cavalry corps to threaten Kleist's left flank and rear. At the same time, the Northern Group's 9th Army, operating south of Mozdok, and Sevast'ianov's 10th Guards Rifle Corps, operating along the Ishcherskaia axis north of the Terek River, east of Mozdok, were to threaten to turn First Panzer Army's left flank and, if possible, encircle the panzer army's entire left wing.[90] Beginning on 2 October and moving primarily at night for 12 days, Kirichenko's 4th Guards Cavalry Corps advanced 150 kilometers across the waterless steppes, so slowly that Maslennikov was forced to postpone his planned offensive. Nevertheless, on 15 October Kirichenko's cavalry corps reached the outskirts of Achikulak, where it conducted attacks on Corps Fermy's defenses over several days. All this was in vain, because Soviet intelligence had underestimated the special corps' strength.

As a postscript to the cavalry corps' initial failure, after being reinforced by 63rd Cavalry Division from the Coastal Group of Forces in late October, Kirichenko made one more attempt to capture Achikulak at month's end, only to fail once again, primarily because of logistical problems. After suffering heavy casualties, 4th Guards Cavalry Corps withdrew eastward, ending Maslennikov's hopes for an offensive against Mozdok and evoking sharp criticism from the Northern Group's commander.[91]

While Kirichenko's cavalry was conducting its fruitless raiding operations against First Panzer Army's left flank, Maslennikov was planning a new offensive to force the Germans back north of the Terek River. However, while doing so he paid scant attention to First Panzer Army's preparations for a new offensive of its own and focused his efforts primarily on the Mozdok sector, neglecting to reinforce his defenses along the Nal'chik axis. Compounding this error, when Mackensen's III Panzer Corps seized small bridgeheads near Maiskii on the southern bank of the upper Terek River on 25 September, neither General Kozlov, commander of 37th Army, nor Maslennikov, Northern Group's commander, reacted forcefully enough to eliminate the bridgeheads because they left only the weak 151st Rifle Division to defend this sector. Further confusing the two Soviet commanders, throughout October First Panzer Army conducted local attacks and raids in the Malgobek region farther east. Meanwhile, Kleist reinforced Romanian 2nd Mountain Division at Baksan with 1st Battalion of 1st Mountain Division's 99th Regiment, increasing his prospective attack force to an estimated 33,894 men, 460 guns and mortars, and roughly 200 tanks, primarily concentrated in the Baksan region and the 20-kilometer-wide bridgehead west of Maiskii.[92]

Throughout this period, however, Trans-Caucasus Front remained overly optimistic, as indicated by a report that its chief of staff, Lieutenant General P. I. Bodin, dispatched to the chief of the Red Army General Staff's Operations Directorate on 6 October:

Assessing Maslennikov's situation, it needs to be said we have succeeded in tying down the enemy on 9th Army's front, and, if he advances, it will be very slowly and with heavy losses. The paucity of our tanks is conducive to an advance. I believe he will begin action in the next few days but then exhaust himself, and, since we have not detected reserves approaching along the Mozdok axis, there is nothing critical in 9th Army's sector. The mood among the troops is combative and confident. The infantry meet tanks boldly, strike them, and remain in their positions when the tanks advance into the infantry's rear. As a rule, the enemy's infantry are cut off [from the tanks]. I must say primarily our artillery perform this mission. If the enemy does not strengthen his air forces opposite Maslennikov, all will be well.[93]

Maslennikov prefaced his proposal for a new offensive, which he sent to the *Stavka* late on 23 October, with his own assessment of the situation and German vulnerabilities:

The main grouping of enemy tanks and infantry on the Northern Group's front is concentrated in the Nizhnii and Verkhnii Kurp, El'khotovo, Arik, and Sled regions southwest of Mozdok. The Northern Group's chief aim and mission is to destroy this enemy group.

The experience of previous combat operations indicates, when our forces activate operations along the northern bank of the Terek River toward Ishcherskaia and Mozdok, the enemy will pull back part of the forces from his main grouping to the northern bank of the Terek River. However, a maneuver by our large forces along that axis is not favorable for us since it will weaken the important axes toward Groznyi and Ordzhonikidze.

In these circumstances it will be more favorable to consider an operation to destroy the enemy's Mozdok grouping by delivering the main attack along the Terek Mountains from east to west, with a secondary attack along the northern bank of the Terek River toward Ishcherskaia and Mozdok and with a simultaneous advance of a cavalry group to the middle reaches of the Kuma River and reinforcement of 37th Army along the Prokhladnyi axis.[94]

Tiulenev then directed Maslennikov to organize and conduct his group's main attack with 337th, 176th, and 317th Rifle Divisions, 3rd Rifle Corps' 9th, 57th, and 60th Rifle Brigades, and 15th, 5th, and 52nd Tank Brigades, all operating under the control of Koroteev's 9th Army. This force was to advance toward Mounts Zhigzapozh and Nizhnii Kurp from the Predgornyi and eastern Malgobek regions, with the immediate mission of capturing the western Malgobek–Nizhnii Kurp line and, subsequently, exploit the attack toward Arik on the Terek River. Meanwhile, 9th Rifle Corps (157th, 43rd, and 256th Rifle Brigades), 10th Guards Rifle Corps, one tank brigade, and 63rd Cavalry Division, operating under the control of Mel'nik's 44th Army, were to conduct the group's secondary attack. Mel'nik's forces were to attack westward toward Mozdok from the Staro-Bukharov and Kapustin regions, east of Ishcherskaia, to draw German forces away from the main attack sector southwest of Mozdok and envelop First Panzer Army's grouping at Mozdok from the north. Finally, Kirichenko's 4th Guards Cavalry Corps was to attack westward from Kizliar to gain First Panzer Army's rear and disrupt its communications and logistical routes. To the west, Kozlov's 37th Army was to hold on to its defensive front and attack eastward toward Arik with at least one rifle division to link up with 9th Army's shock group. Maslennikov retained 11th Guards and 10th Rifle Corps and 414th Rifle Divisions in reserve to reinforce success or to defeat German counterattacks.[95]

The *Stavka* approved Tiulenev's plan late on 25 October, 18 hours after Kleist's forces had initiated their new offensive. Although it mandated several significant changes to Tiulenev's plan, given the Germans' offensive these proved utterly irrelevant.[96] As Maslennikov continued reorganizing his forces for their new offensive, which was to begin on 3 November, they were deployed across a 350-kilometer-wide front from west of Baksan on the Baksan River eastward to Kizliar on the Terek River, as follows:

- **37th Army** (Kozlov), with 11th NKVD, 392nd, 295th, 2nd Guards, 151st, and 275th Rifle Divisions defending along the Baksan and Terek Rivers from Gundelen, 30 kilometers west of Baksan, eastward to Zmeiskaia, five kilometers west of El'khotovo, opposite the Romanian 2nd Mountain, 23rd and 13th Panzer, and 370th Infantry Divisions;
- **9th Army** (Koroteev), with 59th and 164th Rifle Brigades of 10th Rifle Corps (Major General P. E. Loviagin), 19th, 34th, and 131st Rifle Brigades of 11th Rifle Corps (Colonel I. A. Rubaniuk), 9th, 57th, and 60th Rifle Brigades of 3rd Mountain Rifle Corps (Colonel G. N. Perekrestov), 89th, 337th, 417th, 176th, and 347th Rifle Divisions, and 5th Guards, 15th, and 52nd Tank Brigades defending along the front from Darg-Kokh, south of El'khotovo, eastward to Beno-Iurt, northeast of Groznyi, opposite LII Corps' SS "Viking" Motorized and 111th Infantry Divisions;
- **44th Army** (Mel'nik), with 43rd and 157th Rifle Brigades of 9th Rifle Corps (Major General I. T. Zamertsev) and 414th, 402nd, 389th, and 223rd Rifle Divisions defending the southern bank of the Terek River from Beno-Iurt eastward and northeastward to Kizliar;
- **58th Army** (Khomenko), with 271st, 319th, and 416th Rifle and the Makhachkala NKVD Divisions in second echelon protecting the Makhachkala axis; and
- **Group Reserves**, with 9th and 10th Guards and 110th and 30th Cavalry Divisions of 4th Guards Cavalry Corps (Major General N. Ia. Kirichenko) in the region west of Kizliar facing Special Corps Fermy, 4th, 5th, 6th, and 7th Guards Rifle Brigades and 63rd Cavalry Division of 10th Guards Rifle Corps (Colonel I. A. Sevast'ianov) in the region north of the Terek River east of Ishcherskaia, opposite 3rd Panzer Division, and 34th and 62nd Rifle Brigades of 11th Guards Rifle Corps (Major General I. P. Roslyi) in the rear west of Groznyi.[97]

Despite Kleist's careful offensive preparations, the opposing Soviet forces facing his thrust outnumbered his forces in personnel and artillery but not in armor. By selecting as his target the weakest of the Northern Group's armies, Kozlov's 37th, which had no armor whatsoever, Kleist certainly maximized his chances for success. However, his two panzer divisions had to reach their objectives of Nal'chik and Ordzhonikidze rapidly—before Maslennikov managed to regroup his numerically superior forces to protect the region—if they were to have any chance for success. In any case, at dawn on 25 October,

Kozlov's hapless 37th Army, more properly three of its rifle divisions, faced a force three times its size in personnel, nine times as powerful in artillery, and infinitely more superior in armor.

Mackensen's III Panzer Corps began its offensive at dawn on 25 October with a powerful artillery preparation, followed by waves of bomber and fighter aircraft, which pounded the Soviets' forward defenses and deep rear (see Map 81). During this bombardment, a group estimated at 70 German aircraft struck 37th Army's headquarters in Dolinskoe, south of Nal'chik, killing many staff officers, utterly destroying the army's communications system, and forcing Kozlov to move his command post and the remnants of his headquarters to the village of Khasan'e, several kilometers to the south. Following this artillery and aerial bombardment, at 1000 hours Romanian 2nd Infantry Division assaulted 37th Army's defenses at the boundary between its 392nd and 295th Rifle Division in the sector from Baksan eastward to Baksanenek. Supported by waves of Stuka aircraft and spearheaded by 1st Battalion of 1st Mountain Division's 99th Mountain Regiment, the assault propelled the attackers forward 8 kilometers, to the town of Chegem No. 1 on the northern bank of the Chegem River, halfway to Nal'chik. Lacking both communications and reserves, Kozlov lost control of the action as his two rifle divisions rapidly gave ground to the south and east.[98]

The combined Romanian-German force accelerated its advance on 26 October, by nightfall reaching the northern outskirts of Nal'chik. Kozlov responded by launching a counterattack westward from Dokshukino, 18 kilometers northeast of Nal'chik, with 875th Regiment from Colonel Nevr Gevorkovich Safarian's 295th Rifle Division. Safarian, an Armenian by nationality, had commanded the 295th since 15 June 1942.[99] However, Safarian's forces were too fragile to halt the Romanian 2nd Mountain Division's advance.

Compounding Kozlov's problems, attacking abreast from left to right organized in multiple *kampfgruppen*, Boineburg-Lengsfeld's 23rd and Herr's 13th Panzer Divisions unleashed their assaults with about 100 tanks southwestward from their bridgeheads on the western bank of the upper Terek River in the Kotliarevskaia, Maiskii, and Prishibskaia regions. This assault shattered the defenses of 151st Rifle Division's 626th Regiment, as well as the two regiments of Safarian's rifle division, and sent them reeling back to the west and southwest. The two panzer divisions pursued, advancing 20 kilometers by day's end. 23rd Panzer captured the town of Argudan and Lesken Station, midway between Nal'chik and El'khotovo, and 13th Panzer reached Staryi Cherek and Psygansu in the Cherek River valley, 15 kilometers east of Nal'chik.[100]

When he first received word of the new attack, Maslennikov mistakenly believed the Germans were simply trying to liquidate 37th Army's salient

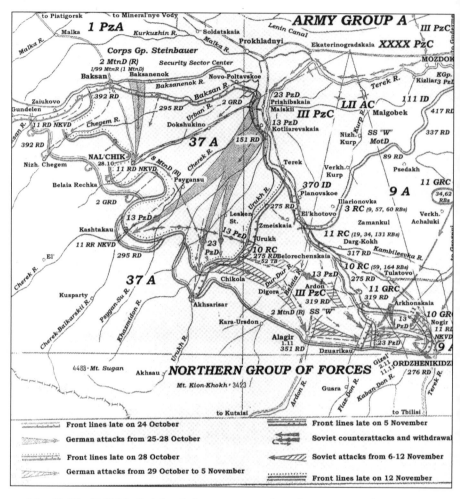

Map 81. The Nal'chik-Ordzhonikidze operation, 25 October–12 November 1942

west of the upper Terek River rather than commencing a major advance to outflank the defenses of Ordzhonikidze from the west. Therefore, he failed to react quickly enough to the assault and finally realized the Germans' ultimate objective only by nightfall. For its part, Army Group A exuded confidence, reporting to Hitler:

Apparently, the enemy was taken unaware in the area of First Panzer Army's offensive toward Nal'chik. On the first day of the offensive, the panzer divisions already advanced to Psygansu, and some of their units turned to the north, creating the prerequisites for encircling approximately four enemy divisions. The destruction of this group must be completed in the next several days. The enemy is being pushed back into the mountains. It appears the advance of the panzer forces to the south and then to the east toward Ordzhonikidze is opening broad perspectives.[101]

Acting quickly to forestall further disaster, the *front* commander, Tiulenev, who was at this time personally directing the defense of Tuapse from the headquarters of the Black Sea Group of Forces, immediately flew back to Northern Group headquarters. At the same time, he ordered 155th Rifle Brigade in Sukhumi and 58th Army's 319th Rifle Division to move northward into the Northern Group's sector. He also directed Major General Petr Ermolaevich Loviagin, commander of the newly formed 10th Rifle Corps, to deploy into the region of German penetration. Loviagin, 45 years old at the time of his appointment, was an experienced commander and staff officer who had served as chief of the Voroshilov Chemical Defense Academy during the first few months of the war and, thereafter, commanded Southern Front's 102nd Rifle Division and served as 24th and 9th Armies' chief of staff during the initial stages of Operation Blau before taking command of 10th Rifle Corps in October.[102]

Loviagin's rifle corps included 59th and 164th Rifle Brigades, reinforced by 275th Rifle Division, two antitank artillery regiments, and three artillery battalions. The corps was to occupy defenses along the eastern bank of the Urukh River (midway between Nal'chik and Ordzhonikidze) from the town of Chikola northward to its confluence with the Terek River overnight on 26–27 October. In addition, Tiulenev directed General Roslyi's 11th Guards Rifle Corps, then in his *front*'s reserve, to man defenses in the Ordzhonikidze Defensive Region proper and Colonel G. N. Perekrestov's 3rd Rifle Corps to concentrate in the Zamankul region, 10 kilometers east of El'khotovo. Like Roslyi, Perekrestov was an experienced commander, but with a record marred by occasional breaches of discipline, who had commanded an airborne brigade in 1941 and, after a brush with military tribunals, a cavalry division in 1942.[103] These measures significantly strengthened the Northern Group's defenses along the Ordzhonikidze axis.

Meanwhile, Mackensen's III Panzer Corps continued its rapid advance on 27 and 28 October, completing the rout of Kozlov's 37th Army. Flanked on the right by Romanian 2nd Infantry Division, whose forces captured Nal'chik on 28 October and pressed 37th Army's 392nd and 2nd Guards Rifle Divisions back into the foothills of the Caucasus Mountains, 23rd and 13th Panzer Divisions advanced southward up to 20 kilometers. Crisolli's panzers seized Lesken, thereby threatening the left wing of Northern Group's new defenses along the Urukh River. At the same time, Herr's panzers helped clear Soviet forces from Nal'chik proper and captured the village of Kash-takau on the Cherek River, where the river passed through an important mountain pass. This advance carved a 20-kilometer-wide gap between 37th Army's forces, which were withdrawing southwestward into the mountain passes, and the prospective defenses of Loviagin's 10th Rifle Corps along the Urukh River, through which the Germans could mount an advance directly southeast to Ordzhonikidze.[104]

Appreciating this opportunity, Mackensen on 29 and 30 October ordered Boineburg-Lengsfeld to wheel 23rd Panzer Division eastward into the Chikola sector along the Cherek River, and Herr to shift his 13th Panzer Division eastward toward Urukh sector along the river on the 23rd Panzer's left. His intent was to launch both divisions in a concerted offensive eastward across the Urukh River toward Ordzhonikidze.[105]

Attacking at dawn on 31 October in two columns with roughly 70 tanks, Boineburg-Lengsfeld's panzer *kampfgruppe* tore through the left wing of 10th Rifle Corps' defenses near Chikola, overran the headquarters of Loviagin's rifle corps, and rushed into the rifle corps' rear area. During the day, 52nd Tank Brigade, which was supporting 10th Rifle Corps, launched repeated counterattacks that first slowed and finally halted 23rd Panzer's advance along the Dur-Dur River, 10 kilometers east of the Urukh River. However, at 1530 hours Herr's 13th Panzer Division, with a force of about 60 tanks and led by teams of Brandenburgers [special forces troops], smashed 10th Rifle Corps' right wing and pushed on rapidly toward the town of Ardon, 20 kilometers to the southeast.

A fierce battle then ensued in the vicinity of the towns of Digora and Ardon on 31 October and 1 November as the two German panzer divisions tried to encircle and destroy 10th Rifle Corps and 52nd Tank Brigade. During this intense fight, the Soviets reported destroying 32 German tanks and significant numbers of troops and weaponry.[106] Unknown to the Soviets, 13th Panzer Division's commander, Herr, was wounded in the fighting and replaced briefly by Colonel Dr. Walter Kuhn on 1 November and, soon after, by Major General Helmut von der Chevallerie, a veteran commander who had commanded 86th Infantry Regiment and 10th Infantry Brigade in 1941 and 1942, and, more recently, served with 22nd Panzer Division.[107]

Once this dramatic struggle ended, Loviagin withdrew the remnants of 10th Rifle Corps to a new defensive line stretching between the towns of Alagir and Kirovo on the Ardon River, 30 kilometers northeast of Ordzhonikidze. Mackensen's panzers pursued, capturing Alagir and nearby crossings over the Ardon River by day's end on 1 November.[108] That same day, the Germans commenced a heavy aerial bombardment of Ordzhonikidze, in the process striking and destroying Trans-Caucasus Front's forward command post and killing the *front*'s chief of staff, Lieutenant General P. I. Bodin, and its commissar, A. N. Sadzhaia. Both sides reportedly suffered heavy aircraft losses during battles in the skies over Ordzhonikidze.[109]

Faced with this increasingly disastrous situation, Tiulenev decided to halt Northern Group's offensive along the northern bank of the Terek River near Ishcherskaia and shift 44th Army's 10th Guards Rifle Corps from that region southward to Ordzhonikidze, a process he expected to take two days. In addition, Tiulenev ordered 9th Army's 2nd Tank Brigade, 11th Guards Rifle Corps' 5th Guards Tank Brigade, and five antitank artillery and three guards-mortar regiments to concentrate in the Ordzhonikidze region. Thanks to these measures Mackensen's advance slowed a bit, although on the morning of 2 November 13th and 23rd Panzer Divisions, with a combined force of perhaps 100 tanks, reached and penetrated Ordzhonikidze's outer defensive line in the vicinity of Fiang-Don and Dzuarikau, fewer than 20 kilometers west of the city. After heavy fighting against forces from Roslyi's 11th Guards Rifle Corps and 11th NKVD Rifle Division, the forward elements of the two panzer divisions by day's end reached and captured Ordzhonikidze's western suburb of Gisel', only 9 kilometers west of the city's center.[110] Overhead, 4th Air Army flew 2,600 air sorties during the German advance, claiming to have destroyed 80 German aircraft.[111]

Mackensen's two panzer divisions continued their assaults on Ordzhonikidze's western perimeter on 3 and 4 November.[112] The day before this, Hitler had formally relinquished control of Army Group A to Kleist, and Mackensen replaced Kleist as First Panzer Army's commander. That same day Mackensen had notified Hitler, "We can presume the enemy forces recently situated in front of the corps' front on the western bank of the Terek River were destroyed. . . . The pursuit of the enemy toward Vladikavkaz [Ordzhonikidze] is continuing."[113] However, as early as 4 November, First Panzer Army's headquarters began tempering its optimism in a report to Army Group A: "We have to halt the offensive toward Ordzhonikidze because the region south of the Terek River has not been cleared of enemy, and this has not removed the danger of an attack against the panzer divisions' flank and rear."[114] In fact, at this time Northern Group still held the eastern bank of the Terek River from just south of El'khotovo southward to Ordzhonikidze with four rifle corps: Colonel I. A. Rubaniuk's 11th, Loviagin's 10th, Roslyi's 11th Guards, and Sevast'ianov's 10th Guards. These sizeable forces threatened the left wing of the narrow German salient projecting southeastward to the Ordzhonikidze region, leaving the two panzer divisions in a potential "sack" of their own.[115]

The precarious position the Germans found themselves in led Tiulenev to conclude:

1. The enemy in front of the Northern Group is striving to penetrate through to the Caspian Sea at all costs and, at the same time, while

supporting an offensive toward Baku, to cut the communications routes linking the Trans-Caucasus with Astrakhan' once and for all and to liquidate the threats to the flanks of the forces operating in front of the Trans-Caucasus and Stalingrad Fronts.

2. The group of forces in front of the Black Sea Group of Forces is trying to encircle our forces operating northeast of Tuapse and cut them off from their supplies by reaching the Black Sea coast in the Tuapse region.

3. To this end, the enemy, who lacks sufficient quantities of ready reserves in the depths, will tailor part of his forces and throw them in to reinforce those forces actively operating along the front, while simultaneously replenishing his operating forces with personnel and equipment (tanks and artillery).[116]

The turning point in the struggle for Ordzhonikidze occurred on 5 November, when the city's defenders definitively halted the forward elements of Chevallerie's 13th Panzer Division in the city's western and northwestern outskirts.[117] That very day, in a moment of prescience, Hitler had sent a message to Kleist: "We can expect large-scale offensive operations along the entire Eastern Front on the Russians' revolutionary holiday on 7 November; the Führer expresses the hope that his forces will defend every inch of ground to the last man."[118] Hitler was indeed correct. That very day, Tiulenev and Maslennikov simultaneously proposed fresh counterstrokes—the former with the entire Northern Group, and the latter with selective forces in key sectors. Once Tiulenev amended Maslennikov's proposal, the new offensive plan called for the conduct of two blows. The first, conducted by Sevast'ianov's entire 10th Guards Rifle Corps and supported by Roslyi's 11th Guards Rifle Corps on its right flank, was to advance from the region north and northwest of Ordzhonikidze to penetrate III Panzer Corps' left (northern) wing. The second, conducted by 276th and 351st Rifle Divisions and 155th Rifle Brigade deployed south and southwest of the city, was to penetrate the defenses on III Panzer Corps' right (southern) wing and advance to link up with the northern assault group.[119]

However, rather than attacking simultaneously, Maslennikov's two shock groups acted in piecemeal fashion, seriously weakening the counterstroke's impact. The 11th Guards Rifle Corps' 10th Guards Rifle, 57th Rifle, 5th Guards Tank, and 63rd Tank Brigades attacked at dawn on 6 November from the Fiang-Don region toward Dzuarikau. However, the 10th Guards Rifle Corps' 4th Guards Rifle and 52nd and 2nd Tank Brigades delayed their assault toward Gizel' until midday. As a result, the latter attack faltered in the face of repeated counterattacks by 23rd Panzer Division. Still, thanks to the successful assault by Roslyi's 11th Guards Rifle Corps, 23rd Panzer Division was forced to withdraw westward toward Dzuarikau, and most of 13th Panzer

Division found itself encircled near Gizel', northwest of Ordzhonikidze. The only possible escape corridor for Chevallerie's panzers ran through the narrow strip of ground stretching from the town of Mairamadag, 12 kilometers west of Ordzhonikidze, westward through Suarskoe Ravine and Mairamadag Valley to Dzuarikau.[120] To reduce the encircled German force, Maslennikov committed the fresh 34th Separate Rifle Brigade to block the road through the Suarskoe Ravine, a task that fully occupied the brigade's experienced naval infantrymen (marines) for the next nine days.

To rescue Chevallerie's beleaguered panzer division, Mackensen reorganized Romanian 2nd Mountain Division and troops from the Brandenburg Regiment, supported by artillery and about 60 tanks from 23rd Panzer Division, and sent them against 34th Rifle Brigade's blocking positions at Mairamadag. A fierce fight erupted around the village as the Germans attacked from three sides, with the ensuing struggle lasting until Northern Group launched its general offensive on 13 November. 34th Rifle Brigade held out stubbornly in the village until relieved by 10th Guards Rifle Brigade on 10 November. Together, the two brigades prevented the Germans from capturing Mairamadag and penetrating through the Suarskoe Gorge, thereby ensuring that 13th Panzer Division remained encircled in the Gizel' region.[121]

Thwarted in his first attempt to rescue 13th Panzer Division, Kleist then hurriedly redeployed Steiner's SS "Viking" Division, one *kampfgruppe* at a time, from the Malgobek sector to the north, to reinforce 23rd Panzer's Division's relief efforts. The "Viking" Division's *Nordland* Regiment began arriving in the region north of Dzuarikau on 10 November, followed the next day by two battalions from the division's *Germania* Regiment. On the afternoon of 11 November, a *kampfgruppe* from *Nordland* Regiment drove eastward against heavy resistance in an attempt to link up with 13th Panzer Division's bedraggled columns. Barely effecting the linkup, the two forces together then ran through the gantlet of intense Soviet artillery, mortar, tank, and machine-gun fire from both sides of the Suarskoe Gorge and succeeded in extracting most of the panzer division's personnel and wounded, less their equipment, to relative safety in the Dzuarikau region by early the next morning.[122]

Although Maslennikov attempted to concentrate enough forces around 13th Panzer Division to prevent its rescue and ensure its destruction, these forces did not operate with sufficient resolution or skill to accomplish their mission. For example, 351st Rifle Division, which was located in defensive positions in Mamisoiskii Pass, just south of the Germans' intended escape route, to protect the Ossetian Military Road, was to play a critical role in reducing the encirclement by attacking northward to block 13th Panzer's withdrawal routes. However, instead of attacking decisively to sever this route, the division remained passively riveted to its defensive positions. This permitted the German relief forces to advance through the deadly corridor on

10–11 November and to extract 13th Panzer Division from its trap the following night.[123] In the wake of 13th Panzer's withdrawal, forces on the left wing of Koroteev's 9th Army smashed through the defenses of 13th Panzer's rear guards and captured Gizel' and, on 12 November, advanced westward through Suarskoe Pass toward the Mairamadag River and Fiang-Don.

In the aftermath of this heavy fighting, Boineburg-Lengsfeld's 23rd Panzer Division also received severe criticism for failing to mount an effective relief effort of its own; however, under attack itself and dispersed over a wide region, the division was simply incapable of mounting such an operation.[124] In fact, every one of First Panzer Army's formations engulfed in the fighting at Ordzhonikidze suffered appalling losses during the intense battle. The heavy fighting to reduce the encirclement and block the relief efforts exacted a heavy toll on 13th Panzer Division, the Brandenburgers' supporting forces (such as 45th White Russian, 7th Engineer, 525th Antitank, and 336th Separate Turkish Battalions), and the cooperating mountain battalion from 1st Mountain Division and inflicted less severe damage on 23rd Panzer and Romanian 2nd Mountain Divisions. During its escape, 13th Panzer Division had no choice but to destroy its tanks, vehicles, and heavy weapons. Including 23rd Panzer Division's losses, the Soviets recorded destroying or capturing 40 tanks, 7 armored personnel carriers, 70 guns, 2,350 vehicles, 183 motorcycles, more than a million rounds of ammunition, and countless other supplies while killing more than 5,000 German and Romanian troops.[125]

As for German records, Army Group A's war diary lists 13th Panzer Division's losses at 507 killed, 1,918 wounded, and 82 missing, with 63 tanks and 1,088 trucks destroyed. In his memoirs, Mackensen claims that German losses included 1,275 killed, 5,008 wounded, and 273 missing and places Soviet losses at 16,100 dead and 188 tanks destroyed or captured. Understandably, therefore, 13th Panzer Division's strength fell from 119 operational tanks on 1 November to only 32 on 17 November.[126] This was the cost of an operation that brought Kleist's panzers within 72 kilometers of their prize—Groznyi—but not a step closer.

The Northern Group of Forces' successful defense of Ordzhonikidze, and in particular its counterstroke at Gizel', ended Army Group A's final offensive in the region and marked the end of Hitler's dreams of reaching the vital Caucasus oil fields. As successful as the Northern Group's defense was, however, Soviet critiques highlighted serious mistakes made by Maslennikov and Kozlov, commander of 37th Army, which collectively led to unnecessarily high casualties and made the victory at the gates of Ordzhonikidze a very close call indeed.

Specifically, at the very outset of the operation, both Maslennikov and Kozlov seriously misinterpreted German offensive intentions, thereby setting up Northern Group for initial defeat. Although Northern Group's commander

Colonel General Ewald von Kleist,
commander of First Panzer Army
and Army Group A.

Army General Ivan Vladimirovich
Tiulenev, commander of Trans-
Caucasus Front.

Red Army cavalrymen in the High Caucasus Mountains.

Soviet submachine gunners fighting in the northern Caucasus region.

Red Army machine gunners fighting in the Mozdok region.

Red Army submachine gunner and antitank rifleman
fighting in the northern Caucasus region.

quickly regained his balance and skillfully regrouped forces to counter the German thrust in the depths, the excessive depth carried German forces to the gates of Ordzhonikidze before their ultimate defeat. Also during the operation, some subordinate commanders, such as that of 351st Rifle Division, failed to act decisively when more initiative and resolve would have produced an even greater victory. In other instances, the relatively green infantry formations failed to operate in close cooperation with supporting tanks and artillery and, as a result, often achieved far less than was possible.

On the German side, at least initially, III Panzer Corps' reconnaissance organs operated with particular effectiveness, as evidenced by their ability to pinpoint and destroy 37th Army's headquarters, thereby opening the path to Nal'chik and Ordzhonikidze and literally eliminating that army from any role in future operations. As in the past, 13th and 23rd Panzer Divisions demonstrated what fully manned and equipped German panzer divisions could accomplish if unleashed into the Soviet rear area, especially when operating in close cooperation with supporting aircraft. Later in the offensive, however, German intelligence failed to detect the forces that Maslennikov had assembled to conduct his counterstroke at Ordzhonikidze.

Nevertheless, 13th and 23rd Panzer Divisions also illustrated how vulnerable these divisions really were when required to operate without adequate numbers of supporting infantry. This reality highlighted the most important mistake that First Panzer Army and its parent army group made—that is, launching a major offensive with inadequate forces. Forgetting the lessons learned at Smolensk, Tikhvin, Rostov, and even Moscow in 1941, Kleist embarked on an adventure when he launched his Nal'chik offensive, an adventure that he and his troops would pay for in blood and defeat on the outskirts of Ordzhonikidze. In this sense, they were simply suffering a fate that Paulus's entire Sixth Army would replicate at Stalingrad in a little more than one week's time.

NORTHERN GROUP'S COUNTERSTROKE

The heavy fighting west of Ordzhonikidze did not end with 13th Panzer's successful escape. No sooner did it reach safety than the *Stavka* ordered Tiulenev and Maslennikov to bring the full weight of their Northern Group's forces to bear against Kleist's troops to prevent them from transferring any forces to the Stalingrad region, where the *Stavka* was in the process of final preparations to mount a major counteroffensive. Therefore, Maslennikov formulated a plan to launch a major concerted counteroffensive of his own along the Nal'chik and Mozdok axes. Conducting the Nal'chik offensive, Koroteev's 9th Army was to "attack toward Ardon, Digora, and Dur-Dur to destroy enemy's Ardon-Alagir grouping and restore defenses along the Urukh River."[127] The operation was to unfold in three stages: first, an advance to reach the Ardon River line by 15 November; second, attacks to capture the Alagir region by 20 November; and third, a drive to reach the Urukh River by 29 November.[128]

As Maslennikov and Koroteev planned their new offensive, Kleist and Mackensen worked frantically to erect coherent defenses to protect their still exposed salient jutting southeastward toward Ordzhonikidze and make it less vulnerable to Soviet counterstrokes that they realized were inevitable. Overnight on 12–13 November, Mackensen withdrew the shaken 13th Panzer Division to the rear to rest and refit and established a new defensive line extending from El'khotovo southward along the Terek River to the Fiang-Don River, southward along the Fiang-Don past Ardon to Dzuarikau, and westward from Dzuarikau past Alagir to just south of Khataldon (Chassnidon) and Nal'chik. He ordered 23rd Panzer Division, reinforced by SS "Viking" Division, whose units were still arriving, to defend the Fiang-Don River line from west of Darg Kokh southward to Dzuarikau and then westward to Alagir. Romanian 2nd Mountain Division was to occupy the sector from Alagir northwestward to Khataldon, and composite Group Steinbauer was to hold the more extended front from Khataldon to west of Nal'chik. However, this line was so weak that Mackensen had no choice but to commit 13th Panzer Division's shopworn forces into defensive positions along the Fiang-Don River near Ardon piecemeal and before they were completely rested.[129]

By this time, both sides were severely worn down by the previous fighting. All of the formations in Koroteev's 9th Army had suffered heavy casualties, perhaps amounting to as much as a quarter of their original strength, and the army's tank strength had diminished significantly because of losses from the fighting on the approaches to Ordzhonikidze. For example, 275th and 319th Rifle Divisions of Perekrestov's 3rd Rifle Corps, whose mission was to attack toward Ardon, numbered a total of only 8,000 men, and on 3rd Corps' left flank Sevast'ianov's 10th and Roslyi's 11th Guards Rifle Corps, which were to assault toward Kadgoron, 8 kilometers south of Ardon, counted a total of only 13,000 men. The five tank brigades (2nd, 15th, 52nd, 63rd, and 5th Guards) designated to spearhead or support Northern Group's attacks fielded a total of 80 tanks, only 8 of them modern T-34s.[130] And 13th and 23rd Panzer Divisions were reduced in strength to fewer than 100 tanks, but the addition of SS "Viking" Division added another 30–40 tanks to the equation.[131]

The shock groups on 9th Army's left wing (10th and 11th Guards and 3rd Rifle Corps, supported by the five tank brigades) began their offensive at dawn on 13 November. However, despite nine days of heavy and costly fighting, they failed to achieve a significant penetration through 23rd Panzer Division's defenses along the Fiang-Don River northwest of Ordzhonikidze.

During this period, a tank group consisting of 44 tanks (mostly Lend-Lease models) from 63rd and 5th Guards Tank Brigades, cooperating with Roslyi's 11th Guards Rifle Corps, was also unable to penetrate 13th Panzer Division's defenses in the Ardon region. However, on 17 November 52nd Tank and 5th Guards Rifle Brigades of Sevast'ianov's 10th Guards Rifle Corps finally managed to drive a 10-kilometer-deep wedge into 13th Panzer's defenses near Rasvet, 10 kilometers east of Khataldon, only to be contained by the SS "Viking" Division's panzer battalion.[132] Soviet critiques of the fighting severely criticize 9th Army's shock groups for failing to concentrate forces properly for the attacks and coordinating attacking forces ineffectively.[133]

On 19 November, the same day that Soviet 5th Tank Army began its famous attack through the defenses of Romanian Third Army northwest of Stalingrad, Kleist subordinated SS "Viking" Division to III Panzer Corps and assigned Steiner's SS grenadiers responsibility for defending the corps' entire right wing. Five days later, after all of Steiner's SS troops finally closed into the region, the OKH ordered 23rd Panzer Division to move northward to the Prokhladnyi region and then entrain for transfer to the Kotel'nikovo region. There, it was to spearhead Army Group B's attempt to rescue Paulus's Sixth Army, by this time encircled in Stalingrad.[134] Although desultory fighting continued in the region south of the Terek River, from this time forward all attention was focused on the titanic battle at Stalingrad—and thereby relegating Army Group A's ambitious operations to near oblivion.

Meanwhile, the *Stavka* was dissatisfied with the Northern Group's performance during its offensive, particularly in light of its own impending counteroffensive at Stalingrad, which was due to begin on 19 November. Therefore, Stalin summoned Tiulenev and Maslennikov to Moscow on 15 November. In Moscow, the dictator ordered the two commanders to mount a fresh and more effective offensive. Northern Group's mission was to "conduct an attack against both flanks of the enemy's Mozdok and Alagir grouping and destroy it, while continuing to defend reliably the main axes toward Groznyi and Ordzhonikidze."[135] Prior to launching his offensive, Maslennikov was to shift 11th and 12th Guards Cavalry Divisions, which had just been transferred to his group from the Black Sea Group of Forces, into the Kizliar region. There they were to join 63rd Cavalry Division, which was already operating in the region, to form a new 5th Guards Don Cossack Cavalry Corps under the command of Major General A. G. Selivanov.[136] Henceforth, Selivanov's corps, together with Kirichenko's 4th Guards Cavalry Corps and 110th Separate Cavalry Division, were to constitute a full Cavalry Army under Kirichenko's overall command. The Cavalry Army's mission was to operate against First Panzer Army's left wing and flank in the region west of Kizliar and north of Mozdok in conjunction with the assault by Koroteev's 9th Army against Kleist's right wing south of Mozdok and west of Ordzhonikidze.

To complement this measure and ensure more effective operational coordination within the Northern Group of Forces, the *Stavka* on 18 November appointed new chiefs of staff for Trans-Caucasus Front, the Northern Group, and the *front's* 18th and 45th Armies. This decision propelled Lieutenant General A. I. Antonov from the post of chief of staff of the Black Sea Group of Forces to his new position as Trans-Caucasus Front's chief of staff. Ultimately, Antonov would become chief of the Red Army's General Staff in Moscow.[137] Then on 20 November, the day after Southwestern and Don Fronts launched the Soviet counteroffensive at Stalingrad, the *Stavka* reshuffled the Northern Group of Forces' organization and command cadre to make it better able to conduct a sustained offensive:

1. Do not create the Cavalry Army but instead form two corps from the existing cavalry divisions: The Kuban' Guards Cossack Cavalry Corps, consisting of 9th and 10th Guards Cavalry Divisions and 30th Cavalry Division; and the Don Guards Cossack Cavalry Corps, consisting of 11th and 12th Guards Cavalry Divisions and 63rd Cavalry Division.

Upon completion of its formation, place 110th Cavalry Division at the disposal of the Northern Group's commander . . .

2. Appoint Lieutenant General Kirichenko as the commander of the Kuban' Guards Cavalry Corps and Major General Selivanov as the commander of the Don Guards Cavalry Corps.

3. Replenish 10th and 11th Guards Rifle Corps and the motorized rifle brigade designated for the cavalry army, 11th NKVD Rifle Division, and the five regiments of NKVD forces (one from Derbent, three from Makhachkala, and one from Groznyi).

4. Disband 295th, 275th, and 319th Rifle Divisions. Use their personnel, weapons, and transport to fill out 2nd Guards Rifle Division.

5. Appoint Major General Khomenko as the commander of 44th Army, freeing him from command of 58th Army.

6. Appoint Major General Mel'nik as the commander of 58th Army, freeing him from command of 44th Army.

7. Upon completion of the operation, withdraw 37th Army's headquarters to the Makhachkala region and employ it at the discretion of the *front* commander.[138]

On 27 November, with this reorganization complete, the forces on the left wing of Koroteev's 9th Army commenced their offensive along the Digora axis, west of Ordzhonikidze, with shock groups advancing along four converging axes from northwest to southwest against III Panzer Corps' salient projecting eastward from the Urukh River to the Fiang-Don River, west of Ordzhonikidze:

- **3rd Mountain Rifle Corps** (Colonel G. N. Perekrestov), with 275th, 389th, and 319th Rifle Divisions and 9th Rifle and 140th and 52nd Tank Brigades, across the Fiang-Don River toward Ardon and Digora;
- **10th Guards Rifle Corps** (Colonel V. V. Glagolev, who replaced Colonel Sevast'ianov on 11 November), with 4th, 5th, 6th, and 7th Guards Rifle and 15th and 207th Tank Brigades, across the Fiang-Don River toward Kadgoron;
- **11th Guards Rifle Corps** (Major General I. P. Roslyi), with 10th Guards, 34th, 57th, and 62nd Rifle and 5th Guards and 63rd Tank Brigades, across the Fiang-Don River toward Nogkai; and
- **One rifle brigade** (probably the 155th) from west of Alagir toward Khataldon.[139]

The new addition to Koroteev's group of corps commanders was 44-year-old Colonel Vasilii Vasil'evich Glagolev, a veteran cavalryman who commanded 42nd Cavalry Division in the Crimea during the first eight months of the war and 24th Army's 73rd Rifle Division, which was encircled and destroyed in the Millerovo region during the first month of Operation Blau. Escaping from encirclement, Glagolev led 9th Army's 176th Rifle Division during the battles for Mozdok and Ordzhonikidze in October and November 1942, before being assigned to command 10th Guards Corps. He would end the war as a successful army commander and be honored as a Hero of the Soviet Union.[140]

Despite three days of intense fighting, Koroteev's shock groups failed to dislodge the defending III Panzer Corps. Although the shock groups resumed their assaults on 4 December, these attacks also failed, forcing the *front* to cease operations and plan yet another offensive. By this time, however, the Red Army's successful counteroffensive at Stalingrad had settled the issue once and for all, leaving Mackensen's panzer army, and all of Army Group A as well, no choice but to begin an arduous withdrawal from the Caucasus region—a withdrawal that ultimately resulted in a race against the clock, as well as against advancing Soviet forces, for the salvation of the entire army group.

THE NORTHERN FLANK

Voronezh Yet Again

Despite the failure of its counterstrokes and other offensive actions in the Voronezh region during July and August, the *Stavka* by mid-September decided to launch new attacks in the region. It considered these attacks as essential for two reasons. First, they would forestall further German counterattacks against the bridgeheads that its forces had seized on the southern bank of the

Don River at Serafimovich and Kletskaia in late August. Second, they would support the counterstrokes that Stalingrad Front was conducting against the defenses of Paulus's Sixth Army between the Don and the Volga Rivers northwest of Stalingrad during the first half of September. In light of this heavy fighting, the *Stavka* thought it sheer folly to allow its armies in the Voronezh region to sit idly by while its armies northwest of Stalingrad were making a maximum effort against the northern flank of Operation Blau. Although it had lost its tank corps to the *Stavka*'s reserve and other sectors of the front, Lieutenant General M. E. Chibisov's 38th Army was still strong, and both Lieutenant Generals I. D. Cherniakhovsky's 60th and M. M. Popov's 40th Armies were formidable forces.[141]

The September offensive was the brainchild of General Nikolai Fedorovich Vatutin, the commander of Voronezh Front who, in addition to being a brilliant young staff officer with a keen strategic perspective, would also prove to be an audacious field commander. In late August Vatutin convinced Stalin that it was essential, in order to prevent replicating previous failures in the Voronezh region, to combine the Red Army's shock groups operating in the region under a unified command. In response to Vatutin's proposal, the *Stavka* on 30 August transferred Chibisov's entire army—four rifle divisions, five rifle and three tank brigades, Major General I. V. Lazarov's 11th Tank and Major General A. S. Zhadov's 8th Cavalry Corps, and a host of artillery and support units—from Briansk Front to Voronezh Front.[142] This gave Vatutin control of 38th, 60th, and 40th Armies and 11th, 18th, and 25th Tank Corps.[143] The new member of Chibisov's command team was General Aleksei Semenovich Zhadov (before 1942, Zhidov), who, though an experienced cavalryman, commanded 4th Airborne Corps during the initial months of Operation Barbarossa and thereafter served as chief of staff of 3rd Army during the battle for Moscow and during the winter campaign of 1941–1942.[144]

Vatutin then developed a plan to encircle German forces in the salient anchored on Voronezh (see Map 82). His plan required Chibisov's 38th Army, supported by Lazarov's 11th Tank Corps, to attack southward west of the Don River to capture Starye Semiluki, 10 kilometers west of Voronezh. East of the Don, Cherniakhovsky's 60th and Popov's 40th Armies, supported by Colonel B. S. Bakharov's 18th and Major General P. P. Pavlov's 25th Tank Corps, were to attack the defenses of German Second Army at Voronezh proper from the north and east, respectively, and then cross the Don to link up with Chibisov's forces at Starye Semiluki. Pride of place in this attack went to Pavlov's 25th Tank Corps, which was to exploit 40th Army's penetration and chop westward across the southern outskirts of Voronezh, seeking to link up with 38th Army at Semiluki.

Regardless of how feasible this plan might have been, it was seriously compromised on 7 September when Moscow detached four rifle divisions

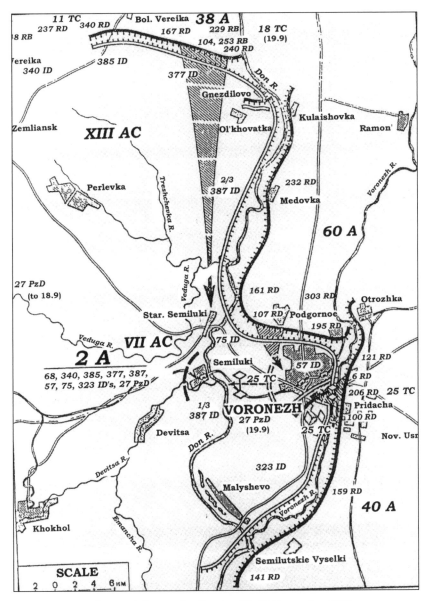

Map 82. Voronezh Front's Voronezh offensive, 15–19 September 1942

from Voronezh Front to reinforce Stalingrad.[145] Indeed, the *Stavka* questioned whether Vatutin's divisions, which averaged only 5,000–5,500 men each, could achieve a penetration given that much stronger forces had failed to do so in July and August. Vatutin had to argue strongly to prevent cancellation of his plan; the start date was moved back from 9 to 15 September.[146] By the date of the assault, Vatutin's forces maintained clear numerical superiority over the defending Germans, who by this time had only the weak 27th Panzer Division in reserve. With a force of three tank corps, 19 rifle divisions, and six rifle, four destroyer (infantry antitank), and seven tank brigades arrayed against six German infantry divisions (XIII Army Corps' 385th and 377th and VII Army Corps' 387th, 75th, 57th, and 323rd), Vatutin's forces had a superiority of 3:1 in infantry and 10:1 in tanks when the offensive began. Nonetheless, Vatutin's September offensive fared no better than previous ones.

Beginning their assaults on 15 September, the attackers lacked sufficient tanks and artillery to penetrate the carefully constructed German defenses. Contrary to the *front* commander's plan, 25th Tank Corps entered battle before 40th Army had broken through at Voronezh. As a result, the tank units became bogged down in urban fighting. In the center, a German artillery counterpreparation disrupted the planned attack of 60th Army just north of the city; west of the Don River, Chibisov's troops ran out of steam after penetrating the first layer of German defenses. Vatutin, however, was determined to succeed. On 19 September, despite the *Stavka*'s advice that he cease his offensive operation, he threw Bakharov's newly arrived 18th Tank Corps into the battle on 38th Army's front but achieved little. The *front* commander persisted, suffering additional casualties until 28 September, when Vasilevsky ordered an immediate halt to the attack and detached further units from Voronezh Front.[147]

Overall, the Soviet offensives at Voronezh cost far more than they achieved. In June and July alone, Briansk Front lost 66,212 casualties, one-third of its force, while the Voronezh Front suffered a further 76,129 losses; the August and September attacks were equally expensive. Meanwhile, the number of German and satellite Axis divisions opposite this sector declined from 16 in mid-July to 11 by September, and the strong 9th and 11th Panzer Divisions were replaced by the much weaker 27th Panzer as an operational reserve. Thus, these offensives failed not only to encircle any German forces but also to tie down German forces that were needed elsewhere.[148]

The Continuing Struggle for Demiansk

Dissatisfied with Northwestern Front's offensive failures at Demiansk in July and August, the *Stavka* insisted that the *front*'s commander, Colonel General

P. A. Kurochkin, begin yet another offensive on 15 September, once again to divert German attention from action in the south. The exhausted troops of Lieutenant General V. Z. Romanovsky's 1st Shock Army, especially 129th and 130th Rifle Divisions, had to attack in the same locations as before, although they received somewhat more artillery and antiaircraft support than in the previous efforts. The results were predictably dismal. Perhaps the most that can be said for the Demiansk offensives is that they provoked a series of German offensives to widen the Ramushevo corridor. The last of these operations, code-named *Winkelried* (Corner Bog), was delayed for two months by the incessant Soviet attacks. It finally began on 27 September with an effort to encircle 1st Shock Army forces lodged in a salient jutting northward at the base of the corridor (see Map 83). By this time, 1st Shock Army's defending 1st Guards Rifle Corps was exhausted—one of its regiments had only 344 soldiers to defend a 6-kilometer front. Although most of the shock army's troops escaped encirclement, *Winkelried* succeeded in loosening the Soviet grip on the Demiansk pocket and brought to a temporary close the sad series of offensives by Northwestern Front.[149]

CONCLUSIONS

The costly offensive operations that the Red Army conducted in the Demiansk and Voronezh regions during the fall of 1942 had little or no impact on the outcome of the more decisive fight persisting at Stalingrad. Yet the same cannot be said of the struggle in the Caucasus. Army Group A launched three major offensives in the Caucasus region during the fall, the first two during September toward Tuapse on the Black Sea and toward Ordzhonikidze and Groznyi, the twin gateways into the Trans-Caucasus oil fields at Baku, and the third toward Ordzhonikidze and Groznyi in late October.

Collectively, these operations sought to realize Hitler's preeminent objective in Operation Blau: the seizure of the oil riches of the Trans-Caucasus region. Therefore, the inability of Army Group A to do so meant the failure of Operation Blau as a whole. Because Army Group A tacitly admitted defeat at the end of the first week of November, Operation Blau actually collapsed prior to Sixth Army's and Army Group B's defeat at Stalingrad. However, just as the struggle at Stalingrad mesmerized the generals on both sides and historians into believing that Operation Blau expired in the ruins of Stalin's namesake city, it also masked the reality that Blau was already a dead issue by the time the Red Army unleashed its armored pincers to encircle Paulus's Sixth Army.

In a strategic sense, Operation Blau replicated Operation Barbarossa the year before. Before the *Wehrmacht* was defeated at the gates of Moscow in early December 1941, it had already suffered major defeats in the Leningrad

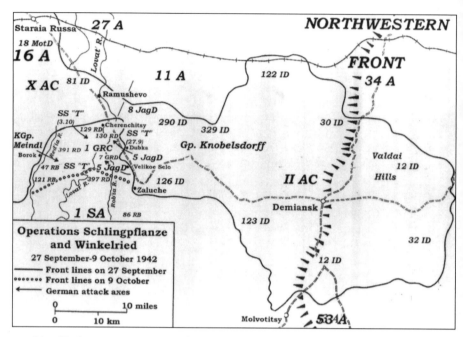

Map 83. Operations at Demiansk, 15 September–9 October 1942

and Rostov regions. Thus, weeks before Army Group Center's offensive had collapsed along the approaches to Moscow, Army Groups North and South had admitted defeat and were already on the defense. Likewise, in the fall of 1942, two weeks before Army Group B suffered its defeat at Stalingrad, Army Group A had admitted defeat and was already on the defense in the Caucasus.

In an operational sense as well, the fighting in the Caucasus also replicated the *Wehrmacht's* operations in the fall of 1941. The year before, as it advanced in the face of determined and ever-increasing Red Army resistance, Army Group South had steadily narrowed its front, pursuing ever more limited objectives with diminishing forces and in increasingly ad hoc fashion before being defeated at Rostov. Similarly, in the fall of 1942, faced with similar resistance and many of the same problems as its predecessor, Army Group A advanced in spasmodic offensive spurts along a diminishing number of axes. In the process, its forces steadily eroded in strength before their defeat along the approaches to Tuapse and the gates of Ordzhonikidze. Thus, just as the *Wehrmacht's* defeats at Tikhvin and Rostov in November 1941 epitomized the ultimate defeat of Operation Barbarossa, Army Group A's defeat at Ordzhonikidze in early November 1942 foretold the ultimate failure of Operation Blau.

Table 39. The Organization of the Trans-Caucasus Front, 1 September–1 November 1942

A. The Organization of the Trans-Caucasus Front on 4 September 1942

Trans-Caucasus Front – Army General I. V. Tiulenev
  Northern Group of Forces – Lieutenant General I. I. Maslennikov
    9th Army – Major General K. A. Koroteev
      11th Guards Rifle Corps – Major General I. P. Roslyi
        8th, 9th, and 10th Guards Rifle Brigade
      151st, 176th, and 389th Rifle Divisions
      62nd Naval Rifle Brigade
      36th and 42nd Separate Armored Train Battalions
    37th Army – Major General P. M. Kozlov
      2nd Guards, 275th, 295th, and 392nd Rifle Divisions
      11th Rifle Division NKVD
      127th Cavalry Regiment (30th Cavalry Division)
    44th Army – Major General M. E. Petrov
      223rd, 414th, and 416th Rifle Divisions
      9th, 10th, and 256th Rifle Brigades
      84th Separate Naval Rifle Brigade
      30th and 110th Cavalry Divisions
      44th Separate Tank Battalion
      66 Separate Armored Train Battalion and 18th Separate Armored Train
    46th Army – Major General K. N. Leselidze
      3rd Mountain Rifle Corps – Colonel G. N. Perekrestov
        9th and 20th Mountain Rifle Divisions
      61st, 394th, and 406th Rifle Divisions
      51st and 155th Rifle Brigades
      63rd Cavalry Division
      51st Fortified Region
      12th Separate Tank Battalion
      11th and 12th Separate Armored Train Battalions and 41st Separate
        Armored Train
    58th Army – Major General V. A. Khomenko
      317th, 328th, and 337th Rifle Divisions
      Makhachkala Rifle Division NKVD
      3rd Rifle Brigade
    4th Air Army – Colonel General of Aviation K. A. Vershinin, Major General of
      Aviation N. F. Naumenko in September 1942
      216th, 217, and 265th Fighter Aviation Divisions
      218th Fighter-Bomber Aviation Division
      219th Bomber Aviation Division
      790th Fighter Aviation Regiment
      4th Reconnaissance Aviation Squadron
      Forming:
        229th Fighter Aviation Division
        230th Assault Aviation Division
        8th and 247th Fighter Aviation Regiments
        103rd Assault Aviation Regiments
        459th Close-range Bomber Aviation Regiment
        647th Mixed Aviation Regiment
        718th, 762nd, and 889th Light Bomber Aviation Regiments
    8th Sapper Army – Colonel I. E. Salashchenko
      11th, 23rd, 24th, 25th, 26th, 28th, 29th, and 30th Sapper Brigades

Table 39. (continued)

10th Guards Rifle Corps – Major General I. T. Zamertsev, Colonel I. A. Sevast'ianov
    on 15 September
    4th, 5th, 6th, and 7th Guards Rifle Brigades
    89th, 347th, and 417th Rifle Divisions
    52nd Tank Brigade
    249th, 258th, and 563rd Separate Tank Battalions
Black Sea Group of Forces – Colonel General Ia. T. Cherevichenko (from North
    Caucasus Front on 4 September)
    12th Army – Major General A. A. Grechko (disbanded on 4 September and
    incorporated into 18th Army as the Tuapse Defensive Region)
        395th Rifle Division
        16th Rifle and 68th and 81st Naval Rifle Brigades
    18th Army – Major General F. V. Kamkov
        31st, 236th, and 383rd Rifle Divisions
        10th Guards Cavalry Division
        1331st Rifle Regiment
    47th Army – Major General A. A. Grechko
        77th and 216th Rifle Divisions
        103rd Rifle, 83rd Naval Rifle, 1st Naval Infantry, and Composite Rifle Brigades
        126th Separate Tank Battalion
        16th Separate Armored Train
    56th Army – Major General A. I. Ryzhov
        30th, 261st, 349th, and 353rd Rifle Divisions
        76th Naval Rifle Brigade
        Rostov Peoples' Militia Rifle Regiment
        7th Separate Armored Train Battalion
    5th Air Army – Lieutenant General of Aviation S. K. Goriunov
        132nd Bomber and 236th and 237th Fighter Aviation Divisions
        742nd Reconnaissance Aviation Regiment
        Forming:
        238th Assault Aviation Division
        763rd Light Bomber and 931st Mixed Aviation Regiments
Front subordinate (from former North Caucasus Front)
    4th Guards Cavalry Corps – Major General N. Ia. Kirichenko
        9th, 11th, and 12th Guards Cavalry Divisions
    32nd Guards, 318th, and 339th Rifle Divisions
    976th Separate Rifle Regiment
    67th Separate Rifle, 323rd Naval Infantry, and Separate Parachute Assault
        Battalions
    1st and 2nd Shock Detachments
    69th and 151st Fortified Regions
    Separate Motorized Rifle Brigade
    1st Separate Motorized Rifle and 62nd Separate Tank Battalions
    53rd Separate Armored Train
Front subordinate (to Trans-Caucasus Front)
    242nd Mountain Rifle and 271st, 276th, 319th, and 351st Rifle Divisions
    19th, 34th, and 43rd Rifle Brigades
    14th Tank Corps – Major General of Tank Forces N. N. Radkevich
        138th and 139th Tank and 21st Motorized Rifle Brigades
    5th Guards, 2nd, 15th, 63rd, 140th, and 191st Tank Brigades
    75th, 562nd, and 564th Separate Tank Battalions
    8th and 19th Separate Armored Train Battalions and 14th and 15th Separate
        Armored Trains

Table 39. (continued)

Non-Operating Forces
    45th Army – Lieutenant General F. N. Remezov
        228th, 320th, 402nd, 408th, and 409th Rifle Divisions
        55th Fortified Region
        151st Tank Brigade
    Forces in Iran
        75th Rifle Division
        15th Cavalry Corps – Major General K. S. Mel'nik
            1st and 23rd Cavalry Divisions
        207th Tank Brigade

Source: Boevoi sostav Sovetskoi armii, Chast 2 (Ianvar'–dekabr' 1942 goda) [Combat composition of the Soviet Army, Part 2 (January–December 1942)] (Moscow: Voenizdat, 1966), 173–174, 182.

B. The Organization of the Trans-Caucasus Front on 1 October 1942

Trans-Caucasus Front – Army General I. V. Tiulenev
    Northern Group of Forces – Lieutenant General I. I. Maslennikov
        9th Army – Major General K. A. Koroteev
            11th Guards Rifle Corps – Major General I. P. Roslyi
                8th, 9th, and 10th Guards Rifle and 57th Rifle Brigades
            89th, 176th, and 417th Rifle Divisions
            19th, 59th, 60th, 131st, and 256th Rifle and 62nd Naval Rifle Brigades
            5th Guards and 52nd Tank Brigades
            75th and 249th Separate Tank Battalions
            41st and 42nd Separate Armored Train Battalions
        37th Army – Major General P. M. Kozlov
            2nd Guards, 151st, 275th, 295th, and 392nd Rifle Divisions
            11th Rifle Division NKVD and 113th Separate Rifle Regiment NKVD
            127th Cavalry Regiment (30th Cavalry Division)
        44th Army – Major General M. E. Petrov, Major General K. S. Mel'nik on 11 October
            223rd, 317th, 337th, and 389th Rifle Divisions
            9th and 157th Rifle Brigades
            Separate Cavalry Regiment (Bn)
            19th, 36th, and 65th Separate Armored Train Battalions
        58th Army – Major General V. A. Khomenko
            271st, 319th, and 416th Rifle Divisions
            Makhachkala Rifle Division NKVD
            43rd Rifle Brigade
        4th Air Army – Major General of Aviation N. F. Naumenko
            216th, 217, and 265th Fighter, 218th Fighter-Bomber, 219th Bomber, and
                230th Assault Aviation Divisions
            4th Reconnaissance Aviation Squadron
            In the process of formation:
                229th Fighter Aviation Division
                8th, 45th, 247th, and 483rd Fighter, 136th, 570th, 590th, and
                    657th Assault, 585th and 762nd Light Bomber, and 647th Mixed
                    Aviation Regiments
        8th Sapper Army – Colonel I. E. Salashchenko
            11th, 23rd, 24th, 25th, 26th, 28th, 29th, and 30th Sapper Brigades
        10th Guards Rifle Corps – Colonel I. A. Sevast'ianov
            4th, 5th, 6th, and 7th Guards Rifle Brigades

Table 39. (continued)

4th Guards Cavalry Corps – Major General N. Ia. Kirichenko
    9th and 10th Guards and 30th and 110th Cavalry Divisions
414th Rifle Division
19th Rifle Division NKVD
10th Rifle Brigade
44th, 258th, and 563rd Separate Tank Battalions
Black Sea Group of Forces – Colonel General Ia. T. Cherevichenko, Major
    General I. E. Petrov on 11 October
    18th Army – Major General F. V. Kamkov, Major General A. A. Grechko on 18 October
        32nd Guards, 31st, 236th, 328th, 383rd, and 395th Rifle Divisions
        68th Naval Rifle Brigade
        12th Guards Cavalry Division and Separate Cavalry Regiment
        40th Motorized Rifle Brigade
    46th Army – Major General K. N. Leselidze
        3rd Mountain Rifle Corps – Colonel G. N. Perekrestov
            9th, 20th, and 242nd Mountain Rifle Divisions
        61st, 351st, 394th, and 406th Rifle Divisions
        51st, 107th, 119th, and 155th Rifle Brigades
        63rd Cavalry Division
        Composite Rifle Regiment (Colonel Semenov)
        1st–10th Mountain Rifle Detachments
        Separate Naval Infantry Battalion
        51st Fortified Region
        562nd Separate Tank Battalion
        11th and 12th Separate Armored Train Battalions
    47th Army – Major General A. A. Grechko, Major General F. V. Kamkov on 18
        October
        216th and 318th Rifle Divisions
        163rd Rifle, 81st and 83rd Naval Rifle, and 255th Naval Infantry Brigades
        672nd Rifle (408th Rifle Division) and 137th Naval Infantry Regiments
        126th Separate Tank and 1st Separate Motorized Rifle Battalions
    56th Army – Major General A. I. Ryzhov
        30th, 339th, and 353rd Rifle Divisions
        76th Naval Rifle Brigade
        Rostov Peoples' Militia Rifle Regiment
        69th Fortified Region
    5th Air Army – Lieutenant General of Aviation S. K. Goriunov
        132nd Bomber, 236th, 237th, and 295th Fighter, and 214th Assault
            Aviation Divisions
        763rd Light Bomber, 718th, 750th, and 931st Mixed, and 742nd
            Reconnaissance Aviation Regiments
77th Rifle Division
16th and 103rd Rifle Brigades
11th Guards Cavalry Division
Separate Parachute Battalion
151st Fortified Region
62nd Separate Tank Battalion
8th Separate Armored Train Battalion
Tuapse Defensive Region
    408th Rifle Division (less 762nd Regiment)
    145th Naval Infantry Regiment
    143rd and 324th Naval Infantry Battalions
    1st Special Designation Detachment

Table 39. (continued)

Front subordinate
   261st, 276th, 347th, and 349th Rifle Divisions
   34th, 164th, and 165th Rifle, and 84th Naval Rifle Brigades
   Separate Mountain Ski Battalion
   2nd, 15th, 63rd, 140th, and 191st Tank Brigades
   132nd, 266th, and 564th Separate Tank Battalions

Non-Operating Forces
   45th Army – Lieutenant General F. N. Remezov
      228th, 320th, 402nd, and 409th Rifle Divisions
      55th Fortified Region
      151st Tank Brigade
   Forces in Iran
      75th Rifle Division
      15th Cavalry Corps – Major General K. S. Mel'nik, Colonel V. F. Damberg on
         16 October
         1st and 23rd Cavalry Divisions
      207th Tank Brigade

Source: Boevoi sostav Sovetskoi armii, Chast 2 (Ianvar'–dekabr' 1942 goda) [Combat composition of the Soviet Army, Part 2 (January–December 1942)] (Moscow: Voenizdat, 1966), 195–197, 204.

C. Organization of the Soviet Forces in the Caucasus Region on 1 November 1942

Trans-Caucasus Front – Army General I. V. Tiulenev
   Northern Group of Forces – Lieutenant General I. I. Maslennikov
      9th Army – Major General K. A. Koroteev
         3rd Rifle Corps – Colonel G. N. Perekrestov
            9th, 57th, and 60th Rifle Brigades
         11th Rifle Corps – Colonel I. A. Rubaniuk
            19th, 34th, and 131st Rifle Brigades
         89th, 176th, 317th, 337th, 347th, and 417th Rifle Divisions
         10th Guards Rifle Brigade
         5th Guards Tank Brigade
         2nd and 15th Tank Brigades
         41st, 42nd, and 66th Separate Armored Train Battalions
      37th Army – Major General P. M. Kozlov
         10th Rifle Corps – Major General P. E. Loviagin
            59th and 164th Rifle Brigades
         2nd Guards, 275th, and 295th Rifle Divisions
         11th Rifle Division NKVD
         113th Separate Rifle Regiment NKVD
         563rd Separate Tank Battalion
      44th Army – Major General K. S. Mel'nik
         9th Rifle Corps – Major General I. T. Zamertsev
            43rd and 157th Rifle Brigades
         10th Guards Rifle Corps – Colonel I. A. Sevast'ianov, Colonel V. V.
            Glagolev on 11 November
            4th, 5th, 6th, and 7th Guards Rifle Brigades
         223rd, 389th, and 402nd Rifle Divisions
         63rd Cavalry Division (to 5th Guards Cavalry Corps on 15 November)
         63rd Tank Brigade

Table 39. (continued)

132nd and 488th Separate Tank Battalions
19th and 36th Separate Armored Train Battalions
58th Army – Major General V. A. Khomenko
    271st and 416th Rifle Divisions
    Makhachkala Rifle Division NKVD
4th Air Army – Major General of Aviation N. F. Naumenko
    216th and 217th Fighter, 218th Fighter-Bomber, 219th Bomber, and 230th
        Assault Aviation Divisions
    647th Mixed Aviation Regiment
    4th Reconnaissance Aviation Squadron
    In the process of formation:
        229th Fighter Aviation Division
        8th, 247th, 483rd, 805th, and 863rd Fighter, 136th, 570th, 590th, and
            657th Assault, 288th Bomber, and 585th Light Bomber Aviation
            Regiments
11th Guards Rifle Corps – Major General I. P. Roslyi
    34th and 62nd Rifle Brigades
4th Guards Cavalry Corps – Major General N. Ia. Kirichenko
    9th and 10th Guards and 30th and 110th Cavalry Divisions
5th Guards Cavalry Corps (created on 15 November) – Major General A. G. Selivanov
    11th and 12th Guards and 63rd Cavalry Divisions
276th, 319th, 320th, and 414th Rifle Divisions
19th Rifle Division NKVD
256th Rifle Brigade
52nd Tank Brigade
44th, 75th, 249th, 258th, and 266th Separate Tank Battalions
37th Separate Armored Car Battalion
20th Separate Armored Train Battalion
Black Sea Group of Forces – Major General I. E. Petrov
    18th Army – Major General A. A. Grechko
        32nd Guards, 328th, 353rd, and 383rd Rifle Divisions
        8th and 9th Guards and 10th, 68th, 107th, 119th, and 165th Rifle Brigades
        Separate Cavalry Regiment
        40th Motorized Rifle Brigade
    46th Army – Major General K. N. Leselidze
        9th, 20th, and 242nd Mountain Rifle Divisions
        61st, 394th, and 406th Rifle Divisions
        Sukhumi Rifle Division NKVD
        51st and 155th Rifle Brigades
        7th and 8th Mountain Rifle Detachments
        51st Fortified Region
        562nd Separate Tank Battalion
        11th Separate Armored Train Battalion
    47th Army – Major General F. V. Kamkov
        216th and 318th Rifle Divisions
        81st Naval Rifle and 255th Naval Infantry Brigades
        137th Naval Infantry Regiment
        69th Fortified Region
    56th Army – Major General A. I. Ryzhov
        30th, 339th, and 395th Rifle Divisions
        76th and 83rd Naval Rifle Brigades
        814th Separate and Separate (Rostov) Peoples' Militia Rifle Regiments
        323rd Naval Infantry Battalion
        151st Fortified Region

Table 39. (continued)

5th Air Army –
    132nd Bomber and 236th and 295th Fighter Aviation Divisions
    718th and 763rd Light Bomber, 750th and 931st Mixed, and 742nd Reconnaissance
        Aviation Regiments
    11th and 12th Guards Cavalry Divisions (to 5th Guards Cavalry Corps on 15 November)
    62nd Separate Tank Battalion
    12th Separate Armored Train Battalion
    Tuapse Defensive Region
        236th and 408th Rifle Divisions
        408th Rifle Brigade
        126th Separate Tank Battalion

Front subordinate
    12th Rifle Corps
        77th, 261st, 349th, and 351st Rifle Divisions
    31st and 151st Rifle Divisions
    16th and 103rd Rifle Brigades
    67th Separate Mountain and 691st Separate Rifle Regiments
    69th–83rd Separate Antitank Battalions
    140th and 191st Tank Brigades
    Separate Motorized Rifle Brigade
    564th Separate Tank Battalion
    8th Separate Armored Train Battalion

Non-Operating Forces
    45th Army – Lieutenant General F. N. Remezov
        228th and 409th Rifle Divisions
        55th Fortified Region
        151st Tank Brigade
    Forces in Iran
        75th Rifle Division
        15th Cavalry Corps – Colonel V. F. Damberg
            1st and 23rd Cavalry Divisions
        207th Tank Brigade

Source: Boevoi sostav Sovetskoi armii, Chast 2 (Ianvar'–dekabr' 1942 goda) [Combat composition of the Soviet Army, Part 2 (January–December 1942)] (Moscow: Voenizdat, 1966), 217–218, 226.

The Assaults on the Barrikady and Krasnyi Oktiabr' Factories, 1–18 November 1942

PLANNING FOR THE GERMANS' "FINAL ACT," 1–8 NOVEMBER

By 1 November, in the wake of its ferocious assaults on Chuikov's defenses in Stalingrad's factory district, Paulus's army controlled more than 90 percent of Stalingrad and was within sight of the Volga at virtually every point along its front but had yet to achieve the objective assigned by Hitler. Instead of allowing Paulus's army to liquidate 62nd Army and drive its remnants into the Volga, the remnants of Chuikov's undermanned and undersupplied army clung stubbornly to multiple elongated bridgeheads along the river's western bank, including (see Maps 84–85):

- **Group Gorokhov** (124th and 149th Rifle Brigades), defending the 1,000-meter-wide and 800-meter-deep enclave between Rynok and Spartanovka, north of the Mokraia Mechetka River;
- **138th Rifle Division** (Liudnikov) and **118th Regiment, 37th Guards Rifle Division**, defending the 1,000-meter-wide and 200–400-meter-deep strip of ground northeast and east of the Barrikady Factory;
- **339th and 344th Regiments, 308th Rifle Division** (Gurt'ev), defending the 400-meter-wide and 300-meter-deep strip of ground east and southeast of the Barrikady Factory;
- **120th Regiment, 39th Guards Rifle Division, 193rd Rifle Division** (Smekhotvorov), and **61st and 253rd Regiments, 45th Rifle Division** (Sokolov), defending the 1,200-meter-wide and 200–500-meter-deep strip of ground between Hall 4 in the Krasnyi Oktiabr' Factory and the ravine south of the Barrikady Factories. On the night of 1–2 November, **161st and 241st Regiments of 95th Rifle Division** reinforced this group;
- **112th Regiment** and part of **120th Regiment, 39th Guards Rifle Division** (Gur'ev), and **10th Regiment, 45th Rifle Division**, defending the 800-meter-wide and 100–500-meter-deep strip of ground from the Bannyi Ravine to Halls 8a and 10 in the Krasnyi Oktiabr' Factory;
- **284th Rifle Division** (Batiuk), defending the 3,600-meter-wide and 100–800-meter-deep strip of ground from the lower Krutoi Ravine past

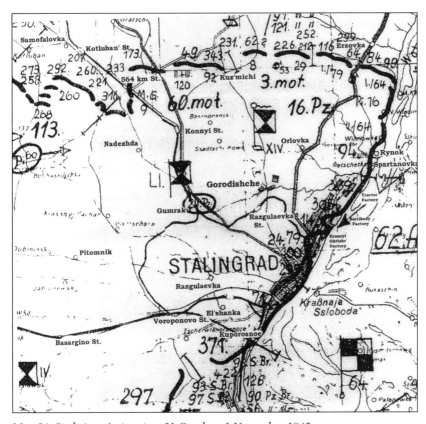

Map 84. Sixth Army's situation, 31 October–1 November 1942

the Dolgii Ravine, the trig point on Hill 102 (Mamaev Kurgan), and the "Tennis Racket" (with Chuikov's headquarters to the east) to the Bannyi Ravine; and

- **13th Guards Rifle Division** (Rodimtsev), defending the 1,200-meter-wide and 200-meter-deep strip of ground in Stalingrad's center city.[1]

Clearly, however, even if the Germans succeeded in securing the entire city, they would go no farther in 1942. From mid-October onward, therefore, pursuant to Paulus's orders, all German units not directly involved in combat devoted their energies to constructing semipermanent buildings in which to pass the winter. Nevertheless, for political reasons the battle had to continue. As Paulus pondered how to fulfill his Führer's wishes, the issue of finding reinforcements for Seydlitz's LI Army Corps remained foremost in

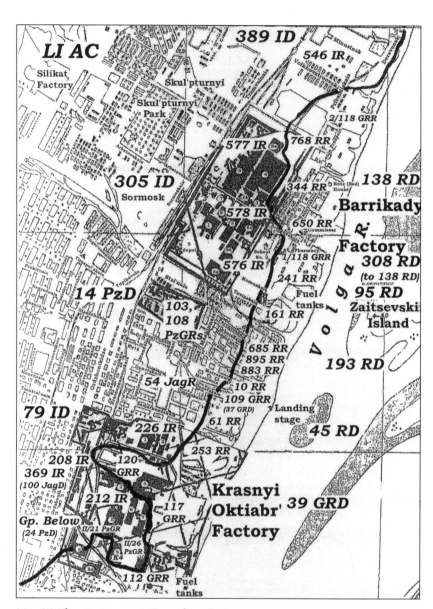

Map 85. The situation on 1 November 1942

his mind. As he considered his army's position, Paulus concluded by the end of October that his most important objective was the Lazur Chemical Factory, situated in the Tennis Racket south of the Krasnyi Oktiabr' Factory and Bannyi Ravine. If his forces could capture this factory, they would cut Chuikov's army in half, thereby rendering 62nd Army's small bridgeheads east of Barrikady and in Krasnyi Oktiabr' virtually irrelevant.

Paulus, Seydlitz, and their respective chiefs of staff met on 1 November at the headquarters of VIII Air Corps in Razgulaevka to discuss the matter of reinforcement and air support with Richthofen, commander of Fourth Fleet, and General Martin Fiebig, commander of VIII Air Corps. At this point, Paulus's principal concern was how the assault on Stalingrad could be "nourished" with fresh forces to support 79th Infantry Division, whose regiments, like those of the neighboring 14th Panzer and 305th Infantry Divisions, could "no longer be considered for larger missions."[2] Paulus's initial concept for resuming the offensive was to replace 305th Infantry Division with 24th Panzer Division, pull 305th from the front lines on 4 and 5 November, and, after resting it for several days, use it to relieve XIV Panzer Corps' 60th Motorized Division on the northern flank of the corridor northwest of Stalingrad on 8 and 9 November. After a week's rest, 60th Motorized, with a force of between three and four reinforced battalions rated "medium strong" but no longer mobile, and nine artillery batteries, would then be available to spearhead an assault on the Chemical Factory on or about 15 November. In addition, Paulus intended to reinforce 60th Motorized Division with a composite regimental-size *kampfgruppe* from 100th Jäger Division and three assault companies pirated from other divisions.

Later on 1 November, Major General Schmidt, the chief of staff of Sixth Army, discussed these matters with Major General Georg von Sodenstern, his counterpart in Army Group B. After informing Sodenstern that 79th Infantry Division could indeed hold on to its positions in the Krasnyi Oktiabr' Factory but was not capable of mounting an assault on the Chemical Factory, Schmidt surfaced the idea of employing 60th Motorized Division to accomplish this task. However, when he described the proposed timeline starting 15 November, Sodenstern declared that that would be "fairly catastrophic."[3] Paulus then telephoned Weichs at 1900 hours, informing him of his plan and telling him the final act in the drama could not occur without further reinforcements. Weichs responded by suggesting that Paulus employ two regiments of 29th Motorized Division (without its artillery), which was then resting and refitting in the Gorodishche region in Fourth Panzer Army's reserve, to reinforce the 79th Infantry Division's assault on the Chemical Factory. This was because 29th Motorized Division's regiments were still rated "above average" in strength. Minutes later, however, Weichs, who had second thoughts about the wisdom of cannibalizing such a critical reserve, suggested that 60th Motorized Division might be used after all or even to replace 29th Motorized.

Ultimately, however, Paulus and Weichs rejected this idea because 60th Motorized itself was understrength after fending off numerous Soviet offensives in the Kotluban' region and would likely be called upon to do so again in the near future. Likewise, they rejected the suggestion that part or all of Fourth Panzer Army's reserve 29th Motorized Division be employed to the same end because it was needed to protect against future offensives by 64th Army from the Beketovka bridgehead. In any case, it would take too much time to move either of these divisions to the Krasnyi Oktiabr' Factory and replace them with other forces.

When these proposals proved unsatisfactory, on 3 November Sodenstern suggested employing five combat engineer (pioneer) battalions from Sixth Army, four of them from divisions defending in the Italian Eighth Army's sector along the Don River and one from the army's reserve, to spearhead an assault on the remaining Soviet strongpoints in the Krasnyi Oktiabr' Factory. In fact, this suggestion had originated from Hitler, whose favorite air force commander, the former World War I ace General von Richthofen, had described to him the key role that this type of battalion had played in the successful assault on the Tractor Factory. Paulus accepted the idea, although his chief of staff, General Schmidt, argued that engineers could "in no way be a substitute for infantry."[4]

The reinforcing forces suggested by Sodenstern included 45th, 50th, 162nd, 294th, and 336th Engineer (Pioneer) Battalions, augmented by an assault company from 44th Infantry Division and a panzer squadron from 24th Panzer Division. The 45th Engineer Battalion, with a strength of 451 men, was directly subordinate to Sixth Army; the 50th, with 539 men, was subordinate to 22nd Panzer Division; the 162nd, with 437 men, was from 62nd Infantry Division; and the 294th and 336th, with 408 and 336 men, respectively, were from the infantry divisions that bore the same numerical designations. The assault company from 44th Infantry Division included about 300 men, and 24th Panzer Division's assault squadron consisted of roughly 150 men.[5]

Even before these discussions, Paulus was taking measures to reinforce Seydlitz's shock group fighting in the vicinity of the Krasnyi Oktiabr' Factory. On 29 October, for example, in accordance with his initial offensive concept, he ordered Lenski's 24th Panzer Division to form an infantry force from its panzer crews and supporting mechanics and to use this force to take over the sector of the adjacent 305th Infantry Division and thereby free up the latter's infantry for employment in further assaults—an order Lenski said he simply could not understand.[6] However, before 24th Panzer could respond to this directive, it received another, this time from LI Corps:

In the night of 30–31 October, 389th Infantry Division will take over the sector of front from 24th Panzer Division. The 24th Panzer Division will prepare to take over the southern front of 79th Infantry Division from the southwest corner of the Steel Factory [Krasnyi Oktiabr'] to the mouth of the gully on the Volga in grid square 71b1 (exclusive). The earliest time for the takeover of this sector is the night of 1 November–2 November.[7]

Overnight on 30–31 October, pursuant to Seydlitz's order, 389th Infantry Division, now commanded by Major General Erich Magnus, who had just replaced Jänecke, relieved 24th Panzer Division's *Kampfgruppe* Below, permitting Below to withdraw his forces back into rear assembly areas near the Gumrak railroad station.[8] There, Lenski's 24th Panzer received fresh orders on 1 November: "On the night of 1–2 November 1942, 24th Panzer Division will replace the employed forces on the southern front of 79th Infantry Division from the boundary with 100th Jäger Division up to and including the southern work hall."[9] Lenski and his troops were not pleased:

This was not what the Division wanted: instead of receiving some well-deserved rest, they were now to relocate to another area of Stalingrad, this time to the grim Krasnyi Oktiabr' Steel Factory. The factory was an immense area of slag-heaps, railway sidings, workshops and huge steel buildings that were now no more than shattered steel skeletons. Shells of large calibers—from both sides—had worked over the factory, ripping up the ground, tearing huge chunks out of the buildings, and creating an indescribable mess of tangled girders, sheet-metal and rubble. . . . Nevertheless, orders were orders.[10]

Lenski's panzer division relieved 79th Infantry Division's 212th Regiment on the night of 1–2 November, taking over its roughly 700-meter-wide front extending from the southern edge of the Krasnyi Oktiabr' Factory's Hall 10 westward around the northern periphery of Hall 8a to the ravine at the factory's southwestern corner, where its right boundary joined 100th Jäger Division's left boundary. At this time, forces from 39th Guards Rifle Division's 112th Regiment occupied the eastern approaches to Hall 10 and all of Hall 8a. As of 31 October, 24th Panzer Division reported a trench strength of 960 combat infantrymen. However, before and after it occupied its positions in the factory, the division was able to raise another 700 combatants, largely by using *Hiwis* (Russian volunteers) to replace German troops in other noncombat positions.[11]

Once in the foreboding confines of the Krasnyi Oktiabr' Factory, Lenski deployed his panzer division's 2nd Battalion, 26th Grenadier Regiment, and

4th Motorcycle Battalion in the sector between the southern edge of Hall 10 and the eastern edge of Hall 8a. He then placed 2nd Battalion, 21st Grenadier Regiment, around the northern edge of Hall 8a westward to the ravine and the boundary with 100th Jäger Division. Colonel Winterfeld's Panzer Detachment, with 20 operational tanks, became the division's reserve deployed in assembly areas in grid square 75 (between the upper Barrikady and Tractor Factory villages).[12] However, to Lenski's chagrin, on 2 November Seydlitz ordered seven of Winterfeld's tanks to provide support to 305th Infantry Division's forces in the sector east of the Barrikady Factory. The 24th Panzer Division's relief effort permitted Schwerin's 79th Infantry Division to concentrate its 208th and 212th Regiments, reinforced by 179th Engineer Battalion and the Croat 369th Regiment (transferred from 100th Jäger Division), to defend the factory's Halls 6 and 7 and organize stronger assault groups to recapture Hall 4. The 79th Division's 226th Regiment was to defend Halls 1 and 2 and also launch attacks eastward north of the factory.

While making these changes in his army's tactical dispositions, Paulus on 2 November made round-robin visits to the command posts of Seydlitz's divisions. Based on what he learned from these visits and on the limited progress and continuing heavy losses being suffered by his assault groups (a total of 400 men killed or wounded) against enemy forces that appeared to be numerically superior, Paulus faced a dilemma. Although his orders to Seydlitz's corps required it to "clean up the enemy breakthrough position at 79th Infantry Division" and "continue the assault with the southern wing of 389th Infantry Division" the following day, additional bloodletting without fresh reserves would clearly be futile.[13] Therefore, Paulus curtailed further major attacks while he continued negotiations with Army Group B over necessary reinforcements—in this case the five engineer battalions. During the extensive exchange of messages during the day, Army Group B confirmed that 29th Motorized Division would definitely not be available for Paulus's use. This meant that the die was cast: LI Corps would have to rely on its own forces, plus the five engineer battalions, if its final act was to succeed. Based on previous experiences, this indeed required relying on a slender reed.

Acquiescing to these realities, Sixth Army issued its initial order for the final act, an operation code-named Hubertus, to Seydlitz's LI Corps at 1825 hours on 3 November. The order required Seydlitz to regroup his forces and attack to capture the northern sector of the Lazur Chemical Factory, an objective Paulus believed was vital to 62nd Army's successful defense, on either 9 or 10 November. The LI Corps' order read:

> The LI Army Corps will initially transition to the defense for a short time, while preparing an attack to wrench the district around the Lazur Chemical Factory out of the enemy bridgehead. . . .

The divisions will hold the positions, fortify them with as much energy as possible and promote the construction of obstacles in front of their lines by all means available. Should the enemy actually carry out an attack on the anniversary of his revolution (7 November), then there is only one thing to do: Not a step back! What has been gained in sacrificial struggle must be unconditionally held under all circumstances.[14]

Seydlitz's order then prescribed his corps' attack formation and task organization (from south to north):

- **295th Infantry Division**—in the "Tennis Racket" and Mamaev Kurgan sectors opposite the Bannyi Ravine and Lazur Chemical Factory;
- **100th Jäger Division** [not specifically mentioned in the order, with 54th Regiment returned from 14th Panzer Division and 294th and 336th Engineer Battalions]—the sector from Mamaev Kurgan to north of the Bannyi Ravine, opposite the southwestern corner of the Krasnyi Oktiabr' Factory;
- **Group Schwerin** (79th Infantry Division, with *Kampfgruppe* Seydel from 14th Panzer Division and *Kampfgruppe* Scheele from 24th Panzer Division, effective at 0800 hours on 5 November)—in the Krasnyi Oktiabr' Factory;
- **14th Panzer Division** (minus)—in the sector between the Krasnyi Oktiabr' and Barrikady Factories opposite 62nd Army's landing stage; and
- **305th Infantry Division** (reinforced by engineer battalions)—along the eastern edge of the Barrikady Factory north of 62nd Army's landing stage.[15]

While Paulus's army and Seydlitz's LI Corps were issuing their initial orders for the final act, Weichs informed Paulus that "the general situation requires the battles around Stalingrad be ended soon."[16] He also informed Paulus that his army would receive five engineer battalions within the next week to be "combined with infantry under panzer-grenadier regimental staffs" and be used in the final assault.[17]

Although Weichs and Paulus had already agreed that the objective would be the Lazur Chemical Plant, which was situated within the Tennis Racket south of the Krasnyi Oktiabr' Factory, the situation changed drastically on 5 and 6 November. At 1430 hours on 5 November, Seydlitz's LI Corps issued Order No. 107, which announced that "'Hubertus' is the attack of the LI Army Corps on X-day on the Lazur Chemical Factory district, with a breakthrough to the Volga. . . . All preparations must be completed so that the attack can begin at daybreak (Y-hour) on 10 November."[18] This order required 100th Jäger Division to conduct the main attack and assigned to it a reinforced regiment from 295th Infantry Division, all five reinforcing engineer battalions, three new assault [*shturm*] companies, and much of the reinforcing artillery and *Werfer* units. Group Schwerin was to join the action against the Krasnyi Oktiabr' Factory once 100th Jäger Division's assault proved successful.

The first indication that Paulus's plans were going awry came at 2315 hours on 5 November, when Weichs's chief of staff, Sodenstern, called Paulus's chief of staff, Schmidt, and informed him that Hitler now questioned the order of his priorities. Specifically, because Hitler felt it necessary to eliminate Soviet resistance in the steel (Krasnyi Oktiabr') and gun (Barrikady) factories before dealing with the chemical factory, the OKH had just asked Army Group B why they wanted to attack the chemical facility first. For his part, Sodenstern had already informed Zeitzler, chief of the Army General Staff, that attacking the steel and gun factories first would sap the army's strength to the point where it would be unable to capture the chemical facility. Agreeing to take the matter up with the Führer, Zeitzler first asked when either of the attacks could be carried out and the rationale for going after the chemical facility first.

In a lengthy response, Paulus stressed the relative weakness of his forces and shared his doubts over the success of either operation. In short, he stated that either operation could begin on 10 November. Listing both the positive and negative aspects of each offensive option, as before, he stressed that the attack on the steel and gun factories would certainly clear the army's northern flank before the attack on the chemical facility; however, it might also sap the army's strength to the extent that it might not be able to conduct the latter. By contrast, an attack on the chemical facility would seize the most decisive objective but might require delay in seizing the two other factories. Summarizing the options, the army commander concluded:

> I again come to the previously expressed opinion that it is not certain whether one solution or the other—with the ultimate objective of the chemical factory—can succeed because the army has very few forces at its disposal and that's why it would be better in any case if the army were provided with more infantry units. This is thought to be necessary because the Russians have again thrown fresh forces into Stalingrad in the last few days.[19]

As he transmitted Paulus's response to Sodenstern, Schmidt added, "Give us a decision and an order, and we'll carry it out."[20] At 1940 hours the operations officer of Army Group B informed his counterpart in Sixth Army, "We've got the decision from the OKH operations department; the Fuhrer has ordered that the first decision [the chemical factory] retains validity, whereby the 'lesser evil' (the bridgeheads east of the gun and metallurgical works) should be eliminated first."[21] At 2010 hours the die was cast when Army Group B informed Sixth Army:

> The Führer has ordered: before resuming the attack to recapture the Lazur chemical factory, the two sections of the city the enemy still holds east of the gun factory and east of the steel factory are to be taken. Only after the bank of the Volga there is entirely in our hands will the assault on the chemical factory begin.[22]

Confirming Paulus's plan for the final act had been aborted, at 1015 hours on 7 November, LI Corps issued its Order No. 108, which announced "Operation Hubertus is postponed."[23] This order also made some adjustments in the task organization of the corps for the forthcoming attack, leaving 336th Engineer Battalion and the assault companies from 44th Infantry and 24th Panzer Divisions subordinate to 100th Jäger Division and the assault company from 79th Infantry Division subordinate to Group Schwerin. Finally, the panzer company from 14th Panzer Division and the panzer squadron from the 24th Panzer Division were at the disposal of the LI Army Corps, and 45th, 50th, and 162nd Engineer Battalions were to support the corps' infantry divisions. Accordingly, LI Corps' Order No. 109, issued at 1030 hours on 7 November, split up the forces assembled to conduct Operation Hubertus into two groups with separate objectives, as follows:

- **Group Schwerin**, with 79th Infantry Division, two engineer battalions, one panzer squadron from 24th Panzer Division, half of an assault gun battalion, and three *Werfer* battalions (one heavy and two light), was to capture the Martin Furnace in the Krasnyi Oktiabr' Factory; and
- **305th Infantry Division**, with two engineer battalions, one assault gun battalion, one panzer company from 14th Panzer Division, and an assault company from 44th Infantry Division, and the right wing of 389th Infantry Division, with one engineer battalion, half of an assault gun battalion, and an assault squadron from 24th Panzer Division, were to crush Soviet forces in the strip of land between the Barrikady Factory and the Volga River.[24]

Finally, *Kampfgruppe* Seydel from 14th Panzer Division was to operate on 305th Division's right to protect its flank and prevent Soviet forces from counterattacking into the gap between the two attacking shock groups.

However, because Seydlitz and many of his subordinates thought that splitting up their forces was a mistake, LI Corps issued a revised Order No. 109 at 1435 hours on 7 November that staggered the sequencing of the assaults, according priority to the seizure of the region east of Barrikady. Now the primary objective was "305th Infantry Division and 389th Infantry Division (southern wing)—after thorough preparation—to conquer the bank of the Volga east of the gun factory on 11 November."[25] This order bolstered the strength of 305th and 389th Infantry Divisions by augmenting the former with a third engineer battalion and the latter with a second engineer battalion and a full assault-gun battalion. Thereafter, Group Schwerin was to capture the Martin Furnace in the Krasnyi Oktiabr' Factory sometime after 14 November.[26]

On the following day, 8 November, Sixth Army allocated necessary reinforcements to 305th and 389th Infantry Divisions, including seven infantry companies from the former's 576th, 577th, and 578th Regiments and the latter's 544th and 546th Regiments, the five newly arrived engineer battalions, the army's two divisional engineer companies, the two assault-gun battalions (244th and 245th), the panzer company from 14th Panzer Division, and the bulk of the artillery from LI Corps. By this time, 244th Assault Gun Battalion reported it had 17 operational assault guns (5 long and 8 short 75mm and 5 new 150mm heavy infantry guns) and 245th Assault Gun Battalion three assault guns (2 long and 1 short 75mm).[27] The attack on the area east of Barrikady was to begin early on 11 November, and after regrouping the one against the Krasnyi Oktiabr' Factory and the area to the east would take place no earlier than 15 November.[28]

Later on 8 November, however, after additional discussions with army headquarters, LI Corps amended its attack order once again, this time making no mention whatsoever about Group Schwerin's attack on the Krasnyi Oktiabr' Factory. According to the new order, Order No. 110, issued at 1400 hours, LI Corps was "to capture the Volga shore east of the gun factory from the fuel installation (inclusive) to the southwestern area of the brick works."[29] Specifically:

> The 305th Infantry Division and the southern wing of 389th Infantry Division will launch a surprise attack at daybreak (Y-hour) along a broad front with grenadier regiments reinforced by strong engineer forces and capture the Volga shore.
>
> Through deep deployment and readiness of strong reserve forces, it will be ensured that they approach the forward line again and again, conserve their fighting strength and maintain sufficient forces to remove bypassed enemy nests and clean out the cellars of conquered houses.
>
> The engineer battalions are not to be employed in a single engineer regiment or battalion, but will be attached to the infantry and will work in the closest cooperation with them and their heavy weapons. . . .
>
> The 71st, 295th, 100th Jäger Divisions and Group Schwerin will carry out well-prepared storm-troop operations to deceive the enemy about

the extent of the assault front. . . . Group Schwerin [also] has the task, from the very beginning of the attack, to eliminate every flanking effect from the area in front of the left wing of Group Schwerin against the right wing of 305th Infantry Division by heavy fire from infantry weapons and artillery.[30]

By virtue of this order, 305th Infantry Division received 50th, 294th, and 336th Engineer Battalions, and 389th Infantry Division received 45th and 162nd Engineer Battalions.

Therefore, the indecision reflected in the discussions between Hitler, the OKH, Weichs, Paulus, and Seydlitz and the frequent changes in Sixth Army's and LI Corps' operational plans set the corps on a course that neither Paulus nor Seydlitz—to say nothing of the rank-and-file German soldier—was confident would produce victory. Instead of trying to crush the entire Soviet bridgehead simultaneously, this time Seydlitz planned to reduce it one bastion at a time.

These frequent changes in plans had a rippling effect within the forces designated to carry out the final act. For example, in 24th Panzer Division, on the morning of 4 November, Lenski replaced Colonel von Below, commander of the *kampfgruppe* of that name, with Colonel Alexander von Scheele, transforming the group into *Kampfgruppe* Scheele, which still consisted of a single grenadier battalion (the 2nd) from 21st and 26th Grenadier Regiments and the division's motorcycle and pioneer battalions.[31] Then, at 1415 hours, a new corps order formed Group Schwerin, headed by the commander of 79th Infantry Division, consisting of the *kampfgruppen* from his own division and 24th Panzer Division's *Kampfgruppe* Scheele, effective at 0800 hours on 5 November. It also reinforced Scheele's force with a squadron of 10 tanks from Panzer Detachment Winterfeld and shifted its left boundary to include the Krasnyi Oktiabr' Factory's Hall 10. This required *Kampfgruppe* Scheele to relieve 79th Infantry Division's *Kampfgruppe* Sobottka in Hall 10 during the night. Finally, the new order warned Schwerin's and Scheele's forces to reckon on "large-scale Russian attacks" on 7 November, the anniversary of the Soviet Union's October Revolution, stating, "Plied with copious amounts of vodka [the troops], the [Russian] assaults were expected to be determined and fierce."[32] Scheele's forces succeeded in relieving Sobottka's group of 105 officers and soldiers in Hall 10 without incident or casualties by 2300 hours.

In addition to this regrouping and similar shifts within other divisions of Seydlitz's corps, LI Corps' order required 14th Panzer, 79th Infantry, and 24th Panzer Divisions to form one assault company [*sturmkompanie*] apiece with which to spearhead their future assaults. Each company was to consist of about 150 soldiers, supported by heavy machine guns, heavy mortars, 37mm antitank guns, and a squad of engineers, all three operating under

100th Jäger Division's control "for an attack in about a week's time."[33] The assault companies were to form in the rear and be prepared to conduct their operations by late on 7 November.

THE CALM BEFORE THE STORM: THE FIGHTING DURING THE OPERATIONAL "LULL," 1–10 NOVEMBER

1 November

As Weichs, Paulus, and Seydlitz adjusted plans to comply with Hitler's demands and slowly reorganized their forces opposite Stalingrad's factory district, desultory yet often fierce and desperate fighting continued across the entire front during the first few days of November. The heaviest fighting on 1 November took place in the so-called central sector of the front along the approaches to the landing stage and within the Krasnyi Oktiabr' Factory. There, according to 62nd Army's daily report, "The enemy repeatedly attacked our positions toward Mezenskaia and Umanskaia Streets, trying to capture the crossings. Simultaneously, the enemy tried once again to capture the halls captured by our units in the Krasnyi Oktiabr' Factory." During this fighting:

138th, 308th, and 193rd RDs, repelling two attacks by the forces of up to a battalion with tanks toward the landing stage, held on to their occupied positions.

45th RD and 39th Gds. RD repelled attacks by enemy infantry and tanks toward Merovsk and the landing stage and continued to hold on to their occupied positions.

39th Gds. RD was fighting on the grounds of the Krasnyi Oktiabr' Factory.[34]

While Seydlitz reshuffled his forces to maintain maximum pressure on 62nd Army, Chuikov threw every last force he could muster across the river to shore up his army's defenses between the Barrikady and Krasnyi Oktiabr' Factories, especially to protect his last vital landing stage on the Volga's western bank. To this end, at 1345 hours on 1 November, the army commander ordered 161st and 241st Regiments of Gorishnyi's 95th Rifle Division, which had been partially rested and refitted on the eastern bank of the Volga during the preceding several days, to cross over to the right bank of the Volga on the night of 1–2 November. Once there, these regiments would occupy defensive positions to prevent the enemy from reaching the bank of the Volga.[35] In addition, Chuikov ordered the headquarters of Zholudev's 37th Guards Rifle Division and the division's 109th Regiment, which he had previously sent across the Volga to support Liudnikov's 138th Rifle Division, to withdraw to the river's eastern bank for rest and refitting. However, Chuikov left all of the division's personnel west of the river under the control of Liudnikov's division.[36] The Red Army General Staff's daily operational summary duly reported:

> **62nd Army**, holding on to its occupied positions, repelled several attacks by enemy infantry and tanks in the vicinity of Mezinskaia and Umanskaia Streets and on the grounds of the Krasnyi Oktiabr' Factory.
> The enemy air force constantly bombed the combat formations of our units in the Krasnyi Oktiabr' Factory-Bannyi Ravine sector and in the vicinity of the Barrikady Factory with groups of 5–12 aircraft during the day on 1 November.
> The units of 138th, 308th, 193rd, and 45th RDs and 39th Gds. RD remained in their previous positions and repelled repeated attacks by enemy infantry and tanks, which were especially fierce in the vicinity of Mezinskaia and Umanskaia Streets and on the grounds of the Krasnyi Oktiabr' Factory.
> 284th RD occupied 6 enemy dugouts as a result of night actions.
> 13th Gds. RD exchanged fire with the enemy in its occupied positions.
> On the army's right wing, as a result of fighting, 300th RD's [amphibious] assault battalion captured the northeastern part of Latashanka, where it dug in and exchanged fire with up to a battalion of enemy infantry with 14 tanks.[37]

Largely discounting the action in the factory district because it considered it inconsequential, the OKW reported that "north of Stalingrad, Soviet forces once again tried unsuccessfully to cross the Volga. Two cannon boats and several large landing cutters were sunk, one cannon boat was damaged, and several hundred prisoners were captured."[38]

As Army Group B and Paulus fenced with one another over the question of reinforcements, on 1 November Sixth Army's commander ordered Seydlitz's LI Corps to seize as much of the region east of the Barrikady Factory as possible with the forces he had at hand. By castling 24th Panzer Division to the right, Paulus hoped that the concentrated 305th Infantry Division, now commanded by Colonel Bernhard Steinmetz, who had replaced Oppenländer only hours before, could clear Soviet forces from the remainder of the Barrikady Factory and the region to the east as quickly as possible.[39]

Issued at 1055 hours on 1 November, LI Corps' order required 305th Infantry Division and the southern wing of 389th Infantry Division to clear Soviet forces (138th and 308th Rifle Divisions) from the remainder of the Barrikady Factory and the swath of land between the factory and the Volga's western bank.[40] To ensure they could do so, Seydlitz reinforced the 305th Infantry with 244th Assault Gun Battalion, a company of self-propelled antitank guns from 14th Panzer Division's 4th Panzer Jäger Battalion, a panzer company from 24th Panzer Division, and 389th Infantry Division with a company of self-propelled antitank guns from 24th Panzer Division's 40th Panzer Jäger Battalion.[41]

For his part, Chuikov, overnight on 1–2 November, took measures to tighten and strengthen defenses east of the Barrikady Factory and between it and the Krasnyi Oktiabr' Factory and to ensure that his forces kept the Germans away from the vital landing stage. For example, at 0105 hours he shifted 45th Rifle Division's left boundary to the line from the letter "B" in the designation Bakinskaia through Kommissarskaia to Dzhankoiskaia Streets, making Colonel Sokolov, commander of 45th Rifle Division, responsible for securing the boundary on its left with 39th Guards Rifle Division.[42] At the same time, Chuikov disbanded his army's headquarters security company, employing its troops and weapons to reinforce 39th Guards Rifle Division.[43] Finally, the army commander ordered 95th Rifle Division's 241st Regiment, which had already crossed the Volga, to defend the crucial sector between 308th and 193rd Rifle Divisions, especially the landing stage. Before its division headquarters arrived, the regiment would be subordinate to Gurt'ev's 308th Rifle Division.[44]

2 November

Seydlitz's forces began their advance at 0900 hours on 2 November, with small *kampfgruppen* from 305th Infantry Division's 578th and 576th Regiments assaulting eastward from the central and southern part of the Barrikady Factory, protected on the left by the division's 577th Regiment. To the north, company-size *kampfgruppen* from 389th Infantry Division's 546th Regiment attacked eastward from the Brick Factory. Attacking on 305th Infantry Division's right wing, 576th Regiment's *kampfgruppen* struck the defenses of Gurt'ev's 308th Rifle Division, which were by now reinforced by 95th Rifle Division's 241st Regiment. After advancing several hundred meters, 576th Regiment's forces came to an abrupt halt short of the fuel depot southeast of the factory. To the north, the attack by 578th Regiment's *kampfgruppen* faltered immediately after it began in the face of strong resistance by 138th Rifle Division's 650th Regiment east of the central section of the factory. Likewise, 389th Infantry Division's 546th Regiment also faced heavy going east of the Brick Factory against 138th Rifle Division's 768th Regiment and attached 118th Guards Regiment.

As 62nd Army reported late on 2 November:

The enemy, having brought up new forces from the depth and having reinforced his operating units, went over to the attack beginning at 0700 hours toward Spartanovka in the northern sector of the front with a force of more than an infantry regiment and tanks and in the central sector with two infantry divisions and 35–40 tanks.

The enemy air force bombed the sectors of attack constantly all day with groups of aircraft and assaulted the combat formations of our forces with groups of up to 30 aircraft simultaneously in separate sectors. . . .

138th RD—the enemy undertook an attack against the sector of the division with a force of more than an infantry regiment with tanks from the Volkhovstroevsk region along the Volga River from the north, but the division repelled four attacks and held on to its occupied positions.

308th RD, with 241st RR (95th RD), drove off four attacks by the enemy, who were trying to reach the bank of the Volga River from the Mezenskaia region, but the units held on to their positions.

During the day, 193rd and 45th RDs repelled repeated attacks by the enemy toward the landing stage and held on to their positions. The 45th RD, counterattacking with its left wing, repelled the attack by the enemy and was fighting along the line of the iron-casting, blooming, and calibrating halls-the finished product warehouse at day's end. The enemy suffered heavy losses.[45]

Seconding 62nd Army's report, the Red Army General Staff recorded:

62nd Army. The Northern Group (124th and 149th RBs) repelled several attacks by an enemy force of more than a regiment of infantry with tanks in the Spartanovka region on 2 November.

138th RD repelled four attacks by the enemy in the Barrikady Factory region and held its occupied positions on 2 November.

308th RD, with 241st RR, 95th RD, repelled four attacks by the enemy attacking from the Mezenskaia region.

193rd and 45th RDs repulsed five attacks by enemy infantry and tanks trying to capture the landing-stage on 2 November. 45th RD's units, while going over to counterattacks, captured several shops in the Krasnyi Oktiabr' Factory.

The army's remaining units occupied their previous positions.[46]

Chuikov, reporting that his forces had inflicted more than 1,200 casualties on the Germans during the day and also destroyed 10 tanks, ordered his supply services to replenish his forces with ammunition and his forces to prepare "to repel the offensive being prepared by the enemy."[47]

Once again, the OKW focused primarily on the fighting north of Stalingrad: "The offensive in Stalingrad is continuing. Heavy street fighting is going on. Dive-bombers are continuing to inflict bombing strikes against centers of fierce enemy resistance in the northern part of the city. Despite desperate resistance, Russian forces are continuing to withdraw. Several enemy counterattacks have been repelled."[48]

3–4 November

While Paulus and Seydlitz were busily formulating their plans for the final act, the intensity of the fighting in the central sector decreased sharply during the next two days as the forces of LI Corps limited their actions to straightening the lines and improving the starting positions for the final offensive to reduce 62nd Army's defenses once and for all. On 3 November, for example, while Stalingrad Front tried to extract its 300th Rifle Division from a precarious foothold on the Volga's western bank north of Rynok, Chuikov's army reported "repelling attacks by enemy infantry and tanks in the central sector," which "were trying to reach the Volga River and capture the landing stage"; the army's forces held on to their occupied positions.[49] Specifically, Liudnikov's 138th Rifle Division repelled attacks by a reinforced enemy company along Derevianskaia Street and another, by a battalion, against the northeastern corner of the Barrikady Factory. At the same time, Gorishnyi's 95th Rifle Division fended off an attack by an infantry battalion and tanks along Stal'naia Street, and Sokolov's 45th Rifle and Gur'ev's 39th Guards Rifle Divisions did the same against small groups between the Barrikady and Krasnyi Oktiabr' Factories and on the grounds of the latter.

The Red Army General Staff reported on the reduced combat activity at day's end:

> **The Stalingrad Front**.
> The battalion of 300th RD conducted a fighting withdrawal from the Latashanka region behind the railroad line and continued to fight in the vicinity of the Nizkovodnaia landing stage.
> **62nd Army** held on to its previous defensive positions and repelled attacks by the enemy on 3 November.
> The units of the Northern Group, remaining in their occupied positions, repulsed two attacks by the enemy.
> 138th RD repelled an attack by up to a company of enemy infantry toward the Derevensk region and up to a battalion of infantry and tanks from the southeastern corner of Barrikady Factory toward Taimyrsk.
> 95th RD repulsed an attack by an enemy force of up to a battalion of infantry along Stal'naia Street.
> 39th Gds. RD repelled an attack by a battalion of enemy infantry in the vicinity of the Krasnyi Oktiabr' Factory.
> The positions of the army's remaining units were unchanged.[50]

At day's end, the OKW simply remarked, "We are continuing to clear the occupied territory in Stalingrad of enemy. While doing so, separate groups of enemy were encircled. Several counterattacks by Soviet forces have been repelled. Dive-bombers conducted bombing strikes against concentrations of enemy forces west of the bend in the Volga. During unsuccessful attempts to cross the river north of Stalingrad, the enemy lost yet another cannon boat."[51]

Chuikov, expecting Sixth Army to resume a large-scale offensive at any time, at 1545 hours on 3 November assigned specific defensive sectors to his subordinate divisions, together with precise instructions regarding how they were to defend them. Most important, all of the divisions were to complete their regrouping by 2300 hours on 3 November and be prepared to repel assaults by 0400 hours on 4 November. During the ensuing 10 hours they were to "widen" their bridgehead by pushing the forward edge of their defenses westward "no fewer than 80–100 meters each day by means of local operations so as to completely clear the enemy from the grounds of the Barrikady and Krasnyi Oktiabr' Factories by day's end on 6 November 1942" and "advance the forward edge in the Volkhovstroevsk-Bannyi Ravine sector up to the main (western) railroad line."[52]

With both sides preparing for what they considered the climactic stage of the struggle for the city, combat action ceased almost entirely on 4 November. 62nd Army reported attacks by only "small groups" of enemy on its front and continued adjusting forces and strengthening defenses. In accordance with Chuikov's orders, 138th Rifle Division withdrew its 118th Guards Regiment into reserve positions, and Chuikov ordered 45th and 193rd Rifle Divisions to conduct local attacks to improve their positions between the Barrikady and Krasnyi Oktiabr' Factories. Reflecting this diminution in fighting, the Red Army General Staff claimed that 62nd Army "repelled probing attacks by the enemy from the direction of Derevensk, the Bannyi Ravine, and Kurskaia Street and in the vicinity of Krasnyi Oktiabr' Factory with part of its forces and held on to its occupied positions on 4 November" although German aircraft "continuously bombed the Barrikady and Krasnyi Oktiabr' Factories during the first half of the day with groups of 5–7 aircraft."[53]

From its vantage point, the OKW reported, "Our combat reconnaissance groups operated successfully in Stalingrad. Enemy strongpoints were eliminated, and enemy attacks were repulsed. A river ferry was sunk by our combat security forces on the Volga. Our aircraft inflicted powerful strikes against enemy strong points west of the Volga bend and on battery positions on the river's eastern bank."[54]

Based on this lull and reports from his intelligence organs, Chuikov concluded that "Paulus had presumably begun preparations for his next offensive before 1 November, but in the thick of the fierce fighting we had not noticed it. . . . It became clear that the battle for the city was not over."[55] More tellingly still, Eremenko informed Chuikov, "The Germans are planning to discontinue the offensive against 62nd Army" and, therefore, had "already started withdrawing forces from the Army's front to the rear and flanks." Based on this information, Chuikov concluded that "the G.H.Q. [General Headquarters], whose plans Eremenko of course knew about, in preparing its counterattack, had decided at any price, principally by active operations in the city, to pin down the enemy group at the Volga."[56] If this judgment proved correct, Chuikov was convinced that Paulus would attempt to complete his operations in Stalingrad as quickly as possible. As he jotted in his diary on 4 November, "In the next few days, the enemy will continue his fierce attacks. He will use fresh forces—up to two divisions. It is obvious, however, that he is making his last efforts."[57]

Late on 4 November, 62nd Army released a remarkably accurate assessment of German forces facing its bridgehead defenses. It began with a conclusion: "In recent days the enemy, by directing his efforts on such a fierce offensive toward the Spartanovka and Barrikady and Krasnyi Oktiabr' Factories with his main forces, has suffered significant losses."[58] Regarding the strength of German forces, the report claimed that 10 enemy divisions were operating along 62nd Army's front, including 295th, 71st, 79th, 94th, 100th, 305th, and 389th Infantry and 14th, 16th, and 24th Panzer Divisions, and Paulus's army could muster up to 200 tanks and up to 1,000 guns. Its appended list of each German division and regiment and, in some instances, even separate battalions and the precise sector each occupied was uncannily accurate. The condition report that Paulus's Sixth Army issued on 9 November confirmed Chuikov's assumptions regarding the weakness of Sixth Army, although it woefully overstated its armor strength (see Table 40).

Although Sixth Army managed to generate one more infantry battalion rated "strong" and increased the number of battalions rated "average" by consolidating its forces, the total number of battalions in the army's forces fighting in and around Stalingrad decreased from 69 to 62. Worse still, by 9 November three of LI Corps' seven divisions (94th, 295th, and 79th Infantry) were rated between "weak" and "exhausted," and two more (389th Infantry and 14th Panzer) maintained ratings approaching "average" only by consolidating their forces into a fewer number of battalions. In addition, by 11 November Sixth Army was able to muster only 21 tanks and 28 assault guns to support LI Corps' final act, including 13 tanks in 14th Panzer Division's Group Seydel and 8 in 24th Panzer's Group Scheele and 18 guns in 244th Assault Gun Battalion and 10 in 245th Assault Gun Battalion.[59] Operating north of Stalingrad, XIV Panzer Corps reported on 11 November that 16th Panzer Division had 55 operational tanks (41 Pz. III long, 3 Pz. IV short, and 11 Pz. IV long) and on 14 November that 3rd and 60th Motorized

Table 40. The Combat Rating of Infantry and Pioneer Battalions Subordinate to Sixth Army's Divisions Fighting in Stalingrad, 26 October–9 November 1942

	26 October	9 November
XIV PANZER CORPS		
3rd Motorized Division		
(4–3 infantry battalions)	4 medium strong	3 medium strong
(1 pioneer battalion)	weak	average
60th Motorized Division		
(7–6 infantry battalions)	2 medium strong, 1 average, 3 weak, and 1 exhausted	1 medium strong, 1 average, 3 weak, and 1 exhausted
(1 pioneer battalion)	weak	weak
16th Panzer Division		
(4–3 infantry battalions)	1 medium strong, 1 average, and 2 weak	1 medium strong and 2 weak
(1 pioneer battalion)	weak	weak
94th Infantry Division		
(7 infantry battalions)	7 weak	2 weak and 5 exhausted
(1 pioneer battalion)	average (with 2 companies and 1 Russian *Hiwi* company attached)	average
LI ARMY CORPS		
24th Panzer Division		
(4 infantry battalions)	1 weak and 3 exhausted	1 medium strong and 3 average
(1 pioneer battalion)	exhausted	exhausted
100th Jäger Division		
(5 infantry battalions)	1 strong, 1 medium strong, 2 average, and 1 weak	2 medium strong and 3 weak
(1 pioneer battalion)	average	average
305th Infantry Division		
(9–6 infantry battalions)	5 weak and 4 exhausted	2 weak and 4 exhausted
(1 pioneer battalion)	exhausted	exhausted
295th Infantry Division		
(7 infantry battalions)	1 average, 4 weak, and 2 exhausted	1 average, 5 weak, and 1 exhausted
(1 pioneer battalion)	weak	weak
389th Infantry Division		
(5–6 infantry battalions)	1 average, 2 weak, and 2 exhausted	4 average and 2 weak
(1 pioneer battalion)	exhausted	weak
79th Infantry Division		
(6 infantry battalions)	3 average and 3 weak	1 average and 5 weak
(1 pioneer battalion)	average	average

Table 40. (continued)

	26 October	9 November
14th Panzer Division		
(4–2 infantry battalions)	4 weak	2 strong
(1 pioneer battalion)	average	average
71st Infantry Division		
(7 infantry battalions)	2 average and 5 weak	5 average and 2 weak
(1 pioneer battalion)	weak	weak
Totals:		
69–62 infantry battalions	1 strong, 8 medium strong, 11 average, 37 weak, and 12 exhausted	2 strong, 8 medium strong, 15 average, 26 weak, and 11 exhausted
12 pioneer battalions	4 average, 5 weak, and 3 exhausted	5 average, 5 weak, and 2 exhausted

Source: Florian *Freiherr* von und zu Aufsess, "Betr.: Zustand der Divisionen, Armee – Oberkommando 6, Abt. Ia, A. H. Qu., 26. Oktober 1942, 10.15 Uhr" and "Betr.: Zustand der Divisionen, Armee – Oberkommando 6, Abt. Ia, A. H. Qu., 09. November 1942, 16.20 Uhr," in *Die Anlagenbander zu den Kriegstagebuchern der 6. Armee vom 14.09.1942 bis 24.11.1942, Band I* (Schwabach: January 2006), 212–216 and 248–253.

Divisions fielded 28 and 23 tanks, respectively.[60] Therefore, contrary to Chuikov's estimate that Sixth Army fielded 200 tanks on 11 November, Paulus's forces in the Stalingrad region actually had 127 operational tanks and 28 assault guns and only 49 in support of LI Army Corps. In fairness to Chuikov, his estimate also included 22nd Panzer and 29th Motorized Divisions.

5–10 November

As Paulus and Seydlitz finalized attack plans and prepared forces for the final assault, both sides conducted reconnaissance and local attacks across the entire front from the Barrikady Factory to the Krasnyi Oktiabr' Factory. The 62nd Army's daily summary noted the continuous German probing attacks by forces from company- to battalion-size, particularly in the sectors of 95th and 45th Rifle and 39th Guards Rifle Divisions. The Red Army General Staff summarized the day's actions:

> The units of **62nd Army** continued to repel all enemy attacks and held on to their positions on 5 November.
> Enemy aviation conducted up to 500 sorties against the Krasnyi Oktiabr' Factory, Bannyi Ravine, Gornaia Poliana State Farm, Beketovka, Svetlyi Iar, and army crossings on 5 November.

95th RD fought with an attacking enemy force of up to a battalion of infantry and tanks attacking [14th PzD] its occupied positions. Enemy infantry and tanks blockaded two of our strong points on Lenin Prospect.

45th RD, repulsing an attack by up to a battalion of enemy infantry and tanks [79th ID] from the northwestern corner of the Krasnyi Oktiabr' Factory toward the Martenovskii Shop, held its previous positions.

39th Gds. RD fought with a battalion of enemy infantry and 10 tanks [79th ID] in the center of the Krasnyi Oktiabr' Factory.

The positions of the army's remaining units were unchanged.[61]

Commenting on the day's action, Chuikov said the fighting on 5 November inflicted 750 casualties on the Germans but also took the lives of two of his commanders, Colonel Bolvinov, commander of Group Gorokhov's 149th Rifle Brigade, and Major Ustinov, commander of 193rd Rifle Division's 895th Regiment, who was fatally wounded along with several members of his staff when a German bomb destroyed their command bunker.[62] In reaction, asserted Chuikov, he ordered his assault groups to intensify their activity, claiming that troops from Batiuk's 284th Rifle Division "captured dug-outs and pill-boxes, [wiping] out the garrisons within them."[63] For its part, the OKW downplayed the day's actions, noting that "German and enemy combat reconnaissance groups operated actively in Stalingrad on 5 November, and several enemy attacks were repelled."[64]

The relative lull persisted on 6 November, although 24th Panzer Division reported repelling vigorous Soviet probing attacks against its defenses in Hall 10 of the Krasnyi Oktiabr' Factory and lesser probes elsewhere along the front. Typical of these skirmishes, in 24th Panzer Division's sector, a "large storm group . . . of 30 men conducted their assault against Hall 10 from the gully and a small group of buildings to the east, but this foray was repulsed after 15 minutes of fighting."[65] 62nd Army's records, however, failed to note these attacks. Heavy rains that began in the afternoon put a damper on further actions, although the weather front accompanying the rain also brought a dose of sharply cold weather.

From the Red Army General Staff's perspective, in the only action worth reporting, "Subunits of 45th Rifle and 39th Guards Rifle Divisions repulsed small groups of enemy infantry trying to attack our positions in the Krasnyi Oktiabr' Factory by fire." Otherwise, "There were no changes in the positions of the army's units."[66] The OKW confirmed this by acknowledging, "Fighting of local importance went on in the Stalingrad region. Bombers, including dive-bombers, launched bombing strikes against battery positions and populated points east of the Volga."[67]

As the first taste of the approaching Russian winter arrived, Chuikov observed, "The temperature dropped sharply. The local inhabitants told us about conditions on the Volga; in November appears 'sludge,' small pieces of ice, which then turn into large pieces, floating down the river. In the period of floating ice, communications across the Volga are halted, as shipping cannot get through it."[68] This raised the commander's concerns about an impending assault, prompting him to conclude, "Paulus was probably waiting for precisely this moment to begin his new offensive." When his intelligence organs informed him that German 44th Infantry Division was en route to Stalingrad, Chuikov feared, "We were going to have to fight on two fronts—against the enemy and the Volga."[69] As erroneous as his intelligence was (44th Infantry Division was still defending along the Don River west of Kletskaia), he was correct that a German assault was indeed imminent.

The continuing lull on 7 November was punctuated by the usual raids on both sides, leading Chuikov to conclude that "the enemy conducted reconnaissance and brought fresh forces forward from the depths," both clear indicators that the Germans were making preparations for some sort of more general assault.[70] In the evening, the Red Army General Staff's operational summary provided a more thorough description of 62nd Army's defenses:

> **62nd Army** repelled several attacks by small enemy groups and held on to its previous positions on 7 November. According to confirmed data, the units of the army occupied [the following] positions:
>
> 124th RB and subunits of 149th RB—the bank of the Volga River 200 meters north of the water tower, the northern and western outskirts of Rynok, three separate buildings in the northern part of Spartanovka village, and the "trapezoid" block in the southern part of Spartanovka village;
>
> 138th RD and 118th RR—the bank of the Volga River in the center of Derevensk, the railroad crossing on Pribaltiiskaia Street, the southeastern part of Volkhovstroevsk, the northeastern part of the Barrikady Factory, and Pribaltiisk;
>
> 95th RD (less one RR)—(incl.) Pribaltiisk, the northwestern slope of the *balka* south of Mezenskaia, Tuvinsk, and the eastern part of Granitnaia Street;
>
> 45th RD—from Granitnaia Street to the northeastern outskirts of the Krasnyi Oktiabr' Factory and further along the grounds of the factory to the southwest;
>
> 39th Gds. RD—along the grounds of the factory [Krasnyi Oktiabr'] to the railroad siding, the southern part of Russkaia Derevnia and Stanislavski Streets, and further along the railroad bed to the Bannyi Ravine;
>
> 284th RD—the southern slope of the Bannyi Ravine, Chernomorskaia, the western outskirts of Stalingradskaia and Tekhnicheskaia Streets, Hill 102.0 [Mamaev Kurgan], and the northern bank of Dolgii Ravine;

13th Gds. RD—the center of the Dolgii Ravine, the eastern part of Nekrasovskaia Street, the center of Tambovskaia Street, the center of 9 January Square, the northern part of Respublikanskaia Street, and the bank of the Volga River 600 meters north of the landing-stage;

84th TB in second echelon—the eastern part of Novosel'skaia and Dolinskaia Streets;

193rd RD is protecting the [ferry] crossing in positions from the southern part of Bakinskii Komissarov [Baku Commissar] to the railroad tower;

The positions of 308th RD are being confirmed.[71]

Early the same day, Sixth Army began an artillery and mortar counterpreparation against Soviet artillery firing positions on the eastern bank of the Volga, a bombardment that lasted off and on for four days but intensified on 10 November. Other than this artillery and air bombardment and occasional outbursts of Soviet artillery in response, ground activity in Stalingrad's factory district remained relatively light from 8–10 November. Nevertheless, both sides continued reconnaissance probes, and as Paulus's attack date neared 62nd Army's forces intensified probing operations in the Krasnyi Oktiabr' Factory—a clear indication that Chuikov understood that a concerted German assault was imminent.

Keeping close track of the action, the Red Army General Staff on 8 November reported, "Defending its previous positions, part of the forces of **62nd Army** repulsed small groups of enemy trying to filter into the depths of our defenses in separate sectors. At 0715 hours enemy aircraft in a group of 35 Ju-87 planes bombed the Bobrov and Krasnaia Sloboda regions (on the left bank of the Volga River east of Stalingrad)."[72] In the wake of the day's fighting, Chuikov ordered his forces to "determine the grouping of enemy forces in front of the army's front by the actions of reconnaissance groups" and—reiterating his previous orders—"drive the enemy from the positions they occupy and broaden the defensive bridgehead of the right bank of the Volga by seizing them through the methodical destruction of strongpoints."[73]

On 9 November 62nd Army's daily report was extremely brief, noting only that 39th Guards Rifle Division was fighting with German forces for possession of the Sortovoi Shop in the Krasnyi Oktiabr' Factory. The General Staff simply reported, "Defending its previous positions, part of 62nd Army's forces repulsed small groups of enemy trying to filter into the depths of our defenses in separate sectors."[74] On the other side, the OKW made no mention of ground fighting whatsoever, although Seydlitz's divisions at the front noted increased probing activities by groups of 30 to 200 Soviet troops, especially in the vicinity of the Krasnyi Oktiabr' Factory.[75]

Underscoring his belief that a German assault was imminent, once again Chuikov ordered his forces to conduct larger-scale probing actions and counterattacks on 10 November to disrupt Paulus's offensive preparations to as great an extent as possible, principally in the vicinity of the Krasnyi Oktiabr' Factory, and to expand their bridgehead defenses wherever possible. The Red Army General Staff duly reported:

> **62nd Army** continued to hold on to its previous positions and repelled repeated attacks by enemy infantry and tanks in separate sectors.
> The positions of the Northern Group's units (124th and 149th RBs) remained unchanged.
> 138th RD exchanged fire with the enemy in its previous positions.
> 95th RD repelled four attacks by up to a battalion of enemy infantry and 2 tanks in the region south of the Barrikady Factory. Four submachine guns and 9000 rounds were seized in the fighting.
> 45th RD occupied its previous positions.
> 39th Gds. RD, remaining in its previous positions, fought with small enemy groups in the vicinity of the Krasnyi Oktiabr' Factory with part of its forces.
> 284th RD repulsed an attack by up to a company of enemy infantry from the Bannyi Ravine region at 1200 hours with part of its forces.
> 92nd RB crossed to the right bank of the Volga River in 284th RD's sector with two battalions.
> The positions of the army's remaining units were unchanged.[76]

According to 62nd Army's daily report, the two battalions of 92nd Rifle Brigade, together with 284th Rifle Division's 1043rd Regiment, assembled in the vicinity of the railroad loop (the Tennis Racket), in the rifle division's second echelon. Presumably, this move was associated with Chuikov's fears about a major German attack on the Chemical Factory, which prompted him to order 92nd Rifle Brigade as follows: "Upon completion of your concentration, after conducting a partial regrouping, go over to active operations to broaden the bridgehead in the Krasnyi Oktiabr' Factory and Krutoi Ravine regions [including Mamaev Kurgan]."[77]

The OKW, however, noted the increased level of Soviet troop activity, reporting on 9 November that "operations by combat reconnaissance groups are continuing actively in Stalingrad"; on 10 November, Army Group B's operations section reported cryptically that "attacks were repulsed on the metallurgical factory from the east and south. The enemy suffered heavy losses."[78] Nevertheless, the army group's intelligence officer continued putting an optimistic face on the ongoing stalemate:

> In spite of stubborn resistance to the attacks by our units in the city of Stalingrad, the enemy was forced to withdraw in the vicinity of the fuel

dump and northeast of the gun factory. Large-scale combat actions did not take place in the remaining sectors of the front . . .

The 6th Army. Supported by individual tanks, the enemy attacked once again in the eastern part of the metallurgical factory. The attacks had no success. Despite a stubborn defense against our attacking units, the enemy abandoned the fuel dump, as well as the sector northeast of the gun factory. In Pechetka, he lost 2 machine gun firing points and several pillboxes and field positions.[79]

From 24th Panzer Division's perspective, however, although not reported in Soviet records, 39th Guards Rifle Division's probes within the Krasnyi Oktiabr' Factory on 10 November appeared far from routine:

At 0730 hours, a violent barrage dropped on Hall 10 and its surroundings, placing a curtain of fire between 26th Panzer Grenadier Regiment's sector and the rest of the factory. Five minutes later, out of the fuel installation area [southeast of the factory] and along the railroad line [south of the factory], several enemy assault groups rushed toward the southern end of Hall 10. There were at least several hundred Russians. The barrage lifted as soon as the assault groups left their starting areas. The grenadiers hardly had time to raise their weapons over the parapets or poke them through loopholes before the tide of Russians washed over the defensive line. A couple of bursts from machine-guns toppled a few Russians, but the fighting quickly degenerated into vicious hand-to-hand combat. Groups of grenadiers, cut off by the advancing enemy, held out until their ammunition was depleted, some fighting to the death with their bayonets and spades, while others hid amongst the rubble, waiting for the immediate danger to pass before they found their way back to their comrades. The attack was directed on Hall 10 and also simultaneously toward the south-east front from out of the oil tanks along the railroad line.

Forced back by the pressure of the attackers, the grenadiers around the southern end of Hall 10 scampered back to reserve positions between Halls 9 and 10, fighting all the way, and the Russians penetrated into the southern three-story end of Hall 10, occupying the vital stairwells within. After an hour of grueling combat, around 0845 hours, the enemy attack was finally halted. The defensive line southwest of Hall 10, in the open ground between Halls 10 and 8a, was held by a few determined squads from 2nd Battalion, 26th Panzer Grenadier Regiment, and 4th Motorcycle Battalion, successfully repelling all attacks. In the northern part of Hall 10, the remainder of 2nd Battalion, 26th Panzer Grenadier Regiment, continued to repel enemy assaults from the east, but they had been forced to bend their southern defensive line to the west, out of the western facade of the work hall, to join up with the reserve positions that now formed the front-line. They now defended against enemy storm groups entering the shambles of the factory floor through the two doors coming from the three-story southern wing. All of these assaults were fought off. At 0945 hours, the enemy renewed his attack just as 2nd Battalion, 26th Panzer Grenadier Regiment, was preparing a counterattack to retake the southern end of Hall 10. The counterattack groups were forced to repel the enemy attack, which they successfully did, but at the expense of the planned counterattack. . . .

While the attack on the previous day was only reconnaissance without substantial enemy artillery support, the enemy artillery support on this day was strong.[80]

This concerted attack, probably conducted by riflemen from 112th Regiment of Gur'ev's 39th Guards Rifle Division, proved too strong for *Kampfgruppe* Scheele to dislodge from Hall 10. Throughout the day, for example, "six times . . . the enemy threw in attacks with 200 and 300 men, the last one at 1800 hours. The Germans were incapable of launching the counterattack."[81] Because of this Soviet attack, Group Schwerin (79th Infantry and 24th Panzer Divisions) now faced the daunting twin tasks of conducting two separate assaults on 11 November, the first by 79th Infantry Division against the Krasnyi Oktiabr' Factory's Hall 10 (which Seydlitz had just rescheduled for 11 November), and the second a simultaneous assault by *Kampfgruppe* Scheele to recapture Hall 10. From Seydlitz's perspective, Gur'ev's counterattack on 10 November also prevented *Kampfgruppe* Scheele from regrouping northward to support 305th Infantry Division's assault in the vicinity of the Barrikady Factory.

Nonetheless, the forces designated to conduct the assaults in LI Corps' final act on 11 November completed their offensive preparations by the evening of 10 November (see Map 86). On the left wing of Seydlitz's shock group, Steinmetz's 305th Infantry Division, flanked on the left by the bulk of Magnus's 389th Infantry Division, deployed their forces from left to right (north to south) in the roughly 2.5-kilometer-wide sector extending from the southwestern corner of the Brick Factory (100 meters from the Volga) southward along the eastern edge of the Barrikady Factory (300–400 meters from the Volga) to the lower part of the ravine south of the factory (300 meters from the Volga). On the shock group's left wing, *kampfgruppen* formed by cannibalizing all three of 389th Infantry Division's six infantry battalions, supported by the division's own 389th Engineer Battalion and 162nd Engineer Battalion (from 62nd Infantry Division), deployed in the sector from the Brick Factory southward to the northeastern edge of the Barrikady Factory

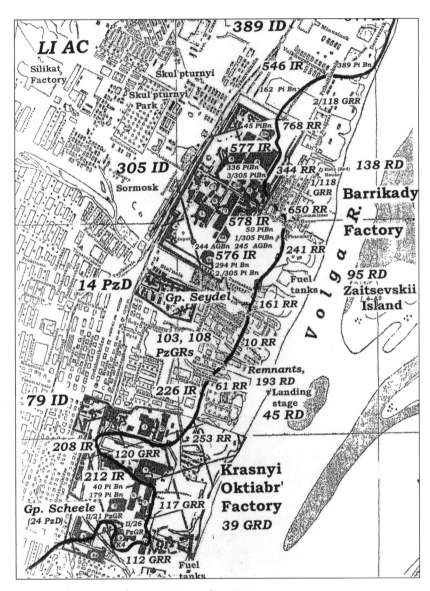

Map 86. The situation late on 10 November 1942

opposite the defenses of 138th Rifle Division's 768th Regiment and attached 118th Guards Regiment.[82]

On 389th Infantry Division's right, 305th Infantry Division deployed its 577th, 578th, and 576th Regiments abreast from left to right along the eastern edge of the Barrikady Factory. 336th Engineer Battalion (detached from 336th Infantry Division) supported 577th Regiment, the 305th's 305th Engineer Battalion and Sixth Army's 50th Engineer Battalion (Motorized) backed up 578th Regiment, and 294th Engineer Battalion (from 294th Infantry Division) did likewise for 576th Regiment. 14th Panzer Division was to reinforce the division's assault with two panzer companies with a total of seven tanks. Each of the engineer battalions fielded about 450 men, except for 305th and 389th Battalions, which had roughly 150 and 220 men, respectively. Steinmetz's forces faced 138th Rifle Division's 344th and 650th Regiments and 95th Rifle Division's 241st Regiment, augmented by the few survivors from 308th Rifle Division. Although comparative strength figures at this stage were indeed problematic, it is likely that 305th and 389th Infantry Divisions were able to muster roughly 3,000 infantrymen for the assault, reinforced by about 2,200 engineers, for a combined strength of about 5,200 men, facing a Soviet force much less than half its size.[83]

Meanwhile, on the right wing of Seydlitz's main shock group, despite the disruptions caused by Chuikov's counterattack on 10 November, during the ensuing evening Group Schwerin (reinforced 79th Infantry Division) and its subordinate *Kampfgruppe* Scheele formed up their forces for the assaults on Halls 4 and 10 in the Krasnyi Oktiabr' Factory. Schwerin deployed his shock group with 208th Regiment on the left, opposite the northern half of Hall 10, and *Kampfgruppe* Scheele on the right, facing the southern half of Hall 10. 226th Regiment protected the shock group's left flank east of Halls 1 and 2 with 2nd Battalion of 24th Panzer Division's 21st Grenadier Regiment, and 4th Motorcycle Battalion defended the shock group's right flank north of Hall 8a.

Schwerin planned to spearhead his attack on Hall 4 with an assault group of 120 men formed from his division's 179th Engineer Battalion, supported by 3rd Company of 24th Panzer Division's 40th Panzer Pioneer Battalion. This assault group was to attack in four combat wedges, each divided into two waves, supported thereafter by 208th Regiment's *kampfgruppe* with about 1,000 men and the remnants of the Croat 369th Regiment with 191 men.[84] According to German reports, this force faced an estimated 400 Soviet troops defending Hall 10, including 135 men from 39th Guards Rifle Division's 120th Regiment, 205 men from 45th Rifle Division's 253rd Regiment, and several antitank companies manned by about 60 men.[85] However, additional Soviet troops, estimated to number in the hundreds, from the two regiments defending Hall 4 manned numerous squad, platoon, and company positions in the eastern part of the factory, complicating Group Schwerin's assault.

On Schwerin's right, 24th Panzer Division's *Kampfgruppe* Scheele faced the difficult task of driving Soviet forces from the factory's Hall 10 and then pushing them into the Volga. Scheele planned to do so with assault parties in squad strength from 2nd Battalion, 26th Grenadier Regiment, reinforced by additional troops obtained from other divisional units and supported by fires from the division's 89th Panzer Artillery Regiment and the panzer division's remaining seven tanks. This pitted a German force of about 400 men against the estimated 100–150 Soviet troops in Hall 10.[86]

Although Heim's 14th Panzer Division played only a small role in this attack, it provided some armor support to Steinmetz's infantry. Organized into the single *Kampfgruppe* Seydel, the forces assigned to its own two grenadier regiments and combat support battalions were responsible for containing Soviet forces in the sector between the Barrikady and Krasnyi Oktiabr' Factories and supporting both wings of Seydlitz's shock group with their fire. Most important, Group Seydel had the task of protecting Steinmetz's right flank south of the Barrikady Factory.

SOVIET PLANS AND AXIS PERCEPTIONS

As Paulus and Seydlitz redeployed their forces for what they hoped, once again, would be the climactic final phase of the fighting in Stalingrad, the pathetically weak strengths of their shock groups indicated how both understood that they were indeed playing their last cards in what would turn out to be the final struggle for possession of the southern half of Stalingrad's factory district. Sharing this understanding, Chuikov stoically prepared his defense. From the vantage point in Moscow, Stalin and the *Stavka* were also doing everything in their power to ensure that 62nd Army's defense was successful and, at the same time, to improve the Red Army's posture and capabilities for conducting fresh and decisive offensive operations of its own. They did so, however, with an equally clear appreciation that on occasions in the past— too numerous to count and too unpleasant to recall—their strenuous efforts to orchestrate decisive offensive operations had always come to naught.

Nevertheless, beginning in late October and accelerating throughout the first two weeks of November, Stalin and the *Stavka* worked unceasingly to realize their offensive dreams. They issued directive after directive aimed at assembling new offensive hosts, this time, however, well distant from the bloody battlefields in the Kotluban' and Erzovka regions. As this process unfolded, on 1 November the *Stavka* ordered the NKO to release three newly formed mechanized brigades and their associated tank regiments to

Stalingrad Front's control. These were 17th, 61st, and 62nd Mechanized Brigades, with their component 44th, 176th, and 163rd Tank Regiments, which were to entrain in the Tambov region, 500 kilometers north of Stalingrad, unload and concentrate in the Kapustin Iar region, 60 kilometers southeast of Stalingrad, and reach the vicinity of Stalingrad proper by mid-November.[87]

Hours before, the *Stavka* strengthened its forces along the Don River front northwest of Stalingrad by redesignating Southwestern Front's 63rd Army as 1st Guards Army, incorporating 63rd Army's 1st, 153rd, and 197th Rifle Divisions into the new guards army, and appointing Lieutenant General D. D. Leliushenko, former commander of Western Front's 30th Army, as the army's new commander.[88] Then, on 5 November, the Red Army General Staff directed Leliushenko to combine his 1st, 153rd, and 197th Rifle Divisions into the new 14th Rifle Corps, effective on 10 November, to improve command and control within his army.[89] In addition, to coordinate operations by the air forces operating along the northern half of the Stalingrad axis more effectively, Stalin on 4 November appointed Lieutenant General G. A. Vorozheikin, 1st Deputy Commander of the Red Army Air Force, to coordinate all air operations in the Voronezh and Southwestern Fronts.[90]

Continuing its efforts to reinforce the Don River front, the General Staff on 9 November assigned three fresh rifle divisions and two rifle brigades to Voronezh Front with instructions it combine the three divisions into a new rifle corps under 6th Army's control to strengthen the *front*'s left wing while retaining the two rifle brigades to constitute 6th Army's reserve.[91] Later still, three days after Paulus and Seydlitz unleashed their final assault in the factory district, on 14 November the General Staff dispatched two additional rifle divisions, the 315th and 87th, to reinforce Eremenko's Stalingrad Front. It instructed him to employ them on the eastern bank of the Volga River to ensure the viability of the *front*'s defenses in the Stalingrad region.[92]

All of these measures, however, were pale reflections of the intensive strategic planning actually under way in Moscow and the equally extensive operational and tactical planning going on in the headquarters of the *Stavka*'s Voronezh, Don, and Stalingrad Fronts and their subordinate armies. Some German intelligence organs at every level of command indeed detected some of these ongoing changes in the Red Army's dispositions and began issuing warnings about possible Soviet offensive activity. However, because they were preoccupied with the struggle in and around Stalingrad, the Germans failed to detect many if not most of these indicators. German aerial reconnaissance and signals-intercept units had some success, but strenuous Soviet camouflage efforts and the paucity of reliable human intelligence made it difficult for German intelligence officers to see into the depths of the Red Army's rear. In addition, German commanders tended to dismiss any such intelligence information and accompanying warnings either because they did not believe them to be valid or, because of overconfidence born of previous experience, they believed that existing German forces could defeat any future Soviet offensive operations.

Beginning as early as 25 October and throughout the first week of November, for example, the OKH's intelligence organ, Foreign Armies East [*Fremde Heere Ost*—FHO], headed by General Reinhard Gehlen, received disturbing intelligence reports from a variety of collection means, including aerial reconnaissance, radio intercepts, and *Abwehr* agents operating in the Red Army's rear. These indicated a "weak but steady flow of reinforcements" moving forward to reinforce Soviet forces facing Romanian Third Army along the Don. Although Gehlen later claimed that "it was not until the latter part of this phase that Soviet intentions became clear to us," on 29 October he informed General Zeitzler, the army's chief of staff, that "there is nowhere any sign of preparation for a major attack, but the entire area needs continued observation."[93]

FHO soon received additional reports, primarily from reconnaissance aircraft, concerning Soviet reinforcements arriving in the Serafimovich region, heavy transport and loading activity along the railroad to Serafimovich, and extensive traffic across the Don River at Kletskaia. Repeating his previous assessment, Gehlen on 31 October warned the OKH that there "might be localized attacks on the Rumanians' position at Serafimovich."[94] During the next few days, FHO received more reports about Soviet reinforcements arriving in the sector west of Serafimovich, as well as other reports about Soviet troops being transferred to the same region from Don Front's 65th and 21st Armies. The sheer volume of these messages and their improved credibility prompted Gehlen to advise his masters at OKH on 2 November, "We must expect there to be continued reinforcement of the enemy confronting the Rumanian Third Army and, possibly, even an attack"; however, as before, he qualified this judgment, adding, "We must await further indications."[95]

The next day, after air reconnaissance reported tanks and field artillery being transferred from the front north of Stalingrad to the Serafimovich region, Gehlen informed the OKH, "There emerges an increasingly clear picture of preparations for an attack on the Rumanian Third Army, though they are in their early stages."[96] Once again, he added a qualifier: "We cannot yet be certain whether the object is an attack designed to lure our forces away from Stalingrad or an operation with a much broader objective" (although Gehlen asserted he favored the former possibility).[97] After detecting reinforcements flowing to the Stalingrad region as well, Gehlen on 4 November decided that "the enemy had by no means given up the fight for the city" and was also reinforcing its forces in the Beketovka bridgehead south of the city. At the same time, however, he informed the OKH that the Soviets were still redeploying forces from the area of the land bridge between the

Don and the Volga to the Serafimovich region and were moving many vehicles—presumably from new rifle and tank divisions—into the region north of Kletskaia.[98]

Based on these intelligence reports and other radio intercepts indicating that a new headquarters—that of Southwestern Front—had taken over control of Soviet forces in the Serafimovich region north of the Don, Gehlen decided that a Soviet offensive was indeed likely. Therefore, on 10 November he flatly warned Zeitzler, "The appearance of the Soviet headquarters for the Southwestern Front somewhere to the northwest of Serafimovich indicates that a major enemy attack is in sight."[99]

Although most German commanders did not question the accuracy of these intelligence reports and accompanying warnings, there were cogent reasons why they tended to discount their importance. First, Soviet forces deployed between the Don and Volga Rivers had conducted major offensive operations against Sixth Army's left wing repeatedly since late August, always with at least two armies and sometimes with as many as four, frequently supported by as many as three tank corps and several hundred tanks. Yet as indicated by the last of these offensives, which had ended in utter failure only days before, on every occasion the German defenders repelled such assaults with relative ease. Furthermore, in September the Soviets had conducted new assaults in the Serafimovich region, and although they still clung to the bridgeheads they had seized on the southern bank of the Don, defending Axis forces had successfully contained these bridgeheads. Finally, Soviet forces had also launched major attacks from the Beketovka bridgehead south of Stalingrad, the last one as recently as late October, but these assaults also quickly collapsed without achieving any significant success. Therefore, experience indicated that one or two German divisions were indeed capable of holding multiple Soviet armies at bay. To those who argued that Romanian and Italian forces might not fare as well against a concerted Soviet offensive, German commanders pointed out that German infantry divisions were supporting these satellite Axis forces, specifically 298th Infantry Division in the Italians' sector east of Novaia Kalitva, 376th Infantry Division east of Kletskaia, and, soon, XXXXVIII Panzer Corps' headquarters with 22nd Panzer Division behind the Romanians' defenses at Serafimovich.

Second, for months Gehlen's FHO had been unable to predict exactly where the Soviets would make their main strategic effort along the Germans' Eastern Front. Acknowledging the virtual certainty of a Soviet winter counteroffensive, the FHO vacillated between Moscow and Stalingrad as the likely regions for the main Soviet effort. On 29 August, for example, Gehlen argued that the Soviets would most probably use their offensive potential "against Army Group Center [in the Rzhev-Viaz'ma salient] to eliminate the threat to Moscow and to gain a success where the configuration of the front would not overtax the tactical capabilities of the lower commanders."[100] By 15 September, however, Gehlen admitted that given the realities in the Stalingrad region, the initial Soviet action would take place in this region because he estimated that the Soviets had the resources to conduct only one major offensive that fall.[101] Based on subsequent heavy Soviet rail movement along the flanks of the Rzhev salient west of Moscow, Gehlen on 17 September reversed himself by again predicting a possible offensive against Army Group Center's Ninth Army in the salient.

Intensified Soviet troop movements in the Rzhev region during early October prompted Gehlen to conclude, first, in early October that "the Russian forces assembling around Ninth Army are combat forces" and, in mid-October, that an attack was probable against both the center and the left wing of Army Group Center in the salient.[102] On 15 October, however, based on its detection through agent reports of a new Southwestern Front "in the Saratov region," the FHO concluded that the Soviets would "eventually" attempt an offensive in Army Group B's sector, but only at the expense of their main effort against Army Group Center.[103] Thereafter, intelligence reports about Soviet troop movements north of the Don River in late October prompted the FHO to forecast only local attacks in the Serafimovich region.

As late as 6 November—even after Gehlen had begun issuing warnings of possible Soviet preparations for an offensive against Romanian Third Army along the Don—the FHO issued another assessment that, while not undermining the credibility of these reports, certainly diminished their impact:

1. The point of main effort of the future Russian operations against the German Eastern Front looms with increasing distinctness in the sector of Army Group Center. However, it is still not clear whether, along with this, the Russians intend to conduct a major operation along the Don or they will limit their aims in the south due to the considerations that they cannot achieve success simultaneously along two axes because of insufficient forces. In any event, we can conclude that the offensive they are preparing in the south is not so far advanced that one must reckon with a major operation here in the near future simultaneously with the expected offensive against Army Group Center. Presently there is no information indicating that the Russians have given up the attack across the Don entirely, an idea which undoubtedly affected their previous intentions. The likely demarcation of this operation according to time will accord them the advantage of, for the time being, holding the forces designated for this attack back as a reserve to throw in against Army Group Center if the situation developing there warrants their use.

Here we are not considering the operational capabilities of the Russians on the southern wing.

Among the reasons which impel the enemy to undertake a decisive operation against Army Group Center before long, the most important can be the following:

a) The necessity of a quick and major success for military and political reasons. The enemy presumes he can finish off an operation against Army Group Center easier than against Army Group B. A successful operation in the sector of Army Group Center would lead to a lessening of the danger of a German offensive toward Moscow. The enemy fears that it will begin next year.

b) The configuration of Army Group Center's front, with the presence of concentration areas suitable from the point of view of transport and advantageous jumping-off regions (the Sukhinichi-Toropets salient) for an operation against Smolensk, is very favorable for the development of a major operation. The Smolensk region ought to be viewed as the first objective of a decisive operation against Army Group Center. In distance, this objective fully corresponds to the resources and capabilities of the Russian command.

c) In the event of success, after destroying the forces in the center of the German front, the possibility will exist to exploit the success by continuing the operation to the west, into the Baltic countries, to cut off German forces on the northern wing.

d) In contradistinction with this are the greater difficulties in controlling the forces and supplying them in an operation against Rostov. In the event such an operation succeeds, although it could lead to the destruction of the southern wing of the German front, it would open fewer opportunities for the further exploitation of success. Notwithstanding, we must expect an operation along the Don together with the main operation against Army Group Center.[104]

Considered alongside Gehlen's previous reports, there were good reasons, therefore, why many German senior commanders in southern Russia remained confused about the Soviets' offensive intentions. Nevertheless, Hitler had been worried since mid-August about what he termed a "standard attack" by the Soviets toward Rostov, that is, one modeled after the Bolshevik's famous raid against General Wrangel's White Army during 1920; he therefore took prudent measures to ensure against such a Soviet attack and insisted that his commanders do so as well.[105] For example, on 26 October he ordered the *Luftwaffe* to move some of its newly formed field divisions, which had limited equipment and training for ground operations, forward to back up his Allied forces along the Don.

After receiving Gehlen's reports about the buildup of Soviet forces near Serafimovich, Hitler on 2 November canceled the movement of the

Luftwaffe divisions eastward, probably because he mistrusted their capabilities. Instead, two days later he ordered that 6th Panzer Division and two infantry divisions be transferred from the French coast to Army Group B to provide a reserve behind the Italian Eighth and Romanian Third Armies. The fact that this move would take four to five weeks to complete, which indicated Hitler "did not expect the offensive to begin before December," underscores the indecision within the German High Command regarding where and when the Soviet blow would fall.[106] Regardless of this continuing uncertainty, during the ensuing weeks Weichs and Paulus undertook measures that they considered prudent to ensure the worst did not occur.

Despite the Germans' nonchalance, by mid-November indicators mounted that the Soviets did indeed intend to embark on some sort of offensive action. However, most of these indicators pertained to sectors where offensives had previously occurred and been repulsed with ease. For example, on 17 November Gehlen's FHO reported that in Army Group B's sector "the positions of the enemy's units are basically unchanged." In addition to identifying the presence of 422nd Rifle Division in 64th Army, which it had already identified on the basis of previous daily combat reports on the fighting in the Beketovka region days before, on the basis of agent reports FHO also identified that 13th Tank Corps' headquarters was subordinate to Stalingrad Front's 57th Army. Yet the corps' 13th, 56th, and 90th Tank Brigades were still in 64th Army's bridgehead at Beketovka. The report also identified 91st and 8th Tank Brigades, the former transferred from 66th to 65th Army and the latter from 65th to 21st Army. Finally, it reported "entrenching work" and "no enemy activity" in the sectors of the satellite Axis armies along the Don.[107]

The threat was much clearer to the satellite commanders along the front. Because of a shortage of troops, the Romanians, unlike the Italian Eighth Army, were not even defending on the Don River itself except at their extreme flanks. Instead, their defensive line dipped as much as 30 kilometers south of the river, granting Southwestern Front large bridgeheads to mass for its forthcoming attack. General Petre Dumitrescu, commander of Romanian Third Army, was no fool: From the moment Dumitrescu received his assignment to defend this sector, he had repeatedly insisted that the river line itself was the only effective defense for a force that was so deficient in antitank weapons. General Weichs's staff at Army Group B agreed with him in principle, but the Stalingrad struggle monopolized the additional troops and fire support that Dumitrescu needed to eliminate the Soviet bridgeheads. On 16 October, Dumitrescu again raised the subject, asking permission to make a minor attack near Blinov. Instead, Army Group B instructed Dumitrescu to extend his frontage to the west, taking over part of the Italian sector so that one Italian division could move into reserve positions.[108] In early November,

Dumitrescu's front-line troops reported signs that Soviet units were moving into the bridgeheads on the western banks of the river.

THE FINAL ACT: SIXTH ARMY'S ASSAULT ON THE BARRIKADY FACTORY SECTOR, 11–15 NOVEMBER

11 November

With the winter cold firmly in place, Paulus and Seydlitz unleashed their long-awaited final offensive against Chuikov's forces in the vicinity of the Barrikady and Krasnyi Oktiabr' Factories at dawn on 11 November (see Map 87). Preceding the general assault, Sixth Army during the early morning hours conducted an extensive series of probes and raids across the entire front from Rynok southward to Stalingrad's central city. These were intended to deceive 62nd Army regarding the real *Schwerpunkt* [center of gravity], strength, and objectives of Paulus's main attack.[109]

Once these preliminaries were over, beginning at 0340 hours Sixth Army softened up 62nd Army's defenses with an artillery and *Werfer* preparation. Then, beginning 15 minutes later and intensifying over the ensuing 30 minutes, the assault groups of 305th and 389th Infantry Divisions advanced, spearheaded by their attached engineer battalions and supported by assault guns from 244th and 245th Assault Gun Battalions. These threadbare elements began Seydlitz's main attack against the defenses of 138th and 95th Rifle Divisions east of the Barrikady Factory. Because it was standard Soviet practice to conduct reconnaissances-in-force and multiple feints prior to a major attack to confuse the enemy, Chuikov's forces undoubtedly recognized the intent of these actions. Thus, 62nd Army later reported:

> The army engaged in heavy fighting with superior attacking enemy forces during the day [on 11 November].
> The enemy, after a strong artillery preparation, went over to an offensive along the Volkhovstroevsk and Bannyi Ravine front at 0630 hours [Moscow time] with the units of five infantry divisions (389th, 305th, 79th, 100th, and 295th) and 24th and 14th Tank Divisions, reinforced by separate units of 294th Infantry Division, transferred on aircraft from Rossosh' on 10 November 1942, and units of 161st Infantry Division flown in on aircraft from the Millerovo region on 10 November 1942, delivering their main attack toward Mezenskaia with the aim of splitting the army's front apart and reaching the Volga River.
> The bitter attacks with increasing strength are continuing in the sector of 138th RD. The enemy committed his reserves into combat and is suffering heavy losses. As a result, the enemy managed to reach the bank

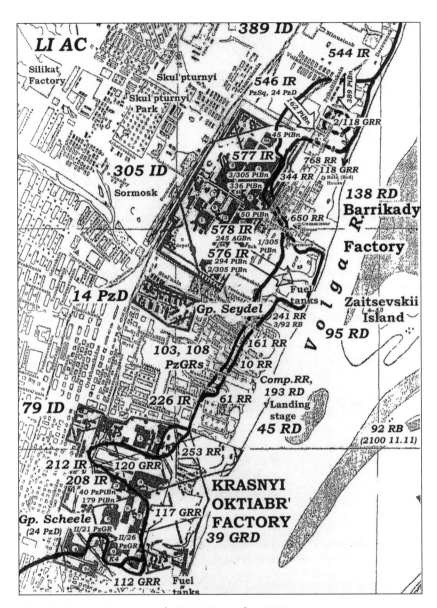

Map 87. LI Army Corps' assault, 11–12 November 1942

of the Volga River in the sector of 241st RR, 95th RD, along a 200 meter front (east of Mezenskaia and Tuvinsk).

The enemy pressed 117th Gds. RR partially back in the sector of 39th Gds. RD.

The air force of the enemy bombed our combat formations and artillery OPs [observation posts] with groups of 4–5 aircraft.[110]

From the perspective of Liudnikov's 138th Rifle Division:

After a strong 30-minute artillery preparation, the enemy went over to the attack along the entire front of the division with a force of up to three infantry regiments and two sapper battalions at 0600 hours [Moscow time]. The 544th Infantry Regiment, 546th Infantry Regiment, and 45th Separate Sapper Battalion of the High Command's reserve attacked the divisions' right wing and center (118th Gds. RR and 768th RR) from the north and northwest. The 577th Infantry Regiment and 336th Sapper Battalion attacked the division's left wing (344th and 650th RRs). . . . The offensive was supported by aircraft, artillery, and tanks.[111]

Summarizing the entire day's actions, including the Germans' preliminary probes and raids, the Red Army General Staff reported:

62nd Army engaged in sustained fighting in all sectors of the front beginning at 0630 hours on 11 November.

The Northern Group of Forces began an attack toward the Tractor Factory at 1000 hours on 11 November and, overcoming stubborn enemy resistance, advanced 400 meters from their jumping-off positions.

138th RD repelled several attacks by more than a regiment of enemy infantry with tanks [305th ID's 578th IR] and held on to their previous positions.

95th RD conducted heavy defensive fighting in the vicinity of Mezenskaia [with 305th ID's 576th IR].

45th RD repelled attacks by the enemy [79th ID] in the region northeast of the Krasnyi Oktiabr' Factory and held on to its previous positions.

39th Gds. RD's subunits in the region of the Krasnyi Oktiabr' Factory abandoned some of the positions they occupied under heavy enemy pressure [24th PzD]. The situation in this sector of the front was being restored by day's end.

284th RD repelled two attacks by enemy forces of up to two battalions each.

13th Gds. RD repelled attacks by groups of submachine gunners and exchanged fire from their previous positions.[112]

The five infantry regiments of 305th and 389th Infantry Divisions, led by their attached engineers and supported by 16 assault guns, began their attack from the Barrikady Factory and the region to the north across "one giant field of rubble, which gently sloped down to the Volga—with a steep embankment straight at the river's edge" (see Table 41).[113]

Advancing in this configuration, Steinmetz's 305th Infantry launched its main attack with 576th and 578th Regiments on his division's right wing and center.[114] The division's main attack, which was designed to capture the fuel depot and reach the Volga, and 389th Infantry Division's supporting attacks north of the Barrikady Factory sought to encircle and destroy all Soviet forces east of the Barrikady Factory in a pincer maneuver.

Commencing Steinmetz's main attack, the assault group on 578th Infantry Regiment's right wing, led by 50th Engineer Battalion and supported by 10 assault guns from 245th Assault Gun Battalion, plowed eastward toward its two key objectives (designated by German nicknames): the "Pharmacy" two blocks due east of the center of the Barrikady Factory and 400 meters from the Volga, and the "Commissar's House," several buildings to the north and the same distance from the Volga (see Map 88). Liudnikov, commander of 138th Rifle Division, had his headquarters in the ruins of the Commissar's House. Simultaneously, on 578th Regiment's right 576th Regiment and 294th Engineer Battalion struck eastward astride Mezenskaia Street and between the ravine and the factory in an attempt to reach and capture the mouth of the ravine and the oil depot just to the north. Two other assault groups from 578th Regiment, the first supported by 1st Company, 305th Engineer Battalion, and the second simply a reinforced infantry battalion, delayed the attack on their objectives, the ravine 400 meters north of the Pharmacy and House No. 78, a building about 400 meters from the factory's northeastern corner, respectively, until the neighbors on their right secured their initial objectives. On the left wing of Steinmetz's division, 577th Regiment and 336th Engineer Battalion, supported on the left by smaller assault parties from 389th Infantry Division, attacked Soviet defenses from the Brick Factory southward toward House No. 78 (these houses were numbered differently by the Germans and Russians).[115]

Catching the Soviets by surprise, the assault group on 578th Regiment's right wing (1st Company, 305th Engineer Battalion) succeeded in smashing through Soviet defenses near the boundary between 95th Rifle Division's 241st Regiment and 138th Rifle Division's 650th Regiment and quickly captured the ruins around the Pharmacy. However, on the right, when the 50th Engineers pushed on another 100 meters to reach the ruins of the Commissar's House, it found all of the entrances into the building blocked by heaps of rubble. Unable to gain access so that it could throw its satchel charges

Table 41. The 305th and 389th Infantry Divisions' Task Organization, Missions, and Objectives on 11 November 1942 (from left to right)

- **389th Infantry Division:**
  - o **544th Infantry Regiment**, spearheaded by 389th Engineer Battalion, attacked eastward from south of the Brick Factory toward the Volga River against 138th Rifle Division's 118th Guards Regiment.
  - o **546th Infantry Regiment**, preceded by 45th and 162nd Engineer Battalions and supported by 24th Assault Squadron (24th PzD) and 244th Assault Gun Battalion, attacked eastward from the Hall 6a (northeastern corner) area of the Barrikady Factory toward the northern end of Pribaltiiskaia Street and Prospect Lenin against 138th Rifle Division's 768th Rifle Regiment.
- **305th Infantry Division:**
  - o **577th Infantry Regiment**, spearheaded by 336th Engineer Battalion, 3rd Company, 305th Engineer Battalion, and 44th Assault Company, attacked from the Hall 4 portion of the Barrikady Factory to seize the buildings along Pribaltiiskaia Street and Prospect Lenin, against the adjoining wings of 138th Rifle Division's 650th and 344th Rifle Regiments (the former with 167 "bayonets" and the latter, 207).
  - o **578th Infantry Regiment**, led by 50th Engineer Battalion and 1st Company, 305th Engineer Battalion and supported by 245th Assault Gun Battalion, struck eastward astride Arbatovskaia Street from the Hall 3 portion of the Barrikady Factory toward its primary objectives, two formidable buildings one–two city blocks away. The first of these buildings, the so-called "Pharmacy," situated on the southern side of Arbatovskaia at the junction with Apothekskaia Street, was defended by the left wing of 95th Rifle Division's 241st Regiment. The second objective, the so-called "Commissar's House," the second building north of Arbatovskaia Street, was a massive U-shaped fortified building whose open end faced Taimyrskaia Street, which was defended by 650th Rifle Regiment on 138th Rifle Division's left wing.
  - o **576th Infantry Regiment**, spearheaded by 294th Engineer Battalion and 2nd Company, 305th Engineer Battalion, attacked eastward from the Hall 6d and 6e (southeastern corner) of the Barrikady Factory astride Mezenskaia Street toward the fuel depot, against 95th Rifle Division's 241st Rifle Regiment (420 men).

into the building's shell, the engineers and supporting infantry withdrew into nearby shell craters, where they were pinned down by heavy enemy fire.

As 578th Regiment pushed toward the Pharmacy and Commissar's House, on its right 576th Regiment and 294th Engineer Battalion made "slow but continuous progress" against 95th Rifle Division's 241st Regiment but ultimately captured the fuel depot and reached the Volga's western bank from the southern end of the depot northward to the mouth of the ravine east of the Pharmacy. Attacking at 0900 hours on 578th Regiment's left wing, two more assault groups quickly penetrated down the ravine east of the Pharmacy, reached the Volga, and then wheeled north to seize the ruins of House No. 79 on the northern side of the ravine from 138th Rifle Division's 650th Regiment. However, heavy flanking fire from the vicinity of the Commissar's House, a position that "controlled the open terrain to the division's front," prevented 578th Regiment from advancing any farther.

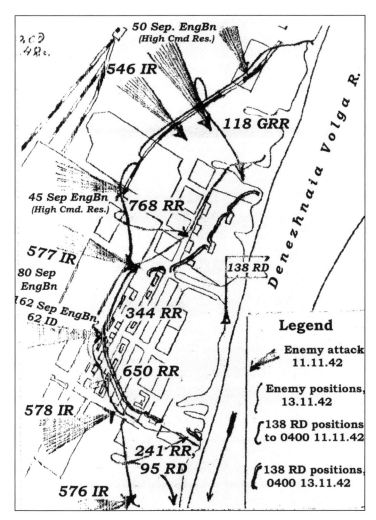

Map 88. 138th Rifle Division's defense, 0400 11–0400 13 November 1942

Meanwhile, on 305th Infantry Division's left wing, its 577th Regiment was unable to advance because of the strong resistance by 138th Rifle Division's 344th Regiment to its front. However, on its left 389th Infantry Division's 546th Regiment, spearheaded by 45th and 162nd Engineer Battalions and supported by 24th Assault Squadron and 244th Assault Gun Battalion, pushed forward to capture several blocks of buildings along Pribaltiiskaia Street and Prospect Lenin from 138th Rifle Division's 768th Regiment, in the process carving a 30-meter-deep wedge in Liudnikov's defenses and reaching to within 200 meters of the Volga. On 546th Regiment's left, 389th Engineer Battalion also drove a wedge toward the Volga, separating 1st and 2nd Battalions of 118th Guards Regiment and forcing the remnants of the 118th to fight their way back to Liudnikov's main bridgehead east of the Barrikady Factory by day's end.

By nightfall on 11 November, 305th Infantry Division reported that it had encircled "2,000 Russians" in the region east of the Barrikady Factory and intended to crown its success by liquidating the encircled Soviets the next morning. However, as one participant observed, "The balance sheet was not cheery. Losses had never been as high as today. Here, all we had gained was two to three houses and three to four hundred meters of ground. We had to admit it; this was another kind of war, which we had to wage here."[116] Substantiating this fact, the 305th reported that it lost 13 men killed and 119 wounded in the day's action. Its attached 245th Assault Gun Battalion saw 7 of its 10 assault guns, including 5 of its 6 150mm models, put out of action, however, some of them for mechanical reasons. Although it managed to cut off and destroy most of the 118th Guards Rifle Regiment, 389th Infantry Division reported even heavier casualties. Although the division itself suffered only 2 killed and 13 wounded, its supporting assault squadron from 24th Panzer Division reported 48 killed, 152 wounded, and 180 missing in action, and its supporting 244th Assault Gun Battalion lost 3 of its 18 guns.[117]

138th Rifle Division's daily report provided a detailed description of the day's confused and costly fighting:

Suffering heavy losses in sustained bloody encounters, 138th RD's units held on to their positions until 1030 hours. Beginning at 1030 hours, the enemy [389th ID's 546th IR] committed fresh forces (45th Engineer Battalion), crushed the numerically inferior remnants of 1st Bn, 118th Gds. RR, and reached the Volga River.

Although half encircled, 118th Gds. RR continued to repel the enemy attacks. Only at day's end, when all of its men had been put out of action, the enemy completely captured 118th Gds. RR's positions, since the regiment had been fully destroyed. A total of 7 men, together with the wounded commander of the regiment, Lieutenant Kolobavnikov, escaped from the fighting.

Striving to cut off 138th RD from the army, a group of enemy reached the Volga River at the junction of 138th and 95th RDs. The 138th RD was cut off from 62nd Army. . . . The 768th RR drove off numerous attacks by the enemy [546th IR], but at 1300 hours the enemy enveloped the right flank of the regiment and filtered into its rear with groups. The advance by the enemy was halted by forces from the headquarters and a company from the division, and the penetrating enemy group was completely destroyed by 1500 hours. At 1530 hours the enemy once again undertook a drunken [sic] attack against 768th RR's subunits. They smashed these subunits and continued to advance toward the Volga River. The remaining 24 men in the regiment, including mortar-men, are continuing to defend the group of buildings 150 meters east-northeast of the corner of the Barrikady Factory.

Beginning at 0600 hours, 344th RR beat off fierce attacks [577th IR] from the direction of Halls 4 and 14. At 1130 hours small groups of enemy submachine gunners [336th Eng. Bn] succeeded in seeping through the forward edge on the regiment's left wing. The fighting with penetrating groups of enemy submachine gunners in the depth of the defense and constant attacks from the flanks continued until 1600 hours. By this time, the penetrating groups of enemy submachine gunners were completely destroyed.

Beginning at 1740 hours, the attacks resumed against the regiment's center. All of the enemy attacks are being repelled.

650th RR, in cooperation with 241st RR, was fighting with an enemy force of up to an infantry regiment and 10 tanks [578th IR] beginning at 0530 hours. The 650th RR repelled all of the attacks by the enemy during the day, destroying up to 400 Hitlerites, and 3 tanks were burned and 1 was destroyed.

Beginning at 1520 hours, having lost its personnel, 241st RR abandoned the positions it occupied [to 576th IR] and, without advance warning, withdrew toward the south, entirely exposing the division's left flank. There is no elbow-to-elbow communication with the neighbor. Nine Hitlerite prisoners have been captured. Up to 750 enemy soldiers and officers have been destroyed by our fire, counterattacks, and hand-to-hand combat.[118]

Grudgingly, Chuikov later acknowledged the devastating impact of Steinmetz's assault, insisting, however, that it was not decisive:

The factory chimneys were tumbling down under air bombing and artillery fire. The enemy's main attack was clearly being made at the junction point of Liudnikov's [138th] and Gorishnyi's [95th] rifle divisions. The 118th Guards Rifle Regiment, which the previous day had had 250 infantrymen, by noon had only six left. The regimental commander was seriously wounded.

At 1130 hours the Germans threw in their reserves, and their infantry and tanks overran our lines on the right flank of Gorishnyi's division and reached the Volga along a front of about 550–650 yards. The army had been split for a third time, and Liudnikov's division was cut off from the main body of the army.[119]

In the Krasnyi Oktiabr' Factory to the south, two separate but equally fierce and costly struggles raged on 11 November: first, the assault by Group Schwerin to capture the Martenovskii Shop (Hall 10), and second, a counterattack by *Kampfgruppe* Scheele to recapture Hall 10, which it had lost the day before. The assault group of Schwerin's 79th Infantry Division, consisting of 179th Engineer Battalion and 24th Panzer Division's 40th Panzer Pioneer Battalion, began its advance against the Soviet forces defending Hall 4 shortly after 0400 hours upon receiving the code-word "Martin" (see Map 89). This assault group was formed into four separate assault parties, termed combat "wedges," and was supported by 14 artillery pieces, including a 210mm mortar battery and two 150mm infantry guns firing over open sights. Ironically, at 0340 hours, 15 minutes before the assault group planned to commence its assault, Chuikov's artillery and guards-mortars placed heavy fire on their assembly areas, in the process killing a squad leader and four of his men in the assault group's third wedge.[120]

Attacking northward from the western part of Hall 3, the assault group's first wedge encountered intense small-arms and machine-gun fire as it approached the southern edge of Hall 4, and it quickly withdrew to the locomotive shed just south of the hall, where it remained pinned down by heavy fire. The second wedge, which had worked its way forward to the western edge of Hall 4 during the night, assaulted into the southwestern corner of the hall but became entangled in the rubble of machinery, masonry, and bent steel before heavy Soviet fire forced it, too, to withdraw to the locomotive shed. The third wedge fared little better. Already weakened by the losses that it suffered in the Soviet artillery counterpreparation, it reached the hall's western face, where its commander fell. Thereafter, a combination of intense enemy fire and impenetrable smoke and flames forced it to withdraw to its jumping-off positions. The same fate awaited the fourth wedge, whose attack faltered along the northwestern face of the hall.

Assessing the causes of its failure, 179th Engineer Battalion concluded, "The concentrated, surprisingly strong enemy defense, as well as the quick artillery preparation, leads to the suspicion that our own attack was launched straight into the preparations for a major enemy offensive. If looked at like this, our own failed attack could be seen as a defensive success."[121] Attesting to the heavy fighting, 179th Engineers lost 54 of 120 men killed, wounded, or missing in the failed assault.[122] In addition, Schwerin reported that his 79th Division lost 23 killed, 101 wounded, and 10 missing.[123]

Meanwhile on 11 November, on the right wing of Group Schwerin, the 400 men of 24th Panzer Division's small *Kampfgruppe* Scheele had their

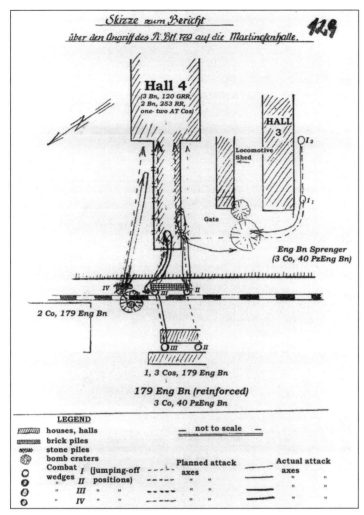

Map 89. Group Schwerin's (79th Infantry Division's) assault on Hall No. 4 (The Martenovskii Shop), 11 November 1942

hands full trying to recapture Hall 10, which it had lost the previous day, much less attempting to mount any more ambitious offensive effort of its own. After repelling several weak Soviet probes before dawn, Scheele formed several assault parties in the northern half of Hall 10, which his *kampfgruppe* still controlled, and in the safety of Hall 9, less than 100 meters to the west. These parties attacked Hall 10 at 0655 hours after a short five-minute mortar bombardment.

Equipped with submachine guns, grenades, and entrenching tools, the parties threaded their way through the grotesque ruins of the three-story hall, forcing the apparently surprised Soviet garrison of slightly more than 100 men to abandon the building by 0700 hours and withdraw eastward through gullies north of the oil tanks southeast of the factory.[124] A brief counterattack by a small group of Soviet troops was easily repulsed by the grenadiers with the help of several accompanying tanks. By 1400 hours Scheele's forces had succeeded in recapturing their former defensive positions. Given his group's weakness, Scheele abandoned all thoughts of conducting further attacks until the next morning. The attacks had cost his force (some 400 men) 12 killed and 26 wounded.[125]

The 62nd Army's daily combat report summarized the action on 11 November:

The Northern Group. After an artillery and air preparation, our infantry went over to the attack on 10 November. Despite strong enemy fire resistance, the infantry slowly advanced forward, and, at the present time, the forward units are located 500 meters south of the railroad bridge at the mouth of the Mokraia Mechetka River.

138th RD, with the attached 118th Gds. RR, repelled attacks by an enemy force of up to three IRs and two sapper battalions and tanks beginning at 0630 hours. As a result of bitter fighting, of the 200 men in 118th Gds. RR, only 6 remain. The commander of the regiment was severely wounded. The division is engaged in bitter fighting with enemy [forces] trying to encircle the units completely from the north and south.

95th RD repelled an attack by an enemy force of up to two infantry regiments and tanks beginning at 0630 hours. At 1030 hours the enemy brought reserves of up to two battalions forward and once again went over to the attack, crushed the right wing of 241st RR, and reached the bank of the Volga. The remaining units engaged in sustained fighting in their previous positions, repelling fierce attacks by enemy infantry.

45th RD, having repelled repeated attacks by the enemy, is holding on to its previous positions and exchanging fire.

39th Gds. RD. The enemy, after two unsuccessful attacks, committed reserves into combat and partially pushed 117th Gds. RR back. Stubborn fighting is going on to restore 117th Gds. RR's positions.

284th RD repelled two attacks by an enemy force of up to an infantry regiment. In the sector of 1045th RR, the enemy succeeded in wedging into the defensive region of 2nd Company, 1st Battalion. The situation is being restored. The fighting is continuing. The positions of the remaining units of the division are as before.

13th Gds. RD, having repelled an attack by two groups of submachine gunners, is holding on to its previous positions.
The positions of the remaining units are unchanged.[126]

At the end of his daily report, in addition to reporting 2,000 German soldiers and officers killed and four tanks destroyed, Chuikov decided "to restore the situation in 241st RR and destroy the forward units of the enemy who have reached the bank of the Volga River and, at the same time, prevent the complete encirclement of 138th RD by combined operations with the two battalions of 92nd RB which have crossed to the right bank of the Volga and the units of 95th RD."[127] To this end, he requested that Eremenko "increase the supply of ammunition for the artillery on the left bank and right bank" and "shift all of the artillery on the left bank and aviation to support 62nd Army on 12 November 1942."[128] In addition, he requested that the *front* dispatch 95th Rifle Division's 90th Regiment across the river to reinforce its parent division in its struggle to eradicate the German penetration to the Volga.

Although Seydlitz's forces recorded some dramatic successes on 11 November, especially southeast of the Barrikady Factory, they fell far short of Paulus's hopes and expectations. And the cost—a total of 445 men killed, wounded, and missing from the 305th and 389th Divisions and their supporting units alone—was a dear price to pay for such meager gains.[129] At nightfall, therefore, Paulus informed the OKH, "The attack east of the gun factory in Stalingrad achieved a partial success against a numerically superior enemy who defended himself bitterly," adding that he would regroup his forces the next day and resume the assaults on 13 November.[130] In the wake of Seydlitz's assault, the OKW's daily communiqué concealed the day's disappointments, simply stating, "In Stalingrad, German assault groups seized several more city blocks and enemy strong points in fierce offensive fighting. Ground force artillery and air force antiaircraft artillery sank five cutters and cargo barges on the Volga. German aircraft delivered massive strikes against enemy artillery firing positions and rear area communications on the eastern bank of the Volga."[131]

On a more ominous note, however, that very same day the FHO issued yet another report detailing the situation opposite Army Group B. This time, on the basis of agent reports, Gehlen identified the presence of Southwestern Front headquarters in the region 15 kilometers northwest of Kumylshenskaia (33 kilometers northeast of Serafimovich) and a new 1st Guards Army, whose composition had yet to be determined, in the vicinity of Kalach (Voronezh).[132] Based on this new intelligence, Gehlen on 12 November presented Zeitzler at the OKH with a chilling (but still highly qualified) assessment of the Red Army's capabilities and intentions for launching a fresh and even larger-scale offensive operation somewhere in the sector of Army Group B. Stating flatly, "In front of the Army Group, the enemy's attack intentions, which we have long suspected, are gradually becoming more clearly defined," the report then presented Gehlen's evidence:

> In addition to establishing two main groups of forces, which we have detected opposite the two wings of the Rumanian Third Army—where the enemy can now be said to be ready to attack—there are growing indications that forces are being concentrated still farther west, primarily in the Kalach area [meaning at Kalach in Voronezh *oblast'*, 50 kilometers northeast of Verkhnyi Mamon] (we have intercepted radio traffic between the Russian 63rd Army and six or seven unidentified formations, and detected the possible transporting sections of the 5th Tank Army; and we also have *Abwehr* reports of reinforcements arriving in Kalach) and possibly in front of the Hungarians as well.[133]

Gehlen, however, tempered this sharp warning with a strong qualification: "The overall picture of the force groupings in relation to place, time, and their strength is still not clear, and there are no indications of a possible offensive."[134] Admitting that "while it is not possible to make any overall assessment of the enemy situation ['intention' in the Russian translation] with the picture as uncertain as it is at present," he then offered a curiously mixed judgment of the enemy capabilities and intent:

> We must expect an early attack against the Rumanian Third Army, with the interruption of our railroad to Stalingrad as its objective so as to endanger all German forces farther to the east and compel our forces in Stalingrad to withdraw. This will thereby reopen the Volga as a waterway. The enemy has too few forces for such a large-scale operation (at present there are approximately 16 rifle divisions and from one up to four tank brigades situated in front of the Rumanian Third Army's right wing, and 7 rifle divisions and 3 cavalry divisions in front of its left wing).
> At present it is still unclear whether we can expect a large-scale offensive across the Don against the Italian Eighth and Hungarian Second Armies—with Rostov as the objective, which, in terms of time, would follow after the operations against the Rumanian Third Army, or whether the enemy, along with an offensive against the Rumanian Third Army, would undertake offensive operations with limited objectives against the Italian Eighth and Hungarian Second Armies.[135]

The report ended by offering some sobering news: "To all appearances, the testimony of one captured officer who designated the Morozovsk-Stalingrad road as the objective of the offensive, confirms this thought."[136] Although on 9 November Weichs had already considered redeploying Fremerey's 29th Motorized Division from Fourth Panzer Army's rear northward to back up the Romanian Third Army, he had quickly abandoned this idea because Hoth objected that it would deprive him of reserves to repulse an anticipated attack by 64th Army from the Beketovka bridgehead.[137] Instead, on 10 November Weichs transferred the headquarters of XXXXVIII Panzer Corps, which was in army group reserve, into Romanian Third Army's rear area and, despite Hoth's objections, alerted 29th Motorized Division to follow "on the shortest notice."[138] Weichs attempted to further bolster the Romanians' defenses on 12 November by ordering Paulus to "squeeze 10,000 men out of his engineer and artillery units to man a support line behind the Rumanians."[139] Also worried about reports of heavy enemy troop movements in front of his Fourth Panzer Army, Hoth remarked that the Russians were certainly not going through all the trouble just to strengthen their defenses.[140]

12 November

Pursuant to Paulus's instructions regarding a temporary halt in the offensive, Seydlitz's forces in the combat area east of the Barrikady dug in on 12 November. As they reorganized to resume their attacks, 305th and 389th Infantry Divisions also conducted new probes to improve their positions or seize key points that would facilitate the next day's assault. However, leaving no chance for respite, Chuikov unleashed violent counterattacks of his own, principally to eliminate the dangerous German corridor to the Volga River. Acknowledging the temporary lull, 62nd Army noted, "The Army repelled attacks by the enemy and fought to restore its positions in the central sector of the front"; more specifically:

> The enemy, after suffering heavy losses in the fighting on 11 November 1942, conducted a partial regrouping during the first half of 12 November and brought fresh forces forward.
>
> Based on documents taken from the dead, the presence of new units was established: 336th IR, 161st ID, 132nd IR, 44th ID, and 162nd Eng. Bn, 162nd ID and 294th Eng. Bn, 294th ID [sic].
>
> Having received reinforcements, during the second half of the day, the enemy resumed his attacks from the Mezenskaia region eastward toward the Volga River.
>
> Simultaneously, a concentration of infantry was detected in the vicinity of Hill 107.5 and Karusel'naia Street.
>
> Artillery and mortars conducted powerful fire raids on the combat formations of the forces and the crossings.

Enemy aircraft carried out reconnaissance, and single aircraft bombed the combat formations.

The Northern Group—exchanged fire from their previous positions. 102 men remain in the detachment operating in the Tractor Factory. According to verified data, the losses for the previous days were 76 killed and 160 wounded.

138th RD engaged in fierce fighting with significantly superior enemy. At a cost of heavy losses, it proved impossible to restore the positions in the division's sector. The composite regiment of 193rd RD became operationally subordinate to the commander of 138th RD at 1800 hours with the mission to restore the situation.

95th RD, having repelled three attacks by an enemy force of up to two battalions, engaged in sustained fighting with the enemy to restore the positions on its right wing. The oil tanks exchanged from hand to hand several times during the day.

At 1600 hours, having brought up reserves, the enemy went over to the attack once again with a force of up to two battalions, and, smashing the right wing of 241st RR, once again captured the oil tanks. The fight to restore the situation is continuing.

45th RD, repelling attacks by small groups of infantry, held on to its previous positions.

39th Gds. RD, after sustained fighting, completely restored the situation in the sector of 117th Gds. RR. The positions of its remaining regiments are unchanged.

284th RD, repelling two attacks by an enemy force of up to a battalion, went over to a counterattack with part of its forces and completely restored the situation in the defensive region of 1st Bn, 1045th RR.

In light of its extreme weakness, a composite regiment (200 men) is being created from **193rd RD**, which will move to the sector of 138th RD to restore the situation on its left wing at 1800 hours.

The positions of the army's remaining units are unchanged.

90th RR [95th RD] failed to reach the region of the crossings, and, of those designated to reinforce the crossings, only the low-powered tugboat "Dena," arrived, which again threatens to disrupt the plan for transferring units and ammunition.[141]

The fighting referred to in this report involved local German attacks as well as frequent counterattacks by 95th Rifle Division to recapture the oil tanks and restore communications with the isolated 138th Rifle Division (see Map 90). This action began at 0730 hours, when 241st Regiment, reinforced by naval infantry from 3rd Battalion, 92nd Rifle Brigade, attacked and seized several dugouts from 305th Infantry Division's 576th Regiment. In a see-

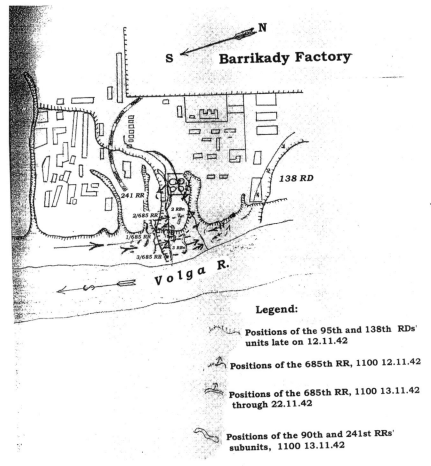

S ← **Barrikady Factory**

138 RD

241 RR

2/685 RR

2 RBn

1/685 RR

3/685 RR

3 RBn

V o l g a   R.

Legend:

⤳ Positions of the 95th and 138th RDs'
    units late on 12.11.42

⤴ Positions of the 685th RR, 1100 12.11.42

⤳ Positions of the 685th RR, 1100 13.11.42
    through 22.11.42

⌒ Positions of the 90th and 241st RRs'
    subunits, 1100 13.11.42

Map 90. Dispositions of 193rd Rifle Division's 685th Regiment and 95th Rifle Division to link up with 138th Rifle Division, 12–22 November 1942

saw battle lasting most of the day, 241st Regiment failed to recapture the oil tanks. After losing roughly 90 percent of its men in the previous day's fighting, the regiment was able to field only 23 bayonets. The division's 161st Regiment had 235 men remaining, and 3rd Battalion, 92nd Rifle Brigade, only 15.[142] 305th Infantry Division's losses amounted to 21 men killed and 21 wounded.[143] Clearly, reinforcements were essential if Chuikov's orders were to be fulfilled.

As the intensity of the fighting waned later in the day, Chuikov rearranged his forces to protect the region east of the Barrikady Factory and the vital landing stage. First, at 1630 hours, in order to "destroy the groups of enemy forces which had reached the Volga River," an order signed by the army's chief of staff, Krylov, directed the composite regiment of 193rd Rifle Division "to concentrate in the region immediately to the north of the mouth of the Bannyi Ravine." Once assembled, operating under 138th Rifle Division's control and cooperating with the units of 95th Rifle Division, it was to "destroy the enemy groups which had reached the Volga River in the vicinity of the oil tanks and Mezenskaia [Streets] and restore the situation at the junction of 138th and 95th Rifle Divisions."[144]

Then, at 1915 hours Chuikov addressed the growing crisis in the Krasnyi Oktiabr' Factory, where, as he described the situation, "the enemy is trying to penetrate the front in the southeastern part of the Krasnyi Oktiabr' Factory and reach the Volga River." To forestall this eventuality, he decided to reinforce the left wing of Zholudev's 39th Guards Rifle Division so it could clear the entire factory of Germans. His order, also signed by Krylov, required Batiuk's 284th Rifle Division "to allocate part of its 1043rd Regiment to relieve the left wing battalion of 112th Regiment [39th Gds. RD] on the night of 12–13 November and prepare its sector for a firm defense." In addition, so he could clear the enemy from the factory, Zholudev was to use the relieved battalion of 112th Regiment "to strengthen the combat formations in his division's center and on its left wing, with the mission to restore the situation completely and clear the factory grounds of enemy."[145] Still later, at 2300 hours, another order signed by Krylov directed Smekhotvorov to withdraw the headquarters of his shattered 193rd Rifle Division and its subordinate regiments back to the Volga River's eastern bank. A composite regiment from the division, with its remaining 289 men, was to become subordinate to Liudnikov's 138th Rifle Division, and his divisional artillery likewise to the chief of 62nd Army's artillery.[146]

At the end of his daily report on 12 November, Chuikov added the lament:

> The absence of replacements and the tardiness of the transfer of the battalions of 92nd RB and 90th RR have placed the army in an extremely difficult condition. Only the exceptional heroism of the personnel and their steadfastness in the fighting has allowed them to hold onto today's positions and, having overcome the offensive by a significantly superior enemy force, inflict heavy losses on him in personnel and equipment.
>
> The units of the army, having suffered great losses in the fierce fighting, require personnel replacements.
>
> The army commander appeals to the Stalingrad Front with a request concerning the dispatch of march-replacements of up to 10,000 men, to facilitate the supply of ammunition, and take measures to increase the army's crossing means [boats].[147]

If Chuikov was worried about the survival of his severely worn-down forces, he also realized that these forces had exacted a terrible toll on their tormenters. For example, a report that his army's intelligence organs prepared on the strength and grouping of opposing German forces on 13 November assessed that 62nd Army had inflicted "up to 45 percent losses on [the enemy's] combat soldiers during the fighting on 11–12 November," a fact gruesomely documented by "the more than three thousand dead soldiers and officers the troops observed on the battlefield."[148] Nevertheless, Chuikov judged, "during the period 13–18 November 1942, the enemy will continue attempts to develop his offensive along the Barrikady and Krasnyi Oktiabr' axes and, simultaneously, begin more active operations toward the Bannyi Ravine with secondary operations to the south." Interestingly enough, Chuikov limited his assessment to the period prior to 18 November—perhaps indicating that something major was in the wind.

Substantiating Chuikov's claim regarding German losses, Sixth Army reported on 12 November on its personnel shortages and recent losses to Army Group B (see Table 42).

This figure indicated that Sixth Army's 12 infantry divisions, after suffering more than 12,000 casualties in October, were short roughly 74,000 men by 1 November. Since these were primarily combat losses, most of them involved infantrymen and combat engineers, the cutting edge of the divisions. Furthermore, 5 of the 12 divisions (79th, 94th, 305th, 389th, and 100th Jäger), all assigned to Seydlitz's LI Corps, suffered 75 percent (9,409) of the army's casualties.

While lamenting such losses, German commanders at all levels also pondered the real meaning of the ominous but often contradictory intelligence assessments produced by FHO and adjusted their dispositions accordingly. Late on 12 November, for example, Paulus ordered Seydlitz to consolidate the gains his forces had made the previous day in Stalingrad's factory district, reorganize them to strengthen their most important shock groups, particularly east of the Barrikady Factory, and resume his assaults on 13 November to crush the remnants of Chuikov's defending forces.[149] Accordingly, on 13 November Seydlitz detached 162nd Engineer Battalion from 389th Infantry Division and assigned it to 305th Infantry Division, directing Steinmetz to use it to reinforce his 578th Regiment's assault on the Commissar's House the next day.[150]

Reflecting the daylong respite in the action, at day's end the OKW announced: "In Stalingrad, German forces combed regions previously occupied, destroying the remnants of defeated enemy units"; to stress the continuing resistance, 62nd Army reported that it "was continuing to fight to restore the situation in the Barrikady Factory . . . and, during the second half of the day, repelled all attacks by enemy forces of up to a regiment in the regions of Mezenskaia Street and the Krasnyi Oktiabr' Factory."[151]

**Table 42. Personnel Shortages in Sixth Army's Infantry Divisions as of
1 November 1942**

Force	Officers	Permanent [*Beamte*]	NCOs	Men	Total	Losses (3-31.10.42)
44th ID	134	27	622	3,270	4,053	185
71st ID	125		1,026	5,928	7,079	274
76th ID	157	24	993	5,591	6,765	226
79th ID	222	31	1,124	4,947	6,324	1,970
94th ID	219	37	1,146	5,600	7,002	1,233
113th ID	140	22	808	3,625	4,595	1,259
295th ID	187	28	1,170	6,928	8,313	724
305th ID	149	16	870	4,609	5,644	2,876
376th ID	158	16	1,125	5,007	6,206	158
384th ID	177	13	1,032	4,643	5,865	72
389th ID	223	28	1,007	5,298	6,556	1,296.
100th JägD	20	21	807	4,757	5,705	2,034
Totals	1,810	263	11,730	60,193	73,996	12,297

Source: Florian *Freiherr* von und zu Aufsess, *"Personeller Fehlbestand der Infanterie
Divisionen (Stand 01.11.42), Armee – Oberkommando 6, Ia Nr. 4534/42 geh., A. H. Qu.,
12. November 1942,"* in *Die Anlagenbander zu den Kriegstagebuchern der 6. Armee vom
14.09.1942 bis 24.11.1942, Band I* (Schwabach: January 2006), 271.

13 November

Because LI Corps' forces in the Krasnyi Oktiabr' Factory were too weak to
conduct attacks of any scale on 13 November, Seydlitz decided to focus his
assaults that day against the region east of the Barrikady Factory (see Maps
91–92). There, while 576th Regiment and 294th Engineer Battalion fended
off Soviet attacks via the oil tanks from the south, 578th and 577th Regiments of Steinmetz's 305th Infantry Division, now supported by three rather
than two engineer battalions and eight tanks in Heim's 14th Panzer Division
and four assault guns in 245th Assault Gun Battalion, were to liquidate the
encircled forces of Liudnikov's 138th Rifle Division and attached 118th Regiment.[152] As before, Steinmetz's key objectives were the Commissar's House,
where Liudnikov had his headquarters, and the open and deadly stretch of
ground between that house and the oil tanks to the south and House No. 78
on Prospect Lenin to the north.

On the shock group's right, 578th Regiment, spearheaded by 50th and
162nd Engineer Battalions and supported by 44th Assault Company and the
12 tanks and assault guns, were to attack northward from House No. 79 and
the northern bank of the ravine between the Pharmacy and the Volga toward
the Commissar's House to widen its foothold on the Volga's western bank. On
Steinmetz's left wing, 577th Regiment, with 336th Engineer Battalion, was
to clear Soviet forces from their fortified houses along Pribaltiiskaia Street

Map 91. LI Army Corps' assault, 13–15 November 1942

and Prospect Lenin as far north as House No. 78 and push them westward to Taimyrskaia Street into the arms of the advancing 578th Regiment.

One observer graphically described the battlefield:

> There were isolated ruins here that had to be eliminated at all cost because of their flanking effect. Between these ruins and the Volga was a flat, undeveloped area that fell away with a steep drop to the river bank. The Russians had built dug outs halfway up this cliff which were protected by emplacements along the top edge of the cliff which could take the open ground in front of them with effective fire. They also received accurate fire support from the other bank of the Volga. An attack here was therefore very difficult.[153]

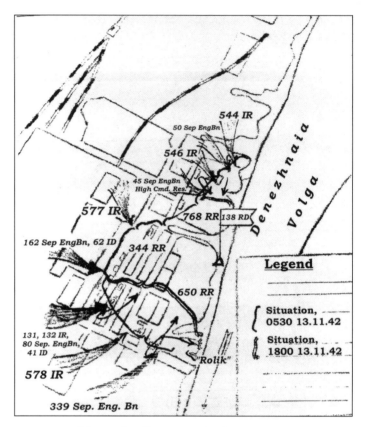

Map 92. Dynamics of the 138th Rifle Division's battle, 0530–1800 13 November 1942

The mission of Liudnikov's 138th Rifle Division was quite simple—to defend his "island" at all costs and prevent the Germans from reaching the Volga. Specifically, his roughly 2,000 men were "to defend the positions they occupied stubbornly and, fighting to the last man, prevent the enemy from reaching the Volga."[154] To this end, Liudnikov ordered his commanders "to mobilize every resource and to fulfill the mission at all costs. Not a step back! Strengthen observation and steadfastly repulse all attacks by the enemy."[155] Complicating 305th Infantry Division's task, all day on 13 November Chuikov's forces south of Liudnikov's island conducted repeated counterattacks in the sector of 95th Rifle Division's hapless 241st Regiment in an attempt to capture the oil tanks and break through to rescue Liudnikov's beleaguered forces.

Steinmetz's forces began their assault at 0345 hours, several hours before sunrise, in an attempt to catch the defenders by surprise. Commencing from the Pharmacy and House No. 79, the attack indeed caught 138th Rifle Division's 650th Regiment off guard and, before they could recover, reached the forbidding wall of the Commissar's House. Major Eberhard Rettenmaier, commander of 2nd Battalion, 578th Regiment, described 305th Infantry Division's assault:

> The assault party of the [50th] engineers was re-ordered [reorganized] and equipped with ladders. Simultaneously with the attack on the Commissar's House, an attack was to be launched from House 79 across the open terrain, and the small toehold on the Volga was to be expanded to both sides [the north and south]. Again . . . the artillery began the battle with its fire. This time the engineers of the 50th had success. With the aid of ladders, they managed to penetrate into the house through the windows. The Russians fled into the cellars and fortified themselves there. The engineers tore up the floors and closed with the enemy with smoke rounds, explosive ammunition [satchel charges], and petrol. The house was smoking from all apertures, and throughout the day explosions could be heard. Only by evening the Russians disappeared from the cellars and escaped through an exit on the side of the enemy. There was general joy at the command post by evening when the first runner came in from there; by day only radio contact had been possible.[156]

138th Rifle Division accurately described the day's action in its report:

> At 0600 hours on the morning of 13 November, the forces of 305th Infantry Division (reinforced by subunits of 131st and 132nd IRs and 80th Sapper Battalion [sic]), 44th ID (reinforced by 45th and 50th Sapper Battalions), and 162nd and 336th Sapper Battalions went over to the attack, delivering their main attack from the direction of Mezenskaia Street on the division's left wing, with the mission to reach the division's rear in the vicinity of the command post. The offensive by the enemy was supported by strong artillery and mortar fire.
>
> By 0730 hours the groups protecting our left wing were completely destroyed by superior enemy forces.
>
> A group of enemy submachine gunners numbering up to 70 men succeeded in seeping into the division's rear in the area of the firing positions of 344th RR's mortar batteries. The firing positions were showered with grenades. The enemy engaged in hand-to-hand fighting with the counterattacking mortar-men.
>
> Part of the enemy submachine gunners began to spread out into the vicinity of the division's command post. By this time, the remnants of 179th Sep.RBn, with 12 men, and the commandant's company of 6 men

threw themselves into a counterattack, shouting "For the Motherland." The group of penetrating enemy was destroyed in hand-to-hand fighting, and, by 1000 hours, the situation was stabilized on the division's left wing. The staff officers of the division participated in the counterattack led by the commander, Colonel Liudnikov.

The fighting continued with increasing ferocity in the division's center and on its right wing. The enemy continuously threw in fresh forces.

At 1200 hours, having concentrated large forces of infantry in the houses of the Barrikady Factory, an enemy force of no fewer than two battalions with tanks once again went over to the attack against 650th RR's left wing.

The repeated attacks by the enemy were repulsed until 1500 hours and, only when the ranks of 650th RR's left wing had been thinned, the enemy threw 10 more tanks into combat, destroyed the upper story of the "P"-shaped building with direct fire, and managed to capture the destroyed upper story of this building.

The mortar-men of 650th RR fought for the ruins of the "P"-shaped building for hours. Only by calling in the fires of our own artillery on "themselves" were they able to continue holding the building in their hands. By day's end, the building was blown up by the enemy. Only a small group of our soldiers, numbering 10 men, the majority of which were wounded and burned, managed to escape the destruction of the "P"-shaped building. The attacks by large forces of enemy infantry and tanks were repeated constantly until nightfall. By the end of the day, the enemy succeeded in destroying the garrisons of Houses Nos. 35 and 36 [German Nos. 66 and 73] and the "P"-shaped building and seized these buildings.[157]

On the left wing of Steinmetz's shock group, and immediately after beginning their attack, 577th Regiment's and 336th Engineer Battalion's assault parties encountered stiff resistance from 138th Rifle Division's 344th Regiment and the right wing of its 650th Regiment in the houses along Pribaltiiskaia Street and Lenin Prospect (Houses Nos. 66 and 67 on the former and No. 73 on the latter). This stout resistance prevented 577th's troops from advancing southward to link up with 578th Regiment's forces struggling around the Commissar's House. Making matters worse, during the ensuing struggle, the former also lost to a Soviet counterattack some houses that they had already captured.

On the shock group's right, after its initial successes, 578th Regiment also faced strong resistance, prompting Rettenmaier to note, despite the success in 578th Regiment's center that "on this day, the small toehold [along the Volga on 305th Infantry Division's left wing] could only be enlarged a little."[158] Commenting on this struggle, another German participant recorded, "On November 13, House 81, close by the 'Commissar's House,' was taken. The first break here took place in the cellars, and again the fight from room to room (man to man) lasted the entire day. On both sides men fought with a bitterness and determination that can hardly be imagined."[159] Claiming that the battles on 13 November were very costly, he added:

> In total, the engineers suffered about 30 percent men killed and wounded in the days between November 9th [should read 11th] and 13th, 1942. Now and again, assault guns were committed with the engineer attacks. But before this commitment, the approach roads had to be carefully checked because of the impassible terrain. The assault guns could not follow the attack of the engineer assault parties and could only provide protective fire from the rear. Even in this, there were losses among our assault guns, as the Soviets had anti-tank weapons in the front line, which had been camouflaged well. In our sector, no flame throwing tanks were used.[160]

As a result of this heavy fighting, 578th Regiment indeed captured the Commissar's House and then pushed northward, almost reaching Liudnikov's new headquarters, which days before had moved about 300 meters northward to a ravine on the bank of the Volga just east of House No. 87 (known to the Germans as the Rote [Red] House) on the eastern side of Taimyrskaia Street.

While the intense fighting swirled around Liudnikov's shrinking perimeter, the Soviets struck once again near the oil tanks, this time at 0900 hours, with the composite regiment of 193rd Rifle Division against the defenses of 305th Infantry Division's 576th Regiment. Although this assault failed, new ones materialized at 1000 hours and even later in the day. 62nd Army described the precarious situation:

> The composite regiment of 193rd RD, operating from behind 95th RD's right wing, was halted along the line of Mezenskaia Street eastward to the Volga River. Fierce fighting is continuing. The situation of the division is very difficult. The transport of ammunition and the evacuation of wounded has ceased over the past two days.
>
> 95th RD. All attempts by the enemy to widen their penetration by attacking southward along the bank have been repulsed. The units are holding on to the positions they occupy but have not restored the situation on the right wing of 241st RR.[161]

After nightfall on 13 November, LI Corps informed Sixth Army that it had conducted "successful shock troop actions," during which it captured two blocks of houses and the Commissar's House and was going to continue its assaults the following day.[162] From its vantage point in Berlin, the OKW reported that "in Stalingrad combat reconnaissance groups of our forces seized several city blocks as a result of intense fighting. Enemy counterattacks were repulsed. Enemy forces in jumping-off positions were destroyed by concentrated fire from artillery and antiaircraft guns, supported by dive-bombers."[163] Acknowledging the growing concerns within the German command about a possible impending Soviet offensive, the communiqué added, "Rumanian forces south of Stalingrad repelled several enemy attacks of local significance," but farther north, "on the Don front, German forces and those of their Allies repelled enemy attacks of local significance and threw them back to their jumping-off positions by counterattacks."[164]

The OKH's daily report summarized the action in Stalingrad: "In Stalingrad, assault groups occupied two blocks of civilian buildings and the Commissar's House east of the 'Krasnyi Barrikady' factory. An attack by an enemy force of 150 men was repelled."[165] It added: "The enemy repeatedly attacked the positions of the Rumanian forces at Lake Tsatsa and south of Stalingrad with forces of from a company to a battalion without success" and, in the Serafimovich region, "with a force of up to two battalions."[166] Although they realized that this type of intense reconnaissance activity was usually indicative of an impending Soviet offensive, German operations officers generally dismissed these actions as insignificant because their forces had repelled all previous Soviet counterstrokes with relative ease.

The 62nd Army's daily situation report late on 13 November confirmed the ferocity of this fighting, emphasizing in particular the precarious predicament faced by Liudnikov's and Gorishnyi's encircled riflemen, which, according to German count, now numbered well less than 2,000 men. Claiming that his forces counted more than 3,000 German dead on 12 November and more than 1,200 on 13 November, Chuikov ordered his forces at day's end "to repel the attacks by the enemy with their existing forces and restore the situation in the Mezenskaia Street region, while preventing any further advance by his units, with the approaching 90th RR and the remnants of 92nd RB, while destroying the enemy that had reached the oil tanks."[167]

The Red Army General Staff then summarized its view of the day's action:

62nd Army. The Northern Group of Forces exchanged fire from its previous positions on 13 November.

138th RD engaged in defensive fighting with an enemy force of up to an infantry division and four sapper battalions with 15 tanks. The enemy on the left wing of the division succeeded in penetrating the forward edge of the defense and advanced forward. The positions of the units of the division are being confirmed.

95th RD, in cooperation with the [composite] regiment of 193rd RD, fought fiercely to restore its previously occupied positions in the vicinity of the oil tanks east of Mezenskaia Street, and, after encountering stubborn enemy resistance, the units of the division were unable to advance.

The army's remaining units exchanged fire with the enemy from their previous positions.[168]

From the vantage point of his command post in the Tennis Racket east of Mamaev Kurgan, Chuikov described the day's fighting in even more dramatic terms:

On the morning of November 12 [should read 13 November], the enemy brought up more reserves, which meant that another attack was on the way. And the attack came at noon that day. Fighting flared up along the whole of the army's front. German soldiers, drunk or mad, came on and on. The Far East seamen who had come to reinforce Gorishnyi's division showed the enemy what was what and how the famous Red Navy men could fight. The petrol tanks of Tuvinskaia Street changed hands several times. In the heat of battle, the Red Navy men threw off their greatcoats and, in singlets [jerseys] and hats, beat off the attacks and then went on the offensive themselves. The fighting in the Krasnyi Oktiabr' and Barrikady Factories and on Mamaev Kurgan was no less fierce. We now felt that our men had become warriors that no force could defeat. . . . The Germans' desperate attacks came to a halt on the evening of November 12 [13].[169]

Parenthetically, Chuikov argued that the bloody assaults were inexorably sapping the Sixth Army's offensive strength. "We could tell from documents taken from dead enemy soldiers that the Germans would not be able to keep up their attack for long," he added, concluding that "they would be exhausted in two to three days."[170] However, it was also uncertain how long 138th Rifle Division could hold out, because, in Liudnikov's words, "ammunition and foodstuffs were running out; only a day's supply remained. During the entire day the enemy delivered intense artillery and mortar fire against the crossings, Zaitsev Island, and the left bank of the Volga River. 500 mines [mortar rounds] were fired."[171]

Furthermore, Chuikov's entire army was suffering immense attrition because of the frenzied fighting. Late on 13 November, for example, some older Soviet sources place his army's overall strength at 47,000 men, supported by 800 guns and mortars, most of them firing from the Volga's eastern bank, and 19 tanks, including 7 heavy and 12 medium models.[172] In reality, however, the army's forces still fighting on the western bank of the Volga likely numbered no more than 8,000 men, the equivalent of one rifle division, subdivided as follows:

- **Group Gorokhov** (124th and 149th Rifle Brigades) defending in the Rynok and Spartanovka region with 500–600 men in each of its brigades, for a total of 1,000–1,200 combat troops;
- **138th Rifle Division** (Liudnikov), with some remnants of **308th Rifle Division's 339th and 344th Regiments** and **118th Guards Rifle Regiment**, defending the 400 by 700 meter strip between the Barrikady Factory and the Volga River with as many as 1,500 men;
- **95th Rifle Division's** (Gorishnyi) **161st and 241st Rifle Regiments**, with the composite regiment of **193rd Rifle Division** (Smekhotvorov) and the remnants of **92nd Rifle Brigade**, defending the 300 by 500 meter sector south of the ravine south of the Barrikady Factory with about 1,500 men [193rd Rifle Division's remnants had been combined into its 685th Rifle Regiment];
- **45th Rifle Division's** (Sokolov) **10th and 61st Regiments** defending the 300 by 500 meter sector northeast of the Krasnyi Oktiabr' factory with roughly 1,200 men;
- **39th Guards Rifle Division's** (Gur'ev) 120th and **112th Regiments and 45th Rifle Division's 253rd Regiment** defending Halls 4 and 8a and the eastern outskirts of the Krasnyi Oktiabr' Factory with about 1,200 men;
- **284th Rifle Division** (Batiuk) defending from the lower Krutoi Ravine to the ravine southwest of the Krasnyi Oktiabr' Factory with about 1,200 men; and
- **13th Guards Rifle Division** (Rodimtsev) defending the sector from Stalingrad's center city to the southern edge of the Krutoi Ravine with about 1,500 men.

As the forces of Seydlitz's LI Corps pounded the remnants of Chuikov's forces in the vicinity of the Barrikady Factory from 11 through 13 November, Army Group B kept close track of troop movements in the Soviets' rear area. Alarmed by an intensification of these troop movements, particularly opposite the sector of the German IV Army Corps south of Stalingrad, early on 14 November the OKH's FHO reported, "The repositioning of enemy forces, with the commitment of new units in a series of sectors of the army group's front and also the appearance of antiaircraft guns between Lakes Tsatsa and Bol'shie Chapurniki, in front of the Rumanian VI Army Corps, bears witness to possible enemy offensive operations in this region."[173] Once again, however, Gehlen qualified this judgment by asserting that "the enemy's situation in the remaining sectors of the army group's front is unchanged."[174] However, buried in the section entitled "Enemy Grouping," the report's author acknowledged the presence north of the Don River of 6th Guards Cavalry Division in the region east of Serafimovich and 21st Cavalry Division in the sector opposite Romanian I Army Corps southeast of Elanskaia. Based on this information, but drawing no further inferences, the report concluded that the Soviets had already regrouped 3rd Guards and 8th Cavalry Corps, the parent formations of these divisions, into this region.[175]

14 November

No longer strong enough to conduct major attacks elsewhere in Stalingrad's northern factory district, Seydlitz's LI Corps once again sought to liquidate the persistent pocket of Soviet forces east of the Barrikady Factory on 14 November (see Maps 93–94). As before, this task fell to the exhausted 305th Infantry Division. For this attack, Steinmetz employed the right wing of 577th Regiment, spearheaded by two companies of 336th Engineer Battalion and supported by as many as 23 assault guns from 244th and 245th Assault Gun Battalions.[176] This force attacked from Halls 3 and 4 in the Barrikady Factory eastward toward House No. 67 and No. 68, striking the right wing of 138th Rifle Division's 344th Regiment. On the right, the 305th's 44th Assault Company led the attack toward House No. 74, which was defended by troops from 650th Regiment. Attacking with a force of little more than 3,000 men, this time at 0930 hours instead of at dawn, Steinmetz's troops and supporting engineers ground their way through the narrow strip of ground between the Commissar's House and the Volga River against a Soviet force that was well less than half the Germans' strength but manned hundreds of strongpoints scattered throughout the rubble.

As one participant in the attack described it:

On 14 November, a renewed attack. As before, 294th Engineer Battalion was defending the [oil] tank farm [with 576th Regiment]. The 50th Engineer Battalion (motorized) attacked toward the east from the Commissar's House [and] 162nd Engineer Battalion toward the north. Here there were individual ruins that had to be taken out because of their enfilading fire. Between the ruins and the Volga, a level field stretched away, which, down by the river bank, fell away steeply towards the Volga. Halfway down the steep slope, the Soviets had built their bunkers, whilst he defended himself from the edge of the steep slope and controlled the terrain in front of him. Furthermore, he had excellent fire support from the other bank of the Volga. An attack here, therefore, was very difficult, nevertheless, we succeeded in getting there through a trench that led down to the Volga and expanded our position on the Volga. Now the Soviets

Map 93. Sixth Army's situation, 14–15 November 1942

were to be thrown out of the remaining bridgehead, but again and again he brought up new men and material. The attacks we launched were unsuccessful, as the enemy was clever and tough. Our hand grenades, which we threw, rolled down the steep slope and exploded without any effect. Any bombardment with heavy weapons had a similar effect. Here also, most shells landed in the Volga. Tunnels often connected the Soviet bunkers halfway up the slope with each other. Here other means had to be employed and gradually mining and explosions made an improvement in our forward position on the Volga.[177]

The assault by 305th Infantry Division's infantrymen and supporting engineers, despite their immense exertions and continuing heavy losses, expired at nightfall on 14 November before Steinmetz's decimated troops could

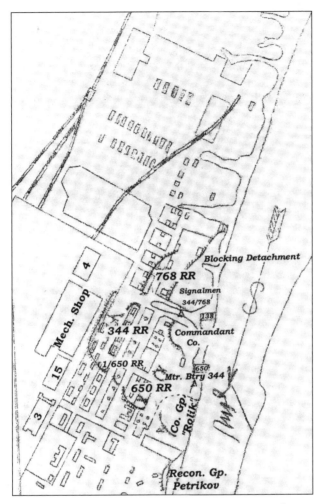

Map 94. Dispositions of 138th Rifle Division, 0400–1900 14 November 1942

accomplish their assigned mission. During the see-saw fighting throughout the day, the Germans measured gains in the tens rather than hundreds of meters. 138th Rifle Division described the day's action, underscoring the extreme privations that Liudnikov's forces were experiencing:

> At 1030 hours the army commander ordered 95th RD and the composite regiment of 193rd RD to restore the front by an attack toward the north and link up with 138th RD, which had been cut off from the remaining

forces of the army, on 14 November. At 1150 hours, trying to reach the Volga River, an enemy force of up to two companies went over to the attack from the vicinity of Halls 14 and 15 in the Barrikady Factory against 650th RR and the left wing of 344th RR. Numerically superior in men and weapons, the enemy destroyed the garrisons of Houses Nos. 37 and 38 [German Nos. 74 and 67] and captured these buildings; but soon the enemy himself in these buildings was destroyed by a group from 344th RR, which occupied these buildings once again.

The actions of this group of 344th RR were supported by our artillery on Zaitsev Island. Our artillery fired 200 shells.

Several covered vehicles arrived in the vicinity of Halls 14 and 15 between 1330 and 1650 hours. Animated troop activity noted among the enemy indicated replacements were arriving.

Enemy aircraft circled over the combat formation of the division all day long, while striking Zaitsev Island, the left bank of the Volga River, and the division's command post.

138th RD had expended all of its resources by 14 November. For five days it has conducted intense fighting with ammunition seized from the enemy.

The parcels which are being dropped by PO-2 aircraft often fall into the hands of the enemy. Despite the shortages of food and ammunition, the division's men are stoutly defending the right bank of the Volga River, displaying exceptional examples of heroism.[178]

Summarizing the fighting over the previous three days, 138th Rifle Division then provided a unique mosaic of the sort of combat that raged in the ruins east of the Barrikady Factory:

The division was completely cut off from the units of the army and its bases. Suffering great losses, the enemy reached the Tuvinsk region and began to control the bank of the Volga River, destroying routine supply of ammunition and foodstuffs, which was reduced to what he had at hand, only adequate for up to 35 percent of the division's personnel. The enemy penetrated to the Volga on 12–13 November.

On 13 November up to 1,500 drunk Hitlerites penetrated through our combat formations. All of 138th RD's forces were thrown in to repel the enemy's attacks. The fighting lasted for 11 hours. In the most intensive fighting, a group of up to 70 enemy submachine gunners penetrated to the vicinity of the division's command post but were halted and destroyed by the steadfastness of 18–20 brave men. The enemy abandoned the bodies of more than 1,000 soldiers and officers on the field of battle along the division's front.

Achieving no success in this fighting, the enemy abandoned massive attacks and went over to the tactic of using small groups to seize individual buildings.

Grenade fighting for individual floors and rooms took on exceptional importance. The Germans often blew up bold soldiers who did not surrender the stairwells.

Cut off from the units of the army, the division increasingly needed replenishment of its ammunition and foodstuffs. By 14 November the ammunition was used up, and there was also no food.[179]

At day's end, the roughly 500 survivors of Liudnikov's 138th Rifle Division, bloodied but unbowed, clung stubbornly to their foxholes, trenches, and bunkers on the Volga's western bank. The OKW acknowledged this fact obliquely, without specifically mentioning the failure: "Enemy counterattacks in Stalingrad were repelled. Aircraft offered effective air support in this fighting, conducting bombing strikes on Soviet artillery firing positions and airfields east of the Volga. Dive-bombers and assault aircraft conducted bombing strikes against enemy field positions and force concentrations in the region of the lower Don."[180]

All the while, south of Liudnikov's isolated island, Chuikov's forces continued their attempts to break through and rescue 138th Rifle Division. In its daily report, 62nd Army emphasized its stoic defense, claiming that its forces "repelled attacks by the enemy during the day and fought to restore the situation on its left wing."[181] At the same time, it heaped praise on Liudnikov's resolute defense and the repeated attempts to rescue his forces, declaring:

138th RD, although half encircled, repelled attacks by enemy forces of up to an IR on its left wing and small groups in the center.

The enemy tried to narrow the ring around the half-encircled division with constant attacks against the flanks and the center. The fighting is continuing. The units are repelling attacks in their previous positions. The division is experiencing acute shortages of ammunition, food, and medical supplies.

95th RD, with 3rd Bn, 92nd RB, and the composite RR of 193rd RD, engaged in intense fighting for the restoration of the situation in 241st RR [95th RD] with the aim of establishing elbow-to-elbow communications with 138th RD's units. The fighting is continuing in the vicinity of the oil tanks. The left wing units of the division are fighting in their previous positions.[182]

This report also ended with a now familiar lament:

The floating resources [boats] have not completely arrived. The plan for supply has been disrupted for three days. The designated reinforcements have not crossed, and the units are experiencing acute shortages of ammunition and food. The convoy of boats arriving from Tumak with the subunits of 90th RR could not make their way through because of drifting ice and have turned back. The floating ice has completely disrupted communications with the left bank in the vicinity of 62nd Army's crossings.[183]

Once again, Chuikov acted forcefully during the day's crisis. While acknowledging that "the enemy, having penetrated the front in the defensive sector of 95th RD, has reached the bank of the Volga River," Chuikov admitted that "having abandoned its positions, 241st RR has uncovered the left wing of 138th RD and, at the same time, created a threat of its encirclement." Chuikov, through Krylov, directed Gorishnyi's 95th Rifle Division to restore the situation by ordering:

95th RD, with the attached 3rd Bn, 92nd RB, an automatic weapons company from 92nd RB, and the composite RR [685th] of 193rd RD, will restore the front lines within 95th RD's boundaries and re-establish elbow-to-elbow communications with the units of 138th RD on 14 November 1942 by an attack northward along the bank of Volga River from behind the right wing.

The chief of the army's artillery will support 95th RD's operations with its fires.[184]

On 14 November, while fighting continued amid the ruins of buildings east of the Barrikady Factory, Stalingrad Front's 64th Army unleashed new offensive operations south of the city (see Map 78). This time attacking by surprise, the army's 96th Rifle Brigade managed to penetrate 371st Infantry Division's defenses at the southern outskirts of Kuporosnoe. As 64th Army's commander, Shumilov, was able to report at day's end, the brigade "was fighting in the center of the Kuporosnoe region at 1500 hours."[185] Although Army Group B and the OKW played down the importance of this attack, it was serious enough for Paulus to order 24th Panzer Division's *Kampfgruppe* Scheele to release 10 of its 20 tanks to reinforce 71st Infantry Division's 211th Regiment, which Paulus had ordered to assemble as a reserve force in the brickworks in Stalingrad's southern suburb of Minina and then move southward to shore up 371st Infantry Division's defenses.[186] The following evening Shumilov reported that "96th RB has fortified itself in the center of Kuporosnoe," where it remained for almost 48 hours more.[187] On 17 November, however, 71st Infantry Division's reserve force counterattacked, forcing the rifle brigade to withdraw from Stalingrad's southern suburbs back to its original positions.

15 November

Undeterred by his failure to crush the Soviet forces dug in along the Volga's western bank on 13 and 14 November, Seydlitz reorganized his forces for a third time in four days and ordered them to resume assaults across the same mangled terrain on 15 November. This time, telescoping their attentions down to single buildings, his forces conducted two more limited attacks, seeking to compress Liudnikov's perimeter from the north and south. In the first of these attacks, 305th Infantry Division's 578th Regiment, supported by the decimated 50th Engineer Battalion and a handful of assault guns, was to assault northward against the defenses of 138th Rifle Division's 650th Regiment, due north of the Commissar's House. In the second, 389th Infantry Division's 546th Regiment, supported by 45th Engineer Battalion, 44th Assault Battalion, and roughly 10 assault guns, was to attack southward toward the Rote House, a sector defended by 138th Division's 768th Regiment.

When the two forces attacked, they once again encountered vigorous counterattacks by Chuikov's shrunken army. The infantry and engineers of Steinmetz's 305th Infantry Division, now operating in platoon-size to company-size assault parties, did all in their power to pry Liudnikov's riflemen from their dense web of defensive positions. Although LI Corps reported a "further narrowing the bridgehead east of the gun factory," to its amazement and chagrin it also had to fend off repeated Soviet counterattacks "along the whole line."[188]

Describing its defense and the critical shortages of both men and ammunition, 138th Rifle Division recorded:

The enemy conducted active offensive fighting during the course of the day, enveloping the flanks of the division. The enemy carried out many fierce attacks, the majority of which were smashed by the steadfastness of our soldiers. The enemy began massing in front of the flanks of the division at nightfall.

The 768th RR was used up [combat ineffective] by the end of the day. Together with its command cadre, 650th RR numbered 31 men, and, together with its command cadre, 344th RR [counted] 123 men. Ammunition: 20–30 rounds per rifle. There are no grenades or PPSh [submachine gun] ammunition. The personnel of the division received one meal. The food has been completely used up. 250 wounded are located at the command post of the division. The command of the division requests the commander of the army take immediate measures to provide the division with ammunition and food and for the evacuation of the wounded.[189]

At the end of the day, the OKW's communiqué reported modestly, "In Stalingrad, combat reconnaissance groups seized three more city blocks and repelled enemy counterattacks."[190] The 62nd Army, for its part, stressed the resoluteness of its defense and its continued counterattacks:

> The army repelled attacks by the enemy on the right wing during the day. Part of the forces fought to restore the situation in the Mezenskaia region.
>
> The enemy continued repeated attacks on our positions in the sector of the Barrikady Factory during the day. Simultaneously, he conducted reconnaissance of our forward edge, particularly in the sector of the Krasnyi Oktiabr' Factory and the Bannyi Ravine. . . .
>
> 138th RD repelled fierce attacks by the enemy along its entire front during the day. The enemy, suffering heavy losses, brought up fresh forces three times during the day. Despite the numerical superiority of the enemy, all of the attacks were repulsed by day's end.
>
> The situation in the division has become extremely difficult. There is no ammunition, replacements have not arrived, and the wounded have not been evacuated. The fighting in half encirclement is continuing.
>
> 95th RD, with 3rd Bn, 92nd RB, and the composite 685th RR went over to the attack with part of their forces at 1330 hours after a 30-minute artillery preparation, with the aim of restoring the situation in the Mezenskaia region. Despite exceptionally strong enemy fire resistance, our units advanced forward slowly. Fierce hand-to-hand fighting raged in the region of the oil tanks. The region of the oil tanks changed hands several times.
>
> The enemy, having brought fresh forces forward, went over to the attack and once again captured the oil tanks by day's end. The fighting is continuing. The situation in 241st RR's sector has not been restored.
>
> 45th RD and 39th Gds. RD, in their previous positions, repelled attacks by small groups of enemy infantry trying unsuccessfully to penetrate into the halls occupied by our units on the grounds of the Krasnyi Oktiabr' Factory.
>
> 284th RD, in its previous positions, exchanged artillery and mortar fire with the enemy, destroying 150 soldiers and officers during the day.[191]

Overnight on 15–16 November, Chuikov ordered Gorishnyi's 95th Rifle Division and the composite 685th Rifle Regiment to "destroy the enemy who have reached the bank of the Volga with night operations" to once again restore the situation east of Mezenskaia Street and reestablish communications with Liudnikov's division. He also asked Eremenko to "oblige the units of the fortified region on Zaitsev Island to provide 138th RD with ammunition and organize the evacuation of wounded across the Denezhnaia Volozhka channel," which separated the island from the river's western bank.[192]

Waxing poetic about his army's gallantry in extreme adversity and the difficulties in mounting effective counterattacks, Chuikov later wrote:

> We had to find, or rather to squeeze out, some resources or other among our units on the right bank. The Army Military Council decided primarily to incorporate the units of Smekhotvorov's [193rd] division into one regiment, the 685th, and, concentrating it on the right flank of Gorishnyi's [95th] division, to counterattack northward along the Volga to join up with Liudnikov's division.
>
> In all of Smekhotvorov's units, we managed to collect only 250 ablebodied men. With this composite regiment and the right flank of Gorishnyi's division, which was gradually reinforced with soldiers and small groups of soldiers coming over from the left bank, we counterattacked northward continuously until November 20, aiming to link up with Liudnikov's men.
>
> Our counterattacks, it is true, did not restore the position, but neither was the enemy able to wipe out Liudnikov's division.[193]

In one of many instances when German and Soviet combat reports coincided perfectly, Chuikov claimed, "On the night of November 15, our nightflying aircraft dropped four bales of provisions and four of ammunition to Liudnikov."[194] Major Rettenmaier, commander of 578th Regiment's 2nd Battalion, confirmed this incident, noting, "In the afternoon of the 15th we were surprised. Two Soviet airplanes circled over the position [near the Commissar's House] at low altitude. Suddenly they dropped something that did not look like bombs at all. They were sacks, of which part also fell in our sector. They contained bread and meat. So the misery of the encircled troops must have been great; we were cheered by this and hoped for an imminent complete success."[195]

TO THE EDGE OF THE ABYSS: 16–18 NOVEMBER

The intense but inconclusive fighting between 11 and 15 November convinced Paulus and Seydlitz that little more could be gained unless they rested, reorganized, and reinforced LI Corps' severely weakened shock groups. This they did during the next three days, with the intention of resuming assaults on 20 November. In the meantime, however, on 16 November the first snows fell, leaving a pale dusting on the grotesquely twisted wreckage of factory machinery and the blackened shells of the destroyed buildings and adding to the misery of soldiers on both sides. Accompanying the first snows of winter, the ice floes on the Volga inexorably thickened, by 20 November forming an impenetrable barrier of ice extending almost 75 meters from the Volga's eastern and western shores. This ice severely impeded Chuikov's efforts to reinforce his forces still struggling on the river's western bank.[196]

As Paulus and Seydlitz prepared their forces for the 20 November assault, Weichs, who was increasingly concerned over the viability of Romanian Third Army's defenses in the event Gehlen's predictions proved correct, took new measures to reinforce the Romanians' defenses. On 16 November he decided to transfer 22nd Panzer Division, which had been backing up the Italian Eighth Army, eastward into the Romanian Third Army's rear area, where, together with the Romanian 1st Armored Division, it would become subordinate to XXXXVIII Panzer Corps' headquarters, which he had moved into the region on 10 November.[197]

Some observers later criticized this move, asserting that it was "nothing of the sort" of the type of "fairly strong reserve" required by the situation. Such was the case because 22nd Panzer Division fielded only 46 tanks. Although the Romanian 1st Armored Division had 122 tanks, only 21 were German Panzer III models; the remainder were captured Czech tanks mounting only light 37mm guns. At the time, demonstrating their superb repair capabilities, Sixth Army's 14th, 16th, and 24th Panzer Divisions fielded 48, 50, and 46 tanks, respectively.[198] Yet given the fact that the final act in the Stalingrad drama remained unfinished, Weichs and Paulus believed that it would be imprudent to release any of these three divisions to support the Romanian and Italian forces along the Don.[199]

As Seydlitz regrouped his forces for yet another stab at the Soviet forces holding out west of the Volga, the infantry and engineers of Steinmetz's 305th Infantry Division conducted local assaults against the remnants of Liudnikov's 138th Rifle Division to improve their jumping-off positions for the 20 November assault (see Map 95).[200] For example, after failing to seize House No. 74, northeast of the Commissar's House, with an assault during the day, overnight on 16–17 November assault parties from the division's 577th Regiment and 336th Engineer Battalion seized two more houses in the 70 Block of houses south of House No. 73 on 17 November and, on 18 November, captured House No. 77, due north of the Commissar's House. As a result of these actions, Major Rettenmaier concluded, "The battles were not as costly anymore. The enemy seemed to be at the end of his strength. Based on this experience, a large-scale attack was planned for the next day [actually 20 November]." Ruefully, he added, "But things turned out differently."[201]

Map 95. The struggle for "Liudnikov's Island," 16–18 November 1942

While Seydlitz's forces prepared for their 20 November attack, Chuikov, although confident of victory, worried about the fate of Liudnikov's forces, trapped as they were between Steinmetz's infantry and the massive ice floes piling up on the western bank of the Volga. "We finally felt," said Chuikov, that "the days of the Germans were numbered. But we were concerned about the fate of Liudnikov's division. We had to come to their rescue. Using every last ounce of energy, our units began to counterattack day after day, round the clock, against an enemy who had occupied the Volga bank between Liudnikov's division and the Army's main forces."[202] Then, engaging in a bit of bravado, Chuikov said, "Our assault groups were step by step winning back buildings and dugouts on other sectors of the Army's front, or, to be more precise, along the whole of the front. Colonel Gorokhov's group attacked toward the Tractor Factory from the north; Sokolov's and Gur'ev's divisions attacked the Krasnyi Oktiabr' Factory; Colonel Batiuk's division attacked

Mamaev Kurgan; and Rodimtsev's division stormed individual buildings in the city."[203]

Combat reports from both sides only partially substantiate Chuikov's account. For example, after the fighting on 16 November, the Red Army General Staff's daily operational summary for that day reported the precise locations of its forces without mentioning any concerted offensive actions:

62nd Army. The Northern Group (124th and 149th RBs) defended the line: Rynok-the western part of the large gully in Spartanovka village-the eastern large pit south of the railroad at Spartanovka-(incl.)-Terskaia Street-(incl.) the reinforced concrete railroad bridge across the Mokraia Mechetka River-farther southeast to the Volga River.

138th RD repelled repeated attacks by enemy forces of up to two battalions of infantry beginning in the morning on 16 November and occupied defenses along the line: the gully southeast of Volkhovstroevsk-500 meters along the eastern edge of the Barrikady Factory-and farther southeast to the Volga River.

95th RD defended the line: the block east of Mezenskaia Street-(incl.) Mashinnaia Street-the northern bank of the gully south of Granitnaia Street.

45th RD occupied defenses along Reztsovaia Street-the northern part of the Krasnyi Oktiabr' Factory and southwestward to the center of this factory.

39th Gds. RD defended from the center of the Krasnyi Oktiabr' Factory to the southeastern part of the factory, farther to the west, south of Vosstaniia Street to the gully, to the north 300 meters along Russkaia Derevnia Street, westward to Stanislavski Street, and southward along Mokhovaia Street and Severnaia and Ovrazhnaia Streets to the Bannyi Ravine.

284th RD occupied defenses along the southern bank of the Bannyi Ravine to the western part of Chernomorskaia and Tekhnicheskaia Streets, Hill 102.0, the northwestern part of the factory 800 meters southeast of Hill 102.0, along Artilleriiskaia Street to the southeastern part of this factory, and farther along Rezervuarnaia [Reservoir] Street to the Volga River.

92nd RB defended along the western and southern part of the factory (800 meters southeast of Hill 102.0).

13th Gds. RD defended the corner of Divizionnaia and Rezervuarnaia Streets, the eastern part of Nekrasovskaia Street, the large buildings on 2nd Naberezhnaia and Tambovskaia Streets, 9 January Square to the corner of Kievskaia and Respublikanskaia Streets, and farther southeast along the line of Orlovskaia Street to the Volga River.[204]

The 62nd Army's daily report echoed the information it passed to the Red Army General Staff but added: "Overnight, from among the cargo dropped by aircraft, the [138th] RD received 4 bails of food, 2 packages of 45mm shells, 2 packages of 82mm mortar rounds and urgently necessary medical supplies, PPSh rounds and hand grenades." More important still, the army reported, "during the night, the armored cutters nos. 11, 12, 13, 61, and 63 and the ferries 'Spartak,' 'Pugachev,' and 'Panfilov' brought across and delivered ammunition, foodstuffs, and reinforcements at the expense of the army's rear."[205]

In one of the most interesting reports during the day, after 138th Rifle Division described the day's action in its combat journal, someone appended a statement (in capital letters and probably after the fact) asserting that German forces were in as desperate circumstances as their own:

The enemy continued his accumulation of forces. 138th RD, holding on to its lines, repelled numerous attacks by small groups of enemy. Assistance, provided by our aircraft, which dropped cargo, was insignificant. There are no grenades or bullets. There is no food. The commander of the division established daily norms for each soldier—25 grams of rusks [bread crust], 12 grams of groats [buckwheat], and 5 grams of sugar.

The commander of the division requested the [army] commander undertake measures to ease the situation in the division in connection with the attack by the enemy we expected beginning on the morning of 17 November.

CLEARLY, THIS DAY WAS THE HIGHEST STAGE OF TENSION FOR 138TH RD. CLEARLY THE ENEMY, WHO WAS ALREADY IN NO CONDITION TO ATTACK WITH SUCH FEROCITY AS HE HAD ON 11 AND 13 NOVEMBER, WAS IN A SIMILAR STATE. THE ENEMY, APPARENTLY DUE TO THE STEADFASTNESS OF 138TH RD, WAS DEFINITELY BLED WHITE AND REQUIRED SEVERAL DAYS SO THAT HE COULD ONCE AGAIN CONDUCT OFFENSIVE OPERATIONS.[206]

Overnight on 16–17 November, Chuikov issued new orders to ensure that Gorishnyi's 95th and Liudnikov's 138th Rifle Divisions held their ground come what may by conducting counterattacks into the teeth of the German assault. This order read:

1. The enemy, after reaching the bank of the Volga River in the region east of Mezenskaia and having cut off the units of 138th RD, are gradually digging in before 95th RD's front with the aim to prevent the restoration of the front and a link up with 138th RD.

2. The Army is continuing to hold on to the positions it occupies and, while preventing a further enemy advance, will counterattack the enemy

in the region east of Mezenskaia with part of its forces on 17 November 1942.

The missions are the destruction of the enemy's units which have reached the Volga River and a link up with 138th RD.

3. 95th RD, with attached reinforcing units, will destroy the enemy in the region east of Mezenskaia-the oil tanks, restore 241st RR's front, and link up with the units of 138th RD with a counterattack at 1400 hours on 17 November 1942.

62nd Army's artillery group will support.

4. Artillery:

a) from 0700 to 1345 hours—the destruction of pillboxes and suppression of enemy firing points in the vicinity of the oil tanks east of Mezenskaia.

b) 1345–1400 hours—a fire raid on the forward edge of the enemy's defenses and a preparation for the attack.

c) 1400 hours—transfer of fires and suppression of the enemy's combat formations in the depth of the defenses (the beginning of the infantry attack).

5. GMCh [Guards-Mortar multiple-rocket launcher units]

a) 1200–1400 hours—the neutralization of the enemy's shock groups and reserves in the southeastern part of the Barrikady Factory.

b) 1400 hours—successive volleys against the forward edge in the vicinity of the oil tanks.

6. Begin the infantry attack at 1400 hours on 17 November 1942. . . .

Chuikov, Gurov, Krylov[207]

Mentioning no ground action whatsoever, the OKW's daily communiqué simply stated, "Bombers launched precise strikes against railroad communications east of the Volga River."[208] 24th Panzer Division seconded this view, reporting, "Apart from this lively artillery fire and infantry fire from light and heavy weapons along the entire sector, there was no enemy ground activity, and enemy air activity remained weak."[209] At 2200 hours the same day, however, in response to an order from Sixth Army, Lenski's panzer division directed preparations for a large-scale counterattack. Sixth Army ordered some of its armored and motorized units (14th and 24th Panzer Divisions) "to prepare themselves for quick extraction from their current positions and be ready to be shifted for counterattacks and mobile defense."[210]

Likewise, on 17 November, 62nd Army reported a strong German assault against Group Gorokhov's defenses at Rynok but only defensive actions elsewhere except for yet another attempt by 95th Rifle Division to break through and rescue Liudnikov's force east of the Barrikady Factory:

The army repelled attacks by the enemy and, simultaneously, fought to restore its position in the Mezenskaia region during the day.

The enemy conducted an attack on Rynok and the western outskirts of Spartanovka with a force of more than an infantry regiment and 18 tanks, and up to two battalions attacked the positions of 138th RD.

In the Rynok sector, the enemy succeeded in wedging into our defense. The fighting to restore the situation is continuing. Along the remaining attack axes, the enemy was driven back with heavy losses. . . .

138th RD fended off fierce attacks by an enemy force of up to two battalions and tanks and, in spite of the enemy's numerical superiority, repelled the attacks with heavy losses to the enemy by day's end.

95th RD, with the forces of 241st RR and 90th and 685th RRs, attacked the enemy in the region east of Mezenskaia at 1400 hours after an artillery preparation. Overcoming strong enemy resistance, 90th RR captured the oil tanks and advanced to the north with separate groups.

241st and 685th RRs captured the ravine 150 meters northeast of Mezenskaia, continuing the attack along the bank of the Volga. The enemy committed his reserves into the fighting. Fierce fighting is intensifying.

45th RD and 39th Gds. RD exchanged fire [with the enemy] on the grounds of the Krasnyi Oktiabr' Factory.

In the remaining sectors of the front, the units held onto their occupied positions while repelling attacks by small groups of enemy infantry.[211]

The OKH's daily operational report verified 62nd Army's report, stating, "In the city of Stalingrad, the enemy group encircled in the Leather Factory [Tannery] in the Kuporosnoe region was completely destroyed. New attempts by the enemy to break through to the fuel dump from the north failed. In the Rynok region north of the city, as a result of our units' attacks, the enemy was forced to abandon the locality. Essentially, combat actions did not occur in other sectors of the army's front."[212] At the same time, 24th Panzer Division, within the vital Krasnyi Oktiabr' Factory, asserted that "the course of the day passed quietly," although the Soviets did intensify their artillery and rocket fire, and 305th Infantry Division continued its house-to-house assaults east of the Barrikady Factory.[213]

Contrary to 62nd Army reports of heavy fighting in 138th Rifle Division's sector, which probably resulted from the breakdown in radio communications with the division, other than 95th Rifle Division's repeated counterattacks to break through to Liudnikov's island from the south the situation remained quiet along the front of Liudnikov's 138th. This was for good reason: If Seydlitz's attack on 20 November was to succeed, then Steinmetz's division—whose combat strength had fallen to 3,530 men, including only 1,600 infantry—clearly needed some rest and replenishment.[214]

This lull was indeed fortunate, because the situation in Liudnikov's division, as the 138th's daily report indicated, was becoming desperate:

The enemy continued the concentration of forces in the vicinity of Halls 14 and 15, the main mechanical shop, Houses Nos. 35 and 36, and, especially, 200 meters east of the central gate of the Barrikady Factory. During the day small groups of submachine gunners repeatedly tried to infiltrate to the Volga River on the left flank of the division. The 138th RD exchanged fire with the enemy during the day. The army command undertook measures to drop small quantities of cargo in by our PO-2 aircraft in the course of the day. However, of the thirteen packages dropped, only eight were received by 138th RD and the remainder fell among the enemy and into the Volga. There are no bullets, mines [mortar rounds], and food in the division.

The commander of the division considers the situation extremely difficult. Measures undertaken for the supply of food and ammunition on boats have been unsuccessful. By the end of the day, there were about 350 wounded in the vicinity of the CP of the division. The enemy, reaching the Volga River on both flanks, rakes the combat formation of the division, which occupies a defensive sector along a 400-meter front and to a depth of 300 meters, through and through with rifle and machine gun fire.

The Volga is swept day and night with concentrated rifle and machine gun fire and artillery and mortar fire. During the last five days, 138th RD has fought chiefly with trophy [captured] weapons and ammunition, and, in these difficult conditions, the division is holding on to its positions, but the enemy has been able to advance only 200 meters at a cost of exceptionally high losses.[215]

If it was quiet in Liudnikov's sector, the same was not the case to the south, where 90th Regiment had finally reinforced its parent 95th Rifle Division. There, in the vicinity of the ravine southeast of the Barrikady Factory and due east of the boundary between 14th Panzer Division's Group Seydel and 305th Infantry Division's 576th Regiment, Gorishnyi's 95th Rifle Division commenced the counterattack mandated by Chuikov the night before (see Map 96). Attacking at 1130 hours after several hours of artillery preparation, 1st Battalion, 90th Regiment, the 241st Regiment, and 193rd Rifle Division's composite 685th Regiment assaulted eastward toward the oil tanks. Unlike previous counterattacks, this one propelled the Soviets through the oil tanks and beyond the mouth of the ravine and inflicted heavy casualties on the defending Germans. However, because his forces also took heavy losses, Gorishnyi was unable to make the clean breakthrough to 138th Rifle Division's lines.[216]

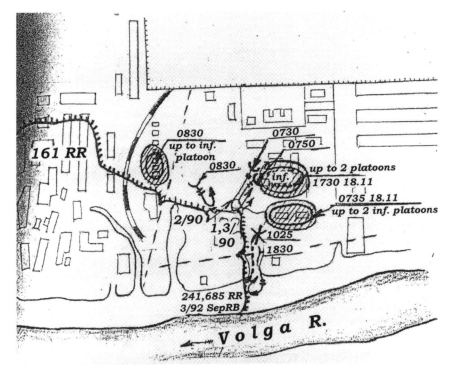

Map 96. 95th Rifle Division's dispositions, 2000 18 November 1942

The heaviest fighting on 17 November took place in the north, near Rynok, where 16th Panzer Division launched yet another assault to capture the stubborn Soviet strongpoint (see Map 60). Some of the division's officers and men considered such an attack pointless because the Soviets were clearly massing behind their front, their own division was worn out, and their division's weapons already dominated Rynok from all sides. Nevertheless, 16th Motorcycle Battalion and 2nd Battalion, 79th Grenadier Regiment, supported by 25 "painstakingly repaired" tanks, assaulted the defenses of Group Gorokhov's 124th Rifle Brigade at Rynok at 0400 hours on 17 November in a driving snowstorm.[217] The XIV Panzer Corps reported on the attack's progress at 1625 hours:

Along the Corps' eastern front, 16th Panzer Division attacked the village of Rynok from the north and west with 2 *kampfgruppen*. Both groups initially succeeded in penetrating into the village. Poor visibility and heavy defensive fire prevented both *kampfgruppen* from making contact with one another. A Russian counterattack, supported by 4 tanks, forced the *kampfgruppen* to withdraw from the northern and western edges of the village. Strong antitank and tank fire, as well as mines, caused numerous losses amongst our own panzers . . . After regrouping, the division renewed the attack at 1300 hours. Combat is still in progress.[218]

Although 16th Panzer Division reported suffering 122 casualties, including 19 dead, during the brief assault on the village, at 1800 hours Sixth Army ordered the division "to continue the attack against Rynok, with the objective of taking the village and bank of the Volga into possession on [18 November]."[219] When it tried to do so the next day, the attack became "hopelessly mired and could not be resumed without reinforcements."[220] Ultimately, the beleaguered German force clung to its positions until the evening of 19 November, when XIV Panzer Corps authorized it to withdraw. The 16th Panzer Division's history provides a fitting epitaph for the division's fight at Rynok, portraying the struggle elsewhere in the Stalingrad region in microcosm: "The operation of the division against Rynok had failed. The heavy losses had weakened its fighting power again. Already 4,000 of its bravest men were lying in the division's graveyard along the Frolow [Frolov]-Stalingrad railroad line. A vast field of crosses spread across the white steppe. At that moment, the battle for Stalingrad had entered into a new phase."[221]

As the fighting raged in Rynok and flared and sputtered elsewhere along Sixth Army's front, Hitler—in a measure of his increasing desperation—on 17 November cabled Paulus a new Führer order, which Sixth Army's operations officer dutifully passed along to the army's weary troops at 1315 hours on 17 November:

Announce the following order verbally to all commanders from army down to regiment fighting in Stalingrad inclusively:

"I am aware of the difficulties of the fighting in Stalingrad and of the decline in combat strengths. But the drift ice on the Volga poses even greater difficulties for the Russians. If we exploit this time span, we will save ourselves much blood later.

I therefore expect that the leadership and the troops will once more, as they often have in the past, devote their energy and spirit to at least getting through to the Volga at the gun factory and the metallurgical plant and taking these sections of the city.

The air force and artillery must do all in their power to prepare and support this offensive."[222]

Paulus endorsed this order with a comment: "I affirm that this order is a new impetus for our courageous forces"; he cabled Hitler in return, "I beg to report to the Führer that the commanders in Stalingrad and I are acting entirely in the sense of this order to exploit the Russians' weakness occasioned during the past several days by the drift ice on the Volga. The Führer's order will give the troops a fresh impetus."[223] Whether or not he agreed with his Führer, Paulus resolved to resume his offensive on 20 November.

Seydlitz, after assuring Hitler of his army's intent to continue the fight come what may, continued to reorganize his forces for what he hoped would be a successful assault on 20 November. As he did so, Sixth Army's forces continued some fighting, primarily to improve their positions in the Rynok sector and opposite Liudnikov's island east of the Barrikady Factory. As before, however, there were no indications that the existing stalemate was about to end.

In the most significant action on 18 November (other than the fighting around Rynok), 305th Infantry Division's 578th Regiment, spearheaded by 50th and 162nd Engineer Battalions and a squadron of 10 tanks from 24th Panzer Division and about 15 assault guns, conducted a meticulously planned assault beginning at 0400 hours, which first captured House No. 77, about 100 meters north of the Commissar's House, from 138th Rifle Division's 650th Regiment. Later in the day, the *kampfgruppe* pushed forward another 100 meters along the Volga's western banks before being halted at nightfall.[224]

138th Rifle Division described this fight in its report:

> In accordance with a decision by the commander of the division, responsibility for the left wing was given inclusively to the commander of 650th RR [Major F. I. Pecheniuk]. A group of Senior Lieutenant Petrenko, an army blocking detachment of NKVD Lieutenant Senchkovsky, and also a group of Captain Zorin was subordinated to the commander of 650th RR.
>
> The enemy began an attack at 0600 hours and, during the day, supported by artillery groups of more than a platoon and 5–7 tanks each, attacked the center and left wing of the division. Despite heavy losses, the enemy tried to reach the vicinity of the command post of the division. These attacks continued all day but each time were halted by the steadfastness and bravery of our soldiers.
>
> The defense preoccupied everyone, right up to the signalmen and the chiefs of staff of the regiments and the division. In light of the impossibility of evacuating the wounded and because of the shortages of medical supplies, the deaths from wounds increased.
>
> The situation of the division became more difficult, even catastrophic. There was no food as before, there was no ammunition, and we had less than half of our combat load of rifle bullets. Our radios did not operate, therefore, it became impossible to summon the fires of our artillery from the left bank of the Volga.[225]

62nd Army in its daily report described 138th Rifle Division's struggle and the action elsewhere along the army's front:

The army repelled attacks by the enemy against its right wing during the day and, in its previous positions, exchanged fire with the enemy in its remaining sectors.

During the day, the enemy repeatedly attacked our positions in the Rynok and the western outskirts of Spartanovka regions with the forces of an IR and tanks and the positions of 138th RD and 95th RD with forces of up to two battalions. All of the attacks were repelled by day's end with heavy losses to the enemy. Simultaneously, the enemy brought up reserves in the vicinity of the Barrikady Factory. Artillery and mortars conducted heavy fire on the combat formations of the forces.

The Northern Group, having repelled attacks by enemy infantry and tanks in a strength of more than an infantry regiment against Rynok and the western outskirts of Spartanovka, went over to a counterattack with part of its forces with the mission of restoring the situation in the Rynok sector. After a prolonged fight, the enemy was expelled from the northwestern outskirts of Rynok, and the situation was fully restored. On 17 and 18 November 1942, 800 [enemy] soldiers and officers and 11 tanks were destroyed, of which 9 burned. The remaining "bayonets" in the group: 124th RB—745, and 149th RB—475. The group urgently needs replenishment of ammunition and food.

138th RD repulsed an attack by an enemy force of up to two battalions and tanks. Bringing fresh troops forward, the enemy managed to push back the left wing of the division and occupy 3 buildings.

95th RD repelled an attack by more than a battalion in the vicinity of the oil tanks. 90th RR is holding on to the region of the oil tanks, where it is digging in. 241st RR and 685th RR are digging in along the line of the ravine 150 meters northeast of Mezenskaia.

45th RD and 39th Gds. RD are fighting with small groups of enemy infantry along their previous lines to improve their positions.

Along the remaining sectors of the front, the units are holding on to their positions, while repelling attacks by small groups of enemy infantry.[226]

At the end of the report, Chuikov related the good news that "replacements of 167 men and food and ammunition for the units were thrown across [the Volga] by one trip by the ferry 'Pugachev' and the armored cutters nos. 11, 12, 61, and 63. 400 wounded were evacuated."[227] He then added his already familiar order: "hold on to the positions you occupy," "prevent any further enemy advance," and "counterattack against the enemy with part of the forces and link up with the units of 138th RD."[228]

At this stage, however, as future events would indicate, such orders were merely academic. Despite the extreme privations suffered by Liudnikov's riflemen and the continuing frustrations of Gorishnyi's riflemen, they, as well as the remaining survivors of Chuikov's army, had already accomplished their mission. These desperate men had held their positions within the ruins of Stalingrad and, by doing so, bled Paulus's army white. By day's end on 18 November, as Sixth Army's condition report indicated, the cream of Sixth Army indeed lay severely wounded in the ruins of the shattered city (see Table 43).

The fact that there were no major changes in the condition of Sixth Army's combat forces fighting in Stalingrad city is no surprise: The damage to that army had already been done. What occurred in November simply confirmed the desperate state that the army had reached in October. That being said, 60th Motorized Division as a whole slipped farther to the "weak" side of "average," 389th and 79th Infantry Division turned more decisively "weak," and 94th and 305th Infantry Divisions remained "exhausted." From Paulus's perspective, the most positive indicator that his army might survive this bloodletting was the reviving strength of his panzer divisions. By Herculean efforts, the mechanics and mobile repair facilities of 14th, 16th, and 24th Panzer Divisions succeeded in restoring the tank strength of those divisions to roughly 50 armored vehicles each. On the negative side of the ledger, Paulus and his commander were perplexed by the Soviets' ability to dispatch a seemingly endless flow of reinforcements into the city's ruins in the form of fresh divisions and personnel replacements organized into dozens of march-battalions and companies. Neither Weichs nor Paulus could match such reinforcements.

Meanwhile, faint warnings of more ominous and dangerous developments rumbled just beyond the horizon. Nonetheless, in the wake of the heavy fighting during the second week of November, Gehlen's FHO issued a daily intelligence summary on 18 November that, even though it was thorough, exuded a distinct air of optimism. It began with a flat declaration: "In the region of the city of Stalingrad and to the north, the enemy has not succeeded in hindering our units' forward progress. In the Rumanian Third Army's sector, the enemy unsuccessfully attacked many points in the bridgehead southwest of Serafimovich. No major combat operations occurred in other sectors of the army group's front."[229] Elaborating, the report stated that Sixth Army had repelled "weak enemy attacks" in the southern sector of the Kuporosnoe region, at the metallurgical factory, and at the fuel dump and that the enemy had "not succeeded in hindering our forces' local progress east of the gun factory" and had been forced to "abandon a group of buildings" on the western outskirts of Rynok.[230]

In regard to the forces of Army Group B's Axis allies, Gehlen noted that Romanian Third Army had "beaten back" operations by several assault

Table 43. The Combat Rating of Infantry and Pioneer Battalions Subordinate to Sixth Army's Divisions Fighting in Stalingrad, 9–16 November 1942

	9 November	16 November
XIV PANZER CORPS		
3rd Motorized Division		
(3–4 infantry battalions)	3 medium strong	3 medium strong and 1 average
(1 pioneer battalion)	average	average
60th Motorized Division		
(6 infantry battalions)	1 medium strong, 1 average, 3 weak, and 1 exhausted	3 average, 2 weak, and 1 exhausted
(1 pioneer battalion)	weak	weak
16th Panzer Division		
(3–4 infantry battalions)	1 medium strong and 2 weak	1 medium strong, 1 average, and 2 weak
(1 pioneer battalion)	weak	weak
94th Infantry Division		
(7 infantry battalions)	2 weak and 5 exhausted	2 weak and 5 exhausted
(1 pioneer battalion)	average	average
LI ARMY CORPS		
24th Panzer Division		
(4 infantry battalions)	1 medium strong and 3 average	1 medium strong and 3 average
(1 pioneer battalion)	exhausted	medium strong
100th Jäger Division		
(5 infantry battalions)	2 medium strong and 3 weak	2 medium strong, 2 average, and 1 weak
(1 pioneer battalion)	average	average
305th Infantry Division		
(6 infantry battalions)	2 weak and 4 exhausted	2 weak and 4 exhausted
(1 pioneer battalion)	exhausted	exhausted
295th Infantry Division		
(7 infantry battalions)	1 average, 5 weak, and 1 exhausted	1 average, 5 weak, and 1 exhausted
(1 pioneer battalion)	weak	weak
389th Infantry Division		
(6 infantry battalions)	4 average and 2 weak	2 average and 4 weak
(1 pioneer battalion)	weak	weak
79th Infantry Division		
(6 infantry battalions)	1 average and 5 weak	6 weak
(1 pioneer battalion)	average	exhausted

Table 43. (continued)

	9 November	16 November
14th Panzer Division		
(2 infantry battalions)	2 strong	2 strong
(1 pioneer battalion)	average	average
71st Infantry Division		
(7 infantry battalions)	5 average and 2 weak	5 average and 2 weak
(1 pioneer battalion)	weak	weak
Totals:		
62–64 infantry battalions	2 strong, 8 medium strong, 15 average, 26 weak, and 11 exhausted	2 strong, 7 medium strong, 18 average, 26 weak, and 11 exhausted
12 pioneer battalions	5 average, 5 weak, and 2 exhausted	1 medium strong, 4 average, 5 weak, and 2 exhausted

Source: Florian *Freiherr* von und zu Aufsess, "Betr.: Zustand der Divisionen, Armee – Oberkommando 6, Abt. Ia, A. H. Qu., 09. November 1942, 16.20 Uhr" and "Betr.: Zustand der Divisionen, Armee – Oberkommando 6, Abt. Ia, A. H. Qu., 16. November 1942, 12.00 Uhr,"in *Die Anlagenbander zu den Kriegstagebuchern der 6. Armee vom 14.09.1942 bis 24.11.1942, Band I* (Schwabach: January 2006), 248–253 and 285–290.

detachments on its right wing, specifically the attacks by up to three enemy battalions east of Kalmykovskii, at Blinov, and to the northwest, and that combat operations did not occur in the sectors of the Italian Eighth, Hungarian Second, and German Second Armies, except for what he termed "usual" reconnaissance activities and failed attacks by assault parties.[231]

Finally, in its section on "Enemy Groupings," Gehlen's report noted that 270th Rifle and 46th Guards Rifle Divisions had just arrived in 6th Army's reserve north of the Don River and detected the repositioning of 17th Mechanized Brigade in Stalingrad Front's reserve southeast of the city, 25th Tank Corps in the Voronezh region, and 44th Guards Rifle Division in 48th Army's reserve near Livny. Although these identifications were not causes for alarm, Gehlen also reported the possible transfer of 9th Guards Rifle Division from 21st Army along the Don to the Belyi region southwest of the Rzhev salient. This seemed to indicate that the Soviets were actually moving troops away from the Stalingrad region and into the Rzhev region, possibly for an offensive west of Moscow.[232]

Flatly contradicting the clearly innocuous contents of his 18 November report, Gehlen later declared in his memoirs: "While the Russian troops confronting the Rumanian Third Army continued to take up their assault positions (according to a deserter, three new tank brigades were being brought into the line opposite the Rumanian VI Army Corps), I reported on the eighteenth that a simultaneous attack from Beketovka, south of Stalingrad, could not be excluded."[233]

Based on the reports his FHO prepared from 9–18 November, Gehlen later accused Hitler and other senior German commanders of "committing basic command errors" by ignoring his warnings of an impending Soviet attack. Retrospectively, for example, in a personal document ostensibly prepared on 10 February 1943, he wrote: "From 9 November onward, our intelligence digest indicated a major offensive was being prepared against the Rumanian Third Army, and, at about the same time, we repeatedly warned of preparations to attack the Italian Eighth and the Hungarian Second Armies, and Voronezh."[234] However, careful examination of FHO intelligence assessments during this period indicates that although they did indeed postulate possible Soviet offensives, particularly against Rumanian Third Army, Gehlen's analysts consistently qualified their warnings with strong caveats about the strength and timing of the attacks. Later still, when Gehlen once again blamed Hitler and these commanders in his memoirs, he conveniently failed to mention his 6 November report, which argued that the Soviets would most likely conduct their main effort against German forces in the Rzhev salient to the north.

Whether or not Gehlen provided Hitler and his senior commanders with sufficient warnings about future Soviet offensive activity, the fact remains that—from the perspective of those commanders who had engaged and defeated countless offensives by numerically superior Soviet forces in the past and had done so with relative ease—it was one thing to predict a Soviet offensive and an altogether different thing to fear its consequences. Because their forces had detected and defeated Soviet offensives on numerous occasions since late August both north and south of Stalingrad, usually with devastating impact on the attacking Red Army forces, in their eyes there was no reason why they should not do so in the future. Even so, remaining ever prudent in the face of Gehlen's qualified warnings, and despite their obvious overconfidence, Weichs and Paulus did take some precautionary measures, albeit modest, to ensure that history would indeed repeat itself should the Soviets attack.

CONCLUSIONS

Sixth Army's struggle for the southern half of Stalingrad's factory district during November was a war of utter and frightening attrition. With maneuver a thing of the past, and despite being reinforced by 79th Infantry Division, the soldiers of Seydlitz's LI Corps had no choice but to engage the remnants of Chuikov's 62nd Army frontally in a brutal contest for possession of the ruins of the Barrikady and Krasnyi Oktiabr' Factories, a fight during which quarter was neither asked for nor received. For a fresh and rested force, this would

Colonel I. I. Liudnikov, commander of 138th Rifle Division, at his command post.

Soldiers of 138th Rifle Division defending in buildings in "Liudnikov's Island"

Soviet communications trenches in "Liudnikov's Island."

A Soviet mortar crew defending "Liudnikov's Island."

Soldiers of 138th
Rifle Division
leave a bunker to
repulse a German
attack during the
fight for "Liudni-
kov's Island."

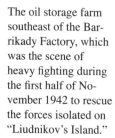

The oil storage farm
southeast of the Bar-
rikady Factory, which
was the scene of
heavy fighting during
the first half of No-
vember 1942 to rescue
the forces isolated on
"Liudnikov's Island."

have been no mean task; for an exhausted one, it was a fight the Germans could not win.

The ensuing struggle was a battle conducted by infantrymen and sappers, in groups of battalion-size or, more often, company-size, supported by individual or small groups of assault guns and, if they were available, tanks and artillery pieces firing over open sights. These assault parties, shock groups, and *kampfgruppen* fought bitterly for days over single buildings and blocks of buildings, often spending hours exchanging fire and assaults for separate rooms, single bunkers and foxholes, cellar positions, and perhaps a single twisted piece of useless machinery. In fighting such as this, casualties were high, and units already as much as 90 percent understrength quickly lost all vestiges of combat effectiveness.

Seydlitz conducted his assault on the Barrikady and Krasnyi Oktiabr' Factories with the surviving infantrymen of his 305th and 79th Infantry Divisions massed abreast and with the remaining panzer-grenadiers of his 14th and 24th Panzer Divisions—now panzer formations in name only because of their paucity of armor—fighting as common infantry either between corps or protecting his corps' flanks. After penetrating into the Krasnyi Oktiabr' Factory in one dramatic but exhausting thrust on 23 and 24 October, thereafter the struggle in this factory and the region east of the Barrikady Factory degenerated into a three-week slugfest, characterized by repeated brief offensive impulses punctuated by attacks and counterattacks by both sides, with progress seldom measured in more than tens of meters. This sort of fighting quickly exhausted the forces on both sides, only reinforcing the state of stalemate.

The assault by Stalingrad Front's 64th Army south of Stalingrad on and after 26 October added to Paulus's miseries by further stretching his army's defenses and drawing part of his dwindling armor and reserves away from his main effort. Although LI Corps skillfully exploited its reinforcing engineer battalions to record significant gains on and after 11 November, Eremenko's commitment of another fresh division, 45th Rifle, into the fight negated the impact of Seydlitz's reinforcements and ensured that the stalemate would continue as long as required.

From the *Stavka's* perspective, the necessity of holding out as long as required meant that Chuikov's army had to defend its shrunken bridgehead until it could mount its long-awaited counteroffensive. As Sixth Army persisted in its assaults against Stalingrad's shattered factories, just as German intelligence reports hinted, the Red Army was indeed up to something. Despite the Germans' apparent confusion over exactly what it entailed, German field commanders—based on their previous experiences—believed that their forces could cope with any eventuality. The question was, however, whether or not the armies of their Axis allies, who were now responsible for defending a large sector along the Don River, would be able to do so as well. By 18 November Weichs and Paulus had taken measures they deemed sufficient to ensure that these armies could perform as expected.

Although German soldiers routinely described the fighting in the northern half of the factory district as hellish, the struggle for the Barrikady and Krasnyi Oktiabr' Factories in November multiplied the horrors, made even worse by the appalling attrition among the German ranks. Describing the attrition in 24th Panzer Division, one soldier said, "According to 'latrine rumours,' often the only source of information for the simple *Landsers* [infantrymen]," his entire regiment had shriveled away to "no more than two companies strong."[235] Countering this declined morale (while coincidentally explaining why German generals were still convinced victory was at hand), Lenski, the division commander, asserted that "education will harden and strengthen [the replacements'] combat morale by emphasizing our feelings of superiority over the Russians."[236]

This air of superiority, however, would soon be tested on a new battlefield—the ruins of the Krasnyi Oktiabr' Factory, which 24th Panzer Division's war diary described as a sector that, "with extremely tangled factory ruins, giant craters, frequent Russian activity, small distance between both opposing fronts and our own negligible combat strengths," still "proves to be difficult."[237] Thus when its panzer-grenadiers assaulted the factory's Hall 4, they found it "a nightmare for any attacker with a confusion of iron parts, remnants of walls, destroyed machinery, twisted girders and metal as well as general rubble" that simply "bewildered" the attackers.[238] Once the heavy fighting in the factory had ended, "the most painful fact for the Germans was that the Russians had not been finished off and were still stubbornly holding their tiny bridgehead in devastated Stalingrad," and it did not help morale to understand that "this [the ruins of Krasnyi Oktiabr'] was where they would spend their winter."[239]

To the north, by early November the soldiers in 16th Panzer Division were calling the Rynok-Spartanovka region "little Verdun" because "there was hardly a square meter that had not been churned up by bombs and shells."[240] Although it was "impossible to deploy panzers in this area," and the enemy's resistance was "still unbroken," a company noncommissioned officer in 94th Infantry Division claimed that "the morale of the men was still high, and we all had complete confidence in our leadership."[241] Days later, after his division's assault failed to break the Soviets' grip on the shrinking bridgehead, the same soldier remarked:

> What the men in the forward line had to perform almost bordered on the superhuman. Most of them still lacked winter clothing. . . . They squatted in fox-holes with only their *Zeltbahne* [shelter halves] as protection

against the damp and cold. There, the hours were an eternity. Many of them emerged from battle with parts of their uniforms shredded and then said laconically, "Never mind. Better the rags than my bones!"

I knew from experience and completely understood the men. And I was sure of one thing: everything we experienced would later be paid for with our health—if we were lucky enough to survive the war at all.[242]

Chuikov's beleaguered soldiers shared these sentiments—in spades. Symptomatic of their plight, on 13 November NKVD Major V. T. Smorodinsky, deputy chief of the NKVD's 2nd Special Section and Colonel Selevanovsky's colleague, presented his chief in Moscow with yet another report on morale and what he termed "anti-Soviet behavior" within Chuikov's 62nd Army based on the censors' review of soldiers' letters. A soldier named Khovsky, who worked in the All-Union Lenin Communist Union of Youth, wrote:

I returned from the front today. The situation at the front is very difficult. Thanks to their strong organization and superior weaponry, the Germans will squeeze us to the end. In my opinion, Hitler will take Moscow this year and take it rather easily if there is no second front. The Germans dominate the skies and bomb relentlessly. Obviously, the Germans will have Stalingrad within a couple of days. . . . Apparently, thanks to our weakness and poor leadership, Hitler will rule over our land.[243]

Another soldier, rifleman A. V. Bakshaevoi, who was lying in a field hospital, added:

Our regiment was smashed in two days. The dead and wounded are too numerous to heed, and capture my heart. To describe everything to you would require a large quantity of paper. What is going on here at the front? The Germans strike so that there is no escape anywhere. We have treachery everywhere. They feed us once every three days in the rear and at the front, and we are never full. Here in the field hospital they feed us two times a day. They give us 600 grams [21 ounces] of bread, bad soup, and a little kasha. Somehow, the women and children manage to live on, thanks to the Lord, evidently by sheer luck.[244]

Finally, sharing his despair with his mother while reflecting on what had occurred weeks before, a guards rifleman emphasized the politics of the situation and his apparent foxhole conversion:

Yes, dear mother, there was a major battle here from 18–20 September, and it is now continuing. The offensive on this front began on 18 September, and the "mincing-machine" was effective. Many were hacked to pieces during these 2–3 days, blood flowed and all of this for what? Because of glory, the authorities and the wealth of some small group of people, nevertheless, as the popular Russian proverb says, "An eye for an eye and blood for blood," and "One must reap as one has sown." For the peoples' suffering, for the bloodshed, and for the widowed, the orphaned and so forth, soon the organizers of this war will pay with their heads and will begin, as was said in days of old, "the retribution of God." Yes, dear mother, after the several days I have spent here, 15–20 days, as they say, they have completely regenerated me, and now I have become entirely different than I was earlier. Only now do I understand all of the politics of this war, for what and whom we pour out our blood and lay down our heads and on what all of our loans, assemblies, donations, and taxes are spent. All of this money is spent on our heads and on our flowing blood and, therefore, not for the peaceful construction of our Motherland. I'll be damned if, upon my return home, I will pay even a single kopeck in loans, donations, etc. Better I spend this money on drink, give it to the destitute, or, finally, throw it in the toilet but never give it in donations. I ask you, go to church for me, spend some time in prayer for me . . . , and burn some candles in front of the icons. Pray to God for the rapidest end to this war, for the suffering Russian people, and for a new peace.[245]

Although his report focused only on the negative, there is no doubt that the excerpts Smorodinsky chose to share with his superiors were symptomatic of the many conflicting moods present throughout 62nd Army's ranks. Regardless of the state of morale of Chuikov's soldiers, thanks to Eremenko's support 62nd Army managed to maintain its tenuous grip on its shrinking bridgeheads in Stalingrad city and the factory district. Despite the battle of attrition, Chuikov's army was able to report that it still defended the city with a force of 35,377 men on 20 November (see Table 44).[246]

EPILOGUE

As Paulus's Sixth Army expended the last vestiges of its rapidly diminishing strength in the brutal, futile struggle over the ruins of Stalingrad's factory district, Stalin, his senior military leaders in the *Stavka*, and the Red Army's *front* commanders were formulating plans for a massive counteroffensive designed to render the Germans' plight utterly superfluous. Set against the backdrop of what had occurred during Operation Barbarossa the year before—especially along the Tikhvin, Moscow, and Rostov axes in late autumn

Table 44. The Personnel Strength of 62nd Army's Rifle Formations Fighting in Stalingrad City on 20 November 1942

- 13th Guards Rifle Division – 5,201 men
- 37th Guards Rifle Division – 2,194 men
- 39th Guards Rifle Division – 2,770 men
- 45th Rifle Division – 4,696 men
- 95th Rifle Division – 2,078 men
- 112th Rifle Division – 659 men
- 138th Rifle Division – 1,673 men
- 193rd Rifle Division – 1,734 men
- 284th Rifle Division – 4,696 men
- 308th Rifle Division – 1,727 men
- 42nd Rifle Brigade – 294 men
- 92nd Rifle Brigade – 3,637 men
- 115th Rifle Brigade – 271 men
- 124th Rifle Brigade – 2,898 men
- 149th Rifle Brigade – 848 men
- **Total – 35,377 men**
- Total strength of 62nd Army – 41,199 men

Source: Isaev, *Stalingrad*, 248–249.

1941—Stalin had been trying to mount a counteroffensive since mid-July 1942, when he had unleashed his three new tank armies in an attempt to halt Hitler's juggernaut across southern Russia. After the Soviets' July counteroffensive failed so dramatically at Voronezh and in the Great Bend of the Don, Stalin tried to launch new counteroffensives—actually counterstrokes with distinctly more limited aims—first from the Kotluban' and Erzovka regions northwest of the city, and later from the Beketovka region to the south. These included counterstrokes on:

- 23–29 August by the Stalingrad Front's Groups Kovalenko and Shtevnev in the Kotluban' region;
- 3–12 September by the Stalingrad Front's 4th Tank, 24th, 1st Guards, and 66th Armies, under Zhukov's control, in the entire sector between the Don and Volga Rivers;
- 18 September–2 October by the Stalingrad Front's 1st Guards, 24th, and 66th Armies in the Kotluban' region;
- 29 September–7 October by the Stalingrad Front's 57th, 51st, and 64th Armies in the Beketovka and lake regions south of Stalingrad;
- 20–26 October by the Don Front's 24th and 66th Armies in the Kotluban' region;
- 24 October–2 November by the Stalingrad Front's 64th Army in the Kuporosnoe region.

Although these counterstrokes did indeed ultimately weaken and slow Sixth Army's assault on Stalingrad, they failed to achieve much more. As a result, Stalin and the Soviet military leadership became convinced of the futility of attacking in such close proximity to Stalingrad. But on 9 October Eremenko presented to the *Stavka* a bold plan that suggested a far broader envelopment operation to destroy German forces throughout the Stalingrad region. Thereafter, Stalin and his key military advisers—reacting to Eremenko's suggestions—focused their efforts on implementing a more ambitious plan. Throughout the remainder of October and the first few weeks of November they did exactly that, in the process giving birth to Plan Uranus: the encirclement and destruction of German Sixth Army throughout the Stalingrad region. In fact, the *Stavka* had completed the planning for Operation Uranus, as well as the companion Operation Mars in the Rzhev region west of Moscow, by early November. The details of this offensive planning are the subject of volume 3 in this series. The important point is that even though German intelligence organizations detected the indicators of Soviet offensive planning, by no means did they comprehend its full scope.

In the wake of the *Stavka*'s strenuous efforts over the previous three weeks to prepare its forces along the Don River northwest of Stalingrad and west of the Volga River south of Stalingrad for decisive counteroffensive action, on 8 November Zhukov dispatched messages to Eremenko and Rokossovsky informing them the counteroffensive would begin on 13 November. Addressed "Personally to Ivanov [the code-name of Eremenko]" and "Personally to Dontsov [the code-name of Rokossovsky]," these cables read, "The 13th is set as the date of the resettlement."[247] The word he used—*pereselenie* (meaning "resettlement" or "move")—was the code-name used by Stalin and the *Stavka* when referring to Uranus. Although the two *front* commanders knew precisely what this code-name meant, there is no evidence that either Chuikov or Shumilov, his colleague in 64th Army, realized what was about to occur.

In addition to underscoring uncertainty on the part of the senior Soviet military leadership regarding precisely when they would be able to begin their new counteroffensives, these messages also justified Gehlen's reluctance to predict when and where the counteroffensives would occur. Exercising their discretion, Zhukov and Vasilevsky ultimately ordered Southwestern Front, as well as Don Front's 65th Army, to begin their assaults on 19 November, and Stalingrad Front to attack on 20 November—decisions that Stalin immediately approved.[248]

As heavy fighting persisted over the ruins of Stalingrad's northern factory district, Stalin—at 1310 hours on 15 November—dispelled all doubt regarding the offensive's timing, by cabling Zhukov (whose code-name was "Konstantinov"):

You can set the day for the resettlement of Fedorov [Vatutin] and Ivanov [Eremenko] at your discretion and subsequently report back to me upon arrival in Moscow. If the thought occurs to you for either of the two to begin the resettlement one or two days earlier or later, I authorize you to decide that matter too at your own discretion.

Vasil'ev [Stalin][249]

Within four days, this brief message would put the confidence of German commanders in the invincibility of their forces to the ultimate test.

CHAPTER 10

Conclusions

THE BATTLE IN STALINGRAD

The intense fighting in Stalingrad's suburbs during the first half of September 1942 set the pattern for the more desperate struggle yet to come. Beset by desperate and ruthless—and costly—counterstrokes from Zhukov's armies in the Kotluban' and Erzovka regions, Paulus's Sixth Army set about capturing the city itself. Convinced that Hitler would employ whatever forces were necessary to seize the city, Stalin, Zhukov, and Eremenko decided to use Chuikov's 62nd and Shumilov's 64th Armies as meat grinders to chew up the attacking German forces in a battle of attrition while they formulated plans for a decisive counteroffensive. In essence, the two Soviet armies became sacrificial bodies whose sole function was to lure combat-ready German forces into the city and, once they were there, sap their strength in the kind of street combat for which German soldiers were neither trained nor accustomed to fighting. By staying close to the German attackers and contesting every block, the Soviet soldiers deprived the Germans of their greatest advantages: firepower and maneuver.

Meanwhile, the struggle in the Kotluban' and Erzovka regions north of the city fulfilled its deadly role by tying down Sixth Army's VIII Army and XIV Panzer Corps and preventing them from reinforcing the fight inside the city.

Although the Germans successfully defeated repeated Soviet assaults in the Kotluban' and Erzovka regions, that fighting adversely affected Sixth Army's fortunes in two important respects. First, in addition to slowing Paulus's initial advance on Stalingrad significantly, it disrupted his offensive plan by preventing his army's northern pincer, Wietersheim's XIV Panzer Corps, from taking part in the assault on the city's factory district. This, in turn, thwarted the German attempt to capture Stalingrad from the march. Second, the repeated victories of Sixth Army's XIV Panzer and VIII Army Corps north of the city were Pyrrhic and, combined with Fourth Panzer Army's later successes in repelling 64th Army's attacks south of the city, lulled German commanders into complacency by convincing them that they could defeat Soviet attacks, counterstrokes, and counteroffensives whenever and wherever they occurred.

Thus, by 26 September the battle for the city had degenerated into a painfully slow, grinding, and immensely costly block-to-block and building-to-building slugging match between Paulus's and Chuikov's troops. German forces clawed their way through the city's streets—but only from the west and south. Stalin's decision to defend the city deprived the Germans of their traditional advantages of mobility, maneuver, and precise, overwhelming, and deadly artillery fire and air support, forcing them to gnaw through Chuikov's defenses in a battle that resembled the fighting on the Somme and at Verdun in 1916 more than it did the familiar blitzkrieg war of the previous three summers. Although it was forced upon them by Hitler, Weichs's and Paulus's decision to take Stalingrad by storm negated all of the Germans' traditional advantages and committed Sixth Army to a struggle it could not win, especially because the issue of who possessed Stalingrad was secondary to the *Stavka*'s principal aim: mounting a general counteroffensive to destroy Paulus's forces.

Regardless of its ultimate outcome, the fighting in Stalingrad was only one element in the strategy that Stalin and his *Stavka* had been pursuing since late July 1942: halt, or at least slow, the momentum of the German advance sufficiently to permit the Red Army to conduct a massive counteroffensive against Axis forces when they became overextended, which the Soviet leadership deemed was inevitable. This strategy had failed to produce victory in late July, August, and early September simply because, at critical moments, German Army Group B was able to restore momentum to Sixth Army's advance despite the Red Army's frequent counterstrokes. By mid-September, however, Hitler's decision to seize Stalingrad by storm stripped Sixth Army of any momentum and handed it over to the Red Army. From the perspective of Stalin and his *Stavka*, the coldhearted sacrifice of Chuikov's 50,000 men in the streets and ruins of Stalingrad—plus whatever reinforcements were required to keep his army operational—was a small price to pay for victory by the million-plus men who would conduct the Red Army's anticipated counteroffensive.

Each piece in the mosaic of military operations taking place after 26 September played a vital role in this strategy. Paulus's assault in Stalingrad committed Sixth Army to a paralyzing set-piece battle. At best, this could produce a Pyrrhic victory and was bound to sap the army's strength and force it to weaken its defenses in other key sectors, for example, by replacing veteran German troops with green and inexperienced Italian and Romanian units. The brutally repetitive Soviet offensives in the Kotluban' and Erzovka regions continued to disrupt the German plan for capturing Stalingrad quickly and bloodlessly by depriving Paulus of his planned northern pincer—XIV Panzer Corps—and did enough damage to his army's VIII Army Corps that Paulus was left with no choice but to divert precious forces earmarked for the battle in Stalingrad (113th Infantry Division) to bolster the defenses on his northern flank.

Once locked in deadly urban warfare, Sixth Army's shock groups suffered so many casualties that Paulus was forced to send a steady stream of fresh divisions into the meat grinder, again at the expense of the defenses on Army Group B's left wing. All the while, the armored strength of Paulus's army—the motive force that had propelled it to Stalingrad in the first place—dwindled dramatically, once again raising the terrible specter of catastrophic defeat when and if the Red Army learned to employ effectively its seemingly endless supply of tanks and tank crews.

Within this context, Paulus employed 24th Panzer Division in one last vestige of maneuver war to penetrate and seize, first, the southern part of Stalingrad city and, second, the western half of the Krasnyi Oktiabr' and Barrikady villages in Stalingrad's northern factory district, during the second half of September. Meanwhile, other forces encircled Soviet forces in the Orlovka salient and captured about half of Mamaev Kurgan. However, attrition finally negated maneuver, leaving 24th Panzer Division's tanks unable to complete their task. As a result, Paulus reinforced his shock group fighting in the factory district with yet another panzer division (the 14th from Fourth Panzer Army) and 389th Infantry Division after its struggle to seize Orlovka. Operating as Group Jänecke, this force managed to sweep southward and capture most of the Barrikady Factory in late October before it, too, succumbed to exhaustion.

The struggle in Stalingrad's northern factory district degenerated steadily and successively into spasmodic fights for workers' settlements and factories, for blocks of buildings and parts of factories, for individual buildings, streets, factory halls, and ravines, and, finally, for separate floors and rooms of buildings and distinct parts of each ravine and gully. With his army bleeding to death, Paulus had no choice but to repeatedly halt his advance throughout October and November to muster forces adequate enough to continue fighting. In this fashion, he fed six relatively fresh divisions into the struggle—389th and 94th Infantry, 14th Panzer and 100th Jäger, 305th Infantry, and finally 79th Infantry—at the expense of weakening his own left wing and that of Army Group B. By November, with no more divisions available, Paulus cannibalized other divisions by taking away their engineer battalions. All the while, Sixth Army carefully documented the devastating attrition affecting its once superb combat capabilities (see Table 45).

Thus, between 14 September and 16 November Paulus's forces fighting in the vicinity of the city received as reinforcements three full infantry divisions (100th Jäger and 305th and 79th Infantry) with 23 infantry battalions. This should have increased the strength of German forces in this region from 59 to 82 battalions. However, because of attrition and the resulting necessity

Table 45. The Combat Rating of Infantry and Pioneer Battalions Subordinate to Sixth Army's Divisions Fighting in Stalingrad, 14 September–16 November 1942

	14 September	16 November
XIV PANZER CORPS		
3rd Motorized Division		
(5–4 infantry battalions)	2 medium strong, 2 average, and 1 weak	3 medium strong and 1 average
(1 pioneer battalion)	weak	average
60th Motorized Division		
(7–6 infantry battalions)	1 medium strong and 6 average	3 average, 2 weak, and 1 exhausted
(1 pioneer battalion)	average	weak
16th Panzer Division		
(5–4 infantry battalions)	3 medium strong and 2 average	1 medium strong, 1 average, and 2 weak
(1 pioneer battalion)	average	weak
94th Infantry Division		
(7 infantry battalions)	7 medium strong	2 weak and 5 exhausted
(1 pioneer battalion)	average	average
LI ARMY CORPS		
71st Infantry Division		
(8–7 infantry battalions)	8 weak	5 average and 2 weak
(1 pioneer battalion)	average	weak
295th Infantry Division		
(7 infantry battalions)	2 medium strong, 3 average, and 2 weak	1 average, 5 weak, and 1 exhausted
(1 pioneer battalion)	average	average
389th Infantry Division		
(6 infantry battalions)	1 medium strong, 3 average, and 2 weak	2 average and 4 weak
(1 pioneer battalion)	average	weak
100th Jäger Division		
(5 infantry battalions)	**(not fighting in the city)**	2 medium strong, 2 average, and 1 weak
(1 pioneer battalion)		average
305th Infantry Division		
(6 infantry battalions)	**(not fighting in the city)**	2 weak and 4 exhausted
(1 pioneer battalion)		exhausted
79th Infantry Division		
(6 infantry battalions)	**(not fighting in the city)**	6 weak
(1 pioneer battalion)		exhausted
24th Panzer Division		
(4 infantry battalions)	2 medium strong and 2 average	1 medium strong and 3 average
(1 pioneer battalion)	average	medium strong

Table 45. (continued)

	14 September	16 November
XXXXVIII PANZER CORPS		
14th Panzer Division		
(4–2 infantry battalions)	4 medium strong	2 strong
(1 pioneer battalion)	average	average
29th Motorized Division		
(6 infantry battalions)	3 medium strong and	**(not fighting in the city)**
	3 average	
(1 pioneer battalion)	strong	
Totals:		
59–64 infantry battalions	25 medium strong,	2 strong, 7 medium strong,
	21 average, and 13 weak	18 average, 26 weak, and
		11 exhausted
10–12 pioneer battalions	1 strong, 8 average, and	1 medium strong,
	1 weak	4 average, 5 weak, and
		2 exhausted

Source: Florian *Freiherr* von und zu Aufsess, "Betr.: Zustand der Divisionen, Armee – Oberkommando 6, Abt. Ia, A. H. Qu., 14. September 1942, 12.35 Uhr" and "Betr.: Zustand der Divisionen, Armee – Oberkommando 6, Abt. Ia, A. H. Qu., 16. November 1942, 12.00 Uhr," in *Die Anlagenbander zu den Kriegstagebuchern der 6. Armee vom 14.09.1942 bis 24.11.1942, Band I* (Schwabach: January 2006), 12–14 and 284–290.

for consolidating ruined battalions to form new combat-ready ones, the real strength of Sixth Army's forces increased by only five battalions (from 59 to 64). Underscoring the debilitating effect on Sixth Army, and despite all the replacements it had received, the number of infantry battalions in the army rated "strong" or "medium strong" *decreased* from 25 to 9, even as the number rated "weak" or "exhausted" *increased* from 13 to 37. Overall, the combat rating of Sixth Army's forces in the region decreased from slightly above "average" to slightly above "weak." Thus, Stalin's and Eremenko's meat grinders achieved the intended goal.

Meanwhile, Chuikov's 62nd Army also suffered appalling attrition as its bridgehead on the Volga's western bank inexorably shrank. Chuikov lost the factory workers' villages and Orlovka by early October, the Tractor Factory by mid-October, and half of the Barrikady and Krasnyi Oktiabr' Factories by the end of October. Yet the mission of 62nd Army was to defend tenaciously, to counterattack whenever and wherever possible, and, if necessary, to die in place. In doing so, its only mission was to inflict as much damage as it could on Paulus's army. Therefore, his army did indeed shrink, first with the loss of its forces fighting in southern Stalingrad, then those defending Mamaev Kurgan, the workers' villages, and Orlovka, and finally many of those defending the factories themselves. To ensure that Chuikov's army accomplished its mission, the *Stavka* and Eremenko gave renewed force to the Stalingrad meat grinder, including an array of divisions and brigades in succession that, although imposing on paper, were formations bloodied in previous fighting, often without adequate weaponry, and barely strong enough to keep Chuikov's attrition machine functioning.

In effect, what happened to Paulus's army in October and November replicated the pattern of late July, August, and September. At the most critical points during its advance, Sixth Army simply lacked the strength necessary to overcome, defeat, and destroy the opposing Soviet forces decisively without additional reinforcements. And by mid-November, the Germans had reached the bottom of their replacement barrel.

Meanwhile, the *Stavka* exploited the idea of attrition by reorganizing and positioning its forces for more decisive offensive operations against Army Group B's forces in the Stalingrad region. Acting on suggestions made by Eremenko, it formed the new Don and Southwestern Fronts along the Don River northwest of Stalingrad, reinforced those *fronts* with fresh forces, and ordered both to prepare for future offensives from the Serafimovich and Kletskaia bridgeheads. At the most critical junctures during the fighting for Stalingrad's factory district, these *fronts*—together with the Soviet armies south of Stalingrad—increased the stress on Sixth Army by renewing their counterstrokes north and south of the city.

Paulus's struggle in the southern half of Stalingrad's factory district during the final week of October and the first half of November degenerated into a desperate and terrible fight for both sides. No longer able to maneuver, Seydlitz's LI Corps engaged the remnants of Chuikov's 62nd Army frontally in a brutal contest of infantry and engineers striving to pry Chuikov's defenders from the ruins of the Barrikady and Krasnyi Oktiabr' Factories like rats from their holes. No quarter was requested nor received. For a fresh and rested force, this would have been no mean task; for an exhausted one, it was a fight they could not win. In this struggle German infantrymen and sappers fought in groups of battalion-size and, more often, company-size, supported by individual or small groups of assault guns and, if they were available, tanks, as well as artillery pieces firing over open sights. *Kampfgruppen*, shock groups, and assault parties spent days fighting for single buildings or blocks of buildings, struggling for hours over separate rooms, single bunkers and foxholes, cellars, and twisted pieces of destroyed machinery. The sheer attrition took a terrible toll on both sides, quickly depriving units of their combat effectiveness.

During this struggle, Chuikov's army held out as long as required, meaning that its shattered remnants, amounting to less than a full-strength division, had to defend a shrunken bridgehead until the Red Army could mount its long-awaited counteroffensive. As for Paulus's Sixth Army, like its parent

Army Group B, it indeed suspected that the Red Army was up to something, but it could never identify what that was. Compounding their confusion over Soviet intent, German field commanders, based on their previous experiences, firmly believed that they could deal with any eventuality.

THE INFLUENCE OF COMBAT ON THE DISTANT FLANKS

Given the strategy that Stalin adopted throughout Operation Blau, the battles waged elsewhere along the Soviet-German front from September through November 1942 were inexorably intertwined with the fighting along the Stalingrad axis. In short, the numerous offensives, counterstrokes, and attacks the Red Army mounted from the Demiansk region in the north to the High Caucasus Mountains in the south were designed to weaken German forces at Stalingrad. In this sense, the Germans' decision to conduct operations deep into the Caucasus region and, to a lesser extent, along the Voronezh axis merely played into the *Stavka's* hands.

Although the offensives the Red Army launched in the Demiansk and Voronezh regions during the fall of 1942 had little or no impact on the outcome of the more decisive fight at Stalingrad, the same cannot be said of the fighting in the Caucasus region to the south and the Rzhev region to the north. Considered collectively, the six major offensives that Army Group A conducted toward Tuapse, Ordzhonikidze, and Grozny during the fall sought to fulfill Hitler's dream of seizing the vital oil riches of the Trans-Caucasus region. The inability of Army Group A to reach the oil fields in early November signaled the failure of Operation Blau as a whole. Just as the struggle at Stalingrad mesmerized the generals on both sides (as well as historians) into believing that Operation Blau expired among the ruins of Stalin's namesake city, it also masked the reality that the failure of Army Group A in the Caucasus rendered the final bloody struggle in Stalingrad virtually irrelevant.

In a strategic sense, Operation Blau replicated Operation Barbarossa's failure from the year before. Before the *Wehrmacht* was defeated at the gates of Moscow in early December 1941, it had already suffered major defeats in the Leningrad and Rostov regions. Thus, weeks before Army Group Center's offensive collapsed along the approaches to Moscow, Army Groups North and South had admitted defeat and were already on the defensive. Likewise, in the autumn of 1942, two weeks before Army Group B suffered its defeat at Stalingrad, Army Group A had admitted defeat and was already on the defensive in the Caucasus.

Operationally as well, the struggle in the Caucasus replicated the *Wehrmacht's* performance in 1941. The year before, as it advanced in the face of determined and increasing Red Army resistance, Army Group South had steadily narrowed its front, pursuing ever more limited objectives with diminishing forces and in increasingly ad hoc fashion before being defeated at Rostov. Similarly faced with persistent resistance and many of the same problems, Army Group A in 1942 advanced in spasmodic offensive spurts along a diminishing number of axes, its forces steadily eroding in strength, before its defeat along the approaches to Tuapse and the gates of Ordzhonikidze. Thus, just as the *Wehrmacht*'s defeats at Tikhvin and Rostov in November 1941 epitomized the ultimate defeat of Operation Barbarossa, Army Group A's defeat at Ordzhonikidze in early November 1942 represented the failure of Operation Blau.

The heavy fighting in the Rzhev region in the late summer and early autumn of 1942 also had a significant impact on the outcome of Operation Blau. In addition to contributing to German overextension and tying down German forces along the Moscow strategic axis, Zhukov's Rzhev-Sychevka Offensive (30 July–23 August) established a clear pattern for future Soviet offensive operations. Based on the progress of his forces during this offensive, Zhukov remained convinced that with one or two more armies at his disposal he could have inflicted a decisive defeat on his old nemesis, German Army Group Center. Thus, his offensive in July and August would become a dress rehearsal for an even grander offensive operation in November.

Regardless of the degree to which these Soviet offensives on the flanks actually absorbed German resources, they contributed to the psychological strain on Hitler and the German military command. This in turn made it more difficult for staff officers to voice any doubts to Hitler and, moreover, encouraged Hitler to mistrust and ultimately dismiss his most experienced subordinates. Unaware of the increasing effectiveness of the Soviet defenders, the dictator became impatient with what he perceived as prevarication and delay among the field commanders. Whether these psychological effects were worth the enormous cost in Soviet blood and materiel remains an entirely subjective judgment.

THE RED ARMY

If the *Wehrmacht* began its first two campaigns in the Soviet Union with dangerous misconceptions, the same might be said of its opponent. In each case, Stalin made the mistake of simply counting numbers of tanks and troops and believing that the Red Army should be able to launch successful offensives against the more experienced Germans. Thus Stalin, like Hitler, became frustrated when his subordinates did not sweep their apparently inferior enemies off the map. Subconsciously, Stalin and Hitler each made the mistake of believing that his side had recovered from the winter battles while his opponent remained as weak as it had been when the front reached a troubled equilibrium in March 1942. Eventually, however, Stalin came to trust at least selected subordinates, allowing them to command even when, like Zhukov, they occasionally failed. The most visible sign of this increased trust in the efficiency and political reliability of Soviet commanders was the reduction in the military authority of commissars in the fall.[1] This occurred at the very time when, on the German side, Hitler openly questioned both the efficiency and the loyalty of his subordinates.

Stalin's underestimation of his opponent, combined with the reluctance of many subordinates to disagree with him, was a key factor in the preliminary victories the Germans achieved in May 1942 at Kerch' in the Crimea and at Khar'kov as well as in June during operations Wilhelm and Fridericus. Thereafter, however, Stalin far more readily heeded the advice of his senior military leaders, in particular Zhukov, Vasilevsky, and Eremenko.

In addition, 1942 witnessed weapons production and force generation for the Red Army like never before—a miracle of industrial output and military might that created the building blocks, especially tank and mechanized corps, of eventual Soviet victory. Unfortunately, the combination of prewar purges and 1941 disasters meant that the Red Army suffered a shortage of senior officers to conduct the 1942 campaign. Thus, the wealth of new units outran the supply of staff officers and commanders capable of maneuvering such large, flexible units. In the course of 1942–1943, enough officers learned through experience so that the Soviet tankists could fulfill their potential, but this experience was purchased at the price of much blood and treasure.

In addition to its initial strategic errors in the spring of 1942, the Soviet leadership suffered from massive impatience, launching literally dozens of counterstrokes and counteroffensives with inadequate penetration. To some extent, this impatience was unavoidable given that the invaders had the initiative and were driving ever deeper into the Soviet Union. Particularly at Stalingrad, the repeated attacks on the German flanks were the obvious course of action for the Soviets, who were seeking to relieve the pressure on Chuikov's beleaguered defenders. Individually, such attacks often failed in their immediate intent. For example, when Stalin insisted that Don Front attack yet again in the Kotluban' area on 19 October, Rokossovsky knowingly sacrificed four rifle divisions and supporting artillery without causing the Germans to withdraw a single battalion from the assault on Tractor Factory village. Frequently, such offensive actions failed because the controlling headquarters had neither the preparation time nor the skilled staffs to assemble troops and supplies for an effective attack. As a result, thousands of Soviet soldiers died, and hundreds of vehicles were lost, without visible effect on the enemy. What's more, the German defenders became overconfident about their ability to stop similar attacks in the future. Cumulatively, however, the persistent counterattacks from Voronezh in July to the Kotluban' from August to October contributed markedly to the effort to pin down the invaders and bleed them white. Thus, even when Paulus traded regiments and divisions in Stalingrad with those defending the flanks, the resulting new units arrived in Stalingrad with only marginally more combat power than those they had replaced.

Meanwhile, the Soviet staffs, as noted above, gradually learned their jobs, and Stalin slowly came to trust his subordinates. Despite repeated failures to achieve a shallow tactical encirclement of German forces, these subordinates by November had planned a much deeper operational-level encirclement, an encirclement that focused the attack not on the German troops on Paulus's immediate left and right but rather the poorly equipped satellite forces that protected the long open flanks of Army Group B. These changes—in combination with sufficient time to prepare an offensive properly—would have enormous consequences for the exhausted Germans in November.

Throughout the Blau campaign, largely because of the poor performance of the Soviet soldier during the summer, the Germans routinely discounted his combat skills and staying power come autumn. Contrary to German stereotypes about the unimaginative Soviet soldier, the defenders of Stalingrad proved remarkably innovative in their tactics. Sometimes these innovations were born of desperation, as when a few small units came together and improvised some type of defense against the hated Germans. Over time, however, the tactics that had first appeared in mid-September became standard, and new soldiers learned them quickly. The Soviet battle groups hugged their opponents, so to speak, staying as close as possible to the Germans at all times. This not only stymied German pilots and artillerymen; it also kept the Germans in a constant state of anxiety—never able to relax or even to stand upright without drawing enemy fire. By preference, the Soviets attacked at night, denying the Germans any rest while increasing their confusion and uncertainty.

Snipers were used on both sides, but the defenders made snipers a systematic part of their campaign to exhaust the Germans. Before dawn, men and women would conceal themselves in the rubble, often waiting all day to take a single shot at an unwary German. The premier sniper of the 284th Rifle Division, Vasilii Zaitsev, became the subject of Soviet propaganda at the time as well as later fiction, including the novel and film *Enemy at the Gates*. Zaitsev claimed more than 300 German deaths before he was wounded in the eye; thereafter he trained other snipers, including Victor Medvedev, who eventually exceeded Zaitsev's score and served with the Red Army all the way to Berlin.[2]

Yet the Soviet defenses involved much more than individual courage and skill. Whereas Paulus had little detailed knowledge about his opponents,

Chuikov and his subordinate commanders consistently used small reconnaissance patrols to locate German troop concentrations and bring back prisoners for interrogation. This raw information allowed the defenders to anticipate major German attacks. Small-scale Soviet counterattacks, often launched at dawn before the *Luftwaffe* was on station, sought to disrupt the German preparations. Failing that, the defenders established a series of killing zones to absorb and defeat the Germans. In addition to booby traps and mines of all kinds, the units of 62nd Army tried to ambush the spearhead of the attack, stripping away the infantry that tanks needed for close-in security in built-up areas. Next, perhaps two blocks down a street, concealed Soviet antitank guns would engage the isolated tanks, while troops armed with short-range antitank weapons allowed the panzers to pass and then fired at the thin armor and engine grill at the rear of each vehicle.

The basic building-blocks of this defense were the assault group of 20–50 men, including machine guns, grenades, and engineer satchel charges, and the strongpoint, a group of buildings organized for all-around defense with antitank obstacles and fields of fire cleared around them. Guns or tanks defended the ground floor, while upper floors contained machine guns and artillery forward observers. Between these strongpoints, the assault groups remained mobile, crawling down sewers and breaking through the walls of adjacent buildings so that they could move behind the German spearheads without exposing themselves on the street. In one instance, an assault group of 45th Rifle Division needed to break through a major building wall in the Krasnyi Oktiabr' sector in order to attack their opponents from an unexpected direction. Piece by piece, the Soviet soldiers moved an entire 122mm howitzer inside the building, then fired it at point-blank range to break through the wall![3]

This combination of intelligence, discipline, and determination enabled 62nd Army to continue the battle of Stalingrad when, by all conventional measures, the Germans had won.

COSTS

Given the immense scale and scope of Operation Blau, it is difficult if not impossible to quantify the cost to both sides. According to official Russian sources, the Briansk, Southwestern, and Southern Fronts began their defense against Operation Blau on 28 June 1942 with 169,400, 610,000, and 522,500 men, respectively. Including the 8,900 sailors of the Azov Flotilla, the strength of Soviet forces operating along the south strategic axis totaled 1,310,000 men. Of this total force, the three *fronts* suffered 568,347 casualties during the Voronezh-Voroshilovgrad defensive operation (28 June–24

July 1942), including 370,522 killed, mortally wounded, captured, or missing in action and 197,825 wounded or sick.[4]

Thereafter, the Stalingrad Front and Volga Flotilla began operations with a force of 447,600 men on 17 July. Counting the several hundreds of thousands of reinforcements it received in the ensuing four months, during the Stalingrad defensive operation (25 July–18 November 1942) it and the Southeastern and Don Fronts lost another 643,842 men, including 323,586 killed, mortally wounded, captured, or missing in action and 319,986 wounded or sick.[5] This brought the casualty toll along the Voronezh and Stalingrad axes (not counting the losses along the Voronezh axis after 24 July) to the staggering total of 1,212,189 men, including 694,108 killed, mortally wounded, captured, or missing in action and 517,811 wounded or sick by 17 November.

In addition, the Southern and North Caucasus Fronts and the Black Sea Fleet began operations along the Rostov and Caucasus axis on 25 July with a total force of 603,200 men. Of this number, counting reinforcements received, these two *fronts*, plus the Northern and Coastal Groups of the Trans-Caucasus Front, suffered 373,911 casualties during the North Caucasus defensive operation (25 July–31 December 1942), including 192,791 killed, mortally wounded, captured, or missing in action and 181,120 wounded or sick.[6] This brought the gruesome tally of casualties the Red Army suffered along the Stalingrad and Caucasus axes to a total of 1,586,100 losses, including 886,899 killed, mortally wounded, captured, or missing in action and 698,931 wounded or sick.

Yet despite these appalling losses, and illustrating the Red Army's immense regeneration capability, the Southwestern, Don, and Stalingrad Fronts mustered a total strength of 1,143,500 men, including 398,100 in Southwestern Front, 307,500 in Don Front, and 429,200 men in Stalingrad Front, plus another 8,700 in the Volga Military Flotilla, at day's end on 18 November 1942.[7]

As far as ancillary operations on the distant flanks were concerned, under Zhukov's direction the Kalinin and Western Fronts committed 345,100 men in the Rzhev-Sychevka offensive (30 July–23 August 1942) and lost 193,683 men, including 51,482 killed, mortally wounded, captured, or missing in action and 142,201 wounded or sick during this offensive.[8] Also by official tally, during its offensive in the Kozel'sk region (22–29 August 1942), the Western Front committed 218,412 soldiers to combat and lost 34,549 men, including 12,134 killed, mortally wounded, captured, or missing in action and 22,415 wounded or sick.[9] The Russians have yet to release official casualty figures for other operations, such as the fighting around Voronezh and at Demiansk in the fall.

In terms of equipment losses, officially the Briansk and Southwestern Fronts lost 2,436 tanks, 13,716 guns and mortars, and 783 combat aircraft during Blau I and II (28 June–24 July 1942); Stalingrad, Southeastern, and Don Fronts lost 1,426 tanks, 12,137 guns and mortars, and 2,063 combat aircraft during the Stalingrad defensive operation (25 July–18 November 1942); and Southern, North Caucasus, and Trans-Caucasus Fronts lost another 990 tanks, 5,049 guns and mortars, and 644 combat aircraft during the North Caucasus defensive operation (25 July–31 December 1942).[10] Thus, the Red Army lost at least 4,852 tanks during the five months of fighting— four times more than the 1,260 tanks the Germans were able to field in Army Group South at the beginning of Operation Blau.

While the precise personnel losses of the German Army during Operation Blau remain relatively opaque, in part because of the frequent changes in the organization of the armies as they advanced, it is clear that Sixth Army suffered 40,068 casualties, including 1,068 officers and 39,000 soldiers, during the period from 21 August through 17 October 1942.[11] With slightly lower losses during the first two months of Blau, and similar casualty rates during the final month of intense fighting in the city, Sixth Army probably suffered more than 100,000 casualties during Operation Blau even before the Soviet counteroffensive of November. Based on the same calculations, the smaller Fourth Panzer Army suffered about 30,000 casualties during its advance on Stalingrad.

The personnel strength returns of the Sixth Army, Fourth Panzer Army, Romanian Third and Fourth Armies, and Army Group B's reserves in mid-November, which vividly underscore the debilitating effects of attrition, substantiate these loss figures (see Tables 46–49). For example, by mid-1942 the establishment (table of organization and equipment—TO&E) personnel strength of a German infantry division was roughly 15,000 men, with motorized and panzer divisions fielding roughly 16,000 and 17,000 men, respectively. The 14 German infantry divisions in Sixth and Fourth Panzer Armies in mid-November ranged in strength from as few as 6,683 men (389th Infantry Division) to as many as 10,601 (44th Infantry Division) but averaged about 8,533; these divisions were short 6,467 (43 percent) of their authorized personnel. At the same time, the four panzer divisions (14th, 16th, 22nd, and 24th), which ranged in strength from 10,950 to 11,051 men, averaged 10,863, for a deficit of roughly 6,137 (36 percent) of their authorized strength, and the four motorized divisions (3rd, 16th, 29th, and 60th) ranged in strength from 8,653 men to about 12,000, for an average of 9,896, a deficit of 6,104 men (38 percent). Even worse for German forces, most of the personnel shortages were in infantry, panzer-grenadier, and combat engineers— the very heart of the *Wehrmacht's* striking power.

A simple tally of the deficit in personnel among Sixth Army's combat divisions on 15 November indicates that the army was short 115,414 men in those forces alone. Given that most of these divisions were already about

15 percent understrength when Blau began (i.e., from 2,225 men per infantry division to 2,550 men per panzer division), Sixth Army began the operation with a deficit of roughly 50,000 men. The deficit then grew to more than 115,000 men during the offensive, an increase of 65,000 soldiers. And because replacements made up for less than 70 percent of the deficit, this would substantiate the army's loss of about 100,000 men.

Similarly, Romanian forces suffered 39,089 losses between 1 July and 31 October, including 13,154 in Third Army and even more in Fourth Army, plus additional losses during the first half of November.[12] With replacements being held back for the winter campaign, these losses also matched Third Army's deficit of roughly 17,000 men and Fourth Army's even more pronounced deficit.

As for German personnel losses elsewhere along the front, they, too, are opaque. However, indicative of these heavy losses, during the fighting at Rzhev Model's Ninth Army suffered 20,000 casualties by 17 August and, with a loss rate of 2,000 per day, 42,000 by 1 September.[13] Thereafter, the fighting continued in the Gzhatsk and Viaz'ma sectors through 22 September, with Model claiming that his army could not sustain such losses much longer without completely losing its combat effectiveness.

In regard to armor losses, because of the German effective evacuation and repair system it is virtually impossible to determine actual losses of tanks and assault guns. However, overall loss figures, as well as the steadily declining number of operational tanks and assault guns in operating panzer and motorized divisions and assault-gun battalions, indicate that attrition was indeed a major problem. Overall figures indicate that the German Army lost a total of 1,613 tanks during the period from 1 July through 30 November 1942, including 20 Pz I, 159 Pz II, 205 38 (t), 33 Pz III short, 936 Pz III long, 257 Pz IV short, and 3 Pz IV long models, at least 1,000 of them by the forces conducting Operation Blau (700 along the Voronezh and Stalingrad axes and 300 in the Caucasus).[14] As a result, after beginning the campaign with up to 125 tanks, by early September the panzer and motorized divisions participating in Operation Blau were fortunate to muster as many as 30–40 operational tanks each, and frequently far fewer, on any given day.

Thus, comparing these gross and often imprecise figures, the Soviets suffered at least 1.2 million casualties in the fighting along the Voronezh and Stalingrad axes from 28 June through 17 November 1942 as compared with a rough Axis casualty toll of about 200,000 (130,000 in Sixth and Fourth Panzer Armies, 30,000 in Romanian Third and Fourth Armies, and the remainder in the German Second and Hungarian Second Armies). During the same period and along the same axes, the Soviets lost in excess of 4,862 tanks as opposed to German losses of fewer than 700 tanks (discounting the losses in the Caucasus region). Meanwhile, during the fighting at Rzhev in late summer, the Soviets lost about 200,000 men compared to Ninth Army's loss of about 42,000. And though the comparative casualty toll incurred in the fighting in the Caucasus is not available, the loss ratios there probably replicated the patterns encountered elsewhere along the front, that is, a loss ratio of roughly 5:1 or 6:1 in the Germans' favor in personnel and a ratio of roughly 5:1 in the Germans' favor in armor.

However, given the Soviets' immense manpower base and production rate (about 2,000 tanks per month as compared with the far more limited German resources in both respects), the Red Army could endure such losses far more readily than could the Germans. In short, as was the case in 1941, it was inevitable that the Soviets would win any war of attrition, particularly if and when they learned to exploit their resources more effectively.

Hitler, who personally orchestrated the campaign, must bear a large measure of the responsibility for this dispersal of effort, the constant shifting of air and ground assets between the Crimea, Stalingrad, and the Caucasus, not to mention Western Europe and Leningrad. Might-have-beens can never be tested or proven in history. In retrospect, however, it appears that Germany, if Hitler had concentrated his forces and resources, might have taken *either* Stalingrad *or* the Caucasus oil fields in 1942 but was incapable of capturing both. The latter goal appears especially possible in retrospect given that the Red Army had its own logistical difficulties in the Caucasus region. Instead, however, each of the two German army groups found its advance dependent on a handful of inadequately supplied mechanized divisions, supported by perhaps a dozen infantry or mountain divisions, while the remaining German and satellite troops had to defend their long open flanks. Stuck at the end of two long and diverging logistical chains, Army Groups B and A suffered separate and nearly simultaneous failures.

Table 46. The Personnel Strength and Weaponry of the Sixth Army's Forces in Mid-November 1942

Force	Personnel Strengths					Weapons	
	Ration	Combat	Non-Combat	Hiwis	Deficit	Antitank Guns (PAKS)	Tanks or Assault Guns
XI Army Corps							
376th ID	8,187	5,269	2,918	4,105	6,464	33	
44th ID	10,601	6,748	3,865	2,365	4,238	28	
384th ID	8,821	5,025	3,796	1,804	5,937	30	
VIII Army Corps							
76th ID	8,023	4,740	3,283	8,033	6,981	24	
113th ID	9,461	5,064	4,397	5,564	5,854	24	
177th AGBn							11
XIV Panzer Corps							
94th ID	7,469	2,924	4,345	2,581	8,233	10	
16th PzD	11,051	4,855	6,196	1,843	7,673	21	28
60th MotD	8,933	4,812	4,121	2,071	5,848	13	27
3rd MotD	8,653	4,498	4,155	4,530	4,831	16	29
LI Army Corps							
71st ID	8,906	4,331	4,575	8,134	7,353	25	
295th ID	6,899	3,459	3,440	50	9,037	18	
100th JgD	8,675	4,688	3,987	2,132	7,739	15	
79th ID	7,980	4,304	3,676	2,018	8,294	49	
305th ID	6,683	2,915	3,768	1,562	8,520	17	
389th ID	7,540	4,021	3,519	2,379	7,852	21	
Gr. Seydel (14th PzD)	—	588	—	934	5,434	8	6
24th PzD	10,950	6,160	4,790	1,675	5,126	—	58
244th AGBn							20
245th AGBn							2

Sources: Manfred Kehrig, *Stalingrad: Analyse und Dokumentation einer Schlacht* (Stuttgart: Deutsche Verlag-Anstalt, 1974), 662–663, citing reports dated 11 and 19 November 1942.

Table 47. The Estimated Personnel Strength and Weaponry of the Romanian Third Army in Mid-November 1942

Force	Personnel Strengths					Weapons	
	Authorized	Combat	Non-Combat	*Hiwis*	Deficit	Antitank Guns (PAKS)	Tanks or Assault Guns
I Army Corps (Romanian)							
7th ID (R)	13,100	ca. 12,000			1,100	12	
11th ID (R)	13,100	ca. 12,000			1,100	12	
II Army Corps (Romanian)							
9th ID (R)	13,100	ca. 12,000			1,100	12	
14th ID (R)	13,100	10,839			2,261	12	
7th CD (R)	7,600	ca. 5,500			2,100	6	
V Army Corps (Romanian)							
5th ID (R)	13,100	ca. 12,000			1,100	12	
6th ID (R)	13,100	ca. 12,000			1,100	12	
VI Army Corps (Romanian)							
13th ID (R)	13,100	9,337			3,763	12	
1st CD (R)	7,600	ca. 5,500			2,100	4	
15th ID (R)	13,100	ca. 12,000			1,100	12	
Total:	155,492						

Note: Based on the establishment (TO&E) strengths of Romanian forces of 13,100 men for an infantry division and 7,600 for a cavalry division.

Source: Mark Axworthy, Cornel Scafeş, Cristian Craciunoiu, *Third Axis/Fourth Ally: Romanian Armed Forces in the European War, 1941–1945* (London: Arms and Armour, 1995), 89–90.

Table 48. The Estimated Personnel Strength and Weaponry of the Fourth Panzer Army in Mid-November 1942

Force	Personnel Strengths					Weapons	
	Ration	Non-Combat	Hiwis	Combat	Deficit	Antitank Guns (PAKS)	Tanks or Assault Guns
VI Army Corps							
371st ID	10,317			ca. 6,000	6,000	25	
297th ID	9,898			ca. 4,500	7,000	24	
20th ID (R)	13,100			6,288 (48%)	6,812		
VI Army Corps (Romanian)							
	Authorized			On-hand	Deficit		
2nd ID (R)	13,100			3,930 (30%)	9,170		
18th ID (R)	13,100			10,218 (78%)	2,882		
1st ID (R)	13,100			3,275 (25%)	9,825		
4th ID (R)	13,100			4,454 (34%)	8,646		
VII Army Corps (Romanian)							
5th CD (R)	7,600			4,332 (57%)	3,268		
8th CD (R)	7,600			4,864 (64%)	2,736		
Total:	75,380						
	Ration			Combat	Deficit	PAKS	Tanks/AGs
16th MotD	ca. 10,000			ca. 6,000	6,000	26	52
29th MotD	ca. 12,000			ca. 7,500	4,000	12	55

Sources: Manfred Kehrig, *Stalingrad: Analyse und Dokumentation ener Schlacht* (Stuttgart: Deutsche Verlag-Anstalt, 1974), 667, citing *Lagekarten* and *Tagesmeldung* dated 11 and 19 November 1942; Mark Axworthy, Cornel Scafeş, Cristian Cracuinoin, *Third Axis/Fourth Ally: Romanian Armed Forces in the European War, 1941–1945* (London: Arms and Armour, 1995), 101.

Table 49. The Estimated Personnel Strength and Weaponry of Army Group B's Reserves in Mid-November 1942

ARMY GROUP B's RESERVE

Force	Personnel Strengths					Weapons	
	Ration	Combat	Non-Combat	Hiwis	Deficit	Antitank Guns (PAKS)	Tanks or Assault Guns
XXXXVIII Panzer Corps							
14th PzD	10,239	4,760	5,050	—	6,000	19	36
22nd PzD	11,211	ca. 5,200	—	—	5,000	8	38 (41)
1st PzD (Rom)	12,196	—	—	—	—	90	105
Gr. Simons	632	—	—	—	—	4	—

Sources: Manfred Kehrig, *Stalingrad: Analyse und Dokumentation ener Schlacht* (Stuttgart: Deutsche Verlag-Anstalt, 1974), 668, citing reports dated 11 and 19 November 1942; Mark Axworthy, Cornel Scafeṣ, Cristian Craciunoiu, *Third Axis/Fourth Ally: Romanian Armed Forces in the European War, 1941–1945* (London: Arms and Armour, 1995).

Notes

Abbreviations

JSMS	*Journal of Slavic Military Studies*
TsAMO	*Tsentral'nyi arkhiv Ministerstva Oborony* [Central Archives of the Ministry of Defense]
TsPA UML	*Tsentral'nyi partiinyi arkhiv Instituta Marksizma-Leninizma* [Central Party Archives of the Institute of Marxism and Leninism]
VIZh	*Voenno-istoricheskii zhurnal* [Military-historical journal]
VV	*Voennyi vestnik* [Military herald]

Chapter 1: The Germans at the Gates

1. Wolfgang Werthen, *Geschichte der 16. Panzer-Division 1939–1945* (Friedberg: Podzun-Pallas-Verlag, 1958), 106–107. For the similar experiences of 3rd Motorized Division, see Gerhard Dieckhoff, *3. Infanterie-Division, 3. Infanterie Division (mot), 3. PanzerGrenadier-Division* (Cuxhofen: Oberstudienrat Gerhard Dieckhoff, 1960).

2. Konstantin K. Rokossovsky, ed., *Velikaia bitva na Volge* [Great Victory on the Volga] (Moscow: Voenizdat, 1965), 124–133.

3. Heinz Schröter, *Stalingrad*, translated from the German by Constantine Fitzgibbon (New York: E. P. Dutton, 1958), 31.

4. Ibid.; Earl F. Ziemke and Magna E. Bauer, *Moscow to Stalingrad: Decision in the East* (Washington, DC: U.S. Army Center of Military History, 1987), 87; and Werthen, *Geschichte der 16. Panzer-Division*, 110–111.

5. See, for example, David M. Glantz and Jonathan M. House, *When Titans Clashed: How the Red Army Stopped Hitler* (Lawrence: University Press of Kansas, 1995), 49–156.

6. Franz Halder, *The Halder Diaries: The Private War Journals of Colonel General Franz Halder*, vol. 2. (Boulder, CO: Westview Press and T. N. Depuy Associates, 1976), 348, 361, and passim.

7. Fedor von Bock, *The War Diary*, ed. Klaus Gerbet, trans. David Johnston (Atglen, PA: Schiffer Military History, 1996), 513.

8. Geoffrey Parker, ed., *The Cambridge Illustrated History of Warfare* (London and Cambridge, UK: Cambridge University Press, 2000), 1–10.

9. See, for example, Horst Boog, Jürgen Forster, Joachim Hoffmann, Ernst Klink, Rolf-Dieter Muller, and Gerd R. Ueberschar, *Germany and the Second World*

War, volume IV: The Attack on the Soviet Union, trans. Ewald Osers, et al. (Oxford, UK: Clarendon Press, 1996.)

10. Klaus Reinhardt, *Moscow—The Turning Point: The Failure of Hitler's Strategy in the Winter of 1941–42*, trans. Karl Keenan (Oxford, UK, and Providence, RI: Oxford University Press, 1992), 367–370. According to Reinhardt, during the 1941 campaign, the Germans lost 13,600 gun tubes, 4,902 aircraft, 41,000 trucks, and 207,000 horses, many of which were not replaced for 1942.

11. Führer Directive No. 41 is reproduced in translation in Hugh R. Trevor-Roper, ed., *Blitzkrieg to Defeat: Hitler's War Directives 1939–1945* (New York and Chicago: Holt, Rinehart and Winston, 1964), see esp. 117 and 119. For the full text of Directive No. 41, see *Sbornik voenno-istoricheskikh materialov Velikoi Otechestvennoi voiny, Vypusk 18* [Collection of materials of the Great Patriotic War, Issue 18] (Moscow: Voenizdat, 1960), 257–262. Prepared by the Military-Historical Department of the General Staff's Military-Scientific Directorate and classified as secret. Hereafter cited as *SVIMVOV*, with appropriate issue number and page(s).

12. Andrei Galushko and Maksim Kolomiets, "Boi za Khar'kov v Mae 1942 god" [The battle for Khar'kov in May 1942], in *Frontovaia illiustratsiia, 6–2000* [Front illustrated, 6–2000] (Moscow: "Strategiia KM," 2000), 73, 220–238; Aleksei Isaev, *Kratkii kurs Istorii Velikoi Otechestvennoi voiny: Nastuplenie Marshala Shaposhnikova* [A short course in the history of the Great Patriotic War: The offensives of Marshal Shaposhnikov] (Moscow: "IAUZA" "EKSMO," 2005), 352–253. For a complete description of this battle, see David M. Glantz, *Kharkov 1942: The Anatomy of a Military Disaster* (Rockville Center, NY: Sarpedon, 1998).

13. G. F. Krivosheev, ed., *Soviet Casualties and Combat Losses in the Twentieth Century* (London: Greenhill Books; Mechanicsburg, PA: Stackpole Books, 1997), 123–124.

14. Bock, *The War Diary*, 512–520.

15. On Bock's dismissal, see Geoffrey Jukes, *Hitler's Stalingrad Decisions* (Berkeley: University of California Press, 1985), 43; and Ziemke and Bauer, *Moscow to Stalingrad*, 347–348.

16. George E. Blau, *The German Campaign in Russia: Planning and Operations, 1940–1942* (Washington, DC: U.S. Army Center of Military History, 1955), 148; and Ziemke and Bauer, *Moscow to Stalingrad*, 351. For full details of the changing German operational plans, see volume one of this study.

17. Führer Directive No. 45 is reproduced in full in *SVIMVOV, Vypusk* 18: 265–267; and Trevor-Roper, *Blitzkrieg to Defeat*, 129–131. See also Blau, *The German Campaign in Russia*, 152–155, for an analysis.

18. See *Stavka* directives nos. 994124 and 994125, dated 2030 hours 22 July 1942, in V. A. Zolotarev, ed., "Stavka VGK: Dokumenty i materialy 1942 god" [The Stavka VGK: Documents and materials of 1942], in *Russkii arkhiv: Velikaia Otechestvennaia 16 (5–2)* [The Russian archives: The Great Patriotic [War], 16 (5–2)] (Moscow: "TERRA," 1996), 320–321. Hereafter cited as Zolotarev, "*Stavka* 1942," with appropriate page(s).

19. V. A. Zolotarev, ed., "*Prikazy narodnogo komissara oborony SSSR, 22 iiunia 1941 g.—1942,*" [Orders of the People's Commissariat of Defense of the USSR, 22 June 1941–1942], in *Russkii arkhiv: Velikaia Otechestvennaia 13 (2–2)* [The Russian archives: The Great Patriotic [War], 13 (2–2)] (Moscow: TERRA, 1997), 276–278.

Hereafter cited as Zolotarev, "NKO 1941–42," with appropriate page(s). This order, which was signed by Stalin, was entitled "Order No. 227 Concerning Measures for Strengthening Discipline and Order in the Red Army and Preventing Unauthorized Retreat from Combat Positions."

20. Blau, *The German Campaign in Russia*, 149–150, 155; See Maksim Kolomiets and Il'ia Moshchansky, "Oborona Kavkaz (iiul'-dekabr' 1942 goda)" [The defense of the Caucasus (July-December 1942)], in *Frontovaia illiustratsiia, 2: 2000* [Front illustrated, 2: 2000] (Moscow: "Strategiia KM," 1999), 5. On infantry equipment, see Horst Boog, Werner Rahn, Reinhard Stumpf, and Bernd Wegner, *Germany and the Second World War, volume VI: The Global War: Widening of the Conflict into a World War and the Shift of the Initiative, 1941–1943*, trans. Ewald Osers, et al. (Oxford, UK: Clarendon Press, 2001), 1035.

21. This account is based largely on the sympathetic biography by Walter Goerlitz, *Paulus and Stalingrad: A Life of Field-Marshal Friedrich Paulus with notes, correspondence, and documents from his papers*, trans. R. H. Stevens (New York: Citadel Press, 1963). See also Samuel Mitcham's analysis in Correlli Barnett, ed., *Hitler's Generals* (New York: Grove Weidenfeld, 1989), 361–373.

22. Goerlitz, *Paulus and Stalingrad*, 21–28, 35.

23. For additional details on Seydlitz's controversial military career, see Helmut Heiber and David M. Glantz, *Hitler and His Generals: The Military Conferences, 1942–1945* (New York: Enigma Books, 2002), 798. Captured by the Soviets in February 1943, Seydlitz cooperated with his captors, becoming president of the German Officers' Association and vice president of the National Committee to Liberate Germany. After the committee was dissolved, he refused to accept a position in the Soviets' occupation administration. Therefore, in 1950 the Soviets tried Seydlitz for atrocities against Soviet prisoners of war and civilians while in *Wehrmacht* service and sentenced him to 25 years' imprisonment. Released from captivity in October 1955, he returned to West Germany and died in 1976.

24. On Kempf, see Heiber and Glantz, *Hitler and His Generals*, 860; "Eichenlaubträger Werner Kempf," in *Generale des Heeres* at http://balsi.de/Homepage-Generale/Heer/Heer-Startseite.htm; and Konstantin Zalessky, *Vermacht: Sukhoputnye voiska i Verkhovnoe komandovanie* [The *Wehrmacht*: Ground Forces and the High Command] (Moscow; "IAUZA," 2005), 232–233. After commanding XXXXVIII Panzer Corps during the Stalingrad campaign, Kempf commanded an *Armeegruppe* bearing his name during the fighting at Khar'kov and Kursk in 1943 and, thereafter, Eighth Army to August 1944, the Armed Forces of the *Ostland* [Eastland] Commissariat (an antipartisan command) until the end of 1944, and the High Command in the Vosges Mountains (France) until he reverted to the OKW's reserve in December 1944. Surviving the war, Kempf died in 1964.

25. For further details, see Heiber and Glantz, *Hitler and His Generals*, 804; and the website www.geocities.com/-orion47/WEHRMACHT/HEER/Generaloberst/Heitz_Walter. Promoted to colonel general on 28 January 1943, the same day he surrendered to the Russians, like so many of his counterpart POWs, Heitz died in Soviet captivity in February 1944.

26. On Wietersheim, see Zalessky, *Vermacht*, 100. Still questioning Wietersheim's reliability, Hitler relieved him of command in September 1942, replacing

him with General Hans Hube, commander of 16th Panzer Division. After his relief, Wietersheim occupied no further command position in the army. At war's end, he was serving as a common soldier in Germany's ragtag *Volksturm* [People's Militia].

27. Richard Woff, "Chuikov," in Harold Shukman, ed., *Stalin's Generals* (New York: Grove Press, 1993), 67–76.

28. See I. N. Rodionov, ed., *Voennaia entsiklopediia v vos'mi tomakh, 3* [Military encyclopedia in eight volumes, 3] (Moscow: Voenizdat, 1995), vol. 3, 165. Hereafter cited as *VE*, with appropriate volume and page(s).

29. Most Soviet sources written after 1964 also credit Zhukov with planning the Stalingrad counteroffensive, although many sources prior to that date accord credit for doing so to Vasilevsky and Eremenko. Certainly, as Deputy Supreme Commander, Zhukov played a considerable role in all *Stavka* strategic planning. See volume 3 (forthcoming) of this study for the historiographical debate about planning the counteroffensive.

30. In addition to his memoirs, A. M. Vasilevsky, *Delo vsei zhizni* [Life's work] (Moscow: Politizdat, 1983), see Geoffrey Jukes, "Alexander Mikhailovich Vasilevsky," in Shukman, *Stalin's Generals*, 275–285.

31. For additional details, see *Komandarmy. Voennyi biograficheskii slovar'* [The Great Patriotic [War]. Army commanders. Military-bibliographical dictionary] (Moscow: Institute of Military History, Russian Federation's Ministry of Defense, OOO "Kuchkovo pole," 2005), 153–155. Moskalenko commanded 38th, 1st Tank, 1st Guards, and 40th Armies during Operation Blau and 38th Army, once again, from October 1943 to the end of the war. While in command, his army figured prominently in many of the Red Army's most important victories in the Ukraine, Poland, and Czechoslovakia. After the war, Moskalenko commanded armies until 1948 and the Moscow Military District's PVO (Air Defense) Forces from 1948 through 1953. After helping thwart an attempted coup by Beriia's NKVD in the wake of Stalin's death in 1953, he commanded the Moscow Military District and became Marshal of the Soviet Union and Deputy Minister of Defense of the USSR in 1955. After retiring in 1962, Moskalenko wrote one of the best of the memoirs penned by wartime Red Army generals and died in 1985.

32. Ibid., 113–114. In the wake of Operation Blau, Kriuchenkin commanded 69th, 10th, and 33rd Armies from March 1943 to the fall of 1944, taking part in the battle for Kursk and the Belorussian offensive in the summer of 1944. Although relieved from command on several occasions for both cause and illness, Kriuchenkin ended the war as deputy commander of 61st Army and, later, 1st Belorussian Front. After serving as deputy commander of the Don Military District, Kriuchenkin retired in 1946 and died in 1976.

33. Ibid., 95–96. After leading 24th Army during its bloody struggles in the Kotluban' region during September 1942, Kozlov served as representative of the *Stavka* during the Red Army's Ostrogozhsk-Rossosh', Voronezh-Kastornoe, and Khar'kov offensives in January–March 1943. Once again discredited when his forces were defeated in the Khar'kov region in March 1943, Kozlov spent the remainder of the war as deputy commander of Trans-Baikal Front, where he remained during the Manchurian campaign in August and September 1945. After war's end, he was deputy commander of the Trans-Baikal Military District. Never fully regaining Stalin's favor, Kozlov died in 1967.

34. Ibid., 139–141. Malinovsky presided over his *front's* near total destruction during Operation Blau but survived the embarrassment to command 66th Army during its many counterattacks in the Kotluban' region northwest of Stalingrad from August into October 1942 and the powerful 2nd Guards Army from October 1942 to February 1943, when his army played a pivotal role blocking German attempts to relieve Sixth Army encircled in Stalingrad. Thereafter, Stalin appointed Malinovsky to command Southern Front in February 1943 and Southwestern Front in March 1943. Malinovsky commanded the Southwestern (renamed 3rd Ukrainian in October 1943) and 2nd Ukrainian Fronts until war's end. Because Malinovsky had planned and conducted most of the Red Army's most significant victories in the Ukraine and southeastern Europe, Stalin appointed him commander of Trans-Baikal Front during the Manchurian campaign against the Japanese Kwantung Army in August and September 1945. After remaining in the Far East as Supreme High Commander from 1947 to 1953 and commander, Far East Military District, from 1953 to 1956, Malinovsky returned to Moscow in March 1956 to become commander of Soviet Ground Forces and 1st Deputy Minister of Defense of the USSR and, in October 1957, Minister of Defense of the USSR, a post he held until his death in 1967.

35. Ibid., 272–273. After commanding 64th Army during Operation Blau, Shumilov commanded the same army (redesignated as 7th Guards) to war's end and fought in the Red Army's famous victories at Kursk in the summer of 1943 and in the Ukraine, Romania, and Hungary in 1944 before ending his wartime career at Vienna in May 1945. After the war, Shumilov commanded 7th Guards Army through 1948 and the Belorussian and Voronezh Military Districts from 1948 until his retirement in 1958. Shumilov died in 1975 at age 80.

36. Timothy A. Wray, *Standing Fast: German Defensive Doctrine on the Russian Front during World War II, Prewar to March 1943* (Ft. Leavenworth, KS: Combat Studies Institute, 1986), 112–113.

37. Halder, *The Halder War Diaries*, vol. 2, 348.

38. See Marcel Stein, *Field Marshal von Manstein, A Portrait: The Janus Head* (Solihull, UK: Helion, 2007), esp. 251–310.

39. Omar Bartov, *The Eastern Front, 1941–45: German Troops and the Barbarization of Warfare* (New York: St. Martin's, 1986), 51, 66, and passim.

40. For a more detailed description of the Red Army soldier, see David M. Glantz, *Colossus Reborn: The Red Army at War, 1941–1943* (Lawrence: University Press of Kansas, 2005), 536–608.

Chapter 2: The Battle in Stalingrad's Suburbs, 3–12 September 1942

1. Compare Army Group B's strength on 3 September 1942 with Army Group South's strength of roughly 1 million German and 300,000 Hungarian, Romanian, Italian, and Slovak soldiers on 28 June 1942. By this time Army Groups A and B had lost more than 547,000 men but had received only 415,000 replacements, for a net reduction in strength of 132,000 men. The figures shown reflect actual strength rather than ration strength.

2. As many as 10,000 troops of XIV Panzer Corps also operated against Stalingrad's northern suburbs, but only a fraction of these forces did so offensively.

3. Rokossovsky, *Velikaia Pobeda na Volge*, 154, asserts that the German forces facing 62nd Army fielded 390 tanks. Moshchansky and Smolinov, *Oborona Stalingrada*, 38, claims the infantry divisions and 14th and 24th Panzer and 29th Motorized Divisions facing 62nd and 64th Armies fielded 500 tanks. However, even including the 30–40 assault guns in Sixth Army's 177th, 244th, and 245th Assault Gun Battalions [*Sturmgeschutz-Abteilung*], these figures are excessive.

4. The *Stavka* transferred 7th and 16th Tank Corps from Voronezh Front. Stalingrad Front's tank strength included 191 tanks in the fresh 7th Tank Corps and slightly more than 100 tanks in 4th and 16th Tank Corps. See V. V. Beshanov, *God 1942—"Uchebnyi"* [The Year 1942—"Training"] (Minsk: Harvest, 2002), 527–529; and Rokossovsky, *Velikaia bitva na Volge*, 154, which also places 62nd and 64th Armies' tank strength at 146.

5. Rokossovsky, *Velikaia bitva na Volge*, 155, places 8th Air Army's strength at 137 operable aircraft, plus 89 aircraft from 16th Air Army.

6. See appropriate daily maps for this period, in "Ia. Lagenkarten Nr. 1 zum KTB Nr. 13, Jul–Oct 1942," *AOK 6, 23948/1a*, in NAM T-312, Roll 1446; and, on the *Luftwaffe*, see Hayward, *Stopped at Stalingrad*, 195. Estimates of the relative strength of the opposing forces vary widely, depending on source and what forces are included in the count. For example, Rokossovsky, *Velikaia pobeda na Volge*, 154, claims the eight Axis divisions (389th, 295th, and 71st Infantry, 24th Panzer, Romanian 20th Infantry, 14th Panzer, 29th Motorized, and 94th Infantry), which were deployed from Kul'stan, northwest of Stalingrad, to Elkhi in the city's southwestern suburbs, numbered 80,240 men, supported by 390 tanks and 1,880 guns and mortars, opposing 62nd Army's 44,970 men, 108 tanks, and 495 guns and mortars. By contrast, Moshchansky and Smolinov, *Oborona Stalingrada*, 38, which includes Fourth Panzer Army's IV Army Corps in its figures, claims the Axis committed 10 divisions (295th, 71st, and 76th Infantry, 24th Panzer, Romanian 20th Infantry, 14th Panzer, 29th Motorized, and 94th, 297th, and 371st Infantry) and 500 tanks against 62nd and 64th Armies' 144 tanks (80 operable and 64 inoperable). In addition, Isaev, *Kogda vnezapnost' uzhe ne bylo*, 80, places 62nd Army's strength on 3 September at 54,000 men and the strength of German forces deployed between the Don River at Kletskaia and Elkhi (VIII and LI Army and XIV and XXXXVIII Panzer Corps) at 100,000 men. The same source claims 24th Panzer Division fielded 41 tanks and 14th and 16th Panzer Divisions were in "even worse" condition.

7. Later still, at Weichs and Hoth's request, on 15 September Hitler transferred Kempf's XXXXVIII Panzer Corps, with its 24th Panzer, 29th Motorized, and 94th Infantry Divisions, to Paulus's command to ensure unity of command and permit Hoth to plan his advance on Astrakhan'. This transfer left Hoth with IV Army Corps' four divisions (14th Panzer and Romanian 20th Infantry and 297th and 371st Infantry), flanked on the right by Romanian VI Army Corps, to contain 64th Army's large bridgehead around Beketovka, south of the city, defend the army group's right flank, and conduct the projected thrust on Astrakhan'.

8. The 12 Axis divisions involved in the city fighting during September included the German 16th, 14th, and 24th Panzer, 29th Motorized, and 389th, 295th, 71st, and 94th Infantry Divisions and the Romanian 20th Infantry Division. In October and November, the German 305th Infantry, 100th Jäger, and 79th Infantry Divisions

joined them, for a total of 12 divisions. Chuikov's history of the fighting, as well as most subsequent Russian and Western histories, erroneously assert that 76th Infantry Division also took part in the assault on the city. See the Soviet order of battle in *Boevoi sostav Sovetskoi armii*, 2: 171–172.

9. See *Stavka* directives nos. 994180–994185, dated 0745 hours 31 August 1942, in Zolotarev, *"Stavka 1942,"* 380–381.

10. See *Stavka* directives nos. 994187, 994188, 994196, 994198, and 994199, dated 31 August 1942, in ibid., 382–383.

11. See *Stavka* directive no. 994186, dated 0745 hours 31 August 1942, in ibid., 381.

12. See *Stavka* directive no. 994197, dated 31 August 1942, in ibid., 383.

13. Born in 1896, Golubev rose to command a company in the Tsar's army during World War I, joined the Red Army in 1918, and led a platoon, company, and regiment during the Civil War. He graduated from the Frunze Academy in 1926, was chief of staff of 29th Rifle Division, and graduated from an officers improvement course (KUVNAS) in 1929. Golubev was an instructor at the Moscow Combined School and commanded 22nd Rifle Division during the 1930s before attending the General Staff Academy in 1937 and 1938. After serving as a senior instructor at the Frunze Academy from 1939 to March 1941, Golubev received command of the Western Special Military District's 10th Army, which he was leading when the German invasion began. During the first two weeks of Operation Barbarossa, the invaders encircled and destroyed this army in the Bialystok and Minsk encirclements. More fortunate than most of his troops, Golubev escaped from the Minsk pocket and was immediately assigned command of Central Front's 13th Army, which he led during the battle for Smolensk in July and August 1941. Relieved of his command on 25 August, Golubev worked on the Peoples' Commissariat of Defense's (NKO) staff until 15 October 1941, when the *Stavka* assigned him to lead Western Front's 43rd Army. Golubev led 43rd Army until October 1943, fighting in the battle for Moscow under Western Front's control, and in the Red Army's Smolensk and Belorussian offensives from August to October 1943 under the Kalinin (1st Baltic) Front's control. After he was seriously wounded during the heavy fighting on the approaches to Vitebsk on 10 October 1943, Golubev spent a year convalescing before he was assigned as deputy and later 1st Deputy Peoples' Commissar for the repatriation of Soviet citizens in Germany and other allied states, a post he occupied until 1949. Thereafter, Golubev taught at the Voroshilov Academy from 1949 to 1953 and, after a brief period in retirement, was secretary of the academy's council from 1956 through his death in 1956. For further details, see *Komandarmy, Voennyi biograficheskii slovar'*, 50.

14. See *Stavka* directive nos. 994189, 994190, and 994192, dated 31 August 1942, in Zolotarev, *"Stavka 1942,"* 384–385.

15. Moskalenko, *Na iugo-zapadnom napravlenii*, 1: 315.

16. Four of 1st Guards Army's rifle divisions were transferred from other sectors of the front, including 24th Division from Kalinin Front, 64th Division from 8th Reserve Army, 84th Division from Northwestern Front, and 116th Division from Western Front. See Aleksei Isaev, *Stalingrad: Za Volgoi dlia nas zemli net* [Stalingrad: There is no land for us beyond Stalingrad] (Moscow: Iauza, Eksmo, 2008), 141.

17. The armored strength of 4th, 16th, and 7th Tank Corps as of 31 August was as follows:

	4th Tank Corps			16th Tank Corps			7th Tank Corps		
Tank Model	45 TB	47 TB	102 TB	107 TB	109 TB	164 TB	3 Gds. TB	62 TB	87 TB
KV	4	3	—	10	—	—	33	—	—
T-34	—	8	5	—	11	28	—	44	30
T-60	1	9	3	23	19	13	27	20	15
T-70	—	3	—	—	—	—	—	—	—
Total	5	23	8	33	30	41	60	64	45
Grand total		36			104			169	

See Isaev, *Stalingrad*, 142, citing *TsAMO, RF,* f. 220, op. 220, d. 71, l. 192 and f. 3401, op. 1, d. 8, l. 2.

18. Moskalenko. *Na iugo-zapadnom napravlenii*, 316.

19. Group Kovalenko's (i.e., 1st Guards Army's) new front extended from 8 kilometers south of Kotluban' to roughly 23 kilometers southeast of Kotluban'.

20. Moskalenko, *Na iugo-zapadnom napravlenii*, 1: 316.

21. Ibid., 318, quoting archival citation *TsAMO*, f. 220, op. 451, d. 26, ll. 202–204. See Zhukov's account in Zhukov, *Reminiscences and Reflections*, Book II, 89.

22. Moskalenko, *Na iugo-zapadnom napravlenii*, 1: 319, quoting *TsAMO*, f. 300, op. 6914, d. 17., ll. 129–130; and Zhukov, *Reminiscences and Reflections*, Book II, 89.

23. Moskalenko, *Na iugo-zapadnom napravlenii*, 1: 319.

24. See German movements in "Ia. Lagenkarten Nr. 1 zum KTB Nr. 13, Jul–Oct 1942," *AOK 6, 23948/1a*, in NAM T-312, Roll 1446.

25. Ibid.; and Langermann, *3. Infanterie-Division*, 199–202.

26. See a scathing critique of 4th Tank Army's offensives in late August and early September prepared by the Special Department of the Stalingrad Front's NKVD, in *Stalingradskaia epopeia: Vpervye publikuemye dokumenty, rassekrechennye FSB RF* [Stalingrad epoch: Declassified documents of the Russian Federation's FSB published for the first time] (Moscow: "Evonnitsa-MG," 2000), 201–203.

27. Rotmistrov's 7th Tank Corps attacked in two-echelon formation, with its 3rd Guards and 62nd Tank Brigades in first echelon and its 87th Tank and 7th Motorized Rifle Brigades in second. When the attack by the two lead brigades faltered largely due to poor coordination with the advancing infantry of 116th Rifle Division, Rotmistrov committed his second-echelon 87th Tank Brigade to break the deadlock. However, its attack also faltered in the face of intense German antitank fire. The day's fighting ultimately cost 7th Tank Corps 53 tanks burned or otherwise destroyed, including 12 KV, 32 T-34, and 9 T-60 tanks. See Isaev, *Stalingrad*, 145, citing *TsAMO RF*, f. 3401, op. 1, d. 3., l. 2. The 23rd Tank Corps' 2nd Motorized Rifle and 189th Tank Brigades and cooperating infantry from 399th Rifle Division, which were supposed to link up with 7th Tank Corps' forces north of Gorodishche, were unable to do so because of strong German resistance and heavy fog that shrouded the battlefield.

28. Moskalenko, *Na iugo-zapadnom napravlenii*, 1: 321–322.

29. For a complete German perspective on this intense fighting, see *3. Infanterie-Division*, 201–202.

30. Moskalenko, *Na iugo-zapadnom napravlenii*, 1: 322.

31. Zhilin, *Stalingradskaia bitva*, 486.

32. See "Ia. Lagenkarten Nr. 1 zum KTB Nr. 13, Jul–Oct 1942," *AOK 6, 23948/1a*, in NAM T-312, Roll 1446.

33. See *Stavka* order no. 170599, dated 2230 hours 3 September 1942, in Zolotarev, "*Stavka 1942*," 387.

34. Zhukov, *Reminiscences and Reflections*, Book II, 90; and Moskalenko, *Na iugo-zapadnom napravlenii*, 1: 325.

35. Zhilin, *Stalingradskaia bitva*, 492.

36. Isaev, *Stalingrad*, 147–148.

37. Zhilin, *Stalingradskaia bitva*, quoting KTB OKW. Bd. II, 1162–1163.

38. Moskalenko, *Na iugo-zapadnom napravlenii*, 1: 326.

39. Ibid. "Ia. Lagenkarten Nr. 1 zum KTB Nr. 13, Jul–Oct 1942," *AOK 6, 23948/1a*, in NAM T-312, Roll 1446.

40. Moskalenko, *Na iugo-zapadnom napravlenii*, 1: 327, citing *TsAMO*, f. 220, op. 451, d. 54, ll. 51–52.

41. Ibid., 329. Zhukov, *Reminiscences and Reflections*, Book II, 91–92, describes the action but does not mention the delay in the assaults by 66th and 24th Armies.

42. Moskalenko, *Na iugo-zapadnom napravlenii*, 1: 329.

43. See a frank discussion of Zhukov's and Eremenko's plan, in ibid., 329–331.

44. Werthen, *Geschichte der 16. Panzer-Division*, 111–112.

45. Zhilin, *Stalingradskaia bitva*, 499–500.

46. Werthen, *Geschichte der 16. Panzer-Division*, 112.

47. Ziemke and Bauer, *Moscow to Stalingrad*, 391.

48. Ibid.

49. See Zolotarev, "*Stavka 1942*," 389.

50. Ibid., 390.

51. Zhilin, *Stalingradskaia bitva*, 511–525.

52. See details concerning the action from 10 to 13 September, in ibid., 529–542.

53. P. A. Rotmistrov, *Stal'naia gvardiia* [The steel guards] (Moscow: Voenizdat, 1984), 124.

54. "Ia. Lagenkarten Nr. 1 zum KTB Nr. 13, Jul–Oct 1942," *AOK 6, 23948/1a*, in NAM T-312, Roll 1446.

55. Werthen, *Geschichte der 16. Panzer-Division*, 111–112.

56. "Ia. Lagenkarten Nr. 1 zum KTB Nr. 13, Jul–Oct 1942," *AOK 6, 23948/1a*, in NAM T-312, Roll 1446.

57. Zhukov, *Reminiscences and Reflections*, Book II, 93.

58. Moskalenko, *Na iugo-zapadnom napravlenii*, 1: 332–333.

59. "Ia. Lagenkarten Nr. 1 zum KTB Nr. 13, Jul–Oct 1942," *AOK 6, 23948/1a*, in NAM T-312, Roll 1446.

60. See these discussions in Zhukov, *Reminiscences and Reflections*, Book II, 93–94.

61. Ibid., 94.

62. Ibid.

63. Zhilin, *Stalingradskaia bitva*, 548.

64. Rokossovsky, *Velikaia pobeda na Volge*, 157.

65. Ibid.
66. Ibid.
67. Moskalenko, *Na iugo-zapadnom napravlenii*, 1: 328.
68. Ibid.
69. Rotmistrov, *Stal'naia gvardiia*, 123.
70. Moskalenko, *Na iugo-zapadnom napravlenii*, 1: 329.
71. Langermann, *3. Infanterie-Division*, 203.
72. "Boevoe rasporiazhenie no. 0075/op, Shtab IuVF, 1. 9. 42. 2215." [Combat order no. 0075/op, headquarters, Southeastern Front, 2215 hours 1 September 1942], in *62nd Army Combat Journal*, copy of the original. Hereafter cited as *62nd Army Combat Journal*.
73. "Vypiska iz boevogo prikaza no. 0078/op, Shtab IuVF, 2. 9. 42. 0300" [Excerpts from combat order no. 0078/op, headquarters, Southeastern Front, 0300 hours 2 September 1942], in ibid.
74. Samsonov, *Stalingradskaia bitva*, 276; and *Geroi Sovetskogo Soiuza, tom 1* [Heroes of the Soviet Union, vol. 1] (Moscow: Voenizdat, 1987), 128. Batrakov's early military career remains obscure. During Operation Barbarossa, Batrakov commanded 211th Rifle Division from 4 August to 13 October 1941. After being severely wounded in the fighting for Stalingrad, he attended the Voroshilov Academy and led 59th Rifle Division from 31 May 1944 to 3 September 1945. Promoted to major general in April 1945, after the European phase of the war ended, Batrakov led his division, under the control of 5th Army, during the Soviet offensive against the Kwantung Army in Manchuria in August and September 1945. Thereafter, he served as military commissar of the Novosibirsk region, retired in 1952, and died in 1995. See the website www.generals.dk.
75. Afanas'ev survived the battle for Stalingrad and was promoted to major general on 1 September 1943. He commanded 244th Rifle Division until 15 August 1944. Thereafter, however, his military career remains obscure.
76. "Boevoi prikaz no. 120. Shtarm 62. 3. 9. 42. 4.00" [Combat order no. 120. headquarters, 62nd Army, 0400 hours 3 September 1942], in *62nd Army Combat Journal*.
77. Ziemke and Bauer, *Moscow to Stalingrad*, 392.
78. Mark, *Death of the Leaping Horseman*, 115.
79. Ibid., 115–116.
80. Born on 1 January 1901, Glazkov joined the Red Army in 1920 and fought on the southern front during the Civil War. A graduate of infantry command courses in 1922 and 1925 and the Leningrad Parachute–Air Assault Course in 1935, Glazkov commanded an infantry platoon and company in the 1920s and a battalion during the first half of the 1930s. After his parachute training, he led a battalion in the Red Banner Far Eastern Army's 12th Rifle Division from October to June 1936, a battalion in the same army's 5th Air Assault Regiment from June 1936 to May 1938, and 1st Separate Red Banner Army's 5th Air Assault Regiment from May to October 1938 and 211th Airborne Brigade from October 1938 to the outbreak of the war. During Operation Barbarossa, Glazkov commanded his airborne brigade until October 1941, when he received command of the Volga Military District's 8th Airborne Corps. After the NKO reorganized his airborne corps into 35th Guards Rifle Division on 6 August

1942, Glazkov led the division during the heavy fighting on the approaches to Stalingrad until his death from German artillery fire in the village of Verkhniaia El'shanka on 8 September 1942. For further details about his life, see *Komkory, Voennyi biograficheskii slovar'*, 2: 10–11; and the website www.generals.dk. The circumstances surrounding his death are found in Maslov, *Fallen Soviet Generals*, 59.

81. Zhilin, *Stalingradskaia bitva*, 485. See also "Ia. Lagenkarten Nr. 1 zum KTB Nr. 13, Jul–Oct 1942," *AOK 6, 23948/1a*, in NAM T-312, Roll 1446. Born in 1897, Pesochin's prewar military career remains obscure. During Operation Barbarossa, he commanded 6th Army's 411th Rifle Division from 15 April 1942 until it was disbanded on 30 June 1942 after being demolished during the Germans' Operation Fridericus. Thereafter, he led 131st Rifle Division from 27 July 1942 to 18 November 1943 and 225th Rifle Division from 29 May 1944 until he was severely wounded on 10 February 1945 during 1st Ukrainian Front's Lower Silesian offensive. Pesochin died in a Red Army field hospital on 3 March and was posthumously promoted to major general in April 1955. For further details about his career and death, see Maslov, *Fallen Soviet Generals*, 240.

82. Wuthmann, most of whose military career remains obscure, commanded 295th Infantry Division from 2 May to 16 November 1942. Presumably, he was either killed or wounded in the city fighting.

Hartmann, who was born on 11 December 1890, joined the *Reichswehr* in 1934, was promoted to lieutenant colonel in 1937, commanded 37th Infantry Regiment from 1937 to 1941 (and was promoted to colonel), and led 71st Infantry Division from 28 March 1941 to 24 January 1943. Promoted to major general in 1941, lieutenant general in September 1942, and general of infantry on 1 January 1943, Hartmann was killed in action on 25 January 1942 during the struggle for the Stalingrad pocket. See Heiber and Glantz, *Hitler and His Generals*, 804.

Born on 9 May 1901, Travnikov joined the Red Army in 1920, fought in the Civil War, and graduated from infantry commanders' courses in 1922 and 1925, the Zhukovsky Air Academy in 1935, and the Voroshilov Academy in 1941. An aviation officer who later transferred to airborne forces, Travnikov commanded a platoon, company, and battalion in 9th Don Rifle Division during the 1920s before attending the Air Academy during the first half of the 1930s. After graduating from the academy, he was chief of staff of 19th Heavy Bomber Aviation Brigade from May 1936 to January 1940 and chief of staff of the Voronezh Reserve Aviation Brigade from January to September 1940. Returning to academe, Travnikov was deputy chief of the operations faculty of the Red Army's Military Academy for Command and Navigator Cadre in September and October 1940 and a student at the Voroshilov Academy until the beginning of the war. During Operation Barbarossa Travnikov was senior assistant head of the Red Army General Staff's Reserve Operations Directorate in September 1941 and, later in the month, became commander of the newly formed 3rd Airborne Corps. He received command of 399th Rifle Division on 1 March 1942 and led his division during the heavy fighting in the Stalingrad region in August and September. After his division was withdrawn from the Stalingrad region for refitting, Travnikov led the new 9th Airborne Corps briefly in November and December 1942 and, after it was redesignated as 5th Guards Airborne Division in December, commanded the guards' division from 8 December 1942 to 30 May 1943, fighting under 68th Army's control in the Demiansk region in the winter of 1942–1943. Travnikov then led 299th Rifle Division from 13 August 1943 to 13 March 1945, when his division took part in many famous operations, including Steppe Front's Belgorod-Khar'kov offensive in August 1943 and the Iasi-Kishinev offensive in August 1944. In March 1944, however, Travnikov was relieved of command, ostensibly because he failed to create a solid enough defense during the German offensive at Lake Balaton in Hungary. He then served as deputy military commandant in Vienna from April 1945 to March 1947 and taught on various faculties at the Voroshilov Academy until June 1950. Travnikov ended his military career as principal adviser to the Chinese Peoples' Army's Officers Command Course (KUKS). He retired in June 1958 and died in 1970. For additional details, see *Komkory, Voennyi biograficheskii slovar'*, 2: 35–36.

Although little is known about Ermolkin's military career, he commanded 112th Rifle Division from 10 August to 15 November 1942 and, while doing so, was promoted to colonel on 31 August. Regardless of his ultimate fate, his division was sent to the Saratov region for rest and refitting in late October or early November 1942.

83. Born on 25 August 1901, Kazartsev joined the Red Army in 1920 and fought on the eastern front in the Civil War. He received his military education at officers' courses in the Siberian Military District in 1923 and 1926, the Frunze Academy in 1936, and the Voroshilov Academy in 1947. A junior commander and political officer in the Siberian Military District during the 1920s, he rose to lead a battalion in 73rd Rifle Division in 1932. After graduating from the Frunze Academy in 1936, Kazartsev served in staff positions in Separate Far Eastern Red Banner Army's 92nd Rifle Division, rising to become the division's chief of staff in late 1940 and chief of staff of 1st Red Banner Army's 26th Rifle Corps in March 1941. After he served as chief of staff of 26th Corps throughout the first year of Operation Barbarossa, the NKO assigned Kazartsev as commander of Stalingrad Front's 87th Rifle Division in July 1942. Although his division was decimated during German Sixth Army's advance to the Volga River in August, he led its remnants during the intense fighting in Stalingrad city in September and October. Surviving his ordeal in Stalingrad, Kazartsev commanded 126th Rifle Division from 5 March 1943 to 10 June 1944. During this period he became a Hero of the Soviet Union in January 1943 for heroism in the defense of Stalingrad and was promoted to major general on 15 September 1943 for his division's effective performance during Southern Front's offensive in the Donbas region in the fall of 1943. Kazartsev then led 72nd Rifle Corps from 11 July 1944 to 3 September 1945, participating in 3rd Belorussian Front's offensives in Belorussia during the summer of 1944 and in East Prussia during January and February 1945. After the European war ended, the *Stavka* transferred Kazartsev's corps to the Far East, where it took part in 1st Far Eastern Front's Manchurian offensive in August and September 1945. Thereafter, he led the Carpathian Military District's 3rd Mountain Rifle Corps until December 1949 and then occupied senior command and staff positions in the Soviet Army's Air Defense Forces until his retirement in 1960. Promoted to colonel general in 1958, Kazartsev died in 1985. For additional details, see *Komkory, Voennyi biograficheskii slovar'*, 1: 250–251.

84. Although little is know about Ivanov's military career, he commanded 196th Rifle Division from 17 August to 8 December 1942 and 10th Guards Airborne Division from 8 December 1942 to 23 December 1943. He was promoted to the rank of major general on 25 September 1943. After a brief interruption, probably to serve

on *front* or army staff, Ivanov ended his wartime service leading 114th Guards Rifle Division from 25 December 1944 to 11 May 1945.

85. Zhilin, *Stalingradskaia bitva*, 484.

86. See entry for 4 September 1942, in *62nd Army Combat Journal*.

87. Kravchenko's counterattack force consisted of his corps' 27th and 99th Tank Brigades (62 tanks) and elements of 112th Rifle Division. The failed attack reduced 27th Tank Brigade's strength to 15 tanks (1 T-34, 1 T-70, and 13 T-60s) and 99th Tank Brigade's to 20 tanks (16 T-34s and 4 T-70s). See Isaev, *Stalingrad*, 154.

88. Ibid.

89. See the details of this fighting and Lopatin's orders, in *62nd Army Combat Journal*.

90. Mark, *Death of the Leaping Horseman*, 118.

91. Zhilin, *Stalingradskaia bitva*, 493. See also "Ia. Lagenkarten Nr. 1 zum KTB Nr. 13, Jul–Oct 1942," *AOK 6, 23948/1a*, in NAM T-312, Roll 1446.

92. See entry for 5 September 1942, in *62nd Army Combat Journal*.

93. Zhilin, *Stalingradskaia bitva*, 494, quoting from *KTB OKW*. Bd. II, 1162–1163.N.

94. Ibid., 498.

95. Mark, *Death of the Leaping Horseman*, 124–125.

96. Ibid., 126. This included 10 Pz. II, 20 Pz. III, and 4 Pz. IV long tanks, plus one command tank.

97. Rokossovsky, *Velikaia bitva na Volge*, 159. Lopatin included the five tank brigades as a reconstituted 2nd Tank Corps. He also formed two army artillery groups to support his army, the first consisting of 266th and 1103rd Gun Artillery Regiments, 1st Battalion, 457th Gun Artillery Regiment, and 47th and 89th Guards-Mortar Regiments, and the second made up of 1105th Gun and 85th Guards Howitzer Artillery Regiments and 83rd and 91st Guards-Mortar Regiments. The 64th and 57th Armies formed one army artillery group each. However, when 62nd and 64th Armies' fronts shrank to a total length of about 30 kilometers, on 13 September Eremenko combined all of the army artillery groups into a single *front* artillery group on the Volga River's eastern bank. Its mission was to conduct massive fires against German forces penetrating into the city. In turn, Eremenko's chief of artillery subdivided the *front*'s artillery into four subgroups as follows:

- **Northern** in support of 62nd Army, including 266th, 457th, 1103rd, and 1105th Gun Artillery Regiments, 3rd Battalion, 85th Guards Howitzer Regiment, and 125th Mortar Regiment, with a total of 86 guns and mortars;
- **Southern** in support of 64th Army, including 1111th, 1104th, and 1159th Gun Artillery and 140th Mortar Regiments, with a total of 64 guns and mortars;
- **Volga Military Flotilla**, with 16 guns; and
- **Antiaircraft**, with 84 85mm guns.

Southeastern Front's *front* artillery group consisted of a total of 250 guns and mortars, including six 76mm guns, 84 85mm guns, four 100mm guns, six 107mm guns, 72 120mm mortars, 33 122mm gun-howitzers, and 45 152mm gun-howitzers.

The Soviets employed the antiaircraft guns, together with the field guns and an-titank rifles, to engage enemy tanks and used the six antiaircraft batteries to protect the crossings over the Volga River. The Volga Flotilla used its guns principally in sup-port of 62nd Army's forces fighting in the Kuporosnoe region and 64th Army's forces defending the Beketovka bridgehead. See ibid., 160.

98. Zhilin, *Stalingradskaia bitva*, 500.

99. Mark, *Death of the Leaping Horseman*, 127. XXXXVIII Panzer Corps as-signed the following missions to its forces on the night of 5–6 September:

> Reinforced 14. Panzer-Division will attack over the railway line from the line 153.2-Barracks over the western edge of Verkhne-Yelshanka [El'shanka] and occupy Hill 144.9. With a progressive attack, an anti-tank defen-sive front will be constructed on the right flank facing the high ground east of Pestshanka [Peschanka]. After the capture of Hill 144.9 by grena-diers, Panzer Abteilung von der Lancken containing all of the Korps' panzers will immediately thrust through to the Volga bridge south of Ku-perossnoye [Kuporosnoe]. For this attack, it is subordinate to 14. Panzer-Division.
>
> 29. Infanterie-Division (mot.) (without panzers) will attack out of the area south-east of 145.8 through Drieckwäden [small triangular forest] to Verkhne-Yelshanka and take it. After clearing this village, the division will next gain the Pestshanka-Stalingrad road.
>
> 24. Panzer-Division (without panzers)—while holding their positions in Square Forest—will attack with the bulk of the Division over Hill 147.5, clean out the area from the southern slope of this hill up to the railway line and in the further course of the attack, cover the eastern flank of Korps and in addition to this, win the eastern edge of the forest south-east of Verkhne-Yelshanka.

Born in December 1905, Utvenko joined the Red Army in October 1924, was released in August 1938, and rejoined the army in December 1938. A 1927 gradu-ate of the Red Commanders School, he received no further higher education until he attended an accelerated course at the Voroshilov Academy in 1945 and the acad-emy's main course in 1947–1948. During the 1920s, Utvenko served as a commander and political officer at company and battalion levels before being released into the reserves in August 1938. Recalled in December of the same year, he was deputy chief of combat training in 19th Rifle Division's 56th Regiment, and from August 1939 until the German invasion he commanded the same division's 315th Rifle Regi-ment. In August 1941, the NKO assigned Utvenko command of 19th Rifle Division of the Reserve Front's 24th Army, which he led during the battle for Smolensk and the ensuing successful attack on the German El'nia bridgehead in September. After being promoted to colonel for his bravery at El'nia, when his division was encircled in the Viaz'ma region in October 1941, Utvenko led a small group of survivors out of the pocket and reconstituted his division under 43rd Army's control. His division then took part in the Moscow counteroffensive and Western Front's offensive in the winter of 1941–1942. Recovering from wounds he received in March 1942, Utvenko took command of 274th Rifle Division in May 1942 and, after it was reorganized into

33rd Guards Rifle Division during the summer, led this division during the German advance to Stalingrad and the intense fighting on the city's outskirts. In late September the *Stavka* withdrew his decimated division from Stalingrad and assigned it to the newly formed 2nd Guards Army in December 1942. Refilled with troops, Utvenko's division then took part in Stalingrad Front's offensive in the Kotel'nikovskii region in December 1942 and Southern Front's subsequent advance to Rostov and pursuit to the Mius River in February and March 1943. Elevated to command 5th Shock Army's 31st Guards Rifle Corps in April 1943, he led this corps until 7 February 1944, in the process becoming a lieutenant general on 17 January 1944. After graduating from the Voroshilov Academy's short course in March 1945, he commanded 9th Guards Army's 38th Guards Rifle Corps through the remainder of the war, participating in the fighting around Lake Balaton, Hungary, and the capture of Vienna in April 1945. After the war ended, Utvenko led the same corps (reorganized as 38th Guards Airborne Corps) until May 1948 and, after graduating from the Voroshilov Academy, commanded 65th Rifle Corps until July 1951. Utvenko ended his military career as a course and faculty chief at the Frunze Academy, retiring in May 1954. He died in 1963. For further details, see *Komkory, Voennyi biograficheskii slovar'*, 1: 581–583.

100. By late on 6 September, 189th Tank Brigade fielded 15 tanks, including 8 T-34s, 5 T-70s, and 2 T-60s, and 60th Motorized Rifle Battalion, with a total of 150 men. The 99th Tank Brigade lost 5 tanks during the day's fighting, 9th Motorized Rifle Brigade had 130 men, and 399th Rifle Division had 494 men, 3 antitank guns, 2 122mm mortars (but no ammunition), and 2 heavy and 5 light machine guns. See Moshchansky and Smolinov, *Oborona Stalingrada*, 38, and Isaev, *Stalingrad*, 155.

101. Zhilin, *Stalingradskaia bitva*, 505.

102. Isaev, *Stalingrad*, 156.

103. Zhilin, *Stalingradskaia bitva*, 511.

104. Ibid., 510; See also "Ia. Lagenkarten Nr. 1 zum KTB Nr. 13, Jul–Oct 1942," *AOK 6, 23948/1a*, in NAM T-312, Roll 1446.

105. Although little is known about Dubiansky's military career before the war, he was chief of staff of 24th Light Tank Brigade in 1940 and deputy commander of 7th Motorized Rifle Division in 1941. He rose to lead 35th Guards Rifle Division on 8 September 1942, after its previous leader, General Glazkov, was killed in action. Prior to commanding the 35th Guards, he had served as its chief of staff after it was formed from 8th Airborne Corps between 1 and 5 August 1942. Once his division's remnants were withdrawn from Stalingrad for rest and refitting, on 20 November Dubiansky returned to Moscow for duty on the NKO's staff. After the war, Dubiansky became commandant of the Suvorov Military School in Voronezh. See the website www.generals.dk.

106. Ziemke and Bauer, *Moscow to Stalingrad*, 392.

107. Ibid. For additional details on these altered plans, see Mark, *Death of the Leaping Horseman*, 129–145. Prior to this reorientation of the corps' main effort, 24th Panzer Division had concentrated on capturing Peschanka and Verkhne-El'shanka, in cooperation with the 29th Motorized and 14th Panzer Divisions. The combined force did so on 9 September, after extremely heavy and costly fighting.

108. Mark, *Death of the Leaping Horseman*, 137.

109. Zhilin, *Stalingradskaia bitva*, 517.

110. Rokossovsky, *Velikaia bitva na Volge*, 159.

111. Zhilin, *Stalingradskaia bitva*, 519.

112. Ziemke and Bauer, *Moscow to Stalingrad*, 392.

113. Zhilin, *Stalingradskaia bitva*, 523.

114. For details of XXXXVIII Panzer Corps' and 24th Panzer Division's fight, see Mark, *Death of the Leaping Horseman*, 143–146. By day's end on 9 September, the armor strength of 24th Panzer Division had eroded to 11 Pz. II, 6 Pz. III short, 10 Pz. III long, and 1 Pz. IV long tanks, plus a command tank.

115. Ibid.

116. Quoted in Goerlitz, *Paulus and Stalingrad*, 191.

117. See *Stavka* directive no. 170603, dated 0440 hour 8 September 1942, in Zolotarev, "*Stavka* 1942," 389, for Stalin's relief of Lopatin.

118. See *Stavka* directive no. 994200, dated 2310 hour 9 September 1942, in ibid., 390.

119. See Chuikov, *The Battle for Stalingrad*, 71–74, for details on Chuikov's hegira to his new command.

120. Ibid., 76.

121. Ibid., 80–81.

122. Born on 1 November 1901, Gurov joined the Red Army in 1919 and served as a junior officer and political worker on the far eastern front during the Civil War. Educated at military-political courses in 1921 and 1928, the infantry school in 1928, and the Military-Political Academy in 1936, he was a political worker in a battalion before rising to become chief military commissar at the Military-Pedagogical Institute in 1940–1941. After the outbreak of war, he served, in succession, as commissar of Western Front's 29th Army during the summer and fall of 1941, of Southwestern Front from January to August 1942, of 62nd Army from August 1942 to March 1943, and of Southern Front and 8th Guards Army from March 1943 until his death from an unspecified illness on 25 August 1943. Gurov rose to the rank of lieutenant general in late 1943. For additional details about Gurov's career, see "Gurov Kuz'ma Akimovich," in *VE*, 2: 534.

123. See, for example, Chuikov, *The Battle for Stalingrad*, 81–82; and NKVD reports about disciplinary matters, in *Stalingradskaia epopeia* [Stalingrad epoch] (Moscow: "Evonnitsa-MG," 2000), 192–208.

124. According to Isaev, *Stalingrad*, 161–162, citing *TsAMO RF*, f. 345, op. 5487, d. 6, l. 3, the numerical strength of 62nd Army's rifle formations on 11 September 1942 was as follows:

| Force | Men | Horses | Rifles | PPSh | Machine Guns | | Mortars | Guns | AT rifles |
					Light	Heavy			
33rd GRD	864	60	189	92	4	—	21	—	11
35th GRD	454	—	271	115	2	1	—	6	28
87th RD	1,819	315	509	40	1	—	13	—	—
98th RD	465	20	219	20	2	—	—	—	1
112th RD	2,297	638	1,181	117	5	6	11	—	—
131st RD	2,540	443	1,918	215	4	3	11	—	14
196th RD	1,004	107	605	162	3	—	3	1	6

229th RD	192	48	73	14	—	—	—	—	—
244th RD	3,685	860	989	141	14	5	115	29	130
315th RD	2,873	333	1,797	260	15	10	6	23	126
399th RD	565	18	—	—	—	—	—	—	—
10th RD NKVD	8,615	406	7,069	1,080	129	38	102	12	63
10th RB	1,912	280	1,148	18	11	34	26	—	24
115th RB	4,868	308	2,625	113	100	40	93	30	69
149th RB	4,125	630	3,472	590	115	29	51	23	78
124th RB	3,607	620	2,438	341	84	22	56	25	68
42nd RB	5,032	336	—	—	—	—	—	—	—
9th MRB	1,073	—	630	82	39	6	13	2	13
38th MRB	2,370	71	1,671	—	119	6	45	21	48
Total	48,360	5,493	26,804	3,400	647	200	566	172	679

125. Lemelson, et al., *29.-Division*, 198. See also Mark, *Death of the Leaping Horseman*, 147.

126. Ziemke and Bauer, *Moscow to Stalingrad*, 392; and Zhilin, *Stalingradskaia bitva*, 532.

127. Zhilin, *Stalingradskaia bitva*, 533, quoting the OKW's information bulletin (Berlin: Viking Verlag, 1943).

128. Zhilin, *Stalingradskaia bitva*, 532.

129. Ziemke and Bauer, *Moscow to Stalingrad*, 393.

130. Ibid.

131. Zhilin, *Stalingradskaia bitva*, 536.

132. Ibid.

133. "Ia. Lagenkarten Nr. 1 zum KTB Nr. 13, Jul–Oct 1942," *AOK 6, 23948/1a*, in NAM T-312, Roll 1446. For details on the 94th Infantry Division's regrouping and subordination, which took longer than anticipated, see Mark, *Death of the Leaping Horseman*, 145–149.

134. Mark, *Death of the Leaping Horseman*, 149–150. On 11 September 24th Panzer Division's 24th Panzer and 21st and 26th Panzer Grenadier Regiments reported combat strengths of 1,174, 1,125, and 1,424, respectively, as compared with their ration strengths of 2,302, 1,440, and 1,797. Its park of serviceable tanks included 4 Pz. II, 6 Pz. III short, 2 Pz. III long, and 2 Pz. IV long tanks, plus 2 command tanks.

135. Zhilin, *Stalingradskaia bitva*, 543.

136. For additional details on the air battle, see Hayward, *Stopped at Stalingrad*, 194–195. Far younger than most of the commanders of the Red Army's combined-arms and tank armies, Khriukin was assigned command of 8th Air Army in June 1942 at the age of 32. Born on 21 June 1910, he joined the Red Army in 1932 and graduated from pilots school in Lugansk (Voroshilovgrad) 1933, General Staff Academy Command Courses (KUKS) in 1939 and 1941, and the Voroshilov Academy in 1950. Khriukin led an aircraft wing and squadron in the early 1930s before commanding an aviation squadron in the service of the Republican government during the Spanish Civil War from August 1936 to March 1937. Returning from Spain, he traveled to China, where he once again led an aircraft squadron and bomber group against

Japanese forces from March 1938 to early 1939, in the process earning the title of Hero of the Soviet Union. Khriukin then honed his combat experience by command- ing 14th Army's air forces during the Finnish War of 1939–1940. Resting after nearly four years of intermittent combat, he became chief of the bomber aviation depart- ment of the Red Army Air Force's Directorate for Combat Training in May 1940 and, in July 1940, deputy General-Inspector of the Air Forces within the USSR's Minis- try of Defense. As war approached, the NKO appointed him commander of the air forces of the Kiev Special Military District's 12th Army, a post he was occupying when war began. Exploiting his combat and organizational experience, the *Stavka* assigned Khriukin as commander of Kalinin Front's air forces in August 1941 and commander of Southwestern Front's air forces, and simultaneously, 8th Air Army in June 1942. He led this army until July 1944, organizing and conducting air operations in the bat- tle for Stalingrad and the Red Army's ensuing offensives across the Donbas in 1943 and the first half of 1944. Thereafter, he led 1st Air Army to war's end, participating in the Belorussian offensive in the summer of 1944 and the East Prussian offensive in January and February 1945. He earned his second Hero of the Soviet Union award in April 1945 for the role his aircraft played in the storming of the German fortress city of Konigsberg. After the war, Khriukin commanded 1st Air Army until August 1946, served as deputy High Commander of the Air Forces for Training until July 1947, commanded 7th Air Army until April 1949, commander of the Baku Air Defense Region until September 1950, and deputy High Commander of the Air Force for Training until his retirement. Khriukin died in July 1953. For additional details, see *Komandarmy, Voennyi biograficheskii slovar'*, 393–394.

137. See *Stavka* directive no. 170600, dated 0235 hours 6 September 1942, in Zolotarev, "*Stavka* 1942," 388. Born in 1901, Stepanov joined the Red Guards in 1917 and the Red Army in 1918 and served as a political officer and military inspector during the Civil War. Schooled at a correspondence course of the Combined Forces School in 1931 and at the Orenburg Pilot-Observer Military School in 1932 and a course at the 1st Military School for Pilots at Kacha in 1935, he spent the 1930s as a deputy commissar or commissar at the regimental, division, and military district levels. He gained his first experience with combat operations while serving as a com- missar to air forces supporting Soviet ground forces during the invasion of eastern Poland in September 1939 and Bessarabia in 1940. Because Stalin considered him to be absolutely politically reliable, the dictator appointed him as deputy chief for political units of the Red Army's Main Directorate for Air Forces in early 1941, a position he occupied during the first few months of Operation Barbarossa. Probably because of Stepanov's presumed reliability, Stalin also chose him to command an avi- ation group and, simultaneously, to coordinate air operations against German Second Panzer Group as it advanced toward Kiev in September 1941. Although these opera- tions failed, in October and November 1941 Stalin once again selected Stepanov to coordinate Western Front's and Kalinin Front's air operations during the defense of Moscow against German forces conducting Operation Typhoon, this time with far greater success. After managing the air forces during the Red Army's successful Mos- cow counteroffensive in December 1941, Stepanov led a special aviation group sup- porting Volkhov Front in January and February 1942 and coordinated air operations

for Briansk and Voronezh Fronts from March to May 1942. He capped his military career by commanding an aviation group and, finally, 16th Air Army during the battle for Stalingrad. However, beginning in September 1942, when political reliability no longer remained the cardinal prerequisite for command, Stalin relegated Stepanov to noncombat command of the air forces of various military districts, posts he filled until war's end and his retirement from military service in 1954. He did receive promotion to lieutenant general in 1943. Stepanov died in 1977. For further details, see *Komandarmy, Voennyi biograficheskii slovar'*, 391–392.

138. By 12 September, between them, XXXXVIII Panzer Corps' 24th and 14th Panzer Divisions each fielded roughly 40 operational tanks, and 29th Motorized Division somewhat fewer. Florian Freiherr von und zu Aufsess, "Tagesmeldung, Armee—Oberkommando 6, Abt. Ia, A. H. Qu., den 14. September 42," in *Die Anlagenbander zu den Kriegstagebuchern der 6. Armee vom 14.09.1942 bis 24.11.1942, Band I* (Schwabach: January 2006), 11, indicates Sixth Army fielded about 180 tanks on 14 September, subdivided as follows:

- **XIV Panzer Corps**
  - o 16th Panzer Division—72 tanks (8 Pz. II short, 52 Pz III long, 3 Pz. IV short, and 9 Pz III 7.5)
  - o 3rd Motorized Division—24 tanks (6 Pz. II, 15 Pz. III long, 1 Pz. IV short, and 2 Pz. III 7.5)
  - o 60th Motorized Division—no operational tanks indicated
- **XVII Army Corps**
  - o 22nd Panzer Division—66 tanks (9 Pz. IV long, 15 Pz. III long, 17 Pz. III 7.5, and 25 Pz. 38 (t)).

In addition, Sixth Army as a whole also included up to 30 assault guns of various types. Virtually every book written on the battle for Stalingrad, Western and Russian alike, all apparently based on Chuikov's appraisal of the fighting in the city, includes 76th Infantry Division in Weichs's assault group attacking Stalingrad city. This is mistaken, since this division was assigned to Sixth Army's VIII Army Corps. Since the 76th took part in defeating the Stalingrad Front's and, later, Don Front's assaults in the Kotluban' region, it was never committed to action against the city itself.

139. According to Moshchansky and Smolinov, *Oborona Stalingrada*, 39, after two days of heavy fighting, Southeastern Front's tank strength on 12 September was as follows:

- **62nd Army**—23rd Tank Corps, with 100 tanks (56 operational), including:
  - o 6th Tank Brigade—24 T-34s (18 operational)
  - o 6th Guards Tank Brigade—25 (15 T-34s and 4 T-70 operational and 3 T-34s and 3 T-60s nonoperational)
  - o 27th Tank Brigade—28 (3 T-34s, 1 T-70, and 1 T-60 operational and 9 T-34s, 7 T-70s, and 7 T-60s nonoperational)
  - o 189th Tank Brigade—23 (8 T-34s and 6 T-70s operational and 5 T-34s, 2 T-70s, and 2 T-60s nonoperational)
- **64th Army**—13th Tank Corps, with 23 tanks (11 operational), including:

   o 13th Tank Brigade—8 (3 T-34s, 2 70s, and 1 T-60 operational and 2
       T-60s nonoperational)
   o 39th Tank Brigade—reforming without tanks
   o 56th Tank Brigade—15 (1 T-34 and 4 T-70s operational and 3 T-34s
       and 9 T-60s nonoperational)
- **Front Subordinates**
   o 99th Tank Brigade—without tanks
   o 137th Tank Brigade—15 T-60s operational
   Total—138 (82 operational)

140. Rokossovsky, *Velikaia pobeda na Volge*, 164, generalizes by stating the 87th, 98th, and 196th Rifle Divisions averaged 800 riflemen each.

141. Beshanov, *God 1942*, 534.

Chapter 3: The Battle for Central and Southern Stalingrad, 13–26 September 1942

1. See German dispositions and troop movements in "Ia. Lagenkarten Nr. 1 zum KTB Nr. 13, Jul–Oct 1942," *AOK 6, 23948/1a*, in NAM T-312, Roll 1446.

2. See "Lagenkarten zum KTB. Nr. 5 (Teil III.), PzAOK 4, Ia, 21 Oct–24 Nov 1942," *PzAOK 4, 28183/12*, in NAM T-313, Roll 359; and Hayward, *Stopped at Stalingrad*, 231. Colonel Stahel escaped from the Stalingrad encirclement in late November 1942 to command another *kampfgruppe* identified by his name along the Chir River in early December. Stahel later played an instrumental role in the defense of Zaporozh'e in mid-February 1943 and served as commander of the German garrison in Warsaw in late summer 1944. The employment of Group Stahel preceded the OKH's fielding and employment of *Luftwaffe* field divisions, which began in December 1942.

3. "Lagenkarten zum KTB. Nr. 5 (Teil III.), PzAOK 4, Ia, 21 Oct–24 Nov 1942," *PzAOK 4, 28183/12*, in NAM T-313, Roll 359.

4. For the 12–13 September conference, see Paulus's own account in Goerlitz, *Paulus and Stalingrad*, 159–160.

5. Zhilin, *Stalingradskaia bitva*, 545, quoting *KTB OKW*. Bd. II, Hb. 2, s. 520.

6. Ibid.

7. Ziemke and Bauer, *Moscow to Stalingrad*, 395; and Blau, *The German Campaign in Russia*, 168.

8. *Boevoi sostav Sovetskoi armii*, 2: 171–172; and Zhilin, *Stalingradskaia bitva*, 542–543.

9. Samsonov, *Stalingradskaia bitva*, 176.

10. Ibid., 176, claims that 62nd and 64th Armies fielded 120 tanks, and the Germans committed 500 tanks in the battle for the city. However, this figure, which includes XIV Panzer Corps' tanks and all of the assault guns available to 177th, 244th, and 245th Assault Gun Detachments in Weichs's shock groups, is vastly inflated.

11. Moshchansky and Smolinov, *Oborona Stalingrada*, 41–43, citing "Doklad o boevykh deistviiakh avtobronetankovykh voisk Stalingradskogo fronta za period s

11 sentiabria po 1 oktiabria 1942 goda" [Report concerning the combat actions of the Stalingrad Front's auto-armored forces for the period 11 September–1 October 1942], in *TsAMO*, f. 38, op. 80038ss, d. 49, l. 5.

12. Jentz, *Panzertruppen*, 1: 248. Mark, *Death of the Leaping Horseman*, 157, places 24th Panzer Division's tank park on 13 September at seven Pz. II, five Pz. III short, six Pz. III long, one Pz. IV short, and three Pz. IV long tanks and one command tank.

13. For the daily strengths of these assault-gun battalions, see Sixth Army's daily strength returns for the period 1 September through 18 November 1942, in NAM T-312, Roll 1453.

14. Rokossovsky, *Velikaia bitva na Volge*, 169.

15. Ibid., 170.

16. XXXXVIII Panzer Corps directed 24th Panzer Division to conduct its main attack eastward along and north of the main railroad line south of the Tsaritsa River, advance into the heart of the southern part of Stalingrad, wheel northward to cross the Tsaritsa River, and then cooperate with LI Corps' 71st Infantry Division in clearing Soviet forces from the central part of Stalingrad. On 24th Panzer's right, 94th Infantry and 29th Motorized Divisions were to liquidate Soviet forces in Stalingrad's southern suburbs of Minina, El'shanka, and Kuporosnoe. See Mark, *Death of the Leaping Horseman*, 156–158.

17. "Chastnyi boevoi prikaz no. 188 Shtarm 62 11. 9. 42" [Individual order no. 188, headquarters, 62nd Army, 11 September 1942], in *62nd Army Combat Journal*.

18. Samsonov, *Stalingradskaia bitva*, 173, which asserts that the authorities evacuated about 125,000 inhabitants of Stalingrad across the Volga River from late August through early October, cites incomplete official statistics indicating that 42,754 of the city's inhabitants perished and that tens of thousands more were wounded during the bombing and artillery and mortar strikes on the city during this period and throughout the remainder of October. After early November, however, in ibid., 275, Samsonov states that only a few thousand inhabitants remained in the city.

19. This artillery included six artillery and mortar regiments belonging to Southeastern Front's artillery group and 2nd Tank Corps' artillery. See Rokossovsky, *Velikaia pobeda na Volge*, 171.

20. Zhilin, *Stalingradskaia bitva*, 549.

21. Ibid., 549.

22. Moshchansky and Smolinov, *Oborona Stalingrada*, 45.

23. For details on General Lenski's arrival, see Mark, *Death of the Leaping Horseman*, 157–158.

24. Ibid., 157.

25. For details, see Chuikov, *The Battle for Stalingrad*, 86–87, who later wrote, "Several bunkers were destroyed, and there were casualties among the army's headquarters' staff." In this sector, Chuikov erroneously identifies 76th Infantry Division as part of LI Army Corps' assaulting force, an error repeated in most subsequent accounts of the battle.

26. "Boevoi prikaz no. 145 Shtarm 62. 13. 9. 42 22.30" [Combat order no. 145, headquarters, 62nd Army, 2230 hours on 13 September 1942], in *62nd Army Combat Journal*. Confusion exists in older Soviet sources over just who commanded 92nd Rifle Brigade. F. I. Golikov, "V Oborona Stalingrada," in A. M. Samsonov, ed.,

Stalingradskaia epopeia [The Stalingrad epoch] (Moscow: "Nauka," 1968), 311, identifies Major V. I. Samodaia as the brigade's commander. However, the NKVD report cited below described Tarasov as the brigade's commander and describes his command neglect, and Chuikov's memoir points out his disobedience without mentioning his fate. No other major Soviet study of the battle refers to either officer. 92nd Brigade's daily maps and reports solve this mystery because Tarasov signed them. These maps also indicated that Major Shtrigol' was in command of the brigade by early November. It is likely that Tarasov was either shot or assigned to a penal battalion or company for his crimes.

27. "Opersvodka no. 150–151" [Operational summary no. 150–151], in *62nd Army Combat Journal*.

28. "Opersvodka no. 151–152" [Operational summary no. 151–152], in ibid. Ziemke and Bauer, *Moscow to Stalingrad*, 394, states the Germans reached the station at 1200 hours and the Volga River at 1500 hours. By contrast, Rokossovsky, *Velikaia bitva na Volge*, 172, claims that the Germans reached the station at 1700 hours.

29. Moshchansky and Smolinov, *Oborona Stalingrada*, 46.

30. See additional details in Chuikov, *The Battle for Stalingrad*, 90–91.

31. Ibid., 87–91; and Ziemke and Bauer, *Moscow to Stalingrad*, 393–394.

32. Zhilin, *Stalingradskaia bitva*, 555.

33. Ibid., quoting OKW informational bulletins.

34. Ibid., 556–557, quoting *KTB OKW*. Bd. II. S. 1245–1246.

35. Ibid.

36. "Opersvodka No. 151–152," in *62nd Army Combat Journal*.

37. Chuikov, *The Battle for Stalingrad*, 91. The 13th Guards Rifle Division was subordinate to Southwestern Front's 28th Army during the fighting in late June and early July when it was almost entirely destroyed during the heavy fighting west of Rossosh'. However, some of the division's cadre was successfully evacuated eastward to the Ural Military District, where the division was re-formed virtually from scratch during late July, August, and early September. Its strength as of 25 July was only 1,235 men. Alerted for duty at Stalingrad well before its training was complete, like many other divisions reinforcing 62nd Army, most of its men were veterans who had recovered from previous wounds or were green conscripts. The 13th Guards Division's strength on 13 September was 9,603 men. Like many other reinforcing divisions, 13th Guards went into battle with far short of its full complement of authorized rifles and heavy weapons, in this instance with 7,774 rifles, 170 PPD and PPSh (submachine guns), 30 light and 16 heavy machine guns, and no antiaircraft machine guns. See I. A. Samchuk, *Trinadtsataia gvardeiskaia* [13th Guards] (Moscow: Voenizdat, 1971), 97–99, and Isaev, *Stalingrad*, 171, citing TsAMO RF, f. 48, op. 451, d. 41, l. 69. Subsequently, however, Chuikov exploited internal resources within his army to increase the weapons strength of Rodimtsev's division. For example, by 15 September, after it suffered its initial losses, 13th Guards fielded 8,009 men, equipped with 5,616 rifles, 325 light and 36 heavy machine guns, 720 PPD and PPSh, and 229 antitank rifles. See Isaev, *Stalingrad*, 173, citing TsAMO RF, f. 48, op. 451, d. 41, l. 67.

38. "Rodimtsev, Aleksandr Il'ich," in *VE*, vol. 7 (Moscow: Voenizdat, 2003), 251. Born in 1905, Rodimtsev joined the Red Army in 1927. Originally a cavalryman, he graduated from a cavalry course at the Moscow Combined Military School in

1932, the Frunze Academy in 1939, the Military Academy for Command and Navigator Cadre of the Red Army's Air Forces in 1941, and, after surviving the war, the Voroshilov Academy in 1947. Rodimtsev commanded platoon and battalion in 36th Cavalry Division from March 1932 to January 1936 and then served for a year as a "volunteer" in the Republican Army in the Spanish Civil War, where he was awarded two Orders of the Red Banner and designated a Hero of the Soviet Union for his bravery. After returning to the Soviet Union, Rodimtsev led 36th Cavalry Division's 61st Regiment in 1937–1938 and was assistant commander of the same division from May 1939 to May 1941, during which period his division participated in the invasion of eastern Poland in September 1939. Appointed to command 3rd Airborne Corps' 5th Brigade in May 1941, he led his airborne troops in the defense of Kiev in August 1941 and 40th Army's attempts to halt German Second Panzer Group's drive south to Kiev in September. After 3rd Airborne Corps, together with Rodimtsev and most of his brigade, escaped encirclement at Kiev, the NKO reorganized the corps as the 87th Rifle Division with Rodimtsev as its commander. He then led the 87th throughout the fall of 1941 and winter campaign of 1941–1942, when it distinguished itself in the fighting east of Kursk. In recognition of that fine performance in the winter, the NKO redesignated the 87th as the 13th Guards Division in March 1942, with Rodimtsev still in command. During Operation Blau the division was nearly destroyed in the summer, only to be resurrected and sent to Stalingrad in September. After the battle for Stalingrad ended in early February 1943, Rodimtsev led the 13th Guards Rifle Division until April 1943 and then 32nd Guards Rifle Corps until the end of the war. As such he participated in some of the Red Army's most famous battles, including Kursk in July–August 1943, in the Ukraine during late 1943 and 1944, the Vistula-Oder offensive in Poland in January 1945, and the Berlin and Prague offensives in the spring of 1945. After the war, Rodimtsev led the 32nd Guards Corps until May 1946 and, after attending the Voroshilov Academy, 11th Guards Rifle Corps from March 1947 until February 1951. Thereafter, he was assistant commander of the Siberian Military District (1951–1953), chief adviser to the Albanian Peoples' Army and military attaché to Albania (1953–1956), 1st deputy commander of the Northern Military District, and commander of 1st Army before retiring into the Soviet Army's Inspectorate in 1966. Rodimtsev died in 1977. For further details, see *Komkory, Voennyi biograficheskii slovar'*, 1: 477–478.

39. Chuikov, *The Battle for Stalingrad*, 92. See the missions Chuikov assigned to Rodimtsev's division in Samsonov, *Stalingradskaia bitva*, 183.

40. Mark, *Death of the Leaping Horseman*, 160–161. 24th Panzer Division fielded 25 tanks in this drive, including 8 Pz. II, 6 Pz. III short, 6 Pz. III long, 1 Pz. IV short, and 4 Pz. IV long tanks, plus 2 command tanks. The division's remaining tanks were in reserve, prepared to reinforce success, whenever and wherever it occurred.

41. Ibid.

42. Ibid.

43. Chuikov, *The Battle for Stalingrad*, 95.

44. For a vivid description of 24th Panzer Division's daring thrust, see Mark, *Death of the Leaping Horseman*, 163–170.

45. Ibid., 163.

46. Ibid., 168.

47. Ibid., 165–166.

48. Ibid., 170.

49. Ibid., 173. The subordination was tactical only, meaning Kempf's corps would still depend on Hoth's panzer army for its supplies and replacements.

50. Ibid., 170.

51. Ibid.

52. "Opersvodka no. 153 Shtarm 62" [Operational summary no. 153, headquarters, 62nd Army], in *62nd Army Combat Journal.*

53. Zhilin, *Stalingradskaia bitva*, 562.

54. "Donesenie OO NKVD STF v NKVD SSSP o khode boev v Stalingrad, 16 sentiabria 1942 g." [Report by the OO [Special Department] of the Stalingrad Front's NKVD to the NKVD of the USSR about the course of battles in Stalingrad, 16 September 1942], in *Stalingradskaia epopeia* [Stalingrad epoch] (Moscow: "Evonnitsa-MG," 2000), 197–199, citing *TsA FSB RF* [Central Archives of the Russian Federations FSB], f. 14, op. 4, d. 326, ll. 220–223.

55. I. V. Kuz'michev, "Shtafniki" [Penal troops], *Serzhant* [Sergeant], No. 14, 2006, 25–34. For greater detail on the formation and employment of penal battalions and companies and blocking detachments, see Vladimir Daines, *Strafbaty i zagradotriady Krasnoi Armii* [Penal battalions and blocking detachments of the Red Army] (Moscow: "Iauza" "Ekso," 2008).

56. The German terms for these ratings are "strong" [*stark*], "medium strong" [*mittelstark*], "average" [*durchschnitten*], and "weak" [*schwach*]. Although ultimately subjective, the rating reflected the combat strength of the divisions, in particular their infantry and pioneer battalions, based on the number of combat soldiers they include. A fifth category, "exhausted" [*abgekampft*], which began appearing in later status reports, meant the battalion was exhausted in manpower, munitions, materiel, and/or morale—in reality, much more than simply not combat-ready. Based on one such "condition" report, an infantry division with a ration strength of 15,097 men and combat strength of 5,906 men, including 3,264 infantrymen, and consisting of five "medium strong" and two "average" infantry battalions, warranted a rating of between "medium strong" and "average." In another instance, an infantry division that had a ration strength of 12,277 men and a combat strength of 4,723 men, including 2,235 infantrymen, and that included two "average" and five "weak" infantry battalions, received a rating between "average" and "weak." As a final example, a division whose ration strength was 10,578 men and combat strength was 3,345 men, including 1,231 infantry, and that contained five "weak" and four "exhausted" infantry battalions, achieved a rating of between "weak" and "exhausted." Expressed in terms of ratio (percentage) comparing the division's combat strength to its ration strength, a "strong" division could be as low as 60 percent strength (fill), a "medium strong" division at 50 percent strength, an "average" division at 40 percent strength, a "weak" division at 30 percent strength, and an "exhausted" division below 30 percent.

Applied at the battalion level, German reports indicate the following combat ratings and average range of line-personnel strengths in types of battalions (sample actual strength in parentheses). Note the subjectivity of the rating by the actual strengths in these categories.

- **Infantry battalions**: Authorized strength—900–1,000 men
  - o Strong 700 or more men
  - o Medium strong—500–700 men
  - o Average—400–500 men
  - o Weak—300–400 men
  - o Exhausted—fewer than 300 men
- **Panzer-grenadier battalions**: Authorized strength—950–1,000 men
  - o Strong—700 or more men
  - o Medium strong—500–700 men (450, 500)
  - o Average—400–500 men (420)
  - o Weak—300–400 men (410, 360, 340, 330)
  - o Exhausted—fewer than 300 men (290, 270)
- **Pioneer battalions**—843–885 men
  - o Strong—600 or more men
  - o Medium strong—400–600 men
  - o Average—300–400 men (365, 233, 294, 201, 256, 242)
  - o Weak—200–300 men (218, 227, 209)
  - o Exhausted—fewer than 200 men (176, 76, 313)

These figures indicate that the Germans, like the Soviets, routinely operated with understrength divisions, regiments, and battalions, often retaining them in combat even after their personnel strengths decreased to well below 30 percent of their authorized strengths.

57. "Opersvodka no. 154 Shtarm 62," [Operational summary no. 154, headquarters, 62nd Army], in *62nd Army Combat Journal.*

58. Zhilin, *Stalingradskaia bitva*, 573–574.

59. The participation of 10th (Stalingrad) Rifle Division NKVD in the battle for Stalingrad is covered in greater detail in V. V. Dushen'kin, ed., *Vnutrennye voiska v Velikoi Otechestvennoi voine 1941–1945 gg.: Dokumenty i materially* [Internal troops in the Great Patriotic War 1941–1945: Documents and materials] (Moscow: Iuridicheskaia literatura, 1975), 362–409. The 10th Rifle Division NKVD consisted of 269th, 270th, 271st, 272nd, and 282nd Regiments and had a total strength of 7,568 men on 1 September. The 269th Regiment fought for 15 days in Stalingrad's center city and the area north of Mamaev Kurgan. The 270th Regiment, which was initially attached to the 269th, later reinforced 272nd Regiment, which was fighting in the city center in support of 13th Guards Rifle Division. The 271st Regiment was deployed in the Minina and Kuporosnoe suburbs and, later, south of the Tsaritsa River, generally in cooperation with 131st Rifle and 35th Guards Rifle Divisions and 133rd Tank Brigade. Finally, 282nd Regiment fought in the northern part of the city, first in the region east of Orlovka as part of Group Gorokhov, and later in the vicinity of the Tractor Factory, where it supported both 115th Rifle Brigade and Group Gorokhov. By 15 September 10th NKVD Rifle Division had only 2,410 men, subdivided as follows: 269th Regiment—435 men; 270th Regiment—540 men; 271st Regiment—135 men; 272nd Regiment—210 men; and 282nd Regiment—1,100 men.

60. Chuikov, *The Battle for Stalingrad*, 90–97; A. M. Samsonov, *Stalingradskaia bitva* [The Battle of Stalingrad] (Moscow: "Nauka," 1983), 184–188; and Ziemke and Bauer, *Moscow to Stalingrad*, 384.

61. Mark, *Death of the Leaping Horseman*, 174.

62. Ibid., 176–181. These included seven Pz. II, three Pz. III short, four Pz. III long, one Pz. IV short, and four Pz. IV long tanks, plus two command tanks.

63. Ibid., 181.

64. "Boevoe rasporiazhenie no. 149 Shtarm 62 16. 9. 42 12.30" [Combat instructions no. 149, headquarters, 62nd Army, 16 September 1942], in *62nd Army Combat Journal*.

65. "Opersvodka No. 154," in ibid.

66. Ibid.

67. Zhilin, *Stalingradskaia bitva*, 572.

68. Ibid., 573–574.

69. Moshchansky and Smolinov, *Oborona Stalingrada*, 47.

70. For a vivid description of this fighting, see Mark, *Death of the Leaping Horseman*, 184.

71. Ibid.

72. Ibid., 184–185.

73. Ibid., 185. Underscoring 24th Panzer Division's increasing weakness, on 21 September the combat strength of its 24th Panzer Regiment and 21st and 26th Panzer-Grenadier Regiments fell to 1,171, 1,049, and 1,095 men, respectively, compared with their respective ration strengths of 2,298, 1,375, and 1,464. See ibid., 196.

74. Chuikov, *The Battle for Stalingrad*, 99.

75. "Opersvodka, 16. 9. 42 Shtarm 62" [Operational summary, headquarters, 62nd Army, 16 September 1942], in *62nd Army Combat Journal*.

76. Ziemke and Bauer, *Moscow to Stalingrad*, 395.

77. The biographies of Tarasov and Udovichenko remain quite obscure. We do know the former's last name but not his first and second names by virtue of his signature on 92nd Brigade's operation maps. Neither officer, apparently, was ever promoted to the rank of major general.

78. Chuikov, *Battle for Stalingrad*, 98–99, 103; Moshchansky and Smolinov, *Oborona Stalingrada*, 47; and Rokossovsky, *Velikaia bitva na Volge*, 173. Chuikov's order, dated 17 September, in *62nd Army Combat Journal*, reads:

> 1. Include 92nd RB and 137th TB, which are arriving in Stalingrad city on the night of 17–18 September, in 62nd Army.
> 2. Upon completion of their crossing over the Volga River, they will be concentrated [as follows]:
>   a) 92nd RB—in the vicinity of the (incl.) railroad station and the railroad bridge over the Tsaritsa River, 3 kilometers southeast of [Marker] 20.7 and 1 kilometer southwest of the landing site. Mission: destroy the enemy detachments penetrating into its concentration region and occupy [the following] defensive sector: on the north—the Tsaritsa River, and on the south—the rectangular railroad [crossing] in the vicinity of Valdaiskaia Street and along the railroad with its front to the west. Prevent the enemy from entering the defended sector along the

valley of the Tsaritsa River from the direction of Sadovaia Station, and destroy the enemy in the region of the [grain] elevator.

b) 137th TB—deploy in the vicinity of the railroad loop 1.5 kilometers northeast of Hill 102.0 [known as the "Tennis Racket"] and occupy an all-round defense with the mission to prevent enemy units from advancing from the defended region to the Volga River and enemy movement northward along the railroad.

79. The Peoples' Commissariat of Defense (NKO) formed "second formation" divisions to replace divisions that had previously been destroyed in combat. These divisions retained the same numerical designation as their destroyed predecessors. Some Red Army divisions went through as many as four separate "formations" during the war.

80. For details on 193rd Rifle Division's wartime experiences record, including its role in the battle for Stalingrad, see *Pomnit Dnepr-reka* . . . [Remember the Dnepr River] (Minsk: "Belarus'," 1986), 7–11, which contains the recollections of its commander, General F. N. Smekhotvorov. Before his appointment as the division's commander on 3 January 1942, Smekhotvorov had led 135th Rifle Division from 13 June 1940 to 27 December 1941. After Operation Blau, Smekhotvorov led the 193rd until 18 March 1943 and 106th Rifle Division from 14 May until 1 August 1943. Although the remainder of his career is obscure, we know Smekhotvorov was born in 1900 and died in 1989. See the website www.generals.dk.

81. Rokossovsky, *Velikaia bitva na Volge*, 173.

82. For Zhukov's wartime itinerary, see S. I. Isaev, "Vekhi frontovogo puti" [Landmarks of a front path], in *VIZh*, No. 10 (October) 1991, 24–25. Zhukov was with Stalingrad Front from 31 August through 11 September, with both Stalingrad and Don Fronts from 29 September to 3 October, with Southwestern Front from 6–12 October, and with Southwestern, Don, and Stalingrad Fronts from 30 October to 16 November. He was also with Kalinin Front from 21–29 October and Western and Kalinin Fronts from 19 November–6 December and from 9–26 December, when he planned and supervised the two *fronts* throughout the duration of Operation Mars. During the intervals between these visits to the field, Zhukov was in Moscow, usually in the General Staff or the Kremlin.

83. Chuikov, *Battle for Stalingrad*, 103.

84. Ibid., 104–106.

85. See 18 September entry from *62nd Army Combat Journal*.

86. Zhilin, *Stalingradskaia bitva*, 581.

87. Chuikov, *Battle for Stalingrad*, 100–102.

88. Mark, *Death of the Leaping Horseman*, 189.

89. Ibid., 191.

90. Ibid.

91. Chuikov, *The Battle for Stalingrad*, 84–85.

92. Senger und Etterlin, *Die 24.-Panzer-Division*, 120.

93. Shtemenko, *Soviet General Staff at War*, Book One, 116.

94. Rokossovsky, *Velikaia bitva na Volge*, 173–174.

95. Moskalenko, *Na iugo-zapadnom napravlenii*, 1: 336–337.

96. Ibid., 337. According to Isaev, *Stalingrad*, 184, the numerical strength of 1st Guards Army's rifle divisions on 15 September 1942 was as follows:

Force	Men	Rifle	Machine Guns		PPSh	Mortars	Guns	AT guns	AT rifles
			Heavy	Light					
173rd RD	7,194	6,179	53	166	679	188	44	30	198
207th RD	4,789	3,882	29	57	583	95	37	20	145
221st RD	5,724	6,341	56	142	653	230	41	28	215
258th RD	13,429	9,174	85	225	746	222	44	30	277
260th RD	13,303	8,913	80	207	649	207	44	30	269
273rd RD	12,770	9,001	81	200	739	222	44	30	279
308th RD	8,671	8,408	56	195	713	260	44	30	275
316th RD	10,495	6,820	46	188	858	180	44	30	239
292nd RD	9,970	6,212	81	210	911	188	44	30	228
Total	86,300	62,930	567	1,590	6,531	1,792	386	258	2,125

97. For the condition of 7th Tank Corps during this period, see Rotmistrov, *Stal'naia gvardiia*, 124–125.

98. Moskalenko, *Na iugo-zapadnom napravlenii*, 1: 341–342; and Zhilin, *Stalingradskaia bitva*, 580–581, 588. For actual German force dispositions and troop movements during this period, see "Ia. Lagenkarten Nr. 1 zum KTB Nr. 13, Jul–Oct 1942," *AOK 6, 23948/1a*, in NAM T-312, Roll 1446.

99. The 246th Tank Brigade consisted of 13 tanks (6 T-34s and 7 T-70s) and 69th Tank Brigade of 5 tanks (4 T-34s and 1 T-70). See Isaev, *Stalingrad*, 187.

100. The total personnel strength of 24th Army was 54,000 men, roughly the same number as 66th Army. See ibid., 192.

101. 3rd Motorized Division fielded a total of 24 tanks (6 Pz. II, 15 Pz. III short, 2 Pz. III long, and 1 Pz. IV long) and 60th Motorized Division 24 tanks (7 Pz. II, 3 Pz. III short, 12 Pz. III long, and 2 Pz. IV long). In addition, 16th Panzer Division's tank park, available to reinforce, if necessary, included 66 tanks (8 Pz. III short, 55 Pz. III long, and 3 Pz. IV long). See Isaev, *Stalingrad*, citing Sixth Army's daily strength records.

102. Zhilin, *Stalingradskaia bitva*, 588; and "Ia. Lagenkarten Nr. 1 zum KTB Nr. 13, Jul–Oct 1942," *AOK 6, 23948/1a*, in NAM T-312, Roll 1446.

103. Isaev, *Stalingrad*, 187.

104. Chuikov, *Battle for Stalingrad*, 112.

105. For details about XIV Panzer Corps' defense, see Langermann, *3. Infanterie-Division*, 204; and Werthen, *Geschichte der 16. Panzer-Division*, 118–120.

106. Zhilin, *Stalingradskaia bitva*, 579.

107. Ibid., 580–581.

108. Ibid., 583.

109. Moskalenko, *Na iugo-zapadnom napravlenii*, 1: 342.

110. Zhilin, *Stalingradskaia bitva*, 583.

111. Moskalenko, *Na iugo-zapadnom napravlenii*, 1: 342.

112. Ibid., 343–344.

113. 16th Panzer Division also reported that 66th Army managed to penetrate its defenses, but only temporarily, with 10 tanks. However, no Soviet reports confirm this fact.

114. Zhilin, *Stalingradskaia bitva*, 595.

115. Ibid., 594, citing *Stavka* order no. 170619, dated 21 September 1942.

116. The strength of Maslov's 16th Tank Corps was 4,519 men and 87 tanks, including 14 KVs, 42 T-34s, and 31 T-60s. See Isaev, *Stalingrad*, 209, citing *TsAMO RF*, f. 3414, op. 1, d. 25, l. 16.

117. Moskalenko, *Na iugo-zapadnom napravlenii*, 1: 344.

118. Zhilin, *Stalingradskaia bitva*, 610. See the Red Army General Staff's daily operational summaries during the intervening period in ibid., 581 and 610.

119. Ibid., 616. See also "Ia. Lagenkarten Nr. 1 zum KTB Nr. 13, Jul–Oct 1942," *AOK 6, 23948/1a*, in NAM T-312, Roll 1446.

120. 7th Tank Corp's 82 tanks included 39 tanks (24 T-34s and 15 T-60s) in the corps' composite 87th Tank Brigade, with 43 tanks from 58th Tank Brigade attached. See Isaev, *Stalingrad*, 208.

121. Zhilin, *Stalingradskaia bitva*, 618. See also Rotmistrov, *Stal'naia gvardiia*, 127, which states, "Our 7th Tank Corps . . . conducted active combat in the Erzovka region until the end of September." The *Stavka* withdrew the corps from combat on 6 October and sent it to the Saratov region for rest and refitting.

122. Zhilin, *Stalingradskaia bitva*, 622.

123. Ibid., 624.

124. Isaev, *Stalingrad*, 209.

125. Zhilin, *Stalingradskaia bitva*, 622.

126. Isaev, *Stalingrad*, 211, citing *TsAMO RF*, f. 3414, op. 1, d. 25, l. 16.

127. Zhilin, *Stalingradskaia bitva*, 632. See Stalingrad Front's daily reports to the Red Army General Staff between 24 September and 4 October, in ibid., 616–676.

128. See details in *3. Infanterie-Division*, 204–206.

129. "Ia. Lagenkarten Nr. 1 zum KTB Nr. 13, Jul–Oct 1942," *AOK 6, 23948/1a*, in NAM T-312, Roll 1446.

130. Ziemke and Bauer, *Moscow to Stalingrad*, 395.

131. "Boevoi prikaz no. 00122, Shtab IuVF 18. 9. 42 18.00" [Combat order no. 00122, headquarters, Southeastern Front, 1800 hours on 18 September 1942], in *62nd Army Combat Journal*. See also Chuikov, *Battle for Stalingrad*, 109–110.

132. "Boevoi prikaz no. 151, KP Shtarm 62 18. 9. 42 23.50" [Combat order no. 151, CP, headquarters, 62nd Army, 2350 hours on 18 September 1942], in *62nd Army Combat Journal*. See also Zhilin, *Stalingradskaia bitva*, 581.

133. Zhilin, *Stalingradskaia bitva*, 588–589.

134. *Komandovanie korpusnogo i divizionnogo zvena Sovetskikh vooruzhennykh sil perioda Velikoi Otechestvennoi voiny 1941–1945 g.* [Commanders at the corps and division level in the Soviet Armed Forces in the period of the Great Patriotic War, 1941–1945] (Moscow: Frunze Academy, 1964), 146, 325. Gorishnyi was born in 1903; his career in the prewar years remains obscure. Before commanding 95th Rifle Division, he had led 13th NKVD Rifle Division earlier in 1942. He commanded this division (redesignated as 75th Guards Rifle Division on 1 January 1943) through the remainder of the war. Gorishnyi ultimately rose to the rank of lieutenant general after war's end and died in 1962.

135. "Boevoe donesenie nos. 122–123, Shtarm 62, 19. 9. 42."

136. For details see, N. I. Afanas'ev, *Ot Volgi do Shpree: Boevoi put' 35-i gvardeiskoi strelkovoi Lozovskoi Krasnoznamennoi, ordena Suvorova i Bogdan Khmel'nitskogo divizii* [From the Volga to the Spree: The combat path of 35th Guards Lozovaia, Red Banner, and Orders of Suvorov and Bogdan Khmel'nitsky Rifle Division] (Moscow: Voenizdat, 1982), 76–77, which also contains Dubiansky's complete withdrawal order.

137. For further details on these actions, see "Boevoe donesenie nos. 122–123, Shtarm 62, 19. 9. 42." [Combat reports nos. 122–123, headquarters, 62nd Army, 19 September 1942], in *62nd Army Combat Journal*.

138. Chuikov, *Battle for Stalingrad*, 113–115.

139. Zhilin, *Stalingradskaia bitva*, 583.

140. "Boevoi prikaz No. 152 Shtarm 62 20. 9. 42" [Combat order No. 152, headquarters, 62nd Army, 20 September 1942], in *62nd Army Combat Journal*.

141. See 24th Panzer Division's *Divisionbefehl* [Division order] Nr. 62, in Mark, *Death of the Leaping Horseman*, 193.

142. Zhilin, *Stalingradskaia bitva*, 593.

143. Samchuk, *Trinadtsetaia gvardeiskaia*, 109–111. 39th Guards Rifle Regiment had just returned from its fight on Mamaev Kurgan.

144. Afanas'ev, *Ot Volgi do Shpree*, 77.

145. Ibid., 78.

146. Ibid.

147. Ibid., 80–81. Colonel Dubiansky was evacuated to Moscow for a rest on 16 November. His division was assigned to 2nd Reserve Army in late September and then to 1st Guards Army's 4th Guards Rifle Corps on 23 October.

148. "Donesenie OO NKVD STF v YOO NKVD SSSP ob obstanovke v Stalingrad, 21 sentiabria 1942 g." [Report by the OO [Special Department] of the Stalingrad Front's NKVD to the Directorate of OO's of the NKVD of the USSR about the situation in Stalingrad, 21 September 1942], in *Stalingradskaia epopeia* [Stalingrad epoch] (Moscow: "Evonnitsa-MG," 2000), 205–206, citing *TsA FSB RF* [Central Archives of the Russian Federations FSB], f. 14, op. 4, d. 326, ll. 229–230.

149. Moshchansky and Smolinov, *Oborona Stalingrada*, 48–49.

150. See the Red Army General Staff's daily operational summary, in Zhilin, *Stalingradskaia bitva*, 600; and *62nd Army Combat Journal*.

151. Thereafter, 94th Infantry Division regrouped northward. For an excellent soldier's-eye description of the division's subsequent role in the fighting, particularly its 276th Infantry Regiment, see Adelbert Holl, *An Infantryman in Stalingrad: From 24 September 1942 to 2 February 1943*, trans. Jason D. Mark and Neil Page (Sydney, Australia: Leaping Horseman Books, 2005).

152. Zhilin, *Stalingradskaia bitva*, 601, quoting OKW informational bulletins.

153. "Boevoe rasporiazhenie no. 156 Shtarm 62 21. 9. 42" [Combat instructions no. 156, headquarters, 62nd Army, 21 September 1942], in *62nd Army Combat Journal*.

154. As a result of 284th Rifle Division's superb combat performance during the fighting in Stalingrad, the division was awarded the designation of 79th Guards Rifle Division on 1 March 1943, and Batiuk was promoted to the rank of major general.

Batiuk would command the division until 28 July 1943, when he died of illness in the Donbas region. Because Batiuk was Ukrainian and Rodimtsev was Russian, the latter received greater praise and attention than the former in Soviet accounts of the battle of Stalingrad.

155. Mark, *Death of the Leaping Horseman*, 202–203. During this assault 295th Infantry Division suffered more than 200 casualties, including 46 men killed, 7 officers and 164 men wounded, and 4 men missing in action, and 24th Panzer Division counted 19 dead and 25 wounded.

156. Ibid., 203.

157. Zhilin, *Stalingradskaia bitva*, 606. See *62nd Army Combat Journal*, for further details.

158. Ibid., 611.

159. For additional details on 13th Guards Rifle Division's fight, see Samchuk, *Trinadtsataia gvardeiskaia*, 120–130.

160. Rokossovsky, *Velikaia pobeda na Volge*, 174.

161. Florian *Freiherr* von und zu Aufsess, "Betr.: Zustand der Divisionen, Armee—Oberkommando 6, Abt. Ia, A. H. Qu., den 14 September 42, 12.35 Uhr" and "Betr.: Zustand der Divisionen, Armee—Oberkommando 6, Abt. Ia, A. H. Qu., den 26 September 42," in *Die Anlagenbander zu den Kriegstagebuchern der 6. Armee vom 14.09.1942 bis 24.11.1942, Band I* (Schwabach: January 2006), 12–13 and 59–62.

162. See Chuikov, *Battle for Stalingrad*, 140, for details of this misreporting.

163. For Chuikov's complete attack order, see "Chastnyi prikaz, Shtarm 62 22. 9. 42" [Separate order, 62nd Army, 22 September 1942], in *62nd Army Combat Journal*.

164. Chuikov, *Battle for Stalingrad*, 132–133.

165. Moshchansky and Smolinov, *Oborona Stalingrada*, 49, provides the following strengths for 23rd Tank Corps and its cooperating units on 23 September 1942:

- 6th Guards Tank Brigade—23 tanks (21 T-34 and 2 T-70 tanks);
- 27th Tank Brigade—8 T-34 tanks (plus another 9 nonoperational tanks);
- 137th Tank Brigade—9 T-60 tanks;
- 189th Tank Brigade—10 tanks (7 T-34 and 3 T-70 tanks);
- 38th Motorized Rifle Brigade—395 men, 10 machine guns, and 9 antitank rifles;
- 9th Motorized Rifle Brigade—280 men, 23 guns, and 13 antitank rifles; and
- 10th NKVD Rifle Division's 269th Regiment—3 infantry battalions.

166. Zhilin, *Stalingradskaia bitva*, 611, 616–617, 622, 627. See also multiple reports in *62nd Army Combat Journal*. The 42nd Rifle Brigade's reports on 25 and 26 September proved erroneous because Tarasov had already withdrawn its remnants and his 92nd Rifle Brigade to islands in the Volga River.

167. Mark, *Death of the Leaping Horseman*, 208. All the while, 24th Panzer Division's casualties mounted, with 32 men killed and 122 wounded on 23 September, 25 killed and 76 wounded on 24 September, and 14 killed and 58 wounded on 25 September. See ibid., 205, 208–209. The 24th Panzer Division's order no. 64 [*Divisionbefehl*

Nr. 64], issued at 2100 hours, informed the panzer division's 4th Motorcycle Battalion and part of its 21st Grenadier Regiment, which occupied the western portion of Mamaev Kurgan, that 100th Jäger Division would relieve them by 1900 hours the next day.

168. Zhilin, *Stalingradskaia bitva*, 624, citing *KTB OKW. Bd. II*, s. 1323.

169. Chuikov, *Battle for Stalingrad*, 133–134.

170. *Freiherr* von und zu Aufsess, "Betr.: Zustand der Divisionen, Armee—Oberkommando 6, Abt. Ia, A. H. Qu., den 14 September 42, 12.35 Uhr," "Betr.: Zustand der Divisionen, Armee—Oberkommando 6, Abt. Ia, A. H. Qu., den 26 September 42," and "Betr.: Zustand der Divisionen, erstmalig nach neu festlegter Bestimmung des Begriffes 'Gefechsstärke,' Armee—Oberkommando 6, Abt. Ia, A. H. Qu., den 5 Oktober 1942," in *Die Anlagenbander zu den Kriegstagebuchern der 6. Armee vom 14.09.1942 bis 24.11.1942, Band I* (Schwabach: January 2006), 12–13, 59–62, and 128–132.

171. Mark, *Death of the Leaping Horseman*, 210.

172. Richthofen, quoted in Goerlitz, *Paulus and Stalingrad*, 192.

173. Rokossovsky, *Velikaia pobeda na Volge*, 178.

174. Ibid., 178.

175. Ibid., 175.

176. Ibid., 175–176.

177. Ibid., 176.

178. Erickson, *The Road to Stalingrad*, 409.

179. Rokossovsky, *Velikaia pobeda na Volge*, 177.

180. Ibid., 176.

181. Ziemke and Bauer, *Moscow to Stalingrad*, 396.

Chapter 4: The Initial Assault on the Workers' Villages and Reduction of the Orlovka Salient, 27 September–3 October 1942

1. For details on 94th Infantry Division's struggle to secure this region, including the fight for the infamous Grain Elevator, see Holl, *An Infantryman in Stalingrad*, 16–70. At 1230 hours on 24 September, Sixth Army had ordered the division, "Once the city sector up to the mouth of the Tsaritsa has been cleared, it is intended to transfer 94th Infantry Division into the area north of Gorodishche, simultaneously positioning them to clear out the area around Orlovka." However, due to the heavy fighting near the mouth of the Tsaritsa River, the division was not able to disengage from combat in the city until late on 28 September. According to LI Corps' report, dated 2320 hours on 28 September, "On the morning of 29 September, 94th Infantry Division will march to join XIV Panzer Corps without the elements already near XIV Panzer Corps and without 276th Infantry Regiment, which is still with LI Corps. . . ." See ibid., 16, 75.

2. Mark, *Death of the Leaping Horseman*, 211.

3. Since it was a *jäger* (light) division, the 100th fielded only two organic German regiments, 54th and 227th Jäger, each with two *jäger* battalions. However, to bring the division to near full combat strength, Army Group B had augmented

Sanne's division with the 369th Croatian Infantry Regiment in the summer of 1941. In reality, however, the Croat regiment fielded only one infantry battalion.

4. Mark, *Death of the Leaping Horseman*, 212–213, 216–218. *Kampfgruppe* Edelsheim consisted of 21st and 26th Grenadier Regiments (the latter without its 1st Battalion), two companies of 40th Panzer Pioneer Battalion, and 1st Company, 40th Panzer Jäger Battalion. *Kampfgruppe* Winterfeld included 24th Panzer Regiment's tanks (organized in one battalion of roughly 25 tanks), the armored personnel carriers of 1st Battalion, 26th Grenadier Regiment, 2nd Company, 4th Motorcycle Battalion, and 1st Battalion, 89th Panzer Artillery Regiment. By this time, the strengths of 21st and 26th Grenadier Regiments and 40th Pioneer Battalion in terms of frontline combat troops were 456, 479, and 156 men, respectively. With a strength of only about 1,000 men, Edelsheim's *kampfgruppe* was forced to attack in a sector roughly 400 meters wide.

5. Ibid., 213.

6. See German dispositions and troop movements in "Ia. Lagenkarten Nr. 1 zum KTB Nr. 13, Jul–Oct 1942," *AOK 6, 23948/1a*, in NAM T-312, Roll 1446; and Rokossovsky, *Velikaia pobeda na Volge*, 179. The 94th Infantry Division's 267th and 274th Regiments were to deploy northward to the Gorodishche region to participate in the reduction of the Orlovka salient.

7. "Ia. Lagenkarten Nr. 1 zum KTB Nr. 13, Jul–Oct 1942," *AOK 6, 23948/1a*, in NAM T-312, Roll 1446.

8. Chuikov, *The Battle for Stalingrad*, 137.

9. "Boevoi prikaz no. 164 Shtarm 62 25. 9. 42" [Combat order no. 164, 25 September 1942], in *62nd Army Combat Journal*. See also Chuikov, *The Battle for Stalingrad*, 137–138, which contains a slightly different translation.

10. "Opersvodka no. 171 Shtarm 62 25. 9. 42" [Operational summary no. 171, headquarters, 62nd Army, 25 September 1942], in *62nd Army Combat Journal*.

11. "Boevoi prikaz no. 166/op, Shtarm 62, 26. 9. 42" [Combat order no. 166/op, headquarters, 62nd Army, 26 September 1942], in ibid. See also Chuikov, *The Battle for Stalingrad*, 149–150.

12. Chuikov, *The Battle for Stalingrad*, 151.

13. Mark, *Death of the Leaping Horseman*, 216.

14. Ibid., 217–218.

15. Ibid., 218.

16. Chuikov, *The Battle for Stalingrad*, 152.

17. Zhilin, *Stalingradskaia bitva*, 636, quoting *KTB OKW. Bd. II*, s. 1332–1333.

18. Ziemke and Bauer, *Moscow to Stalingrad*, 396, quoting *AOK 6, Ia Kriegstagebuch Nr. 13*, 27 Sep 42, in *AOK 6 2394811* file.

19. Zhilin, *Stalingradskaia bitva*, 632. The 62nd Army's complete report, in *62nd Army Combat Journal*, showed the positions of all of the army's formations and units on the following dates:

[Morning, 27 September]

- **124th and 149th RBs, 282nd RR NKVD, 115th RB, and 2nd MRB**—unchanged in the Rynok, Spartanovka, and Orlovka regions.

- **23rd TC, with 38th MRB, 9th MRB, 269th RR NKVD, and 137th TB**—(heavy losses) from the crossroads 1.5 kilometers west of Hill 101.4 eastward to Vishnevaia *Balka*.
  - o 6th Gds. TB and 189th TB from (incl.) the cemetery to Zhmerinskaia Street. The remnants of 27th TB and 38th MRB west of Penskaia Street.
  - o 9th MRB, with 269th RR NKVD and the remnants of 137th TB from Chernorechenskaia Street to the Bannyi Ravine.
- **95th RD** (241st and 161st RRs) from (incl.) the Bannyi Ravine to the western outskirts of the city along Syzranskaia Street, and due west of the railroad line to the northern slope of Hill 102.0.
- **284th RD**—1045th RR (army reserve). 1047th and 1043rd RRs from the eastern slope of Hill 102.0 to the railroad bridge across Dolgii Ravine and the mouth of the Krutoi Ravine.
- **13th Gds. RD, with 685th RR (193rd RD)** in the eastern belt of the center city.
  - o 1st Bn, 42nd RR crossed to the left bank of Volga River and concentrated in the Krasnyi Sloboda region.
- **Remnants of 92nd RB, 42nd RB, and 272nd RR NKVD** crossed to the islands and part to the left bank of the Volga River for rest and refitting.
- **112th RD** formed a second defensive belt along the Vishnevaia *Balka*, east of the Krasnyi Oktiabr' village.
  - o 385th RR (165 men) was smashed by enemy tanks passing through the 524th RR.
- **193rd RD (883rd and 895th RRs)** crossed to the western bank of the Volga River.

[Day's end, 27 September]
- **62nd Army** from the southeastern outskirts of Barrikady village to the western outskirts of Krasnyi Oktiabr' village and the northern slope of Hill 102.0.
- **23rd TC** (heavy losses in men and weapons).
  - o 6th Gds. TB from the crossroads 1.5 kilometers north of Hill 101.4 east-ward to the Vishnevaia *Balka*.
  - o 189th TB from (incl.) the cemetery to Mezenskaia Street.
  - o Remnants of 27th TB and 38th MRB west of Penskaia Street.
  - o 9th MRB, with 269th RR NKVD and remnants of 137th TB from Chernorechenskaia Street to the Bannyi Ravine.
- **193rd RD** from the cemetery on the southern outskirts of Barrikady village southward to the Bannyi Ravine.
- **92nd and 42nd RBs** (remnants) on Hill 102.0 at the junction of 95th and 284th RDs.

20. Mark, *Death of the Leaping Horseman*, 215–228.

21. Ibid., 225–226, claims that 24th Panzer Division captured 550 Soviets and 22 mortars and destroyed 15 tanks on 27 September, at a cost of 36 killed and 221 wounded.

22. Chuikov, *The Battle for Stalingrad*, 152. See an account of 112th Rifle Division's fight in V. Khar'kov, "112-ia strelkovaia diviziia v Bitva za Stalingradom" [The 112th Rifle Division in the battle for Stalingrad], *VIZh*, 3: (March 1980), 36–43; and the division's combat journal. Chuikov erroneously listed Colonel I. P. Sologub as the commander of the division during this fighting, when, in reality, Sologub had been mortally wounded during the August battles and was replaced by Ermolkin.

23. For details on 100th Jäger Division's fight, see Hanns Neidhardt, *Mit Tanne und Eichenlaub: Kriegschronik der 100. Jäger-Division vormals 100. leichte Infanterie-Division* (Graz-Stuttgart: Leopold Stocker Verlag, 1981), 210–211.

24. Chuikov, *The Battle for Stalingrad*, 152.

25. The heaviest fighting for Dom Pavlova [Pavlov's House] took place during the second half of October. Pavlov himself was wounded and evacuated in late November but later returned to service and received the Hero of the Soviet Union award in 1945. Ultimately, 13th Guards Rifle Division's troops defended the house successfully from 27 September through 2 February 1943. For more detail, see Samchuk, *Trinadtsataia gvardeiskaia*, 139–140; and *Geroi Sovetskogo soiuza*, vol. 2, 223.

26. Samchuk, *Trinadtsataia gvardeiskaia*, 139–140.

27. Mark, *Death of the Leaping Horseman*, 224.

28. The mission of Smekhotvorov's two regiments was "to destroy the enemy penetrating into the Krasnyi Oktiabr' village and dig in on its western outskirts." The division's headquarters was to be situated in the House of Specialists adjacent to the Krasnyi Oktiabr' Factory. Once across the river, Smekhotvorov assigned 895th Regiment the mission of occupying defenses along Zhmerinskaia Street and 883rd Regiment to man defenses along Ugol'naia Street, west of the Krasnyi Oktiabr' Factory. The division's training battalion, the batteries of 50th Antitank Battalion, and 184th Separate Machine Gun Battalion were in the division's second echelon or reserve. The division reached its designated positions just in time to contain the Germans' assaults on its defensive lines. The division's 685th Regiment had already reinforced 13th Guards Rifle Division's defenses in Stalingrad's center city. See F. N. Smekhotvorov, "Ispytaniia na stoikost'" [An ordeal in determination], in *Pomnit Dnepr-reka . . . : Vospominaniia veteranov 193-i strelkovoi Dneprovskoi ordena Lenina, Krasnoznamennoi, ordena Suvorova i Kutuzova divizii* [Remember the Dnepr River . . . : Recollections of veterans of the Dnepr, order of Lenin, Red Banner, and orders of Suvorov and Kutuzov 193rd Rifle Division] (Minsk: "Belarus'," 1986), 12.

29. Chuikov, *The Battle for Stalingrad*, 154.

30. Ibid., 154–155.

31. Mark, *Death of the Leaping Horseman*, 228.

32. Zhilin, *Stalingradskaia bitva*, 641, quoting *KTB OKW. Bd. II*, s. 1335–1337.

33. Ziemke and Bauer, *Moscow to Stalingrad*, 396, quoting *AOK 6*, Ia Kriegstagebuch Nr. 13, 28 Sep 42, in *AOK 6 2394811* file.

34. Zhilin, *Stalingradskaia bitva*, 639–640. The 62nd Army's complete report, in *62nd Army Combat Journal*, showed the positions of all of the army's formations and units on the following dates:

[Day's end on 28 September]

- **124th and 149th RBs, 282nd RR NKVD, 115th RB, and 2nd MTB** were firmly holding their positions in the Rynok, Spartanovka, and Orlovka regions.
- **23rd TC** (626 killed, and wounded)
  - o 6th Gds. TB from the northwestern corner of the triangular woods to the western part of Shakhtinskaia Street.
  - o 38th MRB (remnants) from the western part of Zaraiskaia Street and along the western outskirts of Krasnyi Oktiabr' village to Karusel'naia Street.
  - o 9th MRB (remnants) along the western outskirts of Krasnyi Oktiabr' village and (incl.) Karusel'naia Street to the northern bank of the Bannyi Ravine.
  - o 137th TB in the Bannyi Ravine.
  - o 189th TB in between Tsentral'naia Street and Karusel'naia Street.
  - o 27th TB in the *front*'s reserve at the entrance to Tsentral'naia Street.
- **193rd RD** from the cemetery to the training airfield, Zaraiskaia Street, and the Bannyi Ravine.
- **95th RD** (241st and 161st RRs) from (incl.) the Bannyi Ravine to the western outskirts of the city along Syzranskaia Street and due west of the railroad line to the northern slope of Hill 102.0.
- **284th RD** (39 killed, 137 wounded, 127 missing in action) was holding on to its occupied positions.
- **13th Gds. RD** was improving its occupied positions.
- **112th RD** was holding on to its occupied positions. The 416th RR withdrew to the cemetery.

35. For details on 24th Panzer Division's advance on 28 September, see Mark, *Death of the Leaping Horseman*, 228–234.

36. Ibid., 230, 233–234.

37. Ibid.

38. Ibid., 234.

39. Ibid., 160, and map; and Moshchansky and Smolinov, *Oborona Stalingrada*, 56. To avoid confusion in terminology: The Mokraia Mechetka River flowed eastward from the confluence of the Orlovka and Mechetka Rivers to the Volga River south of Rynok and Spartanovka. Before combining to form the Mokraia Mechetka, the Orlovka River flowed southeastward from the Orlovka region and the Mechetka River eastward from the Gorodishche region.

40. For details, see Neidhardt, *Mit Tanne und Eichenlaub*, 211.

41. *Freiherr* von und zu Aufsess, "Betr.: Zustand der Divisionen, Armee—Oberkommando 6, Abt. Ia, A. H. Qu., den 28 September 42, 12.20 Uhr," in *Die Anlagenbander zu den Kriegstagebuchern der 6. Armee vom 14.09.1942 bis 24.11.1942, Band I* (Schwabach: January 2006), 76.

42. Chuikov, *The Battle for Stalingrad*, 155.

43. Ibid.

44. "Boevoi prikaz no. 171 KP Shtarm 62 28. 9. 42 19.30" [Combat order no. 171, CP, headquarters, 62nd Army, 1930 hours 29 September 1942], in *62nd Army Combat Journal*.

45. Chuikov, *The Battle for Stalingrad*, 156.

46. See the appropriate General Staff directives in A. M. Zolotarev, ed., "General'nyi shtab v gody Velikoi Otechestvennoi voiny: Dokumenty i materially, 1942 god, T. 23 (12-2)" [The General Staff in the Great Patriotic War: Documents and materials, 1942, vol. 23 (12-2)], in *Russki arkhiv: Velikaia Otechestvennaia* [The Russian archives: The Great Patriotic [War]] (Moscow: "TERRA," 1999), 334, 339. Hereafter cited as "General Staff, 1942," with appropriate page(s).

47. Ibid., 336–337.

48. See *Stavka* order no. 994209, dated 28 September 1942, in Zolotarev, "*Stavka* 1942," 403–404. The order was accompanied by a directive resubordinating 127th Rifle Division (and its sector) from the Stalingrad Front's former 63rd Army to the Voronezh Front's 6th Army.

49. Zhukov, *Reminiscences and Reflections*, vol. II, 100. While Zhukov claims that he flew back to Moscow on 1 October, his wartime itinerary in *VIZh*, No. 10 (October 1991), 24, shows that he returned to Moscow on 3 October.

50. See *Stavka* directive no. 994215, dated 1 October 1942, in Zolotarev, "*Stavka* 1942," 407.

51. See *Stavka* directive no. 994216, dated 1 October 1942, in ibid., 407–408.

52. Mark, *Death of the Leaping Horseman*, 234.

53. Ibid.

54. Neidhardt, *Mit Tanne und Eichenlaub*, 212.

55. Mark, *Death of the Leaping Horseman*, 235–236.

56. *Pomnit Dnepr-reka*, 16. Because 193rd Rifle Division's objective was Ugol'naia Street, in the western part of Krasnyi Oktiabr' village, the division's assault fell short by two to four city blocks.

57. Ziemke and Bauer, *Moscow to Stalingrad*, 396, quoting *AOK 6*, Ia Kriegstagebuch Nr. 13, 29 Sep 42, in *AOK 6 2394811* file.

58. Zhilin, *Stalingradskaia bitva*, 644–645. The 62nd Army's complete report, in *62nd Army Combat Journal*, shows the positions of all of the army's formations and units on the following dates:

[Day's end on 29 September]

- **124th RB** (3,085 men), **149th RB** (3,958 men), and **282nd RR NKVD** (1,058 men) were holding their positions in the Rynok, Spartanovka, and Orlovka regions.
  o 115th RB and 2nd MRB (5,121 men) (fighting bitterly with superior enemy forces).
  o 1st Bn, 115th RB, and 2nd MRB were almost completely destroyed. The 115th RB lost 453 men, 8 heavy machine guns, 11 light machine guns, 28 antitank rifles, 21 82-mm mortars, 7 120-mm mortars, 4 45-mm guns, and 2 76-mm guns. 57 men remain in 2nd MRB. The composite RR, 196th RD, lost up to 100 men.

- **23rd TC** (17 tanks and 150 soldiers) (was fighting fiercely with enemy tanks and infantry but no longer combat capable) in the cemetery and Barrikady village sector.
- **112th RD** (2,493 men, including 1,327 in rear service subunits) (fighting with superior enemy forces) (416th RR with 39 "bayonets" and 524th RR with 19 "bayonets") withdrew to the northeastern outskirts of the Silikat Factory.
- **193rd RD** (under heavy enemy attack) (suffered heavy losses, including three regimental commanders and three battalion commanders).
- **95th RD** (230 active soldiers)—90th RR held on to the trigonometric point on Hill 102.0. The positions of 241st and 161st RRs are unchanged.
- **284th RD** (6,820 men, including 1,280 in rear service subunits) was holding on to its existing positions.
- **13th Gds. RD** (6,888 men, of which 3,973 are on the right bank of the Volga River) was holding on to its existing positions.
- **42nd and 92nd RBs** (remnants) will cross over to the western bank of the Volga on the night of 29–30 September and defend the Mechetka, Silikat Factory, and Kaluzhskaia Street sector, relieving 23rd TC.
- **685th RR (193rd RD)** will reinforce **193rd RD**, which will then clear out the city center and Krasnyi Oktiabr' and create defensive groups within the city.

59. Samsonov, *Stalingradskaia bitva*, 211.

60. Mark, *Death of the Leaping Horseman*, 237.

61. Ibid., 239.

62. Ibid., 238. This did not count the crews of heavy machine guns, or antitank and infantry guns.

63. Isaev, *Stalingrad*, 225–226.

64. *Pomnit Dnepr-reka*, 16–17. The 685th Regiment left at least one battalion to support Rodimtsev's guards division. After its arrival back at its parent division, 685th Regiment deployed along Zhmerinskaia Street, on the division's right wing, flanked on the left by the division's 895th and 883rd Rifle Regiments. By this time, the division's front extended 3 kilometers.

65. Zhilin, *Stalingradskaia bitva*, 650. The 62nd Army's complete report, in *62nd Army Combat Journal*, showed the positions of all of the army's formations and units on the following dates:

[Day's end on 30 September]
- **124th and 149th RBs, and 282nd RR NKVD** were holding on to their previous positions.
- **115th RB and 2nd MRB** (under heavy enemy attacks)
  - o 1st Bn, 115th RB was in the southeastern outskirts of Orlovka. Displaying cowardice and abandoning his battalion, the battalion commander, Senior Lieutenant Sadikov, fled to the rear and reported falsely about the fighting, for which he was arrested and tried by a court (shot).

o 2nd MRB (with 75 men after suffering heavy losses in intense fighting) was at the railroad bridge and the northern slope of Hill 108.3. The operational group (115th and 2nd MRBs) lost 257 men killed and wounded and 75 missing-in-action, 3 45-mm guns, 3 76-mm guns, 7 82-mm mortars, 8 50-mm mortars, 6 AT rifles. . . .

- **42nd and 92nd RBs** were occupying their previous positions.
- **23rd TC** (with 14 T-34s, including 5 non-operational, 1 T-70, non-operational, and 6 T-60s, 2 non-operational). Consolidated in 6th Gds. TB in the region 300–400 meters northwest and northeast of Silikat.
- **112th RD** (398 "bayonets") was occupying its previous positions.
- **193rd RD** was attacking with small groups to destroy the enemy in the vicinity of the western outskirts of the city (Krasnyi Oktiabr').
- **95th and 284th RDs** (6,515 men, including 1,195 rear service soldiers) were repelling attacks and holding on to their previous positions.
- **13th Gds. RD** was clearing out individual buildings in the center city.
- **39th Gds. RD** began crossing to the right bank of the Volga River.
- **308th RD** was in 62nd Army but on the eastern bank of the Volga River.
- **Decisions**:
  o Reinforce 115th RB with 499th Antitank Regiment (6 guns) and two rifle companies from 124th RB.
  o 39th Gds. RD will occupy the Silikat and Zuevskaia Street sector.
  o Prepare to attack on the evening of 1 October with 39th Gds. RD to capture the cemetery and Barrikady village and with 193rd RD to capture Hill 107.5.

66. Mark, *Death of the Leaping Horseman*, 239.

67. For details on 13th Guards Rifle Division's deployment and struggle, see Samchuk, *Trinadtsataia gvardeiskaia*, 125–130.

68. Isaev, *Stalingrad*, 226, citing *TsAMO RF*, f. 220, op. 220, d. 72, l. 85.

69. See "Vypiska iz boevogo prikaza no. 00142/op Shtab CTF 30. 9. 42 20.46." [Excerpt from Combat order no. 00142/op, headquarters, Stalingrad Front, 2046 hours 30 September 1942], in *62nd Army Combat Journal*, which read:

> The enemy is conducting offensive operations with his main forces on the *front*'s right wing—in the sector of 62nd Army and is trying to capture Stalingrad.
>
> The enemy is conducting secondary fighting along the remaining sectors of the *front*.
>
> The forces of the Stalingrad Front have the immediate mission to destroy the enemy on the approaches to Stalingrad and hold Stalingrad for themselves.
>
> Destroy the enemy's personnel and weapons by frequent offensive operations and brutal and stubborn defense and, simultaneously, prevent the enemy from reaching the city of Astrakhan' and the Volga River. Halt the further advance of the enemy on the army's entire front.
>
> Reinforce 62nd Army with 39th Gds. RD and 308th RD, which will become subordinate at 2000 hours 30 September.

Subsequently, dislodge the enemy from Barrikady village, Krasnyi Oktiabr' village, and from the region of Mamaev Kurgan, with the adjoining blocks south of Mamaev Kurgan by frequent successive operations.
To do so, allocate the main means of fire [artillery and mortars] to each
operation. Neighboring artillery subgroups—1103rd, 457th, 1105th, and
256th Gds. ARs RGK [Gun Artillery Regiments of the Reserve of the
High Command].

The 64th Army, with the aim of weakening the enemy pressure on
62nd Army's front and attracting it away from Stalingrad city, will go over
to the offensive on the night of 1–2 October, attacking on its right wing
toward Peschanka and Vorontsovo.

The immediate mission is to reach the Hill 133.1 and Peschanka
line; and subsequently, reach the railroad in the VPChK, Sadovaia, and
Vorontsovo sector.

70. For details on 39th Guards Rifle Division's wartime record, see A. M. Morozov, *39-ia Barvenkovskaia* [The 39th Barvenkovo] (Moscow: Voenizdat, 1981). The
strength of the division after the fighting in the Kotluban' region was 3,801 men. See
also Samsonov, *Stalingradskaia bitva*, 277.

71. Gur'ev's division was equipped with 2,978 rifles, 695 PPSh, 24 light, 12
heavy, and 2 antiaircraft machine guns, 114 antitank rifles, and 13 field and 7 antitank
guns. See Isaev, *Stalingrad*, 207.

72. *Komandovanie korpusnogo i divizionnogo zvena Sovetskikh vooruzhennykh
sil perioda Velikoi Otechestvennoi voiny 1941–1945 gg.* [Commanders at the corps
and division level of the Soviet Armed Forces in the period of the Great Patriotic
War 1941–1945] (Moscow: Frunze Academy, 1964), 55, 314. Born in 1902, Gur'ev
joined the Red Army in 1919 and fought during the Russian Civil War. A graduate
of the Ivanovo-Voznesensk Infantry School in 1925, the Moscow Military-Political
Course in 1928, the *"Vystrel'"* Officers Command Course in 1937, the Red Army Air
Force's Academy for Command and Navigator Cadre in 1941, and the Voroshilov
Academy in 1944, Gur'ev was a platoon leader and company political officer during
the 1920s. After more political work and command of a battalion in Separate Red
Banner Far Eastern Army's 35th Rifle Division in the early 1930s, he led 57th Rifle
Division's 293rd Regiment in the fighting at Khalkhin Gol in August and September
1939 and became commander of 5th Airborne Corps' 10th Airborne Brigade in the
Baltic Special Military District in March 1941. In the wake of the German invasion,
Gur'ev fought in the border battles and rose to command 5th Airborne Corps on 3
October 1941. After leading his airborne brigade during the battle for Moscow, his
division was reorganized into 39th Guards Rifle Division in August and dispatched to
the Stalingrad region, where it took part in the heavy fighting in the Kotluban' region.
Promoted to major general on 7 December 1942 in recognition of his bravery during the battle in Stalingrad city, Gur'ev led 39th Guards Rifle Division until 17 April
1943, when he was given command of 28th Guards Rifle Corps, which he led until
attending the Voroshilov Academy in December 1943. Gur'ev returned to the field
in April 1944 as commander of 11th Army's 16th Guards Rifle Corps and, thereafter,
led his corps in the Belorussian offensive in the summer of 1944. After becoming a

Hero of the Soviet Union in April 1945 because of his corps' excellent performance in the siege of Konigsberg, Gur'ev's outstanding military career ended when he was shot dead by a German sniper on 22 April 1945. For additional details about his life, see *Komkory, Voennyi biografcheskii slovar'*, 2: 14–16.

73. Zholudev's division was equipped with 5,842 rifles, 1,157 PPSh, 154 light, 82 heavy, and 10 antiaircraft machine guns, 254 antitank rifles, and 41 field and 29 antitank guns. See Isaev, *Stalingrad*, 229.

74. For details on the 37th Guards Rifle Division's wartime record, see N. I. Volostnov, *Na ognennykh rubezhakh* [In firing positions] (Moscow: Voenizdat, 1983).

75. *Komandovanie korpusnogo i divizionnogo zvena*, 54, 313. Born in 1905, Zholudev joined the Red Army in 1922. He was educated at the 2nd Petrograd Infantry School in 1923, a Command Cadre Course in Irkutsk in 1925, the Airborne Officer Command Course (KUKS) at Chita in 1934, and the Frunze Academy in 1934. Although he joined the army too late to fight in the Civil War, Zholudev was a platoon leader and company commander in the Far East during the 1920s. He then rose to lead Separate Red Banner Far Eastern Army's 36th Airborne [Air Assault] Detachment in 1936 and a motorized battalion in 57th Special Rifle Corps during the fight against Japanese forces at Lake Khasan in August 1939. Returning west in September 1938, he commanded 20th and 18th Reserve Rifle Brigades in Kazan' in 1940, 234th Rifle Division in April 1941, and 3rd Airborne Corps' 6th Airborne Brigade in March 1941. During Operation Barbarossa, Zholudev's brigade took part in the defense of Kiev in July and August 1941 when he was wounded. After recovering, he took command of 212th Airborne Brigade in September but shortly thereafter his brigade, together with the entire Southwestern Front, was encircled and destroyed in the Kiev region during September. Although Zholudev was taken prisoner during the Kiev disaster, he escaped and, after making his way back to the Soviet lines, assumed command of 1st Airborne Corps in December. After the *Stavka* reorganized his corps into 37th Guards Rifle Division in August 1942, Zholudev led his guards division throughout the defense of Stalingrad until he was wounded in the fight for the Tractor Factory. Upon recovering from his wounds, Zholudev led his guards division until 8 April 1943, when he was appointed to command 35th Rifle Corps as a lieutenant general. Zholudev perished on 28 July 1944 while leading his corps (then under 65th Army's control) in the Belorussian offensive. For further details, see *Komkory, Voennyi biografcheskii slovar'*, 2: 18–19; and Maslov, *Fallen Soviet Generals*, 147–149.

76. Gurt'ev's 308th Division was equipped with 5,513 rifles, 476 PPSh, 106 light and 33 heavy machine guns, 119 antitank rifles, and 45 field and 20 antitank guns. See Isaev, *Stalingrad*, 227.

77. *Komandovanie korpusnogo i divizionnogo zvena*, 255. Gurt'ev was promoted to major general on 7 December 1942 and commanded 308th Rifle Division until 3 August 1943, when he perished during the battle for Orel. At the time of his death, his division was subordinate to 3rd Army's 41st Rifle Corps. See Maslov, *Fallen Soviet Generals*, 100–101.

78. Samsonov, *Stalingradskaia bitva*, 277; and Rokossovsky, *Velikaia pobeda na Volge*, 184.

79. Chuikov, The *Battle for Stalingrad*, 164.

80. Ibid., 164.

81. Ibid., 164–165; and Samsonov, *Stalingradskaia bitva*, 214.

82. Chuikov, The *Battle for Stalingrad*, 165.

83. Isaev, *Stalingrad*, 228–229, citing *TsAMO RF*, f. 48, op. 451, d. 41, l. 104, lists slightly different strength figures for 62nd Army's combat formations in Stalingrad City as of 1 October, as follows (strengths in 62nd Army's daily report are in [brackets]):

- 13th Guards Rifle Division—6,075 men [5,866]
- 39th Guards Rifle Division—3,745 men [3,741]
- 95th Rifle Division—2,616 men [2,592]
- 112th Rifle Division—2,551 men [2,722]
- 193rd Rifle Division—4,154 men [4,687]
- 284th Rifle Division—2,089 men [3,469]
- 308th Rifle Division—4,055 men [same]
- 42nd Rifle Brigade—1,151 men [same]
- 92nd Rifle Brigade—92 men [1,831]
- 124th Rifle Brigade—4,154 men [same]
- 149th Rifle Brigade—3,138 men [3,312]
- 2nd Motorized Rifle Brigade—1,312 men [1,131]
- 115th Rifle Brigade—3,464 men [same]
- 6th Guards Tank Brigade—913 men [963]
- 282nd Rifle Regiment (NKVD)—1,088 men [1,073]
- **Total—40,598 men [44,201]**

84. Chuikov, The *Battle for Stalingrad*, 160.

85. Ibid.

86. Ibid., 160, and map; and Moshchansky and Smolinov, *Oborona Stalingrada*, 56.

87. See "Ia. Lagenkarten Nr. 1 zum KTB Nr. 13, Jul–Oct 1942," *AOK 6, 23948/1a*, in NAM T-312, Roll 1446.

88. Werthen, *Geschichte der 16. Panzer-Division*, 113.

89. Zhilin, *Stalingradskaia bitva*, 645.

90. Chuikov, *The Battle for Stalingrad*, 162 describes the assault:

> The attack against the salient was made from three sides. Approximately one battalion of infantry with eighteen tanks attacked southward across Hill 135.4, and about a battalion of infantry with fifteen tanks across Hill 147.6 toward the south-east.
>
> Nearly two battalions of infantry with sixteen tanks attacked eastward from Uvarovka, aiming to wheel round the south of Orlovka. . . .
>
> At 3 P.M. some fifty tanks, together with tommy-gunners, attacked Hills 109.4 and 108.9 from Gorodishche, and after overrunning units of the 2nd Battalion of Andriusenko's infantry brigade, approached Orlovka from the south.
>
> At the same time, enemy tanks and infantry, attacking Orlovka from the north, smashed the 1st Battalion of the same brigade. The battalion suffered heavy losses and withdrew to the northern outskirts [of the village]. A threat of encirclement developed for the units fighting west of Orlovka.

91. This detailed description of the fighting around the Orlovka salients is based on Moshchansky and Smolinov, *Oborona Stalingrada*, 57–60.

92. Ibid. asserts the Germans lost up to 1,200 dead and 50 tanks destroyed or damaged during the first two days of fighting.

93. Ibid., 58.

94. Zhilin, *Stalingradskaia bitva*, 650.

95. Ibid., 659.

96. Ibid., 665, 672.

97. Ibid., 660, quoting an OKW information bulletin.

98. Ibid., 676–677.

99. Moshchansky and Smolinov, *Oborona Stalingrada*, 58.

100. Zhilin, *Stalingradskaia bitva*, 684.

101. Ibid., 692.

102. Ibid., 700, 704.

103. Chuikov, *The Battle for Stalingrad*, 166; Moshchansky and Smolinov, *Oborona Stalingrada*, 59, states, "The northern group, consisting of 121 men, withdrew from the encirclement successfully; they united with the forces of the brigade situated in the northern part of the Tractor Factory by 0800 hours on 8 October."

Chapter 5: The Final Assault on the Workers' Villages and Battles on Sixth Army's Flanks, 3–13 October 1942

1. Mark, *Death of the Leaping Horseman*, 239. The order [*Divisionbefehl*] was numbered 67.

2. Holl, *An Infantryman in Stalingrad*, 87. Translated into English by the author.

3. Mark, *Death of the Leaping Horseman*, 242.

4. For a graphic portrayal of this complex regrouping, see "Ia. Lagenkarten Nr. 1 zum KTB Nr. 13, Jul–Oct 1942," *AOK 6, 23948/1a*, in NAM T-312, Roll 1446.

5. Holl, *An Infantryman in Stalingrad*, 95.

6. Moshchansky and Smolinov, *Oborona Stalingrada*, 55.

7. Carell, *Stalingrad, Defeat of the German 6th Army*, 148.

8. Mark, *Death of the Leaping Horseman*, 241.

9. Holl, *An Infantryman in Stalingrad*, 93.

10. Zhilin, *Stalingradskaia bitva*, 659.

11. See *62nd Army Combat Journal*.

12. Mark, *Death of the Leaping Horseman*, 241. See 24th Panzer Division's order No. 69, dated 2125 hours.

13. "Boevoi prikaz no. 179 Shtarm 62 1. 10. 42 18.00" [Combat order no. 179, headquarters, 62nd Army, 1800 hours on 1 October 1942], in *62nd Army Combat Journal*. This order read:

> 1. The enemy is conducting an offensive in the central sector and trying to capture Stalingrad.

2. On the right, the units of the Don Front, whose forward units reached the Sukhaia Mechetka *Balka*, Hill 129.6, and Sukhaia line, are attacking. On the left 64th Army is attacking Voroponovo.

3. The Army has the main mission of holding on to the city of Stalingrad and the Orlovka region and halting any further enemy advance along the army's entire front. Subsequently, by destroying the enemy's men and equipment by successive local operations, drive him from the Barrikady and Krasnyi Oktiabr' villages and from the Mamaev Kurgan region and the adjacent blocks south of Mamaev Kurgan.

4. **124th and 149th RBs, with 282nd RR NKVD** will continue to hold on to the positions they occupy, while fulfilling my combat order no. 171/op.

5. **115th RB, with 2nd MRB, 199th ATR, and subunits of 124th and 149th RBs** will continue to hold on to the Orlovka region and prevent the formations of the enemy's groupings to the northeast and southwest from linking up in the region south of Orlovka.

6. **42nd RB** will attack toward the northwestern outskirts of Barrikady village, with the immediate mission to drive the enemy from the blocks he occupies and reach the southwestern outskirts of Barrikady village. Subsequently, capture the line of the Vishnevaia *Balka*.

   The boundary line to the left is Neudinskaia Street, the intersection of Goncharskaia and Elanskaia Streets, and the southern edge of the triangular woods (900 meters northeast of Hill 101.4).

7. **308th RD** will attack toward Silikat and farther along the high-voltage line with one reinforced RR to capture the southern blocks along Elanskaia Street and the cemetery.

   The boundary on the left is the intersection of Makeevskaia and Goncharskaia Streets, the cemetery, and Hill 101.4.

8. **92nd RB** will attack toward Deputatskaia Street and Iamy (south of the cemetery) and the section of the road (900 meters northeast of Hill 101.4) to capture Iamy and the intersection of Zhmerinskaia and Prokatnaia Streets.

   The boundary on the left is the intersection of Zlatoustovskaia and Aivazovskaia Streets, the intersection of Zhmerinskaia and Prokatnaia Streets, and Shakhtinskaia Street.

9. **193rd RD**, while continuing to clear the city of separate groups of enemy, will fully restore the situation at the forward edge along Zhitomirskaia and Chernorechenskaia Streets.

   By 1500 hours on 2 October, prepare to seize the Hill 107.5 region in an artillery and engineer fashion.

   The boundaries are as before.

10. **95th and 284th RDs and 13th Gds. RD** will continue to hold on to the positions they occupy and fulfill my order no. 171/op.

11. **112th RD** is in my reserve. Prepare the region you occupy for all-round defense and cut off the enemy's routes of attack into the Tractor Factory village.

12. **39th Gds. RD** is in my reserve. Prepare an all-round defense in the regions of: a) Skul'pturnyi Park, with the adjacent stone buildings; b) the vicinity of the confluence of the railroad, Manezhnaia Street, the intersection of Fedoseevskaia and Severnaia Streets, and Stendalia Street; c) the intersection of Dar'ial'skaia Street with the railroad and the railroad along Severnaia Street and the intersection of Tsentral'naia Street along Podgornaia Street and convert them into strong points. Outfit all of the stone buildings as bunkers for street fighting.

13. **6th Gds. TB** will support the 42nd RB's attack with artillery fire and tanks in place.

14. The chief of artillery will create artillery groups to support the 42nd and 92nd RBs and the RR of 308th RD's attacks, with the missions of suppressing enemy firing means in Barrikady village and the cemetery, preventing enemy counterattacks from the vicinity of the Mechetka valley and from the direction of Shakhtinskaia Street, and carrying out fire raids with all artillery and multiple-rocket launchers against the Barrikady village and cemetery region for 10 minutes before the beginning of the infantry attack.

The artillery is to be ready at 0400 hours 2 October.

15. The infantry attacks will begin at 0600 hours 2 October.

16. Organize the infantry attacks with hand-picked groups and detachments armed with submachine guns, hand grenades, Molotov cocktails, and antitank rifles. Behind these groups have consolidation echelons with the missions to consolidate firmly in the regions secured, prepare the buildings seized for defense, and prevent the withdrawal of our [forces] to the rear. . . .

Chuikov, Gurov, Krylov

See also Moshchansky and Smolinov, *Oborona Stalingrada*, 55.

14. Mark, *Death of the Leaping Horseman*, 241.

15. For details, see the *62nd Army Combat Journal*.

16. Zhilin, *Stalingradskaia bitva*, 665.

17. Chuikov, *The Battle for Stalingrad*, 167. For comparison's sake, see Chuikov's actual order, "Boevoi prikaz no. 180 Shtarm 62 2. 10. 42 19.35" [Combat order no. 180, headquarters, 62nd Army, 1935 hours on 2 October 1942], in *62nd Army Combat Journal*, which read:

1. The enemy, while continuing his offensive in the city, tried to reach the valley of the Mechetka River and separate the army's front by an attack toward Hills 109.4 and 97.7.

2. The army, while continuing to fulfill its main mission, defended the city of Stalingrad and the Orlovka region, while repelling fierce enemy attacks on the positions it occupies.

3. **112th RD** will occupy and defend the sector from the railroad bridge across the stream 750 meters south of Hill 75.9, Hill 97.7 to the gully along the western edge of the grove and the bridge across the Mechetka River 700 meters to the north of Barrikady village by 0500 hours on 3 October 1942.

Mission: Prevent the enemy from reaching the western outskirts of the Tractor Factory village.

The boundary on the left is the Mokraia Mechetka River, Orlovka, and farther to the west along the valley of the unnamed stream.

The boundary on the right is 3rd Kolaev, Botkin, and Vodopadnaia [Streets], the bridge across the Mechetka, and farther to the west along the Mechetka River.

Subordinate the elements of 124th and 149th RBs operating in 112th RD's sector [one battalion each] to the commander of 112th RD operationally. The commander of 112th RD is responsible for protecting the junction with the neighbor on his left.

4. **308th RD** will occupy and defend a strong point in Skul'pturnyi Gardens with one RR by 0400 hours on 3 October 1942. Create a second strong point in the vicinity of Verkhneudinskaia Street and Nizhneudinskaia Street.

  42nd and 92nd RBs are subordinate to the commander of 308th RD operationally and, together with 351st RR, will continue to fulfill the previously assigned missions [to attack]. The commander of 92nd RB is responsible for securing the boundary with 39th GRD.

5. **[39th Gds. RD]** will relieve the units of 883rd RR [193rd RR] along its line. Mission: Prevent the enemy from penetrating into the city.

  The boundary to the right is (incl.) Arbatovskaia Street, the upper reaches of the ravine 200 meters south of Izhimsk, (incl.) the cemetery, (incl.), and Hill 101.4.

  The boundary on the left is the Bannyi Ravine and Hill 112.0.

  The commander of 193rd RD is responsible for protecting the boundary with 284th and 95th RDs.

  Keep one RR in second echelon to defend the region along Severnaia Street from the corner of Kazach'ia to the left boundary. Pay particular attention to and reliably defend the approaches along the ravine and along Tsentral'naia Street. The commander of 39th Gds. RD is responsible for securing the boundary with 193rd RD.

6. **193rd RD**, after 39th Gds. RD's units occupy the sector of 685th RR and part of 895th RR's sector, will partially regroup its forces to occupy and defend the sector from the corner of Dzhankoiskaia and Promyshlennaia Streets to the upper reaches of the Bannyi Ravine, 1,500 meters south of Hill 107.5.

  Under no circumstances allow the enemy to penetrate into the city. Form your defense in three echelons and especially protect Karusel'naia Street to the Bannyi Ravine. . . .

Chuikov, Gurov, Krylov

18. Mark, *Death of the Leaping Horseman*, 243.
19. Ibid.
20. Chuikov, *The Battle for Stalingrad*, 168–169.
21. Ziemke and Bauer, *Moscow to Stalingrad*, 397, quoting *AOK 6*, Ia Kriegstagebuch Nr. 13, 2 Oct 42, in *AOK 6 2394811* file.

22. Mark, *Death of the Leaping Horseman*, 241.

23. Ibid., 241–242.

24. Ibid., 243–245.

25. Ibid. The 24th Panzer Division's order was numbered 70.

26. Ibid., 246.

27. The 24th Panzer's tank force numbered 28 tanks, including 8 Pz. II, 4 Pz. III short, 11 Pz. III long, 2 Pz. IV short, and 3 Pz. III. long tanks, plus 2 command tanks. See "Tagesmeldung, Gen. Kdo LI. A. K., meldet 22.40 Uhr, A. O. K. 6 Ia, Datum: 02.10.42," in Florian *Freiherr* von und zu Aufsess, *Die Anlagenbander zu den Kriegstagebuchern der 6. Armee*, 109.

28. Mark, *Death of the Leaping Horseman*, 246.

29. Ibid.

30. See daily entry from *62nd Army Combat Journal*.

31. Mark, *Death of the Leaping Horseman*, 246.

32. Ibid.

33. See daily entry from *62nd Army Combat Journal*.

34. Ibid.

35. Chuikov, *The Battle for Stalingrad*, 167.

36. For the action on 62nd Army's left wing, see daily entry from *62nd Army Combat Journal*.

37. Zhilin, *Stalingradskaia bitva*, 672.

38. Mark, *Death of the Leaping Horseman*, 249.

39. Moshchansky and Smolinov, *Oborona Stalingrada*, 55. The 308th Rifle Division's main body was situated along the railroad line south of Nizhneudinskaia Street, with its left wing along Vinnitskaia Street. During this fighting Major Markelov, one of Gurt'ev's regimental commanders, was seriously wounded. Overnight, Gurt'ev's division fell back to new defensive positions along Mytishchi, Aviatornaia, and Petrozavodskaia Streets. See Chuikov, *The Battle for Stalingrad*, 170; and daily entry from *62nd Army Combat Journal*.

40. Chuikov, *The Battle for Stalingrad*, 170.

41. At this time, 24th Panzer Division fielded 9 Pz. III short, 17 Pz. III long, 5 Pz. IV short, and 5 Pz. IV long tanks, plus 2 command tanks, 244th Assault Gun Battalion had 9 long and 4 short assault guns, and 245th Assault Gun Battalion had 3 long and 4 short assault guns. See "Morgenmeldung LI. A.K. meldet 06.20 Uhr, A.O.K. 6 Ia, Datum: 04.10.42," in Florian Freiherr von und zu Aufsess, *Die Anlagenbander zu den Kriegstagebuchern der 6. Armee*, 116.

42. Mark, *Death of the Leaping Horseman*, 250.

43. Chuikov, *The Battle for Stalingrad*, 171. The 62nd Army's daily report for 4 October, stated, "37th Gds. RD completely crossed the Volga River on the night of 3–4 October (without its artillery) and reached the line from the mouth of the Mokraia Mechetka River to the mouth of the Orlovka River, the cemetery, the ravine, and farther along the railroad up to Skul'pturnaia Street, and along Skul'pturnyi Street to the corner of the garden at the gate to Skul'pturnyi Park." See *62nd Army Combat Journal*.

44. Soon, Skuba's 6th Guards Tank Brigade received orders to withdraw to the rear for rest and refitting.

45. Chuikov, *The Battle for Stalingrad*, 170.

46. Ziemke and Bauer, *Moscow to Stalingrad*, 396, quoting *AOK 6*, Ia Kriegstagebuch Nr. 13, 3 Oct 42, in *AOK 6 2394811* file.

47. Mark, *Death of the Leaping Horseman*, 251–252.

48. Extract from *308th Rifle Division's Daily Combat Journal*, entry for 4 October 1942. A copy of the original.

49. Mark, *Death of the Leaping Horseman*, 252.

50. Ibid., 258.

51. Moshchansky and Smolinov, *Oborona Stalingrada*, 63.

52. For additional details on 37th Guards Rifle Division's initial deployment forward and subsequent struggle, see Volostnov, *Na ognennikh rubezhakh*, 70–77.

53. Zhilin, *Stalingradskaia bitva*, 676–677.

54. Ibid., quoting *KTB OKW. Bd. II*, s. 1344–1345.

55. Ziemke and Bauer, *Moscow to Stalingrad*, 396, quoting "*AOK 6*, Ia Kriegstagebuch Nr. 13, 4 Oct 42," in *AOK 6 2394811* file.

56. Rokossovsky, *Velikaia pobeda na Volge*, 186. See also "Boevoe rasporiazhenie no. 00150/op Shtab STF. 4. 10. 42 10.50" [Combat order no. 00150/op, headquarters, Stalingrad Front, 1050 hours on 4 October 1942], in *62nd Army Combat Journal*, which read:

> The *front* commander orders:
> 1. Transfer 84th TB to 62nd Army effective at 1900 hours on 4 October 1942.
> 2. Send the brigade to the western bank of the Volga River on the night of 4–5 October 1942.
> 3. The *front*'s chief of Engineer Forces, Major General Shestakov, will provide the crossing 84th TB [with] 5 KV, 24 T-34, and 20 T-70 [tanks].
> 4. The commander of 84th TB will concentrate his brigade at the Krasnyi Oktiabr' crossing site no later than 1900 hours on 4 October 1942. Bring the tanks and equipment to the crossing region singly or in small groups and carefully conceal them in the woods near the crossing region. Send the KV and T-34 [tanks] across the Volga River one at a time.
> 5. The commander of 62nd Army will employ the tanks as in-place firing points. Before their arrival, prepare dug out firing positions for them. After crossing, each tank must have a trench leading to its firing position. . . .
> Zakharov, Shevchenko, Dosik

57. Although much of his biography remains obscure, Belyi was born in 1897 and died in 1973. After leading 84th Tank Brigade until 8 December 1942, Belyi was assigned command of 4th Mechanized Corps' 59th Mechanized Brigade in December 1942. He led the 59th Brigade until early 1943, while doing so participating in the Red Army's counteroffensive at Kotel'nikovskii, which thwarted German attempts to relieve Sixth Army, then encircled in Stalingrad. After the conversion of 4th Mechanized Corps into 3rd Guards Mechanized Corps and 59th Mechanized Brigade into 8th Guards Mechanized Brigade, Belyi commanded 8th Guards Brigade throughout the remainder of 1943 and the first half of 1944. He then served briefly as acting commander of 2nd Guards Mechanized Corps late in 1944.

58. See daily entry from *62nd Army Combat Journal*.

59. Mark, *Death of the Leaping Horseman*, 258–259.

60. Ibid.

61. "Vypiska iz chastnogo boevogo prikaza STF no. 00451/op 5. 10. 42 5.00" [Excerpt from combat order of the Stalingrad Front no. 00451/op, 0500 hours 5 October 1942], in *62nd Army Combat Journal*.

62. See Division Order No. 72, in Mark, *Death of the Leaping Horseman*, 261–262.

63. Ibid., 263.

64. Ziemke and Bauer, *Moscow to Stalingrad*, 396, quoting *AOK 6*, Ia Kriegstagebuch Nr. 13, 6 Oct 42, in *AOK 6 2394811* file.

65. For the daily reports on this fighting, see *62nd Army Combat Journal* for the respective dates.

66. Chuikov, *The Battle for Stalingrad*, 171.

67. Zhilin, *Stalingradskaia bitva*, 684. Bracketed strengths are from *62nd Army Combat Journal* for 5 October 1942.

68. Zhilin, *Stalingradskaia bitva*, 692.

69. Chuikov, *The Battle for Stalingrad*, 173.

70. Ibid., 173. For Chuikov's attack order, see "Chastnyi boevoi prikaz no. 183 CP Shtarm 62 7. 10. 42 4.00" [Individual combat order no. 183, CP, headquarters, 62nd Army, 0400 hours on 10 October 1942], in *62nd Army Combat Journal*, which read, in part:

1. The enemy, after capturing the western part of Barrikady village and reaching the Tipograf Street, (incl.), Stadium, Petrozavodskaia Street, and Aivazovskaia Street line, is trying to reach the crossings over the Volga River and, simultaneously, threaten the flank and rear of 37th Gds. RD.

2. The army continues to hold onto its occupied defense line and will attack and destroy the enemy in the region of Tipograf Street, Verkhneudinskaia and Vinnitskaia Streets, and (incl.) the Stadium with part of the forces of 37th Gds. RD and 308th RD and capture the line from Mytishch to the railroad, Makeevskaia Street, and the northern exit from Aivazovskaia Street.

   Begin the attack at 1630 hours on 7 October 1942.

3. **37th Gds. RD, with 112th RD** on its right flank, while holding on to the positions they occupy, will destroy the opposing enemy and capture the line of Tipograf Street and the railroad with part of the forces of 109th and 114th Gds. RRs.

   The boundary on the left is the Barrikady Factory, Vozdukhoplavatel'-naia, and the bridge across the Mechetka River, all points inclusive for 37th Gds. RD.

   The northern artillery group (1105th, 1111th, 457th, and 266th ARs [artillery regiments]) will support.

4. **308th RD, with 42nd and 92nd RBs**, will attack the enemy toward Silikat and capture the line from Makeevskaia Street to the northern exit of Aivazovskaia Street.

The boundary to the left is the Barrikady Factory, the ravine (unnamed), and (incl.) the cemetery.

The northern artillery group (1105th, 1111th, 457th, and 266th ARs) will support.

5. Artillery. Be ready to open fire at 1200 hours. The artillery preparation will be from 1600–1630 hours. Artillery offensive will begin at 1630 hours. . . .

Chuikov, Gurov, Krylov

71. Chuikov, *The Battle for Stalingrad*, 173–174.

72. Ibid., 174.

73. "Boevoe donesenie no. 295, Shtarm 62, 7. 10. 42" [Combat report no. 295, headquarters, 62nd Army, 7 October 1942], in *62nd Army Combat Journal*. Moshchansky and Smolinov, *Oborona Stalingrada*, 64, agrees with 62nd Army's assertion that 90 tanks supported 389th Infantry Division's assault.

74. Moshchansky and Smolinov, *Oborona Stalingrada*, 64, stated that 1st Battalion, 124th Rifle Brigade, whose defensive positions at that time were actually north of the Mechetka River, repulsed 94th Infantry Division's sortie across the Mechetka River.

75. Zhilin, *Stalingradskaia bitva*, 700.

76. For a detailed description of 24th Panzer Division's actions during this period, see Mark, *Death of the Leaping Horseman*, 265–272. During this so-called lull, the division suffered casualties of 86 men dead and 319 wounded, most of which resulted from Soviet artillery and mortar fire, counterattacks, or patrolling actions.

77. Rokossovsky, *Velikaia pobeda na Volge*, 182–183.

78. Samsonov, *Stalingradskaia bitva*, 216.

79. A. Vasilevsky, "Nezabyvaemye dni" [Unforgettable days], in *VIZh*, No. 10 (October 1965), 19.

80. Rokossovsky, *Velikaia pobeda na Volge*, 183; and Samsonov, *Stalingradskaia bitva*, 215.

81. Samsonov, *Stalingradskaia bitva*, 215.

82. Zhilin, *Stalingradskaia bitva*, 645, 650.

83. Axworthy, Scafeç, and Craciunoiu, *Third Axis/Fourth Ally*, 85.

84. Grams, *Die 14. Panzer-Division*, 53.

85. Zhilin, *Stalingradskaia bitva*, 659.

86. I. K. Morozov, "Na iuzhnom uchaske fronta" [In the *front's* southern sector], in *Bitva za Volge* [The battle for the Volga] (Stalingrad: Knizhnoe izdatel'stvo, 1962), 108–109.

87. Zhilin, *Stalingradskaia bitva*, 665–666, 672, 677.

88. Zolotarev, "General Staff 1942," 351.

89. Zhilin, *Stalingradskaia bitva*, 714, 722.

90. Regarding Hitler's motivation and speeches, also see Tarrant, *Stalingrad: Anatomy*, 86–87; on the shortage of troops, see Jukes, *Hitler's Stalingrad Decisions*, 78. In fact, other than Group Stahel, precious few of the reassigned air defense troops would ever reach the manpower-starved German Army; instead, Air Marshal Goering persuaded Hitler to allow the creation of 20 *Luftwaffe* "field divisions," lightly armed air force formations that often paid a high price to learn the skills of ground combat. See Hayward, *Stopped at Stalingrad*, 207.

91. For example, throughout this period, the Red Army General Staff's daily operational summaries recorded:

[8 October]

62nd Army held on to its previous positions, while fortifying them and repelling enemy attacks in the Zhitomirsk region with part of its forces. . . .

37th Gds. RD, with the remnants of 112th RD, repelled attacks by an enemy force of up to two companies of infantry toward Zhitomirsk at 0830 hours on 8 October and by a force of more than a company of infantry at 1300 hours.

There were no changes in the positions of the army's remaining units.

Enemy aircraft in groups of 5–7 planes bombed the combat formations of our units in the vicinity of the Stalingrad Tractor Factory and Barrikady villages, and his artillery and mortars fired intensively on the positions of our army's units and the crossings over the Volga River in the vicinity of the city of Stalingrad all day long.

[9 October]

62nd Army, while remaining in its previous positions, fortified them and conducted a partial regrouping of forces. The enemy displayed no activity along the army's front on 9 October. . . .

112th RD occupied defensive positions along the right bank of the Mechetka River from the Mokraia Mechetka to the cemetery.

95th RD and 42nd RB occupied defenses along the line from the upper reaches of the ravine (southwest of Zhitomirsk village) to Skul'pturnyi and the Stadium.

The positions of the army's remaining units are unchanged.

[10 October]

62nd Army, while remaining in its previous positions, fortified them and conducted reconnaissance.

The units of 193rd and 284th RDs repelled attacks by enemy forces of up to two infantry battalions before 1900 hours on 10 October, inflicting heavy losses on them.

524th RR [112th RD] (newly-formed) finished crossing to the right bank of the Volga and occupied a defense along the line from the Mokraia Mechetka River to Kooperativnaia Street and the (incl.) "Udarnik" Stadium.

[11 October]

62nd Army fought defensive battles with the enemy during the day on 11 October with part of its forces.

124th RB occupied defenses along the line from Rynok to Spartanovka and the southeastern slope of Hill 135.4.

149th RB and 282nd RR NKVD occupied their previous positions.

115th RB and 2nd MRB were defending in the vicinity of the ravine on Zhemchuzhnaia Street and the southern part of that street, with their fronts toward the west.

112th RD occupied its previous positions.

37 Gds. RD fought defensively with enemy infantry and tanks during the day, repelling his frenzied attacks. By day's end, the units of the division abandoned the six-cornered [*Schnellhefter*] block south of the Stadium and were fighting along the (incl.) line from the cemetery to Bakunin, Kotel'nik, and Surkovo Streets to the upper reaches of the ravine north of Zhitomirsk village. Fighting was going on with penetrating groups of enemy machine gunners and tanks in the vicinity of Krasin and Bauman Streets. Up to two battalions of enemy and 20 tanks were destroyed.

Units of 95th RD repelled attacks by enemy infantry and tanks and continued to hold their previous positions.

The positions of the army's remaining units are unchanged.

[12 October]

62nd Army, while holding on to its previous positions, attacked to restore [the situation] in the Tractor Factory village with part of its forces.

37th Gds. RD and a RR of 95th RD attacked to restore lost positions in the vicinity of the six-sided block south of the Stadium on the morning of 12 October. The division had no success as of 1800 hours.

The RR of 95th RD advanced forward 150–200 meters.

524th RR, 112th RD, occupied defenses along the line from the Stadium (north) to the five-sided block and the western extremity of Kul'tarmeiskaia Street.

193rd RD and 39th GRDs, remaining in their previous positions, repelled attacks by small groups of enemy with part of their forces during the day.

339th RR, 308th RD, fought with enemy lodged in buildings (200 meters west of Aeroportovskii [Airport] Park.

[13 October]

62nd Army continued to fight stubbornly to restore its positions in the Tractor Factory village with part of its forces.

37th Gds. RD repelled two counterattacks by enemy infantry and tanks and firmly held on to the region of the six-sided block with the units on its right wing. Its 114th RR captured two large blocks in the village southwest of the six-sided block, and 118th RR captured one block southwest of Zhitomirsk.

The positions of the army's remaining units are unchanged.

See Zhilin, *Stalingradskaia bitva*, 704, 714, 722, 727, 731, and 738.

92. *62nd Army Combat Journal*. The army's daily report also noted that 112th Rifle Division's 524th Regiment numbered 320 men.

93. Ibid.

94. Ibid. This report claimed that 160 men from 2nd Motorized Rifle Brigade and 61 men from 115th Rifle Brigade escaped from the Orlovka encirclement and occupied defenses west of Zhemchuzhnaia Street (north of the Mokraia Mechetka River) and along the ravine west of Martel'sk.

95. See "Boevoi prikaz no. 190 Shtarm 62 11. 10. 42. 21.30" [Combat order no. 190, headquarters, 62nd Army, 2130 hours on 11 October 1942], in ibid.

96. Chuikov, *The Battle for Stalingrad*, 179.

97. See Zhilin, *Stalingradskaia bitva*, 704, 714, 722, 727, 731, and 738.

98. "Ia. Lagenkarten Nr. 1 zum KTB Nr. 13, Jul–Oct 1942," *AOK 6, 23948/1a*, in NAM T-312, Roll 1446.

99. On 5 October 76th Infantry Division included nine infantry battalions, including three rated as "weak" and six as "exhausted." By disbanding three under-strength battalions, the division on 12 October consisted of one battalion rated as "medium strong" and five rated as "average." Despite this manipulation, on 12 October the division as a whole was just as weak as it had been on 5 October.

100. Initially, Romanian Third Army deployed its V Army Corps' 5th, 6th, and 13th Infantry and 1st Cavalry Divisions into this sector. By mid-October, however, Romanian I, II, and IV Army Corps joined Third Army's defenses in this sector. By this time, Third Army consisted of I Army Corps' 11th Infantry Division, II Army Corps' 9th, 14th, and 14th Infantry Divisions, IV Army Corps' 1st Cavalry and 14th Infantry Divisions, and V Army Corps' 5th and 6th Infantry Divisions. The 7th Infantry and 7th Cavalry Divisions were in the army's reserve. In addition, Army Group B retained the Romanian 1st Armored, 18th Infantry, and 5th Cavalry Divisions in its reserve, and the OKH held the German 22nd Panzer Division in its reserve to back up the Romanians. See "Ia. Lagenkarten Nr. 1 zum KTB Nr. 13, Jul–Oct 1942," *AOK 6, 23948/1a*, in NAM T-312, Roll 1446; and Axworthy, Scafes, and Craciunoiu, *Third Axis/Fourth Ally*, 84–85.

101. Axworthy, Scafes, and Craciunoiu, *Third Axis/Fourth Ally*, 86–87.

102. Ibid., 86.

103. These attacks reportedly took place on 13–16, 19–20, and 24–27 October, during which the Romanian Third Army suffered 13,154 casualties, equivalent to the British Eighth Army's losses in the battle of El Alamein. See ibid., 86. Red Army reports indicate that 21st Army's 14th Guards and 124th Rifle Divisions conducted the 13 October assault, 14th Guards Rifle Division the 19 October attack, and 76th Rifle Division the 24 October assault. See Zhilin, *Stalingradskaia bitva*, 738, 776, and 796.

104. Rokossovsky, *Velikaia bitva na Volge*, 191.

105. For example, Moshchansky and Smolinov, *Oborona Stalingrad*, 63, 65, credits 29th and 60th Motorized Divisions and 14th, 16th, and 24th Panzer Divisions with a total of 250 tanks and 14th and 24th Panzer Divisions with employing a force of 90 tanks in their 14 October assault on the factory district. In reality, 24th Panzer fielded 33 tanks on 11 October, including 7 Pz. II, 5 Pz. III short, 12 Pz. III long, 4 Pz. IV short, and 4 Pz. IV long tanks, plus 1 command tank. Two days later, on 13 October, Sixth Army's armored divisions and assault-gun battalions reported the following strengths:

- 24th Panzer Division—33 tanks, including 6 Pz. II, 7 Pz. III short, 13 Pz. III long, 3 Pz. IV short, 2 Pz. IV long, and 2 command tanks.
- 14th Panzer Division—50 tanks, including 3 Pz. II, 9 Pz. III short, 24 Pz. III. long, 6 Pz. IV short, 4 Pz. IV long, and 4 command tanks.
- 16th Panzer Division—53 tanks, including 1 Pz. III short, 38 Pz. III long, 2 Pz. IV short, and 12 Pz. IV long.

- 3rd Motorized Division—33 tanks, including 5 Pz. II, 19 Pz. III long, 5 Pz. IV short, and 4 Pz. IV long.
- 60th Motorized Division—23 tanks, including 4 Pz. II, 1 Pz. III short, 13 Pz. I II long, 3 Pz. IV short, and 2 Pz. IV long.
- 244th Assault Gun Battalion—18 guns, including 9 short and 9 long, with 3 short in repair.
- 245th Assault Gun Battalion—13 assault guns, including 4 short and long, with 13 short and 1 long in repair.

See Florian *Freiherr* von und zu Aufsess, *Die Anlagenbander zu den Kriegstagebuchern der 6. Armee*, 164, 166.

106. The 177th Assault Gun Battalion was supporting VIII Army and XIV Panzer Corps along the northern flank of the sector between the Don and Volga Rivers northwest of the city, and 243rd Assault Gun Battalion was supporting Axis forces in the lake district south of the city.

107. Hayward, *Stopped at Stalingrad*, 206, quoting H. Schröter, *Stalingrad: ". . . bis letzten Patrone"* (Lengerich: Kleins Druck- und Verlagsanstalt, n.d.), 185.

108. *Stavka* directive no. 170634, dated 1430 hours 5 October 1942, in Zolotarev, "Stavka 1942," 411.

109. Born in May 1897, Zakharov served as a noncommissioned officer in the Tsar's army during World War I, joined the Red Army in 1919, and fought as a company commander in the Civil War. He graduated from the Saratov Infantry School in 1920, the "*Vystrel*'" Officers Command Course in 1923, the Frunze Academy in 1933, and the General Staff Academy in 1939. During the interwar years, Zakharov commanded a battalion and regiment before beginning his long career as a senior staff officer by becoming the Ural Military District's chief of staff. After serving as 22nd Army's and Briansk Front's chief of staff in the summer and early fall of 1941, he led Briansk Front during the initial stages of the German advance on Moscow in November and December. Then, as Zhukov's deputy, he directed Western Front's offensive at Moscow from December 1941 through April 1942, after which he became chief of staff of Budenny's North Caucasus Main Direction and, later, North Caucasus Front. Appointed chief of staff of Southeastern (later Stalingrad) Front in August 1942 and its deputy commander in October, he supervised operations during the defense of Stalingrad and the Red Army's ensuing counteroffensive. As a reward for his effective performance, after serving a short stint as deputy commander of Southern Front, Zakharov received command of 51st Army in February 1943 and then 2nd Guards Army in June 1943. He commanded 2nd Guards until June 1944, taking part in the Rostov and Donbas offensive operations. Appointed commander of 2nd Belorussian Front in June 1944, he led this *front* during the Belorussian offensive in the summer of 1944 and the pursuit of German forces to the Narev River in Poland during the fall of 1944. Zakharov, by now a full army general, then led 4th Guards Army from November 1944 to April 1945, when his army spearheaded the Red Army's advance on Budapest. He ended his wartime service as deputy commander of 4th Ukrainian Front. After the war, Zakharov commanded the South Ural and Eastern Siberian Military Districts and was chief of the "*Vystrel*'" Higher Officers Course until April 1954, when he became head of the Soviet Army Ground Force's Combat

Training Directorate, a post he was occupying at the time of his death in January 1957. For additional details, see *Komandarmy. Voennyi biograficheskii slovar'*, 81–82.

110. Very little is known about Varennikov's military career because he fell afoul of Stalin in 1947 and was arrested in one of the dictator's final purges. What is known is that he was born in 1901 and served as chief of staff for 26th and 37th Armies in 1941 and 1942 and for the Stalingrad and Southern Fronts in 1942 and 1943. Apparently, he also served as chief of staff of 40th Army later in the war. Surviving the war, Varennikov was arrested by the NKVD in 1947; however, he was later released, probably after Stalin's death in 1953. Varennikov died in 1971.

111. *Stavka* order no. 0789, dated 5 October 1942, in ibid., 410.

112. *Stavka* directive no. 170640, dated 0300 hours 6 October 1942, in ibid., 413. A subsequent directive (no. 170641, dated 1620 hours on 6 October) added Golodnyi and Sarpinskii Islands to the list to be defended. See ibid., 414. These subunits included 17th, 19th, 147th, 166th, 298th, 303rd, 349th, 400th, and 416th Artillery–Machine Gun Battalions from the Moscow Military District.

113. *Stavka* directives nos. 994226, 170642, and 170643, dated 7 October and 1925 hours and 1930 hours on 7 October 1942, respectively, in ibid., 415–416. The air defense regiment included 12 37mm guns and 20 large-caliber antiaircraft machine guns. Another directive, no. 994228 dated 8 October 1942, instructed Eremenko regarding the place and time of 45th Rifle Division's arrival and reiterated he was to employ the division "only for defense of the islands on the Volga in the Stalingrad region." See ibid., 417.

114. *Stavka* directives nos. 170647 and 170648, dated 1410 hours and 2335 hours on 10 October 1942, respectively, in ibid., 423.

115. *Stavka* directive no. 170644, referred to in ibid., 549. See the directive, dated 2305 hours on 7 October 1942, in Zhilin, *Stalingradskaia bitva*, 694.

116. Report by the commander of the Don Front no. 0028/op, dated 2240 hours on 9 October 1942, in ibid., 549.

117. For Rokossovsky's complete plan, see ibid., 549–550.

118. *Stavka* directive no. 170650, dated 2035 hours on 11 October 1942, in ibid., 424–425.

119. Ibid., 425.

120. Report by the commander of the Stalingrad Front no. 2889, dated 1117 hours on 9 October 1942, in Zhilin, *Stalingradskaia bitva*, 707–709.

121. Rokossovsky, *Velikaia bitva na Volge*, 191. See "Boevoi prikaz no. 185 KP Shtarm 62 8. 10. 42 20.45" [Combat order no. 185, CP, headquarters, 62nd Army, 1045 hours on 8 October 1942], in *62nd Army Combat Journal*, which read:

> 1. The enemy, after concentrating up to two infantry divisions and two tank divisions in the vicinity of Dizel'naia, Barrikady village, and (incl.) Skul'pturnyi, is trying to develop an offensive and attacks in the general direction of the Tractor Factory village to reach the Volga River and split the army's front.
>
> 2. The army, after repelling enemy attacks during the day, is fulfilling its main and primary mission of continuing to defend the city of Stalingrad, while holding on to the positions it occupies.

3. **112th RD** will occupy and defend the Mokraia Mechetka sector and farther to the southwest along the right bank of the Mechetka River to the cemetery inclusively.

Mission: Prevent the enemy from reaching the Tractor Factory.

The boundary on the left is the Mokraia Mechetka [River] and, on the right, the southern edge of the garden east of Mikhalov Street, Komsomol'sk, the southern outskirts of the cemetery, and the Kazennaia *Balka*.

I entrust the protection of the boundary on the right to the commander of 124th RB and on the left to the commander of 112th RD.

4. **95th RD** will occupy and defend the upper reaches of the ravine, 100 meters southwest of letter "O," and the sign "Zhitomirsk and Skul'pturnyi" sector by 0600 hours on 9 October 1942.

Mission: Prevent the enemy from reaching the Volkhovstroevsk region.

92nd RB, operating in this sector, will be subordinate operationally to the commander of 95th RD.

The boundary on the right is Minusinsk, Zhitomirsk, Verkhneudinsk, and the northern outskirts of Barrikady village, all points inclusive for 37th Gds. RD, and the boundary on the left is Taimyrskaia, Skul'pturnyi, (incl.) Silikat, and the intersection of Arbatovskaia and Aeroportovskaia Streets.

I entrust protection of the boundary to the right to the commander of 37th Gds. RD and on the left to the commander of 95th RD.

Position 95th RD's command post at 42nd RB's command post, using the communication of 42nd RB.

5. **37th Gds. RD**, upon the occupation of part of your designated sector by the units of 95th RD, concentrate your combat formations, with your main grouping in the region west of the Tractor Factory village, and be prepared to restore the situation in the Tipograf and Zhitomirsk sector.

6. **284th RD**, after relieving the units of 95th RD, will defend the sector from Bannyi Ravine to Hill 102.0 and the railroad bridge south of Poloton.

The boundary to the right is as before, and the boundary to the left in from the Dolgii Ravine to Kurskaia Street. I entrust protection of the boundary between 193rd and 308th RDs to the commander of 308th RD and protection of the junction between 193rd and 39th Gds. RDs to the commander of 193rd RD. . . .

Chuikov, Gurov, Krylov

122. For these adjustments, see Chuikov, *The Battle for Stalingrad*, 179; and Zhilin, *Stalingradskaia bitva*, 704, 714, 722, 727, 731, and 738.

123. Chuikov, *The Battle for Stalingrad*, 179. See Chuikov's combat order no. 195, dated 1835 hours on 12 October 142, in *62nd Army Combat Journal*.

124. Rokossovsky, *Velikaia pobeda na Volge*, 191.

125. Ibid., 191–193. In addition, Stalingrad Front's official order of battle as of 1 October also included 38th, 131st, 169th, 208th, 226th, 229th, 244th, and 399th Rifle

Divisions and 254th, 6th, 84th, 135th, 163rd, 188th, and 18th Tank and 2nd Motorized Rifle Brigades, all of which were in its reserve. All of these formations, however, were the remnants of forces previously decimated in the battle and withdrawn for rest and refitting.

126. See Isaev, *Stalingrad*, 235.

127. Rokossovsky, *Velikaia pobeda na Volge*, 191.

128. Ibid., 187–188. This counter-preparation, which was personally organized and supervised by Major General of Artillery N. M. Pozharsky, struck a 3-kilometer sector for 40 minutes.

129. Mark, *Death of the Leaping Horseman*, 26. Either Chuikov or Mark confused the date of the counter-preparation by one day.

130. Hardesty, *Red Phoenix*, 93–104. See more details on Sixth Army's response to these Soviet night air raids, in William Craig, *Enemy at the Gates: The Battle for Stalingrad* (New York, 1973), 136–137.

131. Rokossovsky, *Velikaia pobeda na Volge*, 189. Other special groups defended the railroad lines extending from Astrakhan' through Verkhnyi Baskunchak to Akhtuba and from Verkhnyi Baskunchak to Krasnyi Kut.

Chapter 6: The Struggle for the Tractor Factory and Spartanovka, 14–22 October 1942

1. See Holl, *An Infantryman in Stalingrad*, 138, which asserts that the ration and combat strengths of 94th Infantry Division on 13 November totaled 7,469 and 2,981 men, respectively. The division lost 565 men from 18 to 29 October and, presumably, a like number between 30 October and 13 November.

2. Details about General Oppenländer's career are utterly lacking other than the fact that he was born in 1892, he commanded 305th Infantry Division from 12 April until his relief on 1 November 1942, and he died while in a prisoner-of-war camp in Garmisch on 17 March 1947. Obviously, he escaped from the Stalingrad pocket before Sixth Army surrendered on 2 February 1943. See Jason D. Mark, *Island of Fire: The Battle for the Barrikady Gun Factory in Stalingrad, November 1942–February 1943* (Sydney, Australia: Leaping Horseman Books, 2006), 63. The 83 tanks in Group Jänecke included 33 tanks in 24th Panzer Division (6 Pz. II, 7 Pz. III short, 13 Pz. III long, 3 Pz. IV short, and 2 Pz. IV long, plus 2 command tanks) and 50 tanks in 14th Panzer Division (3 Pz. II, 9 Pz. III short, 24 Pz. III long, 6 Pz. IV short, and 4 Pz. IV long, plus 4 command tanks).

3. See Sixth Army's attack order in Hans J. Wijers, *The Battle for Stalingrad: The Battle for the Factories, 14 October–19 November 1942* (Heerenveen, The Netherlands: Self-published, 2003), 11–12. This excellent book contains documents, including orders and reports, and personal accounts of the fighting during this period, although often poorly translated into English.

4. For details on 24th Panzer Division's plans, see Mark, *Death of the Leaping Horseman*, 269–270.

5. Entry for 14–15 October in *37th Guards Rifle Division Combat Journal*. From a copy of the original. After this abbreviated entry appears in the division's journal on

15 October, someone (either the commander or operations officer) prepared another, more lengthy, entry, dated 15 October, but it was clearly prepared after the fact, which elaborates in greater detail on the events of 14–15 October. It read as follows:

1. By the beginning of the Germans' decisive offensive, the division's units were worn down by prolonged fighting, having suffered significant losses in personnel and equipment.

   In addition, after the division's night offensive, it had just begun to dig in along the positions it reached, and the defensive works were not completed by the time the Germans began their offensive. The incomplete work in preparing foxholes along the forward edge and the unsuitability of the local measures for constructing firing points in the sector of 114th and 118th Gds. RRs hindered the conduct of combat by these units.

2. The enemy began a frightening 90-minute artillery preparation in the morning. Aircraft bombed our units' combat formations continuously and, simultaneously, conducted combat reconnaissance of our forward edge with tanks and submachine gunners. At 1030 hours a force of up to 2 infantry divisions and one tank division, with powerful bomber aviation and artillery fire support, conducted a decisive offensive against the combat formations of our units.

   He conducted the main attacks:

   a) At the boundary between 109th Gds. RR and 114th Gds. RR and 524th RR, which was protecting the boundary.

   b) At the boundary between 117th Gds. RR and 90th RR.

3. The division suffered heavy losses in personnel and weapons while repelling the frenzied enemy attacks. We are experiencing shortages of antitank shells for the artillery. The antitank means remaining in the division are not enough to withstand a massive attack by tanks echeloned in depth.

   More than 20 enemy tanks have been destroyed along the forward edge and up to a battalion of infantry have been destroyed. The struggle is going on for every meter, and the infantry, before being cut off behind each charred wreck from the first echelon of tanks, is being supported by a new wave of tanks along the division's entire front.

   At a huge cost in losses, the enemy has penetrated the defenses and begun to exploit the offensive at the boundary between 109th Gds. RR and 114th Gds. RR and at the boundary between 117th Gds. RR and 90th RR.

   2/109th Gds. RR was smashed by enemy tanks and armored personnel carriers. Up to 25 tanks and up to 200 armored personnel carriers have penetrated to the stadium.

   1/109th Gds. RR, 3/109th Gds. RR, and 2/118th Gds. RR, while suffering heavy losses, were cut off from the division's remaining units during the day and were fighting encircled during the evening.

4. The situation of 114th Gds. RR and 118th Gds. RR is difficult. Enemy infantry, tanks, aircraft, and artillery and mortar fire are inflicting heavy losses in personnel and weapons.

The regiments are courageously fighting unequal combat against superior enemy forces, during which they have destroyed:
114th Gds. RR—15 tanks and more than a battalion of infantry.
118th Gds. RR—13 tanks and a battalion of infantry.

5. The 524th RR, not withstanding the attack, withdrew from their occupied positions and, by doing so, made the situation more serious. As a result, 109th Gds. RR's command post was encircled. During the fight for the command post, 2 tanks and up to 2 platoons of submachine gunners have been destroyed by the headquarters' staff and the communications and commandant's platoons.

6. The second group of enemy succeeded in penetrating into Zhitomirsk Ravine at the boundary between 117th Gds. RR and 90th RR. The regiment fought fiercely day and night, while suffering heavy casualties. In the process, the regiment destroyed 11 enemy tanks and up to a battalion of German infantry.

7. The attached antitank artillery, which was situated in the depths of the defenses, did not demonstrate steadfastness in the struggle with the tanks and was crushed.

8. As a result of 524th and 90th RRs withdrawal and the weak struggle of the attached antitank artillery in the depths of the defenses, the division and its command post was threatened with encirclement. During the night, the remnants of the division fought in encirclement broken up into small uncoordinated groups.

6. For example, a panzer squadron of 14th Panzer Division's 36th Panzer Regiment under the command of Major Bernhard Sauvant was cooperating with 1st Battalion, 103rd Grenadier Regiment. See Wijers, *The Battle for Stalingrad*, 14.

7. See details about 37th Guards Rifle Division's fight in Volostnov, *Na ognennykh rubezhakh*, 100–104; and the German perspective of the ordeal of Zholudev's division, in Wijers, *The Battle for Stalingrad*, 32. See also the daily entries in *37th Guards Rifle Division Combat Journal*, which provides detailed data of its struggle and its losses during this period. According to this journal, the division's 114th Regiment alone lost 850 killed and wounded during the day's fighting.

8. For details on 24th Panzer Division's fight, see Mark, *Death of the Leaping Horseman*, 273–278. During the day, 24th Panzer suffered 27 men killed and another 59 men wounded.

9. Wijers, *The Battle for Stalingrad*, 25.

10. Zhilin, *Stalingradskaia bitva*, 749, citing *KTB OKW*. Bd. II, 1456–1457. Army Group B's companion intelligence summary judged, "In the vicinity of Stalingrad city, the enemy has abandoned the territory shown in the section 'General Situation.' His attempts to cross the Volga River to the west in the zone of the weapons factory were driven back by our artillery fire and aircraft. With the loss of the bridge east of the Tractor Factory, the enemy has been deprived of an important supply route from the east bank of the Volga. North of the Orlovka region, the enemy has been forced to withdraw to Pechetka and Rynok." See ibid., 749, citing *TsAMO RF*, f. 500, op. 12462, d. 89, ll. 147–148.

11. Ibid., 746.

12. "Boevoe donesenie no. 198, Shtarm 62, 14. 10. 42." [Combat report no. 181, headquarters, 62nd Army, 14 October 1942], in *62nd Army Combat Journal*.

13. Ibid.

14. Ibid.

15. Ibid. The journal entry read:

> **308th RD**—The enemy conducted heavy mortar against the division's combat formation beginning in the morning. Up to a company of submachine gunners began an attack along the ravine south of Deputatskaia Street at 0840 hours but were halted by artillery and small arms fire and began an attack in the vicinity of the ravine opposite Aivazovskaia Street.
>
> **193rd RD**—The enemy conducted active air operations and fired on the division's combat formation with artillery and mortars in the division's sector all day long. He carried out more than 250 aircraft sorties in the division's sector during the day and dropped a great quantity of bombs in 685th RR's sector. The division's units firmly defended their occupied positions, improved them in an engineer sense, and conducted reconnaissance.
>
> [The Germans shelled and bombed the remainder of the army's front].
>
> ENEMY LOSSES: During the day, up to 40 tanks and 1,500 soldiers and officers; two mortar batteries, and two heavy machine guns were destroyed.

16. Chuikov, *The Battle for Stalingrad*, 181.

17. Ibid., 181–182. The Sixth Army's combat journal recorded the following losses on 14 October:

	Killed	Wounded	Missing
71st Infantry Division	3	12	
295th Infantry Division	3	12	
100th Jäger Division	8	29	
24th Panzer Division	16	31	1
14th Panzer Division	31	102	2
305th Infantry Division	84	283	15

See "Morgenmeldung, A.O.K. 6, Ia, Datum 15. 10. 42," in Florian *Freiherr* von und zu Aufsess, *Die Anlagenbander zu den Kriegstagebuchern der 6. Armee*, 172.

18. Chuikov, *The Battle for Stalingrad*, 182.

19. Entry for 17 October in *37th Guards Rifle Division Combat Journal*.

20. Chuikov, *The Battle for Stalingrad*, 183–184. Chuikov argued that his headquarters could coordinate its artillery fire more effectively if it was located on the Volga River's eastern bank.

21. "Boevoe rasporiazhenie no. 205 Shtarm 62 15. 10 42 01.00" [Combat instructions no. 205, headquarters, 62nd Army, 0100 hours on 15 October 1942], in *62nd Army Combat Journal*.

22. Wijers, *The Battle for Stalingrad*, 34–35, as edited by the author.

23. Zhilin, *Stalingradskaia bitva*, 755, quoting *OKW Information Bulletins*; and Wijers, *The Battle for Stalingrad*, 38.

24. Zhilin, *Stalingradskaia bitva*, citing *KTB OKW*. Bd. II, 1461; as confirmed by Wijer's, *The Battle for Stalingrad*, 38. These reports confirm that 244th and 245th Assault Gun Battalions participated in the struggle for the Tractor Factory and adjacent building blocks.

25. Zhilin, *Stalingradskaia bitva*, 756, citing *TsAMO RF*, f. 500, op. 12462, d. 89, ll. 155–156.

26. Ibid., 752–753.

27. For details, see *37th Guards Rifle Division Combat Journal*, which states that the division suffered heavy losses, 114th Guards Rifle Regiment (GRR) and 118th GRR were in a "difficult situation," and 95th Rifle Division's 524th and 90th Regiments were "threatened with encirclement."

28. Chuikov, *The Battle for Stalingrad*, 183.

29. Ibid., 185.

30. See "Tagesmeldung, Armee—Oberkommando 6, Abt. Ia, A. H. Qu., 15 Oktober 42," in Florian *Freiherr* von und zu Aufsess, *Die Anlagenbander zu den Kriegstagebuchern der 6. Armee*, 174.

31. "Zwischenmeldung, A.O.K. 6, I. a, Datum: 16.10.42," in ibid., 176.

32. Werthen, *Geschichte der 16. Panzer-Division*, 114–115. For the Soviet perspective on this fighting, see *62nd Army Combat Journal* for the respective days.

33. Samsonov, *Stalingradskaia bitva*, 228. Chuikov's order read, "To the commander of 138th RD. Upon alert, immediately bring one regiment to full strength and send it across to the western bank of the Volga no later than 0500 hours on 16 October." See I. I. Liudnikov, *Doroda dlinoiu v zhizn'* [The long road in life] (Moscow: Voenizdat, 1969). For 138th Rifle Division's perspective, see its combat journal, which is entitled, *138-aia Krasnoznamennaia Strelkovaia Diviziia v boiakh za Stalingrad* [The 138th Rifle Division in the battle for Stalingrad]. Hereafter cited as *138th Rifle Division Combat Journal*. The entry for 14 October states, "In light of the shortage of weapons, by order of the division commander, all of the weapons of 344th and 768th RRs were transferred to 650th RR, which was to cross the Volga River first and occupy defenses in the 'Barrikady' Factory." See details concerning 138th (later 70th Guards) Rifle Division's wartime record in B. S. Venkov and P. P. Dudinov, *Gvardeiskaia doblest': Boevoi put' 70-i gvardeiskoi strelkovoi glukhovskoi ordena Lenina, dvazhdy krasnoznamennoi, ordena Suvorova, Kutuzova i Bogdana Khmel'nitskogo diviziii* [Guards valor: The combat path of the 70th Guards Glukhov, Order of Lenin and order of Suvorov, Kutuzov and Bogdan Khmel'nitsky Rifle Division] (Moscow: Voenizdat, 1979).

34. See Isaev, *Stalingrad*, 239.

35. According to ibid., 238, 138th Rifle Division had 1,025 rifles, 224 PPD and PPSh submachine guns, 6 light and 12 heavy machine guns, and 27 antitank rifles.

36. For details on Liudnikov's life and service, see Liudnikov, *Doroda dlinoiu v zhizn'*; and *Komandarmy. Voennyi biograficheskii slovar'*, 81–82. Born in 1902, Liudnikov joined the Red Guards in 1917 and the Red Army in 1919 and fought as an enlisted man in the North Caucasus region during the Civil War. He graduated from the Odessa Infantry School in 1925, the "*Vystrel'*" Officers Command Course in 1930, the Frunze Academy in 1938, and the Voroshilov Academy in 1952. After commanding a platoon and company during the 1920s, he served as chief of staff of

a battalion at the Vladikavkaz Infantry School and as a staff officer in the General Staff during the 1930s. Liudnikov rose to command the Kiev Special Military District's 200th Rifle Division in March 1941. He led this division under 31st Rifle Corps control (Southwestern Front's 5th Army) during the border battles of June and July 1941 and during 5th Army's skillful fighting withdrawal back to the Kiev region in August and early September. Because he was wounded in the heavy fighting east of Kiev on 14 September and evacuated to the rear, he avoided the subsequent encirclement and destruction of his division and the entire 5th Army. After recovering from his wounds, Liudnikov commanded 16th Student Rifle Brigade during the battle for Rostov in November and December 1941. Because his brigade performed effectively in this signal Red Army victory, Liudnikov was awarded the Order of the Red Banner, and the NKO appointed him to command 138th Rifle Division in May 1942. After his division's resolute defense in Stalingrad's factory district during the fall of 1942, the NKO honored his division by designating it as 70th Guards and rewarded Liudnikov with the Order of Lenin for his personal bravery under fire. He led 70th Guards until June 1943, when he was assigned command of 13th Army's 15th Rifle Corps, which he directed effectively during the battle for Kursk in July and August 1943, the advance to the Dnepr River in September 1943, and the intense battles to seize bridgeheads across the river in October 1943, for which Liudnikov became a Hero of the Soviet Union. After commanding his corps successfully during the offensives in the Ukraine during the winter of 1943–1944, Liudnikov was appointed commander of 39th Army in May 1944 and led this army to war's end. During the final year of war, Liudnikov was promoted to colonel general, and his army played a significant role in the Belorussian offensive in the summer of 1944 and the East Prussian offensive in January and February 1945. Once the European war ended in May 1945, the *Stavka* dispatched Liudnikov's army to the Far East, where it participated in the Manchurian offensive against the Japanese Kwantung Army in August and September 1945. After the war, Liudnikov commanded 39th, 10th Guards, and 13th Armies through December 1949, when he became commander of the Group of Soviet Occupation Forces in Germany, a post he occupied until November 1952. Liudnikov then commanded the Odessa and Tavria Military Districts from November 1952 to July 1956, served as chief adviser to the Ministry of Defenses of the Peoples' Republic of Bulgaria from July 1956 to March 1959, and became chief of the "*Vystrel*'" Officers Course and the Voroshilov Academy from March 1959 through his retirement in July 1968. Liudnikov died in 1976.

37. See Mark, *Death of the Leaping Horseman*, 278–280.

38. Ibid., 281.

39. Chuikov, *The Battle for Stalingrad*, 186.

40. Wijer's, *The Battle for Stalingrad*, 43, citing "Zwischenmeldung," Armee-Oberkommando 6, Abt. Ia, A.H.Qu., 16. Oktober 1942.

41. Ibid., 44, citing V.O./OKH. Bei AOK. 6, A.H.Qu., 16.10.142 19:30 Uhr.

42. Zhilin, *Stalingradskaia bitva*, 762, quoting *OKW Informational Bulletins (1 January 1942–31 December 1942)* (Berlin: Viking Verlag, 1943).

43. Zhilin, *Stalingradskaia bitva*, 759; and "Boevoe donesenie no. 200, Shtarm 62, 16. 10. 42" [Combat report no. 200, headquarters, 62nd Army, 16 October 1942], in *62nd Army Combat Journal*.

44. See daily entry in *37th Guards Rifle Division Combat Journal*.

45. Zhilin, *Stalingradskaia bitva*, 762; and "Boevoe donesenie No. 200."

46. Zhilin, *Stalingradskaia bitva*, 762.

47. Werthen, *Geschichte der 16. Panzer-Division*, 115.

48. Ibid.

49. Zolotarev, "General Staff 1942," 372.

50. Chuikov, *The Battle for Stalingrad*, 185.

51. Ibid., 187.

52. See "Chastnyi boevoi prikaz no. 209 Shtarm 62 16. 10. 42 23.50" [Individual combat order no. 209, headquarters, 62nd Army, 2350 hours on 16 October 1942], in *62nd Army Combat Journal*, which read:

> 1. The enemy, having occupied the Tractor Factory, is developing an attack from the Tractor Factory to the south along the railroad and trying to capture the Barrikady Factory.
> 2. The Army is continuing to hold on to its occupied positions, repelling fierce attacks by the enemy.
> 3. 138th RD will occupy and firmly defend the line of the southern outskirts of Derevensk, reliably protect the boundary with 308th RD, and prevent the enemy from reaching the vicinity of Lenin Prospect and the Barrikady Factory.
>   The boundary on the right is the Volga and on the left is Mezenskaia and Skul'pturnyi [Streets].
> 4. 95th RD, after having destroyed the small groups of enemy in your rear and your relief by 138th RD's units, will defend the Sormosk region.
> 5. 37th Gds. RD, reinforced by 650th RR, 138th RD, will occupy the territory of the Barrikady Factory and, having created a network of strong points in it, will prevent the enemy from entering the factory.
>
> Chuikov, Gurov, Krylov

The Sormosk region is occasionally identified as Sormovsk.

53. For additional details, see *Bitva pod Stalingradom, Chast' 1: Strategicheskaia oboronitel'naia operatsiia* [The battle for Stalingrad, Part 1: The strategic offensive operation] (Moscow: Voroshilov Academy, 1953), maps. Classified secret.

54. For details of this plan, see Mark, *Death of the Leaping Horseman*, 281–282; and Holl, *The Battle for Stalingrad*, 51.

55. Mark, *Death of the Leaping Horseman*, 283.

56. Ibid., 284.

57. Ibid.

58. See the entry for 17–18 October 1942 in *308th Rifle Division Combat Journal*. Copy of the original.

59. See "Boevoe donesenie no. 201, Shtarm 62 17. 10. 42" [Combat report no. 201, headquarters, 62nd Army, 17 October 1942], in *62nd Army Combat Journal*.

60. For details on 138th Rifle Division's fight, see *138th Rifle Division Combat Journal*.

61. "Boevoe donesenie no. 201," in *62nd Army Combat Journal*.

62. Holl, *The Battle for Stalingrad*, 51, citing "Zwischenmeldung," Armee-Oberkommando 6, Abt. Ia, A. H. Qu., 17 October 1942.

63. Ibid., 53, citing "Tagesmeldung," Armee-Oberkommando 6, Abt. Ia, A. H. Qu., 17 October 1942.

64. Werthen, *Geschichte der 16. Panzer-Division*, 115. The 62nd Army reported:

> The enemy attacked the Northern Group of Forces from three directions: Latashchanka toward Rynok and toward Spartanovka from the west and south. A group of tanks penetrated into the southern outskirts of Spartanovka. Simultaneously, the enemy continued to attack from the Tractor Factory to the south. . . . The Northern Group is continuing to engage in heavy defensive fighting in encirclement, and the units have suffered great losses (estimated at 90–200 men overall) but are continuing to hold on to Rynok, Spartanovka, and the northern bank if the Mokraia Mechetka River. The fighting is continuing.

See, "Boevoe donesenie no. 201," in *62nd Army Combat Journal*.

65. Chuikov, *The Battle for Stalingrad*, 187.

66. Ibid., 188.

67. Ibid.

68. Ibid.

69. "Morgenmeldung Gen. Kdo. VIII. A.K. meldit 04.08 Uhr, A.O.K. 6 I. a, Datum: 18.10.42," in Florian *Freiherr* von und zu Aufsess, *Die Anlagenbander zu den Kriegstagebuchern der 6. Armee*, 180.

70. Zhilin, *Stalingradskaia bitva*, 766, quoting *OKW Informational Bulletin*.

71. Ibid., 764–765.

72. Ibid., 189.

73. "Boevoe rasporiazhenie no. 210 Shtarm 62 17. 10. 42 [no time indicated]" [Combat instructions no. 210, headquarters, 62nd Army, 17 October 1942], in *62nd Army Combat Journal*.

74. "Boevoe rasporiazhenie no. 211 Shtarm 62 17. 10. 42 17.30" [Combat instructions no. 211, headquarters, 62nd Army, 1730 hours on 17 October 1942], in ibid.

75. Holl, *The Battle for Stalingrad*, 57.

76. Mark, *Death of the Leaping Horseman*, 287, citing 24th Panzer Division's *Divisionbefehl* Nr. 76, issued at 2215 hours on 17 October. See the compete order in Holl, *The Battle for Stalingrad*, 109–111.

77. Mark, *Death of the Leaping Horseman*, 287–288.

78. Ibid., 291.

79. Holl, *The Battle for Stalingrad*, 116–117.

80. See "Boevoe donesenie no. 202, Shtarm 62 18. 10. 42" [Combat report no. 202, headquarters, 62nd Army, 18 October 1942], in *62nd Army Combat Journal*. Note that 62nd Army quotes directly from 308th Rifle Division's daily report (pages 328, 335).

81. Holl, *The Battle for Stalingrad*, 119.

82. Zhilin, *Stalingradskaia bitva*, 769, quoting *OKW Informational Bulletin*.

83. Isaev, *Stalingrad*, 241. The nucleus of Group Gorokhov was 124th Rifle Brigade, with 2,640 men. Gorokhov, however, was seriously concerned about the shortages of 120mm mortars, shells for his 76mm guns, and sniper rifles.

84. Chuikov, *The Battle for Stalingrad*, 189.

85. "Boevoe donesenie No. 202," in *62nd Army Combat Journal*.

86. Zhilin, *Stalingradskaia bitva*, 768.

87. Chuikov, *The Battle for Stalingrad*, 190. See the full order, "Chastnyi boevoi prikaz no. 215 Shtarm 62 18. 10. 42 20.00" [Individual combat order no. 215, headquarters, 62nd Army, 2000 hours on 18 October 1942], in *62nd Army Combat Journal*, which read:

1. The enemy, having smashed through 308th RD's combat formation, has reached the western outskirts of the Barrikady Factory.
2. The Army will hold on to its occupied positions, while repelling frenzied attacks by the enemy trying to capture the Barrikady Factory and reach 62nd Army's crossings.
3. 138th RD, reinforced by 37th Gds. RD, will defend the sector from the right bank of the Volga River to the eastern outskirts of Volkhovstroevsk, the western outskirts of Tramvainaia (400 meters east of Skul'pturnyi), and Sormosk to the fork in the railroad (100 meters north of Stal'naia) and the entire territory of the Barrikady Factory.

    Mission: Prevent the enemy from seizing the Barrikady Factory and reaching 62nd Army's Volga crossings.

    The boundary on the left is Perekopskaia, Stal'naia, and Mezenskaia [Streets].
4. 37th Gds. RD (less 118th RR) will defend the vicinity of crossing no. 62 on the right bank of the Volga River and prevent its seizure by the enemy.
5. 308th RD will occupy and defend the Sormosk and Lugovaia sector by 0400 hours on 19 October and prevent enemy movement to the south at the boundary of 138th and 193rd RDs.
6. 193rd RD, reinforced by 161st RR [95th RD], will defend the sector occupied by the forces of 161st RR and reliably protect its right flank in the Stal'naia and Okhotnaia sector.

    Chuikov, Gurov, Krylov

88 Chuikov, *The Battle for Stalingrad*, 190–191.

89. "Morgenmeldung, Gen. Kdo. VIII. A.K. meldet 04:00 Uhr, A.O.K. 6, I a, Datum: 19.10.42," in Florian *Freiherr* von und zu Aufsess, *Die Anlagenbander zu den Kriegstagebuchern der 6. Armee*, 184.

90. Ziemke and Bauer, *Moscow to Stalingrad*, 460.

91. Ibid., 462.

92. Ibid., 460.

93. Little is known about Schwerin's military career other than that he was born in 1892 and died in 1951. See Mark, *Island of Fire*, 6.

94. Mark, *Death of the Leaping Horseman*, 294–295. The 29 tanks included 6 Pz. II, 3 Pz. III short, 16 Pz. III long, 1 Pz. IV short, and 1 Pz. III long, plus 2

command tanks. At least nine of these tanks were assigned to the panzer squadron supporting 100th Jäger Division.

95. See the entry for 19 October 1942, in *62nd Army Combat Journal*.

96. Mark, *Death of the Leaping Horseman*, 296.

97. Entry for 19 October 1942 in *62nd Army Combat Journal*.

98. Ibid., 298. See a description of the Soviet counterattack in the Barrikady Factory in Venkov and Dudinov, *Gvardeiskaia doblest'*, 40–42.

99. Zhilin, *Stalingradskaia bitva*, 774, quoting *OKW Informational Bulletin*.

100. Ibid., 772.

101. Entry for 19 October 1942 in *62nd Army Combat Journal*.

102. "Morgenmeldung LI. A.K meldet 06.35 Uhr, A.O.K. 6 I. A, Datum: 20.10.42," in Florian *Freiherr* von und zu Aufsess, *Die Anlagenbander zu den Kriegstagebuchern der 6. Armee*, 190. On 19 October 14th Panzer Division included 3 Pz. II, 1 Pz. III short, 4 Pz. III long, 1 Pz. IV short, 2 Pz. IV long, and 4 command tanks, while 24th Panzer Division fielded 1 Pz. II, 3 Pz. III short, 16 Pz. III long, 1 Pz. IV short, 1 Pz. IV long, and 2 command tanks.

103. Zhilin, *Stalingradskaia bitva*, 778, quoting *OKW Informational Bulletin*.

104. Entry for 20 October 1942 in *62nd Army Combat Journal*.

105. Ibid.

106. "Morgenmeldung, LI A.K. meldet 06.10 Uhr, A.O.K. 6, I a, Datum: 21.10.42," in Florian *Freiherr* von und zu Aufsess, *Die Anlagenbander zu den Kriegstagebuchern der 6. Armee*, 194.

107. Zhilin, *Stalingradskaia bitva*, 777.

108. Entry for 20 October 1942 in *62nd Army Combat Journal*.

109. Mark, *Death of the Leaping Horseman*, 301–302; and Holl, *The Battle for Stalingrad*, 102.

110. For details on this fight, see Mark, *Death of the Leaping Horseman*, 301–304.

111. "Boevoe donesenie no. 206, Shtarm 62 21. 10. 42" [Combat report no. 206, headquarters, 62nd Army, 21 October 1942], in *62nd Army Combat Journal*.

112. Ibid.

113. Zhilin, *Stalingradskaia bitva*, 786, quoting *OKW Informational Bulletin*.

114. Ibid., 781–782.

115. "Boevoe donesenie no. 206" in *62nd Army Combat Journal*.

116. Entry for 22 October 1942 in ibid.

117. Zhilin, *Stalingradskaia bitva*, 786.

118. Ibid., 788, quoting *OKW Informational Bulletin*, and 786–787, citing 62nd Army's daily report.

119. Rokossovsky, *Velikaia pobeda na Volge*, 197–198.

120. Ibid.

121. *Stavka* directive no. 994272, dated 21 October 1942, in Zolotarev, "*Stavka* 1942*,*" 439.

122. Moskalenko, *Na iugo-zapadnom napravlenie*, 1: 351.

123. For example, 1st Guards Army's 173rd, 207th, 221st, 258th, 273rd, 292nd, and 316th Rifle Divisions were transferred to 24th Army, 24th Rifle Division joined the new 65th (former 4th Tank) Army, and 4th and 16th Tank Corps were transferred

to the new Southwestern Front and Don Front, respectively. See *Boevoi sostav Sovetskoi armii*, 2: 193, 215.

124. See Glebov's nickname for the army in P. I. Batov, *V pokhodakh i boiakh* [In marches and battles] (Moscow: "Golos," 2000). 153.

125. Born in 1897, Batov fought as a junior officer in the Tsar's army in World War I, when he earned two Georgievskii Crosses for bravery under fire. He joined the Red Army in 1918 and rose to command a company during the Civil War. He graduated from the "*Vystrel*'" Officers Course in 1927 and the Voroshilov Academy in 1950. During the interwar years, Batov led a battalion and regiment and, from December 1936 through August 1937, served as a "volunteer" in the Republican Army during the Spanish Civil War. Returning from Spain, he commanded 10th Rifle Corps from August 1937 to August 1938 and 3rd Rifle Corps from August 1938 to April 1940, when he led his corps successfully during the Finnish War. After serving as deputy commander of the Tran-Caucasus Military District from April through November 1940, Batov received command of the Khar'kov Military District's 9th Special Rifle Corps, which he was leading when the Germans began their Barbarossa invasion. Batov's corps spent the first three months of war preparing defenses in the Crimea, but when the *Stavka* organized the new 51st Army around the nucleus of his corps, he became the army's deputy commander in August 1941 and its commander in November. Shortly after Batov assumed command of the 51st, German Eleventh Army defeated that army in the Crimea and drove it off the peninsula in disorder. Although he was sharply criticized by the *Stavka*, in January 1942 it nonetheless assigned Batov as commander of Briansk Front's 3rd Army and, in February 1942, as deputy commander of Briansk Front, a position he held during the initial stages of Operation Blau. Assigned to command 65th Army in October, he led this army until war's end. During his tenure as commander of the 65th, his army became one of the Red Army's most effective, playing a significant role in the victories at Stalingrad in late 1942, Kursk in the summer of 1943, the advance to the Dnepr River in the fall of 1943, the Belorussian offensive in the summer of 1944, and the East Prussian and Berlin offensives in 1945. In the process, Batov twice became a Hero of the Soviet Union, first in October 1943 for his role in forcing the Dnepr River, and again in June 1945 for his role in the Berlin operation. After the war, Batov commanded 7th Mechanized Army until October 1946, 7th Separate Tank Division from October 1946 to March 1950, and 11th Guards Army from March 1950 through June 1954. Thereafter, he commanded the Group of Soviet Forces in Germany (GSFG) until March 1955 and the Carpathian and Baltic Military Districts until November 1959, served as senior adviser to the Chinese Peoples' Army to January 1961, and commanded the Southern Group of Forces in Hungary until September 1962. Reaching the pinnacle of success, Batov served as 1st deputy chief of the General Staff and chief of staff of the Combined Forces of the Warsaw Pact from September 1962 to October 1965. Retiring into the Group of General Inspectors in 1965, he led the Soviet Committee of War Veterans until 1981 and died in 1985. One of the Red Army's most accomplished army commanders, Batov was also among the few generals admired by his troops because of his unusual care to keep his army's losses at a minimum. For further details, see *Komandarmy. Voennyi biograficheskii slovar'*, 18–20.

126. Kriuchenkin reverted to the NKO's Main Cadres Directorate but was assigned to command 69th Army in March 1943.

127. *Stavka* directive no. 994273, dated 0250 hours on 22 October 1942, in Zolotarev, "*Stavka* 1942," 440–441. See the General Staff's implementing directive, in Zolotarev, "General Staff 1942," 379.

128. The *Stavka* had transferred 5th Tank Army from its reserve to Briansk Front on 22 September, instructing that it be concentrated in the Plavsk region. The same day it assigned Lieutenant General Romanenko to command the army.

129. *Stavka* directive no. 170678, dated 2400 hours on 22 October 1942, in Zolotarev, "*Stavka* 1942," 441–442.

130. Born in 1900, Borisov was a veteran of the Tsar's army during World War I, joined the Red Army in 1918, and fought on the eastern and Turkestan Fronts during the Civil war. He graduated from Kiev Combined Military School in 1926, the Frunze Academy in 1940, and the Voroshilov Academy in 1947. During the interwar years, Borisov commanded a cavalry squadron during the suppression of insurgent bands in central Asia in 1927 and during the Basmachi insurgency in 1930. He was deputy chief of staff and then chief of staff of the Separate Cossack Cavalry Corps from 1931 to 1936, served as a "volunteer" in the Spanish Civil War in 1937–1938, and became chief of staff of 19th Mountain Cavalry Division before attending the Frunze Academy. After the war began, Borisov was chief of staff of 31st Separate Cavalry Division from June to October 1941 and the division's commander from October 1941 through February 1942, leading it effectively during the Moscow counteroffensive in December 1941. He then commanded 9th Cavalry Corps from February to April 1942 and served as chief of staff of 1st Guards Cavalry Corps from April to October 1942, when he became commander of 8th Cavalry Corps. Borisov led the 8th Cavalry throughout the waning stages of Operation Blau, when, under 5th Tank Army's control, his cavalry corps played a vital role in the Red Army's victorious counteroffensive at Stalingrad. Borisov continued commanding 8th Cavalry Corps throughout the Red Army's offensive in the winter of 1942–1943. However, while leading his corps on a daring raid deep into Army Group South's rear area in the Debal'tsevo region in February 1943, only days after his corps earned the honorific designation of 7th Guards, Borisov was captured when counterattacking German forces encircled and severely damaged his isolated corps. As a result, Borisov spend the remainder of the war in German prisoner-of-war camps. After his release in April 1945, Borisov underwent a special NKVD "filtration" process to determine his loyalty and, when approved for further service, studied at the Voroshilov Academy and taught on the military faculty of the Khar'kov State University. Borisov retired in 1958 and died in 1987. For additional details, see *Komandarmy. Voennyi biograficheskii slovar'*, 44–45; and regarding his years in German captivity, see Maslov, *Captured Soviet Generals*, 74–76, 95–96, 98–99, 106, 148, 213, and 308.

131. For assignment details, see *Stavka* directive no. 170679, dated 0100 hours on 25 October 1942, in Zolotarev, "*Stavka* 1942," 443–444.

132. Ibid., 444.

133. *Stavka* directive no. 994275, dated 23 October 1942, in ibid., 442.

134. Born in 1900, Chistiakov joined the Red Army in 1918 and fought as an enlisted man during the Civil War. He graduated from Machine Gun School in 1920,

"*Vystrel*'" Officers Courses in 1927 and 1930, and the Voroshilov Academy in 1949. A platoon leader during the 1920s, Chistiakov commanded a company and battalion in the early 1930s, 92nd Rifle Division's 275th Regiment in 1936, 1st Separate Red Banner Army's 105th Rifle Division in 1938, and 39th Rifle Corps in the Far East in March 1941. After spending the first five months of Operation Barbarossa in corps command in the Far East, Chistiakov was transferred west and assigned command of Western Front's 64th Separate Rifle Brigade in November 1941 and 8th Guards Rifle Division in January 1942. Because he performed effectively during Western Front's Moscow counteroffensive and subsequent winter offensive, the *Stavka* assigned Chistiakov command of 2nd Guards Rifle Corps, which he led during the Northwestern and Kalinin Fronts' defensive operations in the Toropets and Kholm regions in the summer of 1942. At the height of Operation Blau, Chistiakov was assigned command of 1st Guards Army in September and 21st Army in October. After leading the 21st during the Stalingrad counteroffensive, he led the same army (reorganized as 6th Guards Army in April 1943) until the end of the European war. During the last two years of the war, Chistiakov's army played a significant role in the Red Army's victories at Kursk in July and August 1943, the advance to the Dnepr in the fall of 1943, the Belorussian offensive in the summer of 1944, and the destruction of Axis forces in the Baltic region in late 1944 and 1945. After the European war ended, Chistiakov commanded 25th Army during the offensive against Japanese forces in Manchuria during August and September 1945. Chistiakov continued in army command until 1954, when he became 1st deputy commander of the Trans-Caucasus Military District. He ended his military career as General Inspector of Ground Forces in the Ministry of Defenses Main Inspectorate. Chistiakov retired in 1978 and died in 1979. For further details about Chistiakov's life and military career, see I. M. Chistiakov, *Sluzhim otchizne* [In service to the Fatherland] (Moscow: Voenizdat, 1975); and *Komandarmy. Voennyi biograficheskii slovar'*, 261–262.

135. *Stavka* directive no. 994276, dated 23 October 1942, in Zolotarev, "*Stavka* 1942*," 443.

136. Born in 1905 and one of the Red Army's youngest generals to command an army, Kreizer joined the Red Army in 1921 and was a student officer during most of the Civil War. He graduated from the Voronezh Infantry School in 1923, the "*Vystrel*'" Officers Course in 1931, the Frunze Academy in 1941, and courses at the Voroshilov Academy in 1942 and 1949. During the interwar years, Kreizer rose through every level of command to lead 1st Moscow Motorized Division in March 1941. When the war began, he led 1st Moscow Motorized during the chaotic fighting along the Dnepr in the Orsha region in early July 1941, for which he received the designation of Hero of the Soviet Union. He then commanded Briansk Front's 3rd Army during the defense of Moscow in the fall of 1941 and the Red Army's counteroffensive in the winter of 1941–1942, when his army figured prominently in the victory at Elets. After short stints as deputy commander of 57th, 1st Reserve, and 2nd Guards Armies from February to October 1942, he led Stalingrad Front's and, later, Southern Front's 2nd Guards Army during the Stalingrad defense and counteroffensive in November 1942 and served as the army's deputy commander (under Malinovsky) when it blocked German attempts to rescue its Sixth Army encircled in Stalingrad. Kreizer then commanded 51st Army from August 1943 through war's end, leading this army

in its offensive operations in the Donbas and the Crimea in late 1943 and early 1944, in the Belorussian offensive in the summer of 1944, and the fighting in the Baltic region in late 1944 and 1945. After the war ended, Kreizer remained in army command until May 1955, led the Southern Ural, Trans-Baikal, Ural, and Far Eastern Military Districts until November 1963, and served as chief of the *"Vystrel'"* Officers Course from November 1963 to May 1969. He retired into the Ministry of Defense's Group of General Inspectors in May 1969 and died the same year. For further details, see *Komandarmy. Voennyi biograficheskii slovar'*, 110–111.

137. *Stavka* directive no. 994278, dated 0130 hours on 1 November 1942, in Zolotarev, "*Stavka* 1942," 446–447.

138. *Stavka* directive no. 170668, dated 0523 hours on 15 October 1942, in ibid., 434–435. On Stalin's orders, on 7 October the General Staff had directed Rokossovsky's Don Front to plan for yet another offensive by its 1st Guards and 24th and 66th Armies in the Kotluban' and Erzovka regions to tie down German forces in the corridor between the Don and Volga Rivers. Rokossovsky's proposed plan, however, proved unsatisfactory, prompting the *Stavka* on 11 October to order his *front* to "prevent the enemy from regrouping, attract part of his forces operating against Stalingrad, and secure favorable heights to improve his positions." See Zolotarev, "General Staff 1942," 351; and, for the message to Rokossovsky and details on the subsequent local actions on 10 and 11 October, see Zhilin, *Stalingradskaia bitva*, 722–723, 726. This exchange of messages was overtaken by Paulus's 14 October assault, which convinced Stalin to accept many of Rokossovsky's previous recommendations for a far larger-scale attack.

139. *Stavka* directive no. 170669, dated 0530 hours on 15 October 1942, in Zolotarev, "*Stavka* 1942," 435.

140. See Report no. 0053/op by the commander of the forces of Don Front to the deputy Supreme High Commander, dated 1945 hours on 15 October 1942, in ibid., 552.

141. Born in 1899, Galanin joined the Red Army in 1919, fought as an enlisted man in the Civil War, and commanded a squad of student officers in the suppression of the Kronshtadt mutiny in 1921. He graduated from the All-Russian Central Committee's Combined Military School in 1923, the *"Vystrel'"* Officers Course in 1931, and the Frunze Academy in 1936. During the 1920s, Galanin commanded a company at the Combined Military School and a guards company of the Commandant of the Moscow Kremlin. Rising through a series of command and staff positions in the Trans-Baikal Military District during the 1930s, he commanded 57th Rifle Division during the battle against Japanese forces at Khalkhin-Gol in August and September 1939 and became commander of the Kiev Special Military District's 17th Rifle Corps in June 1940. After war began, he led his corps under 18th Army's control during the border battles in late June and early July 1941 and the intense defensive fighting in the Ukraine during July and August. Escaping from the Uman' encirclement, he then commanded 18th Army from August through November 1941 and the Volkhov Front's 59th Army from November 1941 through April 1942, when the latter participated in the Red Army's victory at Tikhvin in November and December 1941. Treated as a virtual firefighter—sent from one vital sector to another—Galanin led a special group of Western Front's 16th Army from April to June 1942 and served as

deputy commander of the same *front's* 33rd Army and Voronezh Front from June to October 1942, when he took command of Don Front's 24th Army. He led the 24th throughout the remainder of the battle for Stalingrad and, after the 24th was reorganized into 4th Guards Army in late January, 4th Guards until March 1943, when he was assigned command of Central Front's 70th (former NKVD) Army. After commanding 70th Army during the battle for Kursk in July and August 1943, he led 4th Guards Army from September 1943 to February 1944, 53rd Army in February 1944, and 4th Guards Army from February to November 1944, participating in most of the Red Army's most significant victories in the Ukraine and Hungary. Thereafter, all of Galanin's biographies are silent about the remainder of his wartime career. This probably means that Galanin was removed from army command for cause, perhaps because his army failed to capture Budapest in timely fashion. In any case, after the war Galanin served as a deputy corps commander until his retirement in September 1946; he died in 1958. For further details, see *Komandarmy. Voennyi biograficheskii slovar'*, 39–40.

142. See Zolotarev, "*Stavka* 1942," 553.

143. Rokossovsky, *A Soldier's Duty*, 137–138. For 66th Army's perspective on the last offensive in the Kotluban' region, see A. S. Zhadov, *Chetyre goda voyny* [Four years of war] (Moscow: Voenizdat, 1978), 54–57.

144. *Stavka* directive no. 170670, dated 0300 hours on 16 October 1942, in Zolotarev, "*Stavka* 1942," 436.

145. Zhilin, *Stalingradskaia bitva*, 772. The General Staff's daily reports on the fighting in the Kotluban' sector are the only current sources available about this heavy fighting.

146. Ibid., 776–777.

147. Ibid., 779, quoting *OKW Informational Bulletin*.

148. Ibid., 781.

149. Ibid., 786.

150. Ibid., 783, quoting *OKW Informational Bulletin*.

151. Dieckhoff, *3. Infanterie-Division*, 206.

152. Zhilin, *Stalingradskaia bitva*, 788, quoting *OKW Informational Bulletin*.

153. Ibid., 790.

154. Ibid., 792, quoting *OKW Informational Bulletin*.

155. Ibid., 796.

156. Ibid., 801.

157. Ibid., 806.

158. Ibid., 793, citing OKH (*Fremde Heere Ost*) [Foreign Armies East] intelligence summary No. 496, in *TsAMO RF*, f. 500, op. 12462, d. 89, ll. 227–228.

159. Ibid., 810.

160. Mark, *Death of the Leaping Horseman*, 293.

161. Ibid., 306.

162. Ibid., 313.

163. Ibid., 311.

164. Ibid., 312.

165. Ibid.

166. Ibid., 294.

167. Ibid., 304.

168. Holl, *An Infantryman in Stalingrad*, 117.
169. Ibid., 122.
170. Ibid., 123.
171. V. K. Vinogradov, et al., *Stalingradskaia epopeia*, 233, quoting letter extracts from No. 54. Working notes of the 2nd Special Section of the USSR's NKVD in the Directorate of OO's of the USSR's NKVD.
172. Ibid.
173. Ibid., 234.
174. Ibid., 239.
175. Ibid., 240.
176. Ibid.
177. Ibid.
178. Ibid., 241–242.
179. Ibid., 251–252.
180. Ibid.
181. Ibid.
182. Ibid.
183. Ibid.
184. Ibid.
185. Ibid., 252–253.
186. Ibid.
187. Ibid.

Chapter 7: The Assaults on the Krasnyi Oktiabr' and Barrikady Factories, 23–31 October 1942

1. See LI Corps' complete deployment order in Wijers, *The Battle for Stalingrad*, 59–60.
2. See LI Corps' attack order in ibid., 74–79.
3. Ibid.; and Carell, *Hitler Moves East*, 616–617.
4. Wijers, *The Battle for Stalingrad*, 87.
5. Ibid., 82–83, 97. For periodic reports on the armor strength of Sixth Army's panzer and motorized divisions and assault-gun battalions, see Florian *Freiherr* von und zu Aufsess, *Die Anlagenbander zu den Kriegstagebuchern der 6. Armee vom 14.09.1942 bis 24.11.1942, Band I* (Schwabach: January 2006), 210; and Sixth Army's *Combat Journal* [Kriegstagebuch], in NAM T-312, Roll 1453.
6. Ibid., 85.
7. Mark, *Death of the Leaping Horseman*, 306–309.
8. Ibid., 307. These included 2 Pz. III short, 10 Pz. III long, and 1 Pz. IV long tanks, plus 2 command tanks. Seven of these tanks were supporting 79th Infantry Division, and six were supporting 305th Infantry Division.
9. Wijers, *The Battle for Stalingrad*, 80.
10. "Boevoe donesenie no. 208, Shtarm 62 23. 10. 42" [Combat report no. 208, headquarters, 62nd Army, 23 October 1942], in *62nd Army Combat Journal*.
11. Ibid.

12. Ibid.

13. For a more detailed description of 193rd Rifle Division's defensive operations in the city, see Ia. A. Lebedev and A. I. Maliutin, *Pomnit Dnepr-reka: Vospominaniia veteranov 193-i strelkovoi Dneprovskoi ordena Lenina, Krasnoznamennoi, ordena Suvorova i Kutuzova divizii* [Remember the Dnepr River: Recollections of veterans of 193rd Dnepr order of Lenin, Red Banner, and orders of Suvorov and Kutuzov Rifle Division] (Minsk: "Belarus'," 1986), 19–20.

14. "Boevoe donesenie no. 208," in *62nd Army Combat Journal.*

15. Chuikov, *The Battle for Stalingrad*, 192.

16. Wijers, *The Battle for Stalingrad*, 89–92.

17. Ibid., 92.

18. Ibid. See another account of 208th Infantry Regiment's fighting by Sergeant Will Heller in ibid., 96.

19. Ibid., 99. For 79th Infantry Division's complete war diary entry for 23 October, see ibid., 98, 105–106, and 108.

20. For additional details about 39th Guards Rifle Division's defensive operations in the city, see Morozov, *39-aia Barvenkovskaia*, 15–17.

21. "Boevoe donesenie no. 208," in *62nd Army Combat Journal.*

22. Wijers, *The Battle for Stalingrad*, 98, 106.

23. "Boevoe donesenie no. 208," in *62nd Army Combat Journal.*

24. Wijers, *The Battle for Stalingrad*, 108.

25. Mark, *Death of the Leaping Horseman*, 308–309.

26. "Boevoe donesenie no. 208," in *62nd Army Combat Journal.* For further details see the daily entries in *138th Rifle Division Combat Journal*, which claims the Germans achieved "some success" and the division received 258 reinforcements during the day.

27. Zhilin, *Stalingradskaia bitva*, 791, quoting *OKW Informational Bulletin.*

28. Ibid., 792, citing *KTB OKW*. Bd. II., 1497–1498.

29. Ibid., 792–793, citing *TsAMO RF*, f. 500, op. 12462, d. 89, ll. 227–228.

30. Ibid., 790–791.

31. "Boevoe donesenie no. 208," in *62nd Army Combat Journal.*

32. Ibid.

33. Wijers, *The Battle for Stalingrad*, 109, citing "Korpsbefehl Nr. 94 fur den Angriff am 24.10.42," in *Gen. Kdo. LI. A.K. Ia Nr. 3373/42 geheim*, 23.10.42 18,55 Uhr.

34. Ibid., 110–111.

35. Ibid., 111.

36. Zhilin, *Stalingradskaia bitva*, 799, quoting *OKW Informational Bulletin.*

37. "Boevoe donesenie no. 209, Shtarm 62 24. 10. 42" [Combat report no. 209, headquarters, 62nd Army, 24 October 1942], in *62nd Army Combat Journal.*

38. Ibid.

39. "Frontfahrt des Oberbefehlshabers am 24.10.1942, A.O.K. 6, I. a, Datum; 24.10.42," in *Die Anlagenbander zu den Kriegstagebuchern der 6. Armee vom 14.09.1942 bis 24.11.1942, Band I* (Schwabach: January 2006), 200.

40. See the full account of the rescue of Gur'ev in Lebedev and Maliutin, *Pomnit Dnepr-reka*, 20–22.

41. "Boevoe donesenie no. 209," in *62nd Army Combat Journal*.

42. Ibid. *138th Rifle Division Combat Journal* added, "The enemy succeeded in capturing the Machine Hall of the Barrikady Factory in 344th RR's sector at 1900 hours after a bloody fight."

43. Wijers, *The Battle for Stalingrad*, 117.

44. "Tagesmeldung, Armee—Oberkommando 6, Abt. I a, A. H. Qu., 24.Oktober 1942," in *Die Anlagenbander zu den Kriegstagebuchern der 6. Armee vom 14.09.1942 bis 24.11.1942, Band I* (Schwabach: January 2006), 210.

45. Chuikov, *The Battle for Stalingrad*, 193.

46. Zhilin, *Stalingradskaia bitva*, 796.

47. See Chuikov's generally correct appraisal of the dispositions of German forces facing his army in "Gruppirovka protivnika pered frontom 62 Armii na 24. 10. 42" [The grouping of the enemy on 62nd Army's front on 24 October 1942], in *62nd Army Combat Journal*.

48. "Boevoe donesenie no. 209," in ibid.

49. Chuikov, *The Battle for Stalingrad*, 194.

50. "Boevoe donesenie no. 209," in *62nd Army Combat Journal*.

51. Ziemke and Bauer, *Moscow to Stalingrad*, 462.

52. Chuikov, *The Battle for Stalingrad*, 193.

53. Wijers, *The Battle for Stalingrad*, 123, as edited by the author. See other firsthand accounts of the fighting in Krasnyi Oktiabr', including the Croat 369th Regiment, in ibid., 124–125, 131–132.

54. "Boevoe donesenie no. 210, Shtarm 62 25. 10. 42" [Combat report no. 210, headquarters, 62nd Army, 25 October 1942], in *62nd Army Combat Journal*.

55. Carell, *Stalingrad*, 149.

56. "Boevoe donesenie no. 210," in *62nd Army Combat Journal*.

57. Ibid.

58. Chuikov, *The Battle for Stalingrad*, 194–195.

59. Ibid., 195.

60. Zhilin, *Stalingradskaia bitva*, 801.

61. Ibid., 802, quoting *OKW Informational Bulletin*.

62. Ibid., 803, citing *KTB OKW*. Bd. II., 1523.

63. Chuikov, *The Battle for Stalingrad*, 194.

64. Werten, *Geschichte der 16. Panzer-Division*, 115. Speaking of the fighting in the Rynok and Spartanovka region, the *62nd Army Combat Journal* recorded on 25 October:

> The fighting on 24 October created an exceptionally difficult situation for the Northern Group: the attacking enemy, with a force of more than an infantry regiment with 10 tanks, supported by aircraft, succeeded in pushing 149th RB back to the east of Iamy and the railroad northeast of Tverskaia Street front. The 1st Bn, 124th RB, occupied an all-round defense in the vicinity of Tverskaia and Sarai Streets, 100 meters south of the landing stage.
>
> Beginning from 1000 hours on 25 October, the group fought with enemy forces resuming their attacks with infantry and tanks. The group

repulsed all of the attacks by the enemy and held on to their positions by day's end. It was determined, that, having suffered heavy losses, the enemy is bringing his reserves forward to the field of battle.

65. See entry for 25 October, in *62nd Army Combat Journal*.

66. Ibid.

67. Carell, *Stalingrad*, 149. See Stempel's personal accounts of these actions in Wijers, *The Battle for Stalingrad*, 125–126, 128–130, and 133. Stempel dates the Soviet counterattack at the mouth of the ravine on 28 October, while Carell, *Stalingrad*, 149, and Chuikov, *The Battle for Stalingrad*, 197, date it on 27 October. Likewise, Carell places the number of replacements at 70 rather than 80.

68. "Boevoe donesenie no. 211, Shtarm 62 26. 10. 42" [Combat report no. 21, headquarters, 62nd Army, 26 October 1942], in *62nd Army Combat Journal*.

69. Ibid.

70. For the OKW communiqué, see Zhilin, *Stalingradskaia bitva*, 807, quoting *OKW Informational Bulletin*. The Red Army General Staff's report is in ibid., 806.

71. "Boevoe donesenie no. 212, Shtarm 62 26. 10. 42" [Combat report no. 212, headquarters, 62nd Army, 26 October 1942], in *62nd Army Combat Journal*.

72. Ibid.

73. Chuikov, *The Battle for Stalingrad*, 195.

74. "Boevoe donesenie no. 212," in *62nd Army Combat Journal*.

75. Zhilin, *Stalingradskaia bitva*, 806, 810.

76. Ibid., 811, quoting *OKW Informational Bulletin*.

77. Ibid., 812, citing *KTB OKW*. Bd. II., 1539.

78. Ibid., 811, citing *TsAMO RF*, f. 500, op. 12462, d. 89, ll. 236–237.

79. *Boevoi sostav Sovetskoi armii*, 2: 124, 158, 180; and *Kommandovanie korpusnogo i divizionnogo zvena*, 123.

80. Although the 45th Rifle Division's precise strength of 26 October is unclear, it fielded 6,358 men on 5 November. See Isaev, *Stalingrad*, 244.

81. Little is known about Sokolov except that he commanded 45th Rifle Division until it became 74th Guards Rifle Division on 1 March 1943 and the 74th Guards until 1 August 1943. Thereafter, probably after a stint at the Frunze Academy, he led 60th Guards Rifle Division from 30 December 1943 through 9 May 1945.

82. Chuikov, *The Battle for Stalingrad*, 196.

83. Ibid., 197.

84. Burdov led 235th Tank Brigade until it was designated 31st Guards Tank Brigade on 7 February 1943 and the 7th Guards until 10 October 1943. Promoted to major general of tank forces on 7 June 1943, he left the field in October 1943 to become commandant of the Gor'ki Tank School during the final two years of the war. After the war, he served as deputy commander of 29th Tank Division until his retirement in 1946. For the sketchy details about his military career, see the website http://www.generals.dk/general/Burdov/Denis_Maksimovich/Soviet_Union.html.

85. Ibid.

86. "Boevoe donesenie no. 213 Shtarm 62 28. 10. 42" [Combat report no. 213, headquarters, 62nd Army, 28 October 1942], in *62nd Army Combat Journal*.

87. Ibid.

88. Zhilin, *Stalingradskaia bitva*, 815.

89. "Boevoe donesenie no. 214 Shtarm 62 29. 10. 42" [Combat report no. 214, headquarters, 62nd Army, 29 October 1942], in *62nd Army Combat Journal*.

90. Zhilin, *Stalingradskaia bitva*, 819.

91. Ibid., 816, 820, quoting *OKW Informational Bulletins*.

92. See these casualty figures in "Morgenmeldung VIII. A.K. meldet 04.30 Uhr, A.O.K. 6, I. a, Datum: 28.10–42," "Morgenmeldung LI. A.K. meldet 06.20 Uhr, A. O. K. 6, I. a, Datum: 29.10.42," and "Morgenmeldung VIII. A.K. meldet 04.10 Uhr, A. O. K. 6, I. a, Datum: 30.10.42," in *Die Anlagenbander zu den Kriegstagebuchern der 6. Armee vom 14.09.1942 bis 24.11.1942, Band I* (Schwabach: January 2006), 212, 229, and 232.

93. Wijers, *The Battle for Stalingrad*, 137.

94. See "Morgenmeldung VIII. A.K. meldet 04.30 Uhr, A.O.K. 6, I. a, Datum: 28.10–42," "Morgenmeldung LI. A.K. meldet 06.20 Uhr, A. O. K. 6, I. a, Datum: 29.10.42," and "Morgenmeldung VIII. A.K. meldet 04.10 Uhr, A. O. K. 6, I. a, Datum: 30.10.42," in *Die Anlagenbander zu den Kriegstagebuchern der 6. Armee vom 14.09.1942 bis 24.11.1942, Band I* (Schwabach: January 2006), 212, 229, and 232.

95. See "Chastnyi boevoi prikaz no. 216 Shtarm 62 29. 10. 42 15.35" [Separate combat order no. 216, headquarters, 62nd Army, 1535 hours on 29 October 1942], in *62nd Army Combat Journal*, which read:

> 1. The enemy, continuing his offensive in the sector between Stal'naia-Merovsk, is trying to capture the landing stage.
> 2. The army, repelling attacks by the enemy, will continue to hold on to its occupied positions.
> 3. **45th RD** will occupy and defend the Mezenskaia-Merovsk line, having its forward edge [along the line] from the western part of Mezenskaia to Gazov and the eastern part of Merovsk. Establish close elbow-to-elbow contact on the right with 308th RD's subunits and on the left with 39th Gds. RD.
>
>   Mission: Within the limits of your defensive sector, do not allow the enemy to the bank of the Volga River. Carry out your approach to the defense line in dispersed fashion prepared to repel enemy ground and air attacks. Leave the divisional artillery on the left bank of the Volga in readiness to support the rifle regiments beginning at 0700 hours on 30 October.
>
>   The boundary on the right is from Mezenskaia [Street] (from the bank of the Volga River) to (incl.) Goncharskaia [Street].
>
>   The boundary of the left is from the ravine 500 meters south of Mostovaia (from the bank of the Volga River) to Tsentral'naia [Street].
> 4. **193rd RD** will continue to defend its occupied positions beginning on 0600 hours 30 October. Transfer 10th RR to the subordination of the commander of 193rd RD.
>
> Chuikov, Gurov, Krylov

96. Chuikov, *The Battle for Stalingrad*, 197.

97. Zhilin, *Stalingradskaia bitva*, 822.

98. Ibid., 827.

99. Chuikov issued this attack order early on 31 October after Sokolov's 45th Rifle Division had moved its forces across the Volga River. See "Chastnyi boevoi prikaz no. 217, Shtarm 62, g. Stalingrad 31. 10. 42 g." [Separate combat order no. 217, headquarters, 62nd Army, Stalingrad city, 31 October 1942], in *62nd Army Combat Journal*, which read:

1. The enemy, after a series of unsuccessful attacks to penetrate the front and reach the Volga River, has hurriedly dug in along the positions he reached and brought up reserves, preparing to resume the offensive.

2. The army, with the approach of 45th RD, will go over to a counteroffensive with part of its forces on 31 October 1942 with the mission to destroy the enemy operating in the Stal'naia and Karusel'naia sector and reach the main (western) railroad line to restore the situation in the sector of 193rd RD and 39th Gds. RD.

3. Decision: Launch your main attack in the sector between the Barrikady and Krasnyi Oktiabr' Factories with the forces of 45th RD and completely clear the grounds of the Krasnyi Oktiabr' Factory of enemy with the forces of 39th Gds. RD and subsequently reach the railroad line.

4. **45th RD** will attack in the sector: on the right from Mezenskaia [Street] to Goncharskaia [Street] and on the left from the ravine 500 meters southwest of [illegible] to Dzhankoiskaia [Street]. . . .

5. **39th Gds. RD** will attack within the limits of your defensive sector. . . .

8. I demand especially careful study of the terrain along the axis of movement of each subunit and detailed working out of cooperation and agreement of close cooperation between the infantry and artillery on the ground from commanders at every level.

9. I demand all attacking infantry subunits and units skillfully and rapidly advance forward without halting to liquidate separate centers of resistance, and entrust their destruction and the complete clearing of the regions of isolated enemy groups on the reserves and 193rd RD's subunits.

Chuikov, Gurov, Krylov

100. Chuikov, *The Battle for Stalingrad*, 199.

101. "Boevoe donesenie no. 216 Shtarm 62 31. 10. 42" [Combat report no. 216, headquarters, 62nd Army, 31 October 1942], in *62nd Army Combat Journal*.

102. Zhilin, *Stalingradskaia bitva*, 823, 828, quoting *OKW Informational Bulletins*.

103. Ibid., 827. Because Chuikov had no contact with 300th Rifle Division, 62nd Army's reports make no mention of its actions.

104. Ibid., 832–833.

105. Ibid., 838, 842.

106. Werthen, *Die Geschichte der 16. Panzer-Division*, 115–116.

107. Isaak Kobyliansky, *By Fire and Wheels . . . : From Stalingrad to Pillau with Three-Inch Field Guns* (Unpublished manuscript edited by Stuart Britton), 94–96.

108. Werthen, *Geschichte der 16. Panzer-Division*, 116–117.

109. Report no. 3264 by the commander of the Stalingrad Front to the deputy Supreme High Commander, dated 1800 hours 17 October 1942, in Zolotarev, "*Stavka* 1942," 570.

110. Ibid.
111. Ibid., 571.
112. Ibid., 570.
113. See Fourth Panzer Army's daily situation map for 24 October, in "Lagen-karten zum KTB. Nr. 5 (Teil III.) PzAK 4, Ia., 21 Oct–24 Nov 1942," *PzAOK 4, 28183/12*, in NAM T-313, Roll 359.
114. *Stavka* directive no. 170676, dated 2030 hours 19 October 1942, in Zo-lotarev, "*Stavka* 1942," 438–439.
115. D. A. Dragunsky, ed., *Ot Volgi do Pragi* [From the Volga to Prague] (Mos-cow: Voenizdat, 1966), 30–31.
116. Zhilin, *Stalingradskaia bitva*, 801.
117. Ibid., 803, citing *KTB OKW. Bd. II.*, 1523.
118. Ibid., 806.
119. Ibid.
120. Ibid., 810.
121. Ibid., 812, citing *KTB OKW. Bd. II.*, 1539.
122. Ibid., 811, citing *TsAMO RF*, f. 500, op. 12462, d. 89, ll. 236–237.
123. Ibid., 815.
124. Ibid., 816, quoting *OKW Informational Bulletin*.
125. Ibid., 819.
126. Ibid., 820, quoting *OKW Informational Bulletin*.
127. Ibid., 822–823.
128. Ibid., 824, quoting *OKW Informational Bulletin*.
129. Ibid., 827.
130. Ibid., 828, quoting *OKW Informational Bulletin*.
131. Ibid., 833.
132. Ibid., 834, quoting *OKW Informational Bulletin*.
133. See "Morgenmeldung LI. A.K. meldet 04.50 Uhr, A. O. K. 6, I. a, Da-tum: 31.10.42," in *Die Anlagenbander zu den Kriegstagebuchern der 6. Armee vom 14.09.1942 bis 24.11.1942, Band I* (Schwabach: January 2006), 234.
134. See "Deistviia i gruppirovka protivnika za period 20. 10 po 1. 11. 42" [The operations and groupings of the enemy for the period from 20 October through 1 No-vember 1942], in *62nd Army Combat Journal*. Chuikov estimated that this German force also fielded 228 heavy guns, 92 light guns, 20 six-barreled mortars (*Werfer*), 340 mortars, 230 antitank rifles, 1,800 automatic weapons, and 17,550 rifles.
135. Ibid.

Chapter 8: The Struggle on the Flanks, 11 September–18 November 1942

1. Jukes, *Hitler's Stalingrad Decisions*, 43–60; and Halder, *The Halder War Di-ary*, 664. On the German failure to use Maikop's petroleum, see Hayward, *Stopped at Stalingrad*, 159–160. See also Field Marshal List's biography in Chapter 1, volume 1, of this study.
2. Ziemke and Bauer, *Moscow to Stalingrad*, 375.
3. Ibid.

4. Ibid., 375–376; Halder, *The Halder War Diary*, 665, and Jukes, *Hitler's Stalingrad Decisions*, 60.

5. Quoted by Gen. Kurt Zeitzler in Seymour Friedin and William Richardson, eds., *The Fatal Decisions* (New York: William Sloane Associates, 1956), 135–136.

6. Ziemke and Bauer, *Moscow to Stalingrad*, 376–379; and Jukes, *Hitler's Stalingrad Decisions*, 63–64.

7. Quoted in Jukes, *Hitler's Stalingrad Decisions*, 67. See also Halder, *The Halder War Diary*, 668–669, 671.

8. Major General Becker replaced Major General Dr. Ernst Klepp as commander of 370th Infantry Division on 15 September. Klepp, a former officer in the Austrian Army, joined the *Wehrmacht* in 1938 after *Anschluss* [Austria's union with Germany] and served on the staff of 45th Infantry Division in 1938 and 30th Infantry Regiment in late 1938 and 1939 and then commanded 526th Infantry Regiment from August 1940 to 1 April 1942. He led the 370th from 1 April 1942, shortly after the division's formation in France. Thereafter, he commanded Fortress-Brigade Crete in 1943, 4th Field Division from late 1943 to January 1944, 133rd Fortress Division from March 1944 to January 1945, and 702nd Infantry Division from January to May 1945, when he was captured by Allied forces. Klepp was released in 1947 and died in 1958. General Backer, who was born in 1892, served in World War I and commanded a battalion and regiment during the interwar years. He was assigned command of 370th Division after leading 60th Infantry Regiment throughout Operation Barbarossa and serving in Senior Field Commandant 365 during the initial stages of Operation Blau. After commanding 370th Infantry Division until July 1944, he temporarily commanded XXXXVI and XXIV Panzer Corps in 1944 and led 389th Infantry Division from September 1944 until 25 March 1945, when he was wounded in an Allied air attack. When he recovered, he served as commander of Bremen Defense District until he was captured by British forces in April 1945. Released from captivity and internment in January 1948, Becker died in 1967. For further details on both officers, see the website www.generals.dk.

9. See Tieke, *The Caucasus and the Oil*; and "Lagenkarten PzAOK 1, Ia, 1–30 Sep 1942," *PzAOK 1, 24906/15*, in NAM T-313, Roll 36.

10. Grechko, *Bitva za Kavkas*, 115; and *Boevoi sostav Sovetskoi armii*, 2: 173–174. See Khomenko's 4 September report about the defenses of 58th Army along the Makhachkala axis in Shapovalov, ed., *Bitva za Kavkaz v dokumentakh*, 200–201.

11. See Zolotarev, *"Stavka 1942,"* 393. The details concerning the *Stavka's* instructions regarding the employment of the cavalry corps are found in *Stavka* directive no. 170617, dated 0225 hours on 20 September 1942, in ibid., 394.

12. V. F. Mozolev, "Mozdok-Malgrobekaia operatsiia 1942" [The Mozdok-Malgrobek operation, 1942], in I. N. Sergeev, ed., *Voennaia entsyklopidiia v vos'mi tomakh*, T. 5 [Military encyclopedia in eight volumes, vol. 5] (Moscow: Voenizdat, 2001), 196.

13. Tieke, *The Caucasus and the Oil*, 149–156, covers the action through 15 September. See also Grechko, *Bitva za Kavkaz*, 116–128.

14. For further details, see Grechko, *Bitva za Kavkaz*, 116–117; Tieke, *The Caucasus and the Oil*, 153–154; and "Lagenkarten PzAOK 1, Ia, 1–30 Sep 1942," *PzAOK 1, 24906/15*, in NAM T-313, Roll 36.

15. Grechko, *Bitva za Kavkaz*, 117, cites the German losses; although Tieke, *The Caucasus and the Oil*, 154, asserts no German tanks were lost in the fighting.

16. Grechko, *Bitva za Kavkaz*, 117; Tieke, *The Caucasus and the Oil*, 155–156; and Kolomiets and Moshchansky, "Oborona Kavkaza," 22–24.

17. For a candid and detailed description of the Northern Group's struggle in late August and early September, as well as its losses, see a report prepared by Beriia and Tiulenev for Stalin on 2325 hours on 9 September, in Shapovalov, ed., *Bitva za Kavkaz v dokumentakh*, 215–219.

18. Tieke, *The Caucasus and the Oil*, 156, claims that 46 Soviet tanks were destroyed and 150 Soviet soldiers captured in this fighting, while Kolomiets and Moshchansky, "Oborona Kavkaz," 22, asserts more than half of the destroyed Soviet tanks simply burned up.

19. Kolomiets and Moshchansky, "Oborona Kavkaz," 22–23. The 52nd Tank Brigade fielded 46 tanks (10 KVs, 20 T-34s, and 16 T-60s) and 75th Tank Brigade 30 American M-3 tanks.

20. Tieke, *The Caucasus and the Oil*, 157. Kolomiets and Moshchansky, "Oborona Kavkaz," 23, claims the Germans lost 20 tanks, 7 guns, 10 mortars, and 800 dead in the four days of heavy fighting.

21. Tieke, *The Caucasus and the Oil*, 157–160.

22. See General Zamertsev's biography in volume 1 of *Year of Stalingrad*.

23. Tieke, *The Caucasus and the Oil*, 161–162; and Kolomiets and Moshchansky, "Oborona Kavkaz," 24–25.

24. Kolomiets and Moshchansky, "Oborona Kavkaz," 25. See Maslennikov's offensive plan in the Northern Group's operational order no. 0100/op concerning the destruction of the enemy's Mozdok grouping, in Shapovalov, ed., *Bitva za Kavkaz v dokumentakh*, 223–225.

25. For details on this fighting, see ibid., 26; and Tieke, *The Caucasus and the Oil*, 162.

26. Mackensen, *Vom Bug zum Kaukasus*, 96–100; and Ziemke and Bauer, *Moscow to Stalingrad*, 379. The Brandenburger incident is retold in Haupt, *Army Group South*, 197–198.

27. Kolomiets and Moshchansky, "Oborona Kavkaz," 26. The 44th Separate Tank Battalion fielded 3 KV, 7 T-34, and 4 BT-7 tanks.

28. "Lagenkarten PzAOK 1, Ia, 1–30 Sep 1942," *PzAOK 1, 24906/15*, in NAM T-313, Roll 36.

29. Born in 1900, Sevast'ianov joined the Red Army in March 1918 and fought on the western front during the Civil War and in the Polish War of 1920, ending the war as a battalion commander in 56th Rifle Division. He received his military education at the 4th Petrograd Command Course in 1919, the 3rd Comintern Higher Tactical-Rifle School in 1922, the Frunze Academy in 1934, and the Voroshilov General Staff Academy in 1950. Sevast'ianov commanded a battalion in 7th Rifle Brigade, the Bukhara Group of Forces, and 4th Rifle Division during the suppression of the Basmachi insurgency in 1922 and 1923 and in 81st Rifle Division from 1924 to 1930. After his studies at the Frunze Academy, he served on 81st Rifle Division's staff from May 1934 to June 1936, as a section chief in the Red Army General Staff in 1936 and 1937, and as chief of staff of the Separate Red Banner Far Eastern Army's

22nd Rifle Division in late 1937 and 1938. After teaching tactics for two years at the Frunze Academy, Sevast'ianov was chief of staff of 106th Rifle Division when war began. During the war, he commanded 156th and 276th Rifle Divisions in the Crimea and Taman' regions during 1941 and early 1942 and served as deputy commander of 1st Rifle Corps before rising to command 10th Guards Rifle Corps, which he led from 15 September until 10 November 1942, figuring prominently in the defense of Ordzhonikidze and Groznyi. Thereafter, Sevast'ianov commanded 276th Rifle Division from 16 November 1942 to 5 December 1943 and 280th Rifle Division from 17 February to 3 April 1944 and was deputy commander of 36th Rifle Corps from April 1944 to war's end. As such he participated in 1st Ukrainian Front's operations in the Ukraine during 1944 and the offensives in East Prussia and Czechoslovakia in 1945. After the war, Sevast'ianov served in staff posts in several military districts and taught at the Frunze and Voroshilov Academies until his retirement in 1953. He died in 1974. For further details, see *Komkory, Voennyi biograficheskii slovar'*, 1: 504–506.

30. "Lagenkarten PzAOK 1, Ia, 1–30 Sep 1942," *PzAOK 1, 24906/15*, in NAM T-313, Roll 36, map for 21 September.

31. Tieke, *The Caucasus and the Oil*, 163–164; and "Lagenkarten PzAOK 1, Ia, 1–30 Sep 1942," *PzAOK 1, 24906/15*, in NAM T-313, Roll 36.

32. Kolomiets and Moshchansky, "Oborona Kavkaz," 26–27. These trains include 1st and 2nd Armored Trains of 36th Separate Armored Train Battalion, 1st and 2nd Armored Trains of 42nd Separate Armored Train Battalion, 17th, 18th, and 66th Separate Armored Trains, and NKVD Separate Armored Train.

33. See *Stavka* directive no. 170622, dated 0100 hours on 23 September 1942, in Zolotarev, "*Stavka* 1942," 395–396.

34. Grechko, *Bitva za Kavkaz*, 122. See the details of Maslennikov's planned counterstroke in Trans-Caucasus Front's directive no. 00662/op, dated 24 September 1942, in Shapovalov, ed., *Bitva za Kavkaz v dokumentakh*, 231–234; and Tiulenev's directive designed to improve his *front*'s combat capabilities in Shapovalov, ed., *Bitva za Kavkaz v dokumentakh*, 232–234.

35. Kolomiets and Moshchansky, "Oborona Kavkaz," 26.

36. For a description of the Soviet defenses around El'khotovo see Grechko, *Bitva za Kavkaz*, 121.

37. Tieke, *The Caucasus and the Oil*, 165.

38. Jentz, *Panzertruppen*, vol. 1, 251.

39. The SS "Viking" Division included about 2,000 non-German volunteers, including Flemings (Belgian), Walloons (Dutch), Scandinavian, and even a few Swiss troops.

40. Tieke, *The Caucasus and the Oil*, 167.

41. Ziemke and Bauer, *Moscow to Stalingrad*, 379.

42. For details on this fighting, see Tieke, *The Caucasus and the Oil*, 167–185; and Kolomiets and Moshchansky, "Oborona Kavkaz," 28–29.

43. Ziemke and Bauer, *Moscow to Stalingrad*, 379.

44. Tieke, *The Caucasus and the Oil*, 180. Hitler implied, after capturing Stalingrad, that he would transfer XXXXVIII Panzer Corps, with 24th Panzer and 29th Motorized Divisions, back to Army Group A.

45. Ibid.

46. See *Stavka* directive no. 170628, dated 0230 hours on 29 September 1942, in Zolotarev, "*Stavka* 1942," 404–405.

47. Tieke, *The Caucasus and the Oil*, 196–197.

48. Grechko, *Bitva za Kavkaz*, 175. For details on 18th Army's operations along the Tuapse axis, see also M. I. Povalyi, *Vosemnadtsataia v srazheniiakh*, 129–158.

49. See Grechko, *Bitva za Kavkaz*, 176–178, for details on this construction work and associated *Stavka* instructions.

50. Born in 1902, Rakhimov commanded 395th Rifle Division until 8 April 1943, and then, as a major general, 37th Guards Rifle Division from 16 November 1944 to March 1945. He perished on 26 March while his troops were storming the seaport of Danzig during the East Prussian offensive. For further details on his life and death, see the website www.generals.dk, and Maslov, *Fallen Soviet Generals*, 174–175.

51. Tieke, *The Caucasus and the Oil*, 199.

52. Born in 1900, Tikhonov joined the Red Army in 1918 and fought as a cavalryman on the southern front during the Civil War. He graduated from the 1st Moscow Cavalry Course in 1919, a cavalry officers course at Khar'kov in 1921, the Frunze Academy in 1930, the Red Army's Air Forces Academy for Pilots and Navigators in 1941, and the Voroshilov Academy in 1953. After leading a cavalry squadron and serving as a senior staff officer at the regimental and division levels in the 1920s, Tikhonov served as an adviser to the Mongolian Peoples' Army and commanded 1st Cavalry Brigade's 1st Regiment in the 1930s and the same brigade's 28th Regiment during the Soviet-Finnish War of 1939–1940. As a reward for his superior performance during the Finnish War, Tikhonov received command of 4th Airborne Corps' 7th Brigade in May 1941. During the initial stages of the Barbarossa invasion, he led his brigade in the intense fighting along the Berezina River, where he was severely wounded. After his convalescence, Tikhonov led the new 2nd Airborne Corps in September 1941 and its successor, 32nd Guards Rifle Division, until 4 March 1943. Thereafter, he commanded 9th Army's 11th Guards Rifle Corps from March to August 1943 and served as deputy commander of 58th Army and 56th Army until November 1943. After being promoted to lieutenant general, Tikhonov headed 42nd Army's 108th Rifle Corps during Leningrad Front's offensive to break the blockade of Leningrad in January and February 1944 and 9th Guards Army's 39th Guards Airborne (later Rifle) Corps from August 1944 through war's end. During the last few months of the war, his corps took part in the liberation of Hungary and capture of Vienna, for which Tikhonov was made a Hero of the Soviet Union. After the war, Tikhonov served on the faculty of the Frunze Academy and, after studying at the Voroshilov Academy, became chief military adviser to the Hungarian Peoples' Army and attaché to Budapest from September 1953 to March 1957. In the latter post, he played a leading role in the suppression of the Hungarian uprising in 1956. After serving on the faculty of the Kuibyshev Military Engineering Academy, Tikhonov retired in October 1962. He died in 1971. For additional details, see *Komkory, Voennyi biograficheskii slovar'*, 1: 568–570.

53. Born in 1901, Nikita Emel'ianovich Chuvakov joined the Red Army in 1919 and served as an infantryman in the Civil War. He graduated from the 3rd Moscow Infantry Officers Course in 1919, the Frunze Academy in 1928, and the Voroshilov General Staff Academy in 1951. During the interwar years, Chuvakov participated in

the suppression of the Kronshtadt [Kronstadt] mutiny in 1921, commanded a company in the early 1920s, served as chief of staff of 4th Turkestan Rifle Division's 11th Alma Ata Regiment in the late 1920s, was chief of staff and commander of 85th Cheliabinsk Rifle Division in the early 1930s, and headed 31st Stalingrad Rifle Division in 1938 and 1939. He then served as deputy chief of staff of the Khar'kov Military District in 1940 and was chief of the Red Army General Staff's Higher Specialist Schools when war began in June 1941. After further senior staff service, Chuvakov became deputy commander of Southern Front's 12th Army in January 1942. Misfortune struck him in August 1942 when a military tribunal tried him for his failure to enforce the provisions of Stalin's Order No. 227 ("Not a Step Back!"), specifically those provisions pertaining to the formation and use of blocking detachments and penal units. Although Chuvakov was sentenced to four years in prison, the Trans-Caucasus delayed his punishment and instead assigned him command of 236th Rifle Division on 2 September 1942. As commander of the 236th until 4 March 1943, he established a reputation as an effective and decisive commander. Because of his excellent performance in command, the *front*'s military tribunal overturned Chuvakov's conviction in February 1943 and recommended he remain in senior command. Accordingly, Chuvakov commanded 23rd Rifle Corps from March 1943 to July 1944, 35th Rifle Corps from March to December 1944, and 18th Rifle Corps from December 1944 through war's end. While in corps command, Chuvakov's forces played a significant role in the Red Army's Belgorod-Khar'kov offensive in August 1943, the battle for the Dnepr in the fall of 1943, most of 1st Ukrainian Front's many victories in the Ukraine in 1944, and the East Prussian, East Pomeranian, and Berlin offensives of 1945. A soldier's soldier who sought to minimize casualties, he also earned the title of Hero of the Soviet Union in October 1943 for his role in forcing the Dnepr River and was promoted to the rank of lieutenant general in 1945. After the war, Chuvakov commanded 18th and 136th Rifle Corps until 1948 and later occupied senior posts in a variety of Soviet Army higher educational institutions. Chuvakov retired in 1955 and died in 1965. For further details, see *Komkory, Voennyi biograficheskii slovar'*, 1: 620–622.

Born in 1906 and, therefore, one of the Red Army's youngest general officers, Konstantin Ivanovich Provalov joined the Red Army in 1928. He graduated from 39th Rifle Division's regimental school in 1929, the Irkutsk Infantry School in 1931, the Frunze Academy in 1941, and the Voroshilov General Staff Academy in 1950. During the interwar years, Provalov led a platoon in the fighting against Chinese troops in Manchuria in 1929 and rose to command 40th Rifle Division's 120th Regiment in 1938, which he led in 1st Separate Red Banner Army's victory over Japanese forces at Lake Khasan. Twice wounded, Provalov became a Hero of the Soviet Union for his bravery during this battle. A student at the Frunze Academy when Operation Barbarossa began, after his graduation in August 1941 Provalov formed and led 383rd Rifle Division from August 1941 to June 1943. During this period, his division participated in 18th Army's defense and counteroffensive in the Donbas and Rostov regions in the fall of 1941 and winter campaign of 1941–1942, during Southern Front's and Trans-Caucasus Front's defense of the Donbas and Caucasus regions in the summer and fall of 1942, and during the counteroffensive in the Caucasus and Taman' regions in the winter of 1942–1943 and spring of 1943. Provalov was promoted to lieutenant general in June 1943 and assigned command of Trans-Caucasus

Front's 16th Rifle Corps, which he led during the offensive to liberate the Taman' and Crimean Peninsulas. Thereafter, Provalov led 31st Army's 113th Rifle Corps from May 1944 to war's end, taking part in the Belorussian offensive in the summer of 1944 and the East Prussian offensive in January and February 1945. He completed his wartime service by leading the same corps in the 1st Ukrainian Front's Prague offensive in April and May 1945. After the war, Provalov commanded 3rd Guards and 9th Guards Rifle Corps until 1948 and, after graduating from the Voroshilov Academy, led 13th and 31st Rifle Corps and 4th Army until 1959, when he became 1st deputy commander of the Carpathian Military District, a post he held until September 1962. Thereafter, Provalov commanded the Southern Group of Forces in Hungary until October 1969 and served as 1st Deputy Chief Inspector in the Ministry of Defense before his retirement into the Ministry's Group of General Inspectors in November 1973. Provalov died in 1981. For additional details, see *Komkory, Voennyi biograficheskii slovar'*, 1: 456–457.

54. Tieke, *The Caucasus and the Oil*, 200.

55. Ibid., 202–203.

56. Grechko, *Bitva za Kavkaz*, 180; and Tieke, *The Caucasus and the Oil*, 204.

57. Tieke, *The Caucasus and the Oil*, 204.

58. See Vasilevsky's directive, numbered 157318 and dated 1705 hours on 29 September 1942 in Shapovalov, ed., *Bitva za Kavkaz v dokumentakh*, 237–238.

59. See *Stavka* directive no. 170631, dated 2240 hours on 2 October 1942, in Zolotarev, "*Stavka 1942*," 408–409.

60. Born in 1895, Gaidukov fought in the Tsar's army during World War I, joined the Red Army in 1918, and served as a commissar and assistant brigade commander in 2nd Cavalry Division on the southern front during the Civil War. He graduated from Elizavetinsk Cavalry School in 1915, a cavalry command course in Novocherkassk in 1927, and the Voroshilov Academy in 1948. During the interwar years, Gaidukov commanded 6th Chongar Cavalry Division's 5th Regiment and 7th Samara Cavalry Division's 38th Regiment and served as deputy commander of 8th Rifle Division, 2nd Caucasus Cavalry Division, and 13th Don Cavalry Division before commanding the Trans-Caucasus Military District's 17th Cavalry Division from January 1939 to the outbreak of war in June 1941. Thereafter, Gaidukov led his cavalry division until January 1942, when he received command of 2nd Cavalry Corps (redesignated as 9th Cavalry Corps on 24 January). After serving as deputy commander of 18th Army from August to November 1942, Gaidukov commanded 16th Rifle Corps from November 1942 to January 1943 and 15th Cavalry Corps along the Iran border from January 1943 to January 1944, when, as a lieutenant general, he served as deputy commander of Trans-Caucasus Front's 34th and 4th Armies. He ended the war as commander of the same *front's* 58th Army, which was responsible for defending the Iran border and the vital Lend-Lease routes through the country. After the war, Gaidukov was deputy commander of 4th Army until March 1947, and, after attending the Voroshilov Academy, he commanded 19th, 27th, and 14th Guards Rifle Corps until his retirement in August 1955. Gaidukov died in 1980. For further details, see *Komkory, Voennyi biograficheskii slovar'*, 2: 49–50.

61. Grechko, *Bitva za Kavkaz*, 180.

62. Ibid.

63. Ibid., 181–182.

64. Ibid., 182.

65. Ibid., 183.

66. See *Stavka* directive no. 170649, dated 11 October 1942, in Zolotarev, "*Stavka* 1942," 423–424.

67. Born in 1900, Mel'nik joined the Red Army in 1918 and commanded a cavalry squadron on the southwestern front during the Civil War. He graduated from a cavalry commanders' course in 1926 and the Frunze Academy in 1933. Mel'nik commanded a cavalry squadron and was chief of staff and commander of a cavalry regiment in the 1920s and served as chief of staff of 4th Separate Cavalry Brigade and 16th Separate Cavalry Division from 1935 to July 1937. He then led 30th Cavalry Division from July to December 1937 and served as deputy chief of staff of Far Eastern Front during the struggle with Japanese forces at Lake Khasan in 1938 and chief of staff of Far Eastern Front's 2nd Red Banner Army from September 1938 to July 1939. After Mel'nik taught at the Frunze Academy from August 1939 through July 1941, the *Stavka* assigned Mel'nik as commander of 53rd Separate Cavalry Brigade (4th Guards in October 1941), which he led during the battles of Smolensk and Moscow. In the process, Mel'nik participated in the famous raid of General Dovator's Cavalry Group into the German rear and earned the Order of the Red Banner. He then led 15th Cavalry Corps in Iran from March to October 1942, 44th Army in the Caucasus from October 1942 until November 1942, 58th Army from November 1942 to October 1943, 56th Army from October to November 1943, and, after a short stint as its deputy commander, the Separate Coastal Army from April 1944 to war's end. As such, he participated in most of the Red Army's defensive and offensive operations in the Caucasus region in late 1942 and 1943 and in the Crimea in 1944. After the war, Mel'nik commanded the Tavria Military District until 1946 and, after a short stint in the Ministry of Defense, was chief adviser to the Romanian People's Army and attaché to Bucharest. He ended his military career as chief of DOSAAF [All-Union Voluntary Society for Cooperating with the Army, Air Force, and Fleet] training and retired in 1961. Mel'nik died in 1971. For further details, see *Komandarmy, Voennyi biograficheskii slovar'*, 148–150.

68. Tieke, *The Caucasus and the Oil*, 204.

69. Ibid., 205.

70. Ibid., 205.

71. Grechko, *Bitva za Kavkaz*, 184.

72. See *Stavka* directive no. 170660, dated 0510 hours on 15 October 1942, in Zolotarev, "*Stavka* 1942," 434.

73. Ibid. The six divisions were to deploy to Novo-Mikhailovskoe, Tuapse, and Lazarevskaia on the Black Sea coast and Alagir, Baku, and Erevan.

74. Grechko, *Bitva za Kavkaz*, 185.

75. See *Stavka* directive no. 170675, dated 1650 hours on 18 October 1942, in Zolotarev, "*Stavka* 1942," 438. See the *Stavka*'s criticism of Kamkov in its directive no. 170673, dated 2140 hours on 17 October 1942, in ibid., 436–437.

76. See ibid., 437–438. The *Stavka* dispatched 165th Rifle Brigade from Baku to help replace the transferred cavalry divisions.

77. Born in 1900, Luchinsky joined the Red Army in 1919 and fought as a cavalryman during the Civil War. He graduated from the Frunze Academy in 1940 and

the Voroshilov General Staff Academy in 1948, rising to the rank of army general in 1955. During the interwar years, Luchinsky commanded at every level from platoon through regiment, culminating in his assignment to lead 83rd Mountain Rifle Division in April 1941. He led this division throughout Operations Barbarossa and Blau, finally relinquishing command on 4 April 1943 when he was assigned command of 3rd Mountain Rifle Corps, which he also led with distinction during operations to liberate the northern Caucasus and Taman' regions and the Crimean Peninsula. Thereafter, he commanded 28th Army during the Belorussian offensive in the summer of 1944, the East Prussian offensive in January and February 1945, the Berlin offensive in April 1945, and the Prague offensive in May 1945. After becoming a Hero of the Soviet Union in April 1945, he completed his wartime career by leading 36th Army during the Manchurian offensive in August and September 1945. After the war, Luchinsky commanded 4th and 28th Armies until 1949 and served as deputy commander of the Group of Soviet Occupation Forces in Germany from 1949 to 1953. He ended his military career as an army general serving as 1st deputy chief inspector of the Ministry of Defense. He retired in 1964 and died in 1990. For further details, see *Komandarmy, Voennyi biograficheskii slovar'*, 132–133.

78. Grechko, *Bitva za Kavkaz*, 186–187. Commanded by Colonel P. N. Kitsuk, whose fate is unknown, 408th Rifle Division was disbanded in November, probably because of its poor performance in the preceding battles.

79. Ibid., 187–188.

80. Ibid., 190–191.

81. Tieke, *The Caucasus and the Oil*, 207–208. Most of these encircled forces escaped.

82. Born in 1894, Kolchuk fought in the Tsar's army in World War I, led a Red Guard's battalion in the revolution in Saint Petersburg in 1917, and joined the Red Army in 1919. While fighting against Admiral Kolchak's White forces and supporting Czech Legion on the eastern front during the Civil War, Kolchuk was captured, spent 10 months in captivity, and was conscripted into Kolchak's White army in March 1919. However, Kolchuk deserted from Kolchak's army in May, rejoined the Red Army, and commanded a battalion on the Turkestan front in 1919 and during the 1920 Polish War, when he was wounded in action. After the Civil War ended, he graduated from the *"Vystrel'"* Officers Course in 1924 and the Frunze Academy in 1931. During the interwar years, he commanded 24th Samara-Simbirsk Iron Rifle Division's 214th, 208th, and 210th Regiments in 1921 and 1922 and 2nd Rifle Division's 4th Turkestan Regiment in 1927 and 1928. Upon his graduation from the Frunze Academy in March 1931, he led Far Eastern Front's 6th Separate Railroad Exploitation Brigade until April 1936, while doing so earning the Order of the Workers Red Banner. However, in July 1938 he was arrested on charges of disloyalty, sentenced to two years' imprisonment, and ultimately released into the reserves in July 1941. After the German Barbarossa invasion, the NKO recalled Kolchuk to service in late July and appointed him, first, as commander of Southern Front's 182nd Reserve Rifle Regiment and, in May 1942, of 353rd Rifle Division. After leading the 353rd Rifle from May 1942 until May 1944, during which he participated in Southern Front's offensives in the northern Caucasus, Donbas, and Ukraine, he became commander of 46th Army's 37th Rifle Corps, which he led during 3rd Ukrainian Front's offensives in Romania,

Hungary, and finally Austria in 1944 and 1945. An accomplished commander despite his imprisonment, after the war Kolchuk commanded rifle corps until 1950, when he ended his military career as chief of the 1st Automobile School. Kolchuk retired in 1953 and died in 1972. For additional details on his fascinating career, see *Komkory, Voennyi biograficheskii slovar'*, 1: 276–278.

83. Tieke, *The Caucasus and the Oil*, 192.

84. Povaly, *Vosemnadtsataia v srazheniiakh*, 148; and Tieke, *The Caucasus and the Oil*, 209–210.

85. Ziemke and Bauer, *Moscow to Stalingrad*, 451, 453.

86. Tieke, *The Caucasus and the Oil*, 221.

87. Ibid. For First Panzer Army's daily dispositions throughout its offensive, see "Lagenkarten PzAOK 1, Ia, 1–31 Oct 1942," *PzAOK 1, 24906/16*, in NAM T-313, Roll 36. For perceived Soviet dispositions, see, "Feindlagekarten, PzAOK 1, Ic, 1–29 Oct 1942," *PzAOK 1, 24906/27*, in NAM T-313, Roll 38.

88. Jentz, *Panzertruppen*, 251, places 13th Panzer Division's armor strength on 20 October at 130 tanks.

89. Ziemke and Bauer, *Moscow to Stalingrad*, 453.

90. Grechko, *Bitva za Kavkaz*, 196. See the *Stavka's* order for this offensive within the context of its overall defense south of the Terek River in *Stavka* directive no. 170628, dated 0230 hours on 29 September 1942, in "Zolotarev," "*Stavka* 1942," 404–405.

91. For details on 4th Guards Cavalry Corps' operations, see Grechko, *Bitva za Kavkaz*, 196–199; Tieke, *The Caucasus and the Oil*, 145–148; and Kirichenko's report no. 00966, dated 5 November 1942, in Shapovalov, ed., *Bitva za Kavkaz v dokumentakh*, 263–266.

92. Grechko, *Bitva za Kavkaz*, 199–200.

93. See Shapovalov, ed., *Bitva za Kavkaz v dokumentakh*, 250–251. See also the Trans-Caucasus Front's report no. 0957/op, dated 9 October 1942, to the chief of the General Staff concerning the *front's* offensive and defensive preparations and requests for reinforcements, in ibid., 251–253, and the *front's* directive no. 00211/op, dated 10 October 1942 to the Northern Group of Forces concerning 37th Army's defenses, in ibid., 253–255.

94. See order no. 00944/op, dated 1940 hours on 23 October 1942, from the commander of the Trans-Caucasus Front to the commander of the Northern Group of Forces on the destruction of the enemy's Mozdok grouping, in Zolotarev, "*Stavka* 1942," 556–557.

95. Ibid.

96. See the *Stavka's* approval and recommended revisions in *Stavka* directive no. 170680, dated 1900 hours on 25 October 1942, in ibid., 445; and the Trans-Caucasus Front's order no. 0170 to the Northern Group on the same date in Shapovalov, ed., *Bitva za Kavkaz v dokumentakh*, 258–259.

97. Ibid., 200–201; and *Boevoi sostav Sovetskoi armii*, 2: 217.

98. Grechko, *Bitva za Kavkaz*, 202–203; and Tieke, *The Caucasus and the Oil*, 221–222.

99. For what little is known about Safarian's military career, see the website www.generals.dk.

100. Grechko, *Bitva za Kavkaz*, 203; and Tieke, *The Caucasus and the Oil*, 222.

101. Grechko, *Bitva za Kavkaz*.

102. Born in 1897, Loviagin served in the Tsar's army during World War I, joined the Red Army in January 1919, and fought on the eastern and southern fronts during the Civil War. He graduated from 4th Moscow Warrant Officers School in 1917, the Khar'kov Course for Command Cadre in 1924, the Frunze Academy in 1929, and the Voroshilov General Staff Academy in 1949. During the interwar years, Loviagin commanded at the battalion level in the 1920s and, after graduating from the Frunze Academy, served as chief of staff of 43rd Rifle Division in 1936 and 1937, chief of the Minsk Military School in 1937, and chief of the Chemical Defense Academy from November 1937 through December 1941. Transferred to the field in December 1941, he commanded Southern Front's 102nd Rifle Division throughout the waning stages of Operation Barbarossa and during the winter campaign of 1941–1942. During Operation Blau, he served as chief of staff of 24th and 9th Armies and, in September 1942, as chief of staff of 10th Guards Rifle Corps during the intense fighting along the Terek River. After commanding the new 10th Rifle Corps during the battle for Ordzhonikidze in October 1942, Loviagin was relieved of his command, tried for failing to follow orders, and sentenced to 10 years' confinement. However, the Supreme Court of the USSR reviewed his case and remitted his sentence in April 1943 because of a lack of credible evidence against him. Restored to command in May 1943, after serving as deputy commander of 31st Rifle Corps in Southern Front's 5th Shock Army in May and June 1943, he took command of the same army's 55th Rifle Corps and led it successfully during the Donbas offensive in the summer of 1944 and the Melitopol' and Crimean offensives in the fall. Loviagin's corps then performed security missions along the Black Sea coast in late 1944. After his promotion to lieutenant general, Loviagin commanded Far Eastern Front's 88th Rifle Corps in March 1945. In that capacity, he led his corps, then under 25th Army's control, in the Manchurian offensive during August and September 1945. After the war, Loviagin commanded 88th and 65th Rifle Corps in the Far East until April 1949. Thereafter he served as chief of the Ministry of Defense's Combat and Physical Training Directorate from April 1949 until December 1953, as adviser to the Chinese Peoples' Army from February 1954 until December 1957, and in several lesser posts until his retirement in 1958. Loviagin died in 1971. For additional details about his career, see *Komkory, Voennyi biograficheskii slovar'*, 1: 331–333.

103. Grechko, *Bitva za Kavkaz*. See Roslyi's biography in volume 1 of this study (see index). Grigorii Nikiforovich Perekrestov, who was born in 1904, joined the Red Army in September 1922 and graduated from the Ukrainian Cavalry School in Krasnograd in 1925, the Zhukovskii Air Force Academy in 1941, and the Voroshilov General Staff Academy in 1944. During the interwar years, Perekrestov served as deputy chief of staff of 1st Cavalry Division's 1st Regiment and the division itself from 1930 to 1935 and commanded 28th Cavalry Division's 110th Cavalry Regiment and 92nd Separate Cavalry Regiment from 1935 to 1938. After his studies at the Air Academy, he headed the Khar'kov Military District's 4th Airborne Brigade until the outbreak of war in June 1941. Once war began, he led his brigade in 2nd Airborne Corps' defensive operations in the Kiev and Cherkassy regions until he was relieved of command in September 1941 for his "inability to command a formation in combat

failure," after two of his brigade's battalions retreated without orders to do so. Although sentenced to 10 years' imprisonment by a military tribunal in October, his case was reexamined and the sentence was remanded. In November 1941, the NKO assigned Perekrestov to command 5th Cavalry Corps' 60th Cavalry Division, which performed well in Southern Front's Barvenkovo-Lozovaia offensive in January and February 1942. After serving briefly as deputy commander of 9th Army in August and September 1942, he received command of 3rd Mountain Rifle Corps in October 1942 and led it successfully in the defensive and offensive fighting in the Caucasus region until January 1943, when he was transferred to command 18th Army's 16th Rifle Corps. He then led that corps and, after his studies at the Voroshilov Academy in 1944, 65th Rifle Corps until war's end. While in corps command, Perekrestov's forces played a significant role in the Belorussian offensive in the summer of 1944, the East Prussian offensive in January and February 1945, and the offensive against the Japanese Army in Manchuria in August and September 1945. Promoted to lieutenant general in 1945, Perekrestov also became a Hero of the Soviet Union because of his outstanding performance in the Manchurian offensive. After the war, he commanded 16th Rifle Corps until August 1946, served as deputy commander of 39th and 1st Red Banner Armies in the Far East from August 1946 until April 1950, and was deputy commander and commander of the Volga Military District until he fell ill in 1953. He completed his military career as deputy chief of the Molotov Military Academy for Rear Services and Supply and assistant commander of the Voronezh Military District. Perekrestov retired in 1958 and died in 1992. For further details, see *Komkory, Voennyi biograficheskii slovar'*, 1: 421–423.

104. Ibid., 204. See Tiulenev's order no. 4405, dated 30 October 1942, to Maslennikov regarding his defense along Urukh River, in Zolotarev, "*Stavka* 1942," 558. See also Tieke, *The Caucasus and the Oil*, 222–223.

105. Tieke, *The Caucasus and the Oil*, 224.

106. Grechko, *Bitva za Kavkaz*, 205; and Tieke, *The Caucasus and the Oil*, 224–225.

107. Born in 1896, Chevallerie joined the Kaiser's army in 1914 and fought in World War I, when he was wounded twice and captured. After serving in several infantry and mounted regiments, he commanded an infantry regiment and *kampfgruppe* in the Polish and French campaigns in 1939 and 1940. Before commanding 13th Panzer, Chevallerie commanded 86th Infantry Regiment and 10th Infantry Brigade in 1941 and 1942 and was assigned to 22nd Panzer Division's staff in October 1941. After commanding 13th Panzer until October 1943, when he was wounded, Chevallerie returned to field command as commander of 273rd Reserve Panzer Division from November 1943 until May 1944 and 233rd Reserve Panzer Division from August to November 1944. He ended the war as commander of West Sudetenland and was then in captivity from May 1945 to June 1947. Released in June 1947, Chevallerie died in 1965. For additional details see the website www.geocities.com/orion47/WEHRMACHT/Heer.

108. Tieke, *The Caucasus and the Oil*, 227.

109. Grechko, *Bitva za Kavkaz*, 205.

110. Ibid., 206; and Tieke, *The Caucasus and the Oil*, 227–228. This German assault on Ordzhonikidze from the north was code-named "Operation Darg Kokh."

111. Grechko, *Bitva za Kavkaz*, 208.

112. For details, see Tieke, *The Caucasus and the Oil*, 229–231. The 13th Panzer Division suffered 14 killed and 88 wounded on 4 November and saw its tank strength decrease to only 70 operational tanks. The 2nd Battalion of 23rd Panzer Division's 201st Panzer Regiment had only 10 tanks remaining.

113. Grechko, *Bitva za Kavkaz*.

114. Ibid.

115. Born in 1896, Colonel Ivan Andreevich Rubaniuk served in the Tsar's army in World War I, joined the Red Army in December 1917, and was a junior officer on the southern front during the Civil War. He graduated from the Senior and Higher Officers course at Khar'kov in 1924, the Command Cadre Course (KUKS) in Moscow in 1928, and the Voroshilov Academy in 1948. During the interwar years, Rubaniuk commanded at company and battalion levels and served on division staffs during the 1920s and commanded 7th Rifle Regiment from 1934 to 1937, when, like so many of his colleagues who served in the Tsar's army, he was caught up in Stalin's purges. More fortunate than others, Rubaniuk, after two years of NKVD investigations, was exonerated in April 1940 and assigned as commander of a student battalion at the Odessa Military School, where he was serving when war began. During Operation Barbarossa, Rubaniuk commanded 131st Reserve and 591st Rifle Regiments but became deputy commander of 12th Army's 176th Rifle Division during Operation Blau in the summer of 1942. His division performed so well during the battles in the Mozdok region that the *Stavka* assigned him to command the new 11th Rifle Corps on 13 October 1942. Promoted to major general on 10 November 1942, Rubaniuk led 11th Rifle Corps until 11 February 1943, participating in the defenses of Ordzhonikidze and subsequent Red Army counteroffensive in the northern Caucasus and Taman' regions. Thereafter, Rubaniuk commanded 11th Guards Rifle Corps from 12 February 1943 to war's end, achieving the rank of lieutenant general in September 1944 and taking part in many of the Red Army's most successful offensives in the Ukraine, Hungary, and Czechoslovakia. Unlike most of his counterparts caught up in Stalin's purges, who saw their careers forever tarnished, after the war Rubaniuk commanded 11th and 20th Guards Rifle Corps until 1952 and 14th and 25th Armies from 1952 to 1957. He ended his military career as a senior adviser to the Chinese Peoples' Army, a post he was occupying when he died in 1959. For further details, see *Komkory, Voennyi biograficheskii slovar'*, 1: 481–483.

116. See Tiulenev's report to the *Stavka* on 3 November 1942 concerning the situation in the *front* as a whole, his assessment of German intentions, and the measures he was taking to defend Ordzhonikidze and resume the offensive, in Shapovalov, ed., *Bitva za Kavkaz v dokumentakh*, 260–263.

117. For details, see Tieke, *The Caucasus and the Oil*, 231–232. During this fight, the mistaken rumor began circulating that Stalin had entered Ordzhonikidze to lead its defense.

118. Grechko, *Bitva za Kavkaz*, 208–209.

119. Ibid., 209. For details about the counterstroke from the German perspective, see Tieke, *The Caucasus and the Oil*, 232–233.

120. Grechko, *Bitva za Kavkaz*, 209.

121. Ibid., 210.

122. Tieke, *The Caucasus and the Oil*, 235–236.

123. Grechko, *Bitva za Kavkaz*, 210–211.

124. Tieke, *The Caucasus and the Oil*, 237.

125. Grechko, *Bitva za Kavkaz*, 211.

126. Tieke, *The Caucasus and the Oil*, 237.

127. Kolomiets and Moshchansky, "Oborona Kavkaza," 64.

128. Grechko, *Bitva za Kavkaz*, 215.

129. Tieke, *The Caucasus and the Oil*, 239.

130. Kolomiets and Moshchansky, "Oborona Kavkaza," 64.

131. Tieke, *The Caucasus and the Oil*, 237. Although Soviet sources credit 13th Panzer with 106 tanks, 23rd Panzer with 154, and SS "Viking" with 60, 13th Panzer actually fielded 32 tanks, 23rd Panzer about 80, and SS "Viking" no more than 40.

132. For further details, see Kolomiets and Moshchansky, "Oborona Kavkaza," 65–66; and Tieke, *The Caucasus and the Oil*, 239–241.

133. Grechko, *Bitva za Kavkaz*, 215.

134. Tieke, *The Caucasus and the Oil*, 242.

135. Grechko, *Bitva za Kavkaz*, 216.

136. Ibid. See also *Stavka* directive no. 170687, dated 0505 hours on 12 November 1942, in Zolotarev, "*Stavka* 1942," 449; and the Trans-Caucasus Front's orders no. 001090/op and 00110/op, dated 13 and 15 November 1942, in Shapovalov, ed., *Bitva za Kavkaz v dokumentakh*, 266–268. See volume one for Selivanov's biography.

137. See *Stavka* directive no. 170690, dated 2120 hours on 18 November 1942, in ibid., 450–451. Born in 1896, Aleksei Innokent'evich Antonov joined the Red Army in 1919 and served as a brigade chief of staff during the Civil War. He graduated from the Frunze Academy in 1931 and the General Staff Academy in 1937. During the interwar years, Antonov served in a variety of command and staff positions, rising to become a major general and deputy chief of staff of the Kiev Special Military District in 1941. After the outbreak of war, Antonov served as chief of staff of Southern Front from August 1941 to July 1942, North Caucasus Front in July and August 1942, and the Black Sea Group of Forces before his assignment as chief of staff of Trans-Caucasus Front in November. In December 1942 Stalin appointed Antonov as 1st deputy chief of the Red Army General Staff and, simultaneously, as chief of the General Staff's vital Operations Directorate. Thereafter, Antonov's star rose precipitously, as he became sole 1st deputy chief of the General Staff in May 1943 and chief of the General Staff from February 1945 and a member of the *Stavka* to war's end. As Stalin's favorite senior staff officer, Antonov helped plan most of the Red Army's most successful offensives from 1943 to 1945 and played a leading role in the Allied "Big Three" conferences at Yalta in the Crimea and Potsdam in 1945. After the war, Antonov continued as chief of the General Staff to 1950 and then commanded the Trans-Caucasus Military District from 1950 to 1954. Thereafter, Antonov was 1st deputy chief of the General Staff and a collegial member of the Ministry of Defense in 1954 and 1955 and also chief of staff of the Armed Forces of the Warsaw Pact Treaty organization. After his retirement, Antonov died in 1962. For additional details, among his many biographies, see *VOV*, 59.

138. See *Stavka* directive no. 170692, dated 20 November 1942, in ibid., 452.

139. Grechko, *Bitva za Kavkaz*, 217; and *Boevoi sostav Sovetskoi armii*, 2: 241.

140. Born in 1898, Glagolev served as a private in the Tsar's army during World War I, joined the Red Army in 1918, and fought in the Urals and northern Caucasus regions during the Civil War. He graduated from the 3rd Baku Command Course in 1921, cavalry officers command courses (KUKS) in Novocherkassk in 1926 and 1931, and the Frunze Academy in 1941. During the 1920s, Glagolev commanded a squadron in 12th Cavalry Division from 1922 to 1924 and in 1st Rifle Division from 1924 to 1929, when he became a regimental chief of staff in the Separate Caucasus Army's 2nd Separate Cavalry Brigade. After completing his cavalry command course, from January 1943 until August 1939 he led 12th Cavalry Division's 76th Regiment and served as the division's chief of staff. During the final two years before the outbreak of war, he led the North Caucasus Military District's 157th Rifle Division and 42nd Separate Cavalry Brigade. After Operation Barbarossa began, Glagolev commanded 42nd Cavalry Division during the campaign in the Crimea, but in February 1942 he assumed command of 24th Army's 73rd Rifle Division, thereby avoiding the destruction of his cavalry division at Kerch' in May 1942. However, when his division was encircled and destroyed in late July, Glagolev escaped death once again and commanded 9th Army's 176th Rifle Division during its successful defense of Ordzhonikidze. Thereafter, Glagolev led 10th Guards Rifle Corps from 11 November 1942 to 11 February 1943, when he rose to replace Koroteev in command of 9th Army. He then led 9th, 46th, and 31st Armies successfully during the battle for the Dnepr in the fall of 1943 and the Belorussian offensive in the summer of 1944, in the process being promoted to the rank of colonel general and becoming a Hero of the Soviet Union for his performance in successfully forcing the Dnepr River. As a reward for his outstanding performance, in January 1945, Glagolev received command of 9th Guards Army, the former elite Airborne Army, which was made up entirely of airborne troops and was sent into Hungary to spearhead operations to capture Austria and its capital city of Vienna. Glagolev commanded the 9th Guards until 1947, when he was appointed as commander of the Soviet Army's Airborne Forces, a position he was occupying at the time of his death in September 1947. For additional details, see *Komandarmy, Voennyi biograficheskii slovar'*, 43–45.

141. See the biographies of most of these Red Army commanders in volume 1.

142. See *Stavka* directive no. 270593, dated 30 August 1942, in Zolotarev, "*Stavka* 1942*,*" 378.

143. See *Stavka* directive no. 170593, dated 1610 hours on 30 August 1942, in ibid., 378.

144. Born in 1895, Zhidov, who changed his name in late 1941 to Zhadov, perhaps because he was Jewish, fought in the Tsar's army during World War I, joined the Red Guards in November 1917 and the Red Army in 1918, and fought as a cavalryman in the Civil War. He graduated from the Khar'kov course for military commissars in 1922, the Higher Tactical School in 1923, the "*Vystrel*'" Officers Command Course in 1926, and the Voroshilov General Staff Academy in 1947. During the interwar years, Zhidov served as both commander and commissar at the regimental and division levels before becoming commander of the Central Asian Military District's 21st Mountain Cavalry Division in 1940. When war began, Zhidov led 4th Airborne Corps during Western Front's defense of Minsk and the Dnepr River line in late June and July 1941 and then served as the chief of staff of 3rd Army during Briansk Front's

defensive operations south of Moscow in the fall of 1941 and the ensuing winter campaign, when he helped organize the *front's* successful counteroffensive in the Elets region. He then led 8th Cavalry Corps from May to October 1942, when he received command of Don Front's 66th Army. Zhadov commanded this force, redesignated as 5th Guards Army in April 1943, to war's end. As such his army played vital roles in the Red Army's defense and counteroffensive at Kursk in the summer of 1943, the advance to the Dnepr in the fall of 1943, and the successful offensives in the Ukraine and Poland in 1944 and early 1945, culminating in the climactic battle for Berlin and Prague in April and May 1945. Zhadov was a colonel general and Hero of the Soviet Union by war's end. After the war, he served as deputy commander for Combat Training of the Soviet Army's Ground Forces from 1945 until 1950, deputy chief and chief of the Frunze Academy from 1950 to 1954, commander of the Central Group of Forces in Czechoslovakia in 1954 and 1955, 1st deputy commander of the Soviet Army from 1956 to 1964, and 1st deputy Chief Inspector of the Soviet Army from 1964 to 1969. He retired into the Ministry of Defense's Group of General Inspectors in 1969 and died in 1977. For additional details, see *Komandarmy, Voennyi biograficheskii slovar'*, 74–75.

145. See *Stavka* directive no. 170601, dated 1810 hours on 7 September 1942, in ibid., 388.

146. For further details, see Glantz, *Forgotten Battles*, vol. III, 76–85.

147. *Stavka* directive no. 170627, dated 28 September 1942, in Zolotarev, "*Stavka* 1942,*"* 403.

148. The casualty figures are from Krivosheev, ed., *Soviet Casualty and Combat Losses*, 123–124. German troop strengths are detailed in Glantz, *Forgotten Battles*, vol. III, 83–84.

149. For details, see Glantz, *Forgotten Battles*, vol. III, 190–193; Ziemke and Bauer, *Moscow to Stalingrad*, 421–422; and Berdnikov, *Pervaia udarnaia*, 111–116.

Chapter 9: The Assaults on the Barrikady and Krasnyi Oktiabr' Factories, 1–18 November 1942

1. See *62nd Army Combat Journal*, entries for 1–2 November.

2. Ziemke and Bauer, *Moscow to Stalingrad*, 463, quoting *AOK 6, Ia Kriegstagebuch Nr. 14*, 3 Nov 42, AOK 6 33224/2 file. For an excellent description of these German planning meetings, see Jason D. Mark, *Island of Fire: The Battle for the Barrikady Gun Factory in Stalingrad, November 1942–February 1943* (Sydney, Australia: Leaping Horseman Books, 2006), which is also the most thorough tactical treatment of this battle from both the German and Soviet perspectives.

3. Mark, *Island of Fire*, 14.

4. Ibid., 464.

5. For a detailed description of these reinforcing engineer battalions and other units, see ibid., 25–49.

6. Mark, *Death of the Leaping Horseman*, 315. Lenski responded by creating an ad hoc *kampfgruppe* designated *Alarmeinheit* [alarm unit] 24th Panzer Regiment, made up of a company each from the panzer regiment's three panzer battalions.

7. Ibid., 316, citing LI Army *Korpsbefehl* Nr. 101.

8. General Erich Magnus was born on 31 July 1892 in Danzig and died in Hamburg on 6 August 1979.

9. Mark, *Death of the Leaping Horseman*, 316, citing VI Army *Korpsbefehl* Nr. 103.

10. Ibid., 335.

11. Ibid., 334. This included 21st Panzer Grenadier Regiment with 410 men, 26th Panzer Grenadier Regiment with 299 men, 4th Motorcycle Battalion with 129 men, and 40th Panzer Pioneer Battalion with 131 men.

12. Ibid., 337. The first battalions of each of 24th Panzer Division's two panzer grenadier regiments remained in the rear resting and receiving replacements.

13. Mark, *Island of Fire*, 20.

14. Ibid., 51–52.

15. Ibid., 52–53.

16. Ziemke and Bauer, *Moscow to Stalingrad*, 465, quoting *AOK 6, Ia Kriegstagebuch Nr. 14*, 3 Nov 42, in AOK 6 33224/2 file.

17. Ibid.

18. Mark, *Island of Fire*, 54–55.

19. Ibid., 56.

20. Ibid.

21. Ibid., 57.

22. Ibid.; and Ziemke and Bauer, *Moscow to Stalingrad*, 465, quoting *AOK 6, Ia Kriegstagebuch Nr. 14*, 6 Nov 42, in AOK 6 33224/2 file.

23. Mark, *Island of Fire*, 57.

24. Ibid., 58.

25. Ibid., 59.

26. Ibid.

27. "Morgenmeldung LI. A. K. meldet 05.45 Uhr, A. O. K. 6, I. a, Datum 09.11.42," in *Die Anlagenbander zu den Kriegstagebuchern der 6. Armee vom 14.09.1942 bis 24.11.1942, Band I* (Schwabach: January 2006), 247. The new infantry assault gun assigned to 244th Assault Gun Battalion was the experimental 150mm infantry assault gun [*Sturminfanteriegeschütz*] model 33B, which had just arrived in Stalingrad. For further details about this gun, see Mark, *Island of Fire*, 43–51.

28. Mark, *Island of Fire*, 60. See also Ziemke and Bauer, *Moscow to Stalingrad*, 465, quoting *AOK 6, Ia Kriegstagebuch Nr. 14*, 8–10 Nov 42, in AOK 6 33224/2 file.

29. Mark, *Island of Fire*, 61.

30. Ibid.

31. Mark, *Death of the Leaping Horseman*, 342. Colonel Below returned to the rear area for a rest.

32. Ibid.

33. See ibid., 344–345, for the precise composition of 24th Panzer Division's assault company.

34. "Boevoe donesenie no. 217, Shtarm 62 1. 11. 42" [Combat order no. 217, headquarters, 62nd Army 1 November 1942], in *62nd Army Combat Journal*.

35. See "Chastnyi boevoi prikaz no. 218 KP Shtarma 62 1. 11. 42 13.35" [Separate combat order no. 218, CP, headquarters, 62nd Army, 1 November 1942], in ibid., which read:

1. The enemy is bringing up fresh reserves with the aim of resuming the offensive and reaching the Volga River in the landing-stage region.
2. The Army, while repelling attacks of the enemy, continues to hold on to the positions it occupies.
3. **95th RD** (without one RR) will cross to the right bank of the Volga River in the vicinity of 62nd Army's crossing on the night of 1–2 November 1942. Occupy and defend the sector: the southern part of the Barrikady Factory-Mezenskaia [Street]-Granit, with the forward edge along the eastern outskirts of the Barrikady Factory and farther to the south along Mashinnaia [Street].

   Mission: prevent the enemy from reaching the bank of the Volga River in the northern sector.

   The boundary on the right is from the courtyard 150 meters south of the letter "T" to Sormosk. All points including Taimyrskaia are for 138th RD.

   The boundary to the left is from the mouth of the ravine 100 meters north of the landing stage to the letter "Sh" in the name "Mashinnaia [Street]" and Prokatnaia [Street]. All points are inclusive for 95th RD.
4. I entrust the commander of 138th RD with securing the boundary on the right and the commander of 95th RD, the boundary on the left.
5. 95th RD's command post will be in the region east of Mezenskaia.
6. When 95th RD occupies its defensive sector, withdraw 308th RD's units operating in 95th RD's sector to 138th RD's sector, and withdraw 193rd RD's subunits into 45th RD's sector.

   Carry out the withdrawal of the units indicated above after the transfer of the sector and its occupation by 95th RD's units.

   193rd RD's units will remain in place with the mission to protect the immediate approaches to the crossings.
7. The commander of 95th RD will report about the course of the crossing and occupation of its defensive sector every two hours beginning at 1700 hours on 1 November 1942.

   Chuikov, Gurov, Krylov

36. "Boevoe rasporiazhenie no. 227, Shtarm 62 1. 11. 42" [Combat instructions no. 227, headquarters, 62nd Army 1 November 1942], in ibid.

37. Zhilin, *Stalingradskaia bitva*, 832–833.

38. Ibid., 834, quoting *OKW Informational Bulletin*.

39. General Bernard Steinmetz, who was born on 13 August 1896, commanded VIII Army Corps in 1940 and rose to command 305th Infantry Division during the waning stages of the battle for the factory district. Apparently, he was evacuated from the Stalingrad region prior to Sixth Army's surrender. Later, Steinmetz commanded the re-formed 94th Infantry Division's 274th Grenadier Regiment in 1943 and the division itself in Italy from 2 January 1944 until the division's surrender to American forces on 22 April 1945. He died on 22 January 1981. For the few details about his career, see Samuel W. Mitcham Jr., *Hitler's Legions: The German Order of Battle, World War II* (New York: Stein and Day, 1985), 110; and the website, Axis History Factbook, Des Heere, available at www.axishistory.com/index.

40. See LI Army Corps' order no. 102 in Mark, *Island of Fire*, 17.

41. Ibid. The Soviets counted German assault guns and self-propelled antitank guns as tanks.

42. "Boevoe rasporiazhenie no. 228 Shtarma 62 2. 11. 42 01.05" [Combat instructions no. 228, headquarters, 62nd Army, 0105 hours on 2 November 1942], in *62nd Army Combat Journal*.

43. "Boevoe rasporiazhenie no. 229 Shtarma 62 2. 11. 42 01.05" [Combat instructions no. 229, headquarters, 62nd Army, 0105 hours on 2 November 1942], in ibid.

44. "Boevoe rasporiazhenie no. 231 KP Shtarma 62 2. 11. 42 01.05" [Combat instructions no. 231, CP, headquarters, 62nd Army, 0105 hours on 2 November 1942], in ibid.

45. "Boevoe donesenie no. 218, Shtarm 62 2. 11. 42" [Combat order no. 218, headquarters, 62nd Army, 2 November 1942], in ibid.

46. Zhilin, *Stalingradskaia bitva*, 838.

47. "Boevoe donesenie no. 218," in *62nd Army Combat Journal*.

48. Zhilin, *Stalingradskaia bitva*, 839, quoting *OKW Informational Bulletin*.

49. "Boevoe donesenie no. 219," in *62nd Army Combat Journal*.

50. Zhilin, *Stalingradskaia bitva*, 842.

51. Ibid., 843, quoting *OKW Informational Bulletin*.

52. See "Boevoi prikaz no. 197 KP Shtarma 62 3. 11. 42 15.45" [Combat order no. 197, CP, headquarters, 62nd Army, 1545 hours on 3 November 1942], in *62nd Army Journal*, which read:

3. **138th RD** [Liudnikov], reinforced by 118th GRR will hold on to the defensive sector it occupies and prevent the enemy from reaching the Taimyrskaia-Arbatovskaia region.

4. **95th RD** (less 90th RR), with a reinforcing company of KV tanks, will hold on to the sector it occupies and prevent the enemy from reaching the Novosel'sk region and the Volga River. Reliably protect the boundary on the left with the units of 45th RD. The boundary on the left is from the mouth of the ravine, 400 meters south of Novosel'sk, to the ravine in the letter "V" (in the name Gazov) and the corner of Kashira and Volkhovstroevsk.

5. **45th RD** will hold on to the defensive sector it occupies, prevent the enemy from reaching the northeastern part of the Krasnyi Oktiabr' Factory, and protect the boundary to the left with 39th Gds. RD. The boundary on the left is from the southern outskirts of the sides of Bakinskaia and Kommissarskaia [streets] to Zaraisk;

6. **39th Gds. RD**, reinforced by a company of KV tanks, will hold on to the defensive sector it occupies and the halls of the factory situated in the division's defensive sector and prevent the enemy from seizing the eastern and southeastern parts of the Krasnyi Oktiabr' Factory and reaching the Volga River east of the factory. The boundary on the left is from the mouth of the Bannyi Ravine and along the Bannyi Ravine to the railroad bridge across the Bannyi Ravine;

7. **284th RD** will hold on to the defensive sector it occupies and prevent the enemy from reaching the Volga River within the limits of the

division's defensive sector. Especially protect the division's flank and the boundary on the left with the units of 13th Gds. RD. The boundary on the left is from the Dolgii Ravine to Dnepropetrovsk.

8. **13th Gds. RD** will hold on to the defensive sector it occupies and prevent the enemy from reaching the Volga River within the limits of the division's defensive sector. Have the main grouping on the division's right wing.

9. **193rd RD** will protect the immediate approaches to the army's crossing by occupying defensive lines along the southern outskirts of the sides of Bakinskaia and Komissarov Streets and along the eastern outskirts of the Krasnyi Oktiabr' Factory up to the railroad, inclusively.

10. Complete all regroupings of the units associated with the fulfillment of this order by 2300 hours on 3 November 1942. The commanders of the divisions will ensure protection of the junctions for which they are responsible and the occupation of the precise sectors assigned to them by their regiments.

11. Commanders at all levels will fortify their positions in an engineer sense and bring all of their units in positions to full readiness to repel possible enemy attacks by 0400 hours on 4 November 1942.

12. Organize reinforced night raids to seize controlled prisoners and detect the grouping of the enemy along the front of each division.

13. I am assigning [the following] overall missions for each division: Widen the defended bridgehead, moving your forward edge forward (to the west) no fewer than 80–100 meters each day by means of local operations so as to completely clear the enemy from the grounds of the Barrikady and Krasnyi Oktiabr' Factories by day's end on 6 November 1942 and push the forward edge in the Volkhovstroevsk-Bannyi Ravine sector up to the main (western) railroad line. . . .

Chuikov, Gurov, Krylov

Writing in his memoirs well after war's end, Chuikov provided added rationale for the measures he undertook on 3 November:

> Carrying out active operations with small storm groups, the Army managed to build up some reserves. On the left bank of the Volga, we had two infantry regiments and the H.Q. staff of Gorishnyi's division [95th Rifle] (having been sent there to be brought back up to strength) and the 92nd Infantry [Rifle] Brigade, which had been reinforced with seamen arrived from the Far East.
>
> When we had ferried these units across to the city, we decided we would regroup our forces. We decided to put Gorishnyi's two regiments along the front lines between Liudnikov's [138th Rifle] and Sokolov's [45th Rifle] divisions, south of the Barrikady Factory (in fact we did only half of this, managing to ferry only one of the regiments); to incorporate the whole rank and file and junior officers of Zholudev's [37th Guards Rifle] division into the 118th Regiment, which we would leave in its present positions under the operational charge of Liudnikov; to transfer the

whole rank and file and junior officers of Gurt'ev's [308th Rifle] division to Liudnikov as reinforcements; to send Zholudev's and Gurt'ev's divisional and regimental H.Q. staffs across to the left bank, and put our artillery on the left bank directly under the Army's Artillery Commander; to disband the Army H.Q. guard (formerly the Army's emergency training regiment), and transfer the weapons and personnel of this battalion to Gur'ev's [39th Guards Rifle] division as reinforcements; and to move Smekhotvorov's [193rd Rifle] division back into a second line of defense, to protect the ferry.

All divisions had the general task of conducting limited operations to expand the bridgehead occupied by the Army, to advance westward by not less than 80–100 yards a day, so as to clear the Barrikady and Krasnyi Oktiabr' factories of the enemy by November 6. Every advance, however insignificant, was to be slowly, surely, and reliably consolidated.

He then correctly concluded:

These measures, which took several days to carry out, made for more coherent defenses in the vicinity of the two factories, strengthened the defending forces by reinforcing them with 1,500–2,000 men, and doubled the depth of the defenses between the two factories. This more than matched the strength of the 24th Panzer Division, which Paulus had dispatched into the Krasnyi Oktiabr' Factory.

53. Zhilin, *Stalingradskaia bitva*, 845.

54. Ibid., 846, quoting *OKW Informational Bulletin.*

55. Chuikov, *The Battle for Stalingrad*, 201.

56. Ibid., 201.

57. Ibid., 203.

58. See the entire intelligence report, "Spravka o gruppirovke i deistviiakh protivnika pered frontom 62 Armii k iskhody 4. 11. 42 g" [Information about the grouping and actions of the enemy in front of 62nd Army's front at day's end on 4 November 1942], in *62nd Army Combat Journal.*

59. As of the morning of 11 November, 24th Panzer Division's 13 tanks included 10 Pz. III long, 1 Pz. IV short, 1 Pz. IV long, and 1 command tank. The 14th Panzer's 8 tanks included 1 Pz. III short, 6 Pz. III long, and 1 command tank. The 244th Assault Gun Battalion's 18 guns included 5 short and 7 long 75mm models and 6 new 150mm assault guns. The 245th Assault Gun Battalion's 10 guns included 2 long and 2 short 75mm models and 6 150mm guns. See "Morgenmeldung LI. A. K. meldet 06.00 Uhr, A. O. K. 6, I. a, Datum 11.11.42," in *Die Anlagenbander zu den Kriegstagebuchern der 6. Armee vom 14.09.1942 bis 24.11.1942, Band I* (Schwabach: January 2006), 257.

60. See "Tagesmeldung XIV. A. K. meldet 20.30 Uhr, A. O. K. 6, I. a, Datum 14.11.42," in ibid., 275.

61. Zhilin, *Stalingradskaia bitva*, 848.

62. "Boevoe donesenie no. 221 Shtarm 62 5. 11. 42" [Combat report no. 221, headquarters, 62nd Army, 5 November 1941], in *62nd Army Combat Journal.*

63. Chuikov, *The Battle for Stalingrad*, 204.

64. Zhilin, *Stalingradskaia bitva*, 849, quoting *OKW Informational Bulletin*.

65. Mark, *Death of the Leaping Horseman*, 346–347.

66. Zhilin, *Stalingradskaia bitva*, 852. Confirmed by the daily report, in *62nd Army Combat Journal*.

67. Zhilin, *Stalingradskaia bitva*, 853, quoting *OKW Informational Bulletin*.

68. Chuikov, *The Battle for Stalingrad*, 206, confirms the arrival of freezing weather on 9 November when a reinforcing cold front passed through the area. The 24th Panzer Division reported, "The thermometer sank to minus 15 degrees [Celsius] and, from this time on, remained below freezing point. An ice-cold wind whistled over the steppe and through the ruins of the city." See also Mark, *Death of the Leaping Horseman*, 352.

69. Chuikov, *The Battle for Stalingrad*, 207.

70. "Boevoe donesenie no. 223, Shtarm 62, 7. 11. 42" [Combat report no. 223, headquarters, 62nd Army, 7 November 1942], in *62nd Army Combat Journal*.

71. Zhilin, *Stalingradskaia bitva*, 854–855.

72. Ibid., 858.

73. "Boevoe donesenie no. 224 Shtarm 62, 8. 11. 42" [Combat report no. 224, headquarters, 62nd Army, 8 November 1942], in *62nd Army Combat Journal*.

74. Zhilin, *Stalingradskaia bitva*, 861.

75. See details on these actions in Mark, *Death of the Leaping Horseman*, 350–351.

76. Zhilin, *Stalingradskaia bitva*, 864.

77. See "Boevoe donesenie no. 226, Shtarm 62 10. 11. 42" [Combat report no. 226, headquarters, 62nd Army, 10 November 1942], in *62nd Army Combat Journal*.

78. Zhilin, *Stalingradskaia bitva*, 862, 864–865, quoting *OKW Informational Bulletin*.

79. Ibid., 867, quoting *OKW Informational Bulletin*.

80. Mark, *Death of the Leaping Horseman*, 353–354.

81. Ibid., 354. By day's end on 10 November, the armor strength of *Kampfgruppe* Scheele had fallen to seven tanks, including one Pz. III short, six Pz. III long, and one command tank, supported by 15 50mm "Pak" guns and seven self-propelled antitank guns.

82. For details on 305th and 389th Infantry Division's combat formation and strengths, see Wijers, *The Battle for Stalingrad*, 160–162, which contains eyewitness reports by German participants in the fighting.

83. This strength figure of 3,000 men is based on 305th and 389th Infantry Divisions' strength returns for 24 October and 15 November, which were as follows:

	24 October	15 November
305th Infantry Division		
Ration strength	10,678 men	6,683 men
Combat strength	3,345 men	2,915 men
Infantry	1,231 men	900 men (estimated)
Pioneers	122 men	80 men (estimated)
389th Infantry Division		
Ration strength	8,604 men	7,540 men

(continued on page 822)

Combat strength	2,736 men	4,021 men
Infantry	903 men	2,079 men
Pioneers	76 men	200 men

See "Meldungen uber Verpflegungs—und Gefechtsstarken der Division, Armee—Oberkommando 6, Ia Nr. 4548/42 geh, A. H. Qu., 24. Oktober 1942, 08.30 Uhr"and "Verpflegungs—und Gefechtsstarken, Oberkommando 6, Ia Nr. 4150/42 geh, A. H. Qu., 13. November 1942," in *Die Anlagenbander zu den Kriegstagebuchern der 6. Armee vom 14.09.1942 bis 24.11.1942, Band I* (Schwabach: January 2006), 201–202 and 268–269.

84. For additional details, see Mark, *Death of the Leaping Horseman*, 356–357; and Wijers, *The Battle for Stalingrad*, 141, 150.

85. Wijers, *The Battle for Stalingrad*, 139.

86. Mark, *Death of the Leaping Horseman*, 356–359.

87. *Stavka* directive no. 994277, dated 0415 hours on 1 November 1942, in Zolotarev, "*Stavka* 1942," 447. Ultimately, these three mechanized brigades formed the nucleus of the new 13th Tank Corps, which, even though designated as a tank corps, was actually a mechanized corps because of its predominant number of mechanized forces.

88. *Stavka* directive no. 994278, dated 0130 hours on 1 November 1942, in ibid., 446–447.

89. Zolotarev, "General Staff 1942," 383–384.

90. *Stavka* directive no. 170685, dated 0955 hours on 4 November 1942, in Zolotarev, "*Stavka* 1942," 448.

91. Zolotarev, "General Staff 1942," 383–384. These forces included the new 72nd and 267th Rifle Divisions, manned by 9,746 and 9,166 men, respectively, 350th Rifle Division from the Western Front, with 7,891 men (5,111 of whom were combat veterans), the re-formed 106th Rifle Brigade, with 6,019 men, and the re-formed 129th Rifle Brigade, with 3,514 men (including 1,661 veterans).

92. Ibid., 390.

93. Reinhard Gehlen, *The Service: The Memoirs of General Reinhard Gehlen*, trans. David Irving (New York: World Publishing, 1972), 56.

94. Ibid.

95. Ibid., 56–57.

96. Ibid., 57.

97. Ibid.

98. Ibid.

99. Ibid.

100. Earl F. Ziemke, *Stalingrad to Berlin: The German Defeat in the East* (Washington, DC: United States Army Office of the Chief of Military History, 1968), 47, citing OKH, GenStdH, Fremde Heere Ost (1) Nr. 2492/42, Gedanken zur Weiterenwicklung der Feindlage im Herbst und Winter, 29.8.42, in *H 3/190* file.

101. Ibid., 48.

102. David Kahn, "An Intelligence Case Study: The Defense of Osuga, 1942," *Aerospace Historian* 28, no. 4 (December 1981), 243.

103. Ziemke, *Stalingrad to Berlin*, 48; and Zhilin, *Stalingradskaia bitva*, 749–750, citing *TsAMO RF*, f. 500, op. 12462, d. 89, ll. 147–148.

104. Zhilin, *Stalingradskaia bitva*, 849–850, citing *KTB OKW. Bd. II*, hb. II, 1305–1306. See a condensed version of Gehlen's report in Kahn, "An Intelligence Case History," 248. Gehlen, in his memoir, omits any mention of his 6 November report, perhaps because it contradicted his claim that he indeed predicted the Russians' ensuing offensive along the Don, leaving the blame for the ensuing debacle at the feet of senior German field commanders alone.

105. Ziemke, *Stalingrad to Berlin*, 48.

106. Ibid., 49.

107. Zhilin, *Stalingradskaia bitva*, 893, citing *TsAMO RF*, f. 500, op. 12462, d. 89, ll. 421–423.

108. Goerlitz, *Paulus and Stalingrad*, 195–196.

109. These probes and raids included assaults by two *kampfgruppen* from 16th Panzer Division north and northeast of Rynok, 94th Infantry Division west of Spartanovka, 305th Infantry Division northeast and southeast of the Barrikady Factory, a larger-scale assault by 79th Infantry Division against Hall 4 (the Martenovskii Furnace) in the Krasnyi Oktiabr' Factory, 100th Jäger Division along the Bannyi Ravine and the northern slope of Mamaev Kurgan, 295th Infantry Division on Mamaev Kurgan itself, and 71st Infantry Division near 9 January Square. See Mark, *Island of Fire*, 98–99, for additional details.

110. "Boevoe donesenie no. 227, Shtarm 62 11. 11. 41" [Combat report no. 227, headquarters, 62nd Army, 11 November 1942], in *62nd Army Combat Journal*.

111. See the entry for 11 November 1942, in *138th Rifle Division Combat Journal*.

112. Zhilin, *Stalingradskaia bitva*, 870.

113. Wijers, *The Battle for Stalingrad*, 161. For a complete, unsurpassed, and superbly detailed description of the fighting in and east of the Barrikady Factory from 11 to 18 November (and, thereafter, to 2 February 1943) from both the Soviet and German perspectives, see Mark, *Island of Fire*, 95–245.

114. For details on the day's fighting east of the Barrikady Factory, see Mark, *Island of Fire*, 101–148.

115. See Wijers, *The Battle for Stalingrad*, 168–172, for more details.

116. Ibid., 169.

117. "Morgenmeldung LI. A.K. meldet 06.45 Uhr, A.O.K. 6, I. a, Datum 12.11.42," in *Die Anlagenbander zu den Kriegstagebuchern der 6. Armee vom 14.09.1942 bis 24.11.1942, Band I* (Schwabach: January 2006), 266.

118. See the 11 November 1942 entry in *138th Rifle Division Combat Journal*.

119. Chuikov, *The Battle for Stalingrad*, 209–210. As usual Chuikov inadvertently exaggerated the strength of the attacking German force, insisting it included 44th Infantry Division, as well as 389th, 305th, 79th Infantry, 100th Jäger, and 14th and 24th Panzer Divisions. This was because his intelligence organs detected the presence of 44th Infantry Division's engineer battalion.

120. For further details, see Mark, *Death of the Leaping Horseman*, 356–362; and Wijers, *The Battle for Stalingrad*, 151, which includes 179th Engineer Battalion's 12 November report on the action.

121. Wijers, *The Battle for Stalingrad*, 152.

122. Ibid., 144–150. The 54 casualties included 7 killed, 38 wounded, 4 missing, and 5 frostbitten. See other accounts of 179th's assault, including the Croat 369th Regiment's role, in the same source.

123. "Morgenmeldung LI. A.K. meldet 06.45 Uhr, A.O.K. 6, I. a, Datum 12.11.42," in *Die Anlagenbander zu den Kriegstagebuchern der 6. Armee vom 14.09.1942 bis 24.11.1942, Band I* (Schwabach: January 2006), 266.

124. For further details on *Kampfgruppe* Scheele's fight, see Mark, *Death of the Leaping Horseman*, 360–361.

125. Ibid., 361.

126. "Boevoe donesenie no. 227," in *62nd Army Combat Journal*.

127. Ibid.

128. Ibid.

129. For the breakdown of these casualties, see Mark, *Island of Fire*, 144–145.

130. Ziemke and Bauer, *Moscow to Stalingrad*, 467.

131. Zhilin, *Stalingradskaia bitva*, 871, quoting *OKW Informational Bulletin*.

132. Ibid., 867, citing *TsAMO FR*, f. 500, op. 12462, d. 89, ll. 365–367.

133. See Gehlen, *The Service*, 58–59; and Zhilin, *Stalingradskaia bitva*, 872, citing *KTB OKW*. Bd. II., hb. 2, 1305–1306. The latter translation adds "the presumed movement of 1st Guards Army" to the Don River front to the list of indicators of impending Soviet offensive action.

134. Zhilin, *Stalingradskaia bitva*, 872. Gehlen omits this qualification from his memoir.

135. Ibid. Gehlen, *The Service*, 59, omits the sentence reading, "The enemy has too few forces for such a large-scale operation (at present there are approximately 16 rifle divisions and from one up to four tank brigades situated in front of the Rumanian Third Army's right wing, and 7 rifle divisions and 3 cavalry divisions in front of its left wing)."

136. Zhilin, *Stalingradskaia bitva*, 872.

137. Ziemke, *Stalingrad to Berlin*, 49.

138. Ziemke and Bauer, *Moscow to Stalingrad*, 466.

139. Ibid., 467.

140. Ibid.

141. "Boevoe donesenie no. 228, Shtarm 62 12. 11. 41" [Combat report no. 228, headquarters, 62nd Army, 12 November 1942], in *62nd Army Combat Journal*. According to *138th Rifle Division Combat Journal*, the composite regiment of 193rd RD numbered 289 men.

142. Mark, *Island of Fire*, 156–157.

143. "Morgenmeldung LI. A.K. meldet 06.10 Uhr, A.O.K. 6, I. a, Datum 13.11.42," in *Die Anlagenbander zu den Kriegstagebuchern der 6. Armee vom 14.09.1942 bis 24.11.1942, Band I* (Schwabach: January 2006), 268.

144. "Boevoe rasporiazhenie no. 237 Shtarma 62 Stalingrad 12. 11. 42 16.30" [Combat instructions no. 237, headquarters, 62nd Army, Stalingrad, 1630 hours on 12 November 1942], in *62nd Army Combat Journal*.

145. "Boevoe rasporiazhenie no. 239 Shtarma 62 Stalingrad 12. 11. 42 19.15" [Combat instructions no. 239, headquarters, 62nd Army, Stalingrad, 1915 hours on 12 November 1942], in ibid.

146. "Boevoe rasporiazhenie no. 240 Shtarma 62 Stalingrad 12. 11. 42 23.00" [Combat instructions no. 240, headquarters, 62nd Army, Stalingrad, 2300 hours on 12 November 1942], in ibid.

147. "Boevoe donesenie no. 228," in ibid.

148. "Gruppirovka i deistviia protivnika pered frontom 62 Armiii na iskhodu 12. 11. 42" [The grouping and actions of the enemy in front of 62nd Army's front at day's end on 12 November 1942], in ibid.

149. Ziemke and Bauer, *Moscow to Stalingrad*, 466, quoting AOK 6, Ia Kriegstagebuch Nr. 14, 11 Nov 42, in *AOK 6 33224/2* file.

150. Wijers, *The Battle for Stalingrad*, 168.

151. Zhilin, *Stalingradskaia bitva*, 874–875, quoting *OKW Informational Bulletin* and the Red Army General Staff's daily summary. For details of the desultory fighting in the Krasnyi Oktiabr' Factory, see Mark, *Death of the Leaping Horseman*, 361–362. Group Schwerin and *Kampfgruppe* Scheele spent the day repelling Soviet reconnaissance probes by groups of 40–50 men and prepared for heavier Soviet counterattacks they considered inevitable the next day. Evidencing its ever-declining strength, Scheele reported the combat strength of his 21st Grenadier Regiment fell to 211 men, including 6 officers, 47 NCOs, and 168 men.

152. On the morning of 14 November, 14th Panzer Division reported it had 8 tanks remaining, including 1 Pz. II short, 6 Pz. III long, and 1 command tank. The 245th Assault Gun Battalion fielded 1 75mm long assault gun and 3 150mm assault guns, while 244th Assault Gun Battalion had 8 75mm long, 5 75mm short, and 6 150mm guns. See "Morgenmeldung LI. A.K. meldet 06.10 Uhr, A.O.K. 6, I. a, Datum 14.11.42," in *Die Anlagenbander zu den Kriegstagebuchern der 6. Armee vom 14.09.1942 bis 24.11.1942, Band I* (Schwabach: January 2006), 274.

153. Mark, *Island of Fire*, 159–160.

154. Entry for 13 November, in *138th Rifle Division Combat Journal*.

155. Ibid.

156. Wijers, *The Battle for Stalingrad*, 171. Reports by veterans of 305th Infantry Division, who participated in its assaults on 11 and 13 November, often confuse the dates. For example, older memoirs place the assault as early as 9 and 10 November, whereas Sixth Army's records and those of 62nd Army and the Red Army General Staff clearly indicate that the assault began on 11 November and resumed on 13 November.

157. Entry for 13 November 1942, in *138th Rifle Division Combat Journal*.

158. Ibid.

159. Wijers, *The Battle for Stalingrad*, 172.

160. Ibid.

161. "Boevoe donesenie no. 229, Shtarm 62 13. 11. 42" [Combat report no. 229, headquarters, 62nd Army, 13 November 1942], in *62nd Army Combat Journal*.

162. Ziemke and Bauer, *Moscow to Stalingrad*, 467–468.

163. Zhilin, *Stalingradskaia bitva*, 878, quoting *OKW Informational Bulletin*.

164. Ibid.

165. Ibid., 878, citing *KTB OKW*. Bd. II., 1700.

166. Ibid.

167. "Boevoe donesenie no. 229," in *62nd Army Combat Journal*.

168. Zhilin, *Stalingradskaia bitva*, 876–877.

169. Chuikov, *The Battle for Stalingrad*, 210–212. As confirmed by the army's records and the Red Army General Staff summaries, Chuikov mistakenly records that the action against the Commissar's House took place on 12 November rather than 13 November.

170. Ibid., 212.

171. Entry for 13 November, in *138th Rifle Division Combat Journal*.

172. See, for example, Rokossovsky, *Velikaia pobeda na Volga*, 201. The 138th Rifle Division ostensibly included 123 riflemen in its 344th Regiment, 31 in its 650th Regiment, and the remainder in its 768th Regiment and attached 118th Guards Regiment.

173. Zhilin, *Stalingradskaia bitva*, 879, citing *TsAMO RF*, f. 500, op. 12462, d. 89, ll. 392–394

174. Ibid.

175. Ibid.

176. "Morgenmeldung LI. A.K. meldet 06.10 Uhr, A.O.K. 6, I.a, Datum 14.11.42," in *Die Anlagenbander zu den Kriegstagebuchern der 6. Armee vom 14.09.1942 bis 24.11.1942, Band I* (Schwabach: January 2006), 274, states that 244th Assault Gun Battalion fielded 8 75mm long, 5 75mm short, and 6 150mm assault guns, and 245th Battalion 1 75mm long and 3 150mm guns.

177. Wijers, *The Battle for Stalingrad*, 172.

178. Entry for 14 November, in *138th Rifle Division Combat Journal*.

179. Ibid.

180. Zhilin, *Stalingradskaia bitva*, 884, quoting *OKW Informational Bulletin*.

181. "Boevoe donesenie no. 230, Shtarm 62 14. 11. 42" [Combat report no. 230, headquarters, 62nd Army, 14 November 1942], in *62nd Army Combat Journal*. See the Red Army General Staff's report, in Zhilin, *Stalingradskaia bitva*, 882–883.

182. Zhilin, *Stalingradskaia bitva*, 883.

183. Ibid.

184. "Boevoe rasporiazhenie no. 241 Shtarma 62 14. 11. 42 10.30" [Combat instructions no. 241, headquarters, 62nd Army, 1030 hours on 14 November 1942], in *62nd Army Combat Journal*.

185. Zhilin, *Stalingradskaia bitva*, 883.

186. Mark, *Death of the Leaping Horseman*, 371. This order, *Divisionsbefehl* Nr. 86, appeared to some of 24th Panzer Division's senior officers to be "just part of the continued misuse and weakening of the Division."

187. Zhilin, *Stalingradskaia bitva*, 888.

188. Ziemke and Bauer, *Moscow to Stalingrad*, 468.

189. Entry for 15 November, in *138th Rifle Division Combat Journal*.

190. Zhilin, *Stalingradskaia bitva*, 888, quoting *OKW Informational Bulletin*.

191. "Boevoe donesenie no. 231, Shtarm 62 15. 11. 42" [Combat report no. 231, headquarters, 62nd Army, 15 November 1942], in *62nd Army Combat Journal*. See the Red Army General Staff's report, in Zhilin, *Stalingradskaia bitva*, 889. ·

192. "Boevoe donesenie no. 231," in *62nd Army Combat Journal*.

193. Chuikov, *The Battle for Stalingrad*, 215.

194. Ibid., 216.

195. Wijers, *The Battle for Stalingrad*, 173.

196. See Mark, *Death of the Leaping Horseman*, 370; and Ziemke and Bauer, *Moscow to Stalingrad*, 468.

197. Ziemke, *Stalingrad to Berlin*, 49.

198. See "Morgenmeldung LI. A. K. meldet 05.55 Uhr, A. O. K. 6, I. a, Datum 16.11.42," "Tagesmeldung XIV. A. K. meldet 20.35 Uhr, A. O. K. 6, I. a, Datum 16.11.42," and "Morgenmeldung LI. A. K. meldet 06.00 Uhr, A. O. K. 6, I. a, Datum 18.11.42," in *Die Anlagenbander zu den Kriegstagebuchern der 6. Armee vom 14.09.1942 bis 24.11.1942, Band I* (Schwabach: January 2006), 284, 291, and 296.

199. Ziemke, *Stalingrad to Berlin*, 50.

200. For details of the fighting from 16–18 November, see Mark, *Island of Fire*, 207–245.

201. Wijers, *The Battle for Stalingrad*, 173.

202. Chuikov, *The Battle for Stalingrad*, 216.

203. Ibid., 216–217.

204. Zhilin, *Stalingradskaia bitva*, 890–891.

205. "Boevoe donesenie no. 232, Shtarm 62 16. 11. 42" [Combat report no. 232, headquarters, 62nd Army, 16 November 1942], in *62nd Army Combat Journal*.

206. Entry for 16 November, in *138th Rifle Division Combat Journal*.

207. "Chastnyi boevoi prikaz no. 220 Shtarma 62 17. 11. 42 01.37" [Separate order no. 220, headquarters, 62nd Army, 17 November 1942], in *62nd Army Combat Journal*.

208. Zhilin, *Stalingradskaia bitva*, 892, quoting *OKW Informational Bulletin*.

209. Mark, *Death of the Leaping Horseman*, 370.

210. Ibid., 371.

211. "Boevoe donesenie no. 233, Shtarm 62 17. 11. 42" [Combat report no. 233, headquarters, 62nd Army, 17 November 1942], in *62nd Army Combat Journal*. Chuikov also reported renewed evacuation of wounded to the eastern bank of the Volga River, amounting to 383 men on 10 November, 356 on 11 November, 720 on 12 November, 357 on 13 November, 180 on 14 November, 543 on 15 November, and, after a delay of one day, 432 on 17 November. See, Zhilin, *Stalingradskaia bitva*, 896, for the Red Army General Staff's daily summary, which read:

> **62nd Army**. The units of the Northern Group (124th and 149th RBs) fought with an enemy force of up to a regiment of infantry with 18 tanks attacking toward Rynok from the north and toward Spartanovka from the southwest beginning at 0800 hours on 17 November. Our units repelled all enemy attacks by 1200 hours. We destroyed 6 tanks and killed 250 enemy soldiers and officers in the fighting. An enemy force of up to 2 battalions of infantry with 14 tanks attacked the group's units once again at 1540 hours.
>
> 138th RD repelled enemy attacks east of the Barrikady Factory and exchanged fire from their previous positions by day's end.
>
> 95th RD went over to the attack at 1400 hours on 17 November and captured the region of the oil tanks, 400 meters east of the southern part of the Barrikady Factory.
>
> The army's remaining units occupied their previous positions.

212. See OKH Intelligence Summary No. 520, in Zhilin, *Stalingradskaia bitva*, 892, citing *TsAMO RF*, f. 500, op. 12462, d. 89, ll. 421–423.

213. Mark, *Death of the Leaping Horseman*, 372.

214. Mark, *Island of Fire*, 216.

215. Entry for 17 November, in *138th Rifle Division Combat Journal*.

216. For details on this fighting, see Mark, *Island of Fire*, 220–222.

217. See Werthen, *Geschichte der 16. Panzer-Division*, 118, which describes the Soviets' defenses at Rynok as "a fire-spitting fortress, a maze of ditches, hidden tanks, minefields, and nests of antitank rifles." After the division's engineer assault groups cleared passages for the tanks, blew up mined barriers in the streets, and smashed the bunkers in the town's cellars, 2nd Battalion, 79th Panzer Grenadier Regiment, secured the flank to the west, while to the south Battalion Mues captured a cemetery and reached the Volga at about 0900 hours, where it erected a protective barrier to the south and formed a front facing north toward Rynok. Although the panzer grenadier battalion managed to seize a foothold in the town, the attack then stalled with heavy losses, supposedly because of the arrival of Soviet reinforcements.

218. Holl, *An Infantryman in Stalingrad*, 144.

219. Ibid., 145.

220. Ibid.

221. Werthen, *Geschichte der 16. Panzer-Division*, 119.

222. Zhilin, *Stalingradskaia bitva*, 892, quoting "Ia, *AOK 6*, No. 4640/42," in *KTB OKW*. Bd. 2, hb. 2.

223. Ziemke and Bauer, *Moscow to Stalingrad*, 468.

224. For details of this fight, see Mark, *Island of Fire*, 228–232.

225. Entry for 18 November, in *138th Rifle Division Combat Journal*.

226. "Boevoe donesenie no. 234, Shtarm 62, 18. 11. 42" [Combat report no. 234, headquarters, 62nd Army, 18 November 1942], in *62nd Army Combat Journal*. See the Red Army General Staff's daily report in Zhilin, *Stalingradskaia bitva*, volume 2, 26, which read:

> **62nd Army**. The units of the Northern Group (124th and 149th RBs) repulsed six attacks by enemy forces of up to two battalions of infantry and tanks in the Rynok and Spartanovka regions and held on to their previous positions on 18 November. During this fight, 11 enemy tanks were destroyed, up to 800 soldiers and officers were killed, 12 machine guns were taken, and 12 enemy soldiers were captured by the units of the group.
>
> 138th RD repelled several attacks by up to a battalion of enemy infantry and 3 tanks in the region east and northeast of the Barrikady Factory. The enemy pushed the left wing of the division back and captured three buildings by day's end on 18 November.
>
> 95th RD, having repelled three attacks by an infantry battalion in the region of the oil tanks (southeast of the Barrikady Factory), dug in along its occupied positions.
>
> The army's remaining units repelled attacks by small groups of enemy infantry and exchanged fire from their previous positions on 18 November.

227. Ibid.

228. Ibid.

229. Zhilin, *Stalingradskaia bitva*, 1: 897–898, citing OKH Intelligence Summary No. 521 in *TsAMO RF*, f. 500, op. 12462, d. 89, ll. 430–432.

230. Ibid.

231. Ibid., 898.

232. Ibid.

233. Gehlen, *The Service*, 59.

234. Ibid., 61.

235. Mark, *Death of the Leaping Horseman*, 317.

236. Ibid., 318.

237. Ibid., 340.

238. Ibid., 359.

239. Ibid., 371.

240. Holl, *An Infantryman in Stalingrad*, 135.

241. Ibid.

242. Ibid., 145.

243. Vinogradov, *Stalingradskaia epopeia*, 258.

244. Ibid.

245. Ibid., 257.

246. Due to the limited space within 62nd Army's bridgeheads, some of these 35,377 men, particularly soldiers in rear service and artillery units, remained on the eastern bank of the Volga River. For example, as of 18 November, 13th Guards Rifle Division had 3,118 of its men defending positions in Stalingrad's center city, while 2,071 men were situated on the Volga's eastern bank. Likewise, at the same time, 95th Rifle Division, which consisted of its own 90th, 161st, and 241st Regiments, 685th Regiment, and 3rd Battalion, 92nd Rifle Brigade, had 705 of its more than 2,100 men in the bridgehead. See Isaev, *Stalingrad*, 249.

247. See Zhilin, *Stalingradskaia bitva*, 1: 856. See archival citations *TsAMO RF*, f. 48a, op. 1640, d. 180, ll. 361–362. Originals.

248. Zhukov, *Reminiscences and Reflections*, vol. 2, 121–122.

249. Order of the Supreme High Commander no. 170688, dated 1310 hours on 15 November 1942, to the representative of the *Stavka* [Zhukov], in Zolotarev, "*Stavka* 1942," 449–450.

Chapter 10: Conclusions

1. See, for example, Kenneth Slepyan, *Stalin's Guerrillas: Soviet Partisans in World War II* (Lawrence: University Press of Kansas, 2006), 244.

2. Chuikov, *Battle for Stalingrad*, 141–145, discusses the snipers and includes the Soviet version of the romanticized duel between Zaitsev and the German "super-sniper."

3. Ibid., 246–247.

4. Krivosheev, *Grif sekretnosti sniat*, 177–178.

5. Ibid., 178–179.

6. Ibid., 179–180.

7. Ibid., 181–182.

8. Ibid., 225.

9. V. V. Gurkin, "Liudskie poteri Sovetskikh Vooruzhennykh sil v 1941–1945 gg.: Novye aspekty" [Personnel losses of the Soviet Armed Forces in 1941–1945: New aspects], *VIZh*, No. 2 (March–April 1999), 6.

10. Krivosheev, *Grif sekretnosti sniat*, 369.

11. Ziemke, *Stalingrad to Berlin*, 462.

12. Axworthy, *Third Axis, Fourth Ally*, 86–87.

13. Ziemke, *Stalingrad to Berlin*, 407.

14. Jentz, *Panzertruppen*, 252, 254–268.

Selected Bibliography

Abbreviations

JSMS	*Journal of Slavic Military Studies*
TsAMO	*Tsentral'nyi arkhiv Ministerstva Oborony* [Central Archives of the Ministry of Defense]
TsPA UML	*Tsentral'nyi partiinyi arkhiv Instituta Marksizma-Leninizma* [Central Party Archives of the Institute of Marxism and Leninism]
VIZh	*Voenno-istoricheskii zhurnal* [Military-historical journal]
VV	*Voennyi vestnik* [Military herald]

Primary Sources

Combat Journals [*Kriegstagebuch*]: German Sixth Army, in National Archives Microfilm (NAM) series T-312, Roll 1453.
Combat Journals [*Zhurnal boevykh deistvii*]: Soviet
    62nd Army, September–November 1942
    95th Rifle Division
    112th Rifle Division
    138th Rifle Division (*138-ia Krasnoznamennaia strelkovaia diviziia v boiakh za Stalingrada*) [The 138th Red Banner Rifle Division in the battle for Stalingrad].
    284th Rifle Division
    308th Rifle Division
    37th Guards Rifle Division
    39th Guards Rifle Division
    10th Rifle Brigade
    42nd Rifle Brigade
    "Anlage 3 zum Tatigkeitsbericht, AOK 17, Ic, 20 Jul–25 Jul 1942." *AOK 17, 24411/33*.
National Archives Microfilm (NAM) series T-312, Roll 679.
Aufsess, Florian *Freiherr* von und zu. *Die Anlagenbander zu den Kriegstagebuchern der 6. Armee vom 14.09.1942 bis 24.11.1942, Band I*. Schwabach: January 2006.
Boevoi sostav Sovetskoi armii, chast' 2 (Ianvar'–dekabr' 1942 goda) [Combat composition of the Soviet Army, part 2 (January–December 1942)]. Moscow: Voenizdat, 1966.
Dushen'kin, V. V., ed. *Vnutrennye voiska v Velikoi Otechestvennoi voine 1941–1945 gg.: Dokumenty i materially* [Internal troops in the Great Patriotic War 1941–1945: Documents and materials]. Moscow: Iuridicheskaia literatura, 1975.

GKO [State Defense Committee] Decrees, *TsPA UML*. f. 644, op. 1, *delo* [file] (d.), 23, *listy* [leaf, pages] (ll.) 127–129 and f. 644, op. 1, d. 33, ll. 48–50.

"Ia, Lagenkarten Nr. 1 zum KTB Nr. 13, Jul–Oct 1942." *AOK 6, 23948/1a*. National Archives Microfilm (NAM) series T-312, Roll 1446.

Kommandovanie korpusnovo i divizionnogo svena Sovetskikh vooruzhennykh sil perioda Velikoi Otechestvennoi voiny 1941–1945 g. [Commanders at the corps and division level in the Soviet Armed Forces in the period of the Great Patriotic War, 1941–1945]. Moscow: Frunze Academy, 1964.

Kriegstagebuch der Oberkommandes der Wehrmacht/Wehrmachtfuhrungsstab: 1940–1945, Bd. II. Frankfurt, 1963.

"Lagenkarten, 8 July–5 October 1942." *AOK II, Ia, 2585/207a*. National Archives Microfilm (NAM) series T-312, Roll 1207.

"Lagenkarten PzAOK 1, Ia, 1–30 Sep 1942." *PzAOK 1, 24906/15*. National Archives Microfilm (NAM) series T-313, Roll 36.

"Lagenkarten PzAOK 1, Ia, 1–31 Oct 1942." *PzAOK 1, 24906/16*. National Archives Microfilm (NAM) series T-313, Roll 36.

"Lagenkarten zum KTB. Nr. 5 (Teil III.), PzAOK 4, Ia, 21 Oct–24 Nov 1942." *PzAOK 4 28183/12*. National Archives Microfilm (NAM) series T-313, Roll 359.

Sbornik materialov po izucheniiu opyta voiny, No. 4 (Ianvar'–fevral' 1943 g.) [Collection of materials for the exploitation of war experiences, no. 4]. Moscow: Voenizdat, 1943.

Sbornik materialov po izucheniiu opyta voiny, No. 6 (Aprel'–mai 1943 g.) [Collection of materials for the exploitation of war experiences, no. 6]. Moscow: Voenizdat, 1943.

Sbornik voenno-istoricheskikh materialov Velikoi Otechestvennoi voiny, Vypusk 14 [Collection of materials of the Great Patriotic War, Issue 14]. Moscow: Voenizdat, 1954.

Sbornik voenno-istoricheskikh materialov Velikoi Otechestvennoi voiny, Vypusk 15 [Collection of materials of the Great Patriotic War, Issue 15]. Moscow: Voenizdat, 1955.

Sbornik voenno-istoricheskikh materialov Velikoi Otechestvennoi voiny, Vypusk 18 [Collection of materials of the Great Patriotic War, Issue 18]. Moscow: Voenizdat, 1960).

Shapovalov, V. A., ed. *Bitva za Kavkaz v dokumentakh i materialov* [The battle for the Caucasus in documents and materials]. Stavropol': Stavropol' State University, 2003.

Zhilin, V. A., ed. *Stalingradskaia bitva: Khronika, fakty, liudi v 2 kn*. [The battle of Stalingrad; chronicles, facts, people in 2 books]. Moscow: OLMA, 2002.

Zolotarev, A. M., ed. "General'nyi shtab v gody Velikoi Otechestvennoi voiny: Dokumenty i materially, 1942 god" [The General Staff in the Great Patriotic War: Documents and materials, 1942]. In *Russki arkhiv: Velikaia Otechestvennaia* [voina], 23 (12–2) [The Russian archives: The Great Patriotic (War), Vol. 23 (12–2)]. Moscow: "TERRA," 1999.

―――. Prikazy narodnogo komissara oborony SSSR, 22 iiunia 1941 g.–1942 [Orders of the People's Commissariat of Defense of the USSR, 22 June 1941–1942].

In *Russkii arkhiv: Velikaia Otechestvennaia [voina], 13 (2–2)* [The Russian archives: The Great Patriotic (War), Vol. 13 (2–2)]. Moscow: TERRA, 1997.

———. "Stavka VGK: Dokumenty i materialy 1942" [The *Stavka* VGK: Documents and materials, 1942]. In *Russkii arkhiv: Velikaia Otechestvennaia [voina], 16 (5–2)* [The Russian archives: The Great Patriotic (War), Vol. 16 (5–2)]. Moscow: "TERRA," 1996.

Secondary Sources: Books

Afanas'ev, N. I. *Ot Volgi do Shpree: Boevoi put' 35-i gvardeiskoi strelkovoi Lozovskoi Krasnoznamennoi, ordena Suvorova i Bogdan Khmel'nitskogo divizii* [From the Volga to the Spree: The combat path of the 35th Guard Lozovaia, Red Banner, and Orders of Suvorov and Bogdan Khmel'nitsky Rifle Division]. Moscow: Voenizdat, 1982.

Axworthy, Mark, Cornel Scafeç, and Cristian Craciunoiu. *Third Axis Fourth Ally: The Romanian Armed Forces in the European War, 1941–1945.* London: Arms and Armour Press, 1995.

Babich, Iu. P. *Podgotovka oborony 62nd Armiei vne soprikosnovaniia s protivnikom I vedenie oboronitel'noi operatsii v usloviiakh prevoskhodstva protivnika v manevrennosti (po opytu Stalingradskoi bitvy)* [The preparation of the 62nd Army's defense in close proximity to the enemy and the conduct of the defensive operation in circumstances of enemy superiority in maneuver (based on the experience of the battle of Stalingrad)]. Moscow: Frunze Academy, 1991.

Babich, Iu P., and A. G. Baier. *Razvitie vooruzheniia i organitzatsii Sovetskikh sukhoputnykh voist v gody Velikoi Otechestvennoi voiny* [Development of the armament and organization of the Soviet ground forces in the Great Patriotic War]. Moscow: Frunze Academy, 1990.

Bagramian, I. K. *Tak shli my k pobeda* [As we went on to victory]. Moscow: Voenizdat, 1977.

Barnett, Correlli, ed. *Hitler's Generals.* New York: Grove Weidenfeld, 1989.

Bartov, Omar. *The Eastern Front, 1941–45: German Troops and the Barbarization of Warfare.* New York: St. Martin's Press, 1986.

Batov, P. I. *V pokhodakh i boiakh* [In marches and battles]. Moscow: "Golos," 2000.

Beevor, Antony. *Stalingrad: The Fateful Siege: 1942–1943.* New York: Viking, 1998.

Berdnikov, G. I. *Pervaia udarnaia* [The First Shock (Army)]. Moscow: Voenizdat, 1985.

Beshanov, V. V. *God 1942—"Uchebnyi"* [The Year 1942—Educational]. Minsk: Harvest, 2002.

Bitva pod Stalingradom, chast' 1: Strategicheskaia oboronitel'naia operatsiia [The battle at Stalingrad, part 1: The strategic defensive operation]. Moscow: Voroshilov Military Academy, 1953.

Bitva za Stalingrad [The battle for Stalingrad]. Volgograd: Nizhne-Volzhskoe knizhnoe izdatel'stvo, 1973.

Blau, George E. *The German Campaign in Russia: Planning and Operations (1940–1942).* Department of the Army Pamphlet No. 20-261a. Washington, D.C.: Department of the Army, 1955.

Boog, Horst, Jurden Forster, Joachim Hoffmann, et al. *Germany and the Second World War*, Vol. 4: *The Attack on the Soviet Union*. Trans. Dean S. McMurry, Ewald Osers, and Louise Wilmot. Oxford, UK: Clarendon Press, 2001.

Bradley, Dermot, Karl-Friedrich Hildebrand, and Markus Rövekamp. *Die Generale des Heeres 1921–1945*. Osnabruk: Biblio Verlag, 1993.

Carell, Paul. *Stalingrad: The Defeat of the German 6th Army*. Trans. David Johnston. Atglen, PA: Schiffer Publishing, 1993.

Chistiakov, I. M. *Sluzhim otchizne* [In service to the Fatherland]. Moscow: Voenizdat, 1975.

———, ed. *Po prikazu Rodiny: boevoi put' 6-i gvardeiskoi armii v Velikoi Otechestvennoi voine* [By order of the Motherland; The combat path of the 6th Guards Army in the Great Patriotic War]. Moscow: Voenizdat, 1971.

Chuikov, Vasili I. *The Battle for Stalingrad*. Trans. Harold Silver. New York: Holt, Rinehart and Winston, 1964.

Craig, William. *Enemy at the Gates: The Battle for Stalingrad*. New York: Reader's Digest Press, 1973.

Demin, V. A., and R. M. Portugal'sky. *Tanki vkhodiat v proryv* [Tanks enter the penetration]. Moscow: Voenizdat, 1988.

Dërr, G. *Pokhod na Stalingrad* [The march on Stalingrad]. Moscow: Voenizdat, 1957.

Dieckhoff, Gerhard. *3. Infantrie-Division, 3. Infantrie-Division (mot), 3. Panzer-Grenadier-Division*. Cuxhaven, Germany: Oberstudienrat Gerhard Dieckhoff, 1960.

Dinardo, Richard L. *Germany's Panzer Arm*. Westport, CT: Greenwood Press, 1997.

Dragunsky, D. A., ed. *Ot Volgi do Pragi* [From the Volga to Prague]. Moscow: Voenizdat, 1966.

Drig, Evgenii. *Mekhanizirovannye korpusa RKKA v boiu: Istoriia avtobronetankovykh voisk Krasnoi Armii v 1940–1941 godakh* [Mechanized corps of the RKKA in battle: A history of the Auto-armored forces of the Red Army in 1940–1941]. Moscow: Transkniga, 2005.

Eremenko, A. I. *Stalingrad: Uchastnikam Velikoi bitvy pod Stalingradom posviatshchaetsia* [Stalingrad: A participant in the great battle at Stalingrad dedicates]. Moscow: AST, 2006.

———. *Stalingrad: Zapiski komanduuishchevo frontom* [Stalingrad: The notes of a *front* commander]. Moscow: Voenizdat, 1961.

Erickson, John. *The Road to Stalingrad: Stalin's War with Germany, Vol. 1*. New York: Harper and Row, 1975.

Friedin, Seymour, and William Richardson, eds. *The Fatal Decisions*. New York: William Sloane Associates, 1956.

Gehlen, Reinhard. *The Service: The Memoirs of General Reinhard Gehlen*. Trans. David Irving. New York: World Publishing, 1972.

Geroi Sovetskogo Soiuza, tom 1 [Heroes of the Soviet Union, Vol. 1]. Moscow: Voenizdat, 1987.

Glantz, David M. *Atlas of Operation Blau: The German Advance on Stalingrad, 28 June–18 November 1942*. Carlisle, PA: Self-published, 1998.

————. *Atlas of the Struggle for Stalingrad City. Vol. 1: 3 September–18 November 1942*. Carlisle, PA: Self-published, 2007.

————. *Colossus Reborn: The Red Army at War, 1941–1943*. Lawrence: University Press of Kansas, 2005.

————. *Combat Documents on the Struggle for Stalingrad City. Vol. 1: 3 September–18 November 1942*. Carlisle, PA: Self-published, 2007.

————. *Forgotten Battles of the German-Soviet War (1941–1945), Vol. 3: The Summer Campaign (12 May–18 November 1942)*. Carlisle, PA: Self-published, 1999.

————. *Red Army Command Cadre (1941–1945), Volume 1: Direction, Front, Army, Military District, Defense Zone, and Mobile Corps Commanders*. Carlisle, PA: Self-published, 2002.

————. *The Role of Intelligence in Soviet Military Strategy in World War II*. Novato, CA: Presidio Press, 1990.

————. *The Strategic and Operational Impact of Terrain on Military Operations in Central and Eastern Europe*. Carlisle, PA: Self-published, 1998.

————. *The Struggle for the Caucasus: Combat Chronology and Documents, vol. 1: 21 July–18 November 1942*. Carlisle, PA: Self-published, 2008.

————. *Stumbling Colossus: The Red Army on the Eve of World War*. Lawrence: University Press of Kansas, 1998.

————. "Nikolai Fedorovich Vatutin." In *Stalin's Generals*. Ed. Harold Shukman, 287–300. London: Weidenfeld and Nicolson, 1993.

Glantz, David M., and Jonathan House. *When Titans Clashed: How the Red Army Stopped Hitler*. Lawrence: University Press of Kansas, 1995.

Goerlitz, Walter. *Paulus and Stalingrad: A Life of Field-Marshal Friedrich Paulus with notes, correspondence, and documents from his papers*. Trans. R. H. Stevens. New York: The Citadel Press, 1963.

Golikov, F. I. "V Oborona Stalingrada" [In the defense of Stalingrad]. In *Stalingradskaia epopeia* [The Stalingrad epoch]. Ed. A. M. Samsonov. Moscow: "Nauka," 1968.

Gorshkov, S. G. *Na Iuzhnom flange, osen' 1941 g.–vesna 1944 g.* [On the southern flank, fall 1941–spring 1944]. Moscow: Voenizdat, 1989.

Grams, Rolf. *Die 14. Panzer-Division 1940–1945*. Bad Nauheim, BRD: Verlag Hans-Henning Podzun, 1957.

Grechko, A. A. *Bitva za Kavkaz* [The battle for the Caucasus]. Moscow: Voenizdat, 1973.

————. *Battle for the Caucasus*. Moscow: Progress Publishers, 1971.

————. ed. *Istoriia Vtoroi Mirovoi voiny 1939–1945 v dvenadtsati tomakh, tom piatyi* [History of the Second World War in twelve volumes, Vol. 5]. Moscow: Voenizdat, 1975.

"Gurov Kuz'ma Akimovich." In *Voennaia Entsiklopediia v vos'mi tomakh, 2* [Military encyclopedia in eight volumes, Vol. 2]. Ed. P. S. Grachev, 534. Moscow: Voenizdat, 1994.

Halder, Franz. *The Halder War Diary, 1939–1942*. Novato, CA: Presidio Press, 1988.

Hardesty, Von. *Red Phoenix: The Rise of Soviet Air Power 1941–1945*. Washington, DC: Smithsonian Institution Press, 1982.

Haupt, Werner. *Army Group South: The Wehrmacht in Russia 1941–1945*. Trans. Joseph G. Welsh. Atglen, PA: Schiffer Press, 1998.

Hayward, Joel S. A. *Stopped at Stalingrad: The Luftwaffe and Hitler's Defeat in the East, 1942–1943*. Lawrence: University Press of Kansas, 1998.

Heiber, Helmut, and David M. Glantz. *Hitler and His Generals: The Military Conferences 1942–1945*. New York: Enigma Books, 2002.

Holl, Adelbert. *An Infantryman in Stalingrad: From 24 September 1942 to 2 February 1943*. Trans. Jason D. Mark and Neil Page. Sydney, Australia: Leaping Horseman Books, 2005.

Isaev, Aleksei. *Kogda vnezapnosti uzhe ne bylo* [When there was no surprise]. Moscow: Moscow: "IAUZA" "EKSMO," 2005.

————. *Kratkii kurs Istorii Velikoi Otechestvennoi voyny: Nastuplenie Marshala Shaposhnikova* [A short course in the history of the Great Patriotic War: The offensives of Marshal Shaposhnikov]. Moscow: "IAUZA" "EKSMO," 2005.

————. *Stalingrad: Za Volgoi dlia nas zemli net* [The is no land for us beyond the Volga]. Moscow: Iauza, Eksmo, 2008.

Istoricheskii podvig Stalingrada [The historical victory at Stalingrad]. Moscow: "Mysl'," 1985.

Iushchuk, I. I. *Odinnatsatyi Tankovyi Korpus v boiakh za Rodinu* [The 11th Tank Corps in combat for the Motherland]. Moscow: Voenizdat, 1962.

Jentz, Thomas L. *Panzertruppen*. Atglen, PA: Schiffer Publishing, 1996.

Jukes, Geoffrey. *Hitler's Stalingrad Decisions*. Berkeley, CA: University of California Press, 1985.

————. "Alexander Mikhailovich Vasilevsky." In *Stalin's Generals*. Ed. Harold Shukman, 275–286. London: Weidenfeld and Nicolson, 1993.

Kehrig, Manfred. *Stalingrad: Analyse und Dokumentation einer Schlacht*. Stuttgart: Deutsche Verlag-Anstalt, 1974.

Keilig, Wolf. *Die Generale des Heeres*. Bad Nauheim, Podzun-Pallas, 1983.

Keitel, Wilhelm. *In the Service of the Reich*. Trans. David Irving. New York: Stein and Day, 1966.

Kobyliansky, Isaak. *By Fire and Wheels . . . : From Stalingrad to Pillau with Three-Inch Field Guns*. Lawrence: University Press of Kansas, 2007.

Kolomiets, Maksim, and Il'ia Moshchansky. "Oborona Kavkaz (iiul'–dekabr' 1942 goda)" [The defense of the Caucasus (July–December 1942)]. In *Frontovaia illiustratsiia* [Front illustrated]. Moscow: "Strategiia KM," 2000).

Komandarmy. Voennyi biograficheskii slovar' (Velikaia Otechestvennaia). [Army commanders. Military-bibliographical dictionary (The Great Patriotic)]. Moscow: Institute of Military History, Russian Federation's Ministry of Defense, OOO "Kuchkovo pole," 2005.

Komandovanie korpusnogo i divizionnogo zvena Sovetskikh Vooruzhennykh Sil perioda Velikoi Otechestvennoi voiny, 1941–1945 gg. [Commanders at the corps and division level in the Soviet Armed Forces in the period of the Great Patriotic War, 1941–1945]. Moscow: Frunze Military Academy, 1964.

Komkory, Voennyi biograficheskii slovar' (Velikaia Otechestvennaia), Tom 1 and 2. [Corps commanders. A military-biographical dictionary (The Great Patriotic), vols. 1 and 2]. Moscow: Institute of Military History, Russian Federation's Ministry of Defense, OOO "Kuchkovo pole," 2006.

Kozlov, M. M., ed. *Velikaia Otechestvennaia voina 1941–1945: Entsiklopediia* [The Great Patriotic War 1941–1945: An encyclopedia]. Moscow: "Sovetskaia entsiklopediia," 1985.

Krasnoznamennyi Chernomorskii Flot [The Red Banner Black Sea Fleet]. Moscow: Voenizdat, 1987.

Krivosheev, G. F., ed. *Grif sekretnosti sniat: Poteri vooruzhennykh sil SSSR v voinakh, boevykh deistviiakh, i voennykh konfliktakh* [The classification secret is removed: The losses of the USSR's armed forces in wars, combat operations, and military conflicts]. Moscow: Voenizdat, 1993.

————. *Rossiia i SSSR v voinakh XX veka: Poteri vooruzhennykh sil, Statisticheskoe issledovanie* [Russia and the USSR in wars of the XX Century: Armed Forces losses, a statistical investigation]. Moscow: "OLMA," 2001.

————. *Soviet Casualty and Combat Losses in the Twentieth Century*. London and Mechanicsburg, PA: Schiffer Books, 1997.

Krylov, N. I. *Stalingradskii rubezh* [The Stalingrad line]. Moscow: Voenizdat, 1984.

Kuhn, George W. S. *Ground Forces Casualty Rate Patterns: The Empirical Evidence, Report FP703TR1*. Bethesda, MD: Logistics Management Agency, September 1989.

Kuznetsov, I. I. *Sud'by general'skie: Vysshie komandnye kadry Krasnoi Armii v 1940–1953 gg.* [The fates of the generals: The higher command cadre of the Red Army 1940–1953]. Irkutsk: Irkutsk University Press, 2002.

Laskin, I. A. *Na puti k perelomu* [On the path to the turning point]. Moscow: Voenizdat, 1977.

Lebedev, Ia. A., and A. I. Maliutin. *Pomnit Dnepr-reka: Vospominaniia veteranov 193-istrelkovoi Dneprovskoi ordena Lenina, Krasnoznamennoi, ordena Suvorova i Kutuzova divizii* [Remember the Dnepr River: Recollections of veterans of the 193rd Dnepr order of Lenin, Red Banner, and orders of Suvorov and Kutuzov Rifle Division]. Minsk: "Belarus'," 1986.

Lemelsen, Joachim, et al. *29. Division: 29. Infanteriedivision, 29. Infanteriedivision (mot), 29. Panzergrenadier-Division*. Bad Nauheim, BRD: Podzun-Verlag, 1960.

Liudnikov, I. I. *Doroda dlinoiu v zhizn'* [The long road in life]. Moscow: Voenizdat, 1969.

Losik, O. A. *Stroitel'stvo i boevoe primenenie Sovetskikh tankovykh voisk v gody Velikoi Otechestvennoi voiny* [The Formation and combat use of Soviet tank units in the years of the Great Patriotic War]. Moscow: Voenizdat, 1979.

Mackensen, Eberhard von. *Vom Bug zum Kaukasus: Das III. Panzerkorps im Feldzug gegen Sowjetrussland 1941/42*. Neckargemund: Kurt Vowinkel Verlag, 1967.

Mark, Jason D. *Death of the Leaping Horseman: 25. Panzer-Division in Stalingrad, 12th August–20th November 1942*. Sydney, Australia: Leaping Horseman Books, 2003.

————. *Island of Fire: The Battle for the Barrikady Gun Factory in Stalingrad, November 1942–February 1943*. Sydney, Australia: Leaping Horseman Books, 2006.

Martynov, V., and S. Spakhov. *Proliv v ogne* [The straits in flames]. Kiev: Izdatel'stvo politicheskoi literatury Ukrainy, 1984.

Maslov, Aleksander A. *Fallen Soviet Generals*. London: Frank Cass, 1998.

McCroden, William. *The Organization of the German Army in World War II: Army Groups, Armies, Corps, Divisions, and Combat Groups, in five volumes.* Draft manuscript, unpublished and undated.

Mellenthin, Friedrich W. von. *German Generals of World War II As I Saw Them.* Norman, OK: The University of Oklahoma Press, 1977.

Morozov, I. K. "Na iuzhnom uchaske fronta" [In the *front's* southern sector]. In *Bitva za Volge* [The battle for the Volga]. Stalingrad: Knizhnoe izdatel'stvo, 1962.

Moshchansky, Il'ia, and Sergei Smolinov. "Oborona Stalingrada: Stalingradskaia strategicheskaia oboronitel'naia operatsiia, 17 iiulia–18 noiabria 1942 goda" [The defense of Stalingrad: The Stalingrad strategic defensive operation, 17 July–18 November 1942]. In *Voennaia Letopis'* [Military chronicle]. Moscow: BTV, 2002.

Moskalenko, K. S. *Na iugo-zapadnom napravlenii* [On the southwestern axis], Vol. 1. Moscow: "Nauka," 1969.

Mozolev, V. F. "Mozdok-Malgrobekaia operatsiia 1942" [The Mozdok-Malgrobek operation, 1942]. In *Voennaia entsyklopediia v vos'mi tomakh*, 5 [Military encyclopedia in eight volumes, Vol. 5]. Ed. I. N. Sergeev, 196–197. Moscow: Voenizdat, 2001.

Müller, Rolf-Dieter, and Gerd R. Ueberschar. *Hitler's War in the East 1941–1945: A Critical Assessment.* Providence, RI, Oxford, UK: Berghahn Books, 1997.

Muratov, Viktor. *The Battle for the Caucasus.* Moscow: Novosti Press, 1973.

Murray, Williamson. *Luftwaffe.* Baltimore: Nautical and Aviation Publishing Company of America, 1985.

Mirzoian, Suren. *Stalingradskoe Zarevo* [The Stalingrad conflagration]. Erevan: Izdatel'stvo "Anastan," 1974.

Neidhardt, Hanns. *Mit Tanne und Eichenlaub: Kriegschronik der 100. Jäger-Division vormals 100. leichte Infanterie-Division.* Graz-Stuttgart: Leopold Stocker Verlag, 1981.

Nikoforov, N. I. et al., ed. *Velikaia Otechestvennaia voina 1941–1945 gg.: Deistvuiushchaia armiia* [The Great Patriotic War 1941–1945: The operating army]. Moscow: Animi Fortitudo, Kuchkovo pole, 2005.

Plato, Anton Detlev von. *Die Geschichte der 5. Panzerdivision 1938 bis 1945.* Regensberg: Walhalla u. Praetoria Verlag, 1978.

Portugal'sky, R. M. *Analiz opyta nezavershennykh nastupatel'nykh operatsii Velikoi Otechestvennoi voyny. Vyvody i uroki* [An analysis of the experience of uncompleted offensive operations of the Great Patriotic War. Conclusions and lessons]. Moscow: Izdanie akademii, 1991.

Pospelov, P. N. *Istoriia Velikoi Otechestvennoi voiny Sovetskogo Soiuza 1941–1945 v shesti tomakh, tom vtoroi* [History of the Great Patriotic War 1941–1945 in six volumes, Vol. 2]. Moscow: Voenizdat, 1961.

Povalyi, M. M. *Vosemnadtsataia v srazhenii za Rodiny* [The 18th (Army) in the defense of the Motherland]. Moscow: Voenizdat, 1982.

Ramanichev, N. M., and V. V. Gurkhin. "Rzhevsko-Sychevskie operatsii 1942 [The Rzhev-Sychevka operation 1942]." In *Voennaia entsyklopidiia v vos'mi tomakh*, 7 [Military encyclopedia in eight volumes, Vol. 7]. Ed. S. B. Ivanov, 233–234. Moscow: Voenizdat, 2003.

Rokossovsky, K. K. *Soldatskii dolg* [A soldier's duty]. Moscow: "GOLOS," 2000.

————, ed. *Velikaia bitva na Volge* [Great victory on the Volga]. Moscow: Voenizdat, 1965.

Rotmistrov, Pavel A. *Stal'naia gvardiia* [Steel guards]. Moscow: Voenizdat, 1984.

Samchuk, I. A. *Trinadtsataia gvardeiskaia* [The 13th Guards]. Moscow: Voenizdat, 1971.

Samsonov, A. M. *Stalingradskaia bitva* [The battle for Stalingrad]. Moscow: "Nauka," 1983.

————, ed. *Stalingradskaia epopeia* [Stalingrad epic]. Moscow: "Nauka," 1968.

Sandalov, A. M. *Pogoreloe-Gorodishchenskaia operatsiia: Nastupatel'naia operatsiia 20-i armii Zapadnogo fronta v avguste 1942 goda* [The Pogoreloe-Gorodishche operation: The offensive operation of the Western Front's 20th Army in August 1942]. Moscow: Voenizdat, 1960.

Sarkis'ian, S. M. *51-ia Armiia* [The 51st Army]. Moscow: Voenizdat, 1983.

Schröter, Heinz. *Stalingrad*. New York: Ballantine, 1958.

————. *Stalingrad: ". . . bis letzten Patrone."* Lengerich: Kleins Druck- und Verlagsanstalt, n.d.

Senger und Etterlin, Ferdinand von. *Die 24. Panzer-Division vormals 1. Kavallerie-Division 1939–1945*. Neckargemünd: Kurt Vowinckel Verlag, 1962.

Shiian, I. S. *Ratnyi podvig Novorossiiska* [Feat of Arms at Novorossiisk]. Moscow: Voenizdat, 1977.

Shtemenko, S. M. *The Soviet General Staff at War, 1941–1945*, Book One. Trans. Robert Daglish. Moscow: Voenizdat, 1985.

Slepyan, Kenneth. *Stalin's Guerrillas: Soviet Partisans in World War II*. Lawrence: University Press of Kansas, 2006.

Soviet Documents of the Use of War Experience, Volume Three: Military Operations 1941 and 1942. Trans. Harold S. Orenstein. London: Frank Cass, 1993.

Speer, Albert. *Inside the Third Reich*. Trans. Richard and Clara Winston. New York: Macmillan, 1970.

Spielberger, Walter J., and Uwe Feist, *Panzerkampfwagen IV: "Workhorse" of the German Panzertruppe*. Berkeley, CA: Feist Publications, 1968.

Stalingrad: Zabytoe srazhenie [Stalingrad: The forgotten battle]. Moscow: AST, 2005.

Stalingradskaia epopeia: Vpervye publikuemye dokumenty, rassekrechennye FSB RF [Stalingrad epoch: Declassified documents of the Russian Federation's FSB published for the first time]. Moscow: "Evonnitsa-MG," 2000.

Stoves, Rolf. *Die Gepanzerten und Motorisierten Deutschen Grossverbande, 1935–1945*. Friedberg: Podzun-Pallas-Verlag, 1986.

————. *Die 22. Panzer-Division, Die 25. Panzer-Division, Die 27. Panzer-Division, und Die 233. Reserve-Panzer-Division*. Friedberg: Podzun-Pallas-Verlag, 1985.

Sukharev, A. Ia., ed. *Marshal A. M. Vasilevsky—strateg, polkovodets, chelovek* [Marshal A. M. Vasilevsky—strategist, military leader, and the man]. Moscow: Sovet Veteranov knigoizdaniia, 1998.

"Tactics of Mobile Units. Operations of the 5th SS Panzergrenadier Division Wiking at Rostov and the Maikop Oilfields (Summer 1942)." Heidelberg, Germany: Foreign Military Studies Branch, Historical Division, Headquarters, United States Army Europe. In OCMH MS # D-248.

Tarrant, V. E. *Stalingrad: Anatomy of an Agony*. London: Leo Cooper, 1992.

Tieke, Wilhelm. *The Caucasus and the Oil: The German-Soviet War in the Caucasus 1942/43*. Trans. Joseph G. Welsh. Winnipeg, CA: J. J. Fedorowicz, 1995.

"Timoshenko, Semen, Konstantinovich." In *Sovetskaia Voennaia Entsiklopediia v bos'mi tomakh, 8* [Soviet military encyclopedia in eight volumes, 8]. Ed. N. V. Ogarkov, 43–44. Moscow: Voenizdat, 1980.

Tiulenev, I. V. *Krakh operatsii "Edel'veis"* [The defeat of Operation Edelweiss]. Ordzhonikidze: Izdatel'stvo "Ir," 1975.

Trevor-Roper, Hugh R., ed. *Blitzkrieg to Defeat: Hitler's War Directives 1939–1945*. New York, Chicago: Holt, Reinhart and Winston, 1964.

Two Hundred Days of Fire: Accounts by Participants and Witnesses of the Battle of Stalingrad. Moscow: Progress Publishers, 1970.

Utkin, Anatolii. *Sorok vtoroi god [1942]*. Smolensk: "Rusich," 2002.

Vaneev, G. I. *Chernomortsy v Velikoi Otechestvennoi voine* [Black Sea sailors in the Great Patriotic War]. Moscow: Voenizdat, 1978.

Vasilevsky, A. M. *Delo vsei zhizni* [Life's work]. Moscow: Izdatel'stvo politicheskoi literatury, 1983.

Venkov, B. S., and P. P. Dudinov. *Gvardeiskaia doblest': Boevoi put' 70-i gvardeiskoi strelkovoi glukhovskoi ordena Lenina, dvazhdy krasnoznamennoi, ordena Suvorova, Kutuzova i Bogdana Khmel'nitskogo diviziii* [Guards valor: The combat path of the 70th Guards Glukhov, Order of Lenin and order of Suvorov, Kutuzov and Bogdan Khmel'nitsky Rifle Division]. Moscow: Voenizdat, 1979.

Vider, Ioakhim. *Stalingradskaia tragediia: Za kulisami katastrofy* [The Stalingrad tragedy: Behind the scenes of a catastrophe]. Trans. A. Lebedev and N. Portugalov. Moscow: Iauza, Eksmo, 2004.

Voennaia entsiklopediia v vos'mi tomakh, 1 [Military encyclopedia in eight volumes, Vol. 1]. Ed. I. N. Rodionov. Moscow: Voenizdat, 1997.

Volkov, A. A. *Kriticheskii prolog: Nezavershennye frontovye nastupatel'nye operatsii pervykh kampanii Velikoi Otechestvennoi voiny* [Critical prologue: Incomplete front offensive operations of the initial campaign of the Great Patriotic War]. Moscow: AVIAR, 1992.

Volostnov, N. I. *Na ognennykh rubezhakh* [In firing positions]. Moscow: Voenizdat, 1983.

Vyrodov, I. Ia., ed. *V srazheniakh za Pobedy: Boevoi put' 38-i armii v gody Velikoi Otechestvennoi voyny 1941–1945* [In battles for the Fatherland: The combat path of the 38th Army in the Great Patriotic War 1941–1945]. Moscow: "Nauka," 1974).

Warlimont, Walter. *Inside Hitler's Headquarters 1939–1945*. Trans. R. H. Barry. Novato, CA: Presidio, 1964.

Werthen, Wolfgang. *Geschichte der 16. Panzer-Division 1939–1945*. Bad Nauheim: Podzun-Pallas-Verlag, 1958.

Wijers, Hans J. *The Battle for Stalingrad: The Battle for the Factories, 14 October–19 November 1942*. Heerenveen, The Netherlands: Self-published, 2003.

Woff, Richard. "Chuikov." In *Stalin's Generals*. Ed. Harold Shukman, 67–76. London: Weidenfeld and Nicolson, 1993.

————. "Rokossovsky." In *Stalin's Generals*. Ed. Harold Shukman, 177–198. London: Weidenfeld and Nicolson, 1993.

Wray, Timothy A. *Standing Fast: German Defensive Doctrine on the Russian Front during World War II, Prewar to March 1943.* Fort Leavenworth, KS: Combat Studies Institute, 1986.

Zakharov, Iu. D. *General armii Vatutin.* Moscow: Voenizdat, 1985.

Zalessky, Konstantin. *Vermacht: Sukhoputnye voiska i Verkhovnoe komandovanie* [The *Wehrmacht*: Ground Forces and the High Command]. Moscow; "Iauza," 2005.

Zaloga, Steve, and Peter Sarson. *T-34/76 Medium Tank, 1941–1945.* London: Osprey/ Reed Publishing, 1994.

Zhadov, A. S. *Chetyre goda voyny* [Four years of war]. Moscow: Voenizdat, 1978.

Zhukov, G. *Reminiscences and Reflections*, Vol. 2. Moscow: Progress Publishers, 1985.

Ziemke, Earl F. *Stalingrad to Berlin: The German Defeat in the East.* Washington, D.C.: United States Army Office of the Chief of Military History, 1968.

Ziemke, Earl F., and Magna E. Bauer. *Moscow to Stalingrad: Decision in the East.* Washington, DC: Center of Military History United States Army, 1987.

Zolotarev, V. A., ed. *Velikaia Otechestvennaia voina 1941–1945, Kniga 1: Surovye ispytaniia* [The Great Patriotic War, Book 1: A harsh education]. Moscow: "Nauka," 1998.

Zvartsev, A. M., ed. *3-ia gvardeiskaia tankovaia armiia* [The 3rd Guards Tank Army]. Moscow: Voenizdat, 1982.

Secondary Sources: Articles

Anoshkin, V., and N. Naumov. "O stabilizatsii fronta oborony na Iuzhnom strategicheskom napravlenii letom 1942 goda" [About the stabilization of the defensive front on the southern axis in the summer of 1942]. *VIZh*, no. 10 (October 1982): 18–24.

Brusin, G., and G. Nekhonov. "Oborona ostrova Zaitsevskii" [The defense of Zaitsevskii Island]. *VIZh*, no. 3 (March 1964): 113–117.

Danilov, F. "Bitva za Kavkaz" [The battle for the Caucasus]. *VIZh*, no. 7 (July 1967): 117–123.

Glantz, David M. "Soviet Mobilization in Peace and War, 1924–42: A Survey." *JSMS* 5, no. 3 (September 1992): 345–352.

Gorter-Gronvik, Waling T., and Mikhail N. Suprun. "Ethnic Minorities and Warfare at the Arctic Front 1939–45." *JSMS* 13, no. 1 (March 2000): 127–142.

Grilev, A. N. "Nekotorye osobennosti planirovaniia letne-osennei kampanii 1942 goda" [Some features of planning for the 1942 summer-autumn campaign]. *VIZh*, no. 9 (September 1991): 4–11.

Gurkin, V. "'Dom Pavlova'—symbol doblesti i geoistva sovetskikh voinov" ["Pavlov's House"—a symbol of the valor and heroism of Soviet soldiers]. *VIZh*, no. 2 (February 1963): 48–54.

————. "214-ia strelkoviai diviziia v bitva na Volge" [The 214th Rifle Division in the battle for the Volga]. *VIZh*, no. 7 (July 1964): 97–100.

Gurkin, V. V. "Liudskie poteri Sovetskikh Vooruzhennykh sil v 1941–1945 gg.: Novye aspekty" [Personnel losses of the Soviet Armed Forces in 1941–1945: New aspects]. *VIZh*, no. 2 (March–April 1999): 2–13.

Gurkin, V. V., and A. I. Kruglov. "Oborona Kavkaza. 1942 god" [The defense of the Caucasus. 1942]. *VIZh*, no. 10 (October 1942): 11–18.

Hayward, Joel. "Hitler's Quest for Oil: The Impact of Economic Considerations on Military Strategy, 1941–1942." *The Journal of Strategic Studies* 18, no. 4 (December 1995): 94–135.

I'lenkov, S. A. "Concerning the Registration of Soviet Armed Forces Wartime Irrevocable Losses, 1941–1945." *JSMS* 9, no. 2 (June 1996): 440–442.

Il'in, P. "Boi za Kalach-na-Donu" [The battle for Kalach-on-the-Don]. *VIZh*, no. 10 (October 1961): 70–81.

Isaev, S. I. "Vekhi frontovogo puti" [Landmarks of a front path]. *VIZh*, no. 10 (October) 1991: 24–25.

Istomin, V. "Inzhenernye voiska v bitve za Kavkaz" [Engineer troops in the battle for the Caucasus]. *VIZh*, no. 10 (October 1963): 86–90.

Kahn, David. "An Intelligence Case Study: The Defense of Osuga, 1942." *Aerospace Historian* 28, no. 4 (December 1981): 242–252.

Kazakov, M. "Na Voronezhskom napravlenii letom 1942 goda" [On the Voronezh axis in the summer of 1942]. *VIZh*, no. 10 (October 1964): 27–44.

Kharitonov, A. "Na gornykh perevalakh Kavkaza" [In the mountain passes of the Caucasus]. *VIZh*, no. 7 (August 1970): 57–59.

Khar'kov, A. "Sovetskoe voennoe iskusstva v bitva za Kavkaz" [Soviet military art in the battle for the Caucasus]. *VIZh*, no. 3 (March 1983): 21–28.

Khar'kov, V. "112-ia strelkovaia diviziia v Bitva za Stalingradom" [The 112th Rifle Division in the battle for Stalingrad]. *VIZh*, no. 3 (March 1980): 36–43.

Kuz'michev, I. V. "Shtafniki" [Penal troops]. *Serzhant* [Sergeant], no. 14 (2006): 25–34.

Lashchenko, P. N. "Prodiktovan surovoi neobkhodimost'iu" [Severe measures are dictated], *VIZh*, no. 8 (August) 1988: 76–80.

Loskutov, Iu. "Boevye deistviia 308-i strelkovoi divizii 10–25 sentiabria 1942 goda" [Combat operations of the 308th Rifle Division 10–25 September 1942]. *VIZh*, no. 8 (August 1982): 40–48.

Luchinsky, A. "Na tuapinskom napravlenii" [On the Tuapse axis]. *VIZh*, no. 11 (November 1967): 69–75.

Muriev, D. "Kontrudar pod g. Ordzhonikidze" [The counterstroke at Ordzhonikidze]. *VIZh*, no. 11 (November 1967): 125–128.

"Nakanune Stalingradksoi bitvy" [On the eve of the battle for Stalingrad]. *VIZh*, no. 8 (August 1982): 27–31.

Nikiforov, V. "Sovetskaia aviatsiia v bitva za Kavkaz" [Soviet aviation in the battle for the Caucasus]. *VIZh*, no. 8 (August 1971): 11–19.

"Operatsiia neispol'zovannykh vozmozhnostei" [Operations of unfulfilled opportunities]. *VIZh*, no. 7 (July 1965): 117–124.

Parot'kin, I. "O plane letnei kampanii Nemetsko-Fashistskogo komandovaniia na Sovetsko-Germanskom fronte v 1942 godu" [Concerning the summer campaign of the German-Fascist command on the Soviet-German front in 1942]. *VIZh*, no. 1 (January 1961): 31–42.

Poplyko, F. "Geroi bitvy za Kavkaz" [Heroes of the battle for the Caucasus]. *VIZh*, no. 3 (February 1983): 57–60.

Rokossovsky, K. K. "Soldatskii dolg" [A soldier's duty]. *VIZh*, no. 2 (February 1990): 47–52.

Runov, V. "Ot oborony—k reidu" [From defense—to a raid]. *VV* [Military herald], no. 5 (April 1991): 42–46.

Shtykov, N. "V boiakh za platsdarmy na Verkhnem Donu" [In combat for the bridgeheads on the upper Don]. *VIZh*, no. 8 (August 1982): 32–39.

Statiev, Alexander. "The Ugly Duckling of the Armed Forces: Romanian Armour 1919–41." *JSMS* 12, no. 2 (June 1999): 225–240.

—————. "When an Army Becomes 'Merely a Burden': Romanian Defense Policy and Strategy (1918–1941)." *JSMS* 13, no. 2 (June 2000): 67–85.

Sverdlov, F. "Boi u Volga i na Kavkaze (Sentiabr' 1942 goda)" [The battle on the Volga and in the Caucasus (September 1942)]. *VV*, no. 9 (September 1992): 35–36.

—————. "Prichiny neudach (Oktiabr' 1942 goda)" [The reasons for the failures (October 1942)]. *VV*, no. 10 (October 1992): 49–52.

Vasilevsky, A. "Nekotorye voprosy rukovodstva vooruzhennoi bor'boi letom 1942 goda" [Some questions on the direction of the armed struggle in the summer of 1942]. *VIZh*, no. 8 (August 1965): 3–10.

—————. "Nezabyvaemye dni" [Unforgettable days]. *VIZh*, no. 10 (October 1965): 13–24.

Zaitsev, V. "Stalingrad—Sud'ba moia" [Stalingrad—My fate]. *Na boevom postu—Zhurnal Vnutrennykh voisk* [At the combat post—Journal of Internal Forces], no. 2 (February 1992): 3–8.

Websites

Axis Biographical Research at http://www.geocities.com/~orion47/.

Axis Fact Book—*Des Heeres*—at http://www.axishistory.com/index.

Die Generale des Heeres at http://balsi.d Homepage-Generale/Heer/Heer-Startseite.html.

Generals of World War II at http://www.generals.dk/generals.php.

Index